HALL'S CRIMINAL LAW

**CONTEMPORARY
LEGAL EDUCATION SERIES**

LAW SCHOOL ADVISORY BOARD

CO-CHAIRS

Howard P. Fink
Isadore & Ida Topper Professor of Law
Ohio State University
College of Law

Stephen A. Saltzburg
Howrey Professor of Trial Advocacy
George Washington University
National Law Center

MEMBERS

Charles B. Craver
Leroy S. Merrifield Research Professor
  of Law
George Washington University
National Law Center

Jane C. Ginsburg
Morton L. Janklow Professor of
  Literary and Artistic
  Property Law
Columbia University School of Law

Edward J. Imwinkelried
Professor of Law
University of California at Davis
School of Law

Daniel R. Mandelker
Howard A. Stamper Professor of Law
Washington University
School of Law

Mark V. Tushnet
Professor of Law
Georgetown University
National Law Center

Hall's Criminal Law

CASES AND MATERIALS

Fifth Edition

JOHN S. BAKER, JR.
Professor of Law
Louisiana State University Law Center

DANIEL H. BENSON
Professor of Law
Texas Tech University School of Law

ROBERT FORCE
Professor of Law
Tulane University School of Law

B.J. GEORGE, JR.
Professor of Law
New York Law School

THE MICHIE COMPANY
Law Publishers
CHARLOTTESVILLE, VIRGINIA

COPYRIGHT © 1949, 1965, AND 1976 BY THE BOBBS-MERRILL COMPANY, INC.
COPYRIGHT © 1982, 1983, 1993 BY THE MICHIE COMPANY

Library of Congress Catalog Card No. 93-86629
ISBN 1-55834-122-6

Printed in the United States of America.
All rights reserved.

1172710

DEDICATION

Some users of this casebook may wonder at its title: *Hall's Criminal Law*. In part that reflects the fact that Professor Hall was the source of the first casebook in the sequence leading to the present edition, which he published in the early 1950s. As the years and the editions ran their course, he enlisted certain others to participate, for example, Professor Gerhard O.W. Mueller, Professor Robert Force and Professor B.J. George. But the controlling structure and underlying philosophy of this new edition remain as Jerome Hall conceived them.

Both bear a strong influence from Continental European systems of penal law theory, in particular, the organization of the material into a general part, which addresses basic concepts applicable to many or all specific crimes, and a special part that focuses on laws defining specific offenses (in this instance, a representative array of specific offenses). Jerome Hall established the importance of comparative law in the study of domestic law in the 1930s, when comparative legal analysis was unusual in any sphere of American law and practically unknown in criminal law and procedure. Thus, Professor Hall was one of the first voices crying out in the parochial world (if not wilderness) of American legal education for the use of the tools of comparative law to enhance understanding not only of other legal systems in the world, but of one's own legal system.[1] Although this new edition is not overtly comparative in content, the structure and modes of analysis are within the orthodoxy of comparative penal law, and thus perpetuate, the editors hope, the jurisprudential patterns for which Jerome Hall was a strong and effective advocate.

In addition to being a noted comparatist, Jerome Hall was a pioneer figure in what has been called the sociology of penal law. His pioneering work, *Theft, Law and Society*,[2] addressed the social and economic circumstances within which penal law concepts delineating various forms of theft offenses had arisen and were being enforced.[3] In the ensuing five decades, such an approach has become commonplace, but it was not so for at least two decades after Professor Hall's work first appeared. If indeed sociological jurisprudence has flourished, to a significant degree it has been because of Jerome Hall's insightful writings.[4]

A brief biographical note seems to the editors in order. Jerome Hall was born in Chicago in 1901. He received a J.D. degree from the University of Chicago in 1923, a J.S.D. degree from Harvard and an S.J.D. degree from Columbia, both of the latter in 1935. After a brief period of law practice, he entered law

---

[1] Professor Hall's views on the significance of the comparative approach are stated succinctly in Jerome Hall, *The Three Fundamental Aspects of Criminal Law*, in ESSAYS IN CRIMINAL SCIENCE 159, 160-62 (Gerhard O.W. Mueller ed. 1961) [hereinafter Jerome Hall]. *See also* JEROME HALL, COMPARATIVE LAW AND SOCIAL THEORY (1963). The influence of Roman law-based modes of analysis on Professor Hall's jurisprudence is clear in his GENERAL PRINCIPLES OF CRIMINAL LAW (2d ed. 1960).

[2] (2d ed. 1952); the original edition appeared in 1935.

[3] *See also* Jerome Hall, *supra* note 1, at 164-66.

[4] A valuable resource continues to be JEROME HALL, LAW, SOCIAL SCIENCE AND CRIMINAL THEORY, the final edition of which appeared in 1982.

teaching at North Dakota and Louisiana State University, and in 1939 joined the Indiana law faculty. He served there until he retired in 1970; he had held the highest rank then available: distinguished professor of law. Upon retirement he became a faculty member of The University of California's Hastings College of Law, where he taught until 1986. He died in San Francisco March 1, 1992.

The four of us serving as editors of this volume have benefitted directly and indirectly from Jerome Hall's scholarship and friendship. In gratitude we dedicate it to his memory.

PREFACE

In conformity with current practice, this book includes the "basic materials" for the introductory course in criminal law. Beyond that minimal objective there are other equally important, perhaps more important, goals; the degree of achievement of these goals is the measure of the value of a casebook as a pedagogical tool. First, the selection of the cases to compose a new edition involves much more than the substitution of new cases for old ones. An opinion by a very able judge in a relatively old case is, because of its clear elucidation of doctrine, far more significant than a recent run-of-the-mill case that assumes familiarity with the earlier decision. While the authors have been mindful of the interest in recent decisions and made considerable use of them in this edition, the primary test of selection has been the doctrinal significance of the decisions. Included among recent cases are some that discuss constitutional issues. The "vagueness" and "overbreadth" aspects of "due process," the interpretation of the first amendment, and the development of a constitutional right of privacy certainly affect substantive criminal law.

Equally important is the arrangement of the cases in ways that advance understanding of the law. Some cases and some subjects should, of course, be studied before others. More importantly, cases should be arranged in ways that encourage comparison. While much criticism has been directed in recent years at "case method," some of it fully warranted, most of it has not been applicable to teachers of criminal law who have used several methods of teaching for many years. For example, in matters of mental illness or addiction, what is called for is not close comparison of cases and derivation of the *ratio decidendi* but, instead, lecture and discussion of problems, options available to counsel, and the use of relevant, nonlegal disciplines.

At the other extreme, so far as case analysis is concerned, are the materials on theft. Nowhere in the entire curriculum are there cases that lend themselves more easily and significantly to case-comparison and analysis than those on larceny, larceny by trick, obtaining property by false pretenses, and embezzlement. Granted that case analysis ("case method") is only one of the basic skills in which lawyers should be proficient, the acquisition of that skill is very important. We have had this in mind wherever the nature of the problem called for, or made helpful, a careful comparison of cases, and we have inserted cross-references to facilitate that important method of instruction. The theft materials have also been organized to facilitate comparisons of modern law with the common law and early statutes.

Of course, the study of theft and each of the topics lends itself to still other approaches. Some teachers will find it desirable in the study of the law of theft to introduce their students to its historical development, perhaps especially in relation to economic and industrial change. Some teachers may wish to introduce their students to relevant social studies; certainly the current interest in white collar crime fully warrants this. But even an introduction to such study requires substantial reading. Accordingly, since there are various books and many articles on the subject, we have not used excerpts from that literature since that might encourage superficiality. We have sought, instead, to provide for the study of legal materials that will develop the student's technical competence and, at the same time, lay the foundation for the study of relevant social research. This has guided us, also, in the selection of cases on mental illness and addiction. We have retained many of the courts' references to the literature, which can be used by students who wish to explore these subjects more fully.

Perhaps the most challenging and certainly the most important objective of a casebook on criminal law concerns the basic organization of the materials. From the hundreds, perhaps thousands, of crimes, each differing from the others, only a relative few can be studied. Unlike some casebooks, however, this casebook covers much more than a few crimes; it systematically covers the typical range of ordinary crimes as well as incidentally covering other crimes in the course of addressing the general principles and doctrines. In this way, the book provides the student with a set of tools that will enable him or her to analyze the law of any crime. If these tools are to serve that purpose, the organization of the materials must reflect the current knowledge of criminal law by interrelating the rules defining the distinctive aspects of specific crimes, the doctrines (insanity, mistake, and so on) that qualify or limit the rules, and the principles of that law comprised of the ultimate concepts of penal law. We recognize that it may not be feasible in the first course in criminal law to explore these interrelations in detail. But it is important and possible to raise these questions there and to indicate their significance. To provide a set of materials that facilitate that has been one of our principal objectives.

The field of criminal law includes many issues of public concern and controversy. It is tempting, especially in this field, to concentrate on questions of policy, particularly those concerned with reform of the criminal justice system. Students are easily led into long discussions of drug laws or "victimless crimes," sometimes at the expense of the rigorous study necessary to equip them with professional skills. A course designed for legislators might pay scant attention to the analysis of cases; but a casebook oriented heavily towards policy inevitably neglects the training that best prepares students for the practice of the law. Questions of policy are obviously important and a law school curriculum should provide courses and seminars in which they can be thoroughly explored. But in our view of the basic introductory courses, maximum effort and time should be devoted to help students get a thorough grasp of criminal law and to acquire the other skills needed in practice. Accordingly, although the discussion of reform and numerous other questions of policy adds interest and although these questions should be raised at strategic places, we have kept the above major objectives in view. We have tried to maintain a proper balance, bearing in mind not only that lawyers have distinctive functions extending beyond the competence of even very intelligent laymen but also that informed lawyers can help to solve our serious problems of crime control. In sum, by providing a sound technical foundation, this book makes it possible for the discussion of reform and other broad policy problems to be pointed and informed.

In compiling these materials we have also been cognizant of the essential role of the teacher. Accordingly, while we have included editorial notes at strategic places in order to raise important issues, we have refrained from summarization of textbook answers that diminish interest and encourage memorization rather than inquiry.

The course in criminal law is to a considerable degree focused on the interpretation of statutes. Many cases include relevant parts of statutes. Where necessary, we have set out statutes at length; where important changes have been made in recent statutes or were recommended in the A.L.I. Model Penal Code, we have included those materials. We have placed them in close juxtaposition to the cases so that discussions of these newly adopted statutes or suggested policies may be readily brought within the main lines of analysis.

The text of the Model Penal Code has been included as Appendix A. This enables those teachers who would like to use the Model Penal Code as the basic statutory tool for the course to do so. For those teachers who prefer to use the code of their state, the Model Penal Code is available for handy reference and comparison. The body of the casebook includes references to sections of the Model Penal Code (with a cross-reference to the text of the section in Appendix A) wherever applicable to the particular topic under discussion. Thus, students have an opportunity not only to learn about statutes in general but to see the comprehensiveness and interrelatedness among the provisions of modern codes. Students who are using a state code as their basic statutory tool rather than the Model Penal Code will benefit by the frequent references to the Model Penal Code which alert them to examine their own codes. Finally, in order to make the subject of statutory interpretation more systematic, the casebook presents the major rules of statutory construction in an organized fashion.

Acknowledgments

Grateful appreciation is extended to the following for their contribution to the editorial work on this edition: Jennifer L. Dodge, LSU Law 1994; and David E. Tippett, LSU Law 1994.

The authors acknowledge with thanks permission to reprint the following material:

American Bar Association, ABA Standards for Criminal Justice: Legal Status of Prisoners 23-1.1 (Supp. 1983). Reprinted by permission of the ABA.

American Bar Association, ABA Standards for Criminal Justice: Mental Health 7-6.1 (2d ed. 1981). Reprinted by permission of the ABA.

American Bar Association, ABA Standards for Criminal Justice: Sentencing Alternatives and Procedures 18-2.1, 18-2.2, 18-3.1, 18-4.1 and 18-4.3 and commentaries (2d ed. 1981). Reprinted by permission of the ABA.

American Law Institute, Model Penal Code (official text and commentaries). Copyright 1985 by The American Law Institute. Reprinted with permission of The American Law Institute.

Fletcher, The Metamorphosis of Larceny, 89 Harv. L. Rev. 469 (1976). Copyright 1976 by the Harvard Law Review Association. Reprinted with permission of the Harvard Law Review.

Hall, Law, Social Science and Criminal Theory (1982). Reprinted with permission of Fred B. Rothman & Co.

Hart, The Aims of the Criminal Law, 23 Law & Contemp. Probs. 401 (1958). Reprinted with permission of Law and Contemporary Problems.

Summary Table of Contents

	Page
Preface	vii
Acknowledgments	xi
Table of Contents	xvii

PART ONE. PRINCIPLES ... 1

CHAPTER 1. GENERAL PRINCIPLES OF CRIMINAL LAW ... 3
Section I.	The Unifying Principles	3
Section II.	Legality	3
Section III.	The Interpretation of Penal Legislation	16
Section IV.	Constitutional Limits on Penal Legislation	26

CHAPTER 2. ELEMENTS OF CRIMES AND THE CONSEQUENCES OF CRIMINALITY ... 67
Section I.	Culpability (*Mens Rea*)	67
Section II.	Conduct (*Actus Reus*)	103
Section III.	Concurrence of *Mens Rea* and *Actus Reus*	127
Section IV.	The Harm	130
Section V.	Causation	138
Section VI.	Punishment	144

PART TWO. RULES — SPECIFIC CRIMES ... 159

CHAPTER 3. ASSAULT, BATTERY AND RELATED CRIMES ... 161
Section I.	The Act and the Harm: Common Law and Current Views of Assault and Battery	161
Section II.	The *Mens Rea*	169
Section III.	Grading: Aggravated Assaults and Batteries	173
Section IV.	An Expanding View of Harm: Terroristic Threats, Harassment, Stalking	179
Section V.	Consent	186

CHAPTER 4. SEXUAL OFFENSES ... 193
Section I.	Forcible Rape	193
Section II.	Proof	205
Section III.	"Nonforcible" Rape	218
Section IV.	Modern Redefinition of Rape and Other Sexual Offenses	225

CHAPTER 5. CRIMINAL HOMICIDE ... 231
Section I.	The Harm: Death of Another Human Being	232
Section II.	Causation	241
Section III.	Classification in Terms of *Mens Rea*	266
Section IV.	Intent Murder	270
Section V.	"Depraved Heart" Murder	286
Section VI.	Felony Murder	295

		Page
Section VII.	Voluntary Manslaughter	315
Section VIII.	Unlawful-Act—Involuntary Manslaughter	334
Section IX.	Criminal-Negligence Involuntary Manslaughter and Negligent Homicide	342

CHAPTER 6. CRIMES AGAINST PROPERTY AND RELATED CRIMES ... 353
Section I.	Traditional Forms of Criminality	353
Section II.	Theft and Related Offenses Under Contemporary Legislation	419
Section III.	Robbery	474
Section IV.	White Collar Crimes	485
Section V.	Burglary and Other Criminal Intrusions	489
Section VI.	Arson and Other Crimes of Property Destruction	499

PART THREE. DOCTRINES ... 505

CHAPTER 7. JUSTIFICATION ... 507
Section I.	Self-Defense	508
Section II.	Defense of Others	527
Section III.	Defense of Property	534
Section IV.	Prevention of Crime — Arrest	542
Section V.	Necessity	551
Section VI.	Duress	562
Section VII.	Entrapment	577

CHAPTER 8. INCAPACITY ... 583
Section I.	Mental Condition	583
Section II.	Intoxication	643
Section III.	Immaturity	655
Section IV.	Condition or Status	657

CHAPTER 9. IGNORANCE AND MISTAKE ... 669
Section I.	Of Fact	669
Section II.	Of Law	680
Section III.	Strict Liability	693

CHAPTER 10. RELATIONAL DOCTRINES ... 721
Section I.	Parties — Principals and Accessories	721
Section II.	Criminal Liability of Corporations	735
Section III.	Solicitation	739
Section IV.	Criminal Attempt	742
Section V.	Conspiracy	785

PART FOUR. SANCTIONS ... 837

CHAPTER 11. PURPOSES, CONSTITUTIONALITY AND FORMS OF CRIMINAL SANCTIONS ... 839
Section I.	General Purposes of Sanctioning	839
Section II.	Constitutional Restrictions: Cruel and Unusual Punishment	854

		Page
Section III.	Patterns of Sentencing	869
Section IV.	Forms of Sanctions	899
Table of Cases		943
Index		955

Table of Contents

	Page
Preface	vii
Acknowledgments	xi
Summary Table of Contents	xiii

PART ONE. PRINCIPLES	1
Editorial Notes on the Study of Criminal Law	1
CHAPTER 1. GENERAL PRINCIPLES OF CRIMINAL LAW	3
Section I. The Unifying Principles	3
Section II. Legality	3
A. The Rule of Law	3
B. Legality: *Nulla Poena Sine Lege*	4
1. Basic Concept	4
2. Common Law	4
Editorial Note	4
State v. Oliver	5
Notes	7
3. The *Nullum Crimen* Concept in Application	11
Lewis v. Commonwealth	11
Notes	12
State v. Meyer	12
4. The *Nulla Poena* Concept In Application	14
City of Portland v. Dollarhide	14
Notes	15
Section III. The Interpretation of Penal Legislation	16
A. General Rules of Construction	16
1. General Principles	16
2. United States Supreme Court Construction of Federal Legislation	17
Moskal v. United States	17
Notes	20
3. Particular Rules of Construction	22
a. *Ejusdem Generis* Clauses	22
United States v. Turkette	22
Notes	23
b. Statutes "*In Pari Materia*"	24
People v. Robbins	24
Notes	25
Section IV. Constitutional Limits on Penal Legislation	26
A. The *Ex Post Facto* Clause	26
Collins v. Youngblood	26
Note	26
Miller v. Florida	27
Notes	28

	Page
People v. Rossi	29
Notes	31
B. The Due Process Clause	32
1. Vagueness	32
Ex Parte Guerrero	32
Notes	33
2. Overbreadth	37
City of Tacoma v. Luvene	37
Notes	41
C. Individual Rights Based Challenges	43
1. The First Amendment	43
United States v. Eichman	43
Notes	46
2. Equal Protection	48
a. Irrational Legislative Classification	48
United States v. Greene	48
Notes	49
b. Discriminatory Enforcement	50
Editorial Note	50
3. Right of Privacy	51
Bowers v. Hardwick	51
Notes	52
D. The Burden of Proof and Presumptions	53
Editorial Note	53
Francis v. Franklin	54
Notes	59
E. Jurisdictional Limits on Proscribing and Punishing Crimes	60
1. Separation of Powers	60
Editorial Note	60
2. Federalism	62
a. State and Federal Crimes	62
Editorial Note	62
b. Occupation of the Field	62
Editorial Note	62
3. Nonenforcement of Foreign Penal Adjudications	63
Editorial Note	63
CHAPTER 2. ELEMENTS OF CRIMES AND THE CONSEQUENCES OF CRIMINALITY	67
Section I. Culpability (*Mens Rea*)	67
A. *Actus Non Facit Reum Nisi Mens Sit Rea*	67
United States v. United States Gypsum Co.	67
Notes	68
B. Culpability Distinguished From Motive	69
State v. Ehlers	69
Note	71

Page

Employment Division, Department of Human Resources of Oregon v. Smith	71
Notes	77
C. Intent or Purpose	79
1. Basic Concept	79
Model Penal Code § 2.02	79
2. Specific and General Intent	79
People v. Glover	79
Notes	83
Regina v. Pembliton	85
People v. Weaver	86
Note	87
Working Papers of the National Commission on Reform of Federal Criminal Laws 132-33 (1970)	87
D. Knowledge	89
Model Penal Code § 2.02	89
United States v. Sanchez-Robles	89
Notes	92
E. Recklessness	95
Model Penal Code § 2.02	95
Model Penal Code, Tentative Draft No. 4, 125-26 (1955)	96
State ex rel. Juvenile Department of Multnomah County v. Anderson	96
F. Negligence	98
Model Penal Code § 2.02	98
Working Papers of the National Commission on Reform of Federal Criminal Laws 127-28 (1970)	98
People v. Futterman	99
Notes	101
Section II. Conduct (*Actus Reus*)	103
A. The Requirement of Voluntariness	103
Model Penal Code § 2.01	103
Working Papers of the National Commission on Reform of Federal Criminal Laws 106-13 (1970)	104
State v. Taft	107
Notes	109
Commonwealth v. Cheatham	109
B. Innocent Agent	112
State v. Thomas	112
Notes	113
C. Special Dimensions of *Actus Reus*	115
1. Omission To Act	115
Model Penal Code § 2.01	115
Pope v. State	115
Notes	117
2. Possession	123
Model Penal Code § 2.01	123

	Page
State v. Lowe	123
Notes	125
3. Solicitation	127
Editorial Note	127
Section III. Concurrence of *Mens Rea* and *Actus Reus*	127
Model Penal Code § 2.02	127
State v. Asberry	127
Notes	128
Section IV. The Harm	130
State v. Laufenberg	130
State v. Quinnam	131
Note	132
Jerome Hall, Law, Social Science and Criminal Theory 208-11 (1982)	133
Editorial Note	135
Section V. Causation	138
Model Penal Code § 2.03	138
Comments	139
Notes	142
Section VI. Punishment	144
United States v. Halper	144
Title 18, United States Code, Section 3553(a)(2) (1988)	150
United States v. Bergman	150
Notes	157
PART TWO. RULES — SPECIFIC CRIMES	159
Introductory Note	159
CHAPTER 3. ASSAULT, BATTERY AND RELATED CRIMES	161
Editorial Note	161
Section I. The Act and the Harm: Common Law and Current Views of Assault and Battery	161
East's Pleas of the Crown 406 (1803)	161
People v. Yslas	162
Notes	162
Chapman v. State	163
Note	164
Robinson v. United States	164
Model Penal Code §§ 210.0, 211.1, 211.2	167
Notes	167
State v. Allen	168
Notes	169
Section II. The *Mens Rea*	169
State v. Davis	169
Notes	171
Section III. Grading: Aggravated Assaults and Batteries	173
Editorial Note	173
Commonwealth v. Henson	173

	Page
Notes	177
Editorial Note on Assaults with Intent to Commit Specific Crimes and Attempts	178
Section IV. An Expanding View of Harm: Terroristic Threats, Harassment, Stalking	179
Editorial Note	179
Model Penal Code § 211.3	180
State v. Gunzelman	180
Notes	182
Model Penal Code §§ 250.2 — 250.5	184
Notes on Harassment and Stalking	184
Section V. Consent	186
Model Penal Code § 2.11	186
State v. Brown	186
Notes	189
Commonwealth v. Gregory	190
Notes	191
CHAPTER 4. SEXUAL OFFENSES	193
Editorial Note	193
Section I. Forcible Rape	193
East's Pleas of the Crown 434 (1803)	193
Notes on "Utmost Resistance"	194
Rusk v. State	196
Note	202
Notes on *Mens Rea*	202
Notes on Parties	204
Section II. Proof	205
A. The Cautionary Instruction	205
People v. Rincon-Pineda	205
B. Prior Acts of Unchastity	208
Notes	208
State v. Green	209
Notes	212
C. Corroboration	214
United States v. Wiley	214
Notes	217
Section III. "Nonforcible" Rape	218
A. Lack of Capacity	218
Notes	218
B. Fraud	219
Note	219
C. Statutory Rape	220
State v. Duncan	220
People v. Hernandez	220
Notes	223
Section IV. Modern Redefinition of Rape and Other Sexual Offenses	225

	Page
Editorial Note	225
Model Penal Code §§ 213.0-213.4, 213.6	227
Notes on Rape and "Incidental" Offenses	227
Editorial Note on Kidnapping	228

CHAPTER 5. CRIMINAL HOMICIDE 231
    Introductory Note 231
  Section I. The Harm: Death of Another Human Being 232
    A. Human Being 232
      State v. Oliver 232
      Notes 232
    B. Death 235
      State v. Olson 235
      Notes 237
    C. By Another 238
      People v. Campbell 238
      Notes 240
  Section II. Causation 241
    A. Direct, Intervening and Supervening Cause 241
      Model Penal Code § 2.03 241
      Commonwealth v. Rementer 241
      Notes 244
      People v. Hamrick 246
      Notes 247
      State v. McClose 251
    B. Culpability in Relation to Causation 253
      State v. Hallett 253
      People v. Brackett 254
      Notes 256
    C. Evidentiary Problems 258
      State v. Doyle 258
      Notes 260
    D. The "Year and a Day" Rule 264
      State v. Pine 264
      Notes 266
  Section III. Classification in Terms of *Mens Rea* 266
    Note 266
    California Penal Code (1988), §§ 187-189, 192 267
    Model Penal Code §§ 210.9, 210.1 — 210.4, 210.2 268
  Section IV. Intent Murder 270
    A. Premeditation, Intent, and Degrees of Murder 270
      Green v. State 270
      Notes 274
      Bullock v. United States 274
      Notes 275
      State v. Standiford 276
    B. Diminished Responsibility 279

	Page
Note	279
State v. Moore	280
Editorial Note	284
Notes	286
Section V. "Depraved Heart" Murder	286
Commonwealth v. Malone	286
Notes	288
Director of Public Prosecution v. Smith	288
Notes	290
People v. Register	291
Notes	294
Section VI. Felony-Murder	295
State v. Glover	295
Notes	299
Commonwealth v. Spallone	303
Note	305
Jackson v. State	305
Notes	308
Commonwealth v. Bowden	309
Notes	312
Notes on "Bootstrapping"	313
Note on Judicial Abrogation of the Felony-Murder Rule	314
Section VII. Voluntary Manslaughter	315
A. Provocation	315
State v. Ross	315
Ex Parte Fraley	318
State v. Nevares	319
Notes	321
B. Extreme Emotional Disturbance	324
Patterson v. New York	324
State v. Elliott	328
Notes	331
C. Imperfect Self-Defense	332
People v. Flannel	332
Notes	334
Section VIII. Unlawful Act—Involuntary Manslaughter	334
State v. Frazier	334
State v. Horton	335
People v. Stuart	336
Commonwealth v. Williams	339
Note on Unlawful Acts and Criminal Negligence	341
Section IX. Criminal-Negligence Involuntary Manslaughter and Negligent Homicide	342
People v. Rodriguez	342
Notes	343
Notes on Proof of Negligent Homicide	344
People v. Haney	345

	Page
Notes	348
Notes on Vehicular Homicide	350

CHAPTER 6. CRIMES AGAINST PROPERTY AND RELATED CRIMES ... 353
Section I. Traditional Forms of Criminality ... 353
    East's Pleas of the Crown 553 (1803) ... 353
  A. Larceny ... 353
    1. Subject Matter of Theft ... 353
    People v. Dillon ... 353
    Notes ... 357
    2. The Harm ... 358
    People v. Zinke ... 358
    Notes ... 361
    Rex v. Turvey ... 362
    People v. Hanselman ... 363
    Notes ... 364
      3. *Actus Reus* ... 367
        a. Trespass; Continuing Trespass ... 367
    Commonwealth v. White ... 367
    Notes ... 368
    People v. Lafka ... 369
    Notes ... 371
    Dunlavey v. Commonwealth ... 372
    Agnew v. State ... 374
    Note ... 375
        b. Asportation ... 376
    State v. Carswell ... 376
    Note ... 377
    State v. Laborde ... 377
    Notes ... 378
        c. Lost or Mislaid Goods and Mistakenly Transferred Goods ... 379
    Brooks v. State ... 379
    State v. Langford ... 381
    Notes ... 385
      4. *Mens Rea* ... 386
        a. General Concept ... 386
    Mitchell v. Territory ... 386
    Notes ... 388
        b. Claim of Right ... 391
    State v. Kelly ... 391
      5. Grading (Value) ... 392
    State v. Jacquith ... 392
    Notes ... 394
  B. Embezzlement ... 396
    1. *Actus Reus* ... 396

	Page
People v. Yannett	396
State v. Stahl	400
State v. Taylor	401
Notes	403
2. *Mens Rea*	405
State v. Brown	405
Notes	407
C. Obtaining Title to Property by False Pretenses	409
1. *Actus Reus*	409
a. "Title"	409
State v. Hamm	409
Notes	411
b. False Representations	412
People v. Cage	412
Notes	414
2. *Mens Rea*	416
State v. Pickus	416
Note	419
Section II. Theft and Related Offenses Under Contemporary Legislation	419
A. Statutory Patterns	419
Model Penal Code § 223.1	419
Comment	420
B. Protected Values (Harm)	422
Model Penal Code § 223.0	422
Comment	422
United States v. DiGilio	425
Notes	425
C. *Actus Reus*	426
1. Prohibited Activities	426
a. Unauthorized Control	426
Model Penal Code § 223.2	426
Comment	426
People v. Olivo	428
Notes	431
b. Misappropriation	433
Model Penal Code § 223.5	433
Comment	433
State v. Woll	433
c. Obtaining by Deception	434
Model Penal Code § 223.3	434
Comment	435
Linne v. State	435
2. Spousal Property	440
Model Penal Code § 223.1	440
Comment	440
3. Grading	440

	Page
Model Penal Code § 223.1	440
Comment	441
Notes	441
D. *Mens Rea*	442
1. Generally	442
People v. Washburn	442
Notes	445
Model Penal Code § 223.0	445
2. Claim of Right	445
Model Penal Code § 223.1	445
Comment	446
E. Special Forms of Theft	446
1. Theft of Services	446
Model Penal Code § 223.7	446
Notes	446
2. Theft of Funds Received	447
Model Penal Code § 223.8	447
Comment	447
Notes	447
3. Credit Card Misuse	447
Model Penal Code § 224.6	447
Comment	448
Notes	448
4. No-Account Check Legislation	448
Model Penal Code § 224.5	448
Comment	449
Notes	449
5. Unlawful Vehicle Use	449
Model Penal Code § 223.9	449
Comment	449
State v. Clark	449
Notes	452
6. Computer Crimes	453
Commonwealth v. Gerulis	453
Notes	458
F. Receiving Stolen Property	458
1. Generally	458
Model Penal Code § 223.6	458
Comment	459
2. The Harm ("Stolen")	459
United States v. Monasterski	459
Notes	464
People v. Kyllonen	465
Notes	468
3. *Actus Reus*	468

	Page
Jordan v. State	468
Notes	471
4. *Mens Rea*	471
People v. Wielograf	471
Note	474
5. Grading	474
Editorial note	474
Section III. Robbery	474
A. Harm	474
Model Penal Code § 222.1	474
Comment	474
B. *Actus Reus*	475
Jarrett v. State	475
Notes	476
People v. Skelton	477
Notes	480
C. *Mens Rea*	481
People v. Reid	481
Notes	484
D. Gradation	484
Model Penal Code § 222.1	484
Comment	484
Section IV. White Collar Crimes	485
Model Penal Code § 223.4	485
Comment	485
Model Penal Code §§ 240.0 — 240.7	485
Notes	486
Section V. Burglary and Other Criminal Intrusions	489
Model Penal Code §§ 221.0-221.2	489
State v. Albert	490
Notes	491
State v. Lozier	493
Notes	495
In re Appeal No. 631 (77) From the District Court of Maryland, Montgomery County, Juvenile Division	497
Note	499
Section VI. Arson and Other Crimes of Property Destruction	499
Model Penal Code §§ 220.1-220.3	499
State v. Shaw	500
Notes	501
PART THREE. DOCTRINES	505
CHAPTER 7. JUSTIFICATION	507
Note on Justification	507
Note on Defense of Person, Property and Arrest	508

	Page
Section I. Self-Defense	508
Model Penal Code §§ 3.04, 3.09, 3.11	508
People v. Williams	509
Notes	511
Coleman v. State	513
Notes	516
Notes on Intramarital Violence: Battered Wives	517
State v. Abbott	519
Notes	523
Notes on Imperfect Self-Defense	526
Section II. Defense of Others	527
Model Penal Code § 3.05	527
Morrison v. Commonwealth	527
State v. Chiarello	529
State v. Gelinas	531
Notes	533
Section III. Defense of Property	534
Model Penal Code § 3.06	534
Montgomery v. Commonwealth	534
Notes	536
People v. Ceballos	536
Notes	541
Section IV. Prevention of Crime — Arrest	542
Model Penal Code § 3.07	542
Tennessee v. Garner	542
Notes	546
Commonwealth v. Klein	548
Notes	551
Section V. Necessity	551
Note	551
Regina v. Dudley & Stephens	552
Notes	554
United States v. Holmes	555
Note	558
Model Penal Code § 3.02	558
Notes	558
State v. Dorsey	560
Notes on Limitations on the Defense of Necessity	561
Problems	562
Section VI. Duress	562
State v. Hunter	562
Notes	566
State v. Toscano	566
Note	570
United States v. Bailey	571
Notes	574
Notes on Coercive Persuasion (Brainwashing)	576

	Page
Section VII. Entrapment	577
Jacobson v. United States	577
Notes	581
CHAPTER 8. INCAPACITY	583
Section I. Mental Condition	583
Introductory Note	583
Law Reform Commission of Canada, a Report to Parliament on Mental Disorder in the Criminal Process 2-4 (1977)	583
A. Legal Tests for Responsibility	585
1. The *M'Naghten* Rule	585
New York Penal Law § 30.05 (McKinney 1975)	585
Notes	585
U.S. Senate Report No. 97-307 to Accompany Criminal Code Reform Act of 1981, S. 1630, 97th Congress, 1st Session 95-97 (1982)	586
State v. Hamann	589
Notes	591
2. Irresistible Impulse; "Control" Tests	593
State v. Hamann	593
Notes	594
3. ALI Test	595
Model Penal Code § 4.01	595
People v. Drew	595
Notes	599
4. Diminished Responsibility	603
5. "*Mens Rea*" or Abolition Test	604
Idaho Code § 18-207	604
Idaho Code § 19-2523	604
Notes	605
6. "Guilty But Mentally Ill"	612
Michigan Compiled Laws § 768.36 (1975)	612
Notes	613
7. Administration of the Tests	614
a. Pleading the Defense	614
Model Penal Code § 4.03	614
Labor v. Gibson	614
Notes	615
b. Diagnostic Commitments and Reports	615
Model Penal Code § 4.05	615
Notes	616
c. Bifurcated Proceedings	617
Editorial Note	617
d. Psychiatric and Lay Opinion Evidence	617
Model Penal Code §§ 4.07, 4.09	617
Note	618
e. Jury Instructions	618
Government of the Virgin Islands v. Fredericks	618

	Page
Notes	621
f. Burden of Persuasion	622
People v. Drew	622
Notes	622
8. Consequences of Acquittals by Reason of Mental Condition	623
a. Commitment Procedures	623
Model Penal Code § 4.08	623
Matter of Lewis	623
Notes	625
b. Release	626
In re Moye	626
Notes	627
B. Procedural Incompetence	628
1. Constitutional Standards	628
Model Penal Code § 4.04	628
Lane v. State	628
Notes	629
2. Procedural Requirements	630
Jackson v. Indiana	630
Notes	636
3. "Chemical Competence"	638
Editorial Note	638
C. Screening and Diversion of Mentally-Ill Arrestees and Defendants	639
United States National Advisory Commission on Criminal Justice Standards and Goals, Courts Report 27-28, 32, 33, 35, 36 (1973)	639
Notes	641
D. Mentally-Ill Prisoners	642
Editorial Note	642
Section II. Intoxication	643
Model Penal Code § 2.08	643
State v. Stasio	643
Director of Public Prosecutions v. Majewski	650
Notes	653
Section III. Immaturity	655
Model Penal Code § 4.10	655
In re Ramon M	656
Section IV. Condition or Status	657
Fenster v. Leary	657
Note on Robinson v. California and Powell v. Texas	659
United States v. Moore	660
Notes on Other Interpretations of Robinson and Powell	667
CHAPTER 9. IGNORANCE AND MISTAKE	669
Section I. Of Fact	669

		Page
	Editorial Note	669
A.	Negating Required Intent	669
	United States v. Bright	669
	Notes	671
	Davis v. State	675
	Notes	677
B.	Negating *Mens Rea*	678
	Gordon v. State	678
	Model Penal Code § 2.04	679
	Notes	679
Section II. Of Law		680
	State v. Boyett	680
	Notes	681
	Editorial Note on Exceptions to the Rule	682
	United States v. Barker	684
	United States v. Martinez	684
	Editorial Note on Notice — Ignorance and Mistake	690
	Editorial Note on Bigamy and Adultery	691
Section III. Strict Liability		693
	United States v. Greenbaum	693
	United States v. Park	695
	Commonwealth v. Koczwara	700
	Notes	703
	Morissette v. United States	703
	Notes	709
	Lambert v. California	710
	Notes	713
	United States v. Robert Wulff	715
	Notes	719

CHAPTER 10. RELATIONAL DOCTRINES ... 721

Section I. Parties — Principals and Accessories ... 721
    Editorial Note ... 721
    18 United States Code § 2 (1976) ... 722
    Model Penal Code § 2.06 ... 723
    Commonwealth v. Perry ... 723
    Notes ... 724
    United States v. Ruffin ... 726
    Notes ... 730
    Editorial Note on "Knowledge" ... 733
    Notes on Accessories After the Fact ... 734
    Model Penal Code §§ 242.3-242.5 ... 734
Section II. Criminal Liability of Corporations ... 735
    Editorial Note ... 735
    Model Penal Code § 2.07 ... 738
    Proposed Criminal Code Reform Act of 1981, s. 1630, 97th Congress, 1st Session (1981) ... 738

	Page
Editorial Note on Personal Liability for Corporate Acts	738
Section III. Solicitation	739
People v. Lubow	739
Model Penal Code § 5.02	741
Notes	742
Section IV. Criminal Attempt	742
Model Penal Code § 5.01	742
A. The Harm	742
Note	742
B. *Mens Rea*	743
Rhode v. State	743
Note on Intentional and Reckless Attempts	746
C. Preparation and Attempt	747
Editorial Notes	747
People v. Rizzo	750
United States v. Stallworth	752
State v. Hurley	754
Notes	755
State v. Gobin	757
D. Attempt in Relation to Solicitation	760
Editorial Note	760
E. Abandonment	761
Editorial Note	761
Notes	761
F. "Attempted" Attempts	761
State v. Wilson	761
Notes	765
G. Impossibility	765
1. Of Fact	765
State v. Damms	765
Notes	767
2. Of Law	768
Foster v. Commonwealth	768
People v. Jaffe	768
People v. Rojas	771
Notes	773
United States v. Berrigan	777
Notes	781
Editorial Note on the Impossibility Problem	782
Problem	785
Section V. Conspiracy	785
A. Conceptual Matters	785
1. The Rationale of Conspiracy	785
Introductory Note	785
2. The Dangers of Conspiracy Prosecutions	786
Krulewitch v. United States	786
B. Overview	789

	Page
State v. Carbone	789
Notes	791
Model Penal Code §§ 5.03-5.05	792
C. *Actus Reus*	793
Garcia v. State	793
Notes	795
D. *Mens Rea*	797
Editorial Note	797
People v. Lauria	797
Notes on Intent to Further the Objective	802
E. Scope of the Conspiratorial Relationship	804
Editorial Note	804
United States v. Varelli	805
Notes	810
Pinkerton v. United States	815
People v. McGee	819
Editorial Note	820
F. Joint Liability — Procedural Problems	821
Gardner v. State	821
Notes	824
G. Organized Crime	826
Introductory Note	826
Editorial Note on Transition from "Conspiracy" to "Enterprise"	827
United States v. Elliott	829
Notes	835
PART FOUR. SANCTIONS	837
CHAPTER 11. PURPOSES, CONSTITUTIONALITY AND FORMS OF CRIMINAL SANCTIONS	839
Section I. General Purposes of Sanctioning	839
Editorial Note — Views on Punishment	839
Henry M. Hart, The Aims of the Criminal Law, 23 Law and Contemporary Problems 401 (1958)	844
Hintz v. State	852
Model Penal Code § 1.02(2)	853
Notes	854
Section II. Constitutional Restrictions: Cruel and Unusual Punishment	854
A. Generally	854
Notes	855
B. Capital Punishment	858
Editorial Note	858
Section III. Patterns of Sentencing	869
A. Indeterminate Sentences: The Rehabilitative Ideal	869
American Bar Association Standards for Criminal Justice (2d ed. 1981) Sentencing Alternatives and Procedures	869

	Page
§ 18-2.1. Commentary pp. 18-33 to 18-35	869
§ 18-4.1. Commentary pp. 18-241 to 18-246	870
§ 18-2.2. Commentary pp. 18-67 to 18-70	874
Notes	786
B. Presumptive Sentencing: "Just Deserts" Theory	877
American Bar Association Standards for Criminal Justice Sentencing Alternatives and Procedures (2d ed. 1981)	877
§ 18-2-2. Commentary pp. 18-59 to 18-63	877
Juneby v. State	881
Note	887
Note on the Federal Sentencing Guidelines and their Application	887
Sentencing Table	889
American Bar Association Standards for Criminal Justice (2d ed. 1981) Sentencing Alternatives and Procedures	895
§ 18-3.1 and Commentary pp. 18-187 to 18-191	895
Standard 18-3.1	895
Note	899
Section IV. Forms of Sanctions	899
A. Probation	899
Model Penal Code § 7.01	899
Title 18, United States Code (1988)	899
Note	900
Bearden v. Georgia	900
Note on Restitution	905
B. Fines	907
Model Penal Code § 7.02	907
Title 18, United States Code	907
Notes	908
Note on Enforcement of Fines	909
C. Forfeitures	915
1. Collateral Profits of Crime	915
Simon & Schuster v. New York Crime Victims Board	915
2. Forfeitures as a Criminal Sanction	918
Title 18, United States Code Section 1983	918
Note on Forfeiture Procedures	919
3. Forfeiture of Attorney's Fees	924
D. Imprisonment	926
1. Circumstances of Imprisonment	926
American Bar Association Standards for Criminal Justice Legal Status of Prisoners (Supp. 1983)	926
2. Extended Terms of Imprisonment; Habitual Offender Statutes	928
Model Penal Code §§ 6.07, 7.03, 7.04	928
United States National Advisory Commission on Criminal Justice Standards and Goals, Corrections Report (1973)	929
Notes	932

	Page
Note on Federal Sentencing Guidelines Provisions Relating to Criminal History and Livelihood and Career Offenders	932
3. Multiple Sentences	937
Model Penal Code § 7.06	937
United States National Advisory Commission on Criminal Justice Standards and Goals, Corrections Report (1973)	937
4. Mandatory Minimum Sentences	939
American Bar Association Standards for Criminal Justice (2d ed. 1981) Sentencing Alternatives and Procedures	939
Table of Cases	943
Index	955

PART ONE
PRINCIPLES

EDITORIAL NOTES ON THE STUDY OF CRIMINAL LAW

Treatises on Anglo-American criminal law began with Bracton's thirteenth-century work, followed in England by Hale (early eighteenth century) and Stephen (nineteenth century), and in this country by Bishop and Wharton (nineteenth century). *See* G. MUELLER, CRIME, LAW AND THE SCHOLARS (1969). The principal advance contributed by twentieth-century scholars in England and the United States has been between the *organization* of the criminal law by distinguishing general "principles" and "specific crimes." This development corresponded to the long-established practice of continental codification regarding the "General Part" and the "Special Part" of European criminal codes.

The organization of criminal law in codes and treatises represents the same logic and methodology that is characteristic of science, especially physical science. There is, accordingly, nothing esoteric about the organization of the materials in this book or in the effort to maximize knowledge of the criminal law by studying the interrelations of various parts of that law — here designated "principles," "doctrines," and "rules." On the contrary, it is simply an application of the kind of thinking that has characterized the advance of knowledge since the ancient Greeks.

In this country, the influence of the case method has been so great that some teachers may prefer to begin with Part Two, the analysis of the cases defining specific crimes. In this approach the instructor performs the essential job of articulating those general principles which underly the particular cases.

Others will prefer to proceed from the beginning of the book with a preliminary analysis of the principles, which thereafter are applied to the study of specific crimes. These principles which shape criminal law are not to be accepted "on faith," but are to be employed critically. Some of them may have to be modified when applied in the laboratory to specific crimes. Some of them *e.g.*, the alleged "principle of harm," are controversial; and perhaps there are other principles than those presented here which qualify for consideration. By studying the materials in this manner, knowledge of criminal law advances to the point where the student has the conceptual tools needed to analyze any crime.

Insofar as possible, students should study the material daily, briefing all the cases in a section as a unit and not simply preparing the four or five cases which may be discussed during an ensuing class hour. Indeed, in many contexts a teacher may use problems or hypothetical questions, rather than individual cases, to develop the materials. This technique of study and presentation provides an overall view of each substantive area which is not only more helpful than fragmented knowledge derived from individual case study, but also tends to make the study of criminal law more interesting. After all the cases and materials in a section have been briefed, it is desirable to read a relevant law review article or pages in a text. Law review references provided in the pages which follow are not intended to be exhaustive, but rather have been selected to serve the needs of busy law students.

Among leading contemporary texts, we particularly recommend the classic by the late Professor Jerome Hall, who originated this casebook and for whom the current edition is named: J. HALL, GENERAL PRINCIPLES OF CRIMINAL LAW (2d ed., 1960). Other important texts include G. FLETCHER, RETHINKING CRIMINAL LAW (1978); W. LaFAVE & A. SCOTT, CRIMINAL LAW (2d ed., 1986); R. PERKINS & R. BOYCE, CRIMINAL LAW (3d ed., 1982). There may well be criminal law texts, aimed at the practicing bar of a given state, which will be of interest to a law student as well. Texts on English law include J. SMITH & B. HOGAN, CRIMINAL LAW (7th ed., 1992); J. Turner's edition of C. KENNY, OUTLINES OF CRIMINAL LAW (19th ed., 1966), and G. WILLIAMS, CRIMINAL LAW (2d. ed., 1961).

Modern criminal law relies heavily on legislation. Thus, it is desirable for each student to acquire a copy of the penal laws of a particular state, *e.g.*, the state in which he or she intends to practice, and to study its text intensively as it bears on each subsection of this casebook. Appendix A to the casebook contains the complete text of Parts I and II of the American Law Institute's Model Penal Code, which may be used as a substitute for or supplement to the criminal statutes of a particular state. References to the Model Penal Code and excerpts from it also appear throughout the casebook. The Model Penal Code, promulgated by the American Law Institute, has been used during the past thirty years as a model by numerous states in adopting codes of criminal law.

The Model Penal Code has been published by the American Law Institute in several forms. The entire code is contained in a document titled Model Penal Code (Proposed Official Draft), dated May 4, 1962. Subject to some minor changes and a revision of the comments, the proposed draft of the Model Penal Code was approved by the Institute and became its official draft in 1962. In 1980, the American Law Institute published in three volumes in MODEL PENAL CODE AND COMMENTARIES Part II, §§ 210.0 — 251.4 (Official Draft and Revised Comments). In 1985, a final, official complete text of the Model Penal Code was published by the American Law Institute. For convenience, citation to sections of the code in this casebook will simply be MODEL PENAL CODE § __. References to Model Penal Code comments are to the 1980 three-volume publication referred to above unless the contrary is indicated.

Although the text is devoted primarily to matters of substantive criminal law, Appendix C presents an outline of American criminal procedure which may prove helpful in promoting an understanding of the procedural framework within which substantive issues are resolved.

Editorial footnotes are indicated by an asterisk. The original footnotes from quoted material are designated by placing the asterisks or footnote numbers in brackets.

Chapter 1
GENERAL PRINCIPLES OF CRIMINAL LAW

SECTION I. The Unifying Principles

The principles of criminal law consist of seven ultimate notions expressing: (1) *mens rea,* (2) act (effort), (3) the "concurrence" (fusion) of *mens rea* and act, (4) harm, (5) causation, (6) punishment and (7) legality.[1]

SECTION II. Legality

A. THE RULE OF LAW

A committee of the American Bar Association defined the rule of law to embrace the following:

> 1. Freedom from private lawlessness provided by the legal system of a politically organized society;
> 2. A relatively high degree of objectivity in the formulation of legal norms and a like degree of evenhandedness in their application;
> 3. Legal ideas and juristic devices for the attainment of individual and group objectives within the bounds of ordered liberty;
> 4. Substantive and procedural limitations on governmental power in the interest of the individual for the enforcement of which there are appropriate legal institutions and machinery.[2]

The "rule of law" has been regarded as the greatest political achievement of our culture, and the relevant principle of legality has maximum significance in the criminal law because the most basic values are involved. Further, these materials introduce the student to problems dealing with statutes and their interpretation, and they also raise important constitutional issues. Finally, and perhaps most importantly, a careful study of these materials will help to develop linguistic competence. Precision and clarity are distinctive characteristics of first-rate lawyering, and the following materials on legality can cultivate those skills. This will facilitate the development of the habit of carefully weighing the meaning of words that is of the utmost importance in the practice of law.

---

[1] JEROME HALL, GENERAL PRINCIPLES OF CRIMINAL LAW 18 (2d ed. 1960) [hereinafter JEROME HALL].

[2] AMERICAN BAR ASSOCIATION SECTION OF INTERNATIONAL AND COMPARATIVE LAW, THE RULE OF LAW IN THE UNITED STATES 29-30 (1958).

B. LEGALITY: *NULLA POENA SINE LEGE*

1. BASIC CONCEPT

The essence of this principle of legality is limitation on penalization by the State's officials, effected by the prescription and application of specific rules. That is the actual meaning of the principle of legality so far as the criminal law is concerned. In Europe, this principle is usually called *nulla poena sine lege.*

Its meaning is expressed in several ways. In a narrow connotation, centered on *poena,* it concerns the sanctions of penal laws: no person may be punished except in pursuance of a statute which prescribes a penalty. Employed narrowly as *nullum crimen sine lege,* the principle means that no conduct may be held criminal unless it is precisely described in a penal law. In order that there be no doubt regarding the meaning of the principle, it has two important corollaries: penal statutes must be strictly construed, and they must not be given retroactive effect.[3]

2. COMMON LAW

EDITORIAL NOTE

In England before the mid-seventeenth century, there were relatively few statutes which proscribed antisocial behavior. Courts imposed penalties not only where a specific statute was violated and not only where in the absence of statute there was case precedent, but also where behavior was considered prejudicial to the public welfare. The courts were considered the *custos morum* of the people and exercised jurisdiction over acts which were *contra bonos mores,* including behavior which threatened the safety, order, and moral welfare of the state. *Shaw v. Director of Public Prosecutions,* 1962 A.C. 220. This approach has been retained in some American states:

> The common law is sufficiently broad to punish as a misdemeanor, although there may be no exact precedent, any act which directly injures or tends to injure the public to such an extent as to require the state to interfere and punish the wrongdoer, as in the case of acts which injuriously affect public morality, or obstruct, or pervert public justice, or the administration of government.[4]

The American colonies, and later the states through reception statutes, adopted as part of their criminal laws the common law of England including both English case law and statutes, except to the extent that such law was superseded by local statute. Currently, the trend in the United States rejects common-law crimes.[5]

It was reported in 1947 that eighteen states had abolished common-law crimes.[6] Today at least twenty-seven states either expressly or by implication

---

[3] JEROME HALL, *supra* note 1, at 28.
[4] *Commonwealth v. Mochan,* 110 A.2d 788 (Pa. Super. 1955).
[5] MODEL PENAL CODE § 1.05, Appendix A; LA. REV. STAT. ANN. § 14:7 (West 1974).
[6] Note, *Common Law Crimes in the United States,* 47 COLUM. L. REV. 1332 (1947).

have abolished common-law crimes. In only eighteen states can it be said with certainty that common-law crimes are affirmatively recognized, and in the remaining states the status is unclear.

The abrogation of common-law crimes has not made the common law irrelevant in American criminal law. Even in states which have rejected common-law crimes, it is not unusual to find, for example, breach of the peace or disorderly conduct statutes which through broad language and catch-all phrases are similar to common-law crimes. Furthermore, the common law is often resorted to for interpreting terms in criminal statutes. Finally, in many states, notwithstanding the adoption of comprehensive codes of criminal law, common-law defenses such as self-defense and insanity are recognized despite their omission from the codes.

STATE v. OLIVER

Supreme Court of Vermont
563 A 2d. 1002 (Vt. 1989)

ALLEN, CHIEF JUSTICE.

Defendant was charged with careless and negligent operation of a motor vehicle resulting in the death of a person, 23 V.S.A. § 1091(c). According to supporting affidavits, the accident caused the death of an *in utero* fetus at a gestational age of 34-35 weeks. The trial court refused to find probable cause for the charge, ruling that an unborn viable fetus is not a person within the meaning of § 1091. The State brings this interlocutory appeal, and the controlling question of law is "whether an unborn viable fetus is a person as contemplated by 23 V.S.A. § 1091(c)." We answer the question in the negative.

Section 1091(c) imposes criminal penalties on any "person who, while engaged in the violation of any law, ordinance or regulation applying to the operation or use of a motor vehicle or to the regulation of traffic, causes, as a result of the violation, the death of any person ...." ... [W]hen interpreting the meaning of the statute, this Court is compelled to give effect to the apparent intent of the legislature, *State v. Baldwin*, 140 Vt. 501, 509, 438 A.2d 1135, 1140 (1981), and must be guided by the fundamental principle that "the common law in force at the time the statute was passed is to be taken into account in construing undefined words of the statute." *Meadows v. State*, 291 Ark. 105, 107, 722 S.W.2d 584, 585 (1987); ...

....

As far back as the 17th century, it was the prevailing view under the common law that only living human beings could be the victims of homicide. The killing of a fetus did not constitute criminal homicide unless it was born alive and later died of injuries inflicted prior to birth. The "born alive" rule has since become and continues to remain the prevailing common law view throughout the United States. *See* discussions in *Commonwealth v. Cass*, 392 Mass. 799, 805, 467 N.E.2d 1324, 1328 (1984); *Keeler v. Superior Court*, 2 Cal. 3d 619, 625, 470 P.2d 617, 619, 87 Cal. Rptr. 481, 483 (1970); 2 W. LaFave & A. Scott, Substantive Criminal Law § 7.1(c), at 185 n.13 (1986). Although this Court has never had occasion to address the issue, the "born alive" rule was widely accepted throughout the country by the time of the enactment of the statutory predecessor to § 1091 (c), and must be taken into account by the Court when assigning meaning to terms contained in the statute. In light of this rule, we interpret the legislature's intent in using the word "person" in § 1091(c) as limiting the application of the statute to circumstances involving the death of individuals who have already been born. The death of a viable fetus falls outside of the purview of the statute.

The State argues that our recent decision in *Vaillancourt v. Medical Center Hospital of Vermont, Inc.,* 139 Vt. 138, 143, 425 A.2d 92, 95 (1980), holding that there may be liability under Vermont's wrongful death statute for negligently causing the death of an unborn, viable fetus, requires this Court to likewise find that death of an unborn, viable fetus may form the basis of a criminal prosecution under § 1091(c). According to the State, "it ... would make no sense to determine a child's personhood, for purposes of being the victim of a crime, by reference to which side of the birth canal the child is on at the time of its victimization."

There exists, however, an important distinction between § 1091(c) and Vermont's wrongful death statute, 14 V.S.A. §§ 1491, 1492. The wrongful death statute is remedial in nature, being designed to allay the harsh common law rule denying liability due to the death of the victim, and must therefore be construed liberally. *Vaillancourt,* 139 Vt. at 141, 425 A.2d at 94. Penal statutes, on the other hand, are to be strictly construed in a manner favorable to the accused. *In re Hough,* 143 Vt. 15, 19, 458 A.2d 1134, 1136 (1983); *State v. Sidway,* 139 Vt. 480, 484, 431 A.2d 1237, 1239 (1981). "The rule of strict construction of criminal statutes is essential to guard against the creation of criminal offenses outside the contemplation of the legislature under the guise of 'judicial construction.'" *People v. Vercelletto,* 135 Misc. 2d 40, 41, 514 N.Y.S.2d 177, 178 (Ulster County Ct. 1987). Application of the rule of strict construction under these circumstances supports the conclusion that an unborn fetus is not a person within the meaning of § 1091(c).

The State makes several additional arguments based on the Supreme Judicial Court of Massachusetts' decision in *Commonwealth v. Cass,* 392 Mass. 799, 467 N.E.2d 1324. The Court in *Cass* determined that a viable fetus is a "person" for purposes of Massachusetts' vehicular homicide statute, G.L. c. 90, § 24G. In coming to its decision, the court distinguished Massachusetts from those jurisdictions comprising the majority view by its assertion that it may develop "common law rules of criminal law" since its body of "criminal law is largely common law." Id. at 803, 467 N.E.2d at 1327. According to the court, the "notion that [it is] unable to develop common law rules of criminal law because the Legislature has occupied the entire field of criminal law" applies only to code jurisdictions. Id.

The State argues that since Vermont is a "common law" state, this Court has the authority to interpret the term "person" in § 1091(c) to mean something other than its common law definition. We disagree with the distinction drawn by the Massachusetts court and thus with the State's argument. The fact that Vermont is a "common law" jurisdiction with regard to the criminal law does not free us from the fundamental principle of separation of powers underlying the structure of our state government. Here, the legislature has expressly enacted a criminal penalty provision, § 1091(c), and we are bound to

B. LEGALITY: *NULLA POENA SINE LEGE*

interpret its language within the context of the adversary proceeding before us in a manner not inconsistent with existing common law. *Meadows,* 291 Ark. at 107, 722 S.W.2d at 585.

We agree with the State that application of the "born alive" rule may lead to irrational or unjust results. It is not difficult to imagine how an individual might be punished for the death of an infant caused by injuries received prenatally, while another escapes prosecution because the victim is stillborn. ==This Court, however, is not the proper forum in which to consider and accomplish the extension of criminal liability that would occur as a result of interpreting the term "person"== in § 1091(c) to include a viable fetus. That task must be accomplished by the legislature.

The controlling question of law is answered in the negative.

NOTES

1. In *Pope v. State,* 396 A.2d 1054 (Md. 1979), the court refused to revive the common-law crime of misprision of felony, although the English House of Lords had done so in *H.L. Sykes v. Director of Public Prosecutions,* [1961] 3 All. E.R. 33. It noted that misprision had not been included as a crime in the Model Penal Code, and that courts in other states had refused to revive the felony after generations of nonuse (desuetude) as wholly unsuitable to American criminal law. The court's opinion advanced several policy arguments in favor of its conclusion:

> Under *Sykes,* no active step need be taken to conceal the felony (it is only thus that it remains quite distinct from the crime of accessory after the fact), and the concealment need bring no benefit to the accused. But three fundamental questions remained: when does the duty to reveal a felony arise; how is that duty discharged; and does a relationship with the felon prevent the duty arising?
>
> It seems that the duty arises when "[one] knows" of the commission of a felony. When, then, can [one] be said to *know* and *what* is it that [one] must know? Lord Goddard held that there must be disclosure when the knowledge [one] has "is so definite that it ought to be disclosed. [One] is neither bound nor would [one] be wise to disclose rumours or mere gossip, but, if facts are within [one's] knowledge that would materially assist in the detection and arrest of a felon, [one] must disclose them as it is a duty [one] owes to the state." *Sykes* at 46. Lord Goddard left the matter to the jury as a question of fact. Glazebrook suggests that "unless the jury is to be entirely uncontrolled, it has to be told how precise and certain the accused's knowledge must have been before [the accused] can be convicted." 25 Mod.L.Rev. at 313. Is the duty to be confined to felonies committed in the presence of the accused, and, if not, is hearsay sufficient? Should the felon's own admission, standing alone, be enough? Knowledge of the commission of a crime is an ingredient of the offenses of accessory after the fact and receiving stolen goods, but, unlike misprision, they require a positive act. It is reasonable, in such circumstance, to require a person who has reason to believe something is wrong to inquire further

before embarking on some course of conduct, and to hold that [one] fails to do so at [one's] peril. "If this rule is applied to misprision, two duties are imposed: a duty to disclose knowledge of a felony, and a duty also to make inquiries to resolve a suspicion concerning the commission of a felony." *Id.* To paraphrase Glazebrook, must the inhabitants of Maryland become detectives as well as informers? ...

When the duty to disclose has arisen, it is not clear how it is discharged. It would be logical that once the authorities are in possession of all the information concerning a felony, a citizen's duty to disclose his own knowledge ceases. So there is an added element of chance — "the chance that the police already know." *Id.* at 315. Lord Denning saw the duty as requiring a citizen "to disclose to proper authority all material facts known to [the citizen] relative to the offence. It is not sufficient to tell the police that a felony has been committed...."

We observe that common law misprision is not only beset with practical defects but may implicate constitutional privileges. To sustain the Fifth Amendment right against self-incrimination, "it need only be evident from the implications of the question, in the setting in which it is asked, that a responsive answer ... might be dangerous because injurious disclosure might result." *Hoffman v. United States,* 341 U.S. 479, 486-487 (1951). The privilege extends not only to information that would itself support a conviction, but "likewise embraces those which would furnish a link in the chain of evidence to prosecute the claimant ...." We note also that it has been suggested that the federal misprision statute may involve the right of privacy.

We have proceeded on the assumption that the House of Lords was correct in concluding in *Sykes* that "there is and always has been an offense of misprision of felony...." We are persuaded, finding no sound reason not to be, that their lordships' definition of the offense and the composition of its elements properly reflected the crime as it existed at common law. We are satisfied, considering its origin, the impractical and indiscriminate width of its scope, its other obvious deficiencies, and its long non-use, that it is not now compatible with our local circumstances and situation and our general code of laws and jurisprudence. Maintenance of law and order does not demand its application, and, overall, the welfare of the inhabitants of Maryland and society as enjoyed by us today, would not be served by it. If the Legislature finds it advisable that the people be obligated under peril of criminal penalty to disclose knowledge of criminal acts, it is, of course, free to create an offense to that end, within constitutional limitations, and, hopefully, with adequate safeguards. We believe that the common law offense is not acceptable by today's standards, and we are not free to usurp the power of the General Assembly by attempting to fashion one that would be. We hold that misprision of felony is not a chargeable offense in Maryland....

2. In *State v. Egan,* 287 So. 2d 1 (Fla. 1973), the defendant had been indicted for the common-law offense of nonfeasance in office, and had moved successfully in the trial court to have the indictment quashed on the grounds

that the statute on which the indictment rested, which provided that "the common law of England in relation to crimes, except so far as the same relates to the modes and degrees of punishment, shall be of full force in this state where there is no existing provision by statute on the subject," was unconstitutional on vagueness grounds. The Florida Supreme Court reversed. It noted, in explaining an earlier ruling that a prisoner could be convicted for the common-law offense of prison break, "if this Court had not had the right to rely on the common law, then the offender would have been able to violate the law with impunity." Is this statement persuasive?

The *Egan* court disposed of the defense contention that the defendant had not had advance notice of the content of prohibited conduct by invoking its earlier precedent that the indictment or information setting forth the details of the offense sufficed for the purpose. Do you agree?

3. *See also State v. Cogdell,* 257 S.E.2d 748 (S.C. 1979), which approved a conviction for the common-law offense of obstruction of justice entered against a town mayor who failed to report traffic convictions to a state agency, as required by statute.

4. *State v. Carson,* 262 S.E.2d 918 (S.C. 1980), reached a contrary conclusion to that in *Pope* about the continued existence in South Carolina of the common-law crime of misprision. A state statute provided that "all, and every part, of the common law of England, where it is not altered by the Code or inconsistent with the Constitution or laws of this State, is hereby continued in full force and effect in the same manner as before the adoption of this section." The court rejected Carson's claim that the statute conflicted with privilege against self-incrimination. *Contrast Holland v. State,* 302 So. 2d 806 (Fla. Dist. Ct. App. 1974), a post-*Egan* decision, which found misprision of felony no longer to be a crime, because it was inconsistent with "our traditional concepts of peace and quietude" and the right of citizens to mind their own business.

5. In *Watkins v. State,* 400 A.2d 464, 467 (Md. App. 1979), the court noted:

> The rule is that where a statute and the common law are in conflict, the common law yields to the statute to the extent of the inconsistency, but where the legislative intent is shown to encompass an entire area, then that statute preempts the common law.... We find that the [escape] statute simplified the common law by consolidating the three types of escape into one statute and making all escape a felony. The statute as adopted represented the entire subject matter of the law of escape in Maryland and thereby abrogated the common law of escape and its several classifications as well as the distinction among various acts of escape as misdemeanors or felonies. We hold that the adoption of the escape statute was, in effect, the equivalent of the wooden stake in the heart of Dracula which made impossible the resurrection of the common law by the declaration of the trial judge that the escape statute was unconstitutional.

6. *People v. Young,* 340 N.W.2d 805, 810, 811 (Mich. 1983):

> It is an elementary principle of construction that we will assign to common-law terms their common-law meaning unless the Legislature

directs otherwise. We have done so with burglary.... In effect, the people ask us to disregard the plain meaning of the word that the Legislature chose to use and find, instead, that the Legislature meant breaking and entering when it said burglary in 1969.... The rationale for such an unusual request is apparently that burglary and breaking and entering have become so entwined over time by virtue of their placement in the same statute that the Legislature failed to see the difference between the two crimes and regarded them as interchangeable....

This legislative action must be viewed against the historical backdrop of almost 150 years of legislative action distinguishing between the crimes of breaking and entering and burglary.... We can only conclude that in 1969 the Legislature intended that the crime of burglary, in its common-law sense, be the aggravating circumstance for purposes of the first-degree murder statute....

We hold that the term burglary in the first-degree murder statute required that the people prove the historic common law elements of that offense. It was that conduct, the breaking and entering of a dwelling house in the nighttime with an intent to commit a felony, that the Legislature proscribed as an aggravating circumstance in the first-degree murder statute....

7. There are no common-law offenses under federal criminal law, which is exclusively statutory. However, it is appropriate for federal courts to look to the common law for the meaning of traditional terms used by Congress without redefinition. *See, e.g., Government of Virgin Islands v. Williams,* 424 F.2d 526 (3d Cir. 1970); *In re Greene,* 52 Fed. 104 (Cir. Ct., S.D. Ohio 1892) (citing early United States Supreme Court precedent).

8. In *Perrin v. United States,* 444 U.S. 37 (1979), the Court had before it the issue of whether the term "bribery" in the Travel Act, 18 U.S.C. § 1952 (1988), included commercial bribery, *i.e.,* corruption of individuals in private enterprises. In *Perrin,* the defendant had suborned confidential oil geographical exploration material from an employee of a private Louisiana firm and had transmitted it to a firm in Texas. His activity was denominated commercial bribery under Louisiana penal law. The Court concluded that Congress had not intended to restrict definitions of bribery in the statute to narrow common-law concepts:

> At early common law, the crime of bribery extended only to the corruption of judges.... By the time of Blackstone, bribery was defined as an offense involving a judge or "other person concerned in the administration of justice" and included the giver as well as the receiver of the bribe.... The writings of a 19th century scholar inform us that by that time the crime of bribery had been expanded to include the corruption of any public official and the bribery of voters and witnesses as well.... And by the 20th century, England had adopted the Prevention of Corruption Act making criminal the commercial bribery of agents and employees....
>
> In this country, by the time the Travel Act was enacted in 1961, federal and state statutes had extended the term bribery well beyond its common-law meaning. Although Congress chose not to enact a general commercial bribery statute, it perceived abuses in the areas it found required

particular legislation. Federal statutes specifically using "bribery" in the sense of payments to private persons to influence their actions are the Transportation Act of 1940, 49 U.S.C. § 1(17)(b) (prohibiting the "bribery" of agents or employees of common carriers), and the 1960 Amendments to the Communications Act, 47 U.S.C. § 509(a)(2) (prohibiting the "bribery" of television game show contestants).

A similar enlargement of the term beyond its common-law definition manifested itself in the States prior to 1961. Fourteen States had statutes which outlawed commercial bribery generally. An additional 28 had adopted more narrow statutes outlawing corrupt payments to influence private duties in particular fields, including bribery of agents, common carrier and telegraph company employees, labor officials, bank employees, and participants in sporting events.

In sum, by 1961 the common understanding and meaning of "bribery" had extended beyond its early common-law definitions. In 42 states and in federal legislation, "bribery" included the bribery of individuals acting in a private capacity. It was against this background that the Travel Act was passed.

... We are ... persuaded that the generic definition of bribery, rather than a narrow common-law definition, was intended by Congress.

444 U.S. at 43-45, 49.

3. THE *NULLUM CRIMEN* CONCEPT IN APPLICATION

LEWIS v. COMMONWEALTH

Supreme Court of Appeals of Virginia
34 S.E.2d 389 (1945)

CAMPBELL, CHIEF JUSTICE. On the 24th day of August, 1944, the defendant, Barbara Lewis, was tried before the trial justice of Nelson county upon a warrant which charged that she "did on the 20th day of August, 1944, unlawfully be disorderly on the bus operated through Nelson county, Virginia, and commit an assault on one J. F. Gardner." The trial justice, J.B. Massie, entered this judgment against her: "Upon the examination of the within charge, I find the accused guilty and impose a fine of $50.00 and costs." From this judgment the defendant appealed to the Circuit Court of Nelson county.

....

It is the contention of defendant that disorderly conduct "on a bus" is not a crime either at common law or under the provision of section 4533 of Michie's Code.

The contention that disorderly conduct is not a common law crime is well founded.

While it is true that the common law obtains in Virginia unless modified by statute, it is also true that unless disorderly conduct was a crime at common law, it is not a crime in Virginia unless made so by ordinance or by statute.

....

In 27 Corpus Juris Secundum, Disorderly Conduct, § 1, p. 277, it is said: "At common law there was no offense known as 'disorderly conduct.'"

Since it is patent that defendant was not guilty of a common law offense, the question then is, was she guilty of a violation of section 4533 of Michie's Code?

The pertinent part of the section is as follows:

"If any person, whether a passenger or not, shall, while in any car, or caboose, or on any part of a train carrying passengers or employees of any railroad or street passenger railway, behave in a riotous or disorderly manner, he shall be guilty of a misdemeanor."

At the time of the enactment of the statute by the Legislature in its session of 1899-1900, the common carrier known as a bus had not come into existence. The fact that, during the period of years following, the statute has not been amended so as to include disorderly conduct on a bus, is no concern of the court. The province of the court is to interpret the law, not enact it. The statute is perfectly plain and only provides for penalties for being disorderly on "any car" or "caboose," or any part of a "train" or "street railway." ...

Since section 4533 of the Code is a penal statute, it must be construed strictly in favor of defendant. *Young v. Commonwealth,* 155 Va. 1152, 156 S.E. 565. To read into the statute something not contemplated by the Legislature would be to contravene the universal rule which is succinctly stated in 25 Ruling Case Law, sec. 218, as follows:

"Courts 'cannot read into a statute something that is not within the manifest intention of the Legislature as gathered from the statute itself. To depart from the meaning expressed by the words is to alter the statute, to legislate and not to interpret.'"

....

Reversed and remanded.

NOTES

1. The remand in the principal case was for retrial on another charge, omitted from this excerpt.

2. At the next session of the Virginia General Assembly, immediately following the *Lewis* decision, an act approved March 26, 1946, Acts of 1946, c. 296, Code Section 4533a, was passed, which amended the code by including "omnibus or other public conveyance." This act was interpreted in *Taylor v. Commonwealth,* 46 S.E.2d 384 (Va. 1948).

STATE v. MEYER

Supreme Court of Hawaii
595 P.2d 288 (1979)

[Meyer was indicted and convicted of promoting a dangerous drug in the first degree through distribution of more than fifty capsules of lysergic acid diethylamide (LSD). The state statute in force at the time of the transactions specified in the indictment referred to "lysergic acid diethlamine" but not to "lysergic acid diethlamide," as in prior legislation.

MARUMOTO, J.

There is sufficient evidence in the record to warrant this court to hold that the words diethlamide in the 1972 Act and diethlamine in the 1974 Act were

B. LEGALITY: *NULLA POENA SINE LEGE*

misspellings of the words diethylamide and diethylamine respectively. In both Acts, the letter "y" was omitted as the sixth letter in the mentioned words.

Prosecution seeks a holding of this court that the word "diethlamine" in the 1974 Act was a misspelling of the word "diethylamide," and that "lysergic acid diethalmine" in Schedule I(d)(12) covered the drug "lysergic acid diethylamide." We decline to so hold, for the reasons stated below.

At the trial, Gilbert Chang, a criminologist of the Honolulu Police Department, was called by the Prosecution as its expert witness. He testified:

(1) that there is a substance known as lysergic acid diethylamine;

(2) that lysergic acid diethylamine is different from lysergic acid diethylamide;

(3) that lysergic acid diethylamine is not LSD;

(4) that lysergic acid diethylamine, as a lysergic acid derivative, has some hallucinogenic properties.

... [I]n the bill as passed by the Legislature and signed by the Governor, the item in Schedule I(d)(12) was spelled "lysergic acid diethlamine."

The legislative history of House Bill No. 2731-74 shows that the Legislature intended to list lysergic acid diethylamide in Schedule I(d)(12).

. . . .

Code of Federal Regulations, Title 21, § 1308.11 lists lysergic acid diethylamide as one of proscribed controlled substances in Schedule I(d)(12).

However, the Legislature did not carry its intention into effect. Only by analogy with the Federal law can it be said that the dangerous drug really listed in Schedule I(d)(12) of the 1974 Act was lysergic acid diethylamide, and the listing of lysergic acid diethylamine was an inadvertent misspelling.

In this connection, reference may be made to Hawaii Penal Code § 701-104, which reads:

> § 701-104 *Principles of construction.* The provisions of this Code cannot be extended by analogy so as to create crimes not provided for herein; however, in order to promote justice and effect the objects of the law, all of its provisions shall be given a genuine construction, according to the fair import of the words, taken in their usual sense, in connection with the context, and with reference to the purpose of the provision.

To hold that distribution of lysergic acid diethylamide was proscribed by the 1974 Act is to extend the provision of that Act by analogy so as to create a crime not provided for therein. To do so will be in violation of the first clause of § 701-104 quoted above.

A holding that distribution of lysergic acid diethylamine was proscribed by the 1974 Act does not violate the second clause of § 701-104. According to the testimony of Gilbert Chang, that substance exists separate and apart from lysergic acid diethylamide.

Thus, the fair import of the words lysergic acid diethylamine, taken in their usual sense is lysergic acid diethylamine and not lysergic acid diethylamide. The use of those words in Schedule I(d)(12) of the 1974 Act was not out of context and was within the purpose of that Act. In Schedule I(d) of the Act, the Legislature intended to proscribe the distribution of hallucinogenic substances. Under the uncontradicted evidence in this case, lysergic acid diethylamine is a hallucinogenic substance.

Hawaii Penal Code § 701-104 sets forth the same principle of construction stated in *Queen v. San Tana,* 9 Haw. 106, 108 (1893), as follows:

> We cannot change the language of the statute, supply a want, or enlarge upon it in order to make it suit a certain state of facts. We do not legislate or make laws. Even where the Court is convinced in its own mind that the Legislature really meant and intended something not expressed by the phraseology of the Act, it has no authority to depart from the plain meaning of the language used.

Queen v. San Tana is an old case. Nevertheless, in the statement quoted above, the court stated a sound principle of law....

4. THE *NULLA POENA* CONCEPT IN APPLICATION

CITY OF PORTLAND v. DOLLARHIDE

Supreme Court of Oregon
714 P.2d 220 (1986)

CARSON, JUSTICE

....

The first issue we must address is the City's contention that a pretrial demurrer was not the proper vehicle to challenge the penalty provision of a city ordinance. The written record of the dismissal consists only of the following notation by the trial court on the face of the complaint: "preemption invalidated statute [ordinance]." From the tape recording of the oral argument on defendant's motion to dismiss, it is clear that the trial court dismissed the complaint because he believed that state law preempted the City's mandatory minimum penalty provision [for prostitution] and that the proscriptive ordinance could not stand without a valid penalty provision.

The validity of ordinance provisions can be challenged pretrial.... Defendant's pretrial motion did not attack solely the penalty provision; defendant's motion also attacked the ordinance prohibiting prostitution on the grounds, inter alia, that (1) the Oregon Criminal Code of 1971 evinces a legislative intent entirely to "preempt" the field of the prohibition of prostitution; and (2) because the City's mandatory minimum penalty provision is invalid, there can be no prosecution under the prohibiting ordinance, for the reason that the offense carries no penalty.

It is beyond dispute that no conviction can be had for the violation of a statute for which no penalty is provided.... A defendant charged under a criminal law for which only an allegedly invalid penalty is provided may challenge the penalty pretrial because, if the challenge is successful, the charge will be dismissed and the defendant will not be made to stand trial. Because defendant's challenge to the penalty provision was linked to her challenge of the prohibitory ordinance under which she was charged, defendant's pretrial challenge of the penalty provision was proper. In these circumstances, because the trial court invalidated the City's prohibitory provision, based upon the court's conclusion that the mandatory minimum penalty provision was displaced by state law, the ruling on the penalty provision was not premature. This case is appropriate for review.

. . . .

... The trial court concluded that the City's prohibitory ordinance could not stand without the applicable mandatory minimum penalty provision. Although neither party has addressed this issue, we conclude, as did the Court of Appeals, that the invalid mandatory minimum penalty section is severable.... In the instant case, nothing in the text of the city ordinances at issue indicates that the City Council intended, if the mandatory minimum were held to be unconstitutional, that the provision defining and prohibiting prostitution would be invalid.... [T]he prohibitory ordinance is neither incomplete nor incapable of being executed absent the mandatory minimum provision because, upon conviction, a defendant could be sentenced to the penalty provided for in the general penalty provision applicable to the City Code, section 14.08.020.[13]

Thus, after the trial court declared the mandatory minimum penalty provision invalid, it erred in dismissing the complaint. Defendant could have been tried and, if convicted, punished pursuant to section 14.08.020 of the City Code.

The decision of the Court of Appeals is affirmed.

NOTES

1. In *State v. LeCompte,* 406 So. 2d 1300 (La. 1981), the Supreme Court of Louisiana found unconstitutional the penal portion of a controlled substances statute which provided a minimum fine with no maximum:

> In the present case, it takes only a little imagination to think of a fine that would be grossly disproportionate to the offense prohibited, especially in view of the fact that the statute in its various gradations carries with it a term of imprisonment which the court is required to impose on top of the unlimited maximum of the fine. However despicable trafficking in drugs, and however admirable the legislative purpose in seeking to put an end to or even a partial cessation of the practice, we cannot uphold a statute that permits an unlimited fine, especially as we have struck down a somewhat similar statute ... on the ground that it violated the excessive punishment clause of this state's Constitution.

2. As in the principal case, a general penalty provision will support a sentence following conviction even if the specific punishment provisions of the predicate are invalid. *See, e.g., Buckingham v. State,* 516 S.W.2d 195 (Tex. Crim. App. 1974) (statutory provision of a fine was invalid because of an improper caption to the enacting legislation, but a fine of from one dollar to $200 was authorized under a general statute, and could be invoked in the particular case).

---

[13] Section 14.08.020 of the Code of the City of Portland provides: "Violation of any provision of this Code is punishable, upon conviction, by a fine of not more than $500, or by imprisonment not exceeding 6 months, or both. However, no greater penalty shall be imposed than the penalty prescribed by Oregon statute for the same act or omission."

SECTION III. THE INTERPRETATION OF PENAL LEGISLATION

A. GENERAL RULES OF CONSTRUCTION

1. GENERAL PRINCIPLES

The canon of construction of penal statutes, required by the principle of legality, includes several species of interpretation, the common result of which is to favor the defendant. One of these is to adhere to the ordinary meaning of the words instead of to the meaning induced from the general purpose or "legislative intention" of the statute. Another is to adhere to the narrower meaning of ambiguous words established in usage or legal precedent. Still another is to invalidate vague statutes.[14]

....

It has been argued that the rule of liberal construction comports with the trend of the states. The argument equates liberal construction with the construction of words according to their "fair import." In fact, liberal construction and construction according to "fair import" derive from opposing attitudes about the proper role of the judiciary. Where liberal construction endorses judicial lawmaking, "fair import" construction is rooted in a reaction to the common law powers of judges.[356] Moreover, the fact that some states may adopt liberal standards of construction does not necessarily justify a liberal standard for federal legislation. States have primarily been concerned with the common law offenses or what are considered "ordinary" crimes. Even though states have generally departed from the common law of crimes in favor of codification and have modified the elements of particular crimes, the codification of crimes follows in large part the content of the common law of crimes. Such crimes present few constitutional problems in terms of notice because the core meanings of crimes such as murder, rape, and robbery are well understood. On the other hand, newly created crimes, whether state or federal, which proscribe conduct in language that is unclear, are more likely to present notice problems.[8]

---

[14]JEROME HALL, *supra* note 1, at 38-39 (footnotes omitted).

[356]The criminal code which Edward Livingston proposed for Louisiana and that of David Dudley Field eventually adopted for New York reflected hostility toward judge-made criminal law.... These two codes provided respectively for construction according to "plain import" and "fair import" of their terms.... "The rule of the common law that penal statutes are to be strictly construed has no application to this Code. All its provisions are to be construed to the fair import of their terms, with a view to effect its objects land to promote justice." ...

[8]John S. Baker, Jr., *Nationalizing Criminal Law: Does Organized Crime Make It Necessary or Proper?*, 16 RUTGERS L.J. 495, 564-66 (1985) (all but one footnote omitted).

A. GENERAL RULES OF CONSTRUCTION

2. UNITED STATES SUPREME COURT CONSTRUCTION OF FEDERAL LEGISLATION

MOSKAL v. UNITED STATES

United States Supreme Court
498 U.S. 103 (1990)

[Moskal participated in a title-washing scheme in which automobile titles that had been altered to reflect rolled-back odometer mileage were sent from Pennsylvania to Virginia. After Virginia authorities, who were unaware of the alternations, issued Virginia titles incorporating the false odometer readings, Moskal received the washed titles in Pennsylvania, where they were used in the course of automobile sales to unsuspecting buyers. Moskal was convicted of receiving two washed titles under 18 U.S.C. § 2314 (1988), which prohibits the knowing transportation in interstate commerce of "*falsely made,* forged, altered, or counterfeited securities" (emphasis added). In affirming Moskal's conviction, the Third Circuit rejected the defense contention that, because the washed titles were genuine, and the Virginia officials who had issued them did not know the falsity of the odometer information, the titles were not "falsely made."]

JUSTICE MARSHALL delivered the opinion of the Court...

Whether a valid title that contains fraudulently tendered odometer readings may be a "falsely made" security for purposes of § 2314 presents a conventional issue of statutory construction, and we must therefore determine what scope Congress intended § 2314 to have. Moskal, however, suggests a shortcut in that inquiry. Because it is *possible* to read the statute as applying only to forged or counterfeited securities, and because *some* courts have so read it, Moskal suggests we should simply resolve the issue in his favor under the doctrine of lenity....

In our view, this argument misconstrues the doctrine. We have repeatedly "emphasized that the 'touchstone' of the rule of lenity 'is statutory ambiguity.'.".. Because the meaning of language is inherently contextual, we have declined to deem a statute "ambiguous" for purposes of lenity merely because it was *possible* to articulate a construction more narrow than that urged by the Government.... Nor have we deemed a division of judicial authority automatically sufficient to trigger lenity .... If that were sufficient, one court's unduly narrow reading of a criminal statute would become binding on all other courts, including this one. Instead, we have always reserved lenity for those situations in which a reasonable doubt persists about a statute's intended scope even *after* resort to "the language and structure, legislative history, and motivating policies" of the statute .... Examining these materials, we conclude that § 2314 unambiguously applies to Moskal's conduct ....

"In determining the scope of a statute, we look first to its language." ... We think that the words of § 2314 are broad enough, on their face, to encompass washed titles containing fraudulently tendered odometer readings. Such titles are "falsely made" in the sense that they are made to contain false, or incorrect, information.

Moskal resists this construction of the language on the ground that the state officials responsible for issuing the washed titles did not know that they were incorporating false odometer readings. We see little merit in this argument. As used in § 2314, "falsely made" refers to the character of the securities being transported. In our view, it is perfectly consistent with ordinary usage to speak of the security as *being* "falsely made" regardless of whether the party responsible for the physical production of the document *knew* that he was making a security in a manner that incorporates false information. Indeed, we find support for this construction in the nexus between the *actus reus* and *mens rea* elements of § 2314. Because liability under the statute depends on *transporting* the "falsely made" security with unlawful or fraudulent intent, there is no reason to infer a scienter requirement for the act of falsely making itself.

Short of constructing "falsely made" in this way, we are at loss to give *any* meaning to this phrase independent of the other terms in § 2314, such as "forged" or "counterfeited." By seeking to exclude from § 2314's scope any security that is "genuine" or valid, Moskal essentially equates "falsely made" with "forged" or "counterfeited." His construction therefore violates the established principle that a court should "'give effect, if possible, to every clause and word of a statute.'" ...

Our conclusion that "falsely made" encompasses genuine documents containing false information is supported by Congress' purpose in enacting § 2314. Inspired by the proliferation of interstate schemes for passing counterfeit securities, ... Congress in 1939 added the clause pertaining to "falsely made, forged, altered or counterfeited securities" as an amendment to the National Stolen Property Act.... Our prior decisions have recognized Congress' "general intent" and "broad purpose" to curb the type of trafficking in fraudulent securities that often depends for its success on the exploitation of interstate commerce. In *United States v. Sheridan*, 329 U.S. 379 (1946), we explained that Congress enacted the relevant clause of § 2314 in order to "com[e] to the aid of the states in detecting and punishing criminals whose offenses are complete under state law, but who utilize the channels of interstate commerce to make a successful getaway and thus make the state's detecting and punitive processes impotent." *Id.* at 384. This, we concluded, "was indeed one of the most effective ways of preventing further frauds." ...

We think that "title washing" operations are a perfect example of the "further frauds" that Congress sought to halt in enacting § 2314. As Moskal concedes, his title-washing scheme is a clear instance of fraud involving securities. And as the facts of this case demonstrate, title washes involve precisely the sort of fraudulent activities that are dispersed among several States in order to elude state detection.

Moskal draws a different conclusion from this legislative history. Seizing upon the references to counterfeit securities, petitioner finds no evidence that "the 1939 amendment had anything at all to do with odometer rollback schemes." ... We think petitioner misconceives the inquiry into legislative purpose by failing to recognize that Congress sought to attack a category of fraud. At the time that Congress amended the National Stolen Property Act, counterfeited securities no doubt constituted (and may still constitute) the most prevalent form of such interstate fraud. The fact remains, however, that Congress did not limit the statute's reach to "counterfeit securities" but instead chose the broader phrase "falsely made, forged altered *or* counterfeited securities," which was consistent with its purpose to reach a class of frauds that exploited interstate commerce.

This Court has never required that every permissible application of a statute be expressly referred to in its legislative history. Thus, for example, in *United States v. Turkette*, 452 U.S. 576 (1981), we recognized that "the major purpose" of the Racketeer Influenced and Corrupt Organizations statute was "to address the infiltration of legitimate business by organized crime." ... Yet, we concluded from the statute's broad language and legislative purpose that the key term "enterprise" must include not only legitimate businesses but also criminal associations....

Our precedents concerning § 2314 specifically reject constructions of the statute that limit it to *instances* of fraud encompassed by its language. For example, in *United States v. Sheridan, supra*, the defendant cashed checks at a Michigan bank, drawn on a Missouri account, with a forged signature. The Court found that such conduct was proscribed by § 2314. In reaching that conclusion, the Court noted Congress' primary objective of reaching counterfeiters of corporate securities but nonetheless found that the statute covered check forgeries "done by 'little fellows' who perhaps were not the primary aim of the congressional fire.... Whether or not Congress had in mind primarily such small scale transactions as Sheridan's," we held, "his operation was covered literally and we think purposively. Had this not been intended, appropriate exception could easily have been made." ...

In *McElroy v. United States*, [435 U.S. 642 (1982)], we similarly rejected a narrow construction of § 2314. The defendant had used blank checks that had been stolen in Ohio to buy a car and a boat in Pennsylvania. Defendant conceded that the checks he had thus misused constituted "forged securities" but maintained his innocence under the federal statute because the checks were not yet forged when they were transported across state boundaries. The Court acknowledged that "Congress could have written the statement to produce this result," ... but rejected such a reading as inconsistent with Congress' "broad purpose" since it would permit "a patient forger easily [to] evade the reach of federal law." ... Moreover, because we found the defendant's interpretation to be contradicted by Congress' intent in § 2314 and its predecessors, we also rejected the defendant's plea for lenity: "although 'criminal statutes are to be construed strictly ... this does not mean that every criminal statute must be given the narrowest possible meaning in complete disregard of the purpose of the legislature.'" ... We concluded that the defendant had failed to "raise significant questions of ambiguity, for the statutory language and legislative history ... indicate that Congress defined the term 'interstate commerce' more broadly than the petitioner contends." ...

Thus, in both *Sheridan* and *McElroy*, defendants who admittedly circulated fraudulent securities among several States sought to avoid liability by offering a reading of § 2314 that was narrower than the scope of its language and of Congress' intent, and in each instance we rejected the proffered interpretation. Moskal's interpretation in the present case rests on a similarly cramped reading of the statute's words, and we think it should likewise be rejected as inconsistent with Congress' general purpose to combat interstate fraud....

To summarize our conclusions as to the meaning of "falsely made" in § 2314, we find both in the plain meaning of those words and in the legislative purpose underlying them ample reason to apply the law to a fraudulent scheme for washing vehicle titles....

NOTES

1. In *Russell v. United States,* 471 U.S. 858 (1985), a unanimous Court held that a two-unit apartment building fell within 18 U.S.C. § 844(i) (1988), making it a federal crime maliciously to damage or destroy, or attempt to damage or destroy, by means of fire or an explosive "any building ... used ... in any activity affecting interstate or foreign commerce." ... "[T]he legislative history suggests that Congress at least intended to protect all business property, as well as some additional property that might not fit that description, but perhaps not every private home.... [T]he local rental of an apartment rental unit is merely an element of a much broader commercial market in rental properties. The congressional power to regulate the class of activities that constitute the rental market for real estate includes the power to regulate individual activity within that class....

2. In *United States v. Rodgers,* 466 U.S. 475 (1984), the defendant was charged with violating 18 U.S.C. § 1001 (1988), which makes it a crime knowingly and willfully to make a false statement "in any matter within the jurisdiction of any department or agency of the United States." Rodgers admittedly had lied in telling the FBI that his wife had been kidnaped when, in fact, as the FBI determined after investigation, she had left him voluntarily. He also lied in telling the Secret Service that his wife was part of a plot to assassinate the President; when Secret Service agents located the wife, she told them she had left home to get away from the defendant. The district court granted Rodgers' motion to dismiss the indictment because the investigations were not matters "within the jurisdiction" of the agencies, because "jurisdiction" imported the power to decide matters or issue binding administrative and regulative determinations. The Eighth Circuit affirmed.

The Supreme Court reversed. "Jurisdiction" in its usual meaning embraces the territorial sphere of the exercise of powers, or the sphere of authority. The statutory language pointed only to the power of a federal agency to exercise authority in given situations. Both the FBI and Secret Service possessed authority, the exercise of which had been affected adversely by Rodgers' knowing false information. The Court concluded its opinion:

> Finally, respondent urges that the rule of lenity in construing criminal statutes should be applied to § 1001.... The rule of lenity is of course a well-recognized principle of statutory construction, ... but the critical statutory language of § 1001 is not sufficiently ambiguous, in our view, to permit the rule to be controlling here....

Do you agree with the latter statement?

A. GENERAL RULES OF CONSTRUCTION

3. In *United States v. Kozminski,* 487 U.S. 931 (1988), the Court construed the term "involuntary servitude" in 18 U.S.C. §§ 241, 1584 (1988) not to embrace psychological compulsion, but rather to be limited to circumstances in which victims are forced to work for defendants by the use or threat of physical restraint or physical injury or by the use or threat of coercion through law or the legal process. "The purposes underlying the rule of lenity — to promote fair notice to those subject to the criminal laws, to minimize the risk of selective or arbitrary enforcement, and to maintain the proper balance between Congress, prosecutors, and courts — are certainly served by its application in this case." *Id.* at 952.

4. In *Dowling v. United States,* 473 U.S. 207 (1985), the government invoked the National Stolen Property Act, 18 U.S.C. § 2314 (1988), discussed in the principal case, to reach persons who had acquired copyrighted material (Elvis Presley recordings) without the consent of the copyright holders, and had issued and marketed bootleg recordings. Dowling was convicted of violating § 2314 and his conviction was upheld in the Ninth Circuit. The Supreme Court reversed. Justice Blackmun's majority opinion stated:

> Federal crimes, of course, "are solely creatures of statute." ... Accordingly, when assessing the reach of a federal criminal statute, we must pay close heed to language, legislative history, and purpose in order strictly to determine the scope of the conduct the enactment forbids. Due respect for the prerogatives of Congress in defining federal crimes prompts restraint in this area, where we typically find a "narrow interpretation" appropriate.... Chief Justice Marshall early observed:
>
> "The rule that penal laws are to be construed strictly, is perhaps not much less old than construction itself. It is founded on the tenderness of the law for the rights of individuals; and on the plain principle that the power of punishment is vested in the legislative, not in the judicial department. It is the legislature, not the Court, which is to define a crime, and ordain its punishment." *United States v. Wiltberger*, 5 Wheat. 76, 95 (1820).
>
> Thus, the Court has stressed repeatedly that "'when choice has to be made between two readings of what conduct Congress has made a crime, it is appropriate, before we choose the harsher alternative, to require that Congress should have spoken in language that is clear and definite.' "...

Id. at 213-14.

The Court took note of the fact that in 1974 Congress had addressed the criminal coverage of the Copyright Act by extending the misdemeanor penalties of the Law to cover sound recordings and by listing the infringing uses that would generate criminal liability. After the time of the activities of Dowling and his collaborators in 1980, Congress had increased the crime of bootlegging and piracy of records to a felony, based on legislative findings that the earlier misdemeanor penalties were insufficient to deter bootlegging. The Court concluded:

> No more than other legislation do criminal statutes take on straitjackets upon enactment. In sanctioning the use of § 2314 in the manner urged by

the Government here, the Courts of Appeals understandably have sought to utilize an existing and readily available tool to combat the increasingly serious problem of bootlegging, piracy, and copyright infringement. Nevertheless, the deliberation with which Congress over the last decade has addressed the problem of copyright infringement for profit, as well as the precision with which it has chosen to apply criminal penalties in this area, demonstrates anew the wisdom of leaving it to the legislature to define crime and prescribe penalties. Here, the language of § 2314 does not "plainly and unmistakably" cover petitioner Dowling's conduct, ... ; the purpose of the provision to fill gaps in state law enforcement does not couch the problem under attack; and the rationale employed to apply the statute to petitioner's conduct would support its extension to significant bodies of law that Congress gave no indication it intended to touch. In sum, Congress has not spoken with the requisite clarity. Invoking the "time-honored interpretive guideline" that "'ambiguity concerning the ambit of criminal statutes should be resolved in favor of lenity,'" ... we reverse the judgment of the Court of Appeals.

Id. at 228-29.

3. PARTICULAR RULES OF CONSTRUCTION

a. Ejusdem Generis Clauses

UNITED STATES v. TURKETTE

United States Supreme Court
452 U.S. 576 (1981)

[The issue addressed in the case was whether the term "enterprise" in the Racketeer Influenced and Corrupt Organizations Act (RICO), 18 U.S.C. § 1961(4) (1988), was broad enough to encompass both legitimate and illegitimate enterprises, or whether it was limited to the former. In the main body of its opinion, the Court held that both the language and legislative history of RICO supported the broader of the two interpretations.]

... The Court of Appeals, however, clearly departed from and limited the statutory language. It gave several reasons for doing so, none of which is adequate. First, it relied in part on the rule of *ejusdem generis,* an aid to statutory construction problems suggesting that where general words follow a specific enumeration of persons or things, the general words should be limited to persons or things similar to those specifically enumerated.... The Court of Appeals ruled that because each of the specific enterprises enumerated in § 1961 (4) is a "legitimate" one, the final catchall phrase — "any union or group of individuals associated in fact" — should also be limited to legitimate enterprises. There are at least two flaws in this reasoning. The rule of *ejusdem generis* is no more than an aid to construction and comes into play only when there is some uncertainty as to the meaning of a particular clause in a statute.... Considering the language and structure of § 1961(4), however, we not only perceive no uncertainty in the meaning to be attributed to the phrase, "any union or group of individuals associated in fact" but we are convinced for another reason that *ejusdem generis* is wholly inapplicable in this context.

A. GENERAL RULES OF CONSTRUCTION

Section 1961(4) describes two categories of associations that come within the purview of the "enterprise" definition. The first encompasses organizations such as corporations and partnerships, and other "legal entities." The second covers "any union or group of individuals associated in fact although not a legal entity." The Court of Appeals assumed that the second category was merely a more general description of the first. Having made that assumption, the court concluded that the more generalized description in the second category should be limited by the specific examples enumerated in the first. But that assumption is untenable. Each category describes a separate type of enterprise to be covered by the statute — those that are recognized as legal entities and those that are not. The latter is not a more general description of the former. The second category itself not containing any specific enumeration that is followed by a general description, *ejusdem generis* has no bearing on the meaning to be attributed to that part of § 1961(4).

NOTES

1. The statute construed in *Turkette* reads:

> (4) "[E]nterprise" includes any individual, partnership, corporation, association, or other legal entity, and any union or group of individuals associated in fact although not a legal entity[.]

18 U.S.C. § 1961(4) (1988).

2. *State v. Hooper,* 386 N.E.2d 1348, 1350 (Ohio 1979):

> R.C. 2907.12(A) prohibits the insertion of "any instrument, apparatus or other object." The statute lists three nouns — two specific and the third, general. The general term is immediately preceded by the word "other" — a word which refers to the two specific nouns in the list and suggests legislative intent to limit the scope of the general noun to those objects having the characteristics of those specific nouns .... In addition, R.C. 2907.12 is a criminal statute which must be strictly construed against the state (R.C. 2901.04[A]).
>
> Since R.C. 2907.12 lists specific terms followed by a catchall word which is linked to those specific terms by the word "other," and since the statute must be construed strictly, it appears to be subject to the doctrine of *ejusdem generis*....
>
> "Under the rule of *ejusdem generis,* where in a statute terms are first used which are confined to a particular class of objects having well-known and definite features and characteristics and then afterwards a term having perhaps a broader signification is conjoined, such latter term is, as indicative of legislative intent, to be considered as embracing only things of a similar character as those comprehended by preceding limited and confined terms."
>
> Once the doctrine of *ejusdem generis* is applied to Ohio's sexual-penetration statute, it becomes clear that a finger is not an "object" within the purview of R.C. 2907.12(A). In general, dictionaries define instruments and apparatuses as implements or tools, or groups of implements or tools. One characteristic common to instruments and apparatuses is that they

are inanimate. (The American Heritage Dictionary, for instance, defines an instrument as a "mechanical implement.") Since, under the doctrine of *ejusdem generis,* nothing may be construed to fall within the catchall term "object" unless it shares the characteristics of instruments and apparatuses, only inanimate objects fall within the purview of R.C. 2907.12(A). A finger is not inanimate. It is part of the human body. Therefore, a finger is not an object under R.C. 2907.12(A), and Ohio's sexual-penetration statute does not encompass digital penetration....

b. Statutes *"In Pari Materia"*

PEOPLE v. ROBBINS
New York Supreme Court, Appellate Division, Fourth Department
443 N.Y.S.2d 1016 (1981)

[Pamela Robbins and defendant Robert Robbins, her husband, were devout "born again" Christians; defendant Stephanski was a self-professed minister of a religious group which the Robbins couple joined. Stephanski preached that God would cure all illnesses of those who had sufficient faith. Pamela, who had suffered for many years from epilepsy and advanced diabetes and who on several occasions had lapsed into diabetic comas requiring immediate hospitalization, announced during a religious meeting that she had received a divine revelation and would cease taking all medications for her conditions. Robert Robbins and Stephanski agreed with her resolve. Thereafter, she had several diabetic seizures, became weak and ill, lapsed into a diabetic coma, and died. Robert Robbins was indicted for criminally negligent homicide, New York Penal Law § 125.10 (McKinney), based on his failure to summon medical assistance for Pamela, and Stephanski was charged as an accessory to that crime under § 20.00. The trial court granted the defendants' motion to dismiss the indictments; the appellate court confirmed.]

DENMAN, J.

It would be an unwarranted extension of the spousal duty of care to impose criminal liability for failure to summon medical aid for a competent adult spouse who has made a rational decision to eschew medical assistance. In New York such a rationale would be in direct conflict with the related rule that a competent adult has a right to determine whether or not to undergo medical treatment .... There is no basis under New York law for denying an adult the right to refuse medical care where such refusal does not pose a threat to the life or health of others.

In this State, however, there is no statute which prohibits a patient from declining necessary medical treatment or a doctor from honoring the patient's decision. To the extent that existing statutory and decisional law manifests the State's interest on this subject, they consistently support the right of the competent adult to make his own decision by imposing civil liability on those who perform medical treatment without consent, although the treatment may be beneficial or even necessary to preserve the patient's life .... (Public Health Law, §§ 2504, 2805-d; CPLR 4401-a). The current law identifies the patient's right to determine the course of his own medical treatment as paramount to what might otherwise be the doctor's obligation to provide needed medical care. A State which imposes civil liability on a doctor if he violates the patient's right cannot also hold him criminally responsible if he respects that right....

A construction of the law which would give Pamela Robbins the right to decline medical aid and would impose civil liability on anyone who subjected her to treatment without her consent, but at the same time would impose criminal sanctions on her husband if he respected that right of refusal, is not only paradoxical, but totally irrational and fundamentally unfair. Although the indictment against Robert Robbins alleges that he failed to seek medical aid "at a time when the said Pamela Robbins was unable to provide or seek the same for herself," it is defective for failure to state that Pamela Robbins was incapacitated or otherwise unable to make a rational decision and indeed the evidence does not support such claim. The record indicates, rather, that up until a very short time before her death, Pamela and Robert Robbins were praying, he was attempting to ease her discomfort, and was behaving in a very solicitous manner. The failure of medical assistance which resulted in her death was unquestionably the consequence of Pamela Robbins' conscious choice to rely on her faith and forgo medical interference.

With respect to Jerome Stephanski the indictment charged that he "caused the death of Pamela Robbins by counseling, urging, suggesting, and directing" that Pamela Robbins withdraw from insulin. The People concede, however, that "counselling, urging, etc." is not an act which would support liability for criminally negligent homicide and that his liability is merely derivative to that of Robert Robbins. Inasmuch as we find that the indictment against Robert Robbins was properly dismissed, there is no basis for imposing predicate liability on Stephanski.

NOTES

1. *State v. Cann,* 595 P.2d 912, 915 (Wash. 1979):

> If the statute embraces speech, the appellant argues further, it punishes as a class C felony the same conduct which is punished as a misdemeanor under RCW 9A.28.030, prohibiting criminal solicitation, and providing for punishment in the same manner as provided in RCW 9A.28.020. This coincidence, he urges, gives the prosecutor an option to charge either a misdemeanor or a felony for the same conduct, rendering the statute invalid.
>
> ....
>
> RCW 9A.28.030 is a general statute covering solicitation, while RCW 9A.88.080 is a special statute, punishing conduct designed to institute, aid, or facilitate prostitution, including solicitation for such purposes. The rule is that where general and special laws are concurrent, the special law applies to the subject matter contemplated by it to the exclusion of the general....
>
> As these cases hold, where a special statute punishes the same conduct which is punished under a general statute, the special statute applies and the accused can be charged only under that statute. Thus the prosecutor

has a basis for distinguishing between persons who can be charged under one or the other statute, and is not at liberty to charge under the general statute a person whose conduct brings his offense within the special statute. Under such circumstances, there is no denial of equal protection of the laws....

2. On rather similar facts to those in *Robbins,* the Pennsylvania Superior Court affirmed an involuntary manslaughter conviction of a spouse who refused to summon medical aid for her husband. *Commonwealth v. Konz,* 402 A.2d 692 (Pa. Super. 1979). The court discussed no state legislation or precedent covering an individual's power to determine not to seek or accept medical treatment for a known serious condition.

3. *See also City of Chicago v. Wilson, infra* p. 43, Note 2.

SECTION IV. CONSTITUTIONAL LIMITS ON PENAL LEGISLATION

A. THE *EX POST FACTO* CLAUSE

COLLINS v. YOUNGBLOOD

Supreme Court of the United States
497 U.S. 37 (1990)

[State legislation does not contravene the *Ex Post Facto* Clause if it] does not punish as a crime an act previously committed, which was innocent when done; nor make more burdensome the punishment for a crime, after its commission; nor deprive one charged with crime of any defense available according to law at the time when the act was committed....

NOTE

The Court overruled all of its precedents with language inconsistent with the *Youngblood* formulation. That appears to include the fourth branch of the dictum in the 1798 probate case of *Calder v. Bull,* 3 Dall. 386 (1798) (Chase, J.):

> 1st. Every law that makes an action done before the passing of the law, and which was *innocent* when done, criminal; and punishes such action. 2d. Every law that *aggravates a crime,* or makes it *greater* than it was when committed. 3d. Every law that *changes the punishment,* and inflicts a *greater punishment,* than the law annexed to the crime, when committed. 4th. Every law that alters the *legal* rules of *evidence,* and receives less, or different testimony, than the law required at the time of the commission of the offence, *in order to convict the offender.*

[Emphasis in original.]

A. THE *EX POST FACTO* CLAUSE

MILLER v. FLORIDA
Supreme Court of the United States
482 U.S. 423 (1987)

[When Miller committed his criminal acts, the Florida sentencing guidelines assigned a certain number of "primary offense points" to sexual offenses and based each sentence on points governing the highest statutory degree among concurrently-committed crimes. During the interim between the commission of the crimes and Miller's conviction for sexual battery with slight force, burglary with an assault and petit theft, the guidelines were amended to define "primary offense" as the crime which resulted in the most severe sentence range, rather than the offense with the highest statutory degree, and the primary offense points assigned to sexual offenses were increased by 20 percent. Because the sexual battery charge carried the most severe sentence range among the three categories of offenses committed by Miller, the prosecution asked that the new guidelines be applied, thus escalating Miller's presumptive sentence from $5^{1}/_{2}$ years to seven. The trial court imposed the latter over the defendant's objections resting on the *Ex Post Facto* Clauses.]

JUSTICE O'CONNOR delivered the opinion of the Court....

A law is retrospective if it "changes the legal consequences of acts completed before its effective date.... Application of the revised guidelines law in petitioner's case clearly satisfies this standard. Respondent nevertheless contends that the *ex post facto* concern for retrospective laws is not violated here because Florida's sentencing statute "on its face provides for continuous review and recommendation of changes to the guidelines." ... [R]espondent argues that it is sufficient that petitioner was given "fair warning" that he would be sentenced pursuant to the guidelines then in effect on his sentencing date.... Here, ... the statute in effect at the time petitioner acted did not warn him that Florida prescribed a $5^{1}/_{2}$- to 7-year presumptive sentence for that crime. Petitioner simply was warned of the obvious fact that the sentencing guidelines law — like any other law — was subject to revision. The constitutional prohibition against *ex post facto* laws cannot be avoided merely by adding to a law notice that it might be changed.

It is "axiomatic that for a law to be *ex post facto* it must be more onerous than the prior law." ... Looking only at the change in primary offense points, the revised guidelines law clearly disadvantages petitioner and similarly situated defendants.... [H]ere respondent has not been able to identify any feature of the revised guidelines law that could be considered ameliorative.

Respondent maintains that the change in guidelines laws is not disadvantageous because petitioner "cannot show definitively that he would have gotten a lesser sentence." ... This argument, however, is foreclosed by our decision in *Lindsey v. Washington*, 301 U.S. 397 (1937).... *Lindsey* establishes "that one is not barred from challenging a change in the penal code on *ex post facto* grounds simply because the sentence [one] received under the new law was not more onerous than that which [one] might have received under the old."
....

Petitioner plainly has been "substantially disadvantaged" by the change in sentencing laws. To impose a seven-year sentence under the old guidelines, the sentencing judge would have to depart from the presumptive sentence range of three and one-half to four and one-half years. As a result, the sentencing judge would have to provide clear and convincing reasons in writing for the departure, on facts proven beyond a reasonable doubt, and [that] determination would be reviewable on appeal. By contrast, because a seven-year sentence is within the presumptive range under the revised law, the trial judge did not have to provide any reasons, convincing or otherwise, for imposing the sentence, and [the] decision was unreviewable. Thus, ... [the guidelines revision] foreclosed [the petitioner's] ability to challenge the imposition of a sentence longer than his presumptive sentence under the old law. Petitioner therefore was "substantially disadvantaged" by the retrospective application of the guidelines to his crime.

....

The law at issue in this case, like the law in *Weaver*, "makes more onerous the punishment for crimes committed before its enactment." ... Accordingly, we find that Florida's revised guidelines law ... is void as applied to petitioner, whose crime occurred before the law's effective date....

NOTES

1. *See* MODEL PENAL CODE § 1.01, Appendix A.

2. In *Weaver v. Graham*, 450 U.S. 24 (1981), the Court applied the Ex Post Facto Clauses to an instance in which Florida had revised its "gain time" statute from a "5-10-15" formula, according to which prisoners without disciplinary infractions received five days credit monthly for the first two years of imprisonment, ten days for the third and fourth years, and 15 days thereafter, to a "3-6-9" formula. Weaver had been convicted and imprisoned before the statute was amended and sought habeas corpus relief against prospective application of the new formula to him, because he would serve about two more years in prison under his 15-year sentence than he would have done under the earlier statute. Justice Marshall's opinion stated:

> For prisoners who committed crimes before its enactment, § 944.275(1) substantially alters the consequences attached to a crime already completed, and therefore changes "the quantum of punishment." ... Therefore, it is a retrospective law which can be constitutionally applied to petitioner only if it is not to his detriment....
>
> Whether a retrospective state criminal statute ameliorates or worsens conditions imposed by its predecessor is a federal question.... The inquiry looks to the challenged provision, and not to any special circumstances that may mitigate its effect on the particular individual.
>
> ....
>
> Under this inquiry, we conclude § 944.275(1) is disadvantageous to petitioner and other similarly situated prisoners. On its face, the statute reduces the number of monthly gain-time credits available to an inmate who abides by prison rules and adequately performs his assigned tasks. By definition, this reduction in gain-time accumulation lengthens the period that someone in petitioner's position must spend in prison.... Here,

A. THE *EX POST FACTO* CLAUSE 29

petitioner is similarly disadvantaged by the reduced opportunity to shorten his time in prison simply through good conduct....

Respondent argues that our inquiry should not end at this point because [§ 944.275(1)] must be examined in conjunction with other provisions enacted with it.... Respondent claims that the net effect of all these provisions is increased availability of gain-time deductions. There can be no doubt that the legislature intended through these provisions to promote rehabilitation and to create incentives for specified productive conduct.... But none of these provisions for extra gain time compensates for the reduction of gain time available solely for good conduct. The fact remains that an inmate who performs satisfactory work and avoids disciplinary violations could obtain more gain time per month under the repealed provision ... than he could for the same conduct under the new provision.... To make up the difference, the inmate has to satisfy the extra conditions specified by the discretionary gain-time provisions. Even then, the award of the extra gain time is purely discretionary, contingent on both the wishes of the correctional authorities and special behavior by the inmate, such as saving a life or diligent performance in an academic program.... In contrast, under both the new and old statutes, an inmate is automatically entitled to the monthly gain time simply for avoiding disciplinary infractions and performing his assigned tasks.... Thus, the new provision constricts the inmate's opportunity to earn release, and thereby makes more onerous the punishment for crimes committed before its enactment. This result runs afoul of the prohibition against *ex post facto* laws.

PEOPLE v. ROSSI

Supreme Court of California
555 P.2d 1313 (1976)

TOBRINER, JUSTICE.

Defendant appeals from a judgment of conviction entered after a nonjury trial in which the court found her guilty of five counts charging violation of section 288a of the Penal Code. Defendant contends that her conviction should be reversed because, before the conviction became final, the Legislature amended section 288a of the Penal Code so as to legalize her conduct. We conclude that in light of the intervening amendment the conviction must be reversed.

The relevant facts are undisputed. Defendant, a part-time instructor in psychology at UCLA, is a married woman with two children. During the filming of several low-budget movies, she committed several sexual acts which constituted violations of former section 288a. After the trial court rendered its judgment of conviction, it suspended proceedings and placed defendant on probation for three years. Defendant has appealed.

At the time defendant committed the charged acts, Penal Code section 288a broadly proscribed all oral copulation, even between consenting adults.[2] On

---

[2] Prior to January 1, 1976, section 288a read in pertinent part: "Any person's participating in an act of copulating the mouth of one person with the sexual organ of another is punishable by

January 1, 1976, after the rendition of judgment but before its finality by the lapse of the period for appeal, amended section 288a took effect.... The People concede that the acts which defendant committed are not criminal under section 288a as amended.[3]

At common law, a statute mitigating punishment applied to acts committed before its effective date as long as no final judgment had been rendered.... Similarly, when a statute proscribing certain designated acts was repealed without a saving clause, all prosecutions for such act that had not been reduced to final judgment were barred.... Until a decade ago, however, a line of California cases ... had interpreted the general saving clause embodied in Government Code section 9608[4] and its predecessors as completely abrogating these common law rules.

In *In re Estrada* [408 P.2d 948 (Cal. 1965)], this court undertook an extensive review of this entire line of authority and concluded that the earlier cases had improperly extended the application of Government Code section 9608 far beyond its intended scope. In *Estrada* we observed that at common law when a statute was passed that *increased* the punishment for a crime, a defendant who committed the proscribed acts prior to the effective date of the new law could not be punished under the old law because it no longer existed, and he could not be punished under the new law because its attempted application would render it an ex post facto law....

Section 9608, we explained in *Estrada,* was enacted simply to authorize prosecutions under the former statute in order to avoid this technically absurd result by which a defendant could be prosecuted under no law, simply because the Legislature had decided to *increase* the punishment for his crime.... We concluded, however, that the provision was not intended to abrogate the well-established common law rule which, in the absence of clear legislative intent to the contrary, accorded a criminal defendant the benefit of a mitigation of punishment adopted before his criminal conviction became final. Thus, we held that "[w]here the amendatory statute mitigates punishment and there is no saving clause, the rule is that the amendment will operate retroactively so that the lighter punishment is imposed." ...

The *Estrada* court's conclusion as to the limited reach of Government Code section 9608 finds direct support in a line of United States Supreme Court decisions construing the comparable language of the general federal "saving" provision. (1 U.S.C., § 109.)[7] .... *Estrada* teaches that section 9608 must

---

imprisonment in the state prison for not exceeding 15 years, or by imprisonment in the county jail not to exceed one year ...."

[3] As amended, section 288a proscribes acts of oral copulation only when affected by force, committed while confined in a state prison, or committed with a minor....

[4] Section 9608 provides in full: "The termination or suspension (by whatsoever means effected) of any law creating a criminal offense does not constitute a bar to the indictment or information and punishment of an act already committed in violation of the law so terminated or suspended, unless the intention to bar such indictment or information and punishment is expressly declared by an applicable provision of law."

[7] The federal provision reads in relevant part: "The repeal of any statute shall not have the effect to release or extinguish any penalty, forfeiture, or liability incurred under such statute, unless the repealing Act shall so expressly provide, and such statute shall be treated as still remaining in force for the purpose of sustaining any proper action or prosecution for the enforcement of such penalty, forfeiture, or liability."

A. THE *EX POST FACTO* CLAUSE

properly be accorded a similar limited scope, and thus is inapplicable in the instant case.

The People contend, however, that the case at bar is distinguishable from *Estrada,* pointing out that in the instant case the intervening amendment has entirely eliminated any criminal sanction for defendant's acts while in *Estrada* the intervening amendment merely reduced the punishment for the conduct. Although it is true that *Estrada* and recent California cases applying *Estrada* have involved intervening enactments which merely reduced, rather than entirely eliminated, penal sanctions, ... numerous precedents demonstrate that the common law principles reiterated in *Estrada* apply a fortiori when criminal sanctions have been completely repealed before a criminal conviction becomes final....

In light of these numerous authorities, it is clear that the People can gain no comfort from the fact that the intervening amendment of section 288a *completely repealed* the provisions under which defendant was convicted instead of simply mitigating the punishment for defendant's conduct. Indeed, in *Estrada* itself we noted that "[i]t is the rule at common law and in this state that when the old law in effect when the act is committed is repealed, and there is no saving clause, all prosecutions not reduced to final judgment are barred." ...

As the United States Supreme Court has observed, it is "the universal common-law rule that when the legislature repeals a criminal statute or otherwise removes the State's condemnation from conduct that was formerly deemed criminal, this action requires the dismissal of a pending criminal proceeding charging such conduct. The rule applies to any such proceeding which, at the time of the supervening legislation, has not yet reached final disposition in the highest court authorized to review it." (*Bell v. Maryland* (1964) 378 U.S. 226, 230.) In the instant case, this "universal common-law rule" mandates the reversal of defendant's conviction.

NOTES

1. In *People v. Oliver,* 134 N.E.2d 197 (N.Y. 1956), the court first held that the accused should be punished under a new statute mitigating punishment (even though New York has a saving clause substantially similar to § 9608 of the California Government Code).

2. Legislation in some states allows prisoners whose crimes were committed under legislation, retained in force by virtue of a savings clause, to elect to be sentenced under replacement legislation. The sentencing court record must show that such prisoners have been informed before sentence is imposed of their right of election, either by court or defense counsel. *State ex rel. Arbogast v. Mohn,* 260 S.E.2d 820 (W. Va. 1979).

3. Treating prisoners convicted under a former statute, covered by a savings clause, more harshly than those later convicted under a less heavily sanctioned replacement statute does not deny equal protection of the laws. *Banton v. State,* 390 N.E.2d 687 (Ind. App. 1979).

4. In *Bradley v. United States,* 410 U.S. 605 (1973), defendant was convicted on May 6, 1971, of narcotics offenses and was given a minimum five-year

sentence, not subject to probation or parole, which was mandatory when the act was committed. Effective May 1, 1971, was a statute which liberalized the law, allowing probation and parole. D appeals, claiming he was entitled to the advantages of the 1971 law. Conviction affirmed. The Comprehensive Drug Abuse Prevention and Control Act of 1970 specifically provides in its saving clause that prosecutions "occurring prior to the effective date of [the Act] shall not be affected by the repeal or amendments...."

B. THE DUE PROCESS CLAUSE

1. VAGUENESS

EX PARTE GUERRERO
Court of Appeals of Texas, Corpus Christi
811 S.W.2d 726 (1991)

DORSEY, JUSTICE.

....

Appellant was indicted under the Controlled Substances Act for the offense of illegal investment.... The indictment, coincident with the elements of the offense set out by § 481.126, alleged that appellant did intentionally and knowingly finance and invest funds, to wit, United States currency, which she knew and believed were intended to further the commission of the offense of aggravated possession of marihuana. Aggravated possession is defined by statute as the possession of more than fifty pounds of marihuana....

In her application for writ of habeas corpus, appellant alleged, *inter alia*, that § 481.126 was void for vagueness because the terms "finance," "invest," and "funds" were not statutorily defined, thereby making the forbidden conduct ambiguous, vague, and indefinite. At the hearing, appellant did not establish the factual context of this prosecution. Instead, she argued generally that the indictment was void. The trial court disagreed and denied relief. In her sole point of error, appellant contends that the trial court erred by not affording relief.

When challenging the constitutionality of a statute, a defendant must show that in its operation the statute is unconstitutional to him in his situation; that it may be unconstitutional as to others is not sufficient.... Because appellant did not establish the factual context of the instant prosecution, we presume that her challenge essentially is that the statute is unconstitutional *per se*.

A statute which forbids or requires the doing of an act in terms so vague that persons of common intelligence must necessarily guess at its meaning and differ as to its application violates the first essential of due process of law.... As a fundamental proposition, all criminal laws must give notice to the populace of what activity is criminal.... In examining a criminal statute for vagueness, the first inquiry is whether the ordinary, law-abiding individual received sufficient information from the statute that his or her conduct risked violating a criminal law.... A second inquiry is whether the statute provided sufficient notice to law enforcement personnel to prevent arbitrary or discriminating enforcement. A vague law impermissibly delegates basic policy matters to policemen, judges, and juries for resolution on an *ad hoc* and subjective basis, with the attendant dangers of arbitrary and discriminating applications.

Appellant complains that the statute is unconstitutionally vague because the terms in question are not statutorily defined. We disagree. A statute is not unconstitutionally vague merely because the words or terms used are not statutorily or specifically defined.... The words challenged must be read in the context in which they are used, according to the rules of grammar and common usage....

The term "finance" is defined as "to supply money for" or "to have the financial management of." Webster's Twentieth New Century Dictionary (1979 ed.). The same dictionary defines the term "invest" as: 1. to clothe; array; adorn. 2. (a) to cover, surround, or envelop like, or as if with, a garment; as fog *invests* the city; (b) to endue. 3. to install in office with ceremony. 4. to furnish with power, privilege, or authority. 5. (a) to vest or settle (a power or right) in a person, legislative body, etc.; (b) to put on; to don. 6. to put (money) into business, real estate, stocks, bonds, etc., for the purpose of obtaining an income or profit. 7. in military usage, to hem in or besiege (a town, port, enemy salient, etc.).

The term "funds" is defined as "money" or "cash." Another dictionary supplies similar definitions of these terms.... Applying the definitions in the context of the Controlled Substances Act, § 481.126 quite clearly proscribes a person from supplying money which the person knows or believes is intended to further the possession of more than fifty pounds of marihuana. The statute clearly provides that the person must intend to further the commission of an unlawful act, *i.e.*, the possession of more than fifty pounds of marihuana. In the present case, the indictment specifically alleged that the "funds" were United States currency, which the defendant must have used to "invest" or "finance" the possession of more than fifty pounds of marihuana. "Invest" and "finance" are terms which can be readily understood by a person of common intelligence. We find that a person of common intelligence can determine with reasonable precision what conduct is prohibited. We also find that the statute provides sufficient notice to law enforcement personnel to prevent arbitrary or discriminatory enforcement.

It is clear that the legislature intended to punish persons who provide money to further the commission of possessing more than fifty pounds of marihuana....

We hold that, on its face, § 481.126 is not unconstitutionally vague. If for some reason, the statute is vague as it applies to appellant's conduct, appellant has not provided this Court with sufficient information *so to* hold. Accordingly, appellant's sole point of error is overruled. The judgment of the trial court is affirmed.

NOTES

1. For many years the leading case on "vagueness" was *Lanzetta v. New Jersey,* 306 U.S. 451 (1939), which held that "gang" and "known to be a member" violated due process because of their vagueness. "No man may be

required at peril of life, liberty or property to speculate as to the meaning of penal statutes."

2. A statute which prohibited the use of "opprobrious words or abusive language" was held unconstitutionally vague and overbroad by the United States Supreme Court in *Gooding v. Wilson,* 405 U.S. 518 (1972). The Court observed that even if defendant's conduct was clearly within the language of the statute, and even if a narrowly drawn statute embracing that conduct might be valid, he or she may raise the issues of vagueness and overbreadth as applied to others. The Court rejected the contention that state appellate decisions had clarified the statute and limited its application only to "fighting words," since an examination of those decisions did not support this contention.

3. In *Colten v. Kentucky,* 407 U.S. 104 (1972), the Court upheld a disorderly conduct statute which prohibited a person from intentionally causing public inconvenience, annoyance and alarm which included congregating in public after refusing to obey a lawful police order to disperse. The state court had interpreted the statute to require that the intent to cause inconvenience, annoyance and alarm must be the "dominant" intent and could be inferred where defendant did not purport to exercise a constitutional right, or even where a constitutional right was involved if the exercise of the right is insignificant compared to the inconvenience, annoyance or alarm which is caused. Both the Supreme Court and the state court found that a person who wanted to obey the statute would have no difficulty understanding it. The Court, in characterizing the vagueness doctrine as embracing the notion of fairness, cautioned that constitutional considerations should not be used to increase the practical difficulties in drafting statutes in language general enough to include a range of conduct yet specific enough to provide fair warning.

4. In *People in Interest of C.M.,* 630 P.2d 593 (Colo. 1981), the Colorado Supreme Court declared unconstitutional a state law making it a petty offense to "loiter in or about a school building or grounds, not having any reason or relationship involving custody of, or responsibility for, a pupil or any other specific, legitimate reason for being there, and not having written permission from a school administrator":

> In *Papachristou v. City of Jacksonville,* 405 U.S. 156 (1972), the United States Supreme Court struck down a vagrancy ordinance that included within its proscription various forms of loitering because the ordinance failed to furnish adequate notice of the proscribed conduct and invited arbitrary enforcement. The Court stressed initially the broad sweep of the ordinance's prohibitions. The inclusion of such conduct as "walking or strolling around from place to place without any lawful object or purpose" makes criminal those activities "which by modern standards are normally innocent" and "historically [are] part of the amenities of life as we have known them." 405 U.S. at 163-64. Secondly, the Court pointed up that "[d]efiniteness is designedly avoided so as to allow the net to be cast at large, to enable men to be caught who are vaguely undesirable in the eyes of police and prosecution," although not engaging in overt criminal conduct. *Id.*

B. THE DUE PROCESS CLAUSE

The People argue that section 18-9-112(2)(d) is susceptible to a construction that restricts loitering to an identifiable area in the interest of maintaining a safe and proper school environment and such construction, in contrast to the ordinance struck down in *Papachristou,* does provide adequate notice of the proscribed conduct to persons of ordinary intelligence and eliminates the danger of selective and arbitrary enforcement. We find this argument legally unsound for several reasons.

First, contrary to the People's reading of the statute, section 18-9-112(2)(d) does not restrict loitering to a readily identifiable area, such as "*in* the school building" or "*on* the school grounds." The use of the preposition "about" in relation to the situs of the loitering illustrates the broad sweep of the statutory proscription. The term "about the school building or grounds" clearly would include a geographical area immediately surrounding these points of reference. However, "about" in this statutory context also is so general in meaning as arguably to encompass any place in the *vicinity* or *neighborhood* of the school building or grounds. *See* WEBSTER'S THIRD NEW INTERNATIONAL DICTIONARY (1961). It is not uncommon for urban school grounds to cover an area that is equivalent in size to a city block. How close to the bounds of the school grounds one must be to be considered "about" those grounds cannot be answered with any degree of certainty.

Second, the People's argument erroneously presupposes that any uncertainty in the statutory proscription is dispelled by the nexus between the proscribed conduct and the maintenance of a safe and proper school environment. Assuming *arguendo* that "loitering or strolling on public property which obstructs the orderly government process ... might be within the scope of [legitimate] legislative prohibition," ... section 18-9-112(2)(d) does not purport to prohibit loitering only when it is likely to have an adverse effect on the educational process. The statute neither requires a demonstrable causality between the conduct and the impairment of school functions nor does it even require that the conduct occur while school is in session. For this court to read such requirements into the statute would implicate us in wholesale legislative revision, a matter within the exclusive province of the General Assembly....

Additional uncertainties exist in the statutory terminology, one of which is the language "not having ... any other specific, legitimate reason for being there." Customary uses of "legitimate" include: genuine; accordant with law or with established legal requirements; conforming to recognized principles or accepted rules and standards; and reasonable. WEBSTER'S THIRD NEW INTERNATIONAL DICTIONARY (1961). The inclusion of such an open-ended element as a qualification of criminal conduct well might be "a trap for innocent acts," *Papachristou v. City of Jacksonville, supra,* 405 U.S. at 164, and only serves to compound the already existing uncertainty in the statutory definition of loitering.

There is also ambiguity with respect to what elements might be essential to criminal liability. In addition to (1) loitering, (2) in or about a school building or grounds, and (3)(a) without any reason or relationship involving custody of, or responsibility for, a pupil, or (3)(b) without any other specific, legitimate reason for being there, this statute requires that an offender not have "written permission from a school administrator." Arguably, the person who remains in or about the school building or grounds for what he or she reasonably believes is a specific, legitimate reason need not obtain written permission from the school administrator to avoid criminal liability. Under this construction, only those in or about the school building or grounds under no reasonable claim of specific, legitimate reason would be required to have written permission to be there. On the other hand, one might contend that unless a person has written permission from the school administrator, he or she has no "specific, legitimate reason for being there." Under this construction, if that person's presence was unrelated to custody of or responsibility for a pupil, he or she would be subject to prosecution under the statute.

One need not resort to bizarre or extreme examples to underscore the infirmity in statutory proscription underlying section 18-9-112(2)(d). The statute prohibits lingering, delaying, wandering or remaining in or about school grounds. A parent "lingering" in the playground facilities of the school with his or her pre-school infant, a teenager "delaying" on the grounds in order to walk home with a student friend who shortly will leave the school building, an adult "wandering" near the school grounds for an evening walk, a youth "remaining" on the school grounds during a weekend afternoon to make use of an outdoor basketball court — none of these persons can claim with reasonable assurance that their conduct is not included within the broad sweep of the statutory prohibition. Statutory language which strikes such an amorphous and uncertain line of demarcation between criminal conduct and what the ordinary person would consider normal and legitimate behavior cannot survive a constitutional challenge under the Due Process Clause of the federal and state constitutions. *U.S.Const.* Amend. XIV; *Colo.Const.* Art. II, Sec. 25.

The absence of objective criteria in the statutory proscription points up the serious potential for arbitrary and discriminatory enforcement. A standardless delegation of discretion in enforcement impinges on basic notions of fairness at the root of the void-for-vagueness doctrine.... "'It would certainly be dangerous if the legislature could set a net large enough to catch all possible offenders, and leave it to the courts to step inside and say who could be rightfully detained, and who should be set at large.'" *Papachristou v. City of Jacksonville, supra,* 405 U.S. at 165....

5. *Grayned v. City of Rockford,* 408 U.S. 104 (1972), sustained the conviction of one participating in a demonstration in front of a high school. The ordinance prohibited noises or diversions disturbing or tending to disturb the peace or good order of a school or a class within it, on "public or private grounds adjacent" to a school building. The Court thought that the word "adjacent" was not impermissibly vague and that the ordinance did not allow persons to be punished because of what they had said during disruptive activities.

6. In *Warren v. State,* 572 So. 2d 1376 (Fla. 1991), the court found the term "ill fame" to be impermissibly vague. The term might have been understand-

able when the legislature first adopted the statute in 1888 prohibiting the keeping of houses of ill fame resorted to for purposes of prostitution or lewdness. Because statutory language must provide a definite warning of the conduct required or prohibited by the statute, "measured by common understanding and practice," a statute must be written "in language which is relevant to today's society." The court thought the words "prostitution" and "lewdness" met that standard, but the term "ill fame" did not, at least in the present era.

7. At times courts will create legislatively unspecified limitations on statutes to avoid the vagueness doctrine. *See, e.g., State v. Degrenier*, 424 A.2d 412 (N.H. 1980) (statute penalizing intercourse with mentally defective woman not one's spouse, with knowledge or reason to know the woman is mentally defective, construed to cover only those whose mental deficiency makes them incapable legally of consenting).

2. OVERBREADTH

CITY OF TACOMA v. LUVENE

Supreme Court of Washington
827 P.2d 1374 (1992)

UTTER, JUSTICE.

[Luvene launched a facial attack on a city ordinance defining and punishing "drug loitering." The ordinance defined the offense thus:

> It is unlawful for any person to loiter in or near any thoroughfare, place open to the public, or near any public or private place in a manner and under circumstances manifesting the purpose to engage in drug-related activity contrary to any of the provisions [of the state controlled substances act].

The ordinance listed ten circumstances that might be considered by a trier in determining whether a purpose to engage in illegal drug-related activity has been manifested:

> ... 1. Such person is a known unlawful drug user, possessor, or seller [based on an arresting officer's knowledge of prior controlled substances convictions, or observable physical characteristics of drug intoxication or usage like "needle tracks," or possession of drug paraphernalia]; 2. Such person is currently subject to an order prohibiting his/her presence in a high drug activity geographic area; 3. Such person behaves in such a manner as to raise a reasonable suspicion that he or she is about to engage in or is then engaged in an unlawful drug-related activity, including by way of example only, such person acting as a 'lookout'; 4. Such person is physically identified by the officer as a member of a 'gang,' or association which has as its purpose illegal drug activity; 5. Such person transfers small objects or packages for currency in a furtive fashion; 6. Such person takes flight upon the appearance of a police officer; 7. Such person manifestly endeavors to conceal himself or herself or any object which could reasonably be involved in an unlawful drug-related activity; 8. The area involved is by public repute known to be an area of unlawful

drug use and trafficking; 9. The premises involved are known to have been reported to law enforcement as a place suspected of drug activity pursuant to [a cited state statute]; 10. Any vehicle involved is registered to a known unlawful drug user, possessor, or seller, or a person for whom there is an outstanding warrant for a crime involving drug-related activity.

At around 8:00 p.m. on a late August evening, a police officer, from a distance of about 30 feet, maintained surveillance near a corner concerning which a number of complaints and telephone calls had been received from citizens stating that it was a place where drug deals were being made with cruising motorists. The officer watched three people, one of whom was Luvene, standing on a corner, pacing two to three steps in various directions, and looking around continuously. The men tried to flag down several cars. Luvene stopped a car with a wave of his arm, summoned a companion, ran to the car, and waved again to the companion to approach. The latter reached into his pocket and pulled out what appeared to be ten or more pieces of rock cocaine. The companion entered the passenger seat of the car, gave the driver what appeared to be some of the cocaine, and received paper money in return; Luvene maintained an active lookout throughout the transaction. A short time later, the officer saw Luvene walking along the sidewalk with someone who appeared to be smoking a crack pipe.

A half-hour or so later in the evening, another car arrived at the intersection; the driver sounded its horn, and the occupants conversed with a number of persons including Luvene. The driver then made several exchanges with a number of persons. At that time police officers approached and arrested five persons, including Luvene, for drug loitering. A search of one of Luvene's companions turned up a glass-tube pipe used to smoke crack cocaine. The car contained a plastic bag of white powder and two additional glass-tube pipes. No drugs or drug paraphernalia were found on Luvene. The municipal court rejected Luvene's motion to dismiss the charges of drug loitering on grounds of overbreadth and vagueness, and Luvene was convicted.]

....

[The Tacoma ordinance] is the most recent addition to a class of local ordinances that use loitering to help define a criminal offense.... While we have not yet had to consider the constitutionality of a drug loitering ordinance, other jurisdictions have considered the vagueness and overbreadth problems of drug loitering ordinances.... In the past we have been called upon to determine the constitutionality of prostitution loitering measures...

In the context of vagueness challenges, this court has stressed the importance of the linguistic and structural similarity between the statutory language at issue and the statutory language contained in earlier cases in determining the appropriate precedents.... This consideration applies with equal force to a challenge that a statute or ordinance is too broad.

The prostitution loitering ordinance upheld in *Seattle v. Slack* [784 P.2d 494 (Wash. 1989)] stated: A person is guilty of prostitution loitering if he or she remains in a public place and intentionally solicits, induces, entices, or procures another to commit prostitution.... The prostitution loitering ordinance

B. THE DUE PROCESS CLAUSE

we upheld in *Slack,* however, identified remaining in public while soliciting, inducing, enticing, or procuring another person to commit prostitution as the criminal conduct prohibited by the ordinance.... It also identified a mens rea component, intent.... Had the Tacoma ordinance utilized wording and structure similar to that of the prostitution loitering ordinance we upheld in *Slack,* this case would not present such difficult questions.

The language and structure of the Tacoma drug loitering ordinance also depart from the language and structure of the prostitution loitering ordinance upheld in *Seattle v. Jones* [488 P.2d 750 (Wash. 1971)]. In *Jones,* the prostitution ordinance that preceded the *Slack* prostitution loitering ordinance was attacked as vague. The ordinance at issue in *Jones* provided: It is unlawful for anyone: ... [t]o loiter in or near any thoroughfare or place open to the public in a manner and under circumstances manifesting the purpose of inducing, enticing, soliciting or procuring another to commit an act of prostitution.... The ordinance then went on to identify "circumstances which may be considered in determining whether such purpose is manifested."

Luvene correctly observes that the ordinance at issue here does not have similar language or structure as the Seattle prostitution ordinance at issue in *Slack.* Although the two Seattle prostitution loitering ordinances differ from each other, they actually referred to behavior commonly identified with prostitution. While the language and structure of the Tacoma drug loitering ordinance more closely resemble that of the prostitution loitering ordinance we upheld in *Jones,* the Tacoma ordinance, unlike any other drug loitering-based ordinance we have upheld, does not on its face refer to the class of actions commonly identified as illegal drug-related conduct.

This linguistic and structural difference lies at the heart of the constitutional challenges in this case. The gravamen of Luvene's vagueness and overbreadth challenges is that the ordinance identifies the *actus reus* of the prohibited criminal conduct in terms of constitutionally protected conduct. Thus, he argues, the ordinance is impermissibly vague because it fails to identify some overt act in addition to mere loitering, an act which, by itself, cannot be constitutionally punished. As a result, he argues, the ordinance is too indefinite to apprise citizens of the prohibited conduct and to prevent arbitrary and discriminatory law enforcement. He also argues that the ordinance is overbroad because criminal liability for drug loitering is indistinguishable from and in fact defined in terms of constitutionally protected conduct. He concludes that the ordinance thus chills a substantial amount of constitutionally protected conduct....

Overbreadth analysis measures how enactments that prohibit conduct fit within the universe of constitutionally protected conduct. *See generally* Fallon, *Making Sense of Overbreadth,* 100 YALE L.J. 853 (1990-1991). A law is overbroad if it sweeps within its prohibitions constitutionally protected free speech activities... The first task is to determine whether the enactment reaches a substantial amount of constitutionally protected conduct... Criminal statutes require particular scrutiny and may be facially invalid if they "'make unlawful a substantial amount of constitutionally protected conduct ... even if they also have legitimate application.'" ... An ordinance which regulates behavior, and not pure speech, "'will not be overturned unless the overbreadth "is both real and substantial in relation to the ordinance's plainly legitimate sweep."'''' ... A statute or ordinance will be overturned only if the court is unable to place a sufficiently limiting construction on a standardless sweep of legislation....

[The court determined that Luvene had standing to attack the ordinance because it chilled or burdened constitutionally protected conduct.] ... We do not require others to risk criminal sanction or forgo constitutionally protected conduct. The ordinance can be read as prohibiting loitering done without the intent to commit an illegal act. Moreover, the act of mere loitering is an inherent component of political canvassing and other non-political forms of expressive association. Also unclear from the face of the ordinance is whether or not any conduct typically associated with the buying, selling or use of illegal drugs done in addition to mere loitering is required for the police to arrest someone for drug loitering.

Given the procedural posture of petitioner's overbreadth challenge, his overbreadth claim raises pure questions of law. As commentators have noted, when a person convicted under a criminal statute or ordinance challenges the law as overbroad, he or she essentially asserts that his or her conviction rests on an unconstitutional law.... In this context, no prudential purpose is served by refusing to entertain a claim that an ordinance is overbroad. When First Amendment and other constitutionally protected forms of conduct are chilled or burdened, there is likely to be no other better plaintiff than one who has been convicted under an allegedly unconstitutional measure....

Petitioner's overbreadth claim raises two important questions. First, does the ordinance prohibit constitutionally protected activity? Second, if it does prohibit constitutionally protected conduct, does it prohibit a "real and substantial" amount of protected conduct? If possible, an enactment must be interpreted in a manner which upholds its constitutionality....

Luvene argues that two aspects of the ordinance create overbreadth problems: lack of a clearly identified mens rea component and no requirement that the police observe action in addition to loitering in order for a person to be arrested for drug loitering. With regard to the need for an identified mens rea element, petitioner argues that on the face of the ordinance, all that is required for arrest is that the police feel that one is loitering "in a manner and under circumstances manifesting the purpose" to engage in violations of the various controlled substance statutes. With regard to the action in addition to loitering, petitioner argues that while the circumstances section of the ordinance sets out 10 categories of factors that may be considered in determining if the purpose is manifested, only 4 of these circumstances identify any overt act in addition to loitering. These two problems, petitioner concludes, impermissibly extend the reach of the ordinance into the constitutionally protected area of expressive association and freedom of movement.

As a general matter, an ordinance that prohibits loitering may survive an overbreadth challenge if it requires the specific intent to engage in an illicit act.... The Tacoma drug loitering ordinance does contain a mens rea component, specifically the "purpose" to engage in drug-related activity. In *Seattle v. Jones, supra,* we construed the word "purpose" in a similar context to require the mental state of intent.... Because of the similar language and context that the Tacoma drug loitering ordinance shares with the *Jones* prostitution loitering ordinance, it is appropriate to transpose that construction of "purpose" from *Jones* to the case now at hand.

Therefore, as construed, we reject the interpretation of the ordinance to prohibit conduct that only appears to be drug related, regardless of the person's actual intent. To be constitutional the ordinance must prohibit loitering while possessing the intent to engage in unlawful drug activity. If the police observe identifiable, articulable conduct in addition to mere loitering that is consistent with the intent to engage in unlawful drug activity, the ordinance is constitutionally valid....

Our interpretation of the Tacoma drug loitering ordinance's mens rea component places an overt act requirement in the ordinance and meets the petitioner's criticisms. The use of the word "manifesting" in the ordinance indicates that some overt conduct performed while loitering is necessary to determine if a person has the intent to engage in illegal drug-related activity. While we do not feel that this deletion [in the Tacoma ordinance of a series of verbs ("solicit, induce, entice, and procure") and pronoun "another" in the prostitution loitering ordinance upheld in *Slack*] expands the universe that is narrowed by the specific intent requirement, the paring down of the language approved in *Slack* and *Jones* concerns us. Tacoma assumes that subtracting the series of specific acts and "another" from the language of the ordinance in *Jones* makes no difference to the overbreadth analysis. While the potential overbreadth of the ordinance is diminished by the intent requirement, it is critical that the culpable mental state coexist with identifiable, articulable conduct reasonably consistent with the intent to buy, sell, or use illegal drugs. Otherwise, the ordinance does not distinguish between the innocent intent to merely loiter and the culpable intent to engage in unlawful drug-related activity.

As interpreted and limited, the Tacoma drug loitering ordinance is not unconstitutionally overbroad. By requiring specific intent and overt acts, the ordinance does not then reach into the arena of constitutionally protected First Amendment conduct. It prohibits soliciting, enticing, inducing, or procuring another to exchange, buy, sell, or use illegal drugs or drug paraphernalia....

[The court then rejected Luvene's vagueness attack on the ordinance. It found sufficient evidence in the trial court record to support a finding beyond a reasonable doubt of Luvene's intent to violate the controlled substances act.] Because petitioner's behavior is consistent with the acts that precede the exchange, sale, and use of illegal drugs and drug paraphernalia by members of criminal street gangs, we find there is sufficient evidence to sustain his conviction for drug loitering....

NOTES

1. In *United States v. Kozminski,* 487 U.S. 931 (1988), the Court considered whether the term "involuntary servitude" in the federal statute prohibiting sale of persons into involuntary servitude, 18 U.S.C. § 1584 (1988), includes general psychological coercion. The Kozminskis had used various coercive

measures including denial of pay, subjection to substandard living conditions, and isolation from others to cause two mentally-impaired adults to believe they had no alternative but to work on the Kozminski farm. In part of the Court's opinion, Justice O'Connor wrote:

> The Government has argued that we should adopt a broad construction of "involuntary servitude," which would prohibit the compulsion of services by any means that, from the victim's point of view, either leaves the victim with no tolerable alternative but to serve the defendant or deprives the victim of the power of choice. Under this interpretation, involuntary servitude would include compulsion through psychological coercion as well as almost any other type of speech or conduct intentionally employed to persuade a reluctant person to work.
>
> This interpretation would appear to criminalize a broad range of day-to-day activity. For example, the Government conceded at oral argument that, under its interpretation, § 241 [the federal conspiracy provision] and § 1584 could be used to punish a parent who coerced an adult son or daughter into working in the family business by threatening withdrawal of affection.... It has also been suggested that the Government's construction would cover a political leader who uses charisma to induce others to work without pay or a religious leader who obtains personal services by means of religious indoctrination.... As these hypotheticals suggest, the Government's interpretation would delegate to prosecutors and juries the inherently legislative task of determining what type of coercive activities are so morally reprehensible that they should be punished as crimes. It would also subject individuals to the risk of arbitrary or discriminatory prosecution and conviction.
>
> Moreover, as the Government would interpret the statutes, the type of coercion prohibited would depend entirely upon the victim's state of mind. Under such a view, the statutes would provide almost no objective indication of the conduct or condition they prohibit, and thus would fail to provide fair notice to ordinary people who are required to conform their conduct to the law. The Government argues that any such difficulties are eliminated by a requirement that the defendant harbor a specific intent to hold the victim in involuntary servitude. But in light of the Government's failure to give any objective content to its construction of the phrase "involuntary servitude," this specific intent requirement amounts to little more than an assurance that the defendant sought to do "an unknowable something." ...
>
> In short, we agree with Judge Friendly's observation that "[t]he most ardent believer in civil rights legislation might not think that cause would be advanced by permitting the awful machinery of the criminal law to be brought into play whenever an employee asserts that his will to quit has been subdued by a threat which seriously affects his future welfare but as to which he still has a choice, however painful." *United States v. Schackney*, 333 F.2d, at 487.

Accordingly, we conclude that Congress did not intend § 1584 to encompass the broad and undefined concept of involuntary servitude urged upon us by the Government....

487 U.S. at 949-50.

2. In *City of Chicago v. Wilson,* 389 N.E.2d 522 (Ill. 1978), the defendants, male transvestites, were arrested shortly after they had left a restaurant where they had eaten breakfast. Both were wearing women's wigs and clothing. At the police station they were photographed in stages of undress, showing that they were wearing brassieres and garter belts but that their genitalia were male. They were charged under a city ordinance punishing anyone appearing in a public place in dress not belonging to his or her sex, with intent to conceal his or her sex. At trial, both defendants testified that at the time of their arrests they were transsexuals undergoing psychiatric therapy in preparation for a sex-reassignment operation and were required to wear female clothing and adopt a female lifestyle. One defendant stated the police had been informed about these facts at the time of arrest. Both defendants said they had been transsexuals for their entire lives and thought of themselves as female. They were convicted, and appealed on grounds of denial of equal protection, vagueness, and overbreadth of legislative coverage. The court sustained the defendants' attack on the statute as unconstitutionally overbroad:

> Through the enactment of section 17(1)(d) of the Vital Records Act (Ill.Rev.Stat.1977, ch. 111½, par. 73-17(1)(d)), which authorizes the issuance of a new certificate of birth following sex-reassignment surgery, the legislature has implicitly recognized the necessity and validity of such surgery. It would be inconsistent to permit sex-reassignment surgery yet, at the same time, impede the necessary therapy in preparation for such surgery. Individuals contemplating such surgery should, in consultation with their doctors, be entitled to pursue the therapy necessary to insure the correctness of their decision.
>
> Inasmuch as the city has offered no evidence to substantiate its reasons for infringing on the defendants' choice of dress under the circumstances of this case, we do not find the ordinance invalid on its face; however, we do find that section 192-8 as applied to the defendants is an unconstitutional infringement of their liberty interest.

C. INDIVIDUAL RIGHTS BASED CHALLENGES

1. THE FIRST AMENDMENT

UNITED STATES v. EICHMAN
Supreme Court of the United States
496 U.S. 310 (1990)

JUSTICE BRENNAN delivered the opinion of the Court.

....

Last Term in [*Texas v. Johnson,* 491 U.S. 397 (1989)], we held that a Texas statute criminalizing the desecration of venerated objects, included the United States flag, was unconstitutional as applied to an individual who had set such a flag on fire during a political demonstration.... We first held that Johnson's flag burning was "conduct 'sufficiently imbued with elements of communication' to implicate the First Amendment.... We next considered and rejected the State's contention that, under *United States v. O'Brien,* 391 U.S. 367 (1968), we ought to apply the deferential standard with which we have reviewed Government regulations of conduct containing both speech and non-speech elements where "the governmental interest is unrelated to the suppression of free expression." ... We reasoned that the State's asserted interest "in preserving the flag as a symbol of nationhood and national unity," was an interest "related 'to the suppression of free expression' within the meaning of *O'Brien"* because the State's concern with protecting the flag's symbolic meaning is implicated "only when a person's treatment of the flag communicates some message." ... We therefore subjected the statute to "'the the most exacting scrutiny,'" ... , and we concluded that the State's asserted interests could not justify the infringement on the demonstrator's First Amendment rights.

After our decision in *Johnson,* Congress passed the Flag Protection Act of 1989. The Act provides in relevant part:

"(a)(1) Whoever knowingly mutilates, defaces, physically defiles, burns, maintains on the floor or ground, or tramples upon any flag of the United States shall be fined under this title or imprisoned for not more than one year, or both. (2) This subsection does not prohibit any conduct consisting of the disposal of a flag when it has become worn or soiled.

(b) As used in this section, the term 'flag of the United States' means any flag of the United States, or any part thereof, made of any substance, of any size, in a form that is commonly displayed." 18 U.S.C.A. § 700 [West Supp. 1990 ed.].

The Government concedes in this case, as it must, that appellees' flag burning constituted expressive conduct, ... but invites us to reconsider our rejection in *Johnson* of the claim that flag burning as a mode of expression, like obscenity or "fighting words," does not enjoy the full protection of the First Amendment.... This we decline to do. The only remaining question is whether the Flag Protection Act is sufficiently distinct from the Texas statute that it may constitutionally be applied to proscribe appellees' expressive conduct.

The Government contends that the Flag Protection Act is constitutional because, unlike the statute addressed in *Johnson,* the Act does not target expressive conduct on the basis of the content of its message. The Government asserts an *interest* in "protect[ing] the physical integrity of the flag under all circumstances" in order to safeguard the flag's identity "'as the unique and unalloyed symbol of the Nation.'" ...

Although the Flag Protection Act contains no explicit content-based limitation on the scope of prohibited conduct, it is nevertheless clear that the Government's asserted *interest* is "related 'to the suppression of free expression,'" ... and concerned with the content of such expression. The Government's interest in protecting the "physical integrity" of a privately owned flag rests upon a perceived need to preserve the flag's status as a symbol of our Nation and certain national ideals. But the mere destruction or disfigurement of a particular physical manifestation of the symbol, without more, does not diminish or otherwise affect the symbol itself in any way. For example, the secret destruction of a flag in one's own basement would not threaten the flag's recognized meaning. Rather, the Government's desire to preserve the flag as a symbol for certain national ideals is implicated "only when a person's treatment of the flag communicates [a] message" to others that is inconsistent with those ideals....

Moreover, the precise language of the Act's prohibitions confirms Congress' interest in the communicative impact of flag destruction. The Act criminalizes the conduct of anyone who "knowingly mutilates, defaces, physically defiles, burns, maintains on the floor or ground, or tramples upon any flag." 18 U.S.C.A. § 700(a)(1) [West Supp. 1990 ed.]. Each of the specified terms — with the possible exception of "burns" — unmistakably connotes disrespectful treatment of the flag and suggests a focus on those acts likely to damage the flag's symbolic value. And the explicit exemption in § 700(a)(2) for disposal of "worn or soiled" flags protects certain acts traditionally associated with patriotic respect for the flag.

As we explained in *Johnson*, ... : "[I]f we were to hold that a State may forbid flag-burning wherever it is likely to endanger the flag's symbolic role, but allow it wherever burning a flag promotes that role — as where, for example, a person ceremoniously burns a dirty flag — we would be ... permitting a State to 'prescribe what shall be orthodox' by saying that one may burn the flag to convey one's attitude toward it and its referents only if one does not endanger the flag's representation of nationhood and national unity." Although Congress cast the Flag Protection Act of 1989 in somewhat broader terms than the Texas statute at issue in *Johnson,* the Act still suffers from the same fundamental flaw: It suppresses expression out of concern for its likely communicative impact. Despite the Act's wider scope, its restriction on expression cannot be "'justified without reference to the content of the regulated speech.'" ... The Act therefore must be subjected to "the most exacting scrutiny," ... and for the reasons stated in *Johnson,* ... the Government's interest cannot justify its infringement on First Amendment rights. We decline the Government's invitation to reassess this conclusion in light of Congress' recent recognition of a purported "national consensus" favoring a prohibition on flag burning.... Even assuming such a consensus exists, any suggestion that the Government's interest in suppressing speech becomes more weighty as popular opposition to that speech grows is foreign to the First Amendment.

... Government may create national symbols, promote them, and encourage their respectful treatment. But the Flag Protection Act of 1989 goes well beyond this by criminally proscribing expressive conduct because of its likely communicative impact.

We are aware that desecration of the flag is deeply offensive to many. But the same might be said, for example, of virulent ethnic and religious epithets, ... , vulgar repudiations of the draft, ... , and scurrilous caricatures, ... "If there is a bedrock principle underlying the First Amendment, it is that the Government may not prohibit the expression of an idea simply because society finds the idea itself offensive or disagreeable." ... Punishing desecration of the flag dilutes the very freedom that makes this emblem so revered, and worth revering. The judgments of the District Court are

Affirmed.

NOTES

1. *See also City of Tacoma v. Luvene, supra* at pp. 37-41.
2. In *Hernandez v. Commonwealth*, 406 S.E.2d 398 (Va. App. 1991), the court affirmed the conviction of a Ku Klux Klan member who appeared in hooded Klan regalia on a public street. The predicate statute made it a misdemeanor "for any person over sixteen years of age while wearing any mask, hood or other device whereby a substantial portion of the face is hidden or covered so as to conceal the identity of the wearer, to be or appear in any public place..." Hernandez lodged a facial attack against the statute as overbroad in First Amendment terms because it deterred or "chilled" constitutionally protected expression. The court rejected Hernandez' attack on the statute:

> The appellant argues that the statute prohibits persons from wearing ski masks in the winter, Muslim women from wearing traditional outfits covering their faces, widows from wearing black veils, and other similar face coverings. He argues that this prohibition is unconstitutional because it criminalizes personal expression. We decline to read [the statute] as broadly as the appellant suggests we should.
>
> The statute makes it illegal for any person over the age of sixteen to appear in a public place wearing a mask covering a substantial part of the face "so as to conceal the identity of the wearer." ... These words ... express a requirement of intent. Therefore, to violate the statute, an individual must *intend* to conceal ... identity by covering [the] face.... So construed, this statute does not prohibit the masking of one's face for a purpose other than concealing one's identity, such as protection from cold weather, expression of grief, or practice of a religion.
>
> The appellant also argues that the statute is unconstitutional as applied to him because it penalizes him for engaging in disfavored symbolic speech. This is so only if the appellant's wearing of the mask constitutes expressive activity permitting him to invoke the first amendment ... In order for appellant's conduct to fall within the scope of first amendment protection, he must have intended to convey a particularized message by wearing the mask, and there must have been a great likelihood that the message would be understood by those who viewed it....
>
> This record does not support a finding that the wearing of a mask conveyed a particularized message that would have been likely to have been understood by those who viewed it. The record does not establish, as the appellant contends, that the mask is so identified with the Ku Klux Klan that it is a symbol of its identity. The robe and the hood may be such symbols, but the mask is not. The mask worn without the robe and the hood would be meaningless. The mask adds nothing, save fear and intimidation, to the symbolic message expressed by the wearing of the robe and the hood. Without the mask, the social and political message conveyed by

the uniform of the Ku Klux Klan is the same as it would be with the mask.

Even if the wearing of the Ku Klux Klan mask constitutes expressive conduct protected by the first amendment, the statute is constitutional if its purpose is unrelated to the suppression of free expression... A statute which restricts expressive conduct because of the message it conveys is subject to "the most exacting scrutiny." .... On the other hand, a statute which is directed at the "secondary effects" of the regulated speech, and whose justification has nothing to do with that speech is content-neutral.... A statute is content-neutral if it is one in which "the governmental interest is unrelated to the suppression of free expression." ... Such a statute is constitutional so long as it furthers an important governmental interest and "the incidental restriction on alleged First Amendment freedoms is not greater than is essential to the furtherance of the interest." ...

We acknowledge that the legislature's original motivation for enacting the anti-mask statute may have been to "unmask the Klan." The statute was, after all, created in the same act with statutes prohibiting cross burning and intimidation, activities historically associated with the Klan.... However, whatever motivation might have prompted the anti-mask statute's enactment, the purpose of the statute is no more than what appears in the plain language of the statute.... The statute simply forbids the wearing of masks under certain circumstances. An obvious justification for such a prohibition is the prevention of violence, crime and disorder by the unmasking of potential criminals. For example, a potential rapist or bank robber wearing a mask could just as easily be prosecuted under this statute as a Klansman....

The plain language of [the statute] indicates no purpose to stifle the Klan's freedom of expression. Further, nothing in the record shows an indiscriminate enforcement of the statute against members of the Klan. The justification for prosecuting an individual under this statute is the same whether or not that individual is a Klansman. The incidental effect of preventing a Klansman, such as the appellant, from wearing his "full costume" is minor when compared to the government's interest in keeping communities safe and free from violence. We conclude therefore, that [the statute] is not unconstitutional as applied to the appellant....

3. In *Video Software Dealers Ass'n v. Webster*, 968 F.2d 684 (8th Cir. 1992), the court invalidated a Missouri statute restricting the rental or sale to minors of videocassettes or other video reproduction devices depicting violence. The statute contained no definition of the word "violence," although the state argued to the appellate court that it was aimed at "slasher" videos, *i.e.*, "'blood and gore movies' displaying 'the most bestial and graphic acts of violence imaginable' such as 'excessive scenes of murder, rape, sadomasochistic sex, autopsies, mutilations, satanism, and assorted perversions.'" The Eighth Circuit agreed with the district court that the statute was not narrowly enough tailored to promote a compelling state interest. The Supreme Court's standard governing obscenity, set forth in *Miller v. California*, 413 U.S. 15, 23 (1973), does not extend to materials depicting violence. Even assuming that

the statute was aimed at protecting minors from the harmful effects of viewing slasher videos (Missouri's contention), the statute was not limited to "slasher videos" and did not define the term "slasher." Although the state asserted that the statute did not apply to animated violence in cartoon shows, simulated violence in western and war movies, real violence in the boxing ring, or psychological violence in suspense stories or "thrillers," the statutory language itself offered no support for those limitations. Accordingly, the court of appeals affirmed the district court's judgment declaring the statute unconstitutional on its face and permanently enjoining its enforcement.

2. EQUAL PROTECTION

a. Irrational Legislative Classification

UNITED STATES v. GREENE

United States Court of Appeals, Sixth Circuit
892 F.2d 453 (1989)

WELLFORD, CIRCUIT JUDGE.

Defendant appeals the imposition of two concurrent sentences of eighteen months for unlawful distribution of marijuana [following the acceptance of a guilty plea conditioned on the reserved right to appeal the district court's denial of a defense motion to dismiss the indictment]. Because we find that the present classification of marijuana as a Schedule I substance is neither arbitrary nor irrational . . . we affirm the decision of the district court.

. . . .

Defendant contends that the indictment should be dismissed because the classification of marijuana as a Schedule I controlled substance under the Federal Controlled Substances Act ("Act") . . . , and the imposition of penalties for its use, possession, or distribution, are irrational and arbitrary, thus violating the due process mandate of the fifth amendment. Basing his conclusions on medical evidence and the testimony of Dr. Lipman, an expert in pharmacology, and various articles dealing with its therapeutic use, defendant argues that marijuana, on pharmacological grounds, does not satisfy the three statutory criteria for inclusion in Schedule I: (a) high potential for abuse; (b) no currently accepted medical use; and (c) lack of accepted safety for use of the drug under medical supervision.... Defendant emphasizes that the placement of marijuana in Schedule I, when compared to the absence in the Schedules of more dangerous substances such as alcohol and nicotine, is particularly indicative of the irrational and arbitrary nature of the Schedules.

Other courts have considered this very issue [citing Fourth, Eighth and Eleventh Circuit precedents]. Emphasizing that the judiciary may not sit as a "superlegislature" in reviewing legislative policy determinations that do not affect fundamental rights, each court concluded that the present classification is not arbitrary or irrational....

The Act authorizes the Attorney General to reclassify a drug if presented with new scientific evidence.... [Other cited courts] concluded that this provision evidences Congressional intent to provide an efficient and flexible mechanism for assuring the continued rationality of the classification of controlled

C. INDIVIDUAL RIGHTS BASED CHALLENGES

substances.... We agree that this mechanism, and not the judiciary, is the appropriate means by which defendant should challenge Congress' classification of marijuana as a Schedule I drug.

Defendant offers various state court decisions in support of his position; however, as his counsel candidly concedes, all federal authority is adverse. We agree with those courts in rejecting this constitutional due process challenge to the classification of marijuana under the Controlled Substances Act....

NOTES

1. Equal Protection Challenges to federal law, such as in *Greene*, are raised under the implied equal-protection component of the Fifth Amendment's Due Process Clause. See *Bolling v. Sharpe*, 347 U.S. 497 (1954).

2. In *Craig v. Boren*, 429 U.S. 190 (1976), the Supreme Court struck down a statute penalizing sale of alcoholic beverages to males at a greater age than females. Other illustrations of legislation invalidated on the basis of irrational classifications based on gender include *Frolik v. State*, 392 So. 2d 846 (Ala. 1981) (statute invalidated which punished abusive, insulting, or obscene language only in the presence or hearing of a girl or woman); *Plas v. State*, 598 P.2d 966 (Alaska 1979) (prostitution statute limited to female prostitution violated state equal protection clause; court cured the difficulty by striking the offending limitation and leaving the rest of the statute in force); *Purvis v. State*, 377 So. 2d 674 (Fla. 1979) (fornication statute invalidated because it punished married men for illicit sexual activity but not married women). *Contrast City of Seattle v. Buchanan*, 584 P.2d 918 (Wash. 1978), which sustained a statute outlawing public exhibition of female breasts but not male breasts. "There being such a difference between the breasts of males and females (however undiscernible to the naked eye of some), and that difference having a reasonable relationship to the legitimate legislative purpose which it serves, the ordinance does not deny equality of rights or impose unequal responsibilities on women. It applies alike to men and women, requiring both to cover those parts of their bodies which are intimately associated with the procreation function." *Id.*, 584 P.2d at 921. *See also State v. Rivera*, 612 P.2d 526 (Haw. 1980) (rejecting equal protection attack on female rape statute as unconstitutionally gender based).

3. However, in *City of Dallas v. Stanglin*, 490 U.S. 19 (1989), the Court refused to invalidate a local ordinance restricting the admission of persons between the ages of 14 and 18 to "Class E" dance halls and limiting hours of dance-hall operation. It saw a rational relationship between the age restrictions in the ordinance and the city's interest in promoting the welfare of teenagers. The ordinance restriction did not reflect an irrational classification because the city reasonably could conclude that teenagers might be more susceptible to corrupting influences if permitted to frequent dance halls with older persons, or that limiting dance-hall contacts between adults and teenagers would make less likely illicit or undesirable juvenile involvement with alcohol, illegal drugs or promiscuous sex. The Court rejected a contention that the Constitution recognizes a generalized right of "social association" that includes chance encounters in dance halls. The fact that the ordinance al-

lowed adults and teenagers to roller-skate together did not render the classification scheme irrational, because skating involves less physical contact than dancing. "The differences between the two activities may not be striking, but differentiation need not be striking in order to survive rational-basis scrutiny." *Id.* at 28.

4. In *Ex parte Boetscher*, 812 S.W.2d 600 (Tex. Crim. App. 1991), the court held that a provision of a criminal nonsupport statute enhancing penalties on the basis of a defendant's nonresident status violated the Equal Protection Clause. The court explained its rationale thus:

> The United States Constitution guarantees the right to travel to, and reside in, any part of our national homeland.... Because of the fundamental importance to our citizens of this right to choice of residence, any governmental classification that penalizes its exercise is presumed invalid under the equal protection clause of the Fourteenth Amendment. Such a classification will be upheld only if the government can show it is truly necessary to the promotion of a compelling governmental interest....

Because the statute "single[d] out, for increased punishment, all defendants who simply exercise their federal constitutional right to reside where they choose, including those who never entered this state," it was invalid in the absence of a showing of a compelling state interest, and the state had not even attempted to make such a showing.

5. A state statute allowing the purchase of deadly weapons only by those who were identified by two freeholders was held to embody an unreasonable legislative classification. *Hetherton v. Sears, Roebuck & Co.*, 652 F.2d 1152 (3d Cir. 1981). The state had a legitimate concern to regulate access to handguns, but "to limit the options of prospective purchases for guns to a requirement that only people who own real estate can identify purchasers is no more constitutionally permissible than a requirement that only Catholics or Blacks or Indians can identify purchasers of handguns." *Id.* at 1160.

6. State constitutions usually prohibit special, private, or local laws. A criminal statute applicable to too narrow a band of cities or counties may fall afoul of that prohibition, independent of equal protection considerations. *See, e.g., Brewster v. State*, 395 So. 2d 1111 (Ala. Crim. App. 1981) (prohibition against sale or use of steel leg-hold traps for capturing wild animals, applicable only in counties with populations between 50,000 and 52,500 population, was an arbitrary classification which also was a local law outlawed by the Alabama Constitution).

b. Discriminatory Enforcement

EDITORIAL NOTE

The Supreme Court has indicated that equal protection might be violated if prosecuting authorities institute criminal charges for the purpose of discouraging the exercise of substantive or procedural constitutional rights by defendants, or on the basis of race, religion, or other criteria impermissible under the federal Constitution. *United States v. Batchelder*, 441 U.S. 114 (1979);

C. INDIVIDUAL RIGHTS BASED CHALLENGES

Bordenkircher v. Hayes, 434 U.S. 357 (1978); *see also United States v. Goodwin,* 475 U.S. 368 (1982). If a defendant meets the procedural burden of showing that the instant prosecution is "selective, invidious, in bad faith or based on impermissible considerations such as race, religion, or his exercise of constitutional rights," *United States v. Hayes,* 589 F.2d 811, 819 (5th Cir. 1979), relief may be given, but not otherwise.

The concept was invoked in *Federov v. United States,* 600 A.2d 370 (D.C. App. 1991), which held that certain political protestors had established their selective prosecution claim by showing that the prosecutor's office had a policy of denying pretrial diversion to political protestors. "[T]he government — absent an adequate explanation — is not free to punish more severely those unlawful entrants who are political demonstrators, while excusing those who also refuse to leave [premises] on demand of lawful authority but are not making a political statement." *Id.* at 381.

A similar approach has been taken in state cases. If a defendant has violated a felony-level statute, and no constitutionally impermissible criteria have been used to single him or her out for prosecution, he or she cannot claim discriminatory enforcement because other persons committing similar acts have been prosecuted only for misdemeanors.

Thus, in *Sears v. State,* 287 N.W.2d 785 (Wis. 1980), the court sustained a felony conviction based on solicitation to commit sexual perversion, even though homosexuals frequently were charged only with disorderly conduct. Although the defendant asserted (and was not contradicted in the assertion) that he was the first person in eight years to be charged with the particular offense in the locality, that was not a sufficient ground for invalidating the criminal charges; personal vindictiveness on the part of police and prosecutor had to be shown. Sears had not met this burden. There was some question whether Sears' conduct in fact fit within the lesser offense. He also had an extensive criminal record based on similar activities (while dressed in women's clothing, he had approached a male plainclothes officer and offered to perform an act of oral sex for money). The district attorney, moreover, had instituted a policy of commencing a felony-level prosecution against anyone who solicited a plainclothes officer of either sex; the commercial nature of Sears conduct also justified more serious charges. Although Sears had asserted that females arrested under similar circumstances would not have been prosecuted for felony, he offered no evidence to support that assertion, and indeed foreclosed witness examination which might have revealed whether female prostitutes in fact had been charged in the same way. Thus, the appellate court did not pursue the issue further.

3. RIGHT OF PRIVACY

BOWERS v. HARDWICK

Supreme Court of the United States
478 U.S. 186 (1986)

JUSTICE WHITE delivered the opinion of the Court.

....

[The case involved the constitutionality of a state criminal statute forbidding homosexual activities under all circumstances, including in private between consenting adults.]

This case does not require a judgment on whether laws against sodomy between consenting adults in general, or between homosexuals in particular, are wise or desirable. It raises no question about the right or propriety of state legislative decisions to repeal their laws that criminalize homosexual sodomy, or of state-court decisions invalidating those laws on state constitutional grounds. The issue presented is whether the Federal Constitution confers a fundamental right upon homosexuals to engage in sodomy and hence invalidates the laws of the many States that still make such conduct illegal and have done so for a very long time. The case also calls for some judgment about the limits of the Court's role in carrying out its constitutional mandate.

We first register our disagreement with the Court of Appeals and with respondent that the Court's prior cases have construed the Constitution to confer a right of privacy that extends to homosexual sodomy and for all intents and purposes have decided this case. The reach of this line of cases was sketched in *Carey v. Population Services International*, 431 U.S. 678, 685 (1977). *Pierce v. Society of Sisters*, 268 U.S. 510 (1925), and *Meyer v. Nebraska*, 262 U.S. 390 (1923), were described as dealing with child rearing and education; *Prince v. Massachusetts*, 321 U.S. 158 (1944), with family relationships; *Skinner v. Oklahoma ex rel. Williamson*, 316 U.S. 535 (1942), with procreation; *Loving v. Virginia*, 388 U.S. 1 (1967), with marriage; *Griswold v. Connecticut* [381 U.S. 479 (1965)], and *Eisenstadt v. Baird* [405 U.S. 438 (1972)], with contraception; and *Roe v. Wade*, 410 U.S. 113 (1973), with abortion. The latter three cases were interpreted as construing the Due Process Clause of the Fourteenth Amendment to confer a fundamental individual right to decide whether or not to beget or bear a child....

Accepting the decisions in these cases and the above description of them, we think it evident that none of the rights announced in those cases bears any resemblance to the claimed constitutional right of homosexuals to engage in acts of sodomy that is asserted in this case. No connection between family, marriage, or procreation on the one hand and homosexual activity on the other has been demonstrated, either by the Court of Appeals or by respondent. Moreover, any claim that these cases nevertheless stand for the proposition that any kind of private sexual conduct between consenting adults is constitutionally insulated from state proscription is unsupportable....

Precedent aside, however, respondent would have us announce, as the Court of Appeals did, a fundamental right to engage in homosexual sodomy. This we are quite unwilling to do....

NOTES

1. Courts generally reject claims that commercial sexual activity falls within a constitutionally protected right of privacy. *See, e.g., Lutz v. United States*, 434 A.2d 442 (D.C. 1981); *Commonwealth v. King*, 372 N.E.2d 196 (Mass. 1977); *Commonwealth v. Dodge*, 429 A.2d 1143 (Pa. Super. 1981).

2. In *People v. Privitera*, 591 P.2d 919 (Cal. App.), *cert. denied*, 444 U.S. 949 (1979), the court rejected a claim by a doctor that legislation forbidding him to prescribe laetrile for cancer patients violated a right of privacy in him and his patients. The right of privacy allowing physicians to provide abortions upon demand during the first trimester of pregnancy, *Roe v. Wade*, 410 U.S. 113 (1973), and access to contraceptives and contraceptive advice, *Eisenstadt v. Baird*, 405 U.S. 438 (1972), did not extend to prescribing a drug which the federal Food and Drug Administration had found to constitute a genuine health problem, because it is ineffective and serves to divert cancer patients from more effective therapy. Privitera's claim that he simply provided terminally ill patients with a substance they had a personal right to obtain was not supported by the record, for he did not perform careful diagnoses on the persons to whom he provided the substance. Therefore, the question of that claimed patient right did not have to be addressed.

D. THE BURDEN OF PROOF AND PRESUMPTIONS
EDITORIAL NOTE

Presumptions can serve several purposes. One is to place on the party against whom the presumption operates a burden of injecting into the proceedings the issue focused upon by the presumption. Procedural statutes or rules may require this burden to be discharged through a special pretrial pleading, for example, a notice of intent to rely on the defense of insanity (mental disease or defect). See pp. 630-638 infra. Unless there is such a specific notice statute in force, however, defendants are not required to do other than plead not guilty or to stand mute, in which case a plea of not guilty is entered on their behalf. If that is so, a defendant injects the issue into the case through cross-examination of prosecution witnesses, the direct examination of defense witnesses, or both.

A presumption also may have the functional effect of placing on the party adversely affected by it a responsibility to go forward with evidence suggesting the contrary to the presumed fact. The distinction between that and a burden of injecting the issue may be illustrated by the presumption of sanity or mental normalcy. Modern statutes, as noted, usually require a special pleading from the defense on the matter. A notice or other procedural act serves to meet the burden of injecting the issue, but not the burden of going forward with evidence in support of a claim of mental abnormality precluding a finding of criminal guilt. If no special notice or pleading is required affecting the presumed matter, then proof sufficient to inject the issue almost certainly will satisfy the burden of going forward with evidence.

A presumption can be used as a form of evidence, in the sense that if the established existence of fact A supports an inference that fact B also exists or existed at the same time, and the jury is allowed to know of the presumption or inference, the presumption itself constitutes a form of proof. See MODEL PENAL CODE § 1.12(5) (Appendix A). The constitutional limits within which presumptions of this sort can be legislated and utilized are the focus of the materials which follow.

A criminal norm can be legislative in the form of a presumption. Suppose, for example, that a legislature wishes to proscribe sale of alcoholic beverages to persons under age eighteen. It can define the crime as (to paraphrase) intentional sale of liquor to one who as a matter of objective fact is seventeen or younger. The constitutionality of such a strict liability offense is discussed infra, pp. 693-719, but may be assumed to be constitutional if it is a misdemeanor bearing no term of imprisonment. But the legislature might, in an effort to be marginally less harsh on liquor vendors by giving them a limited opportunity to explain reasons for their want of actual knowledge, define the offense as the intentional sale of liquor to one known to be under the diacritical age, and then add a provision that the fact a recipient was under age eighteen is presumptive evidence, prima facie evidence, or whatever of a defendant's knowledge of nonage. A permissive presumption in that form will be evaluated under the cases which follow. However, a conclusive presumption of knowledge is likely to be invalidated even though its sole (and intended) effect is to eliminate knowledge of nonage as part of the mens rea or culpability dimension of the offense, an effect in no way functionally different from an orthodox strict liability statute covering the residual conduct. Granted judicial inability or unwillingness to recognize this use of a conclusive presumption format to create a strict liability offense, legislatures are best advised to avoid this as a statutory drafting technique.

FRANCIS v. FRANKLIN
Supreme Court of the United States
471 U.S. 307 (1985)

JUSTICE BRENNAN delivered the opinion of the Court.

This case requires that we decide whether certain jury instructions in a criminal prosecution in which intent is an element of the crime charged and the only contested issue at trial satisfy the principles of *Sandstrom v. Montana*, 442 U.S. 510 (1979). Specifically, we must evaluate jury instructions stating that: (1) "[t]he acts of a person of sound mind and discretion are presumed to be the product of the person's will, but the presumption may be rebutted" and (2) "[a] person of sound mind and discretion is presumed to intend the natural and probable consequences of his acts but the presumption may be rebutted." ... The question is whether these instructions, when read in the context of the jury charge as a whole, violate the Fourteenth Amendment's requirement that the State prove every element of a criminal offense beyond a reasonable doubt. See *Sandstrom, supra; In re Winship*, 397 U.S. 358 (1970).

....

The Due Process Clause of the Fourteenth Amendment "protects the accused against conviction except upon proof beyond a reasonable doubt of every fact necessary to constitute the crime with which he is charged." *In re Winship*, 397 U.S., at 364. This "bedrock, 'axiomatic and elementary' [constitutional] principle," *id.*, at 363, prohibits the State from using evidentiary presumptions in a jury charge that have the effect of relieving the State of its burden of persuasion beyond a reasonable doubt of every

D. THE BURDEN OF PROOF AND PRESUMPTIONS

essential element of a crime. *Sandstrom v. Montana, supra,* at 520-524; *Patterson v. New York,* 432 U.S. 197 (1977); *Mullaney v. Wilbur,* 421 U.S. 684, 698-701 (1975); see also *Morissette v. United States,* 342 U.S. 246, 274-275 (1952). The prohibition protects the "fundamental value determination of our society," given voice in Justice Harlan's concurrence in *Winship,* that "it is far worse to convict an innocent man than to let a guilty man go free." 397 U.S., at 372. The question before the Court in this case is almost identical to that before the Court in *Sandstrom*: "whether the challenged jury instruction had the effect of relieving the State of the burden of proof enunciated in *Winship* on the critical question of ... state of mind," 442 U.S., at 521, by creating a mandatory presumption of intent upon proof by the State of other elements of the offense.

The analysis is straightforward. "The threshold inquiry in ascertaining the constitutional analysis applicable to this kind of jury instruction is to determine the nature of the presumption it describes." *Id.,* at 514. The court must determine whether the challenged portion of the instruction creates a mandatory presumption, *see id.,* at 520-524, or merely a permissive inference, see *Ulster County Court v. Allen,* 442 U.S. 140, 157-163 (1979). A mandatory presumption instructs the jury that it must infer the presumed fact if the State proves certain predicate facts.[2] A permissive inference suggests to the jury a possible conclusion to be drawn if the State proves predicate facts, but does not require the jury to draw that conclusion.

Mandatory presumptions must be measured against the standards of *Winship* as elucidated in *Sandstrom*. Such presumptions violate the Due Process Clause if they relieve the State of the burden of persuasion on an element of an offense. *Patterson v. New York, supra,* 432 U.S., at 215 ("[A] State must prove every ingredient of an offense beyond a reasonable doubt and ... may not shift the burden of proof to the defendant by presuming that ingredient upon proof of the other elements of the offense"). *See also Sandstrom, supra,* 442 U.S., at 520-524; *Mullaney v. Wilbur, supra,* 421 U.S., at 698-70. A permissive inference does not relieve the State of its burden of persuasion because it still requires the State to convince the jury that the suggested conclusion should be inferred based on the predicate facts proved. Such inferences do not necessarily implicate the concerns of *Sandstrom*. A permissive inference violates the Due Process Clause only if the suggested conclusion is not one that reason and common sense justify in light of the proven facts before the jury. *Ulster County Court, supra,* 442 U.S., at 157-163.

Analysis must focus initially on the specific language challenged, but the inquiry does not end there. If a specific portion of the jury charge, considered in isolation, could reasonably have been understood as creating a presumption that relieves the State of its burden of persuasion on an element of an offense, the potentially offending words must be considered in the context of the charge as a whole. Other instructions might explain the particular infirm

---

[2] A mandatory presumption may be either conclusive or rebuttable. A conclusive presumption removes the presumed element from the case once the State has proved the predicate facts giving rise to the presumption. A rebuttable presumption does not remove the presumed element from the case but nevertheless requires the jury to find the presumed element unless the defendant persuades the jury that such a finding is unwarranted. *See Sandstrom v. Montana,* 442 U.S. 510, 517-518 (1979).

language to the extent that a reasonable juror could not have considered the charge to have created an unconstitutional presumption.... This analysis "requires careful attention to the words actually spoken to the jury ..., for whether a defendant has been accorded his constitutional rights depends upon the way in which a reasonable juror could have interpreted the instruction." ....

Franklin levels his constitutional attack at the following two sentences in the jury charge: "The acts of a person of sound mind and discretion are presumed to be the product of the person's will, but the presumption may be rebutted. A person of sound mind and discretion is presumed to intend the natural and probable consequences of his acts but the presumption may be rebutted." ... The Georgia Supreme Court has interpreted this language as creating no more than a permissive inference that comports with the constitutional standards of *Ulster County Court v. Allen, supra*.... The question, however, is not what the State Supreme Court declares the meaning of the charge to be, but rather what a reasonable juror could have understood the charge as meaning. *Sandstrom*, 442 U.S., at 516-517 (state court "is not the final authority on the interpretation which a jury could have given the instruction"). The federal constitutional question is whether a reasonable juror could have understood the two sentences as a mandatory presumption that shifted to the defendant the burden of persuasion on the element of intent once the State had proved the predicate acts.

The challenged sentences are cast in the language of command. They instruct the jury that "acts of a person of sound mind and discretion are presumed to be the product of the person's will," and that a person "is presumed to intend the natural and probable consequences of his acts." These words carry precisely the message of the language condemned in *Sandstrom*, 442 U.S., at 515 ("'The law presumes that a person intends the ordinary consequences of his voluntary acts'"). The jurors "were not told that they had a choice, or that they might infer that conclusion; they were told only that the law presumed it. It is clear that a reasonable juror could easily have viewed such an instruction as mandatory." ... The portion of the jury charge challenged in this case directs the jury to presume an essential element of the offense — intent to kill — upon proof of other elements of the offense — the act of slaying another. In this way the instructions "undermine the factfinder's responsibility at trial, based on evidence adduced by the State, to find the ultimate facts beyond a reasonable doubt." *Ulster County Court v. Allen, supra*, 442 U.S., at 156.

The language challenged here differs from *Sandstrom*, of course, in that the jury in this case was explicitly informed that the presumptions "may be rebutted." ... The State makes much of this additional aspect of the instruction in seeking to differentiate the present case from *Sandstrom*. This distinction does not suffice, however, to cure the infirmity in the charge. Though the Court in Sandstrom acknowledged that the instructions there challenged could have been reasonably understood as creating an irrebuttable presumption, it was not on this basis alone that the instructions were invalidated. Had the jury reasonably understood the instructions as creating a mandatory re-

D. THE BURDEN OF PROOF AND PRESUMPTIONS

buttable presumption the instructions would have been no less constitutionally infirm....

An irrebuttable or conclusive presumption relieves the State of its burden of persuasion by removing the presumed element from the case entirely if the State proves the predicate facts. A mandatory rebuttable presumption does not remove the presumed element from the case if the State proves the predicate facts, but it nonetheless relieves the State of the affirmative burden of persuasion on the presumed element by instructing the jury that it must find the presumed element unless the defendant persuades the jury not to make such a finding. A mandatory rebuttable presumption is perhaps less onerous from the defendant's perspective, but it is no less unconstitutional. Our cases make clear that "[s]uch shifting of the burden of persuasion with respect to a fact which the State deems so important that it must be either proved or presumed is impermissible under the Due Process Clause." ... In *Mullaney v. Wilbur*, we explicitly held unconstitutional a mandatory rebuttable presumption that shifted to the defendant a burden of persuasion on the question of intent. And in *Sandstrom*, we similarly held that instructions that might reasonably have been understood by the jury as creating a mandatory rebuttable presumption were unconstitutional....

When combined with the immediately preceding mandatory language, the instruction that the presumptions "may be rebutted" could reasonably be read as telling the jury that it was required to infer intent to kill as the natural and probable consequence of the act of firing the gun unless the defendant persuaded the jury that such an inference was unwarranted. The very statement that the presumption "may be rebutted" could have indicated to a reasonable juror that the defendant bore an affirmative burden of persuasion once the State proved the underlying act giving rise to the presumption. Standing alone, the challenged language undeniably created an unconstitutional burden-shifting presumption with respect to the element of intent....

The jury, of course, did not hear only the two challenged sentences. The jury charge taken as a whole might have explained the proper allocation of burdens with sufficient clarity that any ambiguity in the particular language challenged could not have been understood by a reasonable juror as shifting the burden of persuasion.... The State argues that sufficient clarifying language exists in this case. In particular, the State relies on an earlier portion of the charge instructing the jurors that the defendant was presumed innocent and that the State was required to prove every element of the offense beyond a reasonable doubt. The State also points to the sentence immediately following the challenged portion of the charge, which reads: "[a] person will not be presumed to act with criminal intention...."

As we explained in *Sandstrom*, general instructions on the State's burden of persuasion and the defendant's presumption of innocence are not "rhetorically inconsistent with a conclusive or burden-shifting presumption," because "[t]he jury could have interpreted the two sets of instructions as indicating that the presumption was a means by which proof beyond a reasonable doubt as to intent could be satisfied." ...

In light of the instructions on intent given in this case, a reasonable juror could thus have thought that, although intent must be proved beyond a reasonable doubt, proof of the firing of the gun and its ordinary consequences constituted proof of intent beyond a reasonable doubt unless the defendant persuaded the jury otherwise.... These general instructions as to the prosecution's burden and the defendant's presumption of innocence do not dissipate the error in the challenged portion of the instructions.

Nor does the more specific instruction following the challenged sentences — "A person will not be presumed to act with criminal intention but the trier of facts, that is, the Jury, may find criminal intention upon a consideration of the words, conduct, demeanor, motive and all other circumstances connected with the act for which the accused is prosecuted," .... — provide a sufficient corrective. It may well be that this "criminal intention" instruction was not directed to the element of intent at all, but to another element of the Georgia crime of malice murder. The statutory definition of capital murder in Georgia requires malice aforethought. GA.CODE ANN. § 16-5-1 (1984). Under state law malice aforethought comprises two elements: intent to kill and the absence of provocation or justification.... At another point in the charge in this case, the trial court, consistently with this understanding of Georgia law, instructed the jury that malice is "the unlawful, deliberate intention to kill a human being without justification or mitigation or excuse." ... The statement "criminal intention may not be presumed" may well have been intended to instruct the jurors that they were not permitted to presume the absence of provocation or justification but that they could infer this conclusion from circumstantial evidence. Whatever the court's motivation in giving the instruction, the jury could certainly have understood it this way. A reasonable juror trying to make sense of the juxtaposition of an instruction that "a person of sound mind and discretion is presumed to intend the natural and probable consequences of his acts," ... and an instruction that "[a] person will not be presumed to act with criminal intention," ... may well have thought that the instructions related to different elements of the crime and were therefore not contradictory — that he could presume intent to kill but not the absence of justification or provocation.

Even if a reasonable juror could have understood the prohibition of presuming "criminal intention" as applying to the element of intent, that instruction did no more than contradict the instruction in the immediately preceding sentence. A reasonable juror could easily have resolved the contradiction in the instruction by choosing to abide by the mandatory presumption and ignore the prohibition of presumption. Nothing in these specific sentences or in the charge as a whole makes clear to the jury that one of these contradictory instructions carries more weight than the other. Language that merely contradicts and does not explain a constitutionally infirm instruction will not suffice to absolve the infirmity. A reviewing court has no way of knowing which of the two irreconcilable instructions the jurors applied in reaching their verdict. Had the instruction "[a] person ... is presumed to intend the natural and probable consequences of his acts," ... been followed by the instruction "this means that a person will not be presumed to act with criminal intention but the jury may find criminal intention upon consideration of all circumstances connected with the act for which the accused is prosecuted," a somewhat stronger argument might be made that a reasonable juror could not have understood the challenged language as shifting the burden of persuasion to the defendant.... Whether or not such explanatory language might have been sufficient, however, no such language is present in this jury charge. If a juror thought the "criminal intention" instruction pertained to the element of intent, the juror was left in a quandary as to whether to follow that instruction or the immediately preceding one it contradicted....

Because a reasonable juror could have understood the challenged portions of the jury instruction in this case as creating a mandatory presumption that shifted to the defendant the burden of persuasion on the crucial element of intent, and because the charge read as a whole does not explain or cure the error, we hold that the jury charge does not comport with the requirements of the Due Process Clause....

NOTES

1. In *County Court of Ulster County v. Allen,* 442 U.S. 140 (1979), alluded to in the principal case, the Court found that the provisions of N.Y. PENAL LAW § 265.15(3) (McKinney 1983), providing that

> The presence in an automobile, other than a stolen one or a public omnibus, of any firearm, defaced firearm, firearm silencer, explosive or incendiary bomb, bombshell, gravity knife, [or] switchblade knife... is presumptive evidence of its possession by all persons occupying such automobile at the time such weapon, instrument or appliance is found...

did not offend against due process because, as the New York Court of Appeals had stated, the statutory presumption was permissive and there was a sufficiently rational connection between the proven facts and the presumed fact to satisfy due process expectations.

2. In *State v. Hudson,* 273 S.E.2d 616 (Ga. 1981), the trial court had granted a plea in bar to an indictment under a criminal statute governing misapplication of payments by architects, contractors, etc., which made nonpayment for material or labor for which diverted funds had been paid "prima facie evidence of intent to defraud." The Georgia Supreme Court reversed. The statute might be constitutional or unconstitutional, depending on trial court instructions in the particular case, so that it was improper to hold the law unconstitutional on its face. In contrast, *State v. McCoy,* 395 So. 2d 319, 323-24 (La. 1980), declared invalid a prima facie evidence provision of a theft of utility services statute because by its terms it was mandatory rather than permissive. *See also State v. Taylor,* 396 So. 2d 1278 (La. 1981), which confirmed a trial court order based on the unconstitutionality of a statutory presumption that persons in possession of firearms with altered or obliterated serial numbers had altered or obliterated them. Possession alone was not otherwise criminal. The Louisiana Supreme Court read the statute as creating a mandatory presumption which could not meet the requisite "beyond a reasonable doubt" standard which governs such a presumption.

3. The use of the formulation "prima facie proof" does not remove a statute from the ambit of *Allen-Sandstrom* concerns. In *State v. Williams,* 400 So. 2d 575, 579 (La. 1981), a statute prohibiting fraudulent use of access (credit) cards stated that use of a card after notice of its cancellation or termination

had been received, or five days after a notice of cancellation or termination had been deposited by registered or certified mail in the postal service, was "presumptive evidence" of use with intent to defraud. The Louisiana Supreme Court declared the provision unconstitutional:

> The term "presumptive evidence" is literally synonymous with the term "prima facie evidence." Each is defined as evidence sufficient to establish a given fact and which, if not rebutted or contradicted, will remain sufficient.... When the words "shall be" immediately precede each term, it becomes quite clear that proof of the facts which constitute the subjects of the verb must be construed as proof of the elemental facts constituting the objects, at least unless the defendant comes forward with evidence sufficient to create a reasonable doubt. This effect is the same where, as here, the term "shall be presumptive evidence" is used to equate certain evidentiary and elemental facts.
>
> Viewed in this light, the presumption at issue here is mandatory. Thus, it can only stand if proof of the evidentiary facts of certified mailing of a cancellation notice, the passage of five days and the use of the revoked Access Card, would, on its face, constitute proof beyond a reasonable doubt of the elemental facts of use of an Access Card with the specific intention to defraud. We hold that it cannot.

4. *Compare Hall v. State,* 259 S.E.2d 41 (Ga. 1979), which sustained the constitutionality of a statute making the fact a drawer had no account in a drawee bank prima facie evidence of knowledge the check would not be honored when presented. The statutory language created only a permissive presumption, and there was a sufficient rational connection between what was proven and what could be inferred to satisfy the Supreme Court's "more probable than not" test of rational relationship. The court reached the same conclusion concerning a permissive presumption that the identity of a person issuing a check, etc., is the same as the one identified on the face of the instrument (through name, residence address, and home telephone number) or in a check-cashing identification card bearing the same information.

5. In *Carella v. California,* 491 U.S. 263 (1989) (per curiam), the Court indicated that erroneous instructions triggering the *Francis v. Franklin,* concerns might nevertheless constitute constitutional harmless error.

E. JURISDICTIONAL LIMITS ON PROSCRIBING AND PUNISHING CRIMES

1. SEPARATION OF POWERS

EDITORIAL NOTE

The doctrine of separation of powers emerges in the criminal law usually under the fair notice doctrine. Recall that one concern about the process of reviving and adapting dormant common-law crimes to modern circumstances rests on the constitutional assignment of responsibility for creating criminal law norms to the legislative branch. *See supra* pp. 1-5. Recall also the unwillingness of courts to limit through judicial definition of terms overbroad criminal statutes and to make vague and indefinite legislation precise, even when courts are fairly sure about the legislative purpose. To do so would arrogate to the courts an excessive exercise of criminal norm-creating powers. *See supra* pp. 32-43.

Federal and state controlled substances laws arrange psychotropic drugs on schedules which bear on the severity of punishment for contraventions. Substances may be added, deleted, or transferred among schedules through administrative action, usually federal but at times state. Defendants have attacked this legislative approach on two bases: (1) The legislative arm has delegated too much discretion to administrative officials, thus abdicating its constitutional responsibility to establish criminal law norms. (2) Use of administratively modified schedules violates fair notice standards.

The United States Supreme Court appears to have resolved the matter within the federal jurisdiction by its holding in *Touby v. United States,* 111 S. Ct. 1752 (1991). The Federal Controlled Substances Act, 21 U.S.C. § 811 (1988), allows the Attorney General to schedule and reschedule substances both temporarily and permanently. The Toubys were indicted for manufacturing and conspiring to manufacture "Euphoria," a designer drug temporarily designated as a Schedule I controlled substance, during the time the temporary order was in effect. They moved unsuccessfully to dismiss the indictment on the grounds that the statute unconstitutionally had delegated legislative power to the Attorney General, an executive branch official, and that the Attorney General in turn had improperly delegated the responsibility to the Drug Enforcement Administration (DEA). The court of appeals affirmed their conviction.

The Supreme Court concluded that the statutory provisions authorizing temporary scheduling had placed "multiple specific restrictions on the Attorney General's discretion to define criminal conduct," so that the nondelegation doctrine had not been violated. Nor did the delegation accord too much power to the Attorney General, who ultimately was responsible for resulting criminal prosecutions. The delegation doctrine addresses only the allocation of responsibilities among the three branches, not the assignment of responsibilities within a given branch. The Court also concluded that the unavailability of judicial review during a period of temporary scheduling did not invalidate the system, because permanent scheduling orders are subject to such review. Finally, the legislation contained no prohibition against a sub-delegation of scheduling authority to the DEA; the statute allows that delegation if no other statute prohibits it, and none does.

States, of course, can construe the separation of powers doctrine embedded in their own state constitutions to reach a contrary result. *See, e.g., State v. Rodriguez,* 379 So. 2d 1084, 1087 (La. 1980); *In re Powell,* 602 P.2d 711 (Wash. 1979). Use of administratively modified schedules has been ruled to violate fair notice standards because citizens may have no awareness that schedule changes are contemplated and cannot readily find the schedules in print should they wish to consult them. The State of Washington has adopted this premise. *State v. Jordan,* 588 P.2d 1155 (Wash. 1979). Such concerns are particularly acute when state legislation adopts by reference schedules developed by federal administrative agencies; state residents should not have to monitor the Federal Register to apprise themselves of current state law coverage. *State v. Dougall,* 570 P.2d 135 (Wash. 1977).

Naturally, it is no solution to the problem for a legislature to try to include "[a]ny combination of depressant, stimulant, or hallucinogenic drugs, not listed by name or trade name in [the statute], that is of a composition substantially similar to any of the drugs or substances listed." Such a statute is unconstitutionally indefinite in coverage and violates due process because it would allow the conviction of a person "for conduct which he did not know, and could not know, was prohibited." *Crutchfield v. State,* 627 P.2d 196, 201 (Alaska 1980).

An illustration that contests over delegation of authority are not limited to controlled substances statutes is found in *State v. Bender,* 382 So. 2d 697, 700 (Fla. 1980), where a defendant attacked a statute directing the state Department of Highway Safety and Motor Vehicles and the Department of Health and Rehabilitation to establish alcohol blood-testing procedures and approve testing devices as embodying an unlawful delegation of authority. The statute was upheld.

2. FEDERALISM

a. State and Federal Crimes

EDITORIAL NOTE

The statement may appear strange that any state criminal code is more comprehensive than the Federal Criminal Code and other federal criminal legislation combined, granted the very substantial bulk of the latter. Nonetheless, to be constitutional, federal legislation must rest ultimately on one or more of the powers delegated to Congress in United States Constitution Art. I, § 8 or otherwise assigned to the federal government under some other provision of the Constitution. State penal legislation is under no similar limitation, so that state legislation can address problems, for example, offenses against the family, that lie beyond the power of Congress to legislate. Moreover, the need to provide in a federal criminal statute the federal constitutional basis for the statute adds elements that federal prosecutors must establish — elements with no counterpart in state legislation. To illustrate, a state penal law can contain a general bank robbery statute, but a federal counterpart must include a reference to a federally-regulated bank as the victim. State criminal homicide statutes (murder and manslaughter) can be plenary, but federal counterpart legislation must rest on the official status of the victim (*e.g.,* the President, an official or employee of the federal government, or a foreign diplomatic or consular official) or the location of the homicide (*e.g.,* in a federal facility or on a military reservation).

b. Occupation of the Field

EDITORIAL NOTE

When Congress in the exercise of one of the powers delegated to it through U.S. CONST. art. I, § 8, or another provision, legislates comprehensively on a matter, conflicting state legislation on the same matter is unconstitutional, because federal legislation has "occupied the field." *See, e.g., Massachusetts v. Westcott,* 431 U.S. 322 (1977); *Douglas v. Seacoast Products, Inc.,* 431 U.S. 265 (1977); *Pennsylvania v. Nelson,* 350 U.S. 497 (1956). At times, Congress specifically legitimates state legislation if it conforms to federal statutory requirement, for example, in the area of eavesdropping and wiretapping. 18 U.S.C. §§ 2510, 2516-2518 (1988). In the absence of a sufficient statement of congressional purpose to allow concurrent state legislation, courts must analyze federal statutes to determine whether the federal regulatory scheme is pervasive, federal interests are dominant, or the need for national uniformity so great that state regulation must be excluded absolutely. *Head v. New Mexico Board of Examiners in Optometry,* 374 U.S. 424, 431 (1963). These considerations govern fully a constitutional evaluation of state criminal legislation. *People v. Gilbert,* 279 N.W.2d 546 (Mich. App. 1979) (sustaining a statute penalizing private citizen possession of radar detectors without a state police permit, against various claims including an occupation of the field argument based on Federal Communications Commission regulation and assignment of radar frequencies; defendant showed no actual conflict between federal regulations and the state law).

One should not overlook the existence of a counterpart state constitutional doctrine affecting local municipal or county ordinances, at times bearing criminal penalties, which conflict with statewide legislation. Under widely recognized doctrines, pervasive state legislation occupies the field and brings about the invalidation of incompatible local laws. *See, e.g., City of Lorain v. Tomasic,* 391 N.E.2d 726 (Oh. 1979); *City of Spokane v. Portch,* 596 P.2d 1044 (Wash. 1979) (citing authorities).

3. NONENFORCEMENT OF FOREIGN PENAL ADJUDICATIONS
EDITORIAL NOTE

It long has been stated that "[t]he courts of no country execute the penal laws of another." *The Antelope,* 23 U.S. (10 Wheat.) 66, 123 (1825) (Marshall, C.J.). That case involved a libel contesting the seizure of 280 slaves found in the hold of a Venezuelan privateer captured in American territorial waters. The fact that both the United States and Great Britain had abolished international slave trading did not mean that the slaves had to be freed.

The validity of this classical doctrine was tested in *Rosado v. Civiletti,* 621 F.2d 1179 (2d Cir.), *cert. denied,* 449 U.S. 856 (1980), and *Pfeifer v. United States Bureau of Prisons,* 615 F.2d 873 (9th Cir.), *cert. denied,* 447 U.S. 908 (1980). Both cases involved prisoner exchange treaties which the United States has entered into with eleven nations, implemented by federal statute. 18 U.S.C. §§ 3244, 4100-4115 (West Supp. 1993). *See generally* B.J. George, *Jurisdictional Bases for Criminal Legislation,* in TRANSNATIONAL ASPECTS OF CRIMINAL PROCEDURE 1983 MICH. Y.B. INT'L L. 3. The habeas corpus relators in *Rosado* and *Pfeifer* had been returned from Mexico, at their request and following compliance with statutory procedures, and were serving time in federal institutions under their Mexican penal sentences. The treaties allow federal litigation contesting compliance with treaty procedures, but require that attacks on underlying penal convictions and procedures antecedent to them be contested in the courts of the nations in which they were entered. Both relators contended that their imprisonment in federal custody pursuant solely to criminal judgments entered in Mexican courts violated due process, on the theory that the principle of nonenforcement of foreign penal judgments in essence was of constitutional weight. Both courts of appeals disagreed.

Chief Judge Kaufman's opinion in *Rosado* dealt with the issue in this way:

> Though no nation may unilaterally bind another sovereign by the sheer force of its statutory enactments, nothing in the doctrine enunciated by Marshall precludes a sovereign power from extending recognition to another's penal laws where it chooses to do so. Nor does Marshall's dictum suggest any principle limiting the power of sovereign nations to enter into mutual compacts or treaties obligating the signatories to honor and enforce the penal decrees of one another. In the United States, the constitutionality of such measures was decided long ago when the Supreme Court upheld an extradition agreement with foreign nations as a valid exercise of the treaty-making power.... Even where the treaty fails to secure to those who are extradited to another country the same constitutional safeguards they would enjoy in an American criminal trial, it does not run afoul of the Constitution.... Moreover, criminal convictions imposed by foreign tribunals have served as predicates for enhanced sentencing under state multi-offender statutes....
>
> The instant Treaty does not call upon the United States to enforce Mexico's penal laws or procedures, but only to execute criminal convictions entered in its courts against American citizens who elect to transfer to United States custody. Thus, once a prisoner has consented to transfer, the United States is bound simply to take custody of the offender and, with a few significant exceptions, detain him as if he had been convicted in a United States court. The Treaty serves to ameliorate the condition of Americans imprisoned in Mexico by offering them an opportunity for repatriation and, hopefully, better prison conditions and more positive means for rehabilitation.

Federal statute, 18 U.S.C. § 1442(a)(1) (1988), allows any "officer of the United States or any agency thereof, or person acting under him," sued civilly or prosecuted criminally in a state court "for any act under color of such office, or on account of any right, title or authority claimed under any act of Congress for the apprehension or punishment of criminals or the collection of revenues," to remove the state action to an appropriate federal district court. The purpose of the statute was elaborated upon in *Arizona v. Manypenny*, 451 U.S. 232, 241-43 (1981), in which the Court affirmed the right of the state prosecution to appeal pre-jeopardy federal district court decisions in removed litigation before federal appellate courts on the same basis it could have done in state courts had the matter not been removed:

> The Court of Appeals concluded that the fact of removal substantially alters the State's right to seek review. Reasoning that a case brought pursuant to § 1442(a)(1) arises under federal law, the court held that state

enabling statutes retain no significance. But a state criminal proceeding against a federal officer that is removed to federal court does not "arise under federal law" in this pre-empting sense. Rather, the federal court conducts the trial under federal rules of procedure while applying the criminal law of the State....

This principle is entirely consistent with the purpose underlying the removal of proceedings commenced in state court against a federal officer. Historically, removal under § 1442(a)(1) and its predecessor statutes was meant to ensure a federal forum in any case where a federal official is entitled to raise a defense arising out of his official duties. The act of removal permits a trial upon the merits of the state-law question free from local interests or prejudice.... It also enables the defendant to have the validity of his immunity defense adjudicated in a federal forum.... For these reasons, this Court has held that the right of removal is absolute for conduct performed under color of federal office, and has insisted that the policy favoring removal "should not be frustrated by a narrow, grudging interpretation of § 1442(a)(1)." ...

At the same time, the invocation of removal jurisdiction by a federal officer does not revise or alter the underlying law to be applied. In this respect, it is a purely derivative form of jurisdiction, neither enlarging nor contracting the rights of the parties. Federal involvement is necessary in order to insure a federal forum, but it is limited to assuring that an impartial setting is provided in which the federal defense of immunity can be considered during prosecution under state law. Thus, while giving full effect to the purpose of removal, this Court retains the highest regard for a State's right to make and enforce its own criminal laws....

Under our federal system, "[i]t goes without saying that preventing and dealing with crime is much more the business of the States than it is of the Federal Government." Patterson v. New York, 432 U. S. 197, 201 (1977). Because the regulation of crime is pre-eminently a matter for the States, we have identified "a strong judicial policy against federal interference with state criminal proceedings." Huffman v. Pursue, Ltd., 420 U. S. 592, 600 (1975). A State's interest in enforcing its criminal laws merits comparable judicial respect when pursued in the federal courts....

Respondent here, by obtaining a federal forum, has fully vindicated the federal policies supporting removal. The plainest evidence of this vindication is the District Court's application of the immunity defense. No further purpose of the removal statute would be served by denying the State a right to seek review when that very right is available under applicable state law. On the contrary, it would be anomalous to conclude that the State's appellate rights were diminished solely because of the removal. The statutory goal of ensuring fair and impartial adjudication is not advanced when the State in effect can be penalized by the defendant's decision to remove a criminal prosecution. Absent any indication that the removal statute was intended to derogate from the State's interest in evenhanded enforcement of its laws, we see no justification for providing an unintended benefit to a defendant who happens to be a federal officer....

Federal correctional institutions likewise may accommodate prisoners received under contracts with states which do not have adequate, usually maximum security, prisons of their own. Prisoners received under such contracts may be treated like any other federal inmates. *See generally Howe v. Smith,* 452 U.S. 473 (1981).

Chapter 2
ELEMENTS OF CRIMES AND THE CONSEQUENCES OF CRIMINALITY

SECTION I. Culpability *(Mens Rea)*
A. *ACTUS NON FACIT REUM NISI MENS SIT REA*
UNITED STATES v. UNITED STATES GYPSUM CO.
United States Supreme Court
438 U.S. 422 (1978)

CHIEF JUSTICE BURGER delivered the opinion of the Court.

We start with the familiar proposition that "[t]he existence of a *mens rea* is the rule of, rather than the exception to, the principles of Anglo-American criminal jurisprudence." ... In a much-cited passage in *Morisette v. United States, supra,* 342 U.S. at 250-251, Mr. Justice Jackson speaking for the Court observed:

> The contention that an injury can amount to a crime only when inflicted by intention is no provincial or transient notion. It is as universal and persistent in mature systems of law as belief in freedom of the human will and a consequent ability and duty of the normal individual to choose between good and evil. A relation between some mental element and punishment for a harmful act is almost as instinctive as the child's familiar exculpatory "But I didn't mean to," and has afforded the rational basis for a tardy and unfinished substitution of deterrence and reformation in place of retaliation and vengeance as the motivation for public prosecution. Unqualified acceptance of this doctrine by English common law in the Eighteenth Century was indicated by Blackstone's sweeping statement that to constitute any crime there must first be a "vicious will."

(Footnotes omitted.)

Although Blackstone's requisite "vicious will" has been replaced by more sophisticated and less colorful characterizations of the mental state required to support criminality, see ALI, Model Penal Code § 2.02 (Prop. Off. Draft 1962), intent generally remains an indispensable element of a criminal offense. This is as true in a sophisticated criminal antitrust case as in one involving any other criminal offense.

This Court, in keeping with the common-law tradition and with the general injunction that "ambiguity concerning the ambit of criminal statutes should be resolved in favor of lenity," ... has on a number of occasions read a state-of-mind component into an offense even when the statutory definition did not in terms so provide.... Indeed, the holding in *Morisette* can be fairly read as establishing, at least with regard to crimes having their original in the common law, an interpretative presumption that *mens rea* is required. "[M]ere omission ... of intent [in the statute] will not be construed as eliminating that element from the crimes denounced"; instead Congress will be presumed to have legislated against the background of our traditional legal concepts which render intent a critical factor, and "absence of contrary direction [will] be taken as satisfaction with widely accepted definitions, not as a departure from them." 342 U.S., at 263.

While strict-liability offenses are not unknown to the criminal law and do not invariably offend constitutional requirements, ... the limited circumstances in which Congress has created and this Court has recognized such offenses ... attest to their generally disfavored status ... Certainly far more than the simple omission of the appropriate phrase from the statutory definition is necessary to justify dispensing with an intent requirement. In the context of the Sherman Act, this generally inhospitable attitude to non-*mens rea* offenses is reinforced by an array of considerations arguing against treating antitrust violations as strict-liability crimes....

The ALI Model Penal Code is one source of guidance upon which the Court has relied to illuminate questions of this type.... Recognizing that "*mens rea* is not a unitary concept," ... the Code enumerates four possible levels of intent — purpose, knowledge, recklessness, and negligence. In dealing with the kinds of business decisions upon which the antitrust laws focus, the concepts of recklessness and negligence have no place. Our question instead is whether a criminal violation of the antitrust laws requires, in addition to proof of anticompetitive effects, a demonstration that the disputed conduct was undertaken with the "conscious object" of producing such effects, or whether it is sufficient that the conduct is shown to have been undertaken with knowledge that the proscribed effects would most likely follow. While the difference between these formulations is a narrow one, ... we conclude that action undertaken with knowledge of its probable consequences and having the requisite anticompetitive effects can be a sufficient predicate for a finding of criminal liability under the antitrust laws....

NOTES

1. In *State v. Brown*, 389 So. 2d 48 (La. 1980), state legislation made it unlawful to possess "unknowingly or intentionally" a controlled dangerous substance. Defendants moved to quash the information charging them with possession of a listed substance, on the ground the statute was unconstitutional. The trial court granted the motion, based on the statute's overbreadth in penalizing unknowing possession of controlled substances. The Supreme Court of Louisiana allowed the defendants to litigate the issue before it despite the state's argument that they were charged only with intentional possession of a substance:

> Having determined that defendants do have standing, we must consider their allegation that the statute is overbroad in its use of the word "unknowing." Initially, we observe the familiar proposition that "[t]he existence of a *mens rea* is the rule of, rather than the exception to, the

principles of Anglo-American criminal jurisprudence." *Dennis v. United States,* 341 U.S. 494, 500 (1951)....

Although strict liability offenses do exist in the criminal law and do not in all instances offend constitutional requirements, these are limited in number and of a nature different from the statute being challenged here. For example, the law making it a crime for one to receive or possess a firearm which is not registered to him in the National Firearm Registration and Transfer Record was upheld because "one would hardly be surprised to learn that possession of hand grenades is not an innocent act. They are highly dangerous offensive weapons...." *United States v. Freed,* 401 U.S. 601, 609 (1971). Thus, even in *Freed,* the defendants were aware of the nature of the instrumentality they possessed. Conversely, the statute at issue here criminalizes *unknowing* possessing. It requires little imagination to visualize a situation in which a third party hands the controlled substance to an unknowing individual who then can be charged with and subsequently convicted for violation of R.S. 40:969(C) without ever being aware of the nature of the substance he was given. A situation such as the above does indeed offend the conscience. The "unknowing" possession of a dangerous drug cannot be made criminal.

Id. at 50-51.

2. The preeminent case which states the preference for *mens rea* and the rationale for this view is *Morissette v. United States,* 342 U.S. 246 (1952). *Morissette* and other cases which discuss whether and when a legislature may punish conduct alone even in the absence of *mens rea* are included in the subsection on strict liability, *infra* pp. 693-719.

B. CULPABILITY DISTINGUISHED FROM MOTIVE

STATE v. EHLERS

Court of Errors and Appeals of New Jersey
119 A. 15 (1922)

WHITE, J. The verdict of the jury found the defendant, a laborer twenty-eight years old, guilty of murder in the first degree as charged in the indictment, and there was no recommendation of life imprisonment. The indictment charged the murder of defendant's son, Walter, who was proved to be between six and seven years of age. There was another indictment against the defendant for murdering his wife, but there has been no trial as yet under this other indictment.

The defendant, who, it appears, did not stay employed very long at any place, and who had moved from Hoboken with his wife and three children into two attic bedrooms in a farmhouse near Woodridge in October, and then, losing his job in February, had left his family at Woodridge and gone to live with his "folks" in Hoboken while seeking work, and came to Woodridge on the afternoon or night in question to see his family, seems to have first shot his wife at about eleven o'clock at night from the landing at the head of the stairs, as she, in answer to his call, came up the stairs to the attic bedroom where he and their three children were. He then stepped back into the bedroom, "broke," — that is, opened the breech of — the single-barrel shotgun with which he had just shot his wife, ejected the exploded shell, took another loaded shell from the box of shells on the shelf, loaded the gun with it, shot his seven year old son Walter, who was getting out of bed as a result of being awakened by the noise of the first shot, again "broke" the gun, ejecting the second exploded shell (there were two freshly-discharged shells found in the room, one on the bed and the other by Walter's body on the floor), took another loaded shell from the box (three shells were missing from the full box after the shooting), put it in the gun, but got the "finger" of the ejector outside or back of the rim of the shell, and in trying to force the gun closed with the shell in this position "jammed" it so tightly as to prevent either another discharge of the gun or a removal of the shell in the usual manner.

....

Under these circumstances the defendant now claims that the court should reverse and set aside the judgment on the ground that the verdict was against the weight of the evidence, in that ... the state by failing, as defendant alleges it did fail, to prove any motive for the murder of defendant's son, has failed to establish that the killing was willful, deliberate, and premeditated....

We do not agree ... [P]roof of motive is not an essential element in a conviction of murder in the first degree. If the proved facts established that the defendant in fact did the killing willfully, that is, with intent to kill (which is presumed from the proof of the killing until the contrary appears ..., and as the result of premeditation and deliberation, thereby implying preconsideration and determination, there is murder in the first degree, no matter what defendant's motive may have been, nor although he in fact had no motive (using the word in its usual sense of self-serving reason) whatsoever. Suppose, for instance, that this defendant, out of work as he was and unable to supply with the cost of the necessities of life his wife and three children, with whom he was not living at the time, had conceived the thought that the burdens, the sufferings and the disappointments of life overbalance its benefits, its happiness and its successes, and that he would be doing a kindness to his little boy by destroying the latter's life and thereby saving him from future suffering and unhappiness, and that having given this idea careful and thorough consideration, defendant finally arrived at the determination to kill the child, and thereupon, with that intent, he did kill him in the manner proved and admitted in this case, the defendant was just as much guilty of murder in the first degree as if his purpose was (as in fact the jury may have found it to have been) to destroy his wife and children so that their support would not thereafter be a burden upon him.

....

The absence of a self-serving purpose or motive in any murder case would, of course, be a very material and persuasive circumstance for consideration in connection with other circumstances, such as marked melancholia, as tending to establish the degree of mental irresponsibility which is recognized by our law. But while it may well be that in such cases the attending conditions and circumstances might be such that a jury might consider a clearly established absence of motive sufficient proof of insanity to warrant acquittal, certain it is that where the jury convicts instead of acquits, this court will not reverse on the ground that such a verdict is against the weight of the evidence, because there was no proof of motive.

....

For the reasons hereinbefore stated the judgment is affirmed.

NOTE

In *Trice v. United States*, 525 A.2d 176 (D.C. 1987), the defendant appealed a conviction for the crime of willful failure to appear in court when required (criminal bail jumping). He claimed that the statute should be interpreted to require a showing of bad purpose or evil intent, as in crimes of moral turpitude. The court declined to do so:

> Appellant's arguments fly in the face of our decision in *Patton v. United States*, 326 A.2d 818 (D.C. 1974). We held in *Patton* that a conviction ... for willful failure to appear requires a showing only of "what is commonly referred to as a general intent of the defendant to commit the act or omission," and that "lack of an evil state of mind does not exculpate a bail jumping defendant." ... We also noted that [the statute], which provides that "[a]ny failure to appear after notice of the appearance date shall be prima facie evidence that such failure to appear is willful," is "irreconcilable with the contention that specific intent or an 'evil mind' is required; rather, the requisite intent is inferable from the omission itself." ...
>
> We held in *Patton* that a specific intent to violate the law is not an element of the offense of bail jumping. This is so because bail jumping is not a common law crime of moral turpitude (*malum in se*), but a statutory crime (*malum prohibitum*) which we characterized in *Patton* as "regulatory in nature." ... To establish willfulness in a bail jumping case, all that the government must prove is that the defendant's failure to appear in court when requested was knowing, intentional, and deliberate, rather than inadvertent or accidental. This is consistent with long-established case law in the District of Columbia on the meaning of willfulness: It is only in very few criminal cases that "willful" means "done with a bad purpose." Generally, it means "no more than that the person charged with the duty knows what he is doing. It does not mean that, in addition, he must suppose that he is breaking the law." ...

Id. at 181.

EMPLOYMENT DIVISION, DEPARTMENT OF HUMAN RESOURCES OF OREGON v. SMITH

Supreme Court of the United States
494 U.S. 872 (1990)

SCALIA, J., delivered the opinion of the Court.

This case requires us to decide whether the Free Exercise Clause of the First Amendment permits the State of Oregon to include religiously inspired peyote use within the reach of its general criminal prohibition on use of that drug, and thus permits the State to deny unemployment benefits to persons dismissed from their jobs because of such religiously inspired use.

I

Oregon law prohibits the knowing or intentional possession of a "controlled substance" unless the substance has been prescribed by a medical practitioner....

The law defines "controlled substance" as a drug classified in Schedules I through V of the Federal Controlled Substances Act, ... as modified by the State Board of Pharmacy.... Persons who violate this provision by possessing a controlled substance listed on Schedule I are "guilty of a Class B felony." ... As compiled by the State Board of Pharmacy under its statutory authority, ... Schedule I contains the drug peyote, a hallucinogen derived from the plant *Lophophora Williamsii Lemaire*....

Respondents Alfred Smith and Galen Black (hereinafter respondents) were fired from their jobs with a private drug rehabilitation organization because they ingested peyote for sacramental purposes at a ceremony of the Native American Church, of which both are members. When respondents applied to petitioner Employment Division (hereinafter petitioner) for unemployment compensation, they were determined to be ineligible for benefits because they had been discharged for work-related "misconduct." The Oregon Court of Appeals reversed that determination, holding that the denial of benefits violated respondents' free exercise rights under the First Amendment.

On appeal to the Oregon Supreme Court, petitioner argued that the denial of benefits was permissible because respondents' consumption of peyote was a crime under Oregon law. The Oregon Supreme Court reasoned, however, that the criminality of respondents' peyote use was irrelevant to resolution of their constitutional claim — since the purpose of the "misconduct" provision under which respondents had been disqualified was not to enforce the State's criminal laws but to preserve the financial integrity of the compensation fund, and since that purpose was inadequate to justify the burden that disqualification imposed on respondents' religious practice. Citing our decisions in *Sherbert v. Verner*, 374 U.S. 398 (1963), and *Thomas v. Review Bd. of Indiana Employment Security Div.*, 450 U.S. 707 (1981), the court concluded that respondents were entitled to payment of unemployment benefits.... We granted certiorari...

Before this Court in 1987, petitioner continued to maintain that the illegality of respondents' peyote consumption was relevant to their constitutional claim. We agreed, concluding that "if a State has prohibited through its criminal laws certain kinds of religiously motivated conduct without violating the First Amendment, it certainly follows that it may impose the lesser burden of denying unemployment compensation benefits to persons who engage in that conduct." *Employment Div., Dept. of Human Resources of Oregon v. Smith*, 485 U.S. 660, 670 (1988) (*Smith I*). We noted, however, that the Oregon Supreme Court had not decided whether respondents' sacramental use of peyote was in fact proscribed by Oregon's controlled substance law, and that this issue was a matter of dispute between the parties. Being "uncertain about the legality of the religious use of peyote in Oregon," we determined that it would not be "appropriate for us to decide whether the practice is protected by the Federal

Constitution." Accordingly, we vacated the judgment of the Oregon Supreme Court and remanded for further proceedings....

On remand, the Oregon Supreme Court held that respondents' religiously inspired use of peyote fell within the prohibition of the Oregon statute, which "makes no exception for the sacramental use" of the drug.... It then considered whether that prohibition was valid under the Free Exercise Clause, and concluded that it was not. The court therefore reaffirmed its previous ruling that the State could not deny unemployment benefits to respondents for having engaged in that practice.

We again granted certiorari....

II

Respondents' claim for relief rests on our decisions in *Sherbert v. Verner*, supra, *Thomas v. Review Bd. of Indiana Employment Security Div.*, supra, and *Hobbie v. Unemployment Appeals Comm'n of Florida*, 480 U.S. 136 (1987), in which we held that a State could not condition the availability of unemployment insurance on an individual's willingness to forgo conduct required by his religion. As we observed in *Smith* I, however, the conduct at issue in those cases was not prohibited by law. We held that distinction to be critical, for "if Oregon does prohibit the religious use of peyote, and if that prohibition is consistent with the Federal Constitution, there is no federal right to engage in that conduct in Oregon," and "the State is free to withhold unemployment compensation from respondents for engaging in work-related misconduct, despite its religious motivation." ... Now that the Oregon Supreme Court has confirmed that Oregon does prohibit the religious use of peyote, we proceed to consider whether that prohibition is permissible under the Free Exercise Clause.

A

The Free Exercise Clause of the First Amendment, which has been made applicable to the States by incorporation into the Fourteenth Amendment, ... provides that "Congress shall make no law respecting an establishment of religion, or prohibiting the free exercise thereof...." U.S. Const., Amdt. 1... The free exercise of religion means, first and foremost, the right to believe and profess whatever religious doctrine one desires. Thus, the First Amendment obviously excludes all "governmental regulation of religious beliefs as such." ... The government may not compel affirmation of religious belief, ... punish the expression of religious doctrines it believes to be false, ... impose special disabilities on the basis of religious views or religious status, ... or lend its power to one or the other side in controversies over religious authority or dogma....

But the "exercise of religion" often involves not only belief and profession but the performance of (or abstention from) physical acts: assembling with others for a worship service, participating in sacramental use of bread and wine, proselytizing, abstaining from certain foods or certain modes of transportation. It would be true, we think (though no case of ours has involved the point), that a State would be "prohibiting the free exercise [of religion]" if it sought to ban such acts or abstentions only when they are engaged in for religious reasons, or only because of the religious belief that they display. It would doubtless be unconstitutional, for example, to ban the casting of "statues that are to be used for worship purposes," or to prohibit bowing down before a golden calf.

Respondents in the present case, however, seek to carry the meaning of "prohibiting the free exercise [of religion]" one large step further. They contend that their religious motivation for using peyote places them beyond the reach of a criminal law that is not specifically directed at their religious practice, and that is concededly constitutional as applied to those who use the drug for other reasons. They assert, in other words, that "prohibiting the free exercise [of religion]" includes requiring any individual to observe a generally applicable law that requires (or forbids) the performance of an act that his religious belief forbids (or requires). As a textual matter, we do not think the words must be given that meaning. It is no more necessary to regard the collection of a general tax, for example, as "prohibiting the free exercise [of religion]" by those citizens who believe support of organized government to be sinful, than it is to regard the same tax as "abridging the freedom ... of the press" of those publishing companies that must pay the tax as a condition of staying in business. It is a permissible reading of the text, in the one case as in the other, to say that if prohibiting the exercise of religion (or burdening the activity of printing) is not the object of the tax but merely the incidental effect of a generally applicable and otherwise valid provision, the First Amendment has not been offended....

Our decisions reveal that the latter reading is the correct one. We have never held that an individual's religious beliefs excuse him from compliance with an otherwise valid law prohibiting conduct that the State is free to regulate. On the contrary, the record of more than a century of our free exercise jurisprudence contradicts that proposition.... We first had occasion to assert that principle in *Reynolds v. United States*, 98 U.S. 145 (1879), where we rejected the claim that criminal laws against polygamy could not be constitutionally applied to those whose religion commanded the practice. "Laws," we said, "are made for the government of actions, and while they cannot interfere with mere religious belief and opinions, they may with practices.... Can a man excuse his practices to the contrary because of his religious belief? To permit this would be to make the professed doctrines of religious belief superior to the law of the land, and in effect to permit every citizen to become a law unto himself." ...

Subsequent decisions have consistently held that the right of free exercise does not relieve an individual of the obligation to comply with a "valid and neutral law of general applicability on the ground that the law proscribes (or prescribes) conduct that his religion prescribes (or proscribes)." ... In *Prince v. Massachusetts*, 321 U.S. 158 (1944), we held that a mother could be prosecuted under the child labor laws for using her children to dispense literature in the streets, her religious motivation notwithstanding. We found no constitutional infirmity in "excluding [these children] from doing there what no other children may do." ... In *Gillette v. United States*, 401 U.S. 437 (1971), we sustained the military Selective Service System against the claim that it violated free

B. CULPABILITY DISTINGUISHED FROM MOTIVE

exercise by conscripting persons who opposed a particular war on religious grounds.

Our most recent decision involving a neutral, generally applicable regulatory law that compelled activity forbidden by an individual's religion was *United States v. Lee*, 455 U.S., at 258-261. There, an Amish employer, on behalf of himself and his employees, sought exemption from collection and payment of Social Security taxes on the ground that the Amish faith prohibited participation in governmental support programs. We rejected the claim that an exemption was constitutionally required. There would be no way, we observed, to distinguish the Amish believer's objection to Social Security taxes from the religious objections that others might have to the collection or use of other taxes. "If, for example, a religious adherent believes war is a sin, and if a certain percentage of the federal budget can be identified as devoted to war-related activities, such individuals would have a similarly valid claim to be exempt from paying that percentage of the income tax. The tax system could not function if denominations were allowed to challenge the tax system because tax payments were spent in a manner that violates their religious belief."...

The only decisions in which we have held that the First Amendment bars application of a neutral, generally applicable law to religiously motivated action have involved not the Free Exercise Clause alone, but the Free Exercise Clause in conjunction with other constitutional protections, such as freedom of speech and of the press ..., or the right of parents, acknowledged in *Pierce v. Society of Sisters*, 268 U.S. 510 (1925), to direct the education of their children, see *Wisconsin v. Yoder*, 406 U.S. 205 (1972) (invalidating compulsory school-attendance laws as applied to Amish parents who refused on religious grounds to send their children to school).

Yoder said that "the Court's holding in *Pierce* stands as a charter of the rights of parents to direct the religious upbringing of their children. And, when the interests of parenthood are combined with a free exercise claim of the nature revealed by this record, more than merely a 'reasonable relation to some purpose within the competency of the State' is required to sustain the validity of the State's requirement under the First Amendment." ...

The present case does not present such a hybrid situation, but a free exercise claim unconnected with any communicative activity or parental right. Respondents urge us to hold, quite simply, that when otherwise prohibitable conduct is accompanied by religious convictions, not only the convictions but the conduct itself must be free from governmental regulation. We have never held that, and decline to do so now. There being no contention that Oregon's drug law represents an attempt to regulate religious beliefs, the communication of religious beliefs, or the raising of one's children in those beliefs, the rule to which we have adhered ever since *Reynolds* plainly controls. "Our cases do not at their farthest reach support the proposition that a stance of conscientious opposition relieves an objector from any colliding duty fixed by a democratic government." ...

B

Respondents argue that even though exemption from generally applicable criminal laws need not automatically be extended to religiously motivated actors, at least the claim for a religious exemption must be evaluated under the balancing test set forth in *Sherbert v. Verner*, 374 U.S. 398 (1963). Under the *Sherbert* test, governmental actions that substantially burden a religious practice must be justified by a compelling governmental interest.... Applying that test we have, on three occasions, invalidated state unemployment compensation rules that conditioned the availability of benefits upon an applicant's willingness to work under conditions forbidden by his religion.... We have never invalidated any governmental action on the basis of the *Sherbert* test except the denial of unemployment compensation. Although we have sometimes purported to apply the *Sherbert* test in contexts other than that, we have always found the test satisfied... In recent years we have abstained from applying the *Sherbert* test (outside the unemployment compensation field) at all... In *O'Lone v. Estate of Shabazz*, 482 U.S. 342 (1987), we sustained, without mentioning the *Sherbert* test, a prison's refusal to excuse inmates from work requirements to attend worship services.

Even if we were inclined to breathe into *Sherbert* some life beyond the unemployment compensation field, we would not apply it to require exemptions from a generally applicable criminal law. The *Sherbert* test, it must be recalled, was developed in a context that lent itself to individualized governmental assessment of the reasons for the relevant conduct.... [W]here the State has in place a system of individual exemptions, it may not refuse to extend that system to cases of "religious hardship" without compelling reason....

Whether or not the decisions are that limited, they at least have nothing to do with an across-the-board criminal prohibition on a particular form of conduct. Although, as noted earlier, we have sometimes used the *Sherbert* test to analyze free exercise challenges to such laws, ... we have never applied the test to invalidate one. We conclude today that the sounder approach, and the approach in accord with the vast majority of our precedents, is to hold the test inapplicable to such challenges. The government's ability to enforce generally applicable prohibitions of socially harmful conduct, like its ability to carry out other aspects of public policy, "cannot depend on measuring the effects of a governmental action on a religious objector's spiritual development.".... To make an individual's obligation to obey such a law contingent upon the law's coincidence with his religious beliefs, except where the State's interest is "compelling" — permitting him, by virtue of his beliefs, "to become a law unto himself,"... — contradicts both constitutional tradition and common sense....

The "compelling government interest" requirement seems benign, because it is familiar from other fields. But using it as the standard that must be met before the government may accord different treatment on the basis of race,... or before the government may regulate the content of speech,... is not remotely comparable to using it for the purpose asserted here. What it produces in those other fields — equality of treatment and an unrestricted flow of contending speech — are constitutional norms; what it would produce here —

a private right to ignore generally applicable laws — is a constitutional anomaly.

Nor is it possible to limit the impact of respondents' proposal by requiring a "compelling state interest" only when the conduct prohibited is "central" to the individual's religion.... It is no more appropriate for judges to determine the "centrality" of religious beliefs before applying a "compelling interest" test in the free exercise field, than it would be for them to determine the "importance" of ideas before applying the "compelling interest" test in the free speech field. What principle of law or logic can be brought to bear to contradict a believer's assertion that a particular act is "central" to his personal faith? Judging the centrality of different religious practices is akin to the unacceptable "business of evaluating the relative merits of differing religious claims." ... Repeatedly and in many different contexts, we have warned that courts must not presume to determine the place of a particular belief in a religion or the plausibility of a religious claim....

If the "compelling interest" test is to be applied at all, then, it must be applied across the board, to all actions thought to be religiously commanded. Moreover, if "compelling interest" really means what it says (and watering it down here would subvert its rigor in the other fields where it is applied), many laws will not meet the test. Any society adopting such a system would be courting anarchy, but that danger increases in direct proportion to the society's diversity of religious beliefs, and its determination to coerce or suppress none of them. Precisely because "we are a cosmopolitan nation made up of people of almost every conceivable religious preference," ... and precisely because we value and protect that religious divergence, we cannot afford the luxury of deeming *presumptively invalid*, as applied to the religious objector, every regulation of conduct that does not protect an interest of the highest order. The rule respondents favor would open the prospect of constitutionally required religious exemptions from civic obligations of almost every conceivable kind — ranging from compulsory military service ... to the payment of taxes, ...; to health and safety regulation such as manslaughter and child neglect laws, ... compulsory vaccination laws, ... drug laws, ... and traffic laws ...; to social welfare legislation such as minimum wage laws, ... child labor laws, ... animal cruelty laws, ... environmental protection laws, ... and laws providing for equality of opportunity for the races.... The First Amendment's protection of religious liberty does not require this....

Because respondents' ingestion of peyote was prohibited under Oregon law, and because that prohibition is constitutional, Oregon may, consistent with the Free Exercise Clause, deny respondents unemployment compensation when their dismissal results from use of the drug. The decision of the Oregon Supreme Court is accordingly reversed.

It is so ordered.

NOTES

1. In *United States v. Berrigan*, 283 F. Supp. 336 (D. Md. 1968), defendants were charged with injuring federal property, mutilating federal records and hindering the administration of the selective service system when they poured

blood into draft office records. In rejecting their asserted defenses, the district court noted:

> The reasonableness of the belief of these defendants that the government is acting illegally in Vietnam is irrelevant to the present case; for, even if it were demonstrable that the United States is committing violations of international law, this violation by itself would afford the defendants no justifiable basis for their acts.
>
> ....
>
> There can be no doubt that the First Amendment protects speech in opposition to national policy in Vietnam and to the Selective Service System. *Bond v. Floyd*, 385 U.S. 116 (1966). But this protection does not shield conduct which collides with a valid criminal statute. And it makes no difference, as this court has pointed out before, that the defendants acted out of the sincerest of motives and the deepest of convictions, be they religious, moral, or political. Only recently the Supreme Court in *Cox* emphasized it could not sanction
>
>> riotous conduct in any form or demonstrations, however peaceful their conduct or commendable their motives, which conflict with properly drawn statutes and ordinances designed to promote law and order, protect the community against disorder, regulate traffic, safeguard legitimate interests in private and public property, or protect the administration of justice and other essential governmental functions.

Id. at 339, 340-41.

2. Anti-abortion groups frequently picket, physically obstruct entrances to, and even physically invade abortion clinics and counseling centers. A great many of these so-called "right to life" demonstrators assert a religious basis for their efforts to prevent lawful abortions. Although peaceful picketing basically is a form of protected speech under the first amendment, the Supreme Court ruled in *Frisby v. Schultz*, 487 U.S. 474 (1988), that a local ordinance could prohibit focused picketing solely in front of a single residence that destroyed the privacy of the inhabitants; the picketing was directed at the residence of a doctor who performed lawful abortions at clinics in adjacent towns. Trespassers and persons blocking access to clinics have been convicted of criminal trespass; appellate courts have affirmed the convictions and rejected claims of the necessity defense allegedly founded on the need to preserve fetal life. See, e.g., *State v. Aguillard*, 567 So. 2d 674 (La. App. 1990); *People v. Stiso*, 416 N.E.2d 1209 (Ill. App. 1981); *State v. O'Brien*, 784 S.W.2d 187 (Mo. App. 1989); *State v. Migliorino*, 442 N.W.2d 36 (Wis.), *cert. denied sub nom. Haines v. Wisconsin*, 493 U.S. 1004 (1989).

3. The New Hampshire Supreme Court construed its choice of evils (necessity) statute, which is substantially the same as MODEL PENAL CODE § 3.02 (see Appendix A), in a manner consistent with the Model Penal Code provision. *State v. Dorsey*, 395 A.2d 855 (N.H. 1978); *see also Gaetano v. United States*, 406 A.2d 1291 (D.C. App. 1979). In *Dorsey* the defendant was arrested and convicted for trespass after he participated in a mass occupation of the construction site of a nuclear power plant. Defendant had been precluded from

utilizing the necessity defense, and on appeal the New Hampshire Supreme Court upheld this decision. The court noted that the New Hampshire legislature had provided for the construction of such plants after evaluation of public health and safety risks. Using the Model Penal Code policy considerations, the court found it "inconceivable that the legislature would intend that nuclear power be considered such a harm as to justify individuals in breaking the law." *Dorsey*, 395 A.2d at 857. Accordingly, as a matter of law defendant's behavior was not within the scope of the necessity statute.

4. In *Frank v. State*, 604 P.2d 1068 (Alaska 1979), the Supreme Court of Alaska overturned Frank's conviction for illegally taking and transporting a moose out of season. The defendant, an Athabascan Indian, killed the animal for consumption at a funeral potlatch ceremony, a practice deeply rooted in tribal religion of which Frank was a devout adherent. The court thought there was no showing that so many moose would be taken under the exception it was asked to create that the animal population would be affected. It noted that administrative regulations could be created to control such takings. In other jurisdictions regulations have been used to allow Indians to take eagles and deer for use in religious ceremonies.

C. INTENT OR PURPOSE

1. BASIC CONCEPT

MODEL PENAL CODE

§ 2.02. General Requirements of Culpability

....

   (2) Kinds of Culpability Defined
     (a) Purposely.
      A person acts purposely with respect to a material element of an offense when:
        (i) if the element involves the nature of his conduct or a result thereof, it is his conscious object to engage in conduct of that nature or to cause such a result; and
        (ii) if the element involves the attendant circumstances, he is aware of the existence of such circumstances or he believes or hopes that they exist.

2. SPECIFIC AND GENERAL INTENT

PEOPLE v. GLOVER

California Court of Appeal
285 Cal. Rptr. 362 (1991)

TURNER, PRESIDING JUSTICE.

I. INTRODUCTION

Defendant Joan Glover appeals from a judgment of conviction for arson of an inhabited structure in violation of Penal Code section 451, subdivision (b).[1] On appeal, defendant contends that the evidence was insufficient to support her conviction of arson of an inhabited structure because defendant did not act with the requisite specific intent to set fire to an inhabited dwelling rather than her personal property and there was instructional error. We find that no prejudicial error has occurred and, as a result, the judgment is affirmed.

II. THE FACTS

On April 17, 1987, defendant lived in apartment 25 at 1170 Murchison Street in Pomona. Previously, in September of 1986, defendant had told her former husband that "she got some insurance and that she was gonna burn her apartment up because she needed some money." Defendant met with several persons including Albert Dukes (Dukes) and asked him to start a fire with kerosene in her apartment. She never stated why she wanted the fire started. Dukes stated that defendant wanted two other residents of the apartment building out of the building at the time the fire was started.

In compliance with her instructions, Dukes started the fire by pouring kerosene over furniture which was placed in the middle of defendant's living room. He poured kerosene "all over the floor and left a trace to the back door." He then dropped a burning paper bag "onto the trace of kerosene" and the fire ignited. He fled the scene of the incident.

Shortly thereafter, Pomona firefighters arrived at defendant's apartment. An arson investigation indicated that the fire had been intentionally set within a six square foot area in the living room of the apartment. A petroleum product was used to start the fire according to an arson investigator and the carpet had burned down to the concrete through the carpet pad. Cupboards in the kitchen had been burned. When the fire ignited, the arson investigator stated that there had been a low level explosion. In the upstairs area of the apartment, there had been smoke damage or residue. Both Dukes and the fire investigator identified words that had been spray painted in the upstairs area of the apartment in an effort to make the fire look as though it was "gang related." After the fire, she applied for fire insurance proceeds and ultimately received an insurance settlement as a result of the fire.

III. DISCUSSION

A. There is substantial evidence that defendant possessed the requisite mental state to commit a violation of section 451, subdivision (b). Defendant contends that the evidence is insufficient to support a conviction for arson of an inhabited dwelling because it is necessary that a defendant possess a specific intent to set fire to the structure.... [D]efendant argues that an essential element of the crime was the existence on defendant's part of a specific intent

---

[1] Penal Code section 451 . . . provides in relevant part: "A person is guilty of arson when he or she willfully and maliciously sets fire to or burns or causes to be burned or who aids, counsels, or procures the burning of, any structure, forest land, or property.

(b) Arson that causes an inhabited structure or inhabited property to burn is a felony punishable by imprisonment in the state prison for three, five, or eight years." All future statutory references are to the Penal Code.

to set fire to the structure. Because we believe that Stonewall F. does not correctly state California law and, in any event, there was substantial evidence of a specific intent, we affirm.

First, we believe that arson remains a general intent crime.... The California Supreme Court has discussed the requisite intent for an arson conviction on several occasions. Prior to the adoption of the Penal Code in 1872, California statutes did not require a specific intent as an element of the offense of arson.... However, upon the adoption of the Penal Code in 1872, former section 447 was enacted to provide, "arson is the willful and malicious burning of a building, with the intent to destroy it." The Supreme Court interpreted former section 447 to require the presence of a specific intent to destroy the property that was burned....

In 1929, the arson statutes were recodified and section 447 was repealed.... The definition of three forms of arson described in new section 447a, 448a, and 449a required that the perpetrator of the offense act "wilfully and maliciously."... Other sections of the 1929 enactment prohibited arson when done with the "intent to injure or defraud the insurer" or by placing a "flammable, explosive or combustible material" in a building "with the intent to eventually willfully and maliciously set [a] fire" did retain an intent requirement.... These two latter sections which contained an "intent" requirement were codified as former sections 450a and 451a. In 1979, section 450a was repealed and the current provisions of section 451, subdivision (b), the offense of which defendant has been convicted, was added to the Penal Code. Section 451a was amended in 1979 and renumbered and is currently found in section 455.... Of the current arson statutes codified in sections 451-457.1, only sections 453 and 455 contain a requirement that a person possess a particular intent.[5]

Since 1899, despite the substantial changes in the arson provisions of the Penal Code, the California Supreme Court has only commented in dicta concerning the issue of whether there is a requirement that a specific intent exist before the crime of arson may be committed.... Other jurisdictions have without exception concluded that there is no specific intent requirement in order to commit the crime of arson unless an arson statute requires the existence of a particular intention.[6] ... In some states, an arson statute requires a specific

---

[5] Section 453, subdivision (a) provides in relevant part:

"Every person who possesses any flammable, explosive, or combustible material or substance, or any device in an arrangement or preparation, with intent to willfully and maliciously use such material, substance or device to set fire to or burn any structure, forest land or property, is punishable by imprisonment in the state prison...."

Section 455 prohibits aiding, counseling, or procuring the burning of any "structure, forest land or property ..." and proceeds to outlaw the "placing or distributing of any flammable, explosive or combustible material or substance, or any device in or about any structure, forest land or property in an arrangement in preparation with intent to eventually willfully and maliciously set fire to or burn same...."

[6] Only one federal court appears to have directly discussed the issue of what mens rea must exist in order to violate the federal arson statute. Title 18 U.S.C. section 81 provides in relevant part: "Whoever, within the special maritime and territorial jurisdiction of the United States, willfully and maliciously sets fire to or burns ... any building ... shall be fined not more that $1,000 or imprisoned not more than five years, or both." In *United States v. M.W.*, 890 F.2d 239, 240 (10th Cir. 1989), the Court of Appeals analyzed the issue not in terms of a general or specific intent; rather, the court discussed whether the perpetrator's state of mind must be purposeful as distinguished from the less strict requirement of a knowing act of starting a fire. The Court of

intent as an element of the crime of arson or one of its related offenses and the statutory language has been interpreted to require that there be more than a mere general intent to commit the crime.... The general rule of law throughout the country has been that unless a jurisdiction's arson statute requires a particular intent, arson is a general intent crime....

In evaluating whether a crime under California law requires a specific or general intent, the California Supreme Court has held that unless the crime defines a specific intent, the offense is a general offense crime.... Section 451 requires that the act be done "willfully and maliciously" but does not indicate that any particular intent such as the intent to burn an inhabited structure is to exist. In order to act willfully, there is no requirement a defendant act with a specific intent.... Furthermore, a defendant who acts maliciously need not possess a specific intent.... Section 450, subdivision (e) defines "maliciously" in terms of the arson statutes as "a wish to vex, defraud, annoy, or injure another person, or an intent to do a wrongful act...." Section 450, subdivision (e) does not define the term "maliciously" as requiring an intent to burn an "inhabited structure, forest land, or property" as that language appears in section 451, subdivision (b), the statute under which defendant was convicted. The definition of "maliciously" in section 450, subdivision (e) which applies to arson prosecutions, is the same language appearing in section 7, subdivision 4. No court has ever interpreted section 7, subdivision 4 to require the presence of a specific intent as an element of a crime. Section 451, subdivision (b) which defines the particular punishment range to be imposed against a person who causes an inhabited structure or inhabited property to burn does not require any specific intent....

However, even if there was a requirement of a specific intent, there was substantial evidence to support the jury's verdict. Defendant's former husband spoke with her in September 1986 before the fire. According to her former husband, defendant said that "she got some insurance and that she was gonna burn her apartment up because she needed some money." Defendant told Dukes she wanted him and several others to start a fire by pushing "all" of her furniture to the middle of the floor. She gave Dukes "two jugs" of kerosene she obtained from her car. The "jugs" of kerosene were poured into a metal bowl while defendant was still in the apartment. The jugs were emptied into the metal bowl in the upstairs portion of the apartment. She instructed Dukes to insure that "Harold and Dicey" were out of the apartment building when the fire was started. Dukes, who was acting on defendant's instructions, poured the kerosene "all over the floor" and created a "trace" or path of the flammable liquid all the way to the back door of the apartment. When the kerosene provided by defendant ignited, Dukes and his accomplice were blown from the apartment through an open door by the force of the sudden ignition. This certainly constituted sufficient evidence of a specific intent to do more

---

Appeals held that a fire, under the federal arson statute, must only be set "with the knowledge that burning of a building is the practically certain result...." (*Id.* at p. 241.) The Court of Appeals rejected defendant's contention that 18 U.S.C. section 81 required he act "purposely" when the crime was committed. Finally, the Court of Appeals relied upon two Arizona appellate court cases which held that the words "willfully and maliciously" in that state's arson statute did not require a specific intent to burn property. (*Ibid.*)

C. INTENT OR PURPOSE

than simply burn personal property as asserted by defendant. Coupled with her statement to her former husband that she was "gonna burn her apartment up," the manner in which she directed that the fire be started so that it was inevitable that there be a burning throughout the apartment constituted substantial evidence of a specific intent to burn the inhabited apartment building....

The judgment is affirmed.

NOTES

1. In *State v. Burroff,* 598 N.E.2d 1081 (Ind. App. 1992), the court held that a defendant could have been convicted of arson, even if he had no insurance coverage, had he believed there was coverage and he burned the property with intent to defraud an insurer. (The trial court had directed a verdict of acquittal, and the state reserved a question of law for the court to resolve in a form of advisory opinion; double jeopardy barred the defendant's retrial.) The court summarized the doctrine thus:

> ... The gravamen of the offense is the accused's intent to defraud, and the essential inquiry is whether the accused believed he was covered, regardless of the true state of his insurance coverage. If the defendant believes there is coverage, and he burns his property with the intent to defraud the insurer, the crime is committed, even if the defendant's intent could not have come to fruition.
>
> The arson statute requires proof of only general criminal intent which may be inferred from the acts committed and the surrounding circumstances.... If the defendant burned his property the jury should determine his intent from the facts and circumstances surrounding the fire....

Id. at 1083.

2. In *State v. D'Amico,* 385 A.2d 1082 (Vt. 1978), the court considered the intent element in a statutory crime of assault with a deadly weapon. On the day of the alleged offense the respondent sat at home drinking beer while his girlfriend attended a local music festival with one James Holiday. When they returned in the early evening, the respondent threatened to "take a gun" to Holiday the next time. After consuming a quantity of wine, the respondent took his shotgun and drove his truck to a neighboring residence where Holiday and others were sitting in front of the house. Respondent approached the residence screaming, threatening to kill someone, and firing at least four shots. Although a piece of flying debris caused by the shotgun fire struck one Donna Arley, no one was injured. The respondent, in his request to charge, asked the trial court to instruct the jury to consider the evidence of his intoxication as bearing upon his capacity to form the requisite criminal intent to commit the crime charged. The trial court, however, instructed that voluntary intoxication is not a defense to the commission of a crime. The appellate court reversed D'Amico's conviction:

> The State argues that the offense charged is simply a common law assault committed with the use of a deadly weapon and that the mental element required for simple assault is controlling.... [I]t contends that

simple assault is a general intent crime. The State urges us to hold that policy and logic dictate that aggravated assault requires the same general intent, and that therefore ... consideration of intoxication should not be permitted. We disagree....

The novel question for this Court is to determine, first, the mental capacity the Legislature intended to require for the commission of the statutory crime charged under 13 V.S.A. § 1024(a)(2), and, secondly, whether evidence of voluntary intoxication is available to diminish the requisite capacity. The statute provides as follows: "A person is guilty of aggravated assault if he ... (2) attempts to cause or purposely or knowingly causes bodily injury to another with a deadly weapon."

It is evident that the intent of the Legislature in enacting [the statute] was to deal with the full range of assault crimes from those requiring the capacity to form only a general intent ... to those requiring the capacity to form specific intent.... The statutory scheme adopted to accomplish this purpose ... is borrowed almost verbatim from the Model Penal Code §§ 211.0-211.2 (1962). Unlike Vermont's former breach of the peace statute, ... now superseded, which relied on the common law to define the elements of the offense, § 1024(a)(2) enumerates the elements within its provisions. Under § 1024(a)(2) the State had the burden of proving beyond a reasonable doubt the following: first, the respondent attempted to do an unlawful act; secondly, the unlawful act attempted was the causing of bodily injury; thirdly, the unlawful act attempted was done with a deadly weapon.

Although the rationale of the Model Penal Code is not binding on this Court, it is indicative of what the General Assembly intended in adopting legislation modeled on the Code. Under the Code the attempt to commit an offense necessarily involves the same mental intent as would be required in the actual commission of that offense. Model Penal Code § 5.01 (1962). Section 1024(a)(2) defines the completed offense as "purposely or knowingly [causing] bodily injury to another with a deadly weapon" thus making the mental element of either purpose or knowledge a necessary element of the crime charged.... The [Model Penal Code] rationale makes evidence of intoxication available to exculpate if it negatives an element of the offense, *Id.* § 208(1), and, according to Code commentary, proof of a mental state characterized as purposeful and knowing may be negated by evidence of intoxication. *Id.* § 2.08, Comment (Tent. Draft No. 9, 1959).

It is evident to us that the Code concept of purpose and knowledge corresponds to the common law concept of specific intent, as we have already had occasion to characterize, in dicta, a § 1024(a)(2) offense as a specific intent crime.... Both of these concepts import a conscious intent or design to act as charged.... We conclude, therefore, that it was the Legislature's intent in enacting 13 V.S.A. § 1024(a)(2) to proscribe an act which included as an essential mental element that the act be done purposefully and knowingly. Furthermore, we hold that voluntary intoxication is available to negate a finding of the requisite mental intent in a charge under this statute. Since there was evidence in the case of respondent's intoxication, it was for the jury to determine the effect on the

C. INTENT OR PURPOSE

respondent's mental processes and whether his mental capacity was so diminished as to prevent him from forming the requisite felonious intent.... The trial court's instruction on voluntary intoxication standing alone was, therefore, error.

The State argues that it is anomalous to allow intoxication to diminish the capacity to commit crimes of assault which occur so frequently in situations involving inebriation, and we are not unmindful of the policy implications if by our decision we leave the State without adequate means to punish drunken behavior that is without question socially harmful.... The statutory scheme generally covering assault, of which 13 V.S.A. § 1024(a)(2) is but a part, does, however, enable the State to punish various unlawful acts without proving that the act was committed with purpose and knowledge. Whether voluntary intoxication is available to exculpate in charges not involving the mental element of purpose and knowledge is not determined by this opinion....

Additional materials on the significance of intoxication as it bears on culpability appear *infra* pp. 643-655.

REGINA v. PEMBLITON
Court of Criminal Appeal
12 Cox Crim. Cas. 607, 2 C.C.R. 119 (1874)

Lord Coleridge, C.J.

I am of the opinion that this conviction must be quashed. The facts of the case are these. The prisoner and some other persons who had been drinking in a public house were turned out of it at about 11 p.m. for being disorderly, and they then began to fight in the street near the prosecutor's window. The prisoner separated himself from the others, and went to the other side of the street, and picked up a stone, and threw it at the persons he had been fighting with. The stone passed over their heads, and broke a large plate glass window in the prosecutor's house, doing damage to an amount exceeding 5 pounds. The jury found that the prisoner threw the stone at the people he had been fighting with, intending to strike one or more of them with it, but not intending to break the window. The question is whether under an indictment for unlawfully and maliciously committing an injury to the window in the house of the prosecutor the proof of these facts alone, coupled with the finding of the jury, will do? Now I think that is not enough. The indictment is framed under the 24 and 25 Vict. c. 97, S. 51. The Act is an Act relating to malicious injuries to property, and section 51 enacts that whosoever shall unlawfully and maliciously commit any damage, etc., to or upon any real or personal property whatsoever of a public or a private nature, for which no punishment is hereinbefore provided, to an amount exceeding 5 pounds, shall be guilty of a misdemeanor.... Without saying that, upon these facts, if the jury had found that the prisoner had been guilty of throwing the stone recklessly, knowing that there was a window near which it might probably hit, that I should have been disposed to interfere with the conviction, yet as they have found that he threw the stone at the people he had been fighting with intending to strike them and not intending to break the window, I think the conviction must be quashed....

BLACKBURN, J.... The question here is can the prisoner be said when he not only threw the stone unlawfully, but broke the window unintentionally, to have unlawfully and maliciously broken the window. I think that there was evidence on which the jury might have found that he unlawfully and maliciously broke the window, if they had found that the prisoner was aware that the natural and probable consequence of his throwing the stone was that it might break the glass window, on the principle that a man must be taken to intend what is the natural and probable consequence of his acts. But the jury have not found that the prisoner threw the stone, knowing that, on the other side of the men he was throwing at, there was a glass window, and that he was reckless as to whether he did or did not break the window. On the contrary, they have found that he did not intend to break the window....

Conviction quashed.

PEOPLE v. WEAVER

California District Court of Appeal
163 P.2d 456 (1945)

[Defendant was convicted of assault with a deadly weapon.]

DESMOND, PRESIDING JUSTICE. .... Eph Lincoln, the man who was assaulted, was engaged in no controversy with the defendant. At the time she stabbed him or slashed him with a knife she was directing her attention not to him, but to her "boy friend," Ernest Spears, known locally as "Trigger," who had just struck her over the head with a garbage bucket which he seized behind the bar of Sarrell's, the establishment where he was employed as bartender. He testified that in his excitement, being pursued by appellant, the blow with the bucket which landed on appellant's head was intended to strike her hand and knock from it the knife which she carried. As his aim was poor, so was appellant's, for the stab which she intended for Trigger landed instead in the chest of Lincoln who was seated quietly on a stool behind the bar and several feet away from Trigger.

While appellant and Trigger had been quarrelling previously, and had left Sarrell's Bar and Grill shortly before the stabbing took place, only to return almost immediately, Lincoln did not participate in the quarrel in any way. He testified that Trigger, when he returned to the saloon, was followed by appellant who "came running back in the place"; that Trigger "stopped at the cigar counter at the end of the bar and she stopped there. I am sitting behind the cigar counter, which is at the bar, too, on a stool, and all at once she comes behind the counter and lunged there with a knife and struck me." Question by Mr. Danoff: "Did you say anything to her? A. I said 'Madam, you cut the wrong man.'"

....

The record in this case indicates that the person engaged in self-defense at the time of the stabbing was not this appellant, but the man whom she was pursuing with a knife in her hand. Therefore, the authority cited by her counsel (30 C.J. 88, 89) as sufficient to excuse her assault upon an innocent bystander, has no application, and since she was not acting in self-defense, the fact that she did not intend to stab Lincoln cannot clear her, under the reasoning of cases cited by respondent in 40 C.J.S., Homicide, § 17, p. 864.

Judgment affirmed.

NOTE

WORKING PAPERS OF THE NATIONAL COMMISSION ON REFORM OF FEDERAL CRIMINAL LAWS 132-33 (1970):[*]

If a person is charged with intentionally causing X by his conduct, it must have been his purpose not only to engage in the conduct but also to cause X. If he is charged with knowingly causing X by his conduct, he must have known not only what he was doing but also have known (or firmly believed) that his conduct would cause X. If he is charged with recklessly engaging in conduct that causes X, it must be shown that he acted "in conscious ... and ... clearly unjustifiable disregard of a substantial likelihood" that his conduct would cause X, which, in view of the result-based nature of the crime, is one of the "relevant facts." Similarly, if he is charged with negligently engaging in conduct that causes X, it must be shown that he acted "in unreasonable disregard of a substantial likelihood" that his conduct would cause X.

The effect of this provision in some cases is a departure from the commonly expressed doctrine of "transferred intent." If A shoots at a person with the intention of killing him and does kill him, the requirement of intention is satisfied, even if A intended to shoot at X and thought he was shooting at X and intended to kill X but was actually shooting at Y (just as if he shot at X and intended to kill X, but learned later that he had killed the "wrong man"). In such cases, there is no need to "transfer" intent, and there is no conflict between the draft provision and the doctrine of "transferred intent." If, on the other hand, A, intending to kill X, shoots at X, but his bullet misses X and hits Y who is killed, since A did not intend to cause the death of Y, under the proposed formulation, A is not liable for the intentional killing of Y. Under

---

[*]Federal criminal law is exclusively statutory. The bulk is found in title 18 of the United States Code, but penalty-bearing provisions may be found in virtually every title of the code. Since the late 1960s efforts have been forthcoming to prepare and enact a completely revised and modernized federal criminal code, influenced heavily by the pattern of the Model Penal Code. The first major step in that direction was the creation by Congress of a National Commission on Reform of Federal Criminal Laws, chaired by former Governor Edmund G. Brown of California, and thus usually referred to as the Brown Commission. The commission produced a draft federal criminal code which soon thereafter was introduced in Congress, as well as three volumes of working papers commissioned from criminal law experts throughout the country. These volumes continue to be valuable reference resources and, indeed, have been incorporated almost verbatim in congressional committee reports in ensuing years.

Through 1983, each legislative session of Congress saw the introduction of and judiciary committee hearings on variant forms of the original proposal, and each presidential administration submitted its own views on the appropriate contents of a federal criminal code. At length, in 1984 Congress enacted not a comprehensive federal criminal code, but massive changes in certain dimensions of federal legislation, designated as the Comprehensive Crime Control Act of 1984. One of the major dimensions of CCCA was the mandating of federal sentencing guidelines, a matter addressed in Chapter 11; *see infra* at pp. 887-895. Other changes in substantive criminal law and procedure were accomplished in the Anti-Drug Abuse Acts of 1986, 1988, and 1990. At this writing, there appear to be no members of Congress who wish to push for a new criminal code, and it is too early to gauge whether the Administration will become interested in proposing one.

the doctrine of "transferred intent," *A*'s intent to kill *X* would be "transferred" to his act of killing *Y*, and *A* would be liable for the intentional killing of *Y*.

The doctrine of "transferred intent" is rejected because it is both conceptually unsound and unnecessary. Had *A* simply missed *X*, he would have been liable for attempted murder of *X*. He is no less liable for the attempted murder of *X* because he happened to kill *Y*. He may also be liable for the murder of *Y* if the crime of murder includes a provision relating to extreme recklessness, and so forth, which causes death, or a provision comparable to that now contained in Federal law that a murder "perpetrated from a premeditated design unlawfully and maliciously to effect the death of any human being other than him who is killed, is murder in the first degree." What *A* has not done is to kill anyone whom he intended to kill, and he should not be liable for that crime. Because an intent to kill and a death have converged and are causally related, it is easy to overlook the fact that the death of *Y* is, with respect to *A*'s intent, wholly fortuitous and, again so far as intentional wrongdoing is concerned, has no bearing on *A*'s culpability. If *Y*'s death makes *A* more culpable than he would be if his bullet had gone astray and hit no one, it is because *A*'s conduct was not only intentional vis-à-vis *X* but also reckless (or wanton) vis-à-vis *Y*. So far as *Y*'s death is concerned, *A*'s culpability is not different than it would be if *A* had intended to shoot a deer and not another person. Parallel reasoning applies to conduct in which a person engages knowingly.

The proposed formulation accepts this analysis as truer to the facts and the actual culpability of the defendant than the doctrine of transferred intent. The community's outrage at the death of *Y* will not be unsatisfied, since *A* will, in any event, be liable for attempted murder and manslaughter and will, in all probability, be liable for murder as well. All that is rejected is the doctrine of "transferred intent," which is a needless fiction.[82] Do you agree with the Commission's conclusion that the doctrine of transferred intent is superfluous?

---

[82] With respect to reckless and negligent conduct, this provision probably does not depart from existing law. The effect of the provision is to limit liability to the consequences which might have been avoided had the person not been reckless or negligent. Thus, if *A* shoots a gun recklessly, he is not liable if the bullet knocks down a branch which lands on a bear who becomes enraged and attacks and kills *X* miles away in the forest. Even though the death was a consequence of *A*'s reckless shooting, *A* did not act "in conscious and clearly unjustifiable disregard of a substantial likelihood" that his conduct would cause *X*'s death. In tort terms, the result was not within the risk. The scope of liability for consequences of reckless conduct need not be drawn very narrowly. Had *X* been hit directly by the bullet fired from *A*'s gun, *A* would surely be liable for *X*'s death, even though *A* did not know that *X* (or anyone) was within shooting distance and the bullet ricocheted off a rock before hitting *X*, *A*'s conduct may well have been "in ... disregard of a substantial likelihood" that someone would be killed. Parallel reasoning applies to conduct in which a person engages negligently.

Where recklessness or negligence is at stake, the scope of the risk is not ordinarily defined in terms of a particular victim or property and there may be no doctrine parallel to that of transferred intent.

The Model Penal Code (§ 2.03(a)) does include a rule parallel to the doctrine of transferred intent. One can imagine a case where *A* acts in conscious disregard of a likelihood that *X* will be in a place of danger and be injured, and in fact *Y* is in the place of danger and is injured. Again, however, this is not a case of "transferred recklessness;" *A*'s recklessness consisted in his acting in disregard of the risk that someone would be injured. If no one was in the place of danger and *Y* was killed by an unforeseeable chain of circumstances, it is doubtful whether *A* would be liable for reckless homicide. If so, the result would be parallel to that reached by the doctrine of transferred intent. See Williams, Criminal Law 110-112 (1953).

D. KNOWLEDGE

MODEL PENAL CODE

§ 2.02. General Requirements of Culpability

....

(2) Kinds of Culpability Defined
  (b) Knowingly
A person acts knowingly with respect to a material element of an offense when:
    (i) if the element involves the nature of his conduct or the attendant circumstances, he is aware that his conduct is of that nature or that such circumstances exist; and
    (ii) if the element involves a result of his conduct, he is aware that it is practically certain that his conduct will cause such a result.

UNITED STATES v. SANCHEZ-ROBLES

United States Court of Appeals for the Ninth Circuit
927 F.2d 1070 (1991)

RYMER, CIRCUIT JUDGE:

A jury found Susana Sanchez-Robles guilty of importing cocaine, importing marijuana and possessing marijuana and cocaine with intent to distribute in violation of 21 U.S.C. §§ 841(a), 952 & 960. She appeals on grounds of insufficiency of the evidence, ... and error in giving a "deliberate ignorance" instruction under *United States v. Jewell*, 532 F.2d 697 (9th Cir.) (en banc), *cert. denied*, 426 U.S. 951 (1976), where the only evidence to support a *Jewell* instruction was her presence in a van which agents said reeked of marijuana. Because there were no circumstances to arouse in Sanchez-Robles's mind a suspicion of illegal activity aside from the strong odor and because that odor, if recognized, would establish only her actual knowledge of illegality and not deliberate ignorance, the *Jewell* instruction was inappropriate. Accordingly, we reverse.

I. Facts

Sanchez-Robles, a mother of five, lived in El Centro, California. She frequently visited friends and relatives in Mexicali, Mexico. She claims that on June 30, 1989, four of her daughters, aged 4 to 17, asked her to take them to Mexico for tacos. A friend named Armando Lopez, whom she said she had known for one month, had left a van at her apartment, so she borrowed it and left for Mexico with her daughters at around 10 p.m. that evening. Sanchez-Robles claims that she did not use her own car that night because her other daughter, Guadalupe, had borrowed it to go out on a date. Guadalupe and her boyfriend testified that they went out together that night, taking the Sanchez-Robles car to Mexicali and returning at around midnight. Sanchez-Robles and the four daughters made the trip to Mexico in the Lopez van.

Upon their return to the United States at 11:50 p.m., a customs official at the Calexico port of entry overheard Sanchez-Robles speaking in Spanish to

90 CH. 2 ELEMENTS OF CRIMES AND THE CONSEQUENCES OF CRIMINALITY

her daughters, all of whom were sitting on the front seats of the van, telling them to be quiet and not say anything. The inspector noticed an odor inside the van, which he recognized as marijuana. When he opened the side door of the van, the odor was stronger. He referred the van to a secondary inspection area, where another officer noticed the odor and took the family inside. A search of Sanchez-Robles found nothing illegal. The officer at the secondary inspection area characterized the odor from the driver's window of the van as a six on a scale of one to ten, with ten being the strongest, and the odor from the rear of the van as an eight-to-nine. Drug-sniffing dogs alerted customs agents to several areas in the van, and when inspectors took the vehicle apart, they found 43 pounds of cocaine and 417 pounds of marijuana hidden throughout. The dismantling process took an hour and a half, and as the inspectors were removing the contraband, they had to take fresh air breaks because the odor was so strong. After the van doors had been open for approximately five minutes, the odor of marijuana carried across to the far side of the secondary inspection lot.

Sanchez-Robles denied any knowledge of the drugs and claimed that she does not recognize the smell of marijuana. The district court's *Jewell* instruction was as follows:

> If you have a reasonable doubt that the defendant actually believed that the vehicle she was in did not contain a controlled substance, then she did not have the requisite knowledge and you must find her not guilty. However, the government can satisfy its burden of proof as to guilty knowledge by proving beyond a reasonable doubt that, although the defendant was not actually aware that there was a controlled substance in the vehicle at the time of her arrest, she nevertheless was aware of a high probability that the vehicle contained a controlled substance, and her ignorance of the presence of a controlled substance was solely and entirely a result of her having made a conscious effort to disregard the nature of that which was in the vehicle, with a conscious purpose to avoid learning the truth.

II. *Jewell* Instruction

Though we consider jury instructions as a whole to evaluate their adequacy, "whether a jury instruction misstated elements of a statutory crime is a question of law and is reviewed de novo." ...

A *Jewell* instruction is premised on the notion that a defendant cannot insulate herself from criminal liability by consciously preserving a lack of actual knowledge of the criminal activity. "To act 'knowingly' ... is not necessarily to act only with positive knowledge, but also to act with an awareness of the high probability of the existence of the fact in question. When such awareness is present, 'positive' knowledge is not required." ... To fall within *Jewell*, a defendant must make "a calculated effort to avoid the sanctions of the statute while violating its substance. 'A court can properly find wilful blindness only where it can almost be said that the defendant actually knew.'" ... Because of the risk that a jury might convict a defendant on mere negligence — "that the defendant should have known his conduct was illegal" —

we have recognized that the instruction should be used sparingly.... "The *Jewell* instruction should not be given in every case where a defendant claims a lack of knowledge, but only in those comparatively rare cases where, in addition, there are facts that point in the direction of deliberate ignorance."... "Thus, even if the circumstances are highly suspicious, the instruction is improper unless the defendant acted deliberately to avoid learning the truth."...

Our cases upholding a *Jewell* instruction involved facts and circumstances creating a high probability of criminal activity that the defendant then ignored. In our cases disallowing a *Jewell* instruction, there were no suspicious circumstances surrounding the activity beyond direct evidence of the illegality itself, which goes only to actual knowledge.

For example, in *Jewell* itself the defendant entered the United States driving a car containing 110 pounds of marijuana concealed in a secret compartment.... He claimed a stranger who had given only his first name had approached him in Tijuana, Mexico and offered to sell him marijuana. When he declined, the stranger offered him $100 to drive a car across the border. He accepted and saw a secret compartment in the trunk of the car, but he declined to investigate further.... Under those circumstances, we held that there was both circumstantial evidence of actual knowledge of the marijuana, ... and evidence that "he deliberately avoided positive knowledge of the contraband to avoid responsibility in the event of discovery." ...

Cases following *Jewell* show a similar pattern of suspicious circumstances that go beyond direct evidence of the criminal activity itself.... In each of these cases, the defendant remained willfully ignorant of the nature of his activity after the facts and circumstances would "have put any reasonable person on notice that there was a 'high probability' that the undisclosed venture was illegal. Any reasonable person would have inquired extensively into the nature of the proposed venture.... unless, of course, he did not want to hear the answers." ... The facts and circumstances creating that high probability, however, did not at the same time give those defendants any direct knowledge of illegality, although actual knowledge could also be proven circumstantially. Thus, "if there is evidence of both actual knowledge and of deliberate ignorance, a *Jewell* instruction is appropriate."...

On the other hand, a *Jewell* instruction is not appropriate where the only evidence alerting a defendant to the high probability of criminal activity is direct evidence of the illegality itself. "[A] *Jewell* instruction should not be given when the evidence is that the defendant had either actual knowledge or no knowledge at all of the facts in question." ...

Thus, the conduct of a defendant who carried a package containing cocaine across a room and showed its contents to an undercover agent did not support a deliberate ignorance instruction.... [The defendant] claimed to have innocently opened a bag, without knowledge of its contents. [The court] found that the defendant's conduct "was inconsistent with conscious avoidance."... [The defendant] saw the cocaine; he either knew it was cocaine, and that he was thus participating in illegal activity, or he did not know and was therefore merely innocently present. "No evidence suggested a middle ground of conscious avoidance." ...

This case is in the [above] rather than the *Jewell* mold. The evidence points, either directly or circumstantially, only to actual knowledge of illegality, not to deliberate ignorance. The government claims the deliberate ignorance theory is appropriate because Sanchez-Robles willfully declined to inspect the van despite the powerful smell. But a strong odor in a van, without more, does not normally arouse suspicions of illegality. If Sanchez-Robles recognized the smell as that of marijuana, then she knew that there was marijuana in the van, just as [someone], if he recognized the look of cocaine, knew that the bag he held contained cocaine. If Sanchez-Robles did not, on the other hand, recognize the smell of marijuana, then she had no reason to be suspicious, just as [someone would have] no reason to be suspicious if he did not recognize cocaine. There is no meaningful distinction based on the difference between sight and smell. In both cases, a defendant's senses either give rise to direct knowledge of illegality, or there is nothing to raise suspicions of illegality at all. Without suspicion of a high probability of criminal activity, the deliberate ignorance theory fails. In this case, Sanchez-Robles either had actual knowledge of the illegality or she had no knowledge at all.... [T]here is no middle ground of conscious avoidance.

We would have a different case if there were evidence that someone had told Sanchez-Robles to drive the van across the border as a favor, or if someone had paid her to do it. One of those facts coupled with the odor might support a theory of willful blindness, because the circumstances would then be suspicious, just as they were in the smuggling cases following *Jewell*. But in this case, there is no evidence that anyone told Sanchez-Robles to do anything. The only way that smell could have aroused suspicion of illegality is if Sanchez-Robles had recognized it. And if she recognized it, then she knew of the illegality directly and was not willfully blinding herself.

Of course, the jury was entitled to disbelieve Sanchez-Robles and find that the circumstantial evidence showed actual knowledge of the illegal drugs. A jury may very well do that at a retrial. But for now, because of the *Jewell* instruction, we have no way of knowing whether or not this particular jury convicted her on an improper theory: that the odor in the van should have alerted her to illegality whether or not she actually recognized that odor.... We cannot say that the evidence against Sanchez-Robles is so overwhelming as to compel a guilty verdict....

NOTES

1. In *State v. Sidway*, 431 A.2d 1237 (Vt. 1981), an unlicensed driver had lost control of her car, which went across open land, struck an automobile parked in a private driveway and veered back onto the highway. She told her mother she had wrecked the car, but thought it had stemmed from driving over rocks in the field. Her brother-in-law, after investigating the matter the next day, informed her she had damaged another car; she contended that was the first she knew of the incident. She was prosecuted for leaving the scene of an accident. The court affirmed the conviction:

> The defendant rested her entire defense on the claim that she did not know at the time of the alleged accident that she had struck and damaged

another car. She contends that the trial court, therefore, should have granted her motion for an acquittal or should have charged the jury, as she requested, that she could not be convicted unless they found from the evidence that she had actual knowledge of the impact.

The trial court denied the defendant's motion for an acquittal and did not charge the jury as she requested. Instead, the trial court gave the following instruction on the issue of knowledge:

[K]nowledge that an accident occurred and some impact of some kind, is an element of the offense of leaving the scene of an accident.... However, it is not absolute or positive knowledge of damage to property or injury to another person that the law requires. Rather, the State must only prove that the circumstances were such that a reasonable person, situated as the defendant was at the time, would have believed that the impact had resulted in damage or injury to another. In other words, if the defendant was aware of an impact or accident under such circumstances as would ordinarily cause a reasonable person to conclude that injuries or damage had resulted, then it was her duty (1) to stop immediately, and (2) to investigate and then obey the Statute.

While perhaps technically correct when examined with extreme care, we feel that the instruction, as presented to the jury, was confusing. It gave the impression that the jury could convict upon a finding of either actual or constructive knowledge of impact on the part of the defendant. As such, it was overly broad and thus incorrect.

Actual knowledge on the part of the accused that she was involved in an accident is an essential element of the offense. However, since direct evidence of actual knowledge on the part of the defendant is not normally available, a majority of jurisdictions ... permit the necessary knowledge to be imputed to the defendant by the use of circumstantial evidence. Evidence, for instance, that the damage or impact was so great that it could be inferred that the defendant must have been aware that she was involved in an accident is enough. In certain circumstances, proof of an impact alone is sufficient to raise an inference of knowledge of injury on the part of the fleeing driver and to thereby permit the prosecution's case to withstand a motion for a judgment of acquittal. It is for the jury to determine whether the probative weight of the inference of knowledge arising from proof of impact outweighs the probative force of the defendant's claim of lack of knowledge.... We therefore hold that the actual knowledge of impact may be proven either by means of direct or circumstantial evidence.

The hit and run statute requires not only knowledge of an accident, but also knowledge of resultant injury to either the person or property of another. With respect to the requisite knowledge of such injury or damage, the burden of proof is not so stringent. We hold that the State need only prove that element of the offense by a showing of constructive knowledge on the part of the defendant. It is not necessary to show, by direct or circumstantial evidence, that the defendant had actual knowledge of any resultant injury or damage. If an impact occurs under such circumstances that a reasonable person would anticipate injury to person or property, knowledge of that fact is imputed to the driver....

Lack of knowledge, however, of the accident and of the resultant injury or damage is a complete defense to a violation of the hit run statute.

Notwithstanding the above holding, the improper jury instruction is not grounds for a reversal in this case. Such error is only grounds for reversal where prejudice is shown, and the burden of proof on the issue of prejudice is on the party alleging error.... In view of the facts of this case, no prejudice is shown.

The defendant was alert enough to navigate her car successfully both to and from the scene of the accident. The impact was sufficient to move the unoccupied car ten feet, seriously damage both cars and shower the defendant with glass. Reasonable minds cannot differ on the issue of actual knowledge. The defendant must have been aware of the impact. Furthermore, the impact was clearly of such severity as to give rise to constructive knowledge of damage to the property of another. All other elements having been sufficiently proven, the conviction must stand.

2. In *Kimoktoak v. State*, 584 P.2d 25 (Alaska 1978), the court confronted a statute penalizing failure to stop, render assistance and provide personal identification after involvement in a motor vehicle accident causing death, personal injury, or property damage, which on its face required no knowledge that such an accident had occurred. In an earlier decision, *State v. Campbell*, 536 P.2d 105 (Alaska 1975), the court had held that intent could be supplied through judicial interpretation in an instance of a legislative restatement or codification of a common-law crime, but intimated that such a process could not be invoked in a purely legislative (noncommon law) crime. *Kimoktoak* eliminated the latter reservation in *Campbell* and proclaimed a broad judicial power to provide through statutory construction of any criminal statute a culpability dimension satisfying constitutional concerns: "Although we can conceive of cases where we may decline to imply such intent into statutes silent in this respect, hereafter we will resolve such questions on a case by case basis." 584 P.2d at 31. Therefore, the stop-and-assist statute was construed to require awareness of the underlying facts giving rise to a duty to aid: "[W]e cannot believe that the legislature could have intended that persons who unknowingly fail to stop and render assistance could be subject to serious criminal penalties.... We must presume that ... the legislature acted with basic notions of fairness and due process in mind." *Id.*

3. In *People v. Yutt*, 597 N.E.2d 208 (Ill. App. Ct. 1992), the defendants were convicted of criminal trespass for refusing to leave an abortion clinic's premises after having been asked to do so. The appellate court affirmed the convictions:

> ... The instant case involves [a] variety of trespass. The elements ... are (1) an individual is on the land of another; (2) she is directed to leave by the owner or occupant; and (3) she does not leave...
>
> ....
>
> ... [In earlier precedent,] the court held that a defendant must have knowledge of the attendant circumstances before he can be found

guilty.... The court held that a defendant must have known that he had notice to depart and remained in spite of this notice.

Here, defendants have no more than their claim that they thought they had a right to be there. By arguing that they were implied invitees of the collective tenants, they tacitly concede that they knew this is private property, i.e., the property of another.

Defendants argue on the basis of [*People v. Ulatowski*, 368 N.E.2d 174 (Ill. App. Ct. 1977)] that they were not personally aware that notice to leave had been given because they did not think that [a clinic official] or the [arresting] officer had the authority to do so. They claim that knowledge of the attendant circumstances includes knowledge that the one giving notice to leave is in fact the owner or [an] authorized agent.

The reasoning in *Ulatowski,* however, is inapplicable to these facts. There the defendant was under the influence of LSD. He did not leave an apartment despite being told to do so, having shoes thrown at him, and then being dragged out by his hair. It was only after the police arrived and arrested him that he first believed he was no longer welcome at the apartment. The appellate court held that it was reversible error to refuse a jury instruction which stated that a person is not criminally responsible if his drugged condition renders him incapable of acting knowingly.

Thus, in *Ulatowski,* the issue was not whether notice was given to vacate, but rather whether such notice was received. Neither of those is truly in question here.... Defendants concede that they knew that they were being asked to leave and that they were not welcome there. Their only contention is that they subjectively did not think that anyone had the power to remove them from this sidewalk.

We reject defendants' argument that the statute requires that they personally believe that the person notifying them to leave is the owner of the property....

Id. at 213-14.

4. Other dimensions of the problem of significance of ignorance or error are covered under the topic of mistake pp. 669-693 *infra.*

E. RECKLESSNESS

MODEL PENAL CODE

§ 2.02. General Requirements of Culpability

(2) Kinds of Culpability Defined
 (c) Recklessly
A person acts recklessly with respect to a material element of an offense when he consciously disregards a substantial and unjustifiable risk that the material element exists or will result from his conduct. The risk must be of such a nature and degree that, considering the nature and purpose of the actor's conduct and the circumstances known to him, its disregard involves a gross deviation from the standard of conduct that a law-abiding person would observe in the actor's situation.

MODEL PENAL CODE

Tentative Draft No. 4, 125-26 (1955)

A broader discrimination is perceived between acting either purposely or knowingly and acting recklessly. As we use the term, recklessness involves conscious risk creation. It resembles acting knowingly in that a state of awareness is involved but the awareness is of risk, that is of probability rather than certainty; the matter is contingent from the actor's point of view. Whether the risk relates to the nature of the actor's conduct or to the existence of the requisite attendant circumstances or to the result that may ensue is immaterial; the concept is the same. The draft requires, however, that the risk thus consciously disregarded by the actor be "substantial" and "unjustifiable"; even substantial risks may be created without recklessness when the actor seeks to serve a proper purpose, as when a surgeon performs an operation which he knows is very likely to be fatal but reasonably thinks the patient has no other, safer chance. Accordingly, to aid the ultimate determination, the draft points expressly to the factors to be weighed in judgment: the nature and degree of the risk disregarded by the actor, the nature and purpose of his conduct and the circumstances known to him in acting.

Some principle must be articulated, however, to indicate what final judgment is demanded after everything is weighed. There is no way to state this value-judgment that does not beg the question in the last analysis; the point is that the jury must evaluate the conduct and determine whether it should be condemned. The draft, therefore, proposes that this difficulty be accepted frankly and the jury asked if the defendant's conduct involved "culpability of high degree." The alternative suggested asks if it "involves a gross deviation from proper standards of conduct." This formulation is designed to avoid the difficulty, inherent in defining culpability in terms of culpability, but the accomplishment seems hardly more than verbal; it does not really avoid the tautology or beg the question less. It may, however, be a better way to put the issue to a jury, especially as some of the conduct to which the section must apply may not involve great moral culpability, even when the defendant acted purposely or knowingly, as in the violation of some minor regulatory measure.

STATE ex rel. JUVENILE DEPARTMENT OF MULTNOMAH COUNTY v. ANDERSON

Court of Appeals of Oregon
513 P.2d 514 (1973)

FOLEY, JUDGE.

This is an appeal from a finding that Cary Anderson, a minor, is within the jurisdiction of the juvenile court. We reverse.

On August 21, 1972, the juvenile involved in this proceeding, Cary Anderson, 13 years old, and Donald Madsen, 12 years old, were playing with Donald's motorcycle in the vicinity of the General Sheet Metal Works in Portland. It is undisputed that the boys entered an open area in the rear of the sheet metal shop to look for gasoline for the motorcycle. The area, which was open and unfenced, was used by the company as a loading dock, for painting, and

E. RECKLESSNESS

for insulating duct work. There were several large cans of paint thinner under or near a work bench.

Donald poured some of the paint thinner onto the concrete floor, making a puddle six to eight inches in diameter. Donald testified that it did not smell like gasoline, but both thought that they could determine whether it was gasoline by seeing whether it would light. Both boys tossed a couple of matches onto the puddle, but the liquid extinguished the matches. Finally, Donald succeeded in lighting the puddle and it began to burn out of control. He stamped on it to put it out but caught his shoe on fire. When the boys saw that the fire was growing large, they ran from the building. Just what happened next is not clear. The boys either ran or rode their bicycles to Donald's house, but it was locked. Then either Donald or his sister pulled a fire alarm at a street box. Meanwhile, the fire had spread to the work bench and some of the cans of paint thinner exploded.

Cary Anderson was found to be within the jurisdiction of the court for commission of acts which, if committed by an adult, would constitute arson in the second degree. ORS 164.315.[1] He contends on appeal, and the state concedes, that arson was not proven. We agree, since there is no evidence of intent to damage the building.

The state contends, however, that the evidence shows that Cary Anderson did commit reckless burning, a lesser included offense, and that we should affirm a conviction conforming to that offense. ORS 164.335(1) states:

> A person commits the crime of reckless burning if he recklessly damages property of another by fire or explosion.

Both parties to this appeal have attempted to define the term "recklessly," but we choose to use the statutory definition which is found at ORS 161.085(9):

> "Recklessly," when used with respect to a result or to a circumstance described by a statute defining an offense, means that a person is aware of and consciously disregards a substantial and unjustifiable risk that the result will occur or that the circumstance exists. The risk must be of such nature and degree that disregard thereof constitutes a gross deviation from the standard of care that a reasonable person would observe in the situation.

The decision in this case depends upon whether the juvenile committed the act recklessly. There is no question that the risk was substantial and unjustifiable. The next question for resolution then is: Was the Anderson boy aware of and did he consciously disregard the risk?

The question of awareness is one not easily answered. There is no direct evidence on that question in the record. There was some testimony by the two

---

[1] ORS 164.315 provides:

(1) A person commits the crime of arson in the second degree if, by starting a fire or causing an explosion, he intentionally damages any building of another that is not protected property.

(2) Arson in the second degree is a Class C felony.

boys from which one might infer that they were unaware of the risk. And at one point the court stated to Cary Anderson:

> ... I don't think that at your age and your lack of knowledge you had any possible thought of the potential danger to yourself or anyone else.

The child urges that the preceding statement is a finding of fact upon which we might rely for a holding that he was not reckless. The statement was made, however, in the context of the court explaining its decision to the 13-year-old boy and not in discussing the statutory definition of recklessness. However, whether the court's statement is a finding of fact as to the child's mental state, we need not here decide. The burden was upon the plaintiff to establish that the child was within the jurisdiction of the court and we are unable to find in the record evidence that Cary Anderson was "aware of and consciously ... [disregarded the] risk." We therefore conclude that the plaintiff has failed in its proof and the finding of jurisdiction must be reversed.

F. NEGLIGENCE

MODEL PENAL CODE

§ 2.02. General Requirements of Culpability

(2) Kinds of Culpability Defined
(d) Negligently
A person acts negligently with respect to a material element of an offense when he should be aware of a substantial and unjustifiable risk that the material element exists or will result from his conduct. The risk must be of such a nature and degree that the actor's failure to perceive it, considering the nature and purpose of his conduct and the circumstances known to him, involves a gross deviation from the standard of care that a reasonable person would observe in the actor's situation.

WORKING PAPERS OF THE NATIONAL COMMISSION ON REFORM OF FEDERAL CRIMINAL LAWS 127-28 (1970)

"*Negligently.*" The lowest degree of culpability is involved when a person acts negligently, that is, "he engages in the conduct in unreasonable disregard of a substantial likelihood of the existence of the relevant facts [, such disregard involving a gross deviation from acceptable standards of conduct]."

It may be argued that negligent conduct should not be criminal, since, there being no consciousness of wrongdoing, the threat of punishment is ineffective and the imposition of punishment inappropriate. We do, however, commonly assume that people can be made to conduct themselves more carefully by adequate threats or admonitions; greater care may involve giving greater attention to the discovery of danger or giving greater weight to dangers that are discovered. In addition, whether or not negligence is precisely a "moral" fault, it is certainly a fault, for which people can and do incur blame. Consequently, whatever response the criminal law ought to make to prohibited conduct in which a person engages negligently, there is little reason to depart from the present inclusion of negligence within the degrees of culpability that are sufficient for criminal liability.

The formulation used distinguishes negligent conduct from reckless conduct by requiring only an "unreasonable" disregard for the former, in comparison with the requirement of "conscious and [plain and] clearly unjustifiable" disregard for the latter. The major difference is that the negligent person need not be aware of the likelihood that he is engaging in the prohibited conduct. Because he may not be aware, it seems more appropriate to talk of "unreasonable" rather than "unjustifiable" disregard; the former word more easily encompasses a negligent failure to be aware of, as well as a negligent failure to give sufficient weight to, the danger involved. In addition, the omission of the word "clearly," which appears in the definition of reckless conduct, emphasizes the difference in degree between the two levels of culpability. Aside from the distinction drawn between recklessness and negligence on the basis of awareness, the formulations allow a jury to conclude that although the defendant was conscious of a risk, the nature and extent of the risk or the manner or degree of the defendant's disregard of it or the reasons for his disregard of it indicate that he was not reckless, but only negligent. Since all of these elements are relevant to the question whether a person was reckless or entirely without fault, it should be possible to reach the middle ground of negligence on the same basis.

Again, the clause "such disregard involving a gross deviation from acceptable standards of conduct" is added in brackets at the end. For the reasons discussed above, its inclusion is not recommended.

Use of the phrase "relevant facts" in the definition of "recklessly" and "negligently" is not intended to confine consideration to questions "of fact" as opposed to questions "of law," such as, perhaps, a person's legal status or the ownership of property. The phrase is used simply as the most neutral phrase to direct attention to all the facts and circumstances of a situation in light of which the determination that a person was or was not reckless or negligent must be made.

PEOPLE v. FUTTERMAN

New York Supreme Court, Appellate Division, Fourth Department
449 N.Y.S.2d 108 (1982)

DENMAN, JUDGE.

Defendant challenges his conviction for criminally negligent homicide on the ground that the evidence was insufficient to support the verdict. The charge arose from the death of David Murphy, a patient in the psychiatric unit of Erie County Medical Center where defendant was the head nurse on the night shift....

The indictment returned against defendant charged him with two crimes: manslaughter in the second degree (Penal Law, § 125.15, subd 1 [reckless manslaughter]) and criminally negligent homicide (Penal Law, § 125.10). At the close of the proof the trial court dismissed the manslaughter count and the jury found defendant guilty on the single count of criminally negligent homicide. Criminally negligent homicide is defined as follows:

> A person is guilty of criminally negligent homicide when, with criminal negligence, he causes the death of another person. (Penal Law, § 125.10.)
>
> A person acts with criminal negligence with respect to a result or to a circumstance described by a statute defining an offense when he fails to perceive a substantial and unjustifiable risk that such result will occur or that such circumstance exists. The risk must be of such nature and degree that the failure to perceive it constitutes a gross deviation from the standard of care that a reasonable person would observe in the situation. (Penal Law, § 15.05, subd 4.)

Criminal negligence has been a constant source of confusion and vexation for the courts and the Legislature. Conceptually it presents a difficult problem because of its apparent internal inconsistency. The type of conduct which we characterize as "criminal" and to which the penal statutes are directed generally requires the element of mens rea or a criminal state of mind. In contrast to the type of awareness usually employed to define criminal action, viz., "intentional" or "knowing," the culpable mental state required for criminal negligence is a state of unawareness, a failure to perceive a risk, which concept, of course, is intrinsic to the law of tort liability.... Instead of evaluating conduct which is easily recognizable and condemned as morally reprehensible, we are forced to scrutinize conduct which consists essentially of an error in judgment. Therein lies the difficulty for it should be troublesome to even the most casual observer that an error in judgment, though perhaps properly resulting in civil liability, is punishable by criminal sanctions. What is there then to distinguish between the kind of judgmental failure common in civil law and that kind of negligence which makes a qualitative leap into the area of criminal law?

Prior to enactment of the present Penal Law commentators and revision commissions had long pondered the problems inherent in criminal negligence statutes. Not only was there a lack of differentiation between civil and criminal negligence but there was substantial confusion and ambiguity in the statutes dealing with recklessness and negligence. For example, the former Penal Law contained certain manslaughter provisions based on negligent conduct,[*] but the statutory language and judicial interpretation was generally in terms of "wanton," "wanton and willful," "gross negligence," ... in short, the language of recklessness.

In the revised Penal Law, the Legislature attempted to clarify and delineate this area of the law.... The definitional section of the revised Penal Law (§ 15.05) provides a clear demarcation between recklessness and criminal negligence. Reckless conduct is that in which the actor is aware of the risk and proceeds in disregard thereof whereas criminally negligent conduct is that in which the actor fails to perceive a substantial risk....

---

[*] Subdivision 3 of section 1052 made negligent conduct criminal in specific circumstances: i.e., woman producing miscarriage; negligent use of machinery; mischievous animals; overloading passenger vessel; persons in charge of steamboats; persons in charge of steam engines; acts of physicians while intoxicated; persons making or keeping gunpowder contrary to law.

F. NEGLIGENCE

Although the Penal Law revisions have in large measure clarified the difference between reckless conduct and criminally negligent conduct, the line separating civil from criminal negligence is still somewhat blurred. The factors which impose the greater degree of culpability on a criminally negligent defendant are that the risk which he fails to perceive is so substantial that his failure to perceive it constitutes a gross deviation from the standard of care that a reasonable person would exercise in those circumstances....

Measuring Mark Futterman's conduct against that background, we do not find that his failure to perceive the risk of death to David Murphy was such gross deviation from the standard of care to be expected from a reasonable person under those circumstances as to constitute criminal liability. All of the testimony bore out that David Murphy was an extremely violent patient of unusual strength. One witness testified that if defendant had not acted very forcefully, the staff would not have been able to bring the patient under control. All of the staff members who witnessed the event testified that they never perceived that the patient could not breathe or was in danger of asphyxiation. This was an emergency situation, fraught with danger, in which defendant was required quickly to assess the situation and pursue a course of action which he deemed advisable. Since there was no time for the weighing of alternatives, he cannot reasonably be held to the same standard as one who has had full opportunity to reflect.... "[W]hen one is confronted with a sudden and unexpected event or combination of events which leave little or no time for reflection or deliberate judgment, this itself may be a significant circumstance which, realistically as well as conceptually, should enter into the determination of the reasonableness of the choice of action pursued.... To stigmatize the defendant with the brand of a criminal for an incident, which though tragic, was the result of an error in judgment, would be wholly inappropriate, inconsistent with the purpose of the criminal law, and totally disproportionate to defendant's inadvertent conduct. We therefore reverse the judgment of conviction and dismiss the indictment.

NOTES

1. JEROME HALL, LAW, SOCIAL SCIENCE AND CRIMINAL THEORY 260-65 (1982):

> The past discussions have made it clear that the issues involve (1) the justice of punishing for inadvertent negligent behavior; (2) the utility of that, *i.e.*, the question of deterrence; (3) the proper scope of criminal law; and (4) the relevance of liability for inadvertent negligence to the construction of a science of criminal law.
>
> 1. Those who espouse the justice of punishment for negligent behavior base their case on the allegation that the defendant *could* have acted with due care and is therefore culpable for not having done so. To my knowledge (and I should be obliged for correction) none of the advocates of punishment for inadvertent negligence has pointed to any evidence or stated why he thinks that a careless person could have been careful in the

situations described in the law reports. In *Williams*,[30] *e.g.*[,] a child died of gangrene and the defendant, his father, was found guilty of negligent homicide. He was a totally uneducated person, greatly devoted to the child but, obviously, from the stated facts, he was simply unable to understand the gravity of the child's illness until it was too late to save its life. In the automobile cases, which make up the bulk of the relevant statistics, it is often the case that the defendant's negligence endangered his own life. If, as is probable, many of those cases are really cases of recklessness (as a German scholar told me some years ago regarding the German cases of "negligence") then the present law may be defended on pragmatic grounds — that juries will acquit of the more serious manslaughter but will convict of the lesser homicide; that the prosecutor should not, therefore, be required to prove recklessness even when the facts provide ample evidence of recklessness. In sum, conviction of negligent homicide is preferable to acquittal on a charge of reckless manslaughter. From this pragmatic reasoning, however, it cannot be inferred that it is *just* to punish *inadvertent* negligent behavior.

It has been argued that since we blame someone for forgetting or coming late to an appointment, a careless person who steps on one's foot and the frequent thoughtless behavior of our children, it is sound to punish a negligent person who bumps into one's car or, especially, one who carelessly kills someone. One answer might be that we are simply wasting time and emotion ("letting off steam") in rebuking the above persons. The other more pointed answer is that it is a very serious matter to impose the label characterizing one a "criminal" and do that in a formal, public, authoritative procedure followed by imprisonment. What is rational tongue-lashing may not be rational when the sanction is not talk but the most severe one that a society can impose — the deprivation of freedom and the ordeal of confinement in a prison....

2. The second issue — the utility of such punishment, specifically, its deterrent effect — is closely tied to the first one. The utilitarian thesis of general deterrence rests on the assumption that newspaper reports that such persons have been punished will cause an otherwise careless person to be careful. But what does that mean? If it means that he will be aware of or alert to risks we deal with recklessness. If knowledge of possible penal liability does not make him sensitive to danger, inadvertency is not reduced. The specific deterrence thesis is that punishing the defendant for his negligent behavior will make him careful in the future. The latter is plainly the more plausible of the two deterrent themes. But the current skepticism of rehabilitation and the obvious inefficiency of the criminal justice system regarding voluntary offenders raise doubts even as regards the stronger of the two claims. Again, if one concludes with another Scottish verdict, that deterrence has neither been proved nor disproved, what policy should be adopted for the criminal law?

3. "Policy" is sufficiently vague to include the pragmatic use of negligent homicide statutes, i.e., that may not be just but it is the best avail-

---

[30] State v. Williams, 4 Wash. App. 908, 484 P.2d 1167 (1971). [*See* Note 5, pp. 119-121 *infra.*]

able treatment. The narrower pertinent question concerns the fact that ==there is wide acceptance of the thesis that if any problem can be equally dealt with by non-punitive methods, that problem should be excluded from penal law==. Certainly if it can be handled better in civil law, *e.g.*, by damage assessed for torts or by an administrative board, it should even more plainly be excluded from penal law. Current efforts that seek restrictions on the scope of penal law, *e.g.*, of the so-called "victimless crimes," the failure of prisons, and the use by judges of extraordinary sentences, *e.g.*, restitution, work in a hospital, compulsory driving lessons and similar nonstatutory sentences indicate a trend toward acceptance of a restrictive penal policy. Alcoholism, drug addiction, mental illness, and the insensitivity characteristic of careless persons have this in common — they reflect deep psychological problems that call for the reconstruction of character or personality regarding which the crude sanctions of the criminal law can play only a small, if any, role.

2. For a conceptual view differing from Professor Hall's, *see* GEORGE FLETCHER, RETHINKING CRIMINAL LAW 504-14 (1980).

3. A legislature can invoke a standard of ordinary negligence in a criminal statute, should it wish. In *State v. Williams*, 484 P.2d 1167 (Wash. App. 1971), reproduced in part, *infra* pp. 119-121, and summarized by Professor Hall in note 1 *supra,* the court in describing state manslaughter legislation stated: "Under these statutes the crime is deemed committed even though the death of the victim is the proximate result of only simple or ordinary negligence." 484 P.2d at 1171. The defendant's omission to provide medical care for his seriously ill stepchild was ... "ordinary or simple negligence, and such negligence is sufficient to support a conviction of statutory manslaughter." *Id.* at 1174.

SECTION II. Conduct *(Actus Reus)*
A. THE REQUIREMENT OF VOLUNTARINESS
MODEL PENAL CODE

§ 2.01. Requirement of Voluntary Act

(1) A person is not guilty of an offense unless his liability is based on conduct which includes a voluntary act or the omission to perform an act of which he is physically capable.

(2) The following are not voluntary acts within the meaning of this Section:

    (a) a reflex or convulsion;

    (b) a bodily movement during unconsciousness or sleep;

    (c) conduct during hypnosis or resulting from hypnotic suggestion;

    (d) a bodily movement that otherwise is not a product of the effort or determination of the actor, either conscious or habitual.

WORKING PAPERS OF THE NATIONAL COMMISSION ON REFORM OF FEDERAL CRIMINAL LAWS 106-13 (1970)

(a) *"Voluntarily engages in conduct."* — This phrase states the minimum condition of criminal liability: that the person held liable has engaged in criminal conduct. A requirement that the liability (and punishment) of *A* be explained and justified by reference to what *A* has done and not what someone else has done or some event caused is primitive to a rational penal Code. A system in which *A* was "held" responsible and penalized for occurrences with which he was in no way connected and a repetition of which he could not prevent would now be regarded not as a Criminal Code fixing the criminal liability of individuals but as filling some other presumed social purpose. All the more refined principles of responsibility presume as a minimum that the liability of *A* is responsive to what *A* has done.

Whatever the general purposes of a Criminal Code, they cannot be served unless this minimum condition of liability is met. It is apparent that individuals cannot be "deterred" from occurrences unconnected with their own conduct, nor will their "rehabilitation" or "reform," defined somehow, affect the recurrence of such happenings. Even the motives of revenge and the more worthy one of responding to a psychological desire for revenge — which is not explicit but may be behind the first clause of section 102(c) of the proposed draft, "to prescribe penalties which are proportionate to the seriousness of offenses" — are not well served by punishing the wholly innocent.

That liability depends on conduct is derived from the same reasoning. It is no more rational to hold a person criminally liable for a condition over which he has no control than to hold him liable for some wholly external event. While the difference between engaging in specified conduct and being in a specified condition may often be largely a matter of expression, particularly if the "condition" is defined by conduct, a Federal Criminal Code should adopt explicitly the principle that a man is liable for what he does and not what he is. That principle was the basis of the Supreme Court's holding in *Robinson v. California,* 370 U.S. 660 (1962), that a conviction which might have been based on a determination that the defendant had the "status" or "chronic condition" of a narcotics addict imposed a cruel and unusual punishment in violation of the due process clause of the fourteenth amendment....

An effect of the provision basing criminal liability on conduct will be to require that statutes defining particular offenses be cast in terms of conduct rather than "status" or "condition" even where the latter is determined by conduct.

Again, the basic axiom of responsibility requires that criminal liability not attach to conduct unless it is voluntary. This principle, too, is so basic that it has generally been taken for granted and expressed only in the expression of some more particular rule distinguishing between voluntary and involuntary conduct.

> For legal purposes it is enough to say that no involuntary action, whatever effects it may produce, amounts to a crime by the law of England. I do not know indeed that it has ever been suggested that a person who in his sleep set fire to a house or caused the death of another would be guilty

of arson or murder. The only case of involuntary action which, so far as I know, has ever been even expressly referred to as not being criminal is the case in which one person's body is used by another as a tool or weapon. It has been thought worthwhile to say that if A by pushing B against C pushes C over a precipice A and not B is guilty of pushing C over the precipice. (2 SIR JAMES STEPHEN, A HISTORY OF THE CRIMINAL LAW OF ENGLAND 100 (1883) (footnote omitted)).

In the few reported cases, none of them in the Federal courts, in which a defendant's criminal liability depended directly on the requirement of voluntariness (rather than culpability, or some established subsidiary principle based on the requirement of voluntariness, such as the defenses of insanity and coercion), the requirement has been accepted without question. The significance of voluntariness is recognized in the familiar jury instruction that a person is presumed to intend "the natural consequences of his voluntary acts (or omissions)," and is made explicit in the Model Penal Code and other recent codifications of State criminal law.

While the Supreme Court has not accepted the argument that the Constitution does not permit conviction for a crime except on the basis of a person's culpable conduct, ... it has in effect accepted the principle that criminal liability can be based only on a person's voluntary conduct. In *Lambert v. California*, 355 U.S. 225 (1957), the Court held that a person could not consistently with due process be convicted for failing to register under a criminal registration statute if he did not know of the duty to register and there was no showing of the "probability of such knowledge."

Argument can be made that inclusion of the word "voluntarily" to modify the phrase "engages in conduct" is unnecessary and that it will cause confusion. In ordinary circumstances, we should not describe blinking or twitching, or rolling over in sleep, or stumbling over a rock, or being shoved into someone, as "conduct." At least the strong use of the word "conduct" contains some notion of a person's conducting himself in a certain way, exercising control over himself, some element of volition. To some extent, therefore, the word "voluntarily" is unnecessary and the entire phrase "voluntarily engages in conduct" redundant. There are, however, weak uses of the word "conduct." As the performance in question becomes more like the kinds of performance which ordinarily are voluntary — a highly involved "twitch," sleepwalking, or talking in one's sleep instead of rolling over or snoring — it is not so clear that the word "conduct" is inapplicable; used weakly, the word connotes simply behavior. Partial redundancy seems clearly preferable in this case to incompleteness.

The possibility of confusion arises from the ambiguity of the word "voluntarily." There are strong uses of that word according to which conduct is not "voluntary" if it is in any substantial sense the product of an identifiable external or nonconscious internal force. In its strongest sense, which stops just short of rejecting the notion of voluntary conduct altogether, a person engages in conduct "voluntarily" only if his conduct is not significantly subject to explanation by any general theory of behavior. The word is not intended to have that use here. It is intended to exclude from the kind of conduct which may be criminal that which, in the ordinary sense, occurs beyond the control of the actor; reflexes and twitches are paradigms.

Omission of the word "voluntarily" would leave a possibility, small to be sure, that a person whose conduct was truly involuntary in the relevant sense — conduct while asleep, for example — would be prosecuted and obliged to defend on the ground of involuntariness, without an explicit statutory peg on which to hang the defense. Including the word may lead occasionally to the assertion of unintended defenses short of the insanity defense which are based on deterministic theories of human conduct. Of the two possibilities, the latter seems less undesirable. Since the element of voluntariness, elusive as it is, is so much a part of the rationale of criminal liability, it is worthwhile to make it explicit in the statement of the basic principle....

As the commentary to section 2.01(2) of the Model Penal Code states, the definition of "voluntary" is partial and indirect. Reflexive and convulsive movements are perhaps identified rather easily, although even some of these will be border cases. How fully unconscious or asleep or under hypnotic suggestion one has to be for conduct to be involuntary is hard to say, however, and subdivisions (b) and (c) of the formulation are useful as examples only aided by the descriptive content of subdivision (d).[21] Subdivision (d), which attempts to formulate the crucial issue, is simply inaccurate, unless one uses the guide to interpretation afforded by the examples. It is easy to think of "voluntary" conduct which is not in the ordinary sense the product of conscious or habitual effort or determination. The commentary notes that the definition corresponds to the reference in section 2 of the Restatement of Torts (Second) (1965) to an "external manifestation of the actor's will." The notion of "willing" without "trying" or "making an effort" or "determining" to do something is what is at stake here, but one can "feel" what is intended more easily than one can state it.

Subsequent codifications based on the Model Penal Code have partially adopted the Code's formulation. The New York Revised Penal Law (§ 15.00(2)) for example, defines "voluntary act" as "a bodily movement performed consciously as a result of effort or determination." It would appear that the definition is intended to exclude the same kinds of conduct excluded by the Model Penal Code.

These formulations do not seem adequate. In precisely those cases in which the question of voluntariness must be answered, reference to the actor's conscious (or habitual) effort or determination is likely not to be helpful, and may mislead by suggesting that more effort or determination must be shown than is actually intended.[23]

---

[21] In Fain v. Commonwealth, 78 Ky. 183 (1879), for example, the defendant was charged with homicide of a man who was trying to wake him from sleep. He claimed that he was asleep when he shot and killed the deceased, even though he listened to and spoke to the deceased before he shot. The court indicated that he was entitled to present a defense of unconsciousness, or partial unconsciousness, such that he perceived his surroundings to some extent but did not comprehend his situation and believed that he had to defend himself.

[23] Many bodily movements which might produce injury and which we might want to characterize as negligent or even reckless do not require effort or determination in any significant sense; *e.g.*, a man might "stretch" without either, and still be acting negligently.

An alternative possibility is to define "voluntary conduct" not in terms of effort or determination, but in terms of ability to control the conduct. For example: "A person does not engage in conduct voluntarily if the conduct is not subject to his control." A test based on a person's ability to control his conduct at the time when he engages in the conduct probably comes closest to the weak sense of voluntariness intended here. A man who is sleepwalking or under hypnosis cannot control his conduct in the relevant sense. Nor are reflexes or convulsions subject to control. But again, the sleepwalker and the subject of hypnosis may exhibit remarkable ability to pursue a course of conduct and to avoid accidents; in that sense, which is a meaningful one, they control what they do. Given notice, a person may be able to control conduct which we would ordinarily regard as reflexive.

Federal cases do not provide helpful analyses of the concept of voluntariness or usable definitions of the word "voluntarily" (or related words, "voluntary," "involuntarily," etc.). The courts have regularly considered whether particular conduct was voluntary, but have not explored the concept generally or in the context now being considered. Nor are the few State cases in which the courts have considered directly the nature of voluntary conduct in this context more helpful. Where a court has had to consider a defense that a person's conduct was not voluntary but was nevertheless not covered by one of the established defenses — insanity, compulsion, and so forth — the court has typically referred to consciousness as the controlling factor. Consciousness is a necessary but not sufficient condition of voluntary conduct. In order to determine the sense of "conscious" relevant for the present purpose, one must refer back to the notion of voluntariness.

Two purposes might be served by a definition of voluntariness in this section of the Code. The definition might give content to the main provision of section 301(1), which would then reflect more precisely the basic principle of liability under Federal criminal law. The definition might also help to resolve a jury's confusion in a case involving the question of voluntariness. For the reasons given above, it is unlikely that either of these purposes would in fact be served. Conceptually, the concept of voluntariness is probably primitive. To the extent that examples provide helpful illustrations, it seems preferable to leave the definition of "voluntariness" "open" and allow the cases to develop concrete illustrations, supported by full descriptions of particular facts. Such an approach will allow Federal law to reflect developing understanding of what is relevantly voluntary conduct. A court presented with this issue will explain it to the jury as well as it can, almost certainly using the facts of the case and some general term like "unconscious" to suggest what must be decided. The main statement of the basis of criminal liability will remain, if incomplete, accurate.

STATE v. TAFT

Supreme Court of Appeals of West Virginia
102 S.E.2d 152 (1958)

GIVEN, JUDGE. Defendant, Burl H. Taft, was indicted by a grand jury of the Circuit Court of Monongalia County, at the January, 1957, Term.... The indictment in the instant case is in two counts. The first count charges defendant with having driven an automobile while "under the influence of intoxicating liquor." The second count alleges that defendant unlawfully drove an automobile while "under the influence of drugs and narcotics to a degree which rendered him incapable of safely driving a motor vehicle." The trial was commenced on February 12, 1957. On the verdict of the jury, the judgment was that defendant serve six months in the county jail, the sentence to run consecutively to the sentence mentioned in case No. 10907.

. . . .

After the jury had considered of a verdict for some time, the foreman requested the trial court to answer the question, "Is there a legal definition for what constitutes driving a car?" Whereupon, over objection of defendant, the court instructed the jury "that the term 'driving' has been defined and construed as requiring that a vehicle be in motion in order for the offense to be committed." Defendant then offered, in writing, an instruction which would have told the jury "that if they believe from the evidence that defendant got in his parked car for the purpose of waiting for someone else, and that the brakes of his car accidentally released and the car drifted some two to three feet into the rear end of a car parked in front of said Taft car, and that the movement of said car was accidental, and not the act and intent of the defendant, then you are authorized to find and determine that the defendant was not then and there driving his said car, and if you so find that the defendant was not then and there driving his said car, you may find the defendant not guilty."

The statute on which the indictment is based ... makes it a criminal offense for a person "to drive any vehicle on any highway of this state" while "under the influence of intoxicating liquor"; or "under the influence of any narcotic drug." The question posed by the action of the court, as related to the instructions mentioned above, is whether the mere motion of the vehicle constituted "driving" of the vehicle, within the meaning of the statute. We think that it does not.

Though movement of a vehicle is an essential element of the statutory requirement, the mere movement of a vehicle does not necessarily, in every circumstance, constitute a "driving" of the vehicle. To "drive" a vehicle necessarily implies a driver or operator and an affirmative or positive action on the part of the driver. A mere movement of the vehicle might occur without any affirmative act by a driver, or, in fact by any person. If a vehicle is moved by some power beyond the control of the driver, or by accident, it is not such an affirmative or positive action on the part of the driver as will constitute a driving of a vehicle within the meaning of the statute.... This being true, the instruction telling the jury that the vehicle must "be in motion in order for an offense to be committed" necessarily, in view of the evidence before the jury, had the effect of telling them that any accidental movement of the vehicle was sufficient to constitute a driving of the vehicle within the meaning of the statute, and constituted prejudicial error. What is said in this respect also indicates prejudicial error in the refusal to give to the jury the instruction offered by defendant, quoted above, after the giving of the instruction first mentioned. We are not, of course, saying that the refusal to give defendant's instruction, at the stage of the trial at which it was offered, had the first instruction not been given, would have constituted error. That question is not before us.

....

NOTES

1. *Cf. People v. Pomeroy*, 276 N.W.2d 904, 908 (Mich. App. 1979):

Where an intoxicated person exercises actual bodily restraining or directing influence over the machinery of an automobile which would put it in motion, that person is in "actual physical control" of that vehicle and may be prosecuted under the drunk driving provisions of the Vehicle Code.

2. *See* Annot., 93 A.L.R.3d 7 (1979).

COMMONWEALTH v. CHEATHAM

Superior Court of Pennsylvania
615 A.2d 802 (1992)

CIRILLO, JUDGE.

James S. Cheatham appeals from a judgment of sentence entered by the Court of Common Pleas of Allegheny County after his conviction in a non-jury trial on charges of homicide by vehicle and aggravated assault.... We affirm.

On August 3, 1990, Cheatham blacked out while driving on Whitaker Street in the Borough of West Mifflin and lost control of his car. The car left the eastbound lane, jumped the curb, and ran into three children sitting on a fence, killing one child and injuring the other two. There were no tire skid marks before the car hit the fence. Cheatham was found lying across the front seat of the car after the accident. He was described as "dazed" and "swaying" when he stood up.

Cheatham has a history of seizure disorder dating to October, 1988, for which he had been treated at Allegheny General Hospital since January, 1989. He was treated first with dilantin and then Tegretol and, finally, phenobarbital, to control seizures which he told his physician occurred as often as once a day without medication. While receiving medication Cheatham reported to his treating physician that he had seizures once a month.

Cheatham's last reported seizure before the accident occurred on April 15, 1990, three and one-half months prior to the incident. Cheatham's treating physician, Dr. Rehka Pawar, testified that, prior to the accident, she had not seen Cheatham since April 19, 1990, but that his prescription for phenobarbital had been renewed by telephone. Dr. Pawar testified that Cheatham had missed some appointments with her, but she did not specify when. She also testified that she was "not sure that all the medications were being taken regularly." She was not asked to elaborate. A blood test after the accident — the record is unclear as to exactly how many hours later — showed Cheatham had a level of phenobarbital in blood slightly under the therapeutic level.[2]

---

[2] A therapeutic level of phenobarbital is 15 to 40 milligrams per liter. His blood measured 14.47 milligrams per liter.

Cheatham's driver's license was recalled in early 1989. A physician at Allegheny General notified the Commonwealth of Pennsylvania, pursuant to 75 Pa.C.S. 1518(b),[3] on January 5, 1989, that Cheatham suffered from seizure disorder and Cheatham's license was recalled.[4] Both the physician and the state Department of Transportation notified Cheatham he was not entitled to drive; Cheatham himself complained before the accident to his treating physician about the recall of his license.

Cheatham raises two questions for our consideration:

1) Whether a seizure-induced blackout is criminal negligence within the standards of culpability applicable to homicide by motor vehicle; ...

The first question presented by this appeal is whether the evidence established a level of culpability sufficient to sustain a criminal conviction. In reviewing a challenge to the sufficiency of the evidence, this court must ask whether the evidence, and all reasonable inferences deducible therefrom, viewed in the light most favorable to the Commonwealth as verdict winner, are sufficient to establish all the elements of the offense beyond a reasonable doubt....

Cheatham argues that a seizure-induced blackout is an involuntary act without the *mens rea* necessary to raise the conduct from negligent to grossly negligent as required for a criminal conviction ....

The statute under which Cheatham was charged, homicide by vehicle, provides in relevant part:

> Any person who unintentionally causes the death of another person while engaged in the violation of any law of this Commonwealth ... is guilty of homicide by vehicle, a misdemeanor of the first degree, when the violation is the cause of death.

75 Pa. C. S. § 3732.

Cheatham was charged with violating section 1543(a) of the Motor Vehicle Code, operating a motor vehicle while his operating privileges were suspended.[5] On the face of it, the charges against Cheatham appear to satisfy

---

[3] Section 1518(b) requires:

All physicians and other persons authorized to diagnose or treat disorders and disabilities defined by the Medical Advisory Board shall report to the department, in writing, the full name, date of birth and address of every person over 15 years of age diagnosed as having any specified disorder or disability within ten days.

Epilepsy is a disability defined at 67 Pa.Code 83.4:

A person suffering from epilepsy may not drive unless their personal licensed physician reports that the person has been free from seizure for a period of at least 1 year immediately preceding, with or without medication.

[4] Section 1519(c) of the Motor Vehicle Code provides:

The department shall recall the operating privilege of any person whose incompetency has been established ... for an indefinite period. 75 Pa.C.S. § 1519(c).

[5] Section 1543(a) of the Motor Vehicle Code provides:

[A]ny person who drives a motor vehicle on any highway or trafficway of this Commonwealth after the commencement of a suspension, revocation or cancellation of the operation privilege and before the operating privilege has been restored is guilty of a summary offense ... 75 Pa.C.S. § 1543(a).

A. THE REQUIREMENT OF VOLUNTARINESS

the elements of the statute. His violation of the law, driving while his license was recalled, caused the death of Ryan Maszle. Our analysis, however, does not end here. We must go on to consider whether driving without a license supplies the requisite but-for causation link to find Cheatham guilty of a criminal charge. If we find that his violation of the law caused the death, then we must continue our analysis to determine whether the act which caused Ryan Maszle's death was sufficiently reckless to supply the *mens rea* necessary to justify a criminal conviction. Only if we establish both cause and the necessary mental state may we convict Cheatham of a criminal charge....

With that standard in mind, we turn first to the statutory requirement that the violation of the law cause the death to impose culpability. We ask whether Cheatham's violation of the law, driving while his license was recalled, caused the death of seven-year-old Ryan Maszle.... [The court concluded that it did.]

Our next inquiry is directed to the mental element necessary to make a person criminally culpable for the fatal result which his acts cause, the *mens rea*.... The applicable mens rea requirements of culpability are those enumerated in 18 Pa.C.S. § 302(a)." ... Section 302(a) establishes four degrees of culpability: "intentionally, knowingly, recklessly or negligently as the law may require, with respect to each material element of the offense." ... "Negligently" is intended to be criminal negligence which is defined as "a gross deviation from the standard of care that a reasonable person would observe."...

The question becomes: Do the facts of the case at hand present a "gross deviation?" Cheatham asks us to frame the question as: Whether an epileptic seizure while driving constitutes a gross deviation. The Commonwealth, on the other hand, asks whether driving when one knows or has reason to believe one is subject to seizures constitutes a gross deviation from the standard of care. For the reasons that follow, we believe the Commonwealth's formulation of the question is most appropriate.

An epileptic seizure while driving and an ensuing fatal accident is an example law school textbooks use to distinguish cases in which there is no criminal culpability from those in which there is criminal responsibility.... The case most often cited is *People v. Decina*, [138 N.E.2d 799 (N.Y. 1956)]. In that case, Decina killed four children when he lost control of his car during an epileptic seizure. The question before the *Decina* court was whether the evidence was sufficient to indict. Decina argued the state had no evidence of the mens rea required to indict for involuntary manslaughter. The New York court held that, assuming the truth of the indictment as it must on demurrer, Decina knew he was subject to epileptic seizures. That knowledge and the choice to drive, the court said, amounted to culpable negligence. The court distinguished Decina's behavior from that of a person for whom the seizure was unexpected. An unexpected attack, the court reasoned, is altogether different, suggesting a lack of criminal culpability....

The defining difference between the epileptic who drives with the knowledge that he or she is seizure prone and the unsuspecting epileptic who drives is choice. One chooses to take the risk; the other does not know he is taking the risk....

In this case, Cheatham knew the frequency of his seizures even with medication, he knew that he had not had medical attention for three months, he knew that his seizures came on without warning, and he knew that the Commonwealth of Pennsylvania required that he be seizure-free for one year before being licensed to drive. Despite that knowledge, Cheatham chose to drive. That choice to drive raises Cheatham's conduct to the level of a gross deviation from the standard of care that a reasonable person would observe....

We find for the foregoing reasons that Cheatham's violation of the law, driving while his license was suspended, caused the death of Ryan Maszle and that Cheatham's disregard for the safety of others was sufficiently reckless and wanton to rise to the level of criminal culpability....

B. INNOCENT AGENT

STATE v. THOMAS

Supreme Court of Tennessee
619 S.W.2d 513 (1981)

DROWOTA, J.

The conviction of the defendant under § 39-3703 poses no problem with regard to the count charging the defendant with forcing the wife to perform fellatio upon himself. When the defendant forced the wife to perform fellatio upon her husband, however, the defendant was not the person who engaged in the direct sexual penetration of the victim. Nevertheless, we hold that the defendant is criminally liable as a principal for the offense with which he was charged.

At common law, the distinction between principals in the first and second degree had important procedural and substantive consequences. A principal in the first degree was one who actually committed the crime. A person who aided and abetted a crime and who was present at the scene of the crime was classified as a principal in the second degree. Although modern statutes have abolished some of the procedural consequences of the distinction, ... in some instances the distinction remains valid. Thus, the defendant here, as the only criminal actor, cannot be convicted as an aider or abettor under T.C.A. §§ 39-109 and 110, because those statutes "presuppose that a principal exists" who can be aided by the defendant....

The defendant is, however, criminally liable under the common law rule regarding the use of innocent agents as the instrumentality of a crime.

> If a person causes a crime to be committed through the instrumentality of an innocent agent, he is the principal in the crime, and punishable accordingly, although he was not present at the time and place of the offense, as is ordinarily required to render one guilty as a principal. As between him and the innocent agent, there is no such relation as principal in the first and second degree or principal and accessary; he alone is the guilty party. Under such circumstances, an exception to the rules applicable to principals and accessaries, in the trial of criminal cases, arises ex necessitate legis.

22 C.J.S. Criminal Law § 84 at 249....

B. INNOCENT AGENT

This rule of criminal liability has not been modified by statute. It cuts across all offenses, for the most part, regardless of the statutory wording of the offense, just as do the rules regarding aiders and abettors, accessaries before the fact and accessaries after the fact. The defendant who forces an innocent party to commit armed robbery, burglary, rape, incest, etc., is guilty as the only principal, even though the defendant does not commit the crime with his own hand.

In the situation before us, both husband and wife were victims and both were used as innocent agents of the defendant in the perpetration of the crime. The defendant committed the act of "sexual penetration" by means of these agents and he was properly found guilty....

NOTES

1. *See also United States v. Ruffin,* 613 F.2d 408 (2d Cir. 1979), discussed in the materials on parties to crime, *infra* pp. 726-733.

2. One also should reconsider the problem of criminality based on activities of those for whom a defendant is responsible, in the context of strict liability, *infra* pp. 693-719.

3. *Lovelace v. State,* 2 So. 2d 796 (Miss. 1941):

> There is no agency, properly so called, in crime. Aside from those cases where there is actual connivance, conspiring or abetting, or where the business conducted by the principal through the agent is itself unlawful, there is no principle by which criminal responsibility may be imputed to a master for the acts of the servant. The civil doctrine of respondeat superior was not conceived, nor is it to be applied, to include responsibility of the master to the state for the independent acts of the servant.

4. In *Anderson v. State,* 91 P.2d 794 (Okla. Crim. App. 1939), Anderson, Goff, and two women went to a dance; before they arrived Anderson gave Goff his pistol. At the dance both Anderson and Goff quarreled with Williams, and shortly thereafter Goff renewed the quarrel; Goff then fired the pistol indiscriminately into the crowd, killing three persons. In a separate trial, Goff was convicted of murder. At his own trial, Anderson was convicted of murder under an aiding and abetting statute, although there was no evidence of conspiracy between Goff and Anderson or of Anderson's knowledge that the shooting was to occur. The conviction was reversed. Mere acquiescence in a criminal act, not communicated in any way to an actor, on the part of one who did not procure or advise its perpetration, who takes no part in it, gives no counsel and utters no words of encouragement to the perpetrator, is not criminal conduct and does not make one a criminal participant. "There is a plain distinction between consenting to a crime and aiding and abetting in its perpetration. Aiding and abetting are affirmative in their character; consenting may be a mere negative acquiescence, not in any way made known to the principal malefactor. Such consenting, though involving moral turpitude," does not bring about criminality.

5. The Supreme Court of New Hampshire, in *State v. Akers,* 400 A.2d 38 (N.H. 1979), invalidated a statute holding parents criminally responsible for

acts of their children violating statutes regulating the operation of off-highway recreational vehicles. The law made no reference to parental conduct, acts, or omissions and made criminality turn on parental status. The court observed:

> It is argued that liability may be imposed on parents under the provisions of RSA 626:8 II(b), which authorizes imposing criminal liability for conduct of another when "he is made accountable for the conduct of such other person by the law defining the offense." This provision comes from the Model Penal Code § 2.04(2)(b). The illustrations of this type of liability in the comments to the Code all relate to situations involving employees and agents, and no suggestion is made that it was intended to authorize imposing vicarious criminal liability on one merely because of his status as a parent. Model Penal Code § 2.04(2)(b), Comment (Tent. Draft No. 1, 1956)....
>
> Without passing upon the validity of statutes that might seek to impose vicarious criminal liability on the part of an employer for acts of his employees, ... we have no hesitancy in holding that any attempt to impose such liability on parents simply because they occupy the status of parents, without more, offends the due process clause of our State constitution....
>
> Parenthood lies at the very foundation of our civilization. The continuance of the human race is entirely dependent upon it. It was firmly entrenched in the Judaeo-Christian ethic when "in the beginning" man was commanded to "be fruitful and multiply." Genesis 1. Considering the nature of parenthood, we are convinced that the status of parenthood cannot be made a crime. This, however, is the effect of RSA 269-C:24 IV. Even if the parent has been as careful as anyone could be, even if the parent has forbidden the conduct, and even if the parent is justifiably unaware of the activities of the child, criminal liability is still imposed under the wording of the present statute. There is no other basis for criminal responsibility other than the fact that a person is the parent of one who violates the law.
>
> One hundred and twenty seven years ago the justices of this court in giving their opinions regarding a proposed law that would have imposed vicarious criminal liability on an employer for acts of his employee stated, "[b]ut this does not seem to be in accordance with the spirit of our Constitution ..." *Opinion of the Justices*, 25 N.H. 537, 542 (1852). Because the net effect of the statute is to punish parenthood, the result is forbidden by substantive due process requirements of N.H. Const. pt. 1, art. 15.

Id. at 40.

C. SPECIAL DIMENSIONS OF *ACTUS REUS*
1. OMISSION TO ACT

MODEL PENAL CODE

§ 2.01. Omission as Basis of Liability

....

(3) Liability for the commission of an offense may not be based on an omission unaccompanied by action unless:
 (a) the omission is expressly made sufficient by the law defining the offense; or
 (b) a duty to perform the omitted act is otherwise imposed by law.

POPE v. STATE
Court of Appeals of Maryland
396 A.2d 1054 (1979)

[Pope allowed Melissa Norris and her three-month old infant, Demiko, to stay with her overnight because she did not want to "put them out on the street." Melissa sporadically indicated signs of mental distress, seeming to be caught up in a religious frenzy and declaring she was God, but then returning to normal. Pope did nothing about several clear signs that Melissa was abusing her child, and summoned no medical aid and made no reports to the police or other authorities. When the three went to church, the child was dead. When officers questioned Melissa in Pope's presence, she did not contradict Melissa's denials that she had abused her child and indeed told the officers that the baby did not fall and that she did not see Melissa strike her baby. The following part of the court's opinion considers Pope's status under the Maryland child abuse statute, covering "any parent, adoptive parent or other person who has the permanent or temporary care or custody of a minor child. MD. CODE ANN. art. 27, § 35 A (1957).]

ORTH, J. A person may have the responsibility for the supervision of a minor child in the contemplation of § 35A although not standing in loco parentis to that child. "Responsibility" in its common and generally accepted meaning denotes "accountability," and "supervision" emphasizes broad authority to oversee with the powers of direction and decision. See American Heritage Dictionary of the English Language (1969); Webster's Third New International Dictionary (1968). As in the case of care or custody of a minor child under the child abuse law, a judicial decree is not necessary to obtain responsibility for the supervision of a minor child under that statute. Had the Legislature wished to narrow application of that law to those who had been charged with responsibility for the supervision of a child by court order, it could readily have done so in explicit language to that end.... Absent a court order or award by some appropriate proceeding pursuant to statutory authority, we think it to be self-evident that responsibility for supervision of a minor child may be obtained only upon the mutual consent, expressed or implied, by the one legally charged with the care of the child and by the one assuming the responsibility. In other words, a parent may not impose responsibility for the supervision of his or her minor child on a third person unless that person accepts the responsibility, and a third person may not assume such responsibility unless the parent grants it. So it is that a baby sitter temporarily has responsibility for the supervision of a child; the parents grant the responsibility for the period they are not at home, and the sitter accepts it. And it is by mutual consent that a school teacher has responsibility for the supervision of children in connection with his academic duties. On the other hand, once responsibility for the supervision of a minor child has been placed in a third person, it may be terminated unilaterally by a parent by resuming responsibility, expressly or by conduct. The consent of the third party in such circumstances is not required; he may not prevent return of responsibility to the parent. But, of course, the third person in whom responsibility has been placed is not free to relinquish that responsibility without the knowledge of the parent. For example, a sitter may not simply walk away in the absence of the parents and leave the children to their own devices.

Under the present state of our law, a person has no legal obligation to care for or look after the welfare of a stranger, adult or child.

> Generally one has no legal duty to aid another person in peril, even when that aid can be rendered without danger or inconvenience to himself.... A moral duty to take affirmative action is not enough to impose a legal duty to do so. W. LaFave & A. Scott, Criminal Law 183 (1972).

...The legal position is that "the need of one and the opportunity of another to be of assistance are not alone sufficient to give rise to a legal duty to take positive action." R. Perkins, Criminal Law 594-595 (2d ed. 1969). Ordinarily, a person may stand by with impunity and watch another being murdered, raped, robbed, assaulted or otherwise unlawfully harmed. "He need not shout a warning to a blind man headed for a precipice or to an absentminded one walking into a gunpowder room with a lighted candle in hand. He need not pull a neighbor's baby out of a pool of water or rescue an unconscious person stretched across the railroad tracks, though the baby is drowning, or the whistle of an approaching train is heard in the distance." LaFave & Scott at 183. The General Assembly has enacted two "Good Samaritan" statutes which afford protection to one who assists another in certain circumstances. Those statutes, however, impose no requirement that assistance be rendered.

In the face of this status of the law we cannot reasonably conclude that the Legislature, in bringing a person responsible for the supervision of a child within the ambit of the child abuse law, intended that such responsibility attach without the consent criteria we have set out. Were it otherwise, the consequences would go far beyond the legislative intent. For example, a person taking a lost child into his home to attempt to find its parents could be said to be responsible for that child's supervision. Or a person who allows his neighbor's children to play in his yard, keeping a watchful eye on their activities to prevent them from falling into harm, could be held responsible for the children's supervision. Or a person performing functions of a maternal nature from concern for the welfare, comfort or health of a child, or protecting it from danger because of a sense or moral obligation, may come within the reach of the act. In none of these situations would there be an intent to grant or assume the responsibility contemplated by the child abuse statute, and it would be incongruous indeed to subject such persons to possible criminal prosecution....

NOTES

1. In *People v. Beardsley,* 113 N.W. 1128 (Mich. 1907), the defendant had been convicted of manslaughter based on his failure to summon aid for a woman with whom he had engaged in a prolonged bout of sexual activity during his wife's absence from the city. Beardsley and the woman had conducted assignations on earlier occasions. The two drank continuously for some hours and during Beardsley's temporary absence she asked an employee of the hotel where Beardsley was manager to buy morphine. She ingested a number of morphine pills, although Beardsley found and destroyed some of them. The woman became unconscious and Beardsley was too drunk to be of help. Employees of the hotel put the woman in another room where she died. The prosecution theory was that Beardsley violated a duty to care for the woman, bringing about her death. The Michigan Supreme Court reversed:

> The law recognizes that under some circumstances the omission of a duty owed by one individual to another, where such omission results in the death of the one to whom the duty is owing, will make the other chargeable with manslaughter. 21 Cyc. p. 770 et seq., and cases cited. This rule of law is always based upon the proposition that the duty neglected must be a legal duty, and not a mere moral obligation. It must be a duty imposed by law or by contract, and the omission to perform the duty must be the immediate and direct cause of death.... One authority has briefly and correctly stated the rule, which the prosecution claims should be applied to the case at bar, as follows: "If a person who sustains to another the legal relation of protector, as husband to wife, parent to child, master to seaman, etc., knowing such person to be in peril, willfully and negligently fails to make such reasonable and proper efforts to rescue him as he might have done, without jeopardizing his own life, or the lives of others, he is guilty of manslaughter at least, if by reason of his omission of duty the dependent person dies." "So one who from domestic relationship, public duty, voluntary choice, or otherwise, has the custody and care of a human being, helpless either from imprisonment, infancy, sickness, age, imbecility, or other incapacity of mind or body is bound to execute the charge with proper diligence, and will be held guilty of manslaughter, if by culpable negligence he lets the helpless creature die." 21 Am. & Eng. Enc. of Law (2d Ed.) p. 192, notes and cases cited.
>
> ... In *Territory v. Manton,* 8 Mont. 95, 19 Pac. 387, a husband was convicted of manslaughter for leaving his intoxicated wife one winter's night lying in the snow, from which exposure she died. The conviction was sustained on the ground that a legal duty rested upon him to care for and protect his wife, and that for his neglect to perform that duty, resulting in her death, he was properly convicted. *State v. Smith,* 65 Me. 257, is a similar case. A husband neglected to provide clothing and shelter for his insane wife. He left her in a bare room without fire during severe winter

weather. Her death resulted. The charge in the indictment is predicated upon a known legal duty of the husband to furnish his wife with suitable protection....

... The case of *Reg. v. Nicholls,* 13 Cox Crim. Cases, 75, was a prosecution of a penniless old woman, a grandmother, for neglecting to supply an infant grandchild left in her charge with sufficient food and proper care. The case was tried at Assizes in Stafford, before Brett, J., who said to the jury: "If a grown up person chooses to undertake the charge of a human creature, helpless either from infancy, simplicity, lunacy, or other infirmity, he is bound to execute that charge without, at all events, wicked negligence, and if a person who has chosen to take charge of a helpless creature lets it die by wicked negligence, that person is guilty of manslaughter." The vital question was whether there had been any such negligence in the case designated by the trial judge as wicked negligence. The trial resulted in an acquittal. The charge of this nisi prius judge recognizes the principle that a person may voluntarily assume the care of a helpless human being, and, having assumed it, will be held to be under an implied legal duty to care for and protect such person; the duty assumed being that of caretaker and protector to the exclusion of all others.

Another English case decided in the Appellate Court, Lord Coleridge, C. J., delivering the opinion, is *Reg. v. Instan,* 17 Cox Crim. Cases, 602. An unmarried woman without means lived with and was maintained by her aged aunt. The aunt suddenly became very sick, and for 10 days before her death was unable to attend to herself, to move about, or to do anything to procure assistance. Before her death no one but the prisoner had any knowledge of her condition. The prisoner continued to live in the house at the cost of the deceased and took in the food supplied by the trades people. The prisoner did not give food to the deceased, or give or procure any medical or nursing attendance for her; nor did she give notice to any neighbor of her condition or wants, although she had abundant opportunity and occasion to do so. In the opinion, Lord Coleridge, speaking for the court, said: "It is not correct to say that every moral obligation is a legal duty; but every legal duty is founded upon a moral obligation. In this case, as in most cases, the legal duty can be nothing else than taking upon one's self the performance of the moral obligation. There is no question whatever that it was this woman's clear duty to impart to the deceased so much of that food, which was taken into the house for both and paid for by the deceased, as was necessary to sustain her life. The deceased could not get it for herself. She could only get it through the prisoner. It was the prisoner's clear duty at the common law, and that duty she did not perform. Nor is there any question that the prisoner's failure to discharge her legal duty, if it did not directly cause, at any rate accelerated the death of the deceased. There is no case directly in point; but it would be a slur and a stigma upon our law if there could be any doubt as to the law to be derived from the principle of decided cases, if cases were necessary. There was a clear moral obligation and a legal duty founded upon it, a duty willfully disregarded, and the death was at least accelerated, if not caused by the nonperformance of the legal duty."

C. SPECIAL DIMENSIONS OF ACTUS REUS

Id. 1129-31.

2. In reconsidering the *Beardsley* case, *supra* note 1, would you expect the same result today? Should it make any difference if Beardsley had not been married and the decedent had been his steady girlfriend, or his fiancée, or if he and the woman, although not married to each other, had lived together for several years?

3. *Jones v. United States,* 308 F.2d 307, 310 (D.C. Cir. 1962):

> There are at least four situations in which the failure to act may constitute breach of a legal duty. One can be held criminally liable: first, where a statute imposes a duty to care for another; second, where one stands in a certain status relationship to another; third, where one has assumed a contractual duty to care for another; and fourth, where one has voluntarily assumed the care of another and so secluded the helpless person as to prevent others from rendering aid.

4. The fourth alternative in *Jones* was invoked in *Flippo v. State,* 523 S.W.2d 390 (Ark. 1975), in which during a deer-hunting expedition out of season a college-age son negligently wounded a person whom he mistook for a deer. The son administered no first aid but ran to a farmhouse to tell the victim's father about the accident. Father and son told the victim's father they would drive to a telephone and summon an ambulance. However, they passed a number of places from which a call could have been made in driving fourteen miles to their home, from which they telephoned an hour after the accident. When an ambulance finally arrived, the victim bled to death on the way to the hospital. Expert evidence suggested that either immediate first aid or prompt summoning of aid would have prevented death. The convictions of both the father and the son for involuntary manslaughter based on criminal negligence were affirmed.

5. Parents have a responsibility to provide or obtain medical care for their children. *Commonwealth v. Gallison,* 421 N.E.2d 757, 761-63 (Mass. 1981). In *State v. Williams,* 484 P.2d 1167 (Wash App. 1971), the defendants were reservation Indians:

> The defendant husband, Walter Williams, is a 24-year old full-blooded Sheshont Indian with a sixth-grade education. His sole occupation is that of laborer. The defendant's wife, Bernice Williams, is a 20-year-old part Indian with an 11th grade education. At the time of the marriage, the wife had two children, the younger of whom was a 14-month son. Both parents worked and the children were cared for by the 85-year-old mother of the defendant husband. The defendant husband assumed parental responsibility with the defendant wife to provide clothing, care and medical attention for the child. Both defendants possessed a great deal of love and affection for the defendant wife's young son.
>
> The court expressly found:
>
> That both defendants were aware that William Joseph Tabafunda was ill during the period September 1, 1968 to September 12, 1968. The defendants were ignorant. They did not realize how sick the baby was. They thought that the baby had a toothache and no layman regards a

toothache as dangerous to life. They loved the baby and gave it aspirin in hopes of improving its condition. They did not take the baby to a doctor because of fear that the Welfare Department would take the baby away from them. They knew that medical help was available because of previous experience. They had no excuse that the law will recognize for not taking the baby to a doctor.

The defendants Walter L. Williams and Bernice J. Williams were negligent in not seeking medical attention for William Joseph Tabafunda.

That as a proximate result of this negligence, William Joseph Tabafunda died....

Dr. Gale Wilson, the autopsy surgeon and chief pathologist for the King County Coroner, testified that the child died because an abscessed tooth had been allowed to develop into an infection of the mouth and cheeks, eventually becoming gangrenous. This condition, accompanied by the child's inability to eat, brought about malnutrition, lowering the child's resistance and eventually producing pneumonia, causing the death. Dr. Wilson testified that in his opinion the infection had lasted for approximately 2 weeks, and that the odor generally associated with gangrene would have been present for approximately 10 days before death. He also expressed the opinion that had medical care been first obtained in the last week before the baby's death, such care would have been obtained too late to have saved the baby's life. Accordingly, the baby's apparent condition between September 1 and September 5, 1968 became the critical period for the purpose of determining whether in the exercise of ordinary caution defendants should have provided medical care for the minor child.

The testimony concerning the child's apparent condition during the critical period is not crystal clear, but is sufficient to warrant the following statement of the matter. The defendant husband testified that he noticed the baby was sick about 2 weeks before the baby died. The defendant wife testified that she noticed the baby was ill about a week and a half or 2 weeks before the baby died. The evidence showed that in the critical period the baby was fussy; that he could not keep his food down; and that a cheek started swelling up. The swelling went up and down, but did not disappear. In that same period, the cheek turned "a bluish color like." The defendants, not realizing that the baby was as ill as it was or that the baby was in danger of dying, attempted to provide some relief to the baby by giving the baby aspirin during the critical period and continued to do so until the night before the baby died. The defendants thought the swelling would go down and were waiting for it to do so; and defendant husband testified, that from what he had heard, neither doctors nor dentists pull out a tooth "when it's all swollen up like that." There was an additional explanation for not calling a doctor given by each defendant. Defendant husband testified that "the way the cheek looked, ... and that stuff on his hair, they would think we were neglecting him and take him away from us and not give him back." Defendant wife testified that the defendants were "waiting for the swelling to go down," and also that they were afraid to take the child to a doctor for fear that the doctor would

C. SPECIAL DIMENSIONS OF *ACTUS REUS*

report them to the welfare department, who, in turn, would take the child away. "It's just that I was so scared of losing him." They testified that they had heard that the defendant husband's cousin lost a child that way. The evidence showed that the defendants did not understand the significance or seriousness of the baby's symptoms. However, there is no evidence that the defendants were physically or financially unable to obtain a doctor, or that they did not know an available doctor, or that the symptoms did not continue to be a matter of concern during the critical period. Indeed, the evidence shows that in April 1968 defendant husband had taken the child to a doctor for medical attention.

In our opinion, there is sufficient evidence from which the court could find, as it necessarily did, that applying the standard of ordinary caution, i.e., the caution exercisable by a man of reasonable prudence under the same or similar conditions, defendants were sufficiently put on notice concerning the symptoms of the baby's illness and lack of improvement in the baby's apparent condition in the period from September 1 to September 5, 1968 to have required them to have obtained medical care for the child. The failure so to do in this case is ordinary or simple negligence, and such negligence is sufficient to support a conviction of statutory manslaughter.

The judgment is affirmed.

Id. at 1169-70, 1173-74.

6. Review Professor Hall's comments on *Williams, supra* pp. 101-103.

7. Review also *People v. Robbins, supra* pp. 24-26, and note 2 to *Robbins*. The scope of the crime of manslaughter is considered in context *infra* pp. 315-341.

8. In *Commonwealth v. Godin*, 371 N.E.2d 438 (Mass. 1977), *cert. denied*, 436 U.S. 917 (1978), defendant, president of a fireworks-manufacturing corporation, was indicted for manslaughter in the death of three employees in a plant explosion. The amount of fireworks stored in the building where the employees were killed had reached unprecedented levels and the defendant had been warned to that effect but did nothing. He moved for a directed verdict of acquittal at the close of evidence, but the motion was denied and the jury convicted as charged. The Supreme Judicial Court affirmed:

> An employer whose acts or omissions constitute a disregard for the probable harmful consequences and loss of life as to amount to wanton or reckless conduct is properly charged with manslaughter where a foreseeable death is caused thereby. The *Welansky* [*Commonwealth v. Welansky*, 55 N.E.2d 902 (Mass. 1944)] case settled any claim that "negligence" and "wanton" and "reckless" conduct were words expressing differences of degree of risk. The differences involved are differences in kind. The interests involved are distinct. The State is the offended party where a death is caused by recklessness. To accept the defendant's arguments here is not only to overlook the fundamentally different purposes of criminal law and tort law but to create a class of persons — employees — as to whom a license to kill by wanton and reckless conduct is given. No such right has

ever existed, nor do we accept such a view now. The indictments were legally sufficient....

Such evidence, if believed, would warrant the jury in concluding that the defendant should have been aware and indeed was aware of the increased risk of harm and thus his failure to remedy the situation was the kind of conduct which constitutes wanton and reckless conduct. It certainly could not be said that such conduct was not reckless as matter of law. Recklessness involves conscious creation of a substantial and unjustifiable risk. See Model Penal Code § 2.02 (c) (Proposed Official Draft 1962); Comments, § 2.02 at 123-125 (Tent. Draft No. 4, 1955). As long as there is proof that the defendant's conduct was reckless as far as the risk of explosion was concerned, he must then be held accountable for the probable consequences of such conduct.

It therefore follows that the motions for the directed verdicts were properly denied.

Id. at 443, 444.

Query, did the court apply correctly the Model Penal Code concept of recklessness? *See supra* pp. 95-96.

9. Problem:

Suppose a toddler at play in a park fell into a lake and became submerged in three feet of water. The child was unable to rise above the water and was obviously in danger of drowning. The only person in a position to save the child was *X,* a full grown, healthy adult, who was also an excellent swimmer. *X,* a visitor at the park, saw the child's peril and could easily have saved the child without exposing herself to any danger. However, she was not related to the child; she was under no contractual obligation to intervene; she in no manner caused the child to fall into the water. If *X* fails to attempt to rescue the child and the child drowns, should *X* be subjected to criminal sanction?

Generally, the common law and the laws of every state save Vermont [VT. STAT. ANN., tit. 12 § 519 (1973)] would impose no legal duty on *X* under these circumstances. Should the law, under threat of punishment, require people to render aid to others who are in serious peril when they can do so without exposing themselves to serious risks? In Europe such is the case. GERMAN PENAL CODE § 330(e), AMERICAN SERIES OF FOREIGN PENAL CODES (G. Mueller & T. Buergenthal trans. 1961). This provision is now contained in § 323(c) of the 1975 Penal Code. *See also* Note, *The Failure to Rescue: A Comparative Study,* 52 COLUM. L. REV. 631 (1952); Franklin, *Vermont Requires Rescue: A Comment,* 25 STAN. L. REV. 51 (1972).

C. SPECIAL DIMENSIONS OF *ACTUS REUS*

2. POSSESSION

MODEL PENAL CODE

§ 2.01. Possession as an Act

....

(4) Possession is an act, within the meaning of this Section, if the possessor knowingly procured or received the thing possessed or was aware of his control thereof for a sufficient period to have been able to terminate his possession.

STATE v. LOWE

Missouri Court of Appeals
574 S.W.2d 515 (1978)

[Marijuana of more than thirty-five grams weight was seized lawfully under warrant from the apartment shared by Lowe and his wife, but from which he had been absent for about five days because of a "domestic tiff." Lowe was convicted and sentenced to imprisonment; the charges against Mrs. Lowe eventually were dismissed.]

SHANGLER, P.J. The charge of unlawful possession of a controlled substance [in this case, marijuana] ... requires proof that the accused had conscious possession of the substance.... For the penal purposes of these statutes actual possession need not be shown but proof of constructive possession will suffice.... The possession which the narcotics law prohibits, therefore, is not proprietary only but also such an exercise of control over drugs not in physical possession as will give rise to an inference of possession. In either case, the possession need not be exclusive but may be shared and is culpable only where the accused knew of the contraband and had control of the substance....

In a case where an accused is in exclusive control of premises the law makes the inference that a contraband substance found there also rests within his possession and control.... This rule rests on the logic that no one other than the exclusive proprietor could control — and so account for — the drugs.... In a case where premises are shared, a like inference of possession of the contraband does not arise in the absence of additional circumstances to inculpate the accused.... This rule rests on the logic that a shared proprietary interest in premises does not render it more likely that an accused either knows of the presence of drugs on the premises or in fact exercises control over the substances....

Nor does the status of husband and wife between the defendant and Brenda found alone on shared premises amidst the marijuana give rise to a presumption that the husband had control of the substance. Those jurisdictions which continue to deem the possession of contraband by the wife that of the husband as head of the household on premises shared by them cling to the common law unity of persons of a husband and wife, a fiction the emergent status of women and contemporary mores no longer allow. The more correct analysis sees no distinction between spouses and other cotenants of premises but directs inquiry only to whether or not the accused was in a position to exercise control over the drugs found on the premises. *Grantello v. United States,* 3 F.2d 117 (8th Cir. 1924)....

In terms of our decisional law, therefore, the question posed on appeal is whether the evidence shows a circumstance, in addition to the joint control of the apartment premises shared with wife Brenda, which renders it more probable than not that the defendant possessed the drugs taken under warrant.

The prosecution contends that seven incidences of evidence prove that the defendant had conscious, albeit constructive, possession and control of the drugs taken by the police: (1) defendant and wife Brenda lived for one year on the premises where the contraband was found; (2) defendant visited the premises the day before the seizure of the marijuana and of his arrest; (3) 115.7 grams of the substance were found throughout the apartment on the next day; (4) some of the marijuana was on the apartment premises for more than the week defendant was continuously absent from those premises; (5) testimony by wife Brenda [so it is asserted] that defendant knew of the presence of the marijuana stalk with leaves intact in the rear room; (6) defendant remained absent from the premises extendedly only for the five days prior to his arrest; and (7) defendant admitted to the officer that he had smoked marijuana and "didn't see any big deal" about it....

In terms of legal theory, constructive possession is figurative actual possession. ==To convict for constructive possession of an unlawful substance, the knowledge of the presence of the drug and dominion over the substance requisite for conviction for actual possession in fact must be proved by evidence of equivalent effect.==... In this proof, knowledge of the substance necessarily precedes possibility of control.... There was no evidence of the knowledge by the defendant of the marijuana on the shared premises — or, if we assume knowledge of the purchase and presence of the stalk — there was certainly no evidence of dominion over that substance.

The rule which requires that an inculpation in addition to joint use of premises be shown for a submissible issue of constructive possession shows judicial wariness that guilt on circumstantial evidence be imputed only on substantial proof.... Thus, ... proximity to the substance by the accused on premises shared by him was not sufficient to convict for a constructive unlawful possession even when the drugs were in his presence; but physical possession of the drug receptacle was a sufficient additional circumstance of guilt ... as was admitted ownership of the drugs taken, ... and also where the drugs were taken from a safe in a room within the exclusive possession of the accused....

The case at bench resembles most nearly the facts in *Grantello v. United States, supra,* where the court held that possession by the wife of morphine on the marital premises from which the husband had been absent for six months was not sufficient to render his guilt of possession of the substance a jury issue. The evidence before us shows an admitted possession of the marihuana by wife Brenda — a possession, for all the record discloses, actual, exclusive and dominant. The rudiments of proof of the constructive possession of the drugs by the defendant husband were not made. Accordingly, the defendant is entitled not only to reversal of judgment but to discharge....

The judgment is reversed and the defendant ordered discharged.

NOTES

1. In *Johnson v. State,* 376 N.E.2d 542 (Ind. App. 1978), the defendants were in possession of a house where, during an all-day barbecue party, heroin was found. Their convictions were reversed because they were not in exclusive possession of the premises and the circumstantial evidence was inadequate to establish beyond a reasonable doubt that they knew of the presence of the controlled substances.

2. In *State v. Lofton,* 256 S.E.2d 272 (N.C. App. 1979), defendant was alone in her apartment when officers with a valid search warrant entered to find marijuana growing in a porch planter and heroin in a matchbox in the kitchen. There were only two avenues of access to the porch, one through defendant's apartment and another through an unoccupied apartment. The evidence was sufficient to support various controlled substances convictions.

3. In *State v. Flaherty,* 400 A.2d 363 (Me. 1979), defendant, an ex-felon, was held not properly convictable of the felony of possessing a firearm found in the car he was driving, because, although he had become aware of its presence, the trial court failed to instruct the jury that defendant had to be "aware of his control of the rifle for a sufficient period to have been able to terminate his possession." The term "sufficient" was held not unduly vague.

4. Brief handling for the purpose of disposal, *United States v. Santore,* 290 F.2d 51 (2d Cir. 1960), *cert. denied,* 365 U.S. 834 (1961), or possession terminated when police saw defendant pick up and then drop a package containing narcotics, *People v. Mijares,* 491 P.2d 1115 (Cal. 1971), has been held not to constitute "possession."

5. In *Jenkins v. State,* 137 A.2d 115 (Md. 1957), defendant admitted possession of a package taken from a service station, but claimed he took it hoping to find something of value and was unaware that it contained drugs. The conviction was affirmed. The public welfare statute does not require knowledge. *See also Commonwealth v. Lee,* 117 N.E.2d 830 (Mass. 1954), where an unopened package received in the mail and claimed by defendant, when opened in the presence of officers, was found to contain marijuana. In *State v. Henker,* 314 P.2d 645 (Wash. 1957), where marijuana was found growing in defendant's yard, the court held that the state was not required to prove he had knowledge of its existence. *Accord, State v. Boggs,* 358 P.2d 124 (Wash. 1961).

6. In *Petty v. People,* 447 P.2d 217 (Colo. 1968), Smith and Petty were convicted of possession of marijuana which was found in an apartment in which they resided or into which they were in the process of moving. The marijuana was found in a box which also contained Petty's discharge papers, and in a cereal box in another room. The conviction of Smith was reversed.

7. A similar approach was used with respect to the driver of a vehicle where evidence pointed only to possession by a passenger. *Hamburg v. State,* 248 So. 2d 430 (Miss. 1971). *Compare Spataro v. State,* 179 So. 2d 873 (Fla. Dist. Ct. App. 1965), where the court held that defendant's knowledge of the presence of marijuana in an apartment which she shared with another person and her ability to reduce it to her personal dominion was sufficient to show constructive possession.

8. In *Commonwealth v. Buckley,* 238 N.E.2d 335 (Mass. 1968), a Massachusetts law which made it a crime for anyone to be "present where a narcotic drug is illegally kept" was interpreted to require knowledge that drugs were illegally kept on the premises.

9. In *State v. Toppan,* 425 A.2d 1336 (Me. 1981), a conviction for "furnishing" marijuana was sustained against the defendant based on his growing marijuana in a joint venture (pun intended) with two friends; all three were to share the harvest. Officers executing a valid search warrant seized over twenty-two pounds of marijuana. Possession of a usable amount of marijuana was only a civil violation, but sale or other transfer was criminal and possession of more than a stated amount created a presumption of illegal sale or other transfer. A legislative purpose to prevent activities like defendant's was discerned by the court:

> In arguing that a furnishing or transfer has not occurred in the instant case, the appellant is asking this Court to treat his conduct and that of his two friends as the type of small-scale personal use and possession that the Legislature has decided to exclude from criminal penalties. To accept the appellant's characterization would ignore the purpose of section 1106 in the criminal code. Generally speaking, section 1103 curbs the spread of marijuana use by penalizing its sale, while section 1106 is intended to curb the spread of marijuana use arising in the context of more informal social encounters. On the other hand, the treatment of possession of a usable amount as a civil violation is intended only to discourage the personal use of a putatively undesirable drug.
>
> Considered in terms of the basic purpose of section 1106, the word "furnish" in that section must be deemed to cover appellant's conduct. Where three persons pool their resources and labor for the purpose of cultivating, harvesting, and ultimately using marijuana, the legislative purpose underlying § 1106 is clearly involved. Each participant, by his efforts, has contributed to an enterprise from which each has gained access to, and the use of, a substance the Legislature has decided to regulate. The appellant's conduct thus involves more than a question of the individual use of a scheduled drug: by contributing land and labor to the project, he has intentionally facilitated the use of marijuana by others as effectively as if he had raised the marijuana alone and given his friends some of it without any prior understandings.

Id. at 1340.

10. For additional cases and analysis of the subject of possession, including joint and constructive possession, *see* 91 A.L.R.2d 810 (1963); Field, *Some Comments on the Actus Reus of Possession in the Criminal Law of Drugs,* 5 U.B.C.L. Rev. 372 (1970); Whitehead & Stevens, *Constructive Possession in Narcotics Cases: To Have and Have Not,* 58 Va. L. Rev. 751 (1972).

3. SOLICITATION

EDITORIAL NOTE

Solicitation by one person to another that the latter commit a crime is criminal, despite its lack of success. Indeed, should there be an affirmative response in the form of commission of one or more crimes, the solicitor will have become an inducer or conspirator and therefore incurs vicarious criminality as a consequence. *See generally* pp. 739-742 *infra*. Solicitation is defined in MODEL PENAL CODE § 5.01, Appendix A.

The interaction between criminal solicitation and protected first amendment speech is explored, *e.g.*, in *People v. Rubin*, 158 Cal. Rptr. 488 (Cal. App. 1979), *cert. denied*, 449 U.S. 821 (1980), in which the court affirmed a solicitation conviction against an officer of the Jewish Defense League who, in a speech in California, offered $500 to anyone who would kill, maim, or injure any American Nazi Party member participating in a party rally to take place in Skokie, Illinois, over a month later; $1,000 would be paid for both ears of a victim. The court found such a statement, made in all seriousness, to lie outside the scope of constitutionally protected speech, and sufficiently imminent and likely to produce action that it could be viewed as criminal.

SECTION III. Concurrence of *Mens Rea* and *Actus Reus*

MODEL PENAL CODE

§ 2.02. General Requirements of Culpability

(1) Minimum Requirements of Culpability. Except as provided in Section 2.05 [relating to strict liability; *see* Appendix A for text], a person is not guilty of an offense unless he acted purposely, knowingly, recklessly or negligently, as the law may require, with respect to each material element of the offense.

STATE v. ASBERRY

Missouri Court of Appeals
559 S.W.2d 764 (1977)

[Asberry was convicted of first-degree burglary of an occupied dwelling of another, with intent to commit rape.]

TITUS, J.

The presence of any part of an alleged burglar's body within the premises is enough entry to prove one essential element of a charge of burglary.... Although there was no evidence of the size of the basement window opening or proof to indicate that the opening minus the screen was sufficiently large to admit defendant into the house, nevertheless, based on the just-cited authorities, if we accept the jury's apparent finding that the naked foot stuck through the L-shaped cut in the screen was that of the defendant, we are constrained to the conclusion that there was proof of an entry.

However, mere entry does not itself constitute burglary. In this case it was necessary to prove that the entry was made to commit the felony of rape. To sustain such a charge, the proof must show beyond a reasonable doubt that defendant intended not merely to have sexual intercourse with the girl but also to use whatever force was necessary to overcome her resistance.... The intent with which an accused breaks and enters is an essential element of the offense of burglary and must be established by evidence beyond a reasonable doubt....

Pared to the bone, these are the facts: Suzette was awakened by a noise while abed in her basement bedroom. She engaged in a two or three minute innocuous conversation (at least she could not remember its context) with one or more unidentified male persons positioned outside the screened basement window. The size of the window's opening is unknown, but the later discovered L-shaped cut in the screen was of insufficient proportion to permit entry of a normal sized adult male. Upon espying a naked foot of unknown sex being put through the cut in the screen, Suzette forsook her bed, ran from the room and screamed. Posthaste, the possessor of the unadorned foot withdrew it from the opening and hied himself away. Subsequently, defendant, suffering the throes of extreme inebriety and accompanied only by a pillow, was discovered 100 yards from the allegedly burgled premises. Intoning his apologies and awaiting, as directed, the return of his captor, defendant with difficulty donned a proffered pair of pants wrong side out and backwards.

Albeit conceded that defendant may have desired sexual intercourse with Suzette, nothing appears of record to indicate that he was intent upon employing whatever degree of force which may have been necessary to accomplish his wants. When defendant's desires were apparently discovered by Suzette and she manifested a disliking therefor, defendant immediately withdrew his foot and fled. If defendant had intended to force himself upon Suzette in any event, situate and armed as he seemingly was, it appears incredible that he would have first engaged her in two or three minutes of harmless conversation and then put a naked foot through an insufficient opening in the screen to telegraph his desires. It does not appear that the means allegedly employed by defendant were adapted to secure the end desired in any event. We can only arrive at the defendant's intentions by his acts and conduct. Regardless of how reprehensible defendant's conduct may have been, the evidence does not disclose that he intended to commit the crime of rape at all costs.

As it is evident that the state presented all available evidence pertinent to the issues and failed to make a submissible case, the judgment below is reversed and the defendant is discharged.

NOTES

1. In *Carr v. Clark County Sheriff,* 601 P.2d 422 (Nev. 1979), the defendant had been charged with burglary and with use of a deadly weapon during its commission. His application for habeas corpus, based on the insufficiency of the evidence at the preliminary examination to establish a prima facie case of the use of a deadly weapon, was denied in the trial court. A majority of the Nevada Supreme Court reversed:

> The essence of Carr's contention is that the crime of burglary was complete upon his alleged unlawful entry of the house and was not accomplished with the use of the knife. We agree.
>
> The offense of burglary is complete when the house or other building is entered with the specific intent designated in the statute.... Thus, Carr's alleged commission of the burglary, having already occurred upon his entry of the house, could not have been perpetrated with the use of a deadly weapon as contemplated by NRS 193.165. In order to use a deadly weapon for purposes of that statute, there need only be conduct which produces a fear of harm or force by means or display of a deadly weapon....
>
> Therefore, although Carr's alleged conduct with the knife after he gained entry into the house may subject him to other criminal charges ... such conduct may not be used to enhance the crime of burglary pursuant to NRS 193.165. Accordingly, the district court's order denying Carr's petition for a writ of habeas corpus which challenges the allegation that he used a deadly weapon in the commission of the burglary is reversed....

Id. at 423-24.

Two justices dissented:

> The majority holds, in effect, that a burglar who is gathering his loot is no longer engaged in the commission of a burglary. According to the majority, the burglary had already been "completed." I doubt if an unsuspecting homeowner, surprised in his own living room by a weapon-wielding burglar, would be able to comprehend or to appreciate the majority's logic. I know that I do not.
>
> In reaching its conclusion, the majority performs a feat of legerdemain, transforming a legal term of art, "complete," into a conception of reality. Of course, the crime of burglary is "complete," in the sense that criminal liability attaches, once an individual enters a house with a felonious intent.... The *commission* of that crime, though, is not "complete" in the sense of being terminated.
>
> This Court has not always been so swayed by a hypertechnical interpretation of the word "complete." In the felony-murder context, this Court has found that the res gestae of a crime embraces the actual facts of the transaction, the matters immediately antecedent to it, and those "acts immediately following it and so closely connected with it to form in reality a part of the occurrence." ... Thus, we held that a robber who was attempting to secure his stolen possessions or who was attempting to effect his escape was still engaged in the perpetration of a robbery even though the robbery had been technically "completed."... The result should be no different with respect to burglary.

Id. at 424.

2. In *Mason v. State*, 603 P.2d 1146 (Okla. Crim. App. 1979), Mason was convicted of the crime of actual physical control of a vehicle while intoxicated;

the crime covered a person who is under the influence of intoxicating liquor who drives, operates, or is in actual physical control of any motor vehicle within the state. The court affirmed the conviction:

> [In earlier precedent,] we found an individual to be in actual physical control of an automobile when the keys were merely in the ignition and the defendant was unconscious behind the wheel of his parked car... [W]e find the legislative intent in enacting the "actual physical control" portion of [the controlling statute] to be the apprehension of the intoxicated driver before he can do any harm....
>
> ... The appellant created a highly dangerous situation by placing himself behind the wheel of his car and starting the engine while intoxicated. By starting the engine, he undoubtedly "directed influence" over the automobile. We cannot allow the appellant to later extricate himself from these self-created dangerous circumstances by being discovered while unconscious. Such a rule would benefit the most blatant violators of the statute, while punishing individuals found in violation of the statute but intoxicated to a lesser extent. The untenable nature of this position is obvious. Accordingly, an intoxicated individual, although unconscious, positioned behind the wheel of a running automobile, is in actual physical control of the automobile.

....

SECTION IV. The Harm

STATE v. LAUFENBERG

Supreme Court of North Dakota
99 N.W.2d 331 (1959)

BURKE, JUDGE. These seven appellants were convicted in the County Court of Cass County of the crime of grossly disturbing the public peace. A motion for a new trial, made by defendants, was denied by the trial court. Defendants have appealed from the order denying a new trial and from the judgment of conviction. They predicate error upon the trial court's refusal to grant a motion to dismiss the action, made at the close of the state's case and upon specifications of error in the admission of testimony and in the instructions to the jury. The motion to dismiss was made upon the ground that there was no evidence in the record that the public peace had been disturbed.

The testimony disclosed that a group of Fargo boys and a group of boys from Dilworth, Minnesota, all of teenage, had engaged in a physical combat on an otherwise deserted street in the business section of Fargo at 12:00 o'clock midnight. The testimony is that the altercation lasted from one to three minutes. There is evidence that some weapons, an iron pipe, an open end wrench and a flash light, were in possession of the Dilworth boys. There is also evidence that the defendant, Laufenberg, was struck by one of these weapons and that he suffered minor cuts about the back of his head.

....

It is conceded by all that an offense of assault and battery was committed. Defendants assert, however, that the offense was committed in such circumstances that the public peace was not disturbed at all, much less grossly disturbed. The altercation was of very short duration. It lasted from one to three minutes. While it was taking place no one, but the participants and their companions, was present or in view. As far as the record shows no one but the participants and their companions saw the fight or had any knowledge that it had taken place until the Fargo boys told their story at St. John's Hospital. The Fargo police department received no reports of the affair except from the boys themselves and there was no testimony offered at the trial except that of some of the boys and that of police officers who could only testify to admissions made by the boys.

Defendants were charged under Section 12-1901 NDRC 1943. This section reads:

> Every person who willfully and wrongfully commits any act which grossly disturbs the public peace, although no punishment is expressly prescribed, is guilty of a misdemeanor.

This offense is a serious one as it is punishable by imprisonment in the county jail for not to exceed one year or by a fine not to exceed $500 or by both such fine and imprisonment. Section 12-0614 NDRC 1943. It is a different and graver offense than ordinary breach of the peace.... Under the clear wording of the statute there must be proof that the public peace was actually and grossly disturbed in order to support a conviction of a person charged thereunder. It is not enough to prove an act from which a disturbance of the peace might reasonably flow. "By 'peace' as used in the law in this connection, is meant the tranquility enjoyed by citizens of a municipality or community where good order reigns among its members, which is the natural right of all persons in political society. It is, so to speak, that invisible sense of security which every man feels so necessary to his comfort, and for which all governments are instituted." Wharton Criminal Law and Procedure, 2, Sec. 802.

There is no proof in this record that the tranquility or the sense of security of any resident of the City of Fargo was disturbed by the incident which gave rise to this prosecution. As far as the record shows, no one but the participants was even aware of the incident while it was taking place. The evidence is insufficient to sustain the conviction. The judgment is reversed and the case ordered dismissed.

STATE v. QUINNAM

Supreme Judicial Court of Maine
367 A.2d 1032 (1977)

[Defendant appealed his conviction after bench trial for violating a statutory requirement that motorcycle operators and passengers wear protective headgear. The court denied the appeal.]

WERNICK, J.

We hold without merit the first facet of defendant's attack: — that 29 M.R.S.A. § 1373 violates the constitutional guarantee of due process of law.

It would be reasonable for the Legislature to believe: (1) a motorcycle, as an unenclosed vehicle, leaves its operator exposed and highly vulnerable to objects kicked up from roadways or falling from trees; (2) only a slight blow to the exposed head of the operator of a motorcycle, as a delicately balanced vehicle frequently driven at high speeds, can cause the operator to lose control of the vehicle's operation; and (3) the wearing of protective headgear tends to reduce such potential dangers to proper control over the operation of motorcycles. These facts, fairly attributable to the knowledge of the Legislature, establish that the requirement that motorcyclists shall wear protective headgear has rational relationship to the furtherance of the Legislature's legitimate police power interest to promote the public safety and, therefore, comports with the constitutional mandate of due process of law....

Also unconvincing is defendant's argument that the statute invidiously discriminates against motorcyclists in violation of the constitutional guarantee of the "equal protection of the laws." The Legislature had warrant to believe: (1) a motorcycle provides much less protection and stability for its operator than an enclosed four-wheeled motor vehicle; and (2) the speed and power capability of a motorcycle is far greater than that of an unmotorized bicycle. Hence, when a motorcycle is operated by a person lacking protective headgear, the dangers to the safety of the public greatly exceed those arising when an unhelmeted person operates either an enclosed four-wheeled motor vehicle or an unmotorized bicycle. Since there is thus rational basis for its action, the Legislature does not invidiously discriminate in requiring motorcyclists to wear protective headgear without imposing a similar requirement upon the operator of enclosed four-wheeled vehicles or unmotorized bicycles....

Defendant fails in his additional claim that the protective headgear statute abridges the constitutional guarantee of freedom of speech. The essence of the activity of operating a motorcycle is not "speech." If it happens to be utilized to express an idea, such fortuitous "speech" overlay does not deny to the State the right to exercise its police power reasonably to regulate the predominant "nonspeech" facets of the conduct of operating a motorcycle. *United States v. O'Brien,* 391 U.S. 367 (1968). Thus, notwithstanding that the operation of a motorcycle may be the means of making a communicative statement, there is no violation of the constitutional guarantee of freedom of speech when, as here, the predominantly "nonspeech" facets of the activity are subjected to regulations reasonably calculated to promote the safety of the public's use of the highways....

Finally, there is no merit in defendant's claim that the protective headgear statute impairs his constitutionally guaranteed right to travel. The constitutional protection of a right to travel from state to state is not contravened when a State enacts and enforces reasonable regulations to promote public safety....

NOTE

In *People v. Goodman,* 290 N.E.2d 139 (N.Y. 1972), the court sustained the validity of a village ordinance banning commercial signs larger than four square feet in area; Goodman had displayed oversized signs on his drugstore. The court stated:

> It is now settled that aesthetics is a valid subject of legislative concern and that reasonable legislation designed to promote the governmental interest in preserving the appearance of the community represents a valid and permissible exercise of the police power.... Under the police power, billboards and signs may be regulated for aesthetic purposes....

JEROME HALL, LAW, SOCIAL SCIENCE AND CRIMINAL THEORY 208-11 (1982)

Victimless Crimes

I turn now to another area, that of the so-called victimless crimes, because it provides a good example of the need for analysis as an essential prerequisite of sound research. The current interest in this area was stimulated by the publication of the Wolfenden Report in 1957 and by many debates, notably those of Professor Hart and Justice Devlin. But the term "victimless crimes" seems to have been popularized by the publication in 1966 of Edwin Schur's *Crimes Without Victims*. Just as in the cases of individualization of treatment and juvenile delinquency, the origin of the thinking or, if one prefers, of the ideology supporting the current position regarding "victimless crimes" goes far back into the past. In 1935, for example, in an article published in the *University of Chicago Law Review* based on my experience as an assistant state's attorney and also as defense counsel, I said, "the vagrant, the drunkard (frequently the chronic alcoholic), the drug addict, the prostitute, the petty thief and others, should be separated in theory as well as in practice from the truly criminal, and given treatment according to their needs."[7] But at least as regards alcoholism and prostitution, challenging voices were raised long before that; for example, almost two hundred years ago Bentham opposed the criminalization of "drunkenness and fornication" on the ground that that would do more harm than those vices left unpenalized.[8]

The Wolfenden Report, recommending the exclusion from the criminal code of homosexual practices among consenting adults, stressed the requirement of privacy. But "privacy" is obviously not limited to sexual conduct and cannot serve as a distinctive criterion of "victimless crimes." The criteria frequently used to distinguish so-called victimless crime are consent of the parties[9] and lack of complaint to the police; but more insistently it is said that there is no victim in the sense that no particular person has been harmed.

That "consent," even if limited to normal adults, does not distinguish victimless crimes from universally recognized crimes is evident by reference to the limitations placed on consent as a defense, for example, consent to a public brawl, to mayhem, to aiding suicide. Indeed, as regards some of the

---

[7] Hall, The Law of Arrest in Relation to Contemporary Social Problems, 3 U. of Chi. L. Rev. 369 (1936).
[8] J. Bentham, The Theory of Legislation 62 (1882).
[9] "[T]his element of consent precludes the existence of a victim...." E. Schur, Crimes Without Victims (1965).

most serious crimes, consent is simply irrelevant because no one can consent, for example, to treason.

The principal issue, however, has centered on the question of harm, and the polemic was unfortunately formulated in terms of harm versus the preservation of social morality. Those who espoused the harm thesis summoned the support of Mill who said, "the sole end for which mankind are warranted ... in interfering with the liberty of action of any of their number is self-protection."[10] Other statements by Mill are inconsistent with the broad interpretation that was made of that statement, for example, Mill's view on roads, compulsory education, and defense of the country.

The use of "harm," meaning harm to specific persons, also encounters serious difficulties not only because "harm" is a vague concept but also because human beings are so interrelated that it is impossible to restrict harm to the person who harms himself. If a man incapacitates himself by use of alcohol or heroin, his family suffers, he may go on welfare, he may steal to support his habit. In every one of the practices called victimless crimes, because of the vagueness and ramification of "harm," it is possible to present a defensible case that there are harms to other persons. When one turns to crimes like treason, the obstruction of justice, pollution, violation of zoning ordinances, and to carrying guns and driving recklessly or while intoxicated, it becomes quite clear that the assumption that every crime has a specific victim is fallacious.

A stronger case for victimless crimes might have been made if its proponents had focused on *mens rea* and causation. If *mens rea* were restricted to intention and recklessness, as has long been urged not only by me but also by Turner and Williams, it would be difficult, say in alcoholism or prostitution, even granting harm to others, to find the required *mens rea,* that is, to find that the resultant harm was sought or recklessly hazarded. Similarly, since proximate cause has been rejected in criminal law, notably in Pennsylvania and also in many other states, the eventual harm of alcoholism or prostitution is not the direct result of the relevant actions; hence it cannot be brought within the restricted, valid concept of causation in criminal law.

Instead of pursuing a vague and ill-conceived notion like victimless crimes,[11] we would do better, I think, if we approached the problem from the other end, that is, from that of the sanction. Since there may be both immorality and harm in the indicated activities, we should concentrate on the limitations, the crudeness, of the penal sanction, and seek more rational ways of dealing with those problems. My present purpose, however, is to emphasize the need for the analysis of concepts if we are to avoid the expensive detours that follow when vague, ill-defined concepts are accepted as valid.

There is a final point to be made in this context: The lumping together of vagrancy, alcoholism, gambling, prostitution, use of narcotics, adultery, bigamy, and others violates one of the principal findings of research that have emerged as sound, namely, the need to distinguish and divide if we are to control. Thus the study of addiction to alcohol or heroin may lead to a solution

---

[10] J.S. Mill, On Liberty 13 (1956).

[11] This has received much fuller analysis in Wertheimer, Victimless Crimes, 87 Ethics 302 (1977).

very different from that required for gambling or prostitution, and each of these may differ in important ways from the other solutions.

It is not my purpose to depreciate the importance of sound empirical research or to ignore the fact that it contributes to conceptual analysis, the discovery of guiding lines of organization and theoretical inquiry. I have submitted: (1) that sound empirical research depends on the above types of analysis; (2) that even the soundest empirical research cannot provide solutions to our problems; it can inform the practical judgment of those who seek solutions of these problems; and (3) that we should discover the extent of our present knowledge by the deliberate use of methods that assure the adequate presentation of opposed perspectives, data, and theories.

EDITORIAL NOTE

"Harm" implies interests or values which have been destroyed, wholly or in part. Lawyers deal with harms that have been described and forbidden by law. An examination of the statutes of your state (which should become a regular part of your preparation) will reveal a vast array of harms described in many specific crimes — the death of human beings, the burning of houses, the loss of property, and many others.

These harms have been classified in several ways: (a) harms to certain interests or values (against life, person, property, reputation, habitation, morality, political institutions, the family, etc.); (b) major and minor harms (felony and misdemeanor); (c) ultimate harms (e.g., murder) and relational harms (e.g., criminal attempt to murder); (d) with reference to jurisdiction and procedure, and in other ways.

If you think about the nature of the harm in treason, perjury, rape, libel, and kidnapping you will see that "harm" is not confined to physical injuries. This suggests the need for a definition of "harm" that can be applied to the more problematic instances of harm met in criminal law, e.g., in assaults, attempts, conspiracies, and bigamy.

Finally, it is necessary to keep in mind that every legal definition of a crime (case law, statute, etc.) describes a more or less specific harm. Analysis must be concerned not only with the legal definition of a harm but also, and equally, with the relevant fact situation. Is the particular effect in the fact situation the kind of harm (within the class) that is forbidden by the criminal law upon which the prosecutor relies? This distinctive aspect of the lawyer's job is worth emphasizing. For the lawyer, whether he or she is prosecuting or defending, the question is not whether in some sense, ethical or sociological, the defendant has committed a harm. Rather, the question is whether the defendant's conduct has caused the harm which the law in question sought to prevent.

For many years it has been maintained that the alcoholic, the drug addict, the prostitute and others "should be separated in theory as well as in practice, from the truly criminal, and given treatment according to their needs." Jerome Hall, *The Law of Arrest in Relation to Contemporary Social Problems,* 3 U. CHI. L. REV. 345, 369 (1936). *See generally* HERBERT PACKER, THE LIMITS OF THE CRIMINAL SANCTION 249-366 (1968). In 1964, the publication in England of The Wolfenden Report gave added impetus to this view of the criminal law; it recommended that homosexual conduct in private among consenting adults be removed from criminal liability; such conduct may be sinful or immoral, but it is not the sort of conduct that is properly within the scope of the criminal law. This was subsequently enacted by Parliament, then adopted in Illinois and, later, in several other states. The Report stimulated much discussion including the well-known debate between Mr. Justice Devlin (*The Enforcement of Morals,* seven essays published in Devlin's book, same title, 1965) and Professor H.L.A. Hart (LAW, LIBERTY AND MORALITY, 1963). *See also* Nagel, *The Enforcement of Morals,* in MORAL PROBLEMS IN CONTEMPORARY SOCIETY: ESSAYS IN HUMANISTIC ETHICS (P. Kurtz ed. 1969) and Rostow, *The Enforcement of Morals,* CAMBRIDGE L.J. 174 (1960). In the United States there has been much emphasis on "victimless crimes." The following comments are mainly intended to raise relevant questions about the aims and scope of criminal law, and not as criticism of particular proposals.

1. The emphasis on sexual morality has had the unfortunate effect of focusing attention on a peripheral problematic aspect of morality; it is necessary to place that in the perspective of the general scope and aims of the criminal law. See H.L.A. Hart, *The Aims of the Criminal Law,* 23 LAW & CONTEMP. PROB. 399, 401 (1958), *infra* pp. 844-852.

2. Some of the literature on "victimless crimes" errs in the suppositions that consent is always a defense and that there must be a specific victim to warrant penal liability. One need only refer to mayhem and assisting one who wishes to commit suicide to see that consent is not always a defense; similarly, perjury, public disorder, many political crimes, obstruction of justice and others have no specific victims. In addition, lumping prostitution, alcoholism, gambling and homosexual practices together clouds the problem because there may be such important differences among them as to require very different solutions.

3. Mr. Justice Devlin, in the above noted lecture, emphasized the importance, for the preservation of society, of the ordinary person's moral attitudes and of consensus on those values; Professor Hart, relying on parts of Mill's classic discussion, emphasized the liberty of the individual and the pluralistic character of modern democratic society with corresponding diversity of attitudes and values. Although these and other discussions seem to proceed in different directions, it is possible to discern or suggest a common agreement, namely, that there must be a "harm" to society. But that does not provide helpful guidance to a legislator not only because "harm" is vague, but also because "no man is an island, entire of it self"; anyone who harms himself or herself harms his or her family and the society of which he or she is a member, e.g., in requiring its financial aid and social services and in the loss of what he might otherwise have contributed to the common good.

4. This indicates that the scope of the criminal law or, in the present context, the meaning of "harm," cannot be determined with sufficient precision for practical purposes unless one compares the relative crudeness of criminal sanctions with other forms of control — individual and social. This would shift discussion from the question of harm to the question of the degree and types of

harm that may feasibly be retained or brought within the scope of the criminal law.

There is an additional factor that needs more emphasis than it has received, namely, that of changes in public attitudes and their effect on legislation and the judicial process. For example, the recent far-reaching changes in the law on vagrancy are largely responses to shifts in public opinion regarding the idleness of able-bodied persons when unemployment is a major problem. Explanation of changes in the law on abortion calls for a more complex set of conditions; among them, again, are changes in public attitudes regarding the value of privacy and the autonomy of women as compared with the loss of fetal life in an "over-populated" planet.

5. Assuming there is "sufficient" harm, the more pertinent and perhaps less subjective question is whether the conduct in question should be controlled through criminalization or regulation. *See* Robert Force, *Administrative Adjudication of Traffic Violation Confronts the Doctrine of Separation of Powers,* 49 TUL. L. REV. 84, 131-38 (1974).

In support of decriminalization it has been said:

> a. The conduct in question does not deserve the stigma of "crime."
> b. The conduct in question does not deserve punishment.
> c. Law enforcement officers, judges, prosecutors, and defense counsel would have added time to devote to problems involving serious harm.
> d. Discriminatory enforcement, nonenforcement, and corruption would be reduced
> e. The integrity of the narrowed criminal law and its effectiveness within the community would be enhanced.

See Robert Force, *Decriminalization of Breach of the Peace Statutes: A Non-Penal Approach to Order Maintenance,* 46 TUL. L. REV. 367, (1972); Sanford Kadish, *The Crisis of Overcriminalization,* 374 ANNALS 157 (1967); RAYMOND NIMMER, TWO MILLION UNNECESSARY ARRESTS (American Bar Foundation, 1971).

The gain sought by decriminalization should not obscure certain possible consequences.

> a. The conduct in question may still be subject to control through regulation.
> b. The costs of regulations may equal or exceed any savings resulting from decriminalization.
> c. The experience with removing child delinquents from the criminal law system and bringing them into the juvenile system indicates only that one stigma replaced another.
> d. Sanctions in the form of "penalties" or "treatment" may be as severe as or more severe than those presently existing under penal law.
> e. All of the constitutional and statutory procedural protections available in the criminal justice process may not be available to persons subject to a regulatory process.
> f. Finally, one should return to some basic questions about criminal theory, specifically, to the place, if any, of the concept of "harm." That

harm is of such central importance in criminal law as to require the adoption of a relevant principle has been supported on several grounds. First, that it is essential if one is to understand the core and major type of criminal law — the felonies and serious misdemeanors, *i.e.*, reference to harm is essential to understanding criminal law as based on a moral foundation. Second, unless "harm" connotes an actual social disvalue, *mens rea* has no social significance (but the common law certainly gives it moral significance); or, at best this is confused with a neutral or even a moral meaning of "*mens rea*." Third, "harm" serves as an essential "organizational construct" in still other respects, *e.g.*, in classifying crimes, in explanation of the causal principle, in making sense of variations in the gravity of penal sanctions, and finally, it seems clear, as exponents of victimless crimes have assumed, that insistence on harm tends to restrict the scope of criminal law.

This thesis has been opposed on several grounds. First, it is asserted there is no harm in some assaults and attempts. This is apart from the above-noted thesis regarding "victimless crimes" and also from similar views of bigamy, incest, adultery, obscenity, euthanasia and suicide. It has also been argued that danger should be distinguished from harm. But it is difficult to see what actual consequences this entails, e.g., should throwing rocks at blind persons be excluded from criminal liability? If it is intended to base punishment solely on dangerousness, there are further complications regarding the measurement or gravity of the danger. Furthermore, why punish someone for something he or she may do in the future? *Compare* Seney, *"Pond as Deep as Hell": Harm, Danger and Dangerousness in Our Criminal Law,* 17 WAYNE L. REV. 1095 (1971) and 18 WAYNE L. REV. 569 (1972).

Criticism of the principle of harm has also been based on the view that the harm actually caused may be a matter of sheer accident and that the rational thing to do is to base the punishment on the mens rea and the action, disregarding any actual harm or lack of harm or its degree. This recalls some very old arguments about unsuccessful criminal attempts and why they are almost always punished much less severely than the successful ones. See Stephen Schulhofer, *Harm and Punishment: A Critique of Emphasis on the Results of Conduct in the Criminal Law,* 122 U. PA. L. REV. 1497 (1974).

What is your view of the above questions? *See* Eser, *The Principle of Harm in the Concept of Crime: A Comparative Analysis of the Criminally Protected Legal Interests,* 4 DUQUESNE L. REV. 345 (1966).

SECTION V. Causation

MODEL PENAL CODE

§ 2.03. Causal Relationship Between Conduct and Result

(1) Conduct is the cause of a result when:
  (a) it is an antecedent but for which the result in question would not have occurred; and

V. CAUSATION

(b) the relationship between the conduct and results satisfies any additional causal requirements imposed by the Code or by the law defining the offense.

(2) When purposely or knowingly causing a particular result is an element of an offense, the element is not established if the actual result is not within the purpose or the contemplation of the actor unless:

(a) the actual result differs from that designed or contemplated, as the case may be, only in the respect that a different person or different property is injured or affected or that the injury or harm designed or contemplated would have been more serious or more extensive than that caused; or

(b) the actual result involves the same kind of injury or harm as that designed or contemplated and is not too remote or accidental in its occurrence to have a [just]* bearing on the actor's liability or on the gravity of his offense.

(3) When recklessly or negligently causing a particular result is an element of an offense, the element is not established if the actual result is not within the risk of which the actor is aware or, in the case of negligence, of which he should be aware unless:

(a) the actual result differs from the probable result only in the respect that a different person or different property is injured or affected or that the probable injury or harm would have been more serious or more extensive than that caused; or

(b) the actual result involves the same kind of injury or harm as the probable result and is not too remote or accidental in its occurrence to have a [just] bearing on the actor's liability or on the gravity of his offense.

(4) When causing a particular result is a material element of an offense for which absolute liability is imposed by law, the element is not established unless the actual result is a probable consequence of the actor's conduct.

Comments[*]

1. This section is concerned with offenses that are so defined that causing a particular result is a material element of the offense, as in the case of homicide, theft, etc. It undertakes to define the causality relationship that should generally be required to establish liability for such offenses and to deal with inevitable problems incident to variations between the actual result of conduct and the result sought or contemplated by the actor or probable under the circumstances of the action. These problems are now faced as issues of "proximate causation" and they present enormous difficulty, especially in homicide, because of the vague meaning of that term. Rather than seek to systematize variant and sometimes inconsistent rules in different areas in which the prob-

---

*Whenever material appears in brackets in the Model Penal Code it signifies that the Institute has presented alternative versions for consideration by the states.
[*]From MODEL PENAL CODE § 2.03, Tent. Draft No. 4, 132-35 (1955).

lem has arisen, the section undertakes a fresh approach to what appear to be the central issues.

2. Paragraph 1(a) treats but-for cause as the causality relationship that normally should be regarded as sufficient, in the view that this is the simple, pervasive meaning of causation that is relevant for purposes of penal law. When concepts of "proximate causation" disassociate the actor's conduct and a result of which it was a but-for cause, the reason always inheres in the judgment that the actor's culpability with reference to the result, *i.e.*, his purpose, knowledge, recklessness or negligence, was such that it would be unjust to permit the result to influence his liability or the gravity of the offense of which he is convicted. Since this is so, the draft proceeds upon the view that problems of this kind ought to be faced as problems of the culpability required for conviction and not as problems of "causation."

Paragraph 1(b) contemplates, however, that this general position may prove unacceptable in dealing with particular offenses. In that event, additional causal requirements may be imposed explicitly, such, for example, as a temporal limitation with respect to causing death.

3. Paragraphs (2) and (3) are drafted on the theory stated. They assume that liability requires purpose, knowledge, recklessness or negligence with respect to the result which is an element of the offense and deal explicitly with variations between the actual result and that designed, contemplated or threatened, as the case may be, stating when the variation is considered immaterial.

4. Paragraph (2) is addressed to the case where the culpability requirement with respect to the result is purpose or knowledge, *i.e.*, where purposely or knowingly causing a specified result is a material element of the offense. Here if the actual result is not within the purpose or the contemplation of the actor, the culpability requirement is not established, except in the circumstances set forth in sub-paragraphs (a) and (b).

Sub-paragraph (a) deals with the situation where the actual result differed from the result designed or contemplated only in the respect that a different person or different property was injured or affected or that the injury or harm designed or contemplated was more serious or more extensive than that caused. Such variations between purpose or contemplation and result are made immaterial, as almost certainly would be the view under existing law.

Sub-paragraph (b) deals with the situation where the actual result involved the same kind of injury or harm as that designed or contemplated but the precise injury inflicted was different or occurred in a different way. Here the draft makes no attempt to catalogue the possibilities, *e.g.* to deal with the intervening or concurrent causes, natural or human; unexpected physical conditions; distinctions between the infliction of mortal or non-mortal wounds. It deals only with the ultimate criterion by which the significance of such possibilities ought to be judged, presenting two alternative formulations. The first proposes that the question to be faced is whether the actual result is "too accidental in its occurrence to have a just bearing on the actor's liability or on the gravity of his offense." The alternative proposes that the issue turn on whether the actual result "occurs in a manner which the actor knows or ought to know is rendered substantially more probable by his conduct."

It may be useful in appraising either treatment of the problem to note that what will usually turn on the determination will not be the criminality of a defendant's conduct but rather the gravity of his offense. Since the actor, by hypothesis, has sought to cause a criminal result or has been reckless or negligent with respect to such a result, he will be guilty of some crime under a well-considered penal code even if he is not held for the actual result, *i.e.*, he will be guilty of attempt, assault or some offense involving risk creation, such as reckless driving. Thus the issue in penal law is very different than in torts. Only in form is it, in penal law, a question of the actor's liability. In substance, it is a question of the severity of sentence which the Court is authorized or obliged to impose. Its practical importance thus depends on the disparity in sentence for the various offenses that may be involved, *e.g.* the sentences for an attempted and completed crime.

How far a Model Code ought to attribute importance in the grading of offenses to the actual result of conduct, as distinguished from results attempted or threatened, presents an issue of some difficulty which is of general importance in the Code. It may be said, however, that distinctions of this order are to some extent essential, at least when the severest sanctions are involved. For juries will not lightly find convictions that will lead to the severest types of sentences unless the resentments caused by the infliction of important injuries have been aroused. Whatever abstract logic may suggest, a prudent legislator cannot disregard these facts of life in the enactment of a penal code.

It may be added that attributing importance to the actual result does not substantially detract from the deterrent efficacy of the law, at least in dealing with cases of purposeful misconduct. One who attempts to kill and thus expects to bring about the result punishable by the gravest penalty, is unlikely to be influenced in his behavior by the treatment that the law provides for those who fail in such attempts; his expectation is that he is going to succeed. *See* [Jerome] Michael and [Herbert] Wechsler, *A Rationale of the Law of Homicide,* 37 COLUMBIA L. REV. 1261, 1294-1298.

Viewed in these terms, it may be said that ... the proposed ... formulation should suffice for the exclusion of those situations where the actual result is so remote from the actor's purpose or contemplation that juries can be expected to believe that it should have no bearing on the actor's liability for the graver offense or, stated differently, on the gravity of the offense of which he is convicted. If, for example, the defendant attempted to shoot his wife and missed, with the result that she retired to her parents' country home and then was killed in falling off a horse, no one would think that the defendant should be held guilty of murder, though he did intend her death and his attempt to kill her was a but-for cause of her encounter with the horse. Both court and jury would regard the actual result as "too accidental in its occurrence to have a just bearing on the actor's liability or on the gravity of his offense." Alternatively, they would regard the actual result as one which did not occur in a manner that the actor knew or should have known was rendered substantially more probable by his conduct when he attempted to shoot his wife to death.

It is in closer cases that a difference in result might be expected. Thus, if the defendant in the case supposed had shot his wife and in the hospital she had contracted a disease which was medically unrelated to the wound (though related to her presence in the hospital), her death from the disease may well be thought to have been rendered substantially more probable by the defendant's conduct, as presumably he should have known. Yet juries might regard it as a too unusual result to justify convicting him of murder. The advantage of putting the issue squarely to the jury's sense of justice is that it does not attempt to force a result which the jury may resist. It also leaves the principle flexible for application to the infinite variety of cases likely to arise. The argument for the alternative is, on the other hand, that flexibility will involve inequality of application; that if the actual result was foreseen or foreseeable as a substantial probability, there can be no injustice in holding the actor responsible for its occurrence, nor is there any reason to expect that jury action will nullify such a rule....

5. Paragraph (3) deals with the case where recklessness or negligence is the required kind of culpability and where the actual result is not within the risk of which the actor was aware, or, in the case of negligence, of which he should have been aware. The principles proposed to govern are the same as in the case where purposely or knowingly causing the specified result is the material element of the crime. If the actual result differed from the probable result only in the respect that a different person or different property was injured or affected, the variation is declared to be inconsequential. In other situations, if the actual result involved the same kind of injury or harm as the probable result, the question asked is whether it was too accidental in its occurrence to have just bearing on the actor's liability or on the gravity of his offense or, if the alternative is preferred, whether the result occurred in a manner which the actor knew or should have known was rendered substantially more probable by his conduct. The governing considerations are the same as in the situation dealt with by paragraph (2).

NOTES

1. Chief Judge Newman, dissenting in *In re J.N., Jr.,* 406 A.2d 1275 (D.C. 1979), extracts from which appear *infra* pp. 248-249, summarized doctrines of causation in criminal law:

> In every criminal case the government must prove each element of the offense charged beyond a reasonable doubt.... As part of this burden, in a homicide case the government must show that the defendant's conduct is both the actual cause and the legal cause — or probable cause — of the result. Actual cause means that the defendant's conduct in fact was the cause of death. Legal or proximate cause means that, although intervening occurrences may have contributed to the death, the defendant can still, in all fairness, be held criminally responsible for that death.... Thus the two, if proven beyond a reasonable doubt, establish that the defendant's act was the cause of death.
>
> In response to fact situations where two or more actors bring about one death, courts, of necessity, fashioned rules of law to determine which actor is culpable for homicide. These rules reflect an accommodation made by the courts to differing societal interests in punishing certain

wrongful acts. Thus, the assailant can be convicted of homicide even though, after inflicting a blow (fatal or nonfatal), (1) the victim fails to receive or accept medical treatment ...; (2) the victim fails to follow physician's instructions ...; (3) the victim, because of his injury, takes his own life ...; (4) a physician administers negligent treatment ...; (5) or a different or more skillful treatment might have saved the victim's life....

The underlying rationale of these decisions is that the intentional wrongdoer should bear the risk of the victim's death because the aforementioned intervening acts are considered foreseeable and natural consequences of his wrongful act.... Implicit in this determination of culpability is a finding that the initial wrongdoer "may fairly be held responsible for the actual result even though it does differ or happens in a different way from the intended or hazarded result." LaFave & Scott ... at 248.

A more complex issue bearing on allocation of risk and punishment is presented when two or more intentional actors, not in concert, bring about the death of one victim. For example, *A* seriously wounds *B*, and, while *B* is dying, *C* shoots and kills *B* instantaneously. Some courts hold that *A* cannot be liable for homicide because to so hold would necessitate finding that the victim was killed twice.... Other courts hold that both *A* and *C* can be culpable for homicide because of the combined effects of the wounds, ... or because the injury inflicted by the first wrongdoer would have also resulted in death without the intervening act.... Nevertheless, as a general rule voluntary infliction of harm by a second actor usually suffices to break the chain of legal cause and protects the original actor from, while exposing the second actor to, culpability for the homicide.... In sum, when both the original actor and the intervenor inflict harm intentionally, courts differ as to whether the first actor is culpable for homicide, but all agree that the second is culpable. The latter act is considered to have shortened the life of the victim, albeit one who is already dying, and therefore, that act becomes the legal cause of the victim's death....

Likewise, rules have been fashioned to allocate risk and punishment between an intentional wrongful act of one person followed by a grossly negligent act of another. As a general rule, gross negligence by an attending physician, which is the *sole* cause of death, will shield the first wrongful actor from homicide culpability on the theory that the wound inflicted cannot be the legal or proximate cause of death since death results from an unforeseen risk and is not a natural consequence of the wrongful act. Thus, as to the assailant, the causation element of the crime of homicide cannot be proved....

2. Causation principles can apply to many crimes. However, the bulk of causation jurisprudence has been generated in the setting of homicide and assault cases. See Chapter 5, section 1, *infra* pp. 241-252.

SECTION VI. Punishment

UNITED STATES v. HALPER
Supreme Court of the United States
490 U.S. 435 (1989)

JUSTICE BLACKMUN delivered the opinion of the Court.

In this case, we consider whether and under what circumstances a civil penalty may constitute "punishment" for the purposes of double jeopardy analysis.[1]

I

Respondent Irwin Halper worked as manager of New City Medical Laboratories, Inc., a company which provided medical service in New York City for patients eligible for benefits under the federal Medicare program. In that capacity, Halper submitted to Blue Cross and Blue Shield of Greater New York, a fiscal intermediary for Medicare, 65 separate false claims for reimbursement for service rendered. Specifically, on 65 occasions during 1982 and 1983, Halper mischaracterized the medical service performed by New City, demanding reimbursement at the rate of $12 per claim when the actual service rendered entitled New City to only $3 per claim. Duped by these misrepresentations, Blue Cross overpaid New City a total of $585; Blue Cross passed these overcharges along to the Federal Government.

The Government became aware of Halper's actions and in April 1985 it indicted him on 65 counts of violating the criminal false-claims statute, 18 U.S.C. § 287, which prohibits "make[ing] or present[ing] ... any claim upon or against the United States, or any department or agency thereof, knowing such claim to be false, fictitious, or fraudulent." Halper was convicted on all 65 counts, as well as on 16 counts of mail fraud. He was sentenced in July 1985 to imprisonment for two years and fined $5,000.

The Government then brought the present action in the United States District Court for the Southern District of New York against Halper and another, who later was dismissed from the case, ... under the civil False Claims Act (Act), 31 U.S.C. §§ 3729-3731. That Act was violated when "[a] person not a member of an armed force of the United States ... (2) knowingly makes, uses, or causes to be made or used, a false record or statement to get a false or fraudulent claim paid or approved." § 3729. Based on facts established by Halper's criminal conviction and incorporated in the civil suit, the District Court granted summary judgment for the Government on the issue of liability....

The court then turned its attention to the remedy for Halper's multiple violations. The remedial provision of the Act stated that a person in violation is "liable to the United States Government for a civil penalty of $2,000, an amount equal to 2 times the amount of damages the Government sustains

---

[1]The Double Jeopardy Clause reads:

"[N]or shall any person be subject for the same offence to be twice put in jeopardy of life or limb...." U.S. Const., Amdt. 5.

because of the act of that person, and costs of the civil action." Having violated the Act 65 separate times, Halper thus appeared to be subject to a statutory penalty of more than $130,000.

The District Court, however, concluded that in light of Halper's previous criminal punishment, an additional penalty this large would violate the Double Jeopardy Clause. Although the court recognized that the statutory provisions for a civil sanction of $2,000 plus double damages for a claims violation was not in itself criminal punishment, it concluded that this civil remedy, designed to make the Government whole, would constitute a second punishment for double jeopardy analysis if, in application, the amount of the penalty was "entirely unrelated" to the actual damages suffered and the expenses incurred by the Government.... In the District Court's view, the authorized recovery of more than $130,000 bore no "rational relation" to the sum of the Government's $585 actual loss plus its costs in investigating and prosecuting Halper's false claims.... The court therefore ruled that imposition of the full amount would violate the Double Jeopardy Clause by punishing Halper a second time for the same conduct. To avoid this constitutional proscription, the District Court read the $2,000-per-count statutory penalty as discretionary and, approximating the amount required to make the Government whole, imposed the full sanction for only 8 of the 65 counts. The court entered summary judgment for the Government in the amount of $16,000....

The United States, pursuant to Federal Rule of Civil Procedure 59(e), moved for reconsideration. The motion was granted. On reconsideration, the court confessed error in ruling that the $2,000 penalty was not mandatory for each count.... It remained firm, however, in its conclusion that the $130,000 penalty could not be imposed because, in the circumstances before it, that amount would violate the Double Jeopardy Clause's prohibition of multiple punishments. [T]he court concluded that, although a penalty that is more than the precise amount of actual damages is not necessarily punishment, a penalty becomes punishment when ... it exceeds what "'could reasonably be regarded as the equivalent of compensation for the Government's loss.'" ... Applying this principle, the District Court concluded that the statutorily authorized penalty of $130,000, an amount more than 220 times greater than the Government's measurable loss, qualified as punishment which, in view of Halper's previous criminal conviction and sentence, was barred by the Double Jeopardy Clause. Because it considered the Act unconstitutional as applied to Halper, the District Court amended its judgment to limit the Government's recovery to double damages of $1,170 and the costs of the civil action....

The United States, pursuant to 28 U.S.C. § 1252, took a direct appeal to this Court....

II

This Court many times has held that the Double Jeopardy Clause protects against three distinct abuses: a second prosecution for the same offense after acquittal; a second prosecution for the same offense after conviction; and multiple punishments for the same offense.... The third of these protections — the one at issue here — has deep roots in our history and jurisprudence.... The sole question here is whether the statutory penalty authorized by the civil False Claims Act, under which Halper is subject to liability of $130,000 for false claims amounting to $585, constitutes a second "punishment" for the purpose of double jeopardy analysis.

The Government argues that in three previous cases, *Helvering v. Mitchell,* 303 U.S. 391 (1938), *United States ex rel. Marcus v. Hess, supra,* and *Rex Trailer Co. v. United States,* 350 U.S. 148 (1956), this Court foreclosed any argument that a penalty assessed in a civil proceeding, and specifically in a civil False Claims Act proceeding, may give rise to double jeopardy. Specifically, the Government asserts that these cases establish three principles: first, that the Double Jeopardy Clause's prohibition against multiple punishment protects against only a second criminal penalty; second, that criminal penalties are imposed only in criminal proceedings; and, third, that proceedings under, and penalties authorized by, the civil False Claims Act are civil in nature. In addition, the Government argues on the basis of these three cases and others, ... that whether a proceeding or penalty is civil or criminal is a matter of statutory construction, and that Congress clearly intended the proceedings and penalty at issue here to be civil in nature.

The Government, in our view, has misconstrued somewhat the nature of the multiple-punishment inquiry, and, in so doing, has overread the holdings of our precedents. Although, taken together, these cases establish that proceedings and penalties under the civil False Claims Act are indeed civil in nature, and that a civil remedy does not rise to the level of "punishment" merely because Congress provided for civil recovery in excess of the Government's actual damages, they do not foreclose the possibility that in a particular case a civil penalty authorized by the Act may be so extreme and so divorced from the Government's damages and expenses as to constitute punishment.

In *Mitchell,* the Commissioner of Internal Revenue determined that the taxpayer fraudulently had asserted large sums as deductions on his 1929 income tax return. Mitchell was indicted and prosecuted for willful evasion of taxes. At trial, however, he was acquitted. The Government then brought an action to collect a deficiency of $728,709.84 in Mitchell's tax and, as well, a 50% additional amount specified by statute on account of the fraud. Mitchell argued that this second action subjected him to double jeopardy because the 50% addition was intended as punishment, and that the supposedly civil assessment proceeding therefore was actually a second criminal proceeding based on a single course of conduct.

This Court did not agree. The Double Jeopardy Clause, it noted, "prohibits merely punishing twice, or attempting a second time to punish criminally, for the same offense." ... Because Mitchell was acquitted (and therefore not punished) in his criminal prosecution, the Court was called upon to determine only whether the statute imposed a criminal sanction — in which case the deficiency proceeding would be an unconstitutional second attempt to punish criminally. Whether the statutory sanction was criminal in nature, the Court held, was a question of statutory interpretation; and, applying traditional canons of construction, the Court had little difficulty concluding that Congress intended that the statute impose a civil penalty and that the deficiency sanction was in fact remedial, providing reimbursement to the Government for investigatory and other costs of the taxpayer's fraud.... Since "in the civil enforcement of a remedial sanction there can be no double jeopardy," ... the Court rejected Mitchell's claim.

Mitchell at most is of tangential significance for our current inquiry. While the opinion makes clear that the Government may impose both a criminal and a civil sanction with respect to the same act or omission, and that whether a given sanction is criminal is a matter of statutory construction, it simply does not address the question we face today: whether a civil sanction, in application, may be so divorced from any remedial goal that it constitutes "punishment" for the purpose of double jeopardy analysis. If anything, Justice Brandeis' carefully crafted opinion for the Court intimates that a civil sanction may constitute punishment under some circumstances. As noted above, the Court distinguished between the Double Jeopardy Clause's prohibition against "attempting a second time to punish criminally" and its prohibition against "merely punishing twice." ... The omission of the qualifying adverb "criminally" from the formulation of the prohibition against double punishment suggests, albeit indirectly, that "punishment" indeed may arise from either criminal or civil proceedings....

The relevant teaching of these cases is that the Government is entitled to rough remedial justice, that is, it may demand compensation according to somewhat imprecise formulas, such as reasonable liquidated damages or a fixed sum plus double damages, without being deemed to have imposed a second punishment for the purpose of double jeopardy analysis. These cases do not tell us, because the problem was not presented in them, what the Constitution commands when one of those imprecise formulas authorizes a supposedly remedial sanction that does not remotely approximate the Government's damages and actual costs, and rough justice becomes clear injustice. That such a circumstance might arise appears to be anticipated not only in *Mitchell*, as noted above, but also in the explicitly case-specific holdings of *Hess* and *Rex Trailer*.

III

We turn, finally, to the unresolved question implicit in our cases: whether and under what circumstances a civil penalty may constitute punishment for the purpose of the Double Jeopardy Clause. As noted above, the Government takes the position that punishment in the relevant sense is meted out only in criminal proceedings, and that whether proceedings are criminal or civil is a matter of statutory construction.... But while recourse to statutory language, structure, and intent is appropriate in identifying the inherent nature of a proceeding, or in determining the constitutional safeguards that must accompany those proceedings as a general matter, the approach is not well suited to the context of the "humane interests" safeguarded by the Double Jeopardy Clause's proscription of multiple punishments.... This constitutional protection is intrinsically personal. Its violation can be identified only by assessing the character of the actual sanctions imposed on the individual by the machinery of the state....

In making this assessment, the labels "criminal" and "civil" are not of paramount importance. It is commonly understood that civil proceedings may advance punitive as well as remedial goals, and, conversely, that both punitive and remedial goals may be served by criminal penalties.[8] The notion of punishment, as we commonly understand it, cuts across the division between the civil and the criminal law, and for the purposes of assessing whether a given sanction constitutes multiple punishment barred by the Double Jeopardy Clause, we must follow the notion where it leads.... To that end, the determination whether a given civil sanction constitutes punishment in the relevant sense requires a particularized assessment of the penalty imposed and the purposes that the penalty may fairly be said to serve. Simply put, a civil as well as a criminal sanction constitutes punishment when the sanction as applied in the individual case serves the goals of punishment.

These goals are familiar. We have recognized in other contexts that punishment serves the twin aims of retribution and deterrence.... Furthermore, "[r]etribution and deterrence are not legitimate nonpunitive governmental objectives." ... From these premises, it follows that a civil sanction that cannot fairly be said solely to serve a remedial purpose, but rather can only be explained as also serving either retributive or deterrent purposes, is punishment, as we have come to understand the term.... We therefore hold that under the Double Jeopardy Clause a defendant who already has been punished in a criminal prosecution may not be subjected to an additional civil sanction to the extent that the second sanction may not fairly be characterized as remedial, but only as a deterrent or retribution.

We acknowledge that this inquiry will not be an exact pursuit. In our decided cases we have noted that the precise amount of the Government's damages and costs may prove to be difficult, if not impossible, to ascertain.... Similarly, it would be difficult if not impossible in many cases for a court to determine the precise dollar figure at which a civil sanction has accomplished its remedial purpose of making the Government whole, but beyond which the sanction takes on the quality of punishment. In other words, as we have observed above, the process of affixing a sanction that compensates the Government for all its costs inevitably involves an element of rough justice. Our upholding reasonable liquidated damages clauses reflects this unavoidable imprecision. Similarly, we have recognized that in the ordinary case fixed-penalty-plus-double-damages provisions can be said to do no more than make the Government whole.

We cast no shadow on these time-honored judgments. What we announce now is a rule for the rare case, the case such as the one before us, where a fixed-penalty provision subjects a prolific but small-gauge offender to a sanction overwhelmingly disproportionate to the damages he has caused. The rule is one of reason: Where a defendant previously has sustained a criminal penalty and the civil penalty sought in the subsequent proceeding bears no rational relation to the goal of compensating the Government for its loss, but

---

[8] As the name indicates, punitive damages, available in civil cases, serve punitive goals. *Day v. Woodworth*, 13 How. 363, 371 (1852). By the same token, strict liability crimes are principally directed at social betterment rather than punishment of culpable individuals. *See United States v. Balint*, 258 U.S. 250, 252 (1922).

rather appears to qualify as "punishment" in the plain meaning of the word, then the defendant is entitled to an accounting of the Government's damages and costs to determine if the penalty sought in fact constitutes a second punishment. We must leave to the trial court the discretion to determine on the basis of such an accounting the size of the civil sanction the Government may receive without crossing the line between remedy and punishment.... While the trial court's judgment in these matters often may amount to no more than an approximation, even an approximation will go far towards ensuring both that the Government is fully compensated for the costs of corruption and that, as required by the Double Jeopardy Clause, the defendant is protected from a sanction so disproportionate to the damages caused that it constitutes a second punishment.

We do not consider our ruling far reaching or disruptive of the Government's need to combat fraud. Nothing in today's ruling precludes the Government from seeking the full civil penalty against a defendant who previously has not been punished for the same conduct, even if the civil sanction imposed is punitive. In such a case, the Double Jeopardy Clause simply is not implicated. Nor does the decision prevent the Government from seeking and obtaining both the full civil penalty and the full range of statutorily authorized criminal penalties in the same proceeding. In a single proceeding the multiple-punishment issue would be limited to ensuring that the total punishment did not exceed that authorized by the legislature.... Finally, nothing in today's opinion precludes a private party from filing a civil suit seeking damages for conduct that previously was the subject of criminal prosecution and punishment. The protections of the Double Jeopardy Clause are not triggered by litigation between private parties. In other words, the only proscription established by our ruling is that the Government may not criminally prosecute a defendant, impose a criminal penalty upon him, and then bring a separate civil action based on the same conduct and receive a judgment that is not rationally related to the goal of making the Government whole.

IV

Returning to the case at hand, the District Court found a "tremendous disparity" between the Government's actual damages and the civil penalty authorized by the Act.... The court approximated the Government's expenses at no more than $16,000, as compared to the asserted liability of Halper in excess of $130,000.... Although the Government apparently did not challenge the District Court's figure — choosing instead to litigate the legal issue we now decide — we think it unfair to deprive the Government of an opportunity to present to the District Court an accounting of its actual costs arising from Halper's fraud, to seek an adjustment of the District Court's approximation, and to recover its demonstrated costs. While we agree with the District Court that the disparity between its approximation of the Government's costs and Halper's $130,000 liability is sufficiently disproportionate that the sanction constitutes a second punishment in violation of double jeopardy, we remand the case to permit the Government to demonstrate that the District Court's assessment of its injuries was erroneous.

The judgment of the District Court is vacated, and the case is remanded for further proceedings consistent with this opinion.

TITLE 18, UNITED STATES CODE, SECTION 3553(a)(2) (1988)

(a) FACTORS TO BE CONSIDERED IN IMPOSING A SENTENCE. — ... The [sentencing] court, in determining the particular sentence to be imposed, shall consider —

....

(2) the need for the sentence imposed —
(A) to reflect the seriousness of the offense, to promote respect for the law, and to provide just punishment for the offense;
(B) to afford adequate deterrence to criminal conduct;
(C) to protect the public from further crimes of the defendant; and
(D) to provide the defendant with needed educational or vocational training, medical care, or other correctional treatment in the most effective manner....

UNITED STATES v. BERGMAN
United States District Court
416 F. Supp. 496 (S.D.N.Y. 1976)

Sentencing Memorandum

FRANKEL, DISTRICT JUDGE.

Defendant is being sentenced upon his plea of guilty to two counts of an 11-count indictment. The sentencing proceeding is unusual in some respects. It has been the subject of more extensive submissions, written and oral, than this court has ever received upon such an occasion. The court has studied some hundreds of pages of memoranda and exhibits, plus scores of volunteered letters. A broad array of issues has been addressed. Imaginative suggestions of law and penology have been tendered. A preliminary conversation with counsel, on the record, preceded the usual sentencing hearing. Having heard counsel again and the defendant speaking for himself, the court postponed the pronouncement of sentence for further reconsideration of thoughts generated during the days of studying the briefs and oral pleas. It seems fitting now to report in writing the reasons upon which the court concludes that defendant must be sentenced to a term of four months in prison.[1]

I. *Defendant and His Crimes*

Defendant appeared until the last couple of years to be a man of unimpeachably high character, attainments, and distinction. A doctor of divinity and an ordained rabbi, he has been acclaimed by people around the world for his works of public philanthropy, private charity, and leadership in educational enterprises. Scores of letters have come to the court from across

---

[1] The court considered, and finally rejected, imposing a fine in addition to the prison term. Defendant seems destined to pay hundreds of thousands of dollars in restitution. The amount is being worked out in connection with a state criminal indictment. Apart from defendant's further liabilities for federal taxes, any additional money exaction is appropriately left for the state court.

this and other countries reporting debts of personal gratitude to him for numerous acts of extraordinary generosity. (The court has also received a kind of petition, with fifty-odd signatures, in which the signers, based upon learning acquired as newspaper readers, denounce the defendant and urge a severe sentence. Unlike the pleas for mercy, which appear to reflect unquestioned facts inviting compassion, this document should and will be disregarded.) In addition to his good works, defendant has managed to amass considerable wealth in the ownership and operation of nursing homes, in real estate ventures, and in a course of substantial investments.

Beginning about two years ago, investigations of nursing homes in this area, including questions of fraudulent claims for Medicaid funds, drew to a focus upon this defendant among several others. The results that concern us were the present indictment and two state indictments. After extensive pretrial proceedings, defendant embarked upon elaborate plea negotiations with both state and federal prosecutors. A state guilty plea and the instant plea were entered in March of this year. (Another state indictment is expected to be dismissed after defendant is sentenced on those to which he has pled guilty.) As part of the detailed plea arrangements, it is expected that the prison sentence imposed by this court will comprise the total covering the state as well as the federal convictions.

For purposes of the sentence now imposed, the precise details of the charges, and of defendant's carefully phrased admissions of guilt, are not matters of prime importance. Suffice it to say that the plea on Count One (carrying a maximum of five years in prison and a $10,000 fine) confesses defendant's knowing and wilful participation in a scheme to defraud the United States in various ways, including the presentation of wrongfully padded claims for payments under the Medicaid program to defendant's nursing homes. Count Three, for which the guilty plea carries a theoretical maximum of three more years in prison and another $5,000 fine, is a somewhat more "technical" charge. Here, defendant admits to having participated in the filing of a partnership return which was false and fraudulent in failing to list people who had bought partnership interests from him in one of his nursing homes, had paid for such interests, and had made certain capital withdrawals.

The conspiracy to defraud, as defendant has admitted it, is by no means the worst of its kind; it is by no means as flagrant or extensive as has been portrayed in the press; it is evidently less grave than other nursing-home wrongs for which others have been convicted or publicized. At the same time, the sentence, as defendant has acknowledged, is imposed for two federal felonies including, as the more important, a knowing and purposeful conspiracy to mislead and defraud the Federal Government.

II. *The Guiding Principles of Sentencing*

Proceeding through the short list of the supposed justifications for criminal sanctions, defense counsel urge that no licit purpose could be served by defendant's incarceration. Some of these arguments are plainly sound; others are not.

The court agrees that this defendant should not be sent to prison for "rehabilitation." Apart from the patent inappositeness of the concept to this individual, this court shares the growing understanding that no one should ever be sent to prison *for rehabilitation.* That is to say, nobody who would not otherwise be locked up should suffer that fate on the incongruous premise that it will be good for him or her. Imprisonment is punishment. Facing the simple reality should help us to be civilized. It is less agreeable to confine someone when we deem it an affliction rather than a benefaction. If someone must be imprisoned — for other, valid reasons — we should seek to make rehabilitative resources available to him or her. But the goal of rehabilitation cannot fairly serve in itself as grounds for the sentence to confinement.[3]

Equally clearly, this defendant should not be confined to incapacitate him. He is not dangerous. It is most improbable that he will commit similar, or any, offenses in the future. There is no need for "specific deterrence."

Contrary to counsel's submissions, however, two sentencing considerations demand a prison sentence in this case:

> *First*, the aim of *general deterrence*, the effort to discourage similar wrongdoing by others through a reminder that the law's warnings are real and that the grim consequence of imprisonment is likely to follow from crimes of deception for gain like those defendant has admitted. *Second*, the related, but not identical, concern that any lesser penalty would, in the words of the Model Penal Code, § 7.01(1)(c), "depreciate the seriousness of the defendant's crime."

Resisting the first of these propositions, defense counsel invoke Immanuel Kant's axiom that "one man ought never to be dealt with merely as a means subservient to the purposes of another."[4] In a more novel, but equally futile, effort, counsel urge that a sentence for general deterrence "would violate the Eighth Amendment proscription against cruel and unusual punishment." Treating the latter point first, because it is a short subject, it may be observed simply that if general deterrence as a sentencing purpose were now to be outlawed, as against a near unanimity of views among state and federal jurists, the bolt would have to come from a place higher than this.[5] As for Dr. Kant, it may well be that defense counsel mistake his meaning in the present context.[6] Whether or not that is so, and without pretending to authority on that score, we take the widely accepted stance that a criminal punished in the interest of general deterrence is not being employed "merely as a means...." Reading Kant to mean that every man must be deemed more than the instrument of others, and must "always be treated as an end in himself,"[7] the

---

[3] This important point, correcting misconceptions still widely prevalent, is developed more fully by Dean Norval Morris in The Future of Imprisonment (1974).

[4] Quoting from I. Kant, Philosophy of Law 1986 (Hastie Trans. 1887).

[5] To a large extent the defendant's eighth amendment argument is that imprisoning him because he has been "newsworthy" would be cruelly wrong. This thought is accepted by the court without approaching the Constitution. (See below.) The reference at this point is meant to acknowledge, if only to reject, a seemingly broader submission.

[6] See H.L.A. Hart, Punishment and Responsibility 243-44 (1968).

[7] Andenaes, The Morality of Deterrence, 37 U. Chi. L. Rev. 649 (1970). See also O. Holmes, Common Law 43-44, 46-47 (1881).

humane principle is not offended here. Each of us is served by the enforcement of the law — not least a person like the defendant in this case, whose wealth and privileges, so long enjoyed, are so much founded upon law. More broadly, we are driven regularly in our ultimate interests as members of the community to use ourselves and each other, in war and in peace, for social ends. One who has transgressed against the criminal laws is certainly among the more fitting candidates for a role of this nature. This is no arbitrary selection. Warned in advance of the prospect, the transgressor has chosen, in the law's premises, "between keeping the law required for society's protection or paying the penalty."[8]

But the whole business, defendant argues further, is guesswork; we are by no means certain that deterrence "works." The position is somewhat overstated; there is, in fact, some reasonably "scientific" evidence for the efficacy of criminal sanctions as deterrents, at least as against some kinds of crimes.[9] Moreover, the time is not yet here when all we can "know" must be quantifiable and digestible by computers. The shared wisdom of generations teaches meaningfully, if somewhat amorphously, that the utilitarians have a point; we do, indeed, lapse often into rationality and act to seek pleasure and avoid pain.[10] It would be better, to be sure, if we had more certainty and precision. Lacking these comforts, we continue to include among our working hypotheses a belief (with some concrete evidence in its support) that crimes like those in this case — deliberate, purposeful, continuing, non-impulsive, and committed for profit — are among those most likely to be generally deterrable by sanctions most shunned by those exposed to temptation.[11]

The idea of avoiding depreciation of the seriousness of the offense implicates two or three thoughts, not always perfectly clear or universally agreed upon, beyond the idea of deterrence. It should be proclaimed by the court's judgment that the offenses are grave, not minor or purely technical. Some attention must be paid to the demand for equal justice; it will not do to leave the penalty of imprisonment a dead letter as against "privileged" violators while it is employed regularly, and with vigor, against others. There probably is in these conceptions an element of retributiveness, as counsel urge. And retribution, so denominated, is in some disfavor as a reason for punishment. It remains a factor, however, as Holmes perceived,[12] and as is known to anyone who talks to judges, lawyers, defendants, or people generally. It may become more palatable, and probably more humanely understood, under the rubric of "deserts" or "just deserts."[13] However the concept is formulated, we have not yet reached a state, supposing we ever should, in which the infliction of punishments for crime may be divorced generally from ideas of blameworthiness, recompense, and proportionality.

---

[8] H. L. A. Hart, *supra* note 6, at 23.

[9] See, e.g., F. Zimring and G. Hawkins, Deterrence 168-71, 282 (1973).

[10] See Andenaes, *supra* note 7, at 663-64.

[11] For some supporting evidence that "white-collar" offenses are somewhat specially deterrable, see Chambliss, Types of Deviance and the Effectiveness of Legal Sanctions, 1967 Wis. L. Rev. 703, 708-10.

[12] See O. Holmes, Common Law 41-42, 45 (1881).

[13] See A. von Hirsch, Doing Justice 45-55 (1976); see also N. Morris, The Future of Imprisonment 73-77 (1974).

III. *An Alternative, "Behavioral Sanction"*

Resisting prison above all else, defense counsel included in their thorough memorandum on sentencing two proposals for what they call a "constructive," and therefore a "preferable" form of "behavioral sanction." One is a plan for Dr. Bergman to create and run a program of Jewish vocational and religious high school training. The other is for him to take charge of a "Committee on Holocaust Studies," again concerned with education at the secondary school level.

A third suggestion was made orally at yesterday's sentencing hearing. It was proposed that Dr. Bergman might be ordered to work as a volunteer in some established agency as a visitor and aide to the sick and the otherwise incapacitated. The proposal was that he could read, provide various forms of physical assistance, and otherwise give comfort to afflicted people.

No one can doubt either the worthiness of these proposals or Dr. Bergman's ability to make successes of them. But both of the carefully formulated "sanctions" in the memorandum involve work of an honorific nature, not unlike that done in other projects to which the defendant has devoted himself in the past. It is difficult to conceive of them as "punishments" at all. The more recent proposal is somewhat more suitable in character, but it is still an insufficient penalty. The seriousness of the crimes to which Dr. Bergman has pled guilty demands something more than "requiring" him to lend his talents and efforts to further philanthropic enterprises. It remains open to him, of course, to pursue the interesting suggestions later on as a matter of unforced personal choice.

IV. *"Measuring" the Sentence*

In cases like this one, the decision of greatest moment is whether to imprison or not. As reflected in the eloquent submissions for defendant, the prospect of the closing prison doors is the most appalling concern; the feeling is that the length of the sojourn is a lesser question once that threshold is passed. Nevertheless, the setting of a term remains to be accomplished. And in some respects it is a subject even more perplexing, unregulated, and unprincipled.

Days and months and years are countable with a sound of exactitude. But there can be no exactitude in the deliberations from which a number emerges. Without pretending to a nonexistent precision, the court notes at least the major factors.

The criminal behavior, as has been noted, is blatant in character and unmitigated by any suggestion of necessitous circumstance or other pressures difficult to resist. However metaphysicians may conjure with issues about free will, it is a fundamental premise of our efforts to do criminal justice that competent people, possessed of their faculties, make choices and are accountable for them. In this sometimes harsh light, the case of the present defendant is among the clearest and least relieved. Viewed against the maxima Congress ordained, and against the run of sentences in other federal criminal cases, it calls for more than a token sentence.[14]

On the other side are factors that take longer to enumerate. Defendant's illustrious public life and works are in his favor, though diminished, of course, by what this case discloses. This is a first, probably a last, conviction. Defendant is 64 years old and in imperfect health, though by no means so ill, from what the court is told, that he could be expected to suffer inordinately more than many others of advanced years who go to prison.

Defendant invokes an understandable, but somewhat unworkable, notion of "disparity." He says others involved in recent nursing home fraud cases have received relatively light sentences for behavior more culpable than his. He lays special emphasis upon one defendant whose frauds appear indeed to have involved larger amounts and who was sentenced to a maximum of six months' incarceration, to be confined for that time only on week nights, not on week days or weekends. This court has examined the minutes of that sentencing proceeding and finds the case distinguishable in material respects. But even if there were a threat of such disparity as defendant warns against, it could not be a major weight on the scales.

Our sentencing system, deeply flawed, is characterized by disparity. We are to seek to "individualize" sentences, but no clear or clearly agreed standards govern the individualization. The lack of meaningful criteria does indeed leave sentencing judges far too much at large. But the result, with its nagging burdens on conscience, cannot be meaningfully alleviated by allowing any handful of sentences in a short series to fetter later judgments. The point is easy, of course, where Sentence No. 1 or Sentences 1-5 are notably harsh. It cannot be that a later judge, disposed to more leniency, should feel in any degree "bound." The converse is not identical, but it is not totally different. The net of this is that this court has considered and has given some weight to the trend of the other cited sentences (though strict logic might call for none), but without treating them as forceful "precedents" in any familiar sense.

How, then, the particular sentence adjudged in this case? As has been mentioned, the case calls for a sentence that is more than nominal. Given the other circumstances, however — including that this is a first offense, by a man no longer young and not perfectly well, where danger of recidivism is not a concern — it verges on cruelty to think of confinement for a term of years. We sit, to be sure, in a nation where prison sentences of extravagant length are more common than they are almost anywhere else. By that light, the term imposed today is not notably long. For this sentencing court, however, for a nonviolent first offense involving no direct assaults or invasions of others' security (as in bank robbery, narcotics, etc.), it is a stern sentence. For people like Dr. Bergman, who might be disposed to engage in similar wrongdoing, it should be sufficiently frightening to serve the major end of general deterrence. For all but the profoundly vengeful, it should not depreciate the seriousness of his offenses.

---

[14] Despite Biblical teachings concerning what is expected from those to whom much is given, the court has not, as his counsel feared might happen, held Dr. Bergman to a higher standard of responsibility because of his position in the community. But he has not been judged under a lower standard either.

V. *Punishment in or for the Media*

Much of defendant's sentencing memorandum is devoted to the extensive barrage of hostile publicity to which he has been subjected during the years before and since his indictment. He argues, and it appears to be undisputed, that the media (and people desiring to be featured in the media) have vilified him for many kinds of evildoing of which he has in fact been innocent. Two main points are made on this score with respect to the problem of sentencing.

First, as has been mentioned, counsel express the concern that the court may be pressured toward severity by the force of the seeming public outcry. That the court should not allow itself to be affected in this way is clear beyond discussion. Nevertheless, it is not merely permissible, but entirely wholesome and responsible, for counsel to bring the expressed concern out in the open. Whatever our ideals and mixed images about judges, it would be naive to doubt that judges have sometimes been swept by a sense of popular demand toward draconian sentencing decisions. It cannot hurt for the sentencing judge to be reminded of this and cautioned about it. There can be no guarantees. The sentencer must confront and regulate himself. But it bears reaffirmance that the court must seek to discount utterly the fact of notoriety in passing its judgment upon the defendant. Defense counsel cite reported opinions of this court reflecting what happens in a large number of unreported cases, by the present sentencer and many others, in which "unknown" defendants have received prison sentences, longer or shorter than today's, for white-collar or comparably nonviolent crimes. The overall run of cases, with all their individual variations, will reflect, it is hoped, earnest efforts to hew to the principle of equal treatment, with or without publicity.

Defendant's second point about his public humiliation is the frequently heard contention that he should not be incarcerated because he "has been punished enough." The thought is not without some initial appeal. If punishment were wholly or mainly retributive, it might be a weighty factor. In the end, however, it must be a matter of little or no force. Defendant's notoriety should not in the last analysis serve to lighten, any more than it may be permitted to aggravate, his sentence. The fact that he has been pilloried by journalists is essentially a consequence of the prestige and privileges he enjoyed before he was exposed as a wrongdoer. The long fall from grace was possible only because of the height he had reached. The suffering from loss of public esteem reflects a body of opinion that the esteem had been, in at least some measure, wrongly bestowed and enjoyed. It is not possible to justify the notion that this mode of nonjudicial punishment should be an occasion for leniency not given to a defendant who never basked in such an admiring light at all. The quest for both the appearance and the substance of equal justice prompts the court to discount the thought that the public humiliation serves the function of imprisonment.

Writing, as judges rarely do, about a particular sentence concentrates the mind with possibly special force upon the experience of the sentencer as well as the person sentenced. Consigning someone to prison, this defendant or any other, "is a sad necessity." There are impulses of avoidance from time to time — toward a personally gratifying leniency or toward an opposite extreme. But there is, obviously, no place for private impulse in the judgment of the court. The course of justice must be sought with such objective rationality as we can muster, tempered with mercy, but obedient to the law, which, we do well to remember, is all that empowers a judge to make other people suffer.

Supplemental Sentencing Memorandum on Adjournment of Surrender

The defendant moves to adjourn his surrender on the ground that interrelated plea bargains by state and federal prosecutors contemplate coordinated sentencing decisions in this and the state court....

This is a case in which two prosecutors, state and federal, brought indictments charging monstrous frauds and larcenies, but then chose to deal away most of the charges in two narrowly drawn plea bargains. It is highly probable that if either prosecutor had proved even a substantial part of his charges in open court, Dr. Bergman would have faced a heavy sentence indeed. Instead of taking these charges to trial, however, the prosecutors entered into interrelated plea bargains with the defendant's counsel. Both agreements were reduced to writing, signed by the parties, and made a part of the public record.

The federal and state plea bargains provided that the Special State Prosecutor was to drop his fraud and larceny indictment altogether and only require the defendant to plead to a much narrower one charging bribery of a state legislator. (That indictment was dismissed as against the legislator. The dismissal is being appealed.) Both plea agreements provided that Dr. Bergman was to plead guilty to only Counts One and Three of the 11-count federal indictment. Although these are serious crimes, they are moderate in comparison to the full panoply of the offenses originally charged. Under the federal agreement, the defendant was permitted to plead guilty by reading a prepared statement of narrowly drawn, tightly limited admissions of fact, which were to be all the defendant would confess (and all he could justly be sentenced for). This statement contained nothing, for example, about $1.2 million or $2.5 million or any other astronomical sums of allegedly fraudulent Medicaid claims. There was certainly nothing about whether the Bergman nursing homes had given good or bad nursing care.

This court's duty was, of course, to sentence defendant for what he had admitted, not upon accusations that were not only unproved, but that the prosecutors had agreed to drop as criminal charges. The general public could easily have misunderstood this. But the plea bargainers certainly had no reason to misunderstand. It appears, however, that there have been, putting the best face upon things, some possible misunderstandings.

....

Nobody should be made to begin serving a sentence in such circumstances. Courts serve the public, to be sure. That cannot mean bowing to passing waves of popular frenzy goaded by misunderstanding.

The motion to postpone surrender is granted.

NOTES

1. Judge Frankel has been an outspoken critic of sentencing practices in the United States. MARVIN FRANKEL, CRIMINAL SENTENCES (1972). *See also*

REPORT OF THE TWENTIETH CENTURY FUND TASK FORCE ON CRIMINAL SENTENCING, FAIR AND CERTAIN PUNISHMENT (1976); ANDREW VON HIRSCH, DOING JUSTICE: THE CHOICE OF PUNISHMENTS (1976); NORVAL MORRIS, THE FUTURE OF IMPRISONMENT (1974).

2. The subject of punishment is discussed more fully *infra* Chapter 11.

PART TWO
RULES — SPECIFIC CRIMES

INTRODUCTORY NOTE

Some contemporary casebooks have virtually abandoned substantial coverage of specific crimes. It may seem that, with the hundreds of state crimes and perhaps an equal number of federal crimes, detailed coverage of specific crimes might have limited value. Nevertheless, the basic crimes covered in this part of the book represent a very large part of the actual business of the criminal courts. Moreover, a study of specific crimes not only serves as good preparation for the trial of criminal cases but also as an introduction to the technical side of drafting and interpreting statutes. Understanding the interaction of statutes and decisions in defining specific crimes provides an appreciation for the trend toward codification of criminal law.

The study of specific crimes develops judgment about the differences between crimes based on the harms, e.g., battery versus rape, and differences based on the grading of harms, e.g., aggravated versus simple assault. The grading of harms serves to adjust the range of permissible punishments according to the culpability of the offender, as in criminal homicide or the degree of harm, as in assault and battery. The study of specific crimes, especially property offenses, also conveys insight into the historical development of the criminal law. Study of this area develops a better understanding of the differences between criminal law and other areas of law such as torts.

Each crime should be studied not only in terms of its defining elements, but also in relation to the general principles discussed in Part I. Thus specific crimes should be analyzed both for the particular rules and also in terms of the principles of *mens rea*, act, harm, and so on. The study of specific crimes reinforces an understanding of those principles. The principles become less abstract when examined in the context of specific crimes. For example, some of the materials on homicide should clarify your understanding of criminal negligence and recklessness. In this "laboratory" where the material elements of specific crimes are viewed against previously studied principles, the principles can be tested and, where necessary, modified or even rejected. This kind of study can lead to an organized knowledge of the criminal law.

Chapter 3
ASSAULT, BATTERY AND RELATED CRIMES*

EDITORIAL NOTE

The common law offenses of assault and battery are distinguishable in terms of the harm. Battery requires touching or injury; assault does not. Nevertheless, "the word 'assault' is sometimes used loosely to include a battery, and the whole expression 'assault and battery' to mean battery." LaFave & Scott, Criminal Law 684 (2d ed. 1986). The Model Penal Code includes assault and what would be a battery under its definition of assault, § 211.1.

The modern criminal law of assault, battery and related crimes involves a proliferation of offenses. The assault crimes show how the "acts" proscribed and the "harms" protected have gradually expanded. A relatively narrow and straightforward prohibition of violence or attempted violence against the person has been augmented by prohibitions which include threats of violence, violence-provoking behavior, acts which create a fear of possible violence, and harassment of various sorts. The criminal law includes not only assaults directed at the body but also those against peace of mind.

This proliferation results in the grading of offenses to allow greater punishment for aggravated offenses. In terms of both culpability and harm, shooting a person is more serious than punching a person although each act involves an assault or battery. A crime of assault or battery may cause such serious harm as to be properly regarded as an aggravated form of the basic crime (even though the conduct may also constitute another crime, e.g., attempted murder). In most states these differences are reflected in a range of basic and aggravated assault and battery crimes.

SECTION I. The Act and the Harm: Common Law and Current Views of Assault and Battery

EAST'S PLEAS OF THE CROWN 406 (1803)

An assault is any attempt or offer with force and violence to do a corporal hurt to another, whether from malice or wantonness; as by striking at him, or even by holding up one's fist at him in a threatening or insulting manner, or with such other circumstances as denote at the time an intention, coupled with a present ability of using actual violence against his person; as by pointing a weapon at him within the reach of it. Where the injury is actually inflicted, it amounts to a battery (which includes an assault) and this, how-

---

*The crimes included in this chapter are discussed comprehensively in the A.L.I. Model Penal Code and Commentaries, part II, vol. 1, art. 211, pp. 172-207, art. 250, pp. 309-446 (Official Draft and Revised Comments 1980).

ever small it may be; as by spitting in a man's face, or any way touching him in anger without any lawful occasion. But if the occasion were merely accidental and undesigned, or if it were lawful, and the party used no more force than was reasonably necessary to accomplish the purpose, as to defend himself against a prior assault, or to arrest the other, or make him desist from some wrongful act or endeavour, or the like; it is no assault or battery in the law, and the party may justify the force.

PEOPLE v. YSLAS

Supreme Court of California
27 Cal. 630 (1865)

The testimony for the prosecution showed that the defendant entered the house of the prosecutrix and called for liquor, and was refused. He insisted, and it was given to him, when he called on the prosecutrix to drink, and upon her declining to do so, throwed [sic] the tumbler on the floor, threatened to kill her, and seized a hatchet and started towards her, having it raised in a threatening attitude. The prosecutrix, when the defendant had approached within seven or eight feet of her, fled through the door into an adjoining room, and locked the door after her. The defendant then went up to the door and struck it with his hatchet....

SANDERSON, C.J.

... In order to constitute an assault there must be something more than a mere menace. There must be violence begun to be executed. But where there is a clear intent to commit violence accompanied by acts which if not interrupted will be followed by personal injury, the violence is commenced and the assault is complete. Thus riding after the prosecutor so as to compel him to run into a garden for shelter, to avoid being beaten, was held to be an assault. *Mortin v. Shoppee*, 3 Car. & P. 374.) So where the defendant was advancing in a threatening attitude, with intent to strike the plaintiff, so that his blow would in a second or two have reached the plaintiff, if he had not been stopped, although when stopped he was not near enough to strike, it was held that an assault had been committed. (*Stephen v. Myers*, 4 Car. & P. 349.) It is not indispensable to the commission of an assault that the assailant should be at any time within striking distance. If he is advancing with intent to strike his adversary and come sufficiently near to induce a man of ordinary firmness to believe, in view of all of the circumstances, that he will instantly receive a blow unless he strike in self-defense or retreat, the assault is complete. In such a case the attempt has been made coupled with a present ability to commit a violent injury within the meaning of the statute....

Judgment affirmed.

NOTES

1. "When the defendant was in the yard, angry words passed between the parties, and the prosecutor ordered him to go out of his yard, and thereupon defendant went out into a lane leading from prosecutor's house to the public road; and in the lane, when about ten or twelve feet from the prosecutor, the

defendant picked up a stone and called the prosecutor a horse thief and other insulting names.... Here, as the defendant did not offer to throw the stone, there certainly was no assault." *State v. Milsaps,* 82 N.C. 549, 550-51 (1880).

2. "The prosecutor was where he had a right to be, and was in no wrong; the defendant drew his pistol from its scabbard, advanced towards the prosecutor who was retiring, threatened to shoot him if he did not leave, was in ten steps of him, and drove him from the place. This was certainly an 'offer' of violence and constituted an assault.

The fact that the pistol was not cocked and pointed makes no difference. That would have been but the work of a moment and was not needed to put the prosecutor in fear, and to interfere with his personal liberty." *State v. Church,* 63 N.C. 15, 16 (1868).

CHAPMAN v. STATE
Supreme Court of Alabama
78 Ala. 463, 56 Am. Rep. 42 (1885)

SOMERVILLE, J.

The defendant was indicted for an assault and battery upon the person of one McLeod, and was convicted of a mere assault.

....

The present conviction ... can be sustained only on the theory, that it was an assault for the defendant to present or aim an unloaded gun at the person charged to be assaulted, in such a menacing manner as to terrify him, and within such distance as to have been dangerous had the weapon been loaded and discharged. On this question, the adjudged cases, both in this country, and in England, are not agreed, and a like difference of opinion prevails among the most learned commentators on the law. We have had occasion to examine these authorities with some care, on more occasions than the present; and we are of the opinion that the better view is, that presenting an unloaded gun at one who supposes it to be loaded, although within the distance the gun would carry if loaded is not, without more, such an assault as can be punished criminally, although it may sustain a civil suit for damages. The conflict of authorities on the subject is greatly attributable to a failure to observe the distinction between these two classes of cases. A civil action would rest upon the invasion of a person's "right to live in society without being put in fear of personal harm;" and can often be sustained by proof of a negligent act resulting in unintentional injury. — *Peterson v. Haffner* [59 Ind. 130], 26 Am. Rep. 81; Cooley on Torts, 161. An indictment for the same act could be sustained only upon satisfactory proof of criminal intention to do personal harm to another by violence. — *State v. Davis,* 23 N.C. 125; s.c., 35 Am. Dec. 735. The approved definition of an assault involves the idea of an inchoate violence to the person of another, with the present means of carrying the intent into effect. — 2 Greenl. Ev. § 82; Roscoe's Cr. Ev. (7th Ed.) 296; *People v. Lilley,* 43 Mich. 521 [5 N.W. 982]. Most of our decisions recognize the old view of the textbooks, that there can be no criminal assault without a present intention, as well as present ability, of using some violence against the person of another.... In *Lawson v. State,* 30 Ala. 14, it was said that, "to constitute an assault, there must be the commencement of an act, which, if not prevented, would produce a battery." ...

It is true that some of the modern textwriters define an assault as an apparent attempt by violence to do corporal hurt to another, thus ignoring entirely all question of any criminal intent on the part of the perpetrator. 1 Whart. Cr. Ev. § 603; 2 Bish. Cr. Law, § 32. The true test can not be the mere tendency of an act to produce a breach of the peace; for opprobrious language has this tendency, and no words, however violent or abusive, can, at common law, constitute an assault. It is unquestionably true, that an apparent attempt to do corporal injury to another may often justify the latter in promptly resorting to measures of self-defense. But this is not because such apparent attempt is itself a breach of the peace, for it may be an act entirely innocent. It is rather because the person who supposes himself to be assaulted, has a right to act upon appearances, where they create reasonable grounds from which to apprehend imminent peril. There can be no difference, in reason, between presenting an unloaded gun at an antagonist in an affray, and presenting a walking-cane, as if to shoot, provided he honestly believes, and from the circumstances has reasonable ground to believe, that the cane was a loaded gun. Each act is a mere menace, the one equally with the other; and mere menaces, whether by words or acts, without intent or ability to injure, are not punishable crimes, although they may often constitute sufficient ground for a civil action for damages. The test, moreover, in criminal cases, can not be the mere fact of unlawfully putting one in fear, or creating alarm in the mind; for one may obviously be assaulted, although in complete ignorance of the fact, and, therefore, entirely free from alarm. — *People v. Lilley*, 43 Mich. 525 [5 N.W. 982]; s.c., 1 Crim. Law Mag. 605.

... [R]eversed and the cause remanded.

NOTE

Some courts have limited the scope of "present ability" by equating it not with whether "the defendant had the actual means to execute the battery, but whether defendant's acts had proceeded far enough toward that end to constitute an assault." "[W]here the intent is formed and some act done in performance thereof, but the party voluntarily abandons his purpose, or is prevented from proceeding farther, *and this while at a distance too great to make an actual assault*, he could not be convicted of an assault." *People v. Smith*, 89 Mich. App. 478, 280 N.W.2d 862, 865 (1979), *cert. denied*, 452 U.S. 714 (1981). (Emphasis added.)

ROBINSON v. UNITED STATES
Court of Appeals of the District of Columbia
506 A.2d 572 (1986)

TERRY, ASSOCIATE JUDGE.

Appellant was convicted of simple assault and carrying a pistol without a license. On appeal he challenges only the assault conviction, contending that the evidence was insufficient to go to the jury. We disagree and affirm.

I

Shortly after 11:00 o'clock one evening, Sergeant Ronald Monroe of the Metropolitan Police was driving to work in his private automobile ... [when] he saw a large number of people running from the 900 block of Farragut Street onto Georgia Avenue. Monroe "cautiously" turned his car into Farragut Street, then stopped in the middle of the street and turned on his high-beam headlights.

Appellant was standing about thirty to forty yards away, holding a pistol. Monroe got out of his car with his service revolver in his left hand, leaving his bright lights on in the hope that appellant would not be able to see him. As he stepped from the car, he unzipped his jacket, identified himself as a police officer, and told appellant, who was now only "two car lengths" from him, to drop the gun. After Monroe shouted, "Police officer; put the gun down," appellant turned toward him and pointed the gun at him.

Monroe again identified himself as a police officer, but received no response from appellant, who by then was crouched behind the rear of a car. Once more Monroe told appellant to put the gun down, and for a few seconds Monroe and appellant moved back and forth behind the parked cars, closely watching each other's movements. Finally, appellant laid his gun on the ground, stood up, and started to walk away rapidly. Monroe again yelled, "Police, stop," [and proceeded to arrest the appellant] ....

II

....

Although assault is a misdemeanor in the District of Columbia, Congress chose not to define it when it enacted the statute that is now D.C. Code § 22-504 (1981). The courts, therefore, have traditionally defined assault as consisting of the following three elements:

> 1. That the defendant made an attempt or effort, with force or violence, to do injury to the person of another;
> 2. That at the time he made such an attempt or effort, he had the apparent present ability to effect such an injury; and
> 3. That, at the time of the commission of the assault, he intended to do the acts which constituted the assault.

Criminal Jury Instructions for the District of Columbia, No. 4.11 (3d ed. 1978), quoted with approval in *Sousa v. United States*, 400 A.2d 1036, 1044 (D.C.), *cert. denied*, 444 U.S. 981 (1979). The standard instruction, which the trial court gave in this case, is all right as far as it goes, but it does not cover all situations.

There are two distinct kinds of criminal assault. The more common is the "attempted-battery" type, described in the standard instruction and in *Sousa*. The other is the "intent-to-frighten" or "tort" type, which consists of some threatening conduct intended either to injure or to frighten the victim. *See* W. LaFave & A. Scott, Handbook on Criminal Law § 82, at 610-612 (1972). Both varieties are recognized in the District of Columbia. The major difference between them is in the nature of the intent that must be proven. Attempted-battery assault requires proof of an attempt to cause a physical injury, which "may consist of any act tending to such corporal injury, accompanied with such circumstances as denote at the time an intention, coupled with the present ability, of using actual violence against the person." *Patterson v. Pillans*, 43 App. D.C. 505, 506-507 (1915). Intent-to-frighten assault, on the other hand, requires proof that the defendant intended either to cause injury or to create apprehension in the victim by engaging in some threatening conduct; an actual battery need not be attempted. *See* W. LaFave & A. Scott, *supra*.

If the trial court in the case at bar had given only the standard instruction, we would have to reverse the conviction because there was no evidence that appellant ever attempted to cause actual physical injury to Sergeant Monroe. To establish an attempted-battery type of assault on the facts of this case, the government would have had to prove that appellant either fired the gun or attempted to fire it. Fortunately, however, the court also instructed the jury:

> To point a dangerous weapon, such as a pistol, at another person in a menacing or threatening manner, or to use a weapon, such as a pistol, in any manner that would reasonably justify the other person in believing that the weapon might be immediately used against him, constitutes an assault under our law.

This was a correct statement of the law.

In *Anthony v. United States*, 361 A.2d 202 (D.C. 1976), this court recognized for the first time that the crime of assault included not only attempted battery but also "such conduct as could induce in the victim a well-founded apprehension of peril." *Id.* at 204 (citations and footnote omitted). We reiterated that holding a few years later in *Williamson v. United States*, 445 A.2d 975 (D.C. 1982). Taking note of "this expanded concept of common law criminal assault," we enlarged the standard three-part definition to include the intent-to-frighten type of assault as well as the attempted-battery type:

> First, there must be an act on the part of the defendant; mere words do not constitute an assault.... The act does not have to result in injury[.] ... [I]t can be either an actual attempt, with force or violence, to injure another, or a menacing threat, which may or may not be accompanied by a specific intent to injure, on the part of the defendant.... [Second], at the time the defendant commits the act, the defendant must have the apparent present ability to injure the victim.... [Third], at the time the act is committed, the defendant must have the intent to perform the acts which constitute the assault.

Id. at 978 (citations and footnotes omitted).

In the case at bar, there was sufficient evidence before the jury to prove each of these three elements beyond a reasonable doubt. First, appellant's act of pointing a gun at Sergeant Monroe constituted "a menacing threat." It is irrelevant whether appellant had a specific intent to injure Monroe. An intent to frighten is sufficient, and that intent can be inferred from the pointing of a gun. Second, from the fact that appellant had a gun in his hand, it is reasonable to infer (it would be unreasonable not to infer) that appellant had the "apparent present ability to injure the victim." *Williamson, supra*, 445 A.2d at 978. *Anthony* makes clear that the victim, in this case Sergeant Monroe, need not "be shown factually to have experienced apprehension or fear in order to establish the offense." 361 A.2d at 206 (footnote omitted). Instead, "the crucial inquiry [is] whether the assailant acted in such a manner as would under the circumstances portend an immediate threat of danger to a person of reasonable sensibility." *Id.* Finally, the jury was free to infer that appellant had the intent to perform the act, in this case the pointing of the gun, that constituted the assault; appellant presented no evidence suggesting that his actions were inadvertent, accidental, or involuntary.

Thus we hold that the evidence was sufficient to permit the case to go to the jury, and that the jury, under proper instructions, validly found appellant guilty of assault....

Affirmed.

MODEL PENAL CODE

§ 210.0. Definitions
§ 211.1. Assault
§ 211.2. Recklessly Endangering Another Person
[The text of these sections appears in Appendix A.]

NOTES

1. The expansion of the term "present ability" by adding the word "apparent" represents a major change in the definition of assault. Does including the "tort" approach as part of definition shift the focus in criminal assault cases from the actor to the victim?

2. Compare the elements of assault under MODEL PENAL CODE § 211.1 with the definition given in *Robinson*.

3. "I think that fright is such bodily harm that to shoot in the general direction of a person, with intent to 'bluff or scare' him, is an assault." *Edwards v. State*, 4 Ga. App. 849, 62 S.E. 565 (1908).

4. In *People v. Pape*, 66 Cal. 366, 5 P. 621 (1885), the information charged assault with intent to murder. Defendant placed a tin box filled with gunpowder in the stove of the prosecuting witness where it exploded.

Held: "An assault is an unlawful attempt, coupled with a present ability, to commit a violent injury on the person of another.... But this does not mean that it must be apparent to the person against whom the assault is made, and it is no defense that the attack is made upon an unconscious person.... He had a present ability to do the act." Conviction of assault with a deadly weapon was affirmed.

5. Problem: *A* and *B* enjoyed terrorizing people. One night they hid in an alleyway wearing ski masks and "armed" with toy guns which looked real. As *C* passed the alley, *A* and *B* jumped out, pointed the toy guns at *C* and shouted "Freeze!" *C* was so drunk that he didn't have the faintest idea of what was going on. He was not in the slightest apprehensive or fearful. He merely ignored *A* and *B* and staggered on home. Have *A* and *B* committed assault under either the Model Penal Code or the definition of assault set out in *Robinson*?

If C had feared for his life and bolted into the street, where he was struck and seriously injured by a car driven by a careful driver, would A and B be guilty of "aggravated assault" under the Model Penal Code? See Elliott, *Frightening a Person into Injuring Himself,* [1974] CRIM. L. REV. 15.

6. In England the Criminal Law Revision Committee recommended that the crime of assault remain as defined at common law but that the battery offenses be redefined to include causing serious injury with intent, causing serious injury recklessly, and causing injury recklessly or with intent. Hogan, *The Fourteenth Report of the Criminal Law Revision Committee: Offences Against the Person, Non-Fatal Offences,* [1980] CRIM. L. REV. 542.

STATE v. ALLEN

Supreme Court of North Carolina
245 N.C. 185, 95 S.E.2d 526 (1956)

PARKER, JUSTICE.

The defendant presents for decision one question: did the trial court commit error in denying his motion for judgment of non-suit made at the close of the State's evidence.

The warrant charges an assault, not an assault and battery.

.... "North Carolina is rightly listed as one of the jurisdictions in which it is not essential to the definition of assault, or to the completion of that crime, that there should be a present ability to carry out the threat or menace if it is sufficient in manner and character to cause the person menaced to forgo some right of conduct he intended to exercise, or to leave a place where he had a right to be." [*State v. McIver*, 231 N.C. 313, 317, 56 S.E.2d 604, 606 (1949).]

....

The rules of law in respect to assaults are plain, but their application to the facts is sometimes fraught with difficulty. Each case must depend upon its own peculiar circumstances.

The defendant ... had been watching Nancy Powers for ten days. Considering the evidence in the light most favorable to the State, and giving to it the benefit of every reasonable inference to be drawn therefrom, as the law requires us to do, when a motion for judgment of nonsuit is made, the facts show the defendant repeatedly day after day stopping his car a few minutes within a few feet of Nancy Powers, while she was standing on a public street corner in the city of Greensboro waiting for her ride to go to work, a place where she had a right to be, gazing at her and moving the lower part of his body back and forth, implying a lustful desire directed particularly toward her. [The defendant said he was engaged in self-pollution, and was trying to get Nancy Powers to look at him, while he was so engaged.] It seems apparent from the defendant's conduct and acts, that he, possessed by his lustful obsession for Nancy Powers, deliberately planned to meet her at the same place on successive mornings. Because of fear of him she quit walking the usual way to the place for her ride, and went a different way.... Considering the defendant's acts there on the morning of 23 January 1956, in connection with similar acts of the defendant there on 19 January 1956 and 20 January 1956, in the light most favorable to the State, can it be said as a matter of law, thereby taking the case away from the jury, that the defendant's acts on 23 January 1956 were insufficient to constitute a show of violence creating in the mind of Nancy Powers a reasonable apprehension that the defendant was planning to get out of his car and inflict upon her immediate bodily harm to satisfy his lust, and thereby put her in fear, and forced her to run from a place where she had a right to be? In our opinion, the answer to the question is, No: it is a case for the jury.

A show of violence, causing "the reasonable apprehension of immediate bodily harm," *State v. Ingram*, 237 N.C. 197, 74 S.E.2d 532, 535, whereby another is put in fear, and thereby forced to leave a place where he has a right to be, is sufficient to make out a case of an assault. *State v. McIver, supra*....

The trial court correctly denied defendant's motion for judgment of nonsuit. In the trial below we find.

No error.

NOTES

1. What was the "threat" or "menace" in *State v. Allen, supra*? Despite the fact that defendant acted in an outrageous manner does his conduct fit comfortably within the modern definition of assault? Would his conduct fit better under a statute drafted with the specific view of prohibiting harassment or annoyance discussed in Section 4, *infra*?

2. In *re D.W.J., Jr.*, 293 A.2d 268 (D.C. 1972) the court held that oral threats without more will not support a conviction of assault.

In *Postell v. United States*, 282 A.2d 551, 553 (D.C. App. 1971), the court, in upholding the conviction of the defendant on a charge of "threats to do bodily harm," a crime unknown to the common law, construed the meaning of "threats" to include words of such a nature as to convey a menace or fear of bodily harm to the ordinary hearer. "It matters not whether or to what degree the threat engenders fear or intimidation in the intended victim or whether the party threatening had or had not the intention to carry out the threat later."

3. *Conditional Threats*: A conditional threat of injury accompanied with an act calculated to put the person assailed in fear and with present ability to inflict the threatened injury was held to constitute an assault in *State v. Mitchell* 139 Iowa 455, 116 N.W. 808 (1908).

SECTION II. The *Mens Rea*

STATE v. DAVIS

Supreme Judicial Court of Maine
528 A.2d 1267 (1987)

CLIFFORD, JUSTICE.

....

The evidence showed that the defendant, a Commissioner of Washington County, assaulted Harold Prescott, the Sheriff of Washington County, on September 17, 1985, at the office of the Washington County Treasurer in Machias. The Treasurer, Sally C. Smith, had died the previous day after an extended illness. Smith's daughter, Susan Mills, and three others entered the Treasurer's office on September 17th in order to remove her mother's personal effects, after first having obtained permission to enter the office from another Washington County Commissioner. Mills, who had assisted her mother in carrying out her duties during her illness, had also requested that Sheriff Prescott witness the inventory and removal of Smith's personal property from the office.

....

Upon Sheriff Prescott's arrival at the Treasurer's office, the defendant became agitated, especially upon seeing Mills and the others near the county safe, which was open. There was also testimony to the effect that there had been preexisting hostilities between Sheriff Prescott and the defendant. ... The defendant viewed the presence of Sheriff Prescott and the others in the Treasurer's office as unauthorized. The defendant refused to comply with Sheriff Prescott's requests to compose himself and to leave the office. Sheriff Prescott then took the defendant by the arm and began to escort him from the office. The defendant turned and struck Sheriff Prescott in the jaw with his fist.

The defendant was subsequently tried for assault. In particular, he was charged with "intentionally, knowingly or *recklessly* caus[ing] bodily injury or offensive physical contact to Harold Prescott" (emphasis added). At trial, the trial justice instructed the jury on self-defense but not on sections 101(3), 102, 104 or 105 of Title 17-A. The jury returned a verdict of guilty.

I.

The defendant contends that although the presiding justice adequately instructed the jury on the issue of self-defense under 17-A M.R.S.A. § 108(1) (1983), his failure to instruct the jury pursuant to 17-A M.R.S.A. § 101(3) (1983) constituted reversible error. The second sentence of section 101(3) provides:

> If a defense provided under this chapter is precluded solely because the requirement that the actor's belief be reasonable has not been met, he may be convicted only of a crime for which recklessness or criminal negligence suffices, depending on whether his holding the belief was reckless or criminally negligent.

If the defendant's honest but objectively unreasonable belief is found to be recklessly held, section 101(3) will have no impact on the assault charge, since recklessness is one of the alternative culpable mental states of that offense under section 207. If, on the other hand, the State fails to prove that the defendant's honestly held but objectively unreasonable belief is reckless, if the jury finds that it rises only to the level of criminal negligence, his conduct will have been justified under sections 108 and 101(3) and he will be acquitted, since criminal negligence is not an element of that offense.

II. THE *MENS REA*

We agree with the defendant's assertion that having been charged with assault, for which a reckless state of mind suffices, an instruction under section 101(3) is essential to his receiving a fair trial....

....

[W]here the issue of self-defense is generated in the evidence and the crime charged is one for which a reckless or criminally negligent state of mind is sufficient, a defendant is entitled to an instruction under section 101(3). Where the issue of self-defense is central to the defendant's case, as it was here, where the defendant admitted the assault and based his entire case at trial on justification, the failure to instruct on section 101(3) amounts to obvious error affecting substantial rights, since it is a defect of omission in the instructions "so misleading to the jury" that the defendant is denied a fair trial. 2 Cluchey & Seitzinger, *Maine Criminal Practice* § 52.4 at 52-10 (1986); *see also State v. Earley*, 454 A.2d 341, 343-44 (Me. 1983).

....

Judgment of conviction vacated.

Remanded to the Superior Court for further proceedings consistent with the opinion herein.

All concurring.

NOTES

1. Review *Robinson v. United States, supra* pp. 164-168. How does intent for attempted-battery assault differ from that for intent-to-frighten assault? Would the definition in *Robinson* allow for an assault based on recklessness?

2. In some states intoxication can be offered to negate the existence of specific intent, but not general intent. Much assaultive behavior is associated with excessive consumption of alcohol, and neither courts nor legislatures have been disposed to allow people who strike or threaten to strike another to defend on the grounds that they were drunk. One way of achieving this result is simply to say that both assault and battery are general intent crimes. The problem is discussed in *People v. Hood*, 1 Cal. 3d 444, 462 P.2d 370, 378, 82 Cal. Rptr. 618 (1969):

> Even if assault requires an intent to commit a battery on the victim, it does not follow that the crime is one in which evidence of intoxication ought to be considered in determining whether the defendant had that intent. It is true that in most cases specific intent has come to mean an intention to do a future act or achieve a particular result, and that assault is appropriately characterized as a specific intent crime under this definition. An assault, however, is equally well characterized as a general intent crime under the definition of general intent as an intent merely to do a violent act. Therefore, whatever reality the distinction between specific and general intent may have in other contexts, the difference is chimerical in the case of assault with a deadly weapon or simple assault. Since the definitions of both specific intent and general intent cover the requisite intent to commit a battery, the decision whether or not to give effect to evidence of intoxication must rest on other considerations.

Intoxication as a defense is discussed *infra* pp. 643-655.

3. In *State v. Warbritton*, 215 Kan. 534, 527 P.2d 1050 (1974), defendant, after shooting his wife, pointed his gun at Mrs. B who was holding defendant's baby. Mrs. B testified that because of the position of the baby in her arms, she had no fear for herself. Conviction reversed as to assault on Mrs. B.

4. Is the statement "every battery includes an assault" true? It is for the common law definition of these crimes. *People v. Greer*, 30 Cal.2d 589, 184 P.2d 512 (1947). *Lamb v. State*, 93 Md. App. 422, 613 A. 2d 402 (1992), *cert. denied*, 329 Md. 110, 617 A. 2d 1055 (1993), however, terms the statement one of several "half-truths" about assault and battery.

> The idea that those half-truths are attempting to communicate, of course, is that every *intended* battery includes an assault. An *intended* battery includes, by its very nature, an antecedent attempt, which is a form of assault.
>
> An unintended battery, on the other hand, does not include such an attempt (or assault) lest it lose its very character of being unintended. An unintended battery, moreover, normally will not include an assault of the intended frightening variety. In rare instances it could, as where in the course of an intended threatening a gun goes off by accident or a frightened victim leaps from a window and suffers harm. Except in such Ripleyesque instances, however, an unintended battery will not include an assault of either variety.

613 A. 2d at 419.

5. It has been held that a battery results from an injury inflicted in the commission of an *act malum in se*. *King v. State*, 157 Tenn. 635, 11 S.W.2d 904 (1928) (driving while intoxicated is an offense *malum in se*, and the resulting injury is a battery); *contra State v. Agnew*, 202 N.C. 755, 164 S.E. 578 (1932): the injury must be intended or the proximate result of "criminal negligence." But it would appear that such cases as the above may be included as "reckless batteries."

6. Where a person is prosecuted under a statute which prohibits an assault on a peace officer engaged in the performance of his duties, must the state prove that the defendant knew that the victim was a peace officer? *Compare United States v. Feola*, 420 U.S. 671 (1975) (no), with *Bundren v. State*, 247 Ga. 180, 274 S.E.2d 455 (1981) (yes).

Statutes which proscribe assaults on peace officers have been enacted to impose a more severe penalty than is authorized for ordinary assaults. What is the objective of such statutes? (1) Protection of peace officers? How will this be furthered if the defendant does not know the identity of the victim? (2) Peace officers more vulnerable; hence offense more serious? Defendants take their victims as they find them?

SECTION III. Grading: Aggravated Assaults and Batteries

EDITORIAL NOTE

Except for murder, manslaughter, and mayhem (injury permanently impairing the victim's ability to defend himself or intentional disfigurement of a permanent character) there were no crimes of aggravated battery or assault at common law. Assault and battery were misdemeanors punishable by short jail sentences. The general crime of "attempt" was also punished in a manner disproportionally lower than the completed offense. Thus, a range of offenses and punishments were needed to reflect the differences, for example, between slapping a person's face and shooting at a person — which itself could be graded in terms of whether the victim was wounded or not.

The result was the development of basically two types of aggravated offenses of the assault or battery variety. The first sought to create a range of personal injury offenses focusing upon the means by which the actor caused or threatened injury [e.g. dangerous weapon], the person upon whom the injury or threat was inflicted [e.g. law enforcement officer] and the seriousness of the injury caused or threatened [e.g. great bodily harm]....

The second development was designed primarily to cure the disparity between the drastic penalties authorized for serious offenses such as murder and rape and the relatively trivial sanctions applied to an attempt to commit those offenses. One convenient way to attack this problem was to create statutory felonies punishing assault with intent to commit murder, rape, or some other serious offense. The result was a series of nominally substantive offenses functionally analogous to specific applications of the law of attempt, though generally requiring closer proximity to actual completion of the offense and carrying heavier penalties.

MODEL PENAL CODE § 211.1, comment at 175, 180-82.

COMMONWEALTH v. HENSON

Supreme Judicial Court of Massachusetts
357 Mass. 686, 259 N.E.2d 769 (1970)

QUIRICO, JUSTICE.

These are appeals under G.L. c. 278, §§ 33A-33G, from convictions on two complaints charging the defendant, respectively, with the crimes of assault on Theodore Finochio by means of a dangerous weapon, to wit: a revolver, and carrying a loaded revolver without a valid license so to do....

The evidence would permit the jury to find the following facts. On December 24, 1968, Theodore Finochio, an off-duty police officer was at a gasoline station in Boston. He was not in uniform, but he had his service revolver in a holster under his coat. Another man and woman also were in the station at that time. The defendant and a female companion entered the station and the female used profane language. Finochio asked the defendant to keep the woman quiet. The defendant reached in his pocket, pulled out a revolver, aimed it at Finochio's stomach and said "Why should I?" Finochio put up his hands and said "No reason at all." He described his state of mind at that time by saying "I thought I was done for." The defendant then turned to go out of the station, holding the revolver at his side. Finochio took out his revolver, pointed it at the defendant and said, "Hold it there, buddy. I am a police officer." The defendant who was then partially out of the door, turned and fired two shots at Finochio from a distance of about five feet. Finochio fired back and chased the defendant out to the street. They exchanged further shots in that chase which lasted about twenty to thirty seconds until the defendant was captured, subdued and handcuffed, and his revolver taken from his hand. The defendant fired a total of five or more shots, and Finochio fired six, one of which struck the defendant. Finochio was not struck by any projectile, and he received no injuries or powder burns in the incident. No projectiles were recovered at the scene. The defendant had taken the revolver from his female companion before going to the gasoline station. Before the shooting he noticed that it was loaded. He removed one shell from the cylinder and recognized it as a blank. He described the revolver as a "phony" gun or "play" gun.

. . . .

On the evidence the jury could find that the defendant, without any legal justification, suddenly drew his revolver from his pocket, pointed it at Finochio's stomach in a threatening manner and thereafter fired it at Finochio five or more times. They could also find that the defendant intended to create, and did create, the impression on the persons present that he had a loaded revolver which was capable of shooting Finochio, and that until the defendant's running gun battle with Finochio was over and he was subdued, no one present except the defendant knew that the defendant's revolver was loaded with blanks. Finally, they could find that all persons present, except the defendant, reasonably believed that the defendant's revolver was loaded with live bullets which he was firing at Finochio.

. . . .

Despite this factual situation, the defendant contends that although he carried the revolver in violation of G.L. c. 269, § 10, as found by the jury, and used it against Finochio thereby committing an assault upon him, his conduct could not, and did not, constitute the aggravated offence of assault by means of a dangerous weapon since the shells in the revolver at the time were blanks. He equates his position to that of a person using a revolver which is capable of firing a bullet, but which is in fact not loaded, or to that of a person using a toy or imitation revolver which in fact cannot fire a bullet. Basically, he argues that because the revolver was not loaded with live ammunition, he did not have the ability to accomplish a battery by means of the revolver, and thus cannot be convicted of assault by means of the revolver.

This aggravated form of assault by means of a dangerous weapon was first made a crime in this Commonwealth by St. 1927, c. 187, § 1, enacting G.L. c. 265, § 15A. It had previously been held in *Commonwealth v. White*, 110 Mass. 407, decided in 1872, that the inability to commit a battery with an unloaded gun was no defence to a charge of simple assault. There, although the defendant was charged with a simple assault, the complaint included reference to a threat "to shoot with a gun ... pointed and aimed at [the victim]." The court said, at 409: "It is not the secret intent of the assaulting party, nor the undisclosed fact of his ability or inability to commit a battery, that is material; but what his conduct and the attending circumstances denote at the time to the party assaulted. If to him they indicate an attack, he is justified in resorting to defensive action. The same rule applies to the proof necessary to sustain a criminal complaint for an assault. It is the outward demonstration that constitutes the mischief which is punished as a breach of the peace."

If this test were applied to the present case, the jury could find that the defendant's conduct and the attending circumstances indicated that the defendant was attacking Finochio by means of a loaded revolver. Thus the defendant's secret intent not to shoot Finochio based on his undisclosed inability to do so with the blank shells is not material. The defendant's acts, judged without the benefit of his secret knowledge that he was firing blanks, constituted a reasonably obvious case of an assault by means of a loaded revolver, involving a violent breach of the public order and setting in motion the normal reaction thereto by Finochio. The issue before us is whether this test should be applied to a case of assault by means of a dangerous weapon. Put another way, should the defendant now be allowed to avoid criminal responsibility for his conduct on the ground that he had only blank shells in his revolver, or that the revolver was only a "phony" gun or "play" gun?

....

An examination of decisions on this question in other jurisdictions shows a considerable conflict of authority, but it may be accurate to state that a majority of the jurisdictions which have spoken on the question have concluded that the crime of aggravated assault by means of a firearm, and in some cases the crime of simple assault is not made out by evidence of the pointing of an unloaded firearm. See Annotation, 79 A.L.R.2d 1412. That applies whether the case is one where it was established that the firearm was not loaded at the time of the alleged assault, or one where there was no proof that the firearm was loaded. Many of these decisions turn on local legal provisions which do not prevail in this Commonwealth, and therefore they do not help us in this case.[1]

It is equally true that a number of decisions holding that one who menacingly points a firearm at another knowing it to be unloaded can be found guilty of assault by means of a dangerous weapon are based on local

---

[1] (a) Some of the decisions are based upon the application of statutory or other definitions of assault which expressly require proof of a present ability to do harm or to accomplish the threatened battery as an element of the crime. *Chapman v. State*, 78 Ala. 463. *People v. Sylva*, 143 Cal. 62, 76 P. 814. *Klein v. State*, 9 Ind.App. 365, 36 N.E. 763. *People v. Wood*, 10 A.D.2d (N.Y.) 231, 199 N.Y.S.2d 342. (b) Others are based upon the application of local laws requiring proof of a specific intent to commit an assault with a dangerous weapon, or to inflict bodily harm, with the result that if the assailant knew the firearm to be unloaded, he could not have the required specific intent. *People v. Katz*, 290 N.Y. 361, 365, 49 N.E.2d 482. *People v. Wood*, 10 A.D.2d (N.Y.) 231, 235, 199 N.Y.S.2d 342. (c) Still others are based upon the application of statutes expressly requiring a specific intent, such as intent to kill or intent to murder, which cannot exist in one who knows the gun he is using is not loaded. *Marshall v. State*, 21 Ala. App. 500, 109 So. 558. *Meriwether v. State*, 104 Ga. 500, 30 S.E. 806. *State v. Mitchell*, 139 Iowa 455, 116 N.W. 808. (d) Finally, some decisions are based on the application of statutes relating to assaults with "deadly weapons" which may mean something different from or more than the words "dangerous weapon" used in our statute. G.L. c. 265, § 15A. *Territory v. Gomez*, 14 Ariz. 139, 125 P. 702. *State v. Bush*, 50 Idaho 166, 295 P. 432. *State v. Napper*, 6 Nev. 113.

legal provisions which do not prevail in this Commonwealth or on factual situations different from ours.[2] However, in one jurisdiction, on facts similar to those before us, it has been decided without reliance on local statutory provisions that an unloaded gun is a dangerous weapon when the offence charged was assault "with a dangerous weapon, to wit: a revolver." *State v. Johnston*, 207 La. 161, 164, 20 So.2d 741, 744.

Our answer to the question before us would seem to depend on whether, under the law of this Commonwealth, proof of a charge of the crime of simple assault or of aggravated assault requires proof of the present ability to accomplish the battery which is threatened or attempted in the assault. As we have indicated above, it was held as to simple assault that "[i]t is not the secret intent of the assaulting party, nor the undisclosed fact of his ability or inability to commit a battery, that is material; but what his conduct and the attending circumstances denote at the time to the party assaulted.... It is the outward demonstration that constitutes the mischief which is punished as a breach of the peace." *Commonwealth v. White*, 110 Mass. 407, 409. That language has been quoted and the decision cited on many occasions in the discussion of "apparent" ability to commit the battery threatened or attempted....

The fundamental reason for permitting a conviction for simple assault on proof of apparent ability of the assailant to accomplish the attempted or threatened battery is that the public peace and order is affected by and dependent upon what is reasonably apparent, and not upon secret fact or reason rendering the assailant incapable of accomplishing the battery. The reason applies with even greater force to a case of apparent ability to accomplish a battery attempted or threatened by means of a firearm. The threat to the public peace and order is greater, and natural reactions thereto by the intended victim and others may be more sudden and violent than in cases where no weapon is involved. There is no reason why the rule of apparent ability should not apply to charges of aggravated assaults by means of weapons. It is sufficient to prove such a charge if the evidence shows an apparent ability to accomplish the battery by means of the particular weapon used. Thus, the mere fact that a firearm brandished by an assailant is known by him to be unloaded, or to be loaded with blank cartridges, does not entitle him to an acquittal on a charge of the aggravated offence of assault by means of a dangerous weapon.

Judgments affirmed.

---

[2](a) Some of these decisions are based on statutes which make it a crime to carry or commit assaults with a "pistol, revolver ... or other offensive or dangerous weapon" or similar words, and have concluded that a firearm is a dangerous weapon whether loaded or not. *State v. Ashland*, 259 Iowa 728, 730, 145 N.W.2d 910. *State v. Atkinson*, 141 N.C. 734, 53 S.E. 228. (b) In some cases where there was no evidence that the firearm was loaded the court held that evidence of an assault by means of the firearm without more made out a prima facie case, or created a rebuttable presumption that the firearm was loaded, and that absent any evidence that it was unloaded it was sufficient to support the conviction. *State v. Herron*, 12 Mont. 230, 235, 29 P. 819. *State v. Lewis*, Ohio App., 186 N.E.2d 487. (c) Some of these decisions noted, in upholding the convictions, that the unloaded firearm was used or could have been used as a bludgeon and thus was a dangerous weapon. *People v. Egan*, 77 Cal.App. 279, 284, 246 P. 337. *People v. White*, 115 Cal.App.2d 828, 832, 253 P.2d 108.

NOTES

1. In determining whether an assault is aggravated because committed with a dangerous weapon some courts have classified "dangerous weapons" into two groups. One group is referred to as "dangerous weapons per se" and includes those which are "specially designed and constructed to produce death or great bodily harm." The other group includes "... objects which are not dangerous per se but which can be used in a dangerous fashion to inflict serious harm."

Commonwealth v. Davis, 406 N.E.2d 417, 419 (Mass. App. Ct. 1980).

Although the term "dangerous" or "deadly" weapon is usually interpreted in inclusive rather than exclusive terms there is some difference in approach in reaching that result.

> An examination of the decisions of the reviewing courts discloses that the courts will indulge in machinations in order to hold that almost any weapon is a dangerous one if it strikes fear into the heart of the victim. It may well be time to face realism and permit the trial court to determine as a matter of law what is a dangerous weapon.
>
> ....
>
> It is regrettable that the reviewing courts have adhered to an objective test in determining whether or not an accused was armed with a dangerous weapon. There is an adherence to the practice of determining the potentially harmful effects of the weapon whether used in the manner intended or in some other harmful manner. By applying the objective test the courts have indulged in the far from satisfactory reasoning that an uncocked air pistol similar in appearance to a .45 caliber automatic pistol is a dangerous weapon because it could be used as a bludgeon.
>
> A subjective test in determining what is a dangerous weapon would be a more realistic approach. "In making the determination the focus should not be so much upon the firearm or the pseudo firearm itself, but upon the intention with which the alleged firearm, or other weapon, was used by the perpetrator and the belief such use instilled, or reasonably could have been expected to instill, in the victim."

People v. Chapman, 73 Ill. App. 3d 546, 392 N.E.2d 391, 394 (1979).

2. Defendant bit off a piece of victim's ear. The court, after a comprehensive analysis of the numerous aggravated assault offenses, held that neither teeth nor other parts of the human body are dangerous weapons under the crime of assault and battery by means of a dangerous weapon. There are other offenses under which prosecution may be brought such as mayhem, assault with intent to maim, and in serious cases, assault with intent to kill. *Commonwealth v. Davis*, supra note 1.

Contra State v. Zangrilli, 440 A.2d 710 (R.I. 1982). A person's hands when used in a manner likely to produce substantial bodily harm may be regarded as a dangerous weapon notwithstanding the fact that the person has had no training in the martial arts or boxing. *See People v. Ross*, 831 P. 2d 1310, 1314 and n. 6 (Colo. 1992) which agrees with *Zangrilli* and rejects *Davis*. Also, a dog (here, a Doberman Pinscher) may be used in such a way as to constitute a "deadly weapon." *State v. Bowers*, 239 Kan. 417, 721 P. 2d 268 (1986).

3. The variety of chemical sprays designed to disable persons against whom they are used has raised a question as to whether they should be classed as "deadly" or "dangerous" weapons. One court has held that chemical "Mace" is not a "deadly weapon."

> A deadly weapon has generally been defined to be one likely to produce death or great bodily injury. The question of whether a particular weapon involved is to be classed as "deadly" is a factual question to be resolved by the jury.... The jury may consider the character of the assault and the way the weapon is used. *Austin v. State*, 336 So. 2d 480, 81-82 (Fla. Dist. Ct. App. 1976).

4. Some states, such as Louisiana, impose an additional penalty on a person who uses a firearm in the commission of a crime. LA. REV. STAT. ANN. 14:95.2 (West 1986).

5. *State v. Everhardt*, 326 N.C. 777, 392 S.E. 2d 391 (N.C. 1990) a case involving assault with a dangerous weapon, held that the statutory requirement of "serious injury" could be proven by evidence of serious mental injury. Under the facts of the case, the victim who was the wife of the defendant did suffer physical injury as a result of the defendant's degrading sexual batteries on her. Nevertheless, the court focused on the fact that "[t]he assaults perpetrated on the victim were in the main psychologically torturous in nature, calculated to inflict mental or emotional injury rather than bodily injury." *Id.* at 393.

EDITORIAL NOTE ON ASSAULTS WITH INTENT TO COMMIT SPECIFIC CRIMES AND ATTEMPTS

In *Marthall v. State*, 34 Tex. Crim. 222, 36 S.W. 1062 (1894), defendant accosted the prosecutrix as she was passing a bluff of the creek en route to a neighbor's. He exposed himself and chased her but never got close enough to touch her. The court reversed his conviction for "assault with intent to rape" because he was never "within such distance of the prosecutrix as to place it within his power to commit a battery upon her by the use of the means with which he attempted it.... If he was at such distance from her as that he could not reach person by use of the means employed, he is not guilty of an assault." *Id.* at 1062. The court suggested there is a difference between the crimes of assault with intent to rape (the crime charged) and the crime of attempted rape, but did not discuss whether defendant could have been convicted of attempted rape because that issue had not been submitted to the jury.

Assaults with intent to commit specific crimes were created to allow more severe punishment than was authorized for simple assault or attempt. But, if assault is defined in part as an "attempted battery," can there be any difference in the elements of the offenses? This question has generated considerable discussion. *State v. Johnson*, 243 Minn. 296, 67 N.W.2d 639 (1954); Note, 21 MINN. L. REV. 213 (1936-37).

Some courts have concluded that an assault with intent to kill or rape is indistinguishable from attempted murder or attempted rape. *State v. Collis*, 243 Or. 222, 413 P.2d 53 (1966); *Commonwealth v. Moon*, 151 Pa. Super. 555, 30 A.2d 704 (1943). Other courts have concluded that while every assault with intent to commit a specific crime includes an attempt, conduct which constitutes an attempt does not necessarily include an assault with intent to commit the crime. The distinction suggested is that attempt merely requires an act which goes beyond preparation, but for assault with intent to commit a specific crime the defendant must do the "last proximate act prior to the consummation of the felony intended to be perpetrated." *State v. Hetzel*, 159 Ohio St. 350, 112 N.E.2d 369, 370 (1953). Another suggested distinction is that certain attempts such as attempted rape may be established by proof of threats, but this would be insufficient for assault with intent to rape. *State v. Hyams*, 64 Utah 285, 230 P. 349 (1924). However, this supposed distinction would not seem to apply in those states where a threat to inflict immediate injury is considered an assault.

Would the result in *State v. Marthall, supra*, be different if the statute had included as part of the definition of assault "placing the victim in apprehension of an impending battery?"

In a case somewhat similar to *Marthall* — although there was no exposure or pursuit — the court upheld a conviction of "an attempt to commit an assault with intent to rape." *Morris v. State*, 32 Ala. App. 278, 25 So. 2d 54 (1946). Is it incongruous to convict a person for an attempted assault? *Christensen v. State*, 33 Md. App. 653, 365 A.2d 562, 566 (1976) stated "[t]here is no such crime as an attempt to commit an assault." Why? Does it make any difference as to how assault is defined? See *supra* pp. 161-162.

SECTION IV. An Expanding View of Harm: Terroristic Threats, Harassment, Stalking

EDITORIAL NOTE

The common-law crimes of assault and battery were aimed at acts of imminent and actual violence. Incorporation of the tort definition of assault enlarged the protected interests to include acts which instill fear or apprehension of imminent violence. This may still leave threats of future violence or acts which otherwise disturb our "peace of mind" outside of the definition of assault and battery. Many states have enacted statutes to prohibit conduct which is frightening or otherwise disturbing to the peace of mind. "Peace of mind" is not as easy to define as brute violence because it is difficult to describe harassment or annoying conduct in specific terms except by drafting a cumbersome catalogue of a wide variety of acts and, when more general terms are used, the risk of overbreadth is ever present. The problem of drafting is made more difficult because the conduct to be prohibited often consists only of spoken words which raises substantial first amendment problems.

MODEL PENAL CODE

§ 211.3. Terroristic Threats

[The text of this section appears in Appendix A.]

STATE v. GUNZELMAN

Supreme Court of Kansas
210 Kan. 481, 502 P.2d 705 (1972)

FROMME, J.

Jack R. Gunzelman was tried and convicted for the crime of battery of a law enforcement officer (K.S.A.1971 Supp. 21-3413) and for the crime of making a terroristic threat against another person (K.S.A.1971 Supp. 21-3419). He appeals from conviction and sentence thereon.

....

The charges arose from an incident which occurred at the home of a highway patrol officer, Bobby L. Norton, in Stockton, Kansas, on the evening of April 5, 1971. A brief recitation of the facts will be helpful. Appellant was in the roofing business and hired employees to drive his roofing trucks. Patrolman Bobby L. Norton had issued a traffic ticket to one of the truck drivers for not having a driver's license. At 9:30 that evening Norton received a call on the telephone from appellant who claimed Norton was picking on the drivers. Appellant warned the patrolman to quit stopping his vehicles. No violence was threatened over the telephone. Later that same evening the appellant and his driver appeared at the patrolman's front door. The following took place on or near the front porch of the home.

The patrolman testified that the appellant was belligerent when he and his driver, Aguilera, came to see the patrolman. The patrolman's wife answered the door bell, then she retreated inside the house. Her husband stepped out on the porch. It was after 9:30 P.M. and the children were in bed. Appellant accused the patrolman of picking on his drivers and said, "I am warning you for the last time that you are not pulling my drivers over for no reason and arresting them; ..." By this time the patrolman's wife was looking out of a darkened bedroom window and was worried about her husband's safety. Appellant said, "You have a wife and family. You had better give some thought to that. You are gone a lot of nights. Where is your bedroom? I will be back." According to the patrolman's testimony appellant walked around and peered into a window south of the porch.

[At this point appellant struck the patrolman and then left.]

....

The patrolman's wife had heard the iron railing on the porch rattle when appellant knocked the patrolman back against the railing. She was able to hear part of the conversation including, "I am warning you for the last time. You had better quit picking on my men." She saw appellant shaking his finger at her husband. She was frightened. She saw the man lunge at her husband and heard the blow. She called the sheriff on the telephone. The appellant was arrested later that night.

The terroristic threat statute under which appellant was charged reads as follows:

> A terroristic threat is any threat to commit violence communicated with intent to terrorize another, or to cause the evacuation of any building, place of assembly or facility of transportation, or in wanton disregard of the risk of causing such terror or evacuation.

According to a comment by the judicial council, which comment appears below the statute, this is a new provision designed to fill a gap in the law. The idea was drawn from the American Law Institute's Model Penal Code, § 211.3.

....

The American Law Institute's comments, which follow this section of the code, may be helpful. In part they read:

> ... Where, as in the present section, the object is to prevent serious alarm for personal safety, such as may arise from letters or anonymous telephone calls threatening death, kidnapping or bombing, the class of threats can be narrowly defined, and the gravity of the offense can be related both to the seriousness of the threat and the disturbing character of the psychological result intended or risked by the actor.... (MPC § 211.3)

Under the constitutional attack lodged by the appellant, he contends the statute was enacted to proscribe threats in connection with campus unrest, fire and bomb threats to public buildings and threats which arise from mob violence. He argues the statute is vague, indefinite and uncertain if it is extended to terroristic threats to person or property of an individual as it does not advise the ordinary citizen of the required nature of the proscribed threats.

....

The main thrust of appellant's constitutional argument is based upon a failure by the legislature to define the words "threat" and "terroristic". In the general definition section of the Kansas Criminal Code (K.S.A.1971 Supp. 21-3110) threat is defined as follows, "(24) 'Threat' means a communicated intent to inflict physical or other harm on any person or on property." Terrorize is not defined therein, so it must be measured by what men of common intelligence would consider it to mean.

Webster's Third New International Dictionary (Unabridged) says to terrorize means to coerce by threat or violence, to rule by intimidation.

The few other jurisdictions which have dealt with "terroristic threat" statutes have had no trouble in finding the common meaning of the term.... In *Armstrong v. Ellington*, 312 F.Supp. 1119 (W.D.Tenn.1970) the court dealt with T.C.A. § 39-2805.

... On page 1126 of the reported case the court defined terrorizing as follows:

> ... It means to reduce to terror by violence or threats, and terror means an extreme fear or fear that agitates body and mind. We hold that "terrorizing" is specific enough and within the appropriate area in which the

State of Tennessee might protect the citizens even though expression might be involved.

A statute creating a new offense must be sufficiently explicit to inform those who are subject to it what conduct on their part will render them liable to its penalties. (*State v. Blaser*, 138 Kan. 447, 26 P.2d 593; *State v. Rogers*, 142 Kan. 841, 52 P.2d 1185; *State v. Carr*, 151 Kan. 36, 98 P.2d 393.) In creating an offense which was not a crime at common law the legislature must make the statute sufficiently certain to show what was intended to be prohibited and punished, otherwise it will be void for uncertainty. But reasonable certainty is all that is required, and liberal effect is always to be given to the legislative intent in view of the evil to be corrected. (*State v. Davidson*, 152 Kan. 460, 105 P.2d 876; *State v. Hill*, 189 Kan. 403, 369 P.2d 365, 91 A.L.R.2d 750.)

The word "threat" as used in K.S.A.1971 Supp. 21-3419 means a communicated intent to inflict physical or other harm on any person or on property. (K.S.A.1971 Supp. 21-3110[24].) The word "terrorize" means to reduce to terror by violence or threats, and terror means an extreme fear or fear that agitates body and mind.

Given limiting definitions for the words "threat" and "terrorize," as those terms are understood by men of common intelligence, K.S.A.1971 Supp. 21-3419 proscribing terroristic threats survives any constitutional challenge for vagueness and uncertainty under Section 10, Bill of Rights, Constitution of the State of Kansas, and under Amendment 14, § 1, Constitution of the United States.

Although the statute may have been directed at campus unrest, fire and bomb threats to public buildings and acts of mob violence, the main elements of the offense are threats communicated with a specific intent to terrorize another. The wording of the statute appears sufficient to proscribe such threats whether directed generally against one or more persons and regardless of the purpose which the terrorist has in mind to accomplish.

NOTES

1. In *People v. Mirmirani*, 30 Cal. 3d 375, 636 P.2d 1130, 178 Cal. Rptr. 792 (1981), the California Supreme Court struck down the state's "terroristic threats" statute. The term "terrorize" was defined as the creation of "a climate of fear and intimidation by means of threats or violent action causing sustained fear for personal safety in order to achieve social or political goals." The crime was one that could be committed by words alone without action or intent to act. As such the offense could consist of pure speech. Applying the strict standards of the first amendment the court found the phrase "social or political goals" to be unconstitutionally vague.

2. In *Kelner v. United States*, 534 F.2d 1020 (2d Cir. 1976), cert. denied, 429 U.S. 1022 (1977), the court upheld defendant's conviction of transmitting in interstate commerce, via a television interview, a threat to assassinate the

IV. AN EXPANDING VIEW OF HARM: TERRORISTIC THREATS, HARASSMENT, STALKING

leader of the Palestine Liberation Organization. Defendant had offered the first amendment as a defense. Judge Oakes in the lead opinion wrote:

> On the most elementary level it would seem possible to conclude that a threat of murder falls within the narrow class of "fighting words" which are so inherently deleterious to social order, see *Chaplinsky v. New Hampshire*, 315 U.S. 568, 572, 62 S.Ct. 766, 769, 86 L.Ed. 1031, 1035 (1942); *Cantwell v. Connecticut*, 310 U.S. 296, 308, 60 S.Ct. 900, 905, 84 L.Ed. 1213, 1220 (1940), and so inherently unrelated to the "robust" political debate necessary to a democratic society, see Watts,* supra, 402 F.2d at 683 n.17, that the umbrella of the First Amendment does not protect the threat from governmental restriction. We do not, however, rest on this simplistic and perhaps misleading proposition. Professor Emerson points out that both Chaplinsky and Cantwell were cases involving the use of expression that might lead to a breach of the peace in the streets, that is to say, they were incitement cases. T. Emerson, The System of Freedom of Expression 313-15 (1970). Here the crime charged is not that appellant was inciting others to assassinate Arafat but that he himself was threatening to do so. The question remains, therefore, whether an unequivocal threat which has not ripened by any overt act into conduct in the nature of an attempt is nevertheless punishable under the First Amendment, even though it may additionally involve elements of expression.
>
> On that question we believe we have help from *Watts, supra*, 394 U.S. at 705-08, 89 S.Ct. at 1399-1400, 22 L.Ed.2d at 664-665. [There] ... the Court construed the word "threat" to exclude statements which are, when taken in context, not "true threats" because they are conditional and made in jest. 397 U.S. at 708, 89 S.Ct. at 1401, 22 L.Ed. at 667.... [W]e believe a narrow construction of the word "threat" in the statute here, 18 U.S.C. § 875(c), as approved in Watts, 394 U.S. at 708, 89 S.Ct. at 1401, 22 L.Ed.2d at 667, is consonant with the protection of First Amendment interests. Even where the threat is made in the midst of what may be other protected political expression, ... the threat itself may affront such important social interests that it is punishable absent proof of a specific intent to carry it into action when the following criteria are satisfied. So long as the threat on its face and in the circumstances in which it is made is so unequivocal, unconditional, immediate and specific as to the person threatened, as to convey a gravity of purpose and imminent prospect of execution, the statute may properly be applied.

Judge Meskill concurring raised some provocative questions. Suppose after the interview but before it was broadcast defendant recanted the threat but the station nevertheless televised it. Suppose the station reported the story by using silent film but quoting defendant.

Judge Mulligan also concurred objecting to the narrow definition of the word threat. He would have upheld the conviction if the threat had been

---

Watts v. United States, 394 U.S. 705 (1969), *rev'g* 402 F.2d 676 (D.C. Cir. 1968), which had upheld defendant's conviction.

phrased, "We plan to kill Arafat a week from today unless he pays us $1,000,000" notwithstanding it "is not immediate, imminent or unconditional." *Id.* at 1029.

The constitutional issues are discussed in Comment, *United States v. Kelner: Threats and the First Amendment*, 125 U. PA. L. REV. 919 (1976-77).

MODEL PENAL CODE

§ 250.2. Disorderly Conduct
§ 250.3. False Public alarms
§ 250.4. Harassment
§ 250.5. Public Drunkenness; Drug Incapacitation
[The text of these sections appears in Appendix A.]

NOTES ON HARASSMENT AND STALKING

1. A Connecticut telephone "harassment" statute provided in part that "[a] person is guilty of harassment when: ... (3) with intent to harass, annoy or alarm another person, he makes a telephone call, whether or not a conversation ensues, in a manner likely to cause annoyance or alarm." The statute was upheld against a constitutional challenge in *Gromley v. Director of Connecticut State Department of Probation*, 632 F.2d 938 (2d Cir., cert. denied, 449 U.S. 1023 (1980). The majority opinion drew a parallel between the "compelling interest" which the Connecticut statute sought to protect and the interest Congress sought to protect in the federal telephone harassment statute, 47 U.S.C. § 223 (1976).

> [I]n enacting § 223 the Congress had a compelling interest in the protection of innocent individuals from fear, abuse or annoyance at the hands of persons who employed the telephone, not to communicate, but for other unjustifiable motives."

Id. at 941 quoting from *United States v. Lampley*, 573, F.2d 783, 787 (3d Cir. 1978).

The majority opinion characterized telephone harassment statutes as regulating "conduct, not mere speech," that is "making a telephone call with the requisite intent and in the specified manner." By characterizing the statute as affecting "conduct" the majority found that overbreadth of the statute was not "substantial" "'in relation to the statute's plainly legitimate sweep.'" *Id.* at 942.

Judge Mansfield concurred but would have upheld the statute only if the Connecticut Supreme Court had narrowly construed it "to apply only to speechless calls or to obscene or threatening calls of the type involved in this case." *Id.* at 943. He found no solace in labeling the state statute as one which prohibits "conduct." "Telephone calls by irate citizens to their Congressmen, by collectors seeking payment of legitimate bills overdue, by customers voicing to a seller dissatisfaction with goods or services purchased, and calls of like tenor, are likely to be annoying, even harassing, to the recipients.... But if the statute here were construed, as it easily could be, to prohibit any telephone calls made 'with intent to annoy,' which had such effect, it would patently violate the First Amendment." *Id.* at 944.

Justice White dissented from the denial of certiorari. 449 U.S. 1023 (1980). Although a state has a valid interest in protecting its citizens against obscenity or threats of physical violence it is important to remember:

> that speech may be "annoying" without losing its First Amendment protection and that the Connecticut statute on its face criminalizes any telephone call that annoys and was intended to do so. It is not difficult to imagine various clearly protected telephone communications that would fall within the ban of the Connecticut statute. As such it is fairly arguable that the statute is substantially overbroad and hence unconstitutional. *Lewis v. City of New Orleans*, 415 U.S. 130, 94 S.Ct. 970, 39 L.Ed.2d 214 (1974); *Gooding v. Wilson*, 405 U.S. 518, 92 S.Ct. 1103, 31 L.Ed.2d 408 (1972).
>
> Beyond the obvious tension between our prior cases and the judgment below is the difference in opinion among those courts that have considered constitutional challenges to similar state statutes. Contrary to the decision reached by the Court of Appeals in this case, state appellate courts have invalidated substantially equivalent provisions as being unconstitutionally overbroad. *People v. Klick*, 66 Ill.2d 269, 5 Ill.Dec. 858, 362 N.E.2d 329 (1977) (invalidating statute making it a crime for anyone who "[w]ith intent to annoy another, makes a telephone call, whether or not conversation thereby ensues"); *Wisconsin v. Dronso*, 90 Wis.2d 149, 279 N.W.2d 710 (Wis.Ct.App. 1979) (same). Another court has invalidated a like statute on the grounds that it was unconstitutionally vague. *State v. Blair*, 287 Or. 519, 601 P.2d 766 (1979) (statute made it a crime to communicate by telephone "in a manner likely to cause annoyance or alarm" to the receiver). On the other hand, various state courts, like the Connecticut court in this case, have rejected overbreadth challenges to telephone harassment statutes. *See, e.g., State v. Elder*, 382 So.2d 687 (Fla. 1980) (statute prohibiting a person from making a telephone call "whether or not conversation ensues, without disclosing his identity and with intent to annoy, abuse, threaten, or harass any person at the called number"); *Constantino v. State*, 243 Ga. 595, 255 S.E.2d 710 (1979) (prohibiting repeated telephoning "for the purpose of annoying, harassing or molesting another or his family"). See generally *United States v. Lampley*, 573 F.2d 783 (CA3 1978); *People v. Smith*, 89 Misc.2d 789, 392 N.Y.S.2d 968 (1977). The above cases demonstrate that the state courts are not in agreement concerning application of First Amendment principles in this area of the law.
>
> The foregoing suggests that even if the Court is of the view that the judgment below is correct, there is sufficient reason to grant certiorari and issue a judgment to this effect. Accordingly, I dissent.

2. California and other states have recently adopted "stalking" statutes. The primary purpose of these statutes is to provide greater protection to any person, but especially to women, who have reason to fear that another person who has either followed or "harassed" them might eventually use force. The statute would apply to situations in which the "stalker" has not yet done anything which would qualify as an assault. Is the California statute broad enough to prosecute a political protestor who "repeatedly follows" and publicly pickets a political candidate or corporate officer? An abortion clinic protestor who "repeatedly follows" the clinic doctor home and pickets on the sidewalk outside the doctor's home? If the "credible threat" requirement adequately limits the statute, why is there the special exemption for labor picketing?

STALKING

(a) Any person who willfully, maliciously, and repeatedly follows or harasses another person and who makes a credible threat with the intent to place that person in reasonable fear of death or great bodily injury is guilty of the crime of *stalking*, punishable by imprisonment in a county jail for not more than one year or by a fine of not more than one thousand dollars ($1,000), or by both that fine and imprisonment.

....

(d) For the purposes of this section, "harasses" means a knowing and willful course of conduct directed at a specific person which seriously alarms, annoys, or harasses the person, and which serves no legitimate purpose. The course of conduct must be such as would cause a reasonable person to suffer substantial emotional distress, and must actually cause substantial emotional distress to the person. "Course of conduct" means a pattern of conduct composed of a series of acts over a period of time, however short, evidencing a continuity of purpose. Constitutionally protected activity is not included within the meaning of "course of conduct."

(e) For the purposes of this section, "a credible threat" means a threat made with the intent and the apparent ability to carry out the threat so as to cause the person who is the target of the threat to reasonably fear for his or her safety. The threat must be against the life of, or a threat to cause great bodily injury to, a person as defined in Section 12022.7.

This section shall not apply to conduct which occurs during labor picketing.

CAL. PENAL CODE § 646.9 (West 1992).

SECTION V. Consent

MODEL PENAL CODE

§ 2.11. Consent

[The text of this section appears in Appendix A.]

STATE v. BROWN

Superior Court of New Jersey, Law Division
143 N.J. Super. 571, 364 A.2d 27 (1976), aff'd,
154 N.J. Super. 511, 381 A.2d 1231 (1977)

BACHMAN, J. S.C.

[T]his opinion is to serve as amplification of this court's ruling on the issue of consent of the victim to the alleged atrocious assault and battery.

V. CONSENT

Specifically, defendant contends that he is not guilty of the alleged atrocious assault and battery because he and Mrs. Brown, the victim, had an understanding to the effect that if she consumed any alcoholic beverages (and/or became intoxicated), he would punish her by physically assaulting her. The testimony revealed that the victim was an alcoholic. On the day of the alleged crime she indulged in some spirits, apparently to Mr. Brown's dissatisfaction. As per their agreement, defendant sought to punish Mrs. Brown by severely beating her with his hands and other objects.

. . . .

Some courts have allowed the defense of consent in civil suits, while denying it in criminal prosecutions for battery (e.g., *Wright v. Starr*, 42 Nev. 441, 179 P. 877 (Sup.Ct. 1919)). According to these courts, there are two different interests at stake. While criminal law is designed to protect the interests of society as a whole, the civil law is concerned with enforcing the rights of each individual within the society. So, while the consent of the victim may relieve defendant of liability in tort, this same consent has been held irrelevant in a criminal prosecution, where there is more at stake than a victim's rights. Love, Criminal Law: Consent as a Defense to Criminal Battery — The Problem of Athletic Contests, 28 Okla. L.Rev. 840 (1975).

Because of the dearth of authority in New Jersey, it will be useful to examine the manner in which other jurisdictions have resolved the issue of consent to criminal assaults. Several of these courts have ruled on the issue of consent in criminal assault cases that did not have sexual overtones but did involve actual batteries. These courts have almost invariably taken the position that since the offense in question involved a breach of the public peace as well as an invasion of the victim's physical security, the victim's consent would not be recognized as a defense, especially where the battery is a substantial or severe one. *Taylor v. State*, 214 Md. 156, 133 A.2d 414, 65 A.L.R.2d 740 (Ct. App. 1957). See generally, 58 A.L.R.3d, Assault and Battery, § 2 at 662. It was very early held to be a crime to cut off the hand of a person at his request and with his full consent. *Wright's Case* (Leicester Assizes 1604), reported in Beale, Cases on Criminal Law (3 ed. 1915), 209. Professor Beale explained that

> Homicide, mayhem and battery may be committed, though the individual injured consented to the injury. The reason for this is clear: The public has an interest in the personal safety of its citizens and is injured where the safety of any individual is threatened, whether by himself or another. [Beale, Consent in the Criminal Law, 8 Harv. L. Rev. 317, 324 (1895)].

. . . .

The reasoning and public interest that is of concern and served by this rule is that of peace, health and good order. An individual or victim cannot consent to a wrong that is committed against the public peace. The state, not the victim, punishes a person for fighting or inflicting assaults. As astutely noted in *Wright v. Starr, supra*, the court, citing with approval 1 Cooley, Torts, 283, "There are three parties involved in criminal assaults, one being the state, which for its own good does not suffer the others to deal on a basis of contract with the public." It has been stated, and perhaps rightly so, that the only true consent to a criminal act is that of the community. Hughes, Criminal Law — Defense of Consent — Test to be Applied, 33 Can.B.Rev. 88, 92 (1955).

This is so because these acts (the physical assaults by defendant upon Mrs. Brown), even if done in private, have an impingement (whether direct or indirect) upon the community at large in that the very doing of them may tend to encourage their repetition and so to undermine public morals.

State v. Fransua, 85 N.M. 173, 510 P.2d 106, 58 A.L.R.3d 656 (App.Ct. 1973), bears further illustration and support for this court's holding, as it is a classic and recent case of an invitation and consent to an aggravated assault. There, as the result of an argument the victim, in compliance with defendant's wishes, produced a loaded pistol, laid it within defendant's reach and said: "there's the gun, if you want to shoot me go ahead." The defendant picked up the pistol and shot the victim, wounding him seriously. In response to defendant's argument of consent on the part of the victim, the court wisely opined,

> We cannot agree. It is generally conceded that a state enacts criminal statutes making certain violent acts crimes for at least two reasons: One reason is to protect the persons of its citizens; the second, however, is to prevent a breach of the peace [citing] *State v. Seal*, 76 N.M. 461, 415 P.2d 845 (1966). While we entertain little sympathy for either the victim's absurd actions or the defendant's equally unjustified act of pulling the trigger, we will not permit the defense of consent to be raised in such cases. Whether the victims of crimes have so little regard for their own safety as to request injury, the public has a stronger and overriding interest in preventing and prohibiting acts such as these. [510 P.2d at 107.]

....

There are a few situations in which the consent of the victim (actual or implied) is a defense. These situations usually involve ordinary physical contact or blows incident to sports such as football, boxing, or wrestling. *People v. Samuels*, 250 Cal. App. 2d 501, 58 Cal. Rptr. 439 (D. Ct. App. 1967), *cert. denied sub nom. Samuels v. California*, 390 U.S. 1024, 88 S. Ct. 1404, 20 L. Ed. 2d 281. But this is expected and understood by the participants. The state cannot later be heard to charge a participant with criminal assault upon another participant if the injury complained of resulted from activity that is reasonably within the rules and purview of the sports activity.

However this is not to be confused with sports activities that are not sanctioned by the state. Thus, street fighting which is disorderly and mischievous on many obvious grounds (even if for a purse and consented to), and encounters of that kind which tend to and have the specific objective of causing bodily harm, serve no useful purpose, but rather tend to breach the peace and thus are unlawful. *Commonwealth v. Collberg*, 119 Mass. 350 (Sup. Jud. Ct. 1876); *Willey v. Carpenter*, 64 Vt. 212, 23 A. 630 (Sup. Ct. 1892). No one is justified in striking another, except it be in self defense, and similarly whenever two persons go out to strike each other and do so, each is guilty of an assault. It is no matter who strikes the first blow, for the law proscribes such striking.

As stated by this court in its ruling and by the court in *People v. Samuels, supra,* it is a matter of common knowledge that a normal person in full possession of his or her mental faculties does not freely and seriously consent to the use upon his or herself of force likely to produce great bodily harm. Those persons that do freely consent to such force and bodily injury no doubt require the enforcement of the very laws that were enacted to protect them and other humans. A general principle of law is that a person cannot contract out of protective legislation passed for his benefit.... The laws of this State and others that have dealt with the question are simply and unequivocally clear that the defense of consent cannot be available to a defendant charged with any type of physical assault that causes appreciable injury. If the law were otherwise, it would not be conducive to a peaceful, orderly and healthy society.

....

Defendant in *Banovitch v. Commonwealth*, [196 Va. 210, 83 S.E.2d 369 (1964)] certainly lacked a hostile or evil disposition or malice, but was denied the defense of consent to the charge of mayhem (atrocious assault and battery) on facts showing that he recklessly applied a corrosive chemical to the victim's person in purporting to treat her for cancer. Nor did defendant in *People v. Samuels, supra*, entertain any malice when he administered a beating to another while making a sadomasochistic film. Yet the defense of consent was unavailable to him. And certainly the court in *Commonwealth v. Farrell*, [322 Mass. 606, 78 N.E.2d 697 (1948)] did not require an evil or hostile disposition on the part of defendant in order to sustain a conviction for assault based on a sadistic burning with a cigarette. In fact, there was no evil or hostile disposition on the part of defendant. Defendant there simply had a perverted notion of branding his female victim by burning his initials on the private parts of her body in order that she would be "his and she would never cheat on him." Similarly, defendants in *People v. Lenti*, [44 Misc.2d 118, 253 N.Y.S.2d 9 (1964)] displayed or harbored no evil or hostile disposition but were merely administering and inflicting a so-called initiation punishment as a requirement for induction of pledges (victims) into a fraternal organization. Nor did any other case that this court studied require malice or hostile or evil disposition, as it is not an element of the crime of criminal atrocious assault and battery.

....

NOTES

1. In the principal case, if Mrs. Brown had consented why did prosecution result? Does the rule which disregards "consent" in serious assault cases simply eliminate difficult evidentiary problems for the prosecution in trying to prove lack of consent especially in one-on-one situations? Or is the rule a statement of substantive law that consent is immaterial to the harm?

2. The principal case, *State v. Brown*, suggests that people in their "right minds" do not consent to violence against their person which could result in serious injury. Consider the following examples of "consent."

   1. Professional football and hockey players and boxers. Note, *Consent in Criminal Law: Violence in Sports*, 75 MICH. L. REV. 148 (1976-77).

2. Victims of rape who have accepted the advice "don't resist." The conflict between insights gained from empirical studies and the legal requirement of nonconsent is discussed in Chapter 4.

3. Persons who consent to be subjects in scientific experiments where there are known risks, or worse, where risks are unknown. B. GRAY, HUMAN SUBJECTS IN MEDICAL EXPERIMENTATION 1 n.1 (1975): J. Katz, Experimentation with Human Beings (1972).

4. Persons who have their fingers amputated to avoid military service or to collect insurance. Comment, *Mayhem-Consent of Maimed Party as a Defense*, 47 IOWA L. REV. 1122, 1130 nn.43-44 (1961-62).

5. Sadists who derive and supply pleasure by beating their masochistic partners. *People v. Samuels*, 250 Cal. App. 2d 501, 58 Cal. Rptr. 439 (1967), *cert. denied*, 390 U.S. 1024 (1968); 81 Harv. L. Rev. 1339 (1967-68); Leigh, *Sado-Masochism, Consent, and the Reform of the Criminal Law*, 39 MOD. L. REV. 130 (1976).

6. The laws of some states recognize that terminally ill patients may refuse treatment. Note, *The California Natural Death Act: An Empirical Study of Physicians' Practices*, 31 STAN. L. REV. 913 (1978-79); President's Comm'n for The Study of Ethical Problems in Medicine & Biomedical & Behavioral Research, *Deciding to Forego Life-Sustaining Treatment*, 43-60, 244-48 (1983). See *Cruzan v. Director, Missouri Department of Health*, 497 U.S. 261 (1990) *infra* p. 241.

COMMONWEALTH v. GREGORY

Superior Court of Pennsylvania
132 Pa. Super. 507, 1 A.2d 501 (1938)

John Lester Gregory was convicted of assault and battery and indecent assault and of practicing medicine and surgery without a license, and he appeals.

PARKER, Judge.

... Marie A. Harkins, a married woman 28 years of age at the time of trial, lived with her father, mother, and sister on Green Street in Philadelphia. One of her legs had been amputated and she was wearing an artificial leg. On July 13, 1936, the defendant secured a card from the Girard Artificial Limb Company and presented it to Mrs. Harkins' father at his residence where he introduced himself as Doctor Gregory and asked for Mrs. Harkins. At this point we quote from the testimony of Mrs. Harkins: "I told him he would have to wait. Dr. Gregory said that would be all right, he would wait. It was in our private dining room — I came downstairs and we were in our private dining room and I told him to come in — it was a taproom and I could not talk in the public part. Dr. Gregory came back and he sat down and asked was I satisfied with the limb, did it fit and how was I getting along. I said I was satisfied, then he asked me to remove my dress. First I hesitated and he said I didn't have to be ashamed, he was a doctor. Then when I took off the dress, he asked me would I lift my slip and walk up and down the room to see how it worked — to see how the knee worked, and I did. Then I was going to sit down and he asked me how the belt fitted me, that went around my waist. Then he pulled down my stepins about three inches, past the hip. Then when I put my hand over the front of me, he said I didn't need to be embarrassed, that he was a doctor. Then he asked me to remove the limb. He felt all around the stump of my leg and he said I was quite flabby but in time that would all disappear.

....

The appellant asks us to assume that this familiarity was all with the consent of Mrs. Harkins and to conclude that it was therefore not assault and battery or indecent assault. We are of the opinion that the evidence warranted a conclusion by the trial court that Dr. Gregory secured such consent as he did in fact obtain to study the mechanics and efficiency of the artificial limb by knowingly and fraudulently leading Mrs. Harkins to believe that he was a doctor of medicine and surgery....

Such being the facts which we must assume the court found, any consent claimed to have been given was obtained by the perpetration of a fraud, was vitiated by such fraud and is not a defense to the charge of assault and battery or indecent assault. The deceit practiced was a fraud on the will of Mrs. Harkins equivalent to force. *Com. v. Stratton*, 114 Mass. 303. The legal reasoning involved is the same as that followed in the consideration of larceny by trick....

The conclusion at which we have arrived is in harmony with that reached in other states. In the case of *Bartell v. State*, 106 Wis. 342, 345, 82 N.W. 142, the defendant under the pretense of giving a massage treatment to a young woman 18 years of age who was afflicted with a nervous ailment, caused her to expose her body to him and permit him to examine and touch her naked form. In addition he took some further undue liberties with her person. The court there sustained a conviction for indecent assault and in that connection said [page 143]: "The law relating to physical violations of the persons of females, accomplished by such a species of fraud or imposition as may be exercised by a person under the pretense of necessity or authority, where the violator, because of his position, has exceptional opportunities for thus imposing upon his victim, is too well known to need any discussion here." ...

The judgment in each appeal is affirmed.

NOTES

1. "At common law, it was generally held that a man who took improper liberties with the person of a female, without her consent, was guilty of assault.... The attempt need not be made violently, insolently, or in anger. Such assaults are not made in that way. Hence, to stand in proximity to a young girl in a state of indecent exposure with intent to ravish has been held to be an assault. *Hays v. People*, 1 Hill [N.Y.] 351. So, too, it was held to be an assault to give a girl figs containing 'love powders,' which she ate and which made her ill. And, again, it was held to be an assault to sit on the bed of a girl and lean over her with a proffer of sexual intercourse. When an assault is committed upon a child, it is immaterial whether there is submission or resistance thereto. Neither is it necessary that such a victim should be aware of the nature of the act or of the danger." Miller, J., in *Beausoliel v. United States*, 107 F.2d 292, 296-97 (D.C. Cir. 1939).

2. "A wife in confiding her person to her husband does not consent to cruel treatment, or to infection with a loathsome disease. A husband, therefore, knowing that he has such a disease, and concealing the fact from his wife, by accepting her consent, and communicating the infection to her, inflicts on her physical abuse, and injury, resulting in great bodily harm; and he becomes, notwithstanding his marital rights, guilty of an assault, and indeed a completed battery." *State v. Lankford*, 29 Del. 594, 596, 102 A. 63, 64 (1917). *Contra Queen v. Clarence*, 22 Q.B. 23 (C.C.R. 1888).

Chapter 4
SEXUAL OFFENSES*

EDITORIAL NOTE

During the past thirty years the law relating to sexual offenses, especially rape, has been significantly changed. Probably there is no other area of criminal law where the substantive changes have been made so quickly and extensively. This phenomenon, which represents a response to a major change in social attitudes is reflected in this chapter. Earlier, in Chapter 3, we saw how criminal law has expanded to include a wider range of harm. This dynamic of change, however, has also affected traditional crimes such as rape, murder, and theft. Changes in the law of rape and other sexual offenses mirror broader changes in the legal status of women including the abolition of numerous distinctions in the law which treated men and women differently.

This chapter also demonstrates the impact of social science research on the law. The law of crimes is premised on certain assumptions about human behavior. Most of these assumptions which underlie traditional as well as new crimes are not based on systematic empirical study. Rather, they are judgments which reflect religious, economic, and social values and are based on history, experience, and sometimes ignorance and prejudice. Scientific investigation has provided an opportunity to test these assumptions. Observe in this chapter how the findings of social science research have led to important changes in legislative definitions of sexual crimes and ancillary judge-made rules as well.

There are four sections in this chapter. The first deals with forcible rape ("aggravated sexual assault" in modern criminal codes) and some definitional problems. This is followed by a section on special requirements of proof in forcible rape cases — the old cautionary instruction, the use that can be made of prior acts of unchastity, and the corroboration requirement — and the trend towards the abrogation or limiting of these requirements. The third section involves "nonforcible" rape, and the final section focuses on recent statutory changes in the definition of rape and other sexual offenses.

SECTION I. Forcible Rape

EAST'S PLEAS OF THE CROWN 434 (1803)

Rape is the unlawful carnal knowledge of a woman by force and against her will....

---

*The crimes included in this chapter are discussed comprehensively in A.L.I. Model Penal Code and Commentaries, part II, art. 213, pp. 271-439 (Official Draft and Revised Comments 1980).

It is no mitigation of this offense that the woman at last yielded to the violence, if such her consent was forced by fear of death or by duress. *Id.* at 444.

... But the least penetration makes it rape ..., although there be no emissio seminis. *Id.* at 436.*

NOTES ON "UTMOST RESISTANCE"

1. "[W]hether carnal knowledge was forcible and against her will or with her consent, is ordinarily indicated by resistance or lack of it by the woman. While the degree of resistance required is also relative, ... the general rule is that a mentally competent woman must in good faith resist to the utmost with the most vehement exercise of every physical means or faculty naturally within her power to prevent carnal knowledge, and she must persist in such resistance as long as she has the power to do so until the offense is consummated." *Cascio v. State,* 147 Neb. 1075, 25 N.W.2d 897, 900 (1947).

2. "[T]he phrase 'by force and against her will' means either that her utmost resistance is overcome or prevented by physical violence or that her will to resist is overcome by threats of imminent physical violence likely to cause great bodily harm." "Resistance to the utmost" is relative and measured by a subjective test. It is erroneous to say "'that the measure of resistance required is absolute and fixed in all cases and must be so great that, when it fails to defeat the purpose of the ravisher, the failure is only by the narrowest possible margin.'" *State v. Muhammad,* 41 Wis. 2d 12, 162 N.W.2d 567, 570 (1968).

3. The victim, Mary, had known defendant for several months and had gone out with him several times. On the night in question she met him at a bar where they had a few drinks. Later at her apartment defendant said he wanted to stay all night. When she asked him to leave he grabbed her, hit her in the face, pressed his thumb into her eye and threatened to push her eyes through her head if she were not silent. He then had intercourse with her.

The claim of improbability is based mainly upon the fact that after defendant talked lewdly to her and attempted to get her to agree to intercourse, Mary made no attempt to run away or arouse the neighbors in the adjoining apartments, and that after he started to attack her she did not cry out. Her testimony clearly shows that until he actually seized her she did not realize that he would attack her. Before she realized what was occurring he seized her throat, threatened her and hit her repeatedly, and also thrust his finger in her eye and threatened to push her eyes out. While she could have screamed, it is evident that she was afraid to. There was nothing inherently improbable in her story. "Proof of her vehement exertion was not necessary to show her resistance. When attacked by a rapist it is primarily for the woman to decide to what extent she can with safety resist."

People v. Merrill, 104 Cal. App. 2d 257, 231 P.2d 573, 577 (1951).

4. "The defendant's contention is that the complaining witness did not resist to the utmost, and that one of her concerns was not to wake her children

---

*Can an impotent man be convicted of rape? The Arizona Court of Appeals stated that only minimal penetration was required, and therefore held that he could. *State v. Kidwell,* 27 Ariz. App. 466, 556 P.2d 20 (1976).

sleeping nearby. The complaining witness did testify that, 'I didn't want my children to get harmed,' and 'Well, if my children would have woke up, he may have done terrible damage.' 'Utmost resistance' in a particular case depends upon the facts and circumstances of that case. It is a relative term, to be measured by a subjective test. Here the mother's concern not to have her children involved, and possibly harmed, in the assault made upon her person is understandable. In no way does it suggest consent or acquiescence." *Madison v. State*, 61 Wis. 2d 333, 212 N.W.2d 150, 152 (1973).

5. Submission to a compelling force or genuine fear is not tantamount to consent, and threats to kill a third person, even when that person is not present, may be sufficient to overcome the victim's resistance. *Fitzpatrick v. State*, 93 Nev. 21, 558 P.2d 630 (1977).

6. The New York statute for first-degree rape and first-degree sodomy required proof of "forcible compulsion" which

> means physical force which is capable of overcoming earnest resistance; or a threat, express or implied, that places a person in fear of immediate death or serious physical injury to himself or another person, or in fear that he or another person will immediately be kidnapped. "Earnest resistance" means resistance of a type reasonably to be expected from a person who genuinely refuses to participate in sexual intercourse, deviate sexual intercourse or sexual contact, under all the attendant circumstances. Earnest resistance does not mean utmost resistance.

N.Y. PENAL LAW § 130.00(8) (McKinney 1981-82 Supp). That was replaced in 1982 by a new definition:

> Forcible compulsion means physical force or a threat, express or implied, which force or threat places a person in fear of immediate death or serious physical injury to himself, herself or another person, or in fear that he, she or another person will immediately be kidnapped.

L. 1982, ch. 560 § 1.

7. Some evidence of resistance by the female may be required in the absence of a showing of fraud in the factum, mental incapacity, or physical incapacity. "There is no clear rule as to how much resistance is required of a woman in order to prove her lack of consent.... The law does not put her life into even greater jeopardy than it is already in. When a woman is dealing with a man bent on rape, how can she know how much resistance she can give without provoking him into killing her? Continuous resistance to an attempted rape is not required." *State v. Glidden*, 165 Mont. 470, 529 P.2d 1384, 1386 (1974). Where, however, the defendant insists on having intercourse with the female and she has no reasonable grounds for believing that violence will be used against her if she does not submit, her submission without any threats or force being used by the defendant will not support a rape conviction. *Gonzales v. State*, 516 P.2d 592 (Wyo. 1973). However, "resistance is not necessary under circumstances where resistance would be futile and would endanger the life of the female, nor where she is overcome by superior strength or paralyzed by fear." Id. at 594.

8. "Thus, the issue was not whether in some abstract sense the victim's resistance was reasonable. The critical inquiry is whether the resistance was

sufficient to 'reasonably manifest' her refusal to [defendant]." *People v. Guthreau*, 102 Cal. App. 3d 436, 162 Cal. Rptr. 376, 378 (1980).

9. The concern reflected in these cases regarding the behavior of the victim, rather than the defendant, is found only in the laws pertaining to rape. In all other offenses, we focus on the behavior of the defendant. While it is true that the issue of consent necessarily requires us to examine the behavior of the victim as it bears on that matter, the issue of consent is not limited to rape cases and can arise in a variety of settings involving other offenses. In those other settings, however, we do not require a showing of "utmost resistance" on the part of a victim (for example, in a case of bank robbery). Is there significant probative value in a showing of the absence of "utmost resistance" in a rape case? If not, is there any justification for retaining the requirement of "utmost resistance" in rape cases?

RUSK v. STATE
Court of Special Appeals of Maryland
406 A.2d 624 (1979)

[The majority reversed a rape conviction* on the ground that the evidence was insufficient to convict. That decision in turn was reversed in *State v. Rusk*, 89 Md. 230, 424 A.2d 720 (1981). In reinstating the conviction the Court of Appeals referred with approval to Judge Wilner's dissenting opinion in the Court of Special Appeals at p. 629 which is set out below.]

WILNER, JUDGE, dissenting.

....

Md. Annot. Code art. 27, § 463(a) considers three types of conduct as constituting second degree rape. We are concerned only with the first: a person is guilty of rape in the second degree if he (1) engages in vaginal intercourse with another person, (2) by force or threat of force, (3) against the will, and (4) without the consent of the other person. There is no real question here as to the first, third, or fourth elements of the crime. The evidence was certainly sufficient to show that appellant had vaginal intercourse with the victim, and that such act was against her will and without her consent. The point at issue is whether it was accomplished by force or threat of force; and I think that in viewing the evidence, that point should remain ever clear. *Consent is not the issue here, only whether there was sufficient evidence of force or the threat of force.*

Unfortunately, courts, including in the present case a majority of this one, often tend to confuse these two elements — force and lack of consent — and to think of them as one. They are not. They mean, and require, different things. See *State v. Studham*, 572 P.2d 700 (Utah 1977). What seems to cause the confusion — what, indeed, has become a common denominator of both elements — is the notion that the victim must actively resist the attack upon her. If she fails to offer sufficient resistance (sufficient to the satisfaction of the judge), a court is entitled, or at least presumes the entitlement, to find that there was no force or threat of force, or that the act was not against her

---

*Defendant had been sentenced to imprisonment for 10 years — Eds. note.

I. FORCIBLE RAPE

will, or that she actually consented to it, or some unarticulated combination or synthesis of these elements that leads to the ultimate conclusion that the victim was not raped. Thus it is that the focus is almost entirely on the extent of resistance — *the victim's acts, rather than those of her assailant.* Attention is directed not to the wrongful stimulus, but to the victim's reactions to it. Right or wrong, that seems to be the current state of the Maryland law; and, notwithstanding its uniqueness in the criminal law, and its illogic, until changed by statute or the Court of Appeals, I accept it as binding.

But what is required of a woman being attacked or in danger of attack? How much resistance must she offer? Where is that line to be drawn between requiring that she either risk serious physical harm, perhaps death, on the one hand, or be termed a willing partner on the other? Some answers were given in *Hazel v. State*, 221 Md. 464, 157 A.2d 922 (1960), although, as in so many cases, they were stated in the context of both the requirement of force and the lack of consent. The Court said, at pp. 469, 470, 157 A.2d at p. 925:

> Force is an essential element of the crime and to justify a conviction, the evidence must warrant a conclusion either that the victim resisted and her resistance was overcome by force or that she was prevented from resisting by threats to her safety. But no particular amount of force, either actual or constructive, is required to constitute rape. Necessarily that fact must depend upon the prevailing circumstances. As in this case force may exist without violence. *If the acts and threats of the defendant were reasonably calculated to create in the mind of the victim — having regard to the circumstances in which she was placed — a real apprehension, due to fear, of imminent bodily harm, serious enough to impair or overcome her will to resist, then such acts and threats are the equivalent of force....*
>
> With respect to the presence or absence of the element of consent, it is true, of course, that however reluctantly given, consent to the act at any time prior to penetration deprives the subsequent intercourse of its criminal character. *There is, however, a wide difference between consent and a submission to the act. Consent may involve submission, but submission does not necessarily imply consent.* Furthermore, *submission to a compelling force, or as a result of being put in fear, is not consent....*
>
> The authorities are by no means in accord as to what degree of resistance is necessary to establish the absence of consent. However, the generally accepted doctrine seems to be that a female — who was conscious and possessed of her natural, mental and physical powers when the attack took place — must have resisted to the extent of her ability at the time, unless it appears that she was overcome by numbers or was so terrified by threats as to overpower her will to resist.... Since resistance is necessarily relative, the presence or absence of it must depend on the facts and circumstances in each case.... *But the real test, which must be recognized in all cases, is whether the assault was committed without the consent and against the will of the prosecuting witness.*

The kind of fear which would render resistance by a woman unnecessary to support a conviction of rape includes, but is not necessarily limited to, a fear of death or serious bodily harm, or a fear so extreme as to preclude resistance, or a fear which would well nigh render her mind incapable of continuing to resist, or a fear that so overpowers her that she does not dare resist. (Citations omitted.) (Emphasis supplied.)

From these pronouncements in *Hazel*, this Court has articulated what the majority refers to as a "rule of reason" — i.e., that "where the victim's story could not be corroborated by wounds, bruises or disordered clothing, the lack of consent could be shown by fear based upon reasonable apprehension." *Winegan v. State,* 10 Md.App. 196, 200, 268 A.2d 585, 588 (1970); *Goldberg v. State,* 41 Md.App. 58, 395 A.2d 1213 (1979). As so phrased, I do not consider this to be a rule of reason at all; it is highly unreasonable, and again mixes the element of consent with that of force. But what I do accept is what the Court of Appeals said in *Hazel*: (1) if the acts and threats of the defendant were reasonably calculated to create in the mind of the victim — having regard to the circumstances in which she was placed — a real apprehension, due to fear, of imminent bodily harm, serious enough to impair or overcome her will to resist, then such acts and threats are the equivalent of force; (2) submission is not the equivalent of consent; and (3) the real test is whether the assault was committed without the consent and against the will of the prosecuting witness.[1]

Upon this basis, the evidence against appellant must be considered. Judge Thompson [in the majority opinion] recounts most, but not quite all, of the victim's story. The victim — I'll call her Pat — attended a high school reunion. She had arranged to meet her girlfriend Terry there. The reunion was over at 9:00, and Terry asked Pat to accompany her to Fell's Point.[2] Pat had gone to Fell's Point with Terry on a few prior occasions, explaining in court: "I've never met anybody [there] I've gone out with. I met people in general, talking in conversation, most of the time people that Terry knew, not that I have gone down there, and met people as dates." She agreed to go, but first called her mother, who was babysitting with Pat's two-year old son, to tell her that she was going with Terry to Fell's Point, and that she would not be home until late. It was just after 9:00 when Pat and Terry, in their separate cars, left for Fell's Point, alone.[3]

They went to a place called Helen's and had one drink. They stayed an hour or so and then walked down to another place (where they had another drink), stayed about a half hour there, and went to a third place. Up to this point, Pat conversed only with Terry, and did not strike up any other acquaintanceships. Pat and Terry were standing against a wall when appellant came over and said hello to Terry, who was conversing with someone else at the time. Appellant then began to talk with Pat. They were both separated, they both had

---

[1] Other courts have stated the rule this way: A rape victim is not required to do more than her age, strength, surrounding facts and all attending circumstances make it reasonable for her to do to manifest her opposition. *See Dinkens v. State,* 92 Nev. 74, 546 P.2d 228 (1976); *State v. Studham,* 572 P.2d 700 (Utah 1977). *See also Schrum v. Com.,* 219 Va. 168, 246 S.E.2d 893 (1978).

[2] Fell's Point is an old section of Baltimore City adjacent to the harbor. It has been extensively renovated as part of urban renewal and, among refurbished homes and shops, hosts a number of cafes and discotheques. It is part of the City's night scene.

[3] Pat said that Terry and she lived at opposite ends of town and that Fell's Point was sort of midway between their respective homes.

I. FORCIBLE RAPE   199

young children; and they spoke about those things. Pat said that she had been ready to leave when appellant came on the scene, and that she only talked with him for five or ten minutes. It was then about midnight. Pat had to get up with her baby in the morning and did not want to stay out late.

Terry wasn't ready to leave. As Pat was preparing to go, appellant asked if she would drop him off on her way home.[4] She agreed because she thought he was a friend of Terry's. She told him, however, as they walked to her car, "I'm just giving a ride home, you know, as a friend, not anything to be, you know, thought of other than a ride." He agreed to that condition.

Pat was completely unfamiliar with appellant's neighborhood. She had no idea where she was. When she pulled up to where appellant said he lived, she put the car in park, but left the engine running. She said to appellant, "Well, here, you know, you are home." Appellant then asked Pat to come up with him and she refused. He persisted in his request, as did she in her refusal. She told him that even if she wanted to come up, she dared not do so. She was separated and it might cause marital problems for her. Finally, he reached over, turned off the ignition, took her keys, got out of the car, came around to her side, opened the door, and said to her, "Now, will you come up?"

It was at this point that Pat followed appellant to his apartment, and it is at this point that the majority of this Court begins to substitute its judgment for that of the trial court and jury. We know nothing about Pat and appellant. We don't know how big they are, what they look like, what their life experiences have been. We don't know if appellant is larger or smaller than she, stronger or weaker. We don't know what the inflection was in his voice as he dangled her car keys in front of her. We can't tell whether this was in a jocular vein or a truly threatening one. We have no idea what his mannerisms were. The trial judge and the jury could discern some of these things, of course, because they could observe the two people in court and could listen to what they said and how they said it. But all we know is that, between midnight and 1:00 a.m., in a neighborhood that was strange to Pat, appellant took her car keys, demanded that she accompany him, and most assuredly implied that unless she did so, at the very least, she might be stranded.

Now, let us interrupt the tale for a minute and consider the situation. Pat did not honk the horn; she did not scream; she did not try to run away. Why, she was asked. "I was scared. I didn't think at the time what to do." Later, on cross-examination: "At that point, because I was scared, because he had my car keys. I didn't know what to do. I was someplace I didn't even know where I was. It was in the city. I didn't know whether to run. I really didn't think, at that point, what to do. Now, I know that I should have blown the horn. I should have run. There were a million things I could have done. I was scared, at that point, and I didn't do any of them." What, counsel asked, was she afraid of? "Him," she replied. What was she scared that he was going to do? "Rape me, but I didn't say that. It was the way he looked at me, and said, 'Come on up, come on up;' and when he took the keys, I knew that was wrong. I just didn't say, are you going to rape me."

---

[4] Her testimony about this, on cross-examination, was: "I said I was leaving. I said, excuse me. It's nice meeting you; but I'm getting ready to leave; and he said, 'which way are you going;' and I told him; at that time, he said, 'Would you mind giving me a lift?'"

So Pat accompanied appellant to his apartment. As Judge Thompson points out, appellant left her in his apartment for a few minutes.[5] Although there was evidence of a telephone in the room, Pat said that, at the time, she didn't notice one. When appellant returned, he turned off the light and sat on the bed. Pat was in a chair. She testified: "I asked him if I could leave, that I wanted to go home, and I didn't want to come up. I said, "Now, I came up. Can I go?"" Appellant, who, of course still had her keys, said that he wanted her to stay. He told her to get on the bed with him, and, in fact, took her arms and pulled her on to the bed. He then started to undress her; he removed her blouse and bra and unzipped her pants. At his direction, she removed his clothes. She then said:

> I was still begging him to please let, you know, let me leave. I said, "you can get a lot of other girls down there, for what you want," and he just kept saying, "no;" and then I was really scared, because I can't describe, you know, what was said. It was more the look in his eyes; and I said, at that point — I didn't know what to say; and I said, "If I do what you want, will you let me go without killing me?" Because I didn't know, at that point, what he was going to do; and I started to cry; and when I did, he put his hands on my throat, and started lightly to choke me; and I said, "If I do what you want, will you let me go?" And he said, yes, and at that time, I proceeded to do what he wanted me to.

He "made me perform oral sex, and then sexual intercourse." Following that:

> I asked him if I could leave now, and he said, "Yes;" and I got up and got dressed; and he got up and got dressed; and he walked me to my car, and asked if he could see me again; and I said, "Yes;" and he asked me for my telephone number; and I said, "No, I'll see you down Fell's Point sometime," just so I could leave.[6]

At this point, appellant returned her car keys and escorted her to her car. She then drove off:

> I stopped at a gas station, that I believe was Amoco or Exon (sic), and went to the ladies' room. From there I drove home. I don't know — I don't know if I rode around for a while or not; but I know I went home, pretty much straight home and pulled up and parked the car.
> I was just going to go home, and not say anything.
> Q. Why?
> A. Because I didn't want to go through what I'm going through now.
> Q. What, in fact did you do then?
> A. I sat in the car, thinking about it a while, and I thought I wondered what would happen if I hadn't of done what he wanted me to do. So I thought the right thing to do was to go report it, and I went from there to Hillendale to find a police car. (Emphasis supplied.)

---

[5] On direct examination, she twice said that he left the room "for a minute" after telling her to sit down. On cross-examination, she said she couldn't remember how long he was gone, but, at counsel's suggestion, said that it was not longer than five minutes.

[6] Pat explained this last comment further: "I didn't know what else to say. I had no intention of meeting him again."

How does the majority Opinion view these events? It starts by noting that Pat was a 21-year old mother who was separated from her husband but not yet divorced, as though that had some significance. To me, it has none, except perhaps (when coupled with the further characterization that Pat and Terry had gone "bar hopping") to indicate an underlying suspicion, for which there is absolutely no support in the record, that Pat was somehow "on the make." Even more alarming, and unwarranted, however, is the majority's analysis of Pat's initial reflections on whether to report what had happened. Ignoring completely her statement that she "didn't want to go through what I'm going through now," the majority, in footnote 1, cavalierly and without any foundation whatever, says:

> If, in quiet contemplation after the act, she had to wonder what would have happened, her submission on the side of prudence seems hardly justified. Indeed, if she had to wonder afterward, how can a fact finder reasonably conclude that she was justifiably in fear sufficient to overcome her will to resist, at the time. (Emphasis in the original.)

It is this type of reasoning — if indeed "reasoning" is the right word for it — that is particularly distressing. The concern expressed by Pat, made even more real by the majority Opinion of this Court, is one that is common among rape victims, and largely accounts for the fact that most incidents of forcible rape go unreported by the victim. See F.B.I. Uniform Crime Reports (1978), p. 14; Report of Task Force on Rape Control, Baltimore County (1975); The Treatment of Rape Victims in the Metropolitan Washington Area, Metropolitan Washington Council of Governments (1976), p. 4. See also Rape and Its Victims: A Report for Citizens, Health Facilities, and Criminal Justice Agencies, LEAA (1975). If appellant had desired, and Pat had given, her wallet instead of her body, there would be no question about appellant's guilt of robbery. Taking the car keys under those circumstances would certainly have supplied the requisite threat of force or violence and negated the element of consent. No one would seriously contend that because she failed to raise a hue and cry she had consented to the theft of her money. Why then is such life-threatening action necessary when it is her personal dignity that is being stolen?

....

I close with this comment taken from 13 Western Australian Law Rev. at 75 (1977), written half a world away, but precisely for this case:

> ....
>
> If the purpose of the law is to protect women from acts of sexual intercourse to which they have not in fact consented, whether by reason of force actually applied, physical or other threat, or fear induced by accused or by others, then the relevant question would appear to be: Did this particular woman, in these particular circumstances, submit to this particular man; or did she in fact freely consent to have intercourse with him? If, on the contrary, the law requires a woman to react in a particular way, that is, by fighting back against her attacker and sustaining a certain degree of damage inflicted by the accused in order to signify the lack

of consent, and if the law deems the woman to have consented to the act despite ample evidence of threats which rendered her submissive but nonconsenting, then the law cannot be said to be serving its true function of protecting individuals from the imposition of nonconsensual sexual intercourse.

....

NOTE

The dissenting opinion in the principal case, *Rusk v. State,* relied heavily on findings from various studies and reports on the subject of rape. These findings include the fact that "[b]etween 1973 and 1977, forcible rape has increased 19%.... Physical force is absent in over half of reported cases.... The most common type of resistance offered by victims is verbal.... [R]ape victims who resisted were more likely to be injured than ones who did not. [Data omitted].... "These results indicate one popular danger of the notion (and some statutory requirements) that a victim of an attack should resist to the utmost.'" *Id.* at 633-34.

Law enforcement agencies throughout the country warn women not to resist an attack haphazardly, not to antagonize a potential attacker, but to protect themselves from more serious injury. The United States Department of Justice, for example, has published a pamphlet warning, among other things.

If you are confronted by a rapist, stay calm and maximize your chances for escape. Think through what you will do. You should not immediately try to fight back. Chances are, your attacker has the advantage. Try to stay calm and take stock of the situation. Id. at 635.

Be on the safe side, LEAA, U.S. Department of Justice. The pamphlet also advises: "Be selective about new acquaintances; don't invite a forcible sexual encounter." See also Let Prevention Be Your Guide, a pamphlet published by the (Baltimore City) Mayor's Coordinating Counsel on Criminal Justice; Rape Prevention, a pamphlet distributed by the Prince George's County Police Department. That pamphlet specifically warns:

Extensive research into thousands of rape cases indicates that attempts at selfdefense, such as screaming, kicking, scratching and use of tear gas devices and other weapons, usually have provoked the rapist into inflicting severe bodily harm on the victim. Since it is unlikely you will be able to overcome the rapist by force, you must think about what he will do after you try and fail. Before you do anything, remember ... IF WHATEVER YOU DO DOES NOT HELP YOU, MAKE SURE THAT IT WILL NOT HARM YOU.

Id. at 635, n. 15.

NOTES ON *MENS REA*

1. What is the *mens rea* for the crime of rape? This issue is presented when a defendant claims that either by mistake or intoxication he thought the victim had consented. According to one view: "'Rape is not a crime which requires a specific intent.' This is in accord with the great weight of authority which holds the crime of rape requires no intent other than that indicated by the commission of the acts constituting the offense." *United States v. Thornton,* 498 F.2d 749 (D.C. Cir. 1974). Cf. *People v. Mayberry,* 15 Cal. 3d 143, 542 P.2d 1337, 125 Cal. Rptr. 745 (1975). But, does this response answer the question? What is the act required and the accompanying intent — intent to have sexual intercourse or intent to have nonconsensual sexual intercourse?

In *D.P.P. v. Morgan,* [1975] 2 All E.R. 347, the House of Lords held: "The crime of rape consisted in having sexual intercourse with a woman with intent to do so without her consent or with indifference as to whether or not she consented. It could not be committed if that essential *mens rea* were absent. Accordingly, if an accused in fact believed that the woman had consented, whether or not that belief was based on reasonable grounds, he could not be found guilty of rape."

Consider Parliament's response to the decision in *D.P.P. v. Morgan*: "(2) It is hereby declared that if at a trial for a rape offence the jury has to consider whether a man believed that a woman was consenting to sexual intercourse, the presence or absence of reasonable grounds for such a belief is a matter to which the jury is to have regard, in conjunction with any other relevant matters, in considering whether he so believed." Sexual Offenses (Amendment) Act 1976, c. 82.

The "subjective" approach used in Morgan has not been applied as a general proposition in other situations, such as self-defense. Cowley, The Retreat from *Morgan,* [1982] CRIM. L. REV. 198.

2. The issue of intent arose in an unusual manner in *State v. Talbert,* 416 So. 2d 97 (La. 1982). At defendant's trial for rape he claimed that on a prior occasion he paid the prosecutrix to have sexual intercourse with him and although she took the money she refused to perform the act. He claimed that on the occasion of the alleged rape he forcibly entered her apartment and demanded that she return the money or do what she had promised. The state, over defendant's objection, introduced evidence that defendant had forcibly raped the prosecutrix on a previous occasion and that there could have been no doubt as to her lack of consent. Although the evidence of a defendant's prior acts of misconduct are ordinarily inadmissible as being unfairly prejudicial, the admission of evidence in this case was sustained as falling within the "intent" exception:

> With respect to intent, it was the defendant who put the question of intent at issue by contending that he only intended to, and did, pay Ms. James to have intercourse with him.
>
> ... Normally if the act is proved, there can be no real question as to intent. However, under the facts of this particular case there is a real issue of the defendant's intent to have intercourse without the victim's consent. Defendant's argument that intent is not an issue because he admits to having intercourse with the victim is incorrect. The issue is intent to perform the act without the victim's consent. Evidence of the prior incident is admissible to prove that intent.

Id. at 100.

3. "If, as a result of self-induced intoxication, appellant believed that the victim was consenting, that belief would not thereby become either 'reasonable' or 'in good faith' ... This rule is entirely consistent with the Supreme Court holding in *People v. Mayberry, supra,* where the diminished capacity defense by virtue of intoxication arose in the context of a charge of assault with intent to commit rape. The latter charge embraces a specific intent crime not present in the prosecution of forcible rape." *People v. Guthreau,* 102 Cal. App. 3d 436, 162 Cal. Rptr. 376, 379 (1980).

NOTES ON PARTIES

1. Rape was and in many states still is defined as an offense committed by a *man* against a *woman not his wife*. Under the so-called "marital exemption," as the Supreme Court of New Mexico explained it in a 1977 case, "a wife is irrebuttably presumed to consent to sexual relations with her husband, even if forcible and without consent," and "[a] husband is legally incapable of raping his wife." *State v. Bell,* 90 N.M. 134, 560 P.2d 925, 931 (1977). The situation is changing, however; many jurisdictions have now abandoned or significantly modified the "marital exemption":

> New Jersey, by statute, has expressly repudiated the so-called "marriage exemption." The earlier statutes had never incorporated the express language "of a female not his wife." The Supreme Court of New Jersey doubted the validity of the view that a husband could under no circumstances be convicted of raping his wife. Notwithstanding there had never been a New Jersey case which said that such a conviction could be had, the Court read the old statute as permitting a conviction of a husband of raping his estranged wife. The court said that the interpretation of the statute did not violate due process.

State v. Smith, 85 N.J. 193, 426 A.2d 38 (1981). Texas has abandoned the "marital exemption" in cases of aggravated sexual assault, but has maintained a remnant of it in cases of non-aggravated sexual assault, through a provision that requires a showing of bodily injury or threat of bodily injury to the victim in a prosecution against a spouse for non-aggravated sexual assault. Tex. Penal Code Ann. § 22.011(g) (West 1991). Does the "marital exemption" which exempts men from prosecution for sexual acts committed against their wives unconstitutionally discriminate against married women by denying them the protections given to all other women? The court in *People v. Brown,* 632 P.2d 1025 (Colo. 1981), held that it did not because of the "legitimate state interest in encouraging the preservation of family relationships" and because it "averts difficult emotional issues and problems of proof inherent in this sensitive area." *Id.* at 1027.

2. "It is now a well-settled rule of law that rape is a felony, and that all persons who are present, aiding, abetting, and assisting a man to commit the offense, whether men or women, are principals, and may be indicted as such.... It is immaterial that the aider and abettor is disqualified from being the principal actor by reason of age, sex, condition, or class." *State v. Flaherty,* 128 Me. 141, 146 A. 7, 9 (1929).

3. A woman may be tried as a principal and convicted of rape. In *People v. Hernandez,* 18 Cal. App. 3d 651, 96 Cal. Rptr. 71 (1971), defendant forced her unwilling husband at rifle-point to have intercourse with an 18-year old girl. The court held that either under a theory of coercion or aiding and abetting that the woman would be guilty of rape. See also Colo. Rev. Stat. § 40-2-25(1)(k) (1964), providing that a female is guilty of rape in the third degree if she solicits intercourse with a male under 18 years of age who was of good moral character prior to the offense. The statute is discussed in *People v. Green,* 183 Colo. 25, 514 P.2d 769 (1973).

4. In *State v. Martin,* 17 N.C. App. 317, 194 S.E.2d 60 (1973), defendant husband held his wife and threatened her, forcing her to have intercourse with the co-defendant. Both convictions of rape were affirmed, the court stating that "[a] husband who counsels, aids, or abets, assists or forces another to have sexual intercourse with his wife, or forces her to submit to sexual intercourse with another, is guilty of rape." 194 S.E.2d at 61. A husband may be convicted as a principal in the rape of his wife even if the perpetrator is later acquitted in a separate trial. *Rozell v. State,* 502 S.W.2d 16 (Tex. Crim. App. 1973).

Aiding another to commit a crime is discussed in Chapter 10 *infra*.

SECTION II. Proof

A. THE CAUTIONARY INSTRUCTION

> It is true, says Lord Hale, rape is a most detestable crime ... but it must be remembered that it is an accusation easily to be made, and hard to be proved; and harder to be defended by the party accused, though ever so innocent.... And these rules have been laid down as some guides to the discovery of the truth; for instance, if the witness be of good fame; if she presently discovered the offence, and made pursuit after the offender; if she shewed circumstances and signs of the injury ... these and the like are concurring circumstances which give greater probability to her evidence. On the other hand, if she be of evil fame and stand unsupported by other evidence; if she concealed the injury for any considerable period of time after she had opportunity to complain; ... these and the like circumstances afford a strong, though not conclusive presumption that her testimony is feigned.

East's Pleas of The Crown 445-46 (1803).

PEOPLE v. RINCON-PINEDA
Supreme Court of California, In Banc
14 Cal. 3d 864, 538 P.2d 247, 123 Cal. Rptr. 119 (1975)

Wright, Chief Justice.

[Defendant was charged with a brutal rape and tried twice. At the first trial which ended in a hung jury the court read to the jury the mandatory cautionary instructions as follows:]

> A charge such as that made against the defendant in this case is one which is easily made and, once made, difficult to defend against, even if the person accused is innocent.

Therefore, the law requires that you examine the testimony of the female person named in the information with caution.

...

[At the second trial] the court refused over defense objection to give the cautionary instruction, CALJIC No. 10.22. The court acknowledged that the instruction was mandatory in sex cases, but noted that its compulsory use had not been authoritatively reexamined for decades.

...

Even if the mandatory instruction here in issue did square with Hale's* analysis, the changes in criminal procedure wrought in the intervening 300 years would suffice of themselves to sap the instruction of contemporary validity. It has been suggested that Hale's concern over fabricated rape prosecutions was a product of the accused's incompetence to testify in his own defense. But the accused's incompetency was one of form only; he was allowed, and indeed was expected to address the jury in an unsworn statement responsive to the evidence against him....

There are other, more dramatic differences in the position of the criminally accused in the United States today from one so accused in 17th century England. The fundamental precepts of due process, that an accused is presumed innocent and is to be acquitted unless proven guilty beyond a reasonable doubt, were recognized as desiderata in Hale's era but had yet to crystallize into rights. The rights of an accused to present witnesses in his defense and to compel their attendance, subsequently enshrined in the Sixth Amendment, were barely nascent in the 17th century. Most importantly of all, in the context of a rape case, one accused of a felony in Hale's day had no right whatsoever to the assistance of counsel, while today he is constitutionally entitled to such assistance regardless of his personal means.

...

We next examine whether such a charge is so difficult to defend against as to warrant a mandatory cautionary instruction in the light of available empirical data. (See generally Note, The Rape Corroboration Requirement: Repeal Not Reform (1972) 81 Yale L.J. 1365, 1378-1384.) Of the FBI's four "violent crime" offenses of murder, forcible rape, robbery, and aggravated assault, forcible rape has the highest rate of acquittal or dismissal. (FBI, Uniform Crime Reports 1973 (1974) table 18, p. 116; see also, id., at p. 35) [same result as to adult suspects only].[3] Equally striking is the ranking of forcible rape at the bottom of the FBI's list of major crimes according to percentage of successful prosecutions for the offense charged.

...

---

*See above.

[3] These figures represent the dispositions of only those cases in which a suspect was actually formally charged. Thus they do not reflect an additional barrier to prosecution of a rape charge: the victim's convincing the police that the legal elements of the crime have occurred. "As a national average, 15 percent of all forcible rapes reported to police were determined by investigation to be unfounded. In other words, the police established that no forcible rape offense or attempt occurred. This is caused primarily due to the question of the use or threat of force frequently complicated by a prior relationship between victim and offender." (FBI, Uniform Crime Reports 1973 (1974) p. 15.)

A. THE CAUTIONARY INSTRUCTION

These findings are consistent with the leading study of jury behavior, which found that "the jury chooses to redefine the crime of rape in terms of its notions of assumption of risk," such that juries will frequently acquit a rapist or convict him of a lesser offense, notwithstanding clear evidence of guilt. (Kalven & Zeisel, The American Jury (1966) p. 254.)

....

The low rate of conviction of those accused of rape and other sexual offenses does not appear to be attributable to a high incidence of unwarranted accusations. Rape in particular has been shown by repeated studies to be grossly under-reported. (See, e.g., FBI Uniform Crime Reports 1973, *supra*, at p. 15; LeGrand, *Rape and Rape Laws: Sexism in Society and Law* (1973) 61 Cal. L. Rev. 919, 921; Note, supra, 81 Yale L.J. at pp. 1374-1375; Amir, Patterns in Forcible Rape (1971) pp. 27-28.) The initial emotional trauma of submitting to official investigatory processes, the fear of subsequent humiliation through attendant publicity and embarrassment at trial through defense tactics which are often demeaning, and a disinclination to encounter the discretion of the police in deciding whether to pursue charges of rape, especially with regard to what may appear to the police to be "victim-precipitated" rapes, are among the powerful yet common disincentives to the reporting of rape. (See *ante,* pp. 9-11; Medea & Thompson, Against Rape (1974) pp. 111-121; Astor, The Charge is Rape (1974) pp. 169-188; Note, *The Victim in a Forcible Rape Case: A Feminist View* (1973) 11 Am. Crim. L. Rev. 335, 348-351; Amir, *supra,* at p. 29; MacDonald, Psychiatry and the Criminal (2d ed. 1969) p. 238; Amir, Victim Precipitated Forcible Rape (1967) 58 J. Crim. L. C. & P.S. 493.) Those victims with the pluck to disregard such disincentives discover the utter fallaciousness of the conventional wisdom that rape is a charge easily made. A large number of reports of rape are deemed "unfounded" by the police and are pursued no further: the percentage has been set variously at 15 percent (see *ante,* fn. 3), 20 percent (see Comment, *Police Discretion and the Judgment That A Crime Has Been Committed — Rape in Philadelphia* (1968) 117 U.Pa.L.Rev. 277, 281), 25 percent (MacDonald, *supra,* at p. 239), and 29 percent (Amir, *supra,* at p. 29).

....

Since it does not in fact appear that the accused perpetrators of sex offenses in general and rape in particular are subject to capricious conviction by inflamed tribunals of justice, we conclude that the requirement of a cautionary instruction in all such cases is a rule without a reason.

....

Whatever might have been its historical significance, the disapproved instruction now performs no just function, since criminal charges involving sexual conduct are no more easily made or harder to defend against than many other classes of charges, and those who make such accusations should be deemed no more suspect in credibility than any other class of complainants.

....

The judgment is affirmed.

B. PRIOR ACTS OF UNCHASTITY

NOTES

1. "[A]re we to be told that previous prostitution shall not make one among those circumstances which raise a doubt of assent? That the triers should be advised to make no distinction in their minds between the virgin and a tenant of the stew? between one who would prefer death to pollution, and another who, incited by lust and lucre, daily offers her person to the indiscriminate embraces of the other sex? And how is the latter case to be made out? How more directly and satisfactorily than by an examination of the prosecutrix herself?

"... And will you not more readily infer assent in the practiced [sic] Messalina, in loose attire, than in the reserved and virtuous Lucretia?

....

"... Shall I be answered that an isolated instance of criminal connection does not make a common prostitute? I answer; yes; it only makes a prostitute, and I admit introduces a circumstance into the case of less moment; but the question is not whether it be of more or less persuasive force, it is one of competency; in other words, whether it be of any force at all.

"...[N]o court can overrule the law of human nature, which declares that one who has already started on the road of prostitution, would be less reluctant to pursue her way, than another who yet remains at her home of innocence and looks upon such a career with horror." *People v. Abbot,* 19 Wendell's Rep. 192, 195-96 (N.Y. 1838).

2. "Almost every jurisdiction permits the substantive use of evidence concerning the unchastity of a prosecutrix where the defense of consent is raised in a forcible rape prosecution. A majority of states limit the scope of this character evidence to a showing of the general reputation of the complaining witness for unchastity, while a minority in addition allow the presentation to extend to specific prior acts of unchastity. The leading case in Arizona is *State v. Wood,* 59 Ariz. 48, 122 P.2d 416 (1942), where we adopted the existing rule in California which admitted both types of evidence on the theory that it "best conforms to logic and the common experience of mankind'."

The court later quoted extensively from *People v. Rincon-Pineda, supra,* and relying on the empirical data cited therein it concluded that "[t]he 'logic' and 'common experience of mankind' upon which we rested our holding in *State v. Wood, supra,* now clearly dictate that the case be overturned. It is no longer satisfactory to argue that we should "more readily infer assent in the practiced [sic] Messalina, in loose attire than in the reserved and virtuous Lucretia.'" *State ex rel. Pope v. Superior Court,* 113 Ariz. 22, 545 P.2d 946, 950, 952 (1976).

3. Not only was the victim subject to cross-examination on acts of prior unchastity but it was the practice for the court to instruct the jury on the importance of such testimony as shown in the following example.

> Evidence was received for the purpose of showing that the female person named in the information was a woman of unchaste character.

A woman of unchaste character can be the victim of a forcible rape but it may be inferred that a woman who has previously consented to sexual intercourse would be more likely to consent again.

Such evidence may be considered by you only for such hearing as it may have on the question of whether or not she gave her consent to the alleged sexual act and in judging her credibility.

People v. Rincon-Pineda, 14 Cal. 3d at 951-52. Cal. Jury Instrs., Crim. No. 10.06 (3d 1970), now superseded by CALIFORNIA EVIDENCE CODE §§ 782 and 1103, which restrict the admission of evidence concerning the victim's unchastity.

STATE v. GREEN
Supreme Court of West Virginia
260 S.E.2d 257 (1979)

[Green appealed from a conviction of second-degree sexual assault. Among other matters he attacked the constitutionality of the "rape shield" law.]

....

III

Is that portion of our sexual assault law which limits defendants from presenting evidence of a victim's previous sexual conduct, constitutional? W. Va. Code, 61-8B-12 provides:

....

>   (b) In any prosecution under this article evidence of specific instances of the victim's sexual conduct with persons other than the defendant, opinion evidence of the victim's sexual conduct and reputation evidence of the victim's sexual conduct shall not be admissible: Provided, that such evidence shall be admissible solely for the purpose of impeaching credibility, if the victim first makes his previous sexual conduct an issue in the trial by introducing evidence with respect thereto.

Green argues that this law violates his right to confront witnesses by restricting cross-examination of his accusers;[3] that the statute is overbroad; and that the alternative to its unconstitutionality should be a case-by-case evaluation of such evidence a defendant seeks to introduce.

The argument that the trial court's interpretation of the law was unconstitutionally overbroad because Green was prevented from examining the victim about other sexual acts with him and his co-defendant has no merit. A rape victim's previous sexual conduct with other persons has very little probative value about her consent to intercourse with a particular person at a particular time. That portion of the law which prohibits such evidence is constitutional.

As to whether he was prevented from examining Ms. McClung about prior sexual relations between them, the record does not support any claim by him

---

[3]The Sixth Amendment to the United States Constitution provides:

In all criminal prosecutions, the accused shall enjoy the right ... to be confronted with the witnesses against him. The same right is in W. Va. Const., art. 3, § 14.

that there was such a relationship.... There is no evidence that Green wanted to introduce evidence of prior sexual relations between himself and Ms. McClung.

Most rape shield statutes that have been judicially examined provide for balancing Sixth Amendment claims against a victim's privacy rights. The common vehicle to decide this balancing is an in camera hearing by the trial court. A typical statute containing this device was upheld in *People v. McKenna,* Colo., 585 P.2d 275, 279 (1978):

> The statute provides specific means by which a defendant may make a formal offer of proof, and a full in camera hearing may be held prior to trial to determine the relevance, if any, of the evidence. If the court finds that the victim's sexual history is relevant and material in the particular case, then the defendant may introduce the evidence at trial. On the other hand, if the court determines in camera that the proffered evidence is irrelevant, the prosecutrix is spared the ordeal of public cross-examination regarding the subject.

The Colorado court thus seems to recognize an in camera screening mechanism to be essential to avoid Sixth Amendment-privacy complaints.

....

Cases upholding statutes such as ours that do not provide for balancing, but simply flatly prohibit the evidence are *People v. Blackburn,* 56 Cal.App.3d 685, 128 Cal. Rptr. 864 (1976), and *Smith v. Commonwealth,* Ky.App., 566 S.W.2d 181 (1978). In Blackburn, a California Court of Appeal decided that a "shield law" similar to ours did not "deny to the defendant the due process rights of a fair trial or confrontation of witnesses against him." See also, *State v. Jalo,* 27 Or.App. 845, 557 P.2d 1359 (1976).

....

We agree with the Supreme Court of Arizona in *State ex rel. Pope v. Superior Court,* 113 Ariz. 22, 28, 545 P.2d 946, 952 (1976), that "[t]he fact that a woman consented to sexual intercourse on one occasion is not substantial evidence that she consented on another ...." We do not agree that her sexual history with other men is never relevant and never admissible. A woman's reputation for unchastity has no probative value because it is neither relevant to her credibility as a witness nor does it prove she consented in any particular instance. But there may be unusual cases where the probative value is precisely demonstrated, and outweighs the prejudicial effect of the testimony, such as "[where] ... the defendant alleges the prosecutrix actually consented to an act of prostitution ...." [Id., 545 P.2d at 953]. A statutory prohibition so broad that it forecloses cross-examination even in instances such as that in Pope, denies a defendant his right to effectively confront his accuser.[10]

---

[10] For further analysis of the issue, see: Rudstein, Rape Shield Laws: Some Constitutional Problems, 18 Wm. & Mary L. Rev. 1 (1976) and Note, Criminal Procedure — Right of Cross-Examination — Sexual Assault Statute, 79 W. Va. L. Rev. 293 (1977).

Also see: Berger, Man's Trial, Woman's Tribulation: Rape Cases in the Courtroom, 77 Colum. L. Rev. 1, 52-69 (1977), which argues that when a defendant says the victim consented, based on a pattern of prior specific sexual conduct with third parties, or where she acted in such a way as to mislead him into believing she consented, the evidence should be admitted.

B. PRIOR ACTS OF UNCHASTITY

We therefore recommend to our legislature that provision be made for in camera trial court determination whereby a judge may decide whether evidence of a victim's past sexual behavior is clearly relevant and material to an accused's "consent" defense.

Reversed on other grounds.

NEELY, JUSTICE, dissenting:

This society's rising consciousness of unjust discrimination against women has brought a rash of enthusiasm for reform. Among the most egregious and intensely felt wrongs is the social tradition which has denied the legitimacy of sexuality in women with the infamous attendant "double standard" for men and women. This Court unanimously concurred in the opinion in *J.B. v. A.B.*, W. Va., 242 S.E.2d 248 (1978) which forbade depriving women of their children for sexual escapades which would be tolerated in men. There are occasions, therefore, when it is possible to eradicate the old law's discrimination; however, there are other occasions, such as our Legislature's attempt at a rape shield law, when alleged reform is mere obeisance to popular enthusiasm — a product of sophisticated lynch-mob mentality. To take liberty for a moment with Cato, McCarthyism in defense of trendy values is still a vice. Lynching in a popular cause is no less lynching.

The confrontation clause of W. Va. Const., art. III, § 14 and its counterpart in the Sixth Amendment to the Constitution of the United States, provides that one may confront his accusers about all issues relevant to his guilt. This constitutional right is absolute and cannot be limited by statute. A prohibition against the introduction of a woman's past sexual conduct where such evidence is relevant is no more legitimate than a prohibition against introduction of alibi evidence in prosecutions for armed robbery.

As stated earlier, there is no question that the policy in this statute is a legitimate one. The protection of the prosecutrix from unnecessary inquiry into her private life and the concomitant encouragement of rape reporting is laudable. However, with cross-examination so severely limited by this statute and with no corroboration requirement, the defendant may be left with no avenue of defense. In weighing the increased reports of rape against the possibility of an unjust conviction it must not be forgotten "that traditionally the penalty for rape has been a severe one; that unlike other crimes carrying severe penalties, there have been no delineated degrees of rape; and that factual circumstances of rape, more than those of any other crime, readily lend themselves to strong and different interpretations depending upon one's station or experiences in life, including age, sex, race and environment." *Arnold v. United States*, 358 A.2d 335, 349 (D.C. App. 1976) (Mack, J., concurring in part and dissenting in part). In this regard it is worth noting that nationwide, 89% of the 455 men executed for rape between 1930 and 1969 were black men and nearly all of the complainants were white. See Note, The Rape Corroboration Requirement: Repeal Not Reform, 81 Yale L.J. 1365, 1380 n. 103 (1972).

....

A trial court in the exercise of its sound discretion can always exclude evidence which is both irrelevant and scandalous; however, on a showing of the least relevance in chambers, and this does not imply a balancing test as suggested in the majority opinion, it would be unconstitutional to deny inquiry into a prosecutrix's past sexual history where such history is likely to lead to the reasonable inference on the part of the jury that the prosecutrix is lying — or more accurately stated — is likely to produce such question concerning her credibility as to raise a reasonable doubt about the defendant's guilt.

While it is true that a prostitute can be raped, it is a denial of human experience to assert that a woman of loose sexual standards is as unlikely to be a party to a fraudulent charge as a woman who is highly circumspect about her sexual activities.

NOTES

1. To which activities, if any, and for what purpose, if any should evidence of the complainant's prior sexual activities be admissible?

    a. Prior sexual activities with the defendant?
    b. To refute physical or scientific evidence such as loss of virginity, the origin of semen, disease, or pregnancy?
    c. In conjunction with an effort to show that the complaining witness had made unsubstantiated charges of rape in the past?
    d. To show acts of prostitution?

State ex rel. Pope v. Superior Court, 113 Ariz. 22, 545 P.2d 946, 953 (1976).

2. When, if ever, should the defendant be able to introduce evidence as to the complainant's reputation for unchastity? Where the prosecutor has offered testimony as to her chastity? Where she is reputed to be a prostitute? *State ex rel. Pope v. Superior Court, supra.*

3. When evidence of prior sexual acts or reputation for unchastity is admitted in evidence, is it for the purpose of "disproving" lack of consent or to impeach the credibility of the complainant or both? Does it make any difference for which purpose the evidence was admitted?

4. Rule 412, Texas Rules of Criminal Evidence, is a typical example of a "rape shield" law:

> Rule 412. Evidence of Previous Sexual Conduct.
>
> (a) In a prosecution for sexual assault or aggravated sexual assault, or attempt to commit sexual assault or aggravated sexual assault, reputation or opinion evidence of the past sexual behavior of an alleged victim of such crime is not admissible.
>
> (b) In a prosecution for sexual assault or aggravated sexual assault, or attempt to commit sexual assault or aggravated sexual assault, evidence of specific instances of an alleged victim's past behavior is also not admissible, unless: (1) such evidence is admitted in accordance with paragraphs (c) and (d) of this rule; (2) it is evidence (A) that is necessary to rebut or explain scientific or medical evidence offered by the state; (B) of past sexual behavior with the accused and is offered by the accused upon the

issue of whether the alleged victim consented to the sexual behavior which is the basis of the offense charged; (C) that relates to the motive or bias of the alleged victim; (D) [that] is admissible under Rule 609 [impeachment by evidence of conviction of crime]; or (E) that is constitutionally required to be admitted; and (3) its probative value outweighs the danger of unfair prejudice.

(c) If the defendant proposes to introduce any documentary evidence or to ask any question, either by direct examination or cross-examination of any witness, concerning specific instances of the alleged victim's past sexual behavior, the defendant must inform the court out of the hearing of the jury prior to introducing any such evidence or asking any such question. After this notice, the court shall conduct an in camera hearing, recorded by the court reporter, to determine whether the proposed evidence is admissible under paragraph (b) of this rule. The court shall determine what evidence is admissible and shall accordingly limit the questioning. The defendant shall not go outside these limits nor refer to any evidence ruled inadmissible in camera without prior approval of the court without the presence of the jury.

(d) The court shall seal the record of the in camera hearing required in paragraph (c) of this rule for delivery to the appellate court in the event of an appeal.

....

TEX. R. CRIM. EVID. 412.

5. In *Olden v. Kentucky*, 488 U.S. 227 (1988), a case involving kidnapping and sexual assault, it was held that an accused's right of confrontation under the Sixth Amendment had been violated by the trial court's ruling prohibiting the accused from cross examining the alleged victim regarding her cohabitation with a third party at the time of the trial. The Supreme Court acknowledged the broad discretion of a trial judge to preclude unduly harassing interrogation of witnesses, but said that the exposure of a witness' motivation in testifying is an important function of the constitutionally protected right of cross examination. Interestingly, the Kentucky Court of Appeals had specifically held in *Olden* that Kentucky's rape shield law did not bar the accused's desired cross examination, and even acknowledged that the evidence in question was relevant to the accused's theory of the case. But the Kentucky Court of Appeals concluded that the evidence should have been excluded because its probative value was outweighed by its possibility for prejudice to the victim-witness. In reversing, the Supreme Court observed that the limitation imposed by the trial court for the purpose of protecting the victim-witness was beyond reason in this instance, under the particular circumstances of the case.

C. CORROBORATION

UNITED STATES v. WILEY

United States Court of Appeals
492 F.2d 547 (D.C. Cir. 1973)

[Defendant's conviction of carnal knowledge of a twelve-year-old girl was reversed, one judge dissenting, because of a lack of corroborating evidence on the question of sexual intercourse. The victim described the event in detail and without inconsistency or contradiction. Two police officers to whom she complained shortly after the event described her as crying and upset, clothing disheveled, and having no coat although it was very cold. The coat was found at the scene of the alleged rape.]

BAZELON, CHIEF JUDGE (concurring):

The requirement of corroboration in sex offenses, particularly rape, has come under sharp attack in recent years.[1] Feminists have found the requirement unjust to women and prosecutors have argued that it makes convictions too difficult to obtain.[3] These criticisms force us to examine the origins of the current views on corroboration.*

....

II

Numerous justifications have been advanced for the requirement of corroboration in sex cases. An examination of these rationales reveals a tangled web of legitimate concerns, out-dated beliefs, and deep-seated prejudices.

The most common basis advanced for the requirement is that false charges of rape are more prevalent than false charges of other crimes. A statement such as this is extremely difficult to prove, and little or no evidence has been adduced to support it.[12] Two reasons are generally given for the belief that unfounded rape charges are common. It is argued, first, that women often

---

[1] See, e.g., Report of the District of Columbia Public Safety Committee Task Force on Rape, at 51-55 (July 9, 1973) [hereinafter Task Force Report]; Note, The Rape Corroboration Requirement: Repeal Not Reform, 81 Yale L.J. 1365 (1972) [hereinafter Repeal Not Reform].

[3] See, e.g., Ludwig, The Case for Repeal of the Sex Corroboration Requirement in New York, 36 Brooklyn L.R. 378 (1970) [hereinafter Ludwig].
Criticism was particularly severe of the pre-1972 New York law which required corroboration of each material element of the offense. This criticism led to modification of the New York requirement. Repeal Not Reform at 1365, 1368.

*Judge Bazelon then observed that the common law did not require corroboration for sex offenses or any other offense except perjury. Also thirty-five states had rejected the corroboration requirement for rape — Eds. note.

[12] The report of the District of Columbia Public Safety Committee Task Force, see note 1, supra, contends that:

> That allegation, by now transformed into an accepted "truth," even judicial doctrine, that women often fantasize or fabricate false charges of rape, has been reported over and over without citing any supporting evidence....
>
> In all offenses, including rape, some false and mistaken accusations will be made. For example it is not uncommon for a person to complain that a friend pointed a gun or waved a knife at him — an assault with a dangerous weapon. It may well be that no weapon is found and the complainant has a motive to lie, but there is no corroboration requirement.

have a motive to fabricate rape accusations and second, that women may fantasize rapes.[13]

It is contended that a woman may fabricate a rape accusation because, having consented to intercourse she is ashamed and bitter, or because she is pregnant and feels pressured to create a false explanation, or because she hates the man she accuses or wishes to blackmail him. It is said to be relatively easy to create a false description of rape in convincing detail.

There are, however, countervailing reasons not to report a rape. One said to be a victim of rape may be stigmatized by society, there may be humiliating publicity, and the necessity of facing the insinuations of defense counsel may be a deterrent. Moreover, those claiming to have been raped may be treated harshly by the police and by hospitals. One result of all of these obstacles is that rape is one of the most under-reported of all crimes.[18]

It is difficult to say whether those inclined to falsify a charge of rape are deterred by the same factors that deter the reporting of actual rapes. A falsifier, for example, may be a seeker of publicity rather than one who shuns it.

In addition to fabricated rapes, it has been suggested that women may report fantasized rapes.[19] Both the causes and prevalence of rape fantasies have been hotly disputed and it is not established that any significant number of rape charges arise out of fantasies. To the extent that rape charges do so arise, that could be the result of an inferior and oppressed status of women that is now being eroded.

With both fabricated and fantasized rapes it appears well-established that what dangers do exist are greatest when the complainant is young. Care must be taken, however, not to blindly look at chronological age when the background and experience of a complainant may make her more or less likely to be prone to the suggestiveness that at times makes the young unreliable witnesses.

In addition to the problem of false charges, the corroboration requirement is justified on the theory that rape is a charge unusually difficult to defend against....

Again, there is little hard evidence with which to test this theory. What studies are available suggest that a defendant is unlikely to be convicted of

---

[13] See, e.g., Coltrane v. United States, 135 U.S.App.D.C. 295, 298-299, 418 F.2d 1131, 1134-1135 (1969) ("We know from the lessons of the past that all too frequently such complainants have an urge to fantacize or even a motive to fabricate ...").

[18] President's Commission on Law Enforcement and the Administration of Justice: The Challenge of Crime in a Free Society 21 (1967); Federal Bureau of Investigation, Uniform Crime Reports 1970 14 (1971). The President's Commission found that forcible rapes occurred at 3 and one-half times the reported rate.

[19] See, e.g., 3A Wigmore § 924(a), at 736-746; Wedmore v. State, 237 Ind. 212, 227-239, 143 N.E.2d 649, 656-662 (1957) (Emmert, J., dissenting). The Wedmore opinion quotes the following statement of Dr. Karl A. Menninger:

> ... fantasies of being raped are exceedingly common in women, indeed one may almost say that they are probably universal. By this I mean that most women, if we may judge from our clinical experience, entertain more or less consciously at one time or another fleeting fantasies or fears that they are being or will be attacked by a man. Of course, the normal woman who has such a fantasy does not confuse it with reality, but it is so easy for some neurotic individuals to translate their fantasies into actual beliefs and memory falsifications that I think a safeguard should certainly be placed upon this type of criminal charge. Wedmore, supra at 658.

rape on the uncorroborated testimony of the complainant in those jurisdictions that do not require corroboration.[26] Thus juries may be more skeptical of rape accusations than is often supposed.

Another justification for the corroboration requirement is the prevalence of severe penalties for rape. For many years rape was punishable by death in many states.[27] Today rape is still among the most severely punished of crimes.[28] One result has been the development of rules such as the corroboration requirement. Proposals that the corroboration requirement be abandoned are at times coupled with proposals that the penalties for rape be reduced. Reformers are subject to certain tensions on this issue. On the one hand, they seek to bring standards of proof and punishment for rape in line with those for other crimes of violence. Thus it is argued that "As long as rape is viewed primarily as a sexual crime rather than as a crime of violence and power, society will continue to react to rape as it has in the past. The goal ... is to normalize the crime of rape."[30] On the other hand, reformers note that rape is an unusually traumatic experience. Special procedures are suggested for rape victims.[31] We are told that "rape is considerably more than mere physical assault. It is a psychic violation also, a serious injury against the victim's emotions and spirit that may cause mental torment difficult or impossible to be eased." In light of this there may well be resistance to lowering the penalties.

Still another basis for the corroboration requirement lies in "the sorry history of racism in America." There has been an enormous danger of injustice when a black man accused of raping a white woman is tried before a white jury.[34] Of the 455 men executed for rape since 1930, 405 (89 percent) were black.[35] In the vast majority of these cases the complainant was white.[36]

All of the safeguards that developed in this context should not be automatically applied today. Juries are more integrated than in the past and racial prejudice may be at a somewhat lower level. Numerous rape victims are black and their interests, as well as those of white women, may have been slighted by the concern for black defendants.

A final theory of the corroboration requirement is that it stems from discrimination against women. It is said that traditional sex stereotypes have resulted in rape laws that protect men rather than women. Penalties are high because a "good" woman is a valued possession of a man. Corroboration is required because to a "good" woman rape is "a fate worse than death" and she should fight to the death to resist it. If no such fight is put up, the woman

---

[26] Repeal Not Reform at 1382-1389.
 The conclusion here is based on an analysis of the Kalven and Zeisel empirical study of criminal juries. H. Kalven and H. Zeisel, The American Jury (1966).
[27] Task Force Report at 6.
[28] Id.
[30] Id. at 35.
[31] Id. at 14.
[34] Repeal Not Reform at 1380.
[35] Id. at note 103.
[36] See Ronald Goldfarb, Rape and Law Reform, The Washington Post, August 2, 1973, p. A24, col. 2. Goldfarb reports the estimate that, although capital punishment is available for crimes other than rape, the single category of rapes of whites by blacks accounts for most sentences to capital punishment in the United States.

must have consented or at least enticed the rapist, who is therefore blameless. In sum it is said to be the "male desire to 'protect' his 'possession' which results in laws designed to protect the male — both the 'owner' and the assailant — rather than protecting the physical well-being and freedom of movement of women."

This point of view, which has been expressed by men as well as women,[39] may well have some validity. It would be surprising if entrenched notions of sexuality did not play a role in the law of crimes dealing with sexual violations. Corroboration rules may be structured, for example, to protect male rather than female defendants. This could explain the fact that conviction for soliciting for homosexual purposes requires corroboration while soliciting for heterosexual prostitution does not.[40]

Ultimately modern notions of sexual equality may help break down those aspects of rape law which stem from unjust discrimination against women.

NOTES

1. As the principal case, *United States v. Wiley*, illustrates, the requirement of corroboration in rape prosecutions traditionally stemmed from popular beliefs on the subject, many of which appear unfounded today, e.g., false charges of rape are much more prevalent than those of other crimes; many reported rapes are actually fabricated or fantasized; charges of rape are unusually difficult to defend against; the penalties for rape are unusually severe. As a result of the reorganization of the courts in the District of Columbia the corroboration requirement was reexamined, this time by the District of Columbia Court of Appeals, in *Arnold v. United States*, 358 A.2d 335 (D.C. 1976). The position of the majority in *United States v. Wiley* was rejected, and the corroboration requirement was abandoned "insofar as mature females are concerned." Id. at 344. The court relied heavily on the analysis and data used in *People v. Rincon-Pineda, supra* pp. 205-207. Judge Mack dissented from the abrogation of the corroboration rule:

> I, too, believe that rape *should* be treated as any other crime of violence. The stark reality is, however, that in our society, it has not been so treated. Rape is thought to be one of the most underreported crimes due primarily to fear and embarrassment but also due to the severity of the sentence. As long as there remains an inordinately severe penalty for rape — as long as there remains racial hostility — I feel as did Chief Judge Bazelon (concurring in *United States v. Wiley*, 160 U.S.App.D.C. 281, 289-90, 492 F.2d 547, 555-56 (1973)), that the liberally applied corroborative rule of this jurisdiction is the best protection against attitudinal judgments which operate in derogation of the protection of the innocent — whether that innocent be a victimized female or a falsely accused

---

[39] *See, e.g.*, Younger at 276, note 105 ("When all is said and done, it just might be that the requirement of corroboration in prosecutions for sex offenses (where, remember, the complainant is usually female and the defendant almost always male) is nothing more than an illustration of the law's unequal treatment of women.")

[40] *Cf.* Kelly v. United States, 90 U.S. App. D.C. 125, 194 F.2d 150 (1952) and Price v. United States, 135 A.2d 854 (D.C. Ct. App. 1957).

male. I would retain the rule in future rape cases and reverse for failure to give the required instruction.

Id. at 352. The court has continued to require corroboration where the victim is a minor. *Hall v. United States,* 400 A.2d 1063 (D.C. 1979).

2. Other cases which have abandoned the corroboration requirement also have relied heavily on empirical data and have used an analysis very similar to that used in *People v. Rincon-Pineda, supra. State v. Byers,* 102 Idaho 159, 627 P.2d 788 (1981); *State v. Cabral,* 410 A.2d 438 (R.I. 1980).

3. Texas has virtually abandoned the corroboration requirement for cases of sexual assault and aggravated sexual assault by a statute which provides that a conviction is supportable on the uncorroborated testimony of the victim if the victim informed any person, other than the defendant, of the offense within six months after the date on which the offense is alleged to have occurred, and the requirement that the victim inform another person of the alleged offense does not apply if the victim was younger than 14 years of age at the time of the alleged offense. TEX. CODE CRIM. PROC. ANN. art. 38.07.

SECTION III. "Nonforcible" Rape

A. LACK OF CAPACITY

NOTES

1. Despite some definitions such as the one given by East *supra* p. 193, "rape" at common law is more accurately defined as "the carnal knowledge of any woman above the age of ten years against her will and of a woman-child under the age of ten years with or against her will." 1 Hale's, PLEAS OF THE CROWN 627 (1st Am. ed. 1847).

2. "Force" and its corollary "resistance" are relevant as evidence of consent or lack thereof when the victim has the capacity to give consent or withhold it. Generally, when a woman lacks the mental capacity to consent she is deemed legally incapable of consenting. Sexual intercourse with her by a man not her husband is rape.

3. "The later decisions have established the rule in England that unlawful and forcible connection with a woman in a state of unconsciousness at the time, whether that state has been produced by the act of the prisoner or not, is presumed to be without her consent, and is rape.

".... If it were otherwise, any woman in a state of utter stupefaction, whether caused by drunkenness, sudden disease, the blow of a third person, or drugs which she had been persuaded to take, even by the defendant himself, would be unprotected from personal dishonor. The law is not open to such a reproach." *Commonwealth v. Burke,* 105 Mass. 376, 7 Am. Rep. 531, 534-35 (1870).

4. "There can be no question but that a copulation with a woman known to be mentally incapable of giving even an imperfect consent is rape. BISHOP'S CRIM. LAW, § 1123; *Reg. v. Ryan,* 2 Cox C.C. 115; *Reg. v. Fletcher,* Bell C.C. 63; *Reg. v. Barratt,* Law Rep. 2 C.C. 81, 12 Cox C.C. 498; *McQuirk v. State,* 84 Ala. 435, 4 So. 775, 5 Am. St. Rep. 381; *State v. Tarr,* 28 Iowa 397. But a noncompos whose infirmity is less profound may consent. BISHOP'S CRIM. LAW, *supra; Reg. v. Pressy,* 10 Cox C.C. 635. The mere fact that a woman is weak-minded does not disable or debar her from consenting to the act. It has been said that a woman with a less degree of intelligence than is requisite to make a contract may consent to carnal connection, so that the act will not be rape in the man. *McQuirk v. State, supra.* We adopt the measure of capacity to consent used by the respondent in his motion for a verdict, and hold that there can be no conviction of rape under the circumstances of this case unless the woman was incapable of understanding the act, its motive and possible consequences." *State v. Jewett,* 109 Vt. 73, 76-77, 192 A. 7, 8 (1937).

5. Is it necessary to prove that defendant either rendered the victim unconscious or that he knew of her lack of capacity or will recklessness suffice? That knowledge of the mental incompetence is required in first degree rape is held and discussed in *State v. Helderle,* 186 S.W. 696 (Mo. 1916). See also MODEL PENAL CODE §§ 213.1(1)(b)(c), 213.1(2)(b)(c), Appendix A *infra.*

B. FRAUD

NOTE

If during the course of a medical "examination" or "treatment" defendant has intercourse with his patient the case may turn on whether the patient knew the defendant was having intercourse with her. If she believed that a surgical operation was taking place and that penetration was effected with the hand or an instrument she has not consented to an act of intercourse and defendant is guilty of rape. Pomeroy v. State, 94 Ind. 96, 48 Am. Rep. 146 (1883), citing *Queen v. Flattery,* 2 L.R., Q.B.D. 410, 21 Eng. Rep. 188 (1877). Where the patient knows that the defendant is having sexual relations with her there must be some other element in the facts to satisfy the requirement of "force." Thus, when the defendant told the patient that if she did not have intercourse he would have to perform an operation on her from which she would probably die the fear and apprehension he created could satisfy the requirement that the sexual intercourse was "by force." *Don Moran v. People,* 25 Mich. 356, 12 Am. Rep. 283 (1872).

Modern statutes punish the procurement of sexual intercourse by means of fraudulent representations or under false pretenses as a lesser crime, e.g., CAL. PENAL CODE § 266 (maximum five years imprisonment). However, rape may be defined as including intercourse procured by wilful impersonation of a husband. CAL. PENAL CODE § 261(5); *State v. Navarro,* 90 Ariz. 185, 367 P.2d 227 (1961).

Fraud in the factum does vitiate "consent," since the victim did not consent to the act performed. *State v. Ely,* 114 Wash. 185, 194 P. 988 (1921); *State v. Atkins,* 292 S.W. 422 (Mo. 1926). The early cases divided on whether one who fraudulently pretends to be the husband of the female and obtains "consent" for an act of intercourse is guilty of rape. The early English cases held that such fraud did not vitiate the consent, since the woman had consented to an act of intercourse, and was merely mistaken in a collateral matter (the identity of the male). *Regina v. Barrow,* 11 Cox C.C. 191 (1868). However, such consent was also viewed as vitiated by a fraud in the factum, in that the woman had consented to a legal act of intercourse with her husband, and not to an illegal act of adultery. *Regina v. Dee,* 15 Cox C.C. 579 (1884). Such frauds are now included in statutes in several states, *e.g.,* CAL. PENAL CODE § 261 (1971); 21 OKLA. STAT. ANN. § 1111 (1951).

C. STATUTORY RAPE

STATE v. DUNCAN
Supreme Court of Montana
82 Mont. 170, 266 P. 400 (1928)

MATTHEWS, J. Jesse Duncan, a man 25 years of age, was convicted of the crime of rape, alleged to have been committed on July 15, 1927, upon one Anna Williamson, a girl of 17. The jury fixed the punishment at not less than 2 nor more than 4 years' imprisonment.

....

Under the law as declared by subdivision 1 of section 11000, Revised Codes 1921, any man who accomplishes an act of sexual intercourse with a female under the age of 18 years, when such female is not his wife, is guilty of the crime of rape. Under this provision, the consent of the female, the lack of knowledge of her age, or even her misrepresentation as to her age, and the lack of chastity of the female, and even the fact that she was at the time an inmate of prostitution, are all immaterial matters; a conviction depends solely upon proof of intercourse, and nonage, and if a man indulge in promiscuity with strange women he has only himself to blame if it later develops that he has unwittingly committed the crime of rape. Such is the law as declared by the lawmaking body of this state, and the province of the courts is to enforce the law as they find it.

....

[Affirmed.]

PEOPLE v. HERNANDEZ
Supreme Court of California
61 Cal. 2d 529, 393 P.2d 673, 39 Cal. Rptr. 361 (1964)

PEEK, JUSTICE. By information defendant was charged with statutory rape. (Pen. Code, § 261, subd. 1.) Following his plea of not guilty he was convicted as charged by the court sitting without a jury and the offense determined to be a misdemeanor.

Section 261 of the Penal Code provides in part as follows: "Rape is an act of sexual intercourse, accomplished with a female not the wife of the perpetrator, under either of the following circumstances: 1. Where the female is under the age of 18 years; ...."

The sole contention raised on appeal is that the trial court erred in refusing to permit defendant to present evidence going to his guilt for the purpose of showing that he had in good faith a reasonable belief that the prosecutrix was 18 years or more of age.

The undisputed facts show that the defendant and the prosecuting witness were not married and had been companions for several months prior to January 3, 1961 — the date of the commission of the alleged offense. Upon that

C. STATUTORY RAPE

date the prosecutrix was 17 years and 9 months of age and voluntarily engaged in an act of sexual intercourse with defendant.

In support of his contention defendant relies upon Penal Code, § 20, which provides that "there must exist a union, or joint operation of act and intent, or criminal negligence" to constitute the commission of a crime. He further relies upon section 26 of that code which provides that one is not capable of committing a crime who commits an act under an ignorance or mistake of fact which disapproves [sic] any criminal intent.

Thus the sole issue relates to the question of intent and knowledge entertained by the defendant at the time of the commission of the crime charged.

....

The assumption that age alone will bring an understanding of the sexual act to a young woman is of doubtful validity. Both learning from the cultural group to which she is a member and her actual sexual experiences will determine her level of comprehension. The sexually experienced 15-year old may be far more acutely aware of the implications of sexual intercourse than her sheltered cousin who is beyond the age of consent. A girl who belongs to a group whose members indulge in sexual intercourse at an early age is likely to rapidly acquire an insight into the rewards and penalties of sexual indulgence. Nevertheless, even in circumstances where a girl's actual comprehension contradicts the law's presumption, the male is deemed criminally responsible for the act, although himself young and naive and responding to advances which may have been made to him.[1]

The law as presently constituted does not concern itself with the relative culpability of the male and female participants in the prohibited sexual act. Even where the young woman is knowledgeable it does not impose sanctions upon her. The knowledgeable young man, on the other hand, is penalized and there are none who would claim that under any construction of the law this should be otherwise. However, the issue raised by the rejected offer of proof in the instant case goes to the culpability of the young man who acts *without* knowledge that an essential factual element exists and has, on the other hand, a positive, reasonable belief that it does not exist.

The primordial concept of *mens rea*, the guilty mind, expresses the principle that it is not conduct alone but conduct accompanied by certain specific mental states which concerns, or should concern the law.... England has now, by statute, departed from the strict rule, and excludes as a crime an act of sexual intercourse with a female between the ages of 13 and 16 years if the perpetrator is under the age of 24 years, has not previously been charged with a like offense, and believes the female "to be of the age of sixteen or over and has

---

[1] The inequitable consequences to which we may be led are graphically illustrated by the following excerpt from *State v. Snow* (Mo. 1923) 252 S.W. 629 at page 632: "We have in this case a condition and not a theory. This wretched girl was young in years but old in sin and shame. A number of callow youths, of otherwise blameless lives ... fell under her seductive influence. They flocked about her, ... like moths about the flame of a lighted candle and probably with the same result. The girl was a common prostitute.... The boys were immature and doubtless more sinned against than sinning. They did not defile the girl. She was a mere 'cistern for foul toads to knot and gender in.' Why should the boys, misled by her, be sacrificed? What sound public policy can be subserved by branding them as felons? Might it not be wise to ingraft an exception in the statute?"

reasonable cause for the belief." (Halsbury's Statutes of England, 2d Ed., Vol. 36, Continuation Volume 1956, at page 219.)[2]

... There can be no dispute that a criminal intent exists when the perpetrator proceeds with utter disregard of, or in the lack of grounds for, a belief that the female has reached the age of consent. But if he participates in a mutual act of sexual intercourse, believing his partner to be beyond the age of consent, with reasonable grounds for such belief, where is his criminal intent? In such circumstances he has not consciously taken any risk. Instead he has subjectively eliminated the risk by satisfying himself on reasonable evidence that the crime cannot be committed. If it occurs that he has been misled, we cannot realistically conclude that for such reason alone the intent with which he undertook the act suddenly becomes more heinous.

. . . .

We have recently given recognition to the legislative declarations in sections 20 and 26 of the Penal Code, and departed from prior decisional law which had failed to accord full effect to those sections as applied to charges of bigamy. (*People v. Vogel, supra,* 46 Cal. 2d 798, 299 P.2d 850.) We held there that a good faith belief that a former wife had obtained a divorce was a valid defense to charge of bigamy arising out of a second marriage when the first marriage had not in fact been terminated. Pertinent to the instant contention that defendant's intent did not suddenly become more criminal because it later developed that he had been misled by the prosecutrix, are the following comments appearing in *Vogel* at page 804 of 46 Cal. 2d, at page 854 of 299 P.2d: "Nor would it be reasonable to hold that a person is guilty of bigamy who remarries in good faith in reliance on a judgment of divorce or annulment that is subsequently found not to be the 'judgment of a competent Court' .... Since it is often difficult for laymen to know when a judgment is not that of a competent court, we cannot reasonably expect them always to have such knowledge and make them criminals if their bona fide belief proves to be erroneous." Certainly it cannot be a greater wrong to entertain a bona fide but erroneous belief that a valid consent to an act of sexual intercourse has been obtained.

Equally applicable to the instant case are the following remarks, also appearing at page 804 of 46 Cal. 2d, at page 855 of 299 P.2d of the Vogel decision: "The severe penalty imposed for bigamy, the serious loss of reputation conviction entails, ... and the fact that it has been regarded for centuries as a crime involving moral turpitude, make it extremely unlikely that the Legislature meant to include the morally innocent to make sure the guilty did not escape."

---

[2] The American Law Institute in its Model Penal Code (1962) provides in part as follows at pages 149 and 150:

Section 213.6. Provisions Generally Applicable (Article 213 [Sexual Offenses].)

(1) *Mistake as to Age.* Whenever in this Article the criminality of conduct depends upon a child's being below the age of 10, it is no defense that the actor did not know the child's age, or reasonably believed the child to be older than 10. When criminality depends upon the child's being below a critical age other than 10, it is a defense for the actor to prove that he reasonably believed the child to be above the critical age.

We are persuaded that the reluctance to accord to a charge of statutory rape the defense of a lack of criminal intent has no greater justification than in the case of other statutory crimes, where the Legislature has made identical provision with respect to intent. "'At common law an honest and reasonable belief in the existence of circumstances, which, if true, would make the act for which the person is indicted an innocent act, has always been held to be a good defense.... So far as I am aware it has never been suggested that these exceptions do not equally apply to the case of statutory offenses unless they are excluded expressly or by necessary implication.'" (*Matter of Application of Ahart,* 172 Cal. 762, 764-765, 159 P. 160, 161-162, quoting from *Regina v. Tolson,* [1889] 23 Q.B.D. 168, s.c., 40 Alb. L.J. 250.) Our departure from the views expressed in *Ratz* is in no manner indicative of a withdrawal from the sound policy that it is in the public interest to protect the sexually naive female from exploitation. No responsible person would hesitate to condemn as untenable a claimed good faith belief in the age of consent of an "infant" female whose obviously tender years preclude the existence of reasonable grounds for that belief. However, the prosecutrix in the instant case was but three months short of 18 years of age and there is nothing in the record to indicate that the purposes of the law as stated in *Ratz* can be better served by foreclosing the defense of a lack of intent. This is not to say that the granting of consent by even a sexually sophisticated girl known to be less than the statutory age is a defense.[4] We hold only that in the absence of a legislative direction otherwise, a charge of statutory rape is defensible wherein a criminal intent is lacking.

For the foregoing reasons *People v. Ratz, supra,* 115 Cal. 132, 46 P. 915, and *People v. Griffin, supra,* 117 Cal. 583, 49 P. 711 are overruled, and *People v. Sheffield,* 9 Cal. App. 130, 98 P. 67 is disapproved to the extent that such decisions are inconsistent with the views expressed herein. [Reversed.]

NOTES

1. Most courts which have considered the *Hernandez* rule have rejected it and retained the common law approach that mistake as to age is no defense. *Vasquez v. State,* 622 S.W.2d 864, 866 (Tex. Crim. App. 1981); *State v. Randolph,* 12 Wash. App. 138, 528 P.2d 1008 (1974) and numerous cases cited therein. Alaska, however, has followed Hernandez. *State v. Guest,* 583 P.2d 836 (Alaska 1978). Refusal by courts to allow mistake as a defense in statutory rape cases does not preclude a legislature from adopting such a rule. As one court observed: "The crime has been defined by the Legislature in terms which negate any element of criminal intent on the part of the actor. It is for that body, not the courts, to change the law if it chooses to subscribe to a more

---

[4]See an article on forcible and statutory rape in 62 Yale Law Journal (1952) which concludes at page 82 as follows:

> The crime of statutory rape is unsupportable in its present form. Neither the policies underlying the law nor public sentiment warrants the imposition of rape penalties solely because of the girl's youth. By making the presumption of the underage girl's incapacity rebuttal, [rebuttable] the law would continue to protect the "naive." But although legally underage, the girl who is past puberty and sexually sophisticated would be capable of granting operative consent to sexual intercourse.

liberal pattern of sex behavior among young females." *State v. Moore,* 105 N.J. Super. 567, 253 A.2d 579, 581 (1969).

Some state legislatures have modified the strict common law rule. *E.g.,* WASH. REV. CODE § 9A.44.030(2) (1979) which provides:

> In any prosecution ... in which the offense or degree of the offense depends on the victim's age, it is no defense that the perpetrator did not know the victim's age, or that the perpetrator believed the victim to be older, as the case may be: Provided, That it is a defense which the defendant must prove by a preponderance of the evidence that at the time of the offense the defendant reasonably believed the alleged victim to be older based upon declarations as to age by the alleged victim.

"Mistake of fact" is considered more fully in Chapter 9, Ignorance and Mistake, *infra.*

2. Statutes which make sexual acts with a person under a specified age an offense regardless of consent, in effect, have created an irrebuttable presumption that such persons are legally incapable of giving consent. For example, the KENTUCKY REVISED STATUTES provide:

> 510.020. Lack of consent
>
> (1) Whether or not specifically stated, it is an element of every offense defined in this chapter that the sexual act was committed without consent of the victim.
>
> ....
>
> (3) A person is deemed incapable of consent when he is:
>   (a) Less than sixteen years old....

The statute withstood constitutional attack in *Payne v. Commonwealth,* 623 S.W.2d 867 (Ky. 1981), *cert. denied sub nom. Payne v. Kentucky,* 456 U.S. 909 (1982).

3. Not only is the age of the victim critical, but under some statutes the age of the defendant also may be critical. For example, in Louisiana, carnal knowledge of a juvenile (statutory rape) is committed when a male over the age of seventeen has consensual sexual intercourse with a female over the age of twelve but under the age of seventeen when there is a difference of more than two years between them. LA. REV. STAT. ANN. 14:80 (West 1980 Supp). Texas recognizes the significance of the age of the defendant through a statute which provides that it is an affirmative defense to prosecution for sexual assault of a child (defined as a person younger than 17 years of age who is not the spouse of the actor) that the actor was not more than two years older than the victim. TEX. PENAL CODE ANN. § 22.011(e) (West 1991).

4. Are statutory rape statutes which punish only males for acts committed with underage females a denial of "equal protection of the laws?" A closely divided Supreme Court in *Michael M. v. Superior Court of Sonoma County,* 450 U.S. 464 (1981), held they are not. The plurality accepted the reasoning of the Supreme Court of California which "found that the classification was "supported not by mere social convention but by the immutable physiological fact that it is the female exclusively who can become pregnant.'" *Id.* at 467. In upholding the statute the plurality found that the state had a strong interest in preventing teenage pregnancies. It referred to numerous reports and studies which revealed both the increase in and adverse effects of such pregnancies. "Only women may become pregnant and they suffer disproportionately the profound physical, emotional and psychological consequences of sexual activity. The statute at issue here protects women from sexual intercourse at an age when these consequences are particularly severe." *Id.* at 471-72.

The statute was not under inclusive in punishing only the male participant because the legislature was trying to protect minor females; risk of pregnancy might deter females, but not males; finally, to punish the female could frustrate enforcement of the statute.

Justice Stewart concurred, pointing out that the statute in question was "but one part of a broad statutory scheme that protects all minors from the problems and risks attendant upon adolescent sexual activity." *Id.* at 477.

The dissenters rejected the need for a gender specific law based on the fact that at least thirty-seven states have enacted gender-neutral statutory rape laws. Furthermore, "a gender-neutral statutory rape law is potentially a greater deterrent, for the simple reason that a gender-neutral law subjects both men and women to criminal sanctions." Id. at 494 (emphasis in original). Thus, they concluded the state has failed to prove that a gender-neutral law would be more difficult to enforce than the gender-based law.

SECTION IV. Modern Redefinition of Rape and Other Sexual Offenses

EDITORIAL NOTE

Judge Bazelon, in *United States v. Wiley, supra* pp. 214-217, almost in passing, adverts to perhaps the most crucial consideration, that is, the basis for making an act of sexual intercourse against the will of a woman a crime. What is the interest which the law seeks to vindicate? Is rape a property crime, an aggravated offense against the person, a sexual offense, an invasion of the sexual privacy of a woman? The answer may not be as straightforward as one might think. Consider Susan Brownmiller's explanation:

> To a woman the definition of rape is fairly simple. A sexual invasion of the body by force, an incursion into the private, personal inner space without consent — in short, an internal assault from one of several avenues and by one of several methods — constitutes a deliberate violation of emotional, physical and rational integrity and is a hostile, degrading act of violence that deserves the name of rape.
>
> Yet by tracing man's concept of rape as he defined it in his earliest laws, we now know with certainty that the criminal act he viewed with horror, and the deadly punishments he saw fit to apply, had little to do with an actual act of sexual violence that a woman's body might sustain. True, the law has come some distance since its beginnings when rape meant simply and conclusively the theft of a father's daughter's virginity, a specialized crime that damaged valuable goods before they could reach

the matrimonial market, but modern legal perceptions of rape are rooted still in ancient male concepts of property.

....

Since marriage, by law, was consummated in one manner only, by defloration of virginity with attendant ceremonial tokens, the act man came to construe as criminal rape was the illegal destruction of virginity outside a marriage contract of his making. Later, when he came to see his own definition as too narrow for the times, he broadened his criminal concept to cover the ruination of his wife's chastity as well, thus extending the law's concern to nonvirgins too. Although these legal origins have been buried in the morass of forgotten history, as the laws of rape continued to evolve they never shook free of their initial concept — that the violation was first and foremost a violation of male rights of possession, based on male requirements of virginity, chastity and consent to private access as the female bargain in the marriage contract (the underpinnings, as he enforced them, of man's economic estate).

....

When rape is placed where it truly belongs, within the context of modern criminal violence and not within the purview of ancient masculine codes, the crime retains its unique dimensions, falling midway between robbery and assault. It is, in one act, both a blow to the body and a blow to the mind, and a "taking" of sex through the use or threat of force.... [M]ore precisely, in rape the threat of force obtains a highly valued sexual service through temporary access to the victim's intimate parts, and the intent is not merely to "take," but to humiliate and degrade.

This, then, is the modern reality of rape as it is defined by twentieth-century practice. It is not, however, the reality of rape as it is defined by twentieth-century law.

S. BROWNMILLER, AGAINST OUR WILL 376-78 (1975) (emphasis in original).

How have contemporary statutes dealt with the problem not only of rape but of sexual offenses generally? Compare the approaches of the MODEL PENAL CODE and the penal code of your state:

1. Are the statutes gender free? What is the significance of defining sexual crimes to include in a single offense the acts of both male and female aggressors against both male and female victims?

2. Are the statutes based on unlawful use of force or on lack of consent? Is "consent" a relevant although unstated issue even in statutes based on "force"?

3. Is there a grading of offenses from more serious to less serious? If so, what are the criteria for distinguishing between less and more serious offenses?

4. What is the interest which the statutes seek to protect?

For an analysis of the modern trends in sexual offense legislation, see Ireland, *Reform Rape Legislation*, 49 U. COLO. L. REV. 184-204 (1977-78).

MODEL PENAL CODE

§ 213.0. Definitions

[The text appears in Appendix A *infra*.]

§ 213.1. Rape and Related Offenses

[The text appears in Appendix A *infra*.]

§ 213.3. Corruption of Minor and Seduction

[The text appears in Appendix A *infra*.]

§ 213.4. Sexual Assault

[The text appears in Appendix A *infra*.]

§ 213.6. Provisions Generally Applicable to Article 213

[This section contains miscellaneous provisions which include mistake of age as a defense, definition of "spouse," evidence of prior sexual misconduct, requirement of prompt complaint, and corroboration required. The text of this section appears in Appendix A.]

NOTES ON RAPE AND "INCIDENTAL" OFFENSES

1. Some states have divided rape into a crime of several degrees based on the presence or absence of aggravating circumstances. Where the aggravating circumstances are separately defined as crimes such as kidnapping or assault can defendant be convicted of those crimes as well? For example, a Washington statute defines rape as forcible sexual intercourse where the perpetrator "uses or threatens to use a deadly weapon" or "kidnaps the victim," etc. By definition, to prove first-degree rape the prosecutor must prove an assault* or kidnapping or both. May the prosecutor "pyramid" the charges to include all three crimes? In *State v. Johnson*, 92 Wash. 2d 671, 600 P.2d 1249 (1979), *cert. denied*, 446 U.S. 948 (1980), the Supreme Court of Washington stated that "the legislature has removed the necessity or occasion for the pyramiding of charges ... by creating more clearly defined degrees of crimes, ... and specifying the types of conduct incidental to the crime which will call forth more severe penalties." 600 P.2d at 1252." [A]n additional conviction cannot be allowed to stand unless it involves some injury to the person ... of the victim ..., which is separate and distinct from and not merely incidental to the crime of which it forms an element." *Id.* at 1254.

---

*Aggravated assaults, such as assaults with intent to rape are discussed in Chapter 2, section 2 *supra*.

2. Expanded definitions of the crime of "kidnapping" have raised questions in some states as to whether every rape is necessarily a kidnapping as well. For example, the Kansas statute provides:

> Kidnapping is the taking or confining of any person, accomplished by force, threat or deception, with intent to hold such person:
> (a) ...
> (b) To facilitate flight or the commission of any crime; or ... K.S.A. 21-3420.

In *State v. Buggs,* 219 Kan. 203, 547 P.2d 720 (1976), defendants compelled shopkeeper and assistant who were outside premises locking-up to return inside. Under threat or force defendants took daily receipts from purse of shopkeeper, and then raped her. Defendants argued that every robbery or rape involves some movement or detention of the victim, and, therefore, an exception should be made for "minor and inconsequential movements" which are merely incidental to the intended crimes.

The Kansas Supreme Court rejected the defense. The statute requires "no particular distance of removal, nor any particular time or place of confinement." 547 P.2d at 730. The court did, however, illustrate the need for some limitations on broad kidnapping statutes. "A standstill robbery on the street is not a kidnapping; the forced removal of the victim to a dark alley for robbery is. The removal of a rape victim from room to room within a dwelling solely for the convenience and comfort of the rapist is not a kidnapping; the removal from a public place to a place of seclusion is. The forced direction of a store clerk to cross the store to open a cash register is not a kidnapping; locking him in a cooler to facilitate escape is." *Id.* at 730.

EDITORIAL NOTE ON KIDNAPPING*

> Kidnaping** is aggravated false imprisonment. At common law kidnaping was defined as the forcible abduction or stealing away of a man, woman or child from his own country and sending him to another. It was a misdemeanor at common law but is a felony under modern statutes.

R. Perkins & R. Boyce, Criminal Law 229 (3d ed. 1982).

The classification of kidnapping as a misdeameanor indicates that it was not regarded as a serious offense at common law. It was defined in narrow terms and only applied when the victim was transported out of the country. Kidnapping, in the United States, is regarded as a very serious offense, and at one time it was commonly punishable by death when a victim kidnapped for ransom was not released unharmed. After the celebrated kidnapping and death of the Lindbergh child,*** a federal kidnapping law was enacted. 18 U.S.C. § 1201 (1976). The Lindbergh Law, as it is called, prohibits the taking

---

*The crimes included in this note are discussed comprehensively in the A.L.I. Model Penal Code and Commentaries, part II, vol. 1, art. 212, pp. 208-70 (Official Draft and Revised Comments 1980).
**Spelling in original text.
***Prosser, Book Review, 46 Minn. L. Rev. 383 (1961-62).

of a kidnapped person from one state to another and holding the person for ransom.

Not only is the offense regarded as serious but in some states the scope of the offense has been greatly expanded. For example, the Wisconsin statute provides:

> 940.31 Kidnapping
> (1) Whoever does any of the following is guilty of a Class B felony:
>   (a) By force or threat of imminent force carries another from one place to another without his consent and with intent to cause him to be secretly confined or imprisoned or to be carried out of this state or to be held to service against his will; or
>   (b) By force or threat of imminent force seizes or confines another without his consent and with intent to cause him to be secretly confined or imprisoned or to be carried out of this state or to be held to service against his will; or
>   (c) By deceit induces another to go from one place to another with intent to cause him to be secretly confined or imprisoned or to be carried out of this state or to be held to service against his will.
> (2) Whoever violates sub. (1) with intent to cause another to transfer property in order to obtain the release of the victim is guilty of a Class A felony; but if the victim is released without permanent physical injury prior to the time the first witness is sworn at the trial the defendant is guilty of a Class B felony.

WIS. STAT. ANN. (West 1982).

The statute is all-inclusive. It does not matter how long the victim is confined (minutes or days), how far the victim is carried or moved (from one room to another or from one part of the state to another), or to how much danger or terror the victim is exposed. With the exception of kidnapping for ransom, which is made a Class A felony, the objective of the actor is irrelevant under the statute. Furthermore, the statute makes no attempt to differentiate between movements or confinements of relatively short distance or duration which are incidental ingredients of some other crimes and those of a more substantial nature. Frequently, in crimes such as rape and robbery the victim may be moved, seized, or confined to a limited extent. See notes 1 and 2 *supra*.

Another example is provided by the Texas statute:

> § 20.04. Aggravated Kidnapping.
>   (a) A person commits an offense if he intentionally or knowingly abducts another person with the intent to:
>   (1) hold him for ransom or reward;
>   (2) use him as a shield or hostage;
>   (3) facilitate the commission of a felony or the flight after the attempt or commission of a felony;
>   (4) inflict bodily injury on him or violate or abuse him sexually;
>   (5) terrorize him or a third person; or
>   (6) interfere with the performance of any governmental or political function.

(b) An offense under this section is a felony of the first degree unless the actor voluntarily releases the victim alive and in a safe place, in which event it is a felony of the second degree.

TEX. PENAL CODE ANN. § 20.04 (West 1973). Note that the Texas statute covers a broad range of possible objectives on the part of the actor, including the intent to use the kidnapping to interfere with the performance of any governmental or political function. It reduces the crime from a first degree felony to a second degree felony if the actor voluntarily releases the victim alive and in a safe place.

The MODEL PENAL CODE and a number of states have departed from the use of very broad kidnapping statutes and utilize several statutes to deal with different types of unlawful movement or confinement. This enables the more aggravated situations to be described with greater specificity and to provide a more structured approach to punishment.

In sections 212.1 through 212.5 the MODEL PENAL CODE deals with the respective crimes of kidnapping, felonious restraint, false imprisonment, interference with custody, and criminal coercion. The text of these sections appears in Appendix A. Kidnapping is limited to situations where a victim is removed from his or her residence or place of business, or is moved a substantial distance, or is confined for a substantial period of time. The movement or confinement must be carried out to achieve one of the following four purposes: to hold the victim for ransom or as a shield or hostage; to further the commission of or escape from a felony; to physically injure or terrorize the victim; to interfere with the operations of the government. The removal or confinement must be accomplished by force, threat, or deception, or in the case of incompetents or children under fourteen, without the consent of their guardian or parent. The use of the qualifying term "substantial" in regard to distance and time precludes a conviction for kidnapping of movement or confinement is merely incidental to the commission of some other felony. Kidnapping is a more serious offense if the victim is not released alive in a safe place.

Another crime, "felonious restraint," is provided for those situations where the victim has been unlawfully restrained and either exposed to risk of serious bodily injury or kept in involuntary servitude. The crime of "false imprisonment" requires that the actor knowingly restrain the victim by unlawful means and in a manner so as to substantially interfere with his or her liberty.

The MODEL PENAL CODE treats as a separate offense, "interference with custody," the taking of a child from the custody of its parents. A defense is provided when the act is done for the welfare of the child. Finally, "criminal coercion" occurs when the actor makes certain specified threats in order to restrict another's freedom of action to his or her detriment.

Congress has enacted the Parental Kidnapping Prevention Act of 1980 to deal with the difficult and not infrequent problem where one parent removes a child from the jurisdiction of the court which had awarded custody of a child to the other parent. 18 U.S.C.A. § 1073 note; 28 U.S.C.A. §§ 1738A, 1738 note.

Chapter 5
CRIMINAL HOMICIDE*

INTRODUCTORY NOTE

The cases in this chapter provide an opportunity to apply the principles examined in Chapter 1, namely, problems of intent, conduct, concurrence, and causation. One might think that the law of homicide would be simple and straightforward. After all, there is only one type of harm — causing death. On the contrary most states have several statutes which deal with criminal homicide. This reflects an intention to vary punishment based on the degree of culpability. The specific intent to kill and negligence are viewed as being at opposite ends of a "culpability spectrum." Both deserve punishment but the intentional killing may result in a sentence of death while the negligent actor may be placed on probation. Not only are the stakes high, but it is not always easy to determine whether a killing was intentional or not, and, even if unintentional, whether it was characterized by reckless or negligent conduct. Also, it is necessary to do more than classify homicides as intentional or unintentional. Depending on the circumstances, an unintentional killing may reveal a more calloused and socially irresponsible attitude than an intentional killing. Compare, for example, a "mercy killer" with a person who shoots into an occupied house. Even when it is apparent that a killing was either intentional or unintentional it is still necessary to distinguish between the "mercy killer" and the "hired killer" and between the person who shoots into the house and a careless driver.

The complex and intricate statutory schemes which enable the decisions on culpability to be made require close attention to the facts and elements of the various crimes. It will also become apparent that while states generally agree on what should be classified as culpable homicide there are variations as to the degree of culpability in regard to particular homicides.

There are two other matters which are important to keep in mind. First, there is the matter of mental illness and culpability. To what extent should the actor's mental and emotional problems be taken into account in evaluating his or her culpability. Although the insanity defense and related matters are covered in Chapter 8, Incapacity, some cases in this chapter also deal with problems of capacity.

Second, the prospect of capital punishment hovers over the crime of murder. The dispute over capital punishment involves more than whether we should have it or not. Since most states authorize capital punishment only for certain homicides, it becomes critically important to define those crimes in the most precise language and to assure by appellate review that the fact finder prop-

---

*The crimes included in this chapter are discussed comprehensively in A.L.I., Model Penal Code and Commentaries, part II, vol. 1, art. 210, pp. 1-90 (Official Draft and Revised Comments 1980).

erly classified the particular case as one which fits the criteria for a capital case. Capital punishment is discussed in Chapter 11, pp. 858-869 *infra*.

The complexity of the "laws" of homicide indicate that the legislature has played a significant role in expressing its views on culpability. Is it appropriate or desirable for the legislature to play this role? Is the role as significant as it seems at first examination, in light of prosecutorial discretion and plea bargaining?

SECTION I. The Harm: Death of Another Human Being
A. HUMAN BEING

STATE v. OLIVER
Supreme Court of Vermont
563 A. 2d 1002 (Vt. 1989)

(Note: Please read *State v. Oliver*, pp. 5-7, before proceeding.)

NOTES

1. Adherence by American courts to the "born alive" rule is based on Lord Coke's statement of the English common law, as follows:

> "If a woman be quick with childe, and by a potion or otherwise *killeth it in her wombe;* or if a man beat her, whereby the *childe dieth in her body,* and she is delivered of a *dead childe,* this is a great misprison, and no murder; but if the childe be *born alive* and dieth of the potion, battery, or other cause, this is murder: for in law it is accounted a reasonable creature *in rerum natura,* when it is born alive ... and so was the law holden in Bracton's time...."

3 COKE, INSTITUTES SO (1648).

2. In *People v. Guthrie,* 97 Mich. App. 226, 293 N.W.2d 775 (1980), a trial court dismissed an information charging Guthrie with negligent homicide, based on the stillbirth of a nine-month fetus after Guthrie collided with a car driven by a pregnant woman. The Michigan Court of Appeals affirmed. It characterized the "born alive" rule as "an archaic legal fiction which no longer serves a legitimate objective." "Modern medical practice has advanced to the point that, unlike the situation when the rule was first developed, the vast majority of viable fetuses will, in the absence of some unexpected event, be born alive and healthy. Further, medical technology can now accurately determine the stages of fetal development and viability. This being so, birth itself in terms of emergence from the mother's body should no longer be held determinative." *Id.* at 778. Nevertheless, "[a]lthough we find that the 'born alive' rule is archaic and should be abolished in prosecutions brought under the negligent homicide statute, the abolition of the rule is a matter for action by the Legislature. For this Court to interpret the statute to include unborn viable fetuses as persons would usurp the Legislature's traditional power of defining what acts shall be criminal and would be contrary to the decisions from other jurisdictions .... Respectfully, we urge the Legislature to make the necessary amendments to the statute." *Id.* at 780-81.

A. HUMAN BEING

3. Twenty-one states do punish the killing of an unborn child as some form of homicide or feticide. All but two of the states have modified the common law "born alive" rule by statute. These statutes vary as to the point during pregnancy when they apply.

Courts have sometimes restrictively interpreted legislative modification of the common law rule. In *State v. Gyles*, 313 So. 2d 799 (La. 1975), the Louisiana Supreme Court followed the common law "born alive" rule in construing the state's criminal homicide statute. Thereafter, the Louisiana Legislature amended the definition of "person" in the state criminal code, LA. REV. STAT. 14:2(7) (West 1986), to read: "'Person' includes a human being from the moment of fertilization and implantation ...." The court considered the meaning of the statute in *State v. Brown*, 378 So. 2d 916 (La. 1979), in which the defendant, charged with murder of a fertilized implanted fetus, pleaded guilty to manslaughter of the fetus. It thought the revised definitional section insufficient to amend the general homicide statute. The statute "does not say that a fetus or a human embryo is a human being, for the purpose of the murder statute, but only that the word 'person' 'includes a human being' and includes a human being 'from the moment of fertilization and implantation.' If the homicide statutes are to be amended to include feticide it must be done with greater clarity and less confusion than the amendment of the definition of the word 'person' reflects, and within the limits fixed in *Roe v. Wade*, ... which prohibits the regulation of voluntary abortions within the first trimester of pregnancy." *Id.* at 918.

Justice Blanche, dissenting, thought the state legislative purpose in redefining "person" clearly was to overturn *Gyles*: "The redefinition of murder by the legislature to include feticide is within the bounds set by *Roe*, since that decision was limited to the regulation of the voluntary abortion. In *Roe*, ... the Court found that a state could not, by adopting one theory of life, override the privacy rights of the mother. The defendant here asserts no countervailing privacy right." *Id.* at 919 (Blanche, J., dissenting).

Louisiana later enacted separate feticide statutes. LA. REV. STAT. 14:32.5-8 (West Supp. 1992).

4. Abortion is the premature termination of pregnancy resulting in destruction of a fetus. Unlike fetal homicide, abortion involves the consent of the pregnant woman.

Until the Supreme Court decisions in *Roe v. Wade*, 410 U.S. 113 (1973), and *Doe v. Bolton*, 410 U.S. 179 (1973), statutes generally prohibited abortions except those performed by medical doctors in order to save the life of the mother. The MODEL PENAL CODE, in § 230.3, proposed to allow abortion when pregnancies might gravely impair the physical or mental health of pregnant women, when children would be born with grave physical or mental defects, or when pregnancies were the result of rape, incest, or other forms of felonious intercourse. Prior to 1973, however, only a few states had loosened their prohibitions against abortion either through modified legislation or judicial interpretation. *See generally* George, *Evolving Law of Abortion*, 27 Case W. Res. L. Rev. 708 (1972).

In *Roe* and *Doe*, the Supreme Court held that, during the first trimester of pregnancy, states may not restrict a pregnant woman's decision in consultation with her physician to have an abortion for whatever reason. The Court found: 1) a fundamental right of privacy inherent in the Fourteenth Amendment which "is broad enough to encompass a woman's decision whether or not to terminate her pregnancy," *Roe v. Wade*, 410 U.S. at 153; and 2) a physician's decision to perform an abortion must rest upon his or her best clinical judgment "exercised in light of all factors — physical, emotional, psychological, familial, and the woman's age — relevant to the well-being of the patient." *Doe v. Bolton*, 410 U.S. at 192. The state retained the power during the second trimester of pregnancy to regulate abortion procedures to protect the health of pregnant women, and after viability and during the final trimester to proscribe abortion when unnecessary to preserve the life or health of a pregnant woman. The Court's jurisprudence did not invalidate criminal prohibitions as applied to abortions performed by nonphysicians, because they "infringe upon no realm of personal privacy secured by the Constitution against state interference." *Connecticut v. Menillo*, 423 U.S. 9, 11 (1975).

Since 1973 the Court has considered an array of legislative restrictions on consensual, medically performed abortions. Prior to 1989, the Court had invalidated almost all of them except for restrictions on funding abortions, *Harris v. McCrae*, 448 U.S. 297 (1980) and requirements for notification of parents of unemancipated, female minors, *H. L. v. Matheson*, 450 U.S. 398 (1981).

Coloutti v. Franklin, 439 U.S. 379 (1979), is of special interest as a matter of substantive penal law. The court struck down on vagueness grounds a Pennsylvania statute with criminal sanctions which required the doctor to test for viability before performing an abortion and, if viability was evident, to use those abortion techniques with the best opportunity for producing the birth of a live child. Thus, the Court restricted a state's ability to prohibit post-viability or third trimester abortions, which *Roe* had allowed (although *Doe's* definition of "health" to include "mental health" seemed to defeat).

In 1989 the Court's approach to abortion seemed to change direction. *Webster v. Reproductive Health Serv.*, 492 U.S. 490 (1989) sustained the provision of a Missouri abortion statute, including a requirement that doctors do viability-testing at twenty weeks or later before performing an abortion. In the following year the Court upheld requirements to notify one parent, and to notify both parents, followed by 48-hour waiting period if an alternative judicial-bypass procedure is provided. See *Ohio v. Akron Center for Reproductive Health*, 497 U.S. 502 (1990) and *Hodgson v. Minnesota*, 497 U.S. 417 (1990). In none of these cases did a majority choose to address directly the status of *Roe* itself.

In *Planned Parenthood v. Casey*, 505 U.S. __, 112 S. Ct. 2791 (1992), however, a joint opinion by Justices O'Connor, Souter, and Kennedy reaffirmed "the essential holding of *Roe*," 112 S. Ct. at 2817, while upholding all but one provision of a Pennsylvania abortion law. The plurality opinion "reject[ed] the trimester framework which [it did] not consider to be part of the essential holding of *Roe*." *Id*. at 2818. The plurality focused on "[t]he woman's right to terminate her pregnancy before viability [as] the most central principle of *Roe v. Wade*." *Id*. at 2817. Justices Blackmun and Stevens adhered to *Roe* and its progeny. Chief Justice Rehnquist joined by Justices White, Scalia and Thomas dissented, urging that *Roe* be overruled.

B. DEATH

STATE v. OLSON

Supreme Court of Minnesota, En Banc
435 N.W.2d 530 (1989)

SIMONETT, JUSTICE.

The trial court asks us the following certified question:

> Whether brain death, defined as irreversible cessation of all functions of the entire brain, including the brain stem, as stated in the Uniform Determination of Death Act constitutes "death" for purposes of Minn. Stat. § 609.20 and Minn. Stat. § 609.19 (1988).

Defendant Duane Olson is charged with second degree murder and first degree manslaughter in the death of his 6-week-old son, Dustin. On January 4, 1988, the police were called to the Olson home because Dustin was not breathing. The child was taken to the hospital, where, according to the complaint, the child "was diagnosed as being brain dead, but was placed upon life support systems which sustained his respiratory functions until January 8, 1988." The baby was diagnosed as having had an intracranial brain injury secondary to "whiplash shaken baby syndrome." The complaint further stated, "On January 8, 1988 at approximately 4:10 p.m., the hospital, after consulting with the family, disconnected the life support systems and the baby was declared dead at 5:25 p.m. on January 8, 1988." According to the complaint, defendant Olson told police that he had been awakened during the early morning hours of January 1, 1988, by the baby's crying; that he had shaken the baby three times to stop the crying, each time harder than the last; and that during the shaking the baby's head moved back and forth unprotected. According to the police, defendant also told them of an earlier shaking incident. The autopsy disclosed cerebral swelling with bilateral subdural hematomas.

...

Traditionally, death has been signified by cessation of breathing and heartbeat. When this occurs, inevitably there is a termination of all vital organ functioning and death is present. If the brain ceases to function, breathing and blood circulation cease too, and death occurs. In the last 30 years, however, medical technology has developed mechanical respirators and cardiac resuscitation methods that will produce breathing and heartbeat in the body even with the brain dead. In such a case, the body is completely unresponsive; there is no movement, no reflexes, no response to any stimulus. The muscles are flaccid, the pupils of the eyes fixed and dilated. There is no central nervous system activity. The body begins to decompose. The condition is irreversible. Even so, the mechanical support system will produce breathing and heartbeat in the body; the skin, for example, stays warm, urine is excreted, and glucose is metabolized. Despite the support system, however, cellular decomposition begins and, in a matter of weeks, all breathing and heartbeat stop.

The brain may be said to consist of two parts: the main cerebral hemispheres, which are the center of intelligence, cognition, emoting, consciousness, and the higher perceptions; and the brain stem, which is the lower middle part of the brain, connecting to the spinal cord and controlling respiration, blood pressure, and other biological functions. "Brain death," as that term is used in the medical community, means the entire brain, including the stem, is dead. This condition must be distinguished from a separate condition known as a persistent vegetative state, where the person is in an irreversible coma, but there is still at least some residual brain activity. (Karen Ann Quinlan was such a case.) A person in a persistent vegetative state is still living and is not dead under any definition of death. Removal of the support system from a patient in this vegetative state raises the question of when may life supports be removed from a dying person, see, e.g., *In re Torres*, 357 N.W.2d 332 (Minn. 1984); removal of the life support system from a brain-dead patient, on the other hand, is considered to be removal of the support system from a person already dead.

The medical profession has recognized the concept of brain death since at least 1968. See A Definition of Irreversible Coma, Report of the Ad Hoc Committee of the Harvard Medical School to Examine the Definition of Brain Death, 205 J. A.M.A. 337 (1968). Since then, other highly reputable organizations have affirmed the concept. Forty states and the District of Columbia have enacted statutes recognizing brain death as death. Seven states without brain death statutes have, by judicial decision, recognized brain death.

In 1980 the National Conference of Commissioners on Uniform State Laws approved the Uniform Determination of Death Act.... This model act was subsequently adopted by the American Medical Association in 1980 and by the American Bar Association in 1981. Also, in 1981, the President's Commission for the Study of Ethical Problems in Medicine and Biomedical and Behavioral Research issued a report in which it defined death and recommended adoption of the Uniform Determination of Death Act in all jurisdictions.

If the concept of brain death as death is accepted, the next question — which is a separate question — is what are the criteria for determining that brain death has, in fact, occurred. Even under the traditional definition of death, it should be remembered, there is a need for procedures to determine that death, indeed, has taken place. The Harvard Report lists four criteria for brain death: unreceptivity and unresponsitivity; no movement or breathing; no reflexes; and a flat EEG. In 1976 the Minnesota Medical Association adopted the following criteria: cerebral unresponsitivity; no breathing for 3 minutes without a respirator; no brain stem reflexes; two separate clinical examinations with at least 12 hours between; irreversibility, specifically excluding the possibilities of hypothermia or intoxication; and, in appropriate cases, such confirmatory tests as a flat EEG or a cerebral angiography showing lack of blood flow to the brain. See Cranford, Minnesota Medical Ass'n Criteria: Brain Death — Concept and Criteria, 61 Minnesota Medicine 561-63 (1978).

...

The concept of brain death is firmly established in the medical community. Defendant does not dispute the medical evidence. The concept has been accepted by an impressive number of state legislatures. No court has denied the validity of the concept. [The court concluded that it was unnecessary to decide the issue of brain death on this pretrial motion to dismiss and that it was preferable for the legislature to address the issue].

NOTES

1. Other appellate decisions invoking the "brain death" concept sustained homicide convictions based on deaths of persons removed from life support systems after massive injuries inflicted by criminal defendants had brought about a complete cessation of brainwave activities. See *State v. Fierro*, 124 Ariz. 182, 603 P.2d 74 (1979); *People v. Driver*, 62 Ill. App. 3d 847, 379 N.E.2d 847 (1978); *Swafford v. State*, 421 N.E.2d 596 (Ind. 1981); and *State v. Shaffer*, 229 Kan. 310, 624 P.2d 440 (1981).

2. National Conference of Commissioners on Uniform State Laws, Uniform Determination of Death Act and Report (1981) provides:

> Section 1. [Determination of Death.] An individual who has sustained either (1) irreversible cessation of circulatory and respiratory functions, or (2) irreversible cessation of all functions of the entire brain, including the brain stem, is dead. A determination of death must be made in accordance with accepted medical standards.

Report

The Uniform Determination of Death Act provides comprehensive bases for determining death in all situations. It is the result of a more than five-year evolution of statutory language on this subject. In 1975, the Law and Medicine Committee of the American Bar Association drafted a Model Definition of Death Act. Upon recommendation from the ABA House of Delegates, in 1978, the National Conference of Commissioners on Uniform State Laws completed the Uniform Brain Death Act which was based on the prior work of the ABA. In 1979, the American Medical Association (AMA) created its own Model Determination of Death statute. In the meantime, some 26 state legislatures adopted statutes based on one or another of the existing models.

The interest in these statutes arises from modern advances in life-saving technology. A person may be artificially supported for respiration and circulation after all brain functions cease irreversibly. The medical profession, also, has developed techniques for determining loss of brain functions while cardiorespiratory support is administered. At the same time, the common law definition of death cannot assure recognition of these techniques. The common law standard for determining death is the cessation of all vital functions, traditionally demonstrated by "an absence of spontaneous respiratory and cardiac functions." There is, then, a potential disparity between current and accepted biomedical practice and the common law.

The proliferation of model acts and uniform acts, while indicating a legislative need, is also confusing. All the existing acts have the same principal goal — extension of the common law to include the new techniques for determination of death. With no essential disagreement on policy, the associations which have drafted statutes met to find common language. This Act contains that common language, and is the result of agreement between the ABA, AMA, and NCCUSL.

Part (1) codifies the existing common law basis for determining death — total failure of the cardiorespiratory system. Part (2) extends the common law to include the new procedures for determination of death based upon irreversible loss of all brain functions. The overwhelming majority of cases will continue to be determined according to part (1). When artificial means of support preclude a determination under part (1), the Act recognizes that death can be determined by the alternative procedures.

Under part (2), the entire brain must cease to function, irreversibly. The "entire brain" includes the brain stem, as well as the neocortex. The concept of "entire brain" distinguishes determination of death under this Act from "neocortical death" or "persistent vegetative state." These are not deemed valid medical or legal bases for determining death.

This Act also does not concern itself with living wills, death with dignity, euthanasia, rules on death certificates, maintaining life support beyond brain death in cases of pregnant women or of organ donors, protection for the dead body, acceptable diagnostic tests and medical procedures, and time of death.

It is unnecessary for the Act to address specifically the liability of persons who make determinations. No person authorized by law to determine death, who makes such a determination in accordance with the Act, should, or will be, liable for damages in any civil action or subject to prosecution in any criminal proceeding for his acts or the acts of others based on that determination. No person who acts in good faith, in reliance on a determination of death, should, or will be, liable for damages in any civil action or subject to prosecution in any criminal proceeding for his acts. There is no need to deal with these issues in the text of this Act.

C. BY ANOTHER

PEOPLE v. CAMPBELL

Court of Appeals of Michigan
335 N.W.2d 27, 124 Mich. App. 333 (1983)

HOEHN, JUDGE.

Defendant, Steven Paul Campbell, was charged with open murder, MCL 750.316; MSA 28.548, in connection with the suicide death of Kevin Patrick Basnaw.... Defendant moved to quash the information and dismiss the defendant on the ground that providing a weapon to a person, who subsequently uses it to commit suicide, does not constitute the crime of murder. The motion to quash was denied by the circuit court, and this Court granted leave to appeal.

....

On October 4, 1980, Kevin Patrick Basnaw committed suicide. On the night in question, Steven Paul Campbell went to the home of the deceased. They were drinking quite heavily.

The testimony indicates that late in the evening the deceased began talking about committing suicide. He had never talked about suicide before.

About two weeks before, the defendant, Steven Paul Campbell, caught the deceased in bed with defendant's wife, Jill Campbell. Some time during the talk of suicide, Kevin said he did not have a gun. At first the defendant, Steven Paul Campbell, indicated Kevin couldn't borrow or buy one of his guns. Then he changed his mind and told him he would sell him a gun, for whatever amount of money he had in his possession. Then the deceased, Kevin Basnaw, indicated he did not want to buy a gun, but Steve Campbell continued to encourage Kevin to purchase a gun, and alternately ridiculed him.

The defendant and the deceased then drove to the defendant's parent's home to get the weapon, leaving Kimberly Cleland, the deceased's girlfriend, alone. Even though she knew of the plan, she did not call anyone during this period of time. She indicated she thought the defendant was saying this to get a ride home.

The defendant and the deceased returned in about 15 minutes with the gun and five shells. The deceased told his girlfriend to leave with the defendant because he was going to kill himself. He put the shells and the gun on the kitchen table and started to write a suicide note.

The defendant and the deceased's girlfriend left about 3 to 3:30 a.m. When they left, the shells were still on the table.

Steven, out of Kevin's presence and hearing, told Kimberly not to worry, that the bullets were merely blanks and that he wouldn't give Kevin real bullets. Kimberly and Steven prepared to leave.

On the way home, Kimberly asked Steven if the bullets he had given Kevin were really blanks. Steven said that they were and said "besides, the firing pin doesn't work." The girlfriend indicated that both defendant and deceased were about equally intoxicated at this point. The deceased's blood alcohol was found to be .26%.

The deceased's girlfriend drove herself to the defendant's home and remained there overnight. The deceased's roommate, Alfred Whitcomb, arrived home at approximately 4 a.m. His testimony indicates that when he arrived home he looked for Kevin Basnaw throughout the home and was unable to find him, but he did see the suicide note on the kitchen table. He waited up about 20 to 30 minutes. The deceased did not come home, so he went to sleep on the couch.

Next morning, one Billy Sherman arrived at about 11:30 a.m. and he and the deceased's roommate found the deceased slumped at the kitchen table with the gun in his hand. ...

The prosecutor and the trial court relied on *People v. Roberts*, 211 Mich 187; 178 NW 690 (1920), to justify trying defendant for open murder. In that case, Mr. Roberts' wife had terminal multiple sclerosis. She was in great pain. In the past, she had unsuccessfully attempted suicide by ingesting carbolic acid. At his wife's request, Mr. Roberts made a potion of water and poison and placed it within her reach. Defendant Roberts was convicted of murder in the first degree.

....

We now consider whether the *Roberts* case still represents the law of Michigan, and we find that it does not. Recent cases of our Supreme Court cast doubt on the vitality of the 1920 *Roberts* decision.

The *Roberts* case, without discussion, assumed that a murder had occurred and considered only the degree of that crime. It then determined that the act of placing poison within the reach of the deceased constituted the administration of poison within the meaning of 1915 CL 15192, now MCL 750.316; MSA 28.548, which provided: "All murder which shall be perpetrated by means of poison, or lying in wait, or any other kind of wilful, deliberate and premeditated killing, or which shall be committed in the perpetration, or attempt to perpetrate any arson, rape, robbery or burglary, shall be deemed murder of the first degree, and shall be punished by solitary confinement at hard labor in the state prison for life."

The prosecutor argues that inciting to suicide, coupled with the overt act of furnishing a gun to an intoxicated person, in a state of depression, falls within the prohibition, "or other wilful, deliberate and premeditated killing."

There exists no statutory definition of the term "murder." That crime is defined in the common law. "Homicide is the killing of one human being by another.... 'homicide' is not a crime. In this state, it is 'murder' and 'manslaughter' that are crimes." *People v. Allen*, 39 Mich. App. 483, 501; 197 NW2d 874 (1972) (Levin, J., dissenting), adopted by the Supreme Court in *People v. Allen*, 390 Mich 383; 212 NW2d 21 (1973).

The term suicide excludes by definition a homicide. Simply put, the defendant here did not kill another person.

....

Incitement to suicide has not been held to be a crime in two-thirds of the states of the United States. In the states where incitement to suicide has been held to be a crime, there has been no unanimity as to the nature or severity of the crime.

Most certainly, Michigan's imposition of a mandatory life sentence, without parole, for this type of conduct stands as the most severe punishment afforded.

No Legislature has classified such conduct as murder.

Lastly, it is not clear that incitement to suicide was ever considered murder at the common law. Certainly, attempted suicide was not held to be attempted murder. *Regina v. Burgess*, 9 Cox Crim. Cas. 247 (1862). Only three cases in the entire history of the United States have held such conduct to be murder, one of those cases having been decided in Massachusetts.

....

[While finding the defendant's conduct "morally reprehensible," the court determined that conduct did not constitute a crime. It therefore reversed the trial court and invited the state legislature to address the issue.]

NOTES

1. In Michigan, where doctor-assisted suicide has been a much publicized issue in recent years, the legislature passed a statute which makes assisting a suicide a felony punishable by up to four years in prison. Act. No 270, Public Acts of 1992 (Dec. 15, 1992). The same legislation also established a commission to make recommendation to the legislature on the subject within fifteen months.

2. *Cruzan v. Director, Missouri Department of Health*, 497 U.S. 261 (1990), addressed for the first time "the issue whether the United States Constitution grants what is ... referred to as a 'right to die.' *Id.* at 277. A majority of the court decided "not to attempt, by any general statement, to cover every possible phase of the subject." *Id.* While recognizing "a constitutionally protected liberty interest in refusing unwanted medical treatment," *Id.*, the court ruled the Constitution does not bar Missouri from requiring clear and convincing evidence of an incompetent's wish to withdraw life-sustaining medical treatment.

3. For a discussion of the relationship between assisted suicide and the *Cruzan* case, see Y. Kamisar, *"Are Laws Against Assisted Suicide Unconstitutional?"*, HASTINGS CENTER REPORT 23, No. 3 (May-June, 1993) 32-41.

SECTION II. Causation

A. DIRECT, INTERVENING AND SUPERVENING CAUSE

MODEL PENAL CODE

§ 2.03. Causal Relationship Between Conduct and Result

[The text of this section appears in Appendix A.]

COMMONWEALTH v. REMENTER

Superior Court of Pennsylvania
598 A.2d 1300 (1991)

BECK, JUDGE.

[The appellant was convicted of third degree murder for the death of Mary Berry. The appellant and Berry, who had gone together to a bar, had an argument and], Berry left the bar and got into her cab, which was parked outside and which she drove for a living. A moment later, appellant followed her, got into the driver's side where Berry was sitting, shoved her into the passenger's seat and drove away.

An out-of-town trucker, Brent Murphy, was taking a break from loading his truck a few blocks from the bar when he saw Berry's cab. Berry was hanging out of the passenger window, screaming "Help me, he's trying to kill me." The driver of the cab, identified as appellant, was holding on to Berry, beating her and pulling her hair. Berry, by "fighting and kicking," had managed to get one leg out of the passenger window, but all the while appellant was "trying to pull her back in by her hair."

While Murphy watched, Berry struggled away from appellant and fell out of the passenger window. Appellant also left the car and continued the assault on Berry, beating her "with his fists in the face" while she was lying on the ground. Murphy ran into a nearby supermarket and told somebody to call the police. ...

Other witnesses testified about their observations of the fight, including Smith and Campbell who saw a station wagon run over the victim.]

The station wagon referred to by Smith and Campbell was driven by Vito Michielli. Michielli and his wife and two small children were on Water Street that evening driving home from a shopping trip. Berry and appellant approached his car forcing him to stop. Berry was screaming "help me" and "let me in" and attempted to open the back door of the station wagon. Michielli and his wife were frightened and the children began to cry. The Michiellis' reaction was to lock all the doors and attempt to close the windows of the car. Mr. Michielli reached out of his window, pushed Berry away and sped off. Not until several days later, when a local newspaper reported the incident and Berry's tragic death, did Michielli realize that in leaving the scene his car had run over Berry.

....

The medical examiner's report revealed that Berry had suffered "blunt head trauma consistent with direct blows to the face, recent contusions to the chin, right and left cheeks near the nose and contused lacerations to the upper and lower lips, on the inside of the mouth." The medical examiner also found that Berry sustained a crush injury of the chest, "consistent with a motor vehicle passing over the body." ... The coroner's report, as stipulated to by the parties at trial, concluded that the crush injury was the cause of death....

At trial, appellant testified on his own behalf. He stated that both he and Berry had injected cocaine earlier on the day of her death. He testified that they were arguing and that they had also been drinking. Appellant stated that he drove Berry's cab out of concern for her welfare because she was "acting schizy from the cocaine." According to appellant, Berry's pleas for help were entirely unprovoked by him. He said that he pulled her back into the cab to prevent her from hurting herself and from "making a scene." Appellant admitted striking Berry but claimed that he did so out of anger because his attempts to calm her down by talking rationally had failed. He also claimed that he hit her only once, did not mean to hurt her and did not intend to kill her.

....

The issue regarding causation plainly arises in the instant case because the immediate cause of Berry's death was the crushing blow received under the wheels of Michielli's station wagon. Appellant argues that by the time Berry ran over to Michielli's car the "unfortunate domestic dispute" had ended and that therefore Berry's death had an accidental and intervening cause. Thus, according to appellant, the chain of causation between his assault on Berry and her resulting death had been broken. As such, he argues, his actions did not constitute a sufficiently direct cause of Berry's death. Moreover, appellant argues that Berry's death was not foreseeable and stemmed not from his assault but from independent actions by Berry for which he, appellant, cannot be held culpable. We reject these claims.

Certain fundamental principles guide our inquiry. First, it is well established that the tort theory of causation will not suffice to impose criminal responsibility. This principle was first explicitly adopted by the supreme court in *Commonwealth v. Root*, 403 Pa. 571, 575, 170 A.2d 310, 311 (1961), which held that "... the accused is not guilty unless his conduct was a cause of death sufficiently direct as to meet the requirements of the *criminal*, and not the

A. DIRECT, INTERVENING AND SUPERVENING CAUSE

tort, law." (emphasis in original). The *Root* court explained: "Legal theory which makes guilt or innocence of criminal homicide depend upon such accidental and fortuitous circumstances as are now embraced by modern tort law's encompassing concept of proximate cause is too harsh to be just." *Root*, 403 Pa. at 576, 170 A.2d at 312. Thus, a "more direct causal connection is required for conviction." 403 Pa. at 580, 170 A.2d at 314.

It is difficult to draw a bright line between causation in the criminal law and in the tort law. Certain principles can, however, be ascertained. In order to impose criminal liability, causation must be direct and substantial. Defendants should not be exposed to a loss of liberty based on the tort standard which only provides that the event giving rise to the injury is a substantial factor. Although typically the tort context refers only to substantial and not to direct and substantial as in the criminal context, the additional language in the criminal law does not provide much guidance. Therefore, criminal causation has come to involve a case-by-case social determination; ...

Many cases have grappled with the concept of what constitutes a legally sufficient causal connection where, as here, the immediate cause of death was not the blow dealt by the defendant's hand. We have concluded, from a careful reading of these cases and from analysis provided by criminal law commentators, that the resolution of the causation issue here and in analogous cases involves a two part inquiry. The first part of the inquiry requires us to decide whether the defendant's conduct was an operative cause of the victim's death. With respect to establishing a causal relationship between conduct and result, our crimes code poses a threshold factual requirement and that is, the conduct must be "an antecedent but for which the result in question would not have occurred." 18 Pa. C.S.A. § 303(a)(1) (Purdon 1983). Thus, if the victim's death is attributable *entirely* to other factors and not at all brought about by the defendant's conduct, no causal connection exists and no criminal liability for the result can attach.[*] The second part of the test raises the question of whether the result of defendant's actions were so extraordinarily remote or attenuated that it would be unfair to hold the defendant criminally responsible.

....

In light of the foregoing principles, we examine appellant's claim that the evidence at trial was insufficient to establish the necessary causal connection between his conduct and Berry's resulting death. Appellant first contends that the argument he was having with Berry was over by the time she approached Michielli's car for aid and that, therefore, her actions in seeking refuge in the station wagon cannot be attributed to him. Berry's actions were not provoked by his assault but were spontaneous and unrelated to the "earlier dispute,"

---

[*]Illustrating this basic concept, one commentator explains:

"Thus if A shoots at B intending to kill but misses, but at that moment B drops dead of some cause wholly unconnected with the shooting, A is not liable for the murder of B, in spite of the simultaneous existence of the two required ingredients, A's intentional conduct and the fatal result. What is missing is the necessary causal connection between the conduct and the result of conduct; and causal connection requires something more than mere coincidence as to time and place."

LaFave and Scott, Substantive Criminal Law, Vol. 1, Ch. 3., at 391-392 (1986).

appellant argues, and therefore, his conduct cannot be said to have caused her death.

This argument that there was no dispute occurring at the time Berry ran to Michielli's car is belied by considerable evidence which, when viewed in the light most favorable to the Commonwealth, establishes quite the contrary. As described above, several witnesses testified to the ferocity and tenacity of appellant's assault on Berry and all the observations attested to occurred within minutes of Berry's death....

Appellant further argues that Berry's death occurred through such an unforeseeable chain of events that his conduct cannot be said to have caused the fatal result. We disagree. The evidence at trial plainly established that appellant subjected Berry to a brutal and persistent assault from which she continually attempted to escape. In the first place, it is completely natural and foreseeable that any victim of an assault would respond to the danger by trying to escape it. In fact, it is difficult to imagine behavior which is more responsive or more predictable than fleeing from a deadly assault. Moreover, Berry's actions were particularly likely in the context of the instant case. Berry was clearly intent upon escaping her assailant at any cost and attempted to do so repeatedly. She tried climbing out of the car window, only to be beaten and pulled back into the car. She ran away from appellant twice after that and each time was violently forced back into the car by appellant. Just before Berry escaped for the last, and fatal, time, the cab was seen moving along the street with the passenger door open. The risk that Berry might suffer serious injury or death either during the assault or in her attempt to avoid it, was inherent in the situation appellant's attack created. In our view, the fatal result of appellant's assault is not rendered unforeseeable merely because the precise agency of death, i.e. the Michielli's station wagon, could not have been foretold. Appellant perpetrated a deadly assault on the decedent in and around an automobile on a public street with other moving vehicles in close proximity. It is absurd to argue that the fatal result was so extraordinary or accidental that appellant should not be held criminally liable for the consequences of his conduct. We find that more than sufficient evidence was adduced at trial from which the factfinder could conclude that appellant's conduct was the legal cause of Berry's death.

Judgment of sentence affirmed.

NOTES

1. *State v. Crocker*, 431 A.2d 1323, 1325 (Me. 1981): "In every case where causing a result is an element of the offense the State must prove beyond a reasonable doubt that the result would not have occurred *but for* the defendant's conduct. The State may prove either that the defendant's conduct, *operating alone*, produced the result or that the defendant's conduct, operating in conjunction with a concurrent causative condition, produced the result. In the latter circumstance, the State must prove beyond a reasonable doubt either (a) that the concurrent cause alone *was not* clearly sufficient to produce the result, or (b) that the conduct of the defendant alone *was not* clearly insufficient to produce the result." (Emphasis in original.)

2. In *State v. Roush*, 95 W. Va. 132, 120 S.E. 304 (1923), the defendant, who was of slight weight and crippled from an industrial accident, struck the decedent (who was taller and nearly twice the defendant's weight) two blows which left slight discolorations of the skin. The decedent, who had been drinking heavily for some time, sank down to the street as if lying down and died a few minutes later. An autopsy showed the cause of death to have been a blood clot at the base of the brain. There was no other sign of traumatic injury to brain tissue, no injury to the skull, and only a slight discoloration of the inside of the skin at the back of the skull, discernible only after the scalp had been removed during autopsy. The prosecution's medical expert, not experienced in brain surgery, testified that death might possibly have resulted from the blows inflicted by defendant. The appellate court reversed a second-degree murder conviction.

A tendered defense instruction, refused by the trial court, stated that it was not sufficient for the jurors "to surmise that the licks struck by Roush might or possibly or probably did result in the death, but that they must believe from all the evidence, beyond a reasonable doubt, that the death was the actual result of the blows, before they could find defendant guilty of involuntary manslaughter. There could be no crime charged to defendant unless the death resulted from his act, not even involuntary manslaughter, much less any higher degree of crime. The instruction correctly states the law applicable to the facts proven. It went to the very heart of the case, and should have been given."

3. *In the Matter of Anthony M.* and *People v. Cable and Godbee*, 63 NY 2d 270 (1984) (consolidated cases), one appellant had attempted to snatch the purse of an elderly victim who as a result was dragged along the sidewalk and the other had robbed at knife-point and struck an elderly victim during a burglary. In both cases the victims died of heart attacks some days afterwards. The court concluded the evidence was sufficient to support a finding of causation:

> While in both cases other possible causes of the heart attacks suffered by the elderly victims were not eliminated, the medical evidence, ... supported the fact-finder's determinations that defendants' acts were at least a contributing cause of both fatalities. In *Anthony M.*, the medical evidence connected the stress of the fall and fractured hip to the consequent stresses and fears of immobility, pain and surgery to correct the condition caused by the fall, leading to cardiac arrest and ultimate death. Similarly, in *Cable* and *Godbee*, there was proof in the medical evidence to support the jury determination that the stress arising from defendants' acts was a cause of the infection that manifested itself two days later. In neither instance was the testimony of the medical expert that there was a causal link so baseless or riddled with contradiction that it was unworthy of belief as a matter of law (see *People v. Stewart*, 40 N.Y. 2d 692, 699, supra; *People v. Ledwon*, 153 N.Y. 10 (1897)) and, despite contrary medical opinion, the jury was entitled to accept this evidence.

4. *Psychological causation.* "Sir James Stephen in his note to article 221 of his Digest of Criminal Law, commenting on the old rule, says: 'Suppose a man

were intentionally killed by being kept awake til the nervous irritation of sleeplessness killed him; might not this be murder? Suppose a man kills a sick man, intentionally, by making a loud noise which wakes him when sleep gives him a chance of life; or suppose, knowing that a man has aneurism of the heart, his heir rushes into his room and roars in his ear "Your wife is dead," intending to kill and killing him, why are not these acts murder? They are no more "secret things belonging to God" than the operation of arsenic. As to the fear that by admitting that such acts are murder people might be rendered liable to prosecution for breaking the hearts of their fathers or wives by bad conduct, the answer is that such an event could never be proved. A long course of conduct gradually "breaking a man's heart," could never be the "direct or immediate" cause of death. If it was, it was intended to have that effect, why should it not be murder?'

....

... [I]t would be unsafe, unreasonable and often unjust for a court to hold as a matter of law that under no state of facts should a prosecution for manslaughter be sustained where death was caused by fright, fear or terror alone, even though no hostile demonstration or overt act was directed at the person of the deceased. Many examples might be called to mind where it is possible for the death of a person to be accomplished through fright, nervous shock or terror as effectually as the same could be done with a knife or gun." *Ex parte Heigho*, 18 Idaho 566, 574-76, 110 P. 1029, 1931-32 (1910).

See *People v. Stamp*, 2 Cal. App. 3d 203, 82 Cal. Rptr. 598 (1970), *cert. denied*, 400 U.S. 819 (1970).

PEOPLE v. HAMRICK
Supreme Court of Colorado
624 P.2d 1320 (1981)

[On a January day, Hamrick and an accomplice went to Baumert's house, ostensibly to borrow money. After some time there, the defendant repeatedly struck Baumert on the head with a club until the club broke, and then kicked him about the body until Baumert became unconscious. Hamrick robbed Baumert of his wallet and watch, and drove away in Baumert's car. Baumert's body was not discovered for several days. Medical experts for prosecution and defense concluded that the immediate cause of Baumert's death was heart failure because of an epileptic seizure. The prosecution pathologist concluded that the seizure had been initiated by multiple trauma to Baumert's head; the neurogenic shock of the assault, coupled with excessive loss of blood from head injuries, started the seizure which in turn produced cardiac arrest. The defense expert hypothesized that there were other possible causes for the seizure including failure by Baumert, who had a history of epilepsy, to take anticonvulsant medication, and ingestion of alcohol. Hamrick was convicted of felony-murder.]

LEE, JUSTICE.

To instruct the jury on supervening cause as requested by the defendant in his tendered instructions, would have been incorrect inasmuch as the facts of the case did not involve a supervening cause. As defendant's tendered instruction No. 1 stated, a supervening cause is an independent intervening cause in which the defendant did not participate and which he could not foresee.... For the defendant to be responsible for the death of a victim, the death must be the natural and probable consequence of his unlawful conduct.

... [I]t is not indispensable to a conviction that the wounds be fatal and the direct cause of death. It is sufficient that they cause death indirectly through a chain of natural effects and causes unchanged by human action.... *Drury v. Burr*, 107 Ariz. 124, 483 P.2d 539 (1971).

The defendant must take his victim as he finds him, and it is no defense that the victim is suffering from physical infirmities. *Swan v. State*, 322 So.2d 485 (Fla. 1975). In *Swan, supra*, the defendant had beaten the victim, an elderly woman, in the course of a burglary of her home. The victim was discovered the next day injured but alive. She died seven days later. The victim had previously suffered a heart attack, stroke, arteriosclerosis and, apparently, diabetes. Defendant tried to show that if the victim had been in good physical condition she would have survived the attack. The court held:

> ... Appellant can not be excused from guilt and punishment because his victim was weak and could not survive the torture he administered. If the jury could have concluded reasonably that the wounds resulting from the beating administered by the Appellant and his codefendant caused or materially contributed to the victim's death, it was proper to find Appellant guilty....

In the present case, defendant attacked an epileptic who had consumed a considerable amount of whiskey and had failed to take his prescribed medication. The question for the jury's determination was whether the injuries inflicted by the defendant began a chain of events which in their natural and probable consequences caused the victim's death.... The jury resolved this question adversely to the defendant and the record of evidence clearly supports the guilty verdict.

NOTES

1. In *State v. Jenkins*, 276 S.C. 209, 277 S.E.2d 147 (1981), the defendant inflicted serious stab wounds on the victim, who was rushed to a hospital. To determine the extent of injuries to major blood vessels, an arteriogram was performed. The victim suffered a rare, fatal reaction to the dye used in the arteriogram procedure. Expert medical testimony indicated the victim probably would have survived had the reaction not occurred, but she would not have survived without medical treatment. Instructions on causation were legally correct and the trial court jury convicted Jenkins of murder. The appellate court affirmed.

2. *State v. Sauter*, 120 Ariz. 222, 585 P.2d 242 (1978):

> Appellant's position is that he was guilty of assault rather than homicide because of the intervening malpractice of the surgeon who did not discover the laceration in Lines' aorta, and he urges that error occurred when the trial court refused to allow evidence of the surgeon's failure to discover the wound to Lines' aorta. We, however, do not think so.

In *State v. Myers*, 59 Ariz. 200, 125 P.2d 441 (1942), we quoted with approval from State v. Baruth, 47 Wash. 283, 91 P. 977, to the effect that where one unlawfully inflicts a wound upon another calculated to endanger his life, it is no defense to a charge of murder to show that the wounded person might have recovered if the wound had been more skillfully treated. We said in *State v. Ulin*, 113 Ariz. 141, 143, 548 P.2d 19 (1976), that medical malpractice will break the chain of causation and become the proximate cause of death only if it constitutes the sole cause of death. We think these cases correctly summarize the law relative to intervening acts arising out of medical treatment in the United States.... For example, in *People v. Stamps*, 8 Ill. App.3d 896, 291 N.E.2d 274, 279 (1972), the court held:

> ... it is the generally recognized principle that where a person inflicts upon another a wound which is dangerous, that is, calculated to endanger or destroy life, it is no defense to a charge of homicide that the alleged victim's death was contributed to by, or immediately resulted from, unskillful or improper treatment of the wound or injury by attending physicians or surgeons.

See also *People v. Stewart*, 40 N.Y.2d 692, 389 N.Y.S.2d 804, 358 N.E.2d 487, 491 (1976), where the court said:

Neither does "direct" mean "unaided" for the defendant will be held liable for the death although other factors, entering after the injury, have contributed to the fatal result. Thus if "felonious assault is operative as a cause of death, the causal co-operation of erroneous surgical or medical treatment does not relieve the assailant from liability for homicide."...

Only if the death is attributable to the medical malpractice and not induced at all by the original wound does the intervention of the medical malpractice constitute a defense.... Such is not the case here.

3. *In re J.N., Jr.*, 406 A.2d 1275 (D.C. 1979):

> The trial judge properly refused to instruct the jury on the defense's theory that discontinuing the "heroic measures"[1] may have constituted an "intervening cause" of death[2] so as to insulate the defendant from homicide liability. Although no specific instruction was requested, the defendant suggests in his brief that the court could have properly instructed the jury as follows:
>
> If you find that the Government has proved beyond a reasonable doubt all the other elements of the offense and that the defendant caused [the victim's] death, it is your duty to find the defendant guilty of murder. If,

---

[1] Heroic measures were defined at trial as

[m]easures that are other than normal supportive care. For example normal supportive care would be assuring that the patient has food to eat, that they have clothing to keep them warm, to prevent pneumonia. What I consider heroic in this case was infusions of drugs in order to reduce the pressure in the head, maintenance of the patient on a machine, when there was no obvious response to those measures of therapy in the sense of improvement in the patient's condition.

[2] All agree that under any legally accepted definition of death, the victim was not dead when the "heroic measures" were discontinued.

on the other hand, you find that the Government has failed to prove beyond a reasonable doubt that the defendant caused [the victim's] death because the actions of [the physician] constituted *intentional or willful malpractice* or were an *abnormal response to the situation* caused by the defendant's acts, then you must find the defendant not guilty of murder. [Emphasis added.]

For such an instruction to have been proper, evidence must have been presented (1) to resolve the issue of what constitutes "intentional or willful malpractice" or an "abnormal response," and (2) to demonstrate that the actions of the attending physician breached that standard.... In this case, there is no evidentiary basis for the kind of instruction now proposed.

The situation is analogous to a tort claim for medical malpractice. With one exception, a jury is permitted to find a physician liable in tort for malpractice only when the standard of care has been established by expert testimony.... The exception to the rule is:

> Where laymen can say, *as a matter of common knowledge and observation*, that the type of harm would not ordinarily occur in the absence of negligence, the jury is allowed to infer negligence without expert testimony being presented....

The medical conduct here involved does not, "as a matter of common knowledge and observation," constitute the requisite malpractice. The exception applies only where "a physician has committed a blunder so egregious that a layman is capable of comprehending its enormity. An example is the case of a surgeon who leaves a sponge in an incision after the removal of a kidney.".... On facts quite similar to those here, however, an Illinois intermediate appellate court recently ruled that a physician's discontinuance of heroic measures was "reasonable" medical care.

Defendant's contention that the evidence failed to prove beyond a reasonable doubt that the victim died of the wounds from the gunshot is without merit. When the victim was brought to the hospital, his pulse was minimal. The neurosurgeon who examined him testified that the bullet had damaged a major portion of his brain and that he then exhibited many signs of death. The doctor's decision to withdraw life support measures was reasonable. [*People v. Olson*, 60 Ill. App. 3d 535, 538, 377 N.E.2d 371, 374-75 (1978).]

We need not hold that the doctor's actions were reasonable because that issue is not before us. It appears clear, however, that they were not so unreasonable, as a matter of common knowledge, as to be grossly negligent or worse.

4. *People v. Eulo,* 63 N.Y.2d 341 (1984) involved gun-shot victims, placed on mechanical respirators, who were later determined to be "brain-dead" and then removed from the respirators. The appellants objected that the jury instructions improperly allowed them to be convicted "if their conduct was the legal cause of the victims' 'brain death' rather than the victims' ultimate state of cardiorespiratory failure." 63 N.Y.2d at 342.

Each defendant correctly notes that the respective trial judges did not expressly instruct the juries concerning the criteria to be applied in determining when death occurred. Whether medically accepted brain-based criteria are legally cognizable became an issue in these cases when the respective juries heard testimony concerning the victims being pronounced medically dead while their hearts were beating and before artificial maintenance of the cardiorespiratory systems was discontinued. To properly evaluate whether these diagnoses of death were legally and medically premature and, therefore, whether the subsequent activities were possibly superseding causes of the deaths, the juries had to have been instructed as to the appropriate criteria for determining death: irreversible cessation of breathing and heartbeat or irreversible cessation of the entire brain's functioning.

The courts here adequately conveyed to the juries their obligation to determine the fact and causation of death. The courts defined the criteria of death in relation to the chain of causation. By specifically charging the juries that they might consider the surgical procedures as superseding causes of death, the courts made clear by ready implication that death should be deemed to have occurred after *all* medical procedures had ended.

The trial courts could have given express instructions that death may be deemed to have occurred when the victims' entire brain, including the brain stem, had irreversibly ceased to function. On the facts of these cases, that would have been the better practice. But, as mentioned, the brain-based criteria are supplemental to the traditional criteria, each describing the same phenomenon of death. In the context of a criminal case for homicide, there is no theoretical or practical impediment to the People's proceeding under a theory that the defendant "cause[d] the death" of a person, with death determined by either criteria.

... If the victims were properly diagnosed as dead, of course, no subsequent medical procedure such as the organ removals would be deemed a cause of death. If victims' deaths were prematurely pronounced due to a doctor's negligence, the subsequent procedures may have been a cause of death, but that negligence would not constitute a superseding cause of death relieving defendants of liability (see *People v. Stewart*, 40 NY 2d 692, 697-698; *People v. Kane*, 213 NY 260, 270). If, however the pronouncements of death were premature due to the gross negligence or the intentional wrongdoing of doctors, as determined by a grave deviation from accepted medical practices or disregard for legally cognizable criteria for determining death, the intervening medical procedure would interrupt the chain of causation and become the legal cause of death (see *People v. Kane, supra*, at pp 270-271; see, also, *State v. Scates*, 50 NC 420).

Thus, the propriety of the medical procedures is integral to the question of causation.

5. *People v. Lewis*, 124 Cal. 551, 57 P. 470 (1899):

But we have reached the conclusion by a course of argument unnecessarily prolix, except from a desire to fully consider the earnest and able argument of the defendant, that the test is — or, at least, one test — whether, when the death occurred, the wound inflicted by the defendant did contribute to the event. If it did, although other independent causes also contributed, the causal relation between the unlawful acts of the defendant and the death has been made out. Here, when the throat was cut, Farrell was not merely languishing from a mortal wound; he was actually dying; and after the throat was cut he continued to languish from both wounds. Drop by drop the life current went out from both wounds, and at the very instant of death the gunshot wound was contributing to the event. If the throat-cutting had been by a third person, unconnected with the defendant, he might be guilty; for, although a man cannot be killed twice, two persons, acting independently, may contribute to his death, and each be guilty of a homicide. A person dying is still in life, and may be killed; but, if he is dying from a wound given by another, both may properly be said to have contributed to his death.

The *Lewis* case is criticized in HALL, GENERAL PRINCIPLES OF CRIMINAL LAW (2d ed. 1960) at 265-67.

STATE v. McCLOSE

Court of Appeals of Wisconsin
95 Wis. 2d 49, 289 N.W.2d 340 (1980)

[A trial court dismissed a complaint charging homicide by reckless conduct on the basis that one who participates in an automobile race on a public road may not be held criminally responsible for a resulting death to a third party when one's own vehicle is not the direct instrument of death. "Recklessness" was defined substantially as in the Model Penal Code. The defendant, Norris McClose, and his brother, George McClose, agreed to race their cars on a rural highway. As they approached an intersection at a high rate of speed, George pulled ahead and Norris slowed his car. George's car crossed the center line and collided with an oncoming car driven by Jerry Langford. Langford and George McClose were killed.]

BROWN, JUDGE.

The criminal responsibility of one racing driver for the death of a third person killed by the other participant's automobile is a matter of first impression in Wisconsin. However, the other jurisdictions that have addressed the issue find that regardless of which vehicle strikes the victim the joint conduct of the participants is what causes the deaths.... The exceptions are twofold. If the facts of the particular case show no causal link between defendant's conduct and the death, the driver is not guilty. *See ... Commonwealth v. Root*, 403 Pa. 571, 170 A.2d 310 (1961). Additionally, if the deceased was a willing passenger in the other racing vehicle, the policy considerations are against imposing responsibility for the death on the surviving racer when his sole contribution to the death is the participation in the mutually agreed upon activity....

The policy behind the general rule is aptly stated in *People v. Kemp*, 150 Cal. App. 2d 654, 659, 310 P.2d 680, 683 (1957). The court stated:

> The evidence here strongly indicates that Kemp and Coffin were *inciting and encouraging one another* to drive at a fast and reckless rate of speed on a residence street and as they closely approached a blind intersection. It was by the merest chance that Kemp was able to avoid hitting the other car, and that Coffin was not. Only the matter of a split second and a few inches made the difference. They were both violating several laws, the acts of both led directly to and were a proximate cause of the result, and the fact that the appellant happened to narrowly escape the actual collision is not the controlling element. The evidence is sufficient to show that *they were not acting independently of each other, and that they were jointly engaged in a series of acts which led directly to the collision.* [Emphasis added.]

The policy language in *Kemp* is compatible with the policy behind our homicide by reckless conduct statute.... It is clear that our statute was designed to make it a felony for death resulting from total disregard for the safety of innocent people. When a driver places a dangerous instrumentality such as an auto on our public highways, he must take care that he does not engage in conduct which he knows is dangerous to himself and others. By taking an unreasonable risk, the driver shirks his duty to the public. By engaging in conduct which produces a high probability of death or great bodily harm to another, the driver is flirting with impending doom. Since racing on public streets creates a risk of death or great bodily injury to innocent people, it is outlawed.... We conclude that a person racing an automobile on a public highway may be found guilty of homicide by reckless conduct even though his automobile is not the direct instrument of death....

... [T]he trial court's decision reasoned that a racing participant, whose auto is not directly involved in the collision, must logically be charged as an aider and abetter or as a conspirator.... [W]e disagree.... [W]hen death results from an illegal race upon a public highway, the drivers may be direct participants in violating the criminal statute. One racer incites and encourages the other. The deceased is a victim of the unreasonable risk created by the race itself — not the carelessness of one of the drivers aided and abetted by another. We hold that when death results, each actor, regardless of which automobile causes the death, directly commits the crime of homicide by reckless conduct.

Secondly, we hold that a person whose vehicle is not a direct instrument of death may, nevertheless, have a defense to the charge of homicide by reckless conduct. If the facts adduced to show that the actor whose vehicle directly caused the death committed an act of wrongful conduct independent of the race or subsequent to the race, this conduct may supersede the original reckless conduct created by the race. Whether the action of the first actor supersedes the joint conduct of the racing participants is a jury question.

B. CULPABILITY IN RELATION TO CAUSATION

STATE v. HALLETT

Supreme Court of Utah
619 P.2d 335 (1980)

[Hallett and his companions were "apparently bent on revelry and mischief." They bent over one stop sign and uprooted another. The following morning, the victim, driving her family to church, failed to see the bent-over stop sign and drove into the intersection. She died later the same day from massive physical injuries when her car was struck by another vehicle entering the intersection with the apparent right-of-way. The defendant was charged with manslaughter on the basis of his unlawful act in destroying the stop sign; the jury convicted him of the lesser included offense of negligent homicide. The Utah penal code defined negligence in Model Penal Code terms.]

CROCKETT, CHIEF JUSTICE.

As to the issue of the defendant's intent: The inquiry is whether from the evidence and the reasonable inferences to be drawn therefrom, the trial court could believe beyond a reasonable doubt that the defendant's conduct met the elements of that statute. In his analysis of the evidence, the trial court was justified in viewing the situation thus: The defendant could not fail to know that stop signs are placed at particular intersections where they are deemed to be necessary because of special hazards; and that without the stop sign, the hazards which caused it to be placed there would exist; and that he should have foreseen that its removal would result in setting a trap fraught with danger and possible fatal consequences to others.

From what has been delineated above, the trial judge expressly found that the defendant should have foreseen that his removal of the stop sign created a substantial risk of injury or death to others; and that his doing so constituted a gross deviation from the standard of care that an ordinary person would exercise in all the circumstances.

Defendant makes a separate argument that the evidence does not support the conclusion that his acts were the proximate cause of Ms. Carley's death. He starts with a uniformly recognized definition: that proximate cause is the cause which through its natural and foreseeable consequence, unbroken by any sufficient intervening cause, produces the injury which would not have occurred but for that cause. His urgence here is that there was evidence that as the deceased approached from the south, she was exceeding the speed limit of 25 mph; and that this was the subsequent intervening and proximate cause of her own death. This is based upon the fact that a motorist, who was also coming from the south, testified that he was going 25 mph and that Ms. Carley passed him some distance to the south as she approached the intersection.

In regard to that contention, there are three observations to be made: The first is that the evidence just referred to would not necessarily compel the trial court to believe that the deceased was exceeding 25 mph as she got close to and entered the intersection, nor did the trial court make any such finding.

Second, even if it be assumed that she was so exceeding the speed limit, the reasonable and proper assumption is that if the stop sign had been there, she would have heeded it and there would have been no collision.

The foregoing provides sufficient justification for the trial court's rejection of the defendant's contentions. But there is yet a third proposition to be considered. It is also held that where a party by his wrongful conduct creates a condition of peril, his action can properly be found to be the proximate cause of a resulting injury, even though later events which combined to cause the injury may also be classified as negligent, so long as the later act is something which can reasonably be expected to follow in the natural sequence of events. Moreover, when reasonable minds might differ as to whether it was the creation of the dangerous condition (defendant's conduct) which was the proximate cause, or whether it was some subsequent act (such as Ms. Carley's driving), the question is for the trier of the fact to determine.

Reflecting upon what has been said above, we are not persuaded to disagree with the view taken by the trial court: that whether the defendant's act of removing the stop sign was done in merely callous and thoughtless disregard of the safety of others, or with malicious intent, the result, which he should have foreseen, was the same: that it created a situation of peril; and that nothing that transpired thereafter should afford him relief from responsibility for the tragic consequences that did occur.

PEOPLE v. BRACKETT

Supreme Court of Illinois
510 N.E.2d 877 (1987)

RYAN, JUSTICE.

The defendant, Randy Brackett, was originally charged in the circuit court of Madison County with the rape, deviate sexual assault and aggravated battery of Mrs. Elizabeth Winslow. Approximately five weeks after the events giving rise to these charges, Mrs. Winslow died. The defendant was then additionally charged with four counts of murder....

On the evening of October 20, 1981, defendant Randy Brackett, age 21, entered the home of Elizabeth Winslow, an 85-year-old widow, for whom he had previously done yard work. During the course of that evening, he raped and severely beat Mrs. Winslow, forced her to write him a check for $125, cooked himself some food and fell asleep for a time in an arm chair. He finally left in the early hours of the morning. The first policeman on the scene found Mrs. Winslow lying naked on the living room hide-a-bed. She was severely bruised about the face and appeared to have a broken arm and various other injuries to her body. She said she had been raped, choked and beaten.

[After being treated at a hospital, the victim was transferred to a nursing home. Already in poor condition, she declined to eat, could not use a nasal feeding tube, and had to be spoon-fed. Less than two weeks later, she died. The immediate cause of death, asphyxiation, resulted from food lodged in the trachea. Her inability to generate a sufficient volume of air to clear the trachea was related to her broken rib and the pain associated therewith.]

....

It is a matter of common knowledge that a person can accidentally choke to death while eating. Moreover, that type of accidental death could be the type of intervening cause which would relieve a defendant of criminal responsibility for death. (W. LaFave & A. Scott, Criminal Law sec. 35, at 257 (1st ed. 1972).) The courts in Illinois have repeatedly held that an intervening cause completely unrelated to the acts of the defendant does relieve a defendant of criminal liability. (*People v. Meyers* (1946), 392 Ill. 355; *Cunningham v. People* (1902), 195 Ill. 550; *People v. Gulliford* (1980), 86 Ill. App. 3d 237; *People v. Paulson* (1967), 80 Ill. App. 2d 44.) The converse of this is also true: when criminal acts of the defendant have contributed to a person's death, the defendant may be found guilty of murder. (*People v. Schreiber* (1982), 104 Ill. App. 3d 618; *People v. Brown* (1978), 57 Ill. App. 3d 528.) It is not the law in this State that the defendant's acts must be the sole and immediate cause of death. *People v. Reader* (1962), 26 Ill. 2d 210, 213.

. . . .

Cases concerning unrelated, intervening causes of death have been problematic in the law for hundreds of years. By the mid-1700's the doctrine was well established that "if a man receives a wound, which is not in itself mortal, but either for want of helpful applications, or neglect thereof, it turns to a gangrene, or a fever, and that gangrene or fever be the immediate cause of his death, yet, this is murder or manslaughter in him that gave the stroke or wound, for that wound, tho [sic] it were not the immediate cause of his death, yet, if it were the mediate cause thereof, and the fever or gangrene was the immediate cause of his death, yet the wound was the cause of the gangrene or fever, and so consequently is *causa causati*." (1 Hale, Pleas of the Crown 428 (S. Emlyn Ed.).) In our technological age, we have come to expect scientific explanations for all types of physical phenomena. In cases such as this, where the causal links are not immediately apparent, we frequently look to medical experts to assist the trier of fact in determining whether the defendant's acts constitute a contributing factor to the victim's death. (*People v. Love* (1978), 71 Ill. 2d 74, 81.) In this case the trier of fact heard factual testimony and opinion testimony from the victim's treating physician, the pathologist who performed the autopsy and the nursing home staff. We are mindful that the weight of medical experts' opinions is gauged by the reasons given for their conclusions and the factual details they marshall to support them. (*People v. Brown* (1978), 57 Ill. App. 3d 528, 532.) ... Here there was uncontradicted evidence that the ability to expel food lodged in the trachea is directly related to the volume of air present in the lungs. The victim, due to her broken rib, was not able to breathe deeply, nor would she have had the capacity to expel the food. There was further uncontradicted evidence that the nasal feeding tube could not be used because of the beating the victim had received. Consequently, the nursing home staff was unable to use a feeding method that would have avoided the possibility of choking. [In], the victim's depressed, weakened, debilitated state ... she became too weak even to swallow.

. . . .

... The trier of fact was entitled to find that the defendant, a 21-year-old male, 6 feet 3 inches tall and 170 pounds, who battered and raped an 85-year-old woman, set in motion a chain of events which contributed to her death.

The defendant argues that the appellate court ignored a long-standing principle in this State, that death is not ordinarily contemplated as a natural consequence of blows from bare fists. (*People v. Crenshaw* (1921), 298 Ill. 412; *People v. Mighell* (1912), 254 Ill. 53; *People v. Gresham* (1979), 78 Ill. App. 3d 1003; *People v. Drumheller* (1973), 15 Ill. App. 3d 418.) He therefore asserts he could not know that blows from his bare fists created a strong probability of death or great bodily harm, as charged under section 9-1(a)(2). We do not see that the appellate court ignored this principle. While Illinois cases do stand for the proposition the defendant recites, these same cases also stand for the proposition that death may be the natural consequence of blows with bare fists where there is great disparity in size and strength between the two parties. Given the disparity in size and strength between the defendant and Mrs. Winslow, we find it difficult to give credibility to this argument that the defendant, who battered this victim with enough force to break bones, did not know that his acts created a strong probability of death or great bodily harm.

Finally, the defendant argues that Mrs. Winslow's death by asphyxiation was not a foreseeable consequence of his felonious acts. There are often cases in which the precise manner of death will not be foreseeable to the defendant while he is committing a felony. This does not relieve the defendant of responsibility. There are cases where the immediate cause of death was meningitis (*People v. Paulson* (1967), 80 Ill. App. 2d 44), or pneumonia (*People v. Gulliford* (1980), 86 Ill. App. 3d 237), or a heart condition (*People v. Fuller* (1986), 141 Ill. App. 3d 737). In each of these cases the defendant's felonious acts contributed to the victim's demise, and in each of these cases the defendant could not foresee the exact manner in which the victim would die. We hold here that the defendant did not have to foresee that this victim would die from asphyxiation in order to be guilty of felony murder.

For the reasons stated, the defendant's conviction is affirmed.

Judgment affirmed.

NOTES

1. Review *State v. McClose*, supra.
2. In *Commonwealth v. Howard*, 265 Pa. Super. 535, 402 A.2d 674 (1979), the defendant persistently failed to intervene when defendant's boyfriend physically abused defendant's five-year-old child. When the child died during the night as a result of a beating, Howard called the police and fabricated a story to account for her child's traumatic injuries. She was indicted and convicted for homicide based on reckless or grossly negligent conduct. The appellate court affirmed the conviction. "While the immediate cause of the child's death was multiple injuries to the head and trunk, inflicted on the child by Watts over a period of several weeks, appellant may still be held culpable for her continuing failure to protect the child during all that time." Based on *Commonwealth v. Root*, 403 Pa. 571, 170 A.2d 310 (1961), "tort concepts of causation have no proper place in criminal homicide prosecutions and ... a conviction requires a more direct causal connection." "In *Root*, the decedent was aware of a dangerous condition created by the defendant's recklessness in operating his automobile, but the decedent nonetheless recklessly swerved his

car into the left lane attempting to pass the defendant. The decedent thereby drove into the path of an oncoming truck, causing his own death. The Court held that this intervening act of recklessness superseded the defendant's antecedent recklessness. Because the defendant's recklessness thus was not a 'direct' cause of the decedent's death criminal culpability could not be imposed."

"However, the Supreme Court distinguished *Root* in *Commonwealth v. Skufca*, ... 457 Pa. 124, 321 A.2d 899, *appeal dismissed*, 419 U.S. 1028 (1974), and upheld an involuntary manslaughter conviction of a parent who went out for a social evening leaving her two minor children locked in a room of an unattended apartment. A fire started in the building, and the children, trapped inside, suffocated. The Court stated: ... 'Although suffocation due to fire was the immediate cause of the children's death, appellant's unlawful conduct in leaving them locked in the room, without supervision, susceptible to numerous foreseeable dangers, was the legal cause of their death....'

"In the instant case, the argument for culpability is even stronger than in *Skufca*, because appellant was present during the several weeks of Watts' abuse of her child and knowingly consented to it. Unlike *Root*, here there was no superseding act of recklessness by the decedent — a helpless child. Thus we hold that appellant's failure to protect her child from Watts' savagery was a direct cause of death sufficient to impose criminal culpability.

"Lastly, we must consider whether appellant's failure to protect her child was, under these circumstances, reckless or grossly negligent.... [The evidence] is sufficient to show that appellant consciously disregarded a manifestly apparent risk to the health and safety of her young child and that this neglect was a gross deviation from the standard of conduct the reasonable parent would observe under the circumstances.... It is this long period of knowing yet apathetic acquiescence in her child's undoubted agony which satisfies the culpability requirements of the involuntary manslaughter statute."

265 Pa. Super. at 538-41, 402 A.2d at 676-77.

3. Compare *Commonwealth v. Youngkin*, 285 Pa. Super. 417, 425-26, 427-28, 427 A.2d 1356, 1360, 1361 (1981):

> In the instant case, death was caused by aspiration of the regurgitated contents of the stomach due to a depressed gag reflex. The jury found that the depression of the gag reflex was caused by ingestion of the drug Tuinal, prescribed to the decedent by appellant. Our review of the record supports the jury's finding that the drug Tuinal caused Ms. Fedder's demise. Dr. Robert Hunter, the pathologist for Berwick Hospital who performed the post-mortem examination of Ms. Fedder, testified that he believed her gag reflex was depressed from the barbiturates present in her system, and this postulation was seconded by Wellon Collom, a toxologist who performed the laboratory tests on sample tissues and serums taken from the decedent. Mr. Collom testified that the specimens taken were tested for the presence of all prescription drugs and several non-prescription drugs including morphine. The only drugs found present in the decedent's body were amobarbital and secobarbital, the components of Tuinal. No traces of alcohol were discovered. Mr. Collom also testified that the

levels of amobarbital and secobarbital discovered in the specimen taken from the decedent were of a sufficient degree of concentration to effectuate depression of Ms. Fedder's gag reflex. On the basis of this evidence, we conclude that the jury's finding that ingestion of Tuinal led to Ms. Fedder's death is sufficiently supported by the record.

However, the mere finding that the decedent died from ingestion of a drug prescribed to her by appellant is insufficient, in itself, to support a conviction for involuntary manslaughter. Prescription of a controlled drug by a licensed physician does not constitute an unlawful act. Therefore, under the Crimes Code, the Commonwealth must prove that appellant executed this lawful act, i.e. prescription, in a reckless or grossly negligent manner and that his conduct was the legal cause of Ms. Fedder's death.

Our review of the evidence leads us to the conclusion that there was sufficient evidence to prove each element of involuntary manslaughter. The evidence indicates that appellant prescribed Tuinal to the decedent in quantities and frequencies termed irresponsible and totally inappropriate in the circumstances. The frequency with which the prescriptions were written should have suggested that the decedent was abusing Tuinal. Moreover, this fact was specifically brought to appellant's attention by a pharmacist who called appellant alarmed over the decedent's physical condition. However, appellant chose to ignore these indications of abuse and continued to prescribe the drug to decedent. In these circumstances the record supports and justifies the jury's conclusion that appellant consciously disregarded a substantial and unjustifiable risk, which disregard involved a gross deviation from the standard of conduct a reasonable person would have observed.

The record also supports the jury's finding that appellant's acts were a direct and substantial factor in producing Ms. Fedder's death. Appellant recklessly overprescribed Tuinal to decedent over the course of several months, he was aware of her abuse of the drug yet took no remedial measures, and her death was attributed to asphyxiation due to a depressed gag reflex caused by ingestion of Tuinal....

C. EVIDENTIARY PROBLEMS

STATE v. DOYLE

Supreme Court of Nebraska
205 Neb. 234, 287 N.W.2d 59 (1980)

[Defendant was observed by neighbors and relatives to be pregnant; a witness testified that she had indicated her expected delivery date as August 8th. After August 5th the same witnesses testified that they had seen Doyle and in their opinion she no longer was pregnant. On August 9th, during the execution of a search warrant, a dead human infant was found in the home occupied by Doyle and her family. At her subsequent trial, a pathologist testified that the infant was at or near term and that in his opinion it had been born alive. However, he had found no evidence of either internal or external trauma, and could not state a cause of death. At the conclusion of the prosecution evidence, defense counsel moved for dismissal of the charges. When the motion was denied, the defense offered no evidence and rested, renewing the motion to dismiss on grounds of insufficiency of the prosecution evidence to establish guilt beyond a reasonable doubt. The trial court denied the motion as to manslaughter, but withdrew a second-degree murder count because it found no evidence of intentional killing. The jury convicted the defendant of manslaughter and the statutory offense of feloniously disposing of a dead human body. The Supreme Court affirmed the latter conviction but reversed the manslaughter conviction.]

KRIVOSHA, CHIEF JUSTICE.

An examination of the record discloses that the trial court was absolutely correct when it determined that there was not sufficient evidence to establish a killing. At best the evidence, almost exclusively circumstantial in nature, disclosed that a child was born to the defendant and that the child died. The pathologist was unable to testify as to any cause of death and could not testify that the cause of death was not from natural causes. Obviously, the trial court had concluded that the State had failed to prove a killing beyond a reasonable doubt as the State was required to do. There is no doubt that a defendant may not be convicted except upon proof beyond a reasonable doubt of every fact necessary to constitute the crime with which the accused is charged. *In Re Winship*, 397 U.S. 358....

The mere fact that a child is born alive and then dies is not sufficient evidence to convict a defendant beyond a reasonable doubt of having killed the child.

In addition, however, for all the reasons for which the trial court concluded it could not submit to the jury the issue of second degree murder, the court was compelled to reach the same conclusion with regard to the charge of manslaughter in this case. The court correctly instructed the jury that in order for the defendant to be guilty of manslaughter, an unlawful act had to have been committed by the defendant in the course of which the infant was killed. The trial court was not able to discover any evidence introduced by the State upon which the jury could find beyond a reasonable doubt that the defendant had been engaged in some unlawful act in the course of which the infant was killed. The court attempted to fill that gap by instructing the jury on the provisions of section 38-116, R.R.S.1943 (endangering the health of a child). However, the elements necessary to constitute a violation of that statute were likewise lacking in the evidence. There was no evidence offered by the State that had the defendant done something, which she did not do, the infant would have lived; nor that had she not done anything, which she did do, the infant would have lived. There was, in short, no evidence that the defendant had willfully or negligently caused or permitted the life of such child to be endangered or the health of such child to be injured, or permitted the child to be placed in such a situation that its life or health may have been endangered. One may speculate on that point, but speculation alone does not constitute evidence. *Reyes v. State*, 151 Neb. 636, 38 N.W.2d 539. There was simply no testimony upon which the jury could have found the defendant guilty under section 38-116, R.R.S. 1943, beyond a reasonable doubt.

The most that could be said, as was said by the State, is that one who has a baby should not have the baby at home. There was, however, no evidence offered that had the child been born in a hospital rather than at home it would not have died. Likewise, there was no evidence that there was an opportunity for the defendant to get to a hospital before the child was born. The only evidence offered by the State was to the effect that a child was born, it lived momentarily, and was thereafter found dead. That was not sufficient to submit a charge of manslaughter to the jury.

The traditional and prevailing view expressed by courts from other jurisdictions is that in a prosecution for killing a newly born baby it is incumbent upon the State to prove that the child was born alive and had an independent and separate existence apart from its mother and that the accused was the criminal agent causing the infant's death....

In the recent case of *State v. Klutts*, 204 Neb. 616, 284 N.W.2d 415, we reviewed our rules with regard to a criminal conviction based upon circumstantial evidence, saying, "Where circumstantial evidence is relied upon, the circumstances proven must relate directly to the guilt of the accused beyond all reasonable doubt in such a way as to exclude any other reasonable conclusion." To justify a conviction on circumstantial evidence, it is necessary that the facts and circumstances essential to the conclusion sought must be proven by competent evidence beyond a reasonable doubt, and, when taken together, must be of such a character as to be consistent with each other and with the hypothesis sought to be established thereby and inconsistent with any other reasonable hypothesis of innocence.... Any fact or circumstance reasonably susceptible of two interpretations must be resolved most favorably to the accused....

In *Reyes v. State, supra*, we said, "[A] conviction should not be based upon suspicion, speculation, the weakness of the status of the accused, the embarrassing position in which he finds himself, or the mere fact that some unfavorable circumstances are not satisfactorily explained."

We believe an examination of this record fails to disclose how the jury could possibly find beyond a reasonable doubt that the defendant had violated section 38-116, R.R.S.1943, or that she was the criminal agent causing the infant's death. In the absence of such evidence, the conviction cannot stand. The trial court should have sustained the defendant's motion to dismiss both the second degree murder and manslaughter charges, and it was error for the court not to do so. Accordingly, we reverse that portion of the court's ruling and remand said matter with instructions to dismiss count I.

NOTES

1. *People v. Brown*, 57 Ill. App. 3d 528, 532-33, 373 N.E.2d 459, 462 (1978):

> In the instant case the testimony of Dr. Pimental more than adequately describes the nature and extent of the injuries inflicted by the defendant upon the decedent. What the State fails to elicit, through this witness, is the essential causative relationship between the wounds and the death of Cheryl Edwards from a pulmonary embolism 11 days later. The sum of the evidence offered by the State is the opinion of the medical expert that,

C. EVIDENTIARY PROBLEMS 261

> he "surmised that the blood clots" which developed into the death of Edwards "originated from the site of injury, either abdomen, chest wall or both arms." This statement by the doctor, coupled with foundations of fact and reasons upon which the opinion could stand would have been sufficient to relate the wounds caused by the defendant to the death of Edwards. Without such underpinnings however, it is incomplete. The weight of an expert's opinion is measured by the reasons given for his conclusion and the factual details which he marshals in support of it.... The credibility of the expert cannot be evaluated by the trier of fact on opinion alone.... [W]ithout facts which explain how the defendant's attack caused or contributed to the ultimate reason for death, an expert's testimony is inadequate to prove the connection, leaving the relation of the act and the cause of death to inference and speculation.

The State argues that the rule in *People v. Myers* (1946), 392 Ill. 355 at 359, 64 N.E.2d 531 at 533 applies:

> ... when the State has shown the existence, through the act of the accused, of a sufficient cause of death, the death is presumed to have resulted from such act, unless it appears death was caused by a supervening act disconnected from any act of the defendant....

This merely means that the State is charged with proving that one act, which was sufficient to cause death, did occur and that the State has no burden to disprove all speculative causes. But application of the presumption in this case begs the question; the issue here is whether the State has demonstrated with adequate evidence the existence of an act on the part of the defendant sufficient to cause death. Unlike the numerous cases cited by the State in support of its arguments, there was no evidence of an autopsy, no descriptions detailing the physical condition found at death relating it to the defendant's act, no explanations of the reasons underlying the cause of death....

2. *People v. Stewart*, 40 N.Y.2d 692, 698-99, 358 N.E.2d 487, 389 N.Y.S.2d 804, 809 (1976):

> The other difficulty in the case is that it was never determined what actually caused the cardiac arrest. Dr. Di Maio acknowledged several possibilities which individually or combined could have created the condition. Most of the factors cited would indicate that the defendant's act was responsible either because it created a physical strain or shock or created the need for an operation which had the same effect. But Dr. Di Maio conceded that there was some evidence that the anesthesiologist failed to provide oxygen to the patient and that this alone could have been the cause of death. In our view if this occurred it was a grave neglect, perhaps gross negligence, but in any event sufficient to break whatever tenuous causal relationship existed at the time of this incidental operation....
>
> Finally, it should be noted that this is not a case where two or more witnesses gave conflicting testimony which simply created a credibility question for the jury. Here all the evidence on this point came from a single prosecution witness who offered irreconcilable testimony pointing

in both directions to guilt and innocence on the homicide charge. There was then no basis for the jury to find that the injury inflicted by the defendant caused the death of Daniel Smith, beyond a reasonable doubt.

3. *People v. Lopez*, 72 Ill. App. 3d 713, 717, 391 N.E.2d 105, 108 (1979):

> We next consider the judgments entered on the guilty verdicts pertaining to the Lopez twin who actually fired the gun. As admitted by the State, although there was evidence proving that the man who fired the gun was one of the Lopez twins, no witness could identify which twin actually crossed the street and fired the gun. As indicated previously, such a failure was not fatal at the trial level because one Lopez brother was held accountable for the conduct of the other. However, having reversed the judgments based on the accountability theory, we must also reverse the judgments entered against the Lopez brother who actually fired the gun due to the State's failure to prove which brother fired the gun.

4. How far should expert witnesses be allowed to go in presenting evidence that a dead child manifested signs of what is known as the "battered child syndrome"? In *State v. Wilkerson*, 295 N.C. 559, 247 S.E.2d 905 (1978), the body of the two-year-old child of the defendant showed indications of multiple injuries of a nonaccidental character. A qualified expert testified that those injuries were compatible with child battering, which usually occurs in the form of purported discipline administered by a parent, guardian, or custodian of a young child. Circumstantial evidence offered by the prosecution showed that no one other than the Wilkersons had physical custody of the child at the time the fatal injuries must have been inflicted, but the expert gave no testimony in that regard. The North Carolina Supreme Court affirmed a manslaughter conviction:

> Upholding the admission of similar testimony, the California District Court of Appeals in *People v. Jackson*, 18 Cal. App. 3d 504, 507, 95 Cal. Rptr. 919, 921 (1971) said:
>
> > A finding, as in this case, of the "battered child syndrome" is not an opinion by the doctor as to whether any particular person has done anything, but, as this doctor indicated, "it would take thousands of children to have the severity and number and degree of injuries that this child had over the span of time that we had" by accidental means. In other words, the "battered child syndrome" simply indicates that a child found with the type of injuries outlined above has not suffered those injuries by accidental means. This conclusion is based upon an extensive study of the subject by medical science. The additional finding that the injuries were probably occasioned by someone who is ostensibly caring for the child is simply a conclusion based upon logic and reason. Only someone regularly "caring" for the child has the continuing opportunity to inflict these types of injuries; an isolated contact with a vicious stranger would not result in this pattern of successive injuries stretching through several months.

As far as our research reveals, all courts which have considered the question, including our own Court of Appeals, have concluded that such expert medical testimony concerning the battered child syndrome as was offered in this case is properly admitted into evidence. *State v. Periman*, 32 N.C.App. 33, 230 S.E.2d 802 (1977); *State v. Loss*, 295 Minn. 271, 204 N.W.2d 404 (1973); *People v. Henson*, 33 N.Y.2d 63, 304 N.E.2d 358 (1973); *State v. Best*, 232 N.W.2d 447 (S.D. 1975).

The cases relied on by defendant, *Hill v. R.R.*, 186 N.C. 475, 119 S.E. 884 (1923); *Mule Co. v. R.R.*, 160 N.C. 252, 75 S.E. 994 (1912); *Summerlin v. R.R.*, 133 N.C. 550, 45 S.E. 898 (1903), are readily distinguishable. In each of these cases the difficulty was that the medical expert was permitted to testify that a certain event had in fact caused the injuries complained of. The court in each case pointed out that it would have been proper to have asked the expert whether the event could or might have caused the injury, but not whether it in fact did cause it. (There may be questions of cause and effect, however, about which an expert should be permitted to give, if he has one, a positive opinion. *Mann v. Transportation Co.*, 283 N.C. 734, 198 S.E.2d 558 (1973).) The Court in Summerlin also relied on the rule that an expert must base his opinion upon facts within his own knowledge or upon facts put to him in a properly phrased hypothetical question.

Defendant's first assignment of error is overruled.

295 N.C. at 570-71, 247 S.E.2d at 911-12.

5. *Christian v. Commonwealth*, 221 Va. 1078, 277 S.E.2d 205, 208 (1981):

Like the body of the crime, criminal agency can be proven by circumstantial evidence. *Graham v. Commonwealth*, 140 Va. 452, 457, 124 S.E. 429, 430 (1924). Were the rule otherwise, many atrocious crimes would go unpunished. Often, the deceased is the only eyewitness to murder. Typically, child abuse is practiced by a parent in the privacy of the home with no one present but the victim and frequently, as here, the victim is an infant too young to testify.

A single circumstance seldom justifies a finding of criminal agency. Thus, mere opportunity to commit an offense raises only "the suspicion that the defendant may have been the guilty agent; and suspicion is never enough to sustain a conviction." *Simmons v. Commonwealth*, 208 Va. 778, 783, 160 S.E.2d 569, 573 (1968). Opportunity is always a relevant circumstance, of course, and, when reinforced by other incriminating circumstances, may be sufficient to establish criminal agency beyond a reasonable doubt. Moreover, where it appears that a criminal assault was made upon a child within a particular period of time, evidence which shows that the accused was sole custodian of the child during that period may be sufficient, standing alone, to prove criminal agency.

But there was no such evidence here. It is true that, after the defendant's father left for work the night of November 28, she had sole custody of her daughter until she placed her on the bus the next morning. Thereafter, however, at least five people had an opportunity to handle the child before Ms. Vaughan discovered that her legs were broken. If, as the Attorney General asks us to infer, the defendant injured her daughter during the night, it is strange the bus driver or his aides or one of Ms. Vaughan's assistants did not discover the painful fractures.

When the only evidence connecting the accused with the crime is circumstantial, the evidence is sufficient to establish criminal agency only when it meets the standard required for proof of other elements of the offense.

All necessary circumstances proved must be consistent with guilt and inconsistent with innocence. It is not sufficient that the evidence create a suspicion of guilt, however strong, or even a probability of guilt, but must exclude every reasonable hypothesis save that of guilt. To accomplish that the chain of circumstances must be unbroken and the evidence as a whole must be sufficient to satisfy the guarded judgment that both the *corpus delicti* and the criminal agency of the accused have been proved to the exclusion of any other reasonable hypothesis and to a moral certainty....

While the defendant's opportunity to injure her daughter and certain other circumstances in this case may raise inferences which "create a suspicion of guilt ... or even a probability of guilt," we are of opinion the evidence is insufficient to exclude a reasonable hypothesis that someone other than the defendant was the criminal agent.

D. THE "YEAR AND A DAY" RULE

STATE v. PINE
Supreme Court of Rhode Island
524 A.2d 1104 (1987)

SHEA, JUSTICE.

This case is before the Supreme Court on appeal by the State of Rhode Island following the grant by the Superior Court of the defendant's pretrial motion to dismiss an indictment for manslaughter. The trial justice dismissed the indictment because the victim died more than a year and a day after the defendant allegedly assaulted him. He held that the common-law year-and-a-day rule was no longer viable but declined to give its abrogation retroactive effect. We affirm.

Although it is unclear when the year-and-a-day requirement in homicide prosecutions concerning the death of the victim first arose, it has been referred to and defined in numerous works compiling and explaining the state of English common law. Indeed, by the early eighteenth century and probably much earlier, there was a general assumption that a homicide could be prosecuted as such only if the victim died within a year and a day of the wrongful act. 381 Mass. at 413-14, 409 N.E.2d at 772-73. Both Sir Matthew Hale and William Hawkins refer to the rule in their treatises on the common law:

"If a man give another a stroke, which it may be, is not in itself so mortal, but that with good care he might be cured, yet if he die of this wound within the year and a day, it is homicide or murder, as the case is, and so it hath been always ruled." 1 Hale, History of the Pleas of the Crown, ch. 33 at 428 (1736).

"Also it is agreed, that no person shall be adjudged by any act whatever to kill another who doth not die thereof within a year and a day after; in the computation whereof, the whole day in which the hurt was done shall be reckoned the first." *Elliott v. Mills*, 335 P.2d at 1107 (quoting 1 Hawkins' Pleas of the Crown, ch. 13, § 9 (8th ed. 1824)).

Since compilation of the criminal law in the early law reports was not so adequate as the compilation of the civil law, Hale's History of the Pleas of the Crown (1736) together with Hawkins' Pleas of the Crown (1716) are said to form the basis of the modern criminal law. H. Potter, An Historical Introduction to English Law, 249 (2d ed. 1943). It is clear, therefore, that the year-and-a-day rule was well known to be part of the common law of England prior to the adoption of the Rhode Island State Constitution in 1842. Article 14, section 1, of our State Constitution holds that "[a]ll charters, contracts, judgments, actions and rights of action shall be as valid as if this Constitution had not been made." We conclude, therefore, that the common-law year-and-a-day rule was in effect and hence accepted by our State Legislature as part of our jurisprudence, both before and after the enactment of our constitution in 1842, as being part of the body of common law that had not been specifically abrogated by the writers of the constitution.

[The court concluded that subsequent legislation had not affected the common-law, year-and-a-day rule in the state.]

... [W]e must now decide whether the rule remains viable in light of the state of modern medical and forensic science and the structure of procedural protections afforded criminal defendants by various statutes, case law and rules of practice and procedure. Medical science has advanced to the point where some lives that in the past would have ended almost immediately can now be sustained or prolonged indefinitely. The reason advanced for the rule at common law was that if the person alleged to have been murdered dies after the expiration of a year and a day, "it cannot be discerned, as the law presumes, whether he died of the stroke, or poison, etc., or a natural death." *Elliott v. Mills*, 335 P.2d at 1108 (citing 1 Warren on Homicide § 60 (1938)). Modern pathologists are able to determine the cause of death with much more accuracy than was possible in earlier times. The causation question therefore presents a far less difficult problem of proof in modern-day criminal prosecutions.

It is true that when the period between the assault and the victim's death is prolonged, problems of proof can be made more difficult. This greater difficulty affects the ability of the state to prove its case and consequently can be said to afford additional protection to the criminal defendant. Since the state must establish the connection between the act and the victim's death beyond a reasonable doubt, any problems of proof serve to benefit the defendant. "A murder conviction which rests upon uncertain medical speculation as to the cause of death is not a case which has been proved beyond a reasonable doubt." *People v. Stevenson*, 416 Mich. at 392-93, 331 N.W.2d at 146. We think this standard is a sufficient safeguard for the criminal defendant. We do not find, therefore, that our abrogation of the year-and-a-day rule requires us to replace it with some other time period within which death must occur.

Our review demonstrates that a majority of jurisdictions retain the common-law year-and-a-day rule. However, we adopt the conclusion of the Supreme Judicial Court of Massachusetts that the long life of the rule may result from the infrequency with which the issue has been raised. Courts therefore have not been given the opportunity to address it. *Commonwealth v. Lewis*, 381 Mass. at 415, 409 N.E. 2d at 773. That is exactly the case in this state.

Some courts have declined to abrogate the rule, holding that the legislature is the proper forum for such change. *State v. Minster*, 302 Md. 240, 241, 486 A.2d 1197, 1197 (1985). We conclude that since murder is a common-law crime and the application of the year-and-a-day rule in criminal prosecutions was originally judicial and not the act of the legislature, it is entirely appropriate for this court to make the change. See *Becker v. Beaudoin*, 106 R.I. 562, 569, 261 A.2d 896, 900 (1970) (*citing Rampone v. Wanskuck Buildings, Inc.*, 102 R.I. 30, 227 A.2d 586 (1967)). "While a deferral to the legislature in the initiation of changes in matters affecting public policy may often be appropriate, it is not required where the concept demanding change is judicial in its origins." 106 R.I. at 570, 261 A.2d at 900 (quoting *Henry v. John W. Eshelman & Sons*, 99 R.I. 518, 527, 209 A.2d 46, 51 (1965)). The Legislature may wish to comment statutorily on the rule at some future time, and it is certainly not precluded from doing so. Nevertheless, that possibility does not render inappropriate our decision to affect the common-law through judicial decision.

[The court, however, declined to give the ruling retroactive effect and therefore affirmed the lower court's dismissal.]

NOTES

1. Some other courts have also abrogated the rule by invoking inherent powers to change the common law. *See, e.g., State v. Vance*, 403 S.E.2d 495 (N.C. 1991), *Swafford v. State*, 421 N.E.2d 596 (Ind. 1981); *Commonwealth v. Lewis*, 409 N.E.2d 771 (Mass. 1980), cert. denied, 450 U.S. 929 (1981).

2. Some state statutes incorporate the rule. *See, e.g.*, Nev. Rev. Stat. § 200.100 (1991). California has adopted a "three years and a day" rule. Cal. Penal Code § 194 (West 1988). However, "most modern statutes are in accord with the Model [Penal] Code in eliminating the express time limitation as a special causal requirement." MODEL PENAL CODE § 210.1, comment at 9-10.

SECTION III. Classification in Terms of *Mens Rea*

NOTE

The following California statutes exemplify those statutes which continue to rely on the common law distinction between murder and manslaughter in terms of malice aforethought. The California statute and the MODEL PENAL CODE represent, with countless variations, the two basic versions of homicide statutes in the United States.

CALIFORNIA PENAL CODE (1988)

§ 187. Murder Defined; Death of Fetus.

(a) Murder is the unlawful killing of a human being, or a fetus, with malice aforethought.

(b) This section shall not apply to any person who commits an act which results in the death of a fetus if any of the following apply:

(1) The act complied with the Therapeutic Abortion Act, Chapter 11 (commencing with Section 25950) of Division 20 of the Health and Safety Code.

(2) The act was committed by a holder of a physician's and surgeon's certificate, as defined in the Business and Professions Code, in a case where, to a medical certainty, the result of childbirth would be death of the mother of the fetus or where her death from childbirth, although not medically certain, would be substantially certain or more likely than not.

(3) The act was solicited, aided, abetted, or consented to by the mother of the fetus.

....

§ 188. Malice, Express Malice, and Implied Malice Defined.

Such malice may be express or implied. It is express when there is manifested a deliberate intention unlawfully to take away the life of a fellow creature. It is implied, when no considerable provocation appears, or when the circumstances attending the killing show an abandoned and malignant heart.

When it is shown that the killing resulted from the intentional doing of an act with express or implied malice as defined above, no other mental state need be shown to establish the mental state of malice aforethought. Neither an awareness of the obligation to act within the general body of laws regulating society nor acting despite such awareness is included within the definition of malice.

§ 189. Murder; degrees*

....

To prove the killing was "deliberate and premeditated," it shall not be necessary to prove the defendant maturely and meaningfully reflected upon the gravity of his or her act.

§ 192. Manslaughter.

Manslaughter is the unlawful killing of a human being without malice. It is of three kinds:

1. Voluntary — upon a sudden quarrel or heat of passion.

---

*(1992).

2. Involuntary — in the commission of an unlawful act, not amounting to felony; or in the commission of a lawful act which might produce death, in an unlawful manner, or without due caution and circumspection. This subdivision shall not apply to acts committed in the driving of a vehicle.

3. In the driving of a vehicle.

(a) In the commission of an unlawful act, not amounting to felony, with gross negligence; or in the commission of a lawful act which might produce death, in an unlawful manner, and with gross negligence.

(b) In the commission of an unlawful act, not amounting to felony, without gross negligence; or in the commission of a lawful act which might produce death, in an unlawful manner, but without gross negligence.*

MODEL PENAL CODE

§ 210.9. *Definitions*

[The text of this section appears in Appendix A.]

§ 210.1. *Criminal Homicide*

[The text of this section appears in Appendix A.]

§ 210.2. *Murder*

[The text of this section appears in Appendix A.]

§ 210.3. *Manslaughter*

[The text of this section appears in Appendix A.]

§ 210.4. *Negligent Homicide*

[The text of this section appears in Appendix A.]

The introductory note to Article 210 and comment of § 210.2 of the Model Penal Code provides an incisive summary of the basic structures of homicide statutes and definitions of terms.

§ 210.2. *Murder*

. . . .

Comment

1. *Common Law Background.* At common law, murder was defined as the unlawful killing of another human being with "malice aforethought." Whatever the original meaning of that phrase, it became over time an "arbitrary

---

*§ 192(3)(a) requires a showing of greater culpability and is punishable by imprisonment in a county jail or state prison, whereas (b) is punishable by imprisonment only in a county jail.

symbol" used by judges to signify any of the number of mental states deemed sufficient to support liability for murder. Successive generations added new content to "malice aforethought" until it encompassed a variety of mental attitudes bearing no predictable relation to the ordinary sense of the two words. . . .*

Various authorities have given different summaries of the several meanings of "malice aforethought."[4] Generally, these definitions converge on four constituent states of mind. First and foremost, there was intent to kill. Common law authorities included in the notion of intent to kill awareness that the death of another would result from one's actions, even if the actor had no particular desire to achieve such a consequence. Thus, intentional or knowing homicide was murder unless the actor killed in the heat of passion engendered by adequate provocation, in which case the crime was manslaughter. A second species of murder involved intent to cause grievous bodily harm. Again, knowledge that conduct would cause serious bodily injury was generally assimilated to intent and was deemed sufficient for murder if death of another actually resulted. A third category of murder was sometimes called depraved-heart murder. This label derived from decisions and statutes condemning as murder unintentional homicide under circumstances evincing a "depraved mind" or an "abandoned and malignant heart." Older authorities may have described such circumstances as giving rise to an "implied" or "presumed" intent to kill or injure, but the essential concept was one of extreme recklessness regarding homicidal risk. Thus, a person might be liable for murder absent any actual intent to kill or injure if he caused the death of another in a manner exhibiting a "wanton and wilful disregard of an unreasonable human risk" or, in confusing elaboration, a "wickedness of disposition, hardness of heart, cruelty, recklessness of consequences, and a mind regardless of social duty." The fourth kind of murder was based on intent to commit a felony. This is the origin of the felony-murder rule, which assigns strict liability for homicide committed during the commission of a felony. These four states of mind exhausted the meaning of "malice aforethought"; the phrase had no residual content.

2. *Antecedent Statutory Variations.* Prior to the recodification effort begun by the Model Penal Code, most American jurisdictions maintained a law of murder built around these common-law classifications. The most significant departure was the division of murder into degrees, a change initiated by the Pennsylvania legislation of 1794. That statute provided that "all murder, which shall be perpetrated by means of poison, or by lying in wait, or by any

---

* "It was generally agreed that the terms 'malice aforethought' and 'legal malice' were technical terms not restricted to the understanding of the word 'malice' or 'malicious' in common usage by ordinary people. 'Malice,' however, as applied to the offense of murder, need not denote spite or malevolence, hatred or ill-will, to the person killed, nor that the slayer killed his victim in cold blood, as with a settled design and premeditation; . . ."

"The term 'malice,' therefore, in its legal sense, does not necessarily import ill-will towards the individual slain, but includes a general malignant recklessness of the lives and safety of others." *Turner v. Commonwealth*, 167 Ky. 365, 180 S.W. 768, 771-72 (1915).

[4] *See* 4 W. Blackstone, Commentaries *198-201; 4 Stephen's Commentaries on the Laws of England 42-48 (21st ed. Warmington 1950); W. LaFave & A. Scott, Criminal Law 528-62 (1972); R. Perkins, Criminal Law 34-36 (2d ed. 1969); Wechsler & Michael, A Rationale of the Law of Homicide I, 37 Colum.L.Rev. 701, 702-17 (1937).

other kind of willful, deliberate or premeditated killing, or which shall be committed in the perpetration, or attempt to perpetrate any arson, rape, robbery or burglary shall be deemed murder in the first degree; and all other kinds of murder shall be deemed murder in the second degree." The thrust of this reform was to confine the death penalty, which was then mandatory on conviction of any common law murder, to homicides judged particularly heinous. Other states followed the Pennsylvania practice until at one time the vast majority of American jurisdictions differentiated degrees of murder and the term "first-degree murder" passed into common parlance.

....

In summary, therefore, it was the pattern in this country prior to the Model Penal Code to incorporate the common law in some jurisdictions and to build upon it in others. Murder was generally defined to include intentional homicides, unintentional homicides committed with callous disregard of human life, and some variant of felony murder. Fewer statutes explicitly specified "intent to injure" as a sufficient *mens rea* for murder, though some decisions included a separate category to this effect. To this extent, the common law survived virtually intact. On the other hand, there was far less agreement concerning the relative gravity of the various forms of murder, and many states enacted grading schemes unknown to the common law. *Id.* at 13-16, 19.

Article 210 [of the Model Penal Code] undertakes a major restructuring of the law of homicide. It abandons the degree structure that has dominated American murder provisions since the Pennsylvania reform of 1794 and classifies all criminal homicides into the three basic categories of murder, manslaughter, and negligent homicide. Article 210 does not rely on the common-law vocabulary to distinguish among these offenses but substitutes the culpability concepts developed in Section 2.02 as the basis for making the appropriate distinctions among criminal homicides. *Id.* at 1.

SECTION IV. Intent Murder

A. PREMEDITATION, INTENT, AND DEGREES OF MURDER

GREEN v. STATE
Court of Criminal Appeals of Tennessee
1 Tenn. Crim. App. 719, 450 S.W.2d 27 (1970)

WALKER, PRESIDING JUDGE.

The defendant below, Thomas Green, was found guilty of murder in the first degree, in the Criminal Court of Hamilton County, and sentenced to 25 years in the penitentiary, from which judgment he appeals to this court. He contends that the evidence did not warrant a conviction for murder in the first degree, particularly that no premeditation was shown.

The deceased, Morris Snow, age 21 and three other young men (Sylvester Hill, Tommy Lee Billups, and Larry Code) were at Velma's Tea Room in Chattanooga in the early morning hours of January 19, 1968. There was some disagreement between Snow and the defendant. Billups says that the defendant and two other people came to Snow's table and the defendant argued

A. PREMEDITATION, INTENT, AND DEGREES OF MURDER

with him, telling Snow: "My brother killed a man the other night, and you're going to mess around here and get killed, too." After this the defendant and Snow shook hands and the defendant said to forget it. He then returned to his table in another part of the room and the deceased, Snow, sat at his table with his three friends and was drinking a bottle of beer.

A short time later, estimated by the witnesses from four to twenty minutes, the defendant returned to the table where Snow was seated and told him to go home, to which Snow replied that he was grown and didn't have to go home. The defendant asked the deceased to repeat himself and he again said he was grown. All of the witnesses agree that the defendant pulled a pistol and shot the deceased while he was seated at the table with his hands on it. The defendant fired several shots, one striking the deceased back of the left ear and another back of the left shoulder. The second shot was fired after Snow had fallen to the floor. The defendant and one of his friends ran out of the building.

The defendant did not testify or present any evidence as to the facts of the case.

Of course, to support a verdict finding a defendant guilty of murder in the first degree, there must be an evidentiary basis for a conclusion that the killing was willful, deliberate, malicious and premeditated, unless effected by poison or lying in wait or in the perpetration of one of the felonies named in the defining statute, in which cases the specified circumstances make it otherwise unnecessary to prove deliberation and premeditation. *Bass v. State*, 191 Tenn. 259, 231 S.W.2d 707.

Here the defendant had had an argument, during which he threatened to kill the deceased. After some minutes and time to become cool, he returned and shot the deceased. The jury was well warranted in concluding the killing came from deliberation and premeditation. It is not necessary that the design or intention to kill should have been conceived or have pre-existed in the mind any definite time anterior to its execution. It is sufficient if it preceded the assault, however short the interval, and the length of time is not the essence of this constituent of the offense. The design may be conceived and deliberately formed in an instant. Hence it is not material that the interval of premeditation was brief.

....

Concerning the weight and sufficiency of evidence to establish premeditation, and particularly with reference to the nature of the act causing death, many courts have held that deliberation and premeditation may be inferred from the manner in which the killing was committed; and that repeated shots, blows, and other acts of violence are sufficient evidence of premeditation. 3 Warren on Homicide, § 273a, pp. 167-168. Such matters as the atrocity, cruelty, and malignity appearing in the circumstances under which the killing took place have been passed on frequently by the courts in considering the sufficiency of the evidence to sustain a conviction for first degree murder. 41 C.J.S. Homicide § 328, p. 71.

In this case the defendant deliberately shot the deceased in the head, mortally wounding him, callously shot him again in the back after he fell from his chair to the floor, and then fled the premises.

In *State v. McNamara*, 116 N.J.L. 497, 184 A. 797, cert. den., 299 U.S. 568, 57 S.Ct. 32, 81 L.Ed. 419, wherein the deceased was killed by multiple close-range revolver shots, the Court held that the repeated firing of a revolver is sufficient to establish premeditation.

....

In *State v. Faust*, 254 N.C. 101, 118 S.E.2d 769, 96 A.L.R.2d 1422, cert. den., 368 U.S. 851, 82 S.Ct. 85, 7 L.Ed.2d 49, the defendant took one officer's gun, while he was being held by members of an angry crowd, and shot and felled another officer and then walked around him and fired five more shots into his body at close range. Affirming a first degree murder conviction, the Court said that among the circumstances to be considered in determining whether a killing was with premeditation and deliberation is the dealing of lethal blows after the deceased has been felled and rendered helpless.

Dowell v. State, 191 Ark. 311, 86 S.W.2d 23, was a case involving the killing of three people; one was shot in the back of the head at close range, a child was also shot in the head, and the third deceased's head was crushed with a blunt instrument, and all the bodies were then thrown into a creek. The Arkansas Supreme Court held that the manner in which a killing is effected is a potent fact and circumstance tending to prove or disprove premeditation and deliberation, ... Affirmed.

GALBREATH, JUDGE (dissenting).

I must dissent.

....

From the facts of the case it would appear the jury, lower court and the majority here presumed premeditation or inferred it from proof that does not seem to this writer to suggest its existence at the time of the killing. Premeditation may not be presumed, it must be proved. True, the defendant killed the deceased with a deadly weapon following a quarrel. But, from these facts only murder in the second degree may be presumed.

....

> Where the state proves the commission of a homicide, there arises a presumption of second degree murder. To reduce homicide from second degree murder there must be evidence of justification or mitigation. The burden is on the state to raise the offense to murder in the first degree. Admission of deliberate killing is sufficient so as to raise the offense, as is evidence of killing in an attempt at robbery, or to otherwise gain deceased's property. The offense is not raised by proof of killing with a deadly weapon. The burden of reducing the offense to manslaughter is on the defendant, but defendant sustains the burden by raising a reasonable doubt in the jury's mind whether defendant is guilty of second degree murder. Underhill's Criminal Evidence, 5th Ed. § 657.

What is the proof in the record that proves premeditation? There is none. On the contrary, there is undisputed proof from which it may plainly be inferred that an instant before the shooting there was no plan in the mind of the defendant to kill the victim. Green walked up to the table at which the victim was seated and said simply, "Go home." It is submitted for logical

A. PREMEDITATION, INTENT, AND DEGREES OF MURDER

consideration that these actions and words mitigate against a previously designed plan to kill. If the defendant had acceded to the imperious request to go home, nothing appears in the record to suggest that he would not be alive today. Of course, he had every right not to go home, and for the defendant to become angry enough to kill him for not obeying his dictatorial order he should be subjected to such punishment as the law provides for taking the life of another under such circumstances. He should not, in my judgment, be subjected to the same punishment reserved for the felon who carefully plans to insure his child's life and then kills it to collect money. Or the depraved killer who lies in wait to slay his victim from ambush. Or the bandit who kills his robbery victim to conceal his guilt of that crime. These are more serious matters than the rash, impulsive, stupid, impetuous act described in the record before us.

True, it is not necessary to prove premeditation existed for any definite period of time. But it is necessary to prove that it did exist. This is a relatively difficult matter to prove. It involves proving the mental state of the killer just prior to the act of killing. The fact that a killing is unexplainable from a reasonable consideration of the facts and circumstances, that it was pointless and useless, that the killer had nothing to gain from his act, that the killing was executed in a particularly bloody manner as in this case by shooting again and again do not constitute facts that tend to prove first degree murder; on the contrary, the more irrational and pointless a killing is, the more likely is it to lack the planning and deliberation necessary to constitute premeditation. . . .

Premeditation should not, as the majority herein seems to do, when their opinion holds that the design or intention to kill need not have pre-existed for any definite time, be treated as synonymous with intent. Intent, unlike premeditation, is also one of the elements of second degree murder and intent must be accompanied by a deliberate preconceived plan to kill in order to raise the degree to the highest level of murder.

. . . .

Premeditation may, of course, be inferred from the acts and words of the killer. Nowhere in the record from the point the defendant shook hands with the deceased and told him to forget an argument they had concluded does anything at all appear to indicate the defendant's state of mind. If he had stood up and announced, "I am going over and kill Snow,"; or if he had taken his pistol out and walked over to Snow's table in a threatening way, these facts would justify the jury in concluding a previously formulated design to kill had taken shape. Instead of such actions or words the circumstances prove without dispute that the defendant walked over and did something that completely dispels the notion that he planned to kill; he told the deceased to leave! . . . The defendant did not indicate by word or deed that he had determined to kill the deceased if his order had been obeyed. It was his almost infantile, petulant reaction to the deceased's perfectly valid reaction to his demand that triggered the anger that resulted in this hot blooded, second degree murder.

. . . I would recommend modification to second degree murder and a sentence of ten years in the penitentiary subject to acceptance by the State.

NOTES

1. In *State v. Morey*, 25 Or. 241, 35 P. 655, 656 (1894), the court held that, as a matter of law, the time elapsing between the defendant's moving from the sidewalk outside a house and into a room inside the house where he shot the deceased, would be sufficient to give opportunity for deliberation and premeditation. The court stated: "it is essential that the deliberate and premeditated design to kill ... precede the killing by some appreciable length of time, sufficient for reflection and consideration upon the matter, and the formation of a definite purpose to kill; and it matters not how short the time is, if it is sufficient for that purpose. The rapidity of mental action is such that the formation of a design may not occupy more than a moment of time, and it is sufficient if it is formed and matured while the mind is in its normal state, and under the control of the slayer, however brief the space of time may be."

2. In *State v. Weddle*, 29 Utah 2d 464, 511 P.2d 733, 735 (1973), defendant claimed that he had shot the deceased police officer in panic because he feared arrest for an armed robbery which he had committed earlier, and had no prior intention of killing the officer. In upholding the conviction for first degree murder, the court stated: "A person may do an act willfully, intentionally, maliciously and deliberately after a moment's reflection as well as after thinking about the matter for a longer period." *See also Wooten v. State*, 104 Fla. 597, 140 So. 474 (1932): "homicide will constitute murder in the first degree, although the design and intent to commit such homicide was formed by the accused immediately before the act is actually committed."

3. "Both premeditation and deliberation may be inferred from the circumstances of a homicide. The design may be conceived and deliberately formed in an instant." *Meazel v. State*, 500 S.W.2d 627, 629 (Tenn. Crim. App. 1973).

4. In states which do not require proof of a "willful, deliberate and premeditated" killing, but adhere to the common law definition of "malice aforethought," an intentional killing usually is regarded as murder despite the fact that there was no appreciable time interval between the formation of the intent to kill and the act of killing. "It is enough that with the intention to commit the act, the appreciation of the result likely to follow appeared to the defendant at the time the act was committed." *Turner v. Commonwealth*, 167 Ky. 365, 180 S.W. 768, 773 (1915).

BULLOCK v. UNITED STATES

United States Court of Appeals
122 F.2d 213 (D.C. Cir. 1941), *cert. denied*, 317 U.S. 627 (1942)

EDGERTON, ASSOCIATE JUSTICE.

This appeal is from a conviction of murder in the first degree. The trial judge instructed the jury that, though "deliberate and premeditated malice" involves turning over in the mind an intention to kill, "it does not take any appreciable length of time to turn a thought of that kind over in your mind." In 1931, this court said as much. But in 1937 we approved the opposite rule, that "some appreciable time must elapse." We adhere to the latter rule. To speak of premeditation and deliberation which are instantaneous, or which take no appreciable time, is a contradiction in terms. It deprives the statutory requirement of all meaning and destroys the statutory distinction between first and second degree murder. At common law there were no degrees of murder. If the accused had no overwhelming provocation to kill, he was equally guilty whether he carried out his murderous intent at once or after mature reflection. Statutes like ours, which distinguish deliberate and premeditated murder from other murder, reflect a belief that one who meditates an intent to kill and then deliberately executes it is more dangerous, more culpable or less capable of reformation than one who kills on sudden impulse; or that the prospect of the death penalty is more likely to deter men from deliberate than from impulsive murder. The deliberate killer is guilty of first degree murder; the impulsive killer is not. The quoted part of the charge was therefore erroneous. The majority of the court think, however, that it was sufficiently corrected by a later charge which in effect contradicted it.

But we all think the evidence insufficient to show that the killing was deliberate and premeditated. When the victim, a police officer, came on the scene, appellant was engaged in a drunken quarrel with another person and had a loaded revolver in his hand. There is no sufficient evidence that appellant was facing in the officer's direction, or knew of his presence, until he spoke. The officer asked "What's the trouble around here?" or "What's all this racket about?" The prosecutor, in his opening statement to the jury, conceded that "as soon as the officer spoke, defendant shot him." Shortly before the close of the trial the court said: "The way it impresses me from the evidence is that the officer was right on top of them, and almost momentarily the man pulled the revolver and shot him." In denying a motion for a new trial the court said: "My view is that the defendant did not realize a police officer was nearby until the officer called out the question 'What's the trouble around here?' and that it was a matter only of a second or two before the defendant fired the two shots in rapid succession which resulted in the death of the police officer." The evidence overwhelmingly supports these statements of the prosecutor and the judge. Accordingly it does not support a conviction of first degree murder. There is nothing deliberate and premeditated about a killing which is done within a second or two after the accused first thinks of doing it; or, as we think the evidence shows, instantaneously, as appellant, interrupted in his quarrel, turned and fired. Appellant's motion for a directed verdict in respect to first degree murder should have been granted.

. . . .

Reversed.

NOTES

1. Under Washington law, premeditation must involve more than a moment in point of time. RCW9A. 32.020(1). As to what more is required, compare *State v. Bingham*, 105 Wash.2d 820, 719. P.2d 109 (1986) (manual strangulation taking 3 to 5 minutes shows an opportunity to deliberate, but alone does not satisfy that element of premeditation) to *State v. Ollens*, 107 Wash. 2d 848, 733 P.2d 984 (1987) (slashing victim's throat following multiple stab wounds provides sufficient evidence to submit premeditation to the jury) which distinguishes *Bingham*.

2. "As much cruelty, as much indifference to the life of others, a disposition at least as dangerous to society, probably even more dangerous, is shown by sudden as by premeditated murders. The following cases appear to me to set this in a clear light. A, passing along the road, sees a boy sitting on a bridge over a deep river and, out of mere wanton barbarity, pushes him into it and so drowns him. A man makes advances to a girl who repels him. He deliberately but instantly cuts her throat. A man civilly asked to pay a just debt pretends to get the money, loads a rifle and blows out his creditor's brains. In none of these cases is there premeditation unless the word is used in a sense as unnatural as 'aforethought' in 'malice aforethought,' but each represents even more diabolical cruelty and ferocity than that which is involved in murders premeditated in the natural sense of the word." 3 STEPHEN, HISTORY OF THE CRIMINAL LAW OF ENGLAND 94 (1883).

3. "I think the distinction is much too vague to be continued in our law. There can be no intent unless there is a choice, yet by the hypothesis, the choice without more is enough to justify the inference that the intent was deliberate and premeditated. The presence of a sudden impulse is said to mark the dividing line, but how can an impulse be anything but sudden when the time for its formation is measured by the lapse of seconds? Yet the decisions are to the effect that seconds may be enough. What is meant, as I understand it, is that the impulse must be the product of an emotion or passion so swift and overmastering as to sweep the mind from its moorings. A metaphor, however, is, to say the least, a shifting test whereby to measure degrees of guilt that mean the difference between life and death. I think the students of the mind should make it clear to the lawmakers that the statute is framed along the lines of a defective and unreal psychology. If intent is deliberate and premeditated whenever there is choice, then in truth it is always deliberate and premeditated, since choice is involved in the hypothesis of the intent. What we have is merely a privilege offered to the jury to find the lesser degree when the suddenness of the intent, the vehemence of the passion, seems to call irresistibly for the exercise of mercy. I have no objection to giving them this dispensing power, but it should be given to them directly and not in a mystifying cloud of words." Cardozo, *Law and Literature* 98-100 in SELECTED WRITINGS 383-84 (1947).

STATE v. STANDIFORD
769 P.2d 254 (1988)
Supreme Court of Utah

STEWART, JUSTICE.

...

Sometime between 3:00 a.m. and 4:00 a.m. on April 27, 1984, Hisae Wood was stabbed to death in an assault during which 107 stab wounds were inflicted on her body. Earlier that night, Standiford had been in his garage with his friend, Joey Granato, painting Granato's Jeep. Twice during the evening, Standiford and Granato went to Wood's residence to purchase cocaine. After each trip, Standiford and Granato freebased the cocaine and then resumed painting the Jeep. Around 4:00 a.m., Standiford told Granato that he was going to a convenience store to buy cigarettes. He took longer than necessary for that errand, and apparently had more cocaine. He denied returning to the Woods' residence and claimed that he had merely saved the cocaine from one of their earlier purchases.

[Standiford later confessed to the killing but claimed he acted in self-defense. He was convicted of second degree murder.]

Standiford asserts that the trial court erred in failing to instruct the jury that second degree murder required proof of "malice aforethought." Prior to the adoption of Utah's current criminal code in 1973, murder was defined as "the unlawful killing of a human being with malice aforethought." Utah Code Ann. § 76-30-1 (1953) (repealed 1973). Defendant relies on *Farrow v. Smith*, 541 P.2d 1107, 1109 (Utah 1975), for the proposition that the trial court should have instructed on malice aforethought. In *Farrow*, the Court stated in dictum: For many years the definition of second degree murder has been the unlawful killing of a human being with malice aforethought, and ... manslaughter was the unlawful killing of a human being without malice. In our opinion the new criminal code has not changed those definitions. In at least one other case, this Court has also referred to "malice aforethought." *State v. Norman*, 580 P.2d 237, 240 (Utah 1978).

The present criminal code abandoned the common law terminology of malice aforethought and adopted more descriptive and precise language describing the requisite culpable mental states in defining the various crimes. Since the term "malice aforethought" is a confusing carry-over from prior law and can lead to confusion, if not error, it should no longer be used. The present second degree murder statute sets forth the necessary mental states required for each type of second degree murder, except as modified by case law. See *State v. Bolsinger*, 699 P.2d 1214 (Utah 1985); *State v. Fontana*, 680 P.2d 1042 (Utah 1984). The statute provides: Murder in the second degree — (1) Criminal homicide constitutes murder in the second degree if the actor: (a) intentionally or knowingly causes the death of another; (b) intending to cause serious bodily injury to another, he commits an act clearly dangerous to human life that causes the death of another; (c) acting under circumstances evidencing a depraved indifference to human life, he engages in conduct which creates a grave risk of death to another and thereby causes the death of another; or (d) while in the commission, attempted commission, or immediate flight from the commission or attempted commission of [certain enumerated felonies], [the actor] causes the death of another person other than a party .... Utah Code Ann. § 76-5-203 (Supp. 1988).

Thus, the culpable mental states included in the second degree murder statute are (1) an intent to kill, (2) an intent to inflict serious bodily harm, (3) conduct knowingly engaged in and evidencing a depraved indifference to human life, and (4) intent to commit a felony other than murder.

These terms are comparable to the old malice aforethought, but are much more precise and less confusing. The statute treats these forms of homicide as having similar culpability. Second degree murder is based on a very high degree of moral culpability. That culpability arises either from an actual intent to kill or from a mental state that is essentially equivalent thereto — such as intending grievous bodily injury and knowingly creating a very high risk of death. The risk of death in the latter two instances must be so great as to evidence such an indifference to life as to be tantamount to that evidenced by an intent to kill. In contrast, the felony-murder provision of the second degree murder statute is something of an exception to the above principle, as it does not require an intent to kill or any similar mental state. [That provision is designated as second degree murder for the purpose of deterring the use of lethal weapons in the commission of other felonies where there is a significant risk of death.]

The trial court framed its second degree murder and manslaughter instructions in the statutory language and correctly refused to give defendant's requested malice aforethought and absence of malice instructions. See *Bolsinger*, 699 P.2d 1214; *Fontana*, 680 P.2d 1042. To the extent that *Farrow v. Smith*, *State v. Norman*, and any other cases have perpetuated the use of malice aforethought with respect to second degree murder, they are disapproved.

. . . .

[Also], defendant argues that instruction No. 21, which defined second degree murder, was an erroneous statement of the law and was inconsistent with instruction No. 20, a general instruction requiring that a specific intent must be proved beyond a reasonable doubt. We disagree.

Instruction No. 21 stated:

> Criminal homicide constitutes murder in the second degree if the actor: (a) intentionally or knowingly causes the death of another; or (b) intending to cause serious bodily injury to another, he commits an act clearly dangerous to human life that causes the death of another; or (c) acting under circumstances evidencing a depraved indifference to human life, he knowingly engaged in conduct which creates a grave risk of death to another and thereby causes the death of another.

Instruction No. 21 was taken verbatim from the statutory definition of second degree homicide in the criminal code, except for subparagraph (c) above, which was modified to conform to our opinion in *Fontana*, 680 P.2d at 1046-47, by adding the term "knowingly." Instruction No. 21 was not erroneous as far as it went but, for reasons explained below, should have been amplified with respect to the magnitude of the risk of death required in depraved indifference murder.

In any event, instruction No. 21 was not inconsistent with instruction No. 20, which stated: "[W]ith respect to an offense such as charged in this case, specific intent must be proved beyond a reasonable doubt before there can be a conviction." Instruction No. 21 did not use the term "specific intent"; nor did it have to.[3] Rather, it specifically incorporated the culpable mental state re-

---

[3] We are aware that the Model Penal Code has abandoned use of the terms "specific intent" and "general intent." See Model Penal Code § 2.02 comment 1, at 230-32 (Official Draft and Revised Comments 1985); W. LaFave & A. Scott, Handbook on Criminal Law § 28, at 202 (1972). We also recognize that the terms "general intent" and "specific intent" have not been altogether free of difficulty in the criminal law. But we do not believe that total abandonment of the terms will serve to clarify this vital corner of the law. We believe, on the contrary, that the term "specific

quirements set out in the statute. Although the jury may have had some doubt about the meaning of the term "specific intent," it was unambiguously instructed on the mental states it had to find to convict, and it was adequately instructed elsewhere on the necessity of proof beyond a reasonable doubt as to all elements.

In the future, trial courts should define the term "specific intent" for the jury, if that term is used; and if it is, it should be expressly defined in terms of the specific mental state required.

B. DIMINISHED RESPONSIBILITY

NOTE

Traditionally defendants who suffered from mental illness or impairment were relegated exclusively to the insanity defense. If the level of impairment was insufficient to meet the standard required by the insanity defense it was considered irrelevant.

> The effort of the defense is to show that the murder was not deliberate and premeditated; that it was not first but second degree murder. A reading of petitioner's own testimony, summarized above, shows clearly to us that there was sufficient evidence to support a verdict of murder in the first degree, if petitioner was a normal man in his mental and emotional characteristics. Cf. *Bostic v. United States*, 68 App.D.C. 167, 94 F.2d 636, 638 (1937), *cert. denied*, 303 U.S. 635 (1938). But the defense takes the position that the petitioner is fairly entitled to be judged as to deliberation and premeditation, not by a theoretical normality but by his own personal traits.... It is the contention of the defense that the mental and emotional qualities of petitioner were of such a level at the time of the crime that he was incapable of deliberation and premeditation although he was then sane in the usual legal sense.
>
> ... Testimony of psychiatrists to support petitioner's contention was introduced. An instruction charging the jury to consider the personality of the petitioner in determining intent, premeditation and deliberation was sought and refused.
>
> ....

---

intent" has utility in describing a culpable mental state, or mind set, that describes a required purpose, knowledge, attitude, or motive, in addition to the mere volitional act, such as pulling a trigger, which has no inherent moral value but causes a killing. A subjective purpose, attitude, motive, or knowledge of acts or consequences makes the critical moral difference in the various degrees of homicide. The second degree murder statute, for example, requires (1) an intent or purpose to kill; or (2) an intent to inflict grievous bodily harm; or (3) knowledge that one's conduct is so threatening to life, that it is highly likely to result in death. For want of a better term, and because of its historic use in the criminal law, we continue to use the term "specific intent" to refer to such mind sets, even though the term "specific intent" is sometimes confused with general intent (or volitional act) and implies an actual intent, when in reality its meaning, as a term of art, also includes mental states that are not intentional. Because the term "specific intent" has an accepted meaning as a term of art and because that term also has special significance in connection with the diminished capacity defense, we decline to abandon it totally. See *State v. DePlonty*, 749 P.2d 621, 625 n.3 (Utah 1987); *State v. Miller*, 677 P.2d 1129, 1131-32 (Utah 1984); *State v. Wood*, 648 P.2d 71, 90 (Utah), *cert. denied*, 459 U.S. 988 (1982); *State v. Sessions*, 645 P.2d 643, 646-47 (Utah 1982).

We express no opinion upon whether the theory for which petitioner contends should or should not be made the law of the District of Columbia. Such a radical departure from common law concepts is more properly a subject for the exercise of legislative power or at least for the discretion of the courts of the District.... *Fisher v. United States*, 328 U.S. 463, 466, 476 (1946).

STATE v. MOORE

Supreme Court of New Jersey
113 N.J. 239, 550 A.2d 117 (1988)

GARIBALDI, J.

In November 1984, a Passaic County jury convicted Marie Moore of the capital murder of Theresa Feury and sentenced her to death. She appeals directly to this Court as of right. *See R*. 2:2-1(a)(3). We reverse both defendant's murder conviction and sentence of death. We reverse defendant's capital murder conviction because the trial court failed to charge the jury regarding diminished capacity and the lesser-included offenses of manslaughter and aggravated manslaughter....

...

On December 22, 1983, the police searched an apartment that the defendant formerly occupied, and discovered in a crawl space behind the bedroom wall the partially mummified body of Theresa Feury. The investigation into the young girl's death revealed the bizarre pattern of conduct that occurred in defendant's household for a period of time commencing in September 1981 and ending in December 1983. Defendant's conduct during this two-year period formed the basis for the thirty-three count indictment that charged defendant with the murder of Theresa Feury, as well as numerous crimes committed against other victims....

[The defendant, through threats and other means, exercised a control over several children, ages 12-14, and one adult who either lived or visited in her home. She directed one of the children, a 14 year old boy, Ricky, to beat and abuse the other children and the adult. She attributed these orders, not to herself, but to another person named "Billy" who spoke through her voice. Finally, one of Ricky's beatings resulted in the death of Theresa Feury.]

The defendant argues that evidence submitted as part of her insanity defense supported the alternative defense of diminished mental capacity, namely, that a disease of the mind prevented her from "knowingly" or "purposefully" murdering Theresa Feury. Defendant claims that the trial court committed reversible error by failing to instruct the jury that diminished capacity could mitigate murder to aggravated manslaughter. The defendant supplemented this argument following this Court's decision in *State v. Ramseur, supra*, 106 N.J. 123, 524 A.2d 188 claiming that because the *Ramseur* jury received an instruction on aggravated manslaughter, the jury below should have received a similar instruction. In *Ramseur*, we rejected the claim that diminished capacity mitigates murder to manslaughter. Instead, we concluded that "diminished capacity does not operate to transform an offense, it can only negate it." *Id*. at 270, 524 A.2d 188. In that connection, we observed that "diminished capacity either negates the state of mind required for a particular offense, if successful, or it does not. It either provides a complete defense, if successful, or it does not." *Id.* at 269, 524 A.2d 188.

In the recent case of *State v. Breakiron,* 108 N.J. 591, 532 A.2d 199 (1987), we had occasion to consider in depth the defense of diminished capacity. There, defendant was convicted of murdering a young woman, as well as other related offenses. He presented an insanity defense to all charges and argued that if insanity were not established, the evidence of mental disease or defect still showed that the killing was not "knowing" or "purposeful." *Id.* at 593, 532 A.2d 199. The trial court instructed the jury on insanity but refused to instruct that the evidence of mental disease or defect could be used to negate the required "knowing" or "purposeful" element for murder. *Id.* at 594, 532 A.2d 199. In reversing the Appellate Division's split decision affirming the conviction, we held that defendant was entitled to a jury charge that the evidence of mental disease or defect could negate the required elements of purposeful or knowing conduct with respect to the murder charge. *Id.* at 617-18, 532 A.2d 199. We thus reversed defendant's murder conviction because the charge to the jury did not allow it to consider whether the evidence presented in the insanity defense negated the elements of murder.

In reversing defendant's conviction in *State v. Breakiron,* we noted that "the diminished capacity defense was designed by the Legislature not as a justification or an excuse, nor as a matter of diminished or partial *responsibility,* but as a factor bearing on the presence or absence of an essential element of the crime as designated by the Code." 108 N.J. at 608, 532 A.2d 199. Breakiron had argued that by characterizing the diminished capacity defense as an affirmative one, N.J.S.A. 2C:4-2 impermissibly shifted to him the burden of disproving an essential element of the crime. We rejected defendant's argument, noting that "when the Code says that mental disease or defect is an affirmative defense that must be proven by a preponderance of the evidence, it does not mean that the defendant must disprove that the act was knowing or purposeful." *Id.* at 611, 532 A.2d 199. In our view, the defendant's burden is simply to "show that he or she suffered from a mental disease or defect that is relevant to the mental state of the offense." *Id.* Moreover, we concluded that it was not impermissibly unfair to impose that burden on a defendant wishing to avail him or herself of the diminished capacity defense. *Id.* at 612-14, 432 A.2d 199. We found support for that conclusion in the fact that "[w]hether or not mental disease or defect is established the State always bears the burden of proving beyond a reasonable doubt the essential mental elements of the crime charged." *Id.* at 613, 432 A.2d 199. The defense's "sole function is to establish the absence of an essential element of the crime...." *Id.* at 612, 432 A.2d 199.

Breakiron also afforded this Court an opportunity to discuss the quality of evidence that would support a charge of diminished capacity: "the only evidence of mental defect or disease that should be admitted on the defense is that relevant to the question of whether the defendant had the requisite mental state to commit the crime." 108 N.J. at 618, 432 A.2d 199. We also advised trial courts as follows:

> Because we agree with the view that diminished capacity as it exists under the Code is "evidence which merely denies the existence of facts which the State must prove to establish [the essential elements of first degree murder]," *State v. DiPaolo, supra,* 34 N.J. [279] at 294 [168 A 2d 401], we believe that the allocation of responsibility between judge and jury requires that competent reliable evidence be submitted to the jury and that a diminished capacity charge be given to the jury when competent reliable evidence has been offered. [*Id.* at 617, 432 A.2d 199.]

....

In the instant case, where defendant did in fact present an insanity defense, the record persuades us that sufficient competent evidence was adduced at trial to support a charge of diminished capacity. As part of her insanity defense, defendant offered evidence that would permit a jury to decide whether she suffered from a condition that diminished her capacity to form the "knowing" or "purposeful" mental state required to convict her of murder. The trial court, however, instructed the jury only on the insanity defense and did not instruct the jury that the evidence presented as part of that defense could be used to negate the elements of count twenty, the purposeful or knowing murder.

As in *State v. Breakiron,* Moore was charged with both purposeful and knowing murder. In *Breakiron,* we noted that "[t]he former state of mind evidences a conscious object and desire, the latter, that the defendant be practically certain that death would result." 108 N.J. at 615, 432 A.2d 199. Moore's insanity defense testimony presented evidence that her diminished mental capacity, though perhaps not full legal insanity, negated the "purposeful" and "knowing" elements of the murder charge.

While the main thrust of Moore's insanity defense involved the issue of multiple personality, the defense also introduced evidence of defendant's psychological history in an effort to demonstrate that her mental illness was not a recent fabrication. Defendant introduced a letter that Moore's aunt sent to a neurologist/psychiatrist whom defendant consulted on only one occasion in 1968. Defendant's aunt observes in that letter to the psychiatrist that defendant exhibited characteristics of "split personality." Although not a trained psychologist, defendant's aunt attributed defendant's radically changing disposition to some form of psychological disorder....

....

The defense produced three expert witnesses in support of its contention that Marie Moore suffered from a multiple personality disorder. Dr. Charles Opsahl, a clinical psychologist and faculty member of the Yale University School of Medicine, conducted intelligence quotient, personality, and neuropsychological tests of defendant. During his interview with defendant, the personality of Billy also appeared. He conducted similar tests of the Billy personality, and observed that those test results differed from the results obtained when he tested Marie. Based on this observation, as well as other observations concerning differences in behavior between Marie and Billy, Dr.

Opsahl believed that defendant suffered from a multiple-personality disorder. He was also persuaded that defendant had some brain damage. Opsahl's professional opinion was that defendant was thus legally insane because she did not know right from wrong when she was Billy.

Dr. Dorothy Lewis, a board certified psychiatrist from New York University, administered similar tests. She also spoke with Billy who informed her that defendant's father raped her during childhood, that her father drank heavily and beat defendant's mother, and that a Mr. Ragusa had also raped defendant. Dr. Lewis concluded that Billy was psychotic, delusional, and was filled with very violent fantasies. After observing that the Billy personality exhibited traits of paranoid schizophrenia, Dr. Lewis explained that this meant that defendant also had such traits in her own personality. Dr. Lewis' expert conclusion was that defendant suffered from a multiple-personality disorder brought on by her history of sexual abuse.

Dr. James Merikangas, also on the faculty of the Yale University School of Medicine, was the final defense expert. He, too, was board certified in neurology and psychiatry. Dr. Merikangas conducted neurological tests of defendant, and interpreted CAT scan results to show that defendant had "significant" atrophy of frontal lobe brain tissue. Dr. Merikangas observed that defendant had hallucinations, grandiose delusions, and was frequently out of touch with reality. Based on his tests and observations, he concluded that defendant was psychotic and suffered from a multiple-personality disorder. He thus determined that she was legally insane.

Given the nature and extent of the testimony elicited with regard to the insanity defense, we are persuaded that ample evidence existed to support a charge to the jury that a finding of diminished capacity could negate the "knowing" and "purposeful" elements of murder. We believe there was sufficient evidence to warrant a diminished capacity charge, particularly when we "'view[ ] the evidence and legitimate inferences to be drawn therefrom in the light most favorable to defendant....'" *Breakiron, supra,* 108 N.J. at 617, 432 A.2d 199. Accordingly, we find that the trial court committed reversible error by failing to charge the jury that diminished capacity could negate the knowing or purposeful elements of the murder count. We so find despite the fact that defendant did not request such an instruction. As we made clear in *Ramseur,* "the trial court has a duty 'to charge the applicable law to the jury based upon facts regardless of what requests counsel may make...,'" 106 N.J. at 270-71 n. 62, 524 A.2d 188. Defendant had presented sufficient evidence at trial to warrant a diminished capacity instruction, an instruction that would have permitted the jury to determine whether the State had proved the "knowing" and "purposeful" elements of murder beyond a reasonable doubt. This is particularly relevant in this case where the defendant sought and was denied a charge on manslaughter and aggravated manslaughter.

We also find reversible error in the trial court's failure to charge the jury with respect to aggravated manslaughter and manslaughter, as defendant had requested. Our review of the record persuades us that the evidence at trial would have warranted the jury's consideration of an aggravated manslaughter charge, particularly if the jury had believed that defendant's diminished capacity negated the knowing and purposeful elements of murder. Because the trial court failed to charge the jury with respect to diminished capacity and the lesser-included offense of manslaughter, we reverse defendant's murder conviction.

It is clear that "[a] charge on a lesser-included offense cannot be automatically given to a jury when the defense of diminished capacity is raised by a defendant." *Ramseur, supra,* 106 N.J. at 269, 524 A.2d 188. However, "negating the mental state for murder by producing evidence of mental disease or defect does not prohibit a conviction for manslaughter provided the essential elements of that crime are present." *Breakiron, supra,* 108 N.J. at 610, 432 A.2d 199. As we noted in *Ramseur,* "the 'included offense' statute, N.J.S.A. 2C:1-8(e), specifically states as to lesser-included offenses that the court shall not charge the jury with respect to an included offense *unless there is a rational basis for a verdict convicting the defendant of the included offense.*" 106 N.J. at 269, 524 A.2d 188.

Our characterization of the interplay between the diminished-capacity and lesser-included offense instructions in *Ramseur* is relevant to our disposition of the instant case. There we found:

> The trial court charged on aggravated manslaughter in this case not because diminished capacity could reduce the offense from murder to aggravated manslaughter, but because evidence warranted consideration of aggravated manslaughter by the jury in the event it was unpersuaded that defendant had acted "purposely" or "knowingly." The trial court determined, and we agree, that if the jurors did not find knowing and purposeful conduct, they should then appraise the evidence to determine whether defendant acted with a "conscious disregard of a substantial and unjustifiable risk," N.J.S.A. 2C:2-2, "under circumstances manifesting extreme indifference for human life," N.J.S.A. 2C:11-4 — the constituent elements of manslaughter. [106 N.J. at 269-70, 524 A.2d 188.]

In the instant case, the trial court should have instructed the jury that if it did not find knowing or purposeful conduct, it should then appraise the evidence to determine whether defendant was guilty of manslaughter.

Our review of the record persuades us that there was sufficient evidence to establish the essential elements of manslaughter — certainly enough to warrant a charge under our law....

EDITORIAL NOTE

Most states which have accepted the defense of diminished responsibility have done so in narrow *mens rea* terms. Where a defendant, for whatever reason did not, because he or she could not, entertain the required *mens rea,* an essential element of the offense is lacking and defendant cannot be convicted of that offense.

There is an alternative approach. Although seemingly based on *mens rea,* it regards the defendant's diminished capacity to entertain *mens rea* as a basis for reducing the gravity of his or her offense. It is not that defendant cannot entertain *mens rea.* Rather, he or she cannot appreciate the circumstances in which he or she acts nor conform his or her behavior to the law in the same manner as can a fully capacitated person. Under this approach diminished capacity may be characterized as an "imperfect insanity defense."

The California courts had moved closest to this latter approach. See *People v. Wells*, 33 Cal.2d 330, 202 P.2d 53 (1949), *People v. Gorshen*, 51 Cal.2d 716, 336 P.2d 492 (1959), *People v. Conley*, 66 Cal.2d 310, 411 P.2d 911, 49 Cal. Rptr. 815 (1966), and *People v. Poddar*, 10 Cal.3d 750, 518 P.2d 342, 111 Cal. Rptr. 910 (1974). In commenting on the bifurcated trial process by which the legislature tried to clearly separate the trial of issues of objective guilt from those involving mental illness, the California Supreme Court noted that "the defense of diminished capacity has obliterated the distinction the legislature sought to enact. The development of that defense has brought it so close to that of insanity that we doubt that the issue of diminished capacity has currently been placed on the proper side of the judicial ledger. Indeed when we *changed the designation of the defense from diminished 'responsibility' to diminished 'capacity' (People v. Anderson, (1965) 63 Cal. 2d 351, 364, 46 Cal. Rptr. 763, 406 P.2d 43) we approached more nearly the concept of inability to conform one's conduct to the requirements of law which is now a facet of the test of insanity.* We said in *Anderson* "Clearly we cannot hold defendant responsible for a crime which requires as one of its elements the presence of a state of mind which he is incapable of achieving because of subjective abnormality or impaired volitional powers." [Citation omitted; emphasis added.] *People v. Wetmore*, 22 Cal. 3d 318, 583 P.2d 1308, 1316-17, 149 Cal. Rptr. 265 (1978).

California, where diminished capacity originated and where the doctrine has had its broadest development, however, has reversed course. By initiative, the state's voters enacted a "Victims' Bill of Rights" which abolishes diminished capacity,

> Sec. 4. Diminished Capacity; Insanity. Section 25 is added to the Penal Code, to read:
>
> 25. (a) The defense of diminished capacity is hereby abolished. In a criminal action, as well as any juvenile court proceeding, evidence concerning an accused person's intoxication, trauma, mental illness, disease, or defect shall not be admissible to show or negate capacity to form the particular purpose, intent, motive, malice aforethought, knowledge, or other mental state required for the commission of the crime charged.
>
> ....
>
> (c) Notwithstanding the foregoing, evidence of diminished capacity or of a mental disorder may be considered by the court only at the time of sentencing or other disposition or commitment.

In *People v. Saille*, 54 Cal. 3d 1103, 2 Cal. Rptr. 2d 364, 820 P.2d 588 (1991), the California Supreme Court considered the effect of the voter initiative and new legislation. It confirmed that the relevant provisions

> repudiate[ ] the expanded definition of malice aforethought in *People v. Conley, supra*, 64 Cal.2d 310, 49 Cal. Rptr. 815, 411 P.2d 911, and *People v. Poddar, supra*, 10 Cal.3d 750, 111 Cal.Rptr. 910, 518 P.2d 342, that express and implied malice include an awareness of the obligation to act within the general body of laws regulating society and the capability of

acting in accordance with such awareness. After this amendment of section 188, express malice and an intent unlawfully to kill are one and the same (*People v. Stress, supra*, 205 Cal. App. 3d at p. 1268, 252 Cal. Rptr. 913).

Pursuant to the language of section 188, when an intentional killing is shown, malice aforethought is established. Accordingly, the concept of "diminished capacity voluntary manslaughter" (nonstatutory manslaughter) recognized in *Conley, supra*, 64 Cal.2d 310, 49 Cal. Rptr. 815, 411 P.2d 911, is no longer valid as a defense.

NOTES

1. Problems raised by the defense of diminished capacity, especially in regard to psychiatric testimony, are discussed in Arenella, *The Diminished Capacity and Diminished Responsibility Defenses: Two Children of a Doomed Marriage*, 77 COLUM. L. REV. 827-65 (1977).

2. Incapacity because of a mental disease may be offered as a complete defense resulting in a verdict of "not guilty by reason of insanity." Mental incapacity is discussed *infra* Chapter 8.

3. The MODEL PENAL CODE § 4.02(1) provides: "Evidence that the defendant suffered from a mental disease or defect is admissible whenever it is relevant to prove that the defendant did or did not have a state of mind which is an element of the offense."

4. For developments in England where, following the Scottish lead, partial responsibility (often erroneously labelled "diminished responsibility") was introduced in reduction of murder charges, see Williams, *Diminished Responsibility*, MED., SC. & LAW 41 (1960); Edwards, *Diminished Responsibility — A Withering Away of the Concept of Criminal Responsibility?*, in ESSAYS IN CRIMINAL SCIENCE 301 (Mueller ed. 1961). Wootton, *Diminished Responsibility: A Layman's View*, 76 L.Q. REV. 224 (1960); Fingarette, *Diminished Mental Capacity as a Criminal Law Defence*, 37 MODERN L. REV. 264 (1974). For more recent developments see R.D. Mackay, *Pleading Provocation and Diminished Responsibility Together*, [1988] CRIM. L. REV. 411.

SECTION V. "Depraved Heart" Murder

COMMONWEALTH v. MALONE

Supreme Court of Pennsylvania
354 Pa. 180, 47 A.2d 445 (1946)

MAXEY, CHIEF JUSTICE.

This is an appeal from the judgment and sentence under a conviction of murder in the second degree. William H. Long, age 13 years, was killed by a shot from a .32 caliber revolver held against his right side by the defendant, then aged 17 years. These youths were on friendly terms at the time of the homicide....

On the evening of February 26th, 1945, when the defendant went to a moving picture theater, he carried in the pocket of his raincoat a revolver which he had obtained at the home of his uncle on the preceding day. In the

V. "DEPRAVED HEART" MURDER

afternoon preceding the shooting, the decedent procured a cartridge from his father's room and he and the defendant placed it in the revolver.

After leaving the theater, the defendant went to a dairy store and there met the decedent. Both youths sat in the rear of the store ten minutes, during which period the defendant took the gun out of his pocket and loaded the chamber to the right of the firing pin and then closed the gun. A few minutes later, both youths sat on stools in front of the lunch counter and ate some food. The defendant suggested to the decedent that they play "Russian Poker."[1] Long replied: "I don't care; go ahead." The defendant then placed the revolver against the right side of Long and pulled the trigger three times. The third pull resulted in a fatal wound to Long. The latter jumped off the stool and cried: "Oh! Oh! Oh!" and Malone said: "Did I hit you, Billy? Gee, Kid, I'm sorry." Long died from the wounds two days later.

The defendant testified that the gun chamber he loaded was the first one to the right of the firing chamber and that when he pulled the trigger he did not "expect to have the gun go off." He declared he had no intention of harming Long, who was his friend and companion. The defendant was indicted for murder, tried and found guilty of murder in the second degree and sentenced to a term in the penitentiary for a period not less than five years and not exceeding ten years. A new trial was refused and after sentence was imposed, an appeal was taken.

Appellant alleges certain errors in the charge of the court and also contends that the facts did not justify a conviction for any form of homicide except involuntary manslaughter. This contention we over-rule. A specific intent to take life is, under our law, an essential ingredient of murder in the first degree. At common law, the "grand criterion" which "distinguished murder from other killing" was malice on the part of the killer and this malice was not necessarily "malevolent to the deceased particularly" but "any evil design in general; the dictate of a wicked, depraved, and malignant heart"; 4 Blackstone 199. Among the examples that Blackstone cites of murder is "coolly discharging a gun among a multitude of people," causing the death of someone of the multitude.

In Pennsylvania, the common law crime of murder is divided into two degrees, and murder of the second degree includes every element which enters into first degree murder except the intention to kill: *Commonwealth v. Divomte*, 262 Pa. 504, 507, 105 A. 821. When an individual commits an act of gross recklessness for which he must reasonably anticipate that death to another is likely to result, he exhibits that "wickedness of disposition, hardness of heart, cruelty, recklessness of consequences, and a mind regardless of social duty" which proved that there was at that time in him "the state or frame of mind termed malice." This court has declared that if a driver "wantonly, recklessly, and in disregard of consequences" hurls "his car against another, or into a crowd" and death results from that act "he ought ... to face the same consequences that would be meted out to him if he had

---

[1] It has been explained that "Russian Poker" is a game in which the participants, in turn, place a single cartridge in one of the five chambers of a revolver cylinder, give the latter a quick twirl, place the muzzle of the gun against the temple and pull the trigger, leaving it to chance whether or not death results to the trigger puller.

accomplished death by wantonly and wickedly firing a gun": *Commonwealth v. Mayberry*, 290 Pa. 195, 199, 138 A. 686, 688, citing cases from four jurisdictions.

....

... In the instant case if the defendant had by some negligent, unintentional act, caused Long to fall off the stool at which he was sitting in the store and if, as a result of that fall, Long had sustained a fatal injury, both the initial act and the death might be correctly characterized as accidental. But when the defendant knowing that a revolver had at least one loaded cartridge in it, pressed the muzzle of that revolver to the side of Long and pulled the trigger three times, his act cannot be characterized as accidental, even if his statement that he had no intention to kill Long is accepted (as the jury accepted it)....

The killing of William H. Long by this defendant resulted from an act intentionally done by the latter, in reckless and wanton disregard of the consequences which were at least sixty per cent certain from his thrice attempted discharge of a gun known to contain one bullet and aimed at a vital part of Long's body. This killing was, therefore, murder, for malice in the sense of a wicked disposition is evidenced by the intentional doing of an uncalled-for act in callous disregard of its likely harmful effects on others. The fact that there was no motive for this homicide does not exculpate the accused. In a trial for murder proof of motive is always relevant but never necessary.

All the assignments of error are overruled and the judgment is affirmed. The record is remitted to the court below so that the sentence imposed may be carried out.

NOTES

1. Cf. *Regina v. Lamb*, [1967] 2 All E.R. 1282.

2. Since an intention to take human life is perfectly consistent with a conviction of voluntary manslaughter or a finding of justifiable or excusable homicide, is it proper to treat this intention as malice? For that matter, recklessness or wantonness toward human life, frequently treated as malice, is consistent not only with murder convictions (in some states) requiring malice, but also with involuntary manslaughter convictions, not requiring malice.

It follows that the essence of malice — namely the completely unjustified, inexcusable, unmitigated attitude toward the taking of life — is something apart from the various forms of mens rea in homicide, namely intention (or near intention) to take life, or recklessness toward human life.

DIRECTOR OF PUBLIC PROSECUTIONS v. SMITH

House of Lords
[1960] 3 All E.R. 161

... The respondent was driving a car in which there was stolen property. The car was stopped by a police officer on point duty in the normal course of traffic control and, while so stopped, another policeman, who was acquainted with the respondent, came to the driver's window and spoke to the respondent. As a result of what the police constable saw in the back of the car, he told the

V. "DEPRAVED HEART" MURDER

respondent to draw in to his near-side. The respondent began to do so, and the constable walked beside the car. However, the respondent suddenly accelerated and made off down an adjoining road. The constable began to run with the car, and, despite the fact that it had no running board, succeeded in hanging on to the car. The car pursued an erratic course and eventually the constable was thrown off in the path of another vehicle which ran over him, causing fatal injuries. At his trial on an indictment for capital murder, the respondent maintained that he had no intention of either causing the constable severe injury or of killing him. The trial judge's final direction to the jury in his summing-up was as follows: "... if you are satisfied that ... he must, as a reasonable man, have contemplated that grievous bodily harm was likely to result to that officer ... and that such harm did happen and the officer died in consequence, then the accused is guilty of capital murder." Moreover, in the course of summing-up, the trial judge referred to the presumption of law that a man intends the natural and probable consequences of his acts without directing the jury that the presumption was rebuttable. The jury returned a verdict of capital murder under the Homicide Act, 1957, s. 5 (1) (d). On appeal.

Held: there had been no misdirection in the summing-up....

Viscount Kilmuir, L.C.: My Lords, the respondent, Jim Smith, was convicted on Apr. 7, 1960, of the wilful murder on Mar. 2, 1960, of Leslie Edward Vincent Meehan, a police officer acting in the execution of his duty. Such a crime constitutes capital murder under s. 5 of the Homicide Act, 1957, and, accordingly, the respondent was sentenced to death. There was never any suggestion that the respondent meant to kill the police officer, but it was contended by the prosecution that he intended to do the officer grievous bodily harm as a result of which the officer died....

The respondent gave evidence at the trial. He said that, when P.C. Meehan jumped on the side of the car, his foot went down on the accelerator and he was scared. "I was scared very much, I was very much frightened." He agreed that he did not take his foot off the accelerator.

"I never thought of it, sir. I was frightened. I was up in the traffic. I never thought of it. It happened too quick." Asked why he did not take his foot off the accelerator, he said: "I would have done, but when he jumped on the side he took my mind off what I was doing." "When he jumped on I was frightened. I was up the road before it happened. It all happened in a matter of seconds." He further said that, when going up Plumstead Road, he didn't realise that the officer was still hanging on to the car.

... Putting aside for a moment the distinction which the Court of Criminal Appeal were seeking to draw between results which were "certain" and those which were "likely," they were saying that it was for the jury to decide, whether, having regard to the panic in which he said he was, the respondent in fact at the time contemplated that grievous bodily harm would result from his actions or, indeed, whether he contemplated anything at all. Unless the jury were satisfied that he in fact had such contemplation, the necessary intent to constitute malice would not, in their view, have been proved. This purely subjective approach involves this, that, if an accused said that he did not in fact think of the consequences and the jury considered that that might well be true, he would be entitled to be acquitted of murder.

My Lords, the proposition has only to be stated thus to make one realise what a departure it is from that on which the courts have always acted. The jury must of course in such a case as the present make up their minds on the evidence whether the accused was unlawfully and voluntarily doing something to someone. The unlawful and voluntary act must clearly be aimed at someone in order to eliminate cases of negligence or of careless or dangerous driving. Once, however, the jury are satisfied as to that, it matters not what the accused in fact contemplated as the probable result, or whether he ever contemplated at all, provided he was in law responsible and accountable for his actions, i.e., was a man capable of forming an intent, not insane within the M'Naghten Rules and not suffering from diminished responsibility. On the assumption that he is so accountable for his actions, the sole question is whether the unlawful and voluntary act was of such a kind that grievous bodily harm was the natural and probable result. The only test available for this is what the ordinary, responsible man would, in all the circumstances of the case, have contemplated as the natural and probable result.

In the result, the appeal should, in my opinion, be allowed and the conviction of capital murder restored.

NOTES

1.   *Criminal Justice Act 1967 (c.80), s. 8.*

Miscellaneous provisions as to evidence, procedure and trial

8. *Proof of criminal intent.* — A court or jury, in determining whether a person has committed an offence, —

(a) shall not be bound in law to infer that he intended or foresaw a result of his actions by reason only of its being a natural and probable consequence of those actions; but

(b) shall decide whether he did intend or foresee that result by reference to all the evidence, drawing such inferences from the evidence as appear proper in the circumstances. [407]

This section arises out of a report of the Law Commission dated 12th December 1966, in which the decision of the House of Lords in *Director of Public Prosecutions v. Smith*, [1960] 3 All E.R. 161; [1961] A.C. 290 at p. 303, was considered.... The question which arose in *Director of Public Prosecutions v. Smith* was whether the intent required had to be subjective or objective, and it was held that the objective test (viz., the test of what a reasonable man would contemplate as the probable result of his acts and, therefore, would intend) was the right test. Following a considerable amount of criticism (and, it has been suggested, misunderstanding) of this decision the Law Commission considered the matter and came to the conclusion that the test of intent in murder should be subjective and that the same subjective test should be applied in regard to all other offences where it was necessary to ascertain the existence of intent or foresight. A draft clause to give effect to these proposals was appended to the Commission's report and the present section is identical with that clause....

47 Halsbury's Statutes of England 376 (2d ed. 1968).

2. In the early hours of the morning appellant set fire to a dwelling house by pouring half a gallon of gasoline through the mailbox and igniting it with a newspaper and match. Of the four persons asleep in the house, Mrs. Booth and one of her children escaped; two other children were asphyxiated. Appellant stated she had only wanted to frighten Mrs. Booth into leaving the neighborhood, and that she did not intend to kill her or cause serious bodily harm. Her motive was jealousy as Mrs. Booth had taken up with her former lover. Is the following instruction proper? The prosecution must prove, beyond all reasonable doubt, that the accused intended to (kill or) do serious bodily harm to Mrs. Booth, the mother of the deceased girls. If you are satisfied that when the accused set fire to the house she knew that it was highly probable that this would cause (death or) serious bodily harm then the prosecution will have established the necessary intent. It matters not if her motive was, as she says, to frighten Mrs. Booth.

Does it make any difference whether murder is defined as requiring (1) an intention to kill, (2) an intention to cause grievous bodily harm or really serious injury, or (3) intentional acts done with knowledge of a serious risk that death or grievous bodily harm will ensue? See *Regina v. Hyam,* [1975] A.C. 55.

PEOPLE v. REGISTER

Court of Appeals of New York
60 N.Y.2d 270, 469 N.Y.S.2d 599, 457 N.E.2d 704 (1983)
cert. denied, 466 U.S. 953, 104 S. Ct. 2159, 80 L. Ed 2d 544

Simons, J.

Defendant appeals from an order of the Appellate Division which affirmed a judgment entered after a jury trial convicting him of murder in the second degree (Penal Law, § 125.25, subd 2 [depraved mind murder]) and two counts of assault in the first degree (Penal Law, § 120.10, subd 1). The charges arose from a barroom incident in which defendant shot and killed one man and seriously injured two others....

....

The shootings occurred about 12:30 a.m. on January 15, 1977 in a crowded barroom in downtown Rochester. The evidence established that defendant and a friend, Duval, had been drinking heavily that day ... [They went to a bar where defendant got into an argument with another party and drew a loaded pistol]. After midnight another argument developed, this time between Duval and Willie Mitchell. Defendant took out the gun again, shot at Mitchell but mistakenly injured Lawrence Evans who was trying to stop the fight. He then stepped forward and shot Mitchell in the stomach from close range. At that, the 40 or 50 patrons in the bar started for the doors. Some of the bystanders tried to remove Mitchell to a hospital and while they were doing so, the decedent, Marvin Lindsey, walked by defendant. ... For no explained reason, defendant turned and fired his gun killing Lindsey.

Defendant did not contest the shootings. In defense, his counsel elicited evidence during the prosecution's case of defendant's considerable drinking that evening and he called as his only witness a forensic psychiatrist who testified on the debilitating effects of consuming alcoholic beverages. The jury acquitted defendant of intentional murder but convicted him of depraved mind murder and the two assault counts.

The murder conviction must be supported by evidence that defendant "[under] circumstances evincing a depraved indifference to human life recklessly [engaged] in conduct which [created] a grave risk of death to another person, and thereby [caused] the death of another person" (Penal Law, § 125.25, subd 2). A person acts recklessly when he is aware of and consciously disregards a substantial and unjustifiable risk (Penal Law, § 15.05, subd 3), but to bring defendant's conduct within the murder statute, the People were required to establish also that defendant's act was imminently dangerous and presented a very high risk of death to others and that it was committed under circumstances which evidenced a wanton indifference to human life or a depravity of mind (see *People v. Poplis*, 30 NY2d 85, 88; *People v. Jernatowski*, 238 NY 188; *Darry v. People*, 10 NY 120, 148; .... The crime differs from intentional murder in that it results not from a specific, conscious intent to cause death, but from an indifference to or disregard of the risks attending defendant's conduct.

....

The evidence in the record supports the verdict. Defendant's awareness of and indifference to the attendant risks was established by evidence that he entered a crowded bar with a loaded gun, he said that he was "going to kill somebody tonight," or similar words, several times, and he had brought the gun out in the bar once before during the evening only to be told to put it away. Ultimately, he fired the gun three times in the "packed" barroom, conduct which presented a grave risk of death and did in fact result in the death of Marvin Lindsey. His conduct was well within that defined by the statute (see Penal Law, § 125.25, subd 2; § 15.05; *People v. Jernatowski*, 238 NY 188, *supra*; Hechtman, Practice Commentaries, McKinney's Cons Laws of NY, Book 39, Penal Law, § 125.25, p 399; LaFave and Scott, Criminal Law, Depraved-Heart Murder, § 70, p 543).

At the conclusion of the evidence and after the charge, defendant requested the court to instruct the jury on the effect of intoxication (see Penal Law, § 15.25). The court complied with the request when discussing the intentional murder and assault counts, but it refused to charge the jury that it could consider defendant's intoxication in determining whether he acted "[under] circumstances evincing a depraved indifference to human life" in causing the death of Marvin Lindsey. The court held that the mens rea required for depraved mind murder is recklessness and that subdivision 3 of section 15.05 of the Penal Law precludes evidence of intoxication in defense of reckless crimes because it provides that "[a] person who creates such a risk but is unaware thereof solely by reason of voluntary intoxication also acts recklessly." That ruling is assigned as error by defendant. He contends that depraved mind murder contains a different or additional element of mental culpability, namely "circumstances evincing a depraved indifference to human life," which elevates defendant's conduct from manslaughter to murder and that this additional element may be negatived by evidence of intoxication (see Penal Law, § 15.25).

V. "DEPRAVED HEART" MURDER

... Depraved mind murder resembles manslaughter in the second degree (a reckless killing which includes the requirement that defendant disregard a substantial risk [Penal Law, § 125.15, subd 1; § 15.05, subd 3]), but the depraved mind murder statute requires in addition not only that the conduct which results in death present a grave risk of death but that it also occur "[under] circumstances evincing a depraved indifference to human life." This additional requirement refers to neither the *mens rea* nor the *actus reus*. If it states an element of the crime at all, it is not an element in the traditional sense but rather a definition of the factual setting in which the risk creating conduct must occur — objective circumstances which are not subject to being negatived by evidence of defendant's intoxication.

The view is supported by an analysis of the statutory development of the crime. Because of an inability to quantify homicidal risks in precise terms, the Legislature structured the degree of risk which must be present in nonintentional killings by providing that in a depraved mind murder the actor's conduct must present a grave risk of death whereas in manslaughter it presents the lesser substantial risk of death (see, also, Penal Law, § 15.05, subd 4 [criminal negligence, a failure to perceive a substantial risk]). The phrase "[under] circumstances evincing a depraved indifference to human life" refers to the wantonness of defendant's conduct and converts the substantial risk present in manslaughter into a *very* substantial risk present in murder (see LaFave and Scott, Criminal Law, § 70, p 542). The predecessor statute referred to "a depraved mind, regardless of human life" (Penal Law, § 1044, subd 2, cited in *People v. Jernatowski*, 238 NY 188, 190, *supra*) and the older cases, in attempting to explicate this factor, speak of a "depraved heart devoid of social duty and fatally bent on mischief" (see LaFave and Scott, Criminal Law, § 70, p 542). Such phrases, suggesting malice aforethought, have provoked statements that malice or intent is inferred in depraved mind murder (see, e.g., *Darry v. People*, 10 NY 120, *supra*). However, the focus of the offense is not upon the subjective intent of the defendant, as it is with intentional murder (Penal Law, § 125.25, subd 1), but rather upon an objective assessment of the degree of risk presented by defendant's reckless conduct (see, e.g., *People v. Jernatowski*, 238 NY 188, *supra* [firing a bullet into a room defendant knew contained several people]; *People v. Poplis*, 30 NY2d 85, *supra* [defendant continually beat 3½-year-old infant over five-day period]; see, also, Hechtman, Practice Commentaries, McKinney's Cons Laws of NY, Book 39, Penal Law, § 125.25 [depraved mind murder committed when one shoots into a crowd, places a time bomb in a public place or opens the door of a lion's cage in a zoo]; 8 Zett, NY Crim Prac, par 69.2 [2] [a], [c], p 69-18).

The present statute is derived from this conceptual base but it contains important differences. Thus, whereas the former penal statutes defined depraved mind murder by referring to defendant's conduct, i.e., "[when] perpetrated by any act imminently dangerous to others," etc., defined *mens rea* "as a depraved mind" and contained no references to recklessness (see Rev Stat of NY [1829], part IV, ch I, tit I, § 5, subd 2; former Penal Law, § 1044, subd 2), the present statute defines the crime by reference to the circumstances under which it occurs and expressly states that recklessness is the element of mental culpability required. The concept of depraved indifference was retained in the new statute not to function as a mens rea element, but to objectively define the circumstances which must exist to elevate a homicide from manslaughter to murder (see *People v. Le Grand*, 61 AD2d 815, cert. den. 439 U.S. 835, *supra*).

....

In *People v. Poplis*, 30 N.Y.2d 85, 330 N.Y.S.2d 365, 281 N.E.2d 167, *supra*, we construed the present statute and pointed out that depraved mind murder is a crime involving recklessness plus aggravating circumstances. While not explicitly drawing the distinction between the depraved mind *mens rea* of the former statute and the "circumstances" clause which qualifies the element of recklessness in the new statute, Judge Bergan writing for a unanimous court noted that the new statute eliminated the "psychiatrically complicating" considerations found in the former statute (at p. 88, 330 N.Y.S.2d 365, 281 N.E.2d 167) and that it was a distinct improvement over the former statutes which spoke in terms of the operation of defendant's mind. Our holding that depraved mind murder is distinguishable from manslaughter, not by the mental element involved but by the objective circumstances in which the act occurs, finds sound support in that decision.

... [t]he statutory requirement that the homicide result from conduct evincing a depraved indifference to human life is a legislative attempt to qualitatively measure egregiously reckless conduct and to differentiate it from manslaughter. It does not create a new and different *mens rea*, undefined in the Penal Law, or a voluntary act which can be negatived by evidence of intoxication. If the objective circumstances under which the crime is committed constitute an element of it, they do so only in the sense that carrying a gun or acting in concert with another are elements of the crime of robbery or that the theft of more than $250 is an element of grand larceny. It is an element which elevates the severity of the offense but it is not an element subject to being negatived by evidence of intoxication as may intent or the physical capacity to act.

....

Accordingly, the order of the Appellate Division should be affirmed.

NOTES

1. "Extreme indifference murder involves conduct that creates a grave risk of death to another. 'Grave' is commonly understood to mean serious or imminent, or likely to produce great harm or danger. We do not view the term 'under circumstances manifesting extreme indifference to the value of human life' as without meaning. What it connotes is a heightened awareness and disregard of a fatal risk. *People ex rel. Russel v. District Court* [185 Colo. 78, 521 P.2d 1254 (1974)] noted that 'an extreme indifference to human life is clearly a more culpable standard of conduct' than the reckless conduct involved in manslaughter but did not describe that standard. Reckless manslaughter requires a conscious disregard of a substantial and unjustifiable risk of death. Before a person can consciously disregard a risk, he must be aware of that risk. A level of culpability that is more than reckless, but less than intentional, traditionally has been characterized as willful conduct. Willful conduct, however, is the equivalent of acting 'knowingly'.... In the context of criminal homicide, therefore, acting under circumstances manifesting extreme indifference to the value of human life must mean acting with the awareness that one's actions are practically certain to cause the death of another ...." *People v. Marcy*, 628 P.2d 69, 79-80 (Colo. 1981). The court held the "extreme indifference murder" section of the first-degree murder statute unconstitutional because it was not sufficiently distinguishable from second-degree murder — "causing death knowingly" — to warrant the substantial differential in penalty. The constitutionality of punishing the same conduct in more than one statute is discussed at p. 62.

2. The common law and the Model Penal Code recognize degrees of recklessness and require a very high degree for conviction of murder. In differentiating the degree of recklessness can distinctions be drawn in terms of degrees of indifference? Criticizing the formulation of recklessness in the Model Penal Code's definition of murder in terms of "extreme indifference," Professor Williams says, "No." G. WILLIAMS, THE MENTAL ELEMENT IN CRIME 92 (1965), cited in *People v. Marcy, supra*, 628 P.2d at 79. Professor Duff, in rebuttal to Williams, says "Yes." R.A. Duff, *Recklessness*, [1980] CRIM. L. REV. 282, 284.

SECTION VI. Felony-Murder

STATE v. GLOVER
Supreme Court of Missouri
330 Mo. 709, 50 S.W.2d 1049 (1932)

ELLISON, J.

The defendant was convicted by a jury in the circuit court of Jackson county of murder in the first degree, and his punishment assessed at life imprisonment in the state penitentiary. His motion for a new trial being overruled, he prosecutes this appeal. The state's theory was and is that the appellant, acting in concert with one or more other persons, perpetrated the crime of arson by placing a large quantity of gasoline in a certain drug store at 6844 Prospect Avenue, Kansas City, and setting fire to the store, fixtures, and stock of merchandise for the purpose of collecting the insurance on the latter. One John R. Morris was a member of the fire department of Kansas City, and with his company responded to an alarm to put out the fire. While he was in the burning building, an explosion took place, and Morris was pinned down in the ruins and burned to death. The contention of the state is, therefore, that the appellant the caused the death of Morris and committed a homicide in the perpetration of an arson, within the meaning of section 3982, R.S. Mo. 1929, which makes such offense murder in the first degree.

The relevant part of the statute is: "Every homicide which shall be committed in the perpetration or attempt to perpetrate any arson, rape, robbery, burglary, or mayhem, shall be deemed murder in the first degree."

The state's evidence tended to show that the appellant and another person bought a stock of drugs and store fixtures in June, 1929, and set up a drug store at the address mentioned. They took out $7,500 in insurance on the merchandise and fixtures....

The appellant admitted in a written confession which was put in evidence by the state that on Friday night, August 3, he and his confederate went to the drug store with the intention of burning it; but they encountered a policeman on the street out in front and desisted. The next night, Saturday, they planned to perpetrate the arson, but found too many people passing, so the crime was again postponed. The next night, Sunday, or, more accurately, Monday morning at 1:30 a.m., they went to the basement of the store and carried out their plan in this way. A small electric stove was placed in a convenient position, and over and around it they piled shredded tissue or crepe paper. They then began to break the bottles of gasoline so the contents would flow out over the basement floor; but, being in a great hurry, they simply pulled the corks out of part of the bottles and tipped them over on their sides. They then turned on the electric stove and fled.

The fire was discovered by a young man waiting for a street car two blocks away. He was attracted by the crash of falling glass and came to the store, where he found the front plate glass window had been blown out so that some of the glass was scattered clear across the street. He turned in a fire alarm at 2:03 a.m., and firemen responded within a few minutes. The fire was soon extinguished, or nearly so, in the storeroom, and firemen, including the deceased, Morris, were on the inside thereof when another explosion occurred. It was so violent that the south wall of the building was blown out, the roof on that side fell down to and partly into the basement, the ground floor of the store buckled up and sagged back down into the basement, and bricks were scattered clear across the street. The building was reduced to a mass of ruins and flames shot high over the whole area. A bystander was blown eighteen feet out into the street between the street car rails. The deceased, Morris, was pinned down in the ruins and burned to death. The fatal explosion occurred a little before 2:30 a.m., all within an hour after the fire was kindled. No one lived in the building or was in it when the appellant and his confederate left.

The appellant stood on his demurrer to the state's evidence, and offered no testimony in his own behalf.

... His contention is that, even though it be conceded he perpetrated the arson, the further fact is established that he left the premises before the fire began to burn and had no intention of injuring or killing any one, or any idea that any one would come to the building and be injured or killed. The position of appellant's counsel in their brief is that, in order to convict a defendant of first degree murder under section 3982, R.S. Mo. 1929, because of a homicide occurring in the perpetration of an arson (or any of the felonies enumerated in the statute), early cases in this state required proof that the defendant intended to *inflict bodily harm*, citing State v. Jennings, 18 Mo. 435; State v. Nueslein, 25 Mo. 111; and State v. Green, 66 Mo. 631.

....

This contention in our opinion is wholly erroneous.

... As is stated in State v. Wieners, 66 Mo. 13, 22, "If one in perpetrating or attempting to perpetrate a felony, kill a human being, such killing is murder, although not specifically intended, for the law attaches the intent to commit the other felony to the homicide. The law conclusively presumes the intent to kill."

Aside from the statute, our Missouri decisions are well supported by general authority on the proposition that at common law an unintentional homicide was murder if committed in the perpetration of a felony. 29 C.J. § 70, p. 1097; 13 R.C.L. § 149, p. 846; 63 L.R.A. 354; note; 1 Hawkins, P.C., c. 29, § 11, p. 112; 1 East, P.C. p. 255; 1 Michie on Homicide, § 22 (1), p. 135. It is even stated that, though the felony were not dangerous to life and the killing accidental, the law made it murder. 2 Bishop on Criminal Law (9th Ed.), § 694 (2), p. 527. This was on the theory that "the common law measures an act which is malum in se substantially by the result produced, though not contemplated." *People v. Olsen*, 80 Cal. 122, 126, 22 P. 125, 126.

But the weight of authority, especially modern authority, does add another qualification. It is said in 29 C.J. § 70, p. 1097, that, in order to make an unintended homicide committed in the perpetration of a felony first degree murder, "the homicide must be an ordinary and probable effect of the felony."...

The foregoing general doctrine can hardly be made more specific. Its application will vary with the facts of the particular case. But it can be asserted with fairness to the accused here that, even though the homicide be unintentional, yet, if it be committed in course of perpetrating the felony, and is a natural and proximate result thereof, such as the defendant reasonably was bound to anticipate — and therefore especially where the felony is dangerous and betokens a reckless disregard of human life — the homicide will be first degree murder under the statute.

....

The doctrine ... is that, if a defendant perpetrate an arson by setting fire to a building in which he knows, or has reason to believe, there are human beings, and if, in consequence, one of the inmates be burned to death, the defendant will be guilty of first degree murder; but, if the burning be only of a thing and at a place where the defendant has no reason to believe any one will be injured, and the person killed come in later, the defendant cannot be charged with murder, for there the homicide will not be regarded as a natural and probable result of the arson, and the act of the deceased in getting into the fire will be treated as an intervening cause.

In the present case, ... the deceased fireman was not in the building or at the place of the arson when the fire was set out, but came later. But can that make any difference if the appellant reasonably was bound to anticipate that people naturally and probably would come to the fire and be injured thereby, especially when its explosive nature is considered? In our opinion, when a person perpetrates an arson, and the life of a human being is destroyed by the fire, it is wholly immaterial whether the deceased was in the building or outside of it at the time the fire started — if only the defendant was chargeable with notice that fatal injury likely would result from his felonious act. And so, in the present case, if the appellant had reason to think members of the fire department of Kansas City and citizens generally would congregate at the drug store to fight the fire, and thus would place themselves within perilous range of the flames and potentially destructive forces that had been set at work, the ensuing homicide was a natural and probable consequence of the arson; and the fact that the deceased fireman came after the fire began to burn did not break the causal relation between the arson and the homicide, or constitute an independent intervening cause.

This is particularly true, since the act of intervention on the part of the deceased fireman was naturally invited by the appellant's act in starting the fire.

....

That it was a highly reckless act to leave a large quantity of gasoline where fire would be communicated to it, and one fraught with great danger to persons who might come within its range, goes without saying.

... It was a wanton act betokening a disregard for human life, if the appellant was reasonably bound to anticipate that human beings might come there and be injured or killed.

That this is so we think is established, not only by the authorities cited above, but by the facts of this particular case. The neighborhood was an inhabited, well-populated metropolitan district, not an isolated farm house, as in the Horsey Case. The thing destroyed was not a straw stack, but a business building stocked with merchandise. There were several fire stations scattered about in that district. Is there not good ground for an inference that the appellant reasonably should have anticipated these fire departments would be summoned, and that people would come, just as they did do?

....

The appellant makes the further point that, even though it be held he did commit the homicide, in the sense that he is legally responsible therefor as a natural and proximate result of his act in setting out the fire, yet the facts do not bring the case within the statute, because the homicide was not committed "in the perpetration" of the arson. Appellant's idea is that, when he communicated fire to the building and left the premises, the crime of arson was *complete* and the death of the fireman occurred afterwards. To this we do not agree. The same contention was made and rejected in *State v. Messino*, 325 Mo. 743, 764, 30 S.W.2d 750, 759, where the defendant and his conspirators robbed a bank and shot a policeman while fleeing with the loot. It was held that, while the act of asportation was sufficiently complete, even before the policeman was encountered, to have supported a prosecution for robbery, yet the crime was nevertheless in course of perpetration throughout the flight of the conspirators until they had reduced the property taken to their own unmolested dominion.

In the present case the arson was committed to defraud insurers of the drug stock and fixtures. Section 4040, R.S. Mo. 1929. That involved the *destruction* of the property, and it can hardly be asserted the appellant could absolve himself from the consequences of his act merely by withdrawing from the scene after he had put fatally destructive forces in motion to accomplish his purpose. The exact question is discussed and so decided arguendo in *Bissot v. State*, 53 Ind. 408, 413, in a long passage which is quoted with approval in *Conrad v. State*, 75 Ohio St. 52, 68, 78 N.E. 957, 6 L.R.A. (N.S.) 1154, 8 Ann. Cas. 966. This point is ruled against appellant....

Finding no error in the record, the judgment of the trial court is affirmed.

NOTES

1. The view taken by Coke is expressed as follows: "Homicide by misadventure is when a man doth an act that is not unlawful, which without any evil intent tendeth to a man's death."

"Unlawful. If the act be unlawful it is murder. As if A. meaning to steal a deer in the park of B., shooteth at the deer and by the glance of the arrow killeth a boy that is hidden in a bush, this is murder, for the act was unlawful, although A. had no intent to hurt the boy and knew not of him. But if B., the owner of the park, had shot at his own deer, and without any ill intent had killed the boy by the glance of his arrow, this had been homicide by misadventure and no felony. So if one shoot at any wild fowl upon a tree, and the arrow killeth any reasonable creature afar off without any evil intent in him, this is per infortunium, for it was not unlawful to shoot at the wild fowl; but if he had shot at a cock or hen, or any tame fowl of another man's, and the arrow by mischance had killed a man, this had been murder, for the act was unlawful. 3rd Institute, p. 56.

This astonishing doctrine has so far prevailed as to have been recognized as part of the law of England by many subsequent writers, although in a modified shape given to it long afterwards by Sir Michael Foster, who limits it to cases where the unlawful act amounts to felony. It has been repeated so often that I amongst others have not only accepted it, though with regret, but have acted upon it.

3 STEPHEN, HISTORY OF CRIMINAL LAW 57 (1883).

2. "There has often been proposed the question whether uncontrollable events should be imputed to an agent if he has engaged in some illicit activity.... The common opinion [of the ecclesiastics] is that there is no imputation of guilt for the uncontrollable event. In the eyes of the moral law the agent is not guilty of the crime, and the eclesiastical [sic] law will not hold him for a criminal offense." MCGRATH, COMPARATIVE STUDY OF CRIME AND ITS IMPUTABILITY IN ECCLESIASTICAL CRIMINAL LAW AND IN AMERICAN CRIMINAL LAW 58-59 (1957).

3. Judicial and Legislative Limitations on the Felony Murder Rule. *People v. Aaron*, 409 Mich. 672, 699-707, 299 N.W.2d 304, 312-16 (1980):

> *III. Limitation of the Felony-Murder Doctrine in the United States*
>
> While only a few states have followed the lead of Great Britain in abolishing felony murder, various legislative and judicial limitations on the doctrine have effectively narrowed the scope of the rule in the United States. Perkins states that the rule is "somewhat in disfavor at the present time" and that "courts apply it where the law requires, but they do so grudgingly and tend to restrict its application where circumstances permit."
>
> The draftsmen of the Model Penal Code have summarized the limitations imposed by American courts as follows:
>
> (1) "The felonious act must be dangerous to life."

(2) and (3) "The homicide must be a natural and probable consequence of the felonious act." "Death must be 'proximately' caused." Courts have also required that the killing be the result of an act done in the furtherance of the felonious purpose and not merely coincidental to the perpetration of a felony. These cases often make distinctions based on the identity of the victim (i.e., whether the decedent was the victim of the felony or whether he was someone else, e.g., a policeman or one of the felons) and the identity of the person causing the death.

(4) "The felony must be malum in se."

(5) "The act must be a common-law felony."

(6) "The period during which the felony is in the process of commission must be narrowly construed."

(7) "The underlying felony must be 'independent' of the homicide."

....

Many state legislatures have also been active in restricting the scope of felony murder by imposing additional limitations.

Kentucky and Hawaii have specifically abolished the felony-murder doctrine. The commentary to Hawaii's murder statute is instructive as to that state's reasoning in abolishing the doctrine:

> Even in its limited formulation the felony-murder rule is still objectionable. It is not sound principle to convert an accidental, negligent, or reckless homicide into a murder simply because, without more, the killing was in furtherance of a criminal objective of some defined class. Engaging in certain penally prohibited behavior may, of course, evidence a recklessness sufficient to establish manslaughter, or a practical certainty or intent, with respect to causing death, sufficient to establish murder, but such a finding is an independent determination which must rest on the facts of each case.
>
> ....
>
> In recognition of the trend toward, and the substantial body of criticism supporting, the abolition of the felony-murder rule, and because of the extremely questionable results which the rule has worked in other jurisdictions, the Code has eliminated from our law the felony-murder rule.

Some of the limitations on the felony-murder doctrine which have been imposed by the courts, as mentioned above, have been codified by statute. These limitations include restrictions on the underlying felony, requiring that it be forcible, violent or clearly dangerous to human life, that death be proximately caused, that death be a natural or probable consequence or a reasonably foreseeable consequence of the commission or attempted commission of the felony, that the felon must have caused the death, and that the victim must not be one of the felons.

Other restrictions of the common-law rule include the enumeration of felonies which are to be included within the felony-murder category, and the reduction to manslaughter of killings in the course of non-enumerated felonies. The commentary following New York's revision of its felony-murder statute, deleting "any felony" and inserting specifically enumerated felonies, states: "The purpose of the indicated limitations is to exclude from felony murder, cases of accidental or not reasonably foreseeable fatality occurring in the course of a non-violent felony." The limitation is a response to a significant aspect of the common-law felony-murder rule — the fact that it ignores the relevance of factors, e.g., accident, which mitigate culpability.

Finally, a limitation of relatively recent origin is the availability of affirmative defenses where a defendant is not the only participant in the commission of the underlying felony. The New York statute provides, as do similar statutes of nine other states, an affirmative defense to the defendant when he:

(a) Did not commit the homicidal act or in any way solicit, request, command, importune, cause or aid the commission thereof; and

(b) Was not armed with a deadly weapon, or any instrument, article or substance readily capable of causing death or serious physical injury and of a sort not ordinarily carried in public places by law-abiding persons; and

(c) Had no reasonable ground to believe that any other participant was armed with such a weapon, instrument, article or substance; and

(d) Had no reasonable ground to believe that any other participant intended to engage in conduct likely to result in death or serious physical injury.

The commentary to the New York statute states that the provision is premised "upon the theory that the felony-murder doctrine, in its rigid automatic envelopment of all participants in the underlying felony, may be unduly harsh...." The comment acknowledges that there may be some cases where it would be "just and desirable to allow a non-killer defendant of relatively minor culpability a chance of extricating himself from liability for murder, though not, of course, from liability for the underlying felony."

The numerous modifications and restrictions placed upon the common-law felony-murder doctrine by courts and legislatures reflect dissatisfaction with the harshness and injustice of the rule. Even though the felony-murder doctrine survives in this country, it bears increasingly less resemblance to the traditional felony-murder concept. To the extent that these modifications reduce the scope and significance of the common-law doctrine, they also call into question the continued existence of the doctrine itself.

4. In *State v. Diebold*, 152 Wash. 68, 277 P. 394 (1929), D stole an automobile, drove it a distance of five miles and went into a tavern where he drank liquor. Emerging intoxicated about two hours later, he drove the stolen car into a crowd of school children, killing one of them. A conviction for second-degree murder, based on the felony-murder rule, was reversed, the court holding: "It cannot be held that at the time appellant drove his car against the unfortunate victims of his carelessness he was committing, or attempting to commit, or withdrawing from the scene of, a felony." The court quoted with approval from *Hoffman v. State*, 88 Wis. 166, 179, 59 N.W. 588, 592-93 (1894). In that case it was said: "It is not enough that the killing occurred soon or

presently after the felony attempted or committed. There must be such a legal relation between the two that it can be said that the killing occurred by reason and as a part of the felony, or, as in this case, that the killing occurred before the assault on Robert Risto was at an end; so that the assault had a legal relation to the killing, and was concurrent with, in part at least, and a part of, it, in an actual and material sense."

5. In *State v. Mauldin*, 215 Kan. 956, 529 P.2d 124, 126 (1974), the court held that an indictment under the felony-murder statute was properly dismissed against a defendant who had sold heroin to the deceased, who subsequently injected the drug and died of an overdose. The deceased's action had been taken voluntarily, out of the presence of the defendant, and without defendant's assistance. The court cited the lower court's decision with approval: "These cases hold in principle that there must be a closer and more direct causal connection between criminal conduct and a homicide than is required by the tort concept of proximate cause, and that to convict of felony-murder it must be shown that the conduct causing the death was done while in the commission of a felony or in furtherance of the design to commit the felony.... In the case before me, the felony involved was the sale of heroin, and it was completed upon consummation of the sale."

6. An "escape may, under certain unities of time, manner, and place, be a matter so immediately connected with the crime as to be part of its commission but ... where there is no reasonable doubt of a complete intervening desistance from the crime, as by the abandonment of the loot and running away, the subsequent homicide is not murder in the first degree without proof of deliberation and intent." *People v. Walsh*, 262 N.Y. 140, 148, 186 N.E. 422, 424 (1933).

7. In California the felony-murder rule was upheld where, after a robbery, defendants "have not won their way even momentarily to a place of temporary safety and the possession of the plunder is nothing more than a scrambling possession.... Robbery, unlike burglary, is not confined to a fixed locus, but is frequently spread over considerable distance and varying periods of time." *People v. Boss*, 210 Cal. 245, 290 P. 881, 883 (1930). Subsequent cases have held that the felony-murder rule requires only that the defendant failed to reach a place of temporary safety. *People v. Kendrick*, 56 Cal. 2d 71, 363 P.2d 13, 14 Cal. Rptr. 13 (1961); *People v. Salas*, 7 Cal. 3d 812, 500 P.2d 7, 103 Cal. Rptr. 431 (1972), *cert. denied,* 410 U.S. 1401 (1973). Justice Peters dissented in *People v. Salas*:

> Although the rule remains the law in this state, I do not believe we should extend its applicability by broadly defining the term robbery; instead in furtherance of the policy to equate criminal liability with culpability we should strictly limit the meaning of the term robbery as used in section 189.
>
> To extend the felony-murder rule until the robber has reached a place of temporary safety, without regard to whether the decedent is a victim or witness of the crime and without regard to whether there has been a break in the pursuit, would mean that the death of victims of automobile collisions or of pedestrians occurring accidentally during an escape may

VI. FELONY-MURDER

constitute first degree murder. In the absence of a direct pursuit by victims or witnesses, such a broad application of the first degree felony-murder rule to accidental killings is not in accord with the purpose of the rule or the language of the statutes." 500 P.2d 7, 19.

8. [M]any courts have pointed out that a homicide is committed during the perpetration of a felony within the meaning of the felony-murder rule if the homicide is committed within the rea gestae of the felony.

> Although the term *res gestae* has been applied in various legal situations, within the context of the felony-murder rule it has been variously described as requiring that the felony and homicide be part of a continuous transaction, that the homicide be incident to the felony, or that there be no break in the chain of events between the felony and the homicide.

COMMONWEALTH v. SPALLONE

Superior Court of Pennsylvania
267 Pa. Super. 486, 406 A.2d 1146 (1979)

ROBERTS, JUDGE.

Appellant, Walter Spallone, entered a plea of guilty to murder generally for killing Michael Valgene, Sr. On May 19, 1976, the trial court determined that appellant was guilty of murder of the second degree for committing a felony-murder. After denying post-verdict motions, the court sentenced appellant to life imprisonment. Appellant's sole contention is that he could not be guilty of felony-murder because the fact finder determined he did not form the intent to rob until after commission of the killing. We agree, reverse judgment of sentence and remand for a new hearing on degree of guilt.

Based on credible evidence, the trial court found that appellant and several friends were visiting Valgene as they often had before, drinking, talking and smoking. Valgene and appellant began to quarrel. Valgene threw a beer bottle at appellant, striking him, and then attacked appellant with a knife, inflicting a deep cut in one of appellant's fingers. Appellant and Valgene grappled, rolling on the floor. Appellant grabbed a pair of scissors and stabbed Valgene 37 times. Two of the stabs were fatal; the others were superficial. After he killed Valgene, appellant ran outside for a few seconds, then ran back in, cut Valgene's pants pocket with the scissors and removed his wallet. Appellant then fled.

The trial court determined that appellant was not guilty of murder of the first degree because he killed out of provocation, thus negating the specific premeditation required. The court determined that appellant was guilty of murder of the second degree because he had killed while perpetrating a robbery. Although the court found as fact that appellant had not formed the intent to rob until after the killing, it nonetheless held him guilty of murder of the second degree for committing a felony-murder. The court concluded that an accused commits a felony-murder while perpetrating a robbery even when the intent to rob forms subsequent to the killing. In this conclusion, on this record, the court erred.

One of the basic concepts of criminal law is that there must be a concurrence of intent with the prohibited act. W. LaFave and A. Scott, Criminal Law § 34 at 237 *infra* (1972). In felony-murder, the malice necessary to sustain a conviction for murder is inferred from the underlying felonious act. See *Commonwealth v. Yukanavich*, 448 Pa. 502, 295 A.2d 290 (1972); *Commonwealth v. Redline*, 391 Pa. 486, 137 A.2d 472 (1958). Accordingly, for an accused to be guilty of felony-murder, he must commit the killing while performing or attempting to carry out the underlying felony. *Commonwealth v. Yukanavich, supra*. Since an accused cannot be perpetrating or attempting to carry out a felony unless, at the time of the prohibited acts, he has formed the intent to commit the felony, a killing cannot be in the course of perpetrating or attempting to perpetrate a felony if the accused, as here found by the court, forms the intent to commit the felony only after the killing.

Of those jurisdictions which have faced this question, an impressive majority has likewise concluded that an accused is not guilty of felony-murder where he forms felonious intent only after he commits the killing. See *United States v. Bolden*, 169 U.S.App.D.C. 60, 514 F.2d 1301 (1975); *United States v. Mack*, 151 U.S.App.D.C. 162, 466 F.2d 333, cert. denied, 409 U.S. 952, 93 S.Ct. 297, 34 L.Ed.2d 223 (1972); *Long v. United States*, 364 A.2d 1174 (D.C.Ct.App. 1976); *People v. Gonzales*, 66 Cal.2d 482, 58 Cal.Rptr. 361, 426 P.2d 929 (1967); *State v. Snow*, 383 A.2d 1385 (Me.1978); *State v. Montgomery*, 191 Neb. 470, 215 N.W.2d 881 (1974); *People v. Joyner*, 26 N.Y.2d 106, 308 N.Y.S.2d 840, 257 N.E.2d 26 (1970); accord, LaFave and Scott, Criminal Law, *supra* § 71 at 558; Note, 42 Dick. L. Rev. 85 (1938). Contra *State v. Craig*, 82 Wash.2d 777, 514 P.2d 151 (1973).

The Commonwealth relies on a series of Pennsylvania decisions stating that an accused is guilty of committing a felony-murder irrespective of when he formed the intent to commit the underlying felony. In each of those cases, however, the statement is dictum.[2] Moreover, our conclusion comports with the rationale of the felony-murder doctrine. ==The purpose of the rule is to deter one about to commit a felony in which a reasonable man knows, or should==

---

[2] In *Commonwealth v. Butcher*, 451 Pa. 359, 304 A.2d 150 (1973), the comment was unnecessary because the jury acquitted the appellant of felony-murder. In each of the other cases, the appellant argued that the intent to rob arose subsequent to commission of the homicide, but the verdict, supported by sufficient credible evidence, disclosed that the jury had rejected the contention. It was therefore unnecessary for the court to state that, even if the facts did not support the verdict, the conviction in each instance was proper. See *Commonwealth v. Stelma*, 327 Pa. 317, 192 A. 906 (1937); *Commonwealth v. Hart*, 403 Pa. 652, 170 A.2d 850 (1961); *Commonwealth v. Dickerson*, 406 Pa. 107, 176 A.2d 421 (1962); *Commonwealth v. Wilson*, 431 Pa. 21, 244 A.2d 734 (1968); *Commonwealth v. Slavik*, 437 Pa. 354, 261 A.2d 583 (1970); *Commonwealth v. Waters*, 445 Pa. 534, 285 A.2d 192 (1971), cert. denied, 406 U.S. 961, 92 S.Ct. 2073, 32 L.Ed.2d 348 (1972); *Commonwealth v. Tomlinson*, 446 Pa. 241, 284 A.2d 687 (1971) (plurality opinion); *Commonwealth v. Martin*, 465 Pa. 134, 348 A.2d 391 (1975) (plurality opinion); *Commonwealth v. Perkins*, 473 Pa. 116, 373 A.2d 1076 (1977) (plurality opinion). *Commonwealth v. Stelma, supra*, the leading case, is criticized in LaFave and Scott, Criminal Law § 71 at 558 (1972) and Note, 42 Dick.L.Rev. 85 (1938).

Moreover, these cases offer as justification for their dicta the fear that a contrary view would prohibit the prosecution from proving existence of the required intent at or before the time of the killing. This fear is unfounded, for the prosecution, as in the cases upon which the Commonwealth relies in this appeal, may prove concurrence of intent from the circumstances. Appellant's is the rare case in which the trier of fact, supported by sufficient credible evidence, has determined that the intent to rob arose only after the killing.

VI. FELONY-MURDER

know, that death may result, by making him criminally responsible for any such deaths. *Commonwealth v. Yukanavich, supra.* Where, as here, the trier of fact determines that the accused, at the time of the killing, has not formed the intent to commit the felony, a rule designed to deter commission of a contemplated felony can have no effect.

Judgment of sentence reversed and case remanded for a new hearing on degree of guilt to determine whether appellant is guilty of murder of the third degree or manslaughter.

NOTE

In *State v. Craig*, 82 Wash. 2d 777, 514 P.2d 151 (1973), appellant at trial admitted he had entered a taxicab intending to rob the driver. He claimed that he had abandoned that intent prior to killing him and that he killed him as a result of a "rage reaction induced by drugs and precipitated when the driver struck at him with a lug wrench." He argued to the jury that he did not have the intent to rob at the time of the killing, and that the felony-murder rule was inapplicable. The court sustained his murder conviction and upheld the trial court's refusal to allow a medical expert to give his opinion that defendant did not intend to commit robbery at the moment he began to stab the driver.

The court concluded that defendant's state of mind at the time of the killing was "immaterial." "Having killed and robbed the victim, the appellant cannot now be heard to say that his *intentions* were pure when he administered the blows which resulted in the death of the victim.... '[T]he robbery and homicide were all part of the *same transaction*, ...'" 514 P.2d at 155 (emphasis added). Is the court saying that if a person is killed and property taken from the body of the decedent it does not make any difference when the intent to steal was formed — the event will be regarded as one transaction? Is the court saying that the jury had a right to disbelieve defendant's explanation?

JACKSON v. STATE

Court of Appeals of Maryland
286 Md. 430, 408 A.2d 711 (1979)

[Jackson and Wells, at gunpoint, robbed Sugar and Forbes, proprietors of a jewelry store. When police appeared at the scene Jackson and Wells compelled Sugar and Forbes to accompany them as "shields" in their attempt to escape in a police car. After a wild chase in which many shots were fired, the police stopped the vehicle by shooting out the tires. A police officer accidently discharged his shotgun, killing Sugar.]

ORTH, JUDGE.

....

As the trial judge observed, the case is unusual in that the fatal shot was fired accidently by a police officer and not by the felons perpetrating the kidnapping. But the case is not unique. Application of the felony-murder doctrine to circumstances other than those in which a death is directly caused by the felon perpetrating the underlying felony or his accomplice has harassed courts and excited commentators to critical analyses. See cases collected in Annot., 56 A.L.R.3d 239 (1974). [Citations omitted.]

Courts have followed tortuous paths endeavoring to arrive at a sound rationale applicable to a variety of circumstances in determining whether those persons perpetrating the underlying felony are responsible for the lethal act. For example, California enunciated as a test to ascertain if a defendant is guilty of murder when, during the perpetration of a felony, someone is killed by a person other than the defendant or an accomplice, whether the killing was in response to malicious conduct additional to the underlying felony. *People v. Washington*, 62 Cal.2d 777, 44 Cal.Rptr. 442, 402 P.2d 130 (1965); *People v. Gilbert*, 63 Cal.2d 690, 47 Cal.Rptr. 909, 408 P.2d 365 (1966). But then it made the test inapplicable to cases where the victim was being used by the defendant or an accomplice as a shield. It declared that the function of the test was "to provide the trier of fact with a guideline for determining whether the malicious conduct, rather than the underlying felony, *proximately* caused the victim's death. In a shield case this determination may be made without employing that test." *Pizano v. Superior Court of Tulare Cty.*, 21 Cal.3d 128, 145 Cal.Rptr. 524, 526, 577 P.2d 659, 661 (1978). Cf. *People v. Antick*, 15 Cal.3d 79, 123 Cal.Rptr. 475, 539 P.2d 43 (1975); *Taylor v. Superior Court*, 3 Cal.3d 578, 91 Cal. Rptr. 275, 477 P.2d 131 (1970).

Pennsylvania, on the other hand, went the other way. By dictum in *Commonwealth v. Moyer*, 357 Pa. 181, 53 A.2d 736 (1947) and by a holding in *Commonwealth v. Almeida*, 362 Pa. 596, 68 A.2d 595 (1949), cert. denied, 339 U.S. 950, 70 S.Ct. 798, 94 L.Ed. 1364 (1950), a defendant could be found guilty of murder even though the fatal bullet was fired by a police officer in opposition to the felony. The proximate cause theory of murder was applied. "[H]e whose felonious act is the *proximate cause* of another's death is criminally responsible for that death ...." *Almeida*, 362 Pa. at 603, 68 A.2d at 599. *Almeida* changed the rule previously followed that in order to convict for felony-murder, the killing must have been done by the defendant or by an accomplice. In *Commonwealth ex rel. Smith v. Myers*, 438 Pa. 218, 261 A.2d 550 (1970), there was a prosecution for murder arising from the death of an off-duty policeman who was shot while attempting to thwart the escape of the defendant and co-participants in an armed robbery. The trial judge had charged the jury that even if the victim was killed by another policeman, who was attempting to prevent the robbery, or was returning the fire of the felons, the felons would be guilty of murder. A majority of the court, over vigorous dissent, held that the instruction denied a fair trial. The way had been paved for this ruling by extending *Almeida* in *Commonwealth v. Thomas*, 382 Pa. 639, 117 A.2d 204 (1955) and by overruling *Thomas* in *Commonwealth v. Redline*, 391 Pa. 486, 137 A.2d 472 (1958). So the court in *Myers* expressly overruled *Almeida*, stating that it gave "Almeida burial, taking it out of its limbo, and plunging it downward into the bowels of the earth." 261 A.2d at 559-560. Thus *Myers* reverted the Pennsylvania law to the pre-*Almeida* rule — to convict of murder under the felony-murder doctrine, the killing must be done by the hand of the felon or an accomplice.

....

VI. FELONY-MURDER

... [I]n *Wilson v. State*, 188 Ark. 846, 68 S.W.2d 100 (1934), the Supreme Court of Arkansas had before it circumstances of a killing substantially the same as those in the case before us....

The court agreed with the principle expressed in cases in other jurisdictions: "A attempts to rob B. B, while resisting the attempted robbery, shoots at A and accidentally kills C who is an innocent third party. A cannot be convicted of the murder of C." The court noted the reason for the principle was that "[i]n order that one may be guilty of homicide, the act must be done by him actually or constructively, and that cannot be, unless the crime be committed by his own hand, or by the hands of someone acting in concert with him, or in furtherance of a common object or purpose." *Id.*, 68 S.W.2d at 101-102, quoting *Commonwealth v. Moore*, 121 Ky. 97, 88 S.W. 1085, 1086 (1905). But the court did not think that the principle was applicable to the facts before it.

Here the robbers compelled [the teller], over his objections and against his will, to accompany them from a place of safety, so far as outsiders were concerned, to a place known by them to be a place of danger from those on the outside. They knew they had been discovered and apprehended danger from the outside, else they would not have taken [the teller] with them. They wished to use him as a breastwork, as it were, or they thought perhaps the outsiders would not shoot at them for fear of killing [the teller]. In doing this they committed another crime, kidnapping, and caused [the teller's] death. [*Wilson*, 68 S.W.2d at 102.]

....

The basic premise is that "[a] person is only criminally liable for what he has caused, that is, there must be a causal relationship between his act and the harm sustained for which he is prosecuted." 1 Wharton's Criminal Law § 68 (Anderson, 1957). But [i]t is not essential to the existence of a causal relationship that the ultimate harm which has resulted was foreseen or intended by the actor. It is sufficient that the ultimate harm is one which a reasonable man would foresee as being reasonably related to the acts of the defendant.... It is not necessary that the defendant personally inflict harm upon the victim.... To constitute the cause of the harm, it is not necessary that the defendant's act be the sole reason for the realization of the harm which has been sustained by the victim. The defendant does not cease to be responsible for his otherwise criminal conduct because there were other conditions which contributed to the same result. [*Id.*]

....

... [T]here can be no doubt that "but for" the acts of Jackson and Wells — committing the armed robbery, kidnapping Sugar and Farber to use them as hostages, forcing them against their will into a position of known grave danger, attempting to elude apprehension by fleeing in stolen automobiles, all the while purposely exposing their hostages to gunfire, and, when ultimately halted in their flight by police action, resisting arrest — "but for" those acts, Sugar would not have been killed. Although the lethal shot was through the actions of a police officer attempting to apprehend the felons, the behavior of that officer was chargeable to Jackson and Wells. They were just as much the cause of Sugar's death as if each had fired the fatal shot. Their acts themselves produced the intervening cause of Sugar's death, and the result is not to be considered remote and was foreseeable.

... The causal relationship between the acts of Jackson and Wells and the death of Sugar for which they were prosecuted is clear and direct.[5]

Judgment affirmed.

NOTES

1. In *People v. Wood*, 8 N.Y.2d 48, 167 N.E.2d 736, 201 N.Y.S.2d 328 (1960), the court held that the statutory definition of felony-murder, punishing a killing committed "by a person engaged in the commission of, or in an attempt to commit, a felony" indicated a legislative intent to punish only those killings committed by the felon or his accomplice. An indictment for murder was dismissed on facts indicating that fatal shots had been fired by a tavern owner coming to the assistance of a police officer who was attempting to prevent the vehicular flight of the defendant from the scene of a felonious assault.

2. Following the decisions in Pennsylvania and New York, the California Supreme Court also decided to restrict the felony-murder statute to killing by a felon. *People v. Washington*, 62 Cal. 2d 777, 402 P.2d 130, 44 Cal. Rptr. 442 (1965). But in *People v. Gilbert*, 63 Cal. 2d 690, 408 P.2d 365, 47 Cal. Rptr. 909 (1965) and *People v. Taylor*, 3 Cal. 3d 578, 477 P.2d 131, 91 Cal. Rptr. 275 (1970), the California Supreme Court modified its Washington decision: if the felon initiates a gun battle and someone is killed by the intended victim or a police officer, i.e. if apart from the felony-murder statute, the felon is guilty of murder (evidently in the second degree) then by reference to the felony-murder statute, he is guilty of murder in the first degree. Thus, a person engaged in a felony may be held responsible for first degree murder for a felony committed by another such as a policeman or victim ... "when the defendant or his accomplice 'for a base, anti-social motive and with wanton disregard for human life does an act that involves a high degree of probability that it will result in death.' [Citations omitted.] Initiating a gun battle is such an act." Furthermore, "[t]he killing must be attributable to the act of the defendant or his accomplice." In other words, the act of the non-felon which causes death must be in response to the felon's life-endangering act and not merely a response to the felony itself. This "reasonable response" test is not used where the felon uses the victim as a shield. The use of a person as a shield is adequate evidence of malice. Curiously, once malice has been demonstrated and the killing determined to be murder, the felony-murder rule may then be applied to determine the degree of murder. *Pizano v. Superior Court of Tulare County*, 21 Cal. 3d 128, 145 Cal. Rptr. 524, 577 P.2d 659, 663 (1978).

Cf. *People v. Antick*, 15 Cal. 3d 79, 539 P.2d 43, 123 Cal. Rptr. 475 (1975). The defendant's co-conspirator initiated a gun battle with the police to escape

---

[5] 1 Wharton's Criminal Law § 253 (Anderson, 1957) suggests that the general rule is that the defendant is not responsible for a death caused by the shots of a police officer, but that "[t]he general rule recognizes two exceptions in which the felon is guilty of first degree murder, namely, when he uses the victim as a shield, and when he compels the victim to occupy a place or position of danger." The authority given for the "exceptions" is *Wilson v. State*, 188 Ark. 846, 68 S.W.2d 100 (1934); *Taylor v. State*, 41 Tex.Crim. 564, 55 S.W. 961 (1900); and *Keaton v. State*, 41 Tex.Crim. 621, 57 S.W. 1125 (1900). We do not read those cases as setting out exceptions to a "general rule" but as deeming such acts to establish a causal relationship with the harm sustained sufficient to make the felon criminally liable.

arrest in flight from a burglary committed by him and the defendant. A police officer responded by killing the co-conspirator. Held: the defendant cannot be held liable for his co-conspirator's death either under the felony-murder rule or on the theory of vicarious liability.

3. In *People v. Hickman*, 59 Ill. 2d 89, 319 N.E.2d 511 (1974), *cert. denied*, 421 U.S. 913 (1975), the defendant was held guilty of felony-murder when, while he was fleeing from a burglary, an officer shot and killed a person later identified as a detective. The shot which killed Detective Locheider was a shot fired in opposition to the escape of the fleeing burglars, and it was a direct and foreseeable consequence of defendants' actions. 319 N.W.2d at 513. The court cited contrary decisions in California and Pennsylvania and said: Our statutory and case law, however, dictate a different, and we believe preferable, result. *Id.* at 514.

4. The Florida Supreme Court has interpreted its first degree felony-murder rule ("... when committed by a person engaged in the perpetration, etc....") as applying to a defendant who personally commits the killing or to one who is actually present aiding and abetting the commission of the underlying felony. Under a separate statute which applies to a killing during the perpetration of a felony "... by a person other than the person engaged in the perpetration of the felony," aiders and abetters who are not physically present are guilty of second degree murder, as are all of the parties to the crime where an innocent victim is killed by a police officer or bystander. *Hite v. State*, 364 So. 2d 771 (Fla. Dist. Ct. App. 1978). *State v. Lowery*, 419 So. 2d 621 (1982), overruled *Hite* "to the extent that it requires presence at the scene of a crime for a person to be guilty of *second-degree* felony-murder." *Id.* at 624 (emphasis added).

COMMONWEALTH v. BOWDEN

Supreme Court of Pennsylvania
456 Pa. 278, 309 A.2d 714 (1973)

EAGEN, JUSTICE.

This is an appeal by the Commonwealth from the granting of a motion in arrest of judgment by the Court of Common Pleas of Philadelphia. The salient facts are as follows:

The appellee, Halford Bowden, was indicted for murder in connection with the death of Alphonso Saunders. The evidence established Saunders invited Bowden to share a bag of heroin with him, and provided the funds for the purchase of the narcotic. Bowden purchased the heroin and injected himself. Saunders was unable to properly inject himself, and requested Bowden to make the injection and Bowden complied. Saunders died from an adverse reaction to the dosage of heroin.

Appellee was ... found guilty of murder in the second degree.... On September 20, 1972, the court reconsidered the disposition of the post-trial motions and after argument granted the motion in arrest of judgment on the ground the trial evidence was insufficient as a matter of law to establish malice, a necessary ingredient of the crime of murder in the second degree.

....

The issue on the merits can be concisely stated as follows: does the injection of another person with the drug heroin, with death resulting, constitute the crime of murder in the second degree.... Saunders, the deceased, inquired of Bowden if he wished to share a bag of heroin with him; Saunders furnished the money for the purchase and Bowden made the buy. Bowden prepared the drug and used half of the quantity himself, leaving the other half for Saunders. Saunders was unable to properly administer the heroin to himself and asked Bowden to inject him, which Bowden did, and Saunders subsequently died. The record established that both Bowden and Saunders were heroin addicts and had used the drug together during the years 1969-1970, and during this period Bowden had injected Saunders with the drug with no adverse reaction.

The Commonwealth produced the medical examiner for the City of Philadelphia who stated that after performing a post-mortem examination on Saunders, he found morphine and quinine in the blood stream and determined death was caused by an adverse reaction to an injection of the drug, heroin. The doctor stated the test showed the amount of narcotic taken by the deceased was consistent with that taken by an addict, and death would be unexpected or unforeseeable from such a dose in an addict.

... All murder perpetrated by poison or lying in wait, or any wilful, deliberate or premeditated murder or murder which is committed in the perpetration of certain felonies is murder in the first degree. Every other kind of murder is murder in the second degree....

Under the facts of the instant case, we do not believe the necessary element of malice can be implied from Bowden's act of injecting Saunders with the drug, heroin. Initially, although we recognize heroin is truly a dangerous drug, we also recognize that the injection of heroin into the body does not generally cause death. Unfortunately, there are thousands of individuals who use or abuse heroin daily....

Moreover, and more importantly, under the facts of the instant case, Bowden knew Saunders was an addict and had used heroin with him for a period of time, he knew the deceased's tolerance to heroin and knew the quantity of heroin he injected into Saunders was his normal dosage, and he knew this dosage had never adversely affected Saunders before in the times he had used the drug. Moreover, the medical testimony established that the amount of heroin taken by Saunders would not normally cause death in an addict. Hence, under the facts of the instant case, Bowden could not "reasonably anticipate that death to [Saunders was] likely to result."

Order affirmed.

....

NIX, JUSTICE, concurring.

The majority opinion ignores the fact that there are two theories under the facts of this case which could be offered to support a verdict of second-degree murder. To support the trial court's granting of the Motion in Arrest of Judgment there must be a finding that the evidence presented was insufficient under either theory. I fully concur with the Court's conclusion that the evidence did not establish malice for traditional common-law murder. I write this

VI. FELONY-MURDER

concurring opinion because I believe the Court failed to dispose of the second possible theory, to wit, common-law felony-murder.

Originally, the English common-law felony-murder rule provided that one who, in the commission or attempted commission of a felony, caused another's death, was guilty of murder, without regard to the dangerous nature of the felony involved. As the number of felonies multiplied so as to include a great number of relatively minor statutory offenses, many of which involved no great danger to life or limb, it became necessary, in order to alleviate the harshness of the rule, to limit it in some fashion.[2]

Many American authorities have also concluded that this theory should be limited to those instances where the felony is inherently dangerous to human life.[3] Under this view the Commonwealth's burden encompasses more than merely showing that death resulted during the commission of a felony, it must, in addition, demonstrate that the felonious conduct posed an unreasonable threat to life or serious bodily harm.

The basic theory underlying the felony murder rule is that the intent to commit the felony is equivalent to the legal malice required for common law murder. See *Commonwealth v. Malone*, 354 Pa. 180, 47 A.2d 445 (1946). For this theory to be tenable the nature of the felony must be such that an intent to commit that crime exhibits a conscious disregard for human life, hardness of heart, cruelty, recklessness of consequences and a mind regardless of social duty. Where, however, the acts which constitute felonious conduct do not possess a sufficient danger to human life to justify the application of the doctrine of common law felony murder, the doctrine is inapplicable because there is a failure to establish the requisite state of mind from the forming of the intention to commit the felony.

The case at bar is one involving a statutory offense with no common-law background.... An injection of heroin into the body of a user of narcotics in a dosage consistent with his prior habit does not represent the serious threat of death or grave bodily harm that would allow a court to conclude that the framing of an intention to perform these acts exhibited the characteristics which would be comparable to the legal malice required for murder.

....

The Supreme Court of California has also reached the same conclusion in *People v. Satchell*, 6 Cal. 3d 28, 98 Cal. Rptr. 33, 489 P.2d 1361 (1971) (violation of statute prohibiting the possession of a concealable weapon by one

---

[2] At the time the felony murder doctrine developed all felonies were punishable by death, so it made little difference whether the felon was hanged for the felony or for murder. Today most felonies are punishable by penalties much less severe than those imposed for murder, so the situation is different from what it was at common law. See Perkins, "A Re-examination of Malice Aforethought," 43 Yale L.J. 537, 557-563 (1934).

[3] Many writers have suggested limits on the broad language which the early cases employed in convictions based on the second degree felony murder rule. Moreland, The Law of Homicide 222 (1952). Moreland assumes the felony murder rule will be used only in prosecutions for deaths resulting from felonies dangerous to human life. Under his analysis "the lawfulness or unlawfulness of the act in the course of which the homicide occurred is not the deciding factor; the test of liability is whether it was of such a nature as to be wantonly disregardful of the lives and safety of others. This will depend upon the *amount of danger involved in the act itself*." (Emphasis added). *Accord*, Holmes, The Common Law 58 (1881); Perkins, "A Re-examination of Malice Aforethought," 43 Yale L.J. 537, 560 (1934); Wechsler and Michael, "A Rationale of the Law of Homicide," 37 Colum.L.Rev. 701, 1261 (1937).

previously convicted of a felony); *People v. Phillips*, 64 Cal. 2d 574, 51 Cal. Rptr. 225, 414 P.2d 353 (1966) (grand theft by false pretenses); *People v. Williams*, 63 Cal. 2d 452, 47 Cal. Rptr. 7, 406 P.2d 647 (1965) (conspiracy to obtain methedrine, a narcotic). In reaching these results the California Court recognized that to extend the felony murder doctrine to include felonies not inherently dangerous to human life would not serve the ends of punishment.[5]

Thus, I conclude the lower court was correct in granting the motion in arrest of judgment.

NOTES

1. The "inherently dangerous" felony construction narrows the applicability of felony-murder statutes expressed in terms of "any felony." In some states killing in the commission of an "inherently dangerous" felony, other than those specified for first degree murder, is murder in the second degree. Possession of a concealed gun by a previously convicted felon was held not an inherently dangerous felony. *People v. Satchell*, 6 Cal. 3d 28, 489 P.2d 1361, 98 Cal. Rptr. 33 (1971); similarly held as to escape from prison, *People v. Lopez*, 6 Cal. 3d 45, 489 P.2d 1372, 98 Cal. Rptr. 44 (1971); and as to furnishing cocaine, *People v. Patterson*, 49 Cal.3d 615, 778 P.2d 549, 262 Cal. Rptr. 195 (1989). In *People v. Nieto-Bewitez*, 4 Cal.4th 91, 840 P.2d 969, 13 Cal. Rptr. 2d 864 (1992), California's Supreme Court upheld a second degree murder conviction which did not satisfy the "inherently dangerous" standard. The act in question, brandishing a firearm, was only a misdemeanor. The court held the "inherently dangerous" analysis inapplicable because the conviction was based on an "implied malice" theory. The court distinguished the analysis appropriate to felony-murder, which "render[s] irrelevant any evidence of actual malice or lack thereof." *Id.* at 872. Under an implied malice theory, even though the act itself was not inherently dangerous, malice could be implied from other circumstances. *Id.* at 875.

2. The former New York statute was replaced in 1967 by § 125.25 of the New York Penal Law, which provides that only killings committed in the perpetration or attempted perpetration of certain specified felonies fall within the felony-murder statute. See p. 300 *supra*. The Texas Penal Code § 19.02(a)(3) (1974) provides that a person commits murder if he "commits or attempts to commit a felony, other than voluntary or involuntary manslaughter, and in the course of and in furtherance of the commission or attempt, he commits or attempts to commit an act clearly dangerous to human life that causes the death of an individual."

3. A Florida statute defines felony murder, inter alia, as "[t]he unlawful killing of a human being ... which resulted from the unlawful distribution of heroin by a person over the age of seventeen years when such drug is proven to be the proximate cause of death of the user." The statute is discussed and

---

[5] In *Williams* the California Court stated that the purpose of the felony murder rule "may be well served with respect to felonies such as robberies or burglary, but has little relevance to a felony which is not inherently dangerous. If the felony is not inherently dangerous it is highly improbable that the potential felon will be deterred; he will not anticipate that any injury or death might arise solely from the fact that he will commit the felony." 63 Cal.2d at 457-458 n. 4, 47 Cal.Rptr. at 10, 406 P.2d at 650.

VI. FELONY-MURDER 313

applied by the Supreme Court of Florida in upholding the murder conviction of appellant who sold heroin to a user who purchased it on behalf of the person who died from it. *Martin v. State*, 377 So. 2d 706 (Fla. 1979).

NOTES ON "BOOTSTRAPPING"

1. A commits an aggravated assault (a felony) against B. B dies. Is A guilty of felony-murder? Every state which has answered the question, except for one, has answered in the negative. The felony-murder rule requires an independent felony, i.e., one whose elements are established independent of the homicide. A felony-murder instruction should not be given "when it is based upon a felony which is an integral part of the homicide and which the evidence produced by the prosecution shows to be an offense included in fact within the offense charged." In many states an assault which results in death merges into the homicide leaving only a crime of culpable homicide. In the above example the state could not prove the homicide without proving the assault; A committed only one crime. To hold otherwise would allow "bootstrapping" which "finds support neither in logic or in law." *People v. Wilson*, 1 Cal. 3d 431, 462 P.2d 22, 26, 82 Cal. Rptr. 494 (1969).

2. Notwithstanding robbery may include an assault, felony-murder applies, as it does in cases of burglary where intent is to steal property of another. *People v. Burton*, 6 Cal. 3d 375, 491 P.2d 793, 99 Cal. Rptr. 1 (1971).

3. Some states apply the felony-murder rule to a felonious entry of building for the purpose of committing an assault. *People v. Miller*, 32 N.Y.2d 157, 297 N.E.2d 85, 344 N.Y.S.2d 342 (1973); *Commonwealth v. Balliro*, 349 Mass. 505, 209 N.E.2d 308, 312 (1965). Contra *People v. Wilson, supra* note 1.

4. Washington may be the only state which allows a felonious assault resulting in death to support a conviction on a felony-murder theory. *State v. Thompson*, 88 Wash. 2d 13, 558 P.2d 202, appeal dismissed, 434 U.S. 898 (1977); *State v. Harris*, 69 Wash. 2d 928, 421 P.2d 662 (1966). Justice Utter dissented in *State v. Thompson, supra*, 558 P.2d at 207-08:

> The only act of the appellant relied upon to establish the felony necessary for conviction of murder in the second degree under RCW 9.48.040 (2) was the shooting itself, which, standing alone, constitutes the crime of second-degree assault. RCW 9.11.020 (4). The application of the felony-murder rule thus eliminated the necessity for proof by the state of the element of specific intent, which is the distinguishing aspect, in our statutory scheme, of murder in the second degree. Absent the proof of acts constituting an assault, the appellant could not have been found guilty of murder. In this situation it is apparent that the single act of shooting the victim can constitute one crime and one crime only. There exists no general malicious intent based upon proof of the commission of a separate felony which may be "transferred" from that crime to an independent homicide committed in the course thereof. The existence of such a separate intent is an analytical necessity to an inference of intent to kill. For this reason the felony-murder rule should not apply where the underlying felony sought to be used as a basis for the operation of the rule is an offense included in fact in the homicide itself. To hold otherwise consti-

tutes, as Chief Justice Cardozo observed, "a futile attempt to split into unrelated parts an indivisible transaction." *People v. Moran*, 246 N.Y. 100, 104, 158 N.E. 35, 36 (1927).

NOTE ON JUDICIAL ABROGATION OF THE FELONY-MURDER RULE

The Supreme Court of Michigan has abolished the felony-murder rule. *People v. Aaron*, 409 Mich. 672, 708, 712, 727-28, 299 N.W.2d 304 (1980):

> If one had to choose the most basic principle of the criminal law in general ... it would be that criminal liability for causing a particular result is not justified in the absence of some culpable mental state in respect to that result....

The most fundamental characteristic of the felony-murder rule violates this basic principle in that it punishes all homicides, committed in the perpetration or attempted perpetration of proscribed felonies whether intentional, unintentional or accidental, without the necessity of proving the relation between the homicide and the perpetrator's state of mind. This is most evident when a killing is done by one of a group of co-felons. The felony-murder rule completely ignores the concept of determination of guilt on the basis of individual misconduct. The felony-murder rule thus "erodes the relation between criminal liability and moral culpability." *People v. Washington*, 62 Cal. 2d 777, 44 Cal.Rptr. 442, 402 P.2d 130 (1965).

....

The failure of the felony-murder rule to consider the defendant's moral culpability is explained by examining the state of the law at the time of the rule's inception. The concept of culpability was not an element of homicide at early common law. The early definition of malice aforethought was vague. The concept meant little more than intentional wrongdoing with no other emphasis on intention except to exclude homicides that were committed by misadventure or in some otherwise pardonable manner. Thus, under this early definition of malice aforethought, an intent to commit the felony would in itself constitute malice. Furthermore, as all felonies were punished alike, it made little difference whether the felon was hanged for the felony or for the death.

....

Our review of Michigan case law persuades us that we should abolish the rule which defines malice as the intent to commit the underlying felony. Abrogation of the felony-murder rule is not a drastic move in light of the significant restrictions this Court has already imposed. Further, it is a logical extension of our decisions as discussed above.

We believe that it is no longer acceptable to equate the intent to commit a felony with the intent to kill, intent to do great bodily harm, or wanton and willful disregard of the likelihood that the natural tendency of a person's behavior is to cause death or great bodily harm.

....

Abrogation of this rule does not make irrelevant the fact that a death occurred in the course of a felony. A jury can properly infer malice from evidence that a defendant intentionally set in motion a force likely to cause death or great bodily harm.

Thus, whenever a killing occurs in the perpetration or attempted perpetration of an inherently dangerous felony, *People v. Pavlic, supra,* in order to establish malice the jury may consider the "nature of the underlying felony and the circumstances surrounding its commission."

SECTION VII. Voluntary Manslaughter
A. PROVOCATION

STATE v. ROSS
Supreme Court of Utah
28 Utah 2d 279, 501 P.2d 632 (1972)

CALLISTER, CHIEF JUSTICE.

Defendant appeals from his conviction by a jury of the crime of second-degree murder. His primary assertion of error is predicated on the ground that there was insufficient evidence to support a finding of malice aforethought, a requisite element of second-degree murder.

In the early morning hours of June 20, 1970, defendant admittedly killed his wife, Juanita, but he contends that it was upon a sudden quarrel or in the heat of passion, i.e., the crime of voluntary manslaughter....

Defendant testified that in the afternoon prior to her death, his wife and he ate a late lunch and then attended a movie. They returned to their apartment, and she informed him that she had an appointment with a customer; she was a prostitute. He protested mildly because the Welfare Department had taken custody of their child, and upon consultation they were informed by a caseworker that they had a good chance of regaining custody if the wife would terminate her activities in prostitution and drug use, and would establish a home for the family. Apparently, defendant accepted his wife's explanation that she needed money to purchase new clothes, and he departed from the premises. He returned to the apartment, according to his testimony, about 2:30 a.m. and discovered a spoon and cotton, which indicated to him that his wife had used the money from her customer for narcotics. He became furious and stormed into the bedroom, demanding to know the location of her "dope kit." She denied the use of narcotics and the existence of a kit. Defendant claims that he slapped her around and threatened to hit her with a leg broken off a coffee table; upon her repeated denials, he ultimately struck her in the head with the leg. She, subsequently, informed him that her "dope kit" was concealed in a dust pan in the bathroom. He ceased his attack and realized that she was injured; he went to summon help but upon arrival of the police, she was dead. Defendant characterized his encounter with his wife as an argument accompanied by scuffling all over the place; however, he did admit that he hit her with his fists. Defendant, at the time of the incident, weighed 220 pounds and was 5 feet 11½ inches tall. His wife weighed 90 to 95 pounds and was 5 feet tall.

The physician, who performed an autopsy, testified as to his findings; he described multiple abrasions, contusions and lacerations which extended over the entire body. There were 500 c.c. of blood (approximately 1/8 of her total blood) in the wife's abdominal cavity from a fractured 10th rib and lacerations of the liver and other soft tissue. He testified that the cause of death was a combination of loss of blood from the torn liver and asphyxiation by strangulation.

During the course of the trial, defendant made a motion to dismiss the charge of second-degree murder and to submit the cause to the jury on the lesser offenses of voluntary and involuntary manslaughter. Defendant asserted that an analysis of the evidence indicated a sudden quarrel and that the beating was administered in the heat of passion, that upon his realization of his actions, he immediately summoned assistance. These facts he urged negate the existence of malice. Defendant proffered the same argument in a motion for a new trial. The trial court responded that the evidence indicated a substantial physical beating, whether it was by fists or club or both, prior to death, followed by strangulation, which was the probable cause of death. The trial court concluded that from this evidence the jury might find a deliberate intention, unlawfully, to take life; and, therefore, the court denied the motion. Defendant appeals from this ruling.

"Murder" is defined as the unlawful killing of a human being with malice aforethought, Sec. 76-30-1, U.C.A.1953. Sec. 76-30-2, U.C.A.1953, provides that such malice is express when there is manifested a deliberate intention unlawfully to take the life of a fellow creature. Manslaughter is the unlawful killing of a human being without malice; it is voluntary upon a sudden quarrel or in the heat of passion, Sec. 76-30-5(1), U.C.A.1953.

In *People v. Catton*[1] this court stated:

> ... It is very difficult, in many cases, to distinguish manslaughter from murder. The act that caused death may have been wilful, but death may not have been intended. The intention to kill may have been formed, and life taken, during or soon after an angry quarrel, or amid or immediately after violence and excitement. In order to determine whether the accused in any given case acted from reason or passion, the provocation, the weapon used, (if any) the preparation for the act, his expressions, and all the circumstances must be considered; and although it appears that the act proceeded to some extent from malice, upon reflection and calculation, and to some extent from passion, that will be held to be the cause which had the preponderating influence. Passion, to some extent, almost always influences the slayer, when the fatal wound is given during or soon after a quarrel or a fight; and, conversely, malice, to some extent, influences the party killing in either case. But the law charges the act to malice or passion as the one or the other is found to be the preponderating cause of the act.... The passion must be such as is sometimes called "irresistible;" yet it is too strong to say that the reason of the party should be dethroned, or he should act in a whirlwind of passion. There must be sudden passion, upon reasonable provocation, to negative the idea of malice; and the pas-

---

[1] 5 Utah 451, 466, 16 P. 902 (1888).

A. PROVOCATION

sion must proceed from what the law accepts as an adequate cause; else it will not reduce the felonious killing to manslaughter....

One aspect which defendant has failed to discuss is the question of provocation. Heat of passion will not reduce a homicide to manslaughter unless it was engendered by adequate provocation. If the element of provocation is either lacking or legally insufficient, the offense is murder. In a determination of whether the element of provocation has displaced the element of malice aforethought and thus effectuated a reduction of the offense, the fundamental inquiry is whether or not the defendant's reason was, at the time of his act, so disturbed or obscured by some passion — not necessarily fear and never the passion for revenge — to such an extent as would render ordinary men of average disposition liable to act rashly or without due deliberation and reflection, and from this passion rather than from judgment.[3]

Where the defendant asserts that he acted in the heat of passion, two variables must be weighed in relation to each other — the degree of provocation and the measures employed by the defendant in response to it. These factors must be weighed by the jury, unless in a particular case there is no reasonable basis in the evidence to justify the submission of this issue by the court to the jury.

... "Heat of passion" and "malice" are at best very vague terms which must be applied in the light of the legislative purpose in differentiating second degree murder and manslaughter. The differentiation apparently was made "out of the indulgence of the frailty of human nature," recognizing that the provocation in some cases may be so great as to warrant a penalty less than that prescribed for murder. In deciding whether the defendant should be given the benefit of this recognition of the "frailty of human nature," his conduct must be measured against the standards of the community. The jury is best equipped to apply that standard. The trial court properly submitted to the jury the question of defendant's malice.

In the instant action, the trial court did not err by denying defendant's motion to dismiss the charge of second-degree murder. There was substantial evidence from which the jury could reasonably infer a purpose and design on defendant's part to take unlawfully the life of his wife. By his own account, defendant's "heat of passion" was sustained from approximately 2:30 a. m. to 5:00 a. m. The cause of death by strangulation contradicts his story that his wife was alive when he departed to call an ambulance. The magnitude of his wife's injuries seriously undermines defendant's account of the alleged altercation. Finally the alleged provocation, her refusal to divulge the location of her "dope kit" appears insufficient or so the jury could have found to render an ordinary man of average disposition liable to act rashly and without due deliberation and reflection. Defendant's alleged fury about the drugs, when contrasted with his weak protest about the prostitution, undermines his alleged concern about the child when both activities were to cease before the couple would be restored custody .... [Affirmed.]

---

[3]*People v. Morse*, 70 Cal.2d 711, 76 Cal. Rptr. 391, 452 P.2d 607, 621 (1969).

Ex Parte FRALEY

Criminal Court of Appeals of Oklahoma
3 Okla. Crim. 719, 109 P. 295 (1910)

RICHARDSON, J.

This is an original application in this court by M. F. Fraley for a writ of habeas corpus, by which he seeks to be let to bail pending the final hearing and determination of a charge of murder.

... The testimony taken, which is uncontradicted in this court, shows: That the deceased, Dan Parker, on April 11, 1910, was sitting upon or leaning against a railing in front of a drug store in the city of Pawhuska. That he had been in that position for some 10 or 15 minutes engaged in conversation with some gentlemen beside him in regard to the sale of certain walnut timber. That the petitioner came around the corner, walked up in front of the deceased, said "Hello Dan," and without further warning immediately fired two shots into the deceased in quick succession. That the deceased jumped up, threw up his hands, staggered, and fell off the sidewalk. The petitioner thereupon walked around an obstruction and fired four more shots into the deceased. That the petitioner then walked off, and, after going some distance, turned and came back, and putting his pistol close to the head of the deceased, snapped it a time or two, and said: "You damned son of a bitch! I told you I'd kill you. You killed my boy." The substance of the foregoing facts are testified to positively by seven eyewitnesses, and they stand in the record undisputed....

The testimony does not show it, but it was stated by counsel for the petitioner in presenting this case, that the deceased, some 9 or 10 months previously, had shot and killed the son of the petitioner, and that the deceased had been tried for the offense and had been acquitted; and it is urged here that, when the petitioner saw the deceased on this occasion, the recollection of that event must have engendered in him a passion which overcame him, that the killing was committed in the heat of such passion, was without premeditation, and therefore not murder. To this we cannot assent, even if we could take the statement of counsel as a proper substitute for testimony tending to prove the facts stated. In *Ragland v. State*, 125 Ala. 12, 27 South. 983, four hours intervening between the provocation and the killing was held as a matter of law to be sufficient cooling time to preclude the reduction of a homicide to manslaughter. *Perry v. State*, 102 Ga. 365, 30 S. E. 903, and *Rockmore v. State*, 93 Ga. 123, 19 S. E. 32, each hold three days as a matter of law sufficient cooling time. *Com. v. Aiello*, 180 Pa. 597, 36 Atl. 1079, holds from 1 to 2 hours sufficient, and *State v. Williams*, 141 N. C. 827, 53 S. E. 823, holds 15 minutes sufficient. And the authorities are all agreed that the question is not alone whether the defendant's passion in fact cooled, but also was there sufficient time in which the passion of a reasonable man would cool? If in fact the defendant's passion did cool, which may be shown by circumstances, such as the transaction of other business in the meantime, rational conversations upon other subjects, evidence of preparation for the killing, etc., then the length of time intervening is immaterial. But if in fact it did not cool, yet if such time intervened between the provocation and the killing that the passion of the average man would have cooled, and his reason have resumed its sway, then still there is no reduction of the homicide to manslaughter.... If the fatal wound be inflicted immediately following a sufficient provocation given, then the question as to whether the defendant's passion thereby aroused had in fact cooled, or as to whether or not such time had elapsed that the passion of a reasonable man would have cooled, is a question of fact to be determined upon a consideration of all the facts and circumstances in evidence; but, when an unreasonable period of time has elapsed between the provocation and the killing, then the court is authorized to say as a matter of law that the cooling time was sufficient.

Ordinarily one day, or even half a day, is in law much more than a sufficient time for one's passion to cool; and a killing committed upon a provocation given some 9 or 10 months before is not, on account of that provocation or any passion, engendered thereby, reduced to manslaughter. A deliberate killing committed in revenge for an injury inflicted in the past, however near or remote, is "murder."

...

Bail is denied, the writ is discharged, and petitioner is remanded to the custody of the sheriff of Osage county to await his trial in due course.

STATE v. NEVARES

Supreme Court of New Mexico
36 N.M. 41, 7 P.2d 933 (1932)

SADLER, J.

The appellant was convicted of murder in the second degree and appeals.

....

... The appellant was a young man twenty-one years of age. The deceased, Miss Eva Smith, was a young girl eighteen years of age, a student in the high school at Las Cruces, residing with her mother and stepfather at Tortugas, about two miles below Las Cruces. The stepfather conducted a store at Tortugas in the rear of which the family resided. For something more than a year prior to the homicide the young couple had been friendly, and it is evident from the record that appellant was enamored of the deceased. An estrangement between them took place during the Christmas holidays in December, 1929, and had continued to the day of the homicide.

On April 13, 1930, the appellant appeared in a car at the home of deceased about 3 o'clock in the afternoon and requested that she go for an automobile drive with him that evening. She declined, saying she must study, and that she was through with him. He responded by saying he would see whether or not she was through with him. He drove away and about an hour and a half later reappeared and sent in a note to deceased by a younger brother. She received the note which is in evidence, and sent out to him by this brother a reply, the contents of which were never disclosed. The appellant drove away but reappeared in about ten minutes and through a brother of the deceased asked her to come out to his car, which he had stopped directly in front of the store. The deceased went out to the car, was seen to be talking to appellant for a few moments and was in the act of returning into the store having one hand on the screen door, for opening same, when appellant jumped from his car with a shotgun, rushed rapidly toward deceased and called upon her to turn toward him. As she did so, he fired directly into her left breast and she fell dead at his feet. The appellant then drove rapidly away.

It is difficult to perceive how on this state of facts an instruction on voluntary manslaughter was warranted or permissible. Counsel for appellant predicate the right to the instruction on the testimony of Alejandro Smith, a younger brother of deceased, that at the time of rushing toward her with the shotgun appellant appeared "angry." Also, that by reason of a disordered mentality, following a head injury in an automobile accident, some two years previously, he was peculiarly susceptible to emotional stress or excitation, likely to result from the circumstances immediately surrounding the homicide for which he was on trial. And the testimony of Dr. S. D. Swope, an expert witness for appellant, that such emotional stress might have been the result of sudden anger, "if anger there was in this particular case."

The defense was insanity. The appellant did not testify, but if the jury had accepted the testimony of his witnesses on the issue of insanity he would have been acquitted. Having been found not to be insane, but capable instead of appreciating and distinguishing between right and wrong in respect to the killing in question, it remains to be determined whether there is some middle ground between insanity, which will render a homicide excusable, and sanity, which renders its perpetrator accountable, within whose compass its commission will be deemed manslaughter rather than murder.

This brings us to an application of the law to the facts. Mere sudden anger or heat of passion will not reduce the killing from murder to manslaughter. There must be adequate provocation. The one without the other will not suffice to effect the reduction in the grade of the offense. The two elements must concur. *McHargue v. Commonwealth*, 231 Ky. 82 [21 S.W.(2d) 115]; *Ballard v. Commonwealth* (Va.), 159 S.E. 222; Wharton's Criminal Law (11th Ed.), § 425, page 614. And words alone, however scurrilous or insulting, will not furnish the adequate provocation required for this purpose. *State v. Trujillo*, 27 N.M. 594, 203 P. 846.

The test of whether the provocation was adequate must be determined by considering whether it would have created the passion offered in mitigation in the ordinary man of average disposition. If so, then it is adequate and will reduce the offense to manslaughter. If not, it is inadequate. Here is shown nothing but words apprising appellant of the fact that the deceased had rejected his suit, except testimony tending to show that by reason of his peculiar, even defective, state of mind, not amounting to insanity, such knowledge likely would result in a state of excitation and anger in him, although not to be expected in the ordinary man of average disposition. This circumstance does not alter the rule. Wharton on Homicide (3rd Ed.) § 172....

We agree with the soundness of the rule adopted in England and followed generally in this country, that different degrees of mental ability in prisoners who are sane cannot be taken into account for reducing a homicide from murder to manslaughter....

We have heretofore held with respect to the plea of self-defense in homicide cases that the standard by which must be determined the reasonableness of accused's belief in the apparent imminence of danger is that of an ordinary

A. PROVOCATION

person of firmness, reason, and prudence; and that the question is not to be determined from the standpoint of the accused.... We have also held that proof of the impaired mental condition of an accused at the time of a homicide resulting from voluntary intoxication may not be employed to reduce the grade of the offense from murder in the second degree to manslaughter, unless elements of the latter offense are otherwise present....

So in the case at bar, the appellant's peculiar susceptibility to excitation, anger, or passion, even though resulting from a defective mentality, which still left him capable of distinguishing between the right and the wrong of the offense with which he stood charged, cannot aid him. He must have applied to him, for determining the adequacy of provocation relied upon, the test of its effect on the ordinary man of average disposition. Measured by this test, the correctness of the trial court's refusal to submit voluntary manslaughter is readily apparent.

[Affirmed.]

NOTES

1. Intent to kill or injure — "Malice." We agree that it is erroneous to charge that "manslaughter is never attended by a direct intent to kill." It is well established in this Commonwealth that voluntary manslaughter may be consistent with an intent to kill. For example, where a defendant acts under an unreasonable fear that he is in danger of serious bodily harm, there may be a direct and specific intent to kill, and yet the offense may constitute voluntary manslaughter. *Commonwealth v. Jordan*, 407 Pa. 575, 585, 181 A.2d 310, 316; *Commonwealth v. Thompson*, 389 Pa. 382, 394, 133 A.2d 207, 214. Moreover, a defendant may be guilty of voluntary manslaughter when he has a direct and specific intent to kill, but the killing is the result of legal passion. *Commonwealth v. Jennings*, 442 Pa. 18, 274 A.2d 767, 769-70 (1981).

   It [malice] excludes the idea of sudden passion aroused by an unanticipated and unprovoked battery inflicted by the assailant without the fault of the person assailed. If in such a case the death of the aggressor results, even if intentional, it cannot be traced to a malignant heart, but is imputable to human frailty. Passion and malice are not convertible terms, so that an act prompted by the one cannot be said to proceed from the other. *State v. Ponce*, 124 W. Va. 126, 19 S.E.2d 221, 222 (1942).

   The law does not sanction the taking of human life even when the spouse is caught in the act of adultery. Out of regard for the frailty of human nature, an immediate slaying solely as a result of sudden passion aroused by personal knowledge of such act, or from information so direct as to engender like passion, the law commits to the jury the question whether malice, or other elements of murder in the first degree, are present. *Sheppard v. State*, 243 Ala. 498, 500, 10 So. 2d 822, 824 (1942).

2. "Passion." From the evidence viewed as a whole the trial judge could well have concluded that defendant was roused to a heat of "passion" by a series of events over a considerable period of time: [deceased's] admitted

infidelity, her statements that she wished she were dead, her attempt to jump from the car . . . her repeated urging that the defendant shoot her . . . and her taunt, "are you chicken." As defendant argues persuasively, "passion" need not mean "rage" or "anger." According to dictionary definition, "passion" may be any "violent, intense, highwrought, or enthusiastic emotion." (Webster's New International Dictionary, 2d ed.)
People v. Borchers, 50 Cal. 2d 321, 325 P.2d 97, 102 (1958).

"Although 'anger' is the passion usually existing in cases of this class, yet any other passion, as sudden resentment or terror, rendering the mind incapable of cool reflection, may reduce the grade of the crime." 21 Cyc. 737....

... Therefore, in addition to the instruction in the law of self-defense, the jury should have been told, if they found that at the time of the shooting the defendant was not actuated by malice, but that he acted under the influence of an uncontrollable mortal fear raised by the threats and conduct of Rocco, and if they thought that the immediate circumstances, though adequate to raise the fear, were not sufficient reasonably to justify a belief on the part of the defendant that he was in immediate danger of death or great bodily harm, the grade of the crime would not rise higher than manslaughter.
Commonwealth v. Colandro, 231 Pa. 343, 351-52, 80 A. 571, 574 (1911).

This court has said that the term "heat of passion" includes an emotional state of mind characterized by anger, rage, hatred, furious resentment or terror.
State v. McDermott, 202 Kan. 399, 499 P.2d 545, 548, *cert. denied,* 396 U.S. 912 (1969).

3. Legal or Adequate Provocation — The "Reasonable Man." The principle involved in the question and which I think clearly deducible from the majority of well considered cases, would seem to suggest is the true general rule, that reason should, at the time of the act, be disturbed by passion to an extent which might render ordinary men, of fair average disposition, liable to act rashly or without due deliberation or reflection, and from passion, rather than judgment. *Maher v. People,* 10 Mich. 212, 219-20, 81 Am. Dec. 781 (1862).

Despite the fact that psychiatry has attained a recognized position in other areas of the law, the criminal courts refuse to consider the application of a subjective test in determining the adequacy of provocation. The application by the courts of an objective doctrine has led to the establishment of certain concrete standards of conduct which a reasonable man is said to adhere to. Unfortunately many of these incidents have ossified into ironclad rules originally evolved in the nineteenth century. Under modern law, the categories of things which provoked the nineteenth century reasonable man continue to provoke the reasonable man of the twentieth century with the addition of a few new but rigid categories.

In general, he is said to be provoked into taking human life when he is violently assaulted; when an unlawful attempt is made to arrest him; when he kills in mutual combat; or when he sees his wife in an act of adultery and kills her or her paramour. On the other hand, he is said not to be provoked by insulting words or gestures, nor, according to some authorities, is he provoked by a trespass against his land or goods. The outcome of the case which clearly falls within one of these rules may be predicted with a high degree of accuracy. However, the situations which develop are seldom clear cut. (Citations omitted.) Comment, *Manslaughter and the Adequacy of Provocation: The Reasonableness of the Reasonable Man*, 106 U. PA. L. REV. 1021, 1023 (1958).

Cf. R. v. Davies, [1975] 1 All E.R. 890, 896. In construing section 3 of the Homicide Act of 1957 the Court of Appeal said:

> ... [I]t seems quite clear to us that we should construe §3 as providing a new test, and on that test that we should give the wide words of §3 their ordinary wide meaning. Thus we come to the conclusion that whatever the position at common law, the situation since 1957 has been that acts or words otherwise to be treated as provocative for present purposes are not excluded from such consideration merely because they emanate from someone other than the victim.

[In determining the adequacy of provocation,] the mental reactions of the accused are standardized....

But how is it when the effort is the other way — that is, when the defendant's prima facie right to invoke manslaughter has been established and it is sought to take it away on the theory that sufficient time had elapsed for his hot blood to cool? Are his reactions then similarly standardized? Generally it seems they are not, though it is said in some jurisdictions that if sufficient cooling time, or presumptively sufficient time, has elapsed, the homicide will not be attributed to heat of passion but to malice, even though the accused's passion actually did not cool. 29 C.J. § 133, pp. 1147-48; 40 C.J.S., Homicide, § 54, pp. 917-918; 26 Am. Jur. § 24, p. 170.

State v. Robinson, 353 Mo. 934, 939-40, 185 S.W.2d 636, 639 (1945).

In recent years there has been some movement away from the purely objective reasonable man standard. Maine, in 1975, redefined its homicide statutes. In regard to "adequate" or "reasonable" provocation as a prerequisite to mitigation, the Comment to section 204 stated: "This section of the code changes that and follows section 630.2 of the New Hampshire Code 1973 by not requiring that there be an inquiry into reasonableness...." In 1977 the offense was redefined again in terms of the traditional "adequate" provocation and reasonableness. ME. REV. STAT. ANN., tit. 17A, § 203 and Comment. (1981 Pamph.).

The House of Lords in *D.P.P. v. Camplin*, [1978] 2 All E.R. 168, 169 said that the jury should be instructed "that the reasonable man ... is a person having the power of self control to be expected of an ordinary person of the sex and age of the accused, but in other respects sharing such of the accused's characteristics as they think would affect the gravity of the provocation to him, and that the question is not merely whether such a person would in like circumstances be provoked to lose his self constraint but also would react to the provocation as the accused did."

B. EXTREME EMOTIONAL DISTURBANCE

PATTERSON v. NEW YORK
Supreme Court of the United States
432 U.S. 197 (1977)

MR. JUSTICE WHITE.

The question here is the constitutionality under the Fourteenth Amendment's Due Process Clause of burdening the defendant in a New York State murder trial with proving the affirmative defense of extreme emotional disturbance as defined by New York law.

I

After a brief and unstable marriage, the appellant, Gordon Patterson, Jr., became estranged from his wife, Roberta. Roberta resumed an association with John Northrup, a neighbor to whom she had been engaged prior to her marriage to appellant. On December 27, 1970, Patterson borrowed a rifle from an acquaintance and went to the residence of his father-in-law. There, he observed his wife through a window in a state of semiundress in the presence of John Northrup. He entered the house and killed Northrup by shooting him twice in the head.

Patterson was charged with second-degree murder. In New York there are two elements of this crime: (1) "intent to cause the death of another person"; and (2) "caus[ing] the death of such person or of a third person." N.Y. Penal Law § 125.25 (McKinney 1975).[1] Malice aforethought is not an element of the crime. In addition, the State permits a person accused of murder to raise an affirmative defense that he "acted under the influence of extreme emotional disturbance for which there was a reasonable explanation or excuse."[2]

New York also recognizes the crime of manslaughter. A person is guilty of manslaughter if he intentionally kills another person "under circumstances

---

[1] References herein to the charge of "murder" under New York law are to this section. Cf. N.Y.Penal Law § 125.27 (McKinney 1975) (murder in the first degree).

[2] Section 125.25 provides in relevant part:

> A person is guilty of murder in the second degree when:
> 1. With intent to cause the death of another person, he causes the death of such person or of a third person; except that in any prosecution under this subdivision, it is an affirmative defense that:
> (a) The defendant acted under the influence of extreme emotional disturbance for which there was a reasonable explanation or excuse, the reasonableness of which is to be determined from the viewpoint of a person in the defendant's situation under the circumstances as the defendant believed them to be. Nothing contained in this paragraph shall constitute a defense to a prosecution for, or preclude a conviction of, manslaughter in the first degree or any other crime.

B. EXTREME EMOTIONAL DISTURBANCE

which do not constitute murder because he acts under the influence of extreme emotional disturbance."[3] Appellant confessed before trial to killing Northrup, but at trial he raised the defense of extreme emotional disturbance.[4]

The jury was instructed as to the elements of the crime of murder. Focusing on the element of intent, the trial court charged:

> Before you, considering all of the evidence, can convict this defendant or anyone of murder, you must believe and decide that the People have established beyond a reasonable doubt that he intended, in firing the gun, to kill either the victim himself or some other human being....
>
> ....
>
> Always remember that you must not expect or require the defendant to prove to your satisfaction that his acts were done without the intent to kill. Whatever proof he may have attempted, however far he may have gone in an effort to convince you of his innocence or guiltlessness, he is not obliged, he is not obligated to prove anything. It is always the People's burden to prove his guilt, and to prove that he intended to kill in this instance beyond a reasonable doubt. App. A-70-A-71.[5]

The jury was further instructed, consistently with New York law, that the defendant had the burden of proving his affirmative defense by a preponderance of the evidence. The jury was told that if it found beyond a reasonable doubt that appellant had intentionally killed Northrup but that appellant had demonstrated by a preponderance of the evidence that he had acted under the influence of extreme emotional disturbance, it had to find appellant guilty of manslaughter instead of murder.

The jury found appellant guilty of murder. Judgment was entered on the verdict, and the Appellate Division affirmed. While appeal to the New York Court of Appeals was pending, this Court decided *Mullaney v. Wilbur*, 421 U.S. 684, 95 S.Ct. 1881, 44 L.Ed.2d 508 (1975), in which the Court declared Maine's murder statute unconstitutional. Under the Maine statute, a person accused of murder could rebut the statutory presumption that he committed

---

[3] Section 125.20(2), N.Y. Penal Law § 125.20(2), (McKinney 1975), provides:

A person is guilty of manslaughter in the first degree when:
....
2. With intent to cause the death of another person, he causes the death of such person or of a third person under circumstances which do not constitute murder because he acts under the influence of extreme emotional disturbance, as defined in paragraph (a) of subdivision one of section 125.25. The fact that homicide was committed under the influence of extreme emotional disturbance constitutes a mitigating circumstance reducing murder to manslaughter in the first degree and need not be proved in any prosecution initiated under this subdivision.

[4] Appellant also contended at trial that the shooting was accidental and that therefore he had no intent to kill Northrup. It is here undisputed, however, that the prosecution proved beyond a reasonable doubt that the killing was intentional.

[5] The trial court's instructions to the jury focused emphatically and repeatedly on the prosecution's burden of proving guilt beyond a reasonable doubt.

The burden of proving the guilt of a defendant beyond a reasonable doubt rests at all times upon the prosecution. A defendant is never obliged to prove his innocence.

Before you can find a defendant guilty, you must be convinced that each and every element of the crime charged and his guilt has been established to your satisfaction by reliable and credible evidence beyond a reasonable doubt. App. A48-A49.

the offense with "malice aforethought" by proving that he acted in the heat of passion on sudden provocation. The Court held that this scheme improperly shifted the burden of persuasion from the prosecutor to the defendant and was therefore a violation of due process. In the Court of Appeals appellant urged that New York's murder statute is functionally equivalent to the one struck down in *Mullaney* and that therefore his conviction should be reversed.

III

We cannot conclude that Patterson's conviction under the New York law deprived him of due process of law. The crime of murder is defined by the statute, which represents a recent revision of the state criminal code, as causing the death of another person with intent to do so. The death, the intent to kill, and causation are the facts that the State is required to prove beyond a reasonable doubt if a person is to be convicted of murder. No further facts are either presumed or inferred in order to constitute the crime. The statute does provide an affirmative defense — that the defendant acted under the influence of extreme emotional disturbance for which there was a reasonable explanation — which, if proved by a preponderance of the evidence, would reduce the crime to manslaughter, an offense defined in a separate section of the statute. It is plain enough that if the intentional killing is shown, the State intends to deal with the defendant as a murderer unless he demonstrates the mitigating circumstances.

The New York law on extreme emotional disturbance follows this pattern. This affirmative defense, which the Court of Appeals described as permitting "the defendant to show that his actions were caused by a mental infirmity not arising to the level of insanity, and that he is less culpable for having committed them," 39 N.Y.2d, at 302, 383 N.Y.S.2d, at 582, 347 N.E.2d, at 907, does not serve to negative any facts of the crime which the State is to prove in order to convict of murder. It constitutes a separate issue on which the defendant is required to carry the burden of persuasion; and unless we are to overturn *Leland* and *Rivera*,* New York has not violated the Due Process Clause, and Patterson's conviction must be sustained.

We are unwilling to reconsider *Leland* and *Rivera*. But even if we were to hold that a State must prove sanity to convict once that fact is put in issue, it would not necessarily follow that a State must prove beyond a reasonable doubt every fact, the existence or nonexistence of which it is willing to recognize as an exculpatory or mitigating circumstance affecting the degree of culpability or the severity of the punishment. Here, in revising its criminal code, New York provided the affirmative defense of extreme emotional disturbance, a substantially expanded version of the older heat-of-passion concept;

---

*In *Leland v. Oregon*, 343 U.S. 790 (1952), the Supreme Court refused to strike down an Oregon law which placed on the defendant the burden of proving the defense of insanity beyond a reasonable doubt. The Court found that the elements of the crime, "premeditation and deliberation," had to be proven by the state beyond a reasonable doubt based on all the evidence including evidence as to defendant's mental condition. Only after finding those elements did the jury consider as a separate issue the question of insanity. Subsequently, the Court in *Rivera v. Delaware*, 429 U.S. 877 (1976), rejected the contention that *Leland* was overruled by *Mullaney v. Wilbur*, when it dismissed the case as not raising a substantial federal question — Eds.

but it was willing to do so only if the facts making out the defense were established by the defendant with sufficient certainty. The State was itself unwilling to undertake to establish the absence of those facts beyond a reasonable doubt, perhaps fearing that proof would be too difficult and that too many persons deserving treatment as murderers would escape that punishment if the evidence need merely raise a reasonable doubt about the defendant's emotional state.

IV

It is urged that *Mullaney v. Wilbur* necessarily invalidates Patterson's conviction. In *Mullaney* the charge was murder, which the Maine statute defined as the unlawful killing of a human being "with malice aforethought, either express or implied." The trial court instructed the jury that the words "malice aforethought" were most important because "malice aforethought is an essential and indispensable element of the crime of murder." Malice, as the statute indicated and as the court instructed, could be implied and was to be implied from "any deliberate, cruel act committed by one person against another suddenly... or without a considerable provocation," in which event an intentional killing was murder unless by a preponderance of the evidence it was shown that the act was committed "in the heat of passion, on sudden provocation." The instructions emphasized that "'malice aforethought and heat of passion on sudden provocation are two inconsistent things'; thus, by proving the latter the defendant would negate the former." 421 U.S., at 686-687, 95 S.Ct. at 1883 (citation omitted).

Wilbur's conviction, which followed, was affirmed. The Maine Supreme Judicial Court held that murder and manslaughter were varying degrees of the crime of felonious homicide and that the presumption of malice arising from the unlawful killing was a mere policy presumption operating to cast on the defendant the burden of proving provocation if he was to be found guilty of manslaughter rather than murder — a burden which the Maine law had allocated to him at least since the mid-1800's.

The Court of Appeals for the First Circuit then ordered that a writ of habeas corpus issue, holding that the presumption unconstitutionally shifted to the defendant the burden of proof with respect to an essential element of the crime. When the judgment of the First Circuit was vacated for reconsideration in the light of *Lafferty*,* that court reaffirmed its view that Wilbur's conviction was unconstitutional. This Court, accepting the Maine court's interpretation of the Maine law, unanimously agreed with the Court of Appeals that Wilbur's due process rights had been invaded by the presumption casting upon him the burden of proving by a preponderance of the evidence that he had acted in the heat of passion upon sudden provocation.

Mullaney's holding, it is argued, is that the State may not permit the blameworthiness of an act or the severity of punishment authorized for its commission to depend on the presence or absence of an identified fact without assuming the burden of proving the presence or absence of that fact, as the case may be, beyond a reasonable doubt. In our view, the *Mullaney* holding should not

---

State v. Lafferty, 309 A.2d 647 (Me. 1973).

be so broadly read. The concurrence of two Justices in *Mullaney* was necessarily contrary to such a reading; and a majority of the Court refused to so understand and apply *Mullaney* when *Rivera* was dismissed for want of a substantial federal question.

Mullaney surely held that a State must prove every ingredient of an offense beyond a reasonable doubt, and that it may not shift the burden of proof to the defendant by presuming that ingredient upon proof of the other elements of the offense. This is true even though the State's practice, as in Maine, had been traditionally to the contrary. Such shifting of the burden of persuasion with respect to a fact which the State deems so important that it must be either proved or presumed is impermissible under the Due Process Clause.

It was unnecessary to go further in *Mullaney*. The Maine Supreme Judicial Court made it clear that malice aforethought, which was mentioned in the statutory definition of the crime, was not equivalent to premeditation and that the presumption of malice traditionally arising in intentional homicide cases carried no factual meaning insofar as premeditation was concerned. Even so, a killing became murder in Maine when it resulted from a deliberate, cruel act committed by one person against another, "suddenly without any, or without a considerable provocation." *State v. Lafferty, supra,* at 665. Premeditation was not within the definition of murder; but malice, in the sense of the absence of provocation, was part of the definition of that crime. Yet malice, i.e., lack of provocation, was presumed and could be rebutted by the defendant only by proving by a preponderance of the evidence that he acted with heat of passion upon sudden provocation. In *Mullaney* we held that however traditional this mode of proceeding might have been, it is contrary to the Due Process Clause as construed in *Winship*.

As we have explained, nothing was presumed or implied against Patterson; and his conviction is not invalid under any of our prior cases. The judgment of the New York Court of Appeals is

Affirmed.

[The dissenting opinion of Justice Powell is omitted.]

STATE v. ELLIOTT

Supreme Court of Connecticut
177 Conn. 1, 411 A.2d 3 (1979)

LOISELLE, ASSOCIATE JUSTICE.

The defendant, Robert L. Elliott, was indicted by a grand jury for the crime of murder in violation of § 53a-54a of the General Statutes. A jury found him guilty as charged. The defendant was sentenced to not less than twenty-five years to life imprisonment and from that judgment he has appealed.

From the testimony, the jury could have found that on the morning of June 22, 1976, the defendant, armed with a loaded revolver, went to the home of his brother, the victim in this case. After failing to gain entrance to the dwelling at the front door, he forced his way in through the kitchen door. Once inside, he threatened his ten-year-old niece with a gun, forcing her to tell him that his brother was upstairs in bed. On the stairs, Elliott encountered his brother's wife. When she saw the defendant she ran down the hallway to the

B. EXTREME EMOTIONAL DISTURBANCE

back door. Elliott pursued her down the hall pointing a gun at her. Mrs. Elliott's path was blocked by a hobbyhorse. She turned and saw that the defendant was only a few feet away from her. She then saw her husband come up from behind the defendant. He called out "Bobby." The defendant then turned around and shot him twice in rapid succession. The defendant said nothing during this whole episode. The victim died from the gunshot wounds. The defendant was apprehended shortly after the shooting about one-half mile away from his brother's house.

After he was apprehended, Elliott was brought to police headquarters and booked. He gave a written statement to the police detailing the events of that morning. The booking police officer testified that the defendant was calm and able to comprehend and answer questions. The officer described Elliott's emotional state at the time of the arrest and interrogation as normal.

The defendant offered into evidence the testimony of a psychiatrist who interviewed the defendant about eleven months after the shooting. The psychiatrist testified that the defendant, at the time of the shooting, was acting under the influence of an extreme emotional disturbance caused by a combination of child custody problems, the inability to maintain a recently purchased home and an overwhelming fear of his brother. The psychiatrist placed particular emphasis on the history of conflict between the two brothers, noting that the defendant referred to his brother as a "ranger killer." The defendant told the psychiatrist that at one time his brother pulled him from a bus and chased him with a tire iron. The defendant stated that this incident was so frightening that it caused him to leave the area for a couple of years. The psychiatrist believed that this incident compounded by many other extenuating circumstances resulted in the defendant's overwhelming fear of his brother. And he testified that these circumstances taken together constituted a reasonable explanation of the defendant's extreme emotional disturbance.

The defendant's one assignment of error is that the trial court erred in its charge on the defense of extreme emotional disturbance, contained in General Statutes § 53a-54a(a).[1] We agree. In explaining the meaning of "extreme emotional disturbance," the court actually gave the substance of the traditional charge on the "heat of passion" defense, which existed prior to the enactment of the present Penal Code. The defenses of extreme emotional disturbance and heat of passion are not interchangeable.

The extreme emotional disturbance defense outlined in General Statutes § 53a-54a(a) is the same as the affirmative defense that appears in the New York murder statute. The fact that a statute is almost a literal copy of a statute of a sister state is persuasive evidence of a practical reenactment of

---

[1] "[General Statutes] Sec. 53a-54a. MURDER DEFINED; AFFIRMATIVE DEFENSES; EVIDENCE OF MENTAL CONDITION; CLASSIFICATION. (a) A person is guilty of murder when, with intent to cause the death of another person, he causes the death of such person or of a third person or causes a suicide by force, duress or deception; except that in any prosecution under this subsection, it shall be an affirmative defense that the defendant acted under the influence of extreme emotional disturbance for which there was a reasonable explanation or excuse, the reasonableness of which is to be determined from the viewpoint of a person in the defendant's situation under the circumstances as the defendant believed them to be, provided nothing contained in this subsection shall constitute a defense to a prosecution for, or preclude a conviction of, manslaughter in the first degree or any other crime."

the statute of the sister state; as such it is proper to resort to the decisions of a sister court construing that statutory language.

....

It is evident from a reading of § 53a-54a(a) that the defense does not require a provoking or triggering event; or that the homicidal act occur immediately after the cause or causes of the defendant's extreme emotional disturbance; or that the defendant have lost all ability to reason. Further, the reasonable man yardstick is only used to determine the reasonableness of the explanation or excuse of the action of the defendant from the viewpoint of a person in the defendant's situation under the circumstances as the defendant believed them to be. Thus, the statute sets forth a standard that is objective in its overview, but subjective as to the defendant's belief.

Before the enactment of the present Penal Code in this state, to establish the "heat of passion" defense a defendant had to prove that the "hot blood" had not had time to "cool off" at the time of the killing. *State v. Rosa*, 87 Conn. 585, 89 A. 163 (1913). A homicide influenced by an extreme emotional disturbance, in contrast, is not one which is necessarily committed in the "hot blood" stage, but rather one that was brought about by a significant mental trauma that caused the defendant to brood for a long period of time and then react violently, seemingly without provocation.

General Statutes § 53a-54a is based on the Model Penal Code of the American Law Institute, Tentative Draft No. 9, § 210.3, on manslaughter. The comments accompanying the Model Penal Code attempt to explain the change from the old common law concept of killing in the "heat of passion" to the new concept of killing under the influence of an "extreme emotional disturbance." The comments seem to be contradictory in that they claim the ultimate test is objective yet the state of mind of the accused is to be evaluated from his viewpoint under the circumstances as he believes them to be. In the draft, there are no attempts to set guidelines to aid the trier of fact. The draftsmen state: "The question in the end will be whether the actor's loss of self-control can be understood in terms that arouse sympathy enough to call for mitigation in the sentence. That seems to be the issue to be faced." The Chief Reporter for the Model Penal Code has noted that "[t]he purpose was explicitly to give full scope to what amounts to a plea in mitigation based upon a mental or emotional trauma of significant dimensions, with the jury asked to show whatever empathy it can." Wechsler, "Codification of Criminal Law in the United States; The Model Penal Code," 68 Colum. L. Rev. 1425, 1446 (1968). Those comments may explain the rationale of the draftsmen but they ignore the realities of the courtroom. So the task of instructing a jury with understandable guidelines is left to the courts to determine. The New York appeals court in *People v. Patterson*, *supra*, utilized the trial court's definition that "extreme" in the affirmative defense precluded mere annoyance or unhappiness or anger. To be "extreme," the disturbance had to be excessive and violent in its effect upon the individual driven to kill under it. *People v. Patterson*, *supra*, 39 N.Y.2d 293, 383 N.Y.S.2d 573, 347 N.E.2d 898. When reading § 53a-54a in conjunction with the comments to the Model Penal Code from which it is drawn, it becomes apparent that an extreme emotional disturbance is one where self-control and reason are overborne by intense feelings such as passion, anger, distress, grief, excessive agitation or other similar emotions.

In *People v. Shelton*, 88 Misc.2d 136, 149, 385 N.Y.S.2d 708 (1976), Justice Bentley Kassal made an exhaustive analysis of the affirmative defense in question. It is this court's opinion that the guidelines for determining extreme emotional disturbance as presented in that opinion with only a slight variation to include the Patterson observation are the ones that should be followed in this state.

Following *Shelton*, we hold that in determining whether the defendant has proven the affirmative defense of an extreme emotional disturbance by a fair preponderance of the evidence as a mitigation of murder to manslaughter the jury must find that: (a) the emotional disturbance is not a mental disease or defect that rises to the level of insanity as defined by the Model Penal Code; (b) the defendant was exposed to an extremely unusual and overwhelming state, that is, not mere annoyance or unhappiness; and (c) the defendant had an extreme emotional reaction to it, as a result of which there was a loss of self-control, and reason was overborne by extreme intense feelings, such as passion, anger, distress, grief, excessive agitation or other similar emotions. Consideration is given to whether the intensity of these feelings was such that his usual intellectual controls failed and the normal rational thinking for that individual no longer prevailed at the time of the act. In its charge, the trial court should explain that the term "extreme" refers to the greatest degree of intensity away from the norm for that individual.

The jury should be instructed that the reasonableness of a defendant's act under an extreme emotional disturbance is to be determined from the viewpoint of a person in the defendant's situation under the circumstances as the defendant believed them to be.

An examination of the court's charge on this issue shows that it was too narrow and was not in accord with the expanded limits of General Statutes § 53a-54a as amended in 1973.

There is error, the judgment is set aside and a new trial is ordered.

NOTES

1. "In the end, the question is whether the actor's loss of self-control can be understood in terms that arouse sympathy in the ordinary citizen. Section 210.3 faces this issue squarely and leaves the ultimate judgment to the ordinary citizen in the function of a juror assigned to resolve the specific case." MODEL PENAL CODE § 210.3, comment p. 63.

2. The Kentucky Supreme Court rejected the "we-know-it when-we-see-it" approach to "extreme emotional disturbance" and defined the term as a temporary state of mind so enraged, inflamed, or disturbed as to overcome one's judgment, and to cause one to act uncontrollably from the impelling force of the extreme emotional disturbance rather than from evil or malicious purposes. It is not a mental disease in itself, and an enraged, inflamed, or disturbed emotional state does not constitute an extreme emotional disturbance unless there is a reasonable explanation or excuse therefor, the reasonableness of which is to be determined from the viewpoint of a person in the defen-

dant's situation under circumstances as defendant believed them to be. *McClellan v. Commonwealth*, 715 S.W.2d 464, 468-69 (1986).

3. The term "extreme emotional disturbance" was carefully examined by the court in *People v. Shelton*, 88 Misc. 2d 136, 385 N.Y.S.2d 708 (N.Y. Sup. Ct. 1976). The term is a legal rather than psychiatric one. Although psychiatric testimony is not required or binding it is relevant and material. In *Shelton*, a nonjury trial, the court asked both psychiatrists to state their understanding of the term and their responses indicate that there may be some difficulties in arriving at a uniform definition.

C. IMPERFECT SELF-DEFENSE

PEOPLE v. FLANNEL

Supreme Court of California
25 Cal. 3d 668, 603 P.2d 1, 160 Cal. Rptr. 84 (1979)

TOBRINER, JUSTICE.

Defendant Charles M. Flannel appeals from a judgment of conviction entered on jury verdicts finding him guilty of second degree murder (Pen. Code, § 187), and finding affirmatively on a firearm use allegation (Pen. Code, §§ 1203, subd. d(6) and 12022.5). He contends that the court erred in failing to instruct the jury sua sponte that defendant's honest but unreasonable belief that he must defend himself from deadly attack negates malice so that the offense is reduced from murder to manslaughter.

....

1. The *facts*.

On June 28, 1976, about 4:15 in the afternoon, defendant shot and killed Charles Daniels. The two men had a history of hostile and violent relations. Daniels objected to defendant's treatment of Daniel's common law daughter, who was defendant's girlfriend, later his wife. Defendant resented Daniels' interference with his romance. Previously, both men had threatened each others' lives. In January 1976 defendant attacked Daniels at a friend's home, kicking Daniels in the chest and head and hitting him with a glass. Rather than prosecute defendant, the district attorney's office held a citation hearing and warned the two men to avoid one another.

On the morning of the killing defendant consumed some four tall cans of beer and a shot or two of whiskey, took his girlfriend shopping and ate lunch. He joined friends in front of a building in Oakland about 2:30 that afternoon. As he talked with friends, defendant shared some beer and whiskey.

About 4 p.m. defendant, observing Daniels approach from nearby, retrieved his gun from the trunk of his car. One friend reassured him that there was no need for a gun, that everybody was "his friend"; when Daniels came close a second time at 4:15 another friend urged defendant to leave in order to prevent trouble. Defendant walked about 12 or 14 feet away but changed his mind and returned to watch Daniels arrive.

Daniels and the group exchanged greetings. Defendant walked up to Daniels and, standing directly in front of him with his hand on the gun in his right front pocket, asked him what was "happening." Daniels graphically told defendant to "stop messing" with him, that they were not supposed to be around each other, and asked him to "get goin."

Daniels began backing away from the car upon which he had been leaning, waving defendant away with his left hand while his right hand remained near his back pocket where he was known to have kept his knife. Defendant followed, saying "Was you going to stick me in the side with a knife?" "Come on, pull your knife." He then drew the gun from his pocket, extended his arm full length and fired one shot into Daniels' temple from a distance of approximately two feet. As Daniels fell, his switchblade knife flew into the air, landing on the ground where it spun around and popped open. No one observed the knife in Daniels' hand.

Defendant immediately told his friends not to touch Daniels but to "leave him right there." He said, "He pulled a knife on me," adding that Daniels "deserved to be dead, nobody cares." Defendant dropped his weapon and waited until the police arrived.

At trial defendant relied on a theory of self-defense. He testified that Daniels came toward him, grabbed his chest to stabilize him, that Daniels then drew his knife from his back pocket. Defendant was "surprised and scared." Seeing the knife, he pulled his gun out of his front pocket, then jerked away from Daniels and, as Daniels came at him again, he fired. Defendant also testified that he thought he was drunk at the time of the killing.

....

To be exculpated on a theory of self-defense one must have an honest and reasonable belief in the need to defend. (Pen. Code, § 197; *Jackson v. Superior Court* (1965) 62 Cal.2d 521, 529, 42 Cal.Rptr. 838, 399 P.2d 374; *People v. Moore* (1954) 43 Cal.2d 517, 526-529, 275 P.2d 485; *People v. Holt* (1944) 25 Cal.2d 59, 65, 153 P.2d 21.) A bare fear is not enough; "the circumstances must be sufficient to excite the fears of a reasonable person, and the party killing must have acted under the influence of such fears alone." (Pen. Code, § 198.)

This rule is not questioned here. Rather, the issue is whether a defender has committed murder or manslaughter when his belief, although honestly held, fails to meet the standard of a "reasonable person."

The People contend that the only factors recognized as negating malice, so as to reduce murder to manslaughter, are sudden quarrel or heat of passion upon reasonable provocation (Pen. Code, § 192) or diminished capacity caused by voluntary intoxication, mental disease or mental defect *People v. Conley* (1966) 64 Cal.2d 310, 49 Cal.Rptr. 815, 411 P.2d 911; *People v. Gorshen* (1959) 51 Cal.2d 716, 336 P.2d 492; *People v. Yanikian* (1974) 39 Cal.App.3d 366, 114 Cal.Rptr. 188). They argue that unreasonable belief does not exist as a partial defense distinct from these two categories. We disagree that the doctrine of unreasonable belief is necessarily bound up with or limited by the concepts of either heat of passion or diminished capacity.

....

The nature of malice is central here for "[m]urder is the unlawful killing of a human being ... with malice aforethought" (Pen. Code, § 187); "[m]anslaughter is the unlawful killing ..., without malice." (Pen. Code, § 192). In *Conley* we examined the meaning of that mental state. We observed that a person who carefully weighs a course of action, and chooses to kill after considering reasons for and against, is normally capable of comprehending his societal duty to act within the law. "If, *despite such awareness*, he does an act that is likely to cause serious injury or death to another, he exhibits that wanton disregard for human life or antisocial motivation that constitutes malice aforethought." (Emphasis added.) Id., p. 322, 49 Cal.Rptr., p. 822, 411 P.2d, p. 918.)

Given this understanding of malice aforethought, we cannot accept the People's claim that an honest belief, if unreasonably held, can be consistent with malice. No matter how the mistaken assessment is made, an individual cannot genuinely perceive the need to repel imminent peril or bodily injury and simultaneously be aware that society expects conformity to a different standard. Where the awareness of society's disapproval begins, an honest belief ends. It is the honest belief of imminent peril that negates malice in a case of complete self-defense; the reasonableness of the belief simply goes to the justification for the killing.

This approach to unreasonable belief expresses the rule at common law. As one scholar notes, "Since manslaughter is a "catch-all' concept, covering all homicides which are neither murder nor innocent, it logically includes some killings involving other types of mitigation, and such is the rule of the common law. For example, if one man kills another intentionally, under circumstances beyond the scope of innocent homicide, the facts may come so close to justification or excuse that the killing will be classed as voluntary manslaughter rather than murder." Perkins On Criminal Law (2d ed. 1969) pp. 69-70. Perkins goes on to add that "some legislative enactments have spoken of voluntary manslaughter in terms only of a killing in "a sudden heat of passion caused by a provocation' and so forth. Such restriction is probably unintentional, being attributable to the fact that this is by far the most common type of mitigation; but it is very unfortunate." *Id.*, at p. 70.)

[A majority of the court found no prejudicial error and affirmed the conviction.]

NOTES

1. In *People v. Saille*, 54 Cal. 3d 1103, 2 Cal. Rptr. 2d 364, 820 P.2d 588 (1991), discussed *supra* at p. 285, the California Supreme Court noted that it was not deciding whether changes in California law eliminating "diminished capacity" had any impact on the "imperfect self defense." 820 P.2d at 590 n. 1.

2. See further discussion of self-defense, *infra* Chapter 7.

SECTION VIII. Unlawful Act—Involuntary Manslaughter

STATE v. FRAZIER

Supreme Court of Missouri
339 Mo. 966, 98 S.W.2d 707 (1936)

ELLISON, JUDGE.

The appellant was convicted of manslaughter and his punishment assessed at a fine of $400 and 6 months in the county jail, for the killing of Daniel I.

VIII. UNLAWFUL ACT—INVOLUNTARY MANSLAUGHTER

Gross.... The deceased was a hemophiliac, or "bleeder." The appellant struck him on the jaw once with his fist. A slight laceration on the inside of the mouth resulted which produced a hemorrhage lasting ten days and ending in death.

Remembering the appellant was convicted of manslaughter, two questions remain: (1) Was it an adequate defense that the appellant did not know the deceased was a hemophiliac, and struck only one moderate blow with his fist, which ordinarily would not have been dangerous to life?; (2) Is he to be excused because the blow producing the hemorrhage would not have resulted fatally if deceased had not been a hemophiliac? Both these questions must be answered in the negative. Section 3988, Revised Statutes 1929 Mo. St. Ann., p. 2793, provides that "every killing of a human being by the act, procurement or culpable negligence of another, not herein declared to be murder or excusable or justifiable homicide, shall be deemed manslaughter." If one commits an unlawful assault and battery upon another without malice and death results, the assailant is guilty of manslaughter, although death was not intended and the assault was not of a character likely to result fatally. 29 C.J. § 137, p. 1150; 13 R.C.L. § 89, p. 784; *State v. Recke*, 311 Mo. 581, 595, 278 S.W. 995, 998.

Neither is it an excuse that appellant did not know the deceased was a hemophiliac, and that death would not have resulted but for that affliction....

[Affirmed.]

STATE v. HORTON

Supreme Court of North Carolina
139 N.C. 588, 51 S.E. 945 (1905)

W. P. Horton was convicted of manslaughter, and appeals. Reversed.

Indictment for manslaughter. The jury rendered a special verdict, and such verdict and proceedings thereon are as follows: "That in the month of November, 1904, to wit, on the day thereof, the defendant, W. P. Horton, was hunting turkeys on the lands of another; that the following local statute, enacted by the General Assembly of 1901, was in force at and in the place in which said defendant was hunting, to wit, chapter 410 of the Laws of 1901; that the said Horton, at the time he was so hunting, had not the written consent of the owner of said land or of his lawful agent; that while so engaged in hunting he killed Charlie Hunt, the deceased, but that said killing was wholly unintentional; that the shooting of the deceased was done while the defendant was under the impression and belief that he was shooting at a wild turkey; that the hunting engaged in by the defendant was not of itself dangerous to human life, nor was he reckless in the manner of hunting or of handling the firearm with which the killing was done; that hunting at that season was not forbidden under the general game law of the state, but was prohibited only by the special statute referred to; that the shooting from which the killing resulted was not done in such grossly careless or negligent manner as to imply any moral turpitude or to indicate any indifference to the safeguarding of human life; that, but for the said statute herein incorporated, the killing of the deceased by defendant does not constitute any violation of the law. If, upon the above findings of fact, the court should be of opinion that the defendant is guilty of manslaughter, we for our verdict find the defendant guilty of manslaughter: but, if the court should be of opinion that the defendant is not guilty, we for our verdict find that the defendant is not guilty." Upon this special finding, the court, being of opinion that the defendant was guilty of manslaughter, so adjudged, and ordered a verdict of guilty of manslaughter to be entered, and gave judgment that the defendant be imprisoned in the county jail of Franklin for a period of four months. Defendant excepted to the ruling of the court, and appealed from the judgment against him.

Hoke, J.

... The statement sometimes appears in works of approved excellence to the effect that an unintentional homicide is a criminal offense when occasioned by a person engaged at the time in an unlawful act. In nearly every instance, however, will be found the qualification that if the act in question is free from negligence, and not in itself of dangerous tendency, and the criminality must arise, if at all, entirely from the fact that it is unlawful, in such case, the unlawful act must be one that is "*malum in se*," and not merely "*malum prohibitum*," and this we hold to be the correct doctrine....

... An offense *malum in se* is properly defined as one which is naturally evil as adjudged by the sense of a civilized community, whereas an act *malum prohibitum* is wrong only because made so by statute. For the reason that acts malum in se have, as a rule, become criminal offenses by the course and development of the common law, an impression has sometimes obtained that only acts can be so classified which the common law makes criminal; but this is not at all the test. An act can be, and frequently is, malum in se, when it amounts only to a civil trespass, provided it has a malicious element or manifests an evil nature or wrongful disposition to harm or injure another in his person or property. Bishop, Cr. Law, *supra*; *Com. v. Adams*, *supra*. The distinction between the two classes of acts is well stated in 19 Am. & Eng. Enc. (2d Ed.), at page 705: "An offense malum in se is one which is naturally evil, as murder, theft, and the like. Offenses at common law are generally *malum in se*. An offense *malum prohibitum*, on the contrary, is not naturally an evil, but becomes so in consequence of being forbidden."

We do not hesitate to declare that the offense of the defendant in hunting on the land without written permission of the owner was malum prohibitum, and, the special verdict having found that the act in which the defendant was engaged was not in itself dangerous to human life and negatived all idea of negligence, we hold that the case is one of excusable homicide, and the defendant should be declared not guilty....

PEOPLE v. STUART

Supreme Court of California
47 Cal. 2d 167, 302 P.2d 5 (1956)

Traynor, Justice.

Defendant was charged by information with manslaughter, Pen. Code, § 192, and the violation of section 380 of the Penal Code. He was convicted of both offenses by the court sitting without a jury. His motions for a new trial

VIII. UNLAWFUL ACT—INVOLUNTARY MANSLAUGHTER

and for dismissal, Pen. Code, § 1385, were denied, sentence was suspended, and he was placed on probation for two years. He appeals from the judgment of conviction and the order denying his motion for a new trial.

Defendant was licensed as a pharmacist by this state in 1946 and has practiced here since that time. He holds a B.S. degree in chemistry from Long Island University and a B.S. degree in pharmacy from Columbia University. In April, 1954, he was employed as a pharmacist by the Ethical Drug Company in Los Angeles.

On July 16, 1954, he filled a prescription for Irvin Sills. It had been written by Dr. D.M. Goldstein for Sills' eight-day-old child. It called for "Sodium phenobarbital, grains eight. Sodium citrate, drams three, Simple Syrup, ounces two. Aqua peppermint, ounces one. Aqua distillate QS, ounces four." ... Sills ... put a teaspoonful of the prescription in the baby's milk and gave it to the baby. The baby died a few hours later.

Defendant stipulated that there was nitrite in the prescription bottle and that "the cause of death was methemoglobinemia caused by the ingestion of nitrite." When he compounded the prescription, there was a bottle containing sodium nitrite on the shelf near a bottle labeled sodium citrate. He testified that at no time during his employment at the Ethical Drug Company had he filled any prescription calling for sodium nitrite and that he had taken the prescribed three drams of sodium citrate from the bottle so labeled....

An analysis made by the staff of the head toxicologist for the Los Angeles County Coroner of the contents of the bottle given to Sills disclosed that it contained 1.33 drams of sodium citrate and 1.23 of sodium nitrite. An analysis made by Biochemical Procedures, Incorporated, a laboratory, of a sample of the contents of the bottle labeled sodium citrate disclosed that it contained 38.9 milligrams of nitrite per gram of material. Charles Covet, one of the owners of the Ethical Drug Company, testified that on the 17th or 18th of October, 1954, he emptied the contents of the sodium citrate bottle, washed the bottle but not its cap, and put in new sodium citrate. A subsequent analysis of rinsings from the cap gave strong positive tests for nitrite.

....

No evidence whatever was introduced that would justify an inference that defendant knew or should have known that the bottle labeled sodium citrate contained sodium nitrite. On the contrary, the undisputed evidence shows conclusively that defendant was morally entirely innocent and that only because of a reasonable mistake or unavoidable accident was the prescription filled with a substance containing sodium nitrite. Section 20 of the Penal Code makes the union of act and intent or criminal negligence an invariable element of every crime unless it is excluded expressly or by necessary implication. *People v. Vogel*, 46 Cal. 2d 798, 299 P.2d 850. Moreover, section 26 of the Penal Code lists among the persons incapable of committing crimes "[p]ersons who committed the act or made the omission charged under an ignorance or mistake of fact, which disproves any criminal intent," subd. 4, and "[p]ersons who committed the act or made the omission charged through misfortune or by accident, when it appears that there was no evil design, intention, or culpable negligence." (Subd. 6; see also Pen. Code, §§ 195, 199.) The question is thus presented whether a person can be convicted of manslaughter or a violation of section 380 of the Penal Code in the absence of any evidence of criminal intent or criminal negligence.

The answer to this question as it relates to the conviction of manslaughter depends on whether or not defendant committed an "unlawful act" within the meaning of section 192 of the Penal Code when he filled the prescription. The Attorney General contends that even if he had no criminal intent and was not criminally negligent, defendant violated section 26280 of the Health and Safety Code and therefore committed an unlawful act within the meaning of section 192 of the Penal Code.

Section 26280 of the Health and Safety Code provides: "The manufacture, production, preparation, compounding, packing, selling, offering for sale, advertising or keeping for sale within the State of California ... of any drug or device which is adulterated or misbranded is prohibited." In view of the analysis of the contents of the prescription bottle and the bottle labeled sodium citrate and defendant's stipulation, there can be no doubt that he prepared, compounded, and sold an adulterated and misbranded drug.

Because of the great danger to the public health and safety that the preparation, compounding, or sale of adulterated or misbranded drugs entails, the public interest in demanding that those who prepare, compound, or sell drugs make certain that they are not adulterated or misbranded, and the belief that although an occasional nonculpable offender may be punished, it is necessary to incur that risk by imposing strict liability to prevent the escape of great numbers of culpable offenders, public welfare statutes like section 26280 are not ordinarily governed by section 20 of the Penal Code and therefore call for the sanctions imposed even though the prohibited acts are committed without criminal intent or criminal negligence. See *People v. Vogel, supra*, 46 Cal. 2d 798, 801, 299 P.2d 850, note 2; Sayre, Public Welfare Offenses, 33 Colum. L. Rev. 55, 72-75; Hall, Prolegomena To A Science of Criminal Law, 89 U. Pa. L. Rev. 549, 563-569.

It does not follow, however, that such acts, committed without criminal intent or criminal negligence, are unlawful acts within the meaning of section 192 of the Penal Code, for it is settled that this section is governed by section 20 of the Penal Code. Thus, in *People v. Penny*, 44 Cal. 2d 861, 877-880, 285 P.2d 926, 936, we held that "there was nothing to show that the Legislature intended to except section 192 of the Penal Code from the operation of section 20 of the same code" and that the phrase "without due caution and circumspection" in section 192 was therefore the equivalent of criminal negligence. Since section 20 also applies to the phrase "unlawful act," the act in question must be committed with criminal intent or criminal negligence to be an unlawful act within meaning of section 192. By virtue of its application to both phrases, section 20 precludes the incongruity of imposing on the morally innocent the same penalty (Pen. Code, § 193), appropriate only for the culpable. Words such as "unlawful act, not amounting to felony" have been included in most definitions of manslaughter since the time of Blackstone (4 Bl. Com. Homicide 191; see Riesenfeld, Negligent Homicide: A Study in Statutory Interpretation, 25 Cal. L. Rev. 21-22) and even since the time of Lord Hale, "unlawful act" as it pertains to manslaughter has been interpreted as meaning an act that aside from its unlawfulness was of such a dangerous nature as to justify a conviction of manslaughter if done intentionally or without due caution. (See, Moreland, Law of Homicide 186-187, 244, citing 1 Hale, Pleas of the Crown (ed. of 1778) 471-475; Foster, Crown Law (2d ed. 1791) 259; 1 East, Pleas of the Crown (1803) 257). To be an unlawful act within the meaning of section 192, therefore, the act in question must be dangerous to human life or safety and meet the conditions of section 20....

It follows, therefore, that only if defendant had intentionally or through criminal negligence prepared, compounded, or sold an adulterated or misbranded drug, would his violation of section 26280 of the Health and Safety Code be an unlawful act within the meaning of section 192 of the Penal Code.

....

The judgment and order are reversed.

COMMONWEALTH v. WILLIAMS

Superior Court of Pennsylvania
133 Pa. Super. 104, 1 A.2d 812 (1938)

RHODES, JUDGE.

Defendant, Wendall Williams, was convicted in the court below of the involuntary manslaughter of one James Vincent, and he has appealed. The death occurred when an automobile operated by appellant collided with a telephone pole. Appellant had been a duly licensed operator for several years prior to 1936, but had failed to renew his operator's license in 1936, and had no such license at the time of the accident of December 25th of that year....

....

The unlawful act proven in the instant case was neither a felony nor did it naturally tend to cause death or great bodily harm.

....

We think that there is merit in appellant's contention that in order to sustain the conviction the Commonwealth is obliged to show that the death was the result of, or happened in consequence of, the unlawful act as we have defined it, and that the Commonwealth failed to do so in the instant case....

In our opinion, the language of the above cited statutes and cases implies more than that the unlawful act should be a remote unit in a sequence of events culminating in a fatality, and requires such act to be something more than a factor which might be denominated more properly as an attendant condition than a cause of the death.

We find no decision of our appellate courts which we consider determinative.

....

But the question has been considered in other jurisdictions, and answered favorably to the position taken by appellant in this case.

In *Potter v. State*, 162 Ind. 213, 70 N.E. 129, 64 L.R.A. 942, 102 Am. St. Rep. 198, 1 Ann. Cas. 32, one of the participants in a friendly struggle was killed by the accidental discharge of a pistol unlawfully carried in the pocket of the other. The Indiana statute (Burns' Rev. St. Ind. 1901, § 1981), provided: "Whoever unlawfully kills any human being without malice, express or implied, either voluntarily, upon a sudden heat, or involuntarily, but in the commission of some unlawful act, is guilty of manslaughter...." Defendant was convicted of manslaughter, and in reversing judgment and awarding a new trial, the court said [page 131]: "It is undoubtedly true, as a general rule of law, that a person engaged in the commission of an unlawful act is legally responsible for all of the consequences which may naturally or necessarily flow or result from such unlawful act. But before this principle of law can have any application under the facts in the case at bar, it must appear that the homicide was the natural or necessary result of the act of appellant in carrying the revolver in violation of the statute."

In *Votre v. State*, 192 Ind. 684, 138 N.E. 257, a conviction of involuntary manslaughter was reversed on appeal, the court holding [page 258]: "Inasmuch as the death was not the natural result or the probable consequence of the commission of the unlawful act, it follows that the evidence is insufficient to sustain the verdict."

In the instant case the proper conclusion would seem to be that the unlawful act must be something more than an attendant condition without which the death could not have occurred; that the death must be the natural result or probable consequence of the unlawful act.

In *State v. Budge*, 126 Me. 223, 137 A. 244, 53 A.L.R. 241, defendant was indicted for the crime of manslaughter by reason of having caused the death of another by improper operation of an automobile on the public highway. The appellate court stated that if "the unlawful act in no way contributed to the injuries, as where a person driving an automobile 17 or even 20 miles per hour, when the statutory limit was only 15 miles per hour, no other element of negligence being present, and the deceased unexpectedly stepped in front of the automobile without warning, and at a point in a street where pedestrians might not be expected to cross, and it could not be found that the excess of the legal limit of speed at which the automobile was being driven in any way contributed to the accident — though the contributory negligence of the deceased is no defense in a criminal prosecution — a homicide under such conditions cannot be held to be more than a mere accident or misadventure." [Page 246.]

....

As stated in *State v. Nichols*, 34 N. M. 639, 288 P. 407, it would be "ridiculous to say that any accidental killing resulting indirectly or remotely while committing an unlawful act is involuntary manslaughter. Our statutes make it unlawful for a person to drive an automobile without a red tail-light or without first having obtained a license. If, while committing such an unlawful act alone, a person is accidentally and unavoidably run over and killed, the unlawful act could have no bearing whatsoever upon the killing. Would any one contend that the driver be guilty of involuntary manslaughter?"

In the instant case, it is true that the death would not have occurred if appellant's automobile had not been on the highway. Its presence was unquestionably a condition without which Vincent's death could not have taken place. But appellant's violation of the Vehicle Code had no direct relationship to the death.

....

In the opinion of the court below, incorporated as part of the agreed statement of facts, it is said: "The testimony was to the effect that while the defendant was driving along a street he saw a car, coming in the opposite direction, swerve from its path and start to move in his direction. and when, with a view to avoiding a collision, he drove farther over upon his side of the street, his wheels encountered some ice or frost, with the result that his car skidded in such a way as to strike a telephone pole and cause the death of Vincent who was a passenger in the car."

It is obvious that the testimony was insufficient to show any relationship between the death and the unlawful act of appellant, or to establish that the death was the natural result or probable consequence of appellant's unlawful act. Appellant was not negligent; he was blameless except for the violation of section 601 of the Vehicle Code, *supra*. It cannot be logically concluded that the death "happened in consequence of" such violation. Until the swerve of the approaching automobile, appellant and deceased were riding in safety. Remove that factor, and it is perceived, without difficulty, that deceased would still be living, despite the fact that appellant operated his automobile without an operator's license.

Judgment of the court below is reversed, and defendant is discharged.

NOTE ON UNLAWFUL ACTS AND CRIMINAL NEGLIGENCE

Unlawful conduct which results in death may be intentional such as when A commits an assault and battery on B and B dies. Often, however, conduct becomes unlawful because of the criminally negligent manner in which it is performed. In such cases the state may have two bases for prosecuting a person for involuntary manslaughter or negligent homicide, i.e., misdemeanor-manslaughter and criminal negligence. The two bases, in reality, are two sides of the same coin. Conduct may become unlawful because it is performed with criminal negligence; conduct may be criminally negligent because it is performed in a manner prohibited by law. This has caused problems in vehicular death cases. Many states require that a prosecution based on negligence be of a higher level than ordinary negligence. See pp. 350-352. However, suppose a person is negligent in the "ordinary" degree, e.g., drives a vehicle 35 miles per hour in a 30-mile zone, and strikes and kills a pedestrian. A manslaughter or negligent homicide prosecution could not be based on a negligence theory in those states which require more than ordinary negligence. Could the state prosecute under an "unlawful act" or misdemeanor-manslaughter approach? In *State v. Vollmer*, 259 S.E.2d 837 (W. Va. 1979), and *King v. Commonwealth*, 217 Va. 601, 231 S.E.2d 312 (1977), the courts concluded that in such cases, notwithstanding an "unlawful" act, the state could not prosecute absent a showing of culpable negligence.

SECTION IX. Criminal-Negligence Involuntary Manslaughter and Negligent Homicide

PEOPLE v. RODRIGUEZ

District Court of Appeal
186 Cal. App. 2d 433, 8 Cal. Rptr. 863 (1960)

VALLEE, JUSTICE.

By information defendant was accused of manslaughter in that on November 8, 1959, she did wilfully, unlawfully, feloniously, and without malice kill Carlos Quinones. In a nonjury trial she was found guilty of involuntary manslaughter. A new trial was denied. She appeals from the judgment and the order denying a new trial.

In November 1959 defendant was living with her four children in a single-family residence at 130 South Clarence Street, Los Angeles. The oldest child was 6 years of age. Carlos Quinones was the youngest, either 2 or 3 years of age.

Olive Faison lived across the street from defendant. About 10:45 p.m. on November 8, 1959, Miss Faison heard some children calling, "Mommy, mommy." For about 15 or 20 minutes she did not "pay too much attention." She noticed the cries became more shrill. She went to the front window and saw smoke coming from defendant's house.... [W]ith the help of neighbors [she] pulled three of the children out of the house....

Firemen arrived at the scene some time after 10 p.m. The front door was open; there was no obstruction. Fireman Hansen went inside and found a baby boy in the back bedroom near the bed. The fire was about 3 feet away from the boy. Hansen took the boy out of the house. "He appeared to be dead at the time." The child was Carlos Quinones. Around 4 or 4:30 p.m. on November 8, 1959, defendant was in "Johnny's Place." She was at the bar drinking "coke." She stayed about an hour. As John Powers, one of the bartenders, was closing the place about 2:30 a.m. on the morning of November 9, he saw defendant outside the building. He had not seen her inside before that time.

Maria Lucero, defendant's sister, ... found her about 2 or 2:30 a.m. in the same block as "Johnny's Place." Defendant was nervous and frightened, said she knew about the fire and that she went over to tell Johnny Powers about it. Defendant had not been drinking.

Carlos Quinones died from "thermal burns, second and third degree involving 50 to 60 percent of the body surface." Defendant did not testify.

....

It appears from the record that guilt was predicated on the alleged "commission of a lawful act which might produce death, in an unlawful manner, or without due caution and circumspection." Pen. Code, § 192.

In *People v. Penny*, 44 Cal. 2d 861, 285 P.2d 926, the defendant was convicted of involuntary manslaughter. While engaged in the practice of "face rejuvenation" she applied a formula containing phenol to the skin. Death was caused by phenol poisoning. The trial court charged the jury that ordinary negligence was sufficient to constitute lack of "due caution and circumspection" under Penal Code, § 192. The court said (p. 869): "It has been held that without 'due caution and circumspection' is the equivalent of 'criminal negligence.'"...

....

It is generally held that an act is criminally negligent when a man of ordinary prudence would foresee that the act would cause a high degree of risk of death or great bodily harm. The risk of death or great bodily harm must be great. (See cases collected 161 A.L.R. 10.) Whether the conduct of defendant was wanton or reckless so as to warrant conviction of manslaughter must be determined from the conduct itself and not from the resultant harm. *Commonwealth v. Bouvier*, 316 Mass. 489, 55 N.E.2d 913. Criminal liability cannot be predicated on every careless act merely because its carelessness results in injury to another. *People v. Sikes*, 328 Ill. 64, 159 N.E. 293, 297. The act must be one which has knowable and apparent potentialities for resulting in death. Mere inattention or mistake in judgment resulting even in death of another is not criminal unless the quality of the act makes it so. The fundamental requirement fixing criminal responsibility is knowledge, actual or imputed, that the act of the accused tended to endanger life.

....

It clearly appears from the definition of criminal negligence stated in *People v. Penny, supra*, 44 Cal. 2d 861, that knowledge, actual or imputed, that the act of the slayer tended to endanger life and that the fatal consequences of the negligent act could reasonably have been foreseen are necessary for negligence to be criminal at all. Must a parent never leave a young child alone in the house on risk of being adjudged guilty of manslaughter if some unforeseeable occurrence causes the death of the child? The only reasonable view of the evidence is that the death of Carlos was the result of misadventure and not the natural and probable result of a criminally negligent act. There was no evidence from which it can be inferred that defendant realized her conduct would in all probability produce death. There was no evidence as to the cause of the fire, as to how or where it started. There was no evidence connecting defendant in any way with the fire. There was no evidence that defendant could reasonably have foreseen there was a probability that fire would ignite in the house and that Carlos would be burned to death. The most that can be said is that defendant may have been negligent; but mere negligence is not sufficient to authorize a conviction of involuntary manslaughter....

The judgment and order denying a new trial are reversed.

NOTES

1. In *People v. Ogg*, 26 Mich. App. 372, 182 N.W.2d 570 (1970), the defendant was found guilty of involuntary manslaughter when a fire of undetermined origin killed her two young sons. The defendant was found "grossly negligent" because she had left her children locked in a small, windowless upstairs room without supervision when she left the house. The children had a known tendency to start fires. "The acts of defendant in placing her children, or allowing them with her knowledge to be locked in a small windowless upstairs room, without proper heat, light, food, clothing or bedding and without means of escape, and in reckless disregard of the consequences of such

action, absenting herself from the home in pursuit of her own business, constitutes, in our opinion, culpable negligence." 182 N.W.2d at 575.

Gross negligence meant "wantonness and disregard of the consequences which may ensue, and indifference to the rights of others that is equivalent to a criminal intent." *Id.* at 577.

2. "Recklessness" has recently been defined by Lord Diplock (although not in a prosecution for criminal homicide) to include a situation where, "if thought were given to the matter by the doer before the act was done, it would have been apparent to him that there was a real risk of having the relevant harmful consequences ...." He concluded that a person charged under the Criminal Damage Act of 1971 is "reckless as to whether or not any property would be destroyed or damaged if (1) he does an act which in fact creates an obvious risk that property will be destroyed or damaged and (2) when he does the act he either has not given any thought to the possibility of there being any such risk or has recognized that there was some risk involved and has nonetheless gone on to do it." *Regina v. Caldwell*, [1981] 1 All E.R. 961, 964, 967.

Should this approach be characterized as objective, subjective or some mixture of the two?

NOTES ON PROOF OF NEGLIGENT HOMICIDE

1. In civil cases violation of a statute often is prima facie evidence of negligence. Some states have statutes which make similar provisions in criminal cases. The Louisiana Criminal Code states: "The violation of a statute or ordinance shall be considered only as presumptive evidence of such [criminal] negligence." LA. REV. STAT. ANN. 14:32 (West 1974). These statutes are valid only when they are used as permissive inferences. Application of the statute so as to create "a mandatory presumption requiring the defendant to produce a 'quantum of proof'" would shift the burden of persuasion to the defendant. This would violate due process because it could relieve the state of proving criminal negligence beyond a reasonable doubt. *Hammontree v. Phelps*, 605 F.2d 1371, 1379-80 (5th Cir. 1979).

2. Does the fact that many criminal statutes require a higher standard of negligence than ordinary negligence raise a question as to the "rationality" of permitting a jury to infer "criminal" negligence from the violation of a statute? This question was raised by the trial judge in *Hammontree v. Phelps*, 462 F. Supp. 366 (W.D. La. 1978), but not addressed by the Court of Appeals.

3. May a state obtain a conviction for negligent homicide by basing a presumption on a presumption? Many states have a statutory presumption of intoxication when the state proves that a driver had more than a certain percentage of alcohol in his blood. This makes a prima facie case of "driving while intoxicated" which is a statutory violation. May a state use blood-alcohol evidence to establish presumptively a violation of the DWI statute and use that violation to invoke the "violation of statute" presumption to prove negligent homicide? The Louisiana Supreme Court held that it could not use the double presumption. *State v. Williams*, 375 So. 2d 931 (La. 1979).

4. Presumptions are discussed in Chapter 1, pp. 53-60.

PEOPLE v. HANEY
Court of Appeals of New York
30 N.Y.2d 328, 284 N.E.2d 564, 333 N.Y.S.2d 403 (1972)

JASEN, JUDGE.

On this appeal, by the People, the question posed concerns the sufficiency of the evidence before a Grand Jury to support an indictment against the defendant for criminally negligent homicide in violation of section 125.10 of the Penal Law. Consol. Laws, c. 40....

The indictment returned against the defendant charged him with criminally negligent homicide "in that, among other things, he drove a vehicle at a high, reckless, dangerous and unlawful rate of speed; in that he failed and neglected to stop said vehicle at the intersection ... although the traffic signal situated at said intersection was red ... and did thereby cause the death of the said Angela Palazzo.

The defendant, after pleading not guilty, made a motion for inspection of the Grand Jury minutes. Supreme Court, Criminal Term, granted the motion and dismissed the indictment, holding that "[t]he evidence before the Grand Jury, even though unexplained and uncontradicted, would not ... justify conviction by a trial jury." ... The Appellate Division, ... unanimously affirmed on the opinion at Criminal Term.

Section 125.10 of the Penal Law provides that a person is guilty of the crime of criminally negligent homicide when, with criminal negligence, he causes the death of another person. Subdivision 4 of section 15.05 of the Penal Law defines "Criminal negligence" as follows: "A person acts with criminal negligence with respect to a result or to a circumstance described by a statute defining an offense when he fails to perceive a substantial and unjustifiable risk that such result will occur or that such circumstance exists. The risk must be of such nature and degree that the failure to perceive it constitutes a gross deviation from the standard of care that a reasonable person would observe in the situation."

It is the People's claim that the indictment was erroneously dismissed since the facts presented to the Grand Jury "fall within" section 125.10. Specifically, it is argued that the statutory test for the support of an indictment was met since the testimony before the Grand Jury would warrant a conviction by a trial jury for criminally negligent homicide. The defendant, on the other hand, urges that the dismissal of the indictment was proper, since the evidence before the Grand Jury established nothing more than ordinary civil negligence on his part, which conduct falls far short of that required to establish the crime of criminally negligent homicide.

A persistent problem, faced by the courts and legislatures alike, has been the formulation of the "extra" qualities that distinguish unintended homicides, which give rise to criminal liability, from those which, at most, produce civil liability for negligence.... The Model Penal Code (Tent. Draft No. 4 [April 25, 1955], Comments to § 2.02, at p. 128) observes, concerning the judicial and statutory definitions of conduct causing death which is criminal, although unintentional: "Thus, under statutes, as at common law, the concept of criminal negligence has been left to judicial definition and the definitions vary greatly in their terms. As Jerome Hall has put it, the judicial essays run in terms of 'wanton and wilful negligence, gross negligence, and more illuminating yet,' that degree of negligence that is more than the negligence required to impose tort liability. The apex of ambiguity is wilful, wanton negligence which suggests a triple contradiction — 'negligence' implying inadvertence; wilful, intention; and wanton, recklessness. [Citation omitted.] Much of this confusion is dispelled, in our view, by a clear-cut distinction between recklessness and negligence, in terms of the actor's awareness of the risk involved."

Cognizant of this problem, and in an endeavor to "crystallize [this] area of culpability and liability," the Legislature incorporated in the revised Penal Law the dichotomy proposed by the Model Penal Code....[3] Thus, the revised Penal Law makes unintended homicide manslaughter in the second degree, when it is committed "recklessly" (Penal Law, § 125.15)[4] and when committed "negligently," though not recklessly, it is criminally negligent homicide. (Penal Law, § 125.10.)

The distinction between these two crimes is provided in section 15.05 (subds. 3,[5] 4) of the Penal Law, which specifically describes the mental state requisite for each. The reckless offender is aware of the proscribed risk and "consciously disregards" it, while the criminally negligent offender is not aware of the risk created and, hence, cannot be guilty of consciously disregarding it.... Since the criminally negligent offender's liability arises only from a culpable failure to perceive the risk, his culpability is obviously less than that of the reckless offender who consciously disregards the risk.... It is, however, "appreciably greater than that required for ordinary civil negligence by virtue of the 'substantial and unjustifiable' character of the risk involved and the factor of 'gross deviation' from the ordinary standard of care."...[7]

Enactment of section 125.10 represents a marked change from prior law as the former Penal Law contained no crime truly equivalent to it.... The present law lacks the moral implication of murder (Penal Law, § 125.25) or manslaughter in the first or second degree (Penal Law, §§ 125.15, 125.20), each of which involves awareness of the harm which will (or in some degree probably will) result from the offender's conduct. Criminally negligent homicide, in essence, involves the failure to perceive the risk in a situation where

---

[3] Other jurisdictions have adopted this statutory scheme. (See, e.g., Ill.Ann.Stat., ch. 38, §§ 4-6, 4-7; Wis.Stat.Ann., §§ 940.06, 940.08; see, also, Prop.Mich.Rev.Crim.Code, §§ 305[c], 305[d] [Final Draft, 1967]; Study Draft, Federal Criminal Code [June, 1970], § 302.)

[4] When homicide committed recklessly becomes murder, see Penal Law, § 125.25 (subd. 2); *People v. Poplis*, 30 N.Y.2d 85, 330 N.Y.S.2d 365, 281 N.E.2d 167.

[5] "§ 15.05 Culpability; definitions of culpable mental states.... 3. 'Recklessly.' A person acts recklessly with respect to a result or to a circumstance described by a statute defining an offense when he is aware of and consciously disregards a substantial and unjustifiable risk that such result will occur or that such circumstance exists. The risk must be of such nature and degree that disregard thereof constitutes a gross deviation from the standard of conduct that a reasonable person would observe in the situation."

[7] Criminal liability for death caused by ordinary negligence is sometimes imposed by statute. It should be noted that most of these statutes are confined to deaths arising out of automobile accidents. (See Riesenfeld, Negligent Homicide, A Study in Statutory Interpretation, 25 Cal.L.Rev. 1. Ann. Automobiles — Negligent Homicide, 20 ALR3d 473; 3 Wharton, Criminal Law and Procedure [R. Anderson ed.], § 976.) For an example of ordinary negligence sufficient to establish liability for a nonvehicular homicide, see *People v. Sandgren*, 302 N.Y. 331, 98 N.E.2d 460, interpreting a paragraph of section 1052 of the former Penal Law.

the offender has a legal duty of awareness. It, thus, serves to provide an offense applicable to conduct which is obviously socially undesirable. "[It proscribes] conduct which is inadvertent as to risk only because the actor is insensitive to the interests and claims of other persons in society." (Model Penal Code, Tent.Draft No. 9, *supra*, at p. 53.) The Legislature, in recognizing such conduct as criminal, endeavored to stimulate people towards awareness of the potential consequences of their conduct and influence them to avoid creating undesirable risks.[9]

What amounts to a violation of this section depends, of course, entirely on the circumstances of the particular conduct. Whether in those circumstances the act or acts causing death involved a substantial and unjustifiable risk, and whether the failure to perceive it was such as to constitute a gross deviation from the standard of care which a reasonable man would have observed under the same circumstances, are questions that generally must be left directly to the trier of the facts. In other words, "[t]he tribunal must evaluate the actor's failure of perception and determine whether, under all the circumstances, it was serious enough to be condemned." (Model Penal Code, Tent.Draft No. 4, *supra*, at p. 126; see also, Moreland, A Re-Examination of the Law of Homicide in 1971: The Model Penal Code, 59 Ky.L.J. 788, 828.)

While it is difficult to clarify further these questions, ... it would seem sufficiently clear that for proper determination of these questions, two main considerations should be emphasized. Firstly, criminal liability cannot be predicated upon every careless act merely because its carelessness results in another's death; and, secondly, the elements of the crime preclude the proper condemnation of inadvertent risk creation unless "the significance of the circumstances of fact would be apparent to one who shares the community's general sense of right and wrong...." (Model Penal Code, Tent.Draft No. 9, *supra*, at p. 53....)

Turning to the case before us, upon consideration of the totality of the circumstances surrounding the defendant's conduct, ... the evidence presented to the Grand Jury was the equivalent of prima facie proof that the crime charged had been committed by the defendant....

The evidence discloses that Mrs. Palazzo was struck by the defendant's car while crossing Castleton Avenue at the intersection of Castleton and Bard Avenues with the traffic signal green in her favor. At the time she was struck, Mrs. Palazzo was half-way across Castleton Avenue. The evidence also indicates that the defendant failed to obey the red traffic signal at the intersection of Castleton and Bard Avenues and stop his motor vehicle, as required by law, before proceeding through the intersection. Additionally, there is evidence that he was traveling at a high rate of speed (approximately 52 mph) just before and at impact. Furthermore, no visual obstruction to the sighting of Mrs. Palazzo, lawfully crossing at the intersection, was apparent. It should be abundantly clear that such conduct cannot be characterized as mere carelessness, sufficient only to establish liability for ordinary civil negligence. Rather, from this evidence, and the reasonable inferences to be drawn therefrom, a

---

[9] Compare Hall, Negligent Behavior Should Be Excluded from Penal Liability, 63 Col.L.Rev. 632; 16 Buff.L.Rev. 749.

jury could find the defendant guilty of criminally negligent homicide.... To hold otherwise, and excuse the flagrant disregard manifested here, would sanction conduct at which the statute was clearly aimed, and, in effect, abolish the crime of criminally negligent homicide in all homicides resulting from a misuse of a motor vehicle... [Order reversed.]

NOTES

1. In *People v. Calvaresi*, 188 Colo. 277, 534 P.2d 316 (1975), the Supreme Court of Colorado held unconstitutional Colorado's 1971 statute on manslaughter because the conduct proscribed could not be distinguished from the less serious offense of "criminal negligence":

> A statute which prescribes different degrees of punishment for the same acts committed under like circumstances by persons in like situations is violative of a person's right to equal protection of the laws.
>
> Under the manslaughter statute in question, a jury must determine if an accused acted "recklessly," i.e., whether he failed to perceive a risk, of which he should have been aware, and whether he acted in wanton and willful disregard of the standard of conduct that a reasonable person would observe in a given situation.
>
> Under the criminal negligence statute, the jury must determine whether the failure to perceive an unjustifiable risk constitutes a gross deviation from the standard of care that a reasonable person would observe in the situation. The distinction between a gross deviation from, and a wanton and willful disregard of, a standard of care is not sufficiently apparent to be intelligently and uniformly applied. The legislative attempt to distinguish between recklessness, and its purportedly less culpable counterpart, criminal negligence, constitutes a distinction without a sufficiently pragmatic difference.

534 P.2d at 318-19.

2. The Colorado legislature responded to the *Calvaresi* decision by amending the definition of "recklessly" to reflect the distinction adopted in the Model Penal Code, § 2.02(2)(c) and (d), *supra* pp. 95, 98. "The definitions of the two terms now differ in that a person acts 'recklessly' when he 'consciously disregards' a risk, while he is criminally negligent when he 'fails to perceive' the risk through a 'gross deviation' from a reasonable standard of care. Section 18-1-501(3) and (8), C.R.S. 1973 (1978 Repl.Vol. 8). Thus the distinction is between becoming aware of a risk yet consciously choosing to disregard it as opposed to negligently failing to become aware of the risk. Recklessness requires a higher degree of culpability than criminal negligence." *People v. Bettis*, 43 Colo. App. 104, 602 P.2d 877-78 (1979).

3. The difference in culpability between "extreme indifference" murder and negligent homicide is discussed in *People v. Jones*, 193 Colo. 250, 565 P.2d 1333, *appeal dismissed*, 434 U.S. 962 (1977).

4. Statutes which use the Model Penal Code approach, such as the New York statute in *People v. Haney*, *supra*, draw a line between recklessness and criminal negligence (gross, culpable, etc.) based on whether the actor was

aware of the risk and consciously disregarded it, or whether or not in the exercise of due care he should have but was not aware of it. Other statutes equate culpable negligence with recklessness. For example, W. VA. CODE ANN. § 17 C-5-1, (1974) defines the crime of "Negligent Homicide":

> (a) When the death of any person ensues within one year as a proximate result of injury received by the driving of any vehicle in *reckless disregard* of the safety of others, the person so operating such vehicle shall be guilty of negligent homicide. (Emphasis added.)

Furthermore, in trying to articulate a distinction between criminal and nonculpable negligent behavior (ordinary negligence) courts frequently blur the distinction between criminal negligence and recklessness. In *People v. Rodriguez, supra,* by way of note, the court listed the following further definitions of criminal and culpable negligence: *State v. Hintz,* 61 Idaho 411, 102 P.2d 639: "The term 'criminal negligence,' as used in that section [the statute identical with Penal Code, section 20], does not mean merely the failure to exercise ordinary care, or that degree of care which an ordinarily prudent person would exercise under like circumstances. It means gross negligence. It is such negligence as amounts to a reckless disregard of consequences and of the rights of others." *State v. Baublits,* 324 Mo. 1199, 27 S.W.2d 16, 21: "Culpable negligence is tantamount to gross carelessness or recklessness incompatible with a proper regard for human life.... One may endanger the life or bodily safety of another through ordinary negligence only, but that degree of negligence is not sufficient to render one criminally responsible." *People v. Carlson,* 176 Misc. 230, 26 N.Y.S.2d 1003, 1005: "Mere lack of foresight, stupidity, irresponsibility, thoughtlessness, ordinary carelessness, however serious the consequences may happen to be, do not constitute culpable negligence. There must exist in the mind of the accused, at the time of the act or omission, a consciousness of the probable consequences of the act, and a wanton disregard of them." Also see *People v. Wells,* 186 Misc. 979, 66 N.Y.S.2d 161, 164. *People v. Brucato,* 32 N.Y.S.2d 689, 691; "Criminal negligence is synonymous with culpable negligence. Such negligence encompasses a reckless and wanton disregard for the safety of life and limb.... In sum, the evidence must disclose what would almost be tantamount to a wilfulness to do harm on the part of the offender." *Cannon v. State,* 91 Fla. 214, 107 So. 360, 363: "[A] gross and flagrant character, evincing reckless disregard of human life, or of the safety of persons exposed to its dangerous effects, or there is that entire want of care which would raise the presumption of a conscious indifference to consequences, or which shows wantonness or recklessness, or a grossly careless disregard of the safety and welfare of the public, or that reckless indifference to the rights of others which is equivalent to an intentional violation of them. ..." (At 8 Cal. Rptr. 867, Note 1).

5. Scholarly debate as to the proper meaning of recklessness has been active. Williams, *Recklessness Redefined,* 40 CAMB. L.J. 252 (1981); Duff, *Recklessness,* [1981] CRIM. L. REV. 282; Greiw, *Reckless Damage and Reckless Driving: Living with Caldwell and Lawrence,* [1981] CRIM. L. REV. 743. Hall, "Negligent Behavior Should Be Excluded From Penal Liability," in LAW, SOCIAL SCIENCE AND CRIMINAL THEORY (Littleton, 1982) Rothman at 244-265.

6. See also the discussion of criminal negligence, *supra* Chapter 2, p. 98.

NOTES ON VEHICULAR HOMICIDE

1. Murder in the Second Degree: On appeal from a judgment of conviction of murder in the second degree, the following jury instruction was approved:

> If the defendant committed on the person of the deceased an act of violence which produced death and at the time he inflicted such act he had the intention to kill or intended to do an act of violence from which ordinarily in the usual course of events death or great bodily harm may be the consequence he may be guilty of murder in the second degree. Our courts have said that where the accused is himself the driver of an automobile and drives in a manner greatly dangerous to the lives of others so as to evidence a depraved mind regardless of human life he may be guilty of murder in the second degree, if his anti-social act results in the death of another, and this though he had no preconceived purpose to deprive any particular human being of life. Under such circumstances his acts are unlawful and without legal excuse, and malice may be inferred therefrom.

Nixon v. State, 268 Ala. 101, 105 So.2d 349, 350-51 (1958).

But this is not the way vehicular homicides ordinarily occur. In most instances the driver has no intent to kill or cause serious harm. How are these unintended homicides classified? As the following cases show, they are classified in various ways.

2. Involuntary Manslaughter: In an opinion affirming a conviction of involuntary manslaughter, the Supreme Court of Florida said: "To support manslaughter as used in § 782.07, Florida Statutes, F.S.A., one's conduct must reveal a reckless disregard or indifference for the life, safety or rights of those exposed to its effects, or it must show an indifference to consequences regardless of who is affected. If one takes no account of the fact that others are on the highway and have as much right to be there as he has or is totally oblivious to their rights, his conduct may be culpable." *Fulton v. State*, 108 So.2d 473, 475 (Fla. 1959).

3. "Experience in many states has demonstrated the difficulty of obtaining convictions on charges of manslaughter arising out of traffic accident deaths." The President's Highway Safety Conference, Report of Committee on Laws and Ordinances 26 (1949). Consequently, many states have enacted Motor Vehicle Homicide statutes, providing for substantially lower punishments than those assessed under manslaughter statutes.

These negligent homicide or vehicular manslaughter statutes have been interpreted by some courts to require only ordinary negligence to support a conviction. *People v. Watson*, 30 Cal. 3d 290, 179 Cal. Rptr. 43, 637 P.2d 279 (1981); *State v. Anderson*, 561 P.2d 1061 (Utah 1977), *overruled, State v. Chavez*, 605 P.2d 1226 (Utah 1979), criminal negligence required; *State v. Miles*, 203 Kan. 707, 457 P.2d 166 (1969).

Other courts either because of the express language of the statute or by judicial construction require a higher degree of negligence sometimes stated

IX. CRIMINAL-NEGLIGENCE INVOLUNTARY MANSLAUGHTER AND NEGLIGENT HOMICIDE

by the court as "recklessness." *State v. Vollmer*, 259 S.E.2d 837 (W. Va. 1979); *Thompson v. State*, 554 P.2d 105 (Okla. Cr. 1976); *State v. Kim*, 55 Hawaii 346, 519 P.2d 1241 (1974). In these statutes the terms "recklessness" and "gross negligence" are usually regarded as similar standards, *State v. Hodgdon*, 244 Or. 219, 416 P.2d 647 (1966), and courts have described the conduct which will satisfy the statute as demonstrating a "reckless, willful or wanton disregard for the safety of others." The courts focus on defendant's conduct and the risks thereby created. The emphasis is on his "indifference" to the risk he has created rather than requiring proof of conscious disregard of known risks. *State v. Vollmer, supra.*

The relationship between the terms "reckless" and "culpable negligence" is referred to in the RESTATEMENT (SECOND) OF TORTS § 282 (1965): "In construction of statutes which specifically refer to gross negligence, that phrase is sometimes construed as equivalent to reckless disregard."

However, the Restatement further provides:

> § 500. "The actor's conduct is in reckless disregard of the safety of another if he does an act or intentionally fails to do an act which it is his duty to the other to do, knowing or having reason to know of facts which would lead a reasonable man to realize, not only that his conduct creates an unreasonable risk of physical harm to another, but also that such risk is substantially greater than that which is necessary to make his conduct negligent."
>
> Comment A ... — "It must involve an easily perceptible danger of death or substantial physical harm, and the probability that it will so result must be substantially greater than is required for ordinary negligence."

Some vehicular or negligent homicide statutes make provision for both gross negligence and simple negligence. CALIF. PENAL CODE § 192 *supra*, pp. 267-268; HAWAII REV. STATS. §§ 707-703, 707-704 (1976).

4. These special vehicular homicide statutes in some cases may but do not necessarily preclude prosecution under murder or manslaughter statutes. In *People v. Watson*, 30 Cal. 3d 290, 637 P.2d 279, 179 Cal. Rptr. 43 (1981), the court held that state was not as a matter of law precluded from prosecuting for second-degree murder so long as the elements of the two offenses were not identical and there was no legislative intent to make the special statute the exclusive basis for prosecution. *People v. Whitfield*, 15 Cal. Rptr. 2d 4 (Cal. App. 4 Dist., 1992), discusses the effect of changes in California's penal code involving intoxication and diminished capacity on the analysis in *Watson*. See also "Diminished Responsibility" *supra* at pp. 279-286.

A conviction for manslaughter, notwithstanding enactment of a special vehicular homicide statute, was held proper in *McCreary v. State*, 371 So.2d 1024 (Fla. 1979), despite the fact that both offenses were defined in terms of recklessness.

5. Compare *Thompson v. State*, 554 P.2d 105 (Okla. App. Cr. 1976), where the court held that "reckless disregard" as used in the negligent homicide statute had the same meaning as "culpable negligence" in the manslaughter statute. Enactment of the negligent homicide statute impliedly repealed manslaughter statute as to vehicular homicides. There are also cases which have

held "implied repeal" because of differences in the elements or penalties of the manslaughter statute and the special vehicular homicide statute. Cases cited in *State v. Vollmer*, 295 S.E.2d 837, 841 (W. Va. 1979).

6. In *State v. Vollmer, supra*, the court held that negligent homicide defined in terms of reckless driving resulting in death was not a lesser included offense of involuntary manslaughter. Both offenses were predicated on reckless conduct and as both carried the same penalty the state could prosecute under either.

7. Contributory Negligence: "Contributory negligence is not available as a defense or an excuse in a criminal prosecution; this doctrine has no place in criminal law, and it cannot in any degree purge an act which otherwise constitutes a public offense of its criminal character. Accordingly the contributory negligence of a person injured or killed by the criminal negligence of another does not relieve the latter from criminal responsibility. Further, it is ordinarily no defense that the victim of the crime ... is punished because of the offense against society." 22 C.J.S. CRIMINAL LAW § 52, pp. 116-17. The above rule is supported by the great weight of authority in other jurisdictions. *State v. Plaspohl*, 239 Ind. 324, 326, 157 N.E.2d 579, 580 (1959).

Chapter 6
CRIMES AGAINST PROPERTY AND RELATED CRIMES*

SECTION I. Traditional Forms of Criminality
EAST'S PLEAS OF THE CROWN 553 (1803)

At common law larceny was defined as "the wrongful taking and carrying away by any person of the mere personal goods of another, from any place, with a felonious intent to convert them to his (the taker's) own use, and make them his own property, without the consent of the owner."

A. LARCENY
1. SUBJECT MATTER OF THEFT

PEOPLE v. DILLON
Supreme Court of California
668 P.2d 697 (1983)

Mosk, Justice.

Defendant appeals from a judgment convicting him of first degree felony murder and attempted robbery. The case presents two principal issues. First, we inquire whether a standing crop can be the subject of robbery; declining to perpetuate an archaic distinction between that crime and larceny, we conclude that it can....

At the time of these events defendant was a 17-year-old high school student living in the Santa Cruz Mountains not far from a small, secluded farm on which Dennis Johnson and his brother illegally grew marijuana. Told by a friend about the farm, defendant set out with two schoolmates to investigate it and to take some of the marijuana if possible. After crossing posted barricades and evading a primitive tin-can alarm system, the three boys reached the farm, a quarter-acre plot enclosed by a six-foot wire fence. In an effort to avoid being seen by Johnson, who was guarding the property, the boys tried several different approaches, then hid in a hollow tree stump. Johnson appeared with a shotgun, cocked the weapon, and ordered them out; defendant remained in hiding, but his companions complied. Johnson demanded to know what they were doing there; disbelieving their story that they were hunting rabbits, he told them to get off the property. He warned them that his brother would have shot them if he had met them, adding that the next time the youths came on his property he might shoot them himself. Defendant overheard these threats.

---

*The crimes included in this chapter are discussed comprehensively in A.L.I., Model Penal Code and Commentaries, Part II, Vol. 2, Arts. 220-24, pp. 3-367 and Vol. 3, Art. 240, pp. 3-89 (1980).

The two boys departed promptly, but defendant stayed inside the tree trunk until it grew dark. Finally emerging, he went to take another look at the plantation. Again Johnson confronted him with a shotgun, pointed the weapon at him, and ordered him to go. He left without further ado.

Some weeks later defendant returned to the farm to show it to his brother. As the latter was looking over the scene, however, a shotgun blast was heard and once more the boys beat a hasty retreat.

After the school term began, defendant and a friend discussed the matter further and decided to attempt a "rip-off" of the marijuana with the aid of reinforcements. Various plans were considered for dealing with Johnson; defendant assertedly suggested that they "just hold him up. Hit him over the head or something. Tie him to a tree." They recruited six other classmates, and on the morning of October 17, 1978, the boys all gathered for the venture. Defendant had prepared a rough map of the farm and the surrounding area. Several of the boys brought shotguns, and defendant carried a .22 caliber semi-automatic rifle. They also equipped themselves with a baseball bat, sticks, a knife, wirecutters, tools for harvesting the marijuana, paper bags to be used as masks or for carrying plants, and rope for bundling plants or for restraining the guards if necessary. Along the way, they found some old sheets and tore them into strips to use as additional masks or bindings to tie up the guards. Two or three of the boys thereafter fashioned masks and put them on.

The boys climbed a hill towards the farm, crossed the barricades, split into four pairs, and spread out around the field. There they saw one of the Johnson brothers tending the plants; discretion became much the better part of valor, and they made little or no progress for almost two hours. Although the testimony of the various participants was not wholly consistent, it appears that two of the boys abandoned the effort altogether, two others were chased away by dogs but began climbing the hill by another route, and defendant and his companion, with the remaining pair, watched cautiously just outside the field of marijuana.

One of the boys returning to the farm then accidentally discharged his shotgun, and the two ran back down the hill. While the boys near the field reconnoitered and discussed their next move, their hapless friend once more fired his weapon by mistake. In the meantime Dennis Johnson had circled behind defendant and the others, and was approaching up the trail. They first heard him coming through the bushes, then saw that he was carrying a shotgun. When Johnson drew near, defendant began rapidly firing his rifle at him. After Johnson fell, defendant fled with his companions without taking any marijuana. Johnson suffered nine bullet wounds and died a few days later....

Defendant next contends that a standing crop of marijuana cannot in any event be the subject of robbery or attempted robbery because it is realty, not personalty.[5] Although defendant's argument finds apparent support in the common law definition of property subject to larceny, we hold that robbery of a standing crop is punishable in California. We reach this conclusion both

---

[5] Defendant apparently concedes that robbery of contraband is subject to penal sanction.... Today the rule is universal that by prohibiting possession of an item, the government does not license criminals to take it by force or stealth from other criminals.

because the Legislature has said as much with regard to the lesser included offense of larceny, and because the common law rule to the contrary is a hypertechnical remnant of an archaic formalism that can no longer be seriously defended.

The common law rule limiting larceny to the unlawful taking of personalty derived from the undeniable fact that realty, in the sense of land subject to description by metes and bounds, cannot be "carried away." ... "Real property under the English law was never the subject of [larceny]. Being incapable of larcenous asportation, it was not regarded as requiring at the hands of the criminal law the same protection as personalty." ... When restricted to land, the logic of the rule was unassailable. But for various reasons unrelated to the criminal law, "realty" was defined in due course to include many items that can be more or less readily detached and removed from the land. Unfortunately, the legal fiction that these objects are "immovable" has never hindered would-be thieves from moving most of them. Nevertheless, probably because larceny was a felony at common law and therefore a capital offense, judges resisted its application to those who had merely pilfered growing food or wood.[6] Courts therefore clung to the artificial distinction between personal property and things that "savour of the realty" (4 Stephen, New Commentaries on the Laws of England (1st Am. ed. 1846) p. 155), and held that if the thief maintained possession continuously during severance and asportation, the property never became personalty in the possession of its owner and hence no larceny could occur. Put conversely, "if a man come to steal trees, or the lead of a church or house, and sever it, and after about an hour's time, or so, come and fetch it away, this hath been held felony, because the act is not continuated but interpolated, and in that interval the property lodgeth in the right owner as a chattel." (1 Hale, Pleas of the Crown (1st Am. ed. 1847) p. 510.) Thus, in a perverse and unintended application of the work ethic, thieves industrious enough to harvest what they stole and to carry it away without pause were guilty at most of trespass, while those who tarried along the way, or enjoyed fruits gathered by the labor of others, faced the hangman's noose.

The rule has long been the subject of ridicule and limitation. Our court first criticized it over a century ago: "This rule involved many technical niceties, which have resulted in what appear to us to be pure absurdities. For example, if the article stolen was severed from the soil by the thief himself and immediately carried away, so that the whole constituted but one transaction, it was held to be only a trespass; but if, after the severance, he left the article for a time and afterward returned for it and took it away on another occasion, then it became a larceny.... We confess we do not comprehend the force of these distinctions, nor appreciate the reasoning by which they are supported. We do not perceive why a person who takes apples from a tree with a felonious intent

---

[6] "'The horribly severe punishment (death) meted out for this offense in earlier times has also been influential in inducing courts to refine and limit the crime. This process frequently enabled them, in cases which they deemed to be meritorious, to avoid the necessity of pronouncing the death penalty. The subject of larceny therefore is the best illustration of the old saying that hard cases make bad law.'" (State v. Day (Me. 1972) 293 A.2d 331, 333, quoting from 2 Bishop, Criminal Law (9th ed.) § 760, p. 584.)

should only be a trespasser, whereas, if he had taken them from the ground, after they had fallen, he would have been a thief; nor why the breaking from a ledge of a quantity of rich gold-bearing rock with felonious intent should only be a trespass, if the rock be immediately carried off; but if left on the ground, and taken off by the thief a few hours later, it becomes larceny. The more sensible rule, it appears to us, would have been, that by the act of severance the thief had converted the property into a chattel; and if he then removed it, with a felonious intent, he would be guilty of a larceny, whatever dispatch may have been employed in the removal." (People v. Williams (1868) 35 Cal. 671, 676.) But while the rule could no longer command the respect of reason, it was nevertheless honored by time, and on that basis alone the court felt compelled to follow it. Reluctantly putting aside common sense in favor of common law, the court confessed that it "adverted to the question mainly for the purpose of directing the attention of the Legislature to a subject which appears to demand a remedial statute."...

The Legislature was quick to respond. In 1872 it adopted a statute redefining detachable fixtures and crops as personalty subject to larceny, "in the same manner as if the thing had been severed by another person at some previous time." ... Contemporaneously, it enacted a statute dividing the crime of larcenous severance of realty into grand larceny, if the object of the theft is worth $50 or more, and petty larceny otherwise.... Defendant argues that because those statutes are explicitly directed at larceny only, they reveal a legislative intent to leave intact the common law rule as it applies to robbery.

[The court refused to hold that the statutory definition of robbery perpetuated a common-law concept of property rejected in larceny.] ... [T]he rule requiring an interruption between severance and asportation has suffered such erosion and criticism during the past century that we no longer feel compelled to preserve it, as this court did in *Williams,* particularly in an area of law not previously marred by its application. Many courts have found the doctrine at odds with reason and have therefore abolished it rather than await legislative intervention.... Of the courts that have hesitated to overrule the doctrine outright, many have found ways of limiting it; some redefine "fixtures" for this purpose to exclude items that the civil law includes in the term ..., while others effectively eliminate the requirement of a separation between severance and asportation by creative reconstruction of the facts to establish a sufficient temporal gap ....

Moreover, in England the rule has been continuously eroded by statute since 1601 (4 Blackstone, Commentaries 233-234), and in those few American jurisdictions in which courts have refrained from adopting the modern rule, lawmakers have often done so.... Hence despite the common law, "it is the generally accepted modern rule that he who by his wrongful act converts a fixture into personal property, and then with larcenous intent forthwith carries it away without the consent of the owner, may be rightfully convicted of larceny." (50 Am.Jur.2d, Larceny, s 73, p. 245.)

Today, the old rule is less justifiable and more mischievous than ever. As the Maine court observed, "In a modern mobile society in which the attachment of all manner of valuable appliances and gadgets to the realty is commonplace, we see no occasion to attribute to the Legislature any intention to so narrowly circumscribe the meaning of the words 'goods or chattels' in our larceny statute as to make the stealing of chattels severed from realty an attractive and lucrative occupation." ... We perceive no reason to reach a different conclusion regarding the words "goods" and "chattels" as they apply to robbery in our statute.... We believe it would come as a great surprise to the potential victim of crime to learn that the more precautions he takes to guard his valuables, and the more violence that must be done to take them from him, the less severe the penalty the law will impose. Because we find no reasoned support for the continued application of the common law rule, even in the narrow context in which it was traditionally invoked, we refrain from extending it to the crime of robbery....

For the reasons stated, we hold that a robbery within the meaning of section 211 is committed when property affixed to realty is severed and taken therefrom in circumstances that would have subjected the perpetrator to liability for robbery if the property had been severed by another person at some previous time. Defendant was properly convicted of attempting to commit such a robbery.

[A majority of the court affirmed the applicability of the felony-murder rule to the case, but reduced the level of the offense to second-degree murder, for reasons not germane to the present context.]

NOTES

1. MODEL PENAL CODE § 223.1, comment at 128-29:

(a) *Development of Traditional Theft Offenses.* Distinctions among larceny, embezzlement, obtaining by false pretenses, extortion, and the other closely related theft offenses are explicable in terms of a long history of expansion of the role of the criminal law in protecting property. That history begins with a concern for crimes of violence — in the present context, the taking of property by force from the possession of another, *i.e.*, robbery. The criminal law then expanded, by means of the ancient quasi-criminal writ of trespass, to cover all taking of another's property from his possession without his consent, even though no force was used. This misconduct was punished as larceny. The law then expanded once more, through some famous judicial manipulation of the concept of possession, to embrace misappropriation by a person who with the consent of the owner already had physical control over the property, as in the case of servants and even bailees in certain particularly defined situations.

At this point in the chronology of the law of theft, about the end of the 18th century, a combination of circumstances caused the initiative in the further development of the criminal law to pass from the courts to the legislature. Among these circumstances were the general advance in prestige and power of parliament and the conversion of the idea of "natural law" from an instrument for judicial defiance of monarchy to a restraining philosophy envisioning judges as interpreters of immemorial custom rather than framers of policy. Perhaps the most direct influence of all was a revulsion against capital punishment, which was the penalty for all theft offenses except petty larceny during much of the 18th century. The severity of this penalty not only made the judges reluctant to enlarge felonious larceny but also may account for the host of artificial limitations that they engrafted on the offense, *e.g.*, the exclusion of growing crops, fixtures, deeds, and dogs.

2. Contemporary law, discussed *infra* in Section 2, becomes meaningful when set against the background of common-law principles, under which there were four "exceptions" to what could be stolen:

  a. Intangible property, such as labor, other services, and use of machines.
  b. Real property. See the principal case.
  c. Things without value.
  d. Wild animals.

Intangibles. Absent curative legislation, it is not larceny to make use of the factory or equipment, or the labor and services, of another. *People v. Ashworth,* 222 N.Y.S. 24 (N.Y. App. Div. 1927) (such "property" is not capable of asportation, and thus not the subject of larceny). In *Chappell v. United States,* 270 F.2d 274 (9th Cir. 1959), a larceny conviction against an Air Force noncommissioned officer was reversed because use of enlisted personnel under his command to paint residences he owned did not involve "property."

Gas and water are tangible and thus subject matter for common-law larceny. Electricity, although probably not tangible, has been held to be within the protection of larceny. *People v. Menagas,* 11 N.E.2d 403 (Ill. 1937). Telephone service, transportation, accommodations and the like were not viewed to be property. Theft of services under modern law is discussed in Section 2(E) below.

Realty and things savoring of realty. As indicated in the principal case, real property could not be the subject of common-law larceny. *See also United States v. Kehoe,* 365 F. Supp. 920 (S.D. Tex. 1973) (indictment alleging that Kehoe had conveyed land, etc., failed to charge a crime under the "other things of value" clause of 18 U.S.C. § 641 [1988]). Deeds and conveyances have been treated as personalty under statutory restatements of common-law larceny. *State v. McCray,* 177 P. 127 (Okla. Crim. App. 1919).

Value. Anything a thief believes worthy of stealing will be considered to have enough intrinsic value to support a larceny charge, at least in the modern era. *People v. Franco,* 84 Cal. Rptr. 513 (Cal. Ct. App. 1970) (empty cigarette carton had "intrinsic value"). Value of the property has significance in grading the offense, however. *See* subsections A(5) and (C)(4) below.

2. THE HARM

PEOPLE v. ZINKE

Court of Appeals of New York
555 N.E.2d 263 (1990)

KAYE, JUDGE.

The single question before us is whether the general partner in a limited partnership can be found guilty of larceny for misappropriating partnership funds. As a matter of statutory interpretation, we answer that question in the negative, leaving the subject of partnership defalcations to be addressed by any other penal provisions that may be applicable, or by civil litigation, or (if deemed appropriate) by legislative reform.

A. LARCENY

Defendant, an investment adviser for small pension and profit-sharing funds, was the sole general partner in Stonehenge Investment Notes 1, Ltd., a limited partnership; defendant himself was a significant investor in the firm. In January 1987, after the limited partners and their insurers exhausted their efforts to recoup the funds defendant had allegedly embezzled, defendant was indicted for two counts of grand larceny in the second degree. Specifically, the indictment accused defendant of stealing $1,050,000 from the partnership by writing two checks on its money market account — one for $250,000 in April 1984, the other for $800,000 three months later. Defendant, who had authority under the partnership agreement to borrow firm funds, claimed that these were partnership investments.

At trial, upon the close of the People's case, defendant moved to dismiss the indictment on the ground that, as a general partner, he was a "joint or common" owner of the partnership's property and, thus, under the Penal Law could not be prosecuted for larceny even if he had misappropriated partnership property. The court reserved decision and submitted the case to the jury, which convicted defendant of both counts of the indictment. After the verdict, Supreme Court denied defendant's motion to dismiss ... and the Appellate Division affirmed the conviction, concluding that the general partner in a limited partnership could be prosecuted for larceny for stealing partnership property.... We now reverse.

Larceny is committed when one wrongfully takes, obtains or withholds "property from an owner thereof" with intent to deprive the owner of it, or appropriate it to oneself or another (Penal Law § 155.05[1]). "Owner" is defined in Penal Law § 155.00(5) as one "who has a right to possession [of the property taken] superior to that of the taker, obtainer or withholder." This broad definition is immediately qualified by the declaration that "[a] joint or common owner of property shall not be deemed to have a right of possession thereto superior to that of any other joint or common owner thereof." (Penal Law § 155.00[5].)

In that partners under the Partnership Law are "co-owners" of firm property (see, Partnership Law §§ 10, 51[1]), defendant contends that he cannot be charged with having committed larceny as against his limited partners, because all of the partners have an equal right of ownership. The People respond that, under Partnership Law § 51(2)(a), partners lose their status as joint owners when they divert firm property to their own purposes. Alternatively, the People contend that defendant's conviction should be sustained because his position as a general partner in a limited partnership is more akin to that of corporate officers and directors, who do commit larceny when they embezzle firm assets, than it is to general partners in other partnerships.

A useful backdrop against which to consider this issue is the historical evolution of the common-law concept of "owner" into its modern statutory form. As with other aspects of larceny, "a proper interpretation of the past can assist us in understanding the technical rules of the crime."...

At common law, no less than today, the requirement that the victim of a theft be an "owner" of the stolen property was an indispensable element of the crime of larceny. The idea behind this requirement was that the property alleged to be stolen had to "belong" to a party other than the accused.... If the defendant was the owner of the property and entitled to possession at the time of the taking, there could be no larceny. From this principle emerged the rule that if property was owned by two or more persons, none of the owners could commit larceny from the others. In the words of Lord Hale: "Regularly a man cannot commit felony of the goods, wherein he hath a property." (Hale, History of Pleas of the Crown, at 513 [1683].)

Consistent with this principle was the common-law view that a partner could not be convicted of larceny for the misappropriation of partnership assets; because each partner held title to an undivided interest in the partnership, the theory was that partners could not misappropriate what was already theirs. This view has been widely recognized throughout the common-law world. Even as States began codifying larceny, the common-law rule continued to flourish. In the absence of a legislative expression to the contrary, courts have ordinarily held that a partner cannot be guilty of larceny for misappropriating firm property, with any such defalcations left for resolution in the civil arena ....

Such has been the history of the law in this State: it is surely no accident that the People cite no reported New York case where a partner has been convicted of larceny for taking partnership property. Since 1881, larceny has been defined by statute in terms of a wrongful taking or withholding from the possession of the "owner" or "true owner."... For more than 80 years the Legislature made no effort to define these terms. As in other States, the courts of this State consistently regarded the common-law definition of owner as controlling, concluding that partners could not be prosecuted for stealing firm property....

In 1965, the Legislature put to rest all possible doubt on this score. The Model Penal Code, completed in 1962, had rejected the common-law view by defining larceny as stealing "property of another," which was in turn defined as property "in which any person other than the actor has an interest ... regardless of the fact that the actor also has an interest in the property." (Model Penal Code § 223.0[7].) The purpose of this provision was to permit "a person ordinarily considered the owner of property ... [to] be convicted of theft ... Thus, a partner may be convicted of theft of partnership property." (Model Penal Code § 223.2, revised comment, at 169 [1980].) In enacting the present Penal Law in 1965, however, the New York Legislature chose to reject the Model Penal Code approach and instead codified its own existing rule. This choice was made clear when the Legislature set forth the common-law rule, in so many words, in Penal Law § 155.00(5): "[a] joint or common owner of property shall not be deemed to have a right of possession thereto superior to that of any other joint or common owner thereof."

....

A decision not to extend the larceny statute to partnership disputes — commonly litigated in civil courts — is, moreover, consistent with the Legislature's reluctance to elevate civil wrongs to the level of criminal larceny ... In particular, the Legislature was concerned both about the effects of criminalizing conduct arising out of legitimate business activities — where there can often be close questions as to intent — and the effects of offering defeated litigants in civil suits the opportunity to seek retaliation by criminal actions

... Allowing larceny prosecutions against partners is, of course, contrary to those legislative concerns.

Thus, it is clear that, in New York, partners cannot be charged with larceny for misappropriating firm assets. Indeed, while not alone in this view, New York is widely recognized as a prime example of a State that has enacted in statutory form the common-law rule that a partner "could not steal partnership property." (Model Penal Code § 223.2, revised comment, at 169, n.15 ... Since 1965, "[s]everal states have followed the lead of New York on this point in recent enactments and proposals" (Model Penal Code § 223.2, revised comment, at 170, n.15 [citing statutes of Ariz., Conn., Ore., Tex., Ill.]), and many other State courts have continued to follow or have recently adopted the New York rule....

Against this backdrop, the People's arguments for criminal liability must fail....

NOTES

1. The Colorado Supreme Court adopted an equivalent position, using common-law principles, in *People v. Clayton,* 728 P.2d 723 (Colo. 1986).

2. In *State v. Smith,* 684 S.W.2d 576 (Mo. App. 1985), defendant Jollie R. A. Smith and his brother, defendant Ricky R. R. Smith, were convicted of stealing after taking an automobile owned by Jollie Smith from a garage where it had recently been repaired. The repair bill had not been paid. In affirming the conviction, the court stated:

> [The Missouri statutes] do not appear to change the rule in effect before their enactment that one can be guilty of stealing property that he had legal title to. Although § 570.010(8) refers to "owner" and § 570.030 refers to "property or services of another," there is no indication that they intended to change the decisions that ownership of property necessary to support a charge of larceny may be "either general or special" and "may be supported by proof of any legal interest or special property in the things stolen, although it may be less than an absolute title." ...
>
> "It has long been established that ownership of stolen property may be charged either to the actual owner or the one rightfully in possession and a showing that the property was taken from one who merely had charge and control thereof is sufficient." ... Lawful custody and control of property is a sufficient attribute of ownership to support an averment and proof of ownership....
>
> "It is a trite saying that one cannot steal from himself, and that may be true, for the expression implies he is in possession at the time of the supposed crime, and asportation would be lacking. But it is generally conceded that one may steal his own property, which at the time is in the possession of someone else, as, for instance, a bailee, pledgee, and the like."... This appears to be the general rule in other jurisdictions as well....
>
> It was admitted by defendants at trial and the evidence established that Johnson had the right of possession of the car by virtue of a common-law artisan's lien.... Jollie Smith had no right to possession of the vehicle

as against Johnson until the discharge of that lien.... By taking the car from Johnson's possession Jollie Smith could be guilty of stealing. If Jollie Smith could be guilty, it necessarily follows that by helping him, Ricky Smith could also be guilty....

3. At common law, one spouse could not commit larceny of the other spouse's separate property, because marriage created a "unity" so that neither spouse could be recognized to have legal possession separate from that of the other. Several courts have abrogated that restriction through interpreting a Married Women's Act. *See, e.g., Fugate v. Commonwealth,* 215 S.W.2d 1004 (Ky. 1948); *Stewart v. Commonwealth,* 252 S.E.2d 329 (Va. 1979) (citing authorities).

4. In *People v. Newsom,* 181 N.W.2d 551 (Mich. App. 1970), the defendants recaptured property taken from them by two prostitutes, as well as the money paid for acts of prostitution. Larceny convictions based on the latter were sustained. "[T]he agreement had been completed and both parties had received the agreed-upon consideration." *Id.* at 552. Public policy requires that those who obtain property from others by criminal means be punished, and it is no defense that the property has been taken from one who obtained it illegally.

5. An indictment or information for larceny must identify the "owner" whose property has been taken, and the prosecution must prove that status beyond a reasonable doubt. *See, e.g., Compton v. State,* 607 S.W.2d 246 (Tex. Crim. App. 1979), *cert. denied,* 450 U.S. 997 (1981).

REX v. TURVEY
Court of Criminal Appeal
[1946] 2 All E.R. 60

Appeal against a conviction for larceny.

LORD GODDARD, L.C.J. The circumstances were these: The appellant was charged that on Dec. 12, 1945, being a servant of His Majesty's Minister of Works, he stole from the Minister a considerable number of table knives, spoons, and so forth. He had got into touch with some foreigner living in Newton Abbot, and found that he would be a ready receiver of goods which could be stolen from the Ministry of Works. Then, being in charge at that time of a depot of the Ministry of Works at Torquay, he approached one Ward, who was in charge of a depot at Exeter. Ward was tempted to steal the property of the Ministry of Works and hand it to the appellant, who would in turn hand it to the man at Newton Abbot. Ward at once communicated with his superiors at Bristol, the people who were really in control of the property, and told them of this plan which had been suggested to him. The officials of the Ministry of Works said it would be a good thing to let this plan go on and catch them at a suitable time, which would enable them to prosecute this appellant for stealing. What they did was this: They told Ward to hand over the property to the appellant, and Ward handed over the property to the appellant. He intended to hand it to the appellant and did hand it to the appellant.

That being so, the question arose whether or not the appellant could be charged with stealing. He could have been charged with conspiracy that he was inciting to commit a felony and other charges, there is no doubt, but could he be charged with the felony of stealing? In this case it is perfectly clear that if he stole the goods, he stole them at Exeter, but he did not take them there against the will of the owner because the owner handed them to him and meant to hand them to him....

R. v. Egginton was a case in which a servant told his master that someone was going to rob the premises. "Very well," said the master, "let them rob the premises and we will catch them;" in other words, to put a homely illustration, a man, knowing that somebody is going to break into his house, leaves the bolts drawn and so makes it easy for the man to come into the house, and when he comes in he catches him and a crime has been committed; he commits the crime none the less that the servant has been told by the person who really had control of these matters, "Let the appellant come in and take the goods," that would have been one thing, but he told him to take the goods and hand them to the appellant, and that makes all the difference.

....

The charge that was put against the appellant was the wrong charge, a charge of which he could not have been convicted because there was no evidence here of what, to use a technical expression, is termed asportation. He did not carry away the goods against the will of the owner but because the owner was willing that he should have the goods and gave them to him. In those circumstances, the conviction will be quashed, so far as this charge is concerned, and the appeal allowed on count 1.

PEOPLE v. HANSELMAN
Supreme Court of California
18 P. 425 (1888)

McFARLAND, J. The defendant, who is appellant here, was convicted of the crime of grand larceny, averred to have been committed by taking three dollars from the person of F. O. Slanker. The motion in arrest of judgment should have been granted. There is no pretense of an averment in the information that the thing alleged to have been taken was the property of any person other than the appellant.

... The appellant claimed that he was not present at the time of the alleged commission of the larceny, and introduced some evidence tending to prove an *alibi*. The jury, however, had a right to believe the testimony of the prosecuting witness, Slanker. But the appellant contends that Slanker's testimony, taken as true, does not make out a case of larceny, because it shows that the money was taken with his (Slanker's) consent. The statement of Slanker was substantially this: He was a constable in the town of Pomona, and, some crimes having been committed in the town, he, for the purpose of detecting the thieves, on the night of the alleged larceny, disguised himself, and feigned drunkenness. After staggering around the streets awhile, he lay down in an alley and pretended to be in a drunken stupor. Shortly afterward, the appellant and another person came to him and took from his person three dollars, which he had put in the pocket of his overalls. He was perfectly conscious at the time and made no resistance, and intended that any thief who tried it should be allowed to take the three dollars, in order that a case of larceny might be made out against him. He had no previous suspicion, however, of the appellant, and was surprised at his participation in the act. And under these circumstances, counsel for appellant contends that the thing done was not larceny, because the money was not taken against the consent of the prosecuting witness. It is, no doubt, true, as a general proposition, that larceny is not committed when the property is taken with the consent of its owner; but it is difficult in some instances to determine whether certain acts constitute, in law, such "consent;" and, under the authorities, we do not think that there is such consent where there is mere passive submission on the part of the owner of the goods taken, and no indication that he wishes them taken, and no knowledge by the taker that the owner wishes them taken, and no mutual understanding between the two, and no active measures of inducement employed for the purpose of leading into temptation, and no preconcert whatever between the thief and the owner.... Bishop, under the head of "Plans to Entrap," sums up the authorities on the subject as follows: "If a man suspects that an offense is to be committed, and, instead of taking precautions against it, sets a watch and detects and arrests the offenders, he does not thereby consent to their conduct, or furnish them any excuse. And in general terms, exposing property or neglecting to watch it, under expectation that a thief will take it, or furnishing any other facilities or temptations to such or any other wrong-doer, is not a consent in law." (1 Bishop on Criminal Law, § 262.) From the authorities, and upon principle, we are of opinion that the conduct of the witness Slanker, as detailed by him in his testimony, did not amount to consent in law, and affords no reason why the act of appellant in taking the money (if he did take it in the manner sworn to by Slanker) was not larceny. If there had been preconcert of action between Slanker and appellant, a different question would have been presented.

We think that the instructions of the court were, upon the whole, correct; but the record does not show any exceptions taken to them. At all events, if there shall be another trial, the court can readily make its instructions comply with this opinion. Judgment and order appealed from reversed, and cause remanded.

NOTES

1. George Fletcher, *The Metamorphosis of Larceny*, 89 Harv. L. Rev. 469, 481-83, 486-87 (1976):

> *The Carrier's Case*,[51] decided in the Star Chamber in 1473, represents the first major judicial extension of the medieval common law of larceny. A carrier had made a bargain with a merchant to carry some bales of dyer's weed to Southampton; instead he took them to another place, broke open the bales and took the contents.[52] All or part of the goods thus taken appear to have fallen into the hands of the Sheriff of London, who was sued by the original owner — an alien merchant who had come with a

---

[51] Y.B. Pasch, 13 Edw. 4, f. 9, pl. 5 (1473), 64 Selden Soc'y 30 (1945) [cited hereinafter to the Selden Society reprint and translation].

[52] *See id.* at 30 (reporter's note).

A. LARCENY

royal safe conduct covering his goods — for the return of his property.[53] The Sheriff's defense was that the goods were forfeit to the King as waif, because the taking had been a felony.[54]

The impediment to treating the taking as a felony was the rule of possessorial immunity. Chief Justice Bryan took this rule to be decisive: The bailee, having lawfully acquired possession of the goods, could not take them *vi et armis* and therefore the taking could not be said to be felony or trespass.[55] Yet in the end the judges were of the opinion that the taking had been a felony. They could not concur on a rationale,[56] but Lord Chokke's opinion developed the argument that eventually became the rule of the case.[57] Chokke argued that[58]

> [T]he things which were in the bale were not given [to the bailee], but the bales as chose entire ..., in which case if he had given away the bales or sold them, it would not be felony, but when he broke open [the bales] and took out of [them] what was inside, he did this without warrant [and it is felony].

This is the language that generated the rule of "breaking bulk," which remained a prominent exception to possessorial immunity until the mid-nineteenth century.[59] In the final stages of the metamorphosis of larceny,

---

[53] *See id.* at 34 (reporter's note).

[54] *Id.* (reporter's note). Waifed goods are those feloniously taken and then abandoned; these are normally forfeited to the Crown. *See* I W. Blackstone, *supra* note 12, at *296-97 (explaining the rule as an inducement to owners to pursue thieves and recapture stolen goods before they are abandoned).

[55] 64 Selden Soc'y at 30-31 (opinion of Bryan, C.J.C.P.).

[56] The various justices advanced several theories on which the bailee's taking could be considered a larceny. Huse, for example, thought that a felony was committed when the carrier "claim[ed] the goods feloniously without cause from the party with intent to defraud him to whom the property belongs...." *Id.* at 31. The Chancellor and Molyneux also seem to have held this position. Vavasour and Laken sought to distinguish between a bailment, in which there is actual delivery and possession in the bailee, and a bargain to carry, which was thought to give only a limited warrant to take the goods. Thus, if the carrier by his conversion revealed an intent not to comply with the terms of the warrant, his initial taking was felonious. *See id.* at 31 (Vavasour), 33 (Laken, J.K.B.). Nedeham took this argument a step further and maintained that possession determined when the carrier went outside the purpose for which he had been given the bales. *See id.* at 33 (Nedeham, J.K.B.). This analysis would have assimilated the case to those in which the taker had custody merely, and not possession....

[57] *See* E. Coke, *supra* note 12, at *107; M. Dalton, The Country Justice 324 (1655); 1 M. Hale, *supra* note 12, at 504-05; 4 W. Blackstone, *supra* note 12, at *230.

[58] 64 Selden Soc'y at 32. This principle does not appear to have been without precedent. Chokke gives as an example: "[I]f a man is given a tun of wine to carry, if he sells the tun, it is not felony or trespass, but if he took out twenty pints it is a felony, for the twenty pints were not given to him ..." *Id.; cf.* Rattlesdene v. Gruneston, Y.B. Pasch., 10 Edw. 2, pl. 37 (1317), 54 Selden Soc'y 140 (1935).

[59] So far as the law of England from roughly 1600 to 1800 is expressed in the leading treatises, *The Carrier's Case* was viewed as establishing two different circumstances in which a carrier or bailee could be found guilty of larceny. In the first, the culprit breaks bulk and carries away the contents *animo furandi*. This was a felony at the time of the breaking and taking, not at the time of initial receipt of the goods. *See* M. Dalton, *supra* note 57, at 324; E. Coke, *supra* note 12, at *107; 1 M. Hale, *supra* note 12, at 505; 1 W. Hawkins, Pleas of the Crown 135 (1716); 4 W. Blackstone, *supra* note 12, at *230. In the second set of circumstances, the carrier, having received the pack and "carr[ied] it to the place appointed, ... take[s] the whole pack *animo furandi* ...." E. Coke, *supra* note 12, at *107. *See* 64 Selden Soc'y at 33 (opinion of Nedeham, J.K.B.); M. Dalton, *supra* note 57, at 324; 1 M. Hale, *supra* note 12, at 505; 4 W. Blackstone, *supra* note 12, at *230. It is important to note that from the beginning, the rationale for this second rule stemming from *The Carrier's Case* was that upon the carrier's delivery of the goods to their destination, "his

Parliament eliminated possessorial immunity in 1857 and brought all defalcating bailees within the bounds of the criminal law....[60]

Whatever the momentum generated by *The Carrier's Case,* further rending of the possessorial veil was to await the close of the eighteenth century. Rather than seek new exceptions to the rule of possessorial immunity, the courts fastened their attention on determining when the veil of immunity fit and when it did not. That meant that courts and commentators undertook as one of their central concerns to determine the boundaries of legal possession.

At early stages of the common law, the concept of possession coincided roughly with actual dominion over an object.[72] In the course of the law's evolution, the courts gradually recognized, and then widened, a gap between actual control and legal possession. In *The Carrier's Case,* it was recognized that a guest in an inn does not acquire possession of eating utensils or bed linen.[73] In the fifteenth and sixteenth centuries there was considerable controversy whether servants enjoyed possessorial immunity for misappropriation of goods acquired from their masters. After some vacillation[74] it was settled that a servant's custody did not amount to possession as long as the servant was on the master's premises or in the master's company.[75] Parliament intervened in this development in 1529 with a statute that subjected servants to the law of larceny as to all valuable property entrusted to them by their masters.[76] In due course, however, this statute was interpreted not to apply to the goods that servants received from third parties.[77]

In these disputes about the scope of possessorial immunity, the underlying factual transaction is always the same. Someone hands the defendant an object or the defendant picks it up with the owner's permission; the question is whether the acquisition of the physical object is sufficient to acquire legal possession. In the cases of crockery and linen in another's inn, the user would not expect eventually to acquire possession or property in the chattel. The problem is more subtle if the transaction is the sort in which the user normally expects to acquire possession or property. This more difficult variation was posed in the mid-seventeenth century

possession is determined," 64 Selden Soc'y at 33 (opinion of Nedeham, J.K.B.), E. Coke, *supra* at *107-08 ("for the delivery had taken his [sic] effect, and the privity of the bailment is determined"); *accord, e.g.,* 1 M. Hale, *supra* note 12, at 505; 4 W. Blackstone, *supra* note 12, at *230.

[60] 20 & 21 Vict., c. 54, § 4 (1857). Regarding similar American legislative revisions of the rule of "breaking bulk," see 2 J. Bishop, Criminal Law 479 (6th ed. 1877).

[72] *See* 3 W. Holdsworth, A History of English Law 336 (6th ed. rev. 1934).

[73] *See* 64 Selden Soc'y at 33 (opinion of Nedeham).

[74] *Compare* Y.B. Mich. 3 Hen. 7 pl. 9 (1488) *with* Y.B. Hil. 21 Hen. 7 pl. 21 (1506) *translated in* C. Kenny, A Selection of Cases Illustrative of the English Criminal Law 216 (8th ed. 1935) [hereinafter cited as Kenny]; *see* 3 W. Holdsworth, *supra* note 72, at 363-64.

[75] *See* Kenny, *supra* note 74, at 216; 3 W. Holdsworth, *supra* note 72, at 365 & n.2.

[76] 21 Hen. 8, c. 7 (1529). The statute does not formally alter the concept of possession; it provides that servants who "go away" with "caskets, jewels, money, goods, or chattels" which had been "delivered to them by their master or mistress ... to the intent to steal the same ... shall be deemed and adjudged [to have committed] felony ...." In time, larceny by servants was molded into the conceptual system by holding that in this class of cases servants did not get possession. *See* The King v. Bass, 168 Eng. Rep. 228 (1782); 2 E. East, *supra* note 70, at 555-60.

[77] *See* 73 Eng. Rep. 12, 12-13 (K.B. 1533) (opinion by Englefielde).

case of *Chisser*,[78] in which the defendant bolted from a store without paying for two cravats the shopkeeper handed him for inspection. The Exchequer found the taking to be felonious; despite the handing over of the cravat, the owner retained legal possession and was therefore protected until actual sale of the ties. In this situation as well as in the cases of the guest and the servant, drawing the line of possession short of physical control meant that one could commit larceny by carrying off an object already in one's hands. Thus the widening of the gap between legal possession and actual control functioned as a way of restricting possessorial immunity....

2. On the historical development of larceny, particularly in terms of protected interests, see JEROME HALL, THEFT, LAW AND SOCIETY chs. 1-3 (2d ed. 1952); Brickey, *The Jurisprudence of Larceny; An Historical Inquiry and Interest Analysis,* 33 VAND. L. REV. 1101 (1980); Paterson, *Consent in the Law of Theft,* 29 U. TORONTO L.J. 366 (1979).

3. ACTUS REUS

a. Trespass; Continuing Trespass

COMMONWEALTH v. WHITE
Supreme Judicial Court of Massachusetts
65 Mass. (11 Cush.) 483 (1853)

Indictment for larceny from a stable, of a horse, wagon, and harness, alleged to have been committed in the county of Bristol. The stable was situated in Easton, in that county, and the property belonged to John McDonald.... The said James White represented to Josiah White, Jr. the other defendant, that he had hired the horse and wagon of the owner, and invited him to go to North Bridgewater. They harnessed the horse about 5 o'clock P. M. and started and met the owner. He called to them to stop, but they passed on without heeding him. They went to North Bridgewater, and stayed there till evening, when they started on their way back. The horse becoming disabled by a fall, they unharnessed him, turned him loose, and took another horse from a pasture near the road, and harnessed him into the wagon, and proceeded into Easton on the road towards the stable of the owner. While riding along in the town of Easton, James White proposed to Josiah to go to Brighton, in the county of Middlesex. Josiah consented, and they, while in the town of Easton, turned from the road leading to the stable of McDonald, and drove to Brighton. And

---

[78] 83 Eng. Rep. 142 (1678). There are three paragraphs to the report. The first paragraph sets forth the facts (essentially that Anne Charteris handed Chisser two "crevats" and that a few moments later he ran out of the shop) and the question whether it should be adjudged felony; the second paragraph presents the reporter Sir T. Raymond's view that the case could be viewed as a felony according to Chisser's intent when he first received the tie; the third paragraph argues that Chisser was guilty as of the moment he ran from the store, for when Anne Charteris handed him the two cravats "they were not out of her possession by such delivery," *id.* at 142-44. The text relies on the third paragraph. Thomas Leach, *see* 1 W. Hawkins, Pleas of the Crown 135 N.1 (6th ed. T. Leach 1787) and Pollock and Wright, *see* F. Pollock & R. Wright, An Essay on Possession in the Common Law 140 (1888), both read *Chisser* according to the third paragraph. Whether one stresses the second or third paragraph of this opinion is of critical importance in construing The King v. Pear, 168 Eng. Rep. 208 (1779)....

there Josiah, under the instruction and direction of James, put the property into the hands of an auctioneer, stating that his name was Johnson, and that the horse belonged to his father, who had given him leave to sell him. The auctioneer sold the same, but something happening to excite his suspicions, he refused to pay over the money. McDonald testified that he did not let the horse, wagon, and harness, or either of them to James White, nor had he ever let to him any horse, wagon, or harness, but that he had sometimes, but not on this occasion let to Josiah White, Sen. the wagon and harness, but never that horse; that he did not use any force to stop defendants, when he met them, because it would have been very inconvenient for him to have got off from his load, and that he expected they would return the horse and wagon.

The counsel for the defendant contended: ... That if the defendant took the property without leave, although the taking was a trespass, but if he intended, when he took it, to return it, there was no larceny, although, while on the way, he should determine to appropriate the property, and should proceed to do with it as appeared from the testimony....

But the court instructed the jury, that if the taking was a trespass, and if the trespasser, at the time of taking, intended to appropriate the property to his own use, the taking would be a larceny of the entire property. If the taking was a trespass, but the defendant intended at the time of taking to return the property, and this intention continued until after the shifting of the horses, there was no larceny of the horse. But if afterwards and before proposing to go to Brighton, the defendant determined to take the property to Brighton and there dispose of it as his own, and he did in pursuance of that determination do that which was stated in the testimony, this would amount to larceny of the wagon and harness.

The jury found the defendant guilty of simple larceny of the wagon and harness, and not guilty of the residue of the charge in the indictment, and to these instructions the defendant excepted.

MERRICK, J.... But if a person by committing a trespass has tortiously and unlawfully acquired possession of personal property belonging to another, and afterwards conceives the purpose of fraudulently depriving the owner of it, and in pursuance of that design, with a felonious intent, carries it away and converts it to his own use, he thereby commits and is guilty of the crime of larceny. 1 Hale P. C. 507; 2 East P. C. 662; *Regina v. Riley,* 1 Dears. C. C. 149. This is the effect and substance of the explanation and statement of the law, made by the presiding judge upon the trial. While the defendant was on his way to North Bridgewater, and also during the time of his return, until he fraudulently determined to appropriate and convert the horse to his own use, and until he did some act in execution of that purpose, he was only a trespasser; but he made himself a thief as soon as he drove or led away the horse, or made any disposition of him, with such a felonious intent....

Exceptions overruled.

NOTES

1. *Regina v. Riley,* 6 Cox. C.C. 88, 169 Eng. Rep. 674 (1853), held an innocent initial trespass and subsequent intent to steal constitutes larceny.

2. In *Regina v. Kindon,* [1957] 41 Crim. App. 208, defendant, with *E* and *F* had been drinking at *P*'s flat. Later defendant took £1,100 belonging to *P* at a time when defendant was incapable of forming the intent to steal because of the influence of alcohol and drugs. When defendant sobered up, *E* produced the money and it was then divided amongst them. It was held that defendant was rightly convicted of stealing her share of the money since defendant had taken by trespass.

3. In *State v. Riggs,* 70 P. 947 (Idaho 1902), defendant was convicted of grand larceny of a horse. The trial court instructed that if defendant "wrongfully and unlawfully" took the horse, not then intending to steal it, and subsequently formed the intent to steal while still in possession, he would be guilty of larceny. *Held:* Error in instructions. Reversed. Defendant's requested instruction should have been given: "If the jury believe from the evidence that the defendant had no felonious intent to steal the property at the time he took it, then you must acquit, even if you believe he subsequently conceived the intent to appropriate it." *Id.* at 951.

4. In *State v. Coombs,* 55 Me. 477, 92 Am. Dec. 610 (1867), the defendant obtained possession of a horse, sleigh and robes from *O* by misrepresenting his ultimate destination. Defendant subsequently formed the intent to steal the property, and a conviction of larceny was affirmed, although there was no evidence of an intent to steal at the time possession was obtained. The court stated, 55 Me. at 481:

> In contemplation of law, the wrongful act was continuous, and, when to that act the prisoner subsequently added the felonious intent, that is, the purpose to deprive the owner of his property permanently, ... the larceny became complete from that moment.... In such case it is not necessary that the felonious intent should exist at the time of the original taking to constitute larceny, the wrongful taking being all the while continuous.

PEOPLE v. LAFKA

District Court of Appeal of California
344 P.2d 619 (1959)

BRAY, PRESIDING JUSTICE. Defendant appeals from a judgment of conviction after jury verdict, of two felonies, violations of section 487, Penal Code, (1) theft of a diamond ring valued in excess of $200, and (2) theft of money in excess of $200.

...

The complaining witness, Alice, met defendant in March, 1957, while both were working at a hotel. In July she started seeing him socially. After about two weeks defendant proposed marriage. The same night after saying that as they were going to get married and that everything that was his was hers, he asked her for money to go to Washington on a business deal. She gave him $300. A few days later at his request she gave him $500 more for the same trip. On August 12 she loaned him $900 in order for him to obtain a license for a bar and a lease at Bush Street and Grant Avenue. August 16, she loaned him $450 for fixtures and supplies. September 3, she loaned him $325 for a license from the Board of Equalization. September 10, she loaned him an additional $300 for the bar. These loans were to be repaid after the first of the year. When Alice informed defendant that was all the money she had, he began to admire her ring, which had cost her $290 in 1940. He told her that he could get some money for it. Defendant promised to return the ring in a week, saying that he intended to use the money from pawning it for the bar. Stating that it was necessary in order for him to be able to pawn the ring, he produced from his pocket a paper which he asked her to sign. It stated: "This is to inform anyone concerned that I have authorized J. Lafka to make a loan on this ring, and to use said monies for himself as he sees fit." Alice stated, "It isn't saying that you are using it for the bar." He again reassured her that it was for the bar, that he would return the ring in a week, and that he had to word the paper that way in order to pawn the ring. Alice then signed the note and gave him the ring. Alice took a trip to Portland and was met by defendant upon her return. Thereafter he no longer visited her or talked of marriage. She called him and inquired about the ring. Toward the end of October as defendant refused to keep his promise of returning the ring, she consulted the district attorney. Alice testified that she would not have loaned defendant the money if it was not to be used for the purposes defendant described. Defendant did not testify.

It is clear that defendant used the device of pretending that he was "negotiating" for a license and a lease to deprive Alice permanently and wholly of her property, and without any intention of using it for the purposes promised. He said he was "negotiating" with the Board of Equalization for a "liquor license." Such licenses are not issued by that board but by the Department of Alcoholic Beverage Control (Bus. & Prof. Code, § 23051). The department had no record of any application or "negotiations" of any sort by defendant. Moreover, the department's supervising agent testified that the department would not accept an application for a liquor license without a particular premise being specified. As to a lease, defendant called Paul Kwan who owned a store at Bush and Grant Avenue. He testified that defendant had expressed interest in renting the store for a bar but did not go so far as to discuss a lease. Kwan could not remember, however, the month in which defendant came to see him. The jury could very well have believed that it was in November or December, after Alice began to stir up trouble for defendant, that he saw Kwan in an attempt to supply proof of defendant's good faith.

Considering defendant's failure to testify, the fact that as soon as Alice's money was gone defendant's romantic interest in her also waned, the fact that defendant did not discuss a lease with Kwan, and all the other circumstances, there was sufficient evidence to amply demonstrate the defendant had no intention of using the money and ring for the purposes specified nor of repaying the money or returning the ring, and therefore extracted the money and ring by trick and device.

"Larceny amounting to grand theft can be committed by trick and device and usually results when the victim of a fraud intends not to pass complete title to his property, but that it shall be applied to a special purpose while the recipient intends to appropriate it to his own use."...

It is well settled that a loan of money induced by a fraudulent representation that it will be used for a specific purpose accompanied by an intend to steal amounts to larceny by trick and device....

The elements of theft by trick or device ((1) the taking (2) asportation (3) of the property of another (4) with a fraudulent intent) are satisfied here. Clearly there was a "taking" and "asportation."

As to the "taking," applicable here is the following language in *People v. Bartges*, ...

> Without again setting forth the evidence in detail, suffice it to say that it clearly shows that appellant with a preconceived design to appropriate the money to his own use, obtain [sic] possession of it by means of fraud and trickery. The fraud vitiated the transaction and the owner is deemed still to retain a constructive possession of the property. The owner does not part with title to the alleged thief where, as here, he delivered it to appellant to be applied by the latter to a particular purpose and the recipient, having obtained possession with the preconceived intention to appropriate the money to his own use, subsequently did convert it to his own use instead of applying it to the purpose contemplated by the owner. Under the facts here present there was in contemplation of the law of larceny a "taking."

Applicable to the "asportation" is the following from the same case: "Asportation is shown by evidence that when appellant obtained delivery of the money from Mr. Simmons he did not intend to devote it to the use for which it was given him but to convert it to his own use. Upon receipt of the money he intended to keep it as his own and the conversion was then complete." No title passed. "Since the money belonged to Mr. Simmons and appellant acquired possession of it by fraud and chicanery, his holding was without right, and title thereto did not pass to him...."

The judgment is affirmed.

NOTES

1. In *Carey v. State*, 313 A.2d 696 (Md. App. 1974), defendant was convicted of false pretenses in that he obtained possession of a rental car by tendering a check drawn on a closed account. On appeal, the conviction was reversed. "Nowhere does the testimony permit an inference that either the appellant or the owner of the goods intended a transfer of the 'property' in the automobile. Had appellant intended at the time of taking permanently to deprive ... [the owner] of the ownership of the vehicle, while [the owner] intended to part only with possession, the offense might have been larceny 'by trick' but not false pretenses." 313 A.2d at 697.

2. In *Allen v. State*, 153 N.E. 218 (Oh. App. 1926), defendant lawfully obtained possession of the owner's money as an agent for the owner, and subsequently obtained title to the money by fraudulent representations. In affirming a conviction for obtaining money by false pretenses, the court held that it was only necessary for the title to be obtained by false pretenses, and that the general rule which requires both possession and title to be obtained by false

pretenses applies only where delivery of possession is necessary to complete the transfer of title.

DUNLAVEY v. COMMONWEALTH

Supreme Court of Appeals of Virginia
35 S.E.2d 763 (1945)

GREGORY, JUSTICE.

Thomas Orval Dunlavey was convicted of larceny of an automobile, and he brings error.

... The evidence ... is as follows:

On Wednesday, November 22, 1944, the automobile designated and described in the indictment against the defendant was stolen by one Louis Hall, aided and abetted by one, Raymond White. Dunlavey, the defendant, had no connection whatsoever with the said larceny of said automobile on said date of November 22, 1944. Later, on Saturday, November 25, 1944, while said automobile was still in the custody of and under the control of the said Louis Hall, the defendant Dunlavey, pushed the stolen automobile with his, Dunlavey's automobile, in order to start the motor of the stolen automobile. This was done pursuant to a previous agreement between the defendant, Dunlavey, and Louis Hall made this date, three days subsequent to the larceny of the said automobile by Hall and White, that he, Dunlavey, would buy certain parts from said stolen automobile. Louis Hall testified that the defendant, Dunlavey, knew at the time he agreed to purchase the said parts that said automobile had been stolen by Hall and White. Dunlavey denied this statement by Hall. The evidence further showed that the stolen automobile was parked on Linden street, Richmond, Virginia, when Dunlavey pushed it with his automobile to get it started and that Hall, White and a fourth unidentified person drove the stolen automobile to a secluded section of Bryan Park, a distance of approximately three miles from Linden street, but still within the corporate limits of the city of Richmond; and that the defendant, Dunlavey, followed them in his own automobile to Bryan Park where the said four persons and two automobiles were later discovered by Poindexter, a park policeman.... When the defendant, Dunlavey, was apprehended, certain parts, which had been removed from the stolen automobile, were found in Dunlavey's automobile....

The position of the accused is that the automobile had been stolen and carried away from the possession of the rightful owner by others (Hall and White), three days before he knew anything about it. Thus he claims to have come into the picture three days after the larceny when he agreed to assist in moving the automobile and to purchase the parts to be taken from it. He therefore contends that his offense is that of receiving stolen goods of less value than $50.

The position of the Commonwealth is that aside and apart from the subsequent purchase and receipt of the parts of the stolen car, and wholly independent of those acts, the accused was guilty of an offense when, with the knowledge that the car had been stolen, he pushed it in an effort to help Hall get it off of a public street and to place it in a secluded spot where it might be safely

A. LARCENY

dismantled. The Commonwealth makes the further contention that where property is stolen, so long as the original thief has possession of it, his trespass against the possession of the true owner is deemed a continuous trespass, and when a later party intervenes to assist in making the asportation more effective, he is deemed to join in with and become a party to the continuous trespass, and therefore he himself becomes a trespasser upon the owner's legal possession.

The crime here consisted of moving the automobile by the accused in order to get it started and not in receiving the parts taken from it of the value of $15. When he moved the automobile the accused knew it had been stolen....

The part taken by the accused was one incident of a continuous transaction. He was in the possession of the automobile when he started it by pushing it, even though his possession might have been a joint one. His conduct amounted to a trespass upon the constructive possession of the true owner with *animus furandi*.

Larceny has been held to be a continuous offense. This seems to be the weight of authority in other jurisdictions. In *Devine v. State*, 132 Miss. 492, 96 So. 696, the contention was made that the larceny was complete when the thief removed the car from the place where it was parked and that if he thereafter rendered him any assistance in making away with the car he did not thereby become guilty of larceny but only an accessory after the fact. The court held that the contention was without merit for the reason that larceny is a continuous offense and is being committed every moment of the time during which the thief deprives the owner of the stolen property or its possession. The court approved the rule that the legal possession of goods stolen continues in the true owner, and every moment's continuation of the trespass and felony amounts in legal contemplation to a new caption and asportation. The court concluded that if the accused aided and assisted the thief in making away with the car, after knowing that it had been stolen, he was guilty of larceny.

...

In 32 Am. Jur., Larceny, § 49, page 948, the general rule is stated thus: "... In most jurisdictions one who assists in transporting or disposing of the stolen property, knowing it to have been stolen, may be held guilty of the larceny as a principal, even though he was not present at the taking and neither instigated the crime nor took part as a conspirator...."

In *Strouther v. Commonwealth*, 92 Va. 789, at page 791, ... it is held: "... It has been a settled principle of the common law, from an early day in England that where property is stolen in one county, and the thief has been found with the stolen property in his possession in another county, he may be tried in either. This practice prevailed notwithstanding the general rule that every prosecution for a criminal cause must be in the county where the crime was committed. The exception to the general rule grew out of a fiction of the law, that, where property has been feloniously taken, every act of removal or change of possession by the thief constituted a new taking and asportation; and as the right of possession, as well as the right of property, continues in the owner, every such act is a new violation of the owner's right of property and possession. There is no principle in respect to larceny better settled than this,

AGNEW v. STATE

Court of Criminal Appeals of Oklahoma
526 P.2d 1158 (1974)

[Defendant was convicted of obtaining property by false pretenses, and appealed.]

BLISS, PRESIDING JUDGE:

Briefly, the facts adduced at trial disclose that on Christmas Day, 1972, the defendant went to the Food Town Market in Tulsa to purchase some beer. He talked to the store manager and stated that he wished to purchase 48 cases. The store manager advised that they did not have that much beer on hand but that he could have what they had. A stock boy was then instructed to load what beer they had, 29 cases, in the defendant's pickup. The defendant then went to the checkout stand manned by Brenda Gail Minniear to pay for the beer. Ms. Minniear testified that when the defendant approached he stated that he had just bought 29 six-packs. She then calculated the purchase price to be $36.83 on a piece of scratch paper and the defendant paid the amount and left.

After the State rested the defendant inter alia demurred "to the evidence introduced by the State of Oklahoma in this case by and for the reason that ... the evidence presented in this case fails to establish the elements of the crime which they have attempted to allege in the information." His counsel did so on the theory that under the State's evidence the 29 cases of beer had already been placed in defendant's pickup before he had any conversation at all with Ms. Minniear and that possession of the beer could not possibly have been obtained by any alleged false representation or pretense made to her, and that no crime had been committed. The State contended its evidence was sufficient to sustain the charge in the Information, Obtaining Property by False Representation. Defendant's demurrer was overruled and the trial proceeded.

The defendant testified that on the day in question he went to Food Town Market to purchase some beer for resale in his wife's bar in Skiatook. The defendant purchased all the Coors beer on hand which amounted to 29 cases. The defendant testified that the beer was loaded on a dolly and placed in his pickup and after confirming that there were 29 cases he walked up to the checker and advised her that he had purchased 29 cases of beer at $1.27 a six-pack. The girl figured up the price on a small slip of paper and charged him approximately $146.00 which he paid in cash. The defendant's father, who accompanied him to Food Town Market, was then called and he testified to substantially the same facts as his son.

At the conclusion of all the evidence, the defendant renewed his demurrer to the evidence "for the reason it fails to state a cause of action as alleged and set forth in the Information." The record reflects the court's ruling, "I will overrule the renewed demurrer and the Motion for Directed Verdict of Acquittal."

A. LARCENY

This Court is of the opinion that the State's evidence, assuming it to be true as did the jury in returning its verdict of guilty, did not prove the crime charged in the Information but not for the reason contended by the defendant. It in fact proved the crime of Grand Larceny by Fraud, the personal property taken being the beer for which defendant did not pay in the amount of $110.47.

This Court held in *Welch v. State*, . . . as follows:

> The distinction between obtaining property by false pretense and larceny by fraud is very narrow. The distinction is: If the owner, in parting with the property by false pretenses, intends to vest accused with the title as well as the possession, the latter has committed the crime of obtaining the property by false pretenses, but if the intention of the owner is to vest accused with the mere possession of the property, and the latter, with the requisite intent, receives it and converts it to his own use, the crime is larceny by fraud.

The evidence does not reflect that Brenda Gail Minniear, the young lady at the checkout stand acting as an employee and agent of the owner, intended to sell and deliver possession of 29 cases of beer to the defendant. Under her testimony she was led to believe the defendant had 29 six-packs of beer, not cases, and she charged him accordingly and parted with ownership thereof; therefore, defendant did not acquire any beer by false representation, as charged in the Information.

On the other hand, 29 cases of beer were put on the dolly and placed in defendant's pickup with intent of the employees of the owner to part with possession only but not with ownership until defendant paid for the same at the checkout counter, which he did not do. He acquired the excess beer by converting it to his own use after receiving it and not paying for it. He committed the crime of Larceny by Fraud. There is a fatal variance between the allegations in the Information and proof.... [Reversed and remanded.]

NOTE

Thieves who carry property across two or more counties or judicial districts within a state can be tried in either or any of them. *See, e.g., Hodges v. Commonwealth,* 614 S.W.2d 702 (Ky. App. 1981). Under double jeopardy principles, however, one prosecution in which a defendant is placed in jeopardy exhausts the power of the state to proceed against a particular defendant. *Waller v. Florida,* 397 U.S. 387 (1970).

The same principle has been uncritically invoked when thieves carry stolen property across state lines. Statutes denominate that conduct larceny in each state into or through which a thief carries that property. *See, e.g., Newlon v. Bennett,* 112 N.W.2d 884 (Iowa), *appeal dismissed,* 369 U.S. 658 (1962); *Younie v. State,* 281 A.2d 446 (Me. 1971). Multiple prosecutions are possible under such circumstances because each state is considered a separate sovereign, and therefore its powers are not abated by a related prosecution in another jurisdiction. *Heath v. Alabama,* 474 U.S. 82 (1985).

This should be contrasted with an instance in which a defendant, pursuant to a single scheme or plan (in this instance, a *Ponzi* or pyramid investment scheme), defrauds different people in different counties. Defrauding each victim is an independent crime, so that multiple prosecutions can be maintained in as many counties as there are victims resident in them. *People v. Luongo*, 391 N.E.2d 1341, 1347 (N.Y. 1979). There should be no difference in analysis if victims are located in two or more states and multiple prosecutions ensue.

b. Asportation

STATE v. CARSWELL
Supreme Court of North Carolina
249 S.E.2d 427 (1978)

[Several rooms of a motel under construction had been entered forcibly during the night, and in one of them a window air conditioner had been pried away from the base on which it rested but had not been removed. The room was placed under surveillance, and the next night defendant and a companion were observed to walk onto the premises and into the room and to take the air conditioner from the window ledge and place it on the floor a few inches closer to the door of the room than it had been. The two then left and were apprehended in a truck in which the defendant had been seen at the motel during the day. The defendant claimed he and his companion had entered the motel room to lie down because they were tired and drunk and had no ride home, left it because the room smelled, and were then yelled at and arrested. The intermediate court of appeals reversed the defendant's larceny and statutory burglary conviction.]

COPELAND, JUSTICE.

Larceny has been defined as "a wrongful taking and carrying away of the personal property of another without his consent, ... with intent to deprive the owner of his property and to appropriate it to the taker's use fraudulently."... "A bare removal from the place in which he found the goods, though the thief does not quite make off with them, is a sufficient asportation, or carrying away." 4 W. BLACKSTONE, COMMENTARIES 231.

In *State v. Green*, 81 N.C. 560 (1879), the defendant unlocked his employer's safe and completely removed a drawer containing money. He was stopped before any of the money was taken from the drawer. This Court found these actions sufficient to constitute asportation of the money, and we upheld the larceny conviction.

The movement of the air conditioner in this case off its window base and four to six inches toward the door clearly is "a bare removal from the place in which the thief found [it]." The Court of Appeals apparently agreed; however, it correctly recognized that there is a taking element in larceny in addition to the asportation requirement.... The Court of Appeals stated that "here the problem with the State's case is that the evidence of asportation does not also constitute sufficient evidence of taking."...

This Court has defined "taking" in this context as the "severance of the goods from the possession of the owner."... Thus, the accused must not only move the goods, but he must also have them in his possession, or under his

A. LARCENY

control, even if only for an instant.... This defendant picked the air conditioner up from its stand and laid it on the floor. This act was sufficient to put the object briefly under the control of the defendant, severed from the owner's possession.

In rare and somewhat comical situations, it is possible to have an asportation of an object without taking it, or gaining possession of it.

> In a very famous case a rascal walking by a store lifted an overcoat from a dummy and endeavored to walk away with it. He soon discovered that the overcoat was secured by a chain and he did not succeed in breaking the chain. This was held not to be larceny because the rascal did not at any time have possession of the garment. He thought he did until he reached the end of the chain, but he was mistaken. R. Perkins, Criminal Law 222 (1957) (*discussing People v. Meyer,* 75 Cal. 383, 17 P. 431 (1888)).

The air conditioner in question was not permanently connected to the premises of Day's Inn Motel at the time of the crime. It had previously been pried up from its base; therefore, when defendant and his companion moved it, they had possession of it for that moment. Thus, there was sufficient evidence to take the larceny charge to the jury.

The defendant's and the Court of Appeals' reliance on *State v. Jones,* 65 N.C. 395 (1871), is misplaced. In that case, the defendant merely turned a large barrel of turpentine, that was standing on its head, over on its side. This Court held that shifting the position of an object without moving it from where it was found is insufficient asportation to support a larceny conviction. The facts of this case show that there was an actual removal of the air conditioner from its base in the window to a point on the floor four to six inches toward the door. Thus, *Jones* is not controlling.

For the reasons stated above, the decision of the Court of Appeals is reversed, and the larceny judgment reinstated.

NOTE

Review *People v. Dillon, supra* pp. 353-358 and *compare People v. Olivo, infra* pp. 428-433.

STATE v. LABORDE

Supreme Court of Louisiana
11 So. 2d 404 (1942)

HIGGINS, JUSTICE.

The accused was indicted, tried and convicted of the crime of cattle stealing.

... In the early part of 1939, the defendant, as the owner, sold a white-faced heifer or yearling, which was grazing on a free range, to Camille A. Bordelon, who took possession of the animal and placed it with his herd on the range; and that on or about June 15, 1939, he (the defendant) sold the same heifer, while on the range, to Sam Jeansonne, who, unaided and unaccompanied by the defendant, carried the animal away and subsequently disposed of it.

... Jeansonne, unassisted, unaided, and unaccompanied by the defendant, and out of the defendant's presence, went on the range and took possession of the heifer and exercised ownership thereof by disposing of it. Under these facts and circumstances, it is difficult to understand under what legal theory it can be said that Jeansonne, as a bona fide purchaser, in taking possession of the heifer and carrying it away, was acting as the agent of the seller. Both parties to the transaction contemplated that Jeansonne was acting for his own account and he did not in any way intend to act as the agent or representative of the defendant. He took possession of the animal and carried it away for his own benefit in his capacity as the purchaser and owner thereof.... The custody of the animal by the vendee certainly cannot be considered as the constructive possession of the vendor, because Jeansonne was at all times holding the animal in the capacity as purchaser for himself. Since the defendant at no time had the actual or constructive possession of the animal, the act of the purchaser in carrying it away for his own account cannot be said in legal contemplation to have been the act of the seller.... Of course, it was a fraud upon Jeansonne for the defendant to obtain his money by false pretense, but this certainly does not warrant the court in holding that Jeansonne was the innocent agent or representative of the defendant. Consequently, it cannot be said that there was any implied or constructive asportation of the heifer by the defendant.... [H]e cannot be convicted of the crime of larceny or theft, because the essential element of asportation is lacking.

This is in keeping with the well-established rules of the construction of criminal laws which are always strictly construed. The State of Texas, which is one of the greatest cattle raising states in the Union, solved this problem by passing an act of the Legislature dispensing with the element of carrying the property away or asportation and for this Court to declare that the bona fide purchaser is the innocent agent of the fraudulent seller in removing the property is equivalent to the court legislating, as Texas did, by dispensing with the element of asportation.

...

For the reasons assigned, the verdict of the jury and the sentence of the court are annulled and set aside and the accused is discharged.

NOTES

1. In the principal case the court discussed and distinguished the case of *Aldrich v. People* [79 N.E. 964 (Ill. 1907)], quoting (with emphasis by the Supreme Court of Louisiana):

> It will thus be seen that an asportation may be effected by means of innocent human agency as well as mechanical agency, or by the offender's own hands. One may effect an asportation of personal property so as to be guilty of larceny by attaching a gas pipe to the pipes of the company and thus draw the gas into his house and consuming it without its passing through the meter.... [Citations omitted.] From these cases the law appears to be well settled that, where, with the intent to steal, the wrongdoer employs or sets in motion any agency, either animate or inanimate, with the design of *effecting a transfer of the possession of the goods of another to him in order that he may feloniously convert and steal them,* the larceny will be complete, if, in pursuance of such agency, *the goods come*

into the hands of the thief and he feloniously converts them to his own use, and in such case a conviction may be had upon a common-law indictment charging a felonious taking and carrying away of such goods. If, in the case at bar, the plaintiff shifted the checks on the trunks, by means of which the servants of the transportation company were innocently led to further the criminal purpose *by delivering the trunk in question to the accused, who received and converted the same to his own use,* and if there was in the mind of the plaintiff in error a felonious intent *to steal this property pervading the entire scheme and attending every step of it, then he is guilty of larceny,* and the instruction under consideration, as applied to such a state of facts, is a correct statement of the law and there was no error in giving it to the jury.

11 So. 2d at 407.

2. In *Sanditen v. State,* 208 P. 1040 (Okla. Crim. App. 1921), the court held that asportation, as a constituent element of larceny, was sufficiently established by a showing that the defendant authorized an innocent purchaser to take absolute control of property which he purported to sell but which did not belong to him, and authorized the vendee to remove it from its location at a distant point, and that removal was accomplished by vendee pursuant to the arrangement. The court said:

> To us it seems that the accused himself need not have moved the article stolen. It is a sufficient asportation if he procured or directed its removal.... We are not unmindful of the fact that there are authorities that hold that the asportation must be by the thief himself or by some one confederating with him, but to us it seems that the best reason and the weight of authority support the doctrine that the asportation may be accomplished by an innocent agent of the accused.

See 144 A.L.R. 1384 (1943).

3. *Smith v. State,* 74 S.E. 1093 (Ga. App. 1912): "But where, in such cases, the purchaser does take the property so sold into his own possession, in good faith, believing that it is the property of the seller, the seller is guilty of larceny, since the purchaser takes as his innocent agent, and the act of the purchaser amounts to a taking by the seller." *See also Cummings v. Commonwealth,* 5 Ky. L. Rep. 200 (1883); *State v. Hunt,* 45 Iowa 673 (1877); *Crutcher v. State,* 246 S.W. 496 (Ark. 1923) and *State v. Patton,* 271 S.W.2d 560 (Mo. 1954). *See supra,* pp. 358-367, concerning the "harm" of larceny.

c. Lost or Mislaid Goods and Mistakenly Transferred Goods

BROOKS v. STATE
Supreme Court of Ohio
35 Ohio St. 46 (1879)

The plaintiff in error, George Brooks, at the February term, 1879, of the Court of Common Pleas of Trumbull county, was convicted of larceny in stealing $200 in bank bills, the property of Charles B. Newton. It appears from the evidence, that Newton resided at Newton Falls, in the county of Trumbull, and that, on the 24th of October, 1878, he came to the city of Warren in a buggy to attend to some business. He fastened his horse to a hitching post on Market street. On his way home, in the forenoon of the same day, he discovered that he had lost the package of bank bills in question.... Notice of the loss was published in the two newspapers printed in Warren, and in one printed in Leavittsburgh, which also had a circulation in Warren.

On Wednesday, the 20th of November following, the defendant, who resided in Warren, while working on Market street, near the post at which Newton hitched his horse, found the roll or package of bank bills. The package was found "five or six feet from the hitching post." He was, at the time, working in company with several other laborers. At the time he found the money one of these laborers was within ten feet and another within twenty feet of him, but he did not let any of them know that he had found the money. He states, in his testimony, that he put it in his pocket as soon as he found it. Just after finding the package, he picked up a one dollar bill, which he did show to them. This bill was wet and muddy, and he sold it to one of them for twenty-five cents, saying if none of them bought it he would keep it himself. He testifies the reason he sold it was that he did not want them to know at the time that he had found the other money. This bill was shown to several persons at the time, and was put on the hitching post to dry. Within a half hour after finding the money, at the time of stopping for dinner, he quit work, and, at his request, was paid off....

Evidence was also given that the defendant, with his wife, shortly afterward left Warren, and that he attempted to secrete himself before he left. The evidence did not show that the defendant saw any of the notices of the loss of the money published in the newspapers, or that he had any notice of the loss by Newton at the time it was found....

WHITE, J. ... The first instruction asked was properly refused. It was not necessary to the conviction of the accused that he should, at the time of taking possession of the property, have known, or have had reason to believe he knew, the *particular person* who owned it, or have had the means of identifying him *instanter*. The charge asked was liable to this construction, and there was no error in its refusal....

Larceny may be committed of property that is casually lost as well as of that which is not. The title to the property, and its constructive possession, still remains in the owner; and the finder, if he takes possession of it for his own use, and not for the benefit of the owner, would be guilty of trespass, unless the circumstances were such as to show that it had been abandoned by the owner.

The question is, under what circumstances does such property become the subject of larceny by the finder?

In *Baker v. The State,* 29 Ohio St. 184, the rule stated by Baron Park, in *Thurborn's Case,* was adopted. It was there laid down, that "when a person finds goods that have actually been lost, and takes possession with intent to appropriate them to his own use, really believing, at the time, or having good ground to believe, that the owner can be found, it is larceny."

It must not be understood from the rule, as thus stated, that the finder is bound to use diligence or to take pains in making search for the owner. His belief, or grounds of belief, in regard to finding the owner, is not to be determined by the degree of diligence that he might be able to use to accomplish that purpose, but by the circumstances apparent to him at the time of finding the property. If the property has not been abandoned by the owner, it is the subject of larceny by the finder, when, at the time he finds it, he has reasonable ground to believe, from the nature of the property, or the circumstances under which it is found, that if he does not conceal but deals honestly with it, the owner will appear or be ascertained. But before the finder can be guilty of larceny, the intent to steal the property must have existed at the time he took it into his possession....

Judgment affirmed.

STATE v. LANGFORD

Supreme Court of Louisiana
483 So. 2d 979 (1986)

CALOGERO, JUSTICE.

On March 19, 1984, defendant John A. Langford was convicted of theft in excess of $500.00 from the Hibernia National Bank of New Orleans. He was sentenced to eight years' imprisonment at hard labor. The Court of Appeal affirmed. We granted writs to consider whether there was adequate proof of a non-consensual taking and/or a permanent intent to deprive the bank of its funds.

FACTS

On March 11, 1981, defendant met with a vice president in charge of lending at Hibernia to discuss borrowing $225,000 to purchase a Metairie restaurant. Two days later the vice president personally informed defendant that the loan was refused, primarily because of defendant's poor credit record. Within a week, defendant returned to the same branch of the Hibernia to open an interest-bearing checking account, known as a NOW account (negotiable orders of withdrawal). A customer service representative supplied defendant the usual forms, including an application, signature card and deposit slip. Defendant exhibited a Louisiana driver's license, listed his place of employment as a company known as Furniture Distributors and deposited $5,362.21 to open the account. He neither inquired about nor requested overdraft privileges; nor was he told that he would be afforded any such privilege.

NOW checking accounts were an innovation for Hibernia. Prior to January, 1981, federal regulations did not permit banking institutions to pay interest on checking accounts. With the change in the regulations, Hibernia joined other area banks in offering interest-bearing checking accounts to their customers. To accomplish this, it was necessary for the bank to purchase, install and modify a computer program within a very short period of time. Hibernia chose to purchase a program which was being offered to the banking community. Since this program was designed to accommodate the needs of numerous banks, it contained some features which were not consistent with the Hibernia's needs. One of the features of the computer program chosen was the incorporation of various options which a particular account could be given concerning the treatment of checks when the account is in an overdraft status. As will be discussed in greater detail below, the computer could be instructed to pay all or none of the checks as to which there were insufficient funds to cover. It could be instructed to establish a credit line, up to a maximum of $4,000. Additionally, the computer might put a "hold" on a check to await authorization by an account officer.

To accommodate these and other services, the computer program came with a set of Out of Balance Processing Codes (OBPs), which instructed the computer on routing and check payment information. Of particular importance were codes "01," "03" and "05." Code "05" instructed the computer to honor a check (apparently within a certain dollar range), but also to charge the account a fee for processing an overdrawn check; code "03" instructed the computer to honor the check (within a certain dollar range), but carried the further instruction not to charge a fee to the account. Code "01" instructed the computer to honor the check, regardless of the amount, at no charge to the customer. In other words, an "01" code gave the customer unlimited overdraft privileges. The coding was an internal matter; individual customers would not be aware, by scrutiny of account numbers or statements, whether their accounts had been assigned to the "01," "03" or "05" codes.

As new checking accounts (both regular and NOW) were opened, relevant information including OBP Codes were input into the computer. The bank did not intend that NOW accounts should be given "01" coding or unlimited overdraft privileges, bank officials testified. Just the opposite occurred, however.

A former customer service representative at Hibernia's main branch testified that she placed checking account information into the computer during March of 1981. Unaware of the significance or meaning of the codes, and pursuant to instructions received from another employee, she used an "01" code on all new accounts. As a result, eighty-four main office checking accounts received the "01" OBP designation. The error was compounded when the bank's monitoring controls failed, notably the routing and handling of Daily and Monthly Overdraft Reports. An "01" coding indicated to the bookkeeping department that any overdraft had already been approved by an account officer. Meanwhile, the Overdraft Reports were not being delivered to the account officers but, instead, were being discarded. The officers, however, had not been told to expect the Reports and, in the absence of inquiries from bookkeeping, had no idea of the status of "01" accounts assigned to them.

Defendant began using his NOW account. After the initial deposit of $5,362.21 on March 18, 1981, defendant made no further deposits. Within two weeks, the account was overdrawn.

Defendant continued writing checks, however. He also began receiving overdraft notices from the bank. According to testimony of Hibernia officials, an overdraft notice is a computer-generated form sent one per check, "whenever there [is] activity that over[draws] the account...." Such a notice did not mean that an account had been reviewed by a bank employee. In defendant's case, these notices were sent daily. By the end of September, 1981 or within about 195 days, 198 such overdraft notices were sent to the defendant, each of them reflecting the amount of a given honored but NSF check, and a correspondingly increased negative, or overdraft, balance. Bank officials conceded the notices did not contain "specific wording ..." telling customers to come in and make a deposit but, as one witness put it, "[t]here are some things that are understood." In ever-increasing amounts over the six and one-half month period, defendant continued writing checks. The first of his overdraft notices showed a negative balance of $237.79; the 198th and last, $848,904.39.

Finally, on the afternoon of September 23, 1981, the bank received a call from a curious teller at Fidelity Homestead. Defendant was attempting to obtain a certificate of deposit with a large check drawn on his Hibernia NOW account. In a routine check of his account balance, officials learned that defendant was overdrawn by $848,904.39. An inquiry made on that date to Furniture Distributors, the company which defendant listed as his employer when he opened the NOW account in March, revealed that defendant was not then, September 23, 1981, employed by that company.

The following day defendant and his attorney met with bank officials. Hibernia's general counsel served written demand for immediate payment of the entire sum. Defendant, and his lawyer, countered with an offer to repay the balance over a five year period, at 8% interest, with interest payments monthly and principal payments annually. Hibernia declined defendant's offer and began civil proceedings in several parishes within the state in an attempt to recover the funds. Additionally, bank officials contacted the Economic Crime Unit of the Orleans Parish District Attorney's Office and assisted in the subsequent investigation. The defendant was thereafter charged with theft.

...

After a bench trial, the judge found the defendant guilty as charged of theft in excess of $500.00, and sentenced him to imprisonment for eight years with the Department of Corrections, with credit for time served.

...

As already noted defendant contends that there was insufficient evidence to prove that the taking was non-consensual. The state, of course, had the burden of proving that the taking of the money was without the consent of Hibernia. First of all, there was a taking. At the least that taking occurred after the NSF checks were honored and the money came into defendant's possession (if that was by virtue of a mistake rather than consent on the bank's part), when defendant diverted or used the funds, instead of returning them. With respect to the bank's non-consent the Court of Appeal found that "[t]he evidence absolutely precludes the possibility that the bank consented to defendant's conduct. The bank was a victim of it's own mistakes, one in the erroneous coding of the account when it was first opened, and the other in the destruction of the computer printouts before they could be reviewed by a responsible official. The bank's intention was to allow no overdrafts on NOW accounts but this was frustrated by its unfortunate errors. That the bank consented to the defendant's taking $848,000 as some sort of loan is not a reasonable hypothesis when its refusal to loan defendant $225,000 one week before the account was opened is considered." ...

With this assessment by the Court of Appeal we agree. The evidence overwhelmingly supports the fact that no human person with the bank ever made a conscious decision to honor defendant's checks notwithstanding the account's overdraft status. Equally supported, and bearing on the aspect of the taking, is the conclusion that the defendant had to have known a mistake was being made. "It is well settled that the recipient of the mistaken delivery who appropriates the property commits a trespass in the taking, and so is guilty of larceny, if, realizing the mistake at the moment he takes delivery, he then forms an intent to steal the property."...

Defendant's argument that the record also supports the opposite conclusion, *i.e.*, that the repeated honoring of the checks by the bank could be reasonably interpreted as consent to loan the money to the defendant, is not persuasive. In [earlier precedent], this Court held that "[w]hen a case involves circumstantial evidence, and the [fact finder] reasonably rejects the hypothesis of innocence presented by the defendant ..., that hypothesis fails, and the defendant is guilty unless there is another hypothesis which raises a reasonable doubt." The trial court acted reasonably in rejecting the defendant's hypothesis that the bank loaned him the money and therefore consented to the taking.

The facts established by the direct evidence and inferred from the circumstantial evidence were sufficient for a rational trier of fact to conclude beyond a reasonable doubt that defendant was guilty of the essential element of the crime of theft that the taking was non-consensual....

By his second assignment of error, defendant contends that the state failed to prove that he intended to deprive the bank permanently of its money. Intent, like any other fact may be proved by circumstantial evidence....

The most favorable aspect of this case from defendant's perspective, concerning proof of intent to permanently deprive, is the manner in which defendant came by the bank's money. Because his NSF checks in ever increasing amounts were routinely being honored, and were simply prompting increasing negative balance overdraft notices (albeit up to $848,000), any reasonable person would assume that sooner or later the mistake would be discovered and the bank would call for repayment. Distinguish this from the embezzler who distorts records to hide a theft, or the robber who wearing a mask takes and absconds with another's property. The probability of discovery has some bearing on whether the defendant likely intended to deprive the bank permanently of its funds. Unlike the robber or embezzler, above, the defendant had to realize that sooner or later the bank would discover their mistake and call upon defendant to return the money. Furthermore, the evidence which the prosecution chose to present at trial does not show any apparent effort on defendant's part to hide the greater part of the money.

On the other hand there was significant evidence that defendant intended to deprive the bank permanently of its money upon receipt, or at least some of it, for in addition to his not giving any of the money back, he spent at least $12,000 on items in the nature of support and disbursed $113,000 in large checks to various payees other than financial institutions. The greater part of the money, $724,000, comprised checks made payable to [Homestead branches] and *apparently* deposited into accounts, *possibly* in defendant's name, in the respective [branches]. The record does not show what happened to any of the money thereafter. When called upon to repay, defendant was unable, or unwilling, to do so. Rather on defendant's behalf the attorney offered defendant's promissory note.

One who takes another's property intending only to use it temporarily before restoring it unconditionally to its owner (*i.e.*, one who normally is found not to have an intent to steal) may nevertheless be guilty of larceny if he later changes his mind and decides not to return the property after all....

The facts established by the direct evidence and inferred from the circumstantial evidence was sufficient for a rational trier of fact to conclude beyond a reasonable doubt that defendant was guilty of the essential element of the crime of theft, that the defendant intended to deprive the bank permanently of more than $500....

NOTES

1. In *United States v. Rogers,* 289 F.2d 433 (4th Cir. 1961), the defendant in cashing a check received more money than he was entitled to, because of a teller's error. The district court instructed the jury that it might convict if it found that the initial receipt of the money by the defendant was innocent, and he thereafter formed the intention to convert the overpayment. *Held:* reversed. "[I]t appears to have become settled in England that, if the initial receipt of the chattel is innocent, its subsequent conversion cannot be larceny, but, if the recipient knows at the time he is receiving more than his due and intends to convert it to his own use, he is guilty of larceny.... That is the established rule of the American cases." *Id.* at 438.

2. In *People v. Dubrin,* 43 Cal. Rptr. 60 (Cal. Dist. Ct. App. 1965), an error was made with the result that defendant received a check from the bank for the net proceeds of an escrow account although he was entitled only to the difference between the net proceeds and the bank's prior lien on the property. The defendant testified that he knew he had received a windfall and made no attempt to return the overpayment until the bank filed suit. The conviction of grand theft was affirmed, the court stating that on these facts, defendant was guilty of embezzlement. "Where one, through mistake, receives money to which he is not entitled he becomes the trustee of that money for the benefit of the one justly entitled to it.... One who fraudulently appropriates property which has been entrusted to him is guilty of theft. (Pen. Code § 484)." 43 Cal. Rptr. at 63.

3. In *Calhoun v. State,* 2 So. 2d 802 (Miss. 1941), appellant discovered a diamond pin lying in the bottom of a laundry basket after the basket had been emptied of suits and clothes belonging to several customers of the laundry in which he was employed. It was the duty of appellant to search clothing for valuable articles, tag any article found with the name of the owner, and place the article in his employer's desk. On this occasion, however, there was no means available to determine the owner of the pin, and appellant put the pin aside for three weeks awaiting it to be claimed. He did not notify his employer, nor did he place the pin in the normal place where discovered articles were held until their owners claimed them. After a three week period, appellant attempted to pawn the diamond pin, but was apprehended and subsequently convicted of larceny. In reversing the conviction, the court stated that

appellant did not relinquish control of the pin to his employer, since he had not placed the pin in the customary place where lost articles were held. He thus committed no trespass against his employer, since the employer had not become a bailee for the benefit of the true owner. The court also held that there could be no larceny from the owner on these facts.

> It is the general rule, moreover, in view of the particular situation of lost property and consistent with the established principles as to rights therein, that a finder thereof may be guilty of larceny where, and only where, he appropriates the same to his own use with knowledge of, or the immediate means of ascertaining, the owner thereof and with felonious intent entertained at the time of the finding. Both elements are essential, and if either is lacking, the finder is not guilty of larceny. The requirement that at the time of finding, the finder's intent to steal must be accompanied by knowledge or notice as to the owner, has been said to constitute the only distinction between theft of lost goods and theft of other property.

2 So. 2d 804.

4. *Mislaid Goods.* "The fact that the property is mislaid and is not lost implies that means are at hand to know or learn who the owner is." *State v. Courtsol,* 94 A. 973, 975-76 (Conn. 1915).

5. Defendant purchased a trunk which he and the salesman supposed was empty. Some time later, defendant opened the trunk and discovered that it contained several articles of clothing, but kept the goods without notifying the store. In affirming the conviction for larceny of the clothing, the court stated that defendant obtained possession of the trunk only, and that the goods inside were essentially lost or mislaid goods.

> As we have seen, defendant did not know that the goods were in the trunk when the trunk was taken; consequently his taking of the goods at the time he took the trunk was, so far as they were concerned, an involuntary act. With regard to them at the time of taking, he did not and could not have entertained any intention at all. His intentions so far as they were concerned, could only be called into exercise and have had being when he found or discovered them in the trunk, and his criminality must attach at that time if at all.

Robinson v. State, 11 Tex. Crim. 403, 40 Am. Rep. 790 (1882). So held, also, in *Russell v. Smith,* [1957] 2 All E.R. 796, which summarizes the leading English cases prior to the Theft Act of 1968.

4. MENS REA

a. General Concept

MITCHELL v. TERRITORY
Supreme Court of Oklahoma
54 P. 782 (1898)

BURFORD, C.J. The plaintiffs in error, Willard P. Mitchell and Scott Mitchell, were convicted of the larceny of three mules, the property of William

A. LARCENY

Wyanco, and on February 20, 1897, sentenced to five years each in the territorial penitentiary at Lansing, Kan. On the trial of the cause, the prosecution proved that William Wyanco was the owner of three mules, of the value of $180, and that they were taken from his premises in the latter part of February, 1892, without his knowledge or permission, and that about three days afterwards the defendants were arrested in the night time, near the northeast portion of the city of Guthrie, with the three mules in their possession. On this proof the Territory rested. The defendants then each testified, and offered other testimony in their behalf in support of their defense. The defendants testified that their father and Wyanco, the owner of the mules, resided near Guthrie, on the same quarter section of land, for which they were adverse claimants and contestants; that the land had been divided so that each was to occupy certain portions, pending their controversy; that Wyanco was plowing upon, and attempting to cultivate, their father's portion of this land, and was using the mules in question to carry on said work; that, to prevent what they deemed Wyanco's trespassing, and to save their father from annoyance, they determined to take these mules, and conceal them temporarily from Wyanco, and within a short time return them to Wyanco's pasture; that they had no intention to deprive Wyanco of his property, or to permanently remove them from his possession, and were only carrying out a previously arranged plan to annoy Wyanco, and to save their father from having his portion of the disputed tract farmed by Wyanco; that they had arranged with other parties to keep the mules until they were ready to return them to Wyanco; that they took the mules out of Wyanco's pasture after night, and kept them three days in a ravine in the vicinity, and were transferring them to the person that was to care for them when they were arrested by the officers, on the night of February 28th.

Our statute defines larceny as follows: "Larceny is the taking of personal property accomplished by fraud or stealth, and with intent to deprive the owner thereof." (St. 1893, sec. 2371). To constitute larceny under this statute, it is not necessary that the taking should be with the purpose to convert the thing stolen to the pecuniary advantage or gain of the taker, but it is sufficient if the taking be fraudulent or by stealth, and with the intent to wholly deprive the owner of the property. The intent must be felonious, and must be to deprive the owner, not temporarily, but permanently, of the property, and need not be *lucri causa*. A taking of personal property with the intent to deprive the owner temporarily of his property, and return the same to him, is not larceny, but is trespass; is not felony, but a misdemeanor. The felonious intent is one of the material ingredients of the crime of larceny, and the burden is on the prosecution to prove this intent to the satisfaction of the jury beyond a reasonable doubt, the same as any other material constituent of the crime. The reason of the law is to secure a man's property to him, and that is to be carried out rather by punishing the thief for feloniously depriving him of it than for any wrongful gain he has made out of it. The wrong which the law directs its prohibition against and punishment to is the wrongful and felonious deprivation. (3 Rice, Ev. 448.) If the theory of the defense in the trial court was true, then the defendants were not guilty of a larceny, but only of a trespass, and the conviction was wrong. They admitted the wrongful taking of the property, but claimed it was taken with no intention to deprive the owner permanently of his property, but only temporarily; that they intended to keep it a short time, and return it to him. This was a proper and legitimate defense to the charge of larceny, and one that they had a right to have the jury pass upon. Any competent evidence which would tend to rebut any inference or presumption of felonious intent that might arise from the possession of the stolen property was proper to go to the jury. Of course, the jury are not bound to believe statements made by the defendants; but they are to weigh such facts, and, from all the circumstances connected with the case, determine whether such statements were made and purposes disclosed in good faith to carry out a plan or scheme not felonious in character, or whether it is part of a concocted plan or matured scheme to conceal and cover up a felonious purpose.

NOTES

1. In *State v. Cooper,* 575 A.2d 1074 (Del. 1990), the defendant was charged with larceny of livestock under a statute apparently overlooked in the list of repealed provisions approved at the time the state adopted a modern criminal code replacing the older categories of property offenses with a single crime of theft. The unrepealed statute provided that anyone who "feloniously steals, takes and carries away any cow, steer, bull, calf, heifer or swine is guilty of larceny and a felony ...." The trial court granted Cooper's motion to dismiss the information, essentially on the ground that it charged him with a felony based on conduct defined only as a misdemeanor under the new law; it rejected the prosecution's contention that the word "feloniously," as used in the context of the livestock statute, should be accorded its common law meaning, *i.e.,* proceeding from an evil heart or purpose with the deliberate intention of committing a crime. The intermediate appellate court affirmed.

The Delaware Supreme Court reversed:

> ... In analyzing the substance of the former statute, the Commentary [to the new Criminal Code] stated:
>
> The word "feloniously" in the statute had important meaning. It imported a specific felonious intent to steal the property, an essential element of the State's case. If the accused did not have the requisite intent, he was not guilty of larceny, no matter how unlawful his intent may otherwise have been (as, for example, where the taking was a trespass). The required felonious intent would appear to have two elements: First, "the intent must be wholly to deprive the owner of the property." An intent to deprive temporarily was insufficient. The second element of intent was the notion of "*lucri causa,*" borrowed from the ancient Roman law and never a part of the common law. The Delaware cases seem to say that a motive of gain or advantage to the taker was a prerequisite for conviction. A fairly wide definition of gain or advantage was, however, adopted. It was not limited to pecuniary gain. But where property was taken simply to deprive the owner of it, without any benefit to the taker (but, perhaps simply out of malice), there was no larceny....
>
> Section 841 [the replaced general larceny provision] defined the state of mind required for theft generally as an intention to deprive or appropri-

A. LARCENY

ate. Section 841 did not define the state of mind required for larceny of livestock. Therefore, there is no language describing the state of mind required to violate Section 859 [the larceny of livestock provision under which Cooper was charged], unless "feloniously" is accorded its definition at common law in Delaware. Thus, "the state of mind required by the law defining the offense," pursuant to Section 251(a) [the new Criminal Code theft provision], is set forth in Section 859 only if feloniously is accorded its common law meaning. Rather than creating an ambiguity, the General Assembly's use of the word "feloniously," given its common law meaning, provided Section 859 with an indispensable element of the crime of larceny of livestock....

In Delaware, feloniously has always only meant proceeding from an evil heart or purpose, with the deliberate intention of committing a crime. The General Assembly's use of the word feloniously in Section 859 is not reasonably susceptible to any other meaning. Therefore, the word feloniously did not create an ambiguity in Section 859.

2. In *State v. Saucier*, 485 So. 2d 584 (La. App. 1986), Saucer entered into a written agreement with McLoughlin to mate his male dog with her female dog; the promised payment was one puppy from the first litter. A veterinarian was unsuccessful at attempts to inseminate the female artificially. After it appeared evident that no puppies would be engendered, Saucier agreed to purchase McLoughlin's dog for an agreed sum. She neither paid nor returned McLoughlin's animal. McLoughlin charged Saucier with attempted theft of property, and a parish court judge found her guilty. The appellate court reversed and set aside the conviction and sentence:

> To commit the crime of attempted theft, the State is required to establish that the defendant had a specific intent to commit theft (which requires an intent to deprive the victim of his property permanently) coupled with an act for the purpose of and tending directly toward the theft....
>
> Cases interpreting the theft statute indicate that a defendant lacks the requisite intent when he makes an effort to pay the victim or to honor a promise made to him. In *State v. Hoffer*, 420 So. 2d 1090 (La. 1982), a defendant was charged with theft by fraud after he misrepresented himself as a bonded and licensed car dealer, signed bank drafts for fourteen cars at an auction, and subsequently paid only three of the drafts. At trial, defendant denied any intention not to pay for the fourteen vehicles when he obtained them at the time of auction. In reversing defendant's conviction, the Supreme Court noted that even though the defendant's eventual failure to pay eleven drafts may have been consistent with a preexisting intent not to pay at the time he signed the drafts, the evidence did not exclude beyond a reasonable doubt the possibility that he had intended to honor all of the drafts when he made them, especially where he had honored three of them after reselling three vehicles....
>
> Applying [such] holdings to the instant case, we conclude the State has failed to prove defendant's requisite criminal intent on August 2, 1982 as charged in the Bill of Information. Saucier's attempt to breed the dogs as

promised negates a specific criminal intent. When viewed in the light most favorable to the State, the evidence is insufficient to support a conviction for the offense as charged.

3. Intentionally creating substantial risk of permanent loss. In *United States v. Sheffield,* 161 F. Supp. 387 (D. Md. 1958), defendant was convicted of interstate transportation of a stolen automobile. The defendant had taken an automobile from New Jersey and driven it to Virginia, and was apprehended the next day in Maryland while driving north. Defendant maintained that he was en route to return the automobile, and that he intended to leave it about six blocks from where he had originally found it, and that this was his intention at the time he had appropriated the automobile. In denying a motion for a new trial, the court stated that, even if defendant's statement of his intention were to be believed, "there is properly a presumption, or at least sufficient evidence, for an inference of fact that [the automobile] is being taken to deprive the owner of the rights and benefits of his property; and the mere statement of a defendant who has so feloniously taken a motor car that he intended to abandon it somewhere in the same city (one of several thousand inhabitants) is not sufficient to destroy the inference unless well supported by collateral facts."

4. A trial court's instruction that "if [you find that the] defendant took the automobile with the intent to appropriate it to his own use and with intent to abandon later the automobile in such circumstances as would render its recovery by the owner difficult or unlikely, then you may find that the taking was with the intent to permanently deprive the owner of the property" was held to be correct in *State v. Langis,* 444 P.2d 959 (Or. 1968).

5. Defendant and two other boys took an automobile from a used car lot five days prior to defendant's date for reporting for induction into the Army. The defendant and his companions drove around the small town of Crystal Springs, and were stopped and given a citation for driving without a license. After being given the citation, they continued to drive around the town until the automobile was recognized by the sheriff. In the subsequent pursuit of the defendant, the automobile was wrecked. The court reversed a conviction of larceny, stating that "[T]he taking of property with the intention of using it temporarily and with no intention of depriving its owner permanently is not larceny." The fact that the defendant was shortly to report to the Army and that he and his companions confined their driving to the city limits indicated that the intent was merely to drive the automobile around the town on this New Year's Eve. *Slay v. State,* 241 So. 2d 362, 364 (Miss. 1970).

6. "The jury could infer — from the breaking into and entering of the building, the carrying away of the stereo equipment, the storing of the equipment in the abandoned house for several days, and the failure of the defendant to attempt to return the equipment — that when Becker entered the high school, he had the intent then and there to commit the crime of theft by permanently depriving the school of its equipment." *People v. Becker,* 531 P.2d 386, 388 (Colo. 1975).

7. After stealing property, defendant turned himself in to the owner and worked for the owner for some time to make restitution for the theft. Defendant subsequently pleaded guilty to the crime of larceny, and later sought to have his plea withdrawn. The motion to withdraw the plea was denied by the trial court. Held: conviction affirmed. Even though the owner had told the defendant that he would have the charge dropped, his failure to do so provided no basis for withdrawal of the plea. "Restitution does not wipe out the crime and does not deprive the State of its right to prosecute for the crime.... If [the owner] ratified or approved defendant's theft, this would not make defendant's conduct any less criminal." *State v. Odom*, 527 P.2d 802, 803 (N.M. 1974).

b. Claim of Right

STATE v. KELLY

Supreme Court of Appeals of West Virginia
338 S.E.2d 405 (1985)

PER CURIAM.

....

Robert Gross and Kelly were charged in a joint indictment with stealing ten oak mantels having a value of more than $200 from two houses located in Parkersburg in April, 1983. The defense admitted that Kelly arranged for the sale of the items, but contended that he had done so at the request of one James Bradley, who he believed owned the houses. As the evidence developed, a James D. Bradley was married to one of the property owners at the time the property was taken.

....

Our common law definition of the crime of larceny is stated [thus]: "To support a conviction for larceny at common law, it must be shown that the defendant took and carried away the personal property of another against his will and with the intent to permanently deprive him of the ownership thereof." ...

"The animus furandi, or the intent to take and deprive another of his property, is an essential element in the crimes of robbery and larceny." ... It is thus fundamental to the definition of larceny that the personal property must be taken without the consent of the owner, otherwise there is no criminal intent....

It is also widely recognized that one who takes property in good faith under fair color or claim of title, honestly believing he is the owner and has a right to take it, is not guilty of larceny, even though he is mistaken in such belief, since in such case the felonious intent is lacking....

This general rule has been held to apply to one who sells the property of another with the consent of an agent or a servant of the owner and to one who takes personal property with the honest belief that he has a right to do so under a contract....

A number of courts have considered cases in which the defendant took property with the consent and at the request of the owner's wife. The general rule is that the defendant is not guilty of larceny, if he believed at the time of the taking that he had a right to do so, at least where the defendant had not sustained an adulterous relationship with the owner's wife....

The intent to steal, being a state of mind, ordinarily must be proven circumstantially by inferences drawn from the defendant's conduct and the circumstances surrounding such conduct....

In this case, we believe the evidence when viewed in the light most favorable to the prosecution, ... does not establish beyond a reasonable doubt that the defendant acted with criminal intent because he believed that he had proper authority to remove the mantels. As we have outlined at some length, both Kelly and his codefendant testified that the oak mantels were sold on behalf of Bradley, who Kelly believed was an owner of the property. Bradley, however, for reasons not shown in the record, did not testify at trial despite the critical importance of his testimony. Bradley was the spouse of one of the owners at the time the mantels were removed from the houses. The sale was made to a local merchant, Maher, through another merchant, Casto, both of whom visited the premises. The taking was done openly and in broad daylight. It is of particular significance in our view that when Casto agreed to buy the mantels at his furniture store, Kelly indicated that he had to make a phone call to make certain that he could accept the money for the sale. This additional evidence came from two of the State's witnesses, Casto and Taylor. Furthermore, Taylor worked for Casto who ran a new and used furniture store and it was Taylor who assisted in removing the mantels. This testimony from the State's witnesses added substantial support to the defendant's claim that he acted in good faith.

Considering all the circumstances, we conclude the State did not present "'substantial evidence upon which a jury might justifiably find the defendant guilty beyond a reasonable doubt.'" ... Consequently, we cannot assent to his conviction.

5. Grading (Value)

STATE v. JACQUITH

Supreme Court of South Dakota
272 N.W.2d 90 (1978)

MORGAN, JUSTICE.

Appellant was convicted of grand larceny and fourth-degree burglary. He appeals only the grand larceny conviction on the grounds that the jury was not given proper instructions as to intent nor was it properly instructed with respect to the value of the stolen property. We reverse the conviction of grand larceny.

Appellant, Norman Jacquith, Jr., was arrested at the scene by members of the Vermillion Police Department on June 22, 1977, for breaking into a van and stealing a pair of prescription sunglasses. He was charged by a two-count information with burglary in the third degree and with grand larceny. Trial was held before a jury on August 1, 1977, and appellant was found guilty of grand larceny and fourth-degree burglary. Appellant now appeals the grand larceny conviction.

Appellant contends that the trial court erred in refusing to accept and give to the jury his proposed instruction which defines "value" as referring to fair

A. LARCENY

market value for the purpose of determining whether or not appellant committed grand larceny.

Appellant was found guilty by the jury of violating SDCL 22-37-1[1] and 22-37-2.[2] The former statute defines the crime of larceny and the latter statute differentiates between petit and grand larceny. It is well settled that when a statute delineates a specific dollar amount as the differentiation between petit and grand larceny, proof of the value of the item(s) stolen in excess of the statutory amount is an essential element of the crime of grand larceny.... Proof of value in excess of the requisite amount is as essential to the prosecution for grand larceny as in the proof of the elements of specific intent, fraud or stealth, and the actual taking of another's property, and the burden is fully upon the State to prove said value beyond a reasonable doubt....

It is also well settled that the determination of said value is strictly within the province of the jury.... As the North Carolina Supreme Court stated in *State v. Jones, supra,* 168 S.E.2d at 383:

> A plea of not guilty to an indictment charging the felony of larceny puts in issue every essential element of the crime and constitutes a denial of the charge that the value of the stolen property was more than [the requisite amount].

To aid the jury in determining value, the courts have offered various tests for the determination of value as used in statutes distinguishing between petit and grand larceny and other similar statutes involving theft of property. The most widely accepted test is the "fair market value" test. This test provides that the value to be proved is the fair market value at the time and place of the theft....

Appellant submitted, and the trial court rejected, a proposed jury instruction which stated in essence, the "fair market value" test. Appellant contends that the trial court's rejection of the proposed instruction was error. The State's proposed instruction on value, using the "replacement value" test as the proper test, was also rejected by the court. The State, on appeal, contends that there is "no market" for prescription sunglasses and thus a fair market value cannot be ascertained and a different test should be used. In looking to the case law of other jurisdictions that use the "fair market value" test, it is apparent that they do indeed, upon a showing that there is no market for a particular item of stolen property, allow another test to be used. However, the burden is upon the prosecution to affirmatively prove that there is "no market" for the item(s) as a prerequisite to allowing the use of any other test. The

---

[1] SDCL 22-37-1 provides:

Larceny is the taking of personal property accomplished by fraud or stealth and with intent to deprive another thereof.

[2] SDCL 22-37-2 provides:

Grand larceny is larceny committed in any of the following cases:
(1) When the property taken is of a value exceeding fifty dollars;
(2) When such property, although not a value exceeding fifty dollars, is taken from the person of another;
(3) When such property is livestock. Larceny in other cases is petit larceny.

prosecution in this case neither alleged nor submitted evidence that no market existed for used prescription sunglasses.

The jury's determination of whether or not the value of the sunglasses stolen exceeded $50.00 is crucial. The maximum sentence for grand larceny is ten years in the state penitentiary, while the maximum sentence for petit larceny is thirty days in the county jail. The former is a felony, the latter is a misdemeanor. It cannot be said that the determination of value in this case is of little consequence. Since the jury was given separate instructions on petit larceny and grand larceny, it is only reasonable that they be given some guidance in determining the distinction between the two crimes.

This court has not had previous occasion to decide which test shall be used for determining "value" in theft or larceny cases such as this, but we find the decisions of those courts that have adopted the "fair market value" test to be sound and well reasoned. Therefore, we adopt the "fair market value" test as herein stated for use in the courts of this state. Further, when it is contended that a stolen item has no fair market value because no market exists for that item, the burden shall be upon the prosecution to affirmatively prove that no market exists and that a different test should be used. If it is determined that no market exists from which a fair market value could be ascertained, then the jury may properly use the "replacement value less depreciation" test.... [4]

The evidence in the record pertaining to the value of the sunglasses is minimal. The glasses were prescription glasses which had been converted to sunglasses by the addition of colored coating after use in their original condition for about a year and a half. They had various pits or chips in the lenses from a burning torch. The owner of the sunglasses stated that his personal feeling was that they were worth $70.00 or $80.00 and an optometrist called by the state testified that the current replacement cost would be "in the neighborhood of $75.00," but the optometrist further testified that considering their condition it was questionable whether they would meet OSHA industrial safety standards. It is certainly conceivable that the jury would have concluded, under proper instruction, that the value of the sunglasses was below $50.00. Accordingly, we reverse the conviction and remand for new trial.

NOTES

1. As more items are included within the subject matter of theft the problem of valuation for purposes of determining the degree of the offense or for sentencing becomes both more important and more difficult. The problem is discussed in *United States v. DiGilio*, 538 F.2d 972 (3d Cir. 1976), which involved copying of government records and their subsequent sale to a third person. The relevant statute, 18 U.S.C. § 641 (1988), defines "value" as "face, par, or market value, or cost price, either wholesale or retail, whichever is greater."Obviously the stolen records had no 'face' or 'par' value. No evidence was introduced as to their 'cost price'. Thus we are concerned with market

---

[4] In *Shaffer, supra*, we state this test as "original cost or replacement cost adjusted by a percentage for depreciation varying with the age and condition of the property." (249 N.W.2d at 258). Although that case presents a different fact situation, we consider its statement of this test to be accurate.

value. As a general rule, that value will be determined by market forces — the price at which the minds of a willing buyer and a willing seller meet.... If no commercial market for particular contraband exists, value may be established by reference to a thieves' market." *Id.* at 979.

Proof that a thieves' market exists is not enough. There must be proof regarding the "exchange price in the thieves' market generally." *Id.*

In this case numerous documents were taken over a period of time and sold in groupings. "Aggregation" was not allowed because the thefts occurred in "installments." The court also declared that where value is important in determining whether an offense is a felony or misdemeanor, or for sentencing, the government must offer some proof as to value. A court may not take judicial notice, nor may a jury speculate as to value based on the appearance of the articles in question.

2. In *United States v. Alberico,* 604 F.2d 1315 (10th Cir. 1979), an army officer had stolen government checks for which an FBI storefront "scam" operation offered him $7,300. The face value of the checks came to about $74,000, but none had been endorsed. Alberico eventually accepted $7,000 for them. On appeal against his conviction for violating 18 U.S.C. § 641 (1976), he argued that the checks had no value except in a thieves' market, and that the government had not otherwise proven under § 641 "value," which "means face, par, or market value, or cost price, either wholesale or retail, whichever is greater." At trial, the FBI agent in charge of the storefront scam operation testified he had no idea what value the checks might have had in a true underworld exchange. The court of appeals affirmed the conviction. "It is clear in this case that the checks were valuable to the Rocky Mountain Arsenal at the time they were stolen. Indeed, the face value of the checks defined their worth to the arsenal. The checks were 'things of value' for purposes of § 641. Their face value was sufficient to engage the more severe sanctions" under the statutory provisions augmenting punishment based on value of the stolen property. *Id.* at 1322.

3. In *People v. Elkhatib,* 599 P.2d 897 (Colo. 1979), defendant solicited a truck driver for Associated Grocers to steal his employer's goods and sell them to defendant for half their value. The driver informed authorities, and on instructions from his employer turned over the goods to defendant and then gave his employer the amounts received from defendant. One delivery was for goods worth less than $50, but two others involved more than $200 each. The trial court reduced two felony counts based on the latter transactions to misdemeanor theft because it thought the stolen property was worth less than $200, the critical amount under the statute. In an advisory opinion issued at the request of the prosecution, the Colorado Supreme Court agreed with the prosecution that the trial court's valuation ruling was wrong. "Except for the driver's loyalty, Associated Grocers would have had a 100% loss, as was the intent of the defendant." *Id.* at 897. There was no justification in reducing the value of the property to reflect the amount paid to the driver as a believed co-conspirator and returned by him to Associated Grocers. Hence, the market value of $330 and $218 controlled and the larceny was charged properly under the felony statute governing theft of goods worth between $200 and $10,000.

4. Review *Rex v. Turvey, supra* pp. 362-363, and *People v. Hanselman, supra* pp. 363-364 on the issue of consent.

B. EMBEZZLEMENT

1. *ACTUS REUS*

PEOPLE v. YANNETT
New York Court of Appeals
401 N.E.2d 410 (1980)

GABRIELLI, JUDGE.

Defendant appeals from an order of the Appellate Division which affirmed a judgment of Broome County Court convicting him of the crime of larceny in the second degree. The conviction is premised upon the claim that defendant embezzled certain funds that were in his possession but were actually owned by certain residents of a nursing home owned and operated by defendant. The dispositive question on this appeal is whether the funds which defendant was convicted of embezzling were held by him on behalf of the residents, or whether those moneys were in fact owned by defendant. For the reasons discussed below, we conclude that defendant was the actual owner of the money in question, although he was otherwise indebted to the residents. Since the mere failure to pay one's debts cannot sustain a conviction for larceny by embezzlement, defendant's conviction must be set aside and the indictment dismissed.

Defendant is the owner-operator of the Endicott Nursing Home. As is true of most such facilities, defendant's nursing home is funded mainly in three ways: payments made by private residents, their families, or some other non-governmental source; payments from local agencies made pursuant to the State Medicaid program on behalf of needy residents; and payments made by Medicare, the Federal health insurance program, for the care of eligible residents. As a condition to participating in the Medicare program, a nursing home is required to obtain certification from the Federal Government and to enter into a Medicare provider agreement in which it agrees that it will charge those persons eligible for Medicare no more than a set rate established by the Medicare program for that particular home. The home is free, however, to charge private residents a higher rate. Furthermore, Medicare provides the full amount of the Medicare rate for the first 20 days of an eligible person's stay at the home, while for the next 80 days, Medicare pays that rate less a coinsurance charge which the eligible resident is required to pay himself. During that full 100-day period, however, the maximum which a home can charge an eligible resident is limited by the provider agreement to the Medicare rate.

As noted above, when a nursing home applies for participation in the Medicare program, it must first be certified and is then required to enter into a Medicare provider agreement. Moreover, before benefits are paid for a particular resident, that person's eligibility must first be determined by Medicare. All this, of course, may and usually does take considerable time, and in the meanwhile the nursing home needs revenue to operate. The home's solution in such a situation is to require even those residents who seem eligible for Medicare to pay their own way pending approval by Medicare. During this period the home may, and defendant did, charge the higher, private resident rates, rather than the lower Medicare rate. However, the provider agreement requires the home, upon being notified that a particular person is eligible for Medicare, to refund to that resident the entire amount which the resident had previously paid the home during the period in which he was actually eligible but had not yet been approved, including the difference between the Medicare rate and the higher private resident rate, less the coinsurance charge when applicable. If the payments have been made by someone other than the resident, the refunds are to be made to that person. If the resident has died in the interim, the payments are to be made to the patient's estate, pursuant to State law. If for some reason the refund cannot be made within 60 days after the nursing home is notified that a particular resident is eligible for Medicare, then the nursing home is required to set aside an amount equal to the refund in a separate account until payment can be made to the proper party. After the nursing home refunds the proper amount to the appropriate person or places it in a separate account if a refund cannot be timely made, then the local Medicare representative (in this State, Blue Cross) reimburses the home at the Medicare rate. It is important to note that under this plan, no payments are required to be made by Medicare to the nursing home until after the nursing home refunds the proper amount to the resident or sets up a separate account when mandated.

In the instant case, the jury by its verdict necessarily found that instead of making full refunds to certain residents as was required by the Medicare agreement, defendant made only partial and in some cases no refunds. During the period prior to Medicare approval of those residents, defendant charged them at the higher private resident rate, as he was apparently allowed to do under the provider agreement. When he was notified that those persons were eligible for Medicare, he was then required by the agreement to refund to them the full amount of the payments they had made to him, less the coinsurance fee for periods after the initial 20 days. Instead, defendant refunded at most only the amount of the reimbursement payments Medicare was obliged to make to him for those persons, and retained the difference between the higher private resident rate and the Medicare approved rate. This was a clear violation of the provider agreement, which mandated full refunds. Unfortunately, despite defendant's failure to refund the full amount due the residents, Medicare, through its agent Blue Cross, forwarded the Medicare payments to defendant although he was not entitled to any money under the agreement until he made full refunds to the residents. Defendant now stands convicted of larceny in the second degree on the theory that he embezzled funds owned by the residents to whom he did not give full refunds (see Penal Law, § 155.05, subd. 2, par. [a]; § 155.35). The Appellate Division affirmed the judgment of conviction, and defendant now appeals to this court. There must be a reversal, since the funds defendant was convicted of embezzling simply were not the property of the residents.

A distinction must be drawn between the refusal to pay a valid debt and the crime of larceny by embezzlement. . . . The essence of the crime of larceny by embezzlement is the conversion by the embezzler of property belonging to another which has been entrusted to the embezzler to hold on behalf of the owner (see Penal Law, § 155.05, subds. 1-2 ...). In the instant case, the money which defendant has been convicted of stealing never belonged to the residents of his nursing home, nor was it entrusted to defendant to hold on behalf of the residents. Although the residents had a contractual right to receive refunds from defendant equal to the full amount they had previously paid him, minus any coinsurance fees, the money from which defendant was required to make those payments belonged to defendant rather than to the residents. Hence, the failure to pay the full refunds did not constitute larceny by embezzlement.

When the residents initially paid the private resident rate to defendant, that money became the defendant's money. It was not given to him in trust, and he was free to use it for any purpose he wished, although he was of course contractually obliged to provide the services which comprised the promised consideration for payment of the fees. The fact that defendant had also assumed an obligation to provide a refund should the residents subsequently be approved for Medicare benefits does not in any way modify the legal conclusion that those funds were the property of defendant and defendant alone.

Nor was defendant divested of his ownership interest in that money when he was notified that the residents had been approved for Medicare benefits. At that point, the provider agreement required defendant to make certain payments to the residents. Those payments, however, were to be made from defendant's own money, not from any property of the residents which was in the possession of defendant. Thus, although the failure to make those payments constituted a breach of the contract, it was not a withholding of moneys owned by the residents, even under the broad definition of "owner" contained in the Penal Law (Penal Law, § 155.00, subd. 5 ...).

Finally, the fact that Medicare funds were actually paid to defendant does not make his failure to provide full refunds to the residents a theft of property owned by the residents, since the Medicare funds were not the property of the residents, but rather the property of defendant. The funds given defendant by Blue Cross on behalf of Medicare were not intended to serve as the source of the refunds due the residents of the home. Rather, the money from Blue Cross was intended to reimburse defendant for the money which he supposedly had previously refunded to the residents from his own funds. In fact, the money paid to defendant by Blue Cross was less than the amount he was obligated to refund to the residents, since he was required to refund the higher private resident rates, minus any coinsurance charge, while Blue Cross reimbursed him only at the Medicare rate. Indeed, the defendant actually did refund the Medicare rate to several of the residents whose funds he now stands convicted of embezzling. Although defendant could perhaps be said to be subject to criminal prosecution for the theft of Medicare funds from Blue Cross upon a showing that he engaged in practices which constitute larceny by false pretenses ..., the present prosecution is for the theft of funds belonging to the residents of the home and not for the theft of funds belonging to Medicare or to Blue Cross. Defendant's receipt of Medicare funds from Blue Cross adds nothing to the claim that he stole funds belonging to the residents of his nursing home.

We note that the result would be different had either the initial payments made by the residents or the funds subsequently paid by Blue Cross been turned over to defendant to hold in trust for the residents or as an agent or bailee for the residents. Were that the case, defendant's withholding of that money from the residents would constitute larceny by embezzlement.... Here, however, no funds belonging to the residents were ever entrusted to defendant. As is noted above, the fees initially paid to defendant by the residents were not to be held in trust for the residents, but rather became the property of the defendant, to be used for his own purposes. Similarly, the funds paid by Blue Cross on behalf of Medicare were not to be held in trust for the residents, but were instead intended to reimburse defendant for the refunds he was previously required to have made to the residents. Although a constructive trust might possibly be imposed upon those funds pursuant to equitable principles applicable in a civil action because of defendant's failure to have made those prior refunds in full, no actual trust was created by the terms of the provider agreement. It has long been true in this State that the "misuse" of funds upon which a constructive trust could be imposed does not comprise the crime of larceny by embezzlement.... This is so because the possible "beneficiaries" of a potential constructive trust simply do not have the requisite pre-existing interest, superior to that of the legal owner of those funds, which is necessary to support a larceny conviction of that legal owner. We see no justification for modifying this rule. It was within the power of the parties to the provider agreement to have created a trust by their agreement, and had they done so defendant might well have been subject to prosecution for the wrongful withholding of trust funds. The parties failed to create such a trust, however, and thus the residents cannot be deemed the owners of any moneys in the hands of the defendant. Accordingly, defendant's conviction for larceny cannot stand.

The People suggest that in fact the provider agreement did create a trust which defendant has breached. This contention is founded upon those provisions of that agreement which require the nursing home, if it is unable to refund the money to the proper person within 60 days, to set aside a special fund containing the full amount of the refund until the proper recipient of the refund may be determined. Those provisions, however, are inapplicable to this case, since the duty to segregate funds pursuant to the agreement arises only if and when the nursing home is unable to locate the proper recipient of the refunds. Where, as here, there is no failure to pay because of some difficulty in locating the proper recipients, but rather a refusal to pay refunds to presumably identifiable residents or their families or estates, that obligation does not arise. The agreement is quite clear that the primary and first obligation of the nursing home is to actually pay the refunds to the proper party. Where that proper party is identifiable, not only is the nursing home under no duty to create a special fund, but such an action would itself be a violation of the agreement since the nursing home is justified in doing so only if the proper recipient of the refund cannot be located. Indeed, there exists some inconsistency between the asserted basis for criminal liability in this case, the withholding of funds from the proper recipients, and the suggestion that defendant was somehow obligated to set aside those funds. The obligation to segregate arises only if the proper recipient cannot be found; if such were the case, the defendant obviously could not be held liable for failing to make payment to that proper recipient, since the failure to do an impossible act generally may not form the basis for criminal liability.

In short, our examination of the provider agreement persuades us that it did not create a trust in the circumstances of this case. Hence, since the funds defendant was accused of embezzling were not owned by the residents, he may not be convicted of larceny pursuant to the theory asserted by the People. In light of this conclusion, we are not required to and do not reach the other issues presented by defendant on this appeal.

Accordingly, the order appealed from should be reversed and the indictment should be dismissed.

STATE v. STAHL

New Mexico Court of Appeal
596 P.2d 275 (1979)

Wood, Chief Judge.

Defendant was convicted of embezzling over $100. To have embezzled the money, defendant must have been entrusted with the money. Section 30-16-8, N.M.S.A. 1978. Defendant contends there is no evidence that he was entrusted with over $100. We agree.

Defendant was a clerk at a store. The store had two cash registers and a drop-box. There was a slit in the counter; money pushed through this slit went into the drop-box. The drop-box was locked with two padlocks, the keys to which were retained by the manager. When money accumulated in the registers, portions of the accumulation were placed in the drop-box through the slit in the counter.

About 7:30 p. m. on the night in question, the manager removed the money from the drop-box. About 11:00 p. m. the clerk on duty closed down one of the registers, placing the money from that register into the drop-box. When defendant went on duty at midnight, the one register being used contained $50 to $75. Defendant's shift was from midnight to 8:00 a.m. At 3:00 a.m., defendant was absent from the store. The drop-box had been pried open and its money removed. There is evidence that defendant took a total of $612 from the drop-box and the register being used.

Defendant was the only clerk on duty when the money was taken; he was "in charge of the whole store" and "responsible for the entire store." The register being used, and its contents, were for defendant's use in performing his duties. Defendant does not claim that he was not entrusted with the money in this register and does not contend that the money he took from this register was not embezzlement. However, there is no proof that the money taken from the register was over $100, and no proof that the amount of money in the register, plus money from sales after defendant went on duty, ever amounted to $100.

The State asserts that defendant was also entrusted with money which defendant took from the register and placed in the drop-box. We need not answer this contention because there is no evidence that defendant placed any money into the drop-box.

To reach a monetary amount over $100, the money taken from the drop-box must be included. Under the evidence, the money in the drop-box was put there by another clerk, and before defendant was on duty. Defendant did not have the keys to the drop-box, he had no permission or authority to get any money out of the box, he had no permission to have possession of the money in the drop-box, or "use it for change or anything...." The only one supposed to take money from the drop-box was the manager. These facts are not disputed.

The trial court denied defendant's motion for a directed verdict on the charge of embezzlement over $100. Because defendant was in charge of the store, the trial court was of the view that defendant had been entrusted with "everything there on the premises" including the drop-box. We disagree; defendant had not been entrusted with the contents of the drop-box.

"Entrust" means to commit or surrender to another with a certain confidence regarding his care, use or disposal of that which has been committed or surrendered.... The money in the drop-box would not have been entrusted to defendant unless the money came into defendant's possession by reason of his employment....

2 Wharton's Criminal Law and Procedure, § 468 (1957) states:

> A clerk taking money or goods from his employer's safe, till or shelves is guilty of larceny unless he is authorized to dispose of such money or goods at his discretion. An employee who feloniously appropriates to his own use property of his master or employer to which he has access only by reason of a mere physical propinquity as an incident of the employment, and not by reason of any charge, care, or oversight of the property entrusted to him, may be guilty of larceny by such act the same as any stranger.

See also Wharton's Criminal Law and Procedure, *supra*, §§ 513, 524 and 525. In *State v. Peke, supra,* the defendant's employment duties involved checks, the proceeds of which defendant converted. In *State v. Konviser, supra,* the defendant was the manager of the property which he converted.

Although defendant was in charge of the entire store, the undisputed facts show that the money in the drop-box was not committed or surrendered to defendant's care, use or disposal; that money was to be handled exclusively by the manager. Defendant was excluded from having anything to do with that money. Defendant's offense, as to the money in the drop-box, was larceny, not embezzlement, because he had not been entrusted with that money....

STATE v. TAYLOR

Supreme Court of Utah
378 P.2d 352 (1963)

CROCKETT, JUSTICE.

Defendant appeals from a conviction after trial to the court upon the charge that he: on or about the 31st day of October, 1961, committed a felony, to-wit: embezzled money of a value exceeding $50.00 from Utah By-Products Company.

Defendant drove a truck for that company picking up scrap fat, meat and bones from butcher shops and cafes on a daily route. He would give each customer a slip showing the poundage of the items picked up and turn in a copy to the company, which would issue checks to the customers in payment. There was one exception to this procedure. Hill Field Air Force Base required payment in cash rather than by check. So the company would issue a check for the value of scraps, payable to the defendant, who would cash the check and make the required payment.

On October 31, 1961, the defendant made out a slip showing a pickup at Hill Field of bones and scraps totaling $84.25. It is undisputed that he delivered these items to the company, for which he received a check for that amount payable to himself. The difficulty exists because those particular scraps did not come from, and the proceeds of the check were not paid to, the Hill Field account. Inquiry brought forth a confession by the defendant that he had, by issuing shorted weight slips to other customers, accumulated that amount of scrap and turned it in to obtain the money for himself.

. . . .

In a criminal proceeding it is not sufficient to show merely that the accused has been dishonest, or that he is a cheater, or otherwise of bad character. He is entitled to be charged with a specific crime so that he may know the "nature and cause of the accusation against him." And the State must prove substantially as charged the offense it relies upon for conviction.

The judgment must stand or fall upon the proof, or lack thereof, of the crime with which the State charged the defendant, essayed to prove, and of which he stands convicted: i.e., that of embezzling $84.25 from the Utah By-Products Company by taking a check for that sum from the company the proceeds of which he was expected to deliver to Hill Field, and failing to do so. It is important to keep in mind that in that transaction the company received the exact items and poundage of scraps its money was intended to pay for; and that Hill Field had no such money coming. It is thus plain that neither lost anything in the transaction so the crime as charged and relied upon for conviction was not proved.

Another significant aspect of this situation is that defendant's only deception or fraud upon the company was in misrepresenting the source from which he obtained the scraps. Fundamental in the nature of embezzlement is the coming into possession of property honestly, "by virtue of one's trust," and then converting it to one's own use in violation of that trust. This is in contrast to situations where, as here, the essential wrong is committed in obtaining possession of the property. Where the intent to take the property of another is formed before the taking, and is coupled with some deception or trick to acquire possession of the property, the crime is not embezzlement. One could not embezzle that which he had already stolen. Since the State did not prove the charge upon which the conviction is grounded, it is reversed.

HENRIOD, CHIEF JUSTICE (Concurring in the result).

A reading of the record shows a highly speculative and loose agency relationship as to purchases for, delivery of products collected from vendors of the bones, and payment therefor. One is impressed with the fact that in carrying out the modus operandi, the defendant's employer primarily was interested in obtaining the animal products from any source at an established price. In doing so, it appears that defendant had wide latitude and freedom in gathering up and delivering the scraps, and that the method of payment was of interest only to the vendors and not the employer. The fact that defendant obtained the scraps from third parties by means of a short-weight theft device unbeknownst to his employer, may have constituted a series of thefts from others, but would not tighten up the above mentioned looseness of the fiduciary relationship, so as to establish, beyond a reasonable doubt, a violation of the trust where any duty as to pickup, payment and delivery to his employer was left almost entirely to the discretion of the employee.

....

I cannot subscribe to the inference in the main opinion, if there is one, that no offense is committed by an employee, if the employer receives a quid pro quo. Such conclusion would exonerate the bank teller who "borrowed" money from the bank, without authority, but who later returned it.

NOTES

1. *State v. Smith*, 98 P.2d 647, 648 (Wash. 1939):

> In embezzlement, the property comes lawfully into possession of the taker and is fraudulently or unlawfully appropriated by him; in larceny, there is a trespass in the unlawful taking of the property. Embezzlement contains no ingredients of trespass, which is essential to constitute the offense of larceny. Moreover, embezzlement does not imply a criminal intent at the time of the original receipt of the property, whereas in larceny the criminal intent must exist at the time of the taking.

2. In *Partain v. State*, 199 S.E.2d 549 (Ga. App. 1973), defendant's conviction of theft by conversion was reversed upon facts which showed that defendant, as a building inspector for the city, had extorted a bribe from a contractor in lieu of the usual inspection fee. Since the defendant had not come into lawful possession of city funds, his subsequent conversion of those funds did not constitute embezzlement.

3. The possession of the defendant may be constructive. In *State v. Lamb*, 310 A.2d 102 (N.J. Super. 1973), defendant was employed as a receiving clerk. His duties involved checking the quantity of bread delivered by his friend and roommate, and signing delivery slips which were later tendered by the bread manufacturer to defendant's employer for payment. Over a period of time, by signing slips for more bread than was actually delivered, defendant enabled his friend to sell the excess and pocket the proceeds. At no time did defendant have actual possession of the bread, nor did he receive any part of the proceeds of the sales. *Held:* conviction of embezzlement affirmed. "Delivery took place here when defendant signed the slips, thus evidencing receipt. Even though

the goods may still have been on the truck at the time, defendant, nevertheless, was able to exercise sufficient measure of control over them so as to be in constructive, if not actual, possession of the goods on behalf of his employer." 310 A.2d at 105.

4. The failure to pay money due a creditor on an obligation, or the appropriation of money to his own use will not subject the debtor to prosecution for embezzlement. In *Kelley v. People,* 402 P.2d 934 (Colo. 1965), defendant's conviction of embezzlement was reversed on facts which showed that, as an operator and owner of a service station, he received gasoline from a company in return for undertaking an obligation to later pay for the amount of gasoline delivered. The court held that there was no agency relation here, where the defendant was obligated to receive and hold money for the gasoline company. Nor was the money the property of the company when it was received and appropriated by the defendant.

5. "Our statutes expressly provide that 'If any clerk or servant of any private person or co-partnership or corporation ... fraudulently appropriates to his own use, or secretes with a fraudulent intent to appropriate to his own use, any property of any other person which has come into his control or care by virtue of his employment as such clerk or servant, he is guilty of embezzlement.'" 21 O.S. 1971, § 1456. Under such a statute, "'It is immaterial whether the property be intrusted to the accused by the owner of the property, or by some other person for such owner.'" *Byrum v. State,* 507 P.2d 1293, 1296 (Okla. Crim. App. 1973).

6. In *United States v. Powell,* 413 F.2d 1037 (4th Cir. 1969), appellant was employed as a postal clerk, and over a period of several months signed receipts for stamps and envelopes having a value in excess of $6,500. After an audit of appellant's accounts, a shortage of $1,393.56 was revealed. The evidence disclosed that no one but the appellant had access to the stock, which was kept in a locked drawer to which only he had the key. *Held:* conviction of embezzlement affirmed. "Where, as here, the defendant alone has access to the property, a substantial shortage is disclosed, and no explanation of the shortage is tendered by the accused, the trier of fact may reasonably infer from the circumstances that the custodian of the property has embezzled the missing funds." *Id.* at 1038.

7. *Lake v. State,* 379 So. 2d 339, 345 (Ala. Crim. App. 1979), *cert. denied,* 397 So. 2d 345 (Ala. 1980):

> Appellant argues that the acceptance by Russell County of a check from Mr. Mack Hornsby for the amount agreed upon by the contract executed by him and Commissioner Lake, with knowledge of all the previous circumstances, constituted a ratification by the interested party, Russell County, of the conduct of Commissioner Lake. Appellant's reliance upon *Wilkinson v. Moseley,* 30 Ala. 562 (1857), is misplaced. There the *tort* of conversion, a civil wrong, was involved; here there was a prosecution for the *crime* of conversion or embezzlement. As to the one, an accord and satisfaction [*i.e.,* an agreement settling a claim of breach of contract or

other obligation] constitutes a valid affirmative defense. As to the other, it is not a defense.

8. MODEL PENAL CODE § 223.1, comment at 129:

> Under legislative initiative, then, the law of theft continued to expand. The earliest statutes dealt with embezzlement by such narrowly defined groups as bank clerks. Subsequent laws extended coverage to agents, attorneys, bailees, fiduciaries, public officers, partners, mortgagors in possession, etc., until at last a few American legislatures enacted fraudulent-conversion statutes penalizing misappropriation by anyone who received or had in his possession or control the property of another or property which someone else "is entitled to receive and have." Indeed, some modern embezzlement statutes go so far as to penalize breach of faith without regard to whether anything is misappropriated. Thus, the fiduciary who makes forbidden investments, the official who deposits public funds in an unauthorized depository, the financial advisor who betrays his client into paying more for a property than the market value, may be designated as an embezzler.

2. *MENS REA*

STATE v. BROWN

Supreme Court of Appeals of West Virginia
422 S.E.2d 489 (1992)

WORKMAN, JUSTICE.

The State of West Virginia appeals from an order of the Circuit Court of Marion County dismissing seventeen felony embezzlement counts against the appellee, Jay Montgomery Brown, the former prosecuting attorney of Marion County. The trial court dismissed the felony embezzlement counts based on its determination that embezzlement by a public official is a crime requiring proof of specific intent. The circuit court ruled that the State's failure to aver intent rendered the embezzlement counts fatally defective. Having fully reviewed the facts of the case in conjunction with the applicable statute, we reverse the circuit court's finding that West Virginia Code § 61-3-20 (1989) requires proof of specific intent to convict a public official of embezzlement.

. . . .

This case presents an issue of first impression regarding whether intent is an element of the crime of embezzlement by a public official.... [The court concluded that the state legislature intentionally had provided two separate embezzlement statutes: (1) a general embezzlement offense and (2) a specific offense covering only public officials.]

Mr. Brown vehemently argues that the crime of embezzlement, as that offense is defined in West Virginia Code § 61-3-20, includes the element of criminal intent to permanently deprive an owner of the use of his property. The recognized definition of embezzlement in its general sense admittedly involves the element of intent to deprive an owner of the use of entrusted property.... But, as we have previously noted, the crime of embezzlement by a public official does not contain as many elements of proof as the general embezzlement crime. It is generally recognized that the Legislature may set higher standards on public officials by defining embezzlement by public officials without all of the elements found in the general embezzlement statutes.... Moreover, it is well-established that the intent element of embezzlement is often watered down when the crime involves public officials....

The simple explanation for reducing or eliminating the intent element of embezzlement where the crime is committed by a public official is the fact that public officials are not as closely monitored by their employer, the public, as employees in the general sector.... As the State posits, because misuse of public funds is a matter of the general public welfare, it is entirely appropriate to hold public officers to an exacting standard of conduct and that standard may, if the Legislature so chooses, eliminate the element of intent necessary to prosecute a non-public official....

Having decided that the crime of embezzlement by a public official, as that offense is set forth in West Virginia Code § 61-3-20, is not a specific intent[4] crime, the next question that arises is what degree of *mens rea* is necessary to convict a public official under our embezzlement statute. The Supreme Court of Nebraska adjudicated this very issue in *Haines v. State* [102 N.W.2d 609 (Neb. 1960)]. The defendant in *Haines,* a justice of the peace, argued that the information charging him with embezzlement of fines collected by him in his official capacity was defective because it did not charge him with intent to defraud the State of Nebraska or Buffalo County. The statute at issue in *Haines* provided, in relevant part, that when: "any officer ... charged with the collection, receipt, safekeeping, transfer or disbursement of the public money, ... belonging to the state or to any county ... shall convert to his own use, or the use of any other person ... in any way whatever, ... any portion of the public money ... received, controlled or held by him for safekeeping, transfer or disbursement, ... every such act shall be deemed and held in law to be an embezzlement...." ... In addressing the degree of intent necessary to convict a public official for embezzlement, the *Haines* court noted that: "[i]f a statute makes it a felony for a public officer knowingly and unlawfully to appropriate to his own use or to the use of any other person money received by him in his official capacity, it is not necessary, to constitute the offense of embezzlement, that there be an intent to appropriate the money so as forever to exclude the rightful owner from its use and possession. The purpose of the statute is to prevent any public official from using the money or property coming to him in his official capacity for any purpose other than the one for which the money or property was intrusted to him."...

The *Haines* court reasoned that if a public official "'does knowingly use it (money or property coming to him in his official capacity), or permit others to

---

[4] We use the terminology "specific intent" in its "most common usage" which "is to designate a special mental element which is required above and beyond any mental state required with respect to the actus reus of the crime." ... To illustrate, common-law embezzlement (and statutory embezzlement pursuant to paragraph one of W.Va.Code § 61-3-20; *i.e.* embezzlement which does not involve a public official) requires as an element of proof that the defendant intended to permanently deprive an owner of the use of his property. This particular element of proof is what renders garden variety embezzlement a specific intent offense. As this opinion explains, embezzlement by a public official is not a specific intent crime because proof that the public official intended to deprive the public of its property is not required.

do so, for other purposes than the one for which it was intrusted to him, then he comes within the provisions of the statue.'" ... Recognizing that "'under some statutes, especially those relating to the embezzlement of public funds, the offense consists in the violation of the statute and not the intent or motive by which the accused is actuated,'" the court ruled in *Haines* that the offense of embezzlement "consists in ... violation of the statute (use of public money for any purpose other than the one for which the money was entrusted to the official), whether or not the public official fraudulently intended to do so.". . .

Although we conclude that the crime of embezzlement by a public official is not a specific intent crime, the intent to commit the act or acts that results in the misappropriation or misuse is still necessary to convict a public official under the second paragraph of West Virginia Code § 61-3-20.... [The court quoted *People v. Dillon*, 248 P. 230 (Cal. 1926)]:

> No one will deny the power or right of the Legislature to provide that embezzlement of public moneys is committed by a public officer when he uses public funds in a manner forbidden by law, even though he may have no fraudulent intent when he does so. To render a person guilty of crime it is not essential to a conviction that the proof should show such person to have entertained any intent to violate law.... It is sufficient that he intentionally committed the forbidden act.... [T]here must be an intent to do the forbidden thing or commit the interdicted act. It furnishes no basis for the claim that there must exist in the mind of the transgressor a specific purpose or intent to violate law. If it were so, innumerable statutes would be rendered ineffectual....

Imposing the requirement that the public official must have intended to commit the act which constitutes a violation of West Virginia Code § 61-3-20 should eliminate Mr. Brown's concern that an unintentional expenditure of public funds by a public official would amount to embezzlement since the statute makes the mere "use" of such funds a crime. If in fact a mistaken and unintentional expenditure was committed, the public official could not be found to have committed the violative act with the requisite intent necessary to find him or her guilty of embezzlement. Accordingly, we rule that while proof of intent to steal or misappropriate is not required, proof that the public official intended to do the act or acts that resulted in the embezzlement is necessary to convict a public official of embezzlement pursuant to the second paragraph of West Virginia Code § 61-3-20....

NOTES

1. Fifteen minutes after renting a motel room for the night, defendant and several accomplices carried a portable television from the room, placed it in the trunk of defendant's car, and drove away. Defendant appealed his conviction of grand larceny, alleging that, if anything, he was guilty of embezzlement or failure to return rented or leased property. *Held:* conviction affirmed:

> If the property in the hands of the taker amounted to a bailment, or if the property went into the possession of the taker with knowledge of the owner on account of any fraudulent representation by the taker, and the

taker received the same intending at the time of its reception to convert the same to his own use and deprive the owner thereof, the crime is larceny. If, on the other hand, the taker receives the property as a bailment of the same, or with the knowledge and consent of the owner, intending at the time a compliance with the terms of the bailment, or to conform to the owner's wishes concerning the property in his possession, and afterwards converts the property to his own use ... the crime is embezzlement.... In the instant case, it is apparent from the evidence presented that defendant had the necessary criminal intent existing at the time of the taking of the room, therefore constituting larceny.

Norton v. State, 492 P.2d 359, 362 (Okla. Crim. App. 1972), *citing Flohr v. Territory,* 78 P. 565 (Okla. 1904).

2. In *Phelps v. State,* 219 P. 589 (Ariz. 1923), defendant hired a rental car under a false name. Later, defendant and his companion were arrested and charged with the embezzlement of the car. The conviction was reversed, the court stating that defendant's actions appeared to indicate that the intent to convert existed before the car was obtained, and therefore that he was guilty of larceny, not embezzlement.

3. Several statutes specifically define the terms "deprive" and "appropriate" to connote an intent permanently to deprive. NEW YORK PENAL LAW §§ 155.00.3, 155.00.4. However, other states hold that embezzlement does not require an intent to deprive the owner permanently of his property. In *State v. Moss,* 487 P.2d 1347 (N.M. 1971), embezzlement was defined under the statute as conversion of property with which the embezzler was intrusted with fraudulent intent to deprive the owner thereof. The court affirmed the conviction of embezzlement, construing the statute as not requiring an intent to permanently deprive. The court reasoned that a legislative intent to require the *mens rea* of larceny for the offense of embezzlement could not be implied by comparing the larceny statute with the embezzlement statute, since larceny is defined in terms of stealing, while embezzlement punishes wrongful appropriation. Using the same reasoning, the court in *State v. Piper,* 477 P.2d 940 (Kan. 1970) held that embezzlement, unlike larceny, did not require an intent to permanently deprive. Instead, the offense is the intentional misappropriation to the use of the defendant, and an intention to return or restore the misappropriated property is thus no defense to the crime.

4. In *People v. Stewart,* 544 P.2d 1317 (Cal. 1976), the court held that a defendant's belief that he has the authority to appropriate and use property excludes the fraudulent intent of embezzlement if the belief is held "in good faith." "[A]lthough defendant may have 'believed' he acted lawfully, he was aware of contrary facts which rendered such a belief wholly unreasonable, and hence in bad faith." *Id.* at 1320.

C. OBTAINING TITLE TO PROPERTY BY FALSE PRETENSES

1. ACTUS REUS

a. "Title"

STATE v. HAMM

Missouri Court of Appeals
569 S.W.2d 289 (1978)

WASSERSTROM, JUDGE.

Defendant pleaded guilty to stealing by deceit in violation of Section 560.161. From a sentence entered pursuant to that plea, defendant appeals on the ground that the amended information failed to state conduct constituting the crime charged. An appeal on that ground is authorized despite the plea of guilty....

The amended information alleges that defendant intentionally stole $800 by deceit over a nine day period by the following means. He obtained an Americash Plus card and the secret personal identification code of James F. Burnham to an automated teller, Docutel machine, operated by the American National Bank. Defendant then went to the machine and according to the instructions inserted the card and pressed buttons labeled with single digits so as to spell out Burnham's personal identification code. Defendant then pressed the buttons to indicate that the machine should dispense $50. The machine did so and defendant took the money. Defendant followed this procedure on 16 separate occasions so that he obtained an aggregate sum of $800 in transactions of $50 each. The information further states that defendant's use of the card and personal identification code was unauthorized by Burnham, that the $800 was the property of American National Bank, and that defendant followed the foregoing procedure with the intent of permanently depriving the bank of the use of the money so obtained by him.

Defendant argues in support of his attack upon the indictment that it "fails to state that Appellant made any representation at all, let alone a fraudulent misrepresentation, and it fails to state that the bank acted in reliance in parting with the EIGHT HUNDRED DOLLARS ($800.00)." This argument is based on the assumption that in order to support the offense, there must have been a verbal misrepresentation by the defrauding party directly to the party defrauded. Not so. The misrepresentation "may consist in any act, word, symbol, or token calculated and intended to deceive. It may be made either expressly or by implication...." 35 C.J.S. False Pretenses § 17, p. 825. 32 Am.Jur.2d False Pretenses Sec. 17, p. 189, similarly states: "... since a false pretense may be made by implication as well as expressly, words, written or spoken, are not essential to a false representation such as will subject one to punishment for obtaining money or property by false pretenses. Acts or conduct may constitute a false representation." ... By his actions here, defendant represented falsely that he did have authority to use the Burnham bank card and personal identification code.

No case has been cited nor found by independent research involving a criminal prosecution arising from a fraudulent manipulation of an automatic bank teller such as here presented. This is probably due to the fact that this application of computer technology is relatively new. However, this situation is analogous to the fraudulent use of a stolen credit card, which numerous cases hold to provide the foundation for prosecution for false pretenses. Thus in *Snipes v. State*, 50 Ala.App. 139, 277 So.2d 413 (1973), the defendant presented the credit card of another person without permission, signed the sales slip and obtained merchandise. The defense was that the defendant had not misrepresented anything except possibly her marital status. The court rejected that contention holding:

> When appellant presented the Bank Americard in payment of the shoes and handbag bearing the name "Melvin Chatman" and signed the sales card "Mrs. Melvin Chatman," she was then and there representing to Mrs. Foster that she was indeed Mrs. Melvin Chatman the same as if she had said, "I am Shirley Chatman and my husband is Melvin Chatman."

So also in *Hymes v. United States*, 260 A.2d 679 (D.C. App.1970), the defendant was prosecuted for obtaining gasoline by false pretenses. The prosecution introduced seven receipts for gasoline obtained by use of a credit card issued to another and used by the defendant without permission. The court held that this evidence was sufficient upon which to convict. The court further held that there was sufficient proof to support "reliance" without the necessity for evidence by the service station attendants who waited upon the defendant....

A like ruling was made in another analogous situation in *State v. Moore*, 189 Wash. 680, 66 P.2d 836 (1937), where the defendant presented a check with a forged endorsement to a bank for payment. The information charged grand larceny by false pretenses. One defense made was the lack of any representation by the defendant. The court held that when defendant presented the check, "he thereby represented that he was a lawful holder of the check, the legal assignee of the true payee, and that he was entitled to possession of the check and the money that it represented.... False pretenses may be made by conduct and actions as well as by word of mouth." Another analogous case is *State v. Kelly*, 27 N.M. 412, 202 P. 524 (1921) where the presentation of a spurious bond for redemption was held to be a false pretense.

Just as the facts here show a misrepresentation by defendant through his conduct, so also the facts clearly show reliance thereon by the bank. The machine was so programmed that no money would be paid out without the insertion of the appropriate card and the corresponding personal identification numbers. When those items were supplied, the response was programmed so as to pay out the money. No difference can be perceived whether the bank gave approval after the presentation of those identification items or whether it programmed its acceptance upon those conditions in advance. In either case, the bank equally relied upon the presentation of the card and personal identification.

The facts alleged in the amended information adequately stated an offense of obtaining money by deceit, and the judgment of conviction is therefore affirmed.

All concur.

C. OBTAINING TITLE TO PROPERTY BY FALSE PRETENSES

NOTES

1. Model Penal Code § 223.3, comment at 180 n.1:

> The offense of theft by false pretenses is statutory in origin. It stems from 30 Geo. 2, ch. 24 (1757), which has been enacted or adapted in all American jurisdictions. For the history and an evaluation of the legislation, *see* Pearce, *Theft by False Pretenses,* 101 U. Pa. L. Rev. 967 (1953), an article based on research compiled for the Model Penal Code. *See also* J[erome] Michael & H[erbert] Wechsler, Criminal Law and Its Administration 415-56 (1940).

2. Can one be convicted of defrauding a thief? The court in *United States v. Benson,* 548 F.2d 42 (2d Cir. 1977), said "yes." "It is accepted that the prostitute may be raped, the burglar's home burgled, the killer murdered and the thief a victim of larceny.... While it is generally held in a civil suit where both parties are guilty of criminal behavior with respect to the cause sued upon, that the court will leave the parties where it finds them and refuse to act as a referee among thieves, a criminal action is on a manifestly different footing" .... The complaining witness' "gullibility or his own criminal background is not relevant to the inquiry as to whether defendants were properly convicted of fraud." *Id.* at 44.

Defendants also had argued that if the complainant himself acquired property by theft he had no title to the property and defendants could be convicted only of larceny by trick and not obtaining by false pretenses. The court found that distinctions between the two offenses generally were extinct in federal jurisprudence." *Id.* at 45.

3. In *People v. LaRose,* 274 N.W.2d 45 (Mich. App. 1978), defendant was prosecuted for and pleaded guilty to a charge of obtaining money by false pretenses with intent to defraud, and sentenced to prison. A second count of the information charging delivering an insufficient funds check with intent to defraud had been dropped. The Michigan Court of Appeals reversed. The only false pretense relied on by the prosecution was the insufficient funds check which carried with it an express or implied representation that the maker then had funds on deposit and that the bank would pay the check on presentation.

> Although the presentation of an insufficient funds check may, if accompanied by additional false representation, justify conviction under the false pretenses statute ..., we hold that the instant facts preclude prosecution under the statute. It was clearly the Legislature's intent, in enacting the insufficient funds statute, to carve out an exception to the false pretenses statute and to provide for a lesser penalty for the particular type of false pretense involved in presentation of an insufficient funds check.... The prosecutor was bound to charge defendant under the statute which fit the particular facts and not under the more general statute....

Id. at 48.

4. In *Williams v. United States,* 458 U.S. 279 (1982), the Supreme Court held that check-kiting did not violate the provisions of 18 U.S.C. § 1014

(1988), prohibiting false statements to certain federally insured financial institutions: "technically speaking, a check is not a factual assertion at all, and therefore cannot be characterized as 'true' or 'false.'" The Court noted that under Uniform Commercial Code § 3-409(1), a check or draft does not itself constitute an assignment of funds in the hands of a drawee available for its payment, and the drawee is not liable on the instrument until acceptance.

b. False Representations

PEOPLE v. CAGE
Supreme Court of Michigan
301 N.W.2d 819 (1981)

PER CURIAM.

The issue presented is whether the crime of false pretenses ... may be predicated upon the misrepresentation of a present intent to do a future act. We conclude that it may not.

The defendant in the instant case pled guilty in Washtenaw Circuit Court to the charge of obtaining property having a value over $100 by false pretenses. During his plea, he admitted that he went to a Lincoln-Mercury dealer in Ypsilanti and obtained possession of a used car by telling a salesman that he would buy the car if he liked it after test driving it and having it "checked out" at a local service station. The defendant admitted that he had no such intention and made the statements in order to get possession of the car so that he could convert it to his own use.

On appeal, the defendant challenged the factual sufficiency of his plea, one of the grounds being that his misrepresentations related solely to future events or facts and not, as required for conviction of false pretenses under Michigan law, to past or present facts or circumstances.

The Court of Appeals, ... affirmed defendant's conviction, [adopting the rule that]" false promises or representations as to future happenings by which a person is induced to part with [the] property may form the basis of the offense of theft by false pretense so long as the proof shows that such promises are false *ab initio*." ...

We hold that the adoption of a rule construing false pretenses to incorporate misrepresentation of present mental state is at odds with Michigan law. The crime of false pretenses in Michigan, as in other jurisdictions, was created by statute. It is universally held, except where the statute specifically provides otherwise, that the pretense relied on to establish the offense must be a misrepresentation as to a present or existing fact, or a past fact or event, and may not be as to some event to take place in the future. Although it is quite possible to view a false statement of intention, such as a promise which the promisor intends not to keep, as a misrepresentation of existing mental state, the great weight of authority holds that a false promise will not suffice for false pretenses, however fraudulent it may be.

C. OBTAINING TITLE TO PROPERTY BY FALSE PRETENSES

A minority of jurisdictions do recognize a false promise or intention as a false pretense and there does appear to be a modern trend in this direction. Professor Perkins has made the following pertinent criticism:

> One writer has suggested that interpreting the statute to exclude false promises crept into the decisions by inadvertence, so to speak. This may be true or it may be that the statute, as interpreted, was as great a step as the social order was prepared to take two hundred years ago. After all, the change from the punishment of fraud perpetrated by the use of false tokens to the punishment of fraud perpetrated by naked deceit was considerable, even if the latter did not include a misrepresentation of one's own state of mind. However that may be the original position has been restated time and again in recent years. The first clear switch from this to the position that a false promise is sufficient to support a conviction of false pretenses (in recent times and without the aid of statute) seems to have been in California although there was a Massachusetts dictum pointing in the same direction. A start has been made toward amending the statute of false pretenses to include promissory fraud within its scope, which is entirely proper. Just as the social order of two hundred years ago had developed to the point where it was necessary to punish the swindler who operated without the aid of false tokens, so today it has developed to the further point where it is necessary to have adequate punishment for promissory fraud, *but the change should be by legislative enactment.* No court would permit such a statute to apply to a misdeed perpetrated before the act was passed, and for a court to convict a man by changing this interpretation which has been so firmly established for generations it is necessary to violate the principle upon which the *ex post facto* bar is grounded. (Footnotes omitted.) Perkins, Criminal Law (2d ed.), pp. 304-305.

Our review of Michigan precedent leaves us convinced that this jurisdiction early aligned itself with the majority rule that false statements of promise or intention may not form the basis for a conviction of false pretenses. In *People v. Winslow,* 39 Mich. 505 (1878), it was held that the fact that the defendants in that case accomplished their fraud by a promise would not preclude their conviction of false pretenses because the promise was accompanied by other misrepresentations relating to existing facts. Similarly, in *People v. Segal,* 180 Mich. 316, 146 N.W. 644 (1914), it was held that although some of the defendant's misrepresentations in that case related to what would occur in the future, and his promises in relation thereto, several other representations referring to existing or past facts provided the basis for the conviction of false pretenses.

In *People v. Widmayer,* 265 Mich. 547, 251 N.W. 540 (1933), it was explicitly held that statements made by the defendants as to events that would occur in the future and their promises as to what they would undertake to do in the future could not sustain convictions under the false pretenses statute. More recently, and more to the point, in *People v. Morrison,* 348 Mich. 88, 81 N.W.2d 667 (1957), a guilty plea was overturned because the defendant's admissions established only that he made a promise relating to what he would do in the future.

The aforementioned decisions of this Court preclude a conviction of false pretenses where the misrepresentation relates only to future events or facts.

Although there may be valid arguments supporting an amendment of the false pretenses statute to incorporate misrepresentation of present mental state within the meaning of the crime of false pretenses, we are convinced that it should be done by legislative enactment....

NOTES

1. A leading case taking the contrary (and minority) position to *Cage* is *People v. Ashley*, 267 P.2d 271 (Cal. 1954). Justice Traynor for the majority noted:

> If false promises were not false pretenses, the legally sophisticated, without fear of punishment, could perpetrate on the unwary fraudulent schemes like that divulged by the record in this case.... To hold that false promises are not false pretenses would sanction such schemes without any corresponding benefits to the public order. The inclusion of false promises within sections 484 and 532 of the Penal Code will not "materially encumber" business affairs. "Ordinary commercial defaults" will not be the subject of criminal prosecution, for the essence of the offense of obtaining property by false pretenses is (as it has always been) the fraudulent intent of the defendant. This intent must be proved by the prosecution; a showing of nonperformance of a promise or falsity of a representation will not suffice.

Id. at 283.

2. Appellant knowingly failed to report changes in her husband's income to the welfare department in order to continue receiving Aid to Dependent Children benefits to which she would otherwise not be entitled. A conviction of theft by false pretenses was affirmed. "Of course, when one is bound to disclose facts relating to eligibility and status and fails to perform that duty, or when one relates certain facts pertaining to eligibility for aid and suppresses other relative and material facts or information as to status and thereby misleads as to the real facts, such conduct generally constitutes the offense of false pretenses." *State v. Robinson*, 183 N.W.2d 190, 192 (Iowa 1971).

3. Compare *Rogers v. People*, 422 P.2d 377 (Colo. 1967), where defendant induced the victim to deposit a large amount of cash in a finance company of which defendant was principal officer. The defendant told the victim that he had never lost a dollar for any of his depositors, and that the victim could probably withdraw his funds in ten days or less if he desired. There was evidence that the defendant failed to disclose the precarious financial condition of the company at the time he accepted the victim's deposit, which was subsequently not recovered. The court, in reversing the conviction for obtaining money under false pretenses stated that there was no misrepresentation of a past or existing fact. Furthermore, "[a]lthough failure to make a disclosure and intentionally remaining silent as to a material fact may form the basis of

a civil action in fraud or deceit, such evidence cannot support a conviction of obtaining money by false pretenses.... The general rule is that the mere nondisclosure of facts known to defendant, even though a disclosure thereof would operate to deter the prosecuting witness from parting with his money, is not a false pretense." *Id.* at 381.

4. MODEL PENAL CODE § 223.3, comment at 187-93 *passim*:

Of the various devices for swindling to which the criminal law traditionally has accorded some measure of immunity, the most strongly supported in precedent is the promise made without intention to perform. Although it has long been recognized in tort law that a promise ordinarily implies that the actor intends to perform and that "the state of a man's mind is as much a fact as the state of his digestion," a majority of American states adhered to a rule of non-liability for false promises at the time the Model Penal Code was drafted. The reason usually given, aside from precedent, was that defaulting debtors would be subject to abusive prosecutions designed to force them to pay. Additionally, there was the fear that conviction would be authorized upon no more evidence than the fact that a contract was not performed, *i.e.*, the fact of breach would be treated as sufficient evidence of an original intent not to perform....

... It is often said and occasionally held that a misrepresentation of opinion, not being a statement of "fact," is excluded from a false-pretenses statute. The contrary has been held under the federal mail-fraud statute and in some states when the proof shows that the opinion was intended to be taken seriously and was not honestly offered. Upon examination, the cases asserting an immunity for representations of opinion usually turn out to involve either honest opinions or "seller's talk" that the actor did not intend to be taken literally and that in context should not have been so understood by the buyer.

"Value" would seem to be simply an example of something on which sellers or buyers frequently give opinions and thus merely a specific instance of the generic category of subjects on which a false impression may be created by statements of opinion. There are indications in some decisions, however, that such statements might be excluded from criminal false-pretense statutes even where the court would otherwise accept "opinions" as the basis for conviction. This view appears to be grounded in the belief that exaggeration of value by a seller or underrepresentation of value by a buyer is incapable of deceiving the other party. This seems, however, to present a situation much like others that have been adverted to above. There obviously are cases where deception as to value should provide the basis for a conviction of theft .... Misstatements of value are thus another occasion where it is improvident to prohibit conviction by a rule of law simply because there are cases where an inclusive principle could be misapplied. Here, as in other cases, there must be reliance on courts and juries to exclude those cases where conviction is inappropriate. Otherwise the clever will be able to steal with impunity by finding shelter in an immunity created in order to prevent abuse.

There are conflicting precedents on criminal liability for obtaining property by false representations as to relevant law. Liability has been denied on the ground that everyone is "presumed" to know the law and that "ordinary vigilance" would disclose the truth. It is not clear why contributory negligence of the victim should be significant when he is tricked by legal misrepresentations, while it is irrelevant for other misrepresentations.... Even courts that exclude misrepresentations of law concede that the rule may be otherwise when a relation of trust and confidence is involved, or when foreign law is the subject of the deception, or when a misrepresentation of fact can be found implicit in the statement of a legal conclusion, as when the actor states that he has done certain things which have the described legal consequence.

5. Suppose a defendant proposes an investment plan to A and B, based on formation of a company to refine and reclaim hydraulic fluid using a secret chemical process known only to N. A and B know that no company yet has been formed, that N is the only person who possesses the secret process, that the success of the venture depends on N agreeing to its use, and that N is under no obligation to allow that to take place. A and B pay money to defendant to cover organizational and promotional expenses of the proposed company. Their checks, endorsed to show this purpose, are deposited in a bank account with defendant's name as escrow agent. N later refuses to make his secret process available, and defendant fails to return on demand the funds given him by A and B. Would defendant be convictable of obtaining title to property by false pretenses? See *Commonwealth v. Bomersbach*, 302 A.2d 472 (Pa. Super. Ct. 1973).

4. In *People v. Davis,* 491 N.E.2d 1153 (Ill. 1986), the court followed the traditional position adopted by many jurisdictions (the precedents of which the Illinois court discussed) "that ... the prosecution must show ... reliance by the victim on the deceptive conduct." *Id.* at 1156. However, the court confirmed that on the record the defendant could have been convicted of attempting theft by deception if a victim passed title although not believing the defendant's misrepresentations.

2. MENS REA

STATE v. PICKUS

Supreme Court of South Dakota
257 N.W. 284 (1934)

[Pickus was a partner in a construction firm doing business with a county. He was charged with obtaining money from the county "with intent to cheat and defraud," through misrepresentations about the amounts of materials used to construct bridges, thus collecting more than he was entitled to.]

CAMPBELL, JUSTICE.
From the earliest days of the common law, the element of scienter, the willful and corrupt mind, has been of the essence of the crime of obtaining money or property by false pretenses. It is specifically preserved, and always has been, in our statute by the use of the word "designedly." This court has

always held, in substance, that "designedly" false means in substance willfully, knowingly, and intentionally false and that a false pretense is designedly made when it is made with knowledge on the part of the maker that it is in fact false.... It was likewise the rule recognized by the learned trial judge in the instant case when, as hereinbefore stated, he instructed the jury in part as follows:

> The three principal elements involved in the crime of obtaining money by false pretenses, are, ... third, that the defendant at the time he presented the false writing or made the false pretense and at the time he received the money knew that the writing or other pretense was false. Each and every one of these elements must be established by the evidence in the case beyond a reasonable doubt before the crime is established.
> The court further instructs the jury that pretense in any of the counts of this indictment could not be designedly false, without at the same time, being knowingly false, and in order to find the defendant guilty of the charges contained in any of the counts of this indictment, it is necessary for the jury to find, beyond a reasonable doubt, that the defendant knew such pretenses were, in fact, false at the time he made them.

To that instruction, however, the learned trial judge, as hereinbefore indicated, added these two sentences:

> If the accused honestly believed in the truth of the representation made although it may have been false, the offense is not committed. But making a statement that is in fact false recklessly without information to justify a belief in its truth is equivalent to making a statement knowing it to be false.

To such addition, and particularly to the second sentence thereof, appellant promptly excepted and has at all times preserved his objection thereto....

Let us now examine somewhat more particularly that portion of the court's instructions wherein he told the jury that "making a statement that is in fact false recklessly without information to justify a belief in its truth is equivalent to making a statement knowing it to be false." Just what the court may have meant or just what the jury may have understood by the word "recklessly" in this instruction offers an almost unlimited field for speculation and conjecture.... But, whatever may be the significance of the word "recklessly" standing alone, in the court's instruction now under consideration, it is either defined or modified and qualified by the immediately following words, "without information to justify a belief in its truth." By that language the court clearly authorized and indeed almost required the jury to disregard the actual state of mind of the appellant at the time he made the representation claimed to be false and imposed upon appellant in a criminal case the objective standard which is frequently applied to determine civil liability in tort. Under that instruction, if the jury or some of the jurors entertained the view that the representation made by appellant was false, that appellant believed the representation when he made it, but that appellant arrived at his belief on information which would not justify a reasonably prudent man in forming the same belief — in other words, if appellant was rash or careless or foolish, although honest, in arriving at the belief which in fact he entertained — then it would be the duty of the jury to hold appellant criminally liable.

The continuance of the word "designedly" in our criminal false pretense statute renders it clear beyond possibility of question that scienter or specific intent is (as it always has been) of the essence of the crime....

To undertake a precise distinction between knowledge and belief or to mark the line where the one begins and the other ends would be difficult if not impossible. Much that we are accustomed to call knowledge is only a thoroughly developed, firmly grounded, highly conventionalized form of belief. Belief has been well defined (and quite sufficiently for the purposes of this discussion) as "an assent of the mind to the truth of a declaration, proposition or alleged fact." *Keller v. State* (1898) 102 Ga. 506, 31 S.E. 92, 95. We believe that to which we give credence; that which we mentally accept as true. Whenever a representation is made that is in fact false, the mental attitude of the declarant with reference thereto must fall within one of four categories. First, he may know that the representation is false. Second, he may believe that the representation is false. Third, he may have neither any knowledge nor any belief whatsoever as to its truth or falsity. Fourth, he may believe the representation to be true. Each of the first three of these categories is distinguishable from the fourth in this — that in each of the first three the affirmative element of belief in the truth of the representation is absent. In the first two not only is the declarant lacking in mental assent to the truth of his declaration, but his condition of mind is precisely the opposite — his mental assent is to the falsity of the declaration. In both the first and second categories it must, of course, be held that the declaration is designedly false. The third category presents a much closer case. A declaration is made; the mental attitude of the declarant toward it is, so to speak, neutral; he has neither knowledge nor belief as to its truth or falsity; he does not know; he has no data upon which to found a belief either one way or the other and he has formed no belief; it develops that the representation is in fact false. Has the declarant made a designedly false representation within the meaning of the criminal law? Possibly he has. Ethically there appears to be little difference when a man makes a false representation for the purpose of inducing another to act for his benefit between the quality of conduct of the man who knows or believes his representation is false and that of the man who has neither knowledge nor belief concerning it, but nevertheless makes the representation, neither knowing nor caring whether it be true or false. Incidentally we may say that it is our view that this third category (as distinct from the fourth) is as far as the courts really intended their language to reach in the California and New York cases hereinbefore considered. The difficulty in the case now before us is that the language of the instruction given is broad enough to include not only the third category but also the fourth and may very well have been so understood by the jury.

... The instruction in the instant case goes too far. It permits, if it does not require, the jury to find the appellant guilty even though he actually believed in his own mind in the truth of the representation he made if they should think that he arrived at that belief "recklessly" (whatever that may mean), or without sufficient information to justify it, whether according to the standard of the jurors or to the standard of the reasonably prudent man.... It permits a juror, who might be convinced that appellant spoke truly when he claimed that he believed his representation to be true when he made it, to find appellant guilty notwithstanding such belief because he, the juror, was of the opinion that appellant's belief though actually existent was not based upon sufficient information to justify the formation of such a belief. The instruction in so permitting runs contrary to the terms of the criminal statute and overlooks design. This cannot be done.

[*Reversed.*]

NOTE

In *People v. Churchill*, 390 N.E.2d 1146 (N.Y. 1979), the defendant had been convicted of larceny under N.Y. PENAL LAW § 155.05(2)(d), which provides that a promise made without intent that it will be performed constitutes a false pretense. His conviction was reversed:

> Stripped of all unseemly innuendos, the People have shown only that defendant had entered into three contracts for which he received substantial down payments and that he had failed to complete performance. The inferences to be drawn from this record certainly do not exclude to a moral certainty every hypothesis but that at the time he entered into the contracts defendant had no intention of meeting his obligations. Indeed, equally strong is the inference that defendant was simply an inexperienced, uneducated tyro whose talents of salesmanship surpassed his ability to manage a business. In all three instances, supplies and equipment were purchased and delivered to the job sites and at least some work was commenced. Significant, too, is the fact that failure to complete performance was due, at least in part, to the actions of the homeowners themselves. Thus, Van Horn, dissatisfied with the progress of the work, terminated the contract; Vicki commenced a civil suit for breach of contract; and Hild's suspicions were aroused after law enforcement officers questioned her about defendant's activities. On this record, it is impossible to conclude that the proof excludes to a moral certainty every hypothesis except guilty intent. *Id.* at 1151.

SECTION II. Theft and Related Offenses Under Contemporary Legislation

A. STATUTORY PATTERNS

MODEL PENAL CODE

§ 223.1. *Consolidation of Theft Offenses*

> (1) *Consolidation of Theft Offenses.* Conduct denominated theft in this Article constitutes a single offense. An accusation of theft may be supported by evidence that it was committed in any manner that would be theft under this Article, notwithstanding the specification of a different manner in the indictment or information, subject only to the power of the

Court to ensure fair trial by granting a continuance or other appropriate relief where the conduct of the defense would be prejudiced by lack of fair notice or by surprise.

Comment [at 132-38]

Nevertheless, consolidation cannot eliminate the necessity for careful drafting, nor can it avoid the necessity for a properly specific delineation of the various types of property deprivations that should be punished by the criminal law. In relation to taking by stealth, there are difficulties in identifying the degree of control which the thief must achieve, and care must be taken to exclude from liability a mere unconsented occupation of another's property or an infringement of his patent. With respect to fraud or extortion, the criminal law still must define carefully what constitutes the "deception" or "coercion" that may safely be penalized. Moreover, consolidation cannot be regarded, as has sometimes been supposed, as a solution for shortcomings in the definition of any branch of theft. For example, a rule that a false promise is not a criminal false pretense will not be changed merely by consolidating false pretenses with larceny. The common law developed elaborate distinctions with respect to the role that a false promise could play in the law of theft. In cases where the actor secured temporary possession of a chattel by a false promise, it was said to be larceny by trick if he subsequently converted the property to his own permanent use. By fiction, the law was prepared in this case to regard the offense as one that was committed against the possession of the owner, as was required for larceny. In cases where the actor secured full ownership rather than temporary custody, however, the offense-category was shifted from larceny to false pretenses, and it was established that a false promise would not suffice for liability. Experience in New York establishes the point that mere consolidation of larceny, embezzlement, and false pretenses into a single crime called larceny did not result in the elimination of this anomalous distinction from the law.

The purpose of consolidation, therefore, is not to avoid the need to confront substantive difficulties in the definition of theft offenses. The appropriate objective is to avoid procedural problems. Even a consolidated offense, as reflected in Sections 223.2 to 223.8 *infra,* will retain distinctions among methods of acquisition and appropriation. The real problem arises from a defendant's claim that he did not misappropriate the property by the means alleged but in fact misappropriated the property by some other means and from the combination of such a claim with the procedural rule that a defendant who is charged with one offense cannot be convicted by proving another.

Examples come readily to mind where an unwary prosecutor might stumble in distinguishing larceny, false pretenses, extortion, and embezzlement. An offender who is prosecuted for fraud might escape by proving that the victim did not believe the representations made to him but was merely frightened by them. Similarly, one who gives a bad check as a down payment on an automobile which is thereupon delivered to him on conditional sale may defeat criminal prosecution for obtaining by false pretenses by arguing that the vendor reserved title and that the vendee could therefore only be guilty of larceny,

A. STATUTORY PATTERNS

the offense against possession. The intricacies of distinguishing between stealing and receiving stolen goods and of the proper procedure for presenting these alternative views of the defendant's involvement may also lead to needless reversals of convictions.

These problems can be partially solved by more modern definitions of the offenses involved, though it will still be necessary to draw what will often be subtle distinctions. There remains a necessity for some device to prevent a charge based on one method of wrongfully obtaining property from being defeated by the defense that the property was acquired by a different wrongful method. While consolidation is not the only way to accomplish this objective, it does seem the most effective way. This judgment is confirmed by the extent to which consolidation has been accepted in recent legislation dealing with theft....

(c) *Implementing Consolidation.* Article 223 recognizes the substantive problems inherent in the different forms of theft by dealing in Sections 223.2 through 223.8 with different methods of acquisitive behavior. Section 223.1(1), however, creates the single offense of "theft" which is committed by violation of any one of the succeeding sections. It was specifically stated in the text of Subsection (1) as published in the Proposed Official Draft of the Model Code, that the consolidated offense was designed to embrace the offenses that were "heretofore known as larceny, embezzlement, false pretense, extortion, blackmail, fraudulent conversion, receiving stolen property, and the like." This language has been omitted so as not to suggest that the common-law content of these offenses is meant to be carried forward. The omission is not intended to change the basic objective of the consolidation — namely, to subsume various forms of acquisitive behavior into a single theft offense and to redefine the scope of conduct that was formerly treated in the separate categories mentioned above.

The second sentence of Subsection (1) provides that an accusation of theft may be supported by evidence that it was committed in any manner that would be theft under Article 223, even though a different manner was specified in the indictment or information. The defendant is thus foreclosed from defending on the basis that his conduct was not larceny as charged but extortion. These offenses are abolished as separate categories of crime and are to be charged as the single theft offense created by this article.

There is, however, the problem of fair notice to the defendant. In general, the Model Code does not deal with the degree of specificity that an indictment or information must contain but reflects the view that the matter is one of procedure beyond the scope of the penal code itself. On the other hand, account must be taken of the possibility that too great a variance between charge and proof may render an indictment or information insufficient to apprise the defendant of the case he must meet. Accordingly, the last clause of Subsection (1) refers to the inherent power of the court to ensure a fair trial by granting a continuance or other appropriate relief where the conduct of the defense would be prejudiced by lack of fair notice or by surprise.

The problem of lack of fair notice in an indictment or information is not, of course, unique to charges of theft. If overly specific charging is required, technical defenses based on inevitable minor variances can be made to a charge of any type of offense. It should be noted here, however, that the success of the effort to consolidate the various forms of theft into a single offense is limited by the extent to which highly detailed charging is perceived to be mandated by constitutional limitations or the fair notice requirement. It is the premise of Subsection (1) that post-charge relief should in most cases suffice to fill in the details of an accusation of theft that the defendant must know in order to meet the case against him. Such relief can come in the form of a bill of particulars or other specification of information following the formal charge or in the form of a continuance of the trial to allow additional time for preparation. If recharging is consistently required, the advantages of consolidation will be significantly impaired.

B. PROTECTED VALUES (HARM)

MODEL PENAL CODE

§ 223.0. *Definitions*

In this Article, unless a different meaning plainly is required:

....

(4) "movable property" means property the location of which can be changed, including things growing on, affixed to, or found in land, and documents although the rights represented thereby have no physical location. "Immovable property" is all other property.

....

(6) "property" means anything of value, including real estate, tangible and intangible personal property, contract rights, choses-in-action and other interests in or claims to wealth, admission or transportation tickets, captured or domestic animals, food and drink, electric or other power.

(7) "property of another" includes property in which any person other than the actor has an interest which the actor is not privileged to infringe, regardless of the fact that the actor also has an interest in the property and regardless of the fact that the other person might be precluded from civil recovery because the property was used in an unlawful transaction or was subject to forfeiture as contraband. Property in possession of the actor shall not be deemed property of another who has only a security interest therein, even if legal title is in the creditor pursuant to a conditional sales contract or other security agreement.

Comment at 168-74

4. *Property of Another.* Section 223.0(7) defines "property of another" to include any property "in which any person other than the actor has an interest which the actor is not privileged to infringe." Obviously, this concept includes any ownership or possessory interest of another. Also included are the various relations of trust that can lead to traditional liability for embezzlement. In contrast to most embezzlement legislation in effect at the time these provisions were drafted, no effort is made to detail the various relations of trust that suffice for this purpose. It is immaterial how the formal or infor-

mal arrangement between the thief and the owner of property might be designated. What is material is that the thief sets out to appropriate a property interest beyond any privilege established by the arrangement. One therefore "exercises unlawful control" over the "property of another" whenever consent or authority is exceeded, just as one would "unlawfully take" the "property of another" whenever control is acquired over an interest in property beyond any consent or authority given.

There are some circumstances when a person ordinarily considered the owner of property may nevertheless be convicted of theft under Section 223.2. This result follows from the provision in the definition of "property of another" that includes an interest in property held by another "regardless of the fact that the actor also has an interest in the property." Thus, a partner may be convicted of theft of partnership property. Parties to joint bank accounts also may be convicted of stealing from each other by unauthorized withdrawals from the account. At common law, and still in some states, convictions were prevented by the conception that each joint owner had title to the whole of jointly owned property, so that one of the parties could not misappropriate what already belonged to him. Whatever the merits of such notions in the civil law, it is clear that they have no relevance to the efforts of the criminal law to deter impairment of the economic interests of other people. There was modern legislation in effect when the Model Penal Code was drafted that expanded the law of theft to reach such situations. Moreover, a number of states have enacted or proposed a broad notion of "property of another" since the promulgation of the Model Code.

Subsection (7) of Section 223.0 also provides that the infringement of an interest in property can constitute theft even though "the other person might be precluded from civil recovery because the property was used in an unlawful transaction or was subject to forfeiture as contraband." This provision substantially restates the law in effect when the Model Code was drafted and has been followed in recent code-revision efforts. It is inconsistent with the objectives of the criminal law of theft to permit one who wrongfully appropriates wealth to escape from liability merely because the victim of the misappropriation has also incurred criminal liability or forfeiture of his rights with respect to the property. Thus, one who steals an obscene book or contraband drugs can be prosecuted under Section 223.2 regardless of the unlawful character of the objects stolen.

There is, however, one situation involving misappropriation by one of several persons having a legal interest in property where it is not appropriate to permit a conviction for theft. This is the case of the debtor in possession of property subject to a security interest. A debtor's fraudulent disposition of encumbered property is dealt with in Section 224.10 and accordingly is excluded from the offense of theft by the last sentence of Section 223.0(7), which provides that "property in possession of the actor shall not be deemed property of another who has only a security interest therein, even if legal title is in the creditor pursuant to a conditional sales contract or other security agreement." To this extent, the coverage of Section 223.2 is less comprehensive than fraudulent-conversion statutes in effect when these provisions were drafted. The broadest of these laws purported to apply to the misappropriation of property held "in any capacity." Most recent codes and proposals have followed the Model Code by excluding security interests from the provisions on theft.

5. *Movable and Immovable Property.* Despite the judgment that real property is appropriately included within the concept of "property," a definition of theft should not be so broad as to include unlawful use or occupancy of land. The immobility and virtual indestructibility of real estate makes unlawful occupancy of land a relatively minor harm for which civil remedies supplemented by mild criminal sanctions for trespass should be adequate. Such penalties are provided in Section 221.2.

Thus, even though a squatter may acquire title to land by exercising adverse control for the prescriptive period, he is not a thief within Section 223.2. He would be excluded from Subsection (1) because that section applies only to "movable" property. The definition of "movable" property in Section 223.0(4) does include, however, "things growing on, affixed to, or found on land," providing only that it is property "the location of which can be changed." Subsection (1) therefore includes anything located on real property — *e.g.,* crops, timber, dirt, oil — which can be removed and converted to the use of one who is not entitled to do so.

Similarly, Subsection (1) does not apply to landlord-tenant relations. Relations between a landlord and a tenant are so minutely regulated and constitute such a delicate socio-political problem that it would be wrong to introduce the possibility of a theft prosecution for unauthorized occupancy by a tenant or improper eviction by a landlord. Again, the limitation of Subsection (1) to "movable" property assures that this result will not occur and leaves to other sources of law the remedies that should be provided for such conduct.

Subsection (2) makes it clear, however, that a trustee, guardian, or other person empowered to dispose of "immovable" property of others subjects himself to theft liability if he misappropriates the property, *i.e.,* if "he unlawfully transfers immovable property of another or any interest therein with purpose to benefit himself or another not entitled thereto." There may well be situations in which civil remedies are ineffective to deal with such conduct, as in the case of a transfer or encumbrance which is made by the holder of legal title to a good-faith purchaser. Such a transfer would convey an effective interest as against beneficial owners. Quite apart from the possibility that civil remedies may be inadequate, it seems clear that criminal liability for theft is appropriate in cases where a person seeks to benefit himself or another through the illegitimate transfer of interests in real property. There is little to distinguish such cases from any other attempt to secure economic benefit at the expense of another.

Most new codes and proposals have not adopted special provisions with respect to the theft of real estate. A few follow the Model Code approach, while others only cover severed property such as crops and timber. Most, however, define "property" or "thing of value" to include real estate and thus permit prosecutions for wrongful "taking," "exercising control," "withholding," or "obtaining," subject to the same theories applicable to personal property. This would appear to open the possibility of theft prosecutions in cases of holdover or eviction in a landlord-tenant relationship, particularly in states such as New Hampshire, which has no explicit claim-of-right provision. There will also be a problem in such states of distinguishing between theft and criminal trespass.

UNITED STATES v. DiGILIO
United States Court of Appeals for the Third Circuit
538 F.2d 972 (3d Cir. 1976)

[DiGiglio, working through intermediaries, obtained unauthorized copies of FBI files pertaining to criminal investigations into his activities, made from time to time by a government clerk-typist using office paper and copying equipment. The clerk-typist returned the originals to the files. DiGiglio was convicted for violating the portion of 18 U.S.C. § 641 (1976 ed.) covering one who "converts to his use or the use of another ... any record, voucher, money, or thing of value of the United States." On appeal, DiGiglio and his codefendants asserted that unauthorized copies of government records are not themselves records within the meaning of § 641, and that Congress did not intend to include within a federal larceny statute protection of a governmental interest in exclusive possession of information. The government relied for a contrary interpretation on *United States v. Bottone,* 365 F.2d 389 (2d Cir.), *cert. denied,* 385 U.S. 974 (1966), holding that microfilming documents pertaining to a scientific process, made on the thieves' own photocopying equipment, and transportation of the copies in interstate commerce violated 18 U.S.C. § 2314 (1976 ed.), prohibiting interstate transportation of stolen goods.]

GIBBONS, CIRCUIT JUDGE.

It is not necessary to accept the government's thesis in its entirety to hold that in this case a § 641 violation was established. This case does not involve memorization of information contained in government records, or even copying by thieves by means of their own equipment. [The clerk-typist] availed herself of several government resources in copying DiGiglio's files, namely, government time, government equipment and government supplies. That she was not specifically authorized to make these copies does not alter their character as records of the government. A duplicate copy is a record for purposes of the statute, and duplicate copies belonging to the government were stolen....

We do not, by resting upon the narrower ground that a technical larceny has been proved, intend to imply a rejection of the government's broader interpretation of § 641.... But since there was an asportation of records owned by the United States we need not in this case decide whether appropriation of information alone falls within § 641. The statute gives fair warning that at a minimum, it proscribes all larceny-type offenses. The indictment charges such an offense, and the government proved such an offense....

NOTES

1. A similar holding appears in *United States v. Girard,* 601 F.2d 69 (2d Cir. 1979), involving unauthorized use of computer terminals to obtain confidential DEA information. "Although the content of a writing is intangible, it is nonetheless a thing of value.... Although we are not concerned here with the laws of copyright, we are satisfied, nonetheless, that the Government has a

property interest in certain of its private records which it may protect by statute as a thing of value.... [T]he defendants herein could properly be found to have converted DEA's computerized records." *Id.* at 71.

2. Statutory redefinition of property for purposes of larceny in the form of itemization without an *ejusdem generis* clause leaves no room for bringing within penal law coverage the clandestine acquisition of intellectual property. *See Commonwealth v. Yourawski,* 425 N.E.2d 298 (Mass. 1981). The court's conclusion was strengthened by the fact that the state legislature had enacted a special statute which penalized the knowing transfer or sale of recorded sounds without consent of the owner, but did not cover receipt of such material. Hence, the defendant's acts of receiving, purchasing and aiding in the concealment of pirated video cassettes of *Star Wars* did not contravene state criminal law.

3. Legislation which singles out theft of certain kinds of property (in this instance, livestock) for heavier punishment than other forms of property with equivalent value does not violate equal protection. *People v. Burns,* 593 P.2d 351 (Colo. 1979); *State v. Webb,* 528 P.2d 669 (Idaho 1974).

C. *ACTUS REUS*

1. PROHIBITED ACTIVITIES

a. Unauthorized Control

MODEL PENAL CODE

§ 223.2. Theft by Unlawful Taking or Disposition

(1) *Movable Property.* A person is guilty of theft if he unlawfully takes, or exercises unlawful control over, movable property of another with purpose to deprive him thereof.

(2) *Immovable Property.* A person is guilty of theft if he unlawfully transfers immovable property of another or any interest therein with purpose to benefit himself or another not entitled thereto.

Comment at 163-66

2. *Unlawful Taking or Exercising Unlawful Control.* Subsection (1) reaches one who "unlawfully takes, or exercises unlawful control" over the movable property of another. This description of the behavior constituting theft of the larceny-embezzlement type replaces the common-law larceny requirements of "caption" and "asportation." "Caption," or taking, occurred when the actor secured dominion over the property of another; additionally, the common-law crime of larceny required as "asportation," or carrying away of the other's property. Also replaced by the Model Code formulation are the many terms added by legislation — *e.g.,* "steal," "take," "remove," "carry away," "receive," "secrete," "conceal," "withhold," "retain," "fail or refuse to pay," "appropriate," "convert," "embezzle," "misapply," "sell," "convey," "transfer," "dispose," "pledge," "use," "purloin," and the like. Most of these terms do no more than illustrate various means of exercising unlawful control. Some of the terms,

such as "steal" and "embezzle," do not define the acts necessary to constitute a crime but depend for their meaning upon reference to pre-existing law.

The common-law larceny requirements of physical seizure and movement were satisfied by a slight change in position of the object of the theft. If the defendant's behavior fell somewhat short of these requirements, as where a pickpocket grasped but had not yet moved the victim's purse, he was guilty of attempt only. Since larceny was generally a felony and attempt a misdemeanor, important differences in procedure and punishment turned on the criminologically insignificant fact of slight movement of the object of the theft. Under Section 5.01 of the Model Code, and in modern criminal law generally, differences in penal consequences between attempt and completed crime are minimized, so that it becomes less important where the line is drawn between them. It is clear, moreover, that similar penalties for the attempt and the completed offense make obsolete any reference to the concept of "asportation"; the same penal consequences follow whether or not an "asportation" has occurred.

Texas eliminated asportation as an element of larceny during the nineteenth century, but it was the only American jurisdiction to have done so when work on the Model Code began. Since the initial formulation of the Model Code provisions on theft, however, the vast majority of new statutes and proposals have adopted the approach reflected in Subsection (1). Most states use the Model Code language "unlawfully takes or exercises unlawful control" or some variation that is substantially similar. New York and several other states, however, use language that could be interpreted to retain an asportation requirement. The New York Court of Appeals, however, recently decided that the New York statute did not require proof of asportation, at least in a situation involving an already-activated car in which "movement or motion" was not essential to the assertion of control.[5]

Statutory or judicial abandonment of the common-law requirement of asportation does not eliminate the necessity of defining the point at which the offense of theft is completed. The words "unlawfully takes" have been chosen to cover the assumption of physical possession or control without consent or authority, which, as noted above, includes the typical common-law category of larceny. The language "exercises unlawful control" applies at the moment the custodian of property begins to use it in a manner beyond his authority and thus includes the typical embezzlement situation. The word "unlawful" in each instance implies the lack of consent or authority and specifically the absence of any defense under Section 2.11, Section 223.1(3), or Article 3. These concepts accurately describe the kind of conduct that should be treated as theft, as well as the objectives which should support conviction for attempt. They are simple, which has importance in the context of jury trials, and they

---

[5] *People v. Alamo*, 34 N.Y.2d 453, 358 N.Y.S.2d 375, 315 N.E.2d 446 (1974). The court held that an individual who had entered an automobile, positioned himself behind the wheel, started the engine, turned on the lights, and was about to move it, was guilty of a completed larceny, even though the car was not moved. The relevant portion of the theft statute punished "a wrongful taking, obtaining or withholding of another's property ... by conduct heretofore defined or known as trespassory taking." N.Y. § 155.05(2)(a). Chief Judge Breitel dissented, maintaining that the majority had misread New York precedents which clearly established that asportation was an element of larceny as "heretofore defined."

are flexible, which is important in their application to the diversity of situations that arise in a modern economy.

Traditionally, larceny required a trespassory taking, whereas embezzlement involved a misappropriation by one in lawful possession. This distinction is no longer significant under the formulation in Subsection (1). The typical charge under the Model Code provision should specify that the actor unlawfully took or exercised unlawful control over the property of another with the requisite purpose, thus making the method of exercising control relevant only to the extent that it sheds light on the authority of the actor to behave as he did. Apart from the requirement of a purpose to deprive another of his property, the critical inquiry is thus twofold: whether the actor had control of the property, no matter how he got it, and whether the actor's acquisition or use of the property was authorized.

PEOPLE v. OLIVO

New York Court of Appeals
420 N.E.2d 40 (1981)

COOKE, CHIEF JUDGE.

These cases present a recurring question in this era of the self-service store which has never been resolved by this court: may a person be convicted of larceny for shoplifting if the person is caught with goods while still inside the store? For reasons outlined below, it is concluded that a larceny conviction may be sustained, in certain situations, even though the shoplifter was apprehended before leaving the store.

I

In *People v. Olivo,* defendant was observed by a security guard in the hardware area of a department store. Initially conversing with another person, defendant began to look around furtively when his acquaintance departed. The security agent continued to observe and saw defendant assume a crouching position, take a set of wrenches and secret it in his clothes. After again looking around, defendant began walking toward an exit, passing a number of cash registers en route. When defendant did not stop to pay for the merchandise, the officer accosted him a few feet from the exit. In response to the guard's inquiry, defendant denied having the wrenches, but as he proceeded to the security office, defendant removed the wrenches and placed them under his jacket. At trial, defendant testified that he has placed the tools under his arm and was in line at a cashier when apprehended. The jury returned a verdict of guilty on the charge of petit larceny. The conviction was affirmed by Appellate Term.

II

In *People v. Gasparik,* defendant was in a department store trying on a leather jacket. Two store detectives observed him tear off the price tag and remove a "sensormatic" device designed to set off an alarm if the jacket were carried through a detection machine. There was at least one such machine at the exit of each floor. Defendant placed the tag and the device in the pocket of another jacket on the merchandise rack. He took his own jacket, which he had been carrying with him, and placed it on a table. Leaving his own jacket, defendant put on the leather jacket and walked through the store, still on the same floor, bypassing several cash registers. When he headed for the exit from that floor, in the direction of the main floor, he was apprehended by security personnel. At trial, defendant denied removing the price tag and the sensormatic device from the jacket, and testified that he was looking for a cashier without a long line when he was stopped. The court, sitting without a jury, convicted defendant of petit larceny. Appellate Term affirmed....

III

In *People v. Spatzier,* defendant entered a bookstore on Fulton Street in Hempstead carrying an attaché case. The two co-owners of the store observed the defendant in a ceiling mirror as he browsed through the store. They watched defendant remove a book from the shelf, look up and down the aisle, and place the book in his case. He then placed the case at his feet and continued to browse. One of the owners approached defendant and accused him of stealing the book. An altercation ensued and when defendant allegedly struck the owner with the attaché case, the case opened and the book fell out. At trial, defendant denied secreting the book in his case and claimed that the owner had suddenly and unjustifiably accused him of stealing. The jury found defendant guilty of petit larceny, and the conviction was affirmed by the Appellate Term....

IV

Modern penal statutes generally have incorporated [earlier expansions upon common-law doctrines] under a unified definition of larceny (*see e.g.,* American Law Institute, Model Penal Code [Tent Draft No. 1], § 206.1 [theft is appropriation of property of another, which includes unauthorized exercise of control]). Case law, too, now tends to focus upon the actor's intent and the exercise of dominion and control over the property (*see, e.g., People v. Alamo,* [315 N.E.2d 446] ...). Indeed, this court has recognized, in construing the New York Penal Law, that the "ancient common-law concepts of larceny" no longer strictly apply (*People v. Alamo, supra* ...).

This evolution is particularly relevant to thefts occurring in modern self-service stores. In stores of that type, customers are impliedly invited to examine, try on, and carry about the merchandise on display. Thus in a sense, the owner has consented to the customer's possession of the goods for a limited purpose .... That the owner has consented to that possession does not, however, preclude a conviction for larceny. If the customer exercises dominion and control wholly inconsistent with the continued rights of the owner, and the other elements of the crime are present, a larceny has occurred. Such conduct on the part of a customer satisfies the "taking" element of the crime.

It is this element that forms the core of the controversy in these cases. The defendants argue, in essence, that the crime is not established, as a matter of law, unless there is evidence that the customer departed the shop without paying for the merchandise.

Although this court has not addressed the issue, case law from other jurisdictions seems unanimous in holding that a shoplifter need not leave the store to be guilty of larceny.... This is because a shopper may treat merchandise in a manner inconsistent with the owner's continued rights — and in a manner not in accord with that of prospective purchaser — without actually walking out of the store. Indeed, depending upon the circumstances of each case, a variety of conduct may be sufficient to allow the trier of fact to find a taking. It would be well-nigh impossible, and unwise, to attempt to delineate all the situations which would establish a taking. But it is possible to identify some of the factors used in determining whether the evidence is sufficient to be submitted to the fact finder.

In many cases, it will be particularly relevant that defendant concealed the goods under clothing or in a container.... Such conduct is not generally expected in a self-service store and may in a proper case be deemed an exercise of dominion and control inconsistent with the store's continued rights. Other furtive or unusual behavior on the part of the defendant should also be weighed. Thus, if the defendant surveys the area while secreting the merchandise or abandoned his or her own property in exchange for the concealed goods, this may evince larcenous rather than innocent behavior. Relevant too is the customer's proximity to or movement towards one of the store's exits. Certainly it is highly probative of guilt that the customer was in possession of secreted goods just a few short steps from the door or moving in that direction. Finally, possession of a known shoplifting device actually used to conceal merchandise, such as a specially designed outer garment or false bottomed carrying case, would be all but decisive.

Of course, in a particular case, any one or any combination of these factors may take on special significance. And there may be other considerations, not now identified, which should be examined. So long as it bears upon the principal issue — whether the shopper exercised control wholly inconsistent with the owner's continued rights — any attending circumstance is relevant and may be taken into account.

....

V

Under these principles, there was ample evidence in each case to raise a factual question as to the defendants' guilt. In *People v. Olivo,* defendant not only concealed goods in his clothing, but he did so in a particularly suspicious manner. And, when defendant was stopped, he was moving towards the door, just three feet short of exiting the store. It cannot be said as a matter of law that these circumstances failed to establish a taking.

In *People v. Gasparik,* defendant removed the price tag and sensor device from a jacket, abandoned his own garment, put the jacket on and ultimately headed for the main floor of the store. Removal of the price tag and sensor device, and careful concealment of those items, is highly unusual and suspicious conduct for a shopper. Coupled with defendant's abandonment of his own coat and his attempt to leave the floor, those factors were sufficient to make out a prima facie case of a taking.

In *People v. Spatzier,* defendant concealed a book in an attaché case. Unaware that he was being observed in an overhead mirror, defendant looked furtively up and down an aisle before secreting the book. In these circumstances, given the manner in which defendant concealed the book and his suspicious behavior, the evidence was not insufficient as a matter of law....

VII

In sum, in view of the modern definition of the crime of larceny, and its purpose of protecting individual property rights, a taking of property in the self-service store context can be established by evidence that a customer exercised control over merchandise wholly inconsistent with the store's continued rights. Quite simply, a customer who crosses the line between the limited right he or she has to deal with merchandise and the store owner's rights may be subject to prosecution for larceny. Such a rule should foster the legitimate interests and continued operation of self-service shops, a convenience which most members of the society enjoy.

NOTES

1. *Lee v. State,* 474 A.2d 537 (Md. App. 1984):

From this perusal of cases, we conclude that several factors should be assessed to determine whether the accused intended to deprive the owner of property. First, concealment of goods inconsistent with the store owner's rights should be considered. "Concealment" is conduct which is not generally expected in a self-service store and may in many cases be deemed "obtaining unauthorized control over the property in a manner likely to deprive the owner of the property." Other furtive or unusual behavior on the part of the defendant should also be weighed. For instance, if a customer suspiciously surveys an area while secreting the merchandise this may evince larcenous behavior. Likewise, if the accused flees the scene upon being questioned or accosted about the merchandise, as in the instant case, an intent to steal may be inferred. The customer's proximity to the store's exits is also relevant. Additionally, possession by the customer of a shoplifting device with which to conceal merchandise would suggest a larcenous intent. One of these factors or any act on the part of the customer which would be inconsistent with the owner's property rights may be taken into account as relevant in determining whether there was a larcenous intent....

An examination of the legislative history relating to the law of theft leads this Court to conclude that the law in Maryland is intended to be no different than the above cited jurisdictions.

Shoplifting in a self-service store constitutes theft by virtue of Md. Code Art. 27, § 342(a): (a) Obtaining or exerting unauthorized control — A person commits the offense of theft when he willfully or knowingly obtains control which is unauthorized or exerts control which is unauthorized over property of the owner, and: (1) Has the purpose of depriving the owner of the property; or (2) Willfully or knowingly uses, conceals, or abandons the property in such manner as to deprive the owner of the property; or (3) Uses, conceals, or abandons the property knowing the use, concealment or abandonment will deprive the owner of the property.

This subsection requires two primary elements to constitute the offense of theft. They are (1) a knowing exertion or obtainment of control (inadvertent or negligent exertion of control is not punished); and (2) a purpose to "deprive" (the mental element prevalent in most thefts).... Most of the activities which previously constituted shoplifting will now be a theft offense through a violation of this subsection....

Lee knowingly obtained unauthorized control over the property of another when he consciously picked up the bottle of cognac and "concealed the bottle in his pants." A person acts knowingly when he is practically certain that the result will be caused by his conduct. When knowledge of the existence of a particular fact is an element of an offense, that knowledge is established if a person is practically certain of its existence.... In this case when Lee placed the bottle of liquor in his pants, there is no question that he acted knowingly. It would be most difficult to negligently hide a bottle of liquor in such a manner. Lee obtained control over the property when he hid it from the owner's view.

The latter portion of the statute requires proof of mental state — did Lee have the purpose to deprive the owner of the bottle of liquor? The requisite mental state is usually inferred from the offender's disposition of the property....

The requisite mental state of having an intent to deprive is most frequently proved by the defendant's handling of the property....

In the instant case, Lee knowingly removed the bottle of liquor from the shelf and secreted it under his clothing. This act in itself meets the requirement of concealment. The fact that this concealment was brief or that Lee was detected before the goods were removed from the owner's premises is immaterial. The intent to deprive the owner of his property can be inferred from his furtive handling of the property. Lee not only placed the bottle in the waistband of his pants, but did so in a particularly suspicious manner by concealing the bottle such that it was hidden from the shopowner's view. It cannot be so as a matter of law that these circumstances failed to establish the elements of theft. Once a customer goes beyond the mere removal of goods from a shelf and crosses the threshold into the realm of behavior inconsistent with the owner's expectations, the circumstances may be such that a larcenous intent can be inferred....

2. Precedent is abundant that concealment of merchandise on the person or in shopping bags and other containers while a perpetrator is still within a store constitutes the necessary control (or caption and asportation under earlier law) for theft; passing beyond checkout counters to a street or parking lot is not necessary from the viewpoint of *actus reus*. See, e.g., *People v. Tijerina*, 459 P.2d 680 (Cal. 1969); *Groomes v. United States*, 155 A.2d 73 (D.C. 1959); *State v. Knowles*, 498 P.2d 40 (Kan. 1972); *People v. Bradovich*, 9 N.W.2d 560

C. ACTUS REUS

(Mich. 1954); *State v. Doherty*, 509 P.2d 351 (Utah 1973). However, to reduce the likelihood that a defendant will advance successfully a factual defense suggesting lack of culpability, *e.g.*, forgetfulness about the presence of merchandise in clothing or purse, or an intent to pay for the merchandise at a cashier's station or checkout stand, store security officers may well delay until suspected shoplifters have left commercial premises before intercepting, detaining and arresting them.

b. Misappropriation

MODEL PENAL CODE

§ 223.5. *Theft of Property Lost, Mislaid, or Delivered by Mistake*

A person who comes into control of property of another that he knows to have been lost, mislaid, or delivered under a mistake as to the nature or amount of the property or the identity of the recipient is guilty of theft if, with purpose to deprive the owner thereof, he fails to take reasonable measures to restore the property to a person entitled to have it.

Comment

[The text of this Comment appears in Appendix B.]

STATE v. WOLL

Court of Appeals of Washington
668 P.2d 610 (1983)

PETRIE, JUDGE.

....

On February 1, 1979 defendant Woll deposited $448 in his checking account at the Aberdeen Branch of the Seattle First National Bank (Sea-First). The bank mistakenly credited Woll's account with $4,448. The defendant discovered this error when he received his next bank statement several days later. Woll testified that he contacted a person, whose name and title he did not obtain, at Sea-First about the mistake and was told to "keep it in limbo until the error has been found." For the next three months, Sea-First continued erroneously to credit Woll's account. Then, on April 18, 1979, Woll closed the Sea-First account by cashing a check in the amount of $4,223.93 and depositing the proceeds in an interest bearing account in another bank. Although Woll denied that he had any "intention to deprive Sea-First of the money" and denied that he had any "intent to permanently take the money," he subsequently spent it all within 2 months.

The Federal Reserve Board detected the bank's mistake on February 21, 1980 and notified Sea-First of its error. The bank then demanded reimbursement from Woll. Because Woll did not timely repay Sea-First, the bank reported the matter to the prosecuting attorney who then initiated these criminal proceedings. On June 11, 1980, Woll was charged with having committed first degree theft "on or about April 18, 1979," by appropriating lost or misdelivered property under RCW 9A.56.020(1)(c). Three days before trial,

Woll repaid the bank from the proceeds of a second mortgage he placed on his house....

The wrongful withholding of property delivered by mistake, with knowledge of the mistake acquired subsequent to the receipt, may be punishable by statute under the name of larceny, but it is an offense distinct from common law larceny....

Thus, the common law of larceny required proof that the defendant's intent to steal concurred with his mistaken receipt of the property, whereas, under [the Washington statute] the "intent to deprive" must exist at the time of the appropriation. In the case at bench, Woll was charged with having committed the crime on or about April 18, 1979. Thus, under the charge and under the trial court's instruction, the prosecution had to prove defendant's intent on the date he transferred the funds — not the date or dates on which he subsequently spent the money. Under Washington law, "the gravamen of the offense is the appropriation of the property after having received it...."

We are persuaded that in order to prove a charge of theft under the statutory offense of appropriation of misdelivered property, the quality of the intent required is the same as that required under the statutory offense of embezzlement. Embezzlement, also, was not larceny at common law. Washington courts have, accordingly, declined to read into the crime of embezzlement the common law requisite for larceny (the intent to deprive permanently). Embezzlement requires proof only of the intent to deprive, and the crime is completed when the accused fraudulently misappropriates the property....

Therefore, we reject the defendant's contention that theft by the appropriation of misdelivered property incorporates the intent to commit common law larceny. We hold that this crime requires proof of the intent merely to deprive, at any time, the property is appropriated and not necessarily coincidental with the wrongful receipt, precisely as the jury was instructed....

c. Obtaining by Deception

MODEL PENAL CODE

§ 223.3. *Theft by Deception*

> A person is guilty of theft if he purposely obtains property of another by deception. A person deceives if he purposely:
> (1) creates or reinforces a false impression, including false impressions as to law, value, intention or other state of mind; but deception as to a person's intention to perform a promise shall not be inferred from the fact alone that he did not subsequently perform the promise; or
> (2) prevents another from acquiring information which would affect his judgment of a transaction; or
> (3) fails to correct a false impression which the deceiver previously created or reinforced, or which the deceiver knows to be influencing another to whom he stands in a fiduciary or confidential relationship; or

(4) fails to disclose a known lien, adverse claim or other legal impediment to the enjoyment of property which he transfers or encumbers in consideration for the property obtained, whether such impediment is or is not valid, or is or is not a matter of official record.

The term "deceive" does not, however, include falsity as to matters having no pecuniary significance, or puffing by statements unlikely to deceive ordinary persons in the group addressed.

Comment

[The text of this Comment appears in Appendix B.]

LINNE v. STATE
Court of Appeals of Alaska
674 P.2d 1345 (1983)

BRYNER, CHIEF JUDGE.

....

Over a period of approximately ten months, Tami Linne and her friend Theresa Brown obtained large sums of money from William Baenen. Baenen was a sixty-two year old Ketchikan resident who had accumulated more than $60,000 in savings over the course of a twenty-year career as a crane operator. According to Baenen, from May 1980, the first time he met Linne, through February 1981, he gave money to Linne on numerous occasions in response to her solicitations. Linne asked for money from Baenen for a variety of purposes, including: $300 to obtain an abortion; $800 for travel to obtain treatment for abortion complications; $400 because she had been robbed; $1,500 to "buy" a lucrative job as a cocktail waitress in Hawaii; $2,000 for travel, room and board for the Hawaii job; $1,200 to charter a helicopter and boat to search for her brother, who had died in a wilderness area; $3,200 for tuition at a beauty school in Seattle; $1,500 for living expenses while at the school; $1,900 to replace money stolen from Linne; $1,600 for an abortion after Linne was raped in Hawaii; $250 for cancer treatment; $1,000 for drug rehabilitation; $1,500 to post bail for Brown, who had purportedly been arrested in Seattle; $1,000 for a tubal ligation; and $700 for an appendectomy.

In late February 1981, Baenen gave Linne and Brown an additional $6,000 after Linne told him that she had received an offer to work as a fashion model in New York City. Linne told Baenen she needed the money to spend on travel and living expenses for herself and Brown, who was to travel with Linne and assist her with her modeling career.

Baenen considered all of the money that he gave to Linne to be a loan. Baenen also indicated that he had fallen in love with Linne. Linne led Baenen to believe she loved him and intended to move into his apartment. According to Baenen, he had been willing to give Linne money because of his affection for her, because he believed the various stories Linne told him when she asked for money, and because he hoped that she would eventually live with him. Baenen indicated that if Linne had moved into his apartment to live with him, he would have been willing to forgive the money she owed him.

Eventually, Baenen realized that Linne was defrauding him. A friend of Baenen's convinced him to contact the police. Investigation soon revealed that the various reasons Linne had given Baenen in order to obtain money from him had been false. Linne actually spent the money she received from Baenen as she pleased. On March 12, 1981, with Baenen's cooperation, police obtained a warrant to monitor a conversation in which Linne asked Baenen to give her $7,000 so that she could pay off two men who had come to Ketchikan to beat her up because of a $15,000 drug-related debt that had not been paid.

Linne was subsequently indicted by the state. All of the transfers from Baenen to Linne from June 1980 through February 1981, with the exception of the $6,000 payment for Linne's New York modeling career, were included in a single count, which charged Linne with theft by deception in the first degree. The $6,000 payment Baenen made to Linne for her New York job was the basis for the third count, which charged Linne with theft by deception in the second degree. The fourth count, charging attempted theft by deception in the second degree, was based on the request for $7,000 Linne made in March 1981.

....

Linne argues that the superior court should have dismissed her indictment because the evidence presented to the grand jury was insufficient. She contends, initially, that the statements she made to Baenen would not have constituted the common law crime of false pretenses. This claim, while technically correct, is of little consequence. Alaska's theft by deception statute was drafted with the specific purpose of encompassing a broader range of conduct than was included in the common law offense of false pretenses. In particular, the definition of "deception" contained in AS 11.81.900(b)(14) was meant to abrogate the common law rule restricting the crime of false pretenses to misrepresentations concerning existing facts....

Linne next alleges that there was insufficient evidence to merit indictment under any of the specific theories relied on by the state.

Addressing the state's first theory of prosecution — that Linne borrowed money from Baenen without intending to repay — Linne argues that there was insufficient evidence to show Baenen ever loaned her money. Linne premises this argument on a belief that the state was required to produce some evidence of formal, written agreements between Baenen and Linne. However, the statutory definition of deception includes false promises, and there is nothing in the definition that would require loans by Baenen to Linne to be reduced to writing.... Accordingly, we find no merit to Linne's argument. The grand jury could have found that Baenen loaned money to Linne, which she agreed to repay while knowing that she would not in fact repay.

Linne nevertheless maintains that she could not be convicted of deception based on mere proof of failure to repay. She relies on AS 11.46.180(b), which provides, in relevant part:

> In a prosecution based on theft by deception, if the state seeks to prove that the defendant used deception by promising performance which he did not intend to perform or knew would not be performed, that intent or

knowledge may not be established solely by or inferred solely from the fact that the promise was not performed.

Here, however, the state did not rely on Linne's failure to repay Baenen as the sole evidence supporting its claim that she never intended to repay. The state established that Linne used a series of false statements to obtain money from Baenen, that she later told Baenen she would seek to obtain employment to earn enough money to repay him, and that these promises to find employment were themselves merely pretexts for obtaining additional money. Thus, the state relied on evidence showing a series of false representations about Linne's reasons for needing money to establish, circumstantially, that Linne had never intended to repay money she obtained from Baenen. We find that sufficient evidence of Linne's lack of intent to repay was presented to the grand jury by the state.

With respect to the state's second theory of prosecution — that Linne's misrepresentations of her need for money could constitute a basis for finding deception — Linne argues her misrepresentations could not constitute deception because they had no pecuniary significance. Linne relies on AS 11.46.180(c), which states, in relevant part: "As used in this section, 'deception' ... does not include falsity as to matters having no pecuniary significance ...." Linne's claim that her misrepresentations had no pecuniary significance assumes an extremely broad reading of the exception created by AS 11.46.180(c). In effect, Linne would have us define "pecuniary significance" to include only statements expressly dealing with the commercial terms of a transaction such as the date of repayment, the interest due, and the existence of collateral.

We disagree. The plain meaning of AS 11.46.180(c) is that deception cannot be found when the significance of a misrepresentation is unrelated to money or value. The significance — or practical effect — of a misrepresentation and not merely its literal meaning is the crux of the exception. As described in AS 11.46.180, theft by deception is characterized by the taking of property by misrepresentation. Any false statement that directly promotes or induces the transfer of valuable property or that relates to the amount or value of the property transferred will thus necessarily have pecuniary significance under the terms of the statute. The exception in AS 11.46.180(c) only applies to misrepresentations that do not directly promote or induce a "taking" of property and that have no direct bearing on the amount or value of the property taken.

Here, there was ample evidence that Linne made numerous misrepresentations to Baenen concerning various reasons why she was in desperate need of money; these misrepresentations directly led Baenen to give Linne the money she requested. The claim that Linne's misrepresentations had no pecuniary significance is thus without merit.

With respect to the state's third theory of prosecution — that Linne committed deception by falsely promising to live with Baenen — Linne again relies on the exception for statements having no pecuniary significance. She insists that her expressions of love for Baenen had no pecuniary significance and thus fall into the exception of AS 11.46.180(c). This argument mischaracterizes the state's theory. The state did not attempt to establish deception merely by proving that Linne claimed to love Baenen when in fact she did not. Rather, the state sought to show that in order to induce Baenen to continue giving her money, Linne knowingly created or confirmed the false impression that she intended to live with him. Evidence of Linne's false expressions of love for Baenen was only relevant insofar as it tended to support Baenen's testimony that Linne led him to believe she intended to live with him. Creation of this type of false impression is squarely within the statutory definition of "deception." AS 11.81.900(b)(14)(A). Linne's argument that the state relied on her statements of love for Baenen as the sole basis for establishing deception is without merit.

In summary, we find no merit to Linne's claim that insufficient evidence of deception was presented to the grand jury; we therefore hold that the trial court properly rejected Linne's motion to dismiss her indictment....

Linne further contends that Judge Schulz improperly refused to give several of her proposed jury instructions. First, Linne maintains, that her proposed instruction describing the essential elements of theft by deception should have been given to the jury. This instruction differed from the instruction actually given primarily in that it defined the terms "pecuniary" and "reasonable person." We first consider Linne's argument with respect to the definition of the word "pecuniary."

As we have already indicated, Linne incorrectly interpreted the language of AS 11.46.180(c), which excludes statements "having no pecuniary significance" from the statutory definition of "deception," to mean that only misrepresentations expressly dealing with the formal terms of a transaction could constitute "deception." Although the definition of "pecuniary" contained in Linne's proposed jury instructions was slightly broader than the narrow interpretation of AS 11.46.180(c) that she argued for prior to trial, it was intended to support that interpretation.

The relevant portion of Linne's proposed instruction stated:

> Deception does not include falsity as to matters having no pecuniary significance. "Pecuniary" means of or relating to money. So, even if you find that the defendant knowingly deceived William Baenen in obtaining or attempting to obtain property of William Baenen, but that any false statement made to Mr. Baenen had no pecuniary significance, then there is no "deception" within the meaning of the law, and that element is not present with regard to the crime charged.

Because Linne's proposed instruction defined only the word "pecuniary," rather than the statutory term "pecuniary significance," it might well have misled the jury to believe, in keeping with Linne's interpretation of AS 11.46.180(c), that an express misrepresentation as to the pecuniary terms of a transaction was required before deception could be established. As previously noted, Linne's reading of AS 11.46.180(c) was mistaken. Based on this finding, we believe Judge Schulz properly refused to give Linne's definition of the word "pecuniary."

Linne's proposed instruction on the elements of theft by deception also contained the following definition of "reasonable person":

> A "reasonable person" is an average one of ordinary prudence, a hypothetical person who is both prudent and careful. As a jury, you are to consider only whether or not such a reasonable person would be deceived by statements alleged to be made by the defendant. You are not asked to consider whether or not William Baenen was actually deceived by any such statements. In other words, the standard for determining whether a reasonable person would be deceived is objective, not subjective.

As is apparent from this definition, Linne believed the crime of theft by deception was governed by an objective standard: a misrepresentation could not amount to deception unless it would deceive a reasonable person. According to the proposed instruction, it was immaterial that Linne actually deceived William Baenen, as long as a reasonable person would not have been deceived. We find that Linne's instruction conflicts with the plain meaning of the law and with the basic policy underlying the prohibition of theft by deception.

The offense of theft by deception is plainly intended to protect unwary members of the public from a broad range of fraudulent or deceptive schemes. To carve out of the offense a blanket exception for victims whose deception might be deemed unreasonable would be anomalous. Those who engage in deception for pecuniary gain quite naturally tend to select as their victims people who are the most susceptible to misrepresentations. The victims of deceptive schemes will frequently be particularly vulnerable people. If guilt of theft by deception were determined by an objective, reasonable person standard, those who stand in greatest need of protection against deceptive schemes would in effect be declared fair game. Instead of discouraging the use of deceptive means to obtain property, the theft by deception statute would do no more than encourage offenders to be selective in their choice of victim.

The statutory definition of "deception" contained in AS 11.81.900(b)(14) provides no support for the proposition that an objective, reasonable person standard should be applied in theft by deception cases. This definition indicates an intent by the legislature to require a subjective standard: the jury need only find that the victim of false claims was actually deceived. The only statutory reference to an objective standard occurs in the portion of AS 11.46.180(c) that provides: "'deception' does not include ... 'puffing' by statements unlikely to deceive reasonable persons in the group addressed." The scope of this provision is limited; it merely applies the reasonable person standard to cases involving 'puffing.'"

We find no basis for Linne's claim that an objective standard should be applied to the entire theft by deception statute, and we therefore conclude that the trial court properly refused to give Linne's proposed instruction describing the reasonable person standard.

Linne additionally disputes Judge Schulz's refusal to give her proposed instructions defining "loan" and "gift." We believe that the ordinary meaning of both words is widely known and is well within the grasp of average jurors. Technical definitions of these words would have been of little relevance to Linne's case. Although Linne maintains that the legal distinctions between a loan and a gift were crucial, her position is based on the faulty premise that the jury would not have been entitled to convict unless they found that Baenen made legally enforceable loans of money to Linne. Applying the statutory definition of "deception" to this case, however, it would make little difference whether Baenen was found to have given money to Linne as a loan or as a gift. The offense of theft by deception focuses on the means used to obtain property, not the actual method by which property is conveyed. As long as the jury found that Linne obtained money from Baenen by means of deception — by creating or confirming a false impression that she did not believe to be true or by promising performance that she did not intend to perform — conviction would be justified regardless of whether Linne obtained the money as a gift, as a formal loan, or as an informal loan — one that did not meet all legal requirements of enforceability.... We hold that the trial court's refusal to define "gift" and "loan" was not an abuse of discretion....

2. SPOUSAL PROPERTY

MODEL PENAL CODE

§ 223.1. Consolidation of Theft Offenses

> (4) *Theft from Spouse.* It is no defense that theft was from the actor's spouse, except that misappropriation of household and personal effects, or other property normally accessible to both spouses, is theft only if it occurs after the parties have ceased living together.

Comment

[The text of this Comment appears in Appendix B.]

3. GRADING

MODEL PENAL CODE

§ 223.1. *Consolidation of Theft Offenses*

> (2) Grading of Theft Offenses.
> (a) Theft constitutes a felony of the third degree if the amount involved exceeds $500, or if the property stolen is a firearm, automobile, airplane, motorcycle, motorboat, or other motor-propelled vehicle, or in the case of theft by receiving stolen property, if the receiver is in the business of buying or selling stolen property.
> (b) Theft not within the preceding paragraph constitutes a misdemeanor, except that if the property was not taken from the person or by threat, or in breach of a fiduciary obligation, and the actor proves by a preponderance of the evidence that the amount involved was less than $50, the offense constitutes a petty misdemeanor.
> (c) The amount involved in a theft shall be deemed to be the highest value, by any reasonable standard, of the property or services which the actor stole or attempted to steal. Amounts involved in thefts committed

pursuant to one scheme or course of conduct, whether from the same person or several persons, may be aggregated in determining the grade of the offense.

Comment

[The text of this Comment appears in Appendix B.]

NOTES

1. Review the materials on value as a grading criterion under traditional larceny law, § 1(A)(5), *supra* pp. 392-396.

2. Theft from the person, *i.e.*, pickpocketing, usually warrants somewhat escalated penalties. State authorities are not in agreement as to whether a taking of property in the owner's possession or control is sufficient, or whether there must be an actual taking from the person. The court in *State v. Crowe*, 384 A.2d 340, 342-43 (Conn. 1977), noted:

> In our view, larceny from the person requires an actual trespass to the person of the victim. Because of the trespass to the person, the offense is a serious crime in itself so that the value of the property stolen does not enter into the magnitude of the crime. On the other hand, the removal of property from the presence or control of the victim lacks such a trespass and is insufficient to constitute larceny from the person. We are, therefore, in accord with the rule that larceny from the person is a separate and distinct offense from that of simple larceny [citing consonant authorities].

3. The court in *State v. Schaaf*, 449 N.W.2d 762, 770-771 (Neb. 1989) addressed the question of consolidation of thefts in minor amounts (here, thefts by misappropriation) into a single crime of theft carrying heavier penalties:

> Nothing in the explicit language of § 28-511(2) compels the conclusion that theft by disposition is a continuing offense. If the Legislature had intended that a series of misappropriations be considered in the aggregate as one offense, such as in the provision which previously existed in the criminal statute defining the former crime of embezzlement in Nebraska (§ 28-538), the Legislature, through the rather simple process of explicit statutory language, could have inserted the "one act," or continuing offense, provision into § 28-511(2) of the Nebraska Criminal Code. In construing a penal statute, a court cannot supply language which is absent from the statutory definition for a criminal offense.... In the absence of language constituting a "continuing offense" provision in § 28-511(2), we must conclude that the Legislature did not intend that a series of separate acts, each of which is a theft proscribed by § 28-511(2), constitutes one criminal act or a continuing offense of theft. Consequently, the offense of theft by disposition, prohibited by § 28-511(2), was committed each time that Schaaf, without authorization, transferred Lenhart Company's funds, or the corporation's interest in the funds, to himself or 4-S Investments with the intent to benefit himself or 4-S Investments, when neither

was entitled to the property transferred. Inasmuch as Schaaf might have been prosecuted for each of the 25 transactions involving a misappropriation or unauthorized transfer of Lenhart Company's funds, the 3-year statute of limitations prescribed by § 29-110, barred prosecution of Schaaf for each transaction in question which occurred before October 16, 1984. Therefore, the only offense of theft by disposition which was subject to timely prosecution was the transaction of January 7, 1985 — Schaaf's unauthorized transfer of $3,500 from the funds and checking account of Lenhart Company and deposit of those funds in the checking account of 4-S Investments.

D. *MENS REA*

1. GENERALLY

PEOPLE v. WASHBURN

Supreme Court of Colorado
593 P.2d 962 (1979)

ROVIRA, JUSTICE.

The People appeal the ruling of the Adams County District Court which dismissed separate prosecutions of the defendants on the basis that section 18-4-402(1)(b), C.R.S. 1973, and section 18-4-402(1)(b), C.R.S. 1973 (1978 Repl. Vol. 8), required no culpable mental state and thus violated the constitution. For the purpose of this appeal, we have consolidated both cases. We reverse and remand with directions that the informations be reinstated.

William Washburn (Washburn) was arrested and charged with theft of rental property, section 18-4-402(1)(b), C.R.S. 1973, which states:

(1) A person commits theft of rental property if he: ...
(b) Having lawfully obtained possession for temporary use of the personal property of another which is available only for hire, *intentionally* fails to reveal the whereabouts of or to return said property to the owner thereof or his representative or to the person from whom he has received it within seventy-two hours after the time at which he agreed to return it. (Emphasis added.)

Howard Stroh (Stroh) was arrested and charged with theft of rental property, section 18-4-402(1)(b), C.R.S. 1973 (1978 Repl. Vol. 8), as amended July 1, 1977, which provides:

(1) A person commits theft of rental property if he: ...
(b) Having lawfully obtained possession for temporary use of the personal property of another which is available only for hire *knowingly* fails to reveal the whereabouts of or to return said property to the owner thereof or his representative or to the person from whom he has received it within seventy-two hours after the time at which he agreed to return it. (Emphasis added.)

The trial court erroneously assumed that both defendants were charged under the statute as amended. The court, after determining that the statute,

D. MENS REA

as amended, was unconstitutional because it contained no element of conscious wrongdoing or criminal intent and no requirement of criminal conduct, dismissed the charges against both defendants. The bases of the court's ruling were the opinions of the United States Supreme Court in *Morissette v. United States,* 342 U.S. 246 (1952), and of the Alaska Supreme Court in *Speidel v. State,* 460 P.2d 77 (Alaska 1969). The trial court read *Morissette, supra,* to require an element of conscious wrongdoing or criminal intent in statutes such as section 18-4-402(1)(b), C.R.S. 1973, as amended, and read *Speidel, supra,* as an application of that doctrine. Although the order of the trial court did not indicate that the basis for its decision was a violation of due process of law under *U.S. Const.* amend. XIV, counsel on appeal argued, and we now decide the issue in terms of due process requirements.

I

Although the ruling of the trial court concerning Washburn was based on the mistaken assumption by the court and counsel that he had been charged under the statute as amended, we must address the issue of the criminal intent required in the statute under which he was charged in reality. Thus, we first address the issue of the culpable mental state required in section 18-4-402(1)(b), C.R.S. 1973, both before and after amendment.

The legislature can proscribe an act without regard to a culpable mental state, but only if it does so pursuant to its police power. *Morissette, supra; People v. Caddy,* 189 Colo. 353, 540 P.2d 1089 (1975). Such is not the statute in this case. Clearly, the theft of rental property, which is punishable by imprisonment in the state penitentiary because it is a felony, is not akin to speeding violations. *Caddy, supra.* As the United States Supreme Court stated in *Morissette,* offenses which have their bases in common law — such as provisions concerning theft — must be construed to require a culpable mental state.

The culpable mental state required in a statute dealing with theft must be more than mere negligence, *People v. Johnson,* 193 Colo. 199, 564 P.2d 116 (1977), but it need not be specific intent. *Morissette, supra; People v. Holloway,* 193 Colo. 450, 568 P.2d 29 (1977).

Washburn argues that section 18-4-402(1)(b), C.R.S. 1973, does not require a culpable mental state because "intentionally" refers to the act, not to the intent of the actor. Such an interpretation is at odds with *Morissette,* in which the United States Supreme Court addressed a similar statute.

In *Morissette,* the defendant was convicted of converting government property to his own use under a statute which did not specify a culpable mental state. The lower court held that his defense of belief that the property had been abandoned could not be submitted to the jury because a culpable mental state was not an element of the offense. The United States Supreme Court reversed, holding that where an offense has been construed in the past to require criminal intent, legislative silence indicates approval of that prior judicial interpretation. The Court then construed the statute at issue to require an element of criminal intent.

It has been well settled in this state that whenever possible a statute should be construed as to obviate or reduce any constitutional infirmities, section 2-4-201(1)(a), C.R.S. 1973; *Bolles v. People,* 189 Colo. 394, 541 P.2d 80 (1975), not to impose them. This was the crux of *Morissette, supra.* The statute in that case was silent on the subject of a culpable mental state. The United States Supreme Court did not declare the statute to be unconstitutional; rather, it found the element of criminal intent implicit in the statute.

Similarly, the language of section 18-4-402(1)(b), C.R.S. 1973, while imprecise, does require a culpable mental state. By the use of the word "intentionally" the legislature has indicated its design to require a culpable mental state as an element of the offense. Section 18-1-501(4), C.R.S. 1973, states that: "'Culpable mental state' means 'intentionally' ... or 'knowingly'...." The use of those terms thus indicates the requirement of a culpable mental state.

Contrary to Washburn's contentions, a defendant must do more than retain the rental property for more than three days after it is due in order to be convicted. The United States Supreme Court stated in *Morissette* that:

> knowing conversion requires more than knowledge that the defendant was taking the property into his possession. He must have had knowledge of the facts, though not necessarily the law, that made the taking a conversion.

Similarly, in order to be convicted under section 18-4-402(1)(b), C.R.S. 1973, the accused must have had the specific intent that his acts constitute a wrongful retention of the rental property....

II

The issue presented on appeal by Stroh is whether the change of "intentionally" to "knowingly" removed the element of criminal intent from the statute, thus rendering the provision unconstitutional.

The change of the word "intentionally" to "knowingly" does not remove the element of a culpable mental state from the statute. The conscious culpability required by the statute remains the wrongful retention of the rental property. Under the statute before it was amended, the wrongful retention had to be with specific intent, as stated in part I above. Under the statute as amended, the wrongful retention need only be with general intent. The change of the statute from a specific intent offense to a general intent offense does not abrogate the necessity of a culpable mental state as an element of the offense. To the contrary, it is a clear indication from the legislature that conviction under the statute requires proof of the culpable mental state.

Thus, in order to be convicted under section 18-4-402(1)(b), C.R.S. 1973 (1978 Repl. Vol. 8) — the statute as amended — the defendant must have had knowledge that his acts would constitute the wrongful retention of the rental property. To make such a determination, the jury would have to be appropriately instructed....

NOTES

1. On the nature of proof of intent to defraud in a theft prosecution based on fraudulent representations, *see People v. Luongo,* 391 N.E.2d 1341 (N.Y. 1979).

2. Is the following statutory presumption constitutional?

> The knowing concealment, upon his person or the person of another, of unpurchased goods or merchandise offered for sale by any store or other business establishment shall give rise to a presumption that the actor took goods with the purpose of depriving the owner, or another person having an interest therein.

See Smith v. State, 575 S.W.2d 677 (Ark. 1979).

3. While attending a theater, *V* placed her handbag on the floor beside her. *D* surreptitiously picked it up, looked through the contents and placed it back onto the floor without having taken anything from it. *D* then left, but was later arrested and charged with theft. His defense was that he examined the contents of the handbag only to see if it contained anything worth stealing. Having found nothing, he returned the handbag to its original place. Should *D* be convictable of theft? Would attempted theft be a more appropriate charge? *Compare Regina v. Easom,* [1971] 55 Crim. App. 410; [1971] 2 Q.B. 315, *with* MODEL PENAL CODE § 2.02(6) (1980). *See generally* Glanville Williams, *Three Rogues' Charters,* [1980] CRIM. L. REV. 263.

MODEL PENAL CODE

§ 223.0. Definitions

> In this Article, unless a different meaning plainly is required:
> (1) "deprive" means: (a) to withhold property of another permanently or for so extended a period as to appropriate a major portion of its economic value, or with intent to restore only upon payment of reward or other compensation; or (b) to dispose of the property so as to make it unlikely that the owner will recover it....

Comment

[The text of this Comment appears in Appendix B.]

Comment to § 223.5

[The text of this Comment discussing culpability appears in Appendix B.]

2. CLAIM OF RIGHT

MODEL PENAL CODE

§ 223.1. Consolidation of Theft Offenses

> (3) *Claim of Right.* It is an affirmative defense to prosecution for theft that the actor:

(a) was unaware that the property or service was that of another; or

(b) acted under an honest claim of right to the property or service involved or that he had a right to acquire or dispose of it as he did; or

(c) took property exposed for sale, intending to purchase and pay for it promptly, or reasonably believing that the owner, if present, would have consented.

Comment

[The text of this Comment appears in Appendix B.]

E. SPECIAL FORMS OF THEFT

1. THEFT OF SERVICES

MODEL PENAL CODE

§ 223.7. *Theft of Services*

(1) A person is guilty of theft if he purposely obtains services which he knows are available only for compensation, by deception or threat, or by false token or other means to avoid payment for the service. "Services" includes labor, professional service, transportation, telephone or other public service, accommodation in hotels, restaurants or elsewhere, admission to exhibitions, use of vehicles or other movable property. Where compensation for service is ordinarily paid immediately upon the rendering of such service, as in the case of hotels and restaurants, refusal to pay or absconding without payment or offer to pay gives rise to a presumption that the service was obtained by deception as to intention to pay.

(2) A person commits theft if, having control over the disposition of services of others, to which he is not entitled, he knowingly diverts such services to his own benefit or to the benefit of another not entitled thereto.

NOTES

1. To trigger a statutory presumption that absconding without paying or offering to pay for food is prima facie proof of intent to defraud, the prosecution must show that a departure from premises was secretive, clandestine or surreptitious; an open departure or failure to establish the circumstances of leaving a restaurant does not suffice. *State v. Wagenius,* 581 P.2d 319 (Idaho 1978).

2. *State v. Gisclair,* 382 So. 2d 914 (La. 1980), holding that employers do not "own" the services of their employees. Therefore, when a county official was assisted by public employees in renovating his own property during their hours of public employment, the state was not deprived of movable property. The employees owned their own services, but the indictment charged that the state and county (parish) owned them, so that the conviction could not be sustained.

3. In *Johnson v. State*, 316 S.E.2d 160 (Ga. App. 1984), the court brought within the crime of cable television services one who attached a "converter box" to a television set in order to permit the reception of cable television channels for which the expected fee had not been paid.

2. THEFT OF FUNDS RECEIVED

MODEL PENAL CODE

§ 223.8. Theft by Failure to Make Required Disposition of Funds Received

A person who purposely obtains property upon agreement, or subject to a known legal obligation, to make specified payment or other disposition, whether from such property or its proceeds or from his own property to be reserved in equivalent amount, is guilty of theft if he deals with the property obtained as his own and fails to make the required payment or disposition. The foregoing applies notwithstanding that it may be impossible to identify particular property as belonging to the victim at the time of the actor's failure to make the required payment or disposition. An officer or employee of the government or of a financial institution is presumed: (i) to know any legal obligation relevant to his criminal liability under this Section, and (ii) to have dealt with the property as his own if he fails to pay or account upon lawful demand, or if an audit reveals a shortage or falsification of accounts.

Comment

[The text of this Comment appears in Appendix B.]

NOTES

1. A corporate official as well as a corporation itself may be prosecuted for violations of statutes patterned on § 223.8. *Butts v. Commonwealth*, 581 S.W.2d 565 (Ky. 1979).

2. A provision shifting to the defense the burden of persuading the trier of fact that property was appropriated under a claim of right made in good faith, N.Y. PENAL LAW § 155.15 (McKinney 1985), was ruled unconstitutional in *People v. Chesler*, 406 N.E.2d 455 (N.Y. 1980), on the basis of *Mullaney v. Wilbur*, 421 U.S. 684 (1975). *See Patterson v. New York*, 432 U.S. 197 (1979) *supra* p. 324.

3. CREDIT CARD MISUSE

MODEL PENAL CODE

§ 224.6. Credit Cards

A person commits an offense if he uses a credit card for the purpose of obtaining property or services with knowledge that:
   (1) the card is stolen or forged; or
   (2) the card has been revoked or cancelled; or

(3) for any other reason his use of the card is unauthorized by the issuer.

It is an affirmative defense to prosecution under paragraph (3) if the actor proves by a preponderance of the evidence that he had the purpose and ability to meet all obligations to the issuer arising out of his use of the card. "Credit card" means a writing or other evidence of an undertaking to pay for property or services delivered or rendered to or upon the order of a designated person or bearer. An offense under this Section is a felony of the third degree if the value of the property or services secured or sought to be secured by means of the credit card exceeds $500; otherwise it is a misdemeanor.

Comment

[The text of this Comment appears in Appendix B.]

NOTES

1. A "credit card" is defined in N.Y. PENAL LAW § 155.00(7) (McKinney 1985) as "any instrument or article defined as a credit card in section five hundred eleven of the general business law."

2. Coexistence of credit card misuse and forgery statutes, the latter bearing heavier penalties than the former, does not offend against equal protection, even though a given credit card transaction may involve a forgery of a charge slip. *Mack v. State,* 286 N.W.2d 563 (Wis. 1980).

3. A statute, LA. REV. STAT. ANN. § 14:67.3 (West Supp. 1993), covered fraudulent use of a credit card to obtain credit or the privilege of making deferred payment for money, goods or services. A conviction of attempted violation of the statute was proper when a defendant was detected by the intended victim before goods were supplied on credit. *State v. Williams,* 389 So. 2d 384 (La. 1980).

4. NO-ACCOUNT CHECK LEGISLATION

MODEL PENAL CODE

§ 224.5. Bad Checks

A person who issues or passes a check or similar sight order for the payment of money, knowing that it will not be honored by the drawee, commits a misdemeanor. For the purposes of this Section as well as in any prosecution for theft committed by means of a bad check, an issuer is presumed to know that the check or order (other than a post-dated check or order) would not be paid, if:

(1) the issuer had no account with the drawee at the time the check or order was issued; or

(2) payment was refused by the drawee for lack of funds, upon presentation within 30 days after issue, and the issuer failed to make good within 10 days after receiving notice of that refusal.

E. SPECIAL FORMS OF THEFT

Comment

[The text of this Comment appears in Appendix B.]

NOTES

1. Worthless check statutes have been sustained as facially valid against contentions they infringe on state constitutional prohibitions against imprisonment for debt. *See, e.g., Commonwealth v. Mutnik,* 406 A.2d 516 (Pa. 1979); *Locklear v. State,* 273 N.W.2d 334 (Wis. 1979). However, if the facts of a given case indicate that a prosecution was initiated solely to force repayment of a debt to a creditor, it may be terminated on such a ground. *Harris v. State,* 378 So. 2d 257 (Ala. Crim. App.), *cert. denied,* 378 So. 2d 263 (Ala. 1979).

2. A claim of unconstitutional discrimination against poor people, based on the fact that payment within five days destroyed a statutory presumption that nonpayment by the expiry of that time supported a presumption of intent that a check should not be paid, was rejected in *Locklear v. State,* note 1 *supra.*

3. Unless there is a special statute to that effect, amounts obtained through a series of worthless check transactions cannot be cumulated in order to support a heavier penalty. *State v. Meyer,* 613 P.2d 132 (Wash. App. 1980).

4. A statutory requirement of "present consideration" is not met by proof of a promise to pay for property in the future. *State v. Mauck,* 270 N.W.2d 56 (S.D. 1978).

5. Is the presumptive language of MODEL PENAL CODE § 224.5 and its commonly encountered state counterparts, discussed in Appendix B, constitutional in light of *County Court v. Allen, Sandstrom v. Montana,* and *Francis v. Franklin, supra* pp. 54-56?

5. UNLAWFUL VEHICLE USE

MODEL PENAL CODE

§ 223.9. Unauthorized Use of Automobiles and Other Vehicles

> A person commits a misdemeanor if he operates another's automobile, airplane, motorcycle, motorboat, or other motor-propelled vehicle without consent of the owner. It is an affirmative defense to prosecution under this Section that the actor reasonably believed that the owner would have consented to the operation had he known of it.

Comment

[The text of this Comment appears in Appendix B.]

STATE v. CLARK

Supreme Court of Washington
638 P.2d 572 (1982)

[Noll gave Clark permission to use his car for part of a day to see Clark's probation officer and inquire about employment. Clark's version of the transaction was that Noll told Clark he could use the car as if it were his own and to take care of his problems, chief among which was trouble with his girl friend who lived in Colorado. Clark did not return the vehicle at noon, and Noll reported it to police as stolen later that afternoon. Clark drove the vehicle to Denver; he claimed that upon arrival he had telephoned Noll to tell him that fact and the fact that he lacked funds to return the car to Yakima. Noll located his car some weeks later in a Colorado wrecking yard where it was in storage. Clark did not return to Washington for about one year. He was prosecuted under Wash. Rev. Code § 9A.56.070(1) (1974 ed.), covering one who "without the permission of the owner or person entitled to the possession thereof intentionally take[s] or drive[s] away any automobile or motor vehicle," the state "joyriding" statute.]

WILLIAMS, JUSTICE.

... In *State v. Boggs,* 181 Iowa 358, 164 N.W. 759 (1917), a statute similar to the one at issue here was considered. In that case, the defendant obtained consent from the owner to use an automobile for "fifteen or twenty minutes."... Instead, he and some companions took the car around town, then to another town and abandoned it there. In holding the statute inapplicable to those circumstances, the court noted:

> As stated by the court, the gist of the offense is the taking and operating, or causing a motor vehicle to be taken or operated, by another without the consent of the owner. *The statute was not designed to punish one who, by misrepresentation or for a fraudulent purpose, obtains consent of the owner to take and operate his motor vehicle, but one who takes possession thereof without permission or consent of the owner.*

(Italics ours.) *Boggs,* at 361, 164 N.W. 759.

People v. Alaboda, 198 App. Div. 41, 189 N.Y.S. 464 (1921), involved slightly different circumstances in that the defendant originally rented a car but failed to return it. He was prosecuted for larceny. Although larceny would require proof of intent to permanently deprive, the court analyzed the case more from the perspective of a breach of contract. The court noted that such conduct was not an offense against society until the legislature clearly indicates that it is criminal, since statutes in contravention of the common law are to be strictly construed. The conviction was reversed.

In *State v. Mularkey,* 195 Wis. 549, 218 N.W. 809 (1928), the Wisconsin Supreme Court relied heavily on the Iowa Supreme Court's decision in *Boggs.* The court held there was no violation of the Wisconsin joyriding statute where the defendant had lawfully obtained the owner's consent to use his automobile and then made an unauthorized or extended use of the car. The substance of the offense aimed at by the Wisconsin statute was the "obtaining of the possession in the first instance without the consent of the owner." *Mularkey,* at 551, 218 N.W. 809.

In contrast to the above three cases, *State v. Williams,* 74 Ohio App. 370, 59 N.E.2d 58 (1943), held the Ohio statute applicable under slightly different circumstances. *Williams* involved a master-servant relationship whereby the employee used his employer's automobile for personal errands, in excess of the

E. SPECIAL FORMS OF THEFT

permission granted by the employer. In upholding the conviction, the court stated:

> When the defendant departed from the use of the car for which the consent and permission of his employer had been given, and thereafter proceeded to use the car for his own purposes entirely dissociated with any business of his employer, he most certainly drove and operated it without the consent of the owner.

Williams, at 371, 59 N.E.2d 58....

Although no legislative history is available from which to discern the statute's intended reach, we are persuaded that the rule enunciated in *Boggs* and *Mularkey* is the better-reasoned interpretation of joyriding statutes in general and RCW 9A.56.070(1) in particular. Instead of charging the appellant with the crime involved in this case, the prosecutor should have charged him with theft under RCW 9A.56.020(1)(a). That section defines theft as wrongfully obtaining or exerting unauthorized influence over the property of another with intent to deprive him of such property. The phrases "wrongfully obtain" or "exert unauthorized control" are defined to mean:

> (a) To take the property or services of another; or
> (b) *Having any property or services in one's possession, custody or control as bailee,* factor, pledgee, servant, attorney, agent, employee, trustee, executor, administrator, guardian, or officer of any person, estate, association, or corporation, or as a public officer, or person authorized by agreement or competent authority to take or hold such possession, custody, or control, *to secrete, withhold, or appropriate the same to his own use or to the use of any person other than the true owner or person entitled thereto;*

(Italics ours.) RCW 9A.56.010(7)(a) and (b). We think the appellant was clearly a bailee of Noll's vehicle since he was entrusted with the car to do certain errands and return. Also, the above theft statute clearly covers the appellant's conduct without having to interpret RCW 9A.56.070(1) expansively. It would seem logical that RCW 9A.56.070(1) is intended only to prevent the initially unauthorized use of a vehicle. Otherwise, the theft statute and the joyriding statute would proscribe the same conduct, yet a defendant potentially could suffer a different penalty depending on which crime was charged. We do not believe such an overlap between RCW 9A.56.020 and RCW 9A.56.070(1) was intended by the legislature. If we were to accept the State's argument that exceeding the scope of permission is violative of RCW 9A.56.070(1), we would be forced to arrive at absurd results. For instance, if a person takes a car with the owner's permission, then exceeds that permission to some degree, we would be compelled to find him guilty even if he returns the car to the owner. We cannot believe the legislature intended such a result.

Since we hold that once a person obtains permission to use an automobile he cannot violate RCW 9A.56.070(1) even if he exceeds the scope of that permission, the appellant was improperly charged under the statute in question. We therefore reverse his conviction.

NOTES

1. In *People v. Andrews,* 632 P.2d 1012 (Colo. 1981), the court sustained as not overbroad a statute defining as aggravated theft of a motor vehicle the knowing obtaining or exercising of control over a motor vehicle of another without authorization, coupled with retention of possession or control for more than 72 hours. The *mens rea* requirement of "knowing" as defined by statute precluded criminality based on negligence.

2. In *State v. Dirker,* 610 P.2d 1275 (Utah 1980), defendant had been convicted of violating a theft statute based on intentional use or operation of a vehicle, received from the owner under an agreement to perform for compensation repair services, without the owner's consent and for personal purposes constituting a gross deviation from the agreed purpose. He had undertaken to rebuild a Porsche 914 which had been severely damaged in a wreck, and apparently was given permission to drive it to and from his place of employment, although he and the owner disagreed over whether other uses were allowed. Dirker drove the car to a club and met his girl friend. Because her jeep was more difficult to drive than the Porsche, he drove her car and she followed him in the Porsche. She drove it into the back of the jeep, rendering it nonrepairable. The appellate court reversed the conviction because what Dirker had done was not a sufficiently gross deviation from the terms of the consent to justify prosecution.

3. In *Speidel v. State,* 460 P.2d 77 (Alaska 1969), a statute making it a felony to "wilfully neglect" to return a rented automobile to the owner at the time and place specified in the rental agreement was held invalid except to the extent that a conscious purpose to injure the owner of the vehicle is entertained by the defendant. The court distinguished "public welfare" offenses, where relatively light penalties are imposed regardless of criminal intent, for the purpose of protecting the health, safety, and welfare of the public. "To make such an act, without consciousness of wrongdoing or intention to inflict injury, a serious crime, and criminals of those who fall within its interdiction, is inconsistent with the general law. To convict a person of a felony for such an act, without proving criminal intent, is to deprive such person of due process of law." *Id.* at 80.

4. A good faith belief in an owner's consent to use is a factual defense to a charge of joyriding, on the analogy of the traditional larceny doctrine. *State v. Williams,* 588 P.2d 1201 (Wash. App. 1978).

5. A moped was held to be a motor vehicle for purposes of a joyriding statute. *United States v. Stancil,* 422 A.2d 1285 (D.C. 1980) (citing authorities).

6. Failure to return forms of rental property other than automobiles did not constitute theft of movables under the Louisiana statute, because that alone does not establish beyond a reasonable doubt the required intent to defraud. Special legislation would be necessary before intentional noncompliance with rental agreements could be penalized. *State v. Bias,* 400 So. 2d 650 (La. 1981).

7. The statutory crime does not require proof beyond a reasonable doubt of intent permanently to deprive, as in traditional larceny. *Ketchum v. Commonwealth,* 403 S.E.2d 382 (Va. App. 1991).

6. COMPUTER CRIMES

COMMONWEALTH v. GERULIS

Superior Court of Pennsylvania
616 A.2d 686 (1992)

KELLY, JUDGE.

....

Appellant was arrested on May 8, 1990, for her alleged infiltration of voice mailbox systems of two organizations, Magee Women's Hospital and Pittsburgh Cellular I Telephone Company. The Commonwealth charged appellant with two counts of unlawful use of computers, 18 Pa.C.S.A. § 3933(a)(1), two counts of theft of services, 18 Pa.C.S.A. § 3926(a)(1), and one count of unlawful use of credit cards, 18 Pa.C.S.A. § 4106(a)(3). After a preliminary hearing, the last charge was dismissed. On May 3, 1991, appellant proceeded to trial. The Commonwealth adduced the following evidence, which the trial court, as factfinder, accepted.

Gayle Ziccardi, manager of telecommunications at Magee Women's Hospital (Magee Hospital), testified that at least forty of the hospital's voice mailboxes had been taken over by unauthorized users. The authorized users were employees of Magee who left messages for one another and for the benefit of hospital patients and the general public. Cracking the secret password, the unauthorized users would access the system and leave messages for other "phone phreakers,"[1] ousting the intended user. The benefit to the intruders was free message space to leave a list of illegally obtained credit and calling card numbers on the boxes.

Ms. Ziccardi heard the code name "Electra" on one mailbox. The operations of Magee Hospital were disrupted, as Ms. Ziccardi "was required to constantly purge the unauthorized interlopers, re-program the [voice mailboxes] and contact authorized users with regard to the next passwords."... Ms. Ziccardi repeated that process for nine months as often as the intruders entered the hospital's system. She could have spent her time conducting her "daily business matters." ... The court concluded that over the nine month period, due to the interruption of forty boxes, Magee Hospital lost $4,300, calculated by the hours which Ms. Ziccardi was forced to spend purging the voice mailbox system.

The other corporate target was Pittsburgh Cellular I Telephone Company (Pittsburgh Cellular Phones). Paul Zanotto, as operations manager, was responsible for maintaining Pittsburgh Cellular Phones' voice mailbox system. Most of the authorized users of those boxes were subscribers of cellular phones, who paid a monthly usage fee and a per-minute retrieval charge. Customers of Pittsburgh Cellular Phones complained that their passwords no longer accessed their voice mailboxes. Investigation then led to the discovery that someone had changed their passwords.

During his investigation, Mr. Zanotto identified "Electra" as the name of the woman who infiltrated one of the boxes, number 298-8139. "He heard

---

[1] A phone-phreaker is one who illegally markets telephone services. *See generally* Flanagan and McMenamin, *For Whom the Bells Toll,* Forbes, Aug. 3, 1992, at 60-64.

'Electra' providing information for other persons in the system and into private branch exchange (P.B.X.) dialing instructions."... The trial court accepted Mr. Zanotto's testimony that Pittsburgh Cellular Phones had lost $2,500 by fixing the mailboxes and appeasing disgruntled customers.

At trial, another prosecution witness, John Bradbury, testified that "Electra" and he were "phone-phreakers." The trial court explained:

> They discussed codes for long distance calls, how to get into VMB [voice mailbox] systems and how to use these codes to get free phone calls using other people's numbers. Bradbury continued as to how he and the [appellant] would trade these numbers in attempts to get free long distance phone service illegally; the term he applied to one who engages in this activity was "phone-phreaker."...

Appellant and Bradbury were able to succeed in the marketing of their illegally obtained information through the use of the voice mailboxes of Magee Hospital and Pittsburgh Cellular Phones.

Posing as a fellow "phone-phreaker," Sergeant John Michalec was able to gain appellant's confidence. Appellant contacted Sergeant Michalec through an undercover voice mailbox at Magee Hospital. She confided in him that she used Magee's system, and others, as a conduit for furthering the unauthorized dissemination of credit card and telephone card numbers. The sergeant verified that appellant was "Electra" when, pretending to be a customer, he contacted her at her place of business.

At trial, Officer Michalec recounted appellant's post-arrest statement: "Yeah, I know I'm in Cellular I and 647-1666 [Magee Hospital] illegally and, yeah, I use people's telephone credit card numbers, but I'm trying to quit."... She again admitted that she had accessed the systems of both organizations and that she used the name "Electra." Appellant explained that she did not obtain authorization to use the voice mailboxes because she did not want to pay the fees.

Based upon the preceding evidence, the trial court found appellant guilty of two counts each of unlawful use of a computer, 18 Pa.C.S.A. § 3933(a)(1), and theft of services, 18 Pa.C.S.A. § 3926(a)((1). The court graded the theft of services as third degree felonies, because it found that appellant's criminal enterprise had caused more than $2,000 worth of damage to each organization. The trial court ordered restitution in the amounts of $4,300 to Magee Hospital and $2,510.25 to Pittsburgh Cellular Phone and sentenced appellant to two consecutive terms of probation of five years each....

Appellant first contends that the Commonwealth did not offer sufficient evidence to convict her of unlawful use of computers, 18 Pa.C.S.A. § 3933(a)(1), with regard to both Magee Hospital and Pittsburgh Cellular Phone. We disagree.

E. SPECIAL FORMS OF THEFT

Appellant was charged and convicted under subsection (a)(1) of 18 Pa.C.S.A. § 3933,[2] which provides:

§ 3933. Unlawful use of computer

(a) Offense defined. — A person commits an offense if he:

(1) accesses, alters, damages or destroys any computer, computer system, computer network, computer software, computer program or data base or any part thereof, with the intent to interrupt the normal functioning of an organization or to devise or execute any scheme or artifice to defraud or deceive or control property or services by means of false or fraudulent pretenses, representations or promises.

The relevant definitions are as follows:

"Access." To intercept, instruct, communicate with, store data in, retrieve data from or otherwise make use of any resources of a computer, computer system, computer network or data base.

"Computer." An electronic, magnetic, optical, hydraulic, organic or other high speed data processing device or system which performs logic, arithmetic or memory functions and includes all input, output, processing, storage, software or communication facilities which are connected or related to the device in a system or network.

"Computer network." The interconnection of two or more computers through the usage of satellite, microwave, line or other communication medium.

"Computer program." An ordered set of instructions or statements and related data that, when automatically executed in actual or modified form in a computer system, causes it to perform specified functions.

"Computer software." A set of computer programs, procedures and associated documentation concerned with the operation of a computer system.

"Computer system." A set of related, connected or unconnected computer equipment, devices and software.

"Data base." A representation of information, knowledge, facts, concepts or instructions which are being prepared or processed or have been prepared or processed in a formalized manner and are intended for use in a computer, computer system or computer network, including, but not limited to, computer printouts, magnetic storage media, punched cards or data stored internally in the memory of the computer.

* * * * * *

"Property." Includes, but is not limited to, financial instruments, computer software and programs in either machine or human readable form, and anything of value, tangible or intangible.

"Services." Includes, but is not limited to, computer time, data processing and storage functions.

---

[2] Appellant was not charged under 18 Pa.C.S.A. § 3933(a)(2), which criminalizes, *inter alia*, the intentional and unauthorized access of computers.

18 Pa.C.S.A. § 3933(c). Our research has discovered no Pennsylvania appellate decision interpreting this statute, and the legislative history sheds no further light on its meaning, parameters, or general purpose.

Despite the lack of previous interpretation, we are not without guidance, as an unambiguous statute is to be given the meaning expressed by its words.... In this case, we must determine whether appellant accessed a computer (or another protected device) with the requisite intent....

The statutory definition of "access" encompasses several acts, including the interception or communication with, the storage of information in, the retrieval of data from, and the use of the resources of a computer or other specified device. 18 Pa.C.S.A. § 3933(c). We find support in the record for the trial court's conclusion that appellant accessed the voice mailboxes herein....

The uncontroverted trial testimony overwhelmingly establishes that appellant altered the passwords of voice mailboxes, thereby gaining entrance into those systems. Her alteration of passwords was via instruction to and communication with the voice mailboxes. Moreover, her use of the voice mailboxes as her own answering services encompassed the storage and retrieval of data. These actions also fall under the plain meaning of "use of any resources of a computer." Consequently, we conclude that the trial court was correct in determining that appellant "accessed" voice mailboxes herein....

In addition to determining that appellant accessed voice mailboxes, we also conclude that a voice mailbox is a "computer, computer system, computer network, computer software, computer program or data base, or any part thereof," as those terms are defined within the statute. The definitions of these terms are broad. For purposes of this criminal statute, a "computer" is:

> [a]n electronic, magnetic, optical, hydraulic, organic or other high speed data processing device or system which performs logic, arithmetic or memory functions and includes all input, output, processing, storage, software or communication facilities which are connected or related to the device in a system or network.

18 Pa.C.S.A. § 3933(c).

One commentator has explained that even an ordinary telephone system is connected with a computer. "Telecommunications systems have become so tightly merged with computer systems that it is often difficult to know where one starts and the other finishes. The telephone system, for example, is highly computerized and allows computers to communicate across long distances." STANLEY S. ARKIN, ET AL., PREVENTION AND PROSECUTION OF COMPUTER AND HIGH TECHNOLOGY CRIME 7-39 (1990)....

The trial court found that a "voice mailbox is a computerized hard disk drive electronic message answering system having a digital interface that is accessed, via a password, and through a touch tone telephone." ... The mailbox is created by computer software, and the messages are stored on computer disks.... The user, usually an employee or subscriber, retrieves his message by entering his personal identification number....

Provided with the foregoing testimony, the trial court did not err in finding that appellant accessed a "computer," as the term is defined in 18 Pa.C.S.A. § 3933(c). The evidence established that the voice mailboxes store messages left by callers. Moreover, the (authorized or unauthorized) users of the voice mailbox services have the ability to alter the outgoing messages. Therefore, the voice mailboxes are "electronic ... or high speed data processing device[s] ... which perform ... memory functions." 18 Pa.C.S.A. § 3933(c). As such, the voice mailboxes are "computers."...

Appellant contends that, even assuming she accessed a computer, the Commonwealth failed to establish that she did so "with the intent to interrupt the normal functioning of an organization or to devise or execute any scheme or artifice to defraud or deceive or control property or services by means of false or fraudulent pretenses, representations or promises." 18 Pa.C.S.A. § 3933(a)(1). We cannot agree.

From the foregoing language, it is evident that the intent element in this statute is disjunctive rather than conjunctive. Our Supreme Court has explained:

> "Or" in its ordinary usage and meaning clearly and undoubtedly means "or." "Or" can only be construed to mean "and" when to give the word "or" its ordinary meaning would be to produce a result that is absurd or impossible of execution or highly unreasonable or would manifestly change or nullify the intention of the legislative body....

When a criminal statute criminalizes two separate actions or intents, the Commonwealth need only prove one intent....

The following evidence is relevant to appellant's "intent to interrupt the normal functioning" of Magee Hospital and Pittsburgh Cellular Phones. Sergeant John Michalec testified with regard to appellant's statement to him:

> [Appellant stated] that she knowingly and intentionally accessed Magee Hospital systems, that she knew she was in there without their knowledge, and she maintained several voice mailbox systems on the same. When I asked her how long she had been in Magee, she stated she had been in there two years....

Ms. Ziccardi testified that several voice mailboxes, including the one on which Ms. Ziccardi recognized appellant's voice, were disrupted. Legitimate callers would dial Magee Hospital, and, instead of hearing a message from a Magee employee, they would "get a list of Master Card numbers and AT & T and Bell Telephone credit cards with expiration dates." ... "[T]hose mailboxes were rendered useless for that period of time." ...

Appellant also linked into the voice mailbox used by the marketing department of Pittsburgh Cellular Phones. There was evidence that, due to appellant's intrusion, the marketing department could not use box 298-8139, and the authorized users had to eventually create a new box.... Appellant had gained access to Pittsburgh Cellular Phones for "personal use" and remained there approximately one year....

The above evidence establishes that appellant used the voice mailboxes, without authority, as a tool in her scheme of marketing unlawfully obtained information. The trial court could have reasonably concluded that appellant knew that she was unauthorized to use those voice mailboxes, but wanted to avoid payment for the raw materials of her enterprise. Appellant not only gained access but insured her domain on the boxes, if only temporarily, by changing the access codes. A necessary step for her successful routing of contraband information was the exclusive control and use of the voice mailboxes. The logical and probable consequence of appellant's unauthorized domain over the voice mailboxes was that authorized users could not simultaneously enjoy using the boxes. Accordingly, the trial court could have inferred that, by preventing authorized users from using their message systems, appellant foresaw that she would interrupt the normal functioning of the two organizations. These foreseeable consequences came to fruition as appellant's unauthorized access of the voice mailboxes actually disrupted both organizations.

The foregoing evidence sufficiently established that appellant acted "with the intent to interrupt the normal functioning of [two] organization[s]." 18 Pa.C.S.A. § 3933(a)(1). Therefore, appellant's sufficiency challenge necessarily fails....

NOTES

1. In *Evans v. Commonwealth,* 308 S.E.2d 126 (Va. App. 1983), the court sustained the facial validity of a statute defining data stored in a computer as property within the crimes of larceny, embezzlement and obtaining title to property by false pretenses. The defendants had taken computerized customer lists from their employer at the time they resigned.

2. The court in *State v. McGraw,* 480 N.E.2d 552 (Ind. 1985), ruled that a city employee's use of municipal computer facilities to further his private sales enterprise did not fall within the statutory offense of exerting unauthorized control over the city's property, because the city was not deprived of any part of the value or use of its computers because of McGraw's conduct.

F. RECEIVING STOLEN PROPERTY

1. GENERALLY

MODEL PENAL CODE

§ 223.6. Receiving Stolen Property

(1) Receiving. A person is guilty of theft if he purposely receives, retains, or disposes of movable property of another knowing that it has been stolen, or believing that it has probably been stolen, unless the property is received, retained, or disposed with purpose to restore it to the owner. "Receiving" means acquiring possession, control or title, or lending on the security of the property.

(2) Presumption of Knowledge. The requisite knowledge or belief is presumed in the case of a dealer who:

(a) is found in possession or control of property stolen from two or more persons on separate occasions; or

(b) has received stolen property in another transaction within the year preceding the transaction charged; or

(c) being a dealer in property of the sort received, acquires it for a consideration which he knows is far below its reasonable value.

F. RECEIVING STOLEN PROPERTY

"Dealer" means a person in the business of buying or selling goods including a pawnbroker.

Comment

[The text of this Comment appears in Appendix B.]

2. THE HARM ("STOLEN")

UNITED STATES v. MONASTERSKI

United States Court of Appeals
567 F.2d 677 (6th Cir. 1977)

CELEBREZZE, CIRCUIT JUDGE.

Appellant, Raymond Walter Monasterski, was found guilty by a jury of possessing goods stolen from an interstate shipment, knowing them to have been stolen, in violation of 18 U.S.C. § 659. Appellant raises four substantial issues in this appeal, including whether the goods in question had lost their status as stolen goods, thus barring Appellant's conviction for possession of stolen goods. We reverse Appellant's conviction on the basis of our disposition of this issue, making it unnecessary to reach the other issues.

In the early morning hours of June 17, 1976, Rodney Szpytek (age 15), David Fusto (age 16) and Greg Ploshehanski (age 18) met with James "Cold Boy" Logan (age 35) in a Detroit restaurant. There it was planned that the three youths would steal some tires from a Conrail boxcar in a nearby railroad yard. Logan left these boys to their own devices and within hours they had managed to carry thirty Firestone tires out of the boxcar and under a fence surrounding the railroad yard. Before they could get much farther their scheme was foiled when they were apprehended by Conrail police. The Conrail police then called the FBI, whose agents arrived on the scene shortly thereafter. Desirous of catching the intended outlet or "fence" for the stolen tires, the Conrail police and FBI agents talked the three young thieves into following through on their intended disposition of the tires. The youths cooperated fully in this scheme which was modeled after events they said would have occurred but for their arrests.

The Conrail police placed identifying marks on all the purloined tires and loaded twenty of them into a van they had supplied. The other ten tires were loaded into Ploshehanski's car. A Conrail police officer then drove the loaded van to a Detroit park, accompanied by the others in Ploshehanski's vehicle. The three youths left the park at the police's direction and delivered the carload of ten tires to the nearby home of Logan and placed them in his basement. Logan had helped plan the theft so he knew what was transpiring except for being totally unaware that the thieves had been caught and were then acting under police orders and were even under police surveillance. The youths returned to the van in the park, picked up another load of ten tires and delivered them to Logan's home. Upon arriving at Logan's home, they found Logan about to leave in his own car. Szpytek joined Logan, who had loaded seven of the initial delivery of tires into his car while the second load was en route. Logan and Szpytek drove to the home of Appellant, whom they knew as

"Cadillac Ray." Fusto and Ploshehanski followed with the second load of ten tires in Ploshehanski's car.

Logan testified at trial that Appellant had been his outlet for stolen tires before and that he had called Appellant on the morning of this theft to arrange delivery of this batch. Logan said that Appellant told him, at least initially, that he did not want this load of tires and that he was getting out of the "business." Nevertheless, Logan got the impression by the end of the conversation that Appellant would try to dispose of the tires and the initial delivery of seventeen tires was made to Appellant's home.

Fusto and Ploshehanski testified in substance that upon arrival with the first seventeen tires Appellant told Logan that he (Appellant) would "take care" of the tires and that Appellant told Logan not to worry about the money if Appellant was not home when the second load was delivered. Appellant testified that upon arrival of the first batch he told Logan and Szpytek that he did not want the tires and that they were left at his home over his objection. This testimony was corroborated by Appellant's daughter-in-law who lived with him. The final delivery of the remaining thirteen tires was made later the same morning, June 17, when Appellant was not home. All the tires were placed in a shed adjacent to Appellant's home. Both deliveries were made under the watchful eye of the Conrail police and FBI agents.

On the afternoon of June 17, FBI agents obtained and executed a search warrant, seizing the tires from Appellant's shed and arresting him. Appellant's indictment and trial followed in due course. Logan was arrested the same day and later pled guilty to possession of stolen goods. The record does not indicate that any criminal or juvenile court charges were ever brought against Szpytek, Fusto, or Ploshehanski.

Appellant argues that these largely uncontested facts compel reversal of his conviction. His reasoning is that the tires in question had lost their status as stolen goods when they were recovered by the Conrail police, thus precluding conviction for possession of stolen goods. We agree.

Appellant was convicted of violating the following portion of 18 U.S.C. § 659:

> Whoever buys or receives or has in his possession any such goods or chattels, knowing the same to have been embezzled or stolen ...
> Shall in each case be fined not more than $5,000 or imprisoned not more than ten years, or both; but if the amount or value of such money, baggage, goods or chattels does not exceed $100, he shall be fined not more than $1,000 or imprisoned not more than one year, or both.

The phrase "such goods or chattels" refers to the preceding paragraph of § 659, which condemns in pertinent part:

> Whoever embezzles, steals, or unlawfully takes, carries away, or conceals, or by fraud or deception obtains from any ... railroad car, ... with intent to convert to his own use any goods or chattels moving as or which are a part of or which constitute an interstate ... shipment of freight, express, or other property....

F. RECEIVING STOLEN PROPERTY

Under the plain terms of the relevant portion of this statute, one can be convicted only if the Government proves beyond a reasonable doubt that, inter alia, the defendant bought, received or possessed *stolen* goods or chattels.

The rule that one cannot be convicted of receiving stolen goods if, before the stolen goods reached the would-be receiver, the goods had been recovered by their owner or his agent had its genesis in two nineteenth century English cases. *Regina v. Schmidt,* L.R. 1 Cr.Cas.Res. 15 (1866); *Regina v. Dolan,* 29 Eng.Law & Eq. 533 (1855).

The rule in *Schmidt* and *Dolan* has been almost universally adopted by the state courts in this country presented with the same question....

The earliest apposite reported federal case our research has uncovered is *United States v. DeBare,* 25 F.Cas. 796 (No. 14,935) (D.C.E.D.Wis.1875). In *DeBare,* postage stamps had been stolen by a thief who intended to purvey them to the defendant. The thief was caught, however, and the stamps returned to the local postmaster. Pursuant to a scheme not unlike that in the instant case, the stamps were subsequently sent along to the defendant, who was charged with receiving stolen goods. The District Court noted that the defendant's *mens rea* was precisely that required for conviction under the statute but held that the defendant had not committed the forbidden act. Under the authority of *Schmidt* and *Dolan,* the Court held that the recovered stamps had lost their status as stolen goods and thus could not support a conviction....

United States v. Cohen, 274 F. 596 (3d Cir. 1921), is often cited as a leading case in the more modern history of the rule. The facts of *Cohen,* legally indistinguishable from this cause, involved a case of goods which had been diverted from its proper course and readdressed so that it would be delivered to the defendant. A suspicious employee of the carrier, however, turned the case over to his superiors. The carrier's detectives ordered that the case be delivered to the altered address, which led to the defendant's arrest and conviction for receiving stolen goods under the predecessor to 18 U.S.C. § 659.... [T]he Court reversed the conviction and expressed the following rule:

> When the actual, physical possession of stolen property has been recovered by the owner or his agent, its character as stolen property is lost, and the subsequent delivery of the property by the owner or agent to a particeps criminis, for the purpose of entrapping him as the receiver of stolen goods, does not establish the crime, for in a legal sense he does not receive stolen property.

274 F. at 599.

The only relatively recent federal appellate case on point is *United States v. Cawley,* 255 F.2d 338 (3d Cir. 1958). The facts of *Cawley* are nearly identical to those in this case. Two thieves were apprehended by postal inspectors in the process of stealing several packages from a railroad mail shipment. The thieves and packages were taken to the post office and the packages were inventoried. The thieves agreed to cooperate with the inspectors in carrying out their intended plan to sell the packages to the defendant. The defendant, unaware of their apprehension, bought the packages from the thieves under circumstances justifying the inference he knew they were stolen. He was convicted of receiving packages known to be stolen from the mails, in violation of 18 U.S.C. § 1708. The Government conceded and the Court agreed

> that it is a legal principle of long standing that when stolen goods are recovered by the owner or his agent before they are sold, the goods are no longer to be considered stolen, and the purchaser cannot be convicted of receiving stolen goods.

255 F.2d at 340 (footnote omitted).

The Government argued in *Cawley*, however, that the rule did not help the defendant there because the packages were stolen from the railroad and then recovered by postal inspectors who were not agents of the railroad. This, the Government argued, meant the packages had not been recovered by their owner or his agent and thus retained their stolen character even after recovery by the postal inspectors. The Court rejected out of hand this reading of the rule. It held that for purposes of the rule the postal inspectors were agents of the owner. The rule applied whenever the stolen goods were "recovered by the owner or anyone who has a right to possession or control over them. *See Regina v. Schmidt*, ..." *Id*. ... On this reasoning the Court reversed the conviction.

The above cases present this Court with substantial authority pointing toward reversal in this case. In the absence of binding authority, however, it is incumbent upon us to undertake an independent review of the rule in question. We conclude that the rule withstands analysis and we adhere to it.

As noted earlier, the portion of 18 U.S.C. § 659 under which Appellant was convicted requires the Government to prove beyond a reasonable doubt that the defendant received *stolen goods*. Just as did the judges of nineteenth century England, we do not believe the words "stolen goods" include goods that were stolen but recovered by their owner or his agent. All would agree that at some point in time the goods in this case ceased being stolen goods.[6] We must decide at what point the goods lost that status in contemplation of the law. We feel the best and only workable rule is the common law rule — *viz.*, the goods lost their stolen character immediately upon being recovered by the owner or his agent. Trying to choose some later point in time to support the conviction in this case would necessitate a strained reading of the words involved and would yield unnecessary uncertainty....

The government in this case has attacked the common law rule by contending that it punishes efficient police work. It points to the important societal value in apprehending the fences who finance the theft of so much property today. In particular, the Government relies upon *United States v. Egger*, 470 F.2d 1179 (9th Cir. 1972). In *Egger*, two thieves robbed a bank. They were caught soon thereafter but the FBI was unaware of the location of one portion of the stolen money. One of the robbers, who decided to cooperate with the FBI, received a communication from one of the defendants (an attorney who had earlier represented her) telling her to surreptitiously obtain the hidden money. The robber followed these instructions and recovered the hidden money but in the presence of FBI agents. These agents then recorded the

---

[6] Lord Campbell pointed out in *Regina v. Dolan*, 29 Eng.Law & Eq. at 535, that the only other possible rule would be that once goods are stolen they can support a conviction for receipt of stolen goods at any subsequent point in their history. We agree that such a rule would go too far.

serial numbers of the stolen bills and accompanied the robber as she delivered the money to the defendant. The defendant was convicted of knowing possession of money taken in a bank robbery. 18 U.S.C. § 2113(c).

The Ninth Circuit affirmed this conviction. It held the well-settled rule on stolen but recovered property, as directly quoted from *Cohen*, inapposite because the "FBI never assumed 'actual, physical possession' of the stolen property." 470 F.2d at 1181. Rather, the Court held, the FBI's traveling with the robber and counting and inventorying the money was mere surveillance.... The Court said "[e]xtension of the common law rule to bar this prosecution would serve no useful purpose, and would merely create a fringe benefit for criminals." *Id.*

We are very sympathetic to the Government's desire to apprehend fences. Their social disutility is notorious. We cannot agree with the Government's position in this case, however, and we are unpersuaded by *Egger*.[11] The Government's arguments ignore the relevant statutory requisite of stolen goods. We fully realize that the beneficiaries of the rule espoused here likely have the precise culpable state of mind required for conviction of receiving stolen goods. Our law does not punish bad purpose standing alone, however; instead we require that *mens rea* accompany the *actus reus* specifically proscribed by statute. It is one of the most fundamental postulates of our criminal justice system that conviction can result only from a violation of clearly defined standards of conduct. We must apply this principle evenhandedly and not be swayed by our attitudes about the moral culpability of a particular defendant. It is the function of legislatures, not courts, to condemn certain conduct. Petitions to punish reprehensible conduct must be addressed to the Congress and not this Court. Being bound by the current statutory language, this case simply does not involve the proscribed criminal act....

We see at least three alternatives open to the Government in its attempt to apprehend fences when faced with facts like those here.[12] First, it can petition the Congress for a statute clearly drawn to encompass the disfavored activity.[13] Second it can employ the method approved in *Copertino*[14] of surveilling

---

[11] With the exception of *Barnes v. United States*, 313 A.2d 106 (D.C.App.1973), *Egger* appears to stand alone in its refusal to follow the common law rule. Neither of these cases rejected the rule but rather struggled to distinguish it.

[12] A fourth alternative is possible in state prosecutions. Many states have charged persons in Appellant's position with attempted receipt of stolen goods. There is a split of authority on the propriety of this. *Compare People v. Jaffe*, 185 N.Y. 497, 78 N.E. 169 (1906) (no conviction allowed for attempt since underlying offense would not be a crime) *with People v. Rojas*, 55 Cal.2d 252, 10 Cal.Rptr. 465, 358 P.2d 921 (1961) (conviction allowed for attempt despite underlying offense being impossible). *See* 85 A.L.R.2d 259. We need not enter this debate as there is no comprehensive attempt statute in Title 18 of the United States Code nor is attempted receipt of stolen goods specifically proscribed.

[13] We note by way of example only Colorado Revised Statutes § 18-4-410 ("Theft By Receiving"). This statute proscribes receiving property that one mistakenly believes is stolen, whether stolen or not. *People v. Holloway*, 568 P.2d 29 (Colo.1977). In *Holloway* the Court noted that this statute replaced a more traditional receiving stolen goods statute and that the legislature clearly intended to broaden the acts covered by the statute.

Another possible change in the law would be enactment of a comprehensive attempt statute. This may or may not be interpreted to apply to facts like those in this cause. *See* note 12, *supra*. *Cf. State v. Neihuser*, 21 Or.App. 33, 533 P.2d 834 (1975), which approved conviction of attempted receipt of stolen goods on similar facts since the relevant attempt statute explicitly stated that impossibility is not a defense to an attempt charge. *Cf. also* Ohio Revised Code § 2923.02(B).

[14] *See also* the opinion of Martin, B., in *Regina v. Schmidt*, L.R. 1 Cr.Cas.Res. at 17.

the stolen goods until delivered to the fence. Third, the Government can charge fences under 18 U.S.C. § 371, the general conspiracy statute, in cases where it can show the necessary elements of a conspiracy.[15] The Government may not be enthusiastic about any of these proposed alternative courses but the record in this case and the current state of the law cannot yield the result it desires.

In summary, we hold that, in accord with the common law rule, one cannot be convicted of receiving stolen goods when actual physical possession of the stolen goods has been recovered by their owner or his agent before delivery to the intended receiver. We further hold, also in accord with the common law rule, that the term "agent" means any person with a right to possession or control over the goods.[16] The judgment of conviction is reversed.

NOTES

1. Review the materials on impossibility in Chapter 10, *infra* pp. 765-785.

2. Generally, to be subject to receiving, what is dealt with must be "property" for purposes of larceny. *See supra* pp. 446-447. *People v. Kunkin*, 100 Cal. Rptr. 845 (Cal. App.), *rev'd on other grounds*, 507 P.2d 1392 (Cal. 1973), confirmed that newspaper reporters could be guilty of receiving stolen property in the form of photocopies of documents made in the office of the California Attorney General, although the original documents were not. *Compare United States v. DiGiglio, supra* pp. 425-426. The information was viewed as compiled information in tangible form, of some value, and did not lose such a character merely through transmutation into some other tangible form. However, receipt of the same information from a thief through telephone conversations would not constitute receiving stolen property. The California Supreme Court assumed, without deciding the issue, that photocopies were property within the meaning of the statute.

3. In *United States v. Turley*, 352 U.S. 407 (1957), the term "stolen" in the Dyer Act, 18 U.S.C. § 2312 (1988), proscribing interstate transportation of stolen motor vehicles or aircraft, was interpreted to extend beyond takings amounting to common-law larceny to comprehend embezzlements and other felonious takings with intent to deprive owners of the rights and benefits of ownership, including obtaining through false pretenses. Because the statute was intended to reinforce state law enforcement, a broader interpretation comprehending all forms of acquisitive conduct was more consonant with legislative intent than a narrow reading. Four Justices dissented.

---

[15] The record in this case suggests a conspiracy charge would have been supportable against Logan if not Appellant. *But cf. People v. Rojas, supra*, for some difficulties possible in a conspiracy charge.

[16] This will generally work to include all types of police officers, such as the Conrail police in the instant case. *See Cawley, Schmidt* and *Rojas, supra*.

F. RECEIVING STOLEN PROPERTY

PEOPLE v. KYLLONEN

Supreme Court of Michigan
262 N.W.2d 2 (1978)

COLEMAN, J.:

These separate criminal cases present a single narrow and unique question of statutory interpretation: When the Legislature enacted [the statute] which proscribes, *inter alia,* "aid[ing] in the concealment of ... stolen ... property," did it intend to provide an alternative statute under which thieves could be convicted; or did it only intend to cast a net of criminal liability over persons who assist thieves or others in the concealment of stolen property?

[Kyllonen worked as a maintenance person at an automobile dealership. On a day on which he failed to report for work, a pickup truck was discovered to be missing from the firm's inventory. He remained absent for two weeks, and then was arrested while driving the truck. He admitted that he had driven the truck to Florida and back and intended to "get rid of it," using it meanwhile for his own purposes. He was charged with concealing under the statute quoted above, and convicted. In his case, and a similar case consolidated on appeal, the Michigan Court of Appeals confirmed the convictions.]

At common law, thieves could be prosecuted for larceny but persons who assisted thieves in disposing of stolen property could only be convicted of misprision of felony[8] or compounding a felony.[9] The two crimes were misdemeanors and the paltry penalties prescribed did little to deter persons from engaging in the societally harmful business of providing a marketplace for stolen goods. There were no separate substantive felony offenses proscribing such conduct. Persons helping to provide the channel to such a marketplace or providing the marketplace itself could not usually even be convicted as accessories after the fact to the larceny. To be guilty of that crime, one had to harbor the thief, not just his stolen goods.

In response to this situation, Parliament tried to close the loophole in the common law by enacting a statute providing that a person who bought or received stolen property could be convicted as an accessory after the fact to the larceny.[10] However, this statute was difficult to enforce because accessories could only be convicted after the principal felon (here, the thief) had been apprehended, tried and convicted. To remedy the problem, Parliament enacted another statute abolishing this procedural requirement.[11] Finally, Parliament completely severed the umbilical cord between larceny and buying or receiving stolen property by enacting a statute making the latter a separate and distinct substantive felony offense.[12] This early history reveals that the statutory crime of buying or receiving stolen property was originally designed and intended to proscribe conduct by persons who helped thieves dispose of their illegal booty. It was born out of a need to change the common law which permitted these persons to escape serious criminal liability. The statutory

---

[8] Failing to report the commission of a known felony.
[9] Agreeing not to report the commission of a known felony in exchange for some valuable consideration.
[10] 3 W & M, c 9, § 4 (1691).
[11] 1 Anne, Stat 2, c 9, § 2 (1702).
[12] 7 & 8 Geo IV, c 29, § 54 (1827).

development was marked by a series of refinements directed towards prosecution and conviction of these offenders. Nowhere is there an indication that the statute also was intended to be an alternate provision under which thieves could be convicted.

The English statute proscribing buying or receiving stolen property crossed the Atlantic and became a fixture of American jurisprudence. In Michigan, it retained its basic form but its scope was somewhat broadened. The Revised Statutes of 1846, Title 30, Chapter 154, § 20 stated:

> Every person who shall buy, receive or *aid in the concealment of* any stolen money, goods or property, knowing the same to have been stolen, shall be punished by .... (Emphasis added.) Likewise, Rev. stat. 1846, title 30, ch. 154, § 23 stated:
>
> In any prosecution of the offense of buying, receiving or *aiding in the concealment of* stolen money or other property, it shall not be necessary to aver, nor on the trial thereof to prove, that the person who stole such property has been convicted. (Emphasis added.)

Although legislative intent often is elusive, the thrust of the statutory wording is clear on its face and consistent with its historical development. It is directed towards those who assist the thief or others in the disposition or concealment of stolen property. The everyday understanding of the language employed excludes the person who committed the larceny.

To interpret the words "buys," "receives" or "aids in the concealment" of stolen property to mean buying or receiving from one's self or aiding one's self in concealment is needlessly to corrupt a forthright and harmonious statute.[13] Other statutes proscribe larcenous activities.

The precepts above as applied to the case at bar lead to the conclusion that the addition to the statute of the words "aids in the concealment of" was intended "to prevent persons from rendering important, efficient services to a felon, in aiding him in the concealment of stolen property" .... The object was to make liable *persons who helped thieves or others conceal* stolen property as well as those persons already covered by the statute who *bought* or *received* stolen property. Limiting the application of these words does no violence to the end result sought to be achieved by the statute or the objectives sought to be effectuated. Also, this interpretation is consistent with the general policy of all previous legislation on this subject.

Therefore, the statute should be strictly construed to exclude thieves who conceal property they have stolen. Under the Michigan statutory scheme,

---

[13] The fact that some other states have broader statutes which encompass both the thief and those assisting in the disposition or concealment of stolen property does not serve to change Michigan's statutory scheme. For example, California Penal Code, § 496(1), employs the operative language "buys ... receives ... *conceals*, sells, *withholds* or aids in concealing, selling or withholding." Seventeen other states have adopted the language "receives, *retains* or *disposes*" from Model Penal Code (Proposed Official Draft, 1962), § 223.6. New York Penal Law, § 165.60 states clearly:

> In any prosecution for criminal possession of stolen property, it is no defense that:
> ....
> (2) The defendant stole or participated in the larceny of the property.

(Emphasis added.)

F. RECEIVING STOLEN PROPERTY

thieves are to be punished for larceny.[14] Persons who help thieves or others conceal stolen property are to be punished for aiding in the concealment of stolen property ....

In each case at bar the prosecution has anticipated a number of potential problems under the foregoing interpretation. However, the problems have solutions.

The prosecution first contends that under today's decision a defendant charged only with buying, receiving or aiding in the concealment of stolen property may escape all criminal liability by simply revealing in midtrial or on appeal after a conviction that he was the thief and therefore not amenable to prosecution for buying, receiving or aiding in the concealment of stolen property. Apparently, this alarm is based on the assumption that reprosecution would be barred by the "same transaction" test adopted in *People v. White,* 390 Mich. 245, 212 N.W.2d 222 (1973).

Even if the crimes of larceny and buying, receiving or aiding in the concealment of stolen property could be said to arise from the same transaction, the prosecution would not be prohibited from reprosecution on the theft charge if the defendant's revelation that he was the thief was truly a surprise....[15]

The prosecution also contends that today's decision will prohibit the prosecution of thieves who sell or otherwise transfer their stolen property to another person and then help that person conceal it.

That conclusion is not warranted. A sale or other transfer of stolen property by the thief marks the end of the original crime of larceny. After this, aid rendered by the thief which has a tendency to conceal the property from the owner's observation may be considered aid rendered to another and may be punishable under M.C.L.A. § 750.535; M.S.A. § 28.803. The transferee may become the principal felon, guilty of buying or receiving as the case may be and the thief may become his assistant. Similarly, if the thief transfers stolen property and then buys or receives it back, he may be prosecuted and convicted under this statute.

Further, the prosecution contends that today's decision requires proof beyond a reasonable doubt that the defendant was not the thief in order to secure a conviction for buying, receiving or aiding in the concealment of stolen property, and that this will be difficult to prove.

This problem will vanish if the prosecution charges the defendant with both larceny and buying, receiving or aiding in the concealment of stolen property.[16] The prosecution then may simply present its proofs and the fact-finder

---

[14] Larceny includes as an essential element an intent to deprive the owner of his property permanently, indicating that indefinite concealment incidental to the theft is a part of and punishable under this crime.

[15] If the revelation of theft by the defendant is not a surprise, we anticipate that a diligent prosecutor would include both counts in the information.

If the defendant's revelation comes in mid-trial, the prosecutor may ask the court's permission to amend the information to include a count of larceny. See M.C.L.A. § 767.76; M.S.A. § 28-1016.

[16] M.C.L.A. § 767.69; M.S.A. § 28.1009 specifically authorizes the prosecution to add an alternate count of larceny to any information charging a defendant with buying, receiving or aiding in the concealment of stolen property, and M.C.L.A. § 767.63; M.S.A. § 28.1003 permits the prosecution to charge both of these crimes in any county into which the stolen property was transported, even if the larceny actually took place in another county.

may convict the defendant of either crime or acquit him altogether, depending upon its perception of the evidence....

NOTES

1. Similar interpretations of traditional statutes have been reached in, *e.g., Guerin v. State,* 396 So. 2d 132 (Ala. Crim. App. 1980), *cert. denied,* 396 So. 2d 136 (Ala. 1981); *State v. Dechand,* 511 P.2d 430 (Or. App. 1973).

2. A thief may be held within the coverage of statutes which include disposing of property known to have been stolen, *State v. Mitchell,* 524 P.2d 206 (N.M. 1974), or concealing property with like knowledge, *State v. Lawrence,* 312 N.W.2d 251 (Minn. 1981). In *Lawrence,* the court noted: "Since [the statute] is directed at trafficking in stolen goods, it might be argued that to use the statute here against the thief is to use it for a purpose for which it was not intended. But the fact that defendant chose to keep and enjoy his stolen merchandise rather than pass it on to a fence only makes him, in a practical sense, his own fence.... [A] prosecutor has the discretion to charge a person who steals with concealing the property rather than with stealing if the available evidence establishes the former." *Id.* at 252.

3. One who is a principal in the second degree or accessory before the fact (*see infra* pp. 721-734) to a theft transaction can be convicted vicariously of both theft and receiving. *See, e.g., People v. Lamirato,* 504 P.2d 661 (Colo. 1972); *State v. Tindall,* 50 S.E.2d 188 (S.C. 1948).

4. In *Barnes v. United States,* 412 U.S. 837 (1973), the Supreme Court affirmed the constitutionality of a common-law and now predominantly statutory presumption that a person in the unexplained possession of recently-stolen property is the thief. *Barnes* seemingly is still good constitutional law under the doctrines laid down by the Court in its subsequent decisions of *County Court v. Allen, Francis v. Franklin* and *Sandstrom v. Montana,* covered, *supra* pp. 54-60.

3. ACTUS REUS

JORDAN v. STATE
Court of Appeals of Maryland
148 A.2d 292, *cert. denied,* 361 U.S. 849 (1959)

PRESCOTT, JUDGE. This is an appeal by George Thomas Jordan from the judgment and sentence of the Circuit Court for Prince George's County upon his conviction by the court, sitting without a jury, of receiving stolen property of the value of $100 or upwards.

...

On the evening of March 6, 1958, at approximately 7:30 p.m., Clifford parked his automobile in the Eastover Shopping Center. When he returned about an hour later it was gone. At 2:30 a.m. in the morning following, while he was on a routine patrol, Pvt. John Nagy of the county police department, observed the automobile of the defendant which had become mired when it was being backed into a pathway in the woods along the 5800 block of Oxon Hill Road in or near Seat Pleasant. As the officer drove up, the defendant

F. RECEIVING STOLEN PROPERTY

came out of the woods to the left of the mired vehicle and requested the officer to tow his automobile out of the mud. When approaching the defendant's vehicle, the officer noticed a floor mat under the right rear wheel; and in flashing his light around he picked up a reflection from an object about fifty or seventy-five feet farther in the woods along the pathway into which the defendant had backed his automobile. Upon investigation, the officer discovered the stolen automobile, or what was left of it. The vehicle had been almost completely stripped. The hood, back seat, back bumper, wheels, radiator, battery, coil and parking and dome lights had been removed. All removed parts, except the back seat and hood, had been stacked in a "neat pile" at the rear of the stolen vehicle. The floor mat had also been removed but it was not included in the pile. Other than the mat, no parts of the stolen vehicle were found near, in or on the defendant's automobile, and the floor mat of the defendant's automobile was in place.

....

The defendant testified that he had driven his "girl friend" to her sister's residence about 2:30 a.m. and had then proceeded along Oxon Hill Road to return to the home of his mother, with whom he was living, in Pomonkey. He realized that, although he "wasn't going in the wrong direction," it would be "nearer home" if he turned around and took another route. He said that he intended to turn into one of the driveways on the populated side of the highway, which lay to his right but "kind of missed the driveway" and backed up to turn around. In some manner which he did not make clear, this maneuver brought his automobile to the opposite side of the road, i.e., the wooded side. He noticed that other vehicles were approaching him and that there "was kind of a driveway, old road" behind him. Although he intended to remain on the road, he backed farther "to avoid an accident" and the rear wheels of his car dropped over the "drop off" on the far side of the shoulder. At this time, his automobile was "about three feet" from the road itself.

Jordan stated that he found he could not pull his car forward and got out with a flashlight to ascertain the difficulty. He discovered that his left wheel was on solid ground but that his right wheel was spinning and "wouldn't catch hold." He thought that if he could find something to put under the wheel, he could back up farther to get enough traction to "spin out." In looking for an object to put under his wheel, he spied the floor mat lying on the edge of the woods and placed it under the right rear wheel. At this moment, he testified, Officer Nagy pulled up, and he requested the officer to help him get out of the mud....

Property must be received. The receipt of stolen goods is a question to be determined from the circumstances indicating whether dominion and control thereof have been transferred to the person accused of being the receiver. This question was recently considered in *Polansky v. State,* 205 Md. 362, at page 366, 109 A.2d 52, at page 54, where it was said:

> Manual possession is not necessary to constitute receiving. However, one is guilty of so receiving as soon as one obtains a measure of control or dominion over the custody of the goods. And such receiving may be by an

agent or through the instrumentality of another. It is not necessary that the accused should have actually seen the goods.

In that case it was held that there was sufficient evidence of possession where the facts showed that the defendant, though never in proximity to the stolen goods, had directed their distribution to several persons. And, even where actual possession is alleged, it is unnecessary to prove the possession by direct or visual observation thereof; provided the facts and circumstances established are sufficient to support a reasonable and rational inference of such possession.

In the instant case, these facts stand out prominently: that the defendant was found, in the early hours of the morning, on a pathway (not a public highway) in a wooded area just a few feet from where the stolen property had been taken; that the stolen property was necessarily taken there a very short time prior thereto; that the stolen car had been dismantled; that the defendant admitted actual possession of the floor mat and that he had seen the stolen car in the woods; that the defendant was coming out of the woods to the left of his car when the officer arrived (a fact testified to by both the officer and the defendant), although the defendant testified elsewhere that at the time he had completed the purpose for which he had left his car, namely, to place the mat under the right rear wheel; that glove marks were found upon parts of the stolen car and gloves were found in the defendant's automobile, although no positive identification of the marks as having been made by the defendant's gloves could be made; that the physical facts — the removal of the stolen vehicle from where the owner had left it and its dismantling to the extent that it was — in such a short period of time, just a few hours, together with the further fact that the defendant's hands and gloves were clean, clearly indicated, as found by the court, that there was more than one person involved in the larceny and dismantling of the stolen car; and that there was not a shred of corroboration of the fact that he had taken his "girl friend" home, or that he had one who lived in the community.

Of less significance, perhaps, but matters that could have been considered by the trier of facts were the possession of the flashlight and the fact that the defendant had backed his car into the pathway. They were, at least, consistent with the theory that the defendant went to the scene of the dismantled vehicle for the purpose of removing parts thereof, and, in case of an emergency, a quicker exit could be made with his car headed toward the highway than if he were required to back out.

His very implausible account of his close position with relation to the stolen vehicle, together with his previous convictions of serious crimes which the trial court was entitled to consider in weighing the defendant's testimony, may well have led the court to conclude that his story was concocted out of the whole cloth. His story about an attempt to turn around although he "wasn't going in the wrong direction"; the maneuver which resulted in his winding up upon the opposite side of the highway, where there was no convenient place to turn around, when by his own admission he stated, "of course there were numerous places where I could have pulled off"; his terminal point 15 feet off the road as the result of an attempt to avoid oncoming traffic where it ap-

F. RECEIVING STOLEN PROPERTY

peared that the shoulder was sufficiently wide to accommodate his automobile; and the "coincidence" of finding himself on the only path in an otherwise wooded area justified the trial judge in not believing the defendant's explanation as to why he was found at the scene of the stolen car.

Viewed as a whole, the evidence warranted a finding by the court below that the defendant was in actual possession of the floor mat, and at the very least, justified a rational inference that he was also in constructive or potential possession of the remainder of the stolen vehicle....

NOTES

1. In *State v. Ashby,* 459 P.2d 403 (Wash. 1969), defendant was convicted of statutory grand larceny, when he received grain stolen from a logging company. Defendant appealed the conviction on the basis that there was no evidence showing beyond a reasonable doubt that he had received possession of the stolen property, although there was substantial evidence that he had purchased the grain from the thief. In affirming the conviction, the court stated:

> [N]either a manual possession nor an actual touching of the goods by the receiver is a necessary prerequisite to the *receipt* of stolen goods.... Control is the criterion. A purchaser of stolen goods may be said to have received the goods when they are delivered at his direction to a third person or purposefully left with the seller, even though the purchaser never acquired actual physical possession of the goods... Under the evidence, the jury could have found that the defendant had actual or constructive possession of the stolen goods, either of which finding is legally sufficient to support the conviction.

Id. at 405 (emphasis in original).

2. A receiving transaction can extend across state lines, resulting in multiple crimes and therefore the possibility of multiple prosecutions. *Commonwealth v. Farrar,* 413 A.2d 1094 (Pa. Super. 1979). *See also McElroy v. United States, supra* p. 19, relating to interstate theft transactions.

4. *MENS REA*

PEOPLE v. WIELOGRAF

California District Court of Appeals
161 Cal. Rptr. 680 (1980)

LINDSAY, J. — Defendant was charged with receiving stolen property in violation of Pen. Code, § 496, subd. 1. The charge arose out of defendant's agreement to store a stolen antique automobile in his garage indefinitely, although at trial defendant contended that he had intended to return the car to its rightful owner. The trial court instructed the jury on the elements of the offense, the definition of the word "knowingly," general criminal intent, and reasonable doubt. Defense counsel did not request an "innocent intent" instruction, and the trial court did not so instruct the jury *sua sponte.* The jury found defendant guilty....

The Court of Appeal affirmed. The court held that the trial court was under no duty to instruct the jury *sua sponte* that an intent to return stolen property to its rightful owner is a defense to the charge of receiving stolen property. In so holding, the court noted that defendant had had ample time and opportunity after receiving the stolen car to execute his professed innocent intentions, but did not do so....

In urging reversal of his conviction, defendant places almost complete reliance upon *People v. Osborne* (1978) 77 Cal. App. 3d 472 [143 Cal. Rptr. 582]. In *Osborne*, an undercover police officer sold certain items of jewelry to defendant Osborne for $520 cash at Osborne's coin and stamp store. The officer told him before the sale that the jewelry had been stolen by him when, in fact, the jewelry had never been stolen. Osborne testified that he believed the property was stolen and that the officer was really the thief. He claimed twice in his testimony that he purchased the jewelry from the officer because he (Osborne) was going to try to arrest the suspected thief for selling stolen merchandise. However, as soon as the officer counted the money paid him by Osborne, he was arrested.

In analyzing the innocent intent issue, the appellate court discussed the 1951 legislative changes to statutes making the receiving, concealing or withholding of stolen property a crime; reviewed the three elements necessary to establish guilt of the offense ...; concluded that though the present Penal Code section 496 did not require the prosecution to prove a specific fraudulent intent by a perpetrator as an element of the offense, the absence of a guilty intent, if proved, disproved the charge; considered the duty of a trial court to instruct, *sua sponte*, on defenses not inconsistent with the defendant's theory of the case ...; and held that there was substantial evidence supportive of a defense of innocent intent, and that the trial court's failure to instruct, *sua sponte* on the defense of innocent intent (to return the property to its owner) constituted reversible error.

The *Osborne* case involved an *attempt* to receive stolen property, which requires specific intent to commit the substantive offense.... In *Osborne*, the trial court had instructed the jury on specific intent as an element of the offense of attempted receiving stolen property, but on appeal the court discussed the defendant's asserted innocent intent as a defense to the substantive crime of receiving stolen property rather than as a defense to the crime of attempted receiving of stolen property....

There may be trials were [sic] the defendant is charged with receiving, or concealing, or withholding stolen property in which the giving of an "innocent intent" instruction as outlined in *Osborne* is appropriate either in response to a request from defendant's counsel or *sua sponte*. This is not one of them.

The trial court instructed the jury on the elements of the offense, the definition of the word "knowingly" (CALJIC No. 1.21), general criminal intent (CALJIC No. 3.30) and reasonable doubt (CALJIC No. 2.90). On appeal defendant freely concedes that his own testimony admitted each element of the offense, but contends that both his direct testimony concerning his intent and the circumstantial evidence on this point were to the effect that he intended to return the property to the owner. Relying on *People v. Osborne, supra*, 77 Cal. App. 3d 472, defendant argues that the trial court erred in failing to in-

F. RECEIVING STOLEN PROPERTY

struct, *sua sponte,* that the intent to return the property to its true owner is a defense to a charge of receiving stolen property.

As the court stated in *Osborne,* under Penal Code section 496 specific fraudulent intent is not an element of the crime which the prosecution must prove. Under our statute the defendant is obliged to prove that his intent was innocent. Although no other reported California case has been cited or found by independent research wherein the courts of this state have discussed the requisite criminal intent or *mens rea* necessary to sustain a conviction for receiving or concealing stolen property, it has been considered a "general intent" rather than a "specific intent" crime. Thus, despite the language of the statute (Pen. Code, § 496, subd. 1), the mere receipt of stolen goods with knowledge that they have been stolen is not itself a crime if the property was received with intent to restore it to the owner without reward or with any other innocent intent.... The critical factor is the defendant's intent at the time he receives or initially conceals the stolen property from the owner. The intent to restore must exist at the moment the stolen property is accepted by the receiver if he is to be acquitted. If the defendant received or concealed stolen property with general criminal intent to aid the thief, or to deprive the owner of possession, or renders more difficult a discovery by the owner, or to collect a reward, he possesses the requisite wrongful intent, and it is no defense that he *subsequently* intended to return the stolen property to the owner....

It is important to contrast the factual situation and the time element in the instant case and in *Osborne.* In the latter case the defendant was arrested without delay upon his receiving the property and the counting of the money by the officer. In the absence of the passage of time no further conduct nor utterance on the part of the "receiver" was available to directly or circumstantially assist in determining his actual intent. His testimony supplied this element. Osborne testified that he bought the "stolen" property only to effect the arrest of the thief. He had no opportunity to carry out his stated purpose as he himself was arrested immediately. In our case, in addition to the testimony of the defendant, days went by and events provided activity and speech which could be appropriately and properly evaluated by the jury under the instructions actually given by the court. The case against the defendant was overwhelming and the facts are wholly inconsistent with defendant's protestations at trial of worthy motives and righteous intents. He had ample time and opportunity to execute his guiltless "intents." By defendant's own testimony he in effect had no defense.

We do not understand *Osborne* to hold, nor the law to be, that an instruction on innocent intent is necessary whenever a defendant disclaims guilty intent. Otherwise, it would be mandatory almost without exception whenever a defendant denied the charges. In the few instances where such an instruction is warranted, it must of necessity turn on the particular factual situation before the trial court. The evidence in this case did not impose on the trial court the duty to instruct the jury, *sua sponte,* that the defendant's intent to return the stolen car to its owner is a defense to the charge of receiving stolen property....

NOTE

On culpability requirements, *see* MODEL PENAL CODE § 223.6, Comment, which appears in Appendix B.

5. GRADING

EDITORIAL NOTE

Under the Model Penal Code, receiving as a form of theft is subject to the general grading provisions of § 223.1(2), *infra* Appendix A. Value of the property received is frequently a grading factor under modern state legislation, but status of a defendant as a pawnbroker or person otherwise in the business of buying, selling or otherwise dealing in the type of property in question may also govern the severity of the crime. *See, e.g.,* N.Y. PENAL LAW § 165.45(3) (McKinney 1985). The nature of the property also may govern penalties. *See id.* § 165.45(2) (credit cards), (4) (firearms).

General provisions authorizing aggregation of values in thefts committed by a defendant as part of a scheme or plan may not be invoked to escalate penalties against receivers unless they are made applicable specifically to receiving statutes. *State v. Post,* 286 N.W.2d 195 (Iowa 1979).

The standards for ascertaining value generally, *see supra* pp. 392-396, govern determination of value under receiving legislation. *See generally United States v. Perry,* 638 F.2d 862 (5th Cir. 1981).

SECTION III. Robbery

A. HARM

MODEL PENAL CODE

§ 222.1. Robbery

> (1) *Robbery Defined.* A person is guilty of robbery if, in the course of committing a theft, he:
> (a) inflicts serious bodily injury upon another; or
> (b) threatens another with or purposely puts him in fear of immediate serious bodily injury; or
> (c) commits or threatens immediately to commit any felony of the first or second degree.
>
> An act shall be deemed "in the course of committing a theft" if it occurs in an attempt to commit theft or in flight after the attempt or commission.

Comment

[The text of this Comment appears in Appendix B.]

B. *ACTUS REUS*

JARRETT v. STATE

Supreme Court of Arkansas
580 S.W.2d 460 (1979)

GEORGE ROSE SMITH, JUSTICE.

At the time of the offenses police officer Baer, off duty, was acting as a security guard at a grocery store. From a place of concealment the officer saw Jarrett and three other men load a grocery cart with packages of meat. The other three went toward the front of the store, but Jarrett pushed the loaded cart into a storeroom, marked Employees Only. There, within the officer's sight, Jarrett began to put the packages of meat into two large sacks that had been stuck in the back of his pants. When Jarrett saw the officer he started to run, but he stopped when the officer drew his revolver and ordered him to stop. Baer tried to handcuff Jarrett and succeeded in getting one bracelet on his left wrist. The officer's testimony then continues:

> I ... was attempting to put the other bracelet on his right wrist when the fight started.... He broke and tried to run, and of course I was holding on to the one bracelet, and I've got a gun in the other hand, which means I can't grab him. We started fighting, bouncing off. There's all kinds of merchandise, boxes, there's an ice machine, a baler. We bounced off the ice machine and the baler. I tried to handcuff him to the baler, because my car was out front with two more suspects. We continued to fight, wrestle, he was continually trying to break and get away, pushed me away, knocked me away.... We got up closer to the baler, and of course we are still fighting and I was trying to handcuff him to it.

At that point the officer's gun went off accidentally. Both men stopped fighting, and Jarrett was handcuffed and taken into custody.

First, the proof supports the court's finding that Jarrett was guilty of theft of property. Under the new Criminal Code a person commits theft of property if he knowingly exercises unauthorized control over the property of another person with the purpose of depriving the owner thereof. Ark.Stat.Ann. § 41-2203 (Repl.1977). It was reasonable for the trial judge to believe that if Jarrett meant to buy the large quantity of packaged meat he would have taken it to the check-out counter. Instead, he rolled the cart into a storeroom, where the public was not supposed to be, and began putting the meat into sacks. The trial judge could infer from the evidence that Jarrett was exercising unauthorized control over the property with the intention of taking it out of the store in sacks, as if it had been paid for. In fact, no other explanation for Jarrett's conduct is readily apparent.

The proof also supports the conviction for robbery, because the crime of robbery has been materially changed by the Criminal Code. As pointed out in the Commentary to Section 41-2103, under prior law robbery consisted of the felonious taking of money or other valuable thing from the person of another by force or intimidation. That definition put the primary emphasis upon the taking of property. But the Code redefines robbery to shift the focus of the offense from the taking of property to the threat of physical harm to the victim. As the Commentary states: "One consequence of the definition is that the offense is complete when physical force is threatened; no transfer of property need take place."

Under the Code robbery is defined in this language:

> A person commits robbery if with the purpose of committing a theft or resisting apprehension immediately thereafter, he employs or threatens to immediately employ physical force upon another. [§ 41-2103.]

"Physical force" means, among other things, any bodily impact or the threat thereof. § 41-2102.

Needless to say, it is our duty to enforce the new statute as it is written, which we have actually already done in *Wilson v. State,* 262 Ark. 339, 556 S.W.2d 657 (1977). Here the proof supports a finding that Jarrett, immediately after committing a theft, resisted apprehension by employing or threatening to employ physical violence upon Officer Baer. The evidence therefore sustains the conviction.

NOTES

1. *Commonwealth v. Ostolaza,* 406 A.2d 1128, 1131 (Pa. Super. 1979):

> The test for determining whether an offense is a lesser included offense is whether all the essential elements of the lesser offense are included in the greater offense.... Here the greater offense is subsection (ii) robbery, which occurs when the defendant, in the course of committing a theft, threatens the victim or puts him in fear of serious bodily injury. Subsection (v) robbery occurs when the defendant, in the course of committing a theft, takes or removes property from the person of the victim by force. Thus, an essential element of subsection (v) robbery is a taking from the person of the victim. Since subsection (ii) robbery does not contain this element, a conviction under subsection (ii) would not necessarily include proof of this element. To be sure, there may be a case where both types of robbery would be proved, as where the defendant snatches the victim's purse, and at the same time threatens her with a revolver. But there also may be a case where a subsection (ii) robbery is proved on evidence that would not prove a subsection (v) robbery. Suppose, for example, that the victim is standing across the room from her purse and the defendant takes it, telling the victim to stay back or he will shoot her. There would be no subsection (v) robbery, for there was no taking "from the person of another by force," but there would be a subsection (ii) robbery, for there was a threat of serious bodily injury to the victim during the theft. Since a subsection (ii) robbery may be proved without necessarily proving a subsection (v) robbery, we cannot hold that subsection (v) robbery is a lesser offense included in the greater offense of subsection (ii) robbery.
>
> This conclusion does not mean that appellant must be discharged, however, for the Commonwealth's evidence did prove that appellant committed theft, which is a lesser offense included in the greater offense of subsection (ii) robbery....

2. *See* the discussion in the nature of harm perpetrated or threatened for purposes of robbery, in the Comment to MODEL PENAL CODE § 221.2, Appendix B *infra*.

PEOPLE v. SKELTON

Supreme Court of Illinois
414 N.E.2d 455 (1980)

[Skelton was convicted of robbery while armed with a dangerous weapon, a "class X" felony carrying severely aggravated penalties in comparison with unarmed robbery. A plastic toy revolver was taken by police from the defendant's waistband when they found defendant lying on the ground a short distance from the site of the robbery and shortly afterwards. Except for a cylinder of thick, tinny metal, the toy was made entirely of hard plastic; it weighed very little and was a little over four inches in length.]

UNDERWOOD, JUSTICE.

At common law, there was no distinction between simple robbery and a robbery accomplished by use of some weapon. Legislative action generally has made the latter the more serious crime, and our criminal laws provide for a greater penalty when a dangerous weapon is used.... The intent of the more severe punishment provided in such statutes is, of course, to deter the use of dangerous weapons and prevent the kind of violence that often attends the use of a deadly weapon in the perpetration of a robbery.

There is general agreement that "one who puts his victim in fear by the use of a toy gun or the simulation of a gun may be convicted of unarmed robbery." ... Broadly speaking, however, the authorities which have considered the question whether a toy gun may qualify as a dangerous weapon under the armed or aggravated robbery statutes tend to divide into two groups — those adopting a "subjective" test and those favoring an "objective" rule — neither of which is completely free of logical and practical difficulties in its application. The State urges that we adopt the former, arguing that whether armed robbery has occurred is determined by ascertaining whether the robber intended to instill in the victim the belief and fear that the robber had a dangerous weapon and whether the victim in fact so believed....

The problem with the subjective test when carried to its logical extreme is that the victim may very well believe, and the robber may very well intend that the victim believe, that a dangerous weapon is being used in a robbery when in fact the robber has a finger or some innocuous object in his pocket. Some jurisdictions with statutory language making the victim's belief or fear relevant have upheld armed robbery convictions for a finger in the pocket.... The superior court there held the statute contemplated punishment based on the victim's perception of the object in defendant's possession, rather than what defendant actually had. Our statute appears to preclude this result, for it provides:

> Sec. 18-2. Armed Robbery
>
> (a) A person commits armed robbery when he or she violates Section 18-1 [Robbery] while he or she carries on or about his or her person, or is otherwise armed with a dangerous weapon. (Ill.Rev.Stat.1979, ch. 38, par. 18-2(a).)

A fair reading of this language seems to require something more than a finger in the pocket, and to this extent, at least, it would appear that the legislature has rejected the subjective test. The victim's belief concerning the nature of the weapon does not appear to have been an important factor in our earlier decisions, and the subjective test was disapproved in *People v. Greer* (1977), 53 Ill.App.3d 675, 11 Ill.Dec. 388, 368 N.E.2d 996, decided prior to the 1978 amendment. The majority and dissenting opinions in that case contain a review of the Illinois decisions construing the "dangerous weapons" phrase.

There are also logical problems with the objective test proposed by the defendant. That test requires that there be literal compliance with the statute, and asks whether the instrumentality was actually dangerous in the circumstances in which it was used. This standard, however, seems to us to run afoul of logic and common sense in the case where the intended victim is behind bullet-proof glass. Presumably, an armed robbery has occurred if property is actually taken, although even a loaded gun would not be dangerous in such circumstances. Too, the weight of authority permits application of the armed robbery statute to unloaded guns, a result which has been criticized:

> The great weight of authority holds that an unloaded pistol, not used as a bludgeon, is nevertheless a dangerous or deadly weapon for armed-robbery purposes. (Some jurisdictions even hold that a toy pistol is such a weapon.) The majority view seems wrong, however: intimidation by some means is a necessary ingredient of simple robbery without violence; something additional in the way of dangerousness is needed for aggravated robbery; but the robber's use of an unloaded (or toy) gun adds nothing extra to the bare fact that he intimidated the victim. (Footnotes omitted.) (W. LaFave and A. Scott, Criminal Law sec. 94, at 703 (1972).)

In a footnote, LaFave and Scott add:

> Perhaps another way to express the matter is this: the greater punishment is awarded for armed robbery so as to deter the dangerous person who is actually capable of inflicting death or serious bodily harm. The robber with the unloaded or toy gun is not nice — is guilty in fact of (simple) robbery — but he is not the dangerous type for whom the greater penalty is reserved. W. LaFave and A. Scott, Criminal Law sec. 94, at 703 n.67 (1972).

We agree that "something additional in the way of dangerousness is needed" for armed robbery. Our statute requires that "something" to be a dangerous weapon. Despite the quoted material, however, we believe a weapon can be dangerous, even though used in a manner for which it was not designed or intended. Thus, a rifle or shotgun, whether loaded or not, may be used as a club with devastating effect. Similarly, a handgun, when gripped by the barrel and used as a bludgeon, is equally dangerous whether loaded or unloaded. It is, at least in part, for these reasons that application of the armed robbery statute has been permitted even when the firearm used is unloaded....

There are policy considerations to be weighed which have been well stated in Greer:

> On the one hand, to require the State to prove that a firearm used to commit a robbery was loaded and operable would greatly restrict the applicability of the armed robbery statute. Under such a requirement, a defendant could be convicted of armed robbery only if he were apprehended at the scene of the crime or immediately thereafter with the loaded and operable gun in his possession, or if the gun itself were discovered, identified, and found to be loaded and operable, or if the defendant actually fired the weapon. On the other hand, it would be illogical and, perhaps, unfair to convict a person of robbery "while armed with a dangerous weapon" in the face of evidence indicating that his weapon was, in fact, not dangerous....

We believe, however, that these concerns are not irreconcilable. As we earlier noted, many objects, including guns, can be dangerous and cause serious injury, even when used in a fashion for which they were not intended. Most, if not all, unloaded real guns and many toy guns, because of their size and weight, could be used in deadly fashion as bludgeons. Since the robbery victim could be quite badly hurt or even killed by such weapons if used in that fashion, it seems to us they can properly be classified as dangerous weapons although they were not in fact used in that manner during the commission of the particular offense. It suffices that the potential for such use is present; the victim need not provoke its actual use in such manner.

In the great majority of cases it becomes a question for the fact finder whether the particular object was sufficiently susceptible to use in a manner likely to cause serious injury to qualify as a dangerous weapon. Where, however, the character of the weapon is such as to admit of only one conclusion, the question becomes one of law for the court.... The toy gun in this case, in our judgment, falls into the latter category. It does not fire blank shells or give off a flash as did the starter pistols in *Ratliff* and *Trice*; it is entirely too small and light in weight to be effectively used as a bludgeon as could the metal air pistol in *Hill*; it fires no pellets as did the gas pellet pistol in *Greer*; and, except that it could, conceivably, be used to poke the victim in the eye (and a finger could be used for that purpose), it is harmless. It simply is not, in our opinion, the type of weapon which can be used to cause the additional violence and harm which the greater penalty attached to armed robbery was designed to deter....

NOTES

1. A general part definition of "deadly weapon," *e.g.*, "any firearm or other weapon, device, instrument, material or substance, whether animate or inanimate, which in the manner it is used or is intended to be used, is known to be capable of producing death or serious bodily injury," precluded bringing use of a simulated weapon within an aggravated robbery statute requiring that a perpetrator be armed with, use or threaten immediate use of a deadly weapon. *State v. Butler*, 428 A.2d 559 (N.J. Super. 1981).

2. The state armed robbery statute applied to perpetrators armed with a dangerous weapon "or any article used or fashioned in a manner to lead the person so assaulted to reasonably believe it to be a deadly weapon." MICH. COMP. L. § 750.529. In *People v. Krist*, 287 N.W.2d 251 (Mich. App. 1979), the court interpreted the language to require, "in addition to proof of the victim's fear, competent evidence purporting to establish some attempt by defendant, aside from mere oral insinuations, to physically communicate the existence of a dangerous weapon. A verbal statement, without more, is insufficient.... [T]he result of this interpretation does not relieve a defendant of criminal liability, but rather, only effects conviction under another, albeit lesser, statute, i.e., unarmed robbery." *Id.* at 255.

3. Assault is not necessarily a lesser-included offense to a charge of robbery, because some robberies can be committed without an assault. *Thoreson v. State*, 69 Okla. Crim. 128, 100 P.2d 896 (1940).

4. *State v. Thompson*, 254 S.E.2d 526, 528 (N.C. 1979):

> Whether an instrument is a dangerous weapon or a firearm can only be judged by the victim of a robbery from its appearance and the manner of its use. We cannot perceive how the victims in instant case could have determined with certainty that the firearm was real unless defendant had actually fired a shot. We would not intimate, however, that a robbery victim should force the issue merely to determine the true character of the weapon. Thus, when a witness testifies that he was robbed by use of a firearm or other dangerous weapon, his admission on cross-examination that he could not positively say it was a gun or dangerous weapon is without probative value.
>
> We conclude that when the State offers evidence in an armed robbery case that the robbery was attempted or accomplished by the use or threatened use of what appeared to the victim to be a firearm or other dangerous weapon, evidence elicited on cross-examination that the witness or witnesses could not positively testify that the instrument used was in fact a firearm or dangerous weapon is not of sufficient probative value to warrant submission of the lesser included offense of common law robbery. When a person perpetrates a robbery by brandishing an instrument which appears to be a firearm, or other dangerous weapon, in the absence of any evidence to the contrary, the law will presume the instrument to be what his conduct represents it to be — a firearm or other dangerous weapon....
>
> *People v. Hildebrand* (1923), 307 Ill. 544, 555, 139 N.E. 107, had held that no question of intent to kill or maim, required by the robbery statute

since 1874, was involved because that "second intent" of the robbery statute had been deleted in 1919 by the legislature (1919 Ill.Laws 427, 431; Hurd's Rev.Stat.1919, ch. 38, par. 246). *People v. Emerling* (1930), 341 Ill. 424, 428-29, 173 N.E. 474, then cited *Hildebrand* as authority for its holding that specific intent to rob or deprive need not be charged or proved. This court, in *White,* concluded that, on the contrary, specific intent to deprive had always been a requisite element of robbery; that *Hildebrand* had not held otherwise; and that *Emerling,* accordingly, was incorrect. This court also concluded, therefore, that at the time the Criminal Code of 1961 was adopted, specific intent had been a requisite element of robbery. Because the legislature intended no change (Ill.Ann.Stat., ch. 38, par. 18-1, Committee Comments, at 213 (Smith-Hurd 1970)), this court reasoned in *White* (67 Ill.2d 107, 114-15, 8 Ill.Dec. 99, 365 N.E.2d 337) that specific intent to deprive has remained a requisite element.

Although the analysis in *White* is enticing, this court attributed to the legislature knowledge or an intention it never had when enacting the Criminal Code of 1961. Decisions prior to (and after) the enactment have held that specific intent is not an element of robbery: ... What is relevant is the legislature's intention at the time it enacted the Code. At that time robbery was considered a general intent crime; and the legislature intended no change.... Other jurisdictions have interpreted similarly worded robbery statutes as requiring only general intent.... Neither section 18-1 nor section 18-2 enumerates a requisite element of specific intent. (Ill.Rev.Stat.1975, ch. 38, pars. 18-1, 18-2.) The committee comments to section 18-1, prior to this court's holding in *White,* unquestionably state there is no such requirement: "This section codifies the law in Illinois on robbery and retains the same penalty. No change is intended.... No intent element is stated as the taking by force or threat of force is the gist of the offense and no intent need be charged.... We feel compelled to rectify our error and defer to legislative prerogative. For these reasons, we hold that robbery does not require specific intent. *People v. White* ... is overruled....

5. Review the materials on aggravated assaults in Chapter 3 *supra* pp. 173-178.

C. *MENS REA*

PEOPLE v. REID

Court of Appeals of New York
508 N.E.2d 661 (1987)

SIMONS, JUDGE.

The common issue presented by these two appeals is whether a good-faith claim of right, which negates larcenous intent in certain thefts ... also negates the intent to commit robbery by a defendant who uses force to recover cash allegedly owed him. We hold that it does not....

The convictions stem from defendant's forcible taking of money from three others. The evidence established that defendant and his stepbrother, Andre

McLean, approached Arthur Taylor, Donnie Peterson and Donald Thompson, while the three men were standing on a street corner in The Bronx. Defendant and McLean were holding pistols when defendant demanded that the three men hand over money "that belonged to him," apparently referring to money owed him as the result of prior drug transactions. Taylor and Thompson gave defendant money but Peterson responded that he had none and would have to go upstairs to his apartment to get some. As the men walked up the stairs, toward Peterson's apartment, defendant "snatched" McLean's pistol, placed it in his waistband and demanded that McLean turn over money he was holding for him. McLean handed defendant $300. A moment later, he rushed at defendant, a "shot went off" striking McLean and defendant fled. McLean subsequently died from a single gunshot wound to his chest....

Defendant Walter Riddles was indicted for robbery in the second degree and assault in the second degree. He was convicted after a bench trial of robbery in the third degree for forcibly taking money from Genevieve Bellamy on November 10, 1982. Bellamy and defendant both testified at trial, each providing different descriptions of events. Bellamy maintained that while she was waiting for a taxi at a street corner in The Bronx, defendant, whom she did not know, drove up to the curb and asked for directions. According to Bellamy, when she leaned into defendant's automobile to help him, defendant grabbed her, forced her into the car and demanded money from her. Bellamy stated she did not have any, but defendant struck her in the face, searched her pockets, and, upon discovering $50, took the money and ordered her out of the automobile.

Defendant disputed her story. He testified that he knew Bellamy prior to the incident and that she owed him $25. He stated that he met her on the evening of November 10 and she offered to pay him $15 toward her debt if he drove her downtown so she could pick up a package. Defendant maintained that he took Bellamy downtown, as she asked, but that she was unable to obtain her package so he drove her back uptown. Defendant testified that during the return trip, Bellamy again offered to pay him $15 toward her debt, but upon seeing her counting a large sum of money, he took the full amount she owed him, $25, and no more....

A person "commits robbery when, in the course of committing a larceny, he uses or threatens the immediate use of physical force" (Penal Law § 160.00 ...).[1] The larceny statute, in turn, provides that an assertion that "property was appropriated under a claim of right made in good faith" is a defense to larceny (see Penal Law § 155.15[1] ...). Since a good-faith claim of right is a defense to larceny, and because robbery is defined as forcible larceny, defendants contend that claim of right is also a defense to robbery. They concede

---

[1] Penal Law § 160.00 provides:

"Robbery defined;

"Robbery is forcible stealing. A person forcibly steals property and commits robbery when, in the course of committing a larceny, he uses or threatens the immediate use of physical force upon another person for the purpose of:

"1. Preventing or overcoming resistance to the taking of the property or to the retention thereof immediately after the taking; or

"2. Compelling the owner of such property or another person to deliver up the property or to engage in other conduct which aids in the commission of the larceny."

the culpability of their forcible conduct, but maintain that because they acted under a claim of right to recover their own property, they were not guilty of robbery, but only some lesser crime, such as assault or unlawful possession of a weapon.

Defendants' general contention is not without support. Several jurisdictions have held that one who acts under a claim of right lacks the intent to steal and should not be convicted of robbery.... That logic is tenable when a person seeks to recover a specific chattel: it is less so when [asserted] to recover the proceeds of crime ... [or] to recover cash to satisfy a debt....

We have not had occasion to address the issue but the Appellate Divisions to which it has been presented have uniformly ruled that claim of right is not a defense to robbery.... Their determinations have been based upon the interpretation of the applicable statutes and a policy decision to discourage self-help and they are consistent with what appears to be the emerging trend of similar appellate court decisions from other jurisdictions .... For similar reasons, we conclude that the claim of right defense is not available in these cases. We need not decide the quite different question of whether an individual who uses force to recover a specific chattel which he owns may be convicted of robbery. It should be noted, however, that because taking property "from an owner thereof" is an element of robbery, a person who recovers property which is his own (as compared to the fungible cash taken to satisfy a claimed debt in the cases before us) may not be guilty of robbery....

The claim of right defense is found in the larceny article of the Penal Law, which provides that a good-faith claim of right is a defense to trespassory larceny or embezzlement.... The defense does not apply to all forms of larceny. For example, extortion is a form of larceny, but the Legislature, consistent with a prior decision of this court, has not authorized a claim of right defense to extortion.... The exception is significant for extortion entails the threat of actual or potential force or some form of coercion. Thus, the inference may reasonably be drawn that in failing to authorize a claim of right defense for extortion in Penal Law § 155.15(1), and by failing to incorporate it in article 160 of the statute, which governs robbery, the Legislature recognized that an accused should not be permitted to invoke it in crimes involving force. We assume that if the Legislature intended to excuse forcible taking, it would have said so.[2]

Our decision also rests upon policy considerations against expanding the area of permissible self-help. Manifestly, a larceny, in which the accused reacquires property belonging to him without using force, differs from a robbery in which the defendant obtains money allegedly owed to him by threatening or using force. "The former is an instance of mistake, not subjected to penal sanctions because the threat to private property is not so serious as to warrant intervention by the criminal law. The latter is a species of self help and whether or not the exponent of force or threats is correct in estimating his rights, he is resorting to extra-judicial means in order to protect a property interest."... Since such forcible conduct is not merely a transgression against

---

[2] In U.C.C. § 9-503, the Legislature has expressly authorized self-help by a secured party in taking possession of collateral after a debtor's default but only if the taking can be accomplished without breach of the peace.

property, but also entails the risk of physical or mental injury to individuals, it should be subjected to criminal sanctions. Consequently, we find the courts [below] correctly denied defendants' requests to assert claim of right defenses....

NOTES

1. A federal bank robbery conviction under 18 U.S.C. § 2113 (1988) had to be reversed because of a failure to prove beyond a reasonable doubt an intent to take property from its rightful owner. *United States v. Bell*, 649 F.2d 281 (5th Cir. 1981). Bell had opened an account in a bank under his own name, using a nonexistent home address and incorrect date of birth and social security number. He then went to another branch of the same bank and deposited a check for $10,000 in the new account, giving a second false home address. After the twenty-day hold period on the check expired, he returned to the original branch and withdrew the total amount of deposit in cash, giving a third false home address. Although there was strong reason to suspect that the $10,000 check had been stolen, the government did not succeed in proving so. Therefore, the government could not prove beyond a reasonable doubt that he had withdrawn the check proceeds with intent to steal; one cannot steal or purloin one's own property. Giving false personal information about himself did not prove defendant's criminal intent.

2. An intent to hold property temporarily has been held insufficient to meet the culpability requirements of the New York robbery statute. *People v. Guzman*, 416 N.Y.S.2d 23 (N.Y. App. Div. 1979).

3. A claim of right even to specific property cannot be asserted in the context of robbery in some jurisdictions. *State v. Madry*, 529 P.2d 463 (Wash. App. 1974). Even if dictum indicates a contrary position, it will not benefit defendants who take property beyond that to which a specific claim lies, *State v. Kvale*, 302 N.W.2d 650 (Minn. 1981), or who have only general, unliquidated claims against the victim, *State v. Martin*, 516 P.2d 753 (Or. App. 1973); *Commonwealth v. Sleighter*, 433 A.2d 469 (Pa. 1981); *State v. Larsen*, 596 P.2d 1089 (Wash. App. 1979); *Edwards v. State*, 181 N.W.2d 383 (Wis. 1970).

4. *See* the discussion on culpability for robbery in MODEL PENAL CODE § 222.1, Comment which appears in Appendix B.

D. GRADATION

MODEL PENAL CODE

§ 222.1. Robbery

(2) *Grading.* Robbery is a felony of the second degree, except that it is a felony of the first degree if in the course of committing the theft the actor attempts to kill anyone, or purposely inflicts or attempts to inflict serious bodily injury.

Comment

[The text of this Comment appears in Appendix B.]

SECTION IV. White Collar Crimes

MODEL PENAL CODE

§ 223.4. Theft by Extortion

A person is guilty of theft if he purposely obtains property of another by threatening to:

(1) inflict bodily injury on anyone or commit any other criminal offense; or

(2) accuse anyone of a criminal offense; or

(3) expose any secret tending to subject any person to hatred, contempt or ridicule, or to impair his credit or business repute; or

(4) take or withhold action as an official, or cause an official to take or withhold action; or

(5) bring about or continue a strike, boycott or other collective unofficial action, if the property is not demanded or received for the benefit of the group in whose interest the actor purports to act; or

(6) testify or provide information or withhold testimony or information with respect to another's legal claim or defense; or

(7) inflict any other harm which would not benefit the actor.

It is an affirmative defense to prosecution based on paragraphs (2), (3) or (4) that the property obtained by threat of accusation, exposure, lawsuit or other invocation of official action was honestly claimed as restitution or indemnification for harm done in the circumstances to which such accusation, exposure, lawsuit or other official action relates, or as compensation for property or lawful services.

Comment

[The text of this Comment appears in Appendix B.]

MODEL PENAL CODE

§ 240.0. Definitions
§ 240.1. Bribery in Official and Political Matters

[The text of these sections appears in Appendix A.]

Comment

[The text of this Comment appears in Appendix B.]

§ 240.2. Threats and Other Improper Influence in Official and Political Matters

[The text of this section appears in Appendix A.]

Comment

[The text of this Comment appears in Appendix B.]

§ 240.3. Compensation for Past Official Behavior

[The text of this section appears in Appendix A.]

Comment

[The text of this Comment appears in Appendix B.]

§ 240.4. Retaliation for Past Official Action

[The text of this section appears in Appendix A.]

Comment

[The text of this Comment appears in Appendix B.]

§ 240.5. Gifts to Public Servants by Persons Subject to Their Jurisdiction

[The text of this section appears in Appendix A.]

Comment

[The text of this Comment appears in Appendix B.]

§ 240.6. Compensating Public Servant for Assisting Private Interests in Relation to Matters Before Him

[The text of this section appears in Appendix A.]

Comment

[The text of this Comment appears in Appendix B.]

§ 240.7. Selling Political Endorsement; Special Influence

[The text of this section appears in Appendix A.]

Comment

[The text of this Comment appears in Appendix B.]

NOTES

1. Review *United States v. Turkette, supra* pp. 22-24, on the interpretation of the RICO statute.

2. In *United States v. Myers*, 635 F.2d 932 (2d Cir.), *cert. denied*, 449 U.S. 956 (1980), a member of Congress had been convicted of bribe receiving in violation of 18 U.S.C. § 201 (1988), based on his response to tenders by federal undercover operatives conducting the famed Abscam operation. His appeal was based principally on alleged unconstitutionality of the Abscam technique. However, he advanced the following point as well:

> Appellant also contends that the indictment fails to allege an offense covered by § 201 because of the fictitious circumstances surrounding the

corrupt promise allegedly made. This claim is without merit. The offense described by § 201 is complete upon a Congressman's corrupt acceptance of money in return for his promise to perform any official act. The elements of the offense are the receipt of money, the making of the promise, and the corrupt purpose with which these things are done. *United States v. Brewster, supra,* 408 U.S. at 526-27. The promise does not cease to relate to an official act simply because the undercover agent offering the bribe knows that the subject of the promised legislative action is fictitious and that the promise will not actually be performed. The statute condemns the Congressman's actions and state of mind. His alleged promise to introduce private immigration bills is a promise to perform "any official act." 18 U.S.C. § 201(c).

3. In *United States v. Arthur,* 544 F.2d 730 (4th Cir. 1976), the conviction of a bank officer for criminal misapplication of bank funds under 18 U.S.C. § 656 (1988), based on alleged misuse of bank funds to entertain, do favors and buy gifts for state party officials who might prove influential in obtaining government deposits for his bank, was reversed because the trial court's instructions of law to the jury failed to distinguish bribery from legally innocent conduct:

> Not every gift, favor or contribution to a government or political official constitutes bribery. It is universally recognized that bribery occurs only if the gift is coupled with a particular criminal intent.... That intent is not supplied merely by the fact that the gift was motivated by some generalized hope or expectation of ultimate benefit on the part of the donor.... "Bribery" imports the notion of some more or less specific *quid pro quo* for which the gift or contribution is offered or accepted....
>
> This requirement of criminal intent would, of course, be satisfied if the jury were to find a "course of conduct of favors and gifts flowing" to a public official *in exchange for* a pattern of official actions favorable to the donor even though no particular gift or favor is directly connected to any particular official act.... Moreover, ... it is sufficient that the gift is made on the condition "that the offeree act favorably to the offeror when necessary." It does not follow, however, that the traditional business practice of promoting a favorable business climate by entertaining and doing favors for potential customers becomes bribery merely because the potential customer is the government. Such expenditures, although inspired by the hope of greater government business, are not intended a *quid pro quo* for that business: they are in no way conditioned upon the performance of an official act or pattern of acts or upon the recipient's express or implied agreement to act favorably to the donor when necessary....
>
> The crucial difference between "goodwill" expenditures and bribery is, then, the existence or nonexistence of criminal intent that the benefit be received by the official as a *quid pro quo* for some official act, pattern of acts, or agreement to act favorably to the donor when necessary. In instructing on bribery, the District Court in this case was obliged to set forth that distinction with sufficient clarity to enable the jury to determine the legality of appellant's expenditures.... This was not accomplished by the instruction that "payment of money to Government offi-

cials for the purpose of obtaining deposits of government funds in the bank and to influence the judgment of such officials in connection with such deposits ... constitutes ... bribery...." If "influence" is given its broadest common meaning, it is clear that "goodwill" gifts and favors to and entertainment of government officials are intended to influence the judgment of such officials. That is, such expenditures are made with the hope that the officials will be more likely to award government business to the donor if a favorable business climate is created than if such a climate is not established. But, as is apparent from the discussion above, this type of influence does not amount to bribery.

4. In *Commonwealth v. Froelich,* 326 A.2d 364 (Pa. 1974), the defendant, a justice of the peace, accepted an unlawful fee to perform one of his duties of office, or to refrain from performing it, depending on the view the jury might have taken of the transaction. He was convicted after jury trial of the statutory offenses of blackmail and extortion by a public official. The trial court thereafter granted a post-trial motion in arrest of judgment and the prosecution appealed:

> The court below, however, interpreted our decision in *Commonwealth v. Burdell,* 380 Pa. 43, 110 A.2d 193 (1955) as requiring a degree of consent on the part of the victim in cases of extortion and blackmail that would be incompatible with any element of coercion or duress. Such a view is obviously erroneous and at variance with the very essence of the crimes of blackmail and extortion.
>
> In *Commonwealth v. Burdell, supra,* we observed:
>
>> In robbery the taking of property is *against the will by means of force or violence,* while in extortion the taking is *with the consent* of the victim, induced, as it may be, by the threat of some exposure or the making of some criminal charge whether false or otherwise....
>
> In *Burdell, supra,* we were merely restating the traditionally accepted distinction between robbery and extortion. This statement, however, is not to imply that for the transfer of possession from the victim to the accused to possess the requisite consent for extortion it must necessarily be free of all compulsion. Extortion and blackmail have always been recognized as embracing an element of coercion or intimidation. However, as has been noted by some text writers, the use of the concept of consent in this context is not necessarily the most informative method of distinguishing between the crimes.
>
> It is sometimes said that robbery differs from statutory extortion in those states which require property acquisition in that in the former the taking of property must be "against the will" of the victim, while in the latter the taking must be "with the consent" of the victim, induced by the other's unlawful threat; but, in spite of the different expressions, there is no difference here, for both crimes equally require that the defendant's threats induce the victim to give up his property, something which he would not otherwise have done. [WAYNE] LAFAVE & [AUSTIN] SCOTT, CRIMINAL LAW, 707 (1972).

The historical development of these crimes best explains what may otherwise appear to be an inconsistency. Robbery at common law was a taking from the person accomplished by violence or intimidation and, as a felony, it was punishable by death. Because of the severity of the punishment upon conviction the common law courts were most circumspect, in robberies by intimidation, in limiting the type of threats to be included therein. Where the threat was of immediate personal violence the earlier courts were satisfied that the punishment provided was appropriate. Later, the lesser crimes of extortion and blackmail evolved to cover other types of intimidation which were apparently viewed as presenting a lesser threat to personal security and thus not requiring the same severe punishment — doubtless because the severe penalty for robbery, long a capital offense, restrained the courts from expanding robbery to include the acquisition of property by means of other effective threats — such as a threat to inflict future rather than immediate bodily harm, or to destroy the victim's property other than his house, or to accuse him of some crime other than sodomy, or to expose his failings or secrets or otherwise damage his good name or business reputation. To fill this vacuum practically all states have enacted statutes creating what is in effect a new crime — in some states called statutory extortion, in others blackmail, and generally carrying a penalty less severe than for robbery. [*Id.* at 705].

Thus, whether we attempt to distinguish robbery from extortion and blackmail on a theory of "consent" to transfer possession of the property in question or look to the historical development of the crimes, it is evident that the crimes of extortion and blackmail do encompass a degree of coercion or intimidation. Therefore, the fact that Kaufman may well have been moved to allow Froelich to take possession of the $200, because of a fear of the effect of further prosecution upon his family life and general reputation, provides no basis for concluding that the crimes of extortion and blackmail had not been made out by the evidence. Under all of the evidence it is our view that the jury reached a justifiable verdict under an accurate charge on the law.

SECTION V. Burglary and Other Criminal Intrusions
MODEL PENAL CODE

§ 221.0. Definitions
§ 221.1. Burglary

[The text of these sections appears in Appendix A.]

Comment to § 221.1

[The text of this Comment appears in Appendix B.]

§ 221.2. Criminal Trespass

[The text of this section appears in Appendix A.]

Comment

[The text of this Comment appears in Appendix B.]

STATE v. ALBERT

Supreme Judicial Court of Maine
426 A.2d 1370 (1981)

GODFREY, JUSTICE.

The evidence presented at trial tended to show that the structure Albert was accused of burglarizing was a summer cottage. The burglary occurred in the dead of winter, at a time when the utilities were disconnected from the cottage and the furniture was piled up and covered in the middle of the rooms. No one was present at the cottage when it was burglarized; the owner had left Maine in September and did not expect to return to the cottage until June. She had arranged for a caretaker to watch the cottage.

The Maine Criminal Code distinguishes between types of structures in classifying burglaries for the purpose of determining penalties. 17-A M.R.S.A. § 401 (1980). Simple burglary is a Class C crime. When the burglarized structure is a dwelling place, however, the offense is elevated to Class B. Subsection 2(B) of section 401. "Dwelling place" is defined elsewhere in the code as "a structure which is adapted for overnight accommodation of persons ..."; expressly excluded are "structures formerly used as dwelling places which are uninhabitable." 17-A M.R.S.A. § 2(10) (1980).[4] It is immaterial whether a person is actually present. *Id.*

On appeal, Albert contends that there was insufficient evidence to support his conviction for burglary, Class B, because the trial testimony unequivocally showed that the summer cottage was not, at the time of the burglary, within the code definition of a "dwelling place." While conceding that the cottage was adapted to overnight accommodation of persons, Albert argues that in midwinter it fell within the exclusion because it was then only "formerly used" as a dwelling place and was uninhabitable. The statutory exclusion is not to be read so broadly.

Coupled with the careful definition of "dwelling place," the provision for enhanced penalty in section 401(2)(B) expresses a legislative decision that burglary of a dwelling, even when the burglar is unarmed and non-violent, is more serious than burglary of other types of structures. That decision reflects the sense of outrage with which hostile intrusions into the home have been regarded for centuries in English and American law.

For classification as a "dwelling place," it suffices that a structure be adapted for overnight accommodation of persons; it is immaterial whether any person actually be present in the structure at the time of the burglary. It is clear from the definition that the temporary absence of occupants does not

---

[4] Section 2(10) provides as follows:

"Dwelling place" means a structure which is adapted for overnight accommodation of persons, or sections of any structure similarly adapted. A dwelling place does not include garages or other structures, whether adjacent or attached to the dwelling place, which are used solely for the storage of property or structures formerly used as dwelling places which are uninhabitable. It is immaterial whether a person is actually present.

necessarily change the character of a dwelling place; only when it has become uninhabitable and is no longer used as a dwelling place does it lose its special status.

The exclusion of "structures formerly used as dwelling places which are uninhabitable" does not serve to remove a temporarily vacated summer cottage from the definition of "dwelling place." Appellant argues that the cottage could not be used during the winter months for lack of heat and other utilities and was therefore "uninhabitable" within the meaning of the statute. That argument ignores the import of the word "formerly" in the statutory exclusion of "structures formerly used as dwelling places which are uninhabitable." In context, the implication of "formerly" is that the exclusion is limited to structures which were once used as dwelling places but, being now uninhabitable, will not be so used again.

In brief, the meaning of the exclusion is that, for practical purposes, the use of the structure as a dwelling place must have ceased permanently because it has become uninhabitable. The exclusion was aimed at structures that were once dwelling places but have been abandoned by their owners and allowed to deteriorate to the point that they can no longer be used as places of human habitation.

The trial court left to the jury the characterization of the burglarized cottage. On the evidence, the jury could rationally have found beyond a reasonable doubt that, although unoccupied for the winter, the cottage was still a structure adapted for overnight accommodation of persons and still inhabitable. The evidence thus sufficed to support the jury's conclusion that it remained a "dwelling place" within the meaning of 17-A M.R.S.A. §§ 2(10) and 401....

NOTES

1. *Litton v. Commonwealth*, 597 S.W.2d 616, 617-18 (Ky. 1980):

> Litton was convicted of the second degree burglaries of the Virgie Pharmacy and the adjoining Virgie Clinic. He was sentenced to two consecutive ten year terms of imprisonment. He appeals. We reverse and remand.
>
> This case requires us to judicially define the term "inhabited building" as it is used in the burglary statutes, KRS 511.010-.040. The word "inhabited," added by the 1978 Legislature, is not statutorily defined. Commonly, to inhabit means "to occupy as a place of settled residence or habitat: live or dwell." Webster's Third New International Dictionary 1163. However, the statute uses "dwelling" to mean "a building which is usually occupied by a person lodging therein." KRS 511.010(2). Therefore, a somewhat different meaning must have been intended by the Legislature.
>
> The 1971 commentary to the penal code reveals the attitude of the Legislature toward burglary:
>
>> The crime must be committed in a "building," defined in KRS 511.010(1) in such a way as to include all structures in which people lodge, work, or otherwise conduct business. With this definition, burglary is designed to encompass all unlawful intrusions which are accompanied

by alarm and danger to occupants. It is not intended to provide sanctions for intrusions into things such as vending machines, silos and other structures which do not house persons.

The 1978 amendment provides three distinct categories of burglary: first degree when a dwelling (or other circumstances not here relevant) is involved; second degree when there is unlawful entry into an inhabited building; and third degree when there is unlawful entry into an uninhabited building. These crimes are made Class B, C, and D felonies respectively. In order to give effect to this statutory scheme, we conclude that the drafters of the 1978 amendment meant to base the second degree/third degree distinction on the presence or absence of persons in the building at the time of the burglary, because the potential for physical injury is made greater by the presence of other persons who may be encountered in the process of the burglary. *See* K. Brickey, Kentucky Criminal Law, Secs. 12.04 & 12.05 (1978 Supp.); J. Palmore, I Instructions to Juries in Kentucky, Sec. 3.02 comment (1979 Supp.). This usage of "inhabited building" is in accord with *People v. Warwick*, 135 Cal. App. 476, 27 P.2d 396 (1933), a case which interpreted a statute making "every burglary of an inhabited dwelling house or building" a first degree burglary. That court held that while a dwelling house does not cease to be "inhabited" when persons are temporarily absent, a building such as a place of business is "inhabited" only when some person is there.

The trial judge defined "inhabited building" in his instructions in terms which would permit conviction of second degree burglary on the basis that the building "is routinely or regularly occupied by a person or persons for periods of time." However as we have demonstrated, second degree burglary is committed only when a person or persons, other than the burglar or burglars, are present in the building at the time of the burglary. Consequently, these convictions must be reversed and a new trial granted. If the evidence is substantially the same on this point at the new trial, the jury should be instructed only on third degree burglary.

2. *See also State v. Ervin*, 630 P.2d 765 (N.M. App. 1981), which held that an owner's intent to return to a structure at some undetermined future time meant that a structure continued to be a "dwelling house" even though the house had been unoccupied and without utility services for more than a year, and the owner was elderly and physically infirm. The record was bare of evidence that the owner had abandoned the building.

3. A husband physically but not legally separated from his wife committed burglary of her separate apartment when he entered without consent with intent to assault her. *Cladd v. State*, 398 So. 2d 442 (Fla. 1981).

4. Parents had told their minor son, who had an extensive juvenile delinquency record and who was addicted to drugs, to stay away from them and their home until he cured his drug habit. He was adjudicated delinquent on the basis of acts which would have been burglary had they been done by an adult, when he returned to the family home and stole cash and weapons from the parental bedroom. *In re G.L.*, 391 N.E.2d 1108 (Ill. App. 1979).

5. One cannot be convicted of the burglary of property in which he or she has a current possessory interest. *See, e.g., People v. Gauze,* 542 P.2d 1365 (Cal. 1975); *In re M.E.,* 370 So. 2d 795 (Fla. 1979).

6. A house is not a home. *See Jennings v. United States,* 431 A.2d 552 (D.C. 1981), which held that defendant did not commit first-degree burglary of a dwelling house when he robbed two prostitutes and their customers occupying rooms rented to prostitutes for periods of fifteen to thirty minutes.

STATE v. LOZIER

Supreme Court of Louisiana
375 So. 2d 1333 (1979)

[Lozier's accomplice locked an apartment owner in his bathroom and let Lozier in; Lozier stole a pistol. In a separate transaction, Lozier and an accomplice impersonated city police officers by wearing police uniforms and demanding entry into an apartment to look for counterfeit. They discovered currency, declared it counterfeit, and appropriated it. Lozier was charged with and convicted of two counts of burglary.]

CALOGERO, JUSTICE.

The issue presented by defendant's assignment of error number three has never been directly confronted by a Louisiana court: Does entry by misrepresentation constitute "unauthorized entry," an essential element of aggravated burglary.[4] Generalization about the law of burglary in other states is difficult, because most states have replaced the common law "breaking and entering" requirement with varied entry requirements. These include Louisiana's "unauthorized" entry, La.R.S. 14:60; Nebraska's "willful and malicious" entry, Neb.R.S. of 1943, 28-532; Oregon's "unlawful" entry, Or.R.S. 164:205, et seq. and California's liberal entry with felonious intent. Cal.Pen.C. Sec. 459 et seq.

Traditionally consent to enter is a defense against burglary, but this consent may be vitiated by fraud or threat of force. 2 Wharton's Criminal Law and Procedure, Roland Anderson (ed.), 1957, Sec. 415, p. 39. *LaFave and Scott* states that an entry gained through fraud or threat of force was a constructive breaking, but if the occupant had a reasonable chance to close the opening procured in this manner then no breaking would have occurred. LaFave and Scott, Criminal Law, Sec. 96, p. 709.

Fraud and deceit are irrelevant under California type statutes which require an "entry," although the jurisprudence in those states sometimes requires that the entry be without the consent of the occupant. *People v. Gauze,* 15 Cal.3d 709, 125 Cal.Rptr. 773, 542 P.2d 1365 (1975). In a long line of cases

---

[4]R.S. 14:60 provides:

Aggravated burglary is the unauthorized entering of an inhabited dwelling, or of any structure, water craft, or movable where a person is present, with the intent to commit a felony or any theft therein, if the offender,
(1) Is armed with a dangerous weapon; or
(2) After entering arms himself with a dangerous weapon; or
(3) Commits a battery upon any person while in such place, or in entering or leaving such place.
Whoever commits the crime of aggravated burglary shall be imprisoned at hard labor for not less than one nor more than thirty years.

beginning with *People v. Barry,* 94 Cal. 481, 29 P. 1026 (1892), California courts have held that a person can be convicted of burglary even if his entry was not trespassory. A person who enters a store with the intent to commit a felony therein can be convicted of burglary even if he enters during business hours and never strays from areas open to the public. *People v. Brittain,* 142 Cal. 8, 75 P. 314 (1904). The California courts have upheld burglary convictions for shoplifting, *People v. Corral,* 60 Cal.App.2d 66, 140 P.2d 172 (1940), and for flim-flam artists who shortchange cashiers. *People v. Stone,* 155 Cal.App.2d 259, 318 P.2d 25 (1957).

Several states have criticized the California rule on the grounds that it is overbroad, or they have disregarded California cases on the grounds that their state statutes require more than "entry" with intent to commit a crime therein....

This Court rejected the California rationale that an entry with felonious intent is an unauthorized entry in *State v. Dunn,* 263 La. 58, 267 So.2d 193 (1972):

> We conclude that an entry into a building open to the public at the designated hours and within the designated confines is not an unauthorized entry regardless of the intent of the person so entering. See, *Smith v. State of Alaska,* (Alaska), 362 P.2d 1071, 93 A.L.R.2d 525.

The court stated that "unauthorized" entry is an entry without consent, express or implied. In the case of a building open to the public, authorization to enter is implied.

In the case of a private dwelling a person must have the consent of an occupant or an occupant's agent to constitute a defense to "unauthorized" entry. This consent must be given by a person with authority and capacity to consent. 1 Wharton's Criminal Law, Charles Torcia, (ed.), 14th edition, 1978, § 46, p. 231. The consent must be voluntary and intelligent, that is, based on a reasonable understanding of the identity and purpose of the intruder. *Id. Wharton,* p. 231. Obviously, a child who admits a total stranger would not necessarily have sufficient understanding of the circumstances of the entry to give valid consent to an entry. On the other hand once a maid, friend, or employee is given general consent to enter a house at certain times, that consent will generally remain valid until revoked or the terms of the consent exceeded....

The significance of the consent of the occupant in a burglary offense grows out of the rationale behind burglary statutes — that a man's home is his castle. (2 Blackstone Commentaries [Jones ed. 1916] § 258, p. 2430). Burglary laws are not designed primarily to protect the inhabitant from unlawful trespass and/or the intended crime, but to forestall the germination of a situation dangerous to the personal safety of the occupants.... This concern is reflected in the Reporter's Comments to La.R.S. 14:60: "there may also be *great danger to human life* in the burglarization of vessels, trailers, and the like." (emphasis provided)

In the archetypal burglary an occupant of a dwelling is startled by an intruder who may inflict serious harm on the occupant in his attempt to commit the crime or to escape from the house. The frightened occupant, not knowing whether the intruder is bent on murder, theft, or rape, may in panic or anger react violently, causing the burglar to retaliate with deadly force....

This violent scenario is far less likely to unfold where the intruder with felonious intent is known to the occupant and has expressed or implied consent to be on the premises. Thus in *Dunn, supra,* a thief's entry into a business during business hours with the intent to steal did not in itself provoke the defensive reaction of the occupant or owner that may have led to further violence to the occupant or bystanders. Similarly where an employee or friend is on the premises with the consent, express or implied, of an occupant, the discovery of the crime is far less likely to provoke the violence that the burglary statute is designed to discourage.

In regard to the first count, Lozier did not have the consent of the occupant to enter. Angela Clay, the accomplice who let him in, did not have the right to authorize his entry. It was clearly "unauthorized." In the second count Lozier entered with the apparent consent of the occupant, Mr. Havhuburg. That consent was based solely on the understanding that Lozier and his accomplice were police officers. It is clear from the record that Mr. Lozier's misrepresentation prevented Havhuburg from having a sufficient understanding of the circumstances of the entry to validly consent to Lozier's entry. While Lozier's entry did not immediately create a situation that would precipitate violence, the discovery of the fraud by Havhuburg might have created the potentially deadly situation that R.S. 14:60 protects people against. We conclude that Carl Lozier's entry into the Havhuburg residence was "unauthorized."...

NOTES

1. In *State v. Hill,* 520 P.2d 946 (Wash. App. 1974), a conviction of burglary was reversed on facts showing that the defendant entered a building through a broken window, but without a showing that the defendant had broken the window to gain entrance. The court held that "breaking" is a technical legal term of art which must be defined by the trial court on instructing the jury, and cited *State v. Rosencrans,* 167 P.2d 170, 172 (Wash. 1946), in defining the term:

> The gist of burglarious breaking is the application of force to remove some obstacle to entry, and the amount of force employed is not material. The exercise of the slightest force is sufficient. The breaking consists of the removal by the intruder, by the exercise of force, of an obstruction which, if left untouched, would prevent entrance. Hence, the application of force to push further open an already partly open door or window to enable a person to enter a room or building, is a breaking sufficient to constitute burglary if the other essential elements of the offense are present.

Id. at 948.

2. Proof of breaking may be shown by circumstantial evidence. In *State v. Larson,* 475 P.2d 896 (Wash. App. 1970), defendant was apprehended after fleeing from an automobile showroom when he was discovered attempting to open a safe in the office. Except for two open windows, one of which had a glass pane broken out of it, there was no evidence of breaking. The State did not offer proof of the size of the openings, and the defendant maintained that he could have squeezed through either of the two open windows without enlarging the opening. A conviction of burglary was affirmed, however, the court stating: "[W]e believe based upon visual examination of the photographs [of the windows] and the defendant who was present in court, the jury could find that it would have been impossible for defendant to have entered or left the building without the use of some force in expanding the openings. Force, however slight, constitutes a 'breaking.'" *Id.* at 897.

3. In *Commonwealth v. Tilley*, 246 N.E.2d 176 (Mass. 1969), a conviction of breaking and entering a dwelling house was affirmed on facts which showed both doors of the house had been locked, and no evidence that the locks had been forced by the defendants. The proof did not foreclose the possibility that entry had been made through an open window. The court held that the owner's testimony of locking both doors warranted an inference that she had intended to completely secure the house, and was not likely to have left a window open which would afford entrance without removing a screen or window sash. It was also likely that even if one of the intruders had entered through an open window, his confederate had entered through the rear door which could be opened only by his confederate.

4. Under statutes and, sometimes, on the ground that a statute of 12 Anne c. VII (1713) became part of the common law, it is held that breaking out of a building in making an exit is sufficient. *Lawson v. Commonwealth*, 169 S.W. 587 (Ky. 1914); *People v. Toland*, 111 N.E. 760 (N.Y. 1916).

5. Going through the chimney is a breaking because "the chimney is as much shut as the nature of the thing will admit." *State v. Willis*, 52 N.C. 190 (1859).

6. An entry does not occur if the instrument used to create access to a protected structure intrudes into the inner space. *State v. Johnson*, 587 S.W.2d 636 (Mo. App. 1979). If, however, an instrument is inserted through an aperture in order to snare property, there has been entry. *Id. See also Walker v. State*, 63 Ala. 49, 35 Am. Rep. 1 (1879), in which the defendant drilled a hole in the bottom of a corn-crib, allowing grain to flow into a sack which he held below the hole. The entry requirement of common-law burglary was held to have been satisfied.

7. Entry occurs if any part of an offender's body intrudes into the inner space of the protected structure. *People v. Palmer*, 404 N.E.2d 853 (Ill. App. 1980); *Tanner v. State*, 473 S.W.2d 936 (Tex. Crim. App. 1971).

8. Concerning the traditional requirement that burglary be committed in the nighttime and evidentiary standards for determining the issue, *see, e.g., State v. Dougherty*, 352 P.2d 1031 (Kan. 1960); *State v. Hammond*, 616 S.W.2d 890, 893-94 (Tenn. Crim. App. 1981).

9. Review the burglary decisions illustrating the traditional requirement of concurrence of *actus reus* and *mens rea* in Chapter 2 at pp. 127-130 *supra*.

10. Proof of intent to commit an offense may be circumstantial, but requires something more than mere entry. *See, e.g., State v. Barclay*, 196 N.W.2d 745 (Wis. 1972). It is unnecessary, however, to show that intended crime actually was committed. *See People v. Robles*, 24 Cal. Rptr. 708 (Cal. Dist. Ct. App. 1962), in which the court sustained a conviction of burglary despite the fact

that the jury failed to reach a verdict on a rape count. "Proof of intent at the time of entry does not depend upon the subsequent commission of the felony or even an attempt to commit it." *Id.* at 710.

11. Is a presumption constitutionally valid that one caught in possession of goods taken in a burglary is the burglar? *See People v. King,* 397 N.E.2d 905 (Ill. App. 1979), and compare the materials on constitutionality of presumptions in Chapter 1 *supra* pp. 53-60.

IN RE APPEAL NO. 631 (77) FROM THE DISTRICT COURT OF MARYLAND, MONTGOMERY COUNTY, JUVENILE DIVISION

Court of Appeals of Maryland
383 A.2d 684 (1978)

[Respondents, former junior high school students, were told by a vice-principal to stay off school property. They returned later and were taken into custody and charged with delinquency on the basis of the state criminal trespass statute. The adjudication was found improper on this ground, but was sustained because the record showed the respondents had maliciously destroyed school property.]

ELDRIDGE, J.

A mere trespass to real property is not a crime at common law unless it amounts to a breach of the peace.... Thus, criminal trespass is for the most part a statutory creation. The Maryland statutory scheme concerning criminal trespass, Code (1957, 1976 Repl.Vol., 1977 Cum. Supp.), Art. 27, §§ 576-580, involves both public and private property and deals with various situations.

Article 27, § 576, provides that anyone who "*enters* or *trespasses*" on property conspicuously posted against trespassers is guilty of a misdemeanor. Article 27, § 577, makes criminal either *entering* or *remaining* on privately owned property after being notified by the owner not to do so.

Article 27, § 577A, on the other hand, which is concerned generally with public lands and buildings, is more narrow in its scope than the provisions relating to posted property and private property. Although the statute makes "refusing or failing to leave a public building or grounds ... upon being requested to do so by ... [an] authorized employee" a criminal offense, there is no provision whereby mere *entrance* into a public building, following a prior notification, amounts to a criminal trespass under § 577A. Unlike owners of posted property who can forbid *entry* by posting, or owners of non-posted private property who can forbid *entry* by notifying specific persons in advance that they may not have access to their property, public officials under § 577A can only notify people, in specified circumstances, that they may not *remain*.

It was in this context that the General Assembly in 1969 enacted Art. 27, § 577B. See Chap. 627 of the Acts of 1969. Unlike § 577A, § 577B provides for the denial of access to the premises of public educational institutions to certain individuals:

> The highest official or governing body of the University of Maryland, any of the State colleges, any community college or public school may deny

access to the buildings or grounds of the institution to persons who are not bona fide, currently registered students, staff, or faculty at the institution, and who have no lawful business to pursue at the institution, or who are acting in a manner disruptive or disturbing to the normal educational functions of the institution.

Thus, for the first time (other than, perhaps, by posting) the General Assembly provided a means whereby individuals could be forbidden *entry* into public institutions. However, to deny a citizen access to a public institution is an unusual step, and the General Assembly was careful to insure that a step of such magnitude would be taken only by that person or entity responsible for making the major policy decisions for the institution.

The General Assembly then went on, in the same paragraph, to set forth the criminal offenses created under § 577B:

> [a] Whoever shall trespass upon the grounds of the University of Maryland, any of the State colleges, any community or public school or
>
> [b] who refuses or fails to leave the buildings or grounds of these institutions after being requested to do so by an authorized employee of the institution or
>
> [c] who wilfully damages or defaces any of the buildings ... on the grounds of such institutions shall be guilty of a misdemeanor.

The third prong of § 577B concerns property damage, and the second, like § 577A, concerns remaining on premises after being requested to leave. In the first prong, however, the General Assembly has only used the term "trespass." "Trespass" can reasonably only refer to those entries upon public lands which have been barred by reason of a "denial of access" by an authorized official as provided in the first sentence of § 577B. This construction is consistent with the general statutory scheme in which certain types of entries — after "posting" or, with regard to private property, after notification — are proscribed. Moreover, it is difficult to know what meaning "trespass" could possibly have separate from the access provisions of § 577B. There is not, as we have noted, a common law crime of trespass whose elements might aid in interpretation. Further, since this statute concerns lands and buildings to which large segments of the public have regular and general access, it would seem that the elements of the tort of trespass would have little if any application. We conclude, therefore, that an entrance upon the grounds of a public educational institution after having been denied access by the highest official of that institution is a "trespass" in violation of § 577B.

Turning to the instant case, the defendant can only be found to have violated Art. 27, § 577B, if (1) he entered onto the premises of the Randolph Junior High School after having been denied access as specified in the statute, or (2) he refused to leave the school's premises after being requested to do so by an authorized official.

First, under the statute only the "highest official or governing body," that is, the principal of Randolph Junior High School, could have denied the defendant access to the school's premises. There is no suggestion that any action at all regarding the defendant was ever taken by the school's principal. The only warnings or requests to leave which were given were those uttered by the vice-principal. Since, therefore, the defendant had not been denied access to the Randolph Junior High School by the principal, his entrance onto the school's premises was not a trespass in violation of the first criminal offense created by Art. 27, § 577B.

With respect to the second prong of § 577B, the State concedes that at no time on January 19, 1977, was the defendant asked to leave the school premises. He was, rather, immediately arrested after failing to disclose to the vice-principal reasons sufficient to justify his presence. No request having been given, there was none to disobey. It is true that the vice-principal had twice previously warned the defendant that he was "not to be on this property." These requests to leave, however, were given on occasions one or two weeks prior to the subject incident, and Art. 27, § 577B, makes a person's conduct criminal only when he "refuses or fails to *leave* the buildings or grounds of these institutions *after* being requested to do so by an authorized employee of the institution." (Emphasis supplied.) ...

NOTE

A claim of right is a factual defense to a charge of criminal trespass. *State v. Batten*, 578 P.2d 896 (Wash. App. 1978) (but claim of right must be based on reasonable grounds).

SECTION VI. Arson and Other Crimes of Property Destruction

MODEL PENAL CODE

§ 220.1. Arson and Related Offenses

[The text of this section appears in Appendix A.]

Comment

[The text of this Comment appears in Appendix B.]

§ 220.2. Causing or Risking Catastrophe

[The text of this section appears in Appendix A.]

Comment

[The text of this Comment appears in Appendix B.]

§ 220.3. Criminal Mischief

[The text of this section appears in Appendix A.]

Comment

[The text of this Comment appears in Appendix B.]

STATE v. SHAW

Supreme Court of North Carolina
289 S.E.2d 325 (1982)

MEYER, JUSTICE.

...

Of the other questions brought forward on this appeal, only two present matters which are likely to recur on retrial. First, defendant contends that he was entitled to a directed verdict because he cannot be guilty of arson for the reason that he lived in the dwelling he is accused of burning — that is, that the dwelling was not the "dwelling of another." ...

Common law arson is the willful and malicious burning of the dwelling house of another person....

Was the dwelling here "the dwelling house of another person"? We conclude that it was. The fact that defendant resided in the house does not, under the circumstances here, prevent his conviction for the arson of that dwelling. The dwelling in question was rented by Thomas E. Boswell. Mr. Boswell lived there with his twenty-two year old daughter, who is defendant's wife, and his three female grandchildren. "Sometimes [the defendant] was there and sometimes he wasn't." Defendant was living there on the evening of the fire and had all of his personal effects in the house. At best defendant can be considered no more than a joint occupant of the Boswell house. Moreover, at the time of the fire defendant had been forced at gunpoint to leave the house by Mr. Boswell. The defendant testified that, after leaving the Boswell house to avoid the police, he "was going to go out to my mother's house because I didn't have anywhere to stay that night."

In *State v. Jones*,[5] Justice Exum said:

> [T]he main purpose of common law arson is to protect against danger to those persons who might be in the dwelling house which is burned. Where there are several apartments in a single building, this purpose can be served only by subjecting to punishment for arson any person who sets fire to any part of the building....

The rationale expressed by Justice Exum in *Jones*, to wit, the protection of persons who might be in the dwelling, is equally applicable to joint occupancy of a single dwelling unit as to separate apartments in the same building. The need for protection of Mr. Boswell, Glenda Shaw, and the three grandchildren was just as compelling, and perhaps more so, in this joint occupancy situation as it would have been had they been occupants of an adjoining apartment. The wisdom of applying that rationale to joint occupancy situations is highlighted by the facts of this case. At the time defendant is alleged to have set the fire and the entire rear of the house became engulfed in flames, it was occupied by Glenda Shaw and Boswell's three grandchildren. They were able to escape by running out the front door. Fortunately, police officer Mark Adams saw several females screaming and running towards him, called for help, and used his

---

[5] In *Jones*, defendant was convicted of arson for the burning of his own apartment, which he shared with another man in a homosexual relationship, and which was located in a building in which there were three other occupied apartments.

fire extinguisher in an attempt to extinguish the blaze until fire department personnel arrived.

While there is some authority in older cases from other jurisdictions to the contrary, we find the need for protection from willful and malicious burning of a dwelling house so compelling that we hold that the common law arson requirement that the dwelling burned be that of "another" is satisfied by a showing that some other person or persons, together with the defendant, were joint occupants of the same dwelling unit....

NOTES

1. In *State v. Durant*, 674 P.2d 638 (Utah 1983), the court affirmed a conviction of aggravated arson despite a defense claim that the defendant had set fire to the house at the direction of the owner of the house. The court stated:

> Under Utah's earliest statutes, as under the common law, arson was a crime against possession rather than ownership of property. To constitute arson it is not necessary that a person other than the accused should have had ownership in the building set on fire. It is sufficient that at the time of the burning another person was rightfully in possession of, or was actually occupying such building or any part thereof....
>
> ....
>
> This is not to say that the [aggravated arson] statute absolutely prohibits an owner from setting fire to his own property. Section 76-6-103 states that a person is guilty only if he acted "intentionally and unlawfully." ... Thus, the person who carelessly burns a pile of trash in a high wind, setting fire to his own home or another's, might be found guilty under the reckless burning statute, but could not be found guilty of aggravated arson. Similarly, a homeowner who accidentally sets fire to his garage with his welding torch could not be said to have "intentionally" damaged a habitable structure. The word "unlawfully" also limits the reach of the aggravated arson statute. Although the term is not defined by statute, it appears often in the Criminal Code meaning without justification, license or privilege.... Many municipalities have fire safety regulations.... If a property owner complied with such regulations, obtained any necessary permit, notified the fire department, warned the neighbors, obtained assistance in organizing safety precautions, or assured an adequate supply of water, an owner could demonstrate the lawful nature of his activity.
>
> ....
>
> In the instant case the defendant, who was in possession of the house, and his friend apparently fired some shots in the kitchen very late one night. The friend then left, and the defendant apparently used a fire accelerant to set the house on fire. There is no suggestion that the fire was accidental or that there was any justifiable or beneficial purpose for the fire that occurred at approximately 1:50 a.m. The defendant intentionally created the risk that neighbors, firefighters and police [officers]

would be exposed to danger, all without any demonstrated justification or lawful purpose....

....

In summary, it is clear that many states have shifted the emphasis in arson law from a system classifying the offense according to type or ownership of the building to a system based on probability of danger to human life. Some of these states, including Utah, have incorporated a presumption of danger to human life whenever a habitable structure is damaged by an intentionally set fire or explosion without inquiry into the actual intent or knowledge of the accused. We have held that it is the intent of the legislature to penalize more severely any person who intentionally damages by fire a habitable structure actually occupied by a person without regard for whether that structure is owned or possessed by the accused.... Therefore, in the absence of evidence indicating accident or lawful purpose and safety measures, an owner of property may be convicted of aggravated arson for the burning of his own property.... The defendant's argument that he cannot be convicted because he acted at the owner's direction is without merit....

Id. at 640, 641-42, 645.

2. In *DeBettencourt v. State,* 428 A.2d 479 (Md. App. 1981), the defendant set fire to his own residence in a suburban neighborhood and was convicted under a statute covering arson of dwelling houses and their outbuildings, a felony carrying a maximum penalty of 30 years' imprisonment. The appellate court affirmed the conviction:

We simply decide (all that is necessary for this decision) that the intentional setting of a dangerous fire with reckless and wanton disregard of the consequences in terms of the danger of bringing harm to others is part of the content of that aggravating psychic element known as malice. We do not suggest necessarily that this is all there is to malice. We simply state that there is no less than this.

3. In *State v. Troiano,* 421 A.2d 41 (Me. 1980), the court affirmed the conviction under the aggravated arson statute of state prison inmates who had burned out the cell of another prisoner believed by the defendants to be a police informer.

4. In *Hancock v. Commonwealth,* 407 S.E.2d 301 (Va. App. 1991), the defendant had been convicted of arson and attempted capital murder by arson. The appellate court rejected his claim that the evidence of arson was lacking because insufficient damage had occurred to constitute the "burning" required for the crime:

The arson expert testified that while the boards used by the victims to put out the fire were charred because of those efforts to extinguish the fire, damage to the center pole supporting the roof of the structure was due to the fire set by [the principal actor] and his accomplices.... [T]he arson expert testified the center pole was, in fact, charred.... [W]e find the evidence supports the finding that the fire, which was of incendiary origin, did damage to the building.

"The amount of 'burning' necessary to be shown is any amount, provided there is a perceptible wasting of the fiber of the building or object which is a subject of arson, or some part of that building or object, by fire." ... While no Virginia case has directly addressed this proposition, we follow the precedent set by a majority of other states which hold that only a slight burning is necessary....

Id. at 303-04. The historical basis for the "some charring" concept in common-law arson is discussed in *State v. Oxendine,* 286 S.E.2d 546, 547-48 (N.C. 1982).

PART THREE
DOCTRINES

You have not as yet completed the study of the law of the crimes dealt with in Part Two. There is a large and equally important part of the criminal law which modifies and amplifies everything you have learned about those crimes. For example, if an infant or an insane person has done everything which, according to your present knowledge, constitutes larceny, he or she is, nonetheless, not guilty of larceny. This is so because certain doctrines regarding incapacity and mental disease are included in the meaning of "larceny," *i.e.*, these doctrines are part of the law of larceny and, indeed, of all other crimes. Because doctrines have general significance they can be studied at one time and applied to all crimes.

The following materials focus on the ways in which the doctrines modify the law defining specific elements of crimes, *e.g.*, complete exculpation as in the above instances or to reduce liability as regards gross intoxication and they concern the relation of the doctrines to the principles (Part One). It will be noticed that many of the doctrines involve the principle of *mens rea*, others, *e.g.*, self-defense, involve justification while still others, the relational doctrines, *e.g.*, attempt and conspiracy, are especially relevant to the principle of harm. Many of the doctrines are frequently treated simply as "defenses" and, of course, they are defenses. But it will advance knowledge of the criminal law if the reasons for their being defenses are pursued to the point of discovering the relevant substantive law, *i.e.*, the doctrines and principles of that law.

Finally, questions should be raised regarding any differences between justification and excuse. For example, is one privileged to defend against an attack by an insane person, but not against one who is properly exercising a right of self-defense? There are similar questions regarding charges of conspiracy when one of the two defendants is insane. And there are, of course, differences in civil liability with reference respectively to harms caused by justified action and those committed by persons who are exculpated from criminal liability on the ground of infancy or insanity.

Finally, given the various situations dealt with in the following chapters, whether labelled "justification" or "excuse" (they sometimes seem to overlap), analysis should be carried to the point of reference to the relevant principle or principles which ultimately determine the decisions.

Chapter 7
JUSTIFICATION

NOTE ON JUSTIFICATION

This chapter, Justification, and the following chapters on Excuse involve questions as to whether a person who has committed an ostensibly harmful act should be held criminally responsible. Justification and excuse* are defenses to a criminal prosecution, but they are not defined so distinctly as to avoid any doubt as to whether a particular situation falls within one category or the other.

> Claims of justification concede that the definition of the offense is satisfied, but challenge whether the act is wrongful; claims of excuse concede that the act is wrongful, but seek to avoid the attribution of the act to the actor. A justification speaks to the rightness of the act; an excuse, to whether the actor is accountable for a concededly wrongful act.

G. FLETCHER, RETHINKING CRIMINAL LAW 759 (1978). Self-defense, defense of others, defense of property, prevention of crime and arrest, necessity and coercion are included in this chapter; insanity, intoxication, ignorance, and mistake are discussed in subsequent chapters.

Notwithstanding disputes among scholars as to whether a particular situation should be classified as justification or excuse, it would be rare to find an American or English judge discussing the distinction in a judicial opinion and even rarer for the distinction to have any practical effect on the outcome of a case.

> [A]s a matter of criminal practice, Stephen's statement that the common law distinction between justification and excuse "involves no legal consequences"[1] still seems to be valid, at least in the sense that it may be of some procedural value but is "fallacious and misleading"[2] for establishing separate categories of substantive law.

Eser, *Justification and Excuse*, 24 AM. J. COMP. L. 621 (1976). See also Hall *Comment on Justification and Excuse*, 24 AM. J. COMP. L. 638 (1976).

This chapter and the two following chapters will examine various defenses with emphasis on when and why these defenses exist. The subject of defenses

---

*The theory of justification and excuse is examined in G. Fletcher, RETHINKING CRIMINAL LAW 759-875 (1978).

[1] 3 J. Stephen, HISTORY OF THE CRIMINAL LAW OF ENGLAND 11 (1883).

[2] J. Hall, GENERAL PRINCIPLES OF CRIMINAL LAW 233 (2d ed. 1960). *See also Hart*, Punishment and Responsibility 13 (1968): "To the modern [English] lawyer this distinction [between justification and excuse] has no longer any legal importance.... But the distinction between these two different ways in which actions may fail to constitute a criminal offense is still of great moral importance."

has received comprehensive analysis in Robinson, *Criminal Law Defenses: A Systematic Analysis*, 82 COLUM. L. REV. 199 (1982).

NOTE ON DEFENSE OF PERSON, PROPERTY AND ARREST

People are justified under the law to cause harm to others in order to protect certain legally recognized interests including life, bodily integrity, property and public order. As a general proposition people may use as much force, other than deadly force, as is actually required to protect the interest. This does not mean that there are no legal problems when less than deadly force is used. Questions arise as to whether the situation is one in which force may be used, whether defendant used only as much force as appeared necessary, and whether defendant's subjective belief as to both the need for and amount of force necessary to protect his or her interest should be measured against a standard of objective reasonableness.

Many of the cases involve the use of deadly force. Special rules apply in deadly force cases. It will be helpful, therefore, to separate cases in which death or serious injury was inflicted from those where less force was used.

Also it will be helpful to understand that a single act may threaten several different kinds of harms. For example, the act of breaking into a defendant's home for the purpose of killing defendant threatens life, sanctity of dwelling, and public order. Situations often are fluid. What starts out as an attempted petty theft with the resultant attempt to protect property by reasonable, non-deadly force, may suddenly escalate into the highest form of self-defense if the thief tries to stab the resisting property owner. Thus, it is important to identify specifically the harm which defendant claims justified his or her action. Not all harms justify the use of deadly force.

SECTION I. Self-Defense[*]

MODEL PENAL CODE

§ 3.04. *Use of Force in Self-Protection*

§ 3.09. *Mistake of Law as to Unlawfulness of Force or Legality of Arrest; Reckless or Negligent Use of Otherwise Justifiable Force; Reckless or Negligent Injury or Risk of Injury to Innocent Persons*

§ 3.11. *Definitions*

[The text of these sections appears in Appendix A.]

---

[*]The incidence of victim-precipitated crime is difficult to gauge; precipitative conduct may be overlooked or not appreciated in the reconstruction of a crime. As part of a major study, the National Commission on the Causes and Prevention of Violence attempted to assess the extent of victim-precipitated violent crimes. The Commission defined victim-precipitated homicides as those in which the victims were the first to employ physical force. Using this definition, it calculated that victim precipitation occurred in 22% of all homicides, and played no part in 33.8%. In the remaining 44.2%, no authoritative determination could be made. Gobert, *Victim Precipitation*, 77 Colum. L. Rev. 511, 516 (1977).

PEOPLE v. WILLIAMS

Appellate Court of Illinois
56 Ill App. 2d 159, 205 N.E.2d 749 (1965)

...

LYONS, JUSTICE.

This is an appeal from a conviction of involuntary manslaughter with punishment fixed at two to eight years in the penitentiary.

On April 12, 1963, at about eight o'clock in the evening, defendant, while driving a Yellow Cab south on Princeton Avenue, stopped for a traffic light at the corner of 51st Street in Chicago. He observed a group of young men on the northeast corner, beating an old man, later identified as one Joseph Bell. The victim of the assault, while lying on the sidewalk, called to defendant for help. When defendant shouted to the boys to leave the victim alone, the boys shouted back insults. When the traffic light turned green, defendant turned west on 51st Street for about one half block, made a U-turn and drove east, back to the same corner. As he was re-crossing the intersection his cab was struck by a rock or brick. Defendant stopped his cab near the boys, who at this time were standing on the southeast corner. He fired two shots in their direction. The boys ran. Defendant drove away. One of the boys, Kenneth Boatner, age 16, was killed, the result of a bullet wound in the brain.

....

He did not report the shooting to his superiors at the cab company, nor to the police. He did, however, report the damage inflicted on the cab by the brick to the company. Defendant was indicted. He waived a jury trial.

....

Defendant's theory is that there was sufficient evidence of self-defense submitted, to leave reasonable doubt of his guilt in the mind of the trier of fact. Ill. Rev. Stat. 1963, Chap. 38, Sec. 7-1 of the Criminal Code states as follows:

> A person is justified in the use of force against another when and to the extent that he reasonably believes that such conduct is necessary to defend himself or another against such others imminent use of unlawful force. However, he is justified in the use of force which is intended or likely to cause death or great bodily harm only if he reasonably believes that such force is necessary to prevent imminent death or great bodily harm to himself or another, or the commission of a forcible felony.

At the outset, it is settled law that the burden of proof never shifts to the defendant, no matter what his defense may be, and where he pleads self-defense, it is sufficient to acquit him, if his evidence on self-defense, together with all other evidence in the case, creates a reasonable doubt of his guilt....

Bearing this in mind, we now turn to the elements, which if present, justify the use of force in the defense of a person. These elements are: (1) that force is threatened against a person; (2) that the person threatened is not the aggressor; (3) that the danger of harm is imminent; (4) that the force threatened is unlawful; (5) that the person threatened must actually believe: (a) that a danger exists, (b) that the use of force is necessary to avert the danger; (c) that the kind and amount of force which he uses is necessary; and (6) that the above beliefs are reasonable. There is a further principle involved, when, as in the instant case, the defendant uses deadly force. This principle limits the use of deadly force to those situations in which, (a) the threatened force will cause death or great bodily harm or (b) the force threatened is a forcible felony.

It is uncontroverted that a brick was thrown at defendant. Thus, the use of force was threatened against defendant. Furthermore, the State does not contend that defendant was the aggressor. Thus, we can proceed to the third element.

The State contends that the danger to defendant was not imminent. The State reasons that the deceased did not have the present ability of carrying out the alleged threat. This contention is invalid. There were several boys in the gang and they had just thrown a cement block and a brick at defendant's cab, the latter causing substantial damage to the right door (a picture of the damage to the cab was introduced in evidence). The gang was a short distance from defendant. They had the present ability to carry out the threatened use of force. The deceased, identified as part of the gang that damaged the cab, also had the present ability to carry out the threatened harm.

The evidence that the gang threw a brick against the cab of defendant was sufficient to show that the threatened force was unlawful as such conduct is both criminal and tortious. Thus, we can proceed to the fifth and sixth elements.

To satisfy the fifth and sixth elements it must be determined whether or not defendant actually believed that a danger existed; that the use of force was necessary to avert the danger; that the kind and amount of force used was necessary; and that such belief was reasonable. A belief is reasonable even if the defendant is mistaken. Defendant had just seen an elderly man beaten up. Furthermore, we again emphasize the fact that the gang, consisting of a number of young men, had just thrown a cement block and a brick at defendant's cab and that they caused substantial damage to the cab. Defendant testified that when he stopped his cab, the gang started to move toward him. There is only one conclusion that can be reached — defendant actually believed that a danger existed.

Next, defendant, if the State failed to do so, had to introduce evidence that he reasonably believed that the use of force was necessary to avert the danger. The State contends that defendant could have driven away from the scene of the incident with his cab and thus the use of force was unnecessary. We disagree with this contention. When a defendant is where he has a lawful right to be, he has a right to stand his ground, and if reasonably apprehensive of injury is justified in taking his assailant's life. *People v. Bush*, 414 Ill. 441, 111 N.E.2d 326 (1953). *People v. Durand*, 307 Ill. 611, 139 N.E. 78 (1923). Defendant was under no duty to flee. Furthermore, defendant testified that he had not left the area, because of his desire to help the victim of the assault, Joseph Bell. We will take judicial notice of the fact, that recently there have been a number of publicized assaults and homicides, in which the victims called upon their fellow citizens to render aid. In many instances these fellow citizens refused to get involved. Here we have a man who took it upon himself to get involved, when a victim called for help. In addition to the cases cited above, public policy forbids us to say a person must leave the victim of a

I. SELF-DEFENSE

brutal beating lie on the street when called upon to render aid. A citizen must feel free to help the victim of an assault. The State alleges that there was no danger to the victim Bell, as the gang of young men had already walked away from Bell and apparently had terminated the beating. They conclude that defendant should have left the scene of the incident. This allegation does not take into consideration the fact that the gang could have returned and further assaulted the victim after defendant left. We must also consider the language in the stipulation that if Bell testified, he would say of defendant, "the only thing I know, *He saved my life.*" (Emphasis supplied.)

Next we must determine the difficult question of whether or not defendant reasonably believed that the kind and amount of force which he used was necessary. Again we stress the principle that belief is reasonable even if the defendant is mistaken. In reviewing the facts we must sustain defendant's contention that he believed the use of a gun was necessary. Defendant had been robbed several weeks before the incident. He was a cab driver approaching a vicious gang of youths. It was night time. Defendant had just observed Bell being beaten up and stomped on. The gang told him to mind his own business. Upon returning to help the victim, Bell, his cab was hit by a brick. The gang of young men were obviously hostile to him because of his intrusion. He had no other weapon. Furthermore, what is really important is defendant's state of mind at the time of the incident. He testified that he was afraid that he would be beat up like Bell. He knew that the gang was aware that, as a cab driver, he had money on his person. Defendant in using the gun reasonably believed that the kind of force used was necessary. Furthermore, defendant testified that he shot up in the air to scare the boys off. The trial judge believed this portion of defendant's testimony. We can only conclude that defendant reasonably believed that both the kind and amount of force used was necessary under the circumstances.

Finally, we must determine if the use of deadly force by defendant was justified. Such force is justified if the threatened force would cause death or great bodily harm or is a forcible felony. It is apparent that the throwing of bricks at defendant could have caused death or great bodily harm if defendant was struck by one of them. Defendant was justified in using deadly force to protect his person.

In this case we only hold that when a person comes to the aid of another who has been the victim of a battery, said person has the right to use deadly force, if the parties who were the assailants attack him and if the other requirements of self-defense are met. The circumstances of this case present a situation in which we approach the minimum borderline of self-defense. The circumstances are such, however, that the judgment must be reversed.

Judgment reversed.

NOTES

1. In *Commonwealth v. Kendrick*, 351 Mass. 203, 218 N.E.2d 408 (1966), the defendant was convicted of murder in the second degree. He was in an amorous relationship with a Mrs. G. and went to the G. household to tell Mr. G. that Mrs. G. wanted a divorce so that she could marry the defendant. The

defendant took an army knife with him because he feared there might be trouble.

The defendant knocked at the front door of the G. dwelling and when no one answered he walked along the front of the house and looked in the windows. Mr. G. came around the side of the house with a fireplace poker. There was a fight in which Mr. G. was killed by stab wounds in the neck and chest.

The trial judge instructed the jury on self-defense but refused to give a manslaughter instruction. Reversed.

If the defendant used excessive force in defending himself he was guilty of manslaughter. "In passing upon the reasonableness of the force used by the defendant, again on the hypothesis that he was acting in self-defense, the jury should consider evidence of the relative physical capabilities of the combatants, the characteristics of the weapons used, and the availability of maneuver room in, or means of escape from, the doorway area." 351 Mass. at 212, 218 N.E.2d at 414. Annot., 9 A.L.R.3d 933 (1966). A reoccurrence of the facts in *Kendrick* might be affected by the change in Massachusetts law which eliminates the duty of retreat for the occupant of a dwelling as against one unlawfully in the dwelling. See *Commonwealth v. Gregory*, 17 Mass. App. 651, 461 N.E.2d 831, 833 N. 2 (1984). See also n. 4 *infra*.

2. In *Sikes v. Commonwealth*, 304 Ky. 429, 200 S.W.2d 956 (1947), overruled on other grounds, *White v. Commonwealth*, 360 S.W.2d 198 (Ky. 1962), the defendant was at the Fourth of July picnic in Paducah and fought with William Hogan who, according to the defendant, had precipitated their quarrel. Wheatley, who seems to have been a stranger to all the parties, came towards Sikes, "acting like he was going to strike me." Sikes hit him on the jaw with his fist; Wheatley died from a cerebral hemorrhage caused by the blow.

The trial court's instruction on self-defense was that defendant should be acquitted if "he believed and had reasonable grounds to believe that he was then and there in danger of death or the infliction of some great bodily harm at the hands of Wheatley ...." 200 S.W.2d at 958. The conviction was reversed.

"Where a homicide was committed by the use of the fist alone without a weapon, the defendant's right to justify the act as having been committed in self-defense is not confined to a situation so grave that the danger to be averted was great bodily injury or the loss of life." *Id.* at 960. Where the evidence requires an instruction on involuntary manslaughter, a reciprocal instruction on self-defense should be given.

3. In *State v. Graham*, 260 S.C. 449, 196 S.E.2d 495 (1973), defendant and deceased had quarrelled prior to the day of their gun fight. Defendant saw deceased on the street holding a gun and placed himself in a position where an encounter could be expected. Both parties fired at each other, the deceased was mortally wounded and died shortly thereafter. Conviction of manslaughter was affirmed. Where a person voluntarily participates in mutual combat for purposes other than protection he cannot justify his actions on the basis of self-defense.

4. In *State v. Leos*, 7 Or. App. 211, 490 P.2d 521 (1971), the defendant was fighting with his wife who pointed a pistol at him. He asked her to give him a cigarette, and when she turned to get matches, he threw a blanket over her,

I. SELF-DEFENSE

seized her hand with one hand and threw his other arm around her neck. Defendant told her to drop the gun and when she refused he put pressure on her neck, causing her death. Defendant said he did not intend to kill or seriously injure his wife.

A conviction of manslaughter was reversed because the trial judge's instructions did not clearly distinguish self-defense and excusable homicide. "In self-defense the use of *deadly* force is purposeful. In excusable homicide the use of *deadly* force is accidental or mistaken, ..." and "must have been committed by the defendant in doing a lawful act, by lawful means, with usual and ordinary caution." 490 P.2d at 523. "The defendant testified that he was acting in defense of himself when he unintentionally killed his wife. This testimony was sufficient to justify an instruction on excusable homicide." *Id.* at 524.

5. In *Martin v. Ohio*, 480 U.S. 228 (1987), the Supreme Court upheld an Ohio rule requiring a defendant to prove self-defense. The Court relied on *Patterson v. New York*, 432 U.S. 197 (1977). See *supra* pp. 324-328.

> As we noted in *Patterson*, the common-law rule was that affirmative defenses, including self-defense, were matters for the defendant to prove. "This was the rule when the Fifth Amendment was adopted, and it was the American rule when the Fourteenth Amendment was ratified." 432 US, at 202, 53 L Ed 2d 281, 97 S Ct 2319. Indeed, well into this century, a number of States followed the common-law rule and required a defendant to shoulder the burden of proving that he acted in self-defense. Fletcher, Two Kinds of Legal Rules: A Comparative Study of Burden-of-Persuasion Practices in Criminal Cases, 77 Yale L.J. 880, 882, and n 10 (1968). We are aware that all but two of the States, Ohio and South Carolina, have abandoned the common-law rule and require the prosecution to prove the absence of self-defense when it is properly raised by the defendant. But the question remains whether those States are in violation of the Constitution; and, as we observed in *Patterson*, that question is not answered by cataloging the practices of other States. We are no more convinced that the Ohio practice of requiring self-defense to be proved by the defendant is unconstitutional than we are that the Constitution requires the prosecution to prove the sanity of a defendant who pleads not guilty by reason of insanity.

Id. at 235-36.

COLEMAN v. STATE

Supreme Court of Delaware
320 A.2d 740 (1974)

HERRMANN, CHIEF JUSTICE.

The defendant seeks review of his conviction for assault and battery on the ground that the Trial Court improperly charged the jury as to the defense of justification. The instruction included the following:

> ... The use of force upon or towards another is justifiable when the defendant reasonably believes that such force is admittedly necessary for

the purpose of protecting himself against the use of unlawful force by the other person at the time.

... [W]here one is assaulted in a sudden affray, and in the judgment of the jury honestly believes on reasonable grounds that he was in imminent [sic] danger of suffering great bodily harm, he has in such case the right to use a weapon against his assailant; ...

....

... In order to justify the accused it is sufficient that he at the time reasonably believed himself to be in danger at the hands of the injured, but the circumstances must have been such in your judgment so as to justify a reasonable man in such belief and further belief that there was no reasonable way of avoiding or escaping from such danger except by striking his assailant.

The defendant contends that the charge was improper for the reason that the correct test under present law is not what a reasonable man would believe, but rather what the defendant actually believed. As support for this position, the defendant maintains that 11 Del.C. § 464(a), the portion of the new Criminal Code[1] dealing with the use of self-protective force as a defense, creates such subjective standard in lieu of the "reasonable man" objective test formerly prevailing in this jurisdiction. The new § 464(a) provides:

§ 464. Justification; use of force in self-protection.

(a) The use of force upon or toward another person is justifiable when the defendant believes that such force is immediately necessary for the purpose of protecting himself against the use of unlawful force by the other person on the present occasion.

The defendant points out that the word "reasonable" nowhere appears in § 464(a). Further, the defendant points to the codifiers' Commentary on § 464(a):

Section 464 sets generally the permissible limits on the use of force in self-protection. Subsection (a) permits the use of force against another person only when the actor believes the force is immediately necessary for the purpose of protecting himself against that other's use of force on the present occasion. The actor must show that he did believe that force was necessary and that his response was an immediate reaction to a present necessity. Note, however, that a reasonable belief is not required. All that is relevant to the actor's guilt is that he did honestly believe it necessary to use force in his own defense. A person with such a belief presents no criminal threat to social order. Of course, one who is reckless or negligent in ascertaining the facts which give rise to a need for self-protection presents a different problem which is covered expressly by § 469. To the extent possible the criminal law ought to be determining guilt in individ-

---

[1] Although the instant offense occurred prior to the adoption of the new Criminal Code, the defendant elected, as was his option under § 102(b)(2) of the new Code, to use defenses made available thereunder.

I. SELF-DEFENSE

ual terms, and deviations from the "reasonable man" norm ought to be determinative of guilt only when they indicate that the actor threatens social order in the way which the criminal law seeks to prevent. Thus if it has been decided to justify self-defensive force (presumably because it is socially desirable), the man who employs force in self-defense has done nothing wrong; nor does his act suggest any criminal propensity to deviate from social norms. Note that this section is consistent with § 441, relating to mistake of fact, which does not require reasonableness. Of course, if the actor's reaction deviates too substantially from the norm, he runs the risk that the jury will not believe him. But if he honestly believes he needs to act in self-defense, the criminal law will be powerless to stop him, no matter how unreasonable his belief. It is best, then, that the official statement of the law be realistic.

The provision of § 464(a) must be read in the light of § 307(a) of the new Criminal Code which provides in pertinent part:

The defendant's ... belief at the time of the offense for which he is charged may be inferred by the jury .... In making the inference ..., the jury may consider whether a reasonable man in the defendant's circumstances at the time of the offense would have had or lacked the requisite ... belief.

The Commentary on § 307(a) includes the following:

One of the most important underlying premises of this Criminal Code is that criminal guilt ought to turn on the subjective criminality of the accused. Thus, for example, in defining the defense of justification, the defense turns on what the defendant himself believed as to the necessity of taking certain protective action....

Subsection (a) ... applies to cases in which the defendant's mental state is a matter of defense. Thus, if defendant claims that a killing was justified because he believed it necessary for the protection of his own person (note that § 464 requires only proof of belief, not reasonable belief), the jury, in determining whether the defendant actually had the asserted belief, are permitted to test the defendant's credibility by considering what a reasonable man under [the] circumstances would have believed....

It should be emphasized that proof of what would have been the state of mind of a reasonable man will not, in itself, satisfy the prosecution's burden of persuasion. The question in every case is what the accused believed or intended. If the jury have a reasonable doubt about the defendant's own culpability, they must acquit. Section 307 is merely intended to aid the State in getting to the jury without having literally to prove what was going on in the defendant's mind. Likewise where a state of mind is a matter of defense, the Court should instruct the jury that the standard of defense is purely subjective (unless the relevant definition of the defense contains the word "reasonably" or some other objective standard), but that the jury may consider, in determining whether the accused did in fact entertain the asserted belief, what a reasonable man would have believed under the circumstances. If the jury are satisfied that the accused entertained the asserted belief, regardless of what a reasonable man would have believed, they should acquit.

Upon the basis of the foregoing, we have concluded that the new Criminal Code has changed the standard to be applied by the trier of fact in determining the issue of justification. The former objective test of what a reasonable man would have believed under the circumstances, as to the necessity of using force in self-defense, has been supplanted by the subjective test of what the defendant actually believed as to such necessity. In applying the subjective standard and in testing the defendant's actual belief as to the necessity of force for self-protection, it is important to note that § 307(a) of the new Code provides that "the jury may consider whether a reasonable man in the defendant's circumstances at the time of the offense would have had or lacked the requisite ... belief." Thus, the "reasonable man" test is retained as a factor to be considered with all others in the determination of the issue of justification; but it is not necessarily the controlling factor as heretofore.

It follows that the jury instruction in the instant case, based upon the formerly prevailing objective standard, must be declared error.

We are unable to say, in this case in which self-defense was the sole defense, that the error was harmless beyond a reasonable doubt.... Accordingly, the judgment below must be reversed and the cause remanded for new trial.

NOTES

1. "[W]hen facts are present which give rise to a plea of self-defense, it is not unreasonable that if the plea fails, the accused should be found guilty of voluntary manslaughter." *State v. Lopez*, 79 N.M. 282, 285, 442 P.2d 594, 597 (1968). The underlying rationale for this principle of law stems from the difference between self-defense and provocation supporting a conviction for voluntary manslaughter. Self-defense is a belief by a reasonable man in the necessity to save himself from death or great bodily harm. *State v. Kidd, supra.* Provocation supporting a conviction for voluntary manslaughter, on the other hand, is an act "committed under the influence of an uncontrollable fear of death or great bodily harm, caused by the circumstances, but without the presence of all the ingredients necessary to excuse the act on the ground of self-defense". *Id.* at 579, 175 P. at 774. (Emphasis added.) The two principles of law are therefore not mutually incompatible, as the decision of the Court of Appeals imports.

State v. Melendez, 97 N.M. 738, 643 P.2d 607, 609 (1982).

2. In *State v. Wanrow*, 88 Wash. 2d 221, 559 P.2d 548 (1977), the trial judge instructed the jury that before a deadly weapon can justifiably be used to repel an attack by an unarmed person, the jury must find that defendant believed her life was in danger and that this belief was reasonable. Held: the instruction was erroneous.

In our society women suffer from a conspicuous lack of access to training in and the means of developing those skills necessary to effectively repel a

I. SELF-DEFENSE

male assailant without resorting to the use of deadly weapons. [The] instruction does indicate that the "relative size and strength of the persons involved" may be considered; however, it does not make clear that the defendant's actions are to be judged against her own subjective impressions and not those which a detached jury might determine to be objectively reasonable.

The instruction was defective not only in using *apportionality*

[an] objective standard, but through the persistent use of the masculine gender leaves the jury with the impression the objective standard to be applied is that applicable to an altercation between two men. The impression created — that a 5'4" woman with a cast on her leg and using a crutch must, under the law, somehow repel an assault by a 6'2" intoxicated man without employing weapons in her defense, unless the jury finds her determination of the degree of danger to be objectively reasonable — constitutes a separate and distinct misstatement of the law and, in the context of this case, violates the respondent's right to equal protection of the law. The respondent was entitled to have the jury consider her actions in the light of her own perceptions of the situation, including those perceptions which were the product of our nation's "long and unfortunate history of sex discrimination."...

Until such time as the effects of that history are eradicated, care must be taken to assure that our self-defense instructions afford women the right to have their conduct judged in light of the individual physical handicaps which are the product of sex discrimination.

88 Wash. 2d at 238-40, 559 P.2d at 558-59.

NOTES ON INTRAMARITAL VIOLENCE: BATTERED WIVES

1. For self-defense to apply a defendant must be threatened with imminent injury. Where defendant is threatened with future harm defensive force is not ordinarily recognized because defendant may be able to escape future harm. However,

> [t]he failure of the imminence standard to consider the certainty of the threatened harm has a serious impact on the rights of a victim of marital abuse to take defensive action. Many parties to intramarital assaults have had previous violent encounters. This pattern of behavior makes future harm more certain and the avenues of escape less available than in other assault situations.

Note, *Limits on the Use of Defensive Force to Prevent Intramarital Assaults*, 10 RUT.-CAM. L.J. 643, 651 (1978-79).

2. The ability of a jury to consider intramarital violence depends on the admissibility of evidence. This involves the possibilities of evidence from expert testimony and from the defendant herself. In *State v. Hennum*, 441 N.W. 2d 793 (Minn. 1989), the state supreme court upheld the admission of expert

[margin note: No imminence of danger]

testimony on battered Woman Syndrome but disapproved requiring the defendant to submit to a medical examination.

This court has never specifically addressed the question of the admissibility of battered woman syndrome evidence. In *dicta*, the court of appeals stated the admission of such evidence in this case was error since it would not serve to aid the jury. We disagree with this reasoning and choose to address the issue in order to set forth a standard for the admissibility of battered woman syndrome evidence.

The court of appeals relied on this court's decision in *State v. Saldana*, 324 N.W.2d 227 (Minn. 1982), which held it was error for a trial court to admit expert testimony as to "rape trauma syndrome" in a rape case. In *Saldana* we set forth guidelines for the admission of expert testimony:

To be admissible, expert testimony must be helpful to the jury in reaching its decision:

The basic requirement of Rule 702 is the helpfulness requirement. If the subject of the testimony is within the knowledge and experience of a lay jury and the testimony of the expert will not add precision or depth to the jury's ability to reach conclusions about that subject which is within their experience, then the testimony does not meet the helpfulness test.

... If the jury is in as good a position to reach a decision as the expert, expert testimony would be of little assistance to the jury and should not be admitted.

Saldana, 324 N.W.2d at 229 (citation omitted). This court found in *Saldana* that the "scientific evaluation of rape trauma syndrome has not reached a level of reliability that surpasses the quality of common sense evaluation present in jury deliberations." *Id.* at 230.

The majority of states which have examined the admissibility of battered woman syndrome evidence have held it is admissible. Under standards similar to our own, other courts have held that battered woman syndrome is beyond the understanding of the average person and therefore expert testimony should be allowed. *State v. Allery*, 101 Wash. 2d 591, 597, 682 P.2d 312, 316 (1984); *Smith v. State*, 247 Ga. 612, 619, 277 S.E.2d 678, 683 (1981); *Hawthorne v. State*, 408 So.2d 801, 807 (Fla. Dist. Ct. App. 1982); *Ibn-Tamas v. United States*, 407 A.2d 626, 634-35 (D.C. 1979). These courts have admitted expert testimony on this subject (1) to dispel the common misconception that a normal or reasonable person would not remain in such an abusive relationship, (2) for the specific purpose of bolstering the defendant's position and lending credibility to her version of the facts, and (3) to show the reasonableness of the defendant's fear that she was in imminent peril of death or serious bodily injury. Mather, *The Skeleton in the Closet: The Battered Woman Syndrome, Self-Defense, and Expert Testimony*, 39 Mercer L. Rev. 545, 576-77 (1988). We agree expert testimony on this issue is admissible since it would help to explain a phenomenon not within the understanding of an ordinary lay person. In addition we find that this case differs from the rape trauma syndrome in *Saldana*, since the theory underlying the bat-

[margin note: Guilt & fear prevents defendant from leaving]

tered woman syndrome is beyond the experimental stage and has gained a substantial enough scientific acceptance to warrant admissibility.

In allowing the admission of battered woman syndrome evidence, we set some limits on the use of expert testimony on this subject. We hold that in future cases expert testimony regarding battered woman syndrome will be limited to a description of the general syndrome and the characteristics which are present in an individual suffering from the syndrome. The expert should not be allowed to testify as to the ultimate fact that the particular defendant actually suffers from battered woman syndrome. This determination must be left to the trier of fact. Each side may present witnesses who may testify to characteristics possessed by the defendant which are consistent with those found in someone suffering from battered woman syndrome. This restriction will remove the need for a compelled adverse medical examination of the defendant. Since the expert will only be allowed to testify as to the general nature of battered woman syndrome, neither side need conduct an examination of the defendant.

441 N.W. 2d at 797-799.

STATE v. ABBOTT

Supreme Court of New Jersey
36 N.J. 63, 174 A.2d 881 (1961)

WEINTRAUB, C. J.

Frank Abbott was convicted of atrocious assault and battery. The Appellate Division affirmed, 64 N.J.Super. 191, 165 A.2d 537 (1960)....

Abbott shared a common driveway with his neighbors, Michael and Mary Scarano. The Scaranos engaged a contractor to pave their portion. Abbott obtained some asphalt from the contractor and made a doorstop to keep his garage door from swinging onto the Scaranos' property. Nicholas Scarano, who was visiting with the Scaranos, his parents, objected to Abbott's innovation. After some words between them a fist fight ensued.

Although Abbott managed to land the first punch, with which he sent Nicholas to the ground, a jury could find Nicholas was the aggressor. At this point Michael Scarano came at Abbott with a hatchet. Michael said the tool had just been returned to him by the contractor, and denied he meant to use it as a weapon. According to Abbott, Mary Scarano followed, armed with a carving knife and large fork. The actors gave varying versions of what happened, but the end result was that all of the Scaranos were hit by the hatchet. Nicholas received severe head injuries. Abbott claimed he too suffered a laceration.

Abbott admitted he finally wrested the hatchet from Michael but denied he wielded it at all. Rather he insisted that the Scaranos were injured during a common struggle for the instrument. A jury could, however, find Abbott intentionally inflicted the blows.

Abbott was separately indicted for atrocious assault and battery upon each of the Scaranos. There was a common trial of these indictments. The jury acquitted Abbott of the charges relating to Michael and Mary, but found him guilty as to Nicholas.

I

The principal question is whether the trial court properly instructed the jury upon the issue of self-defense. The trial court charged upon the subject of excessive force, as to which Abbott does not complain. It charged also upon the subject of retreat, and it is here that error is alleged. Although the jury could have found Abbott used excessive force, we cannot know whether the jury found for him on that subject and convicted because he had failed to retreat in accordance with the trial court's instruction.

As to retreat, the trial court charged upon two hypotheses. One was that the critical events occurred upon Abbott's property. Upon that basis, the court said Abbott could stand his ground, and, of course, of this Abbott does not complain. The second hypothesis was that the alleged offense occurred upon the common driveway. Presumably on the authority of *State v. Pontery*, 19 N.J. 457, 475, 117 A.2d 473 (1955), the trial court held that since all the principals were equally entitled to be on the driveway, Abbott could not claim immunity from the ordinary retreat rule. Abbott does not question that thesis, but disputes the court's statement of the conditions under which an obligation to retreat would arise.

The subject of retreat usually arises in homicide matters. We will first discuss it in that context, and then consider whether the principles apply to a charge of atrocious assault and battery, and if they do, whether the trial court correctly guided the jury in this difficult area.

We should make it clear that we are discussing the doctrine of retreat and not the subject of the use of excessive force. If the force used was unnecessary in its intensity, the claim of self-defense may [fail] for that reason. In the discussion which follows we assume a defendant used no more force than he believed necessary to protect himself in the circumstances as they reasonably appeared to him, and consider only whether the claim of self-defense should be denied because he could have avoided the use of that force by retreating.

The question whether one who is neither the aggressor nor a party to a mutual combat must retreat has divided the authorities. Self-defense is measured against necessity. *Brown v. State*, 62 N.J.L. 666, 708, 42 A. 811 (E. & A.), affirmed, 175 U.S. 172, 20 S.Ct. 77, 44 L.Ed. 119 (1899); *State v. Hipplewith*, 33 N.J. 300, 316-318, 164 A.2d 481 (1960). From that premise one could readily say there was no necessity to kill in self-defense if the use of deadly force could have been avoided by retreat. The critics of the retreat rule do not quarrel with the theoretical validity of this conclusion, but rather condemn it as unrealistic. The law of course should not denounce conduct as criminal when it accords with the behavior of reasonable men. Upon this level, the advocates of no-retreat say the manly thing is to hold one's ground, and hence society should not demand what smacks of cowardice. Adherents of the retreat rule reply it is better that the assailed shall retreat than that the life of another be needlessly spent. They add that not only do right-thinking men agree, but further a rule so requiring may well induce others to adhere to that worthy standard of behavior....

Other jurisdictions are closely divided upon the retreat doctrine. It is said that the preponderant view rejects it. Perkins, Criminal Law 899 (1957); 1

Warren, Homicide § 157, at pp. 767-68 (perm. ed. 1938); Model Penal Code § 3.04, comment 3, at p. 24 (Tent. Draft No. 8, 1958).... Our Court of Errors and Appeals deliberately adopted the retreat rule.... The Model Penal Code embraces the retreat rule while acknowledging that on numerical balance a majority of the precedents oppose it. Model Penal Code § 3.04, comment 3, at p. 24 (Tent. Draft No. 8, 1958).

We are not persuaded to depart from the principle of retreat. We think it salutary if reasonably limited. Much of the criticism goes not to its inherent validity but rather to unwarranted applications of the rule. For example, it is correctly observed that one can hardly retreat from a rifle shot at close range. But if the weapon were a knife, a lead of a city block might well be enough. Again, the rule cannot be stated baldly, with indifference to the excitement of the occasion. As Mr. Justice Holmes cryptically put it, "Detached reflection cannot be demanded in the presence of an uplifted knife." *Brown v. United States*, 256 U.S. 335, 343, 41 S.Ct. 501, 502, 65 L.Ed. 961, 963 (1921). Such considerations, however, do not demand that a man should have the absolute right to stand his ground and kill in any and all situations. Rather they call for a fair and guarded statement of appropriate principles.

We believe the following principles are sound:

1. The issue of retreat arises only if the defendant resorted to a deadly force. It is deadly force which is not justifiable when an opportunity to retreat is at hand. Model Penal Code § 3.04(2)(b)(iii)....

Hence it is not the nature of the force defended against which raises the issue of retreat, but rather the nature of the force which the accused employed in his defense. If he does not resort to a deadly force, one who is assailed may hold his ground whether the attack upon him be of a deadly or some lesser character. Although it might be argued that a safe retreat should be taken if thereby the use of *any* force could be avoided, yet, as the comment in the Model Penal Code observes (at p. 23), "The logic of this position never has been accepted when moderate force is used in self-defense; here all agree that the actor may stand his ground and estimate necessity upon that basis." Cf. Prosser, Torts § 19, at p. 90 (2d ed. 1955); Restatement, Torts § 63 (1934). Hence, in a case like the present one, the jury should be instructed that Abbott could hold his ground when Nicholas came at him with his fists, and also when Michael and Mary came at him with the several instruments mentioned, and that the question of retreat could arise only if Abbott intended to use a deadly force.

2. What constitutes an opportunity to retreat which will defeat the right of self-defense? As § 3.04(2)(b)(iii) of the Model Penal Code states, deadly force is not justifiable "if the actor *knows* that he can avoid the necessity of using such force *with complete safety* by retreating ...." We emphasize "knows" and "with complete safety." One who is wrongfully attacked need not risk injury by retreating, even though he could escape with something less than serious bodily injury. It would be unreal to require nice calculations as to the amount of hurt, or to ask him to endure any at all. And the issue is not whether in retrospect it can be found the defendant could have retreated unharmed. Rather the question is whether he knew the opportunity was there, and of course in that inquiry the total circumstances including the attendant excite-

ment must be considered. We add that upon a retrial the facts as developed in the light of this principle may be such that Abbott would be entitled to an instruction that if his version of the approach by Michael and Mary is accepted, the issue of retreat must be resolved in Abbott's favor.

3. There has been some uncertainty in the language of our cases upon the burden of proof with respect to self-defense. The decisions are treated in *State v. Chiarello*, N.J.Super., 174 A.2d 506 (1961) where the Appellate Division correctly said that although the burden is upon a defendant to adduce evidence to support the defense, yet if such evidence appears either in the State's case or upon the defendant's case, the issue must be left to the jury with this instruction: that the burden is upon the State to prove beyond a reasonable doubt that the defense is untrue, and hence there must be an acquittal if there is a reasonable doubt as to whether defendant did act in self-defense within the definition of that defense. Accordingly, if the issue of retreat is raised in connection with the defense of self-defense, the jury should be instructed that the burden is also the State's to prove beyond a reasonable doubt that defendant knew he could have retreated with complete safety, and that if a reasonable doubt upon that question should exist, the issue of retreat must be resolved in defendant's favor.

C

As we have said, the subject of retreat arises most often in homicide cases. It is equally pertinent if the charge is assault with intent to kill (N.J.S. 2A:90-2, N.J.S.A.). *State v. Centalonza, supra* (18 N.J.Super. 154, 86 A.2d 780). Here the charge is atrocious assault and battery (N.J.S. 2A:90-1, N.J.S.A.), a crime which involves vicious or brutal conduct.... An intent to kill is not an ingredient of that offense, but an intent to do serious bodily harm would seem to be implicit. The doctrine of retreat reflects a policy with respect to the use of deadly force, and the same policy considerations equally obtain if the end result is something less than murder. The Appellate Division held the doctrine applicable to atrocious assault and battery. The comment to Article 3 of the Model Penal Code (at p. 3) expresses the same view, saying, "If the particular force, for example, would be unjustifiable in a prosecution for homicide it should be equally unjustifiable if the victim survives and what is charged is an assault." This seems sound, and hence an instruction upon the subject is appropriate in a trial for atrocious assault and battery, but the instruction should be expressly centered about the use of deadly force.

D

We turn to the instruction of the trial court. It reads:

> ... If you find the charges involved or either of them happened on the joint or common driveway and that the defendant had an available opportunity to retreat and you also find that he was or appeared to be threatened by assault and battery with imminent danger of life or serious bodily harm, again there is no duty to retreat. On the other hand, under the latter circumstances, if you find that he did not appear to be threatened

I. SELF-DEFENSE

by assault and battery with imminent danger of life or great bodily harm, he had a duty to retreat and if he failed to retreat the defense of self-defense would not avail him and would not constitute a defense to these charges or any of these charges if you find that he had a duty to retreat.

It is at once apparent that the charge consists of abstract propositions, unanchored to the factual setting. It will be recalled the encounter had two phases, although one quickly followed the other. The first phase was an unarmed attack by Nicholas which Abbott met in kind; the second involved, as the jury could find, an attack or apparent attack by hatchet in the hands of Michael and by kitchen utensils allegedly wielded by Mary, both aided by Nicholas who had arisen from the initial punch. We have no way of knowing whether the jury understood Abbott was required to retreat when first assailed by Nicholas alone. The jury may well have so gathered since the instruction excluded self-defense "if you find that he [Abbott] did *not* appear to be threatened by assault and battery with imminent danger of life or great bodily harm," and of course Nicholas's attack with his fists readily fitted within those terms.

The State asks us to assume the jury understood an unarticulated premise, i.e., that the court was referring solely to the hatchet affair. If we could so assume, still under the instruction the obligation to retreat would depend upon the nature of the attack upon Abbott rather than the amount of force Abbott intended to employ. In short, there was no reference to the use of a deadly force by Abbott. And if we should read the charge in still another way, to wit, that the court was merely defining its prior reference to "an available opportunity" to retreat and hence meant that the opportunity was not "available" if retreat would have subjected Abbott to imminent danger to his life or of great bodily harm but was "available" if he could get away with a hurt of lesser character, still the charge would be incorrect. This is so because there is no obligation to retreat unless retreat can be effected "with complete safety," and indeed with knowledge that retreat can be so effected. Further, upon that interpretation, the instruction would be devoid of any statement of the facts prerequisite for consideration of the subject, i.e., an intent by the defendant to use a deadly force.

We have said enough to indicate the insufficiency of the charge. Even upon study and restudy we are not sure we can extract the thesis the trial court held. A jury which listens to a single reading of an instruction cannot be expected to debate its meaning and reach a correct view of it. A charge should be a clear, unambiguous guide related to the evidence in the case. The conviction must be reversed.

NOTES

1. In *Commonwealth v. Johnston*, 438 Pa. 485, 263 A.2d 376 (1970), the defendant was approached by deceased who held a knife in his upraised hand. Defendant was in his place of business with an open door leading outside just a few feet from where he stood. The defendant shot and killed his attacker. Conviction of voluntary manslaughter was reversed. There is an exception to the duty to retreat. There is no duty to retreat when one is attacked in his own

dwelling house by a person not a member of his household. The court extended this exception to include the place of business of the person attacked.

2. The long established rule in Massachusetts had been that the occupant of a dwelling had a duty to retreat before resorting to the use of deadly force in self defense. *See Commonwealth v. Shaffer*, 367 Mass. 508, 326 N.E.2d 880 (1975). That rule, which was contrary to most other jurisdictions, was modified by a statute which eliminates the duty "to retreat from [a] person unlawfully" in the dwelling. MASS. GEN. LAWS ANN. C. 278, § 8 A. *See Commonwealth v. Gregory*, 17 Mass. App. 651, 461 N.E. 2d 831 (1984). Nevertheless, the Rhode Island Supreme Court later adopted the rationale of *Shaffer*. *State v. Quarles*, 504 A.2d 473, 476 (R.I., 1986).

3. The common law imposed a duty to retreat "to the wall" before killing in justifiable self-defense, except in defense of one's habitation. Thus, in *State v. Donnelly*, 69 Iowa 705, 27 N.W. 369 (1886), defendant fatally shot his father, who was pursuing him with a pitchfork, intending to kill defendant. Conviction of manslaughter was affirmed. Defendant could have retreated with safety....

Certain exceptions incorporating and expanding the common-law rule are, however, generally recognized. In *People v. Tomlins*, 213 N.Y. 240, 243, 107 N.E. 496, 497 (1914), defendant, attacked in his home by his son, inflicted a mortal wound. A conviction of murder in the first degree was reversed, Cardozo, J., saying: "It is not now, and never has been the law that a man assailed in his own dwelling, is bound to retreat.... He is under no duty to take to the fields and highways, a fugitive from his own home." A similar holding is *Beard v. United States*, 158 U.S. 550 (1895).

Generalization regarding the duty to retreat is rendered difficult because, as indicated above, insistence on a general duty to retreat is usually limited by the fact that the killing occurred in a place "where defendant had a right to be." *Gibson v. Commonwealth*, 237 Ky. 33, 34 S.W.2d 936 (1931). On the other hand, in Holmes' well-known opinion in *Brown v. United States*, 256 U.S. 335, 343 (1921), there is the famous statement that a person attacked "may stand his ground and that if he kills he has not exceeded the bounds of lawful self-defense." What is often forgotten is that Brown was attacked at his place of employment. The crucial question to be determined in any jurisdiction, therefore, concerns the extent to which the common-law exception has been enlarged. If "defense of home" has been expanded to include any place where defendant "has a right to be," it is evident that the common-law rule has been largely repudiated, even though lip-service is rendered to an abstract "duty to retreat."

In *State v. Cox*, 138 Me. 151, 23 A.2d 634 (1941), defendant, a Jehovah's Witness, canvassing for the sect with a friend, shot deceased who had ordered him to leave his premises. Defendant pleaded self-defense, asserting that deceased was about to strike him with an iron bar. In affirming the conviction, the court distinguished the present situation in which the deceased was killed on his own premises from Beard v. United States, *supra*, where the deceased was killed on the land of defendant; from *Rowe v. United States*, 164 U.S. 546 (1896), where the killing occurred in a hotel office; and from *Brown v. United*

States, supra, where it happened at the place of defendant's work. See Annot., 41 A.L.R.3d 508 (1972).

4. Some states reject outright the common-law duty to retreat.

> Under the old common law, no man could defend himself until he had retreated, and until his back was to the wall; but this is not the law in free America. Here the wall is to every man's back. It is the wall of his rights; and when he is at a place where he has a right to be, and he is unlawfully assailed, he may stand and defend himself; and cases sometimes arise in which he has the right, when unlawfully assailed, to advance and defend himself until he finds himself out of danger.

Fowler v. State, 8 Okla. Crim. 130, 126 P. 831, 833 (1912).

5. In *Bailey v. Commonwealth,* 200 Va. 92, 104 S.E.2d 28 (1958), the defendant planned to marry Mrs. Pittman after she secured a divorce from her husband. She and Bailey were sitting in the bedroom of her mother's apartment when Pittman crashed through the front door and rushed into the bedroom. The defendant warned Pittman that he was armed and fired past him, striking a television set. Pittman continued towards Bailey preparing to hit him with a heavy wrench. Bailey then fired the second and fatal shot.

Defendant's conviction of voluntary manslaughter was reversed. Even if the defendant's relation to Mrs. Pittman constituted a provocation or a bringing on of the fight, that did not deprive him of the right of self-defense. "When the infuriated husband crashed through the door and advanced on the defendant ..., the defendant retreated as afar as he could...." 104 S.E.2d at 32.

6. *Aggressor's duty to retreat.*

> Where one is the first wrongdoer, but his unlawful act is not felonious, as a simple assault upon the person of another, or a mere trespass upon his property, even though forcible, and this unlawful act is met by a counter-assault of a deadly character, the right of self-defense to the first wrongdoer is not lost; for, as his acts did not justify upon the part of the other the use of deadly means for their prevention, his killing by the other would be criminal, and one may always defend himself against the criminal taking of his life. But in contemplation of the weakness and passions of men, and of the provocation, which, though inadequate, was wrongfully put upon the other, it is the duty of the first wrongdoer, before he can avail himself of the plea, to have retreated to the wall, to have declined the strife, and withdrawn from the difficulty, and to have killed his adversary, under necessity, actual or apparent, only after so doing. If, however, the counter-assault be so sudden and perilous that no opportunity be given to decline or to make known to his adversary his willingness to decline the strife, if he cannot retreat with safety, then, as the greater wrong of the deadly assault is upon his opponent, he would be justified in slaying forthwith in self-defense....

People v. Hecker, 109 Cal. 451, 464, 42 P. 307, 312 (1895).

NOTES ON IMPERFECT SELF-DEFENSE

1. The doctrine of imperfect self-defense is set forth in Sec. 940.05(2), Stats., and is denominated as a type of manslaughter.... Sec. 940.05(2) defines manslaughter as the killing of another human being "unnecessarily, in the exercise of his privilege of self-defense...." ... It is thus apparent that the privilege of self-defense may be a conditional one. If a defendant believes that intentional use of deadly force is necessary to protect himself and he uses deadly force when he could reasonably believe that deadly force was necessary, there is a complete privilege. There may, however, be occasions where a defendant used deadly force when his belief, though his at the time, was unreasonable. Or there may be the circumstance where his belief that the necessity of self-defense was reasonable, but the deadly force used was unnecessary.

An instruction in respect to self-defense and an instruction in regard to manslaughter were not mutually exclusive.

Ross v. State, 61 Wis. 2d 160, 211 N.W.2d 827, 830 (1973).

2. In *State v. Mayberry*, 360 Mo. 35, 226 S.W.2d 725 (1950), a conviction of murder in the first degree was reversed. Defendant, a small man, attacked deceased (a 200 pounder) with a knife, then put the knife back into his pocket and ran away, chased by deceased. Unable to escape through a kitchen door, and being choked by deceased, defendant took out his knife, and stabbed and killed deceased. Held: Defendant had right of self-defense, despite the fact that he was initially the aggressor and entered the encounter with felonious intent, when he sought in good faith to withdraw from the combat. "We are treating here with a theory of self-defense justifying homicide. This theory must be distinguished from the theory of imperfect self-defense in which a defendant is the aggressor but enters into a difficulty without felonious intent during which encounter defendant is obliged to kill to save his own life. Shown facts supporting the latter theory do not justify the homicide, but reduce the grade of the offense. Such latter theory contemplates a continuous encounter, and not a factual situation of 'withdrawal in good faith.'" 226 S.W.2d at 728 (emphasis in original.).

3. The typical case to be imagined is this: *A* attacks *B* with his fists; *B* defends himself and knocks *A* down, then starts to batter *A*'s head savagely against the floor. *A* manages to rise and, since *B* is still attacking him and *A* now reasonably fears that if he is thrown again he will be killed, he uses a knife. *B* is killed or seriously wounded.

If no special rule is devised for the case, the solution under the Model Penal Code provisions is as follows:

B is entitled to defend himself against *A*'s attack but only to the extent of using moderate, non-deadly force. He exceeds the bounds of necessary force, however, when, reducing *A* to helplessness he batters his head on the floor. Since this excessive force is, in its turn, unlawful, *A* is entitled to defend himself against it and, if he believes that he is then in danger of death or serious bodily harm without apparent opportunity for safe retreat, to use his knife in self-protection. Thus A is criminally liable for his initial battery on B but not for the ultimate homicide or wounding.

This conclusion — that an initial aggressor is accountable for his original unlawful use of force but not for his defense against a disproportionate return of force by his victim — is surely not unreasonable on its face. There is, however, much authority, both common law and statutory, demanding that a person claiming self-defense be free from fault in bringing on the difficulty. Model Penal Code § 3.04, comment at 21-22 (Tent. Draft No. 8, 1958).

4. Review *People v. Flannel*, Chapter 5, *supra* pp. 332-334.

SECTION II. Defense of Others

MODEL PENAL CODE

§ 3.05. Use of Force for the Protection of Other Persons

[The text of this section appears in Appendix A.]

MORRISON v. COMMONWEALTH

Court of Appeals of Kentucky
24 Ky. L. R. 2493, 74 S.W. 277 (1903)

HOBSON, J.

Appellant, William Morrison, was indicted for the murder of Alex Dean. He was convicted of manslaughter, and his punishment was fixed at confinement in the penitentiary for 11 years. The proof shows that Ida Dean, a sister of the deceased, had borrowed an umbrella on the afternoon of the day of the homicide, promising to return it that evening. About half past 8 o'clock she came up the street with the umbrella and, meeting George Turner, asked him if he had seen Morrison. They went on together, and soon met Alex Dean, who took hold of his sister and told her to go home, upbraiding her for being out looking for Morrison. There is a conflict of evidence as to what followed. The proof for the commonwealth is that Alex Dean went along the street with his sister, pushing her along about 90 feet, when she stopped, declining to go any further, and about this time Morrison, seeing them, ran down to where they were[,] on his tiptoes, and stabbed Dean in the back; that [Dean] immediately fell to the ground, uttering no sound except a groan, and died in a few minutes. The proof for the defendant is that Morrison heard someone say that Alex Dean was beating his sister, and ran out to where they were, putting his hand on Alex Dean's shoulder, and saying: "You can't beat her where I am;" that Dean immediately drew a pistol, and said with an oath, "I will kill you both;" that Morrison caught the pistol, and they clinched, and as they fell, he stabbed Dean in the back with his knife. This proof is made by Morrison himself; and also by Ida Dean, who testified on his behalf, and by Turner. No pistol was found on Dean's person, or on the ground where he fell, nor is it shown by any other proof that he had a pistol....

The court allowed the commonwealth to prove by both Morrison and Ida Dean, on cross-examination, in effect, that Morrison was, and had been for some time past, living in improper relations with Ida Dean. This evidence was objected to, but was properly admitted, for it explained the circumstances of the parties and illustrated their motives. The evidence also went to the interest of the witness Ida Dean, and to show bias.

. . . .

So, the case comes to this: Did Morrison, when he saw Alex Dean committing an assault on his sister, and pushing or striking her against the house, have a right to intervene between the brother and sister for her protection from a simple battery? In 1 Bishop on Criminal Law, § 877, it is said: "The doctrine here is that whatever one may do for himself he may do for another. The common case, indeed, is where a father, son, brother, husband, servant, or the like, protects by the stronger arm the feebler. But a guest in a house may defend the house, or the neighbors of the occupant may assemble for its defense; and, on the whole, though distinctions have been taken and doubts expressed, the better view plainly is that one may do for another whatever the other may do for himself." The statement of the law, as applied to simple batteries and breaches of the peace, is broader than it is usually put in the authorities. Thus, in 3 Blackstone, 3, it is said: "The defense of one's self or the mutual and reciprocal defense of such as stand in relations of husband and wife, parent and child, master and servant. In these cases, if the party himself, or any of these, his relations, be forcibly attacked in his person or property, it is lawful for him to repel force by force; and the breach of the peace which happens is chargeable upon him only who began the affray." In a note to this it is added: "When a person does not stand in either of these relations, he cannot justify an interference on behalf of the party injured, but merely as an indifferent person to preserve the peace." ...

When a felony is apparently about to be committed, as where there is apparent danger of loss of life by the person assailed or of great bodily harm to him, a different rule prevails, and there any third person may lawfully intervene for his protection, using such means for his defense as the person assaulted himself may lawfully use. But where the assault is not felonious, and the person intervening does not stand in any of the relations to the one assaulted excepted out of the common-law rule, then he who intervenes can only act for the preservation of the peace. He cannot come into the difficulty for the purpose of taking the place of the person assailed, and continuing the fight. This is the common-law rule, as we understand the authorities, and we cannot depart from it or extend it.

It is conceded on all hands that Morrison ran down on tiptoe to where Alex Dean and his sister were, some 90 feet away. If, when he got there, he at once stabbed Dean in the back, as stated by the witnesses for the commonwealth, he was the aggressor. The instruction of the court, which submitted to the jury the question whether Morrison believed, or had reasonable grounds to believe, himself in danger of death or great bodily harm at the hands of Dean, when he stabbed him, was more favorable to Morrison than the law warranted, as the court did not submit to the jury the question whether Morrison was the aggressor. Morrison knew that the illicit relations between him and Ida Dean were the foundation of the animosity of Alex Dean to him. He also knew that this was the cause of the quarrel between the brother and sister. With this knowledge he ran on tiptoe down to where they were, armed with a dirk, and if, as he says, he caught Alex Dean by the shoulder and shoved them apart, saying to him, "You can't beat her where I am," his interference was not as an indifferent person to preserve the peace, for his first act was to commit a battery on Alex Dean by taking him by the shoulder, and this was followed up by a declaration which he could but know, under all the circumstances, would make Alex Dean regard him as an assailant. To hold that he intervened, under the evidence, as an indifferent person to preserve the peace, would be to give no real effect to the common-law rule allowing greater rights to parent and child, husband and wife, master and servant, or the like, than to other persons in cases of simple batteries or breaches of the peace. According to his own testimony, the manner of his approach, his conduct on reaching Alex Dean, and his declaration to him, under the circumstances, were not those of one bent on peace, but of one proposing to champion the woman and fight her battles for her. He was therefore the aggressor, and the court did not err in refusing to admit the proof as to the bad character of Alex Dean or his previous threats; and this evidence, if admitted, could not have been of material service to the defendant under the view of the law which we have indicated, for the jury might have inferred that when he interfered with knowledge of the previous threats and the character of Dean he anticipated the result that ensued. The verdict of the jury finding him guilty of manslaughter, and fixing his punishment at 11 years in the penitentiary, seems to have been due to their accepting the version of the transaction as given by the witnesses for the commonwealth, and their believing that Morrison acted in sudden heat on seeing the woman assailed by her brother.

Judgment affirmed.

STATE v. CHIARELLO

Superior Court of New Jersey, Appellate Division
69 N.J. Super. 479, 174 A.2d 506 (1961)

CONFORD, S.J.A.D.

This is an appeal from a conviction of the defendant for atrocious assault and battery with a dangerous weapon, contrary to N.J.S. 2A:90-1 and 2A:151-5. The defendant shot and seriously wounded Louis Walker and Roland Houle, in order, as he claims, to prevent their murdering William J. Edwards. All four were employees of Camp Harmony in Somerset County. An affray had begun among the others, who had been drinking, awakening the defendant. From his testimony ... a jury could have properly found that defendant in good faith reasonably deemed it necessary to physically disable Walker and Houle in order to save Edwards' life. But from proofs adduced as to what had transpired before defendant's attention was drawn to the melee, it might have been concluded by a jury that it was not in fact necessary to shoot Walker and Houle to prevent death or serious injury to Edwards, and that Edwards himself would not in the circumstances have been justified in using such measures as a matter of self-defense.

The principal question for resolution on this appeal is the correctness of the trial court's charge to the jury that the defendant's justification in defending

Edwards in the manner he did depended upon whether Edwards himself would have been legally justified, on the basis of the circumstances known to Edwards, in using the same force and violence on Walker and Houle [alter ego rule]. It is and was the defendant's position at the trial that he had the right to act upon his own reasonable judgment on the basis of the appearances as manifested to him, without imputation to him of Edwards' peculiar knowledge of the circumstances. There is no completely satisfactory appellate decision on the point in this State.

. . .

The clearly defined issue disclosed by the differences between the charge as given, and those requested by defendant, has split the American jurisdictions which have ruled on the matter substantially equally....

. . . .

The American Law Institute rejects the "alter ego" rule as repugnant to the fundamental principle of Anglo-American criminal jurisprudence that the defendant must be shown to have a *mens rea,* or guilty intent. Model Penal Code, Sec. 3.05(1), (Tent. Draft No. 8, 1958). Indeed, the Code goes so far as to eliminate any requirement that the actor's belief in the necessity for the use of force for the protective purpose in question be arrived at without negligence or recklessness, unless the prosecution is for an offense for which recklessness or negligence suffices to establish culpability. Sec. 3.09(2). This is on the theory that negligence is not equatable [sic] ... with guilty intent in relation to a crime for which *mens rea* must be established. The scholars in this field are not uniformly in accord that the range of immunity is, or should be, that broad. Compare Hall, Principles of Criminal Law (2d ed. 1960), pp. 366-372; Smith, "The Guilty Mind in the Criminal Law," 76 L.Q. Rev. 78, 98 (1960); and Williams, Criminal Law (1953), § 49, p. 163, with Sayre, "The Present Signification of Mens Rea in the Criminal Law," Harvard Legal Essays (1934) 399, at p. 403; Sayre, "Public Welfare Offenses," 33 Colum. L. Rev. 55, at p. 70 (1933); Mueller, "Mens Rea and the Law Without It," 58 W. Va. L. Rev. 34, at pp. 34, 35 (1955). See also Nord, "The Mental Element in Crime," 37 U. Det. L.J. 671, at p. 683 (1960); Note: "Justification for the Use of Force in Criminal Law," 13 Stan. L. Rev. 566, 591-598 (1961). But without exception, they deprecate the imputation of criminal liability in the range of serious common-law offenses, including aggravated assault, where there is neither guilty intent nor criminal negligence.

. . . .

The problem of justification for force exerted in defense of others is frequently studied in relation to the common-law principles that one may kill to prevent a felony or in the defense of a member of his household. See 1 Wharton, Criminal Law and Procedure, § 206, p. 453; § 218, p. 480 (1957). In this State those principles are codified by N.J.S. 2A:113-6. However, they are obviously not directly pertinent where the defensive act does not involve homicide. Moreover, our statute is not broad enough to cover defense of strangers, or, apparently, the prevention of an assault, no matter how aggravated. The statute and the common-law principles, consequently, should properly be considered as generic precursors of the development of the right to use non-deadly force in defense of strangers, not as limitations, by analogy, of the scope of that principle. See Note: "Justification for the Use of Force in Criminal Law," op. cit. *supra* (13 Stan. L. Rev., at pp. 573 et seq.); Model Penal Code, op. cit. *supra,* at p. 17, comments to Sec. 3.05.

The State stresses that the "alter ego" rule is the "majority rule" in this country. This may well be doubted, even if the appraisal is in number of jurisdictions expressing approval of it, as against those which condemn it.... As already noted, the rule is roundly rejected by substantial unanimity of the scholars in the field. Moreover, a careful reading of the so-called majority decisions shows that in many of them the issue was not sharply defined on the facts presented....

The State also argues, *ab inconvenienti,* that admeasuring responsibility on the basis of what reasonably appeared necessary to the intervenor-defendant will unduly hamper law enforcement, since police sometimes have to function in plainclothes and might be mistaken by a well-meaning but uninformed newcomer as wrongful aggressors.... In the absence of ... legislation, one would hardly be warranted in making a criminal out of a person selflessly attempting, without negligence, to protect the victim of an apparently unjustified assault — merely because the assailants are police in disguise carrying out an arrest. Much less does the stated argument of the State justify imposing the stigma and punishment of criminality upon one who reasonably, but mistakenly, goes to the rescue of an apparent victim of assailants other than the police.

....

In the light of the foregoing considerations, we are satisfied that the application of sound principle in the area of crimes of assault precludes liability in the absence of either guilty intent or negligence. Consequently, we hold the charge of the trial court, in conditioning this defendant's exculpating justification for his acts upon the premise that Edwards would have been legally justified in taking like defensive measures on the facts as Edwards knew them to be, rather than excusing defendant if his conduct was justified upon the basis of the facts as he reasonably concluded them to be, both in relation to the gravity of the threat to Edwards and to the extent of the force necessary to protect him therefrom, was prejudicially erroneous. This must lead to a reversal of the conviction.

....

Reversed and remanded for a new trial.

STATE v. GELINAS

417 A.2d 1381 (R.I., 1980)
Supreme Court of Rhode Island

BEVILACQUA, CHIEF JUSTICE.

[Police officers seized alcoholic beverages from four juveniles and ordered them into a patrol car. One of the four, the defendant's brother, walked away and refused to get into the car. When an officer tried to seize him, the young man hit the officer. A struggle ensued in which the defendant and another brother (who were not among the four ordered into the patrol car) joined].

....

The issue before us ... is whether the trial justice properly instructed the jury on the right of an individual to come to the aid of another whom uniformed police officers are arresting through the alleged use of excessive force. The defendant contends that the trial justice gave inadequate instructions on the use of force in protection of another. The trial justice in effect instructed the jury that they must decide that the officer in fact used excessive force against defendant's brothers at the time defendant attacked the officer before they could find that defendant committed a justifiable act. If the jury believed that excessive force was not actually used, they had to reject defendant's alleged defense and, on satisfaction of the other elements, return a guilty verdict.

It is a well-accepted principle that in effecting an arrest an officer has the right to use such force as he may reasonably believe necessary in order to discharge properly his duty. General Laws 1956 (1969 Reenactment) § 12-7-8; see *State v. Ramsdell*, 109 R.I. at 326, 285 A.2d at 404; *Tessier v. LeNois*, 97 R.I. 414, 417, 198 A.2d 142, 143 (1964). When there is evidence tending to show the law-enforcement officer's use of excessive force, the trial justice must instruct the jury that the force used against the law-enforcement officer was justified provided the defendant limited his assault to the use of reasonable force in defending himself from excessive force. *State v. Ramsdell*, 109 R.I. at 327, 285 A.2d at 404.

There are two contrasting principles that control the defense of another as it exists in other jurisdictions.[5] One rule adopted by a number of states takes the position that a third party intervenor stands in the shoes of a person whom he is aiding. Under this view it is immaterial whether the intervenor defendant acted as a reasonable person would have; the right attaches to the defendant only when the person being defended would have had the right of self-defense. See, *e.g., People v. Booher*, 18 Cal. App. 3d 331, 95 Cal. Rptr. 857 (1971); *Purdy v. United States*, 210 A.2d 1 (D.C. 1965) (dictum); *State v. Anderson*, 40 N.C. App. 318, 253 S.E.2d 48 (1979); *State v. Wenger*, 58 Ohio St. 2d 336, 390 N.E.2d 801 (1979). In contrast, other jurisdictions focus on the conduct of the intervenor without regard to the self-defense claim of the arrestee and hold that an intervenor may aid another if it appears to be necessary, though he acts on a mistaken belief, even in a situation in which the person who is aided would not have had the right to claim self-defense. See, *e.g., United States v. Ochoa*, 526 F.2d 1278 (5th Cir. 1976); *United States v. Grimes*, 413 F.2d 1376 (7th Cir. 1969); *Coleman v. State*, Del., 320 A.2d 740 (1974); *Commonwealth v. Martin*, 369 Mass. 640, 341 N.E.2d 885 (1976); *State v.*

---

[5]Some jurisdictions adhere to the somewhat antiquated view that a person may only defend others to whom he is somehow related, either by consanguinity, employment, marriage, or acquaintance. *E.g., Tipton v. State*, 1 Md.App. 556, 562, 232 A.2d 289, 291 (1967); *Carter v. State*, 507 P.2d 932, 934 (Okla. Crim. 1973).

Apparently, these states believe that the relationship between the protector and his charge not only compels action but also minimizes the likelihood that the actor will misinterpret the situation and intercede on behalf of the wrongdoer. While we do not question the utility of allowing family members to protect one another, we believe that restricting the privilege only to family members ignores the important social goal of crime prevention, a duty of every citizen. See *Commonwealth v. Martin*, 369 Mass. 640, 650, 341 N.E.2d 885, 891 (1976). See generally Note, Justification: The Impact of the Model Penal Code on Statutory Reform, 75 Colum. L. Rev. 914, 932-33 (1975).

Andrews, 199 Neb. 60, 255 N.W.2d 875 (1977); Ky. Rev. Stat. § 503.070 (1975).

Up until now, this court has never been asked to decide under what conditions a defendant may claim justifiable use of force when intervening on behalf of a third party. Being confronted with different schools of thought, we must decide which theory of law we shall follow.

After reviewing the available authorities, we hereby adopt the rule that one who comes to the aid of an arrestee must do so at his own peril and should be excused only when the individual would himself be justified in defending himself from the use of excessive force by the arresting officer. *Purdy v. United States*, 210 A.2d at 2; *State v. Anderson*, 40 N.C. App. at 323-325, 253 S.E.2d at 52; *State v. Wenger*, 58 Ohio St. 2d at 340-41, 390 N.E.2d at 804. A third party intervenor stands in the shoes of the person whom he is aiding. The defendant may use such force to prevent injury to the person he aids as defendant would use in self-defense. See Del. Code tit. 11, § 469 (1979), Model Penal Code § 3.05 (Tent. Draft No. 8, 1958). Furthermore, the jury must resolve the factual issue raised by this defense when it is properly raised by the evidence at trial. See *State v. Small*, R.I., 410 A.2d at 1338.

The defendant before us was entitled to an instruction that presented the jury with the choice of findings that defendant was justified in interfering with the arrest of his brother if the arrestee was himself justified in resisting arrest. In reading the trial justice's instructions we are of the opinion that he adequately charged the jury as to the rights of a person who defends another against the use of excessive force. He told the jury in clear language that unless they found that Officer LeDuc has used excessive force against defendant's brother, they could not find that defendant had acted justifiably. This instruction is consistent with the rule we adopt today since if Officer LeDuc had not used excessive force, Edward could have had no right to resist the arrest, and, accordingly, defendant could not have been privileged to come to Edward's defense. The jury therefore resolved this factual issue in the light of a charge that properly set out the controlling law in this jurisdiction.

. . . .

The defendant's appeal is denied and dismissed, and the judgment of conviction is affirmed.

NOTES

1. On a right to resist an unlawful arrest, see p. 547, n. 5, *infra*.

2. Under modern statutes, one may defend a third person from "what he reasonably believes to be the use or imminent use of unlawful physical force." N.Y. PENAL CODE § 35.15(1) (McKinney 1987); see also similar provisions in LA. REV. STAT. ANN. 14:22 (West 1986).

3. In *State v. Wenger*, 58 Ohio St. 2d 336, 390 N.E. 2d 801, 803 (1979), the Supreme Court of Ohio held: "A person who intervenes in a struggle and has no duty to do so, acts at his own peril if the person assisted was in the wrong."

4. In *State v. Graves*, 18 N.C. App. 177, 196 S.E.2d 582 (1973), the defendant had witnessed the entry of Samuel into Price's Danceland and had seen Beverly forced to accompany Samuel against her will for several blocks. He knew that Samuel had threatened to kill Beverly and that he was a dangerous, violent man. The court reversed his conviction of felonious assault on Samuel. "A private citizen has a right to go to the defense of another if he has a well grounded belief that a felonious assault is about to be committed upon such other person. In fact, it is his duty to interfere to prevent the supposed crime." 196 S.E.2d at 584. (Emphasis added.)

5. *State v. Marley*, 54 Hawaii 450, 509 P.2d 1095 (1973), involved on appeal from conviction of criminal trespass. Defendants entered the Honolulu office of the Honeywell Corporation. A statement concerning Honeywell's participation in the Indo-China war was read, pictures were hung on the wall and defendants sang and talked among themselves. The activities disrupted normal business but were nonviolent. The defendants refused to leave the office at closing time and were arrested. The evidence established that Honeywell was a major defense contractor and manufactured weapons used in Indo-China. None of these weapons was produced at the Honolulu office.

The defense was that defendant's conduct was a justified attempt to prevent or terminate the commission of crimes committed by the Honeywell Corporation.

The conviction was affirmed. The criminal act sought to be prevented must occur in the presence of the actor. "The inevitable requirement of presence stands, even where the criminal acts done to prevent harm to self, others, or property do not involve force. Failure of the courts to require presence would license persons to violate the criminal statutes far more frequently ... it would make each citizen a judge of the criminality of all the acts of every other citizen, with power to mete out sentence." 509 P.2d at 1108. See also *United States v. Berrigan*, infra p. 777.

SECTION III. Defense of Property

MODEL PENAL CODE

§ 3.06. *Use of Force for the Protection of Property*

[The text of this section appears in Appendix A.]

MONTGOMERY v. COMMONWEALTH

Supreme Court of Appeals of Virginia
98 Va. 840, 36 S.E. 371 (1900)

One Montgomery was convicted of a felonious assault, and brings error.

HARRISON, J.

... The prisoner went upon the lands of Davidson for the purpose of selling a gun to Reed Tyler, one of the hands on the place. While in conversation with Tyler and John Randolph, a tenant on the premises, Davidson, who was riding by, was called up by Randolph, who said to him: "Here is a man who says he is going to hunt anyhow." Davidson then told the prisoner that he could not hunt, that the land was posted to white and black. The prisoner replied that he was not hunting, but that he had seen no notices of posting, and if he had seen anything would have shot at it. Davidson then asked the prisoner what

III. DEFENSE OF PROPERTY

business he had, and was told that he had come to sell his gun, and that Reed Tyler had bought it. Davidson said, "If you have transacted your business you must leave," and motioned his hand to him to go. The prisoner replied that he would go when he got ready. Davidson then dismounted, and started towards the prisoner, saying, "I will see about that." The prisoner with his gun in hand, stepped back some 10 or 15 feet, saying, "If you hurt me, I'll shoot you, damn you." Davidson picked up a corn cutter recently ground and sharp, ran to the prisoner, and they clinched. In the scuffle, the gun was discharged in the air, and Davidson received, it does not clearly appear how, a cut and some abrasions on the head. They fell to the ground, Davidson on top. After some scuffle, the prisoner cried, "Take him off," and they were separated....

The first error assigned is the action of the court in refusing certain instructions asked for by the prisoner, and giving of its own motion in lieu thereof the following:

"The court instructs the jury that W. E. Davidson had the right to require the accused to leave his premises, and that if the accused refused to leave when so requested, the said Davidson had the right to use such force as was necessary to eject him from his premises."

The theory of the prosecution is that the prisoner, having refused to leave immediately upon being ordered to do so, thereby became a trespasser, and as such, Davidson had a right to use any force necessary to remove him, even to the extent of assaulting him with a deadly weapon.

The prisoner contends that, if he was a trespasser at all, the trespass was of the most trivial character, as he was neither doing or threatening to do any harm to Davidson or his property, and that his act did not justify the assault made upon him with a deadly weapon, and that he had a right to defend himself from such assault.

The instruction as given contains the general rule, which is sound as an abstract proposition, that every man has the right to defend his person or property, but it ignores the well-settled and important modification of the rule that in defense of person or property one cannot, except in extreme cases, endanger human life or do great bodily harm. The law is clearly stated by a learned judge in *State v. Morgan*, 25 N.C. 186, 38 Am. Dec. 714, as follows: "When it is said that a man may rightfully use as much force as is necessary for the protection of his person and property, it should be recollected that this rule is subject to this most important modification, that he shall not, except in extreme cases, endanger human life or do great bodily harm. It is not every right of person, and still less of property, that can lawfully be asserted, or every wrong that may rightfully be redressed by extreme remedies. There is a recklessness — a wanton disregard of humanity and social duty — in taking or endeavoring to take, the life of a fellow being, in order to save one's self from a comparatively slight wrong, which is essentially wicked, and the law abhors. You may not kill, because you cannot otherwise effect your object, although the object sought to be effected is right. You can only kill to save life or limb, or prevent a great crime, or to accomplish a necessary public duty." See, also, 1 Bish. New Cr. Law, §§ 839, 841, 850.

In the light of these elementary principles, and in view of the facts of this case, it is clear that the instruction given by the court was erroneous, calculated to mislead the jury, and very prejudicial to the rights of the prisoner. Conceding that the prisoner was a trespasser, and that he ought to have promptly left the premises when ordered to do so, still, this did not justify the assault made upon him. Davidson, armed with a recently sharpened corn-cutter, advancing upon the prisoner and saying that he would see about his leaving, was well calculated to excite in the prisoner apprehension of great bodily harm. Under such circumstances the prisoner had the right to defend himself, within the limits of the law, and the jury should have been so instructed....

... [R]eversed, the verdict set aside, and a new trial awarded....

NOTES

1. With exception of defense of habitation discussed *infra* pp. 541-542, deadly force may not be justified as a defense of property. *Commonwealth v. Emmons*, 157 Pa. Super. 495, 43 A.2d 568 (1945). Furthermore,

> [W]hile one rightfully in possession of property may defend his possession against an attack, and while one lawfully entitled to the possession of real property may, if he can, enter and take peaceable possession, yet, no matter what lawful right to possession one out of the actual possession of real property may have, he will not be justified in making a forcible entry and committing a breach of the peace in ejecting by force an actual occupant.

State v. Bradbury, 67 Kan. 808, 74 P. 231, 232 (1903).

2. The rule is similar in regard to personal property. As the court succinctly stated in *Lockland v. State*, 45 Tex. Crim. 87, 73 S.W. 1054 (1903):

> The law accords one in possession of property the right to protect such possession; but the possession must be actual, and not merely constructive; and when one has parted with the possession of personal property he may not regain it by such means as result in homicide or assault.

3. The rules and pertinent cases are discussed in *State v. Rullis*, 79 N.J. Super. 221, 191 A.2d 197 (1963). But see *State v. Clothier*, 242 Kan. 796, 753 P.2d 1267 (1988), noted *infra* at p. 551, n. 2.

PEOPLE v. CEBALLOS

Supreme Court of California
Cal. 3d 470, 526 P.2d 241, 116 Cal. Rptr. 233 (1974)

BURKE, JUSTICE.

Don Ceballos was found guilty by a jury of assault with a deadly weapon (Pen.Code, § 245). Imposition of sentence was suspended and he was placed on probation. He appeals from the judgment, contending primarily that his conduct was not unlawful because the alleged victim was attempting to commit burglary when hit by a trap gun mounted in the garage of defendant's dwelling and that the court erred in instructing the jury. We have concluded that the former argument lacks merit, that the court did not commit prejudicial error in instructing the jury, and that the judgment should be affirmed.

III. DEFENSE OF PROPERTY

Defendant lived alone in a home in San Anselmo. The regular living quarters were above the garage, but defendant sometimes slept in the garage and had about $2,000 worth of property there.

In March 1970 some tools were stolen from defendant's home. On May 12, 1970, he noticed the lock on his garage doors was bent and pry marks were on one of the doors. The next day he mounted a loaded .22 caliber pistol in the garage. The pistol was aimed at the center of the garage doors and was connected by a wire to one of the doors so that the pistol would discharge if the door was opened several inches.

The damage to defendant's lock had been done by a 16-year-old boy named Stephen and a 15-year-old boy named Robert. On the afternoon of May 15, 1970, the boys returned to defendant's house while he was away. Neither boy was armed with a gun or knife. After looking in the windows and seeing no one, Stephen succeeded in removing the lock on the garage doors with a crowbar, and, as he pulled the door outward, he was hit in the face with a bullet from the pistol.

....

Defendant contends that had he been present he would have been justified in shooting Stephen since Stephen was attempting to commit burglary (Pen.Code, § 459), that under cases such as United States v. Gilliam, 25 Fed.Cas. p. 1319, No. 15,205a, defendant had a right to do indirectly what he could have done directly, and that therefore any attempt by him to commit a violent injury upon Stephen was not "unlawful" and hence not an assault. The People argue that the rule in Gilliam is unsound, that as a matter of law a trap gun constitutes excessive force, and that in any event the circumstances were not in fact such as to warrant the use of deadly force.

The issue of criminal liability under statutes such as Penal Code section 245 where the instrument employed is a trap gun or other deadly mechanical device appears to be one of first impression in this state, but in other jurisdictions courts have considered the question of criminal and civil liability for death or injuries inflicted by such a device.

....

In the United States, courts have concluded that a person may be held criminally liable under statutes proscribing homicides and shooting with intent to injure, or civilly liable, if he sets upon his premises a deadly mechanical device and that device kills or injures another. *Katko v. Briney* (Iowa), 183 N.W.2d 657, 660; *State v. Plumlee*, 177 La. 687, 149 So. 425, 429; *State v. Beckham*, 306 Mo. 566, 267 S.W. 817, 819 [disapproved on another issue in *State v. Tatum*, Mo., 414 S.W.2d 566, 568]; *State v. Childers*, 133 Ohio St. 508, 14 N.E.2d 767, 769; *Marquis v. Benfer* (Ct. of Civ.App., Tex.), 298 S.W.2d 601, 603; *Pierce v. Commonwealth*, 135 Va. 635, 115 S.E. 686, 687 et seq. However, an exception to the rule that there may be criminal and civil liability for death or injuries caused by such a device has been recognized where the intrusion is, in fact, such that the person, were he present, would be justified in taking the life or inflicting the bodily harm with his own hands.... The phrase "were he present" does not hypothesize the actual presence of the person (see Rest. 2d Torts, § 85, coms. (a), (c) & (d)), but is used in setting forth in an indirect manner the principle that a person may do indirectly that which he is privileged to do directly.

Allowing persons, at their own risk, to employ deadly mechanical devices imperils the lives of children, firemen and policemen acting within the scope of their employment, and others. Where the actor is present, there is always the possibility he will realize that deadly force is not necessary, but deadly mechanical devices are without mercy or discretion. Such devices "are silent instrumentalities of death. They deal death and destruction to the innocent as well as the criminal intruder without the slightest warning. The taking of human life [or infliction of great bodily injury] by such means is brutally savage and inhuman." (See *State v. Plumlee, supra,* 149 So. 425, 430.)

It seems clear that the use of such devices should not be encouraged. Moreover, whatever may be thought in torts, the foregoing rule setting forth an exception to liability for death or injuries inflicted by such devices "is inappropriate in penal law for it is obvious that it does not prescribe a workable standard of conduct; liability depends upon fortuitous results." (See Model Penal Code (Tent. Draft No. 8), § 3.06, com. 15.) We therefore decline to adopt that rule in criminal cases.

Furthermore, even if that rule were applied here, as we shall see, defendant was not justified in shooting Stephen. Penal Code section 197 provides: "Homicide is ... justifiable ... 1. When resisting any attempt to murder any person, or to commit a felony, or to do some great bodily injury upon any person; or, 2. When committed in defense of habitation, property, or person, against one who manifestly intends or endeavors, by violence or surprise, to commit a felony...." (See also Pen. Code, § 198.) Since a homicide is justifiable under the circumstances specified in section 197, a fortiori, an attempt to commit a violent injury upon another under those circumstances is justifiable.

By its terms subdivision 1 of Penal Code section 197 appears to permit killing to prevent any "felony," but in view of the large number of felonies today and the inclusion of many that do not involve a danger of serious bodily harm, a literal reading of the section is undesirable. (See 1 Witkin, Cal. Crimes (1963) p. 159; Justification for the Use of Force in Criminal Cases, 13 Stan. L. Rev. 566, 578-579.) *People v. Jones,* 191 Cal. App. 2d 478, 481, 12 Cal. Rptr. 777, in rejecting the defendant's theory that her husband was about to commit the felony of beating her (Pen. Code, § 273d) and that therefore her killing him to prevent him from doing so was justifiable, stated that Penal Code section 197 "does no more than codify the common law and should be read in light of it." Jones read into section 197, subdivision 1, the limitation that the felony be "some atrocious crime attempted to be committed by force." Jones (at p. 482, 12 Cal. Rptr. at p. 780) further stated, "the punishment provided by a statute is not necessarily an adequate test as to whether life may be taken for in some situations it is too artificial and unrealistic. We must look further into the character of the crime, and the manner of its perpetration (see *Storey v. State* [71 Ala. 329]). When these do not reasonably create a fear of great bodily harm, as they could not if defendant apprehended only a misdemeanor assault, there is no cause for the exaction of a human life." (Italics added; see also Harper and James, The Law of Torts (1956) pp. 1441-1442, fn. 38: but see 1 Bishop's Criminal Law (9th ed.) p. 608.)

III. DEFENSE OF PROPERTY

Jones involved subdivision 1 of Penal Code section 197, but subdivision 2 of that section is likewise so limited. The term "violence of [sic] surprise" in subdivision 2 is found in common law authorities (see *Flynn v. Commonwealth*, 204 Ky. 572, 264 S.W. 1111, 1112; 9 Cal.L.Rev. 375, 384), and, whatever may have been the very early common law see *Storey v. State, supra*, 71 Ala. 329, 340; 35 Yale L.J. 525, 542), the rule developed at common law that killing or use of deadly force to prevent a felony was justified only if the offense was a forcible and atrocious crime. (See *Storey v. State, supra*; II Cooley's Blackstone, p. 1349; Perkins on Criminal Law, supra, pp. 989-993; 1 Hale, Pleas of the Crown (1847), p. 487.) "Surprise" means an unexpected attack — which includes force and violence (See *Perkins, supra*, p. 1026, fn. 3), and the word thus appears redundant.

Examples of forcible and atrocious crimes are murder, mayhem, rape and robbery.... In such crimes "from their atrocity and violence human life [or personal safety from great harm] either is, or is presumed to be, in peril...."

Burglary has been included in the list of such crimes.... However, in view of the wide scope of burglary under Penal Code section 459, as compared with the common law definition of that offense, in our opinion it cannot be said that under all circumstances burglary under section 459 constitutes a forcible and atrocious crime.[2]

Where the character and manner of the burglary do not reasonably create a fear of great bodily harm, there is no cause for exaction of human life. *State v. McIntyre*, 106 Ariz. 439, 477 P.2d 529, 534-535; *cf. People v. Jones, supra*, 191 Cal.App.2d 478, 482, 12 Cal.Rptr. 777), or for the use of deadly force (see generally 13 Stan.L.Rev. 566, 577). The character and manner of the burglary could not reasonably create such a fear unless the burglary threatened, or was reasonably believed to threaten, death or serious bodily harm.

In the instant case the asserted burglary did not threaten death or serious bodily harm, since no one but Stephen and Robert was then on the premises. A defendant is not protected from liability merely by the fact that the intruder's conduct is such as would justify the defendant, were he present, in believing that the intrusion threatened death or serious bodily injury. (See *State v. Green*, 118 S.C. 279, 110 S.E. 145, 147-148; Rest. 2d Torts, § 85, com. d; 35 Yale L.J. 525, 544-545.) There is ordinarily the possibility that the defendant, were he present, would realize the true state of affairs and recognize the intruder as one whom he would not be justified in killing or wounding. (See 35 Yale L.J. 525, 545.)

We thus conclude that defendant was not justified under Penal Code section 197, subdivisions 1 or 2, in shooting Stephen to prevent him from committing burglary.

....

---

[2] At common law burglary was the breaking and entering of a mansion house in the night with the intent to commit a felony.... Burglary under Penal Code section 459 differs from common law burglary in that the entry may be in the daytime and of numerous places other than a mansion house (see 1 Witkin, supra, pp. 416-418), and breaking is not required (see *People v. Allison*, 200 Cal. 404, 408, 253 P. 318). For example, under section 459 a person who enters a store with the intent of committing theft is guilty of burglary. (See *People v. Corral*, 60 Cal.App.2d 66, 140 P.2d 172.) It would seem absurd to hold that a store detective could kill that person if necessary to prevent him from committing that offense. (See 13 Stan.L.Rev. 566, 579.)

Several cases contain broad language relating to justification for killing where a person acts in defense of his habitation or property to prevent "a felony" (see, e.g., *People v. Hecker*, 109 Cal. 451, 461-462, 42 P. 307; *People v. Flanagan*, 60 Cal. 2, 3-4; *People v. Hubbard*, 64 Cal.App. 27, 35, 220 P. 315), but in those cases also it does not appear that any issue was raised or decided as to the nature of the felony coming within that doctrine.

We recognize that our position regarding justification for killing under Penal Code section 197, subdivisions 1 and 2, differs from the position of section 143, subdivision (2), of the Restatement Second of Torts, regarding the use of deadly force to prevent a "felony ... of a type ... involving the breaking and entry of a dwelling place" (see also Perkins on Criminal Law, supra, p. 1030, which is in accord with the foregoing section of the Rest. 2d Torts) but in view of the supreme value of human life (see *People v. Jones, supra*, 191 Cal.App.2d 478, 482, 12 Cal. Rptr. 777), we do not believe deadly force can be justified to prevent all felonies of the foregoing type, including ones in which no person is, or is reasonably believed to be, on the premises except the would-be burglar.

. . . .

Defendant does not, and could not properly, contend that the intrusion was, in fact, such that were he present, he would be justified under Penal Code sections 692 and 693 in using deadly force. By its terms section 692 authorizes merely "lawful" resistance to an offense by the party about to be injured. The circumstances in which resistance by such party is lawful are set forth in Penal Code section 693, which provides, "Resistance sufficient to prevent the offense may be made by the party about to be injured: 1. To prevent an offense against his person, or his family, or some member thereof. 2. To prevent an illegal attempt by force to take or injure property in his lawful possession." Subdivision 1 of section 693 manifestly does not apply, since in the instant case there was no attempt to commit "an offense against [defendant's] person, or his family, or some member thereof." Nor does subdivision 2 of that section apply. Section 693, like Penal Code section 197, should be read in the light of the common law, and, as heretofore stated, the rule developed at common law that deadly force to prevent a felony was justified only if the offense was a forcible and atrocious crime. Here the asserted attempted larceny, like the asserted attempted burglary, was not such a crime because the offense did not threaten death or serious bodily harm.

Defendant also does not, and could not properly, contend that the intrusion was in fact such that, were he present, he would be justified under Civil Code section 50 in using deadly force. That section provides, "Any necessary force may be used to protect from wrongful injury the person or property of oneself ...." This section also should be read in the light of the common law, and at common law in general deadly force could not be used solely for the protection of property. (See Model Penal Code, supra, § 3.06, com. 8; Perkins on Criminal Law, supra, p. 1026, fn. 6; 13 Stan.L.Rev. 566, 575-576.) ... Thus defendant was not warranted under Civil Code section 50 in using deadly force to protect his personal property.

Affirmed.

NOTES

1. In *State v. Miller*, 267 N.C. 409, 148 S.E.2d 279 (1965), defendant was convicted of manslaughter. Defendant refused entry to his home to Browning because of previous commotions he had caused. Browning threatened to "tear the place up" and began to rip the screen out of the door. Defendant got his pistol, returned to the hall, and said, "I told you not to tear my screen out." He fired one shot which killed Browning. The trial judge explained the law of self-defense but failed to instruct regarding defense of one's habitation especially if there was reasonable belief that the intruder intended to commit a felony. "The rules governing the right to defend one's habitation against forcible entry by an intruder are substantially the same as those governing his right to defend himself...." 148 S.E.2d at 282 (emphasis in original). "The law does not require such householder to flee or remain in his house until his assailant is upon him, but he may open his door and shoot his assailant, if such course is apparently necessary for the protection of himself or family.... A householder will not, however, be excused if he employs excessive force in repelling the attack, whether it be upon his person or upon his habitation." *Id.* at 281.

2. The law in regard to defense of habitation is far from clear. Part of the confusion stems from the factual context in which the defense is invoked. When a burglar invades an inhabited dwelling and is killed by the occupant, justification may be argued on several bases: self-defense, prevention of felony, and defense of habitation. Thus, many cases do not discuss defense of habitation or property. Instead the analysis proceeds along the lines of self-defense or prevention of a violent felony or both. Even where a court gratuitously asserts the bold proposition that deadly force may be used in defense of habitation, the rationale for the court's decision often is based on self-defense and prevention of felony. Some cases which refer to both defense of habitation and prevention of felony assume that the felony involved threat of injury to the occupants of the building. In other words self-defense is at the core of the defense of habitation.

One court has characterized the defense of habitation as "nothing more than accelerated self-defense." *State v. Ivicsics*, 604 S.W.2d 773, 777 (Mo. App. 1980). A student commentator has concluded: "In the absence of statute, by the weight of authority, deadly force may be used only when there is a reasonable belief that a threatened invasion involves danger to some inmate of the dwelling place." Comment, *Is a House a Castle?*, 9 Conn. L. Rev. 110, 126 (1976-77). A similar conclusion is reached by another student commentator in Comment, *Dwelling Defense Law in Missouri: In Search of Castles*, 50 U.M.K.C. L. Rev. 64 (1981).

However, a number of states have enacted statutes which purport to recognize a specific defense of habitation. The statutes are summarized in Posner, *Killing or Wounding to Protect a Property Interest*, 14 J. Law & Econ. 201, 228-32 (1971). These statutes often qualify the use of force by authorizing the protection of the habitation *for the purpose of preventing a felony*.

When protection of dwelling is limited to self-defense and, to some extent, to prevention of felony it may mean nothing more than that occupants need not "retreat" from their dwellings before using deadly force. One should remember that even in cases of self-defense and prevention of felony, deadly force can be used only where necessary.

The spring gun cases do not really test whether defense of habitation provides an independent reason for taking life because the use of spring guns also implicates the issue of risk to innocent persons. Many states prohibit the use of spring guns. Posner, *supra*. For a tragic example of protection of habitation see *Law v. State*, 21 Md. App. 13, 318 A.2d 859 (1974), where a once-victimized burglary victim mistook a police officer who was looking for prowlers for a burglar, and killed him. Reversed and remanded for new trial on the basis of a *Miranda* error, but with the court holding that the trial judge did not err in instructing to the effect that "[A] defendant is not justified in taking a life '[i]f a cautious and prudent man, under the same circumstances, would not believe the danger to be real'." 318 A.2d at 869-70.

SECTION IV. Prevention of Crime — Arrest

MODEL PENAL CODE

§ 3.07. Use of Force in Law Enforcement

[The text of this section appears in Appendix A.]

TENNESSEE v. GARNER

471 U.S. 1 (1985)

JUSTICE WHITE delivered the opinion of the Court.

This case requires us to determine the constitutionality of the use of deadly force to prevent the escape of an apparently unarmed suspected felon. We conclude that such force may not be used unless it is necessary to prevent the escape and the officer has probable cause to believe that the suspect poses a significant threat of death or serious physical injury to the officer or others.

I

At about 10:45 p.m. on October 3, 1974, Memphis Police Officers Elton Hymon and Leslie Wright were dispatched to answer a "prowler inside call." Upon arriving at the scene they saw a woman standing on her porch and gesturing toward the adjacent house. She told them she had heard glass breaking and that "they" or "someone" was breaking in next door. While Wright radioed the dispatcher to say that they were on the scene, Hymon went behind the house. He heard a door slam and saw someone run across the backyard. The fleeing suspect, who was appellee-respondent's decedent, Edward Garner, stopped at a 6-feet-high chain link fence at the edge of the yard. With the aid of a flashlight, Hymon was able to see Garner's face and hands. He saw no sign of a weapon, and, though not certain, was "reasonably sure" and "figured" that Garner was unarmed. App. 41, 56; Record 219. He thought Garner was 17 or 18 years old and about 5'5" or 5'7" tall. While Garner was crouched at the base of the fence, Hymon called out "police, halt" and took a few steps toward him. Garner then began to climb over the fence.

IV. PREVENTION OF CRIME — ARREST

Convinced that if Garner made it over the fence he would elude capture, Hymon shot him. The bullet hit Garner in the back of the head. Garner was taken by ambulance to a hospital, where he died on the operating table. Ten dollars and a purse taken from the house were found on his body.

In using deadly force to prevent the escape, Hymon was acting under the authority of a Tennessee statute and pursuant to Police Department policy. The statute provides that "[i]f, after notice of the intention to arrest the defendant, he either flees or forcibly resists, the officer may use all the necessary means to effect the arrest." Tenn Code Ann § 40-7-108 (1982).[3] The Department policy was slightly more restrictive than the statute, but still allowed the use of deadly force in cases of burglary. App 140-144. The incident was reviewed by the Memphis Police Firearm's Review Board and presented to a grand jury. Neither took any action. Id., at 57.

Garner's father then brought this action in the Federal District Court for the Western District of Tennessee, seeking damages under 42 USC § 1983 for asserted violations of Garner's constitutional rights. [The district court found for the defendants. Afterwards, the case was appealed, remanded, and appealed again. The Court of Appeals held the Tennessee Statute violated the Fourth Amendment, "The right of the people to be secure in their persons ... against unreasonable searches and seizures, shall not be violated...." U.S. Const., Amdt. 4].

....

II

Whenever an officer restrains the freedom of a person to walk away, he has seized that person. *United States v Brignoni-Ponce*, 422 US 873, 878, 45 L Ed 2d 607, 95 S Ct 2574 (1975). While it is not always clear just when minimal police interference becomes a seizure, see *United States v Mendenhall*, 446 US 544, 64 L Ed 2d 497, 100 S Ct 1870 (1980), there can be no question that apprehension by the use of deadly force is a seizure subject to the reasonableness requirement of the Fourth Amendment.

[The Court summarized its jurisprudence regarding the application of the Fourth Amendment to arrests and applied it to the use of deadly force]

The use of deadly force to prevent the escape of all felony suspects, whatever the circumstances, is constitutionally unreasonable. It is not better that all felony suspects die than that they escape. Where the suspect poses no immediate threat to the officer and no threat to others, the harm resulting from failing to apprehend him does not justify the use of deadly force to do so. It is no doubt unfortunate when a suspect who is in sight escapes, but the fact that the police arrive a little late or are a little slower afoot does not always justify killing the suspect. A police officer may not seize an unarmed, nondangerous suspect by shooting him dead. The Tennessee statute is unconstitutional insofar as it authorizes the use of deadly force against such fleeing suspects.

It is not, however, unconstitutional on its face. Where the officer has probable cause to believe that the suspect poses a threat of serious physical harm,

---

[3] Although the statute does not say so explicitly, Tennessee law forbids the use of deadly force in the arrest of a misdemeanant. See Johnson v. State, 173 Tenn. 134, 114 S. W. 2d 819 (1938).

either to the officer or to others, it is not constitutionally unreasonable to prevent escape by using deadly force. Thus, if the suspect threatens the officer with a weapon or there is probable cause to believe that he has committed a crime involving the infliction or threatened infliction of serious physical harm, deadly force may be used if necessary to prevent escape, and if, where feasible, some warning has been given. As applied in such circumstances, the Tennessee statute would pass constitutional muster.

III

A

It is insisted that the Fourth Amendment must be construed in light of the common-law rule, which allowed the use of whatever force was necessary to effect the arrest of a fleeing felon, though not a misdemeanant. As stated in Hale's posthumously published Pleas of the Crown:

> "[I]f persons that are pursued by these officers for felony or the just suspicion thereof... shall not yield themselves to these officers, but shall either resist or fly before they are apprehended or being apprehended shall rescue themselves and resist or fly, so that they cannot be otherwise apprehended, and are upon necessity slain therein, because they cannot be otherwise taken, it is no felony." 2 M. Hale, Historia Placitorum Coronae 85 (1736).

See also 4 W. Blackstone, Commentaries *289. Most American jurisdictions also imposed a flat prohibition against the use of deadly force to stop a fleeing misdemeanant, coupled with a general privilege to use such force to stop a fleeing felon. [citations omitted]

The State and city argue that because this was the prevailing rule at the time of the adoption of the Fourth Amendment and for some time thereafter, and is still in force in some States, use of deadly force against a fleeing felon must be "reasonable." It is true that this Court has often looked to the common law in evaluating the reasonableness, for Fourth Amendment purposes, of police activity. *See, e. g., United States v Watson,* 423 US 411, 418-419, 46 L Ed 2d 598, 96 S Ct 820 (1976); *Gerstein v Pugh,* 420 US 103, 111, 114, 43 L Ed 2d 54, 95 S Ct 854 (1975); *Carroll v United States,* 267 US 132, 149-153, 69 L Ed 543, 45 S Ct 280, 39 ALR 790 (1925). On the other hand, it "has not simply frozen into constitutional law those law enforcement practices that existed at the time of the Fourth Amendment's passage." *Payton v New York,* 445 US 573, 591, n 33, 63 L Ed 2d 639, 100 S Ct 1371 (1980). Because of sweeping change in the legal and technological context, reliance on the common-law rule in this case would be a mistaken literalism that ignores the purposes of a historical inquiry.

B

It has been pointed out many times that the common-law rule is best understood in light of the fact that it arose at a time when virtually all felonies were punishable by death. "Though effected without the protections and formalities of an orderly trial and conviction, the killing of a resisting or fleeing felon resulted in no greater consequences than those authorized for punishment of the felony of which the individual was charged or suspected." American Law Institute, Model Penal Code § 3.07, Comment 3, p. 56 (Tentative Draft No. 8, 1958) (hereinafter Model Penal Code Comment). Courts have also justified the common-law rule by emphasizing the relative dangerousness of felons. *See, e.g., Schumann v McGinn*, 307 Minn, at 458, 240 NW2d, at 533; *Holloway v Moser, supra*, at 187, 136 SE, at 376 (1927).

Neither of these justifications makes sense today. Almost all crimes formerly punishable by death no longer are or can be. *See, e.g., Enmund v Florida*, 458 US 782, 73 L Ed 2d 1140, 102 S Ct 3368 (1982); *Coker v Georgia*, 433 US 584 53 L Ed 2d 982, 97 S Ct 2861 (1977). And while in earlier times "the gulf between the felonies and the minor offences was broad and deep," 2 Pollock & Maitland 467, n 3; *Carroll v United States, supra*, at 158, 69 L Ed 543, 45 S Ct 280, 39 ALR 790, today the distinction is minor and often arbitrary. Many crimes classified as misdemeanors, or nonexistent, at common law are now felonies. Wilgus, 22 Mich L Rev, at 572-573. These changes have undermined the concept, which was questionable to begin with, that use of deadly force against a fleeing felon is merely a speedier execution of someone who has already forfeited his life. They have also made the assumption that a "felon" is more dangerous than a misdemeanant untenable. Indeed, numerous misdemeanors involve conduct more dangerous than many felonies.

There is an additional reason why the common-law rule cannot be directly translated to the present day. The common-law rule developed at a time when weapons were rudimentary. Deadly force could be inflicted almost solely in a hand-to-hand struggle during which, necessarily, the safety of the arresting officer was at risk. Handguns were not carried by police officers until the latter half of the last century. L. Kennett & J. Anderson, The Gun in America 150-151 (1975). Only then did it become possible to use deadly force from a distance as a means of apprehension. As a practical matter, the use of deadly force under the standard articulation of the common-law rule has an altogether different meaning — and harsher consequences — now than in past centuries. See Wechsler & Michael, A Rationale for the Law of Homicide: I, 37 Colum L Rev 701, 741 (1937).

One other aspect of the common-law rule bears emphasis. It forbids the use of deadly force to apprehend a misdemeanant, condemning such action as disproportionately severe. See *Holloway v Moser*, 193 NC, at 187, 136 SE, at 376; *State v Smith*, 127 Iowa, at 535, 103 NW, at 945. See generally Annot, 83 ALR3d 238 (1978).

In short, though the common-law pedigree of Tennessee's rule is pure on its face, changes in the legal and technological context mean the rule is distorted almost beyond recognition when literally applied.

C

In evaluating the reasonableness of police procedures under the Fourth Amendment, we have also looked to prevailing rules in individual jurisdictions.... Some 19 States have codified the common-law rule, though in two of these the courts have significantly limited the statute. Four States, though without a relevant statute, apparently retain the common-law rule. Two States have adopted the Model Penal Code's provision verbatim. Eighteen others allow, in slightly varying language, the use of deadly force only if the suspect has committed a felony involving the use or threat of physical or deadly force, or is escaping with a deadly weapon, or is likely to endanger life or inflict serious physical injury if not arrested. Louisiana and Vermont, though without statutes or case law on point, do forbid the use of deadly force to prevent any but violent felonies. The remaining States either have no relevant statute or case law, or have positions that are unclear.

It cannot be said that there is a constant or overwhelming trend away from the common-law rule. In recent years, some States have reviewed their laws and expressly rejected abandonment of the common-law rule. Nonetheless, the long-term movement has been away from the rule that deadly force may be used against any fleeing felon, and that remains the rule in less than half the States.

This trend is more evident and impressive when viewed in light of the policies adopted by the police departments themselves. Overwhelmingly, these are more restrictive than the common-law rule....

D

Actual departmental policies are important for an additional reason. We would hesitate to declare a police practice of long standing "unreasonable" if doing so would severely hamper effective law enforcement. But the indications are to the contrary. There has been no suggestion that crime has worsened in any way in jurisdictions that have adopted, by legislation or departmental policy, rules similar to that announced today....

....

... We hold that the statute is invalid insofar as it purported to give Hymon the authority to act as he did.

The judgment of the Court of Appeals is affirmed, ...

So ordered.

[Justice O'Connor, along with Chief Justice Burger and Justice Rehnquist, dissented.]

NOTES

1. In *People v. Couch*, 436 Mich. 414, 461 N.W.2d 683 (1990), the Michigan Supreme Court held "that *Garner* did not change this State's criminal law with respect to the use of deadly force to apprehend a fleeing felon." *Id.* at 687, and that any change was a matter for the State legislature. According to the Court,

> the prosecution's argument that *Garner* applies directly to change this state's fleeing-felon rule fails because it is premised upon the notion that the United States Supreme Court can require a state to criminalize certain conduct. Clearly, the power to define conduct as a *state* criminal offense lies with the individual states, not with the federal government or

even the United States Supreme Court. While the failure to proscribe or prevent certain conduct could possibly subject the state to *civil* liability for its failure to act, or for an individual's actions, if that state, for whatever reason, chooses not to criminalize such conduct, it cannot be compelled to do so.

Moreover, we fail to see how *Garner* can be applied "directly" in any event, since the Court in that case concluded only that the use of deadly force to apprehend a fleeing felon who posed no harm to the officer or others was "unreasonable" for purposes of the *Fourth Amendment*. In other words, *Garner* was a *civil* case which made no mention of the officer's criminal responsibility for his "unreasonable" actions. Thus, not only is the United States Supreme Court without authority to require this state to make shooting a nondangerous fleeing felon a *crime*, it has never even expressed an intent to do so. *Id.* at 684.

2. In *State v. Dunning*, 177 N.C. 559, 98 S.E. 530 (1919), the defendant was constable and chief of police of the town of Aulander. When he tried to arrest C. T. White for disorderly conduct White attacked him with a drawn knife. The defendant shot White although he could have withdrawn with safety. The court held that while private individuals may have a duty to retreat, "The law does not require an officer with a warrant for an arrest for an offense to retreat or retire, but he must stand his ground and perform his duty...." 98 S.E. at 532.

3. In *State v. Elder*, 67 Ohio L. Abs. 385, 120 N.E.2d 508 (1953), the village chief of police was prosecuted for unlawfully discharging his revolver on a public highway. He was standing at the side of the road when Bobby Mock's automobile approached. Defendant signalled Mock to stop and when he failed to do that he fired his revolver at or in the direction of Mock's vehicle. The conviction was affirmed. "[I]t is the general rule that a Peace Officer may use a firearm, even to the extent of taking life, if necessary, to effect the arrest of a felon, but he may not do so, except in self-defense, to effect an arrest for a misdemeanor, such as travelling at a high rate of speed or reckless operation of an automobile, whether his purpose is to kill or merely stop the misdemeanant's flight, even though the latter cannot be taken otherwise." 120 N.E.2d at 510.

4. At common law a police officer or citizen who killed to prevent a felony or apprehend a felon did so at his peril. An arrest was lawful if a police officer had a reasonable belief that the person arrested committed a felony; a private person had authority to make an arrest if a felony had been committed and the person had reason to believe the arrestee committed the felony. Reasonable force, including deadly force, to effect an arrest was permissible. However, killing a suspect in the mistaken belief that he attempted or committed a felony was not justifiable. Prior to *Garner*, some states had relaxed this rule and recognized the privilege in cases in which a person acts under a reasonable mistake. Day, *Shooting the Fleeing Felon: State of the Law*, 14 Crim. L. Rev. 285 (1978).

5. *Resisting arrest*. May a person use force to resist an unlawful arrest? At common law and in some states a person may use reasonable, nondeadly force

to resist an unlawful arrest. Under a more recent approach followed by some states a person must peaceably submit even to an unlawful arrest where he knows or has good reason to believe that the one attempting to make the arrest is a police officer engaged in the performance of his duties. See *Commonwealth v. Moreira*, 388 Mass. 596, 447 N.E.2d 1224 (1983). The purpose of this requirement is to allow the legal issue to be fought in the courts and not on the street corner. Regardless of the legality of the arrest, however, a person may resort to reasonable force in order to protect his person where a police officer uses excessive force which threatens serious injury. *State v. Mulvihill*, 57 N.J. 151, 270 A.2d 277 (1970); *State v. Westlund*, 13 Wash. App. 460, 536 P.2d 20 (1975). *Commonwealth v. French*, 611 A.2d 175 (Pa. 1992).

COMMONWEALTH v. KLEIN

Supreme Judicial Court of Massachusetts
372 Mass. 823, 363 N.E.2d 1313 (1977)

[Defendant was convicted on two counts of assault and battery with a dangerous weapon as a result of shooting two burglars. The burglars had broken into a drugstore across from defendant's home and had stolen money and cigarettes. There were three different versions of what had occurred thereafter. One burglar testified that someone shot into the store without warning and continued to shoot at them as they ran away. Defendant testified that he ordered the burglars to halt but that they charged at him with a tire iron and metal object he believed to be a gun. A police officer's version was that defendant told him he was sitting home watching the store, gun in hand, because of recent burglaries of the store. He saw the thieves enter and called the police. When the police failed to appear, he approached the store and saw the burglars emerge. He ordered them to halt, and when they threw cigarettes at him and ran back toward the store, he shot at them. Later when the burglars left the store and ran away, he emptied his gun, firing at them.]

HENNESSEY, CHIEF JUSTICE.

....

The central question in this case is whether the defendant was justified in using deadly force. We define deadly force as force intended or likely to cause death or great bodily harm....

The defendant's first contention is that his conduct in shooting the two men was justifiable on the ground of self-defense.

The jury was instructed in substance that, in order to create a right to defend oneself with a dangerous weapon likely to cause serious injury or death, it must appear that the person using the weapon had a reasonable apprehension of great bodily harm and a reasonable belief that no other means would suffice to prevent such harm.... Although there was some testimony by the defendant from which the jury could have concluded that the defendant acted reasonably in an attempt to prevent great bodily harm to himself, there was also evidence which warranted the jury in deciding that the defendant did not act in self-defense at all....

....

IV. PREVENTION OF CRIME — ARREST

We turn now to consideration of the defendant's claim that he was justified in using deadly force to prevent the escape of the two men from his attempt to make a citizen's arrest.

....

... Our common law has long recognized a private citizen's right to arrest.... [*breach of peace or felony*] Nevertheless, limits must be set, as to the use of deadly force, against the dangers of uncontrolled vigilantism and anarchistic actions ... and particularly against the danger of death or injury of innocent persons at the hands of untrained volunteers using firearms. In our view, for example, there would be no wisdom in approving the unqualified right of a private citizen to use deadly force to prevent the escape of one who has committed a crime against property only.

Some jurisdictions have adopted such limiting rules. See 32 A.L.R.3d 1072-1077, Annot., 1078-1119 (1970). In *Commonwealth v. Chermansky*, 430 Pa. 170, 242 A.2d 237 (1968), for example, it was held that the prerequisites to justify the use of deadly force by a private person in order to effect the arrest or prevent the escape of a felon are that the person must be in fresh pursuit of the felon and that he must give notice of his purpose to make the arrest for the felony if the attendant circumstances are themselves insufficient to warn the felon of the intention of the pursuing party to arrest him; that such felony must actually have been committed by the person against whom the force is used; and the felony must be one which normally causes or threatens death or great bodily harm.[5] [*felony committed in presence of private citizen*]

We have examined comparable law elsewhere, and we think the relevant provisions of the Model Penal Code will best serve this Commonwealth.... Accordingly, we establish as the law of Massachusetts the rules (in so far as [sic] they are material to the instant case) as found in § 3.07 of the Model Penal Code (Proposed Official Draft 1962). They are as follows:

> Section 3.07. Use of Force in Law Enforcement.
>
> (1) *Use of Force Justifiable to Effect an Arrest*. Subject to the provisions of this Section and of Section 3.09, the use of force upon or toward the person of another is justifiable when the actor is making or assisting in making an arrest and the actor believes that such force is immediately necessary to effect a lawful arrest.
>
> (2) *Limitations on the Use of Force*.
>
> (a) The use of force is not justifiable under this Section unless:
>
> (i) the actor makes known the purpose of the arrest or believes that it is otherwise known by or cannot reasonably be made known to the person to be arrested; and
>
> (ii) when the arrest is made under a warrant, the warrant is valid or believed by the actor to be valid.
>
> (b) The use of *deadly* force [emphasis supplied] is not justifiable under this Section unless:
>
> (i) the arrest is for a felony; and

---

[5] The Pennsylvania court, at 173-174, 242 A.2d 237 included, among such felonies, the crimes of treason, murder, voluntary manslaughter, mayhem, arson, robbery, common law rape, common law burglary, kidnapping, and assault with intent to murder, rape, or rob.

A private citizen "deputized" stands in place of the officer

(ii) the person effecting the arrest is authorized to act as a peace officer or is assisting a person whom he believes to be authorized to act as a peace officer; and

(iii) the actor believes that the force employed creates no substantial risk of injury to innocent persons; and

(iv) the actor believes that:

(1) the crime for which the arrest is made involved conduct including the use or threatened use of deadly force; or

(2) there is a substantial risk that the person to be arrested will cause death or serious bodily harm if his apprehension is delayed.[7]

We further hold that, since the right of the defendant to arrest and prevent the escape of the victims was raised in the evidence, the burden of disproving this defense beyond a reasonable doubt rested on the Commonwealth....

....

As measured by the principles which we have now established and the judge's charge, it is clear that the Commonwealth met its burden of proving beyond a reasonable doubt that the shootings were not justified.[8]

....

[Judgments of Conviction were reversed because the Court refused to apply the Model Penal Code rule retroactively.]

---

[7] The American Law Institute's Model Code of Pre-Arraignment Procedure (1975) carried forward the determinations of the Institute in § 3.07 of the Model Penal Code regarding the use of force and of deadly force in making an arrest. In summary, § 120.7 of the Model Code of Pre-Arraignment Procedure provides that a law enforcement officer authorized to make an arrest may use such force as is reasonably necessary to effect the arrest, and the officer may use deadly force only if (a) the arrest is for a felony; (b) the officer reasonably believes that the force employed creates no substantial risk to innocent persons; and (c) the officer reasonably believes that (1) the crime for which the arrest is made involved conduct including the use or threatened use of deadly force; or (2) there is a substantial risk that the person to be arrested will cause death or serious bodily harm if his apprehension is delayed.

[8] The issue presented in this case is a narrow one; whether deadly force can be used to prevent the flight from arrest of persons who have committed crimes concerned with property only. It is probably useful to stress some of the issues with which we are not concerned here.

For example, this is not a case involving physical resistance to arrest. Almost inevitably, principles relating to self-defense are involved in such a case. We have said that the person attempting a valid arrest has the right to use the force which is reasonably necessary to overcome physical resistance by the person sought to be arrested....

Likewise, we do not face here the issue of the right of the person attempting an arrest to carry a gun or other dangerous weapon, whatever the nature of the crime which gave rise to the right of arrest. The likelihood of a violent confrontation and a consequent necessity for self-defense by the person making the arrest are factors to be considered in such a case.

Finally, insofar as the defendant's assertion that he was entitled to directed verdicts of not guilty is concerned, the instant case is not concerned with the protection of property. The jury were warranted in concluding that the wounding of the two men occurred after the crime involving the drug store. See, e.g., the provisions in the Model Penal Code concerning the protection of property, particularly § 3.06(3)(d), and the justification of the use of deadly force to resist an unlawful attempt to dispossess an owner of his dwelling, or to prevent an act of arson, burglary, or other act of felonious theft or property destruction.

NOTES

1. *People v. Whitty*, 96 Mich. App. 403, 292 N.W.2d 214, 220 (1980) noted:

> "Despite the fact that some jurisdictions have cut back on the justifiable use of deadly force, many others have maintained the common law rule, and there is good reason for doing so. The fact remains that the police cannot be everywhere they are needed at once. The occasion may arise where the private citizen is confronted with the choice of attempting a citizen's arrest, or letting the felon escape. In order to make the citizen's arrest, it is regrettable, but sometimes necessary, to make use of deadly force. The common law in Michigan recognizes this but still stops far short of granting the private citizen a license to hunt down and kill those suspected of committing a felony. The use of deadly force is not justified if the person to be arrested is not in fact a felon. Additionally, and most importantly, the use of deadly force must be necessary either to meet deadly force or to prevent the felon's escape."

In *People v. Couch*, 176 Mich. App. 254, 439 N.W. 2d 354 (1989), the Michigan Court of Appeals reconsidered *Whitty* and decided to adopt a more restrictive standard. On appeal, however, the Michigan Supreme Court reversed that part of the decision which would have adopted a new standard, 436 Mich. 414, 461 N.W. 2d 683 (1990), discussed *supra* at pp. 546-547, n.1.

2. *State v. Clothier*, 242 Kan. 796, 753 P.2d 1267 (1988), found *Tennessee v. Garner*, 471 U.S. 1 (1985), inapplicable to a criminal charge against a private person who, in accord with a state criminal statute, used deadly force in defending property although life was not immediately threatened.

SECTION V. Necessity

NOTE

Many affirmative defenses, except those which involve incapacity, are based on situations where the defendant has asserted that it was necessary to act in order to protect some important interest. Self-defense, for example, is necessary to protect one's person or life. The "defense of necessity," however, applies to a narrower range of situations. A question of "necessity" is presented when physical circumstances are such that the only way defendant can avoid harm to himself or herself is by inflicting harm on some innocent person. This may occur in two kinds of situations. The first is where defendant acts to protect a higher interest, such as by trespassing on someone's property to avoid death or serious injury, or when an ambulance or police vehicle disobeys a traffic law in an emergency situation. The second situation is where defendant acts under "pressure that an ordinary person could not be expected to tolerate."*

---

*Huxley, *Proposals and Counter Proposals on the Defense of Necessity*, 1978 Crim. L. Rev. 141, 143-44.

In both situations defendant had a choice between suffering personal harm or violating the law.** Should there be a defense of necessity, and if so, under what circumstances?

REGINA v. DUDLEY & STEPHENS
Queen's Bench Division
14 Q.B.D. 273 (1884)

[Dudley and Stephens were the master and mate of the yacht *Mignonette*. They were indicted at Exeter assizes before Huddleston, B., for the murder of a cabin-boy named Parker. At the suggestion of the judge, the jury found a special verdict; they added a strong expression of compassion for the sufferings that the prisoners had undergone.

The special verdict was to the following effect: the prisoners, with one Brooks, all able-bodied seamen, and the boy Parker were in an open boat after the shipwreck of the yacht *Mignonette*. They had no food or water in the boat. After eighteen days during which the only food they had had was one small turtle, and the water they caught in their oilskin capes, the prisoners suggested to Brooks that someone should be sacrificed to save the rest. Brooks refused to agree and the boy, to whom they were understood to refer, was not consulted. On the twentieth day Dudley, with the consent of Stephens but not of Brooks, killed the boy. The three fed upon the boy for four days when they were picked up. It was found that if the men had not fed upon the body of the boy they would probably not have survived, to be so picked up, and rescued, but would within the four days have died of famine [sic]; that the boy, being in a much weaker condition, was likely to have died before them; that there appeared to the prisoners every probability that unless they then or very soon fed upon the boy or one of themselves they would die of starvation, and that there was no appreciable chance of saving life except by killing someone for the others to eat; and that, assuming any necessity to kill any one, there was no greater necessity for killing the boy than any of the other three men.

The question argued before the Divisional Court was whether the legal effect of the above special verdict was that the accused were guilty of murder.]

LORD COLERIDGE, C.J.

... First it is said that it follows from various definitions of murder in books of authority, which definitions imply, if they do not state, the doctrine, that in order to save your own life you may lawfully take away the life of another, when that other is neither attempting nor threatening yours, nor is guilty of any illegal act whatever towards you or anyone else. But if these definitions be looked at they will not be found to sustain this contention....

Is there, then, any authority for the proposition which has been presented to us? Decided cases there are none.... The American case cited by my brother Stephen in his Digest, from Wharton on Homicide, in which it was decided, correctly indeed, that sailors had no right to throw passengers overboard to save themselves, but on the somewhat strange ground that the proper mode of determining who was to be sacrificed was to vote upon the subject by ballot,

---

**W. LaFave & A. Scott, CRIMINAL LAW 442 (2d. ed., 1986).

can hardly, as my brother Stephen says, be an authority satisfactory to a court in this country. The observations of Lord Mansfield in the case of *R. v. Stratton and Others,* striking and excellent as they are, were delivered in a political trial, where the question was whether a political necessity had arisen for deposing a governor of Madras.

....

Now it is admitted that the deliberate killing of this unoffending and unresisting boy was clearly murder, unless the killing can be justified by some well-recognized excuse admitted by law. It is further admitted that there was in this case no such excuse, unless the killing was justified by what has been called "necessity." But the temptation to the act which existed here was not what the law has ever called necessity. Nor is this to be regretted. Though law and morality are not the same, and many things may be immoral which are not necessarily illegal, yet the absolute divorce of law from morality would be of fatal consequence; and such divorce would follow if the temptation to murder in this case were to be held by law an absolute defence of it. It is not so. To preserve one's life is, generally speaking, a duty, but it may be the plainest and the highest duty to sacrifice it.... It is not correct, therefore, to say that there is any absolute or unqualified necessity to preserve one's life.... It is not needful to point out the awful danger of admitting the principle which has been contended for. Who is to be the judge of this sort of necessity? By what measure is the comparative value of lives to be measured? Is it to be strength, or intellect, or what? ... In this case the weakest, the youngest, the most unresisting was chosen. Was it more necessary to kill him than one of the grown men? The answer must be "No'.... It is not suggested that in this particular case the deeds were "devilish," but it is quite plain that such a principle once admitted might be made the legal cloak for unbridled passion and atrocious crime. There is no safe path for judges to tread but to ascertain the law to the best of their ability and declare it according to their judgment; and, if in any case the law appears to be too severe on individuals, to leave it to the Sovereign to exercise that prerogative of mercy which the Constitution has entrusted to the hands fittest to dispense it.

It must not be supposed that in refusing to admit temptation to be an excuse for crime it is forgotten how terrible the temptation was; how awful the suffering; how hard in such trials to keep the judgment straight and the conduct pure. We are often compelled to set up standards we cannot reach ourselves, and to lay down rules which we could not ourselves satisfy. But a man has no right to declare temptation to be an excuse, though he might himself have yielded to it, nor allow compassion for the criminal to change or weaken in any manner the legal definition of the crime. It is therefore our duty to declare the prisoners' act was wilful murder, that the facts as stated in the verdict are no legal justification.*

---

*Sentence of death was passed, but was commuted by the Crown to six months' imprisonment without hard labor.

NOTES

1. The Law Commission [England] as part of the process of "codification" of the law has concluded "that there should be no general defence of necessity in the Code. We indicated at the outset that it is very improbable that any such defence exists at common law. For the avoidance of doubt, we recommend that, if any such defence does exist, it should be abolished." Law Comm. Rep., No. 83, p. 38 (1979). A working paper had been prepared for the Commission recommending adoption of a defense of necessity much along the lines of the MODEL PENAL CODE § 3.02, Appendix A *infra*, but this was rejected. Since then, the Law Commission has not attempted to resurrect a general necessity defense. Padfield, *Duress, Necessity and the Law Commission*, [1992] CRIM. L. REV. 778, 786.

Commentators have criticized the action of the Commission, Williams, *Necessity*, [1978] CRIM. L. REV. 128; Huxley, *supra* p. 551. Glanville Williams states that the defense has been recognized in English Law. CRIMINAL LAW: THE GENERAL PART 724 (1961).

2. The rejection of a general defense of necessity and the statement that such defense did not exist at common law did not mean that the Commission believed necessity has not been and should not ever be a defense. The Commission stated that necessity has been recognized:

> (a) through statutory construction — the statute was not intended to apply in this situation —;
>
> (b) by express statutory provisions which create exceptions to the statute — prescription of drugs, abortion;
>
> (c) by use of qualifying language in statutes — requirement that act be "unlawful" or that it be done "without reasonable excuse."

Furthermore "necessitous circumstances" have been considered relevant to mitigation of sentence. In the case of minor offenses, especially where strict liability is provided, the Commission suggested that prosecutorial discretion is the proper vehicle for considering matters of necessity. Law Comm. Rep. *supra* note 1, pp. 20-22, 26.

As to necessity and murder the Commission was concerned with the problem of euthanasia and noted that the Criminal Law Revision Committee had included in its Working Paper a new offense, "mercy killing," which

> would apply to a person who, from compassion unlawfully kills another person who is or is believed by him to be (1) permanently subject to great bodily pain or suffering, or (2) permanently helpless from bodily or mental incapacity or (3) subject to rapid and incurable bodily or mental degeneration. The defendant should have reasonable cause for his belief that the victim was suffering from one of the conditions mentioned in (1), (2) or (3) and consideration should be given to the inclusion within the definition of a requirement that the killing was with the consent or without the dissent of the deceased. Law Comm. Rep. at 29. The mercy killing provision was withdrawn as "too controversial" and not included in the Criminal Law Revision Committee Report on Offences Against the Person. [1980] CRIM. L. REV. 331.

UNITED STATES v. HOLMES

United States Circuit Court of Appeals
1 Wall. Jr. 1, 26 Fed. Cas. 360 (E.D. Pa. No. 15383 (1842)

The American ship William Brown, left Liverpool on the 13th of March, 1841, bound for Philadelphia, in the United States. She had on board (besides a heavy cargo) 17 of a crew, and 65 passengers, Scotch and Irish emigrants. About 10 o'clock on the night of the 19th of April, when distant 250 miles southeast of Cape Race, Newfoundland, the vessel struck an iceberg, and began to fill so rapidly that it was evident she must soon go down. The long-boat and jolly-boat were cleared away and lowered. The captain, the second mate, 7 of the crew, and 1 passenger got into the jolly-boat. The first mate, 8 seamen, of whom the prisoner was one (these 9 being the entire remainder of the crew), and 32 passengers, in all 41 persons, got indiscriminately into the long-boat. The remainder of the passengers, 31 persons, were obliged to remain on board the ship. In an hour and a half from the time when the ship struck, she went down, carrying with her every person who had not escaped to one or the other of the small boats. Thirty-one passengers thus perished. On the following morning (Tuesday) the captain, being about to part company with the long-boat, gave its crew several directions, and, among other counsel, advised them to obey all the orders of the mate, as they would obey his, the captain's. This the crew promised that they would do. The long-boat was believed to be in general good condition; but she had not been in the water since leaving Liverpool, now thirty-five days; and as soon as she was launched, began to leak. She continued to leak the whole time; but the passengers had buckets, and tins, and, by bailing, were able to reduce the water, so as to make her hold her own....

... Without going into more detail, the evidence of both these officers [the captain and the second mate] went to show that, loaded as the long-boat was on Tuesday morning, the chances of living were much against her. But the captain thought, that even if lightened to the extent to which she afterwards was, "it would have been impossible to row her to land; and that the chances of her being picked up, were ninety-nine to one against her."

.... It is probable that by Tuesday night (the weather being cold, the persons on the boat partially naked, and the rain falling heavily), the witnesses had become considerably overpowered by exhaustion and cold, having been 24 hours in the boat. None of them spoke in a manner entirely explicit and satisfactory in regard to the most important point, viz., the degree and imminence of the jeopardy at 10 o'clock on Tuesday night, when the throwing over began. As has been stated, few words were spoken. It appeared, only, that, about 10 o'clock of Tuesday night, it being then dark, the rain falling rather heavily, the sea somewhat freshening, and the boat having considerable water in it, the mate, who had been bailing for some time, gave it up, exclaiming: "This work won't do. Help me, God. Men, go to work." Some of the passengers cried out, about the same time: "The boat is sinking. The plug's out. God have mercy on our poor souls." Holmes and the crew did not proceed upon this order; and after a little while, the mate exclaimed again: "Men, you must go to work, or we shall all perish." They then went to work; and ... threw out, before they ended, 14 male passengers, and also 2 women. The mate directed the crew "not to part man and wife, and not to throw over any women." There was no other principle of selection. There was no evidence of combination among the crew. No lots were cast, nor had the passengers, at any time, been either informed or consulted as to what was now done. Holmes was one of the persons who assisted in throwing the passengers over....

The prisoner was indicted under the act of April 30, 1790, "for the punishment of certain crimes against the United States" (1 Story's Laws, 83 [1 Stat. 115]), an act which ordains (section 12) that if any seaman, &c., shall commit manslaughter upon the high seas, &c., on conviction, he shall be imprisoned not exceeding three years, and fined not exceeding one thousand dollars....

BALDWIN, CIRCUIT JUSTICE.

... It is one thing to give a favorable interpretation to evidence in order to mitigate an offence. It is a different thing, when we are asked, not to extenuate, but to justify, the act. In the former case, as I have said, our decision may in some degree be swayed by feelings of humanity; while, in the latter, it is the law of necessity alone which can disarm the vindicatory justice of the country. Where, indeed, a case does arise, embraced by this "law of necessity," the penal laws pass over such case in silence; for law is made to meet but the ordinary exigencies of life. But the case does not become "a case of necessity," unless all ordinary means of self preservation have been exhausted. The peril must be instant, overwhelming, leaving no alternative but to lose our own life, or to take the life of another person.... For example, suppose that two persons who owe no duty to one another that is not mutual, should, by accident, not attributable to either, be placed in a situation where both cannot survive. Neither is bound to save the other's life by sacrificing his own, nor would either commit a crime in saving his own life in a struggle for the only means of safety. Of this description of cases are those which have been cited to you by counsel, from writers on natural law, — cases which we rather leave to your imagination than attempt minutely to describe. And I again state that when this great "law of necessity" does apply, and is not improperly exercised, the taking of life is devested [sic] of unlawfulness.

But in applying this law, we must look, not only to the jeopardy in which the parties are, but also to the relations in which they stand. The slayer must be under no obligation to make his own safety secondary to the safety of others. A familiar application of this principle presents itself in the obligations which rest upon the owners of stages, steamboats, and other vehicles of transportation. In consideration of the payment of fare, the owners of the vehicle are bound to transport the passengers to the place of contemplated destination. Having, in all emergencies, the conduct of the journey, and the control of the passengers, the owners rest under every obligation for care, skill, and general capacity; and if, from defect of any of these requisites, grievous injury is done to the passenger, the persons employed are liable.

... The passenger stands in a position different from that of the officers and seamen. It is the sailor who must encounter the hardships and perils of the voyage. Nor can this relation be changed when the ship is lost by tempest or other danger of the sea, and all on board have betaken themselves, for safety, to the small boats; for imminence of danger cannot absolve from duty. The sailor is bound, as before, to undergo whatever hazard is necessary to preserve the boat and the passengers. Should the emergency become so extreme as to call for the sacrifice of life, there can be no reason why the law does not still remain the same.

The captain, indeed, and a sufficient number of seamen to navigate the boat, must be preserved; for, except these abide in the ship, all will perish. But if there be more seamen than are necessary to manage the boat, the supernumerary sailors have no right, for their safety, to sacrifice the passengers. The sailors and passengers, in fact, cannot be regarded as in equal positions. The sailor (to use the language of a distinguished writer) owes more benevolence to another than to himself. He is bound to set a greater value on the life of others than on his own. And while we admit that sailor and sailor may lawfully struggle with each other for the plank which can save but one, we think that if the passenger is on the plank, even "the law of necessity" justifies not the sailor who takes it from him. This rule may be deemed a harsh one towards the sailor, who may have thus far done his duty, but when the danger is so extreme, that the only hope is in sacrificing either a sailor or a passenger, any alternative is hard; and would it not be the hardest of any to sacrifice a passenger in order to save a supernumerary sailor?

But, in addition, if the source of the danger have [sic] been obvious, and destruction ascertained to be certainly about to arrive, though at future time, there should be consultation, and some mode of selection fixed, by which those in equal relations may have equal chance for their life. By what mode, then, should selection be made? The question is not without difficulty; nor do we know of any rule prescribed, either by statute or by common law, or even by speculative writers on the law of nature. In fact, no rule of general application can be prescribed for contingencies which are wholly unforeseen. There is, however, one condition of extremity for which all writers have prescribed the same rule. When the ship is in no danger of sinking, but all sustenance is exhausted, and a sacrifice of one person is necessary to appease the hunger of others, the selection is by lot. This mode is resorted to as the fairest mode, and, in some sort, as an appeal to God, for selection of the victim. This manner, obviously, was regarded by the mate, in parting with the captain, as the one which it was proper to adopt, in case the long-boat could not live with all who were on board on Tuesday morning. The same manner, as would appear from the response given to the mate, had already suggested itself to the captain. For ourselves, we can conceive of no mode so consonant both to humanity and to justice; and the occasion, we think, must be peculiar which will dispense with its exercise. If, indeed, the peril be instant and overwhelming, leaving no chance of means, and no moment for deliberation, then, of course, there is no power to consult, to cast lots, or in any such way to decide; but even where the final disaster is thus sudden, if it have been foreseen as certainty about to arrive, if no new cause of danger have arisen to bring on the closing catastrophe, if time have existed to cast lots, and to select the victims, then, as we have said, sortition should be adopted. In no other than this or some like way are those having equal rights put upon an equal footing, and in no other way is it possible to guard against partiality and oppression, violence and conflict....

When the selection has been made by lots, the victim yields of course to his fate, or, if he resists, force may be employed to coerce submission....

After a few remarks upon the evidence, the case was given to the jury, who, about 16 hours afterwards, and after having once returned to the bar, unable to agree, with some difficulty, found a verdict of guilty. The prisoner was, however, recommended to the mercy of the court....

When the prisoner was brought up for sentence, the learned judge said to him, that many circumstances in the affair were of a character to commend him to regard, yet, that the case was one in which some punishment was demanded; that it was in the power of the court to inflict the penalty of an imprisonment for a term of three years, and a fine of $1,000, but, in view of all the circumstances, and especially as the prisoner had been already confined to gaol several months, that the court would make the punishment more lenient. The convict was then sentenced to undergo an imprisonment in the Eastern Penitentiary of Pennsylvania, (solitary confinement) at hard labor, for the term of six months, and to pay a fine of $20.*

NOTE

In the United States some courts have been unwilling to recognize a general defense of necessity in the absence of statute. *Commonwealth v. Koons*, 216 Pa. Super. 402, 268 A.2d 202 (1970). In *Butterfield v. State*, 167 Tex. Crim. 64, 317 S.W.2d 943 (1958), defendant, who had been drinking, struck his head. When he awoke alone in his apartment in a pool of blood he concluded that he needed immediate medical attention. Because he had no telephone to summon assistance he set out for the hospital. On the way he fainted and was involved in an accident. The defense of necessity was rejected: "We are aware of no such defense and decline to hold that an intoxicated driver of an automobile upon a public highway commits no offense if it be shown that a necessity existed, or that it appeared to him to be necessary that he make the journey." There may, however, be another explanation for the court's decision. See note, *infra* p. 561, n. 2. The issue is more fully discussed in Sullivan, *The Defense of Necessity in Texas: Legislative Invention Come of Age*, 16 Hous. L. Rev. 333 (1979).

MODEL PENAL CODE

§ 3.02. Justification Generally: Choice of Evils

[The text of this section appears in Appendix A.]

NOTES

1. The Model Penal Code provision on general justification accepts the rule of necessity. However, it is limited to "choice of evils" situations and only to

---

*Considerable sympathy having been excited in favor of Holmes, by the popular press, an effort was made by several persons, and particularly by the Seamen's Friend Society, to obtain a pardon from the executive. President Tyler refused, however, to grant any pardon, in consequence of the court's not uniting in the application. The penalty was subsequently remitted.

those in which it is necessary to violate the law in order to avoid a greater evil. It is not enough that the harms are of equal value. Unlike the common-law rule of *Regina v. Dudley & Stephens, supra,* that necessity cannot justify the taking of human life in order to save oneself (other than in self-defense), the Model Penal Code does not exclude the defense from criminal homicide prosecutions. It can be used only to justify avoidance of a greater harm and would not be available, as the comments of the code explicitly state, to a defendant "who acted to save himself at the expense of another, as by seizing a raft when men are shipwrecked." MODEL PENAL CODE — comment at 8 (Tent. Draft 8, 1958). Yet under the common law such an act of survival (e.g., where the defendant saved himself, but did not do so by an act which itself directly killed others) would not necessarily have constituted murder because the defendant may have lacked specific intent to kill or because his actual act may not have caused the death. See J. Hall, GENERAL PRINCIPLES OF CRIMINAL LAW (2d ed. 1960) at 419-436. The Model Penal Code focuses on the physical harm rather than on the moral harm as discussed in *Dudley* and *Stephens*. Thus where taking a life saves the lives of several people the greater harm has been avoided according to the MODEL PENAL CODE.

The general defense of justification in the Model Penal Code does not refer to "cause" which compels a person to make a choice between evils. It includes all causes whether physical phenomena or coercive acts of other persons. As such it cuts across the traditional defenses of necessity and duress.

2. A number of states have followed the lead of the Model Penal Code and legislated a necessity defense based on choice of evils. Tiffany & Anderson, *Legislating the Necessity Defense in Criminal Law,* 52 DEN. L.J. 839 (1975); Arnolds & Garland, *The Defense of Necessity in Criminal Law: The Right to Choose the Lesser Evil,* 65 J. CRIM. L. & CRIMINOLOGY 289 (1974).

3. Cases such as *Regina v. Dudley & Stephens* and *United States v. Holmes* present the most provocative context for a discussion of necessity. More often the defense is asserted in prosecutions for minor offenses, notably traffic cases: defense available — *People v. Moore,* 42 A.D.2d 268, 346 N.Y.S.2d 363 (1973); *State v. Matthews,* 30 Or. App. 1133, 569 P.2d 662 (1977); defense not available, *Commonwealth v. Koons* and *Butterfield v. State, supra* note, p. 558.

4. A defendant charged with unlawful possession of marijuana admitted the elements of the charge and presented evidence that he suffered from glaucoma, a disease of the eyes. Marijuana smoke alleviated his symptoms. Conventional medication had become ineffective and surgery involved risk of blindness. The Superior Court of the District of Columbia held that use of marijuana was a medical necessity and dismissed the charge. In a subsequent case the court extended the defense to a glaucoma victim who grew and used marijuana. Note, *Medical Necessity as a Defense to Criminal Liability: United States v. Randall,* 46 GEO. WASH. L. REV. 273 (1978).

These cases illustrate that the common law requirement that immediate harm be threatened relates to the existence of alternatives. The action was justified even though there was no medical emergency because the action taken was the only practical response to avoid an inevitable adverse result. Compare the claim by drug addicts of "pharmacological duress" in the context of robberies committed to obtain funds to procure more narcotics, thus avoiding withdrawal symptoms. The defense of duress was rejected in *Love v. State*, 393 N.E.2d 178 (Ind. 1979). See also *Castle v. United States*, 347 F.2d 492 (D.C. Cir. 1964), *cert. denied*, 381 U.S. 929 (1965) (jury could consider drug dependency in context of "mental disease or defect" under insanity defense; pharmacological duress issue was not properly preserved for appeal).

STATE v. DORSEY

Supreme Court of New Hampshire
118 N.H. 844, 395 A.2d 855 (1978)

GRIMES, JUSTICE.

The issue we decide in this criminal trespass case is whether the trial court erred in ruling that the statutory defense of competing harms, RSA 627:3, is not available to one charged with criminal trespass for occupying the construction site of a nuclear power plant. We hold that no error was committed.

Defendant was arrested during a mass occupation of the construction site of the Seabrook Nuclear Power Plant. He was charged with criminal trespass, RSA 635:2, elected to represent himself, and was tried before a jury, and convicted.

. . . .

The trial court was correct in ruling that the competing harms defense did not apply to this case. RSA 627:3 I reads in part as follows:

> Conduct which the actor believes to be necessary to avoid harm to himself or another is justifiable if the desirability and urgency of avoiding such harm outweigh, according to ordinary standards of reasonableness, the harm sought to be prevented by the statute defining the offense charged....

It establishes a statutory defense akin to the common-law defense of necessity.... These and other early cases elsewhere deal with simple situations, such as killing mink out of season to protect valuable geese, and keeping a child from school without permission because of serious illness. They, like the classic situations contained in the comments to RSA 627:3, relate to factual matters that laymen sitting as a jury have the competence to decide. They deal with dangers that the average person can recognize and about which there can be no dispute.

RSA 627:3 "is based largely on N.Y. § 35.05(a) and states what the Model Penal Code calls the 'choice of evils' doctrine." Report of the Commission to Recommend Codification of Criminal Laws § 572:3 at 19 (1969).

The pertinent comment to the Model Penal Code states that for the defense to be available, the issue of competing values must not have been foreclosed by a deliberate legislative choice. Model Penal Code § 3.02, Comment No. 1 (Tent. Draft Nos. 8, 19). In the context of the present dispute, however, both the legislature of the State and the Congress of the United States have made deliberate choices regarding nuclear power.... [Congress] established an Energy Facility Evaluation Committee to determine, among other things, whether any proposed site and facility will "unduly interfere with ... the public health and safety." [State legislation] mandates that "undue delay in construction of any needed facilities be avoided." Having spoken so forcefully in support of nuclear power, it is inconceivable that the legislature would intend that nuclear power be considered such a harm as to justify individuals in breaking the law. We are confident that it was not intended that such matters be included within the scope of RSA 627:3.

Nor were matters of this sort contemplated under the common-law defense of necessity. The common-law defense dealt with imminent dangers from obvious and generally recognized harms. It did not deal with nonimminent or debatable harms; nor did it deal with activities that the legislative branch of government had expressly sanctioned and found not to be harms. See G. Williams, Criminal Law: The General Part § 232, at 729 (2d ed. 1961) and cases cited therein. To allow nuclear power plants to be considered a danger or harm within the meaning of that defense either at common law or under the statute would require lay jurors to determine in individual cases matters of State and national policy in a very technical field. Competing factions would produce extensive expert testimony on the danger or lack of danger of nuclear power plants, and jurors in each case would then be asked to decide issues already determined by the legislature. The competing harms statute is intended to deal only with harms that are readily apparent and recognizable to the average juror.

Defendant and others who oppose nuclear power have other lawful means of protesting nuclear power; therefore, they are not justified in breaking the law. LaFave and Scott, Criminal Law § 50, at 387 (1972). The act of criminal trespass was a deliberate and calculated choice and not an act that was urgently necessary to avoid a clear and imminent danger.

....

Exception overruled.

NOTES ON LIMITATIONS ON THE DEFENSE OF NECESSITY

1. The defense is generally not allowed where defendant's motive in violating the law is based on moral grounds or on a protest against a statute. *United States v. Simpson*, 460 F.2d 515 (9th Cir. 1972); *State v. Marley*, 54 Hawaii 450, 509 P.2d 1095 (1973). Attempts to raise the defense have generally been unsuccessful against charges growing out of protests such as those at military installations against nuclear policy, *see United States v. Kabat*, 797 F. 2d 580 (8th Cir. 1986), *cert. denied*, 481 U.S. 1030 (1987), and at abortion clinics, *see State v. Sahr*, 470 N.W. 2d 185 (N.D. 1991) and *State v. Clowes*, 310 Or. 686, 801 P.2d 789 (1990).

2. It is not uncommon to preclude the defense when defendant's actions were made necessary by his or her own negligence or recklessness, or where otherwise he or she could have avoided the situation. *State v. Johnson*, 289 Minn. 196, 183 N.W.2d 541 (1971). Sullivan, *infra* p. 562, at 347 n. 57.

3. The defense of necessity should be distinguished from cases where a force of nature intervenes directly and causes certain consequences without any conscious decision or action of the defendant. For example, if a ship is blown off course during a storm and enters a prohibited area this is not a case which

evokes the defense of necessity, but rather a claim of lack of *actus reus*. If the captain ordered the ship to make for the prohibited area to avoid the storm, the defense of necessity is appropriate. J. HALL, GENERAL PRINCIPLES OF CRIMINAL LAW 421-25 (1960).

PROBLEMS

1. Defendant has been charged with carrying a concealed deadly weapon. May he assert necessity on the ground that he lives in a high crime area and carries it for his own protection? Would your answer be different if defendant had recently been robbed and beaten? Finally, suppose defendant had been threatened with death or serious injury by a neighborhood thug who previously had been convicted of serious assaults and was known to carry a gun. Does the right of self-defense together with the inability of police to provide adequate protection justify arming oneself? The answer is "yes" and grounded in the Constitution according to Cottrol And Diamond, *The Second Amendment: Toward an Afro-Americanist Reconsideration*, 80 GEO. L. REV. 309 (1991).

The authors observe: "today the state seems powerless in the face of the tragic black-on-black violence that plagues the mean streets of our inner cities, and at times seems blind to instances of unnecessary police brutality visited upon minority populations." *Id.* at 359-360 (footnote reference is to the beating of Rodney King in Los Angeles, March 3, 1991). The authors conclude "that a society with a dismal record of protecting a people has a dubious claim on the right to disarm them." *Id.* at 361.

2. Defendant was charged with "welfare fraud" by failing to report earned income. She offered the defense of necessity supported by three experts. Both a doctor and nurse testified that her children suffered from malnutritional deficiencies because of a lack of resources. An economist testified as to the inadequacy of the welfare payments and of the loss of buying power for welfare recipients. Should the trial court instruct on "necessity"? The case is discussed in Sullivan, *The Defense of Necessity in Texas: Legislative Invention Come of Age*, 16 HOUS. L. REV. 333, 346 (1979).

During the depression of the 1930s, a group of unemployed people met with officials and demanded more food. When their request was refused they went to a local store and took some food. Held: "economic necessity has never been accepted as a defense to a criminal charge." *State v. Moe*, 174 Wash. 303, 24 P.2d 638, 640 (1933). *Accord Harris v. State*, 486 S.W.2d 573 (Tex. Crim. App. 1972).

SECTION VI. Duress*

STATE v. HUNTER

Supreme Court of Kansas
241 Kan. 629, 740 P.2d 559 (1987)

LOCKETT, JUSTICE.

---

*The terms "duress," "coercion" and "compulsion" are used interchangeably by courts and commentators.

VI. DURESS

Defendant James C. Hunter appeals his convictions of two counts of felony murder, two counts of aggravated kidnapping, one count of aggravated robbery, one count of aggravated battery on a law enforcement officer, and one count of aggravated battery. Hunter raises numerous issues, among them that the trial judge committed reversible error by refusing Hunter's requested instruction on his defense of compulsion. We reverse and remand for a new trial.

[While hitchhiking Hunter got a ride with Mark Walters, Lisa Dunn and Daniel Remata. During the drive, Remata displayed two weapons, a .357 Magnum and a .22 pistol, and fired the .22 out of the car window several times. At one point when Hunter asked unsuccessfully to be let out of the car, Remata told of a prior hitchhiker he wished he had killed.

Later, a police car driven by Undersheriff Albright stopped the car. One of the passengers exited, fired several shots at and wounded Albright. The group drove on and later stopped at a grain elevator in Levant, Kansas where they seized a pickup truck and two hostages. Remata shot one person there and later killed the two hostages. The police eventually captured Remata, Dunn and Hunter after a shoot-out in which Walters was killed.]

....

Hunter contends that the trial court committed reversible error by refusing to instruct the jury on his defense of compulsion. We agree. K.S.A. 21-3209 provides for the defense of compulsion to crimes other than murder or manslaughter, stating:

(1) A person is not guilty of a crime other than murder or voluntary manslaughter by reason of conduct which he performs under the compulsion or threat of the imminent infliction of death or great bodily harm, if he reasonably believes that death or great bodily harm will be inflicted upon him or upon his spouse, parent, child, brother or sister if he does not perform such conduct.

(2) The defense provided by this section is not available to one who willfully or wantonly places himself in a situation in which it is probable that he will be subjected to compulsion or threat.

Defendant's requested instruction, taken from PIK Crim. 2d 54.13, stated:

It is a defense to the charges of Aggravated Battery Against a Law Enforcement Officer, Aggravated Robbery and Aggravated Kidnapping, if the defendant acted under compulsion or threat of immediate infliction of death or great bodily harm, and if said defendant reasonably believed that death or great bodily harm would have been inflicted upon said defendant had he or she not acted as he or she did.

The trial court refused to give the compulsion instruction because the defendant was charged with premeditated and felony murder. The judge was unsure if the instruction was applicable where an individual is charged under the felony-murder rule, but determined that one who aids and abets felony murder is not entitled to the instruction.

Whether the defense of compulsion is available to a criminal defendant charged with felony murder under K.S.A. 21-3401 is an issue of first impression. Most modern statutes providing for a defense of compulsion evolved from the common-law policy that a person, when faced with a choice between suffering death or serious bodily harm and committing some lesser crime, could not be punished for committing the lesser offense. LaFave and Scott have explained the rationale of this "choice of evils" approach as follows:

> "One who, under the pressure of an unlawful threat from another human being to harm him (or to harm a third person), commits what would otherwise be a crime may, under some circumstances, be justified in doing what he did and thus not be guilty of the crime in question.... The rationale of the defense is not that the defendant, faced with the unnerving threat of harm unless he does an act which violates the literal language of the criminal law, somehow loses his mental capacity to commit the crime in question. Rather it is that, even though he has the mental state which the crime requires, his conduct which violates the literal language of the criminal law is justified because he has thereby avoided harm of greater magnitude." LaFave and Scott, Handbook on Criminal Law 374 (1972).

However, even early cases refused to recognize any compulsion as sufficient to excuse intentional killing. See *Arp v. State*, 97 Ala. 5, 12 So. 301 (1893); *State v. Nargashian*, 26 R.I. 299, 58 A. 953 (1904). The rationale is that, when confronted by a choice between two evils of equal magnitude, the individual ought to sacrifice his own life rather than escape by the murder of an innocent. See Perkins, Criminal Law 951 (1969), citing 4 Blackstone, Commentaries 30.

A number of jurisdictions, including Kansas, have incorporated by statute the common-law denial of the compulsion defense in crimes of murder. See e.g. Ariz. Rev. Stat. Ann. § 13-412 (1978); Colo. Rev. Stat. § 18-1-708 (1986); Ga. Code Ann. § 16-3-26 (1984); Ind. Code Ann. § 35-41-3-8 (Burns 1985); Ky. Rev. Stat. Ann. § 501.090 (Michie 1985); Me. Rev. Stat. Ann. tit. 17-A, § 103-A (1983); Mo. Rev. Stat. § 562.071 (1986); Or. Rev. Stat. § 161.270 (1985); Wash. Rev. Code § 9A.16.060 (1985). While not all jurisdictions have considered the applicability of these statutes to crimes of felony murder, we note that both Arizona and Missouri have held that defendants are barred from claiming the compulsion defense in felony-murder cases. They reason that the person charged need only have the required intent to commit or participate in the underlying felony and no other mental state on his part need be demonstrated because of the strict liability imposed by the felony-murder rule. See *State v. Berndt*, 138 Ariz. 41, 672 P.2d 1311 (1983); *State v. Rumble*, 680 S.W.2d 939 (Mo. 1984).

We are not, however, persuaded by the reasoning of these decisions. The better view, consistently adhered to by commentators, is that any limitation to the defense of duress be confined to crimes of intentional killing and not to killings done by another during the commission of some lesser felony. As LaFave and Scott have explained:

> "[I]f *A* compels *B* at gunpoint to drive him to the bank which *A* intends to rob, and during the ensuing robbery *A* kills a bank customer *C*, *B* is not

guilty of the robbery (for he was justified by duress) and so is not guilty of felony murder of C in the commission of robbery. The law properly recognizes that one is justified in aiding a robbery if he is forced by threats to do so to save his life; he should not lose the defense because his threateners unexpectedly kill someone in the course of the robbery and thus convert a mere robbery into a murder." p. 377.

See Perkins at 952; accord Hitchler, *Duress as a Defense in Criminal Cases*, 4 Va. L. Rev. 519, 528-30 (1917).

This reasoning was adopted in *Tully v. State*, 730 P.2d 1206 (Okla. 1986), where the Court of Criminal Appeals of Oklahoma recently held that the defense of compulsion was available to a defendant charged with first-degree felony murder. *Tully* involved a defendant who allegedly was compelled to rob a man fatally beaten by Tully's threatener. The trial court refused defendant's requested instruction on compulsion, and on appeal the State argued that the defense was foreclosed in cases of felony murder. The Oklahoma court disagreed, reversed defendant's conviction, and remanded for a new trial.

While Oklahoma does not statutorily preclude the compulsion defense in murder cases, the Oklahoma court found that, although the common law proscribes the defense of compulsion in cases of intentional killing, the defense should attach where the defendant commits the underlying felony and not the killing, as long as the defendant has reason to believe his life is in danger unless he participates. 730 P.2d at 1210. We agree and believe that the limitation to the use of the compulsion defense is restricted to crimes of intentional killing and that, where compulsion is a defense to an underlying felony under K.S.A. 21-3209 so that the felony is justifiable, compulsion is equally a defense to charges of felony murder.

....

In order to constitute the defense of compulsion, the coercion or duress must be present, imminent, and impending, and of such a nature as to induce a well-grounded apprehension of death or serious bodily injury if the act is not done. The doctrine of coercion or duress cannot be invoked as an excuse by one who had a reasonable opportunity to avoid doing the act without undue exposure to death or serious bodily harm. *State v. Milum*, 213 Kan. 581, 582, 516 P.2d 984 (1973). In addition, the compulsion must be continuous and there must be no reasonable opportunity to escape the compulsion without committing the crime. *State v. Myers*, 233 Kan. at 616.

The only opportunity Hunter would have had for escape would have been when he was out of sight of Remeta at the point when he went around the north side of the building at the Levant elevator. Hunter testified that Remeta came around the building and ordered him to return to the pickup. There was testimony that the total time which elapsed at the grain elevator was approximately five minutes. From the record, it is impossible to tell how long Hunter remained out of sight of Remeta. Viewed in the light most favorable to Hunter, however, and particularly in light of the fact that it was undisputed that Remeta had possession of the .357 Magnum at all times, it cannot be said that Hunter had a reasonable opportunity to escape.

....

Here, the record is replete with testimony that Daniel Remeta was a person to be feared. It was the function of the jury as the exclusive trier of fact to determine if it was believable that Hunter was afraid for his life, if such fear was reasonable, and if such fear justified any criminal acts which Hunter may have performed. When the trial judge refused the requested compulsion instruction, he effectively prevented the jury from considering the evidence presented in Hunter's defense. This denial of the jury's right to determine the facts constitutes reversible error. We reverse and remand this case for a new trial in accordance with this opinion....

NOTES

1. The Model Penal Code and states which have similar statutes have departed from the common law by not denying necessity or duress as a defense even when defendant has taken the life of an innocent person. See MODEL PENAL CODE § 2.09 (Appendix A). Dennis, *Duress, Murder and Criminal Responsibility*, 96 L. Q. REV. 208, 220-28 (1980).

2. In England, the House of Lords held by a 3-2 vote in 1975 that a defendant charged with murder as an aider and abettor should not be precluded, as a matter of law, from relying on the defense of duress. *Lynch v. D.P.P. for Northern Ireland*, [1975] 1 All E.R. 913. Defendant claimed that he was forced by members of the I.R.A. to steal a car and then drive them to a place where they killed a police officer. He knew they intended to kill the policeman but said he was afraid they would kill him if he refused to comply.

The following year, the Privy Counsel determined that as a matter of law the defense of duress was not available to a principal in the first degree to murder, i.e., one who actually did the killing. *Abbott v. The Queen*, [1976] 3 All E.R. 140. Later in *R. v. Howe*, [1987] 1 All E.R. 771, the House of Lords reversed *Lynch*.

STATE v. TOSCANO

Supreme Court of New Jersey
74 N.J. 421, 378 A.2d 755 (1977)

PASHMAN, JUDGE.

Defendant Joseph Toscano was convicted of conspiring to obtain money by false pretenses in violation of N.J.S.A. 2A:98-1. Although admitting that he had aided in the preparation of a fraudulent insurance claim by making out a false medical report, he argued that he had acted under duress. The trial judge ruled that the threatened harm was not sufficiently imminent to justify charging the jury on the defense of duress. After the jury returned a verdict of guilty, the defendant was fined $500.

The Appellate Division affirmed the conviction.... It stressed that defendant had ample opportunity between the time of the threat and the commission of the allegedly coerced act to report the matter to the police or to avoid participation in the conspiracy altogether. Relying on *State v. Churchill*, 105 N.J.L. 123, 143 A. 330 (E. & A. 1928) and *State v. Palmieri*, 93 N.J.L. 195, 107 A. 407 (E. & A. 1919), it also concluded that defendant failed to satisfy the threshold condition that the threatened harm be "present, imminent and impending."

We granted certification to consider the status of duress as an affirmative defense to a crime.... We hold that duress is an affirmative defense to a crime other than murder, and that it need not be based upon an alleged threat of immediate bodily injury. Under the standard announced today, we find that this defendant did allege sufficient facts to warrant charging the jury on his claim of duress. Accordingly, we reverse his conviction and remand for a new trial.

....

III

Since New Jersey has no applicable statute defining the defense of duress,[6] we are guided only by common law principles which conform to the purposes of our criminal justice system and reflect contemporary notions of justice and fairness ....

At common law the defense of duress was recognized only when the alleged coercion involved a use or threat of harm which is "present, imminent and pending" and "of such a nature as to induce a well grounded apprehension of death or serious bodily harm if the act is not done."

....

It was commonly said that duress does not excuse the killing of an innocent person even if the accused acted in response to immediate threats.[7] ... Aside from this exception, however, duress was permitted as a defense to prosecution for a range of serious offenses, see e.g.... [Cases which involved the crimes of treason, kidnapping, cited.]

To excuse a crime, the threatened injury must induce "such a fear as a man of ordinary fortitude and courage might justly yield to." ... Although there are scattered suggestions in early cases that only a fear of death meets this test, ...[8] an apprehension of immediate serious bodily harm has been considered sufficient to excuse capitulation to threats.... Thus, the courts have assumed as a matter of law that neither threats of slight injury nor threats of destruction to property are coercive enough to overcome the will of a person of ordinary courage....

---

[6] The majority of states have no statutory provision defining duress. For a discussion of the statutory sections of the 20 states which have enacted laws on the subject, see Model Penal Code, (MPC) § 2.09, Comment 1 at 2-4. (Tent. Draft No. 10, 1960).

[7] The broad assertion that duress is unavailable as a defense to homicide appears repeatedly in the cases and treatises, but several commentators have observed that the decisions have involved murder as opposed to manslaughter. In repeating this adage, moreover, courts have typically gone on to stress the opportunities for resistance or escape. See Hitchler, *Duress as a Defense in Criminal Cases*, 4 Va.L.Rev. 519, 528 (1917); Hall, General Principles of Criminal Law, 525 (1947). The Model Penal Code draftsmen point out that duress instructions have sometimes been given in murder cases. Model Penal Code, § 2.09. Comment 1, at 4 n. 24. (Tent. Draft No. 10, 1960).

[8] Several states, by statute, continue to require that the actor have reasonable cause to believe that his life was in danger. See, e.g., Arizona Rev.Stat.Ann., Tit. 13-134 (1956); Arkansas Stat.Ann. § 41-117 (1947); Deering's California Penal Code § 26(8) (1960); Colorado Rev.Stat.Ann. Ch. 40-1-11 (1960); Idaho Code, § 18-101 (1947); Montana Rev.Code Ann., Tit. 94-201 (1947). Minnesota limits the defense to situations in which "instant death" is threatened. Minn.Stat. 609.08 (1965).

A "generalized fear of retaliation" by an accomplice, unrelated to any specific threat, is also insufficient....

More commonly, the defense of duress has not been allowed because of the lack of immediate danger to the threatened person. When the alleged source of coercion is a threat of "future harm," courts have generally found that the defendant had a duty to escape from the control of the threatening person or to seek assistance from law enforcement authorities ....

Assuming a "present, imminent and impending" danger, however, there is no requirement that the threatened person be the accused. Although not explicitly resolved by the early cases, recent decisions have assumed that concern for the well-being of another, particularly a near relative, can support a defense of duress if the other requirements are satisfied. See *United States v. Gordon*, 526 F.2d 406 (9th Cir. 1975) (friends imperiled); *United States v. Stevison*, 471 F.2d 143 (7th Cir. 1972) (suicide threat by defendant's daughter); *Hood v. State*, 313 N.E.2d 546 (Ind.App. 1974); *Kootz v. State*, 204 So.2d 224 (Fla.App. 1967) (threats to mother and sister); cf. *State v. Gann*, [N.D., 244 N.W.2d 746 (1976)] (need to support family).

....

The insistence under the common law on a danger of immediate force causing death or serious bodily injury may be ascribed to its origins in early cases dealing with treason, *see, e.g., Respublica v. M'Carty*, [2 U.S. 86, 2 Dall. 86 1 L.Ed. 300 (Pa.Supr.Ct. 1781)]; *Rex v. McGrowther*, 168 Eng.Rep. 8 (1746), to the proclivities of a "tougher-minded age," *R. I. Recreation Center v. Aetna Casualty & Surety Co.*, [177 F.2d 603, 605 (1st Cir. 1949)], or simply to judicial fears of perjury and fabrication of baseless defenses. We do not discount the latter concern as a reason for caution in modifying this accepted rule, but we are concerned by its obvious shortcomings and potential for injustice. Under some circumstances, the commission of a minor criminal offense should be excusable even if the coercive agent does not use or threaten force which is likely to result in death or "serious" bodily injury. Similarly, it is possible that authorities might not be able to prevent a threat of future harm from eventually being carried out. As shown by *Commonwealth v. Reffitt*, [149 Ky. 300, 148 S.W. 48 (1912)], and *Hall v. State*, [136 Fla. 644, 187 So. 392 (1939)], the courts have not wholly disregarded the predicament of an individual who reasonably believes that appeals for assistance from law enforcement officials will be unavailing, but there has been no widespread acknowledgement of such an exception.... Warnings of future injury or death will be all the more powerful if the prospective victim is another person, such as a spouse or child, whose safety means more to the threatened person than his own wellbeing. Finally, as the drafters of the Model Penal Code observed, "long and wasting pressure may break down resistance more effectively than a threat of immediate destruction." § 2.09, Comment at 8 (Tent. Draft No. 10, 1960).

Commentators have expressed dissatisfaction with the common law standard of duress. Stephen viewed the defense as a threat to the deterrent function of the criminal law, and argued that "it is at the moment when temptation is strongest that the law should speak most clearly and emphatically to the contrary." Stephen, *2 History of the Criminal Law in England* 107 (1883). A modern refinement of this position is that the defense should be

VI. DURESS

designed to encourage persons to act against their self-interest if a substantial percentage of persons in such a situation would do so. Hall, *General Principles of Criminal Law* (2 ed. 1960), 446-47. This standard would limit its applicability to relatively minor crimes and exclude virtually all serious crimes unless committed under threat of imminent death.

Others have been more skeptical about the deterrent effects of a strict rule. As the Alabama Supreme Court observed in an early case:

> That persons have exposed themselves to imminent peril and death for their fellow man, and that there are instances where innocent persons have submitted to murderous assaults, and suffered death, rather than take life, is well established; but such self-sacrifices emanated from other motives than the fear of legal punishment. [*Arp. v. State*, [97 Ala. 5, 12, 12 So. 301, 303 (1893)].]

Building on this premise, some commentators have advocated a flexible rule which would allow a jury to consider whether the accused actually lost his capacity to act in accordance with "his own desire, or motivation, or will" under the pressure of real or imagined forces. See Newman & Weitzer, "Duress, Free Will and the Criminal Law," 30 S.Cal.L.Rev. 313, 331 (1957); Fletcher, "The Individualization of Excusing Conditions," 47 S.Cal.L.Rev. 1269, 1288-93 (1974). The inquiry here would focus on the weaknesses and strengths of a particular defendant, and his subjective reaction to unlawful demands. Thus, the "standard of heroism" of the common law would give way, not to a "reasonable person" standard, but to a set of expectations based on the defendant's character and situation....

The drafters of the Model Penal Code and the [proposed] New Jersey Penal Code sought to steer a middle course between these two positions by focusing on whether the standard imposed upon the accused was one with which "normal members of the community will be able to comply...." They stated: "... law is ineffective in the deepest sense, indeed it is hypocritical, if it imposes on the actor who has the misfortune to confront a dilemmatic choice, a standard that his judges are not prepared to affirm that they should and could comply with if their turn to face the problem should arise. Condemnation in such case is bound to be an ineffective threat; what is, however, more significant is that it is divorced from any moral base and is unjust. Where it would be both 'personally and socially debilitating' to accept the actor's cowardice as a defense, it would be equally debilitating to demand that heroism be the standard of legality." [Model Penal Code § 2.09, Comment at 7 (Tent. Draft No. 10, 1960), quoting Hart, "The Aims of the Criminal Law," 23 *Law & Contemp. Prob.* 401, 414 and n. 31 (1958); *New Jersey Model Penal Code* § 2C:2-9, Commentary at 71 (1971).]

Thus, they proposed that a court limit its consideration of an accused's "situation" to "stark, tangible factors which differentiate the actor from another, like his size or strength or age or health," excluding matters of temperament. They substantially departed from the existing statutory and common law limitations requiring that the result be death or serious bodily harm, that the threat be immediate and aimed at the accused, or that the crime committed be a non-capital offense. While these factors would be given evidential weight, the failure to satisfy one or more of these conditions would not justify the trial judge's withholding the defense from the jury. *Model Penal Code, supra*, at 7-8; *New Jersey Penal Code, supra*, at 71.

....

For reasons suggested above, ... a per se rule based on immediate injury may exclude valid claims of duress by persons for whom resistance to threats or resort to official protection was not realistic. While we are hesitant to approve a rule which would reward citizens who fail to make such efforts, we are not persuaded that capitulation to unlawful demands is excusable only when there is a "gun at the head" of the defendant. We believe that the better course is to leave the issue to the jury with appropriate instructions from the judge.

....

Exercising our authority to revise the common law, *cf. Faber v. Creswick*, 31 N.J. 234, 241, 156 A.2d 252 (1959); we have decided to adopt this approach as the law of New Jersey. Henceforth, duress shall be a defense to a crime other than murder if the defendant engaged in conduct because he was coerced to do so by the use of, or threat to use, unlawful force against his person or the person of another, which a person of reasonable firmness in his situation would have been unable to resist.

....

IV

Defendant's conviction of conspiracy to obtain money by false pretenses is hereby reversed and remanded for a new trial.

....

NOTE

Accord Regina v. Hudson & Taylor, [1971] 2 All E.R. 244. Defendants, two teenage girls, witnessed a fight in a pub. Before the trial of the combatants the girls were approached by a group of men and told that they would be "cut up" if they told on one of the men who was involved in the fight. They decided to lie in court to avoid being physically injured after the trial. At their trial for perjury, the recorder (trial judge) told the jury that the defense of duress was not available because there was no threat of immediate injury and because they could have sought police protection. Reversed:

> When ... there is no opportunity for delaying tactics, and the person threatened must make up his mind whether he is to commit the criminal act or not, the existence at that moment of threats sufficient to destroy his will ought to provide him with a defence even though the threatened injury may not follow instantly, but after an interval.

Id. at 247. As to police protection, the court of appeals said:

> The argument does not distinguish cases in which the police would be able to provide effective protection from those when they would not, and it would, in effect, restrict the defence of duress to cases where the person

threatened had been kept in custody by the maker of the threats, or where the time interval between the making of the threats and the commission of the offence had made recourse to the police impossible. We recognise the need to keep the defence of duress within reasonable bounds but cannot accept so severe a restriction on it.

Id. at 247.

UNITED STATES v. BAILEY

United States Supreme Court
444 U.S. 394 (1980)

MR. JUSTICE REHNQUIST delivered the opinion of the court.

In the early morning hours of August 26, 1976, respondents Clifford Bailey, James T. Cogdell, Ronald C. Cooley, and Ralph Walker, federal prisoners at the District of Columbia Jail, crawled through a window from which a bar had been removed, slid down a knotted bed sheet, and escaped from custody. Federal authorities recaptured them after they had remained at large for a period of time ranging from one month to three and one-half months. Upon their apprehension, they were charged with violating 18 U.S.C. § 751(a), which governs escape from federal custody.[1] At their trials, each of the respondents adduced or offered to adduce evidence as to various conditions and events at the District of Columbia Jail, but each was convicted by the jury. The Court of Appeals for the District of Columbia Circuit reversed the convictions by a divided vote, holding that the District Court had improperly precluded consideration by the respective juries of respondents' tendered evidence. We granted certiorari, and now reverse the judgments of the Court of Appeals.

....

The prosecution's case-in-chief against Bailey, Cooley, and Walker was brief. The Government introduced evidence that each of the respondents was in federal custody on August 26, 1976, that they had disappeared, apparently through a cell window, at approximately 5:35 a. m. on that date, and that they had been apprehended individually between September 27 and December 13, 1976.

Respondents' defense of duress or necessity centered on the conditions in the jail during the months of June, July, and August 1976, and on various threats and beatings directed at them during that period. In describing the conditions at the jail, they introduced evidence of frequent fires in "Northeast One," the maximum-security cellblock occupied by respondents prior to their escape. Construed in the light most favorable to them, this evidence demonstrated

---

[1]Title 18 U.S.C. § 751(a) provides:

Whoever escapes or attempts to escape from the custody of the Attorney General or his authorized representatives, or from an institution or facility in which he is confined by direction of the Attorney General, or from any custody under or by virtue of any process issued under the laws of the United States by any court, judge or magistrate, or from the custody of an officer or employee of the United States pursuant to lawful arrest, shall, if the custody or confinement is by virtue of an arrest on a charge of felony, or conviction of any offense, be fined not more than $5,000 or imprisoned not more than five years or both; or if the custody or confinement is for extradition or by virtue of an arrest or charge of or for a misdemeanor, and prior to conviction, be fined not more than $1,000 or imprisoned not more than one year, or both.

that the inmates of Northeast One, and on occasion the guards in that unit, set fire to trash, bedding, and other objects thrown from the cells. According to the inmates, the guards simply allowed the fires to burn until they went out. Although the fires apparently were confined to small areas and posed no substantial threat of spreading through the complex, poor ventilation caused smoke to collect and linger in the cellblock.

Respondents Cooley and Bailey also introduced testimony that the guards at the jail had subjected them to beatings and to threats of death. Walker attempted to prove that he was an epileptic and had received inadequate medical attention for his seizures.

....

[A majority of the court of appeals had held that "intent to escape confinement" was an element of the offense. That majority said defendants who introduce evidence of violence, threats of violence, or other dangerous conditions which are beyond lawful conditions of confinement are entitled to an instruction to the effect that the jury must decide whether defendants escaped to avoid confinement or whether they escaped to avoid only the adverse, "non-confinement" conditions. If the latter, the defendants would not have had the intent to leave custody voluntarily with intent to avoid "confinement." On the separate issue of the duress-necessity defense the court also held that the trial court erred by refusing to give a duress instruction where there was no evidence to show that the defendants had returned or offered to return to custody once they were out of immediate danger. *United States v. Bailey*, 585 F.2d 1087 (D.C. Cir. 1978) — Eds.]

II

A

The majority of the Court of Appeals, ... imposed the added burden on the prosecution to prove as a part of its case-in-chief that respondents acted "with an intent to avoid confinement." ... [T]he majority left little doubt that it was requiring the government to prove that the respondents acted with the purpose — that is, the conscious objective — of leaving the jail without authorization. In a footnote explaining their holding, for example, the majority specified that an escapee did not act with the requisite intent if he escaped in order to avoid "non-confinement conditions" as opposed to "normal aspects of 'confinement.'" 190 U.S.App.D.C., at 148, 585 F.2d, at 1093, n.17.

We find the majority's position quite unsupportable. Nothing in the language or legislative history of § 751(a) indicates that Congress intended to require either such a heightened standard of culpability or such a narrow definition of confinement. As we stated earlier, the cases have generally held that, except in narrow classes of offenses, proof that the defendant acted knowingly is sufficient to support a conviction. Accordingly, we hold that the prosecution fulfills its burden under § 751(a) if it demonstrates that an escapee knew his actions would result in his leaving physical confinement without permission.

....

B

Respondents also contend that they are entitled to a new trial because they presented (or, in Cogdell's case, could have presented) sufficient evidence of duress or necessity to submit such a defense to the jury.

....

We need not decide whether such evidence as that submitted by respondents was sufficient to raise a jury question as to their initial departures. This is because we decline to hold that respondents' failure to return is "just one factor" for the jury to weigh in deciding whether the initial escape could be affirmatively justified. On the contrary, several considerations lead us to conclude that, in order to be entitled to an instruction on duress or necessity as a defense to the crime charged, an escapee must first offer evidence justifying his continued absence from custody as well as his initial departure and that an indispensable element of such an offer is testimony of a bona fide effort to surrender or return to custody as soon as the claimed duress or necessity had lost its coercive force.

... [W]e think it clear beyond peradventure that escape from federal custody as defined in § 751(a) is a continuing offense and that an escapee can be held liable for failure to return to custody as well as for his initial departure. Given the continuing threat to society posed by an escaped prisoner, "the nature of the crime involved is such that Congress must assuredly have intended that it be treated as a continuing one." *Toussie v. United States*, 397 U.S. 112, 115, 90 S.Ct. 858, 860, 25 L.Ed.2d 156 (1970).

....

We therefore hold that, where a criminal defendant is charged with escape and claims that he is entitled to an instruction on the theory of duress or necessity, he must proffer evidence of a bona fide effort to surrender or return to custody as soon as the claimed duress or necessity had lost its coercive force. We have reviewed the evidence examined elaborately in the majority and dissenting opinions below, and find the case not even close, even under respondents' versions of the facts, as to whether they either surrendered or offered to surrender at their earliest possible opportunity. Since we have determined that this is an indispensable element of the defense of duress or necessity, respondents were not entitled to any instruction on such a theory. Vague and necessarily self-serving statements of defendants or witnesses as to future good intentions or ambiguous conduct simply do not support a finding of this element of the defense.

Reversed.

MR. JUSTICE BLACKMUN, with whom MR. JUSTICE BRENNAN joins, dissenting.

....

II

The real question presented in this case is whether the prisoner should be punished for helping to extricate himself from a situation where society has abdicated completely its basic responsibility for providing an environment free of life-threatening conditions such as beatings, fires, lack of essential medical care, and sexual attacks. To be sure, Congress in so many words has not enacted specific statutory duress or necessity defenses that would excuse or justify commission of an otherwise unlawful act. The concept of such a defense, however, is "anciently woven into the fabric of our culture." J. Hall, General Principles of Criminal Law 416 (2d ed. 1960), quoted in Brief for United States 21. And the Government concedes that "it has always been an accepted part of our criminal justice system that punishment is inappropriate for crimes committed under duress because the defendant in such circumstances cannot fairly be blamed for his wrongful act." *Id.*, at 23.

. . . .

I, too, conclude that the jury generally should be instructed that, in order to prevail on a necessity or duress defense, the defendant must justify his continued absence from custody, as well as his initial departure. I agree with the Court that the very nature of escape makes it a continuing crime. But I cannot agree that the only way continued absence can be justified is evidence "of a bona fide effort to surrender or return to custody." *Ante* at 636, 637. The Court apparently entertains the view, naive in my estimation, that once the prisoner has escaped from a life or health-threatening situation, he can turn himself in, secure in the faith that his escape somehow will result in improvement in those intolerable prison conditions. While it may be true in some rare circumstance that an escapee will obtain the aid of a court or of the prison administration once the escape is accomplished, the escapee, realistically, faces a high probability of being returned to the same prison and to exactly the same, or even greater, threats to life and safety.

The rationale of the necessity defense is a balancing of harms. If the harm caused by an escape is less than the harm caused by remaining in a threatening situation, the prisoner's initial departure is justified. The same rationale should apply to hesitancy and failure to return. A situation may well arise where the social balance weighs in favor of the prisoner even though he fails to return to custody. The escapee at least should be permitted to present to the jury the possibility that the harm that would result from a return to custody outweighs the harm to society from continued absence.

Even under the Court's own standard, the defendant in an escape prosecution should be permitted to submit evidence to the jury to demonstrate that surrender would result in his being placed again in a life or health-threatening situation. The Court requires return to custody once the "claimed duress or necessity had lost its coercive force." *Ante*, at 636, 637. Realistically, however, the escapee who reasonably believes that surrender will result in return to what concededly is an intolerable prison situation remains subject to the same "coercive force" that prompted his escape in the first instance. It is ironic to say that that force is automatically "lost" once the prison wall is passed.

NOTES

1. The respondents referred to their defense as one of "duress or necessity." Which defense were they raising? A hybrid? Does it matter? Dissenting in the

court of appeals decision in *United States v. Bailey,* 585 F.2d 1087 (D.C. Cir. 1978), Judge Wilkey observed:

> Necessity is usually distinguishable from duress because the emergency situation compelling a choice between evils is caused by forces of nature rather than coercion by other human beings. Some commentators have suggested that this is the only real difference between the defenses. Others claim that there are further conceptual differences between the two. Whether or not they are actually distinct, they have been hopelessly commingled in case law. The result has been the development of a hybrid defense — a "duress-necessity" defense — which retains the basic features of the duress defense, but which encompasses compulsion arising from natural forces in addition to coercion by other persons.

585 F.2d at 1111.

In statutory schemes which follow the MODEL PENAL CODE there is a major difference between duress and necessity. Section 3.02, Justification Generally, applies in "choice of evils" situations regardless of whether the situation is caused by natural forces or the coercive acts of another person. However, where defendant is coerced by another to cause harm under circumstances which satisfy the requirements of section 2.09, Duress, he or she has a defense, even though the harm inflicted may be greater than the harm avoided. Here, however, the coercion must be such as would overcome the resistance of a person of "reasonable firmness" taking into account factors such as size, strength, age, or health of the defendant, but not temperament. MODEL PENAL CODE comment at 7 (Tent. Draft No. 10, 1960).

2. The majority of the Supreme Court in *United States v. Bailey, supra,* used a fixed, uniform standard for evaluating the defense. The dissent argued for a more individualized approach such as is discussed in Fletcher, *The Individualization of Excusing Conditions,* 47 S. CAL. L. REV. 1269 (1974).

3. Where the defense of coercion fails it may be considered as a mitigating factor in sentencing, but it is not regarded as mitigating the degree of offense. *State v. Nargashian,* 26 R.I. 299, 58 A. 953 (1904). Stephen was of the view that it should only mitigate punishment. 2 J. STEPHEN, HISTORY OF THE CRIMINAL LAW 107 (1831). That mitigation of punishment should be the sole effect of duress was rejected by the Law Commission, Law Comm. Rep. No. 83, p. 13. The Commission proposed legislation similar to the MODEL PENAL CODE § 2.09.

4. As a general proposition a "necessity-duress" defense based on intolerable prison conditions has not been allowed in prison escape cases. The cases reiterate that for the defense to be applicable there must be threat of immediate death or serious injury and there must be no available alternative such as an appeal to prison officials. Gardner, *The Defense of Necessity and the Right to Escape from Prison — A Step Towards Incarceration Free from Sexual Assault,* 49 S. CAL. L. REV. 110 (1975). Fletcher, *Should Intolerable Prison Conditions Generate a Justification or an Excuse for Escape?,* 26 U.C.L.A. L. REV. 1355 (1978-79).

Some courts have allowed the defense to be submitted to the jury when defendants introduce evidence that they fled to avoid serious physical injury or homosexual assaults. *People v. Lovercamp*, 43 Cal. App. 3d 823, 118 Cal. Rptr. 110 (1974), set out the prerequisites for the defense which have been followed in other states. A limited defense is available if, "(1) The prisoner is faced with a specific threat of death, forcible sexual attack or substantial bodily injury in the immediate future; (2) there is no time for a complaint to the authorities or there exists a history of futile complaints which make any result from such complaints illusory; (3) there is no time or opportunity to resort to the courts; (4) there is no evidence of force or violence used towards prison personnel or other "innocent" persons in the escape; and (5) the prisoner immediately reports to the proper authorities when he has attained a position of safety from the immediate threat. 118 Cal. Rptr. at 115. Other courts which have recognized this defense have generally adopted these limitations. *See e.g., State v. Ottwell*, 784 P. 2d 402 (Mont. 1989); *People v. Hocquard*, 64 Mich. App. 331, 236 N.W. 2d 72 (1975).

NOTES ON COERCIVE PERSUASION (BRAINWASHING)

1. The celebrated Patty Hearst trial in 1975 presented, among other issues, the question of the legal effect, if any, that should be given to a claim by defendant that she had been coercively persuaded — "brainwashed" — into committing a robbery with a group of people who had kidnapped her ten weeks earlier. "Brainwashing" currently is not recognized as a defense.

> Simply stated, a true case of coercive persuasion cannot fit under the duress rubric. The coercive aspects of the indoctrination process may occur long before the commission of the crime for which the accused stands charged. At the time of the commission of the offense — i.e., the making of a false confession of war crimes, the recording of a propaganda broadcast, or the participation in a robbery — the defendant may be under no immediate duress. In such a case, the absence of the immediacy of threatened harm may prevent the defendant from even achieving an instruction by the court on duress.
>
> ....
>
> The central flaw in pairing an argument of "brainwashing" with a claim of duress is that the defense may be forced to argue inconsistent states of mind for the defendant at the time of the offense. The gist of the coercion and duress defense is that the defendant clearly perceives that the act is wrong but commits that act out of fear of consequences for herself if she does not act. In contrast, the basis of a defense of coercive "persuasion" or "impairment" secondary to "brainwashing" is that, due to a variety of factors, the defendant is incapable of perceiving that the act is wrong or is incapable of forming the requisite mental states of the crime.

Lunde & Wilson, *Brainwashing as a Defense to Criminal Liability: Patty Hearst Revisited*, 13 CRIM. L. BULL. 341, 358-59 (1977).

The authors of this article, one of whom was among the court-appointed psychiatrists in the case, concluded that brainwashing does not fit within either the mental defenses (insanity, unconsciousness, diminished responsibility) or duress and therefore should be considered as a factor in mitigation of punishment. *Id.* at 377.

2. A more radical approach is suggested by Delgado in *Ascription of Criminal States of Mind: Toward a Defense Theory for the Coercively Persuaded ("Brainwashed") Defendant*, 63 Minn. L. Rev. 1 (1978-79). The author proposes a defense of coercive persuasion when it is established that defendant's conduct was the proximate result of coercive persuasion and "exculpation is morally justified." He suggests that where all or many of the following factors are present defendants should be excused:

> a. The defendant's mental state results from unusual or abnormal influences....
>
> b. The induced mental state represents a sharp departure from the individual's ordinary mode of thinking....
>
> c. The state is one that is imposed on the subject....
>
> d. The criminal acts benefit the captors....
>
> e. The actor, when apprised of the manner in which he came to hold his beliefs, rejects them and sees them as inauthentic or foreign....
>
> f. The actor evidences symptoms typical of the coercively persuaded personality....

Id. at 19-20. The proposed "brainwashing" defense is criticized by Dressler in *Professor Delgado's "Brainwashing" Defense: Courting a Determinist Legal System*, 63 Minn. L. Rev. 335 (1978-79); and defended in Delgado, *A Response to Professor Dressler*, 63 Minn. L. Rev. 361 (1978-79). Such a defense was unsuccessfully raised in *Neely v. State*, 494 So. 2d 669, 677 and 682 (Ala. Cr. App. 1985), *affirmed* 494 So. 2d 697 (1985), *cert. denied*, 488 U.S. 1020 (1989).

SECTION VII. Entrapment

JACOBSON v. UNITED STATES

503 US —, 112 S. Ct. 1535 (1992)

[At a time when federal law did not prohibit such conduct, Jacobson ordered and received from a bookstore two magazines containing photographs of nude preteen and teenage boys. Later, Congress passed the Child Protection Act of 1984 (18 USCS §§ 2251 et seq.), which criminalized the receipt through the mails of sexually explicit depictions of children. While enforcing the act, postal inspectors found Jacobson's name on a bookstore mailing list. The Postal Service sought to explore Jacobson's willingness to place a mail order that would violate § 2252(a)(2)(A), by mailing him letters from three fictitious organizations — which letters discussed (1) protection and promotion of sexual freedom and freedom of choice, and (2) funding of lobbying efforts by catalog sales — and from a bogus pen pal who stated an interest in materials depicting the sexual activities of young men. Jacobson responded to the letters by answering questionnaires and expressing interest in the organizations' goals. Twenty-six months after the Postal Service had commenced sending the mail, the Customs Service, using the name of a fictitious organization, mailed him an advertisement for photographs of young boys engaging in sex, in response to which advertisement he placed an order that was never filled. The Postal Service, posing as yet another fictitious organization that sold sexually explicit materials, then mailed Jacobson a letter that called concerns about pornography hysterical nonsense and decried international censorship. After he ordered and received from this fictitious organization, through the mail, a pornographic magazine depicting young boys engaged in various sexual activities, Jacobson was arrested. A search of his home revealed the magazines bought from the bookstore and the materials sent by the government during its investigation, but did not discover any other materials indicating that he collected or was actively interested in child pornography.]

JUSTICE WHITE delivered the opinion of the Court.

....

There can be no dispute about the evils of child pornography or the difficulties that laws and law enforcement have encountered in eliminating it. See generally *Osborne v. Ohio*, 495 U.S. 103, 110, 110 S. Ct. 1691, 1696, 109 L. Ed. 2d 98 (1990); *New York v. Ferber*, 458 U.S. 747, 759-760, 102 S. Ct. 3348, 3355-3356, 73 L. Ed. 2d 1113 (1982). Likewise, there can be no dispute that the Government may use undercover agents to enforce the law. "It is well settled that the fact that officers or employees of the Government merely afford opportunities or facilities for the commission of the offense does not defeat the prosecution. Artifice and stratagem may be employed to catch those engaged in criminal enterprises." *Sorrells v. United States*, 287 U.S. 435, 441, 53 S. Ct. 210, 212, 77 L. Ed. 413 (1932); *Sherman v. United States*, 356 U.S., at 372, 78 S. Ct., at 820; *United States v. Russell*, 411 U.S. 423, 435-436, 93 S. Ct. 1637, 1644-1645, 36 L. Ed. 2d 366 (1973).

In their zeal to enforce the law, however, Government agents may not originate a criminal design, implant in an innocent person's mind the disposition to commit a criminal act, and then induce commission of the crime so that the Government may prosecute. *Sorrells, supra*, 287 U.S., at 442, 53 S. Ct. at 212; *Sherman, supra*, 356 U.S., at 372, 78 S. Ct. at 820. Where the Government has induced an individual to break the law and the defense of entrapment is at issue, as it was in this case, the prosecution must prove beyond reasonable doubt that the defendant was disposed to commit the criminal act prior to first being approached by Government agents. *United States v. Whoie*, 288 U.S. App. D.C. 261, 263-264, 925 F.2d 1481, 1483-1484 (1991).

Thus, an agent deployed to stop the traffic in illegal drugs may offer the opportunity to buy or sell drugs, and, if the offer is accepted, make an arrest on the spot or later. In such a typical case, or in a more elaborate "sting" operation involving government-sponsored fencing where the defendant is simply provided with the opportunity to commit a crime, the entrapment defense is of little use because the ready commission of the criminal act amply demonstrates the defendant's predisposition. See *United States v. Sherman*, 200 F.2d 880, 882 (CA2 1952). Had the agents in this case simply offered petitioner the opportunity to order child pornography through the mails, and petitioner — who must be presumed to know the law — had promptly availed himself of this criminal opportunity, it is unlikely that his entrapment defense would have warranted a jury instruction. *Mathews v. United States*, 485 U.S. 58, 66, 108 S. Ct. 883, 886, 99 L. Ed. 2d 54 (1988).

But that is not what happened here. By the time petitioner finally placed his order, he had already been the target of 26 months of repeated mailings and communications from Government agents and fictitious organizations. Therefore, although he had become predisposed to break the law by May 1987, it is our view that the Government did not prove that this predisposition was independent and not the product of the attention that the Government had directed at petitioner since January 1985. *Sorrells, supra,* 287 U.S., at 442, 53 S. Ct. at 213; *Sherman,* 356 U.S., at 372, 78 S. Ct. at 820.

. . . .

Petitioner's ready response to these solicitations cannot be enough to establish beyond reasonable doubt that he was predisposed, prior to the Government acts intended to create predisposition, to commit the crime of receiving child pornography through the mails. See *Sherman,* 356 U.S., at 374, 78 S. Ct. at 822. The evidence that petitioner was ready and willing to commit the offense came only after the Government had devoted 2 1/2 years to convincing him that he had or should have the right to engage in the very behavior proscribed by law. Rational jurors could not say beyond a reasonable doubt that petitioner possessed the requisite predisposition prior to the Government's investigation and that it existed independent of the Government's many and varied approaches to petitioner. As was explained in Sherman, where entrapment was found as a matter of law, "the Government [may not] pla[y] on the weaknesses of an innocent party and beguil[e] him into committing crimes which he otherwise would not have attempted." *Id.,* at 376, 78 S. Ct. at 822.

Law enforcement officials go too far when they "implant in the mind of an innocent person the *disposition* to commit the alleged offense and induce its commission in order that they may prosecute." *Sorrells v. U.S.,* 287 U.S. 435, at 442, 53 S. Ct. 210, at 212-213, 77 L. Ed. 413 (emphasis added). Like the *Sorrells* court, we are "unable to conclude that it was the intention of the Congress in enacting this statute that its processes of detection and enforcement should be abused by the instigation by government officials of an act on the part of persons otherwise innocent in order to lure them to its commission and to punish them." *Id.,* at 448, 53 S. Ct. at 215. When the Government's quest for convictions leads to the apprehension of an otherwise law-abiding citizen who, if left to his own devices, likely would have never run afoul of the law, the courts should intervene.

Because we conclude that this is such a case and that the prosecution failed, as a matter of law, to adduce evidence to support the jury verdict that petitioner was predisposed, independent of the Government's acts and beyond a reasonable doubt, to violate the law by receiving child pornography through the mails, we reverse the Court of Appeals' judgment affirming the conviction of Keith Jacobson.

It is so ordered.

JUSTICE O'CONNOR, with whom THE CHIEF JUSTICE and JUSTICE KENNEDY join, and with whom JUSTICE SCALIA joins except as to Part II, dissenting.

....

I

This Court has held previously that a defendant's predisposition is to be assessed as of the time the Government agent first suggested the crime, not when the Government agent first became involved. *Sherman v. United States*, 356 U.S. 369, 372-376, 78 S. Ct. 819, 820-823, 2 L. Ed. 2d 848 (1958). See also, *United States v. Williams*, 705 F. 2d 603, 618, n. 9 (CA2), *cert. denied*, 464 U.S. 1007, 104 S. Ct. 524, 78 L. Ed. 2d 708 (1983). Until the Government actually makes a suggestion of criminal conduct, it could not be said to have "implant[ed] in the mind of an innocent person the disposition to commit the alleged offense and induce its commission ...." *Sorrells v. United States*, 287 U.S. 435, 442, 53 S. Ct. 210, 212-213, 77 L. Ed. 413 (1932). Even in *Sherman v. United States, supra*, in which the Court held that the defendant had been entrapped as a matter of law, the Government agent had repeatedly and unsuccessfully coaxed the defendant to buy drugs, ultimately succeeding only by playing on the defendant's sympathy. The Court found lack of predisposition based on the Government's numerous unsuccessful attempts to induce the crime, not on the basis of preliminary contacts with the defendant.

Today, the Court holds that Government conduct may be considered to create a predisposition to commit a crime, even before any Government action to induce the commission of the crime. In my view, this holding changes entrapment doctrine. Generally, the inquiry is whether a suspect is predisposed before the Government induces the commission of the crime, not before the Government makes initial contact with him. There is no dispute here that the Government's questionnaires and letters were not sufficient to establish inducement; they did not even suggest that Mr. Jacobson should engage in any illegal activity. If all the Government had done was to send these materials, Mr. Jacobson's entrapment defense would fail. Yet the Court holds that the Government must prove not only that a suspect was predisposed to commit the crime before the opportunity to commit it arose, but also before the Government came on the scene. *Ante*, at 1540.

The rule that preliminary Government contact can create a predisposition has the potential to be misread by lower courts as well as criminal investigators as requiring that the Government must have sufficient evidence of a defendant's predisposition *before it ever seeks to contact him*. Surely the Court cannot intend to impose such a requirement, for it would mean that the Government must have a reasonable suspicion of criminal activity before it begins an investigation, a condition that we have never before imposed. The Court denies that its new rule will affect run-of-the-mill sting operations, *ante*, at 1541, and one hopes that it means what it says. Nonetheless, after this case, every defendant will claim that something the Government agent did before soliciting the crime "created" a predisposition that was not there before. For example, a bribe taker will claim that the description of the amount of money available was so enticing that it implanted a disposition to accept the bribe later offered. A drug buyer will claim that the description of the drug's purity and effects was so tempting that it created the urge to try it for the first time.

In short, the Court's opinion could be read to prohibit the Government from advertising the seductions of criminal activity as part of its sting operation, for fear of creating a predisposition in its suspects. That limitation would be especially likely to hamper sting operations such as this one, which mimic the advertising done by genuine purveyors of pornography. No doubt the Court would protest that its opinion does not stand for so broad a proposition, but the apparent lack of a principled basis for distinguishing these scenarios exposes a flaw in the more limited rule the Court today adopts.

The Court's rule is all the more troubling because it does not distinguish between Government conduct that merely highlights the temptation of the crime itself, and Government conduct that threatens, coerces, or leads a suspect to commit a crime in order to fulfill some other obligation. For example, in *Sorrells*, the Government agent repeatedly asked for illegal liquor, coaxing the defendant to accede on the ground that "one former war buddy would get liquor for another." *Sorrells v. United States, supra*, at 440, 53 S. Ct. at 212. In *Sherman*, the Government agent played on the defendant's sympathies, pretending to be going through drug withdrawal and begging the defendant to relieve his distress by helping him buy drugs. *Sherman, supra*, 356 U.S., at 371, 78 S. Ct. at 820.

....

II

[The dissent went on to say the majority had redefined "predisposition," by in effect requiring proof of specific intent to commit a crime which only requires proof of knowing receipt of the outlawed materials.]

....

NOTES

1. The defense of entrapment originated in the states but has been developed largely in federal courts. LaFave and Scott, Criminal Law (2d ed., 1986).

2. Two approaches have been taken to the defense. The "subjective" approach, in *Sorrells v. United States*, 287 U.S. 435 (1932) and in *Sherman v. United States*, 356 U.S. 369 (1958) focuses on the defendant's predisposition to commit the crime. A majority of courts follow this view. The second or "objective" approach focuses on the actions of the government agents. The objective approach is adopted by the Model Penal Code, § 2.13 (See Appendix A). Does *Jacobson* follow the subjective or the objective approach?

Chapter 8
INCAPACITY

SECTION I. Mental Condition

INTRODUCTORY NOTE

Jerome Hall observed that "The problem of mental disease and criminal responsibility has... the appearance of utter simplicity," and he stated clearly the fundamental concepts involved:

> If the defendant was insane at the time of the conduct in issue, the requisite *mens rea* was lacking and no crime was committed. Punishment presupposes normal competence and the relevant causing (authorship) of a proscribed harm; hence there can be no question of responsibility or punishment of insane persons. A psychotic harm-doer should, instead, be placed in a hospital.

J. HALL, GENERAL PRINCIPLES OF CRIMINAL LAW 449 (2d ed. 1960).

But as Hall also noted, there are numerous difficulties associated with disagreements about what constitutes mental disease, whether and to what extent mental disease is like physical disease, and the degree to which philosophical viewpoints affect our decisions about how to treat offenders who are mentally ill. Furthermore, this is an area of the criminal law in which psychiatrists and psychologists, as expert witnesses, have a large role to play, and although we need the assistance they can provide, we are properly reluctant to give them final authority in the fact-finding process. Several considerations bearing upon some of these matters are discussed in the following excerpt from the 1977 report of the Law Reform Commission of Canada:

LAW REFORM COMMISSION OF CANADA, A REPORT TO PARLIAMENT ON MENTAL DISORDER IN THE CRIMINAL PROCESS 2-4 (1977)

The impact of mental disorder in the criminal process may only be properly assessed where there is agreement as to what that process is to achieve. We therefore briefly restate our view on the aims and purpose of the criminal process.

(1) The criminal law, the foundation of the process, serves to protect us from the harmful effects of criminality and to promote and underline values shared by Canadians. This is done through education, by furnishing a necessary social response when basic values such as personal security, honesty and protection of property are infringed. Such a view of the criminal law treats people as responsible individuals with rights and obligations, who may choose to do wrong and risk the consequences.

(2) The criminal trial is the institution through which persons accused of crimes are brought to account or exonerated and the threatened values reaffirmed. Its procedure is adversarial, structured as a dispute between the state and the accused and arbitrated by an impartial judge. The accused's presence and participation is essential; not only is he the reason for the proceeding, he also is an active party, answering the charge, engaging and dismissing counsel and suffering the consequences if convicted.

(3) From conviction flows sentencing and punishment, the final stage of the process. In our view criminal sanctions should further underline the dignity and well-being of the individual, both offender and victim. They should be humane, proportional to the offence and treat like cases in a like manner. As well, account should be taken of the need to reconcile the offender with the victim and society through restitution and compensation.

(4) Underlining the entire criminal process should be a principle of restraint. Because the criminal law is society's most destructive and intrusive form of intervention, it should only be invoked with caution and with full recognition of its moral and practical limitations. It is society's last resort to be used only when milder methods have failed....

Given this view of the criminal process, when is it relevant to consider an individual's mental disorder?

(1) At the outset, mental disorder may affect the exercise of the principle of restraint in the use of the criminal law. An individual's mental disorder might influence the decision whether the criminal law should be used at all.

(2) At the beginning of and during trial mental disorder may affect the exercise of the principle that parties to a criminal proceeding should be aware and be able to participate. Where an accused is so mentally disordered as not to realize the personal import of the proceedings or direct his defence, the question arises as to whether he should stand trial at all.

(3) Mental disorder may also affect the exercise of the principle of responsibility from which springs the presumption that individuals can control and be held accountable for their acts. For individuals so afflicted by mental disorder as to be unable to understand the consequences of their acts or exercise a minimum of control over their behaviour, the question arises whether they should be held criminally accountable in court.

(4) After conviction mental disorder may affect the principle that dispositions should be humane and just. A sentence depriving a mentally disordered offender of essential psychiatric services that would otherwise have been available would be both inhumane and unfair.

It follows that a person's mental state becomes relevant in different ways at each phase of the criminal process.

> Before trial — The relevant question is whether the criminal process should be used at all or whether some other nonpenal procedure would be more appropriate.
>
> At trial — There are two questions: Is the accused mentally fit to stand trial? And, if so, was he mentally capable, entirely or partially, of being held responsible for his acts.

After trial — To what extent should mental disorder be taken into consideration when sentencing a convicted offender?

A. LEGAL TESTS FOR RESPONSIBILITY

Several legal tests for responsibility have been formulated and employed over the years to determine when and under what circumstances a defendant should be considered legally insane. We shall turn now to an examination of these tests, beginning with the so-called *M'Naghten* Rule stated by the English House of Lords in 1843 in *M'Naghten's Case*, 8 ENG. REP. 718 (House of Lords, 1843).

1. THE *M'NAGHTEN* RULE

The following New York statute represents that jurisdiction's adoption of the *M'Naghten* Rule:

NEW YORK PENAL LAW § 30.05 (McKINNEY 1975)

>   1. A person is not criminally responsible for conduct if at the time of such conduct, as a result of mental disease or defect, he lacks substantial capacity to know or appreciate either:
>   (a) The nature and consequence of such conduct; or
>   (b) That such conduct was wrong.
>   2. In any prosecution for an offense, lack of criminal responsibility by reason of mental disease or defect ... is a defense.

NOTES

1. "The *M'Naghten* Rules were a synthesis of *Rex v. Arnold* (1724), 16 How. St. Tr. 695; *Ferrers' Case* (1760), 19 How. St. Tr. 886; *Hadfield's Case* (1800), 27 How. St. Tr. 1282; and *Bellingham's Case* (1812) in 1 COLLINSON, A TREATISE ON THE LAW CONCERNING IDIOTS, LUNATICKS AND OTHER PERSONS NON COMPOTES MENTIS 636 (1812). In *Ferrers' Case* the Solicitor General, purporting to summarize Hale, stressed: 'a faculty to distinguish the nature of actions; to discern the difference between moral good and evil....' *Supra* at 948. In *Hadfield's Case,* Erskine minimized the 'right and wrong' test and emphasized knowledge of the nature of the act. In *Bellingham's Case,* Mansfield said: 'If a man were deprived of all power of reasoning, so as not to be able to distinguish whether it was right or wrong to commit the most wicked transaction, he could not certainly do an act against the law.' 1 COLLINSON, op. cit. *supra* at 671.... Cockburn's argument in defense of *M'Naghten* contains an excellent summary of the earlier leading cases and of the medico-legal treatises. 4 St. Tr. (n.s.) 872-892. Shortly after the *M'Naghten* Rules were announced, and apparently without having seen them, Shaw, C. J., held: 'In order to be responsible, he must have sufficient power of memory to recollect the relation in which he stands to others, and in which others stand to him; that the act he is doing is contrary to the plain dictates of justice and right, injurious to others, and a violation of the dictates of duty.' *Commonwealth v.*

Rogers, 7 Metc. 500, 502 (Mass. 1844)." J. Hall, General Principles of Criminal Law 472 n.67 (2d ed. 1960).

2. Prior to 1984, Congress had never set forth a test for legal insanity to be used in federal courts. Instead, the situation was as described in the following Senate Report:

U.S. SENATE REPORT NO. 97-307 TO ACCOMPANY CRIMINAL CODE REFORM ACT OF 1981, S. 1630, 97th Congress, 1st Session 95-97 (1982):

Congress has never enacted legislation on the insanity defense. The Supreme Court has generally left development of standards to the courts of appeal and those courts, over many years, have gradually broadened the defense.

The foundation of the defense was established in *M'Naghten's Case*[23] in which the "right-wrong" test was introduced:

> To establish a defense on the ground of insanity, it must be clearly proved that, at the time of the committing of the act, the party accused was labouring under such a defect of reason, from disease of the mind, as not to know the nature and quality of the act he was doing; or, if he did know it, that he did not know he was doing what was wrong.

The next step was the widespread adoption of an additional volition test, exculpating a defendant who knew what he was doing and that it was wrong, but whose actions were deemed, because of mental disease, to be beyond his control.[24] This is sometimes called the "irresistible impulse" addition to the *M'Naghten* test. However, because its formulation frequently does not require that the abnormality be characterized by sudden impulse as opposed to brooding and reflection, it is more appropriate to term it a "control" or "volitional" test.

A third stage was the repudiation of both *M'Naghten* and its volitional supplement by the famous decision of *Durham v. United States*.[25] There, the court enunciated the formulation: "[A]n accused is not criminally responsible if his unlawful act was the product of mental disease or mental defect."[26] The court did not define the terms of the new rule in that decision. After numerous appellate opinions, refining, clarifying, expanding, and limiting Durham over a period of eighteen years, the District of Columbia circuit overruled it in *United States v. Brawner*.[27]

Meanwhile, the other Federal courts of appeals, with some modifications and hesitations, had moved from *M'Naghten* and its volitional modification to the proposal of the American Law Institute's Model Penal Code ...[28] Adoption of the A.L.I. formulation marks the fourth and latest stage of development of

---

[23] Clark & F. 200, 8 Eng. Rep. 718 (House of Lords, 1843).
[24] See Davis v. United States, 165 U.S. 373, 378 (1897).
[25] 214 F.2d 862 (D.C. Cir. 1954).
[26] *Id.* at 874.
[27] 471 F.2d 969 (D.C. Cir. 1972). See generally Symposium on United States v. Brawner, 1973 Wash. U.L.Q. 17-154.
[28] Model Penal Code, § 4.01 (P.O.D. 1962).

A. LEGAL TESTS FOR RESPONSIBILITY

Federal decisional law on the subject, although minor differences among the circuits continue to exist.[29] In the *Brawner* case, *supra,* the District of Columbia Circuit joined the other circuits in embracing this approach.[30]

Although the defenses have not been included in the Code, thereby retaining the common law development of an insanity defense, the Committee believes the report should reflect some of the varying views brought out in hearings with respect to the desirability of the insanity defense concepts.

The knowledge tests: M'Naghten *and its progeny*

While criticism of *M'Naghten* in terms of obsolescence is not in itself an argument for its repudiation, the test does tend to ignore the distinction between a medical concept of mental illness or defect and a normative legal standard focusing on legal purposes rather than the identification of medical or psychological entities. Moreover, as noted in *Durham v. United States*:[31]

> The science of psychiatry now recognizes that a man is an integrated personality and that reason, which is only one element in that personality, is not the sole determinant of his control. The right-wrong test, which considers knowledge or reason alone, is therefore, an inadequate guide to mental responsibility for criminal behavior.
>
> ....
>
> By its misleading emphasis on the cognitive, the right-wrong test requires court and jury to rely upon what is, scientifically speaking, inadequate, and most often, invalid and irrelevant testimony in determining criminal responsibility.

Related to the foregoing is the criticism that *M'Naghten* does not lead to the acquittal of an appropriate number of mentally ill persons. When strictly applied it probably exempts from criminal responsibility only persons who are grossly mentally deficient and psychotics with blurred perception and consciousness, together with some paranoid schizophrenics.[32] This is the most common and the most realistic objection to *M'Naghten*. Frequently it has led to interpretation of key terms of the rules in such a manner as to encompass volitional impairment. "Know" is expanded to include a substantial emotional component together with the possibility of acting upon knowledge. "Wrong" may be expanded to include moral wrong as well as violation of criminal law. More commonly today the approach may be to add a control test to the knowledge test of *M'Naghten* and to exculpate those who are said to be volitionally impaired.

It is sometimes stated that the rule asks questions which a psychiatrist cannot answer since they are said to be directed to moralistic rather than

---

[29] The positions of the various circuits are surveyed in United States v. Brawner, *supra* note 27 at 979-981. The most notable departure from uniformity is the Third Circuit where the court has eliminated the cognitive aspect of the A.L.I. test. See United States v. Currens, 290 F.2d 751 (3d Cir. 1961); cf. Government of Virgin Islands v. Bellott, 495 F.2d 1393 (3d Cir. 1974).

[30] Both the National Commission (Final Report, § 503) and S. 1 as introduced originally (§ 1-302) proposed the enactment of the A.L.I. insanity defense, with minor textual variations.

[31] *Supra* note 25 at 871-872.

[32] See Waelder, Psychiatry and the Problem of Criminal Responsibility, 101 U. Pa. L. Rev. 378, 379 (1952).

scientific concerns. While it must be conceded that there is ample ambiguity in the language of *M'Naghten,* one may suspect that much of the criticism of vagueness, and perhaps of language regarded as prescientific, is actually directed at the narrow scope of the rule more intensely than at its vagueness. For example, Dr. Gregory Zilborg has stated:[33]

> To force a psychiatrist to talk in terms of the ability to distinguish between right and wrong and of legal responsibility is — let us admit it openly and frankly — to force him to violate the Hippocratic Oath, even to violate the oath he takes as a witness to tell the truth and nothing but the truth, to force him to perjure himself *for the sake of justice.* For what else is it if not perjury, if a clinician speaks of right and wrong, and criminal responsibility, and the understanding of the nature and quality of the criminal act committed, when he, the psychiatrist, really knows absolutely nothing about such things.

The dispute must be seen as disagreement by psychiatrists with a legal, not a medical, standard.

3. On March 30, 1981, John W. Hinckley, Jr., shot and wounded President Ronald Reagan and three other persons in Washington, D.C. Hinckley was charged with several federal and District of Columbia offenses. He was given a jury trial which began on May 4, 1982, and lasted for seven weeks. The jury returned a verdict of not guilty by reason of insanity under the then-applicable ALI (Model Penal Code) test which provides that a person is not responsible for criminal conduct if at the time of such conduct as a result of mental disease or defect he lacks substantial capacity either to appreciate the criminality (wrongfulness) of his conduct or to conform his conduct to the requirements of law. There was a nationwide reaction of outrage at the jury's verdict, calls were issued for abolition of the insanity defense, and several bills were introduced in Congress and in state legislatures to modify or abolish the insanity defense. In response, and as a part of the Comprehensive Crime Control Act of 1984, Congress enacted the Insanity Defense Reform Act of 1984, which sets forth the present federal test for insanity:

§ 17. Insanity Defense.

> (a) Affirmative defense. It is an affirmative defense to a prosecution under any Federal statute that, at the time of the commission of the acts constituting the offense, the defendant, as a result of a severe mental disease or defect, was unable to appreciate the nature and quality or the wrongfulness of his acts. Mental disease or defect does not otherwise constitute a defense.
>
> (b) The defendant has the burden of proving the defense of insanity by clear and convincing evidence.

18 U.S.C. § 17 (1986)(initially codified in 1984 as 18 U.S.C. § 20, but redesignated as § 17 in 1986). The federal statute eliminates the "volitional" portion of the ALI (Model Penal Code) test, which had become the dominant insanity

---

[33] Guttmacher and Weihofen, Psychiatry and the Law, pp. 400-407 (1952) (emphasis supplied).

A. LEGAL TESTS FOR RESPONSIBILITY

defense test in use by the federal circuits in one form or another up to the time of the Insanity Defense Reform Act of 1984. Under the present federal test, "not guilty by reason of insanity" verdicts are allowed only on the basis of cognitive impairment. That is, even if a person lacks the capacity, because of severe mental disease or defect, to conform his or her conduct to the requirements of the law, such a condition, standing alone and without the requisite cognitive impairment, does not come within the scope of the present federal insanity defense.

STATE v. HAMANN
Supreme Court of Iowa
285 N.W.2d 180 (1979)

HARRIS, J.

The defendant, John R. Hamann, shot and killed Richard Slattery at Slattery's Davenport park board office on May 10, 1977. Defendant's father and Slattery were co-employees and apparently rivals for leadership of the department.

The trial centered on the defendant's insanity defense. Both sides introduced expert psychiatric testimony on the question. Defendant's witness, Dr. Paul Frahm, testified defendant's ability to know right from wrong was impaired by a delusion that his father's life was endangered by a malicious adversary and that defendant alone could enforce justice. Dr. Frahm also testified of defendant's belief that, after he killed Slattery, society would "understand that a great injustice had been righted." Dr. Thomas Garside testified for the defense that, although defendant knew his act was criminal, his illness led him to believe he was doing right in shooting Slattery. Dr. James N. Lyons testified for the State that defendant believed society would be better off without Slattery and that this belief was not a delusion but an opinion....

The defendant argues that the court should have instructed that "right" and "wrong," as used in the *M'Naghten* rule refers to right and wrong in a moral as distinguished from a legal sense. The *M'Naghten* case itself does not answer the question. Cases from other states are divided on the issue and the question seems to be one of first impression in Iowa.

There is some doubt of defendant's standing, on this record, to raise the issue. The division of authority on whether the term is to be taken in a legal or in a moral sense will be explained in more detail later. But this defendant is in a poor position to ask us to adopt the interpretation he supports because the authorities he cites would not aid him. Those states which believe the right or wrong test should be conducted with a view to moral right or wrong are quite uniform in rejecting a subjective test. That is, the test in those jurisdictions is conducted in accordance with society's general mores and not in accordance with an accused's personal views on morality. *See People v. Irwin*, 166 Misc. 751, 761, 4 N.Y.S.2d 548, 558 (1938).

Yet, defendant's insanity defense is peculiarly subjective and stands not at all on the mores of society generally. In his brief he argues:

> It is submitted that such a holding as in *U.S. v. McGraw* [515 F.2d 758, 760 (9th Cir. 1975)], is not a minority view point. It is submitted that the majority of states adhere to the conclusions enunciated above; that in the concept of right and wrong, wrongfulness means moral wrongfulness rather than criminal wrongfulness, and *thus where the defendant is under a delusionary belief produced by mental disease that the act is not morally wrong, such belief transcends the defendant's understanding of the law and nullifies criminal responsibility.* [Emphasis added.]

Of course defendant is driven to argue for a subjective view of morality in the right or wrong test. There is no practical distinction between moral and legal right or wrong in a murder case. Under any rational legal system ever devised murder would be prohibited. And under any rational moral system ever imagined murder would be reprehensible. This defendant's delusion is his only explanation for the killing. That delusion, being personal to him, is irrelevant even under the interpretation he supports....

... We believe the words "right" or "wrong" under the *M'Naghten* rule should be understood in their legal and not in their moral sense.

In this world of revolutionary and often violent change it is futile to pretend that our society maintains a consensus on moral questions beyond what it writes into its laws. Contemporary philosophers and theologians ponder mightily but without notable success to reach agreement on the "general mores" of our society. National debates rage over a myriad of moral issues. Few are resolved with anything approaching unanimity. Impossible uncertainty over the so-called general mores renders the appreciation of morality a tool unfit for the task of measuring sanity.

This is not to say, as has sometimes been suggested, that sanity would thereby be measured by legal knowledge. The test is not how much law a person claiming an insanity defense actually knows. The determination is to be made on the basis of a person's ability to understand it when something is prohibited by law. This is clear from *M'Naghten* itself:

> If the question were to be put as to the knowledge of the accused solely and exclusively with the reference to the law of the land, it might tend to confound the jury, by inducing them to believe that an actual knowledge of the law of the land was essential in order to lead to a conviction, whereas the law is administered upon the principle that everyone must be taken conclusively to know it, without proof that he does know it. If the accused was conscious that the act was one which he ought not to do, and if that act was at the same time contrary to the law of the land, he is punishable....

But the so-called majority rule calls for application of what seems to us an amorphous and shifting standard. It therefore invites the functional equivalent of jury nullification. Obviously, if we were to apply the so-called majority rule we would thereby assume that society's "general mores" were known because they are a part of the ultimate criteria for that insanity test. Yet, the

A. LEGAL TESTS FOR RESPONSIBILITY

courts can only pretend to possess knowledge on general mores. Courts have no way of controlling or monitoring a jury determination on the question. Jury nullification is disallowed by Iowa law....

Only a part of a society's moral standards becomes so fixed and agreed upon as to become law. Until a moral standard becomes law it is an unreliable test for sanity. We believe it is far more workable and a more accurate measure of mental health to test a defendant's ability to understand what society has fixed and established as law.

We hold the words "right" or "wrong" under the *M'Naghten* rule refer to legal right or wrong. The defendant's contention to the contrary is without merit.

NOTES

1. Similar holdings were entered in *State v. Law,* 270 S.C. 664, 244 S.E.2d 302 (1978), and *State v. Crenshaw,* 27 Wash. App. 326, 617 P.2d 1041 (1980). Judge Ringold, dissenting in the latter case, stated:

> My view of the proper interpretation of *M'Naghten's Case* was expressed by Justice Cardozo in *People v. Schmidt,* 216 N.Y. 324, 110 N.E. 945, 947 (1915), when speaking for the New York Court of Appeals, he stated:
>
> The judges [in answering questions two and three in *M'Naghten's Case*] expressly held that a defendant who knew nothing of the law would none the less be responsible if he knew that the act was wrong, by which, therefore, they must have meant, if he knew that it was morally wrong. Whether he would also be responsible if he knew that it was against the law, but did not know it to be morally wrong, is a question that was not considered. In most cases, of course, knowledge that an act is illegal will justify the inference of knowledge that it is wrong. But none the less it is the knowledge of wrong, conceived of as moral wrong, that seems to have been established by that decision as the controlling test. That must certainly have been the test under the older law when the capacity to distinguish between right and wrong imported a capacity to distinguish between good and evil as abstract qualities. There is nothing to justify the belief that the words right and wrong, when they became limited by *M'Naghten's Case* to the right and wrong of the particular act, cast off their meaning as terms of morals, and became terms of pure legality.

The New York court goes on to reconcile the apparent conflict between the first question of *M'Naghten's Case* and the second and third by pointing out that

> [t]he answer to the first question, though it seems to make the knowledge of the law a test, presupposed the offender's capacity to understand that violation of the law is wrong.... A delusion that some supposed grievance or injury will be redressed, or some public benefit attained, has no such effect in obscuring moral distinctions as a delusion that God himself has issued a command. The one delusion is consistent with knowledge that the act is a moral wrong, the other is not.

People v. Schmidt, supra at 948.

Further, I believe our Supreme Court has adopted the moral rather than the legal definition. As pointed out by Professor Arval Morris, the Supreme Court expressly approved a jury instruction providing that the accused was legally insane if his mind was diseased to such an extent that he was "*unable to perceive the moral qualities of the act with which he is charged,* and was unable to tell right from wrong with reference to the particular act charged." (Emphasis added). A. Morris, *Criminal Insanity,* 43 Wash. L. Rev. 583, 603 (1968), quoting from *State v. Davis,* 6 Wash.2d 696, 708, 108 P.2d 641 (1940).... I think that neither statutory nor case-law changes vitiate the clear implication that the Supreme Court understands "right and wrong" in the insanity test to mean *moral* right and wrong.

The concept of right and wrong must be an objective standard of right and wrong. The Arizona Supreme Court upheld in *State v. Corley,* 108 Ariz. 240, 495 P.2d 470, 472-73 (1972), the following instruction:

> Knowledge that the action was wrong, as the phrase is used in these instructions, means knowledge that the act was wrong according to generally accepted moral standards of the community and not the defendant's own individual moral standards. Knowledge that an act is forbidden by law will permit the inference of knowledge that the act is wrong according to generally accepted moral standards of the community.

I am not troubled by the majority's suggestion that according to this formulation one who knew his acts were unlawful could still be found insane, and thereby exculpated. As pointed out above, if we are to be consistent in our application of the maxim that ignorance of the law excuses no man, then a person's knowledge of the law must be immaterial to culpability. The fact that the law is, for the most part, an expression of the collective morality justifies the permissive inference that a defendant knows an act is immoral from his knowledge that it is unlawful. Whether such an inference is to be drawn, however, should be left to the jury. In limiting the definition of right and wrong to the legal sense the court imposed on the jury a mandatory inference that the defendant was not insane, thereby directing a verdict.

2. In *State v. Malumphy,* 105 Ariz. 200, 461 P.2d 677 (1969), Justice McFarland summarized the opposing views and concluded:

> It is my belief that even where a defendant is aware that a particular act is a violation of the law, if he harbors a delusory belief, which is the product of mental disease of such magnitude that he believes that the act is not morally wrong, and that as a result of such mental disease he is unable to understand that it is wrong for him to violate the law prohibiting the act, then he is not criminally responsible.

461 P.2d at 689.

3. In Florida where the *M'Naghten* test applies, a defense predicated upon "involuntary subliminal television intoxication" was rejected and an expert witness was not permitted to testify as to the effect of television on adolescents generally. Her testimony was deemed irrelevant because she could not say that watching violent television programs to excess would preclude an individual from distinguishing between right and wrong. *Zamora v. State,* 361 So. 2d 776 (Fla. Dist. Ct. App. 1978).

2. IRRESISTIBLE IMPULSE; "CONTROL" TESTS

STATE v. HAMANN

Supreme Court of Iowa
285 N.W.2d 180 (1979)

HARRIS, J.:

Defendant also contends that the trial court erred in finding want of substantial evidence to support an instruction on irresistible impulse. We approved the following instruction on the issue of irresistible impulse in *State v. Buck,* 205 Iowa 1028, 1034-35, 219 N.W. 17, 19 (1928):

> In order to be an excuse and defense for a criminal act, the person accused, and who claims insanity as a defense, must prove that the crime charged was caused by mental disease or unsoundness which dethroned, overcame, or swayed her reason and judgment with respect to that act, which destroyed her power rationally to comprehend the nature and consequences of that act ... [and] which, overpowering her will, irresistibly forced her to its commission....

Although sufficient evidence was introduced on the subject of defendant's insanity to justify an instruction to the jury on that subject, this alone does not entitle defendant to an instruction on irresistible impulse. The record must also contain substantial evidence that the illness was "overpowering" so that the defendant was "irresistibly forced" to commit the act.

We do not find substantial evidence in the record to justify a finding that defendant's will was overpowered so that he was irresistibly forced to kill Slattery. Counsel cites the testimony of Dr. Thomas Garside as support for such a finding:

> Q. Doctor, in your examination of Jack Hamann did you find any evidence — indication of compulsion? A. There was evidence of internal struggle, indecisiveness and pro and con types of thinking, prior to the act and at the time of the act. There was a direct quote that he stopped and prayed for courage and felt as though he were forcing himself to do something. You know how it is when your conscience says no but you think you should do something.
>
> .....
>
> Q. Do you believe this compulsion was of such a character that you can tell the jury whether or not he felt he was compelled to act? A. I think only [to] the extent of that sentence that he stated that you know how it is when you — your conscience says no and yet you feel you should or have to do something.

We think this testimony tends to dispute rather than support the request for an irresistible impulse instruction. The doctor did not testify that defendant's will was overborne so that he could not prevent the commission of the act. Rather, he testified defendant was indecisive and "felt as though he was forcing himself to do something." This testimony is evidence, not that defendant's will was overcome, but that defendant's acts were considered and chosen. Defendant's decision to act may have been based on an erroneous perception of right or wrong. But this does not entitle him to an instruction on *irresistible impulse*. Irresistible impulse requires the second step which is not shown here.

The trial court did not err in refusing to instruct on irresistible impulse.

NOTES

1. *State v. Harrison*, 36 W. Va. 729, 751-52, 15 S.E. 982, 989-90 (1892):

> This "irresistible-impulse" test, ... while it is supported by plausible arguments, ... is rather refined, and introduces what seems to me a useless element of distinction for a test, and is misleading to juries, and fraught with great danger to human life, so much so that even its advocates have warningly said that it should be very cautiously applied, and only in the clearest cases. What is this "irresistible impulse?" How shall we of the courts and juries know it? Does it exist when manifested in one single instance, as in the present case, or must it be shown to have been habitual, or at least to have evinced itself in more than a single instance, as Chief Justice Gibson said must be the case? We have kleptomania and pyromania, which better works on medical jurisprudence tell us cannot excuse crime where there is capacity to know the character of the act.... Shall we introduce homicidal mania, and allow him of the manslaying propensity to walk innocent through the land while yet not insane, but capable of knowing the nature and wrong of his murderous act? For myself I cannot see how a person who rationally comprehends the nature and quality of an act and knows that it is wrong and criminal, can act through irresistible innocent impulse. Knowing the nature of the act well enough to make him otherwise liable for it under the law, can we say that he acts from irresistible impulse, and not criminal design and guilt? And if we are sure he was seized and possessed and driven forward to the act wholly and absolutely by *irresistible impulse,* his mind being diseased, how can we say he rationally realized the nature of the act, — realized it to an extent to enable us to hold him criminal in the act? How can the knowledge of the nature and wrongfulness of the act exist along with such impulse as shall exonerate him? Can the two coexist? The one existing, does not the other nonexist?

2. Evidence of the XYY syndrome was barred in *People v. Tanner,* 13 Cal. App. 3d 596, 91 Cal. Rptr. 656 (1970), and in *People v. Yukl,* 83 Misc. 2d 364,

372 N.Y.S.2d 313 (1975) as not "satisfactorily established [in] either the scientific or legal communities."

3. *Gardner v. State,* 419 N.E.2d 749, 751-52 (Ind. 1981):

> [T]he jury was warranted also in inferring that appellant, in spite of the diseased state of his mind, nevertheless retained a substantial capacity to resist the compulsion he felt to kill. A stern reprimand by his mother caused him to suppress it. He had held it in abeyance on a previous occasion until he could call for support from friends. When confronted with superior opposing force at the police station interrogation, he did not act in response to it. Appellant's brother with whom he was close found him to be normal and natural in speech and act. Given the evidence, the jury was warranted in concluding that appellant retained the will to reject and suppress the compulsion arising from his illness and conform his conduct to the law. The evidence is therefore sufficient to sustain the conclusion beyond a reasonable doubt that appellant was sane at the time of this tragedy, in the legal sense.

3. ALI TEST

MODEL PENAL CODE

§ 4.01. Mental Disease or Defect Excluding Responsibility

(1) A person is not responsible for criminal conduct if at the time of such conduct as a result of mental disease or defect he lacks substantial capacity either to appreciate the criminality [wrongfulness] of his conduct or to conform his conduct to the requirements of law. (2) As used in this Article, the terms "mental disease or defect" do not include an abnormality manifested only by repeated criminal or otherwise antisocial conduct.

PEOPLE v. DREW

Supreme Court of California
22 Cal. 3d 333, 583 P.2d 1318, 149 Cal. Rptr. 275 (1978)

TOBRINER, J.

The trial court instructed the jury that "Legal insanity ... means a diseased or deranged condition of the mind which makes a person incapable of knowing or understanding the nature and quality of his act, or makes a person incapable of knowing or understanding that his act was wrong." We explain that this instruction, based on the *M'Naghten* test, was erroneous, and on the record before us constitutes prejudicial error requiring reversal of the judgment.

The purpose of a legal test for insanity is to identify those persons who, owing to mental incapacity, should not be held criminally responsible for their conduct. The criminal law rests on a postulate of free will — that all persons of sound mind are presumed capable of conforming their behavior to legal requirements and that when any such person freely chooses to violate the law, he may justly be held responsible.... From the earliest days of the common law, however, the courts have recognized that a few persons lack the mental capacity to conform to the strictures of the law. Thus in 1582 William

Lambart of Lincoln's Inn wrote that "If ... a mad man or a natural fool, or a lunatic in the time of his lunacy, or a child who apparently had no knowledge of good or evil, do kill a man, this is no felonious act ... for they cannot be said to have any understanding will." (Lambart, Eirenarcha (1582) Cat. 21.218. (Spelling modernized).) The principle that mental incapacity constitutes a defense to crime is today accepted in all American jurisdictions....

The California Penal Code codifies the defense of mental incapacity. Section 20 states that "[i]n every crime ... there must exist a union ... of act and intent." Section 21 provides as to persons of sound mind "[t]he intent ... is manifested by the circumstances connected with the offense" and that "All persons are of sound mind who are neither idiots nor lunatics, nor affected with insanity." Finally section 26 specifies that "All persons are capable of committing crimes except those belonging to the following classes" and includes among those classes "Idiots" and "Lunatics and insane persons."

Although the Legislature has thus provided that "insanity" is a defense to a criminal charge, it has never attempted to define that term. The task of describing the circumstances under which mental incapacity will relieve a defendant of criminal responsibility has become the duty of the judiciary. Despite its widespread acceptance, the deficiencies of *M'Naghten* have long been apparent. Principal among these is the test's exclusive focus upon the cognitive capacity of the defendant, an outgrowth of the then current psychological theory under which the mind was divided into separate independent compartments, one of which could be diseased without affecting the others. (See *United States v. Currens* (3d Cir. 1961) 290 F.2d 751, 766.) As explained by Judge Ely of the Ninth Circuit: "The *M'Naghten* rules fruitlessly attempt to relieve from punishment only those mentally diseased persons who have no cognitive capacity .... This formulation does not comport with modern medical knowledge that an individual is a mentally complex being with varying degrees of awareness. It also fails to attack the problem presented in a case wherein an accused may have understood his actions but was incapable of controlling his behavior. Such a person has been allowed to remain a danger to himself and to society whenever, under *M'Naghten,* he is imprisoned without being afforded such treatment as may produce rehabilitation and is later, potentially recidivistic, released." (*Wade v. United States* (9th Cir. 1970) 426 F.2d 64, 66-67.) (Fns. omitted.)[7]

M'Naghten's exclusive emphasis on cognition would be of little consequence if all serious mental illness impaired the capacity of the affected person to know the nature and wrongfulness of his action. Indeed, the early decision of *People v. Hoin* (1882) 62 Cal. 120, 123, in rejecting the defense of "irresistible impulse," rested on this gratuitous but doubtful assumption. Current psychiatric opinion, however, holds that mental illness often leaves the individual's intellectual understanding relatively unimpaired, but so affects his emotions or reason that he is unable to prevent himself from committing the act....

---

[7] Numerous other cases and writers have criticized *M'Naghten's* failure to include a volitional element in its test of insanity. (See, e.g., United States v. Freeman, *supra,* 357 F.2d 606, 618; Dusky v. United States (8th Cir. 1961) 295 F.2d 743, 759; Durham v. United States (1954) 94 U.S.App.D.C. 228, 236-237, 214 F.2d 862, 870-871; State v. White (1969) 93 Idaho 153, 456 P.2d 797, 801; Guttmacher & Weihofen, Psychiatry and the Law (1952) p. 409.)

"[I]nsanity does not only, or primarily, affect the cognitive or intellectual faculties, but affects the whole personality of the patient, including both the will and the emotions. An insane person may therefore often know the nature and quality of his act and that it is wrong and forbidden by law, and yet commit it as a result of the mental disease." (Rep. Royal Com. on Capital Punishment, 1949-1953, p. 80.)

The annals of this court are filled with illustrations of the above statement: the deluded defendant in *People v. Gorshen, supra,* 51 Cal.2d 716, 336 P.2d 492, who believed he would be possessed by devilish visions unless he killed his foreman; the schizophrenic boy in *People v. Wolff, supra,* 61 Cal.2d 795, 40 Cal.Rptr. 271, 394 P.2d 959, who knew that killing his mother was murder but was unable emotionally to control his conduct despite that knowledge; the defendant in *People v. Robles* (1970) 2 Cal.3d 205, 85 Cal.Rptr. 166, 466 P.2d 710, suffering from organic brain damage, who mutilated himself and killed others in sudden rages. To ask whether such a person knows or understands that his act is "wrong" is to ask a question irrelevant to the nature of his mental illness or to the degree of his criminal responsibility.

Secondly, "*M'Naghten's* single track emphasis on the cognitive aspect of the personality recognizes no degrees of incapacity. Either the defendant knows right from wrong or he does not .... But such a test is grossly unrealistic .... As the commentary to the American Law Institute's Model Penal Code observes, "The law must recognize that when there is no black and white it must content itself with different shades of gray.'" (*United States v. Freeman, supra,* 357 F.2d 606, 618-619, quoting ALI, Model Pen.Code, Tent.Drafts, Nos. 1, 2, 3, and 4, p. 158.)

In short, *M'Naghten* purports to channel psychiatric testimony into the narrow issue of cognitive capacity, an issue often unrelated to the defendant's illness or crime. The psychiatrist called as a witness faces a dilemma: either he can restrict his testimony to the confines of *M'Naghten,* depriving the trier of fact of a full presentation of the defendant's mental state ..., or he can testify that the defendant cannot tell "right" from "wrong" when that is not really his opinion because by so testifying he acquires the opportunity to put before the trier of fact the reality of defendant's mental condition.... As Justice Frankfurter stated before the Royal Commission on Capital Punishment, "I think to have rules which cannot rationally be justified except by a process of interpretation which distorts and often practically nullifies them ... is not a desirable system.... [T]he *M'Naghten* Rules are in large measure shams. That is a strong word, but I think the *M'Naghten* Rules are very difficult for conscientious people and not difficult enough for people who say "We'll just juggle them." " (Royal Com. on Capital Punishment, *op. cit. supra,* p. 102.)

Even if the psychiatrist is able to place before the trier of fact a complete picture of the defendant's mental incapacity, that testimony reaches the trier of fact weakened by cross-examination designed to show that defendant knew right from wrong ... and limited by the *M'Naghten* instruction. As a result, conscientious juries have often returned verdicts of sanity despite plain evidence of serious mental illness and unanimous expert testimony that the defendant was insane....

Conscious of the inadequacies of the *M'Naghten* test, California decisions have modified that test in two significant respects. First in *People v. Wolff, supra,* 61 Cal. 2d 795, 40 Cal. Rptr. 271, 394 P.2d 959, we held that the mere capacity to verbalize socially acceptable answers to questions did not prove sanity; the defendant must not only know but also "appreciate" or "understand" the nature and wrongfulness of his act. (pp. 800-801, 40 Cal. Rptr. 271, 394 P.2d 959.) Second, in a series of decisions dating from *People v. Wells* (1949) 33 Cal. 2d 330, 202 P.2d 53 and *People v. Gorshen, supra,* 51 Cal. 2d 716, 336 P.2d 492, we developed the concept of diminished capacity, under which a defendant can introduce evidence of mental incapacity to negate specific intent, malice, or other subjective elements of the charged crime. Recently in *People v. Cantrell* (1973) 8 Cal. 3d 672, 105 Cal. Rptr. 792, 504 P.2d 1256, we expressly held that "irresistible impulse" — a concept evolved to supply the volitional element lacking in the *M'Naghten* test — can be utilized to prove diminished capacity....

But these innovative modifications to the *M'Naghten* rule fail to cure its basic defects. *Wolff* ameliorates only one of the rigid categories of *M'Naghten;* as Professor Sherry explains: "It still ... falls short of acknowledging the teaching of psychiatry that mental aberration may not only impair knowledge of wrongfulness but may very well destroy an individual's capacity to control or to restrain himself." (Sherry, *Penal Code Revision Project — Progress Report* (1968) 43 State Bar J. 900, 916.) The doctrine of diminished capacity, once hailed as a possible replacement for the defense of insanity (see Diamond, *Criminal Responsibility of the Mentally Ill* (1961) 14 Stan. L. Rev. 59), can now be seen to create its own problems.

....

A defendant whose criminal activity arises from mental illness or defect usually requires confinement and special treatment. Penal Code sections 1026 and 1026a provide such confinement and treatment for persons acquitted on grounds of insanity. A successful diminished capacity defense, on the other hand, results either in the release of the defendant or his confinement as an ordinary criminal for a lesser term. Because the diminished capacity defense thus fails to identify the mentally disturbed defendant, it may result in the defendant not receiving the care appropriate to his condition. Such a defendant, who may still suffer from his mental disturbance, may serve his term, be released and thus permitted to become a danger to the public....

In our opinion the continuing inadequacy of *M'Naghten* as a test of criminal responsibility cannot be cured by further attempts to interpret language dating from a different era of psychological thought, nor by the creation of additional concepts designed to evade the limitations of *M'Naghten*. It is time to recast *M'Naghten* in modern language, taking account of advances in psychological knowledge and changes in legal thought.

The definition of mental incapacity appearing in section 4.01 of the American Law Institute's Model Penal Code represents the distillation of nine years of research, exploration, and debate by the leading legal and medical minds of the country. (*United States v. Freeman, supra,* 357 F.2d 606, 622.) ...[8]

---

[8]The American Law Institute takes no position as to whether the term "criminality" or the term "wrongfulness" best expresses the test of criminal responsibility; we prefer the term "criminality."

A. LEGAL TESTS FOR RESPONSIBILITY 599

Adhering to the fundamental concepts of free will and criminal responsibility, the American Law Institute test restates *M'Naghten* in language consonant with the current legal and psychological thought.... It has won widespread acceptance, having been adopted by every federal circuit for the first circuit[9] and by 15 states.

"In the opinion of most thoughtful observers this proposed test [the ALI test] is a significant improvement over *M'Naghten*." ... The advantages may be briefly summarized. First the ALI test adds a volitional element, the ability to conform to legal requirements, which is missing from the *M'Naghten* test. Second, it avoids the all-or-nothing language of *M'Naghten* and permits a verdict based on lack of substantial capacity.... Third, the ALI test is broad enough to permit a psychiatrist to set before the trier of fact a full picture of the defendant's mental impairments and flexible enough to adapt to future changes in psychiatric theory and diagnosis. Fourth, by referring to the defendant's capacity to "appreciate" the wrongfulness of his conduct, the test confirms our holding in *People v. Wolff, supra,* 61 Cal. 2d 795, 40 Cal. Rptr. 271, 394 P.2d 959, that mere verbal knowledge of right and wrong does not prove sanity. Finally, by establishing a broad test of nonresponsibility, including elements of volition as well as cognition, the test provides the foundation on which we can order and rationalize the convoluted and occasionally inconsistent law of diminished capacity....

[The court then concluded that it had the power to institute a new rule through an overturning of earlier precedent, without violating separation of powers limitations.]

NOTES

1. In 1982, California voters approved an initiative proposal which rejected the Drew adoption of the ALI test by adding a new § 25(b) to the California Penal Code:

> In any criminal proceeding, including any juvenile court proceeding, in which a plea of not guilty by reason of insanity is entered, this defense shall be found by the trier of fact only when the accused person proves by a preponderance of the evidence that he or she was incapable of knowing or understanding the nature and quality of his or her act and of distinguishing right from wrong at the time of the commission of the offense.

Subpart 2 of the American Law Institute test provides that "the terms 'mental disease or defect' do not include an abnormality manifested only by repeated criminal or otherwise antisocial conduct." The language, designed to deny an insanity defense to psychopaths and sociopaths, is not relevant to the present case. The question whether to adopt subpart 2 of the ALI test is one which we defer to a later occasion.

[9] Federal Circuits. (2d Cir.: United States v. Freeman, *supra,* 357 F.2d 606. 3d Cir.: United States v. Currens, supra, 290 F.2d 751. 4th Cir.: United States v. Chandler (1968) 393 F.2d 920. 5th Cir.: Blake v. United States (1969) 407 F.2d 908. 6th Cir.: United States v. Smith, *supra,* 404 F.2d 720. 7th Cir.: United States v. Shapiro (1967) 383 F.2d 680. 8th Cir.: Pope v. United States (1967) 372 F.2d 710. 9th Cir.: Wade v. United States, supra, 426 F.2d 64. 10th Cir.: Wion v. United States (1963) 325 F.2d 420. D.C.Cir.: United States v. Brawner (1972) 153 U.S.App.D.C. 1, 471 F.2d 969.)

1982 Cal. Adv. Legis. Serv. 537 (Deering).

2. *State v. Smith,* 136 Vt. 520, 396 A.2d 126, 128 (1978):

> The raising of a defense to criminal responsibility based on insanity as defined by law has a history antedating the founding of this nation, but has always had grudging acceptance. The popular concern that it might open the way to easy acquittal of criminals was noted in State v. Hanson, 134 Vt. 227, 232, 356 A.2d 517 (1976). Implicit in that concern is the concept that there will be easy and early release from confinement for mental treatment, leaving a crime inadequately punished and, presumably, society unprotected. This understanding does not necessarily comport with the facts....
>
> Even so, the remedy is not to undercut or deny a defendant the right to present an issue related to his defense, sanctioned by statute, and so long acknowledged as validly part of our law. The consequences of a valid insanity defense with respect to confinement, treatment and discharge, if to be changed, are to be addressed in other governmental arenas. State v. Warner, 91 Vt. 391, 393 101 A. 149, 150 (1917), written more than sixty years ago, reminds us that: "It is as much the duty of the state to protect an insane man from conviction, as it is to prevent a sane man from escaping that result."

3. In *Government of Virgin Islands v. Fredericks,* 578 F.2d 927, 930-33 (3d Cir. 1978), the defendant complained that the trial court had rejected his request for an instruction, based on *United States v. Currens,* 290 F.2d 751, 774 (3d Cir. 1961), which had established the insanity standard for the Third Circuit. The language of the requested instruction was:

> Mental disease (or defect) includes any abnormal condition of the mind, regardless of its medical label, which substantially affects mental or emotional processes and substantially impairs behavior controls. The term "behavior controls" refers to the processes and capacity of a person to regulate and control his conduct and his actions.
>
> In considering whether the defendant had a mental disease (or defect) at the time of the unlawful act with which he is charged, you may consider testimony in this case concerning the development, adaptation and functioning of these mental and emotional processes and behavior controls. [The trial judge refused to present the language, stating that expert witnesses and counsel had given them what was needed to understand the concept of mental disease or defect. The Third Circuit affirmed on the point:]
>
> Much of the substance of the proposed instruction was already covered in the judge's charge to the jury under Currens . The requested instruction contained the concept of a mental disease or defect as an abnormal condition of the mind which substantially impairs "behavior controls." It also defined "behavior controls" as the capacity of a person to regulate and control his conduct or actions. Both of these aspects of the requested charge are contained in the Currens instructions given during Fredericks' trial that defendant should be acquitted if

at the time of the alleged conduct, the Defendant, as a result of mental disease or defect, lacked substantial capacity to conform his conduct to the requirements of the law.

The part of the requested charge that directed the jury not to be bound by the medical labels used by the experts and to consider all evidence bearing on "the development, adaptation, and functioning of ... mental and emotional processes and behavior controls" is covered by the following part of the jury charge:

In considering the issue of insanity, you may consider all of the circumstantial evidence just prior to the incident, during the incident, and after the incident. You should consider all of the lay testimony, that is, all the non-expert testimony that you had presented to you. You should consider all the evidence that has been admitted as to the Defendant's mental condition before and after the offense charged, as well as the testimony as to the Defendant's mental condition at the time of the incident....

....

[Y]ou are not bound by the experts' opinion and you may accept or reject their opinions. You are not bound by their definitions, their labels as to what is or what is not a mental illness. It is for you to decide ... whether Mr. Fredericks was, at the time [of the homicide], mentally ill.

Further, even if the contents of the requested instruction were not substantially covered by the charge to the Fredericks' jury — specifically the fixing of a medico-legal definition of mental disease or defect as an "abnormal condition of the mind which substantially affects mental or emotional processes" — we do not believe that such a charge should be mandated. The proposed instruction would not illuminate the charge given and could conceivably confuse the jurors in their application of it. We do not think it self-evident that the concepts of "mental or emotional processes" and "behavior controls" would be more intelligible to a jury than the concept now embodied in Currens of a mental disease or defect which deprives defendant of the substantial capacity to conform his conduct to the requirements of the law. Additionally, the evidence adduced during the Fredericks' trial did not bear closely on these terms of the requested charge. Indeed, we are not convinced that this specification of psychiatric terminology is correct in light of current (let alone future) psychiatric thought.

We also believe that requiring that defendant's proposed instruction be given would conflict with the responsibility of the jury in considering an insanity defense. As this court indicated in the Currens opinion, the decision of whether a defendant is affected by a mental disease or defect rests with the jury's evaluation of all lay and medical evidence in the case.... The requested instruction, insofar as not covered by the Currens charge, directs the jury to trial testimony given in terms of "mental or emotional processes" and "behavior controls" as the determinate of this decision. The definition of mental disease or defect is essentially a factual, medical question, not a legal issue. The court should not encroach upon the jury's function of resolving possibly competing psychiatric views of this definition.

The development of the law regarding the insanity defense in federal courts supports our conclusion. While almost all the courts of appeals have adopted a standard for insanity similar to that of our circuit in Currens, only the Court of Appeals for the District of Columbia has insisted that instructions to the jury contain a "legal definition" of mental disease or defect.

The first appearance of the sort of instruction requested by defendant was in *McDonald v. United States,* 114 U.S.App. D.C. 120, 312 F.2d 847 (1962) (en banc). At that time the District of Columbia court was following the insanity test of *Durham v. United States,* 94 U.S.App.D.C. 228, 214 F.2d 862 (1954), which required the jury to determine whether the acts charged were the "product" of a mental disease or defect.[3] In McDonald, the court noted that its experience under Durham had shown that a "judicial definition" of disease or defect was needed to emphasize that "neither the court nor the jury is bound by ad hoc definitions or conclusions as to what experts state is a disease or defect." 114 U.S.App.D.C. at 824, 312 F.2d at 851.

The American Law Institute in its Model Penal Code and this court in its decision in Currens similarly noted the problems of vagueness in the Durham "product" test. Instead of attempting to define more closely the term "mental disease or defect," both the Institute and this court departed from Durham.[4] ... This court's rule in Currens was derived in part from the ALI's test. 290 F.2d at 774 n.32.

Under both the ALI and the Currens rule, the problem of vagueness in the Durham test is ameliorated. As the dissent points out, the jury still faces two distinct issues: 1) whether the defendant suffers from a mental disease or defect and 2) whether that condition deprives him of the substantial capacity to conform his conduct to the requirements of the law. Nevertheless, the insertion of the second step gives guidance to the jury which was lacking in *Durham.* The jury, when informed of the result of a mental disease or defect which would constitute legal insanity, is able better to understand what a mental disease or defect is.

The approach of the ALI and this circuit, which has omitted the McDonald definition of mental disease or defect, is now widely accepted among federal courts.[6] Although some of these courts have discussed the criti-

---

[3] "[A]n accused is not criminally responsible if his unlawful act was the product of mental disease or defect." Durham v. United States, 94 U.S.App.D.C. 228, 240-41, 214 F.2d 862, 874-75 (1954).

[4] ALI Model Penal Code § 4.01, Comments 5, 6 (Tent. Draft No. 4, 1955); United States v. Currens, 290 F.2d 751, 771 (3d Cir. 1961).

[6] See United States v. Freeman, 357 F.2d 606 (2d Cir. 1966); United States v. Chandler, 393 F.2d 920 (4th Cir. 1968) (en banc); Blake v. United States, 407 F.2d 908 (5th Cir. 1969) (en banc); United States v. Smith, 404 F.2d 720 (6th Cir. 1968); United States v. Shapiro, 383 F.2d 680 (7th Cir. 1967) (en banc); United States v. Frazier, 458 F.2d 911 (8th Cir. 1972); Wade v. United States, 426 F.2d 64 (9th Cir. 1970) (en banc); Wion v. United States, 325 F.2d 420 (10th Cir. 1963) (en banc), *cert. denied,* 377 U.S. 946, 84 S.Ct. 1354, 12 L.Ed.2d 309 (1964). See also Amador Beltran v. United States, 302 F.2d 48, 52 (1st Cir. 1962).

cism of the Durham test raised in McDonald, they have assumed that the ALI test would eliminate the problem.[7]

The sole exception currently is the District of Columbia court. When that court adopted the ALI standard, it ruled that the McDonald definition should be retained to cure the "inherent ambiguity" of the term "mental disease or defect." *United States v. Brawner,* 153 U.S.App.D.C. 1, 15-16, 471 F.2d 969, 983-84 (1972) (en banc). As we mentioned above, we do not find inherently ambiguous the concept of a mental disease or defect which deprives defendant of the substantial ability to conform his conduct to the requirements of the law. We therefore agree with the majority of circuits which have not inserted the McDonald instruction into the ALI test. We hold that under a Currens charge as was given in this case, the trial judge was not required to give the instruction requested by Fredericks on the "legal definition" of mental disease or defect.

4. *In re Ramon M.,* 22 Cal. 3d 419, 584 P.2d 524, 530, 149 Cal. Rptr. 387 (1978):

In sum, it is unnecessary for us to fashion separate standards for the [statutory] defenses of insanity and idiocy or to encounter the difficult theoretical and practical problems which such separate standards would create. The ALI test, already adopted by this court in *Drew,* serves to define all defenses of mental incapacity, and thus encompasses both idiocy and insanity. We conclude that the defense of idiocy proffered by the defendant in the present case is defined by the ALI standard, and that defendant's mental retardation constitutes a defense to criminal conduct if "at the time of such conduct as a result of mental disease or defect he lacks substantial capacity either to appreciate the criminality of his conduct or to conform his conduct to the requirements of law."

5. Automatism can impair volition so as to render persons unable to conform their conduct to the requirements of law. *People v. Grant,* 71 Ill. 2d 551, 377 N.E.2d 4 (1978); *People v. Gaines,* 93 Ill. App. 3d 71, 416 N.E.2d 1156 (1981); *cf. Fulcher v. State,* 633 P.2d 142 (Wyo. 1981) (evidence of automatism bearing on culpability could be tendered by the defense despite a defense refusal to file a pretrial plea of mental illness or deficiency).

6. On "pathological gambling" as a mental disease or defect, *see United States v. Gilliss,* 645 F.2d 1269 (8th Cir. 1981).

7. On the interrelationship between intoxication and mental disease or defect, *see infra* p. 654, n.5.

4. DIMINISHED RESPONSIBILITY

[*See* Chapter 5, *supra* pp. 279-286.]

---

[7]See, e.g., Wade v. United States, 426 F.2d 64, 68-69, 71-73 (9th Cir. 1970) (en banc); Blake v. United States, 407 F.2d 908, 914, 916 (5th Cir. 1969) (en banc); United States v. Smith, 404 F.2d 720, 726, 727 (6th Cir. 1968); United States v. Chandler, 393 F.2d 920, 925-26, 928-29 (4th Cir. 1968) (en banc).

5. "*MENS REA*" OR ABOLITION TEST

IDAHO CODE § 18-207*

(a) Mental condition shall not be a defense to any charge of criminal conduct.

(b) If by the provisions of section 19-2523, Idaho Code, the court finds that one convicted of crime suffers from any mental condition requiring treatment, such person shall be committed to the board of correction or such city or county officials as provided by law for placement in an appropriate facility for treatment, having regard for such conditions of security as the case may require. In the event a sentence of incarceration has been imposed, the defendant shall receive treatment in a facility which provides for incarceration or less restrictive confinement. In the event that a course of treatment thus commenced shall be concluded prior to the expiration of the sentence imposed, the offender shall remain liable for the remainder of such sentence, but shall have credit for time incarcerated for treatment.

(c) Nothing herein is intended to prevent the admission of expert evidence on the issues of mens rea or any state of mind which is an element of the offense, subject to the rules of evidence.

IDAHO CODE § 19-2523**

(1) Evidence of mental condition shall be received, if offered, at the time of sentencing of any person convicted of a crime. In determining the sentence to be imposed in addition to other criteria provided by law, if the defendant's mental condition is a significant factor, the court shall consider such factors as:

(a) The extent to which the defendant is mentally ill;

(b) The degree of illness or defect and level of functional impairment;

(c) The prognosis for improvement or rehabilitation;

(d) The availability of treatment and level of care required;

(e) Any risk of danger which the defendant may create for the public, if at large, or in the absence of such risk;

(f) The capacity of the defendant to appreciate the wrongfulness of his conduct or to conform his conduct to the requirements of law at the time of the offense charged.

(2) The court shall authorize treatment during the period of confinement or probation specified in the sentence if, after the sentencing hearing, it concludes by clear and convincing evidence that:

(a) The defendant suffers from a severe and reliably diagnosable mental illness or defect resulting in the defendant's inability to appreciate the wrongfulness of his conduct or to conform his conduct to the requirements of law;

---

*Added by Idaho Session Laws ch. 368 (April 2, 1982), effective July 1, 1982.
**Added by Idaho Session Laws ch. 368 (April 1, 1982), effective July 1, 1982.

A. LEGAL TESTS FOR RESPONSIBILITY

(b) Without treatment, the immediate prognosis is for major distress resulting in serious mental or physical deterioration of the defendant;

(c) Treatment is available for such illness or defect;

(d) The relative risks and benefits of treatment or nontreatment are such that a reasonable person would consent to treatment.

(3) In addition to the authorization of treatment, the court shall pronounce sentence as provided by law.

NOTES

1. The constitutionality of the Idaho statute was upheld by the Idaho Supreme Court in a decision stating that there is no due process right to present an affirmative defense of insanity. *State v. Searcy*, 798 P.2d 914 (Idaho 1990). Alabama, L. 82-888 (Aug. 13, 1982), and Montana, MONT. CODE ANN. §§ 45-2-101(28); 46-14-101; 46-14-201, have adopted a similar approach. The constitutionality of the Montana statute was upheld in *State v. Korell*, 690 P.2d 992 (Mont. 1984).

2. U.S. Senate Report No. 97-307 to Accompany Criminal Code Reform Act of 1981, S. 1630, 97th Congress, 1st Session (1982):

The Mens Rea Test

One suggested formulation of an insanity test would provide a defense if the defendant, as a result of mental disease or defect, lacked the state of mind required as an element of the offense charged. Mental disease or defect would not otherwise constitute a defense.[47] This concentrates attention on the defendant's mental condition insofar as it relates to determining whether the offender acted with the mental states necessary to commit the offense charged.[48] Thus the focus of initial inquiry in criminal trials would be on such questions as "Did the defendant intend to hijack an aircraft?" in a case of air piracy, rather than "Could he have conformed his conduct to the requirements of law?" The Model Penal Code commentary illustrates the proper subject of an insanity defense by posing the example of a madman who believes that he is squeezing lemons when he is actually choking his wife. Under the mens rea test he would not be guilty of murder, not because he fell within a special defense, but because he lacked the state of mind required by the offense, that is, he did not knowingly cause the death of another person.

The critical issue is seen as one of disposition. Assuming a finding of an intent to hijack the aircraft and of the requisite conduct, the question at the time of sentencing would be whether, in light of all the circumstances, the

---

[47] Such language was contained in S. 1400 and S. 1 of the 94th Congress and was approved by the New York City Bar Association's Special Committee, Hearings, pp. 3490-3491. In the present 97th Congress, Senator Hatch has introduced two bills, S. 818 and S. 1558, which propose this same formulation.

[48] While the provisions are treated in depth in that part of the report dealing with subchapter B of chapter 36, it is worth mentioning here that one who intends to rely upon a defense of insanity must give notice of the defense under Rule 12.2 of the Federal Rules of Criminal Procedure. Cf. Williams v. Florida, 399 U.S. 78 (1970). The provisions of section 3612 allow for comprehensive psychiatric examinations and a special verdict of not guilty by reason of insanity.

defendant should be committed to prison, to a mental hospital, or to some other program.

Apart from its bearing on the defendant's commission of an element of the offense, his mental state or condition at the time of the offense would not provide an excuse for his conduct.

Advocates of a mens rea test recognize that certain persons who may be found not guilty by reason of insanity under traditional insanity tests[49] but who have in fact committed a criminal offense as a result of mental disease or defect, may objectively be found to have committed the offense — and thus to be "guilty" — under this standard.[50] The undesirability of labeling such persons as "guilty" of a crime — given the term's collateral moral connotations — should be weighed against two factors. First, the test would put an end to the abuses which have arisen under the older, more confusing insanity standards and which have in the past allowed those actually guilty of crimes to go free, e.g., those who "cannot" control their behavior because they do not choose to make the effort to do so. Second, though such persons may be technically guilty of an offense under the new standards, the stigma attached to a determination of criminality will be materially mitigated at the sentencing stage by publicly adjudging them to be deserving of proper medical care rather than deserving of a punitive sentence of imprisonment. The nature of the disposition provided by the sentence will constitute society's recognition of the defendant's lack of moral culpability for his offense.

The *mens rea* test is quite simple. In fact this simplicity, when compared to existing law, is one of its major virtues. However, as the hearings before this Committee reveal, the proposal has been the subject of a significant amount of controversy. Support for the mens rea test is based on three factors: fair treatment for the offender; protection of society; and the proper administration of criminal justice.

Fair treatment for the offender: Dealing with the mentally ill offender, as the history of the insanity defense illustrates, has proven to be a difficult matter. The person has committed the conduct forbidden by law. He has offended social norms and may well do so again. Yet, there is a natural reluctance to punish an abnormal person for failure to conduct himself in normal fashion.

On the other hand if the traditional criteria for confinement are considered, then the mentally ill offender is particularly in need of confinement. He is in need of treatment and rehabilitation. Society may well be protected by his

---

[49] The number of persons raising the defense in a given year has been estimated at less than 1% of serious felons with less than 100 persons successfully raising the defense. The Federal portion would be considerably less. See Hearings, p. 7023 (testimony of Seymour Pollack, M.D., President, American Academy of Psychiatry and the Law). Another expert has stated that the defense is successful in only 2% of the cases. See Hearings, p. 7007 (testimony of Stanley Portnow, M.D., Chairman, Committee on Psychiatry and the Law, American Psychiatric Association).

[50] While the categories of such individuals cannot be completely ascertained in advance of a body of decisions under the standard proposed here, for general purposes it can be stated that those who would not be exculpated under this kind of formulation, but who probably would be judged not guilty by reason of insanity under traditional tests, include a person who asserts that he cannot control his behavior, e.g., he is driven by an overpowering urge to steal, and a person who operates under a delusion that what he does is not morally wrong, e.g., he is told by a voice to kill in order to rid the world of an "evil" person.

A. LEGAL TESTS FOR RESPONSIBILITY

incapacitation. His confinement may provide as much deterrent effect as the confinement of any other offender. Only retribution seems to be an inappropriate basis for his confinement since his moral fault may in some cases be considered to be non-existent or at least less than that of the "normal" offender.

If focus is placed on conviction rather than disposition the question becomes even more difficult, for under traditional analysis only the "blameworthy" should be branded as criminals. The question then reduces itself to the inquiry as to when is a mentally ill offender blameworthy? This approach answers that question by stating that all offenders are blameworthy to the extent that they may be found guilty of committing an offense when their mental state as to the proscribed conduct and the circumstances surrounding that conduct is that state required by the offense. In that sense, i.e., with regard to the state of mind of the defendant, the mentally ill offender is treated fairly for he is treated the same as all other offenders.[51]

It has been persuasively argued that the mentally ill offender possibly may presently be treated better than some who also have a colorable claim to lack of blameworthiness. Professor Norval Morris has stated the case as follows: [52]

> It too often is overlooked that one group's exculpation from criminal responsibility confirms the inculpation of other groups. Why not permit the defense of dwelling in a Negro ghetto? Such a defense would not be morally indefensible. Adverse social and subcultural background is statistically more criminogenic than is psychosis; like insanity, it also severely circumscribes the freedom of choice which a nondeterministic criminal law (all present criminal law systems) attributes to accused persons. True, a defense of social adversity would politically be intolerable; but that does not vitiate the analogy for my purposes. You argue that insanity destroys, undermines, diminishes man's capacity to reject what is wrong and to adhere to what is right. So does the ghetto — more so. But surely, you reply, I would not have us punish the sick. Indeed I would, if you insist on punishing the grossly deprived. To the extent that criminal sanctions serve punitive purposes, I fail to see the difference between these two defenses. To the extent that they serve rehabilitative, treatment, and curative purposes I fail to see the need for the difference.

The question arises whether it is still not unfair to impose the stigma of criminality on those few who would be exculpated under some current tests but not under the restricted view and whether they ought to be afforded medical rather than penal treatment.

---

[51] The present insanity defense also tends, more than would the formulation under discussion, in a practical sense to discriminate against the poor defendant. Insanity is frequently and probably properly called a "rich man's defense," for the wealthy can sift the pool of potential expert witnesses for those who will produce favorable testimony in a convincing manner. Poor men, on the other hand, have typically had to rely on public mental hospital experts, or those selected by the court whose reports commonly have been made available to the prosecution as well as the defense. Signs of change are detectable, see 18 U.S.C. 3006A(e), authorizing payment of expert witnesses selected privately by an indigent defendant, but they do not appear to be likely to result in total equality of advantage in litigation of insanity issues.

[52] Morris, Psychiatry and the Dangerous Criminal, 41 S. Cal. L. Rev. 514, 520 (1968).

As to the first of these, it is argued that it is altogether uncertain that the criminal label stigmatizes more than does the label of criminal insanity.[53]

As to the question of treatment or disposition, the same latitude in meeting the needs of the defendant should be available in the sentencing process as in a mental commitment procedure.

Indeed, as to therapeutic treatment, it has been suggested that it is more desirable to treat mentally ill offenders as responsible for their actions than it would be to excuse their conduct entirely.[54]

Protection of society: To the extent that the mens rea test holds forth greater promise of rehabilitative treatment, it affords greater protection for society in general. To the extent that the proposal requires a direct relationship of the defendant's overall mental state to his criminal culpability it removes nebulous and extraneous issues from the determination of guilt. To the extent that it precludes spurious and fabricated claims it makes justice more swift but no less just.

While the actual effects would only be determined by implementation, it is reasonable to believe that a *mens rea* test would do much to achieve the objectives stated above and that the achievement of those objectives would do much to protect the public interest.

Administration of criminal justice: The various insanity defenses currently in use impeded the administration of justice in two significant ways. First, they focus upon terms which are hopelessly vague to the courts, the lawyer, the psychiatrist, and the layman. Second, they allocate psychiatric resources in a manner that is largely inappropriate and frequently unseemly.

The following dialogue between Dr. Karl Menninger and a trial judge is illustrative of the first point:[55]

> Judge. Well, what about the question of whether or not this man is responsible under the law? He committed a crime; that we know. But there is still the question of his intentions and his capacity for knowing right from wrong, his capacity to refrain from the wrong if he knows what wrong is. If he is not responsible, then technically he is not guilty.
>
> Answer [Dr. Karl Menninger]. Your Honor, responsible is another one of these functionally undefined words....
>
> Judge. But your colleagues have often testified in this court that in their opinion a certain prisoner was or was not responsible.
>
> Answer. Yes, your Honor, because the word responsible is in everyday use. But this use is different from the legal use, as you well know, and that fact is not always clear to your witnesses.
>
> ....
>
> What you want to know, I suppose, is whether this man is capable of living with the rest of us and refraining from his propensity to injure us.

---

[53] See generally Farina et al, *Mental Illness and the Impact of Believing Others Know About It*, 71 J. Abn. Psych., Feb. 1971, pp. 1-6; Farina, Holland, and Ring. *The Role of Stigma and Set in Interpersonal Interaction*, 71 J. Abn. Psych., Dec. 1966, pp. 421-428; Enis, *Civil Liberties and Mental Illness*, 7 Crim. L. Bull. 101 (1971); Grazia Report on Pretrial Diversion of Accused Offenders to Community Health Treatment Programs (Georgetown U. School of Medicine, 1972).
[54] Working Papers, p. 251.
[55] Menninger, *The Crime of Punishment*, pp. 136-137 (1968).

A. LEGAL TESTS FOR RESPONSIBILITY

You want to know whether he is dangerous, whether he can be treated and cured — whether we must arrange to detain him in protective custody indefinitely.

Judge. Exactly. This is indeed what the court would like to know. But it seems we do not know how to communicate with one another, and our laws do not permit us to ask you. How, I beg of you, may I obtain direct, nonevasive answers to precisely these questions?

Answer. Your Honor, by asking for them. As you say yourself, you are not permitted by precedent and custom to do so.

Chief Judge Bazelon, a prolific writer on the subject of the insanity defense, has himself cast doubt as to its utility simply because of the difficulty in stating the terms in a comprehensible manner.[56]

While the *mens rea* test, dependent as it is on the use of the phrase "mental disease or defect," may be said to suffer from some of the same vagueness problems, it should be noted that the reduction in availability of the defense reduces the harm and impact of the necessary vagueness. Moreover, juries have traditionally dealt with the existence or non-existence of *mens rea* and this formulation, unlike the traditional insanity defense, poses no additional burdens on them.

The misallocation of psychiatric and psychological resources is an additional consideration favoring a mens rea approach. The question has three aspects: first, the shortage of psychiatric resources; second, the unseemly battle of the experts; and third, the desirability of using such personnel functionally, by explicitly directing their attention to the crucial questions whether defendants should be institutionalized and, if so, to what sort of facility.

As to the first, it is of some interest that in response to a survey conducted some years ago by the Committee staff, some 62% of the Departments of Mental Health in the several States favored either total abolition of an insanity defense or abolition of a separate insanity defense.[57] Many of the responses favoring some form of abolition emphasized the burden that the defense creates on their departments and the time it takes away from the therapy.[58]

Not only do the present defenses place a burden on resources, they also misuse them, for as one psychiatrist wrote to the Committee: "I have felt for a long time that psychiatry does not belong in the adversary proceeding. There is nothing in the training of a psychiatrist which prepares him for this type of

---

[56] Washington v. United States, 390 F.2d 444, 457 n.33 (D.C. Cir. 1967). See also the English case of Regina v. Byrne, [1960] 2 Q.B. 396, 404: "In a case where the abnormality of mind is one which affects the accused's self-control the step between 'he did not resist his impulse' and 'he could not resist his impulse' is, as the evidence in this case shows, one which is incapable of scientific proof. A fortiori there is no scientific measurement of the degree of difficulty which an abnormal person finds in controlling his impulses."

[57] Hearings, pp. 6381-6409.

[58] The terminology "abolition of the insanity defense" is commonly used by writers in the field as a shorthand reference designed to include the modified form of an insanity defense. A more accurate reference would be "abolition of the separate insanity defense" or "abolition of the traditional insanity defense." Most of the writers utilizing such terminology have in mind a formulation under which psychiatric testimony could be introduced with regard to the defendant's possession of the mental state required as an element of the offense charged — a possibility which is not generally available under the approach of current law.

business. I think his primary training has to do with the diagnosis and treatment of mentally and emotionally sick people.[59] Moreover, it can hardly be said to be therapeutically valuable to have a patient view psychiatrists as advocates for or against the patient.

Several other persons who have appeared before or corresponded with the Committee have expressed a distaste for the "battle of the experts."[60] They concluded that it can be of little good to the general view of the psychiatric profession and the criminal justice system to require psychiatrists to testify against each other in an advocate form on matters on which many of them argue they have no expertise.[61]

Continuation of an insanity defense based on amorphous concepts of blameworthiness may ultimately be detrimental to the administration of the criminal justice system and is a waste of judicial and psychiatric resources.[62]

The ultimate question, posed by one expert in the field, is "why an insanity defense?"[63] Exceptions to criminal liability should be based on sound policy grounds, for such special and unequal treatment should not be lightly permitted. A focus on the culpability of the defendant as defined by the state of mind elements is one answer to the question posed. The Committee has found widespread support for the mens rea test since its initial proposal by the National Commission's consultant on the subject, its recommendation by a substantial minority of the members of the National Commission, and its adoption in S. 1400 of the 93d Congress.

. . . .

A study in comparative law of the Swedish experience under laws similar to a mens rea test illustrates that the approach is not only workable but effective.[70] The reported bill, by deleting any reference to the issue, will leave the further development of the appropriate approach to this problem to the courts in the light of experience and the accumulating insights of the varied disciplines involved.

3. "Statement of Richard J. Bonnie, Professor of Law and Director, Institute of Law, Psychiatry and Public Policy, University of Virginia, Submitted to the Committee on the Judiciary of the United States Senate, Concerning the Insanity Defense and Proposed Bills S. 2572, S. 1558, S. 818, S. 1106, S. 2658, S. 2669, S. 2672 and S. 2678, 97th Cong., 1st Sess. (July 19, 1982) (mimeograph):

Abolition: The Mens Rea Approach. The third option is the one I have characterized as abolition of the defense. Technically, this characterization is

---

[59] Hearings, p. 6391 (letter of Zigmond M. Lebensohn, M.D.)

[60] E.g., letter of Dr. Ethel Bonn, *id.* at 6388; letter of Dr. Reginald White, *id.* at 6396.

[61] *Id.* at 6385.

[62] A fairly extreme example is Wright v. United States, 250 F.2d 4 (D.C. Cir. 1957), in which eleven psychiatrists examined the defendant and testified before the jury. In the District of Columbia a committee of the Judicial Conference reported that some psychiatrists were avoiding hospital staff conferences evaluating persons facing criminal charges to avoid being subpoenaed. Judicial Conference of the District of Columbia Circuit, Report of the Committee on Problems Connected with Mental Examination of the Accused in Criminal Cases Before Trial, p. 32 (1966).

[63] Goldstein, The Brawner Rule — Why? Or No More Nonsense on Non Sense in the Criminal Law, Please!, 1973 Wash. U.L.Q. 17.

[70] See Moyer, The Mentally Abnormal Offender in Sweden: An Overview and Comparisons With American Law, 22 Am. J. Comp. L. 71 (1974).

accurate because the essential substantive effect of the so-called 'mens rea' approach (or 'elements' approach) would be to eliminate any criterion of exculpation, based on mental disease, which is independent of the elements of particular crimes. To put it another way, the bills taking this approach[*] would eliminate any separate exculpatory doctrine based on proof of mental disease; instead mentally ill (or retarded) defendants would be treated just like everyone else. A normal person cannot escape liability by proving that he did not know or appreciate the fact that his conduct was wrong, and — under the mens rea approach — neither could a psychotic person.[**]

"*The Case Against the Mens Rea Approach.* Most of the bills now before you would adopt the mens rea option, the approach recently enacted in Montana and Idaho. As I have already noted, this change, abolishing the insanity defense, would constitute an abrupt and unfortunate departure from the Anglo-American legal tradition.

"If the insanity defense were abolished, the law would not take adequate account of the incapacitating effects of severe mental illness. Some mentally ill defendants may be said to have 'intended' to do what they did — that is, their technical guilt can be established — but they nonetheless may have been so severely disturbed that they were unable to appreciate the significance of their actions. These cases do not frequently arise, but when they do, a criminal conviction — signifying the societal judgment that the defendant deserves punishment — would offend the basic moral intuitions of the community. Judges and juries would then be forced either to return a verdict which they regard as morally obtuse or to acquit the defendant in defiance of the law. They should be spared such moral embarrassment.

....

"I believe that ... the mens rea approach does not take sufficient account of the morally significant aberrations of mental functioning associated with severe mental disorder. I readily concede, however, that these technical points may make little practical difference in the courtroom. If ... expert testimony ... were admitted to disprove the existence of mens rea, juries may behave as many observers believe they do now — they may ignore the technical aspects of the law and decide, very bluntly, whether the defendant was too crazy to be convicted. However, I do not believe that rational criminal law reform is served by designing rules of law in the expectation that they will be ignored or nullified when they appear unjust in individual cases.

---

[*] S. 1558, S. 818, S. 2669 and S. 1106 would all adopt the mens rea approach, although they differ on the label for the verdict. Under S. 1558 and S. 2669, the defendant who lacks mens rea due to mental disease would be found "not guilty by reason of insanity." Under S. 1106, the defendant who lacks mens rea due to mental disease would be found "guilty but insane"; however, because such an offender is not sentenced for the crime and is subject only to therapeutic restraint, the verdict label has only symbolic importance. Finally, S. 818 does not address the verdict form.

[**] Of course, a normal person can escape liability or reduce the grade of his offense by showing that he did not have the intention, awareness or belief required in the definition of the offense and, under these bills, so could a crazy person. A review of decisional law in the federal judicial circuits indicates that this is now the law: evidence concerning the defendant's abnormal mental condition is admissible whenever it is relevant to prove that the defendant did or did not have the "specific intent" required in the definition of the offense. Cf. § 4.02(1) of the Model Penal Code.

"Also, another danger of the mens rea approach is that courts will attempt to soften its impact by reinterpreting the concepts of intention, knowledge and recklessness in order to give them qualitative meanings and thereby achieve exculpatory results in cases where criminal liability seems ethically offensive. This would be a particularly unfortunate response because it would undermine the modern trend toward greater precision and coherence in the definition of mens rea. Again, I believe the cause of criminal law reform ... is best served by retaining the insanity defense as a safety valve for qualitative claims of severe mental impairment rather than by squeezing these claims into the generic states of mind defined in the penal law."

6. "GUILTY BUT MENTALLY ILL"

MICHIGAN COMPILED LAWS § 768.36 (1975)

(1) If the defendant asserts a defense of insanity in compliance with section 20a [the notice and diagnostic evaluation provision], the defendant may be found "guilty but mentally ill" if, after trial, the trier of fact finds all of the following beyond a reasonable doubt:

(a) That the defendant is guilty of an offense.

(b) That the defendant was mentally ill at the time of the commission of that offense.

(c) That the defendant was not legally insane at the time of the commission of that offense.

(2) If the defendant asserts a defense of insanity in compliance with section 20a and the defendant waives his right to trial, by jury or by judge, the trial judge, with the approval of the prosecuting attorney, may accept a plea of guilty but mentally ill in lieu of a plea of guilty or a plea of nolo contendere. The judge may not accept a plea of guilty but mentally ill until, with the defendant's consent, he has examined the report or reports prepared pursuant to section 20a, has held a hearing on the issue of the defendant's mental illness at which either party may present evidence, and is satisfied that the defendant was mentally ill at the time of the offense to which the plea is entered. The reports shall be made a part of the record of the case.

(3) If a defendant is found guilty but mentally ill or enters a plea to that effect which is accepted by the court, the court shall impose any sentence which could be imposed pursuant to law upon a defendant who is convicted of the same offense. If the defendant is committed to the custody of the department of corrections, he shall undergo further evaluation and be given such treatment as is psychiatrically indicated for his mental illness or retardation. Treatment may be provided by the department of corrections or by the department of mental health after his transfer [under cited statutes; statutes governing retransfer to correctional custody also apply.] When a treating facility designated by either the department of corrections or the department of mental health discharges such a defendant prior to the expiration of his sentence, that treating facility shall transmit to the parole board a report on the condition of the defendant

which contains the clinical facts, the diagnosis, the course of treatment, and the prognosis for the remission of symptoms, the potential for recidivism and for the danger to himself or the public, and recommendations for future treatment. In the event that the parole board pursuant to law or administrative rules should consider him for parole, the board shall consult with the treating facility at which the defendant is being treated or from which he has been discharged and a comparable report on the condition of the defendant shall be filed with the board. If he is placed on parole by the parole board, his treatment shall, upon recommendation of the treating facility, be made a condition of parole, and failure to continue treatment except by agreement with the designated facility and parole board shall be a basis for the institution of parole violation hearings.

(4) If a defendant who is found guilty but mentally ill is placed on probation under the jurisdiction of the sentencing court pursuant to law, the trial judge, upon recommendation of the center for forensic psychiatry, shall make treatment a condition of probation. Reports as specified by the trial judge shall be filed with the probation officer and the sentencing court. Failure to continue treatment, except by agreement with the treating agency and sentencing court, shall be a basis for the institution of probation violation hearings. The period of probation shall not be for less than 5 years and shall not be shortened without receipt and consideration of a forensic psychiatric report by the sentencing court. Treatment shall be provided by an agency of the department of mental health, or with the approval of the sentencing court and at individual expense, by private agencies, private physicians, or other mental health personnel. A psychiatric report shall be filed with the probation officer and the sentencing court every 3 months during the period of probation. If a motion on a petition to discontinue probation is made by the defendant, the probation officer shall request a report as specified from the center for forensic psychiatry or any other facility certified by the department of mental health for the performance of forensic psychiatric evaluation.

NOTES

1. The Michigan statute was sustained as constitutional against due process and equal protection attacks in People v. McLeod, 407 Mich. 632, 288 N.W.2d 909 (1980).

2. The following statistics were compiled by the Kentucky Legislative Research Commission for presentation to the Kentucky General Assembly, summarizing Michigan experience with its GBMI verdict. The Kentucky legislature added GBMI provisions to Ky. Rev. Stat. ch. 504 through HB 32, signed into law March 26, 1982, effective July 15, 1982.

	1976	1977	1978	1979	1980	Average
Evaluations for Criminal Responsibility [1]	401	561	746	948	1,183[2]	767.8

[1] A new center for evaluations opened in 1976. In the year prior to its opening, only 92 evaluations were performed.

[2] Based on average 24.8% yearly increase.

	1976	1977	1978	1979	1980	Average
Recommendations — Excusable	57	48	140	84	N/A	82.3
Not Guilty by Reason of Insanity Verdicts[3]	32	47	51	68	N/A	49.5
Guilty But Mentally Ill Verdicts[4]	20	20	29	38	34[5]	28.2
Percent Guilty But Mentally Ill to Total Evaluations	4.9	3.5	3.8	4.0	2.8	3.8

3. *See generally* Smith & Hall, *Evaluating Michigan's Guilty But Mentally Ill Verdict: An Empirical Study,* 16 MICH. J. LAW REFORM 77 (1982).

4. Other states which have adopted the guilty but mentally ill alternative include Alaska, Delaware, Georgia, Illinois, Indiana, and New Mexico.

5. *See generally* Note, *Criminal Responsibility: Changes in the Insanity Defense and the Guilty But Mentally Ill Response,* 21 WASHBURN L.J. 515, 542-53 (1982).

7. ADMINISTRATION OF THE TESTS

a. Pleading the Defense

MODEL PENAL CODE

§ 4.03. Mental Disease or Defect Excluding Responsibility Is Affirmative Defense

[The text of this section appears in Appendix A.]

LABOR v. GIBSON

Supreme Court of Colorado
195 Colo. 416, 578 P.2d 1059 (1978)

LEE, JUSTICE.

Petitioner David Manual Labor brings this original proceeding ... and seeks a writ prohibiting the respondent trial judge from entering a plea of not guilty by reason of insanity on his behalf. ...

There are several important consequences of being acquitted of an offense by reason of insanity. The issues raised by a plea of not guilty by reason of insanity are tried separately from the criminal charges to a different jury and the insanity issue is tried first. ... If a defendant is found by the trier of fact to be not guilty by reason of insanity, "the court shall commit the defendant to the custody of the department of institutions until such time as he is found eligible for release." ... Although a procedure is provided ..., by which a defendant can gain his release from commitment, it is certainly possible that

---

[3] The ratio of NGRI verdicts to evaluations remains fairly constant, averaging 7.5%.

[4] The number of determinations of guilty but mentally ill for the period 8/1975 to 6/1978 was 57; 6/1978 through 12/1979 was 57. Figures in the table represent yearly averages. An average of 3.8% of the evaluations result in GBMI verdicts.

[5] Based on 6 months actual determination of 17.

he might be committed for a longer period of time than he would serve in a correctional institution under a sentence for the second-degree assault.

Thus, a defendant may strategically decide not to enter a plea of guilty by reason of insanity, due to the possible greater length of confinement as well as to the probable social stigma of being adjudged to be insane. So long as the defendant is determined to be presently mentally competent, it should be left up to the defendant and his counsel to make the tactical choice of whether to utilize this affirmative defense.... Only in the limited circumstances [when judicial entry of a plea is "necessary for a just determination of the charge against the defendant"] is the trial court authorized to enter a plea of not guilty by reason of insanity on behalf of a defendant.

NOTES

1. *Frendak v. United States*, 408 A.2d 364 (D.C. 1979), advanced as additional reasons justifying a defendant's decision not to plead the defense "the quality of treatment or the type of confinement to which he or she may be subject in an institution for the mentally ill," *id.* at 376; collateral consequences of an insanity acquittal which might follow a defendant through life, *e.g.*, a disability to serve as a juror or to obtain a driver's license, vulnerability to impeachment as a witness in later proceedings, or use of the adjudication in later civil commitment proceedings, *id.* at 377; opposition to "the imposition of an insanity defense because he or she views the crime as a political or religious protest which a finding of insanity would denigrate," *id.*; or "a feeling that he or she is not insane, or that raising the defense would be equivalent to an admission of guilt." *Id.* Such reasons outweighed the opposing considerations "that some abstract concept of justice is satisfied by protecting one who may be morally blameless from a conviction and punishment which he or she might choose to accept." *Id.* at 378. Trial courts, however, must determine that defendants understand the consequences of such a choice and make their waiver decisions voluntarily. *Id.*

2. If a statutorily required plea is not entered, there is no jurisdictional basis to enter a judgment of not guilty by reason of mental disease or defect and order a civil commitment. *United States v. Henry*, 600 F.2d 924 (D.C. Cir. 1979).

3. Even if a formal plea of not guilty by reason of insanity has been abolished, defendants still may be required by statute to give notice of a purpose to rely on the defense, and may be denied an opportunity to present evidence supporting it for failure to give notice without adequate cause. *State v. La Goy*, 136 Vt. 39, 383 A.2d 604 (1978).

b. Diagnostic Commitments and Reports

MODEL PENAL CODE

§ 4.05. Psychiatric Examination of Defendant with Respect to Mental Disease or Defect

[The text of this section appears in Appendix A.]

NOTES

1. In *Estelle v. Smith,* 451 U.S. 454 (1981), Smith had been indicted for capital murder based on a killing perpetrated by an accomplice during an armed robbery. Because the trial court doubted Smith's competency to stand trial, it arranged informally for him to be given a psychiatric examination by Dr. James P. Grigson. Grigson interviewed Smith for about ninety minutes in the county jail where Smith was confined and reported by letter to the court that Smith was "aware of the difference between right and wrong and [was] able to aid an attorney in his defense." Smith subsequently was tried for and convicted of felony-murder. At a bifurcated death penalty hearing, after overruling defense objections, the trial court allowed Grigson to testify on direct examination "(a) that Smith 'is a very severe sociopath'; (b) that 'he will continue his previous behavior'; (c) that his sociopathic condition will 'only get worse'; (d) that he has no 'regard for another human being's property or for their life, regardless of who it may be'; (e) that '[t]here is no treatment, no medicine ... that in any way at all modifies or changes this behavior'; (f) that he 'is going to go ahead and commit other similar or same criminal acts if given the opportunity to do so'; and (g) that he 'has no remorse or sorrow for what he has done.'" 451 U.S. at 450-60. The jury's findings required judicial imposition of the death penalty.

The Supreme Court reversed. Smith's privilege against self-incrimination was infringed through the psychiatric examination and the later use of Grigson's testimony in the capital penalty hearing. Smith was in custody and therefore was within the protection of *Miranda v. Arizona,* 384 U.S. 436 (1966). The failure by Grigson to give the prescribed *Miranda* warnings was fatal to the use of Smith's statements. Moreover, Smith was represented by an attorney, so that all interrogation in the absence of counsel violated his sixth amendment right to counsel, *United States v. Henry,* 447 U.S. 264 (1980), and rendered Smith's statements and testimony based on them inadmissible at Smith's trial.

The Court, however, did not rule out entirely the possibility that some psychiatric examinations can conform to fifth amendment standards. Indeed, there is no constitutional concern as long as statements and evidence derived from them are not used to support either a determination of guilt or an assessment of punitive sanctions. For example, a psychiatric examination related to and considered solely in connection with mental capacity to stand trial, or one bearing on the transferability of a prison inmate to or from a civil mental health institution, poses no fifth amendment difficulties.

Beyond that, if a defendant interjects into the case the issue of culpability based on mental condition and offers evidence in support of the defense, the prosecution cannot be denied all forensic access to that defendant. Hence, invocation of the insanity defense can be taken as a waiver of privilege objections even though the material gotten under compelled prosecution examinations could be tendered on the issue of guilt. However, presentation of expert evidence about mental condition ordinarily comes during and in rebuttal to the defense case, not as a part of the prosecution's case-in-chief, and recitals of statements made to an examiner by a defendant are proper only as background data to an examiner's expert conclusions. Use of defendant statements as confessions or admissions is prohibited, and precautionary instructions to that effect should be available as a matter of course at defense request.

The Court did not need to elaborate on the details of counsel protection for a defendant undergoing psychiatric examination, because Texas had not allowed Smith's attorney to become involved. The Court intimated strongly, however, that counsel has no claim to be present during psychiatric examinations. Nonetheless, counsel should be given adequate advance notice that a psychiatric interview is to be conducted, and should be afforded a suitable opportunity to discuss with a client the scope of fifth amendment controls over the content of an examination and the extent to which information can be withheld from an examiner. If, following proper warnings and advice, a client chooses to cooperate, sixth amendment concerns will have been satisfied.

2. On statutory limitations on use of competency examinations for other purposes, see *State v. Strubberg*, 616 S.W.2d 809 (Mo. 1981).

c. Bifurcated Proceedings.

EDITORIAL NOTE

An unvarying requirement that defendants present defenses based on abnormal mental condition along with other defenses, *e.g.*, self-defense, or a generalized effort to raise a reasonable doubt about the sufficiency of the prosecution's case, can create both logical and functional difficulties: "I did not commit the offense but if I did I was suffering from a mental disease or defect." "I shot in self-defense, but in any event I was insane." Consequently, a number of jurisdictions provide the option of a bifurcated proceeding, in which the issue of guilt or innocence, excluding consideration of the insanity defense, is tried to conclusion. If a guilty verdict is returned, a separate trial ensues on the insanity defense. *See, e.g., Kleinbart v. United States*, 426 A.2d 343 (D.C. 1981); *Montague v. State*, 266 Ind. 51, 360 N.E.2d 181 (1977); *State v. Bragg*, 235 S.E.2d 466 (W. Va. 1977); *Steele v. State*, 97 Wis. 2d 72, 294 N.W.2d 2 (1980). Fairness seems to dictate that a second jury be used in the second stage. *Noble v. State*, 505 S.W.2d 543 (Tex. Crim. App. 1974).

Conversely, however, statutes mandating bifurcation over defense objection have been ruled unconstitutional because they foreclose an ability to use evidence of mental condition to contest the existence of culpability. *Sanchez v. State*, 567 P.2d 270 (Wyo. 1977). New Hampshire resolves the matter by giving a defendant a claim to bifurcation while reserving an opportunity to establish mental condition tending to negate culpability. *Novosel v. Helgemoe*, 118 N.H. 115, 384 A.2d 124 (1978).

d. Psychiatric and Lay Opinion Evidence

MODEL PENAL CODE

§ 4.07. Determination of Irresponsibility on Basis of Report
§ 4.09. Statements for Purposes of Examination or Treatment Inadmissible Except on Issue of Mental Condition

[The text of these sections appears in Appendix A.]

NOTE

The orthodox position has been that juries are allowed to disregard any witness, even a single witness, offered by either party. Therefore, a guilty verdict can be returned even though the prosecution offered no contrary evidence, or no scientific evidence, to rebut defense expert evidence. *State v. Ward,* 374 So. 2d 1128 (Fla. Dist. Ct. App. 1979); *Brooks v. State,* 247 Ga. 744, 279 S.E.2d 649 (1981); *State v. Sanders,* 225 Kan. 147, 587 P.2d 893 (1978); *Graham v. State,* 566 S.W.2d 941 (Tex. Crim. App. 1978). There is other authority, however, which calls for reversal of conviction if no qualified prosecution evidence is advanced. This may be based on a finding that a contrary practice ignores the burden of persuasion on the prosecution, *United States v. Bass,* 490 F.2d 846 (5th Cir. 1974), or that under the circumstances the state did not establish criminality beyond a reasonable doubt, *State v. Doyle,* 117 Ariz. 349, 572 P.2d 1187 (1977). Under the latter approach, however, a jury verdict can be upheld if cross-examination of defense witnesses coupled with other evidence can support a finding of sanity and criminality. *State v. Sanchez,* 117 Ariz. 369, 573 P.2d 60 (1977). A court cannot use a "jury common sense" instruction in effect to counter defense expert data. *Williams v. State,* 354 So. 2d 266 (Miss. 1978).

e. Jury Instructions.

GOVERNMENT OF THE VIRGIN ISLANDS v. FREDERICKS

United States Court of Appeals
578 F.2d 927 (3d Cir. 1978)

JAMES HUNTER, III, CIRCUIT JUDGE.

Defendant attempted to direct the jury's attention to the disposition of a defendant after an insanity verdict during two phases of the trial. First, during *voir dire,* he requested that the jury be told that, following a verdict of not guilty by reason of insanity, a defendant would be committed to a public institution. This information would be followed by the question, whether any juror, knowing this, would find it difficult voting for such a verdict.

The requested question was discussed during a conference in chambers. The prosecutor objected on the grounds that it was improper to inform the jury of the consequences of a verdict, since these should not influence their deliberations on the evidence. The defense counsel answered that he feared that a juror would hesitate to agree to a verdict of not guilty by reason of insanity if he felt that defendant would thereafter be allowed to "walk out."

The court ruled that the question would be given. The trial judge expressed two reasons for his decision. First, if a juror disagreed with the idea of institutional confinement, he might be unwilling to assent to an insanity verdict. Next, the judge expressed his concern over the common misapprehension that an insanity verdict allows defendant to go free.[9] The judge therefore made

---

[9]The court stated in part:

I think most people say "Well, an insanity defense, I wouldn't allow that because all that happens is he goes to an institution and he is there about half year and then he is free."

A. LEGAL TESTS FOR RESPONSIBILITY 619

the following statement to the array from which all of Frederick's jurors were selected:

> If your verdict, if the jury's verdict comes out not guilty by reason of insanity, the Defendant must be committed to a public institution for custody and care and will not be discharged from that institution until the Court is satisfied that he has regained his capacity for judgment, discretion and control so that he no longer represents a danger to himself or to others.
>
> Now, having that in mind, is there anyone who would have difficulty returning a verdict such as an insanity verdict, not guilty by reason of insanity, if it is warranted, if the facts warrant such a verdict, is there anyone here that would have difficulty with such a verdict if it is warranted? If so, please stand.
>
> I might elaborate a little bit, some people feel that just going to an institution is not enough if a person had done some act that a person should normally, a sane person would be punished for, so if anyone has that difficulty or has that position, would you please stand?

There was no affirmative response.

The second attempt to inform the jury came when the court entertained requests for instructions. The defendant submitted the following proposed instruction:

> You are instructed that if you find the defendant not guilty by reason of mental illness, you must state that fact in your verdict. If you do so find, the law in this jurisdiction requires that the court shall thereupon commit the defendant to a suitable public institution for custody, care and treatment from which he shall not be discharged until the court is satisfied that he has regained his capacity for judgment, discretion and control of his affairs and social relations. The charge was not given. The jury was directed not to consider what punishment might result from a guilty verdict.

Defendant objected to the omission of the instruction, which contained the same information as was given all jurors during voir dire. The court answered,

> I am denying that because I don't feel that, that was important to find out the state of mind of jurors on voir dire, but that it is not a proper instruction to tell them what might happen as a result of their verdict.

In this appeal defendant argues that the instruction informing the jury of the consequences of a verdict of not guilty by reason of insanity should be given to insure that jurors do not labor under the misapprehension that the defendant would go free after such a verdict. Defendant contends that jurors, from common knowledge, know the general consequences of the verdicts of guilty and not guilty but often carry with them into deliberations a misunderstanding of the consequences of an insanity verdict. He concludes that, if jurors wrongly believe that an insane and possibly dangerous defendant will be released after a verdict of not guilty by reason of insanity, they will feel constrained by fear for the public safety to return a guilty verdict. Fredericks relies on cases in the District of Columbia[10] and in a growing number of states[11] which require that an instruction substantially like the one requested be given....

....

Resolution of this issue poses a difficult balance of the functions of the judge and jury. It is clear that the consequences following any verdict are solely a matter for the judge and for the legislature. What is done with defendant after any verdict should not in the slightest affect the decision of the jury on whether that defendant is guilty or innocent....

Nonetheless, the requested instruction on the consequences of the insanity verdict presents a *unique* situation where there may be a common misunderstanding, not of the particulars of the result of a verdict, but of the nature of the verdict itself.[14] The words "not guilty" contained in the insanity verdict invoke the idea that a potentially dangerous defendant will be unconditionally released after trial, while in fact he faces mandatory corrective proceedings. A juror who feels that a verdict importing freedom for defendant will endanger the community might, out of his sense of social responsibility, be swayed from rational deliberation and be unwilling to weigh properly the evidence of defendant's mental condition.... This type of problem arises solely with respect to the insanity verdict.

To accept defendant's reasoning, however, would be a substantial departure from the usual rules for allocating responsibility between the judge and jury.... He asks, in effect, that we assume that the jury will disregard its instructions to ignore the consequences of its verdict and then allow erroneous extraneous information to affect its judgment. The cure proposed is to give the jury the correct information, which it should then be instructed to ignore.

Further, we note that accepting this reasoning could be prejudicial to a criminal defendant. A juror who is convinced that a defendant is dangerous, but who believes that he did not in fact commit the act charged, might be

---

[10] Lyles v. United States, 103 U.S. App.D.C. 22, 254 F.2d 725 (1957) (en banc); *cert. denied,* 356 U.S. 961, 78 S.Ct. 997, 2 L.Ed.2d 1067 (1958). *See also* United States v. Brawner, 153 U.S. App.D.C. 1, 18-20, 471 F.2d 969, 996-98 (1972) (en banc).

[11] Commonwealth v. Mutina, 366 Mass. 810, 323 N.E.2d 294 (1975); State v. Babin, La., 319 So.2d 367, *on rehearing,* 319 So.2d 379 (La. 1975); Schade v. State, 512 P.2d 907 (Alaska 1973); People v. Cole, 382 Mich. 695, 172 N.W.2d 354 (1969); Bean v. State, 81 Nev. 25, 398 P.2d 251 (1965), *cert. denied,* 384 U.S. 1012, 86 S.Ct. 1932, 16 L.Ed.2d 1030 (1966); State v. Hamilton, 216 Kan. 559, 534 P.2d 226 (1975) (based on state statute); State v. Pike, 516 S.W.2d 505 (Mo.App. 1975) (same). *See also* State v. Hammonds, 290 N.C. 1, 224 S.E.2d 595 (1976); State v. Krol, 68 N.J. 236, 344 A.2d 289 (1975); State v. Shoffner, 31 Wis. 2d 412, 143 N.W.2d 458 (1966) ("prefer" that instruction be given).

We note, however, that the majority of states either forbid the instruction or merely permit it to be given in the trial judge's discretion. *See* State v. Wallace, 333 A.2d 72, 78 (Me. 1975); Lonquest v. State, 495 P.2d 575, 584 (Wyo.), *cert. denied,* 409 U.S. 1006 (1972); People v. Adams, 26 N.Y.2d 129, 309 N.Y.S.2d 145, 151, 257 N.E.2d 610, *cert. denied,* 399 U.S. 93 (1970).

[14] Cases which have required the instruction on the consequences of an insanity verdict have emphasized that this verdict is unique and, unless guided by statute, have consistently and firmly distinguished this requirement from informing the jury of consequences of other verdicts. *See, e.g.,* State v. Hammonds, 290 N.C. 1, 224 S.E.2d 595, 602 (1976); State v. Babin, 319 So.2d 367, 379-80 (La. 1975); People v. Cole, 382 Mich. 695, 172 N.W.2d 354, 365 (1969); Lyles v. United States, 103 U.S.App. D.C. 22, 25, 254 F.2d 725, 728 (1957) (en banc), *cert. denied,* 356 U.S. 961 (1958).

willing to compromise on a verdict of not guilty by reason of insanity rather than insist on an acquittal....

The premise of defendant's argument is not that the judge made an erroneous statement of the law, but rather that he failed to rebut a misconception possibly held by jurors before they entered the courtroom. In this case, however, each juror was informed during voir dire questioning that the defendant must be civilly committed after a verdict of not guilty by reason of insanity. This information was given upon defendant's request for the express purpose of informing the jurors of these consequences. Thus, whatever the belief of the jurors before their involvement with this case, all of them were told the correct knowledge from an authoritative source before the trial began.

We therefore find no prejudice to defendant in this case. Even if the judge did commit an error in failing to give the instruction, the error would have been harmless. We have no doubts that the jury reached its verdict based solely on the evidence. Since the judge gave the jurors the information which defendant requested, this is not an appropriate case to decide whether, as a matter of Virgin Islands law, an instruction on the consequences of an insanity verdict must be given when requested by defendant.

NOTES

1. Recent decisions adhering to the orthodox, "no instruction," rule include *Curry v. State*, 271 Ark. 913, 611 S.W.2d 745 (1981); *State v. Hamann*, 285 N.W.2d 180, 185-86 (Iowa 1979); *State v. Smith*, 136 Vt. 520, 396 A.2d 126 (1978). Colorado has followed the Lyles approach. *People v. Thomson*, 197 Colo. 232, 591 P.2d 1031 (1979), applied retroactively in *People v. Hardin*, 607 P.2d 1291 (Colo. 1980). On the practical problems of crafting complete instructions under the Lyles doctrine, *see State v. Boyd*, 280 S.E.2d 669 (W. Va. 1981).

2. Doubt has been expressed about the propriety of instructing juries about a presumption of sanity because of a perceived danger that this might confuse jurors about allocation of the burden of persuasion, discussed in subpart (f) *infra*. See, e.g., *United States v. Hendrix*, 542 F.2d 879 (2d Cir. 1976), *cert. denied*, 430 U.S. 959 (1977); *State v. Rossier*, 175 Conn. 204, 397 A.2d 110 (1978); *United States v. Tyler*, 376 A.2d 798 (D.C. 1977); *Kind v. State*, 595 P.2d 960 (Wyo. 1979). In light of United States Supreme Court doctrine on the constitutionality of presumptions, see *supra* pp. 53-60, and allocation of the burden of persuasion to the defense, see subpart (f) *infra*, there probably is no federal constitutional objection to giving the presumption evidentiary weight and allowing it to go to a jury under suitable instructions. See *Walker v. Butterworth*, 599 F.2d 1074 (1st Cir.), *cert. denied*, 444 U.S. 937 (1979); *State v. McKenzie*, 177 Mont. 280, 581 P.2d 1205, 1230-35 (1978), *vacated on other grounds*, 443 U.S. 903 (1979); *State v. Gokey*, 136 Vt. 33, 383 A.2d 601 (1978).

f. Burden of Persuasion

PEOPLE v. DREW

Supreme Court of California
22 Cal. 3d 333, 583 P.2d 1318, 149 Cal. Rptr. 275 (1978)

TOBRINER, JUSTICE.

Evidence Code section 522 provides explicitly that "The party claiming that any person, including himself, is or was insane has the burden of proof on that issue." The trial judge in the present case accordingly charged the jury that "the defendant has the burden of proving his legal insanity by a preponderance of the evidence."

Drew contends that the court's instruction denied him due process of law under the Fourteenth Amendment. He relies on *Mullaney v. Wilbur* (1975) 421 U.S. 684 in which the United States Supreme Court struck down a Maine statute which required a homicide defendant to prove that he acted in the heat of passion to reduce the offense to manslaughter; the court's language suggested broadly that the state must prove beyond a reasonable doubt every fact critical to the guilt of the offender. More recent decisions of the Supreme Court have confirmed, however, that notwithstanding the broad dictum of *Mullaney,* "it remained constitutional to burden the defendant with proving his insanity." (*Patterson v. New York, supra,* 432 U.S. 197, 205; see *Rivera v. State* (Del. 1976) 351 A.2d 561, app. dism. *sub nom. Rivera v. Delaware* (1976) 429 U.S. 877.

Drew further contends that requiring him to bear the burden of proving insanity violates the due process clause of the California Constitution. (Cal. Const., art. I § 7.) California courts, however, have consistently upheld the constitutionality of our rule placing the burden of proof on the defendant.... Recently in *People v. Miller, supra,* 7 Cal.3d 562, 574, 102 Cal.Rptr. 841, 498 P.2d 1089, we unanimously rejected a defendant's contention that the rule conflicted with due process requirements. The validity of this settled line of authority was called into question only because of the broad language of the United States Supreme Court opinion in *Mullaney v. Wilbur, supra,* ... following that court's narrow interpretation of *Mullaney* in *Patterson v. New York, supra,* and its confirmation that a state may constitutionally require a defendant to prove insanity, doubts respecting the constitutionality of the California rule have been laid to rest.[13]

NOTES

1. The Drew allocation of burden of persuasion was overturned by initiative in 1982, which added a new § 25(b) to the CALIFORNIA PENAL CODE. The text appears at Note 1, *supra* pp. 599-600.

---

[13] Defendant points out that the federal courts (see Davis v. U.S. (1895) 160 U.S. 469, 16 S.Ct. 353, 40 L.Ed. 499) and about half of the states (see Note (1976) 64 Geo.L.J. 871, 890, fn. 114; Annot. (1968) 17 A.L.R.3d 146) require the prosecution to prove sanity beyond a reasonable doubt. We are not, however, concerned with the wisdom of placing the burden of proof on the prosecution or the defendant. The Legislature has resolved that issue by enacting Evidence Code section 522.

2. Other recent decisions in accord include *State v. Claibon,* 395 So. 2d 770 (La. 1981); *State v. Roy,* 395 So. 2d 664 (La. 1981); *State v. Moore,* 360 S.E.2d 293 (W.Va. 1979).

3. Jury trial problems. If there is conflicting evidence, a trial court cannot properly take the issue of substantive insanity away from the jury. *United States v. Tyler,* 376 A.2d 798 (D.C. App. 1977). Courts also must take care not to apply evidentiary rules narrowly so as to prevent the defense from mustering data bearing on mental condition. *Patty v. State,* 556 S.W.2d 776 (Tenn. Crim. App. 1977) (business records exception to hearsay rule, bearing on hospital records).

8. CONSEQUENCES OF ACQUITTALS BY REASON OF MENTAL CONDITION

a. Commitment Procedures

MODEL PENAL CODE

§ 4.08. Legal Effect of Acquittal on Ground of Mental Disease or Defect

[The text of this section appears in Appendix A.]

MATTER OF LEWIS

Supreme Court of Delaware
403 A.2d 1115 (1979)

[Lewis had been acquitted by reason of insanity after trial on charges of sexual assault and kidnapping. The trial judge ordered Lewis' immediate commitment to a state mental hospital. Lewis sought habeas corpus on the ground that equal protection was denied him because he did not receive the same procedural safeguards as those involuntarily hospitalized under civil commitment statutes. Similar attacks on earlier legislation had been rejected by the Delaware Supreme Court in *Mills v. State,* 256 A.2d 752 (Del. 1969), but Lewis renewed his attack on the constitutionality of replacement statutes.]

McNEILLY, JUSTICE.

Focusing first on the commitment procedure [under the statute], we find no merit to either the due process or equal protection arguments posed by the appellant. As in *Mills,* our conclusion is based in part on the presumption that mental illness which a defendant has alleged and proven by a preponderance of the evidence to have existed at the time he performed the criminal acts, continues until such time as the presumption is satisfactorily rebutted....

> ... [E]qual protection does not require that the appellant here must have the same procedural safeguards for commitment (the certificates of two physicians) as pertain to one civilly committed under 16 *Del. C.* § 5125, so long as there is a reasonable basis for the distinction made. We find such reasonable basis for distinction in the judicial determination by judge and jury of the mental illness of a § 4702 patient. This is a safeguard against improvident commitment of a higher order than the two certificates required for a civil commitment. 256 A.2d, at 756.

Public policy considerations yield another reasonable distinction between insanity acquitees and involuntary civil commitees for purposes of initial commitment:

> ...[T]he finding by the jury that a defendant, because of his mental disease or defect, shall be held blameless for an act otherwise subject to criminal sanctions puts such a defendant into an exceptional class. The special interest which the public has acquired in the confinement and release of people in this exceptional class results from the fact that there has been a judicial determination that they have already endangered the public safety and their own as a result of their mental conditions as distinguished from people civilly committed because of only potential danger. *Chase v. Kearns,* Me.Supr., 278 A.2d 132, 138 (1971).

Appellant argues that 16 *Del.C.* Ch. 50, governing involuntary commitments to the Delaware State Hospital, supports his proposition that there is no rational distinction between insanity acquitees and involuntary civil commitees for purposes of their initial commitment procedures. Appellant asserts that, under the definition of a "mentally ill person" provided in 16 *Del.C.* § 5001(1), the class of persons suffering from a mental disease or condition which "poses a real and present threat, based upon manifest indications, that such person is likely to commit ... serious harm to ... others," necessarily includes insanity acquitees, thereby requiring commitment procedures for insanity acquitees identical to those afforded involuntary civil commitees. See 16 *Del.C.* § 5001(1). In support of his argument, appellant cites *Baxstrom v. Herold,* 383 U.S. 107 (1966); *Humphrey v. Cady,* 405 U.S. 504 (1972); and *Jackson v. Indiana,* 406 U.S. 715 (1972).

We reject this argument based on the observation of the Supreme Judicial Court of Maine: That insanity acquitees constitute an "exceptional class" because "they have already endangered the public safety ... as a result of their mental conditions as distinguished from people civilly committed because of only potential danger." *Chase,* 278 A.2d, at 138. Although the definition of a "mentally ill person" provided in 16 *Del.C.* § 5001(1) appears broad enough to include insanity acquitees for purposes of potential future behavior, it fails to account for this one important distinction based on past conduct, i.e., insanity acquitees have performed acts which, but for the existence of a mental disease or defect that the time of the acts, would otherwise have subjected them to criminal sanctions. These past criminal acts are sufficient to justify the procedural differences in initial commitment between the two groups. Furthermore, Baxstrom, Humphrey, and Jackson are inapposite because none of the three dealt with the constitutional validity of procedures for initial commitment of an insanity acquitee.

We also reject appellant's contention that he was denied due process of law in that he was not afforded a judicial determination, with accompanying safeguards, as to the existence of any mental illness at the time of his commitment. As in *Mills,* "[w]e hold that in adjusting the delicate balance between a society's right to be protected from potentially mental ill and dangerous individuals, on the one hand, and the individual's right to be protected from improvident confinement on the other, it was not a denial of due process to commit the appellant" under § 403(a) without a separate hearing of the type provided involuntary civil commitees pursuant to 16 *Del.C.* § 5006....

Unlike the involuntary civil commitee who generally denies the existence of the mental condition for which he is committed, the insanity acquitee has been provided a judicial hearing at which he has alleged and proven by a preponderance of the evidence the very mental condition which he has manifested in past criminal action and for which, by reason of the presumption of continuing mental illness, he is committed. We believe this provides a rational basis for the insanity acquitee's immediate commitment. Moreover, "[n]othing in § 403 is meant to limit the right of the committed person or someone acting on his behalf to move the Court for release *at any time*." Delaware Criminal Code with Commentary, Commentary on § 403 (1973) (emphasis added). Thus, the insanity acquitee's right to move the Court for his release at any time following his initial commitment is an additional safeguard which provides him with an adequate opportunity to rebut the presumption of his continuing mental illness....

And finally, although 11 *Del.C.* § 403(a) provides that "... the court shall, upon motion of the Attorney General, order that the [insanity acquitee] shall forthwith be committed ...," the statute does not preclude the Court from ordering immediate commitment upon its own motion where the circumstances warrant it, as the Court in the instant case did.

NOTES

1. *Application of Jones,* 228 Kan. 90, 612 P.2d 1211 (1980), sustained the constitutionality of state automatic commitment legislation. Principal cases holding the contrary include *Wilson v. State,* 259 Ind. 375, 287 N.E.2d 875 (1972); *People v. McQuillan,* 392 Mich. 511, 221 N.W.2d 569 (1974).

2. Equal protection would appear to preclude use of a different standard for commitment or continuation of involuntary hospitalization following acquittal based on mental condition than governs involuntary mental health commitments generally. This includes "danger to others," in the form of serious physical harm, *In re Torsney,* 66 A.D.2d 281, 412 N.Y.S.2d 914 (2d Dept), *rev'd on other grounds,* 47 N.Y.2d 667, 394 N.E.2d 262, 420 N.Y.S.2d 192 (1979) (construing the NGRI-based procedure in pari materia with civil commitment legislation), and danger to the patient himself or herself. *People v. Blackwell,* 117 Cal. App. 3d 372, 172 Cal. Rptr. 636 (1981). The danger must be "imminent." *Suzuki v. Yuen,* 617 F.2d 173 (9th Cir. 1980). *Suzuki* also ruled that a civil commitment statute allowing compelled hospitalization based on danger to any property was unconstitutionally overbroad.

Mental retardation can support commitment after acquittal. *United States v. Jackson,* 553 F.2d 109 (D.C. Cir. 1976).

3. Post-acquittal commitment hearings presumably are within the constitutional requirement of *Addington v. Texas,* 441 U.S. 418 (1979), that commitment grounds be established by some variant on the "clear and convincing proof" standard. "Given the lack of certainty and the fallibility of psychiatric diagnosis, there is a serious question as to whether a state could ever prove beyond a reasonable doubt that an individual is both mentally ill and likely to be dangerous." *Id.* at 429. Hence, a legislatively selected formula must "inform the factfinder that the proof must be greater than the preponderance of the evidence standard applicable to other categories of civil cases." *Id.* at 433. *Dorsey v. Solomon,* 604 F.2d 271 (4th Cir. 1979), so construes *Addington.*

4. If the respondent prevails, collateral estoppel forestalls relitigation under the original petition even though later acquired evidence suggests a basis for commitment. A later petition must be submitted resting on different facts. *Commonwealth v. Travis,* 372 Mass. 238, 361 N.E.2d 394 (1977).

b. Release

IN RE MOYE

Supreme Court of California
22 Cal. 3d 457, 584 P.2d 1097, 149 Cal. Rptr. 491 (1978)

RICHARDSON, JUSTICE.

Specifically, we hold that principles of equal protection require ... that persons committed to a state institution following acquittal of a criminal offense on the ground of their insanity cannot be retained in institutional confinement beyond the maximum term of punishment for the underlying offense of which, but for their insanity, they would have been convicted....

As in the case of [mentally disabled sex offenders] and other dangerous offenders, persons in petitioner's class properly, and consistent with equal protection principles, may be subjected to a period of extended commitment once the maximum term of punishment has expired, in the event the people (or other committing authority) can establish that the person committed remains a danger to the health and safety of himself or others .... [Under the MDSO statute], for example, the commitment of MDSOs may be extended only if a specified procedure is followed, involving the filing of a petition for an extended commitment of one year, notice to the person committed of his right to an attorney and a jury trial, and a hearing on the issue of dangerousness.... The extended commitment period is one year, subject to annual renewal following similar notice and hearing.... To the extent practicable, and in the absence of further legislation on the subject, the procedure for the extended commitment of persons committed following their acquittal on the ground of insanity should conform to the [above] procedures....

The People urge that the paramount interest of the state in protection of the public justifies the commitment and release procedure [under the Penal Code provisions, invalidated in *Moye,* calling for indefinite commitment]. Nevertheless, the availability of an extended commitment procedure akin to [the MDSO statutory proceedings], or the institution of civil commitment proceedings [under governing statutes], would appear to constitute adequate protection against the premature release of dangerous persons to society. If, after a substantial period of confinement and treatment equivalent in duration to the maximum term for the offense committed, petitioner remains demonstrably dangerous, an additional commitment may be sought as discussed above. Although the burden of proof on the issue of dangerousness will have shifted to the People once confinement for the maximum term of the underlying offense has occurred, upon a proper showing the petitioner may be retained in confinement and will not be "loose" or "at large."

It must be remembered that, except for their own plea of insanity, even the most dangerous of offenders are released to society upon serving their maximum term. Under such circumstances, the possibility of an indefinite, lifetime confinement provided [under the Penal Code] may well deter from entering an insanity plea those very persons most in need of hospital treatment. Such a result serves neither the interest of the public nor those like petitioner who have entered insanity pleas.

NOTES

1. Equal protection also has been invoked to require the same periodic review of continued dangerousness which civilly committed patients may claim, *Gibbs v. Helgemoe,* 116 N.H. 825, 367 A.2d 1041 (1976); *State v. Fields,* 77 N.J. 282, 390 A.2d 574 (1978), and equivalent procedures for provisional release on outpatient status. *People v. Gann,* 94 Ill. App. 3d 1100, 419 N.E.2d 613 (1981). It does not deny equal protection, however, to allow judicial review of administrative release decisions at the instance of the state, even though civil committees generally are not subject to such requirements. *People v. Valdez,* 79 Ill. 2d 74, 402 N.E.2d 187 (1980). Judicial approval has been required for release. *State v. Nielson,* 97 Idaho 330, 543 P.2d 1170 (1975).

2. *In re Lewis,* 403 A.2d 1115 (Del. 1979), adopts a contrary constitutional analysis to *Moye, Gibbs* and *Fields,* and therefore found no infirmity in more onerous release requirements for NGRI patients than those governing civil committees generally.

3. Patients must be released when no basis remains for a belief that they continue to pose a threat to the safety of the community (or themselves). *Warner v. State,* 309 Minn. 333, 244 N.W.2d 640 (1976), *and see* note 2, *supra* p. 625. Some courts have found no constitutional bar to placing on involuntarily committed patients, including those committed following NGRI acquittals, the burden of persuasion to establish nondangerousness warranting release. *State v. Alto,* 589 P.2d 402 (Alaska 1979); *In re Torsney,* 66 A.D.2d 281, 412 N.Y.S.2d 914 (2d Dept.), *rev'd on other grounds,* 47 N.Y.2d 667, 394 N.E.2d 262, 420 N.Y.S.2d 192 (1979); *State ex rel. Allen v. Radack,* 246 N.W.2d 611 (S.D. 1976). California legislation discussed in *Moye,* and the law in certain other jurisdictions, however, places the burden on state authorities to show a continuation of the state of dangerousness which originally justified involuntary commitment. This context would seem to require a harmonization of *Addington v. Texas,* 441 U.S. 418 (1979), and *Patterson v. New York,* 432 U.S. 197 (1977) *supra* pp. 324-328 which the Supreme Court has not yet undertaken.

B. PROCEDURAL INCOMPETENCE

1. CONSTITUTIONAL STANDARDS

MODEL PENAL CODE

§ 4.04. Mental Disease or Defect Excluding Fitness to Proceed

[The text of this section appears in Appendix A.]

LANE v. STATE
Supreme Court of Florida
388 So. 2d 1022 (1980)

[Lane, a mental retardate, was convicted of capital murder and sentenced to death by the trial court as recommended by the trial jury which convicted him. Counsel had asserted both procedural incapacity and the insanity defense.]

PER CURIAM

The law in this area has been established by a series of cases of both the United States Supreme Court, *Drope v. Missouri,* 420 U.S. 162 (1975); *Pate v. Robinson,* 383 U.S. 375 (1966); *Dusky v. United States,* 362 U.S. 402 (1960); *Bishop v. United States,* 350 U.S. 961 (1956), and this Court in *Jones v. State,* 362 So.2d 1334 (Fla.1978); and *Fowler v. State,* 255 So.2d 513 (Fla.1971). We implemented the constitutional mandate in Dusky in our Rule of Criminal Procedure 3.210.

The United States Supreme Court in *Dusky* restated the historical rule that a person accused of a crime who is incompetent to stand trial shall not be proceeded against while he is incompetent. The law is now clear that the trial court has the responsibility to conduct a hearing for competency to stand trial whenever it reasonably appears necessary, whether requested or not, to ensure that a defendant meets the standard of competency set forth in *Dusky.* The United States Supreme Court reiterated this directive in *Drope* and said:

> The import of our decision in *Pate v. Robinson* is that evidence of a defendant's irrational behavior, his demeanor at trial, and any prior medical opinion on competence to stand trial are all relevant in determining whether further inquiry is required, but that even one of these factors standing alone may, in some circumstances, be sufficient. There are, of course, no fixed or immutable signs which invariably indicate the need for further inquiry to determine fitness to proceed; the question is often a difficult one in which a wide range of manifestations and subtle nuances are implicated....
>
> ....
>
> Even when a defendant is competent at the commencement of his trial, a trial court must always be alert to circumstances suggesting a change that would render the accused unable to meet the standards of competence to stand trial.

420 U.S. at 180-181.

This requirement for a competency hearing was addressed by us in *Fowler v. State*, where we held that it is obligatory on the trial court to fix a time for a competency hearing if there are reasonable grounds to believe that the defendant is not competent to stand trial.

The trial court at a hearing to determine competency to stand trial must apply the *Dusky* test which requires a determination of (1) whether the defendant has a sufficient present ability to consult with his lawyer with a reasonable degree of rational understanding, and (2) whether he has a rational as well as a factual understanding of the proceedings against him. We adopted this competency test almost verbatim in our Rule of Criminal Procedure 3.210(a)(1). It should also be recognized that *Dusky* held that it was *not* sufficient for a trial judge to find that "the defendant is oriented to time and place and has some recollection of events." 362 U.S. at 402.

In the instant case none of the three medical experts who testified at the continuance hearing were able to say that the appellant was competent to stand trial. The state urges that the appellant had previously been found competent, and that even if he was incompetent it was by his own actions. The finding of competence to stand trial made nine months prior to the hearing does not control in view of the evidence of possible incompetency presented by the experts at the hearing on the motion for continuance. In *Bishop v. United States*, 223 F.2d 582 (D.C. Cir. 1955), *reversed*, 350 U.S. 961 (1956), the facts in the lower court opinion reflected that the defendant had no mental disorder a month prior to the trial. The United States Supreme Court reversed, requiring the trial court to have a hearing on the sanity of the defendant at the time of trial. Further, the issue of competency to stand trial clearly can be raised at any time, including during the trial proceedings. In *Drope*, the defendant shot himself in the foot during the course of the trial. Although the state asserted that this conduct was intentionally done to avoid trial, the court held that such conduct contributed to the need for a competency hearing. What activates the need for a competency hearing is some type of irrational behavior or evidence of mental illness that would raise a doubt as to the defendant's present competence....

NOTES

1. Competence must exist at all stages of a proceeding. *Saddler v. United States*, 531 F.2d 83 (2d Cir. 1976). Therefore, a determination that a defendant is fit to undergo preliminary examination does not discharge a court at a later stage of the proceeding from the responsibility to ascertain trial competence. *United States ex rel. McGough v. Hewitt*, 528 F.2d 339 (3d Cir. 1975); *State v. Bauer*, 310 Minn. 103, 245 N.W.2d 848 (1976).

2. A defendant's wish to be tried, whatever his or her mental condition, does not govern, *United States v. Johnson*, 527 F.2d 1104 (4th Cir. 1975), so that the issue cannot be waived, *Commonwealth v. Hill*, 375 Mass. 50, 375 N.E.2d 1168 (1978); *Ex parte Hagans*, 558 S.W.2d 457 (Tex. Crim. App. 1977), or competence stipulated. *State v. Fox*, 112 Ariz. 375, 542 P.2d 800 (1975).

3. Amnesia is insufficient of itself to sustain a finding of incompetence based on inability to consult counsel. *United States v. Swanson*, 572 F.2d 523

(5th Cir.), *cert. denied,* 439 U.S. 849 (1978); *Davis v. State,* 354 So. 2d 334 (Ala. Crim. App. 1978); *Morrow v. State,* 47 Md. App. 296, 423 A.2d 251 (1980), *aff'd,* 293 Md. 247, 443 A.2d 108 (1982); *Commonwealth v. Lombardi,* 378 Mass. 612, 393 N.E.2d 346 (1979); *Commonwealth v. Barky,* 476 Pa. 602, 383 A.2d 526 (1978). *See also* Law Reform Commission of Canada, Report to Parliament on Mental Disorder in the Criminal Process 14 (1977):

> The third criterion, an ability to communicate with counsel, has created problems in some jurisdictions where amnesia is considered, of itself, a cause of unfitness. We do not feel this should be the case. The fitness rule is concerned with present mental ability to communicate. If the accused is rational and is able to tell his lawyer that he does not remember any of the circumstances of the alleged offence, he should be considered fit to stand trial.

4. Competency must be established under *Drope* principles before a defendant can plead guilty. Because a guilty plea waives a number of important procedural guarantees, the ability to understand and make a reasoned choice between or among alternatives is controlling. *See, e.g., Chavez v. United States,* 656 F.2d 512 (9th Cir. 1981); *United States v. Masthers,* 539 F.2d 721 (D.C. Cir. 1976); *People v. Matheson,* 70 Mich. App. 172, 245 N.W.2d 551 (1976). Failure to advance the competency issued under such circumstances can constitute sixth amendment incompetence of counsel. *DeKaplany v. Enomoto,* 540 F.2d 975 (9th Cir. 1976), *cert. denied,* 429 U.S. 1075 (1977).

5. Mental condition can bear on the validity of a confession under *Miranda v. Arizona,* 384 U.S. 436 (1966). *See, e.g., State v. Glover,* 343 So. 2d 118 (La. 1976); *State v. Mercer,* 625 P.2d 44 (Mont. 1981); *State v. Green,* 613 S.W.2d 229 (Tenn. Crim. App. 1980); *State v. Boyd,* 280 S.E.2d 669 (W. Va. 1981).

2. PROCEDURAL REQUIREMENTS

JACKSON v. INDIANA

United States Supreme Court
406 U.S. 715 (1972)

[Jackson, a mentally-retarded deaf person aged 27 at the time of prosecution, was charged with robberies, which on the record appear to have been purse-snatchings. The trial court found him incompetent to stand trial, based on "almost nonexistent communication skill, together with his lack of hearing and his mental deficiency," and ordered him committed until he should be certified triable. In fact, there was expert testimony the "prognosis appears rather dim" that Jackson's condition would ever change. Jackson's counsel sought a "new trial" on the constitutional premise that Jackson in effect had been detained for life without due process and equal protection in comparison to mentally-ill persons committed civilly. The trial court denied the motion and the state supreme court affirmed. The Supreme Court reversed, the seven sitting Justices agreeing.]

MR. JUSTICE BLACKMUN delivered the opinion of the Court....

II

Equal Protection

Because the evidence established little likelihood of improvement in petitioner's condition, he argues that commitment under § 9-1706a in his case amounted to a commitment for life. This deprived him of equal protection, he contends, because, absent the criminal charges pending against him, the State would have had to proceed under other statutes generally applicable to all other citizens: either the commitment procedures for feeble-minded persons, or those for mentally ill persons. He argues that under these other statutes (1) the decision whether to commit would have been made according to a different standard, (2) if commitment were warranted, applicable standards for release would have been more lenient, (3) if committed under § 22-1907, he could have been assigned to a special institution affording appropriate care, and (4) he would then have been entitled to certain privileges not now available to him.

In *Baxstrom v. Herold,* 383 U. S. 107 (1966), the Court held that a state prisoner civilly committed at the end of his prison sentence on the finding of a surrogate was denied equal protection when he was deprived of a jury trial that the State made generally available to all other persons civilly committed. Rejecting the State's argument that Baxstrom's conviction and sentence constituted adequate justification for the difference in procedures, the Court said that "there is no conceivable basis for distinguishing the commitment of a person who is nearing the end of a penal term from all other civil commitments." 383 U.S., at 111-112.... The Court also held that Baxstrom was denied equal protection by commitment to an institution maintained by the state corrections department for "dangerously mentally ill" persons, without a judicial determination of his "dangerous propensities" afforded all others so committed.

If criminal conviction and imposition of sentence are insufficient to justify less procedural and substantive protection against indefinite commitment than that generally available to all others, the mere filing of criminal charges surely cannot suffice.... The *Baxstrom* principle also has been extended to commitment following an insanity acquittal, ... and to commitment in lieu of sentence following conviction as a sex offender. *Humphrey v. Cady,* 405 U.S. 504 (1972).

Respondent argues, however, that because the record fails to establish affirmatively that Jackson will never improve, his commitment "until sane" is not really an indeterminate one. It is only temporary, pending possible change in his condition. Thus, presumably, it cannot be judged against commitments under other state statutes that are truly indeterminate. The State relies on the lack of "exactitude" with which psychiatry can predict the future course of mental illness, and on the Court's decision in what is claimed to be "a fact situation similar to the case at hand" in *Greenwood v. United States,* 350 U. S. 366 (1956).

Were the State's factual premise that Jackson's commitment is only temporary a valid one, this might well be a different case. But the record does not support that premise. One of the doctors testified that in his view Jackson would be unable to acquire the substantially improved communication skills that would be necessary for him to participate in any defense. The prognosis for petitioner's developing such skills, he testified, appeared "rather dim." In answer to a question whether Jackson would ever be able to comprehend the charges or participate in his defense, even after commitment and treatment, the doctor said, "I doubt it, I don't believe so." The other psychiatrist testified that even if Jackson were able to develop such skills, he would *still* be unable to comprehend the proceedings or aid counsel due to his mental deficiency. The interpreter, a supervising teacher at the state school for the deaf, said that he would not be able to serve as an interpreter for Jackson or aid him in participating in a trial, and that the State had no facilities that could, "after a length of time," aid Jackson in so participating. The court also heard petitioner's mother testify that Jackson already had undergone rudimentary outpatient training in communications skills from the deaf and dumb school in Indianapolis over a period of three years without noticeable success. There is nothing in the record that even points to any possibility that Jackson's present condition can be remedied at any future time....

We note also that neither the Indiana statute nor state practice makes the likelihood of the defendant's improvement a relevant factor. The State did not seek to make any such showing, and the record clearly establishes that the chances of Jackson's ever meeting the competency standards of § 9-1706a are at best minimal, if not nonexistent. The record also rebuts any contention that the commitment could contribute to Jackson's improvement. Jackson's § 9-1706a commitment is permanent in practical effect.

We therefore must turn to the question whether, because of the pendency of the criminal charges that triggered the State's invocation of § 9-1706a, Jackson was deprived of substantial rights to which he would have been entitled under either of the other two state commitment statutes. *Baxstrom* held that the State cannot withhold from a few the procedural protections or the substantive requirements for commitment that are available to all others. In this case commitment procedures under all three statutes appear substantially similar: notice, examination by two doctors, and a full judicial hearing at which the individual is represented by counsel and can cross-examine witnesses and introduce evidence. Under each of the three statutes, the commitment determination is made by the court alone, and appellate review is available.

In contrast, however, what the State must show to commit a defendant under § 9-1706a, and the circumstances under which an individual so committed may be released, are substantially different from the standards under the other two statutes.

Under § 9-1706a, the State needed to show only Jackson's inability to stand trial. We are unable to say that, on the record before us, Indiana could have civilly committed him as mentally ill under § 22-1209 or committed him as feeble-minded under § 22-1907. The former requires at least (1) a showing of mental illness and (2) a showing that the individual is in need of "care, treatment, training or detention." § 22-1201(1). Whether Jackson's mental deficiency would meet the first test is unclear; neither examining physician addressed himself to this. Furthermore, it is problematical whether commitment for "treatment" or "training" would be appropriate since the record estab-

B. PROCEDURAL INCOMPETENCE

lishes that none is available for Jackson's condition at any state institution. The record also fails to establish that Jackson is in need of custodial care or "detention." He has been employed at times, and there is no evidence that the care he long received at home has become inadequate. The statute appears to require an independent showing of dangerousness ("requires ... detention in the interest of the welfare of such person or ... others ..."). Insofar as it may require such a showing, the pending criminal charges are insufficient to establish it, and no other supporting evidence was introduced. For the same reasons, we cannot say that this record would support a feeble-mindedness commitment under § 22-1907 on the ground that Jackson is "unable properly to care for [himself]." § 22-1801.

More important, an individual committed as feeble-minded is eligible for release when his condition "justifies it," § 22-1814, and an individual civilly committed as mentally ill when the "superintendent or administrator shall discharge such person, *or* [when] cured of such illness." § 22-1223 (emphasis supplied). Thus, in either case release is appropriate when the individual no longer requires the custodial care or treatment or detention that occasioned the commitment, or when the department of mental health believes release would be in his best interests. The evidence available concerning Jackson's past employment and home care strongly suggests that under these standards he might be eligible for release at almost any time, even if he did not improve. On the other hand, by the terms of his present § 9-1706a commitment, he will not be entitled to release at all, absent an unlikely substantial change for the better in his condition.

Baxstrom did not deal with the standard for release, but its rationale is applicable here. The harm to the individual is just as great if the State, without reasonable justification, can apply standards making his commitment a permanent one when standards generally applicable to all others afford him a substantial opportunity for early release.

As we noted above, we cannot conclude that pending criminal charges provide a greater justification for different treatment than conviction and sentence. Consequently, we hold that by subjecting Jackson to a more lenient commitment standard and to a more stringent standard of release than those generally applicable to all others not charged with offenses, and by thus condemning him in effect to permanent institutionalization without the showing required for commitment or the opportunity for release afforded by § 22-1209 or § 22-1907, Indiana deprived petitioner of equal protection of the laws under the Fourteenth Amendment.[9]

---

[9] Petitioner also argues that the incompetency commitment deprived him of the right to be assigned to a special "institution for feeble-minded persons" to which he would have been statutorily directed by a § 22-1907 commitment. The State maintains two such institutions. The Indiana Supreme Court thought petitioner "failed to understand the statutory mechanisms" for assignment following commitment under the two procedures. 253 Ind., at 490, 255 N.E.2d, at 517. It observed that since the mental health department now administers, in consolidated fashion, all the State's mental facilities including the two special institutions, ... and since the special institutions are "appropriate psychiatric institutions" under § 9-1706a, considering Jackson's condition, his incompetency commitment can still culminate in assignment to a special facility. The State, in argument, went one step further. It contended that in practice the assignment process under all three statutes is identical: the individual is remanded to the central state authority, which assigns him to an appropriate institution regardless of how he was committed.

III

Due Process

For reasons closely related to those discussed in Part II above, we also hold that Indiana's indefinite commitment of a criminal defendant solely on account of his incompetency to stand trial does not square with the Fourteenth Amendment's guarantee of due process....

In a 1970 case virtually indistinguishable from the one before us, the Illinois Supreme Court granted relief to an illiterate deaf mute who had been indicted for murder four years previously but found incompetent to stand trial on account of his inability to communicate, and committed. *People ex rel. Myers v. Briggs,* 46 Ill. 2d 281, 263 N. E. 2d 109 (1970). The institution where petitioner was confined had determined, "[I]t now appears that [petitioner] will never acquire the necessary communication skills needed to participate and cooperate in his trial." Petitioner, however, was found to be functioning at a "nearly normal level of performance in areas other than communication." The State contended petitioner should not be released until his competency was restored. The Illinois Supreme Court disagreed. It held:

> This court is of the opinion that this defendant, handicapped as he is and facing an indefinite commitment because of the pending indictment against him, should be given an opportunity to obtain a trial to determine whether or not he is guilty as charged or should be released. 46 Ill. 2d, at 288, 263 N. E. 2d, at 113....

The States have traditionally exercised broad power to commit persons found to be mentally ill. The substantive limitations on the exercise of this power and the procedures for invoking it vary drastically among the States. The particular fashion in which the power is exercised — for instance, through various forms of civil commitment, defective delinquency laws, sexual psychopath laws, commitment of persons acquitted by reason of insanity — reflects different combinations of distinct bases for commitment sought to be vindicated. The bases that have been articulated include dangerousness to

---

If true, such practice appears at first blush contrary to the mandate of § 22-1907, requiring the court clerk to seek assignment at one of the two special institutions. However, the relevant statutes, including that effecting consolidation of all mental health facilities under one department, have been enacted piecemeal, and older laws often not formally revised. Since the department of mental health has sole discretionary authority to transfer patients between any of the institutions it administers at any time, § 22-5032(6) and § 22-301, there is evidently adequate statutory authority for consolidating the initial assignment decision.

Moreover, nothing in the record demonstrates that different or better treatment is available at a special institution than at the general facilities for the mentally ill. We are not faced here, as we were in Baxstrom, with commitment to a distinctly penal or maximum-security institution designed for dangerous inmates and not administered by the general state mental health authorities. Therefore, we cannot say that by virtue of his incompetency commitment, Jackson has been denied an assignment or appropriate treatment to which those not charged with crimes would generally be entitled.

Similarly, Jackson's incompetency commitment did not deprive him of privileges such as furloughs to which he claims a feeble-mindedness commitment would entitle him. The statutes relate such privileges to particular institutions, not to the method of commitment. Thus patients assigned to the Muscatatuck institution are entitled to furloughs regardless of the statute under which they were committed; and persons committed as feeble-minded would not be entitled to furloughs if assigned to a general mental institution.

self, dangerousness to others, and the need for care or treatment or training. Considering the number of persons affected, it is perhaps remarkable that the substantive constitutional limitations on this power have not been more frequently litigated.

We need not address these broad questions here. It is clear that Jackson's commitment rests on proceedings that did not purport to bring into play, indeed did not even consider relevant, *any* of the articulated bases for exercise of Indiana's power of indefinite commitment. The state statutes contain at least two alternative methods for invoking this power. But Jackson was not afforded any "formal commitment proceedings addressed to [his] ability to function in society," or to society's interest in his restraint, or to the State's ability to aid him in attaining competency through custodial care or compulsory treatment, the ostensible purpose of the commitment. At the least, due process requires that the nature and duration of commitment bear some reasonable relation to the purpose for which the individual is committed.

We hold, consequently, that a person charged by a State with a criminal offense who is committed solely on account of his incapacity to proceed to trial cannot be held more than the reasonable period of time necessary to determine whether there is a substantial probability that he will attain that capacity in the foreseeable future. If it is determined that this is not the case, then the State must either institute the customary civil commitment proceeding that would be required to commit indefinitely any other citizen, or release the defendant. Furthermore, even if it is determined that the defendant probably soon will be able to stand trial, his continued commitment must be justified by progress toward that goal. In light of differing state facilities and procedures and a lack of evidence in this record, we do not think it appropriate for us to attempt to prescribe arbitrary time limits. We note, however, that petitioner Jackson has now been confined for three and one-half years on a record that sufficiently establishes the lack of a substantial probability that he will ever be able to participate fully in a trial.

. . . .

IV

Disposition of the Charges

Petitioner also urges that fundamental fairness requires that the charges against him now be dismissed. The thrust of his argument is that the record amply establishes his lack of criminal responsibility at the time the crimes are alleged to have been committed. The Indiana court did not discuss this question. Apparently it believed that by reason of Jackson's incompetency commitment the State was entitled to hold the charges pending indefinitely. On this record, Jackson's claim is a substantial one. For a number of reasons, however, we believe the issue is not sufficiently ripe for ultimate decision by us at this time.

A. Petitioner argues that he has already made out a complete insanity defense. Jackson's criminal responsibility at the time of the alleged offenses, however, is a distinct issue from his competency to stand trial. The competency hearing below was not directed to criminal responsibility, and evidence relevant to it was presented only incidentally. Thus, in any event, we would have to remand for further consideration of Jackson's condition in the light of Indiana's law of criminal responsibility.

B. Dismissal of charges against an incompetent accused has usually been thought to be justified on grounds not squarely presented here: particularly, the Sixth-Fourteenth Amendment right to a speedy trial, or the denial of due process inherent in holding pending criminal charges indefinitely over the head of one who will never have a chance to prove his innocence. Jackson did not present the Sixth-Fourteenth Amendment issue to the state courts. Nor did the highest state court rule on the due process issue, if indeed it was presented to that court in precisely the above-described form. We think, in light of our holdings in Parts II and III, that the Indiana courts should have the first opportunity to determine these issues.

C. Both courts and commentators have noted the desirability of permitting some proceedings to go forward despite the defendant's incompetency. For instance, § 4.06 (3) of the Model Penal Code would permit an incompetent accused's attorney to contest any issue "susceptible of fair determination prior to trial and without the personal participation of the defendant." An alternative draft of § 4.06 (4) of the Model Penal Code would also permit an evidentiary hearing at which certain defenses, not including lack of criminal responsibility, could be raised by defense counsel on the basis of which the court might quash the indictment. Some States have statutory provisions permitting pretrial motions to be made or even allowing the incompetent defendant a trial at which to establish his innocence, without permitting a conviction. We do not read this Court's previous decisions to preclude the States from allowing, at a minimum, an incompetent defendant to raise certain defenses such as insufficiency of the indictment, or make certain pretrial motions through counsel. Of course, if the Indiana courts conclude that Jackson was almost certainly not capable of criminal responsibility when the offenses were committed, dismissal of the charges might be warranted. But even if this is not the case, Jackson may have other good defenses that could sustain dismissal or acquittal and that might now be asserted. We do not know if Indiana would approve procedures such as those mentioned here, but these possibilities will be open on remand.

Reversed and remanded.

NOTES

1. In federal practice, a defense motion for a psychiatric examination bearing on competency cannot be denied "unless the court correctly determines that the motion is frivolous or not made in good faith." *Chavez v. United States,* 656 F.2d 512, 516 (9th Cir. 1981) (citing precedent).

2. Review the material on diagnostic commitments and reports, *supra* pp. 615-617, which apply in the present context as well. Under Jackson, diagnostic commitments must be of relatively brief duration. *See, e.g., State ex rel. Walker v. Jenkins,* 157 W. Va. 683, 203 S.E.2d 353 (1974). If there are successive assertions of the competency issue, the same time limits govern all ensuing diagnostic commitments. *State ex rel. Porter v. Wolke,* 80 Wis. 2d 197, 257 N.W.2d 881 (1977).

3. Psychiatric diagnostic labels in psychiatric reports do not, standing alone, provide an adequate basis to adjudge nontriability. *State v. Morris,* 340 So. 2d 195 (La. 1976). The issue is whether a defendant's symptoms comport with a finding of lack of procedural competence, *Bruce v. Estelle,* 536 F.2d 1051 (5th Cir. 1976), *cert. denied,* 429 U.S. 1053 (1977), and experts should be allowed freedom to describe a defendant's mental condition in their own professional terms. *Raithel v. State,* 280 Md. 291, 372 A.2d 1069 (1977).

4. The competency issue must be decided by a court, *State v. Milam,* 226 S.E.2d 433 (W. Va. 1976), and the defendant has a constitutional right to be present at hearings on the issue unless that right is validly waived by defendant or defense counsel. *State v. Blier,* 113 Ariz. 501, 557 P.2d 1058 (1976). The issue, however, can be reserved and determined retroactively in light of experiences at trial. *Williams v. State,* 378 A.2d 117 (Del. 1977), *cert. denied,* 436 U.S. 908 (1978); *Commonwealth v. Lombardi,* 378 Mass. 672, 393 N.E.2d 346 (1979). It is, though, error to allow the prosecution to submit evidence about the crime charged against a defendant in pending proceedings, *Martin v. Estelle,* 546 F.2d 177 (5th Cir.), *cert. denied,* 431 U.S. 971 (1977), or to enter a judgment of acquittal in favor of a defendant on grounds of mental defect or disorder. *State v. Coville,* 88 Wash. 2d 43, 558 P.2d 1346 (1977) (but that judgment was not to be vacated until the defendant was determined to be procedurally competent).

The trier on the incompetency issue cannot find competency in the face of virtually uncontradicted defense evidence showing nontriability. *People v. Samuel,* 29 Cal. 3d 489, 629 P.2d 485, 174 Cal. Rptr. 684 (1981).

5. It is not a denial of equal protection if persons awaiting a determination of triability are considered ineligible for mental health treatment. *People v. Zahn,* 71 Ill. App. 3d 585, 390 N.E.2d 93 (1979).

6. Placing the burden of persuasion on the defense to establish nontriability has been sustained. *State v. Lopez,* 91 N.M. 779, 581 P.2d 872 (1978). Does this comport with *Drope* and *Jackson? See United States v. DiGilio,* 538 F.2d 972 (3d Cir. 1976), *cert. denied sub nom. Lupo v. United States,* 429 U.S. 1038 (1977); *People v. McCullum,* 66 Ill. 2d 306, 362 N.E.2d 307 (1977).

7. It is insufficient under Jackson simply to find nontriability; the court must be presented with a diagnosis and treatment plan which will result in triability "soon." Consequently, a trial court's findings must cover both elements. *Ex parte Kent,* 490 S.W.2d 649 (Mo. 1973). Because an incompetency commitment is conditioned on treatment, *Scott v. Plante,* 641 F.2d 117, 125-27 (3d Cir. 1981), *vacated,* 102 S. Ct. 3474 (1982), the institution to which an incompetent defendant has been committed must make periodic reports to the committing trial court about the defendant's progress. *In re Davis,* 8 Cal. 3d 798, 505 P.2d 1018, 106 Cal. Rptr. 178, *cert. denied,* 414 U.S. 870 (1973). A committing trial court should set the frequency of reporting; according to *Davis,* it is not incumbent on a defendant-patient to demand reports and periodic judicial review of commitment.

8. Recall that *Jackson* left open for consideration on remand the matter of conditional trial or other interlocutory proceedings to protect a defendant

against harm flowing from delayed proceedings, citing for comparison *People ex rel. Myers v. Briggs,* 46 Ill. 2d 281, 263 N.E.2d 109 (1970). The California Supreme Court in *In re Davis,* 8 Cal. 3d 798, 505 P.2d 1018, 106 Cal. Rptr. 178, *cert. denied,* 414 U.S. 870 (1973), was asked to approve such a proceeding for mental incompetents, but thought such a procedure should be authorized through legislation.

9. If the period of hospitalization based on incompetency is reasonable within Jackson, the sixth amendment right to a speedy trial is not impaired. *United States ex rel. Little v. Twomey,* 477 F.2d 767 (7th Cir.), *cert. denied,* 414 U.S. 846 (1973); *State ex rel. Haskins v. County Court,* 62 Wis. 2d 250, 214 N.W.2d 575 (1974). If a period of hospitalization becomes constitutionally excessive, however, a court may dismiss the prosecution on constitutional grounds. *United States v. Pardue,* 354 F. Supp. 1377 (D. Conn. 1973).

10. The Supreme Court in *Jackson* imposed no maximum limit on the period of compulsory hospitalization based on procedural incompetence, other than to indicate that triability must occur "soon." Some decisions have invoked a six-month limitation on that form of hospitalization. *State ex rel. Walker v. Jenkins,* 157 W. Va. 683, 203 S.E.2d 353 (1974); *State ex rel. Matalik v. Schubert,* 57 Wis. 2d 315, 204 N.W.2d 13 (1973). It has been ruled that incompetency commitments cannot continue beyond the period of the maximum sentence which could have been imposed following conviction of pending charges. *United States v. DeBellis,* 649 F.2d 1 (1st Cir. 1981); *State ex rel. Deisinger v. Treffert,* 85 Wis. 2d 257, 270 N.W.2d 402 (1978). After maximum limits have been reached, a civil commitment proceeding must ensue if a defendant continues to be nontriable. On permitted departures from civil commitment procedures in such instances, *see Estate of Hofferber,* 28 Cal. 3d 161, 616 P.2d 836, 167 Cal. Rptr. 854 (1980).

3. "CHEMICAL COMPETENCE"

EDITORIAL NOTE

Chemotherapy, often through administration of tranquilizers, frequently succeeds within a relatively brief time in eliminating or controlling symptoms which have produced nontriability. Such medications can be administered to defendants without their formal consent, *State v. Law,* 270 S.C. 664, 244 S.E.2d 302, 307 (1978), and there is no constitutional bar to placing them on trial while under medication. *United States v. Hayes,* 589 F.2d 811, *reh'g denied,* 591 F.2d 1343 (5th Cir. 1979), *cert. denied,* 444 U.S. 847 (1979); *Lane v. State,* 388 So. 2d 1022, 1026 (Fla. 1980); *State v. Hancock,* 247 Or. 21, 426 P.2d 872 (1967); *State v. Stacy,* 556 S.W.2d 552 (Tenn. Crim. App. 1977); *State v. Murphy,* 56 Wash. 2d 761, 355 P.2d 323 (1960). Due process questions might be present, however, if medication interferes with the defense of abnormal mental condition by obscuring the defendant's abnormal mental symptoms. This concern is discussed, *e.g.,* in *State v. Hayes,* 118 N.H. 458, 389 A.2d 1379 (1978); *State v. Jojola,* 89 N.M. 489, 553 P.2d 1296 (1976); *State v. Law,* 270 S.C. 664, 244 S.E.2d 302, 306-07 (1978); *In re Pray,* 133 Vt. 253, 336 A.2d 174 (1975).

C. SCREENING AND DIVERSION OF MENTALLY-ILL ARRESTEES AND DEFENDANTS

UNITED STATES NATIONAL ADVISORY COMMISSION ON CRIMINAL JUSTICE STANDARDS AND GOALS, COURTS REPORT 27-28, 32, 33, 35, 36 (1973)

The term, "diversion," as used in this report, refers to halting or suspending before conviction formal criminal proceedings against a person on the condition or assumption he will do something in return. Screening, on the other hand, involves the cessation of formal criminal proceedings and removal of the individual from the criminal justice system. Action taken after conviction is not diversion, because at that point the criminal prosecution already has been permitted to proceed to its conclusion, the determination of criminal guilt....

Diversion may occur at many points as a case progresses through the criminal justice system. A police officer who assumes custody of an intoxicated person and releases him to the custody of his family or a detoxification center diverts. A prosecutor who holds formal charges in abeyance while the defendant participates in psychiatric treatment diverts. But in all situations, diversion involves a discretionary decision on the part of an official of the criminal justice system that there is a more appropriate way to deal with the particular defendant than to prosecute him.

Diversion programs tend to fall into two patterns. In one, the defendant is diverted into a program run by agencies of the criminal justice system. In the other, the accused is channeled into a program outside the criminal justice system. Suspension of bad check charges on the condition that the offender make restitution is an example of diversion into a program operated by the criminal justice system; often the only supervision to which such an offender is subjected is that of the prosecutor's staff, aided by the victim. Suspension of prosecution on the condition that the defendant enter a psychiatric hospital for treatment is an example of diversion into a program operated by agencies having no formal relationship to the criminal justice system....

Standard 2.1

General Criteria for Diversion

In appropriate cases offenders should be diverted into noncriminal programs before formal trial or conviction.

Such diversion is appropriate where there is a substantial likelihood that conviction could be obtained and the benefits to society from channeling an offender into an available noncriminal diversion program outweigh any harm done to society by abandoning criminal prosecution. Among the factors that should be considered favorable to diversion are: .... (3) any likelihood that the offender suffers from a mental illness or psychological abnormality which was related to his crime and for which treatment is available ....

Commentary

Diversion occurs most often following the commission of crimes considered to pose little danger to society. However, in some situations cases are diverted even though the behavior is violent (such as intrafamily assault) or the person is potentially dangerous (such as violent, mentally ill persons).... With respect to mentally ill persons who are potentially dangerous, diversion in the form of commitment to public mental health facilities provides more appropriate treatment for the offender as well as a potentially longer term of confinement than is available under criminal statutes....

Diversion ordinarily should not be an ad hoc matter. Occasionally a defendant may on his own initiative arrange for a diversion program, as by obtaining private psychiatric treatment. Defense counsel should be encouraged to develop possible alternatives to formal prosecution and to present these alternatives to the prosecutor with a request that formal charges be suspended. By virtue of his professional and personal contacts in the community, a prosecutor sometimes may become aware of assistance that could be offered on a diversion basis....

In one category of situations, the diversion decision ordinarily will be made before the case is presented to the prosecutor. Usually it is made by the police .... [For example, if] an individual who is clearly mentally ill commits a minor criminal act, there is no legitimate reason to delay his entry into the mental health system pending an acquittal on grounds of insanity or even pending a prosecutor's decision that the defendant should be diverted. Diversion of such individuals should be a police task....

If a police officer encounters a person he would otherwise arrest for a misdemeanor, and the person appears to be mentally ill, the officer should be authorized to refer the individual to a mental health facility for evaluation. The mental health facility should have authority to seek nonvoluntary hospitalization of the individual when appropriate, but such commitment should not be a prerequisite for diversion....

In the situations described above, diversion would be effectuated by the police. In other situations, diversion should occur at a later stage of the criminal justice process, and the decision as to whether to divert a particular offender should be made by the prosecutor's staff....

Several factors characterize situations in which diversion should be delayed .... First, they tend to involve serious offenses. Since the offender has actually demonstrated that he presents a significant danger to the community, the decision to divert him from the criminal justice system poses an even greater threat to community security. Thus the diversion decision should be delayed until more information is available and until the prosecutor himself can evaluate the desirability of prosecution. Second, the programs into which offenders are diverted tend to involve more significant deprivations of liberty than those discussed above. In view of the negative result of an unjustified diversion and the corresponding need to protect defendants, more formality is appropriate. This greater formality can only be provided if diversion is postponed until the case reaches the more formal stages of processing....

C. SCREENING OF MENTALLY-ILL ARRESTEES AND DEFENDANTS

2. *Mentally Ill Serious Offenders.* In theory, a defendant who was mentally ill at the time of his offense is entitled to be channeled into the mental health system by asserting at trial the defense of insanity. If he is still mentally ill and dangerous at the time of acquittal on insanity grounds, he is subject to post-acquittal commitment. In addition, mentally ill defendants often are diverted by informal means, many times on the grounds that they are incompetent to stand trial. Following treatment, prosecutions often are dropped or the charges drastically reduced ....

NOTES

1. Prosecuting or district attorneys usually are competent to institute civil commitment procedures against unconvicted or unconvictable suspects or defendants. *See State v. Milam,* 260 S.E.2d 295, 303 (W. Va. 1979) (double jeopardy barred retrial of defendant on charges relating to which the insanity defense had been interposed in an earlier trial).

2. In *State ex rel. Smith v. Scott,* 280 S.E.2d 811, 813 (W. Va. 1981), it was noted:

> When the issue of sanity has been fully developed at trial and it conclusively appears that the defendant was not criminally responsible at the time the crime was committed, the trial judge may, and in many instances must, direct the verdict in favor of the defendant. Furthermore, neither judges nor prosecutors are usually interested in going through the vain act of a trial where there is overwhelming pretrial psychiatric evidence that the defendant was not criminally responsible at the time the crime was committed. When it appears obvious that a trial court will direct a verdict in favor of the defendant on the issue of criminal responsibility, the proper course is for the prosecutor to move to nolle the indictment and where appropriate, to proceed with a motion for a civil commitment. However, there is no statutory or common law machinery for compelling such a result.

3. A state constitutional due process clause was violated by a statute allowing grand juries to decline to indict if they believed accused persons were insane and to certify to courts that such persons were insane. Grand jury procedures are secret and nonadversarial, witnesses are not cross-examined, a written record on which appeal can be based is not required, accused persons can be compelled to attend without counsel present with them, hearsay evidence is permitted, and the burden of persuasion is at the level of probable cause only. *Kanteles v. Wheelock,* 439 F. Supp. 505 (D.N.H. 1977); *Novosel v. Helgemoe,* 118 N.H. 115, 384 A.2d 124 (1978).

4. LAW REFORM COMM'N OF CANADA, REPORT TO PARLIAMENT ON MENTAL DISORDER in the CRIMINAL PROCESS 11 (1977):

> We feel that considering an accused's mental state in the granting of bail is proper and, in some cases, vital. It is important, however, to try to minimize the tendency of refusing bail to mentally disordered persons who would not otherwise be detained under the usual bail criteria.... In principle no mentally disordered accused should be refused bail if his

disorder is unrelated to the offence charged and he would not otherwise be detained by the civil authorities. If his psychiatric state, although unrelated to the offence, makes him a danger to himself or others, the appropriate [civil commitment] legislation should be used. If the accused's psychiatric state is directly related to his crime, pre-trial detention criteria under the criminal law would be appropriate.

D. MENTALLY ILL PRISONERS

EDITORIAL NOTE

States can create psychiatric wards or hospitals within their prison systems if they choose. If they do so, however, the eighth amendment requires that prisoners receive adequate health care, *Estelle v. Gamble*, 429 U.S. 97, 104-05 (1976), which includes psychiatric treatment for mentally-ill prisoners. *Woodall v. Foti*, 648 F.2d 268 (5th Cir. 1981); *Inmates of Allegheny County Jail v. Peirce*, 612 F.2d 754 (3d Cir. 1979); *Bowring v. Godwin*, 551 F.2d 44 (4th Cir. 1977). Failure to provide a constitutionally acceptable level of health care in federal facilities creates a direct civil cause of action under the eighth amendment itself. *Carlson v. Greene*, 446 U.S. 14 (1980). *See generally* Klein, *Prisoners' Rights to Physical and Mental Health Care: A Modern Expansion of the Eighth Amendment's Cruel and Unusual Punishment Clause*, 7 FORDHAM URB. L.J. 1 (1978).

Should prison administrators wish to transfer mentally ill prisoners to state mental health facilities not administered by the prison system itself, administrative due process governs the procedures they must follow. *Vitek v. Jones*, 445 U.S. 480 (1980). As in mental health commitments generally, mental hospitalization of prisoners entails "a massive curtailment of liberty," *id.* at 491 (*quoting Humphrey v. Cady*, 405 U.S. 504, 509 (1972)), which "can engender adverse social consequences to the individual." *Id.* at 492 (*quoting Addington v. Texas*, 441 U.S. 418, 425-26 (1979)). Conviction of crime legitimates imprisonment but constitutes no determination that a defendant is mentally ill and is to be hospitalized involuntarily. 445 U.S. at 493-94.

Accordingly, due process requires: (1) written notice that a transfer to a mental health facility is under consideration; (2) a hearing, sufficiently after notice to enable a prisoner to prepare, at which time evidence relied upon to support a transfer must be disclosed to the prisoner and an opportunity offered for the prisoner to be heard and to present documentary evidence; (3) an opportunity at the hearing for a prisoner to offer witnesses and to confront and cross-examine witnesses for the prison administration (unless a finding is made, not arbitrarily and based on good cause, that presentation, confrontation or cross-examination cannot be permitted); (4) an independent decisionmaker; (5) a written statement by the fact-finder of the evidence relied upon and the reasons for authorizing inmate transfer; and (6) effective and timely notice to inmates about these rights. Although the federal district court also had included a requirement of legal counsel for inmates, furnished at state expense if they were indigent, a majority of the Supreme Court refrained from endorsing that as a requirement. The Court found its inspiration for its administrative due process analysis in *Wolff v. McDonnell*, 418 U.S. 539 (1974), governing prisoner disciplinary proceedings which may result in loss of good-time credits.

Jones did not present the issue of return of prisoners from mental health facilities to prison, but it appears appropriate to provide them with at least the same administrative and judicial review of a hospital administrative decision to discharge patients permanently or on outpatient status that protects an involuntary civil committee. *See Burchett v. Bower*, 355 F. Supp. 1278 (D. Ariz. 1973); *In re Hurt*, 437 A.2d 590, 595 (D.C. 1981).

Jones requirements cannot be evaded by denominating a portion of a state mental hospital a "prison annex" and transferring prisoners back and forth. *See Liles v. Ward*, 424 F. Supp. 675 (S.D.N.Y. 1976) (pre-*Jones* litigation). Equal protection is denied if mentally ill convicts are transferred administratively to civil patient status at the expiration of their maximum sentences without the same judicial procedures that govern involuntary civil commitment. *Baxstrom v. Herold*, 383 U.S. 107 (1966). Under elementary due process standards, no civil committee, however dangerous, can be transferred from a civil mental hospital to prison except pursuant to a valid criminal conviction. *Kesselbrenner v. Anonymous*, 33 N.Y.2d 161, 305 N.E.2d 903, 350 N.Y.S.2d 889 (1973).

SECTION II. Intoxication

MODEL PENAL CODE

§ 2.08. Intoxication

[The text of this section appears in Appendix A.]

STATE v. STASIO

Supreme Court of New Jersey
78 N.J. 467, 396 A.2d 1129 (1979)

SCHREIBER, J.

The major issue on this appeal is whether voluntary intoxication constitutes a defense to a crime, one element of which is the defendant's intent. Defendant Stasio was found guilty by a jury of assault with intent to rob, in violation of N.J.S.A. 2A:90-2, and of assault while being armed with a dangerous knife, contrary to N.J.S.A. 2A:151-5....

This Court last considered the culpability of an individual who had committed an illegal act while voluntarily under the influence of a drug or alcohol in *State v. Maik*, 60 N.J. 203, 287 A.2d 715 (1972)....

On appeal Chief Justice Weintraub, writing for a unanimous Court, began by discussing generally the concept of criminal responsibility. After pointing out that although there was a difference in the treatment of sick and bad offenders, he noted that notwithstanding that difference "the aim of the law is to protect the innocent from injury by the sick as well as the bad." 60 N.J. at 213, 287 A.2d at 720. It was in that context that a decision would have to be made whether the voluntary use of alcoholic beverages or drugs should support a viable defense. He then stated the generally accepted proposition that criminal responsibility was not extinguished when the offender was under the influence of a drug or liquor and the reasons for that rule:

> It is generally agreed that a defendant will not be relieved of criminal responsibility because he was under the influence of intoxicants or drugs voluntarily taken. This principle rests upon public policy, demanding that he who seeks the influence of liquor or narcotics should not be insulated from criminal liability because that influence impaired his judgment or his control. The required element of badness can be found in the intentional use of the stimulant or depressant. Moreover, to say that one who offended while under such influence was sick would suggest that his sickness disappeared when he sobered up and hence he should be released. Such a concept would hardly protect others from the prospect of repeated injury. [60 N.J. at 214, 287 A.2d at 720].

The Chief Justice set forth four exceptions to the general rule. First, when drugs being taken for medication produce unexpected or bizarre results, no public interest is served by punishing the defendant since there is no likelihood of repetition. Second, if intoxication so impairs a defendant's mental faculties that he does not possess the wilfulness, deliberation and premeditation necessary to prove first degree murder, a homicide cannot be raised to first degree murder.... Under this exception the influence of liquor "no matter how pervasive that influence may be, will not lead to an acquittal. It cannot reduce the crime below murder in the second degree, and this because of the demands of public security." *State v. Maik, supra,* 60 N.J. at 215, 287 A.2d at 721. Third, a felony homicide will be reduced to second degree murder when intoxication precludes formation of the underlying felonious intent. Parenthetically, it may be noted that since voluntary intoxication does not eliminate responsibility for the felony, it could be contended that the defendant should remain liable for first degree felony murder. On the other hand, considerations of fairness indicate that such a defendant should be treated the same as one charged with ordinary first degree homicide requiring premeditation. Fourth, the defense of insanity is available when the voluntary use of the intoxicant or drug results in a fixed state of insanity after the influence of the intoxicant or drug has spent itself. Since the defense in *Maik* may have fallen into the fourth category, the charge as given was erroneous and the cause was remanded for a new trial on the issue of whether the defendant had been insane at the time of the killing and whether that condition continued thereafter.

... In *State v. Del Vecchio,* 142 N.J.Super. 359, 361 A.2d 579 (App.Div.), certif. den. 71 N.J. 501, 366 A.2d 657 (1976), a conviction for breaking and entering with intent to steal was reversed on the ground that the jury had improperly been charged that voluntary intoxication was not a defense to a crime requiring a specific intent. The Appellate Division reasoned that, when a specific intent was an element of an offense, voluntary intoxication may negate existence of that intent. Since intoxication may have prevented existence of that specific intent, an acquittal might be in order....

In our opinion the Chief Justice in *Maik* enunciated a principle applicable generally to all crimes and, unless one of the exceptions to the general rule is applicable, voluntary intoxication will not excuse criminal conduct. The need to protect the public from the prospect of repeated injury and the public policy demanding that one who voluntarily subjects himself to intoxication should not be insulated from criminal responsibility are strongly supportive of this result. We reject the approach adopted by *Del Vecchio* because, although it has surface appeal, it is based on an unworkable dichotomy, gives rise to inconsistencies, and ignores the policy expressed in *Maik*.

Del Vecchio would permit the intoxication defense only when a "specific" as distinguished from a "general" intent was an element of the crime. However, that difference is not readily ascertainable. "The distinction thus made between a 'specific intent' and a 'general intent,'" wrote the Chief Justice in *Maik*, "is quite elusive, and although the proposition [that voluntary intoxication may be a defense if it prevented formation of a specific intent] is echoed in some opinions in our State ... it is not clear that any of our cases in fact turned upon it." 60 N.J. at 215, 287 A.2d at 721. Professor Hall has deplored the attempted distinction in the following analysis:

> The current confusion resulting from diverse uses of "general intent" is aggravated by dubious efforts to differentiate that from "specific intent." Each crime ... has its distinctive mens rea, e.g. intending to have forced intercourse, intending to break and enter a dwelling-house and to commit a crime there, intending to inflict a battery, and so on. It is evident that there must be as many mentes reae as there are crimes. And whatever else may be said about an intention, an essential characteristic of it is that it is directed towards a definite end. To assert therefore that an intention is "specific" is to employ a superfluous term just as if one were to speak of a "voluntary act." [J. Hall, *General Principles of Criminal Law* 142 (2d ed. 1960)].

....

Moreover, distinguishing between specific and general intent gives rise to incongruous results by irrationally allowing intoxication to excuse some crimes but not others. In some instances if the defendant is found incapable of formulating the specific intent necessary for the crime charged, such as assault with intent to rob, he may be convicted of a lesser included general intent crime, such as assault with a deadly weapon. N.J.S.A. 2A:90-3. In other cases there may be no related general intent offense so that intoxication would lead to acquittal. Thus, a defendant acquitted for breaking and entering with intent to steal because of intoxication would not be guilty of any crime — breaking and entering being at most under certain circumstances the disorderly person's offense of trespass. N.J.S.A. 2A:170-31. Similarly, if the specific intent to rob were not demonstrated because of intoxication, then the defendant may have no criminal responsibility since assault with intent to rob would also be excused.

Finally, where the more serious offense requires only a general intent, such as rape, see J. Hall, *General Principles of Criminal Law* 143 (2d ed. 1960), and sources cited, intoxication provides no defense, whereas it would be a defense to an attempt to rape, specific intent being an element of that offense. Yet the same logic and reasoning which impels exculpation due to the failure of specific intent to commit an offense would equally compel the same result when a general intent is an element of the offense....

The *Del Vecchio* approach may free defendants of specific intent offenses even though the harm caused may be greater than in an offense held to require only general intent. This course thus undermines the criminal law's primary function of protecting society from the results of behavior that endangers the public safety. This should be our guide rather than concern with logical consistency in terms of any single theory of culpability, particularly in view of the fact that alcohol is significantly involved in a substantial number of offenses.[3] The demands of public safety and the harm done are identical irrespective of the offender's reduced ability to restrain himself due to his drinking.[4] "[I]f a person casts off the restraints of reason and consciousness by a voluntary act, no wrong is done to him if he is held accountable for any crime which he may commit in that condition. Society is entitled to this protection." *McDaniel v. State,* 356 So.2d 1151, 1160-1161 (Miss. 1978).

Until a stuporous condition is reached or the entire motor area of the brain is profoundly affected,[5] the probability of the existence of intent remains. The initial effect of alcohol is the reduction or removal of inhibitions or restraints. But that does not vitiate intent. The loosening of the tongue has been said to disclose a person's true sentiments — "in vino veritas." One commentator has noted: The great majority of moderately to grossly drunk or drugged persons who commit putatively criminal acts are probably aware of what they are doing and the likely consequences. In the case of those who are drunk, alcohol may have diminished their perceptions, released their inhibitions and clouded their reasoning and judgment, but they still have sufficient capacity for the conscious mental processes required by the ordinary definitions of all or most specific mens rea crimes. For example, a person can be quite far gone in drink and still capable of the conscious intent to steal, which is an element of common law larceny. [Murphy, "Has Pennsylvania Found a Satisfactory Intoxication Defense?," 81 Dick.L.Rev. 199, 208 (1977) (citations omitted).] ...

The new Code of Criminal Justice* provides that a person is not guilty of an offense unless he acted purposely, knowingly, recklessly or negligently, as the

---

[3] See Wilentz, "The Alcohol Factor in Violent Deaths," 12 Am.Pract. Digest 829 (1961); Goodwin, Crane & Guze, "Felons Who Drink," 32 Q.J.Stud.Alc. 136 (1971); McGeorge, "Alcohol and Crime," 3 Med.Sci. & L. 27 (1963). A study in 77 rape cases reflected that 50% of the offenders had been drinking. Rada, "Alcoholism and Forcible Rape," 132 Am.J.Psychiatry 4 (1975). Analysis of many studies reflects a high ratio of offenders who have imbibed to those who have not in violent crimes. See K. Pernanen, "Alcohol and Crimes of Violence," in 4 The Biology of Alcoholism 351 (B. Kissin & H. Begleiter eds. 1976).

[4] This position is consistent with the treatment accorded voluntary intoxication in tort law. Restatement (Second) of Torts § 283C, Comment d (Tentative Draft No. 4, 1959); W. Prosser, Torts § 32 at 154 (4th ed. 1971).

[5] There is some evidence that at 0.20% of alcohol in the blood, the typical individual would normally fall into that category. Greenberg, "Intoxication and Alcoholism: Physiological Factors," 315 Annals Am.Acad.Pol. & Soc.Sci. 22, 27 (1958). The motor vehicle statute presumes a driver is under the influence of liquor if the percentage is 0.10% or more. N.J.S.A. 39:4-50.1(3). Of course, the precise effects of a particular concentration of alcohol in the blood varies from person to person depending upon a host of other factors. See generally Perr, "Blood Alcohol Levels and 'Diminished Capacity'," 3 (No. 4) J.Legal Med. 28-30 (April 1975).

*The court refused to apply the new code because it was not in effect when the defendant acted. Moreover, the state during oral argument suggested that the code provision invoked by the defendant might be repealed — Eds.

II. INTOXICATION

law may require. N.J.S.A. 2C:2-2. It also states that intoxication is not a defense "unless it negatives an element of the offense," N.J.S.A. 2C:2-8(a), and that "[w]hen recklessness establishes an element of the offense, if the actor, due to self-induced intoxication, is unaware of a risk of which he would have been aware had he been sober, such unawareness is immaterial." N.J.S.A. 2C:2-8(b). These provisions were taken from the Model Penal Code of the American Law Institute, § 2.08 (Prop.Off. Draft 1962). The American Law Institute Committee has explained that in those instances when the defendant's purpose or knowledge is an element of a crime, proof of intoxication may negate the existence of either. Tent. Draft No. 9 at 2-9 (1959). The distinction between specific and general intent has been rejected. *Id.* at 4.

. . . .

Our holding today does not mean that voluntary intoxication is always irrelevant in criminal proceedings.[7] Evidence of intoxication may be introduced to demonstrate that premeditation and deliberation have not been proven so that a second degree murder cannot be raised to first degree murder or to show that the intoxication led to a fixed state of insanity. Intoxication may be shown to prove that a defendant never participated in a crime. Thus it might be proven that a defendant was in such a drunken stupor and unconscious state that he was not a part of a robbery. See *State v. Letter,* 4 N.J.Misc. 395, 133 A. 46 (Sup. Ct. 1926). His mental faculties may be so prostrated as to preclude the commission of the criminal act. Under some circumstances intoxication may be relevant to demonstrate mistake. However, in the absence of any basis for the defense, a trial court should not in its charge introduce that element. A trial court, of course, may consider intoxication as a mitigating circumstance when sentencing a defendant.

. . . .

The judgment of Appellate Division is affirmed [on an unrelated issue].

HANDLER, J., concurring.

If a defendant's state of mind is a material factor in determining whether a particular crime has been committed — and if a degree of intoxication so affects the defendant's mental faculties as to eliminate effectively a condition of the mind otherwise essential for the commission of a crime — intoxication should be recognized as a defense in fact.

When dealing with the issue of intoxication, the focus at trial should be upon the mental state which is required for the commission of the particular crime charged. This should not ordinarily call for desiccated refinements between general intent and specific intent. I subscribe to the reasoning expressed in *State v. Maik,* 60 N.J. 203, 287 A.2d 715 (1972), and endorsed by

---

[7] While we recognize that the rule we announce here is at odds with the rule in a number of other jurisdictions, see Annot., 8 A.L.R.3d 1236 (1966), it is in accord with the holding in several other states. See McDaniel v. State, 356 So.2d 1151 (Miss. 1978) (armed robbery; court made rule); State v. Vaughn, 268 S.C. 119, 232 S.E.2d 328 (1977) (house-breaking and assault with intent to ravish; court made rule); Commonwealth v. Geiger, 475 Pa. 249, 380 A.2d 338 (1977) (by statute); McKenty v. State, 135 Ga.App. 271, 217 S.E.2d 388 (1975) (by statute); State v. Cornwall, 95 Idaho 680, 518 P.2d 863 (1974) (by statute); Rodriguez v. State, 513 S.W.2d 594 (Tex.Cr.App.1974) (by statute); State v. Richardson, 495 S.W.2d 435 (Mo.1973) (second degree murder; court made rule); Chittum v. Commonwealth, 211 Va. 12, 174 S.E.2d 779 (1970) (kidnapping and attempted rape; court made rule). See also Ark.Stat.Ann. § 41-207 (1977).

this Court, which denigrated the attempted differentiation between so-called specific intent and general intent crimes. It is an unhelpful, misleading and often confusing distinction. See *People v. Hood,* 1 Cal.3d 444, 456-457, 82 Cal.Rptr. 618, 625-626, 462 P.2d 370, 377-378 (1969); J. Hall, *General Principles of Criminal Law* 142 (2d ed. 1960); G. Williams, *Criminal Law — The General Part* (2d ed. 1961); Hall, "Intoxication and Criminal Responsibility," 57 Harv.L.Rev. 1045, 1064 (1944), authorities cited by the majority opinion. *Ante* at 1132-1133. For the most part, the inquiry at a criminal trial should be directed toward the general guilty condition of mind or mens rea necessary to append responsibility for criminal conduct. See *State v. Savoie,* 67 N.J. 439, 454-461 341 A.2d 598 (1975).

. . . .

The Model Penal Code of the American Law Institute has eschewed this distinction. It deals with mens rea primarily in terms of purpose and knowledge and calls for an analysis of the elements of the criminal offense in relation to these components. See Model Penal Code § 2.02, Comments (Tent. Draft No. 4, 1955); Id., § 2.08, Comments (Tent. Draft No. 9, 1959). The recently enacted New Jersey Code of Criminal Justice, N.J.S.A. 2C:1-1 et seq., similarly abandons the distinctions between specific and general intent in addressing the area of the mental components of crime. N.J.S.A. 2C:2-2. This approach, in my view, enables a trier of fact to assimilate proof of a defendant's intoxication in a more realistic perspective and to reach a more rational determination of the effect of intoxication upon criminal responsibility, particularly in terms of consciousness and purpose. N.J.S.A. 2C:2-2.

. . . .

The criminal laws need not be impotent or ineffective when dealing with an intoxicated criminal. The question should always be whether under particular circumstances a defendant ought to be considered responsible for his conduct. This involves a factual determination of whether he has acted with volition. Intoxication, in this context, would constitute a defense if it reached such a level, operating upon the defendant's mind, so as to deprive him of his will to act.... I would accordingly require, in order to generate a reasonable doubt as to a defendant's responsibility for his acts, that it be shown he was so intoxicated that he could not think, or that his mind did not function with consciousness or volition....

. . . .

PASHMAN, J., concurring in result only and dissenting.

In this and the companion case of *State v. Atkins,* 78 N.J. 454, 396 A.2d 1122 (1979), the majority rules that a person may be convicted of the crimes of assault *with intent* to rob and breaking and entering *with intent* to steal even though he never, in fact, intended to rob anyone or steal anything. The majority arrives at this anomalous result by holding that voluntary intoxication can never constitute a defense to any crime other than first-degree murder even though, due to intoxication, the accused may not have possessed the mental state specifically required as an element of the offense. This holding not only defies logic and sound public policy, it also runs counter to dictates of prior caselaw and the policies enunciated by our Legislature in the new criminal code. I therefore dissent from that holding although I agree that the defendant is entitled to a new trial.

I

The majority's heavy reliance upon *State v. Maik*, 60 N.J. 203, 287 A.2d 715 (1972), as supportive of its holding is wholly misplaced. The sole issue presented in Maik was whether a defendant's use of narcotics could be utilized to assert the insanity defense. In dicta the Court did state that as a general rule "a defendant will not be relieved of criminal responsibility because he was under the influence of intoxicants or drugs voluntarily taken." *Id.* at 214, 287 A.2d at 720. The Court, however, also explicitly remarked that most jurisdictions deem this "general rule" inapplicable where intoxication "prevent[s] the formation of a "specific intent' required in the definition of a particular offense." *Id.* Although the Maik Court acknowledged the difficulty of distinguishing between specific and general intent, it in no way indicated that the general rule should be abandoned.[1]

....

The foregoing evidences the Legislature's recognition that alcoholism is a disease and should be dealt with through rehabilitation and treatment rather than imprisonment. The Legislature has thus abandoned the common law's premise that one who becomes intoxicated necessarily harbors an "evil" intent.

II

Today's holding by the majority not only departs from precedent, it also stands logic on its head. This Court and the Legislature have long adhered to the view that criminal sanctions will not be imposed upon a defendant unless there exists a "'concurrence of an evil-meaning mind with an evil-doing hand.'" *State v. Williams*, 29 N.J. 27, 41, 148 A.2d 22, 29 (1959). The policies underlying this proposition are clear. A person who intentionally commits a bad act is more culpable than one who engages in the same conduct without any evil design. The intentional wrongdoer is also more likely to repeat his offense, and hence constitutes a greater threat to societal repose. A sufficiently intoxicated defendant is thus subject to less severe sanctions not because the law "excuses" his conduct but because the circumstances surrounding his acts have been deemed by the Legislature to be less deserving of punishment.

It strains reason to hold that a defendant may be found guilty of a crime whose definition includes a requisite mental state when the defendant actually failed to possess that state of mind. Indeed, this is the precise teaching of cases allowing the intoxication defense in first-degree murder prosecutions.

---

[1] As Part IV of my opinion makes clear, *infra*, I, as does the majority, reject the illogical and unworkable "specific intent/general intent" dichotomy. Maik and other cases which speak in such terms are utilized herein solely to refute the majority's contention that New Jersey precedent supports the view that voluntary intoxication is a defense only in a first degree murder prosecution. My usage of such cases therefore should not be interpreted as indicating any acceptance of that dichotomy on my part.

To sustain a first-degree murder conviction, the State must prove that the homicide was premeditated, willful, and deliberate. *State v. King,* 37 N.J. 285, 293-294, 181 A.2d 158 (1962). If the accused, due to intoxication, did not in fact possess these mental attributes, he can be convicted of at most second-degree murder .... (Citations omitted.)... That offense, however, can be sustained on a mere showing of recklessness, *State v. Gardner,* 51 N.J. 444, 242 A.2d 1 (1968), and the necessary recklessness can be found in the act of becoming intoxicated.

Just as the lack of premeditation, willfulness, or deliberation precludes a conviction for first-degree murder, so should the lack of intent to rob or steal be a defense to assault and battery with intent to rob, or breaking and entering with intent to steal. The principle is the same in both situations. If voluntary intoxication negates an element of the offense, the defendant has not engaged in the conduct proscribed by the criminal statute, and hence should not be subject to the sanctions imposed by that statute....

Although the distinction between specific intent and general intent would be erased by the rule enunciated herein, this does not mean that the different mental states implicit in our criminal law would become irrelevant. Some crimes — battery, for example — only require that the defendant intend the act that he has committed, while others — such as assault and battery with intent to kill — require that he also intend to bring about certain consequences. Certainly it would take a greater showing of intoxication to convince one that defendant had no intent to strike the victim than to show that he did not intend to kill. In the former case, one might well conclude that he must have intended his act unless he was unconscious. Indeed, this is the main reason why the "specific intent/general intent" dichotomy was first formulated.

DIRECTOR OF PUBLIC PROSECUTIONS v. MAJEWSKI

House of Lords
[1976] 2 All E.R. 142

[Defendant was convicted of "assault occasioning actual body harm" and "assault on a police officer." The convictions grew out of a bar-room fight in which defendant struck the proprietor and law enforcement officers who were called to the scene. Defendant claimed that because of his consumption of alcoholic beverages in conjunction with drugs that he had no conscious understanding of his acts at the time and that thereafter he had no recollection of the events. The defense was rejected and he appealed.

Defendant's legal position was summarized in the opinion of Lord Elwyn-Jones L.C.:]

> I. No man is guilty of a crime (save in relation to offences of strict liability) unless he has a guilty mind.
> II. A man who, though not insane, commits what would in ordinary circumstances be a crime when he is in such a mental state (whether it is called "automatism" or "pathological intoxication" or anything else) that he does not know what he is doing, lacks a guilty mind and is not criminally culpable for his actions.

III. This is so whether the charge involves a specific (or "ulterior") intent or one involving only a general (or "basic") intent.

IV. The same principle applies whether the automatism was the result of causes beyond the control of the accused or was self-induced by the voluntary taking of drugs or drink.

V. Assaults being crimes involving a guilty mind, a man who in a state of automatism unlawfully assaults another must be regarded as free from blame and be entitled to acquittal.

VI. It is logically and ethically indefensible to convict such a man of assault; it also contravenes section 8 of the Criminal Justice Act 1967.

VII. There was accordingly a fatal misdirection.... [The Lord Chancellor in rejecting defendant's position relied in part on a previous opinion of Lord Denning:]

....

... "Another thing to be observed is that it is not every involuntary act which leads to a complete acquittal. Take first an involuntary act which proceeds from a state of drunkenness. If the drunken man is so drunk that he does not know what he is doing, he has a defense to any charge, such as murder or wounding with intent, in which a specific intent is essential, but he is still liable to be convicted of manslaughter or unlawful wounding for which no specific intent is necessary...."

....

... If a man of his own volition takes a substance which causes him to cast off the restraints of reason and conscience, no wrong is done to him by holding him answerable criminally for any injury he may do while in that condition. His course of conduct in reducing himself by drugs and drink to that condition in my view supplies the evidence of mens rea, of guilty mind certainly sufficient for crimes of basic intent. It is a reckless course of conduct and recklessness is enough to constitute the necessary mens rea in assault cases.... The drunkenness is itself an intrinsic, an integral part of the crime, the other part being the evidence of the unlawful use of force against the victim. Together they add up to criminal recklessness. On this I adopt the conclusion of Stroud[8] that:

> "It would be contrary to all principle and authority to suppose that drunkenness" (and what is true of drunkenness is equally true of intoxication by drugs) "can be a defence for crime in general on the ground that 'a person cannot be convicted of a crime unless there was mens rea.' By allowing himself to get drunk and thereby putting himself in such a condition as to be no longer amenable to the law's commands, a man shows such regardlessness as amounts to mens rea for the purpose of all ordinary crimes." ...

[Lord Simon of Glaisdale while rejecting the appeal referred to a possible legislative solution:]

...

---

[8] (1920) 36 L.Q.R. at 273.

The Butler Committee on Mentally Abnormal Offenders[3] recognized that even the traditional view of the effect of intoxication in relation to conduct prohibited by law left a gap in the protection which the criminal law should afford to innocent citizens; this required, in their view, to be closed by legislation. Their recommendation 56 was: "... We propose that it should be an offence for a person while voluntarily intoxicated [to] do an act (or make an omission) that would amount to a dangerous offense if it were done or made with the requisite state of mind for such offense."

The maximum sentence recommended for such offence was imprisonment for one year for a first offence or for three years on a second or subsequent offence.[4]

Lord Salmon:

....

A number of distinguished academic writers support this [defendant's] contention on the ground of logic. As I understand it, the argument runs like this: Intention whether special or basic (or whatever fancy name you choose to give it) is still intention. If voluntary intoxication by drink or drugs can, as it admittedly can, negative the special or specific intention necessary for the commission of crimes such as murder and theft, how can you justify in strict logic the view that it cannot negative a basic intention, *e.g.*, the intention to commit offences such as assault and unlawful wounding? The answer is that in strict logic this view cannot be justified. But this is the view that has been adopted by the common law of England, which is founded on common sense and experience rather than strict logic. There is no case in the nineteenth century when the courts were relaxing the harshness of the law in relation to the effect of drunkenness upon criminal liability in which the courts ever went so far as to suggest that drunkenness, short of drunkenness producing insanity, could ever exculpate a man from any offence other than one which required some special or specific intent to be proved.

....

As I have already indicated, I accept that there is a degree of illogicality in the rule that intoxication may excuse or expunge one type of intention and not another. This illogicality is, however, acceptable to me because the benevolent part of the rule removes undue harshness without imperilling safety and the stricter part of the rule works without imperilling justice. It would be just as ridiculous to remove the benevolent part of the rule (which no one suggests) as it would be to adopt the alternative of removing the stricter part of the rule for the sake of preserving absolute logic. Absolute logic in human affairs is an uncertain guide and a very dangerous master. The law is primarily concerned with human affairs. I believe that the main object of our legal system is to preserve individual liberty. One important aspect of individual liberty is protection against physical violence....

---

[3] (1975) Cmnd. 6244.
[4] *Ibid*, para 18.85.

NOTES

1. More recent decisions preserving the dichotomy between general and specific intent crimes include *People v. DelGuidice,* 199 Colo. 41, 606 P.2d 840 (1979) (defense available only for first-degree, not second-degree, murder); *Norris v. State,* 419 N.E.2d 129, 132-33 (Ind. 1981); *Commonwealth v. Hicks,* 483 Pa. 305, 396 A.2d 1183 (1979) (unavailable to reduce third-degree murder, based on recklessness, to manslaughter); *Harrell v. State,* 593 S.W.2d 664 (Tenn. Crim. App. 1979) (robbery); *State v. D'Amico,* 136 Vt. 153, 385 A.2d 1082 (1978) (available in relation to charges of attempted crime if available for completed offense). Evidence must focus on the intent required for conviction. Therefore, the trial court properly excluded general evidence on the effect of heroin withdrawal symptoms in creating a need to obtain drugs through robbery. *State v. Mishne,* 427 A.2d 450, 455 (Me. 1981).

2. *Commonwealth v. Bridge,* 495 Pa. 568, 573-74, 435 A.2d 151, 154 (1981):

In some instances, intoxication is an element of the offense, e.g., driving under the influence, and therefore proof of intoxication (or some degree thereof) is necessary to prove the crime.... It is also true that there are certain instances where intoxication is not an element of the offense, and yet evidence of intoxication is nevertheless accepted as being relevant, for instance, if the accused seeks to offer his intoxication to prove that he did not perform the physical act required by the crime — that he was unconscious at the time and therefore did not commit the deed — this evidence is germane to the factfinders' inquiry and is properly submitted for their evaluation. In such cases, the issue can be neatly confined to the question of whether the accused was the perpetrator of the deed charged.

3. *O'Leary v. State,* 604 P.2d 1099, 1103 (Alaska 1979):

[The court's earlier precedent] thus clarifies what mental state is required to relieve a chronic alcoholic from criminal responsibility for his acts based on his inability to control his drinking, distinguishing the mental effect of intoxication which is the result of a particular alcoholic bout and "alcoholic psychosis" which occurs as a result of long continued habits of excessive drinking. Only the latter may constitute legal insanity. The test is not whether the defendant can refuse to take the first drink on any particular occasion but, rather, whether the accused's state of mind, before he initiates a drinking episode, has so deteriorated because of his chronic alcoholism (or for any other reason, for that matter) as to constitute a preexisting condition rendering him legally insane....

We think that this test has considerable merit and should be retained. It is consistent with our general reluctance to take account of lessened responsibility brought about by intoxication, in that it focuses on the results of alcoholism as a disease or a mental defect but refuses to consider a particular bout of intoxication as a defense to a crime. Also, by requiring a long period of excessive drinking and recognizable brain syndrome, "a degree of objective evidential corroboration is attained which reduces the possibility of fraud which may be present, in ordinary cases of intoxication." Note, Intoxication as a Criminal Defense, [50 COLUM. L.

Rev. 1210, 1221 (1955)]. There is no dispute here that O'Leary's pre-existing alcohol-related condition was not tantamount to legal insanity. Thus, as a matter of law, we conclude that the trial judge was correct in refusing to instruct the jury on the insanity defense.

4. *Commonwealth v. Hicks*, 483 Pa. 305, 311-12, 396 A.2d 1183, 1186 (1979): "Even accepting the remote possibility of the existence of a pathological disorder, it was at best a passive condition triggered by the ingestion of alcohol. [If so,] appellant was not entitled to escape the responsibility for his conduct under the *M'Naghten* rule."

5. *State v. Freitas*, 62 Haw. 17, 608 P.2d 408 (1980), following Ninth Circuit precedent, held that "mental disease or defect" under the ALI test must be determined without considering the factor of intoxication at the time of the act charged. Defense experts would not respond to prosecution cross-examination about whether, with a reasonable degree of medical certainty, they could say that defendant's capacity would have been impaired at the time of the offense, if the fact of alcohol ingestion were excluded from their consideration. Consequently, the jury need not have formed a reasonable doubt about defendant's sanity.

A similar analysis, in the context of the significance of drug addiction, appears in Commonwealth v. Sheehan, 376 Mass. 765, 772, 383 N.E.2d 1115, 1120 (1978) (rejecting "both drug addiction and the normal consequences of the consumption of drugs as a basis for a claim of lack of criminal responsibility").

6. *O'Leary v. State*, 604 P.2d 1099, 1103-04 (Alaska 1979):

> The court's instructions informed the jury that unconsciousness is a defense unless it is the result of a particular alcoholic bout stemming from voluntarily incurred intoxication. The instructions further defined voluntariness as follows:
>> The consumption of intoxicating liquor is voluntary under the law that applies to this case when a person knowingly introduces such a substance into his body and knows or ought to know that it has a tendency to cause intoxication, unless he induces it pursuant to medical advice.
>
> We think the court's instructions were adequate for the same reasons causing us to reject O'Leary's insanity defense. If he had substantial capacity to appreciate the consequences of his actions before he began to become intoxicated on a particular occasion, he cannot avoid responsibility for acts committed in a blackout state during the alcoholic bout. Therefore, the instructions given by the trial judge regarding the unconsciousness defense were correct.

7. If evidence of intoxication or influence of controlled substances is relevant, the defense must show not only the fact of intoxication but impairment of mental capacity before a trial court need instruct the jury on the matter. *Harrell v. State*, 593 S.W.2d 664, 672-73 (Tenn. Crim. App. 1979).

8. *State v. Schulz*, 102 Wis. 2d 423, 307 N.W.2d 151, 156 (1981):

> Although the accused may not be required to assume a burden of persuasion relative to his "defense" of intoxication, this is not to say that in

every case the state must prove the absence of intoxication beyond a reasonable doubt. The principles of due process are not violated if a burden of production — as opposed to a burden of persuasion — is placed upon the accused to come forward with "some" evidence in rebuttal of the state's case.... In order to place intoxication in issue in a given case, it will be necessary for the defendant to come forward with some evidence of his impaired condition. This evidence must be more than a mere statement that the defendant was intoxicated. The evidence must be credible and sufficient to warrant the jury's consideration of the issue as to whether the defendant was intoxicated to the extent it materially affected his or her ability to form the requisite intent.... ==Upon the production of such evidence the burden will be upon the state to prove beyond a reasonable doubt that the defendant's consumption of alcohol or drugs did not negate the existence of a state of mind necessary to fix criminal liability....==

State v. Correra, 430 A.2d 1251, 1255 (R.I. 1981) (citing authorities), adopts a similar analysis of the ultimate burden of persuasion.

9. Compare *United States ex rel. Goddard v. Vaughn,* 614 F.2d 929 (3d Cir.), cert. denied, 449 U.S. 844 (1980), with *Goddard v. State,* 382 A.2d 238 (Del. 1977), which sustained the constitutionality of a state statute making voluntary intoxication an affirmative defense which a defendant must establish by a preponderance of the evidence. Both courts thought the defense was like the diminished responsibility concept dealt with in Patterson v. New York, 432 U.S. 197 (1977). See *supra* pp. 324-328.

10. California voters by initiative have added § 25(a) to the California Penal Code which outlaws the use of evidence about a defendant's or juvenile court respondent's intoxication bearing on capacity to form the mental state required for the commission of the crime charged. See *supra* p. 285. The Texas Penal Code provides:

§ 8.04. Intoxication.

(a) ==Voluntary intoxication does not constitute a defense to the commission of crime.==

....

TEX. PENAL CODE ANN. § 8.04(a) (West 1973).

Are these approaches constitutional in light of United States Supreme Court decisions like *Chambers v. Mississippi,* 410 U.S. 284 (1973), and *Davis v. Alaska,* 415 U.S. 308 (1974)?

SECTION III. Immaturity

MODEL PENAL CODE

§ 4.10. Immaturity Excluding Criminal Conviction

[The text of this section appears in Appendix A.]

IN RE RAMON M.

Supreme Court of California
22 Cal. 3d 419, 584 P.2d 524, 149 Cal. Rptr. 387 (1978)

[Ramon M. was a 14-year-old youth with an IQ of 40-42, an extremely low level of intelligence, and a mental age equivalent to a five or six-year old child. A clinical psychologist who examined Ramon found that he could not read or tell time and was entirely incapable of abstract thought. Ramon M. along with two other youths attacked a pedestrian with their belts; they were apprehended shortly thereafter. Ramon M. was adjudicated a juvenile delinquent and declared a ward of the juvenile court. A portion of the California Supreme Court opinion relating to mental retardation as a mental defect under the ALI test for criminal responsibility appears *supra* p. 603, note 4. The delinquency adjudication was reversed because the juvenile court did not anticipate the *Ramon M.* doctrinal position, but the Supreme Court nevertheless considered the issue of immaturity as a basis of nonresponsibility.]

Tobriner, Justice

3. Defendant is not entitled to the presumption of incapacity applicable to children under the age of 14.

Penal Code section 26 provides that among those incapable of committing crimes are "children under the age of 14, in the absence of clear proof that at the time of committing the act charged against them, they knew its wrongfulness." Defendant maintains that section 26 should be interpreted to refer to mental age, not chronological age; he argues that his mental age of five renders him incapable of committing crimes. Defendant's proposed interpretation of section 26, however, conflicts with the decisions interpreting that section; moreover, since it would exempt from criminal responsibility a substantial proportion of the adult and adolescent population, it is unworkable.

Arguments essentially identical to those raised by defendant today were presented to this court in *People v. Oxnam, supra,* 170 Cal. 211, 149 P. 165, and *People v. Day* (1926) 199 Cal. 78, 248 P. 250. In *Oxnam* the trial court rejected a defense based on mental deficiency; defendant then moved for a new trial, submitting an affidavit showing him to have a mental age of eight. We affirmed the trial court's order denying that motion. In *People v. Day* defendant also moved for a new trial based upon affidavits showing that his mental age was that of a child under 14. We responded that "Section 26 of the Penal Code, subdivision (1), is not susceptible of the constrained construction contended for by the defendant.... Said section clearly refers to the physical age of a *child* and has no reference to the mental or moral age of an adult." (199 Cal. 78, 87, 248 P. 250, 253.)

The concept of "mental age" derives from intelligence testing. Although a person may grow in wisdom and experience throughout life, one's capacity to learn does not significantly increase beyond the age of 18. Thus the "mental age" of the average adult under present norms is approximately 16 years and 8 months. (See Terman & Merrill, Stanford Binet Intelligence Scale with revised 1972 tables of norms by Robert L. Thorndike (1973) p. 426.) Approximately 16 percent of the adult population and a much higher percentage of adolescents between ages 14 and 18 have "mental ages" below 14 years. Under defendant's proposed interpretation of section 26 all such persons would be presumed incapable of committing crimes.

Contrary to defendant's assertion we find nothing unreasonable in interpreting section 26 to refer to chronological age. Experience and maturity play as important a part as intelligence in determining an individual's ability to conform to the law. The Legislature could reasonably presume that any person of sound mind who reaches the age of 14 has acquired the ability to observe legal requirements; if by reason of mental disease or defect a particular individual has not acquired that ability his remedy is a defense based on idiocy or insanity.[13]

SECTION IV. Condition or Status

FENSTER v. LEARY

Court of Appeals of New York
20 N.Y.2d 309, 229 N.E.2d 426, 282 N.Y.S.2d 739 (1967)

BURKE, J. On three occasions in late 1964, each about a month apart, the plaintiff, Charles Fenster, was arrested by the New York City police and charged with violation of subdivision 1 of section 887 of the Code of Criminal Procedure (New York's vagrancy statute).

. . . .

We are in agreement with plaintiff that subdivision 1 of section 887 of the Code of Criminal Procedure is unconstitutional, on the ground that it violates due process and constitutes an overreaching of the proper limitations of the police power in that it unreasonably makes criminal and provides punishment for conduct (if we can call idleness conduct) of an individual which in no way impinges on the rights or interests of others and which has in no way been demonstrated to have anything more than the most tenuous connection with prevention of crime and preservation of the public order (on which ground the Attorney-General would have us sustain the statute), other than, perhaps, as a means of harassing, punishing or apprehending suspected criminals in an unconstitutional fashion.

. . . .

The Attorney-General of New York, appearing herein pursuant to section 71 of the Executive Law ... in defense of the statute's constitutionality, cites to us various statements from our own decisions and from the decisions of our lower courts in support of vagrancy statutes as a valid exercise of the police power. The general thrust of these decisions is that in order to prevent there coming into existence a "class of able-bodied vagrants ... [supporting] themselves by preying on society and thus [threatening] the public peace and security" *People ex rel. Stolofsky v. Superintendent,* 259 N.Y. 115, 118), to

---

[13] Our interpretation of section 26 is consistent with the common law, under which a minor "who has reached the age of fourteen has the same criminal capacity as an adult, that is, he is fully accountable for his violations of law unless incapacity is established on some other basis such as insanity." (Perkins, Criminal Law (2d ed. 1969) p. 837.) (Fns. omitted.)

"compel individuals to engage in some legitimate and gainful occupation from which they might maintain themselves, and thus remove the temptation to lead a life of crime or become public charges." *People v. Banwer,* 22 N.Y.S.2d 566, 569 [Magistrate's Ct., Brooklyn, 1940], the able-bodied poor may be made, subject to the sanctions of the criminal law, to accept available employment.... [W]e feel the statute is defective on the ground that, whatever purpose and role it may or may not have served in an earlier day, and however valid or invalid may be the proposition that the able-bodied unemployed poor are a likely source of crime, in this era of widespread efforts to motivate and educate the poor toward economic betterment of themselves, of the "War on Poverty" and all its varied programs, it is obvious to all that the vagrancy laws have been abandoned by our governmental authorities as a means of "persuading" unemployed poor persons to seek work (the Attorney-General does not even suggest that the vagrancy laws would be invoked against such people today). It is also obvious that today the only persons arrested and prosecuted as common-law vagrants are alcoholic derelicts and other unfortunates, whose only crime, if any, is against themselves, and whose main offense usually consists in their leaving the environs of skid row and disturbing *by their presence* the sensibilities of residents of nicer parts of the community, or suspected criminals, with respect to whom the authorities do not have enough evidence to make a proper arrest or secure a conviction on the crime suspected.... As to the former, it seems clear that they are more properly objects of the welfare laws and public health programs than of the criminal law and, as to the latter, it should by now be clear to our governmental authorities that the vagrancy laws were never intended to be and may not be used as an administrative short cut to avoid the requirements of constitutional due process in the administration of criminal justice....

The judgment below should be reversed, with costs against the intervenor-respondent, and judgment directed to be entered for plaintiff as demanded in the complaint.

SCILEPPI, J. (dissenting). I disagree and would affirm. A strong presumption of validity attaches to a statute and the heavy burden of proving its invalidity rests upon the appellant who is attacking its constitutionality....

In my opinion, the appellant has not discharged his burden.

... There can be no doubt that the State has a legitimate interest in discouraging able-bodied men who are capable of working from becoming loafers and public charges. *People v. Sohn,* 269 N.Y. 330; *Hicks v. District of Columbia,* 197 A.2d 154 [D.C. Ct. App., 1964], *cert. denied,* 383 U.S. 252. The State has chosen to achieve that end by imposing criminal penalties on those who are vagrants. It is argued that this end might be better achieved through social welfare legislation rather than through criminal sanctions. This may be so, but the relative merit of one approach over another is for the Legislature to decide and not the courts. As long as the exercise of the State's police power bears a reasonable relationship to the ends sought to be accomplished, the constitutionality of the statute must be upheld. We cannot strike down the statute because we feel another approach would be better. In my opinion, the appellant has failed to prove that there is no reasonable relationship between the statute in question and the ends it seeks to accomplish. Accordingly, the statute must stand and the judgment below should be affirmed.

....

Judgment reversed, etc.

NOTE ON ROBINSON v. CALIFORNIA and POWELL v. TEXAS

In *Robinson v. California,* 370 U.S. 660 (1962), the defendant was convicted of violating a California statute making it a criminal offense to be addicted to the use of narcotics. Acknowledging that "a state might impose criminal sanctions against the unauthorized manufacture, prescription, sale, purchase or possession of narcotics within its borders," the Supreme Court reversed, holding that punishment for the status of being addicted to narcotics is unconstitutional.

> It is unlikely that any state ... would attempt to make it a criminal offense for a person to be mentally ill, or a leper, or to be afflicted with a venereal disease ... [A] law which made a criminal offense of such a disease would ... be an infliction of cruel and unusual punishment in violation of the Eighth and Fourteenth Amendments.
>
> We cannot but consider the statute before us as of the same category.

Id. at 666-67. The court noted that a state could establish a program of involuntary civil confinement for treatment of those addicted to narcotics. Justice Harlan, concurring in the majority opinion, said that it had not been proved that the defendant used or possessed narcotics in California. Justice Douglas, also concurring, said, "The addict is a sick person."

Justice Clark dissented; in his view the statute applies only to the first stage of addiction, i.e., only to addicts who can control their use of narcotics. "The proceeding is clearly civil in nature with a purpose of rehabilitation and cure." California has a statute on commitment to a hospital for two years of addicts who have lost their power of control. "The majority acknowledges, as it must, that a state can punish persons who purchase, possess or use narcotics."

Justice White also dissented on the ground that the appellant was not convicted for a mere status or condition, but for the use of narcotics. "To find addiction in this case the jury had to believe that the appellant had frequently used narcotics in the recent past."

In *Powell v. Texas,* 392 U.S. 514 (1968), the defendant was convicted of public drunkenness and he appealed on the ground that the punishment was cruel and unusual, citing *Robinson.* The defendant's experts testified that he was a chronic alcoholic, and that chronic alcoholics have a compulsion to drink. Furthermore, although there is considerable medical dispute regarding alcoholism, it is generally recognized that alcoholism is a disease. The conviction was affirmed.

Justice Marshall, writing the opinion of the Court, said there is no agreement among experts regarding alcoholism. The criminal justice system does, in part, deal with the societal problem. At least it provides a bed and food while the present lack of medical facilities for alcoholics make the only present alternative much less desirable than brief imprisonment. The case does not fall within the scope of *Robinson* since the defendant was convicted, not for being a chronic alcoholic, but rather for being in a public place while intoxicated. Justice Marshall also disagreed with the dissenters regarding the *Robinson* decision: "It thus does not deal with the question of whether certain conduct cannot constitutionally be punished because it is, in some sense, 'involuntary' or 'occasioned by compulsion.'" 392 U.S. at 533. The court refused to establish a standard of constitutional criminal responsibility as to what acts, "voluntary" or "involuntary," are punishable. It rejected the thesis of "compulsion" not only because the concept is unclear and the experts are divided on the subject but, also, because of the logic of acceptance, namely, that it would be a defense to assault, theft, robbery or murder.

Justices Black and Harlan, concurring, held that *Robinson* was limited to proscribing punishment where no act of any kind was involved. They stated that the test urged by the dissent would, in effect, make unconstitutional the punishment of anyone who is not morally blameworthy. Such questions are better left to the legislatures of the respective states. Justice Black also cautioned against the expansion of *Robinson* on the ground of "compulsion." "The result ... would be to require recognition of 'irresistible impulse' as a complete defense to any crime."

Justice White, concurring in the result, did so solely for the reason that there was no showing that the defendant had a compulsion to be on the public streets while drunk. Had such a showing been made, an "irresistible compulsion" would preclude punishment under *Robinson*; thus he appears to have agreed with the policy advocated by the dissenters.

Justices Fortas, Douglas, Brennan and Stewart dissented. Justice Fortas, who wrote the dissenting opinion, emphasized that the issue is limited to the public appearance of an intoxicated person who is "suffering the disease of 'chronic alcoholism.'" In this case, the defendant was in a condition which he was powerless to avoid; he could not prevent his appearing in public places since this was symptomatic of the disease. "[A]lcoholism is caused and maintained by something other than the moral fault of the alcoholic, something that ... cannot be controlled by him."

> *Robinson* stands upon a principle which, despite its subtlety, must be simply stated and respectfully applied because it is the foundation of individual liberty and the cornerstone of the relations between a civilized state and its citizens: Criminal penalties may not be inflicted upon a person for being in a condition he is powerless to change.

Id. at 567.

UNITED STATES v. MOORE

United States Court of Appeals
486 F.2d 1139, *cert. denied,* 414 U.S. 980 (D.C. Cir. 1973)

[Defendant was convicted of possession of heroin. On appeal his defense of "addiction" with "overpowering need to use heroin" was rejected by five of the nine judges. The conviction was affirmed, but the sentence was vacated and

IV. CONDITION OR STATUS

[the case was remanded for further consideration of the Narcotic Addict Rehabilitation Act.]

WILKEY, CIRCUIT JUDGE.

....

According to appellant this case has one central issue:

> Is the proffered evidence of Appellant's long and intensive dependence on (addiction to) injected heroin, resulting in substantial impairment of his behavior controls and a loss of self-control over the use of heroin, relevant to his criminal responsibility for unlawful possession....

In other words, is appellant's addiction a defense to the crimes, involving only possession, with which he is charged? Arguing that he has lost the power of self-control with regard to his addiction, appellant maintains that by applying "the broad principles of common law criminal responsibility" we must decide that he is entitled to dismissal of the indictment or a jury trial on this issue. The gist of appellant's argument here is that "the common law has long held that the capacity to control behavior is a prerequisite for criminal responsibility."

It is inescapable that the logic of appellant's argument, if valid, would carry over to all other illegal acts of any type whose purpose was to obtain narcotics for his own use, a fact which is admitted by Judge Wright [*infra*] in his opinion. Appellant attempts to justify only the acts of possession and purchase of narcotics, both illegal, and both prohibited because if successfully prohibited they would eliminate drug addiction. The justification is on the basis that the addict has lost the power of control over his choice of acts. Appellant argues that the same rationale, justifying a tolerance of these two illegal acts by this court, or a strained construction of the statute that Congress really did not intend to prohibit such acts, or that it is constitutionally impermissible to prohibit such acts, would not carry over to other actions for the same purpose of obtaining narcotics for his own use.

In the case of any addict there are two factors that go to make up the "self-control" (or absence thereof) which governs his activities, and which determines whether or not he will perform certain acts, such as crimes, to obtain drugs. One factor is the physical craving to have the drug. The other is what might be called the addict's "character," or his moral standards.

... Under appellant's theory, adopted by the dissenters, only if there is a resulting loss of self-control can there be an absence of *free will* which, under the extension of the common law theory, would provide a valid defense to the addict. If there is a demonstrable absence of free will (loss of self-control), the illegal acts of possession and acquisition cannot be charged to the user of the drugs.

> *But if it is absence of free will which excuses the mere possessor-acquirer, the more desperate bank robber for drug money has an even more demonstrable lack of free will and derived from precisely the same factors as appellant argues should excuse the mere possessor.*

....

By definition we have assumed crimes of two classes — first, simple possession and acquisition, or second, greater crimes such as robbery — both motivated by the compulsive need to obtain drugs resulting in loss of self-control. If we punish the second, we can do so only because we find *free will*. If *free will* can exist for the second, it likewise must exist for the first class. If, like appellant, one takes the position that any addict who commits crimes (*i.e.* robbery) to feed his habit may be punished, one is making a judgment that this addict possesses *free will*, that he is somehow guilty in a way that the addict who does not commit such crimes to feed his habit (other than the crimes of acquisition and possession) is not. In other words, it follows necessarily that the quality that makes this addict commit such crimes to obtain the drugs is not the compulsion of addiction and the loss of "self-control," but is something apart from his addiction — but if we are dealing with a motivating factor other than drugs, this is another case, it is not the example called for by appellant's rationale. What the analysis just made demonstrates, even in the case of the addict-robber, is that his crime is caused by the same compulsion, his loss of self-control, due to his addiction.

Although attempted by appellant here, there can be no successful differentiation between the source of the drive, the compulsion and resulting loss of control which, appellant argues, vitiates legal accountability, hence the same compulsion would necessarily serve as the basis of the defense for each of the posited illegal acts. It is only a matter of degree. In fact, it seems clear that the addict who restrains himself from committing any other crimes except acquisition and possession, assuming he obtains his funds by lawful means, has demonstrated a greater degree of self-control than the addict who in desperation robs a bank to buy at retail. If the addict can restrain himself from committing any other illegal act except purchase and possession, then he is demonstrating a degree of self-control greater than that of the one who robs a pharmacy or a bank, and thus his defense of loss of control and accountability is even less valid than that of the addict who robs the pharmacy or the bank....

The obvious danger is that this defense *will* be extended to all other crimes — bank robberies, street muggings, burglaries — which can be shown to be the product of the same drug-craving compulsion....

....

Where the asserted analogy with *Powell** breaks down, however, is, first, that the acts in *Powell* were held to be punishable, as Justice White's separate opinion for the majority makes clear. Second, here the acquisition and possession of the addictive substance by Moore are *illegal* activities, whereas in Powell the "addict" induced his addictive state through *legal* means. Powell's violation was in actions taken later, which to four members of the Court were punishable without question, and which to Justice White were punishable so long as the acts had not been proved to be the product of an established irresistible compulsion. In *Moore,* however, the acquisition and possession of the addictive substance (narcotics) are themselves illegal, whether considered as initial acts *causing* addiction or acts *resulting* from addiction.

---

*Powell v. Texas, *supra* p. 659.

IV. CONDITION OR STATUS

....

Moore could never put the needle in his arm the first and many succeeding times without an exercise of will. His *illegal acquisition and possession* are thus the direct product of a *freely willed illegal act.*

... Although the narcotics user may soon through continued use acquire a compulsion to have the drug, and thus be said to have lost his self-control (insofar as he must take the drug regularly) due to a "disease," it is a disease which he has induced himself through a violation of the law. In contrast to the alcoholic Powell, the drug addict Moore has contracted a disease which virtually always commences with an illegal act.

... Thus it would appear that according to the Supreme Court, "rightly or wrongly," an addict is not under an "irresistible compulsion" to possess narcotics, but retains some ability to extricate himself from his addiction by ceasing to take the drugs. Thus it would certainly not be "cruel and unusual punishment" to convict him for possessing the narcotics, since the decision to possess is one that he makes at least in part of his own volition, especially at the beginning of his habit.

On the other hand, once a person has taken a certain amount of narcotics his body develops a craving for more (this, of course, is "addiction" as Justice Harlan defined it), a physical craving which he cannot prevent, and for which, the Supreme Court has said in *Robinson,*** he may not be punished. Taking into account this view of addiction, which view seems to us to be the one taken by the Supreme Court in *Robinson,* it is not inconsistent to say that an addict may not be punished for his craving (his "addiction") but may be punished when he makes the decision not to subject himself to the admittedly painful process of withdrawal, gives in to his craving and commits acts in violation of law and which continue his addiction.... There is no Eighth Amendment defense for the addict-possessor.

[Considering the Narcotic Addict Rehabilitation Act of 1966, the court concluded that "while Congress has *not* explicitly provided that addiction shall not be an affirmative defense to a charge of possessing illicit narcotics, the congressional intent to prosecute drug users ... demonstrates that *Congress has preempted this court's authority to create a common law defense.*" In response to Judge Wright's assertion that punishing addict possessors bears no reasonable relationship to the goal of eliminating the drug traffic and rehabilitating addicts, the court found that Congress' judgment was logical and should prevail over that of the court. 486 F.2d at 1152-56.]

LEVENTHAL, CIRCUIT JUDGE. [Concurring.]

Untenability of impaired control concept as universal and absolute defense negativing criminal responsibility

Appellant's key defense concepts are impairment of behavioral control and loss of self-control....

Appellant's presentation rests, in essence, on the premise that the "mental disease or defect" requirement of *McDonald* and *Brawner* is superfluous....

** Robinson v. California, *supra* p. 659.

The broad assertion is that in general the mens rea element of criminal responsibility requires freedom of will, which is negatived by an impairment of behavioral control and loss of self-control.

If drug dependence really negatived mens rea, it would be a defense not only to the offense of possession or purchase of prohibited drugs but to other actions taken under the compulsion of the need to obtain the drug....

Under common law doctrine the courts did recognize defenses as applicable to some but not all offenses. Thus, the defense of duress was not applicable to murder, and originally not applicable to any capital crime. But these are not defenses of lack of the "free will" or mens rea that is an ethical and moral requisite of criminality, but are affirmative defenses of justification and excuse that are based on policy assessment of the needs and limits of social control, a policy appraisal that has been resolved by the legislature for the heroin offenses.

Appellant's surface logic loses luster with analysis. It does not follow that because one condition (mental disease) yields an exculpatory defense if it results in impairment of and lack of behavioral controls the same result follows when some other condition impairs behavior controls.

The criminal law expresses the requirements of personal and official discipline needed to protect society. By long tradition of the penal law, an actor's behavior is "involuntary" and there is no criminal responsibility, when he is overwhelmed by force, as when his arm is physically moved by someone else. By long tradition, too, the criminal law reaches only acts that are not only voluntary but also accompanied by a mental element, a "mens rea." ... The elements that our basic jurisprudence requires for criminal responsibility — a voluntary act, and a mental state — are plainly fulfilled by an offense of knowing possession of a prohibited article.

The legal conception of criminal capacity cannot be limited to those of unusual endowment or even average powers. A few may be recognized as so far from normal as to be entirely beyond the reach of criminal justice, but in general the criminal law is a means of social control that must be potentially capable of reaching the vast bulk of the population. Criminal responsibility is a concept that not only extends to the bulk of those below the median line of responsibility, but specifically extends to those who have a realistic problem of substantial impairment and lack of capacity due, say, to weakness of intellect that establishes susceptibility to suggestion; or to a loss of control of the mind as a result of passion, whether the passion is of an amorous nature or the result of hate, prejudice or vengeance; or to a depravity that blocks out conscience as an influence on conduct.

The criminal law cannot "vary legal norms with the individual's capacity to meet the standards they prescribe, absent a disability that is both gross and verifiable, such as the mental disease or defect that may establish irresponsibility. The most that it is feasible to do with lesser disabilities is to accord them proper weight in sentencing."

Only in limited areas have the courts recognized a defense to criminal responsibility, on the basis that a described condition establishes a psychic incapacity negativing free will in the broader sense. These are areas where the courts have been able to respond to a deep call on elemental justice, and to

IV. CONDITION OR STATUS

discern a demarcation of doctrine that keeps the defense within verifiable bounds that do not tear the fabric of the criminal law as an instrument of social control.

[The opinion then discusses the doctrines defining the defenses of duress and necessity, concluding that the defense of duress is "inapplicable to a purely internal psychic incapacity," and that the necessity defense is likewise unavailable. The opinion then proceeds to a discussion of the differences between the mental disease defense and the proposed drug dependence defense.]

....

In our view, the rule for drug addiction should not be modeled on the rule for mental disease because of crucial distinctions between conditions. The subject of mental disease, though subject to some indeterminacy, and difficulty of diagnosis when extended to volitional impairment as well as cognitive incapacity, has long been the subject of systematic study, and in that framework it is considered manageable to ask psychiatrists to address the distinction, all-important and crucial to the law, between incapacity and indisposition, between those who can't and those who won't, between the impulse irresistible and the impulse not resisted....

As to the subject of drug dependence and psychic incapacity to refrain from narcotics, even the 1970 Study Draft of the Staff of the National Commission on Reform of Federal Criminal Laws, which favors on balance a drug dependence defense to the crime of possession, for incapacity to refrain from use, candidly recognizes the problems involved.... More important, for present purposes, is the Staff's caution first, that even physical symptoms might "be successfully feigned," and, more broadly, that there is considerable difficulty of verification of the claim of a drug user that he is unable to refrain from use....

There is need for reasonable verifiability as a condition to opening a defense to criminal responsibility. The criminal law cannot gear its standards to the individual's capacity "absent a disability that is both gross and verifiable, such as the mental disease or defect that may establish irresponsibility."

....

WRIGHT, CIRCUIT JUDGE, dissenting....

These "evolving standards of decency," the Eighth Amendment, and the problem of narcotic addiction met head on in *Robinson v. California, supra*....

[T]he [*Robinson*] opinion might also be interpreted as holding that narcotics addiction, like mental illness, leprosy and venereal disease, is an illness and as such cannot constitutionally be punished as a crime. The implications of this interpretation are far-reaching, for if punishment for having a common cold (to use the Court's example) is constitutionally prohibited, it would make little sense to permit a legislature to punish one who has a cold for sneezing or taking medicine. Similarly, this interpretation would seem logically to prohibit not only the criminalization of the status of "being addicted," but also punishment of an addict for those acts, such as possession or use of narcotics, which are symptomatic of the disease and therefore beyond his power to avoid.[166]

....

[Considering *Powell,* Judge Wright stated that, since the Court was split 4-4, the deciding opinion was that of Mr. Justice White.]

Justice White voted to affirm the conviction, however, on the narrow ground that this *particular* alcoholic had failed to prove that he was compelled by his disease to be drunk *in public.*

Thus, as this court noted in *Watson,* because of the absence of a majority opinion, "*Powell* has left this matter of criminal responsibility, as affected by the Eighth Amendment, in a posture which is, at best, obscure." 141 U.S. App. D.C. at 344, 439 F.2d at 451. But insofar as five members of the Court accepted the Fortas-White position, *Powell* and *Robinson* would seem to stand for the proposition that an addict cannot constitutionally be subjected to criminal process for engaging in conduct which is itself inherent in the disease of addiction. Possession of heroin, of course, is just such conduct, for it is logically impossible for a person to be a heroin addict without also purchasing, possessing and using the drug in order to satisfy his addiction. This being so, it is clear that an interpretation of the federal narcotics statutes which would permit prosecution and conviction of addicts who simply possess the drug for their own use would, at the very least, raise serious questions of constitutionality....

....

The basic question of criminal responsibility under the addiction defense is a legal, and not a purely medical, determination. Not all drug users are "addicts" and, as with any compulsion, the degree of dependence may vary among different individuals and, indeed, even in a given individual at different stages of his addiction. Thus what we are concerned with here is not an abstract medical or psychiatric definition of addiction which sets forth a clinical checklist of relevant symptoms but, rather, a behavioral model, based upon traditional legal and moral principles, which tests the ability of the defendant to control his behavior. The essential inquiry, then, is simply whether, at the time of the offense, the defendant, as a result of his repeated use of narcotics, lacked substantial capacity to conform his conduct to the requirements of the law.

....

BAZELON, CHIEF JUDGE (concurring in part and dissenting in part):

... On the issue of guilt or innocence, Judge Wright's views are closest to my own. I cannot, however, accept his view that the addiction/responsibility defense should be limited to the offense of possession. I would also permit a jury

---

[166] It is true, of course, that the Court suggested in dicta that a state might constitutionally "impose criminal sanctions ... against the unauthorized manufacture, prescription, sale, purchase, or possession of narcotics within its borders." 370 U.S. at 664, 82 S.Ct. at 1419. But as Justice White points out in dissent, the Court's failure to include in this listing the states' power to punish the "use" of narcotics could hardly have been inadvertent. *Id.* at 688, 82 S.Ct. 1417. Moreover, since an addict cannot possibly use narcotics without also purchasing, receiving or possessing them, it is only logical to assume that this dictum in *Robinson* was not intended to include possession by addicts not engaged in trafficking.

to consider addiction as a defense to a charge of, for example, armed robbery or trafficking in drugs, to determine whether the defendant was under such duress or compulsion, because of his addiction, that he was unable to conform his conduct to the requirements of the law.

....

NOTES ON OTHER INTERPRETATIONS OF ROBINSON AND POWELL

1. *People v. Davis,* 27 Ill. 2d 57, 188 N.E.2d 225 (1963), declared unconstitutional the provisions of the Narcotic Drug Act which made it a criminal offense to be "under the influence of or be addicted to unlawful use of narcotic drugs." But *Salas v. State,* 365 S.W.2d 174 (Tex. Crim. App.), *appeal dismissed,* 375 U.S. 15 (1963), upheld a conviction for being "unlawfully under the influence of a narcotic drug"; "appellant was charged with the 'act' of being under the influence," not the status or condition of being addicted, as was the defendant in *Robinson.*

2. *State v. Fearon,* 283 Minn. 90, 166 N.W.2d 720 (1969), avoided conflict with Powell (not "a majority opinion") by interpreting a statute prohibiting voluntary drinking of intoxicating liquors so as to exclude the chronic alcoholic whose drinking was due to his illness and thus involuntary. A 1967 Minnesota statute providing hospitalization for alcoholics was also persuasive.

3. But *Vick v. State,* 453 P.2d 342 (Alaska 1969), refused to follow this approach, agreeing with *Powell* that: "We are unable to conclude ... on the current state of medical knowledge, that chronic alcoholics in general ... suffer from such an irresistible compulsion to drink and to get drunk in public that they are utterly unable to control their performance of either or both of these acts and thus, cannot be deterred at all from public intoxication." *Id.* at 345.

4. In *People v. Jones,* 43 Ill. 2d 113, 251 N.E.2d 195 (1969), the defendant, convicted of deviate sexual assault, argued that "his conduct was involuntary and a manifestation of his disease of homosexuality," citing *Robinson.* The court upheld the conviction, stating that: "Defendant here was not convicted and punished for his condition or status of being a homosexual, any more than the defendant in *Jackson* was punished for being a narcotics addict, or the defendant in *Powell* was punished for being an alcoholic. The crime punished here was the act of a sexual deviate assault, involving oral copulation inflicted by force. Punishment for that act should not be precluded because defendant was a homosexual, any more than punishment for 'possession' of narcotics would be barred because defendants were addicts in the Jackson and Nettles cases." 251 N.E.2d at 198.

5. In *Blondheim v. State,* 84 Wash. 2d 874, 529 P.2d 1096 (1975), a 17-year-old girl was committed to the Department of Social and Health Services as an "incorrigible dependent." The court conceded that incorrigibility is "a condition or state of being" but said "it was not the 'status' of being incorrigible for which petitioner was given a suspended commitment and placed on probation. Rather it was her *conduct* which placed her beyond the lawfully exercised

control or power of her mother, that led to her being found to be incorrigible, and, thus, resulted in the suspended commitment." 529 P.2d at 1101 (emphasis in original).

6. There are many references to the literature on addiction in the footnotes in Moore, supra. *See also* Fingarette, *The Perils of Powell: In Search of a Factual Foundation for the "Disease Concept of Alcoholism,"* 83 HARV. L. REV. 793 (1970), *and* Fingarette, *Addiction and Criminal Responsibility*, 84 YALE L.J. 413 (1975).

Chapter 9
IGNORANCE AND MISTAKE

SECTION I. Of Fact

EDITORIAL NOTE

The relevance of defendant's misperception of facts has already been seen in a variety of contexts. Usually, mistakes of fact are regarded as relevant to defendant's guilt. In offenses against the person, *D.P.P. v. Morgan* illustrates how mistake of fact may negate specific intent, *supra* p. 203. The privileges of self-defense and defense of others are not lost when defendant mistakenly apprehends an immediate attack, at least when his or her mistake is reasonable, *supra* pp. 513-517. In property crimes a good faith but mistaken belief that the property is his or hers prevents defendant's conviction for theft, *supra* pp. 391-396. Yet mistake of fact is not always a defense. In statutory rape, for example, mistake as to age no matter how reasonable is irrelevant in many states, *supra* pp. 220-225.

The cases in this section building on the previous cases, provide a more comprehensive analysis of the doctrine of ignorance and mistake.

A. NEGATING REQUIRED INTENT

UNITED STATES v. BRIGHT

United States Court of Appeals
517 F.2d 584 (2d Cir. 1975)

GURFEIN, CIRCUIT JUDGE.

Catherine Bright appeals from a judgment of conviction entered on November 6, 1974, after a jury trial in the United States District Court for the Southern District of New York, Hon. Constance Baker Motley. She was found guilty on three counts of possession of stolen mail in violation of Title 18, United States Code, Section 1708, and received a six month suspended sentence and six months probation.

. . . .

It is uncontested that appellant had been in possession of some nine welfare checks at various dates during 1972, and that these checks had been stolen from the mail. The checks had been in the possession of one Fred Scott, an acquaintance of appellant's "boyfriend" Leslie; Scott gave Bright the checks to cash for him on the pretense that he had no bank account of his own. Appellant admitted at trial that she had cashed or deposited the checks in question in the two accounts she had at her bank, but swore that she had not known that they were stolen. She testified that Scott had told her that he had received the checks in payment for debts or rent owed to him.

She testified that on one occasion, when a check she had cashed had been returned unpaid and her account charged accordingly, she confronted Scott who made good on the loss. After that incident, she cashed three more checks for Scott. The three counts of her conviction are based on her cashing the latter three checks.

I

At trial, the appellant's defense was based upon her purported lack of knowledge that the checks had been stolen and her naive belief that everything Scott told her was true. Appellant testified in her own behalf accordingly.

. . . .

II

We turn then to the contention that the District Judge erred in charging the jury on the element of knowledge required under 18 U.S.C. § 1708, and that this constituted reversible error. In the circumstances we agree.

The issue of knowledge was the only issue in dispute at appellant's trial. In all cases involving the receipt or possession of stolen goods, the definition of the requisite "knowledge" that the goods were stolen, required for a conviction, makes the difference between guilt and innocence. The test is not a technical one requiring a grudging adherence to some abstract standard. The standard should always embrace the ultimate concept of *mens rea*. A negligent or a foolish person is not a criminal when criminal intent is an ingredient. On the other hand, the lack of direct proof that the defendant knew that the goods were stolen is, in the nature of the case, not fatal to conviction. Circumstantial evidence may suffice, but the jury must understand that to convict it must find beyond a reasonable doubt that the defendant willfully and knowingly possessed the goods, knowing them to have been stolen. Without that abiding belief on the part of the jury, there should be no conviction.

. . . .

The draft of the Model Penal Code of the American Law Institute, *supra*, provides:

> When knowledge of the existence of a particular fact is an element of an offense, such knowledge is established if a person is aware of a high probability of its existence, unless he actually believes that it does not exist. § 2.02(7)

This coupling of the "high probability" test with its negation by an actual belief of the non-existence of the fact has been accorded "at least nodding approval in *Leary v. United States*, 395 U.S. 6, 46 n. 93, 89 S.Ct. 1532, 23 L.Ed.2d 57 (1969) and perhaps more than that in *Turner v. United States*, 396 U.S. 398, 416 & n. 29, 90 S.Ct. 642, 24 L.Ed.2d 610 (1970)." *United States v.*

A. NEGATING REQUIRED INTENT

Jacobs, 475 F.2d 270, 287 (2 Cir.), *cert. denied* sub nom. *Lavelle v. United States*, 414 U.S. 821, 94 S.Ct. 116, 38 L.Ed.2d 53 (1973).

In *Jacobs*, the trial court charged:

> ... [G]uilty knowledge cannot be established by merely demonstrating negligence or even foolishness on the part of a defendant. However, it is not necessary that the government prove to a certainty that a defendant knew the bills were stolen. Such knowledge is established if the defendant was aware of a high probability that the bills were stolen, *unless the defendant actually believed that the bills were not stolen....*
> Thus if you find that a defendant acted with reckless disregard of whether the bills were stolen *and* with a conscious purpose to avoid learning the truth the requirement of knowledge would be satisfied, *unless the defendant actually believed they were not stolen*. (Emphasis added). 475 F.2d at 287, n.37.

This court affirmed a conviction based on this charge because it was a balanced charge which had not permitted the "reckless disregard" portion of the charge to stand in isolation.

....

We turn to the record on appeal.

In the main charge, the District Judge properly charged that "before you find the defendant guilty, you must find beyond a reasonable doubt that she knew the checks were stolen at the time she possessed the checks. If you find that the defendant did not know the checks were stolen, then of course you must acquit the defendant."

The court also charged ... as follows:

> You may also find that the defendant had the requisite knowledge if you find that she acted with reckless disregard as to whether the checks were stolen, but with a conscious effort to avoid learning the truth, even though you may find that she was not specifically aware of the fact which would establish the stolen character of the checks.

This was in no way balanced by an instruction that if the jury nevertheless found that "the defendant actually believed that the bills were not stolen" they should acquit.

....

We are constrained to reverse this conviction, however, since we are not convinced that the jury applied the proper standard in weighing appellant's "knowledge," and, hence, her guilt or innocence.

Judgment reversed and remanded for a new trial.

NOTES

1. "[W]here knowledge is an essential element, specific knowledge is not always necessary; rather purposeful ignorance may suffice.... [A] conscious avoidance charge must include references to a purposeful avoidance of the truth ..., an awareness of high probability, ... and the absence of a defendant's actual belief in the nonexistence of the crucial fact." *United States v. Aulet*,

618 F.2d 182, 190, 191 (2d Cir. 1980). Government reliance on defendant's so-called "willful blindness" to prove knowledge occurs frequently in drug smuggling cases where the courier or "mule" claims that he knew he was doing something wrong, i.e. smuggling something, but did not know he was smuggling drugs. Ignorance or mistake as to the specific drug carried is no defense. *United States v. Morales*, 577 F.2d 769 (2d Cir. 1978).

2. A state may not preclude a negligent or foolish mistake from negating a required intent such as knowledge by defining the required intent in terms which exclude such mistakes. The following Washington statute was considered in *State v. Van Antwerp,* 22 Wash. App. 674, 591 P.2d 844 (1979):

> RCW 9A.08.010(1)(b) provided:
>
> (b) *Knowledge.* A person knows or acts knowingly or with knowledge when:
>
> (i) he is aware of a fact, facts, or circumstances or result described by a statute defining an offense; or
>
> (ii) he has information which would lead a reasonable man in the same situation to believe that facts exist which facts are described by a statute defining an offense.

The court of appeals held that defendant could be convicted of taking a motor vehicle without permission:

> if a reasonable person in the same situation as the defendant would believe that the car was stolen, even if the defendant had no subjective or actual knowledge of that fact.... 591 P. 2d at 847.
>
> ... The legislature may even declare an act criminal irrespective of the intent or knowledge of the doer of the act. (Citations omitted.) As such, the State may criminalize certain forms of negligence and it may define knowledge on the basis of a prudent or reasonable man standard. *Id.* at 848.

The Washington Supreme Court reversed because to give the statute that meaning "is inconsistent with the statutory scheme which creates a hierarchy of mental states for crimes of increasing culpability. Knowledge is intended to be a more culpable mental state than recklessness, which is a subjective standard, rather than the equivalent of negligence, which is an objective standard." *State v. Shipp,* 93 Wash. 2d 510, 610 P.2d 1322, 1325 (1980).

3. In *Commonwealth v. Rosenberg,* 379 Mass. 334, 398 N.E.2d 451 (1979), the owner and manager of a general merchandise store, not held out to the public as an adult bookstore or containing an "adults only" section, was convicted of violating MASS. GEN. LAWS ANN. ch. 272, § 29 (West Supp. 1981), which made it a felony to disseminate obscene matter "knowing it to be obscene." Police officers purchased copies of *Penthouse and Hustler* magazines from a publications rack in the store. The supreme judicial court reversed the conviction and directed an acquittal:

> *Proof of scienter.* The Commonwealth contends that the fact that Rosenberg was the active owner and manager of Sam's Spa supports an inference that he had actual knowledge of the magazine's contents, and

therefore knowingly disseminated obscene material. Beyond this, the Commonwealth argues that the jury could reasonably have inferred that Rosenberg had constructive knowledge of the magazine's contents from viewing the magazine's cover at the time it was sold. Finally, the Commonwealth suggests that as owner and manager of the Spa, Rosenberg had constructive knowledge of the contents of his entire stock-in-trade, including the May, 1976, issue of Hustler magazine. We disagree.

As a general matter, proof of knowledge must be personal to the defendant but may be had "by inference from all the facts and circumstances developed at the trial."...

More specifically the "knowing" required by G.L. c. 272, § 29, is defined by G.L. c. 272, § 31, as "a general awareness of the character of the matter" disseminated. We have had occasion to construe this statutory language ... [and] have noted that "[t]he Massachusetts definition of 'knowledge' ... emphasizes that knowledge of legal obscenity is not required.."... "To require proof of a defendant's knowledge of the legal status of the materials would permit the defendant to avoid prosecution by simply claiming that he had not brushed up on the law." *Hamling v. United States*, 418 U.S. 87, 123 (1974).

We have also stressed, however, that the Massachusetts definition "does not dispense ... with the constitutional requirement that a defendant have knowledge of the matter's contents and general character before a criminal conviction for its dissemination may be obtained."... Absent evidence of such knowledge, "a criminal case will not pass the directed verdict stage."...

Proof of scienter is required in order "to avoid the hazard of self-censorship of constitutionally protected material and to compensate for the ambiguities inherent in the definition of obscenity." *Mishkin v. New York*, 383 U.S. 502, 511 (1966). In holding that protection of First Amendment rights requires proof of scienter even in the case of sales to minors, we noted that "[a]bsent the scienter requirement, booksellers, unable to familiarize themselves with all the material on their shelves, would tend to restrict sales ... to the relatively few books of which they had some knowledge of the contents or character. The result would be an impediment to the sale ... not only of unprotected matter but also of that which is constitutionally protected...."

While knowledge of both the character and contents of the material disseminated is thus a required element of the offense described in G.L. c. 272, § 29, the "knowing" called for by the statute may be something less than actual knowledge. Just as the Supreme Court reasoned that requiring knowledge of the legal status of the material sold would immunize all those who conscientiously avoided "brush[ing] up on the law," *Hamling v. United States*, 418 U.S. 87, 123 (1974), the adoption of a requirement of actual knowledge would allow a disseminator of obscenity to immunize himself by studiously maintaining his ignorance regarding the specific contents of the materials he sells....

The Commonwealth need not produce an eyewitness to testify that an alleged disseminator such as Rosenberg actually read or viewed the materials at issue.... Rather, "[t]he prosecution must produce evidence from which a jury could conclude beyond a reasonable doubt that the defendant had seen, or should have seen, or otherwise had knowledge of, the material's contents."

In light of this standard, the Commonwealth may satisfy the statutory and constitutional requirement that a defendant be aware of the contents of the disseminated material in one of two ways.

First, the Commonwealth may prove that the defendant had actual knowledge of the material's contents. Such actual knowledge may have been obtained by the defendant directly by a first-hand examination of the material ("had seen" in the words of the *Thureson* court) or indirectly ("otherwise had knowledge of").

The Commonwealth may also demonstrate the requisite scienter without any proof of actual knowledge by showing that a disseminator "should have seen" the material's contents, i.e., that, on the basis of all the surrounding facts and circumstances, the disseminator was subject to an affirmative duty to inquire further as to the material's contents. It is on such alternative proof, whether it be referred to as "reason to know" (*Ginsberg v. New York*, 390 U.S. 629, 643-644 [1968]), or constructive knowledge (*Ballew v. Georgia*, 435 U.S. 223, 228 [1978]), that the Commonwealth must rely in the present case.

There is simply no evidence that Rosenberg had actual knowledge of the contents of the May, 1976, issue of Hustler magazine. Detective Addonizio testified that Rosenberg did not examine the magazine. In addition, in response to the prosecutor's obvious attempt to elicit any other indication that Rosenberg may have been familiar with the contents of the magazine by asking if, at the time of sale, Rosenberg "did anything," Addonizio replied that he did not.

This case is therefore different from those cases where a seller recommends material as "better" than other available films or publications ... , or answers questions concerning the contents of the material sold, ... or states that the material would not have been sold to minors ... or examines a portion of the contents....

Furthermore, there is also an absence in the Commonwealth's case of any of those additional factors which have been cited as at least partially responsible for placing other sellers on notice as to a publication's contents. The magazine was not labelled "adults only," ... and was not wrapped in plastic, ... or stapled shut.... The magazine was not sold from a place of business "clearly labelled" as an "adult book" store, ... or from a store that charged admission.... And there was no indication that a far higher price was paid for this magazine than for normal periodicals....

4. The subject of criminal intent is discussed generally in Chapter 2, section II, *supra*.

DAVIS v. STATE

Supreme Court of Indiana
265 Ind. 476, 355 N.E.2d 836 (1976)

DE BRULER, JUSTICE.

Appellant, Robert L. Davis, was charged by information in the Monroe Superior Court, with the offenses of kidnapping, Ind. Code § 35-1-55-1 (Burns 1975), and rape, Ind. Code § 35-13-4-3 (Burns 1975). Appellant entered a plea of guilty to the rape charge and was convicted of kidnapping after trial by jury. He was sentenced to a term of seventeen years imprisonment for the rape conviction and life imprisonment for kidnapping. Appellant filed a motion to correct errors which was overruled and, he appeals, raising the following two questions:

(1) Whether the trial court erred in refusing to give a tendered instruction on the defense of mistake of fact; ...

I

The appellant tendered his final instruction (7a) which stated:

> Ignorance or mistake of fact is a defense when it negatives the existence of a mental state essential to the crime charged. If the jury believes, from the evidence, that the conduct of the prosecutrix was such towards the defendant, at the time of the alleged kidnapping, as to create in the mind of the defendant the honest and reasonable belief that she had consented, or was willing to go with the defendant, then you must acquit the defendant.

The trial court refused this instruction....

....

The tendered instruction relates to the defense of "mistake of fact." Indiana has long recognized that an honest and reasonable mistake concerning a fact or facts, excuses criminal conduct which would not be criminal if facts were as the actor reasonably believed. *Noble v. State*, (1967) 248 Ind. 101, 223 N.E.2d 755; *Squire v. State*, (1874) 46 Ind. 459.[1]

To sustain a conviction of kidnapping it is necessary that it be shown that the accused intended to do the prohibited thing, to forcibly or fraudulently carry off a person from any place within the state. *White v. State*, (1963) 244 Ind. 199, 191 N.E.2d 486; *Boatman v. State*, (1956) 235 Ind. 623, 137 N.E.2d 28; *Sweet v. State*, (1941) 218 Ind. 182, 31 N.E.2d 993. An honest, reasonable belief that his victim freely consented to accompany him would negate any intent to "forcibly carry off" the victim. It need not negate an intent to "fraudulently carry off," because the statute also prohibits the procurement of a person's voluntary accompaniment by fraudulent means. See *Shipman v. State*, (1962) 243 Ind. 245, 183 N.E.2d 823.

---

[1] Under the revised penal code which takes effect July 1, 1977, this rule is codified as follows:

Mistake of Fact. It is a defense that the person who engaged in the prohibited conduct was reasonably mistaken about a matter of fact if the mistake negates the culpability required for commission of the offense. (Acts 1976, P.L. 148 at p. 725, adding Ind. Code § 35-41-1-7).

The information in this case charged appellant with "unlawfully, feloniously, and forcibly carry[ing] away, decoy[ing] and kidnap[ping]" his victim. While the word "decoy" seems to suggest that the State had charged appellant with kidnapping by alternative means, force and fraud, there was no evidence at the trial that appellant "decoyed" the victim. We believe that the information charges appellant with committing the crime of kidnapping by forcible asportation. Therefore if appellant was under the honest and reasonable mistaken impression that the victim accompanied him voluntarily, his mistake would ... constitute a defense. We must now determine whether there is sufficient evidence to warrant the giving of the instruction.

Appellant was charged with the kidnapping of a woman from a laundromat in Bloomington in the early morning hours of September 17, 1975. The victim was a nurse who worked the late shift at Bloomington Hospital and did her laundry after work because her irregular hours made her unable to sleep. The victim was alone in the laundromat when appellant entered. She testified that he seized her arm, twisted it behind her back, and thus forced her out of the laundromat, saying "Move, or I'll blow your head off." The victim had her purse in her hands as she left but left her laundry. She was pushed into appellant's car with her arm still behind her back.

Appellant testified that he entered the laundromat intending to steal the victim's purse, and that he had been drinking. Appellant said that after he asked the victim for a match, he "took hold of her hand and ... asked her to go with [him]." As they left, she asked where appellant was taking her, to which he replied, "I don't know." The victim said, "Don't hurt me," and appellant said he would not.

Appellant denied forcing the victim's arm behind her back, but admits not releasing his grip on her arm until she entered his car. After entering his car, the victim said to appellant, "I'll do anything you want; bring me back." Appellant testified that he did not force the victim out of the laundromat, in the following colloquy:

Direct Examination

Q. O.K. Are you saying, are you telling me that you didn't force her out of that bus station?
A. I didn't force her out of the laundromat, no.
Q. Was she scared, do you know? Frightened?
A. She didn't act scared, but ninety per cent of people would be frightened.
Q. At least, in your confession, you said she wasn't scared at first; is that right?
A. At first, no, she wasn't scared.
Q. And she said she'd do anything as long as you took her back to the laundromat?
A. Yes.
Q. Why do you suppose she would walk out of that bus station with you, a perfect stranger, at 2:30 or 3:00 in the morning?
A. I don't know.

A. NEGATING REQUIRED INTENT

In order for a mistake of fact to excuse appellant from criminal liability, that mistake must be honest and reasonable. Honesty is a subjective test dealing with what appellant actually believed. Reasonableness is an objective test inquiring what a reasonable man situated in similar circumstances would do. To require the giving of appellant's instruction, we must find some evidence of both.

Appellant's assertion that he did not "force" the victim out of the laundromat provides some evidence that he honestly so believed. It is, however, no evidence of the reasonableness of that belief. Appellant was properly allowed to testify as to his own state of mind, which was in issue, but his statement also constituted an opinion as to the victim's state of mind, and as such was not competent evidence. *McKee v. Hasler*, (1951) 229 Ind. 437, 98 N.E.2d 657. Apart from this statement we find nothing in the record to suggest that a reasonable man in appellant's position would have interpreted the victim's actions as indicative of her free consent to accompany appellant. By appellant's own version of the encounter the facts are such that no reasonable person could have believed as appellant alleges he did. In spite of our preference to leave determinations of reasonableness to the jury, which embodies the values of the community, we find no evidence here from which the jury could have determined that appellant's belief was reasonable. It is not the law that the victim of a kidnapping must resist with force when the victim is reasonably in fear of her kidnapper. *Johnson v. State*, (1974) Ind., 319 N.E.2d 126. We find no error in the trial court's refusal to give appellant's instruction (7a).

....

We find no error, and the conviction of appellant Robert L. Davis, is affirmed.

ARTEBURN, HUNTER and PRENTICE, JJ.
GIVAN, C. J.

NOTES

1. *Davis v. State*, includes this instruction to the jury: "In order to convict the defendant of the crime of kidnap [sic], it is necessary to satisfy the jury beyond a reasonable doubt that defendant *entertained the specific intent to kidnap his accuser*." 355 N.E.2d at 840. (Emphasis added.) Does it make any difference whether defendant's mistake was reasonable or not? Can it be said that either he had specific intent to kidnap or not? Compare *United States v. Bright, supra* at pp. 669-671: "A negligent or foolish person is not a criminal when criminal intent is an ingredient."

2. Cases such as *Davis v. State*, which require that all mistakes be reasonable, do not distinguish between a mistake offered to negate the existence of a required intent, e.g. knowledge or specific intent, and a mistake offered as an excuse to negate a "mens rea." Compare *D.P.P. v. Morgan, supra* p. 203.

B. NEGATING *MENS REA*

GORDON v. STATE

Supreme Court of Alabama
52 Ala. 308, 23 Am. Rep. 575 (1875) Brickell, C.J.

... The first count charges that the appellant, not being of the age of twenty-one years, voted at the last general election in this State. The second count is a general accusation of illegal voting, not specifying in what the illegality consisted, whether in a want of legal qualification, or in voting more than once, or in depositing more ballots than one, and is not sufficient to support a conviction. 2 Bish. Cr. Pr. § 275. The evidence, as disclosed in the bill of exceptions, tended only to support the charge contained in the first count. Two witnesses were examined on the behalf of defendant; one, his mother, and the other an acquaintance who had known him from his birth, and resided in the same neighborhood, and for a long time a member of the same family with defendant, and they testified the defendant was of the age of twenty-one years, in the August preceding the election, that they had frequently told defendant he would be of full age in that month, and subsequently and before the election told him he was of age. The court refused to charge the jury that if the defendant, in reliance on these statements, honestly believed he was of full age when he voted, he should not be convicted, if the evidence convinced the jury he was not of age.

"All crime exists, primarily, in the mind." A wrongful act and a wrongful intent must concur, to constitute what the law deems a crime. When an act denounced by the law is proved to have been committed, in the absence of countervailing evidence, the criminal intent is inferred from the commission of the act. The inference may be, and often is removed by the attending circumstances, showing the absence of a criminal intent.

Ignorance of law is never an excuse, whether a party is charged civilly or criminally. Ignorance of fact may often be received to absolve a party from civil or criminal responsibility. On the presumption that every one capable of acting for himself knows the law, courts are compelled to proceed. If it should be abandoned, the administration of justice would be impossible, as every cause would be embarrassed with the collateral inquiry of the extent of legal knowledge of the parties seeking to enforce or avoid liability and responsibility.

The criminal intention being of the essence of crime, if the intent is dependent on a knowledge of particular facts, a want of such knowledge, not the result of carelessness or negligence, relieves the act of criminality.... The precise time when a man arrives at the age of twenty-one years is a fact, knowledge of which he derives necessarily from his parents, or other relatives or acquaintances having knowledge of the time of his birth. If acting in good faith, on information fairly obtained from them under an honest belief that he had reached the age, he votes, having the other necessary qualifications, illegal voting should not be imputed to him. The intent which makes up the crime cannot be affirmed. Whether he had the belief that he was a qualified voter, and the information was fairly obtained, should be referred to, and determined by the jury. The whole inquiry should be directed to the voter's knowledge of facts, and to his diligence in acquiring the requisite knowledge. If he votes recklessly or carelessly, when the facts are doubtful or uncertain, his ignorance should not excuse him, if the real facts show he was not qualified. If ignorant of the disqualifying fact, and without a want of diligence, under an honest belief of his right to vote, he should be excused, though he had not the right....

The charge given by the Circuit Court, and several of the refusals to charge, were according to these views erroneous, and the judgment must be reversed, and the cause remanded....

MODEL PENAL CODE

§ 2.04. Ignorance or Mistake

[The text of this section appears in Appendix A.]

NOTES

1. *Gordon v. State* involved a general intent crime and defendant's good faith and reasonableness were necessary to rebut the inference of general intent, a sense of wrongdoing, which stemmed from defendant's conduct. To excuse defendant's acts it is not enough that he or she be mistaken, but he or she also must not be culpable in making the mistake. Recklessness or negligence may satisfy the culpability requirement in general intent crimes.

> No man can be acquitted of responsibility for a wrongful act, unless he employs "the means at command to inform himself." Not employing such means, though he may be mistaken, he must bear the consequences of his negligence. If he relies on information obtained from others, he should have some just reason to believe that from them he could obtain information on which he may safely rely.

Dotson v. State, 62 Ala. 141, 144, 34 Am. Rep. 2, 3 (1878).

2. Where defendant demonstrates that he or she acted under a mistake, even a reasonable mistake, he or she does not necessarily have a defense. The mistake must negate the required mental element. Thus, if a person is charged with receiving stolen goods, his mistake in thinking the goods were television sets when they were actually radios will avail nothing. W. LaFave & A. Scott, Criminal Law 407 (2d ed. 1986).

3. Generally, when a person attempts to commit one crime, but because of a mistake of fact he or she violates another law, he or she can be convicted of the crime he actually committed. "Deeply entrenched in the common law is the concept of risk-assumption by intentional wrongdoing. Conduct with intent to commit one crime may result in guilt of another crime if the latter does not require some special mental element that is lacking."* Perkins, *Ignorance or Mistake of Law Revisited,* 1980 Utah L. Rev. 473, 483. "A mistake relating only to the degree of crime or the gravity of the offense will not shield a deliberate offender from the full consequences of the offense actually committed." *Id.* at 485.

---

* Copyright © Utah Law Review Society 1981.

The MODEL PENAL CODE, § 2.04(2) would change this where the mistake is as to the degree of the offense. For example, where a person makes an unauthorized entry into a structure to commit theft believing the structure to be a store, he or she should be convicted of that offense and not of the greater offense (if there is such a distinction) of burglary of a dwelling if unbeknownst to him or her the structure was also used as a dwelling. "The doctrine that when one intends a lesser crime he or she may be convicted of a graver offense, committed inadvertently, leads to anomalous results if it is generally applied in the penal law; and while the principle obtains to some extent in homicide, its generality has rightly been denied. See G. WILLIAMS, CRIMINAL LAW pp. 156-161." MODEL PENAL CODE, comment at 137 (Tent. Draft No. 4, 1955). This approach is consistent generally with the Code's emphasis on "subjective guilt" and is intended to introduce a change in the law. Even under the code, however, the grade of theft is determined by the actual value of the property taken and not by what defendant believed. MODEL PENAL CODE, § 223.1(2). See Appendix A.

SECTION II. Of Law

STATE v. BOYETT

Supreme Court of North Carolina
32 N.C. 336 (1849)

The defendant was indicted for voting, knowingly and fraudulently, at a constable's election, held for one of the captain's districts in the county of Johnston, in January, 1849. On the trial, it was proved, that the defendant voted for constable in the district mentioned in the indictment, having been a resident in the said district for less than six months, immediately preceding the said election....

PEARSON, J.

"*Ignorantia legis neminem excusat.*" Every one competent to act for himself is presumed to know the law. No one is allowed to excuse himself by pleading ignorance. Courts are compelled to act upon this rule, as well in criminal as civil matters. It lies at the foundation of the administration of justice. And there is no telling to what extent, if admissible, the plea of ignorance would be carried, or the degree of embarrassment that would be introduced into every trial, by conflicting evidence upon the question of ignorance.

In civil matters, it is admitted, the presumption is frequently not in accordance with the truth. The sales of property are complicated systems — the result, "not of the reason of any one man, but of many men put together;" hence, they are not often understood, and more frequently not properly applied, and the presumption can only be justified upon the ground of necessity.

But in criminal matters the presumption most usually accords with the truth. As to such as are *mala in se,* every one has an innate sense of right and wrong which enables him to know when he violates the law, and it is of no consequence if he be not able to give the name by which the offense is known in the law books, or to point out the nice distinctions between the different grades of offense. As to such as are "*mala prohibita,*" they depend upon statutes printed and published and put within the reach of every one; so that no one has a right to complain, if a presumption, necessary to the administration of the law, is applied to him. To allow ignorance as an excuse would be to offer a reward to the ignorant.

The defendant voted, when he was not entitled by law to vote. He is presumed to know the law. Hence, he voted knowing that he had no right, and acting with this knowledge, he necessarily committed a fraud upon the public — in the words of the act, he knowingly and fraudulently voted when he was not entitled to vote. It being proved on the part of the State that he voted, not having resided within the bounds of the [county] for six months next preceding the election, a case was made out against him.

He offered to prove, for the purpose of rebutting the inference of fraud, that he had stated the facts to a respectable gentleman, who advised him he had a right to vote. His Honor held the testimony inadmissible. We concur in that opinion. The evidence had no tendency to rebut the inference of fraud, for the inference was made from his presumed knowledge of the law and that presumption could not be met by any such proof, without introducing all the evils which the rule was intended to avoid....

It would be a different question, if the defendant had stated the facts to the judges of the election, and they had decided in favor of his right to vote, for their decision would rebut the presumption of knowledge on his part, in a manner contemplated by law.... PER CURIAM. There is no error in the Court below and the same must be so certified.

NOTES

1. *The rationale for the rule.*

> The rule that ignorance of the criminal law is no defence is capable of causing hardship; yet it has been widely adopted by the penal systems of the world. The justification advanced for it is the effect it has in compelling people to learn the standard of conduct required of them. As Holmes expressed it, "public policy sacrifices the individual to the general good. To admit the excuse at all would be to encourage ignorance where the law-maker has determined to make men know and obey." The rule is a useful weapon where the legislature intends to change the social mores, for the most effective way of bringing the new rule to the public's notice is by convictions reported in the Press.

G. WILLIAMS, CRIMINAL LAW 289 (2d ed. 1961).

> To permit an individual to plead successfully that he had a different opinion or interpretation of the law would contradict the above postulates of a legal order, for there is a basic incompatibility between asserting that the law is what certain officials declare it to be after a prescribed analysis, and asserting, also, that those officials must declare it to be, *i.e.*, that the law is, what defendants or their lawyers believed it to be. A legal order implies the rejection of such contradiction. It opposes objectivity to subjectivity, judicial process to individual opinion, official to lay, and

authoritative to non-authoritative declarations of what the law is. This is the rationale of ignorantia juris neminem excusat.

This rationale can also be expressed in terms of the ethical policy of ignorantia juris neminem excusat, namely, that the criminal law represents certain moral principles; to recognize ignorance or mistake of the law as a defense would contradict those values. J. HALL, GENERAL PRINCIPLES OF CRIMINAL LAW 383 (2d ed. 1960).

Both of these views are questioned in G. FLETCHER, RETHINKING CRIMINAL LAW 732-36 (1978), where the author discusses the relationship between mistake and culpability. See also O'Connor, Mistake and Ignorance in Criminal Cases, 39 MOD. L. REV. 644 (1976) where the author suggests that non-negligent mistake or ignorance should be an excuse.

2. *Everyone is presumed to know the law.* Frequently it is stated that

> "'[e]very person is presumed to know the law.' This does not mean that the probabilities are sufficient to raise an inference that everyone knows the law. That would be absurd. Nor does it refer to a procedural device that may be overcome by evidence to the contrary. The explanation is that the law sometimes uses the word 'presumption' to mean 'conclusive presumption.' ... It is a postulate used in the determination of a case regardless of the actual facts. What it means is that except for ... rare exceptions ... a *criminal case* will be decided as if the defendant had full knowledge of the *pertinent criminal law* without any consideration of the actual facts in this regard."* Perkins, *Ignorance or Mistake of Law Revisited,* 1980 UTAH L. REV. 473, 474-75 (emphasis in original).

Does such a "presumption" conflict with the holding in *Sanstrom v. Montana,* 442 U.S. 510 (1979), discussed in *Francis v. Franklin,* 471 U.S. 307 (1985), *supra* pp. 54-60? Or does the law presume nothing here? Does it simply refuse to consider or attach any weight to defendant's ignorance or mistake? Should ignorance of the law simply not excuse anyone? See Cass, Ignorance of the Law: A Maxim Re-examined, 17 WM. & MARY L. REV. 671 (1975-76).

EDITORIAL NOTE ON EXCEPTIONS TO THE RULE

The rule, although stated in universal terms, does admit to some exceptions. The Model Penal Code § 2.04 and states which follow it expressly so provide. These fit into two major categories: (1) mistake which negates a required intent, and (2) reliance.

(1) Mistakes which negate required intent. Some offenses are defined to include as an element a defendant's knowledge of a lack of a legal right to act. Thus, the words "knowingly," "fraudulently," "corruptly," and "maliciously," common definitional terms, often may be rebutted by showing good faith predicated upon a mistaken understanding of the law found to be reasonable under the circumstances. For example, those who take property from others under a mistaken but honest (nonperjured) belief that they have a right to do so lack the required intent to steal, *i.e.,* to deprive owners permanently of

---

*Copyright © Utah Law Review Society 1981.

their property. See pp. 391-392 *supra*; *Scott v. State*, 29 Ala. App. 110, 192 So. 288 (1939).

It is "accepted as a general rule that if the offense charged requires any specific intent, a mistake as to *non-penal law* that negatives that intent leaves the defendant innocent." Perkins, Ignorance or Mistake of Law Revisited, 1980 UTAH L. REV. 473, 476 (emphasis supplied).

(2) Reliance. It is generally agreed that when the highest court of a state rules that a statute is invalid or by construction announces the meaning of a statute, people are entitled to rely on these decisions and to act in conformity with them. If a court holds a statute unconstitutional, a person who engages in conduct proscribed by that statute cannot be prosecuted. If the court later overrules its prior decision and resurrects the statute or the legislature enacts a new statute, a subsequent mistake stemming from reliance on the first decision is no defense. A person may rely on the law as it is at the time he acts. However, reliance on decisions of inferior courts which are subject to revision on appeal or which are not generally binding may not have the same result. *State v. O'Neil*, 147 Iowa 513, 126 N.W. 454 (1910); *State v. F.W. Post No. 3722*, 215 Kan. 693, 527 P.2d 1020 (1974). Cf. *State ex rel. Williams v. Whitman*, 116 Fla. 196, 150 So. 136 (1933), 116 Fla. 198 156 So. 705 (1934).

Courts also have allowed defendants to offer in defense evidence that they relied on interpretations of law by nonjudicial officers or government officials responsible for interpreting statutes or regulations, particularly when required to do so as a predicate for official action. Thus, in *State v. Pearson*, 97 N.C. 434, 1 S.E. 914 (1887), a defendant could not be convicted of illegal voting when election judges had ruled him eligible to vote after he had revealed all germane facts. In *People v. Ferguson*, 134 Cal. App. 41, 24 P.2d 965 (1933), the court reversed a conviction for selling securities without a permit, since a state corporations commissioner had told the defendant he required no permit to sell trust shares because they were not securities. The court noted:

> The regulation which has not been complied with is malum prohibitum and not malum in se. It covers one of the most complicated phases of modern commercial life. The statute can be read strictly or liberally, according to the type of mind applied to it. It is under the administration of the commissioner and his decisions in most cases are final. If the appellant early in his real estate career found himself in honest doubt, notwithstanding his high education and legal accomplishments, went to the fountain head itself for information and was there advised that such organizations were not under the department's jurisdiction, and if after he had this identical organization ready to launch, he went to the corporation commissioner himself and was advised in the same manner, we cannot believe the law so inexorable as to require the brand of felon upon him for following the advice obtained. 24 P.2d at 970.

24 P.2d at 970.

Other cases are quite strict, however. *Hopkins v. State*, 193 Md. 489, 69 A.2d 456, appeal dismissed, 339 U.S. 940 (1950), affirmed the defendant's conviction under a statute making it unlawful to erect or maintain any sign intended to aid in the solicitation and performance of marriages, despite the fact that a state's (prosecuting) attorney had advised him before he erected the signs that he would not violate the law in doing so. *People v. Marrero*, 69 N.Y.2d 382, 515 N.Y.S.2d 212, 507 N.E.2d 1068 (1981), upheld the conviction of a federal corrections officer for having a loaded .38 caliber pistol in his possession. The officer originally contended that he fell within the statute's exemption for "peace officers." See 515 N.Y.S.2d at 220 (Hancock, J., dissenting). The trial court agreed with his contention and dismissed the indictment. By a 3-2 vote the appellate court reversed, holding that the "peace officer" exemption applied to state, but not federal, corrections officers. On remand the defendant was not allowed to claim a mistake of law based on the opinion of teachers and fellow federal officers.

UNITED STATES v. BARKER
UNITED STATES v. MARTINEZ

United States Court of Appeals
546 F.2d 940 (D.C. Cir. 1976)

PER CURIAM

The mandate of the court is that the Judgment of the District Court is reversed and the case is remanded for a new trial. Judges Wilkey and Merhige have filed separate opinions. Judge Leventhal dissents.

WILKEY, CIRCUIT JUDGE.

I

Facts

During the summer of 1971, following the publication of the now famous "Pentagon Papers," a decision was made to establish a unit within the White House to investigate leaks of classified information. This "Room 16" unit, composed of Egil Krogh, David Young, G. Gordon Liddy, and E. Howard Hunt — and under the general supervision of John Ehrlichman — determined, or was instructed, to obtain all possible information on Daniel Ellsberg, the source of the Pentagon Papers leak.[1] After Ellsberg's psychiatrist, Dr. Fielding, refused to be interviewed by FBI agents, the unit decided to obtain copies of Ellsberg's medical records through a covert operation.

[Hunt, who had been a career CIA agent recruited Barker and Martinez to break into Dr. Fielding's office to secure the records. Barker had also been in the CIA and Hunt, at one time, had been his immediate supervisor. Martinez also worked for the CIA and was on CIA retainer when contacted. Hunt gave Barker an unlisted White House phone number where he could be reached and wrote to Barker on White House stationery. Barker had one meeting with Hunt in the Executive Office Building. Hunt told Barker he was working for an organization at the White House level with greater jurisdiction than the FBI and the CIA. In enlisting Barker, Hunt asked him to help conduct a surreptitious entry to obtain national security information on "a traitor to

---

[1] A more detailed discussion of the organization and purpose of the "Room 16" unit is in our opinion in *United States v. Ehrlichman*, 546 F.2d 910, at pp. 914-915.

this country who was passing ... classified information to the Soviet Embassy." He suggested the person in question possibly was a Soviet agent. All of this information was passed on to Martinez. On these representations Barker and Martinez joined the team and carried out the break-in which failed to yield the much sought Ellsberg medical records.]

On 7 March 1974 the defendants were indicted under 18 U.S.C. § 241, along with Ehrlichman, Liddy and deDiego for conspiring to violate the Fourth Amendment rights of Dr. Fielding by unlawfully entering and searching his office. On 7 May 1974 the defendants filed a Motion for Discovery and Inspection with an accompanying memorandum outlining, *inter alia*, their proposed defense of absence of *mens rea* due to a mistake of fact mixed with law attributable to their reasonable reliance on apparent authority. On 24 May 1974, in a memorandum order, the District Court rejected the defendant's position on the ground that "a mistake of law is no defense."

On 12 July 1974 the jury returned verdicts of guilty against both Barker and Martinez.

....

... The jury was advised that to convict they need find only that the purpose of the break-in was to enter and search Dr. Fielding's office without a warrant or his permission, and for governmental rather than purely private purposes; a mistake as to the legality of such an operation was no defense.

....

IV

*The Defense of Good Faith, Reasonable
Reliance on Apparent Authority*

A

The primary ground upon which defendants Barker and Martinez rest their appeal is the refusal of the District Court to allow them a defense based upon their good faith, reasonable reliance on Hunt's apparent authority. They characterize this defense as a mistake of fact "coupled with" a mistake of law which negated the *mens rea* required for a violation of section 241. "The mistake of fact was the belief that Hunt was a duly authorized government agent; the mistake of law was that Hunt possessed the legal prerequisites to conduct a search — either probable cause or a warrant."

It is a fundamental tenet of criminal law that an honest mistake of fact negatives criminal intent, when a defendant's acts would be lawful if the facts were as he supposed them to be. A mistake of law, on the other hand, generally will not excuse the commission of an offense. A defendant's error as to his *authority* to engage in particular activity, if based upon a mistaken view of legal requirements (or ignorance thereof), is a mistake of law. Typically, the fact that he relied upon the erroneous advice of another is not an exculpatory circumstance. He is still deemed to have acted with a culpable state of mind.

....

... As the District Court instructed the jury, only a mistake as to whether a *valid* warrant has been obtained would excuse the defendant's action, and that is a mistake of law. That the recipient of the warrant may have relied upon the opinion of a judge in determining that he had legally adequate probable cause to make a search does not, under traditional analysis, alter the situation. His mistake remains one of law, and, under a strict construction of the rule, will not excuse his unlawful act.

It is readily apparent that few courts would countenance an instruction to a jury — even assuming a criminal prosecution were brought against government agents in such a situation[19] which advised that since the mistake in acting on an invalid warrant was one of law, it would not excuse the agent's unlawful search. It is neither fair nor practical to hold such officials to a standard of care exceeding that exercised by a judge. Moreover, although the basic policy behind the mistake of law doctrine is that, at their peril, all men should know and obey the law,[20] in certain situations there is an overriding societal interest in having individuals rely on the authoritative pronouncements of officials whose decisions we wish to see respected.[21]

For this reason, a number of exceptions to the mistake of law doctrine have developed where its application would be peculiarly unjust or counterproductive. Their recognition in a particular case should give the defendant a defense similar to one based upon mistake of fact, I submit, with one important difference. His mistake should avail him only if it is *objectively reasonable* under the circumstances.[23] The mistake of a government agent in relying on a magistrate's approval of a search can be considered virtually *per se* reasonable.... Similarly, if a private person is summoned by a police officer to assist in effecting an unlawful arrest, his reliance on the officer's authority to make the arrest may be considered reasonable as a matter of law. The citizen is under a legal obligation to respond to a proper summons and is in no position to second guess the officer's determination that an arrest is proper. Indeed, it is society's hope in recognizing the reasonableness of a citizen's mistake in this situation to encourage unhesitating compliance with a police officer's call.[25]

---

[19] Police officers, receiving and acting on such defective warrants, are rarely prosecuted. See Model Penal Code § 2.04 (P.O.D. 1962).

[20] For a full discussion of the various rationales which have been forwarded to support the mistake of law doctrine, see *United States v. Barker*, 168 U.S.App.D.C. 312, 331-41, 514 F.2d 208, 227-37 (1975) (Bazelon, J., concurring).

[21] See Hall & Seligman, [Mistake of Law and Mens Rea, 8 U. Chi. L. Rev. 641 (1941)] at 675-83. In support of the general proposition that in compelling circumstances the law will not deny a defense to individuals who have mistakenly relied on the authority of a public official, see *Cox v. Louisiana*, 379 U.S. 559, 85 S.Ct. 476, 13 L.Ed.2d 487 (1965), *Raley v. Ohio*, 360 U.S. 423, 79 S.Ct. 1257, 3 L.Ed. 2d 1344 (1959), and *United States v. Mancuso*, 139 F.2d 90 (3rd Cir. 1943). See also Perkins, [Criminal Law (2nd ed. 1969)] at 926-27.

[23] In view of the strong public policy backing the mistake of law doctrine and the necessity for compelling justification to overcome it, it would appear rarely tenable to allow a defense based upon an irrational reliance on the authority of a public official. See Hall & Seligman, *supra* note [21], at 647. In contrast, although there is some authority to the effect that a mistake of fact must be reasonable to negate intent (Wharton's Criminal Law and Procedure § 157 (Cum. Supp. 1974)], at 382 n.19), the better, and more widely held view is that even an unreasonable mistake of fact, if honest, constitutes a valid defense. Williams, [Criminal Law: The General Part (2nd ed. 1961)], at 201; Model Penal Code, Tentative Draft No. 4, at p. 136 (Commentary on § 2.04 (1) (1953)).

[25] This common law exception to the mistake of law doctrine is codified in section 3.07(4)(a) of the Model Penal Code, which states:

> (a) A private person who is summoned by a peace officer to assist in effecting an unlawful arrest, is justified in using any force which he would be justified in using if the arrest were lawful, provided he does not believe the arrest is unlawful.

Other situations in which a government official enlists the aid of a private citizen to help him perform a governmental task are not so obviously reasonable on their face.[26] If the official does not *order* the citizen to assist him, but simply asks for such assistance, the citizen is not under a legal compulsion to comply. Also, if the circumstances do not require immediate action, the citizen may have time to question the lawfulness of the planned endeavor. Nevertheless, the public policy of encouraging citizens to respond ungrudgingly to the request of officials for help in the performance of their duties remains quite strong. Moreover, the gap (both real and perceived) between a private citizen and a government official with regard to their ability and authority to judge the lawfulness of a particular governmental activity is great. It would appear to serve both justice and public policy in a situation where an individual acted at the behest of a government official to allow the individual a defense based upon his reliance on the official's authority — *if* he can show that his reliance was *objectively reasonable* under the particular circumstances of his case.

....

... It was error for the trial court to bar this defense in the admission of evidence and instructions to the jury, and the convictions must accordingly be

Reversed.

MERHIGE, DISTRICT JUDGE.

....

The district judge advised the jury that a mistake of law is no excuse, and, therefore, that a mistake as to the legality of the search in issue was not a defense to the charges contained in the indictment. In that regard, the district judge was applying the general rule on mistake of law that has long been an integral part of our system of jurisprudence.... The most commonly asserted rationale for the continuing vitality of the rule is that its absence would encourage and reward public ignorance of the law to the detriment of our organized legal system, and would encourage universal pleas of ignorance of the law that would constantly pose confusing and, to a great extent, insolvable issues of fact to juries and judges, thereby bogging down our adjudicative system.... The harshness of the rule on the individual case is responded to by either or both of two thesis [sic]: individual justice and equity is outweighed by the larger social interest of maintaining a public knowledge about the law so as to discourage and deter "illegal" acts; as discussed by Judge Leventhal in his view of this case, the rule is subject to mitigation by virtue of prosecutorial discretion, judicial sentencing, executive clemency, and/or jury nullification.

Exceptions to the rule, however, have developed in situations where its policy foundations have failed to apply with strength, and alternative policy consideration strongly favor a different result. The exceptions have been both statutory, *e.g.*, Act of August 22, 1940, § 49, 15 U.S.C. § 80a-48; Public Utility Holding Company Act of 1935, § 29, 15 U.S.C. § 79z-3, and judicial. *E.g.*, *United States v. Mancuso*, 139 F.2d 90 (3d Cir. 1943); *Moyer v. Meier*, 205 Okl.

---

[26] See the discussion of *People v. Weiss*, 276 N.Y. 384, 12 N.E.2d 514 (1938), in the opinions of Chief Judge Bazelon, concurring, and Judges MacKinnon and Wilkey, dissenting, in *United States v. Barker*, 168 U.S.App.D.C. 312, 338-40, 346-47, 369-74, 514 F.2d 208, 234-36, 242-43, 265-70.

405, 238 P.2d 338 (1951); Annot. 29 A.L.R.2d 825 (1953). See also Model Penal Code §§ 2.05(3), 3.07(4)(a). The instant case fits the pattern of a set of circumstances that has been recognized by some, and that in my view should be endorsed by this court as an exception to the general rule. Defendants Barker and Martinez contend that they were affirmatively misled by an official interpretation of the relevant law, and are entitled to an instruction to that effect, permitting the jury to assess the reasonableness and sincerity of their alleged reliance. The Model Penal Code states the defense as follows:

> A belief that conduct does not legally constitute an offense is a defense to a prosecution for that offense based upon such conduct when: ... (b) he acts in reasonable reliance upon an official statement of the law, afterward determined to be invalid or erroneous, contained in (i) a statute or other enactment; (ii) a judicial decision, opinion or judgment; (iii) an administrative order or grant of permission; or (iv) an official interpretation of the public officer or body charged by law with responsibility for the interpretation, administration or enforcement of the law defining the offense. § 2.04(3)(b).

See also Proposed New Federal Criminal Code, Final Report of a National Commission on Reform of Federal Criminal Laws § 610 (1971). The rationale of the section is well illustrated by the case of *United States v. Mancuso*, 139 F.2d 90 (3d Cir. 1943). The legal issue therein was whether a defendant could be punished for failure to obey an order made by a local draft board when its issuing of such an order to the defendant was interdicted by a judicial decree which was itself, erroneous and subject to reversal. The court in that case stated:

> We think the defendant cannot be convicted for failing to obey an order, issuance of which is forbidden by the court's injunction. While it is true that men are, in general, held responsible for violations of the law, whether they know it or not, we do not think the layman participating in a lawsuit is required to know more than the judge. 139 F.2d at 92. (Footnote omitted)

The introduction of an "official" source for an individual's reliance on a mistaken concept of the law in acting "illegally" significantly diminishes the strength of the policy foundations supporting the general rule on mistake of law, and adds policy considerations of grave import that would favor an apposite result. In my view, the defense is available if, and only if, an individual (1) reasonably, on the basis of an objective standard, (2) relies on a (3) conclusion or statement of law (4) issued by an official charged with interpretation, administration, and/or enforcement responsibilities in the relevant legal field. The first three issues are of course of a factual nature that may be submitted to a jury; the fourth is a question of law as it deals with interpretations of the parameters of legal authority.

....

II. OF LAW

The defense has been most commonly accepted when an individual acts in reliance on a statute later held to be unconstitutional,[3] or on an express decision of unconstitutionality of a statute by a competent court of general jurisdiction that is subsequently overruled.[4] Most jurisdictions will not permit a defense based on reliance upon the advice of counsel.[5] The defense, however, is not limited to those which have been most commonly accepted as I have heretofore made reference. It has been extended to cases of reliance on official advisory opinions....

....

Accordingly, while I concur with Judge Wilkey that the jury should have been instructed on a limited mistake of law defense, I believe any such instruction should, in the event of a retrial, be couched consistent with the views herein expressed.

LEVENTHAL, CIRCUIT JUDGE. Dissenting.

....

The general principle that rejects the defense of ignorance of the requirements of the criminal law, or of mistake as to those requirements, is not a casual or happenstance feature of our legal landscape. It formed a part of English and canon law for centuries and all the time with recognition that it derived from an approach of subjective blameworthiness. Its continuing vitality stems from preserving a community balance, put by Holmes as a recognition that "justice to the individual is rightly outweighed by the larger interests on the other side of the scales."[26] Great minds like Holmes and Austin have struggled with the tension between individual injustice and society's need and have concluded that recognition of the mistake of law defense would encourage ignorance rather than a determination to know the law, and would interfere with the enforcement of law, because the claim would be so easy to assert and hard to disprove.

In some aspect the doctrine may be viewed as a doctrine of negligence, holding individuals to minimal conditions of responsibility and making acting without legal knowledge blameworthy for the failure to obtain that knowledge. Hall suggests in addition that the rationale can be expressed in terms of ethical policy — that the criminal law represents certain moral principles and that to recognize ignorance or mistake of law as a defense would contradict those values.[29] Still, it must in the last analysis be recognized that at its core,

---

[3] *E.g., Claybrook v. State*, 164 Tenn. 440, 51 S.W.2d 499 (1932); *State v. Godwin*, 123 N.C. 697, 31 S.E. 221 (1898); *But see Dupree v. State*, 184 Ark. 1120, 44 S.W.2d 1097 (1932).

[4] *E.g., United States v. Mancuso*, 139 F.2d 90 (3d Cir. 1943); *State v. O'Neil*, 147 Iowa 513, 126 N.W. 454 (1910); *State v. Chicago, M. & St. P. Ry. Co.*, 130 Minn. 144, 153 N.W. 320 (1915); *State v. Longino*, 109 Miss. 125, 67 So. 902 (1915); *State v. Jones*, 44 N.M. 623, 107 P.2d 324 (1940). *But see Hoover v. State*, 59 Ala. 57 (1877).

[5] *E.g., Staley v. State*, 89 Neb. 701, 131 N.W. 1028 (1911); *State v. Whiteaker*, 118 Ore. 656, 247 p. 1077 (1926).

[26] Holmes, The Common Law 48 (1881).

[29] "The criminal law represents an objective ethic which must sometimes oppose individual convictions of right. Accordingly, it will not permit a defendant to plead, in effect, that although he knew what the facts were, his moral judgment was different from that represented in the penal law." Hall, Ignorance and Mistake in Criminal Law, 33 Ind.L.J. 1, 21 (1957), quoted in Report of the Senate Committee on the Judiciary, Criminal Justice Codification, Revision and Reform Act of 1974, Vol. II, p. 96.

the basic mistake of law doctrine imposes liability even though defendant acted in good faith and made a "reasonable" mistake. Otherwise, criminal statutes would be in suspense on any point not authoritatively settled.[30] In a particular case adherence to a generally formulated rule may seem to work injustice, but the jurists pondering the general doctrine have both deemed such individual hardships outweighed by the common good, and have taken into account that certain features of the overall system of criminal justice permit amelioration and relief.[31] These flexible opportunities for mitigating the law's impact — through prosecutorial discretion, judicial sentencing, and executive clemency — avoid the necessity of bending and stretching the law, at the price of undermining its general applicability.

Every mature system of justice must cope with the tension between rule and discretion. Rules without exceptions may grind so harsh as to be intolerable, but exceptions and qualifications inflict a cost in administration and loss of control. The balance struck by the doctrine with which we are now concerned provides for certain rigorously limited exceptions (inapplicable to defendants' claim) but otherwise leaves amelioration of harsh results to other parts of the system of justice. In my view, history has shaped a rule that works, and we should be slow to tinker. Consequently, defendants here must be held to a responsibility to conform their conduct to the law's requirements. To hold otherwise would be to ease the path of the minority of government officials who choose, without regard to the law's requirements, to do things their way, and to provide absolution at large for private adventurers recruited by them.

. . . .

I dissent.

. . . .

EDITORIAL NOTE ON NOTICE — IGNORANCE AND MISTAKE

The requirement that people know the law or act at their peril has a corollary which requires that the law should be capable of being known, at least to the extent required by the notice requirement of the legality principle.

> Fundamental fairness no doubt requires that an individual be given the opportunity to discover a statute's existence, applicability and meaning. Not every layman will read the Penal Code from cover to cover. But, if the statute in question is either clear in meaning upon reading, or sufficient to warn the layman that he should seek legal advice as to its applicability

---

[30] It would fairly be argued that no liability attaches for e.g., action taken under a "reasonable," though erroneous, forecast of how far the courts might go in confining a statute through the doctrine of strict construction. Litigation could come to depend not on what the statute meant, but on the reasonableness of a legal view of its meaning.

[31] If the social harm in a particular case is slight and the ignorance of the law on the part of the offender is fairly obvious, the state may wisely refrain from prosecution in his case. In certain other cases ignorance of law may be considered by the court in mitigation of punishment, or may be made the basis of an application for executive clemency. But if such ignorance were available as a defense in every criminal case, this would be a constant source of confusion to juries, and it would tend to encourage ignorance at a point where it is peculiarly important to the state that knowledge should be as widespread as is reasonably possible.

R. Perkins, Criminal Law 925 (2d ed. 1969). (footnotes omitted).

and meaning, it is proper to charge the potential violator with such knowledge of a law's applicability as he could obtain through competent legal advice. Note, 62 Harv. L. Rev. 77, 80 (1948). If a competent lawyer is consulted, he should be able to predict whether the statute might be used as a basis for prosecuting his client. If the words of the statute and other related law make it impossible to make such a prediction, a statute comes close to inadequate advance notice. Of course, in this particular case, it is patently improper to hold that the inability of a lawyer to predict the jury deliberation of the question of negligence is the basis for ruling lack of adequate notice.... For it is not the duty of the legislature or the courts to advise defendants of the likely reaction of juries in the areas in which defendants engage in business.

Ketchum v. Ward, 422 F. Supp. 934, 941 (W.D.N.Y. 1976).

In *United States v. Squires*, 440 F.2d 859 (2d Cir. 1971), defendant was charged with knowingly making false statements in obtaining a firearm on a form supplied to dealers by the government. The form states: "I certify that I am not prohibited by the provisions of Chapter 44 of Title 18, United States Code, or Title VII of the Omnibus Crime Control and Safe Streets Act of 1968 (citation omitted) from receiving a firearm in interstate or foreign commerce." Defendant claimed he did not knowingly make a false statement because he was ignorant of the law which prohibited him as a convicted felon from receiving the weapon. The trial judge refused to instruct the jury on this point. *Reversed*:

It can safely be said that many lawyers would not have understood, without the benefit of research, the import in the original form of the certification provision. To require a layman, without any explanation, to sign such a certification at his peril appears to us to be quite unrealistic. While it is possible that a defendant may be shown to have sufficient familiarity with the cited statutes, all that we are saying here is that the obscure language of the certification provision was highly relevant to Squires's knowledge, and the trial court should have so instructed the jury.

Id. at 865.

EDITORIAL NOTE ON BIGAMY AND ADULTERY

In interpreting statutory provisions defining certain crimes, for example, bigamy and adultery, courts have taken a strict approach disallowing the defense of mistake. By characterizing these crimes as strict liability offenses requiring no specific intent, courts have rendered immaterial claims that defendants lacked intent or knowledge. This has extended to mistakes of both fact or law. Thus, it has not been a defense under traditional bigamy legislation that persons have remarried because they erroneously believed their spouses were dead at the time or legally divorced from them. *See generally* Comment, Mistake of Fact and Mistake of Law as Defenses to a Prosecution for Bigamy, 15 MERCER L. REV. 275 (1963).

Other courts recognize mistake as a defense, but only when the mistake is of fact and not law. Under Professor Perkins's rationale, *supra* pp. 682-683, no distinction should be drawn here between fact and law because the mistake, if one of law, is a mistake as to non-penal law.

Should the law treat in the same way remarried defendants who act in good faith on reasonable, but mistaken, information? Consider (1) information that spouses have died; (2) information from spouses that they have obtained a divorce; and (3) advice of counsel that earlier marriages have been terminated by valid divorces. Mistakes about spousal death appear to be accepted as errors of fact. *Regina v. Tolson*, 23 Q.B.D. 168 (1889). As to errors about divorces obtained by spouses, *People v. Vogel*, 46 Cal. 2d 798, 299 P.2d 850 (1956), regarded as a leading case in support of the mistake defense," concluded that defendant is not guilty of bigamy, if he had a bona fide and reasonable belief that facts existed that left him free to remarry." *Id.* at 855. *Contra: Regina v. Wheat*, 2 K.B. 119 (1921).

Reliance on advice of counsel has come to be more accepted as divorce has become a much more common occurrence. Older cases did not allow defendants to rely on advice of counsel. In *Staley v. State*, 89 Neb. 701, 131 N.W. 1028 (1911), defendant was advised by three attorneys that his marriage to his cousin was void and needed no annulment or divorce. A deputy county attorney also had advised him so and threatened to prosecute him for his unlawful relations with his cousin. Subsequently defendant married another woman. A prosecution for bigamy followed in which it was determined that the first marriage had been valid. A conviction for bigamy was affirmed. "That one accused of crime had endeavored to ascertain the law and had been misled by counsel or a magistrate is not generally a defense." 131 N.W. at 1029. The same result was reached in a prosecution for adultery where a divorce decree which defendant believed to be valid was declared invalid subsequent to his remarriage. *State v. Whitcomb*, 52 Iowa 85, 2 N.W. 970, 35 Am. Rep. 258 (1879).

This approach was rejected in *Long v. State*, 44 Del. 262, 65 A.2d 489 (1949). There the court recognized mistake of law as a defense where defendant had sought advice of counsel both before he obtained an out-of-state divorce and before he remarried. The court said that it would continue to disallow a defense where

> ignorance or mistake consists merely in (1) unawareness that such conduct is or might be within the ambit of any crime; or (2) although aware of the existence of criminal law relating to the subject of such conduct, or to some of its aspects, the defendant erroneously concludes (in good faith) that his particular conduct is for some reason not subject to the operation of any criminal law. But it seems to us significantly different to disallow mistake of law where (3) together with the circumstances of the second classification, it appears that before engaging in the conduct, the defendant made a bona fide, diligent effort, adopting a course and resorting to sources and means at least as appropriate as any afforded under our legal system, to ascertain and abide by the law, and where he acted in good faith reliance upon the results of such effort. It is inherent in the way our legal system functions that the criminal law consequences of any particular contemplated conduct cannot be determined in advance with cer-

tainty. Not until after the event, by final court decision, may the consequences be definitely ascertained.

65 A.2d at 497. Would this approach encourage attorneys to act unethically to provide their clients with a defense? The court believed that disciplinary measures would deter such actions.

In *State v. DeMeo*, 20 N.J. 1, 118 A.2d 1 (1955), a case involving a "quickie divorce" obtained in Mexico, the court refused to apply the rule of *Long v. State*, because the defendant failed to demonstrate that "he took reasonable steps towards ascertaining the legal validity of the divorce." 118 A.2d at 8. It did not foreclose the possibility that it would follow *Long* in an appropriate case.

It may be that situations involve both mistakes of fact and of law. For example, when persons rely on erroneous advice of counsel as to marital status and eligibility to remarry, is the problem simply one of ignorance or mistake of law? Those prosecuted later for bigamy do not deny knowing at the time of remarriage that bigamy is prohibited, that bigamy means remarriage while a spouse is alive and undivorced, and that remarriage is legally impossible until earlier marriages have been dissolved by valid divorces. The critical error in such instances is that of counsel's interpretation of the law — although their clients arguably have erred as to a critical fact, namely, that counsel have conveyed accurate information to them. The reluctance to allow advice of counsel to establish a defense of mistake of law traditionally has reflected the seriousness of an obligation not to remarry without legal certainty as to one's eligibility to do so.

Under MODEL PENAL CODE § 230.1, reproduced in Appendix A infra, one who reasonably believes he or she is legally eligible to remarry cannot be convicted of bigamy.

SECTION III. Strict Liability

UNITED STATES v. GREENBAUM

United States Circuit Court of Appeals
138 F.2d 437 (3d Cir. 1943)

BIGGS, CIRCUIT JUDGE.

An information was filed against the appellant, Samuel Greenbaum, president of the Bakery Mart of Newark, Inc., and against that company, charging him and it, in two counts, with unlawfully introducing and delivering for introduction in interstate commerce cans of adulterated (i.e., rotten) eggs.... The appellant and the company were found guilty on both counts. Greenbaum was sentenced to pay a fine of $300 and to three months imprisonment. He has appealed.

The information did not charge that he knew that the eggs were rotten when he shipped them into interstate commerce. No proof was offered of guilty knowledge on his part. He contends that for these reasons the judgment should be reversed.

Whether allegation and proof of *mens rea* is requisite to a conviction for a crime which carries with it a possible sentence to penal servitude depends upon the legislative intent evidenced by the statute which defines and punishes the particular offense. *United States v. Balint,* 258 U.S. 250, 252, 42 S. Ct. 301, 66 L. Ed. 604. The constitutional requirement of due process is not violated merely because *mens rea* is not a required element of a prescribed crime. *Shevlin-Carpenter Co. v. Minnesota,* 218 U.S. 57, 69, 70, 30 S. Ct. 663, 54 L. Ed. 930; *United States v. Balint, supra,* 258 U.S. at page 252, 42 S. Ct. at page 302, 66 L. Ed. 604.

While the absence of any requirement of *mens rea* is usually met with in statutes punishing minor or police offenses (for which fines, at least in the first instance, are ordinarily the penalties), we think that interpretation of legislative intent as dispensing with the knowledge and wilfulness as elements of specified crimes is not to be restricted to offenses differentiable upon their relative lack of turpitude. Where the offenses prohibited and made punishable are capable of inflicting widespread injury, and where the requirement of proof of the offender's guilty knowledge and wrongful intent would render enforcement of the prohibition difficult if not impossible (*i.e.,* in effect tend to nullify the statute), the legislative intent to dispense with *mens rea* as an element of the offense has justifiable basis. Notable among such offenses are dealings in adulterated foods and drugs....

The statute under which the appellant was indicted, convicted and sentenced, makes no specific requirement of allegation or proof of the offender's knowledge and wilfulness. While the failure so to provide does not necessarily determine that guilt of the offense may be established without such allegation and proof, we conclude that the requirement of § 335, that, before criminal prosecution for a violation of the statute may be instituted, the person against whom such proceeding is contemplated shall be given an opportunity by the Administrator to present his views with regard to such contemplated proceeding, negatives any idea that proof of guilty knowledge and wrongful intent at trial of an offense under § 333(a) is necessarily implicit. The prescribed inquiry, a preliminary requisite to prosecution, is designed to search out the possible innocent mind of the particular offender by establishing before trial, his good faith or the extent of his actual knowledge and wilfulness.

... [W]e conclude that the construction of the statute before us presents no more than a question of legislative intent and we perceive an intent in § 333(a) to punish persons who introduced adulterated foods into interstate commerce regardless of their lack of knowledge or wilfulness.

In construing Section 2 of the Food and Drugs Act of 1906, 21 U.S.C.A. § 2, courts have held that guilty knowledge was not necessary to sustain a conviction. See *Strong, Cobb & Co. v. United States,* 6 Cir., 1939, 103 F.2d 671, and *United States v. Sprague,* D.C.E.D.N.Y. 1913, 208 F. 419. The analogy is obvious.

....

The judgment will be affirmed.

III. STRICT LIABILITY

UNITED STATES v. PARK

United States Supreme Court
421 U.S. 658 (1975)

[Acme Markets, Inc. and its president, respondent Park, were charged with violations of 21 U.S.C. § 331(k) (1971), in allowing food shipped in interstate commerce to become adulterated by rodents while stored in the corporation's warehouses. Government inspectors had notified respondent of the unsanitary conditions in the warehouse, and respondent had delegated responsibility for correcting the violations to one of the vice presidents. The corporation pleaded guilty; respondent pleaded not guilty. Both were convicted and fined in the district court. The court of appeals reversed, and the Supreme Court reversed that decision, reinstating the conviction.]

MR. CHIEF JUSTICE BURGER delivered the opinion of the Court.

... There was testimony by Acme's Baltimore division vice president, who had responded to the letter on behalf of Acme and respondent and who described the steps taken to remedy the insanitary conditions discovered by both inspections. The Government's final witness, Acme's vice president for legal affairs and assistant secretary, identified respondent as the president and chief executive officer of the company and read a bylaw prescribing the duties of the chief executive officer. He testified that respondent functioned by delegating "normal operating duties," including sanitation, but that he retained "certain things, which are the big, broad, principles of the operation of the company," and had "the responsibility of seeing that they all work together."

....

Respondent was the only defense witness. He testified that, although all of Acme's employees were in a sense under his general direction, the company had an "organizational structure for responsibilities for certain functions" according to which different phases of its operation were "assigned to individuals who, in turn, have staff and departments under them." He identified those individuals responsible for sanitation and related that upon receipt of the January 1972 FDA letter, he had conferred with the vice president for legal affairs, who informed him that the Baltimore division vice president "was investigating the situation immediately and would be taking corrective action and would be preparing a summary of the corrective action to reply to the letter." Respondent stated that he did not "believe there was anything [he] could have done more constructively than what [he] found was being done."

On cross-examination, respondent conceded that providing sanitary conditions for food offered for sale to the public was something that he was "responsible for in the entire operation of the company," and he stated that it was one of many phases of the company that he assigned to "dependable subordinates." Respondent was asked about and, over the objections of his counsel, admitted receiving, the April 1970 letter addressed to him from FDA regarding insanitary conditions at Acme's Philadelphia warehouse.

... The relevant portion of the trial judge's instructions to the jury challenged by respondent is set out in the margin.[9]

II

The rule that corporate employees who have "a responsible share in the furtherance of the transaction which the statute outlaws" are subject to the criminal provisions of the Act was not formulated in a vacuum. Cases under the Federal Food and Drug Act of 1906 reflected the view both that knowledge or intent were not required to be proved in prosecutions under its criminal provisions, and that responsible corporate agents could be subjected to the liability thereby imposed. Moreover, the principle had been recognized that a corporate agent, through whose act, default, or omission the corporation committed a crime, was himself guilty individually of that crime. The principle had been applied whether or not the crime required "consciousness of wrongdoing," and it had been applied not only to those corporate agents who themselves committed the criminal act, but also to those who by virtue of their managerial positions or other similar relation to the actor could be deemed responsible for its commission.

In the latter class of cases, the liability of managerial officers did not depend on their knowledge of, or personal participation in, the act made criminal by the statute. Rather, where the statute under which they were prosecuted dispensed with "consciousness of wrongdoing," and omission or failure to act was deemed a sufficient basis for a responsible corporate agent's liability. It was enough in such cases that, by virtue of the relationship he bore to the corporation, the agent had the power to have prevented the act complained of....

The rationale of the interpretation given the Act in *Dotterweich* [320 U.S. 277], as holding criminally accountable the persons whose failure to exercise the authority and supervisory responsibility reposed in them by the business organization resulted in the violation complained of, has been confirmed in our subsequent cases. Thus, the Court has reaffirmed the proposition that "the public interest in the purity of its food is so great as to warrant the imposition of the highest standard of care on distributors." In order to make

---

[9] In order to find the Defendant guilty on any count of the Information, you must find beyond a reasonable doubt on each count ....

Thirdly, that John R. Park held a position of authority in the operation of the business of Acme Markets, Incorporated.

....

The statute makes individuals, as well as corporations, liable for violations. An individual is liable if it is clear, beyond a reasonable doubt, that the elements of the adulteration of the food as to travel in interstate commerce are present. As I have instructed you in his case, they are, and that the individual had a responsible relation to the situation, even though he may not have participated personally.

The individual is or could be liable under the statute, even if he did not consciously do wrong. However, the fact that the Defendant is pres[id]ent and is a chief executive officer of the Acme Markets does not require a finding of guilt. Though, he need not have personally participated in the situation, he must have had a responsible relationship to the issue. The issue is, in this case, whether the Defendant, John R. Park, by virtue of his position in the company, had a position of authority and responsibility in the situation out of which these charges arose. App. 61-62.

"distributors of food the strictest censors of their merchandise," ... the Act punishes "neglect where the law requires care, or inaction where it imposes a duty." ... [T]he Courts of Appeals have recognized that those corporate agents vested with the responsibility, and power commensurate with that responsibility, to devise whatever measures are necessary to ensure compliance with the Act bear a "responsible relationship" to or have a "responsible share" in violations.

Thus *Dotterweich* and the cases which have followed reveal that in providing sanctions which reach and touch the individuals who execute the corporate mission — and this is by no means necessarily confined to a single corporate agent or employee — the Act imposes not only a positive duty to seek out and remedy violations when they occur but also, and primarily, a duty to implement measures that will insure that violations will not occur. The requirements of foresight and vigilance imposed on responsible corporate agents are beyond question demanding, and perhaps onerous, but they are no more stringent than the public has a right to expect of those who voluntarily assume positions of authority in business enterprises whose services and products affect the health and well-being of the public that supports them. Cf. Wasserstrom, Strict Liability in the Criminal Law, 12 Stan. L. Rev. 731, 741-745 (1960).

The Act does not, as we observed in Dotterweich, make criminal liability turn on "awareness of some wrongdoing" or "conscious fraud." The duty imposed by Congress on responsible corporate agents is, we emphasize, one that requires the highest standard of foresight and vigilance, but the Act, in its criminal aspect, does not require that which is objectively impossible. The theory upon which responsible corporate agents are held criminally accountable for "causing" violations of the Act permits a claim that a defendant was "powerless" to prevent or correct the violation to "be raised defensively at a trial on the merits." ...

III

We cannot agree with the Court of Appeals that it was incumbent upon the District Court to instruct the jury that the Government had the burden of establishing "wrongful action" in the sense in which the Court of Appeals used that phrase. The concept of a "responsible relationship" to, or a "responsible share" in, a violation of the Act indeed imports some measure of blameworthiness; but it is equally clear that the Government establishes a prima facie case when it introduces evidence sufficient to warrant a finding by the trier of the facts that the defendant had, by reason of his position in the corporation, responsibility and authority either to prevent in the first instance, or promptly to correct, the violation complained of, and that he failed to do so. The failure thus to fulfill the duty imposed by the interaction of the corporate agent's authority and the statute furnishes a sufficient causal link. The considerations which prompted the imposition of this duty, and the scope of the duty, provide the measure of culpability.

. . . .

Reading the entire charge satisfies us that the jury's attention was adequately focused on the issue of respondent's authority with respect to the conditions that formed the basis of the alleged violations. Viewed as a whole, the charge did not permit the jury to find guilt solely on the basis of respondent's position in the corporation; rather, it fairly advised the jury that to find guilt it must find respondent "had a responsible relation to the situation," and "by virtue of his position ... had ... authority and responsibility" to deal with the situation....

IV

....

Respondent testified in his defense that he had employed a system in which he relied upon his subordinates, and that he was ultimately responsible for this system. He testified further that he had found these subordinates to be "dependable" and had "great confidence" in them. By this and other testimony respondent evidently sought to persuade the jury that, as the president of a large corporation, he had no choice but to delegate duties to those in whom he reposed confidence, that he had no reason to suspect his subordinates were failing to insure compliance with the Act, and that, once violations were unearthed, acting through those subordinates he did everything possible to correct them.[18]

Although we need not decide whether this testimony would have entitled respondent to an instruction as to his lack of power, had he requested it,[19] the testimony clearly created the "need" for rebuttal evidence. [The rebuttal evidence consisted in part in the introduction of a letter addressed to respondent from the Food and Drug Administration regarding unsanitary conditions at the company's Philadelphia warehouse. The letter predated the Baltimore violations which were the subject of this prosecution. Respondent testified that the same subordinates were responsible for sanitation in both Philadelphia and Baltimore.] That evidence was not offered to show that respondent had a propensity to commit criminal acts ...; its purpose was to demonstrate that respondent was on notice that he could not rely on his system of delegation to subordinates to prevent or correct insanitary conditions at Acme's warehouses, and that he must have been aware of the deficiencies of this system before the Baltimore violations were discovered. The evidence was therefore relevant since it served to rebut respondent's defense that he had justifiably relied upon subordinates to handle sanitation matters....

Reversed.

---

[18] In his summation to the jury, counsel for respondent argued:

> Now, you are Mr. Park. You have his responsibility for a thousand stores — I think eight hundred and some stores — lots of stores, many divisions, many warehouses. What are you going to do, except hire people in whom you have confidence to whom you delegate the work?
>
> ....
>
> ... What I am saying to you is that Mr. Park, through his subordinates when this was found out, did everything in the world they [sic] could. Record, vol. 3, pp. 201, 207.

[19] Assuming, arguendo, that it would be objectively impossible for a senior corporate agent to control fully day-to-day conditions in 874 retail outlets, it does not follow that such a corporate agent could not prevent or remedy promptly violations of elementary sanitary conditions in 16 regional warehouses.

III. STRICT LIABILITY

MR. JUSTICE STEWART, with whom MR. JUSTICE MARSHALL and MR. JUSTICE POWELL join, dissenting.

Although agreeing with much of what is said in the Court's opinion, I dissent from the opinion and judgment, because the jury instructions in this case were not consistent with the law as the Court today expounds it.

As I understand the Court's opinion, it holds that in order to sustain a conviction under § 301(k) of the Federal Food, Drug, and Cosmetic Act the prosecution must at least show that by reason of an individual's corporate position and responsibilities, he had a duty to use care to maintain the physical integrity of the corporation's food products. A jury may then draw the inference that when the food is found to be in such condition as to violate the statute's prohibitions, that condition was "caused" by a breach of the standard of care imposed upon the responsible official. This is the language of negligence, and I agree with it.

To affirm this conviction, however, the Court must approve the instructions given to the members of the jury who were entrusted with determining whether the respondent was innocent or guilty. Those instructions did not conform to the standards that the Court itself sets out today.

The trial judge instructed the jury to find Park guilty if it found beyond a reasonable doubt that Park "had a responsible relation to the situation .... The issue is, in this case, whether the Defendant, John R. Park, by virtue of his position in the company, had a position of authority and responsibility in the situation out of which these charges arose." Requiring, as it did, a verdict of guilty upon a finding of "responsibility," this instruction standing alone could have been construed as a direction to convict if the jury found Park "responsible" for the condition in the sense that his position as chief executive officer gave him formal responsibility within the structure of the corporation. But the trial judge went on specifically to caution the jury not to attach such a meaning to his instruction, saying that "the fact that the Defendant is present [sic] and is a chief executive officer of the Acme Markets does not require a finding of guilt." "Responsibility" as used by the trial judge therefore had whatever meaning the jury in its unguided discretion chose to give it.

The instructions, therefore, expressed nothing more than a tautology. They told the jury: "You must find the defendant guilty if you find that he is to be held accountable for this adulterated food." In other words: "You must find the defendant guilty if you conclude that he is guilty." The trial judge recognized the infirmities in these instructions, but he reluctantly concluded that he was required to give such a charge under *United States v. Dotterweich,* 320 U.S. 277, which, he thought, in declining to define "responsible relation" had declined to specify the minimum standard of liability for criminal guilt.[1]

---

[1] In response to a request for further illumination of what he meant by "responsible relationship" the District Judge said:

> Let me say this, simply as to the definition of the "responsible relationship." Dotterweich and subsequent cases have indicated this really is a jury question. It says it is not even subject to being defined by the Court. As I have indicated to counsel, I am quite candid in stating that I do not agree with the decision; therefore, I am going to stick by it.

COMMONWEALTH v. KOCZWARA

Supreme Court of Pennsylvania
397 Pa. 575, 155 A.2d 825 (1959),
cert. denied, 363 U.S. 848 (1960)

COHEN, JUSTICE.

This is an appeal from the judgment of the Court of Quarter Sessions of Lackawanna County sentencing the defendant to three months in the Lackawanna County Jail, a fine of five hundred dollars and the costs of prosecution, in a case involving violations of the Pennsylvania Liquor Code.

... We, therefore, must determine the criminal responsibility of a licensee of the Liquor Control Board for acts [sale of liquor to minors] committed by his employees upon his premises, without his personal knowledge, participation, or presence, which acts violate a valid regulatory statute passed under the Commonwealth's police power.

While an employer in almost all cases is not criminally responsible for the unlawful acts of his employees, unless he consents to, approves, or participates in such acts, courts all over the nation have struggled for years in applying this rule within the framework of "controlling the sale of intoxicating liquor." See Annotation, 139 A.L.R. 306 (1942). At common law, any attempt to invoke the doctrine of respondeat superior in a criminal case would have run afoul of our deeply ingrained notions of criminal jurisprudence that guilt must be personal and individual.[1] In recent decades, however, many states have enacted detailed regulatory provisions in fields which are essentially noncriminal, *e.g.,* pure food and drug acts, speeding ordinances, building regulations, and child labor, minimum wage and maximum hour legislation. Such statutes are generally enforceable by light penalties, and although violations are labelled crimes, the considerations applicable to them are totally different from those applicable to true crimes, which involve moral delinquency and which are punishable by imprisonment or another serious penalty. Such so-called statutory crimes are in reality an attempt to utilize the machinery of criminal administration as an enforcing arm for social regulations of a purely civil nature, with the punishment totally unrelated to questions of moral wrongdoing or guilt. It is here that the social interest in the general well-being and security of the populace has been held to outweigh the individual interest of the particular defendant. The penalty is imposed despite the defendant's lack of a criminal intent or *mens rea*.

....

In the instant case, the defendant has sought to surround himself with all the safeguards provided to those within the pale of criminal sanctions. He has

---

[1] The distinction between respondeat superior in tort law and its application to the criminal law is obvious. In tort law, the doctrine is employed for the purpose of settling the incidence of loss upon the party who can best bear such loss. But the criminal law is supported by totally different concepts. We impose penal treatment upon those who injure or menace social interests, partly in order to reform, partly to prevent the continuation of the anti-social activity and partly to deter others. If a defendant has personally lived up to the social standards of the criminal law and has not menaced or injured anyone, why impose penal treatment?

III. STRICT LIABILITY

argued that a statute imposing criminal responsibility should be construed strictly, with all doubts resolved in his favor. While the defendant's position is entirely correct, we must remember that we are dealing with a statutory crime within the state's plenary police power. In the field of liquor regulation, the legislature has enacted a comprehensive Code aimed at regulating and controlling the use and sale of alcoholic beverages. The question here raised is whether the legislature intended to impose vicarious criminal liability on the licensee-principal for acts committed on his premises without his presence, participation or knowledge.

....

As the defendant has pointed out, there is a distinction between the requirement of a mens rea and the imposition of vicarious absolute liability for the acts of another. It may be that the courts below, in relying on prior authority, have failed to make such a distinction.[5] In any case, we fully recognize it.[6] Moreover, we find that the intent of the legislature in enacting this Code was not only to eliminate the common law requirement of a *mens rea,* but also to place a very high degree of responsibility upon the holder of a liquor license to make certain that neither he nor anyone in his employ commit any of the prohibited acts upon the licensed premises. Such a burden of care is imposed upon the licensee in order to protect the public from the potentially noxious effects of an inherently dangerous business. We, of course, express no opinion as to the *wisdom* of the legislature's imposing vicarious responsibility under certain sections of the Liquor Code. There may or may not be an economic-sociological justification for such liability on a theory of deterrence. Such determination is for the legislature to make, so long as the constitutional requirements are met.

Can the legislature, consistent with the requirements of due process, thus establish absolute criminal liability? Were this the defendant's first violation of the Code, and the penalty solely a minor fine of from $100-$300, we would have no hesitation in upholding such a judgment. Defendant, by accepting a liquor license, must bear this financial risk. Because of a prior conviction for violations of the Code, however, the trial judge felt compelled under the mandatory language of the statute, Section 494(a), to impose not only an increased fine of five hundred dollars, but also a three month sentence of imprisonment. Such sentence of imprisonment in a case where liability is imposed vicariously cannot be sanctioned by this Court consistently with the law of the land

---

[5] We must also be extremely careful to distinguish the present situation from the question of corporate criminal liability, such as was involved in *Commonwealth v. Liberty Products Company,* 84 Pa. Super. 473 (1925). For a penetrating inquiry into this latter subject, *see* Mens Rea And The Corporation, 19 U. Pitt. L. Rev. 21 (1957).

[6] For an extremely interesting and incisive analysis of the mens rea requirement in criminal offenses, see Mueller, *On Common Law Mens Rea,* 42 Minn. L. Rev. 1043 (1958). While we sympathize fully with the author's eloquent plea for a return to the moral implications of criminal guilt, we await further determination by the Supreme Court of the United States as to whether the rationale of *Lambert v. California,* 355 U.S. 225, 78 S. Ct. 240 (1957) will be extended to all statutory offenses which have been interpreted as not requiring a criminal mens rea. See also Allen, Book Review, 66 Yale L.J. 1120 (1957); Mueller, *Mens Rea And The Law Without It,* 58 W. Va. L. Rev. 34 (1955).

clause of Section 9, Article I of the Constitution of the Commonwealth of Pennsylvania.[7]

The Courts of the Commonwealth have already strained to permit the legislature to carry over the civil doctrine of *respondeat superior* and to apply it as a means of enforcing the regulatory scheme that covers the liquor trade. We have done so on the theory that the Code established petty misdemeanors involving only light monetary fines. It would be unthinkable to impose vicarious criminal responsibility in cases involving true crimes. Although to hold a principal criminally liable might possibly be an effective means of enforcing law and order, it would do violence to our more sophisticated modern-day concepts of justice. Liability for all true crimes, wherein an offense carries with it a jail sentence, must be based exclusively upon personal causation. It can be readily imagined that even a licensee who is meticulously careful in the choice of his employees cannot supervise every single act of the subordinates. A man's liberty cannot rest on so frail a reed as whether his employee will commit a mistake in judgment. See Sayre, Criminal Responsibility for Acts of Another, 43 Harv. L. Rev. 689 (1930).

This Court is ever mindful of its duty to maintain and establish the proper safeguards in a criminal trial. To sanction the imposition of imprisonment here would make a serious change in the substantive criminal law of the Commonwealth, one for which we find no justification. We have *no* case in any jurisdiction which has permitted a *prison term* for a vicarious offense. The Supreme Court of the United States has had occasion only recently to impose due process limitations upon the actions of a state legislature in making unknowing conduct criminal. *Lambert v. California*, 355 U.S. 225 (1957). Our own courts have stepped in time and again to protect a defendant from being held criminally responsible for acts about which he had no knowledge and over which he had little control. *Commonwealth v. Unkrich*, 142 Pa. Super. 591, 16 A.2d 737 (1940); *Commonwealth v. Schambers*, 105 Pa. Super. 467, 161 A. 624 (1932); *Commonwealth v. Rovnianek*, 12 Pa. Super. 86 (1889). We would be utterly remiss were we not to so act under these facts.

In holding that the punishment of imprisonment deprives the defendant of due process of law under these facts, we are not declaring that Koczwara must be treated as a first offender under the Code. He has clearly violated the law for a second time and must be punished accordingly. Therefore, we are only holding that so much of the judgment as calls for imprisonment is invalid, and we are leaving intact the five hundred dollar fine imposed by JUDGE HOBAN under the subsequent offense section.

. . . .

Judgment, as modified, is affirmed.

BELL, JUSTICE.

I would affirm the judgment and the sentence on the opinion of JUDGE HIRT, speaking for a unanimous Superior Court.

[Justices Musmanno and McBride dissented and would have reversed the conviction.]

---

[7] Sec. 9. "... nor can he be deprived of his life, liberty or property, unless by the judgment of his peers or the law of the land."

NOTES

1. In *State v. Gunter*, 87 N.M. 71, 529 P.2d 297 (1974), *cert. denied*, 421 U.S. 951 (1975), the defendant appealed from a conviction of contributing to the delinquency of a minor. Affirmed. "A reading of the statute indicates the legislature did not intend that criminal intent be an element of the offense of contributing to the delinquency of a minor." 529 P.2d at 298. The dissenting opinion argues that since the statute does not require criminal intent and does not require the act in which an accused engages to be criminal, then a person may be guilty of a crime "by virtue of engaging in a lawful act which had an unintended consequence." *Id.* at 299.

2. In *State v. Cutshaw*, 7 Ariz. App. 210, 437 P.2d 962 (1968), the court held that an act contributing to the delinquency of a minor must have been committed with criminal intent. "When a person does an act which reasonable persons should recognize will harm the health or morals of a youth, there is sufficient criminal intent to warrant conviction though the actor for good reason does not know the child is below [the statutory age].... However, no case has come to our attention holding that a person may be convicted ... for influencing the minor to do something which, if the surrounding circumstances were as the actor honestly believed them to be, would be completely moral and righteous for the minor to do, regardless of his age." 437 P.2d at 962.

MORISSETTE v. UNITED STATES
United States Supreme Court
342 U.S. 246 (1952)

MR. JUSTICE JACKSON delivered the opinion of the Court.

This would have remained a profoundly insignificant case to all except its immediate parties had it not been so tried and submitted to the jury as to raise questions both fundamental and far-reaching in federal criminal law, for which reason we granted certiorari.

On a large tract of uninhabited and untilled land in a wooded and sparsely populated area of Michigan, the Government established a practice bombing range over which the Air Force dropped simulated bombs at ground targets. These bombs consisted of a metal cylinder about forty inches long and eight inches across, filled with sand and enough black powder to cause a smoke puff by which the strike could be located. At various places about the range signs read "Danger — Keep Out — Bombing Range." Nevertheless, the range was known as good deer country and was extensively hunted.

Spent bomb casings were cleared from the targets and thrown into piles "so that they will be out of the way." They were not stacked or piled in any order but were dumped in heaps, some of which had been accumulating for four years or upwards, were exposed to the weather and rusting away.

Morissette, in December of 1948, went hunting in this area but did not get a deer. He thought to meet expenses of the trip by salvaging some of these casings. He loaded three tons of them on his truck and took them to a nearby farm, where they were flattened by driving a tractor over them. After expending this labor and trucking them to market in Flint, he realized $84.

Morissette, by occupation, is a fruit stand operator in summer and a trucker and scrap iron collector in winter. An honorably discharged veteran of World War II, he enjoys a good name among his neighbors and has had no blemish on his record more disreputable than a conviction for reckless driving.

The loading, crushing and transporting of these casings were all in broad daylight, in full view of passers-by, without the slightest effort at concealment. When an investigation was started, Morissette voluntarily, promptly and candidly told the whole story to the authorities, saying that he had no intention of stealing but thought the property was abandoned, unwanted and considered of no value to the Government. He was indicted, however, on the charge that he "did unlawfully, wilfully and knowingly steal and convert" property of the United States of the value of $84, in violation of 18 U.S.C. § 641, which provides that "whoever embezzles, steals, purloins, or knowingly converts" government property is punishable by fine and imprisonment. Morissette was convicted and sentenced to imprisonment for two months or to pay a fine of $200. The Court of Appeals affirmed, one judge dissenting.

On his trial, Morissette, as he had at all times told investigating officers, testified that from appearances he believed the casings were cast off and abandoned, that he did not intend to steal the property, and took it with no wrongful or criminal intent. The trial court, however, was unimpressed, and ruled: "[H]e took it because he thought it was abandoned and he knew he was on government property.... That is no defense.... I don't think anybody can have the defense they thought the property was abandoned on another man's piece of property." The court stated: "I will not permit you to show this man thought it was abandoned.... I hold in this case that there is no question of abandoned property." The court refused to submit or to allow counsel to argue to the jury whether Morissette acted with innocent intention. It charged: "And I instruct you that if you believe the testimony of the government in this case, he intended to take it.... He had no right to take this property.... [A]nd it is no defense to claim that it was abandoned, because it was on private property.... And I instruct you to this effect: That if this young man took this property (and he says he did), without any permission (he says he did), that was on the property of the United States Government (he says it was), that it was of the value of one cent or more (and evidently it was), that he is guilty of the offense charged here. If you believe the government, he is guilty.... The question on intent is whether or not he intended to take the property. He says he did. Therefore, if you believe either side, he is guilty." Petitioner's counsel contended, "But the taking must have been with a felonious intent." The court ruled, however: "That is presumed by his own act."

The Court of Appeals suggested that "greater restraint in expression should have been exercised," but affirmed the conviction because, "As we have interpreted the statute, appellant was guilty of its violation beyond a shadow of doubt, as evidenced even by his own admissions." Its construction of the statute is that it creates several separate and distinct offenses, one being knowing conversion of government property. The court ruled that this particular offense requires no element of criminal intent. This conclusion was thought to be required by the failure of Congress to express such a requisite and this

Court's decisions in *United States v. Behrman*, 258 U.S. 280, and *United States v. Balint*, 258 U.S. 250.

I

In those cases this Court did construe mere omission from a criminal enactment of any mention of criminal intent as dispensing with it. If they be deemed precedents for principles of construction generally applicable to federal penal statutes, they authorize this conviction. Indeed, such adoption of the literal reasoning announced in those cases would do this and more — it would sweep out of all federal crimes except when expressly preserved, the ancient requirement of a culpable state of mind. We think a résumé of their historical background is convincing that an effect has been ascribed to them more comprehensive than was contemplated and one inconsistent with our philosophy of criminal law.

The contention that an injury can amount to a crime only when inflicted by intention is no provincial or transient notion. It is as universal and persistent in mature systems of law as belief in freedom of the human will and a consequent ability and duty of the normal individual to choose between good and evil. A relation between some mental element and punishment for a harmful act is almost as instinctive as the child's familiar exculpatory "But I didn't mean to," and has afforded the rational basis for a tardy and unfinished substitution of deterrence and reformation in place of retaliation and vengeance as the motivation for public prosecution.[5] Unqualified acceptance of this doctrine by English common law in the Eighteenth Century was indicated by Blackstone's sweeping statement that to constitute any crime there must first be a "vicious will." Common-law commentators of the Nineteenth Century early pronounced the same principle, although a few exceptions not relevant to our present problem came to be recognized.

Crime, as a compound concept, generally constituted only from concurrence of an evil-meaning mind with an evil-doing hand, was congenial to an intense individualism and took deep and early root in American soil. As the states codified the common law of crimes, even if their enactments were silent on the subject, their courts assumed that the omission did not signify disapproval of the principle but merely recognized that intent was so inherent in the idea of the offense that it required no statutory affirmation. Courts, with little hesitation or division, found an implication of the requirement as to offenses that were taken over from the common law. The unanimity with which they have adhered to the central thought that wrongdoing must be conscious to be criminal is emphasized by the variety, disparity and confusion of their definitions of the requisite but elusive mental element. However, courts of various jurisdictions, and for the purposes of different offenses, have devised working formulae, if not scientific ones, for the instruction of juries around such terms as "felonious intent," "criminal intent," "malice aforethought," "guilty knowl-

---

[5] In *Williams v. New York*, 337 U.S. 241, 248, we observed that "Retribution is no longer the dominant objective of the criminal law. Reformation and rehabilitation of offenders have become important goals of criminal jurisprudence." We also there referred to "... a prevalent modern philosophy of penology that the punishment should fit the offender and not merely the crime." *Id.*, 337 U.S. at 247. Such ends would seem illusory if there were no mental element in crime.

edge," "fraudulent intent," "wilfulness," "scienter," to denote guilty knowledge, or "mens rea," to signify an evil purpose or mental culpability. By use or combination of these various tokens, they have sought to protect those who were not blameworthy in mind from conviction of infamous common-law crimes.

However, the Balint and Behrman offenses belong to a category of another character, with very different antecedents and origins. The crimes there involved depend on no mental element but consist only of forbidden acts or omissions. This, while not expressed by the Court, is made clear from examination of a century-old but accelerating tendency, discernible both here[11] and in England, to call into existence new duties and crimes which disregard any ingredient of intent. The industrial revolution multiplied the number of workmen exposed to injury from increasingly powerful and complex mechanisms, driven by freshly discovered sources of energy, requiring higher precautions by employers. Traffic of velocities, volumes and varieties unheard of came to subject the wayfarer to intolerable casualty risks if owners and drivers were not to observe new cares and uniformities of conduct. Congestion of cities and crowding of quarters called for health and welfare regulations undreamed of in simpler times. Wide distribution of goods became an instrument of wide distribution of harm when those who dispersed food, drink, drugs, and even securities, did not comply with reasonable standards of quality, integrity, disclosure and care. Such dangers have engendered increasingly numerous and detailed regulations which heighten the duties of those in control of particular industries, trades, properties or activities that affect public health, safety or welfare.

While many of these duties are sanctioned by a more strict civil liability, lawmakers, whether wisely or not, have sought to make such regulations more effective by invoking criminal sanctions to be applied by the familiar technique of criminal prosecutions and convictions. This has confronted the courts with a multitude of prosecutions, based on statutes or administrative regulations, for what have been aptly called "public welfare offenses." These cases do not fit neatly into any of such accepted classifications of common-law offenses, such as those against the state, the person, property, or public morals. Many of these offenses are not in the nature of positive aggressions or invasions, with which the common law so often dealt, but are in the nature of neglect where the law requires care, or inaction where it imposes a duty.... Hence, legislation applicable to such offenses, as a matter of policy, does not specify intent as a necessary element. The accused, if he does not will the violation, usually is in a position to prevent it with no more care than society might reasonably expect and no more exertion than it might reasonably exact from one who assumed his responsibilities. Also, penalties commonly are relatively small, and conviction does no grave damage to an offender's reputation. Under such considerations, courts have turned to construing statutes and regulations which make no mention of intent as dispensing with it and hold-

---

[11] This trend and its causes, advantages and dangers have been considered by Sayre, Public Welfare Offenses, 33 Col. L. Rev. 55; Hall, Prolegomena to a Science of Criminal Law, 89 U. of Pa. L. Rev. 549; Hall, Interrelations of Criminal Law and Torts, 43 Col. L. Rev. 753, 967.

III. STRICT LIABILITY

ing that the guilty act alone makes out the crime. This has not, however, been without expressions of misgiving.

....

It was not until recently that the Court took occasion more explicitly to relate abandonment of the ingredient of intent, not merely with considerations of expediency in obtaining convictions, nor with the malum prohibitum classification of the crime, but with the peculiar nature and quality of the offense. We referred to "... a now familiar type of legislation whereby penalties serve as effective means of regulation," and continued, "such legislation dispenses with the conventional requirement for criminal conduct — awareness of some wrongdoing. In the interest of the larger good it puts the burden of acting at hazard upon a person otherwise innocent but standing in responsible relation to a public danger." But we warned: "Hardship there doubtless may be under a statute which thus penalizes the transaction though consciousness of wrongdoing be totally wanting." *United States v. Dotterweich,* 320 U.S. 277, 280, 281, 284.

Neither this Court nor, so far as we are aware, any other has undertaken to delineate a precise line or set forth comprehensive criteria for distinguishing between crimes that require a mental element and crimes that do not. We attempt no closed definition, for the law on the subject is neither settled nor static. The conclusion reached in the Balint and Behrman cases has our approval and adherence for the circumstances to which it was there applied. A quite different question here is whether we will expand the doctrine of crimes without intent to include those charged here.

Stealing, larceny, and its variants and equivalents, were among the earliest offenses known to the law that existed before legislation; they are invasions of rights of property which stir a sense of insecurity in the whole community and arouse public demand for retribution, the penalty is high and, when a sufficient amount is involved, the infamy is that of a felony, which, says Maitland, is "... as bad a word as you can give to man or thing." State courts of last resort, on whom fall the heaviest burden of interpreting criminal law in this country, have consistently retained the requirement of intent in larceny-type offenses. If any state has deviated, the exception has neither been called to our attention nor disclosed by our research.

Congress, therefore, omitted any express prescription of criminal intent from the enactment before us in the light of an unbroken course of judicial decision in all constituent states of the Union holding intent inherent in this class of offense, even when not expressed in a statute. Congressional silence as to mental elements in an Act merely adopting into federal statutory law a concept of crime already so well defined in common law and statutory interpretation by the states may warrant quite contrary inferences than the same silence in creating an offense new to general law, for whose definition the courts have no guidance except the Act. Because the offenses before this Court in the Balint and Behrman cases were of this latter class, we cannot accept them as authority for eliminating intent from offenses incorporated from the common law. Nor do exhaustive studies of state court cases disclose any well-considered decisions applying the doctrine of crime without intent to such enacted common-law offenses,[20] although a few deviations are notable as illustrative of the danger inherent in the Government's contentions here.

The Government asks us by a feat of construction radically to change the weights and balances in the scales of justice. The purpose and obvious effect of doing away with the requirement of a guilty intent is to ease the prosecution's path to conviction, to strip the defendant of such benefit as he derived at common-law from innocence of evil purpose, and to circumscribe the freedom heretofore allowed juries....

....

Congress, by the language of this section, has been at pains to incriminate only "knowing" conversions. But, at common law, there are unwitting acts which constitute conversions. In the civil tort, except for recovery of exemplary damages, the defendant's knowledge, intent, motive, mistake, and good faith are generally irrelevant. If one takes property which turns out to belong to another, his innocent intent will not shield him from making restitution or indemnity, for his well-meaning may not be allowed to deprive another of his own.

Had the statute applied to conversions without qualification, it would have made crimes of all unwitting, inadvertent and unintended conversions. Knowledge, of course, is not identical with intent and may not have been the most apt words of limitation. But knowing conversion requires more than knowledge that defendant was taking the property into his possession. He must have had knowledge of the facts, though not necessarily the law, that made the taking a conversion. In the case before us, whether the mental element that Congress required be spoken of as knowledge or as intent, would not seem to alter its bearing on guilt. For it is not apparent how Morissette could have knowingly or intentionally converted property that he did not know could be converted, as would be the case if it was in fact abandoned or if he truly believed it to be abandoned and unwanted property.

....

... The court thought the only question was, "Did he intend to take the property?" That the removal of them was a conscious and intentional act was admitted. But that isolated fact is not an adequate basis on which the jury should find the criminal intent to steal or knowingly convert, that is, wrongfully to deprive another of possession of property. Whether that intent existed, the jury must determine, not only from the act of taking, but from that together with defendant's testimony and all of the surrounding circumstances.

Of course, the jury, considering Morissette's awareness that these casings were on government property, his failure to seek any permission for their removal and his self-interest as a witness, might have disbelieved his profession of innocent intent and concluded that his assertion of a belief that the casings were abandoned was an afterthought. Had the jury convicted on

---

[20] Sayre, Public Welfare Offenses, 33 Col. L. Rev. 55, 73, 84, cites and classifies a large number of cases and concludes that they fall roughly into subdivisions of (1) illegal sales of intoxicating liquor, (2) sales of impure or adulterated food or drugs, (3) sales of misbranded articles, (4) violations of antinarcotic Acts, (5) criminal nuisances, (6) violations of traffic regulations, (7) violations of motor-vehicle laws, and (8) violations of general police regulations, passed for the safety, health or well-being of the community.

III. STRICT LIABILITY

proper instructions it would be the end of the matter. But juries are not bound by what seems inescapable logic to judges. They might have concluded that the heaps of spent casings left in the hinterland to rust away presented an appearance of unwanted and abandoned junk, and that lack of any conscious deprivation of property or intentional injury was indicated by Morissette's good character, the openness of the taking, crushing and transporting of the casings, and the candor with which it was all admitted. They might have refused to brand Morissette as a thief. Had they done so, that too would have been the end of the matter.

Reversed.

MR. JUSTICE DOUGLAS concurs in the result.

MR. JUSTICE MINTON took no part in the consideration or decision of this case.

NOTES

1. See *United States v. United States Gypsum Co.*, 438 U.S. 422 (1978), *supra* pp. 67-68.

2. Citing *Morissette* and *Gypsum,* the Supreme Court interpreted the federal statute governing food stamp fraud, 7 U.S.C. § 2024(b)(1), to require proof "that the defendant knew that his acquisition or possession of food stamps was in a manner unauthorized by statute or regulations, *Liparota v. United States*, 471 U.S. 419, 433 (1985) (footnote omitted).

3. *State v. Keian*, 542 N.E.2d 963 (Ind. 1989), considered the crime of driving while one's license is suspended. Citing *Gypsum* and *Liparota*, the state supreme court interpreted the statute to require proof of defendant's knowledge of the suspension.

4. In the case of conspiracy, as with other common law crimes, it is necessary that criminal intent be shown. Speaking in general terms, there must be an intent to do wrong. Selling the shares on installments was not in itself wrong. It need involve no deceit or other element detrimental to the individual purchaser or to the public interest. So long as the contracts had not been approved, sale of the shares was malum prohibitum because of the statute, and nothing more. While no decision in this commonwealth directly in point has been called to our attention, it has been held by excellent authority in other jurisdictions that in order to sustain an indictment for conspiracy to commit an offense which, like that here involved, is malum prohibitum only, belonging to a general type of offenses which has been greatly extended by modern legislation in many fields, it must appear that the defendant knew of the illegal element involved in that which the combination was intended to accomplish. *People v. Powell*, 63 N.Y. 88; *Landen v. United States* (C.C.A.) 299 F. 75. See *Commonwealth v. Adams*, 114 Mass. 323, 19 Am. Rep. 362; *Vogel v. Brown*, 201 Mass. 261, 87 N.E. 686; *People v. Flack*, 125 N.Y. 324, 26 N.E. 267; 11 L.R.A. 807. We believe that this is sound law, where the charge is conspiracy. We do not imply that proof of criminal intent is required to sustain a complaint or indictment for the substantive offense prohibited by the statute.

To constitute the criminal intent necessary to establish a conspiracy there must be both knowledge of the existence of the law and knowledge of its actual or intended violation. *Commonwealth v. Benesch,* 290 Mass. 125, 134-35, 194 N.E. 905, 910 (1935).

LAMBERT v. CALIFORNIA

United States Supreme Court
355 U.S. 225 (1957)

MR. JUSTICE DOUGLAS delivered the opinion of the Court.

Section 52.38(a) of the Los Angeles Municipal Code defines "convicted person" as follows:

> Any person who, subsequent to January 1, 1921, has been or hereafter is convicted of an offense punishable as a felony in the State of California, or who has been or who is hereafter convicted of any offense in any place other than the State of California, which offense, if committed in the State of California, would have been punishable as a felony.

Section 52.39 provides that it shall be unlawful for "any convicted person" to be or remain in Los Angeles for a period of more than five days without registering; it requires any person having a place of abode outside the city to register if he comes into the city on five occasions or more during a 30-day period; and it prescribes the information to be furnished the Chief of Police on registering.

Section 52.43(b) makes the failure to register a continuing offense, each day's failure constituting a separate offense.

Appellant, arrested on suspicion of another offense, was charged with a violation of this registration law.[1] The evidence showed that she had been at the time of her arrest a resident of Los Angeles for over seven years. Within that period she had been convicted in Los Angeles of the crime of forgery, an offense which California punishes as a felony. Though convicted of a crime punishable as a felony, she had not at the time of her arrest registered under the Municipal Code. At the trial, appellant asserted that § 52.39 of the Code denies her due process of law and other rights under the Federal Constitution, unnecessary to enumerate. The trial court denied this objection. The case was tried to a jury which found appellant guilty. The court fined her $250 and placed her on probation for three years. Appellant, renewing her constitutional objection, moved for arrest of judgment and a new trial. This motion was denied. On appeal the constitutionality of the Code was again challenged. The Appellate Department of the Superior Court affirmed the judgment, holding there was no merit to the claim that the ordinance was unconstitutional. The case is here on appeal. 28 U.S.C. § 1257(2). We noted probable jurisdiction, 352 U.S. 914, and designated *amicus curiae* to appear in support of appellant. The case having been argued and reargued, we now hold that the registration provisions of the Code as sought to be applied here violate the Due Process requirement of the Fourteenth Amendment.

---

[1] For a recent comprehensive review of these registration laws see Note, 103 U. of Pa. L. Rev. 60 (1954).

III. STRICT LIABILITY

The registration provision, carrying criminal penalties, applies if a person has been convicted "of an offense punishable as a felony in the State of California" or, in case he has been convicted in another State, if the offense "would have been punishable as a felony" had it been committed in California. No element of willfulness is by terms included in the ordinance nor read into it by the California court as a condition necessary for a conviction.

We must assume that appellant had no actual knowledge of the requirement that she register under this ordinance, as she offered proof of this defense which was refused. The question is whether a registration act of this character violates due process where it is applied to a person who has no actual knowledge of his duty to register, and where no showing is made of the probability of such knowledge.

We do not go with Blackstone in saying that "a vicious will" is necessary to constitute a crime, 4 Bl. Comm. *21, for conduct alone without regard to the intent of the doer is often sufficient. There is wide latitude in the lawmakers to declare an offense and to exclude elements of knowledge and diligence from its definition. See *Chicago, B. & O.R. Co. v. United States*, 220 U.S. 559, 578. But we deal here with conduct that is wholly passive — mere failure to register. It is unlike the commission of acts, or the failure to act under circumstances that should alert the doer to the consequences of his deed. *Cf. Shevlin-Carpenter Co. v. Minnesota*, 218 U.S. 57; *United States v. Balint*, 258 U.S. 250; *United States v. Dotterweich*, 320 U.S. 277, 284. The rule that "ignorance of the law will not excuse" (*Shevlin-Carpenter Co. v. Minnesota, supra,* p. 68) is deep in our law, as is the principle that of all the powers of local government, the police power is "one of the least limitable." *District of Columbia v. Brooke*, 214 U.S. 138, 149. On the other hand, due process places some limits on its exercise. Engrained in our concept of due process is the requirement of notice. Notice is sometimes essential so that the citizen has the chance to defend charges. Notice is required before property interests are disturbed, before assessments are made, before penalties are assessed. Notice is required in a myriad of situations where a penalty or forfeiture might be suffered for mere failure to act. Recent cases illustrating the point are *Mullane v. Central Hanover Bank & Trust Co.*, 339 U.S. 306; *Covey v. Town of Somers*, 351 U.S. 141; *Walker v. Hutchinson City*, 352 U.S. 112. These cases involved only property interests in civil litigation. But the principle is equally appropriate where a person, wholly passive and unaware of any wrongdoing, is brought to the bar of justice for condemnation in a criminal case.

Registration laws are common and their range is wide. *Cf. Bryant v. Zimmerman*, 278 U.S. 63; *United States v. Harriss*, 347 U.S. 612; *United States v. Kahriger*, 345 U.S. 22. Many such laws are akin to licensing statutes in that they pertain to the regulation of business activities. But the present ordinance is entirely different. Violation of its provisions is unaccompanied by any activity whatever, mere presence in the city being the test. Moreover, circumstances which might move one to inquire as to the necessity of registration are completely lacking. At most the ordinance is but a law enforcement technique designed for the convenience of law enforcement agencies through which a list of the names and addresses of felons then residing in a given community is compiled. The disclosure is merely a compilation of former convictions already publicly recorded in the jurisdiction where obtained. Nevertheless, this appellant on first becoming aware of her duty to register was given no opportunity to comply with the law and avoid its penalty, even though her default was entirely innocent. She could but suffer the consequences of the ordinance, namely, conviction with the imposition of heavy criminal penalties thereunder. We believe that actual knowledge of the duty to register or proof of the probability of such knowledge and subsequent failure to comply are necessary before a conviction under the ordinance can stand. As Holmes wrote in The Common Law, "A law which punished conduct which would not be blameworthy in the average member of the community would be too severe for that community to bear." Id., at 50. Its severity lies in the absence of an opportunity either to avoid the consequences of the law or to defend any prosecution brought under it. Where a person did not know of the duty to register and where there was no proof of the probability of such knowledge, he may not be convicted consistently with due process. Were it otherwise, the evil would be as great as it is when the law is written in print too fine to read or in a language foreign to the community.

Reversed.

MR. JUSTICE BURTON dissents because he believes that, as applied to this appellant, the ordinance does not violate her constitutional rights.

MR. JUSTICE FRANKFURTER, whom MR. JUSTICE HARLAN and MR. JUSTICE WHITTAKER join, dissenting.

The present laws of the United States and of the forty-eight States are thick with provisions that command that some things not be done and others be done, although persons convicted under such provisions may have had no awareness of what the law required or that what they did was wrongdoing. The body of decisions sustaining such legislation, including innumerable registration laws, is almost as voluminous as the legislation itself. The matter is summarized in *United States v. Balint*, 258 U.S. 250, 252: "Many instances of this are to be found in regulatory measures in the exercise of what is called the police power where the emphasis of the statute is evidently upon achievement of some social betterment rather than the punishment of the crimes as in cases of *mala in se*."

... [W]hat the Court here does is to draw a constitutional line between a State's requirement of doing and not doing. What is this but a return to Year Book distinctions between feasance and non-feasance — a distinction that may have significance in the evolution of common-law notions of liability, but is inadmissible as a line between constitutionality and unconstitutionality. One can be confident that Mr. Justice Holmes would have been the last to draw such a line. What he wrote about "blameworthiness" is worth quoting in its context:

"It is not intended to deny that criminal liability, as well as civil, is founded on blameworthiness. Such a denial would shock the moral sense of any civilized community; or, to put it another way, a law which punished conduct which would not be blameworthy in the average member of the community would be too severe for that community to bear." (This passage must be read in the setting of the broader discussion of which it is an essential part. Holmes, The Common Law, at 49, 50.)

If the generalization that underlies, and alone can justify, this decision were to be given its relevant scope, a whole volume of the United States Reports would be required to document in detail the legislation in this country that would fall or be impaired. I abstain from entering upon a consideration of such legislation, and adjudications upon it, because I feel confident that the present decision will turn out to be an isolated deviation from the strong current of precedents — a derelict on the waters of the law. Accordingly, I content myself with dissenting.

NOTES

1. A statute which imposes strict liability is particularly susceptible to challenge where the prohibited conduct involves speech. In *Smith v. California*, 361 U.S. 147 (1959), the Supreme Court held that the imposition of strict responsibility on the proprietor of a book store for possessing obscene books was unconstitutional.

> By dispensing with any requirement of knowledge of the contents of the book on the part of the seller, the ordinance tends to impose a severe limitation on the public's access to constitutionally protected matter. For if the bookseller is criminally liable without knowledge of the contents, and the ordinance fulfills its purpose, he will tend to restrict the books he sells to those he has inspected; and thus the State will have imposed a restriction upon the distribution of constitutionally protected as well as obscene literature. It has been well observed of a statute construed as dispensing with any requirement of scienter that: "Every bookseller would be placed under an obligation to make himself aware of the contents of every book in his shop. It would be altogether unreasonable to demand so near an approach to omniscience." The *King v. Ewart*, 25 N.Z.L.R. 709, 729 (C.A.). And the bookseller's burden would become the public's burden, for by restricting him the public's access to reading matter would be restricted.... The bookseller's self-censorship, compelled by the State, would be a censorship affecting the whole public, hardly less virulent for being privately administered. Through it, the distribution of all books both obscene and not obscene, would be impeded.

Id. at 153-54.

2. In *Reyes v. United States*, 258 F.2d 774 (9th Cir. 1958), the defendant was convicted of a violation of the Federal Narcotics Act which required any person with a prior narcotics conviction to register with a customs official upon entering or leaving the United States. On March 4, 1957, defendant, who had been convicted of possession of marijuana in 1943, left the United States for Mexico and returned the same day without registering either on his departure or re-entry. Held: conviction affirmed. No criminal intent was necessary to

violate the statute, nor was knowledge of the statute required. The court distinguished Lambert v. United States, on the following grounds:

> (1) Lambert concerned only a nonfeasance, i.e., mere presence in California, while the present case requires misfeasance, i.e., crossing the border.
> (2) Lambert concerned a "common act" — living in a community — while crossing a border should "'alert the doer' and is attended by circumstances which 'move one to inquire as to necessity of registration.'"
> (3) The statute under consideration here is not merely for police bookkeeping but is intended to reduce the illegal transportation of narcotics across the border.

3. In *United States v. Freed*, 401 U.S. 601 (1971), a majority of the Supreme Court held that a prosecution under 26 U.S.C. § 5861(d) (1976) does not require proof that a person who possesses certain types of weapons (in this case, hand grenades) which have not been registered as required by the Act knew that they were unregistered. Justice Brennan, concurring in the judgment, stated:

> If the ancient maxim that "ignorance of the law is no excuse" has any residual validity, it indicates that the ordinary intent requirement — mens rea — of the criminal law does not require knowledge that an act is illegal, wrong, or blameworthy. Nor is it possible to decide this case by a simple process of classifying the statute involved as a "regulatory" or a "public welfare" measure. To convict appellees of possession of unregistered hand grenades, the Government must prove three material elements: (1) that appellees possessed certain items; (2) that the items possessed were hand grenades; and (3) that the hand grenades were not registered. The Government and the Court agree that the prosecutor must prove knowing possession of the items and also knowledge that the items possessed were hand grenades. Thus, while the Court does hold that no intent at all need be proved in regard to one element of the offense — the unregistered status of the grenades — knowledge must still be proved as to the other two elements. Consequently, the National Firearms Act does not create a crime of strict liability as to all its elements.

Id. at 612.

4. In *State v. Hatch*, 64 N.J. 179, 313 A.2d 797 (1973), the defendant's conviction for unlawfully possessing a rifle and shotgun was affirmed. Defendant was a resident of Massachusetts driving through New Jersey on his way to Pennsylvania, when he was stopped for a traffic violation, The police officer saw a rifle and shotgun in the rear seat of the defendant's car. Defendant had a Massachusetts hunting license and his conduct conformed to Massachusetts law.

> While there is much to be said in favor of the wide recognition of lack of scienter as a defense, there are fields in which the dangers are so high and the regulations so prevalent that, on balance, the legislative branch

III. STRICT LIABILITY

may ... declare the act itself unlawful without any further requirement of mens rea or its equivalent. Gun control is clearly such a field....

313 A.2d at 799-800.

5. In *United States v. International Minerals & Chemicals Corp.*, 402 U.S. 558, 563 (1971), the defendant was charged with shipping sulfuric acid in interstate commerce and knowingly failing to show on the shipping papers the classification "Corrosive Liquid" as required under an administrative regulation. Held: Lack of knowledge of the regulation is not a defense.

> The principle that ignorance of the law is no defense applies whether the law be a statute or a duly promulgated and punished regulation....
>
> So far as possession, say, of sulfuric acid is concerned the requirement of *"mens rea"* has been made a requirement of the Act as evidenced by the use of the word "knowingly." A person thinking in good faith that he was shipping distilled water when in fact he was shipping some dangerous acid would not be covered.
>
> ... But where, as here and as in Balint and Freed, dangerous or deleterious devices or products or obnoxious waste materials are involved, the probability of regulation is so great that anyone who is aware that he is in possession of them or dealing with them must be presumed to be aware of the regulation.

UNITED STATES v. ROBERT WULFF

United States Court of Appeals
758 F.2d 1121 (6th Cir. 1985)

MILBURN, CIRCUIT JUDGE.

The United States appeals the judgment of the district court dismissing an indictment that charged the defendant, Robert Wulff, with offering to sell migratory bird parts in violation of the Migratory Bird Treaty Act ("MBTA"), 16 U.S.C. § 703 *et seq.* This case raises the question of whether a felony conviction for the sale of a migratory bird part in violation of the MBTA is violative of the due process clause of the Fifth Amendment of the United States Constitution. Because a felony conviction under the Act does not require proof of scienter, because the crime is not one known to the common law, and because the felony penalty provision is severe and would result in irreparable damage to one's reputation, we affirm the decision of the district court and declare the felony provision of the Act, § 707(b)(2), unconstitutional.

I.

On September 15, 1983, a federal grand jury returned a one-count indictment charging the defendant with selling migratory bird parts in violation of 16 U.S.C. §§ 703 and 707(b)(2). Section 707(b)(2) provides as follows:

(b) Whoever, in violation of sections 703 to 711 of this title, shall —

....

(2) sell, offer for sale, barter or offer to barter any migratory bird shall be guilty of a felony and shall be fined not more than $2,000 or imprisoned not more than two years, or both.

The indictment was based on a sale made by the defendant to a special agent of the United States Fish and Wildlife Service of a necklace made of red-tailed hawk and great horned owl talons. Both birds are protected species under the Migratory Bird Treaty Act. The indictment charged, as an element of the offense, that the defendant acted "knowingly."

The defendant filed a "Motion to Strike Surplusages in Indictment" asking the district court to strike the word "knowingly" as not being required under section 707(b)(2) of the MBTA. The United States agreed to the elimination of the word.

The defendant also filed a "Motion to Dismiss Indictment or Enter Order Directing Charge of Misdemeanor," arguing that because section 707(b)(2) does not require guilty knowledge, imposition of a felony conviction would be a violation of due process. The district court agreed and directed that if the defendant was convicted of a violation, he would be sentenced under the misdemeanor provision of the Act, rather than the felony provision. In response to a motion by the United States, however, the district court ultimately dismissed the felony indictment and this appeal followed.

In arriving at its decision, the district court began with the principle that "the existence of a *mens rea* is the rule of, rather than the exception to, the principles of Anglo-American criminal jurisprudence." *Dennis v. United States*, 341 U.S. 494, 500, 71 S. Ct. 857, 862, 95 L. Ed. 1137 (1951). The district court noted, however, that the constitutional requirement of due process is not violated merely because *mens rea* is not an element of a proscribed crime, citing *United States v. Greenbaum*, 138 F.2d 437, 438 (3rd Cir. 1943). The court further noted that there is no precise or easily applied formula available to resolve the present controversy and turned for guidance to the Supreme Court opinion in *Morissette v. United States*, 342 U.S. 246, 72 S. Ct. 240, 96 L. Ed. 288 (1952): [quote omitted]

The district court next turned to the case of *Holdridge v. United States*, 282 F.2d 302 (8th Cir. 1960):

> [W]here a federal criminal statute omits mention of intent and where it seems to involve what is basically a matter of policy, where the standard imposed is, under the circumstances, reasonable and adherence thereto properly expected of a person, where the penalty is relatively small, where conviction does not gravely besmirch, where the statutory crime is not taken over from the common law, and where congressional purpose is supporting, the statute can be construed as one not requiring criminal intent. The elimination of this element is then not violative of the due process clause.

Id. at 310. The court noted that this articulation of the governing distinctions was approved by Justice Brennan in his concurrence in *United States v. Freed*, 401 U.S. 601, 613 n.4, 91 S. Ct. 1112, 1120 n.4, 28 L. Ed. 2d 356 (1971).

Applying these legal precedents to the facts before it, the district court noted that the felony statutory penalty involved in this case included a maximum sentence of two (2) years' imprisonment or a fine of Two Thousand ($2,000.00) dollars, or both. The district court felt that these were not "relatively small penalties." The district court further noted that a convicted felon loses his right to vote, his right to sit on a jury and his right to possess a gun, among other civil rights, for the rest of his life. The district court was of the opinion that a felony conviction irreparably damages one's reputation.

Based on these findings, the district court held that the MBTA felony penalty provisions did not meet the criteria of *Holdridge, supra,* and, accordingly, concluded that section 707(b)(2) is violative of due process of law. As further support for its decision, the district court quoted *United States v. Heller,* 579 F.2d 990 (6th Cir. 1978):

> Certainly, if Congress attempted to define a *malum prohibitum* offense that placed on onerous stigma on an offender's reputation and carried a severe penalty, the Constitution would be offended....

Id. at 994.

II.

Dilemmas similar to the one presented in this case have been resolved in the past by reading a requirement of scienter into an otherwise, silent statute. See, *e.g., Morissette, supra,* 342 U.S. at 263, 72 S. Ct. at 250. However, this court has previously held that Congress did not intend for scienter to be an element of the offense under the MBTA. See *United States v. Catlett,* 747 F.2d 1102 (6th Cir. 1984); *United States v. Brandt,* 717 F.2d 955 (6th Cir. 1983); and *United States v. Green,* 571 F.2d 1 (6th Cir. 1978). Other courts that have addressed the issue are in accord. See *United States v. Ireland,* 493 F.2d 1208 (4th Cir. 1973); *United States v. Wood,* 437 F.2d 91 (9th Cir. 1971); *United States v. Ardoin,* 431 F. Supp. 493 (W.D. La. 1977); *United States v. Bryson,* 414 F. Supp. 1068 (D. Del. 1976); and *United States v. Schultze,* 28 F. Supp. 234 (W.D. Ky. 1939).

These cases are distinguishable in that the convictions therein were under the misdemeanor penalty provisions of the MBTA or the regulations promulgated thereunder. Accordingly, nothing in this opinion is to be construed as in any way overruling or modifying those decisions. Rather, we are concerned with the construction of the felony provision of the MBTA, viz., 16 U.S.C. § 707(b)(2). In our opinion, we cannot read a requirement of scienter into section 707(b)(2) because the crime is not one known to the common law. An element of scienter can be read into an otherwise silent statute only where the crime is one borrowed from the common law. See *Morissette, supra,* 342 U.S. at 252, 262, 72 S. Ct. at 244, 249; *Holdridge, supra,* 282 F.2d at 310.

The question thus becomes whether, given that a violation of the MBTA is a strict liability offense, a conviction under the Act operates to deny a defendant his right to due process under the Fifth Amendment. The United States argues that this court's decision in *Heller, supra,* does not compel the result reached by the district court. In *Heller,* the defendant was indicted under 18 U.S.C. § 875 of having willfully and knowingly transmitted in interstate commerce a communication containing a request for ransom and reward for the release of a kidnapped person. The defendant had argued that because the government had not charged that he acted with the intent to extort and because the punishment was severe, the statute was unconstitutional. This court held that the legislative history of the statute demonstrated that Congress intended the crime to include the intent to extort. The court cured any asserted defect by ruling that the indictment was insufficient because it did not correctly charge that the defendant acted with the requisite intent to extort and remanded the case to the district court.

The United States argues that the legislative history of the felony provision of the MBTA requires a different result here. The government notes that both before and after the 1960 amendment to the Act adding section 707(b)(2), scienter was not an element of an offense under the statute. Therefore, the 1960 amendment did not change the elements of an offense under the statute. The United States further argues that the crime with which the defendant was charged here, that is, the sale of a necklace made from the parts of two protected species, is exactly the type of commercialization of protected birds Congress sought to punish as a felony.

This argument misses the point. The question before us today is not whether scienter is an element of the offense or whether Congress made a rational choice in legislating a felony conviction for the commercialization of protected birds. Rather, we must decide whether the absence of a requirement that the government prove some degree of scienter violates the defendant's right to due process.

We believe the proper guidance for the resolution of this issue can be found in Judge, now Justice, Blackmun's opinion in *Holdridge, supra*, Extrapolating from *Holdridge*, the proper test would appear to be as follows: The elimination of the element of criminal intent does not violate the due process clause where (1) the penalty is relatively small, and (2) where conviction does not gravely besmirch. As the district court held, section 707(b)(2) does not meet these criteria. The felony penalty carries a maximum sentence of two (2) years' imprisonment or Two Thousand ($2,000.00) Dollars fine, or both. "This is not, in this Court's mind, a relatively small penalty." *United States v. St. Pierre*, 578 F. Supp. 1424, 1429 (D.S.D. 1983) (concluding that imposition of felony penalty under section 707(b) would violate due process and, therefore, directing that if convicted, the court would sentence under the misdemeanor provision). In addition, as the district judge noted, a felony conviction irreparably damages one's reputation, and in Michigan a convicted felon loses, among other civil rights, his right to sit on a jury and his right to possess a gun. *See, e.g.*, Mich. Comp. Laws § 27A.1307(1)(e) (jury); and 18 U.S.C. app. § 1202 (firearms).

III.

We are of the opinion that in order for one to be convicted of a felony under the MBTA, a crime unknown to the common law which carries a substantial penalty, Congress must require the prosecution to prove the defendant acted with some degree of scienter. Otherwise, a person acting with a completely innocent state of mind could be subjected to a severe penalty and grave damage to his reputation. This, in our opinion, the constitution does not allow.

. . . .

III. STRICT LIABILITY

For the reasons stated herein, the judgment of the district court is AFFIRMED.

NOTES

1. Despite the government's concession "that the absence of a scienter requirement in the felony provision of the Migratory Bird Treaty Act violates the due process clause," the Court of Appeals for the Third Circuit held that lack of such did not constitute a due process violation. *United States v. Engler*, 806 F. 2d 425, 433 (3rd Cir., 1986). The court disagreed with *Wulff's* reading of the Supreme Court's jurisprudence regarding the constitutionality of strict liability offenses.

2. *United States v. Williams*, 872 F.2d 773 (6th Cir. 1989), involved a conviction for willingly and knowingly transferring an unregistered fully automatic weapon in violation of 26 U.S.C. § 5861(e). The court discussed and distinguished *United States v. Freed*, 401 U.S. 601 (1971) which had addressed another part of the same statute, see *supra* p. 714, n. 3. Relying on a passage from Justice Brennan's concurring opinion *Id.* at 773 (quoted *supra* p. 714, n. 3) and citing "the due process concerns advanced in *Morissette* [*supra* pp. 703-709] and refined in later cases such as *United States v. Wulff*," *id.* at 777, the court interpreted the statute to require proof "the defendants knew that a 'firearm' as legislatively defined was being transferred." *Id.*

Chapter 10

RELATIONAL DOCTRINES

SECTION I. Parties — Principals and Accessories

EDITORIAL NOTE

At common law, parties were divided into four categories:

(1) *Principals in the first degree:* those actors who are the actual perpetrators of the crime.

(2) *Principals in the second degree:* those actors who are present at the scene, aiding and abetting the perpetrator of the crime.

(3) *Accessories before the fact:* those actors who are absent from the scene of the crime, but who procure, counsel, or assist another to commit a crime.

(4) *Accessories after the fact:* those actors who, with knowledge that a felony has been committed, render assistance to the felon in an effort to hinder his detection, arrest, trial or punishment.

4 W. BLACKSTONE, COMMENTARIES *34-39.

An accessory before the fact could not be arraigned until a final judgment of conviction had been entered against the principal. The rule has been universally rejected in the United States. *Lewis v. State,* 285 Md. 705, 404 A.2d 1073 (1979) abolished most distinctions. Modern statutes have also abolished most distinctions between principals in the first degree, principals in the second degree, and accessories before the fact for purposes of pleading. For example, the Texas Penal Code provides:

§ 7.01. Parties to Offenses.

(a) A person is criminally responsible as a party to an offense if the offense is committed by his own conduct, by the conduct of another for which he is criminally responsible, or by both.

(b) Each party to an offense may be charged with commission of the offense.

(c) All traditional distinctions between accomplices and principals are abolished by this section, and each party to an offense may be charged and convicted without alleging that he acted as a principal or accomplice.

TEX. PENAL CODE ANN. § 7.01 (West 1973).

Under the Texas statutes, accessories are no longer included as parties. Criminal conduct that would have been classified as "accessorial" under the common law is now prosecuted as a separate crime: obstructing governmental operation (interference with the administration of justice) by hindering the apprehension or prosecution of another. TEX. PENAL CODE ANN. § 38.05 (West 1991).

Although most of the common-law distinctions between principals and accessories have been abolished in modern codes, not every jurisdiction handles this matter in the same way. The California Penal Code provides:

> § 971. Abrogation of distinction between accessories and principals, and between principals in first and second degree; effect upon pleadings.
>
> The distinction between an accessory before the fact and a principal, and between principals in the first and second degree is abrogated; and all persons concerned in the commission of a crime, who by the operation of other provisions of this code are principals therein, shall hereafter be prosecuted, tried and punished as principals and no other facts need be alleged in any accusatory pleading against any such person than are required in an accusatory pleading against a principal.

CAL. PENAL CODE § 971 (West 1971).

An accessory after the fact is punished for a crime which is separate and distinct from the felony itself. *People v. Mitten,* 37 Cal. App. 3d 879, 112 Cal. Rptr. 713 (1974). Thus, one charged as a principal cannot be convicted by proof that he was an accessory after the fact. *People v. Zierlion,* 16 Ill. 2d 217, 157 N.E.2d 72 (1959).

In *People v. Ah Gee,* 37 Cal. App. 1, 174 P. 371 (1918), defendant and two others were separately tried for murder. Defendant was convicted of murder in the first degree after the state presented its case on two alternative theories: (1) that Ah Gee aided, abetted and assisted in the murder; (2) that Ah Gee himself actually killed the victim. The evidence was conflicting as to whether the defendant shot at the victim and missed, or whether he fired the shot which killed the victim. The court affirmed the conviction, stating that while the evidence was conflicting concerning the role which defendant had in the killing, it established that he was a principal in the killing under California Penal Code § 31, which states that "all persons concerned in the commission of a crime, whether it be felony or misdemeanor, and whether they directly commit the act constituting the offense, or aid and abet in its commission, or, not being present, have advised and encouraged its commission ... are principals in any crime so committed."...

Federal criminal law, taking basically the same approach as modern state codes, treats as a principal anyone who aids, abets, counsels, commands, induces or procures the commission of an offense.

18 UNITED STATES CODE § 2 (1976)

Principals

> (a) Whoever commits an offense against the United States or aids, abets, counsels, commands, induces or procures its commission, is punishable as a principal.

I. PARTIES — PRINCIPALS AND ACCESSORIES

(b) Whoever willfully causes an act to be done which if directly performed by him or another would be an offense against the United States, is punishable as a principal.

MODEL PENAL CODE

§ 2.06. Liability for Conduct of Another; Complicity

[The text of this section appears in Appendix A.]

COMMONWEALTH v. PERRY

Supreme Judicial Court of Massachusetts
357 Mass. 149, 256 N.E.2d 745 (1970)

QUIRICO, JUSTICE.

The defendant was found guilty by a jury on two indictments returned on May 6, 1969, alleging ... that the defendant being armed with a revolver assaulted George Salibe with intent to rob him....

At 9:30 P.M. on November 6, 1968, Kempner and Salibe were working as clerks at the Murray Kempner Company liquor store in the Dorchester district of Boston. Three men entered the store. One of the men had a gun, and they robbed Kempner of his wallet and some money and assaulted Salibe with the intent to rob him. Both clerks testified that the defendant was not one of the three robbers who entered the store, and that they had never seen him before.

The defendant did not testify.... [Police testimony based on the defendant's confession showed that] on November 6, 1968, he was at the apartment of one Carlson on Beacon Street in Boston, and that one Wiggins and Gary Murphy were also there. Wiggins and Murphy talked about holding up a liquor store later that night. Murphy had formerly been a truck driver in the area of the Kempner liquor store and he suggested that they holdup that store. They all agreed and they went to that area by public transit. The defendant had formerly lived with a sister in that area and on occasions he had made purchases at the Kempner store. In view of this he feared that he would be recognized. He therefore arranged with the other three that after the holdup they would pick him up at the Y.M.C.A. which was a block away from the store. He waited at the Y.M.C.A. for them, but they did not come. He then went to his home in Boston by the public transit system. Wiggins came to his home about 11 P.M. that evening. They discussed the holdup and Wiggins said they got no money from the store. Wiggins told him that Murphy stayed near the door with a gun and Carlson went to the register looking for money. Two or three days later the defendant met Carlson who also told him they got no money.

... There was no evidence whether the Y.M.C.A. was on the same street as the liquor store, or whether it was possible to see from one place to the other.

....

There was evidence that the defendant knew the three persons who entered the liquor store and committed the robbery and assault, that he associated with them, and that he was in their company both before and after the robbery. But that, without more, is not enough to convict the defendant on either charge. There can be no finding of guilt by association....

There was also evidence that the defendant knew before the robbery and assault that Carlson, Wiggins and Murphy were going to the liquor store to commit those crimes, and that he knew later that they had committed them. But mere knowledge that a crime is to be committed, even when coupled with subsequent concealment of the completed crime, does not make one guilty as an accessory before the fact or as a principal to the crime about which he has knowledge....

The Commonwealth's evidence is also deficient in that it does not show that the defendant counseled, hired or otherwise procured the three other persons to commit the robbery or the assault with intent to rob, or that he did any other act which would make him an accessory before the fact to such crimes. It appears that it was Murphy who counseled and procured the others to rob the liquor store. Moreover, the Commonwealth made no showing that there was an agreement for the defendant to stand by, at or near the scene of the crimes to render aid, assistance or encouragement to the perpetrators if it became necessary, or to assist them in making their escape from the scene. Finally, there was no showing that he was in any location or position where he could aid in any way in the commission of the crimes.... He did not act as a lookout or decoy for the perpetrators of the crimes. He had no car or other means by which he could assist them to escape....

There may possibly be enough evidence to warrant the jury in finding that the defendant conspired with Carlson, Wiggins and Murphy to commit the robbery and the assault charged in the indictments. But even that, without more, would not be sufficient to convict the defendant on the basis that he was either an accessory before the fact or a principal to the substantive crimes charged. If the defendant agreed with the other persons to commit the crimes of robbery and assault and did nothing more, he is guilty of criminal conspiracy; but he was not charged with that crime. That alone does not make him an accessory before the fact or a principal to the substantive crime which was the objective of the conspiracy.... [Exceptions sustained. Judgment for defendant.]

NOTES

1. In *Commonwealth v. Benders,* 361 Mass. 704, 282 N.E.2d 405 (1972), the defendant was convicted of assault and battery with a dangerous weapon. Defendant and two companions stole ice cream and candy from a store, and when pursued by the owner, defendant's companions assaulted the owner and struck him with an empty bottle. Defendant did not strike the victim, and the evidence indicated that he may have attempted to intervene. The trial court refused to give an instruction to the effect that defendant's mere presence at the scene was insufficient to establish his liability as an accomplice, and that there must be shown to have been "an active engagement in the common enterprise." Defendant excepted to the refusal to give the charge. *Held:* exceptions sustained. "In these circumstances it was essential to conviction that the defendant and his companions were jointly engaged in the commission of the assault and that the defendant associated himself with that venture and participated to some extent in the commission of that offence.... But mere presence at the commission of the wrongful act and even failure to take affirmative steps to prevent it do not render a person liable as a participant." 361 Mass. at 706-707, 282 N.E.2d at 408. *Accord People v. Turner,* 86 Cal. App. 2d 791, 195 P.2d 809 (1948).

2. Appellant was celebrating at a New Year's Eve party when catsup was spilled on her dress. Thinking that the victim had spilled the catsup, she importuned her boyfriend to "do something about it," and that he "didn't love her if he wouldn't defend her and take up for her." Her boyfriend subsequently called the victim outside, argued with him, then took a pistol from his pocket and killed the victim. Appellant was convicted of third degree murder on the theory that she had urged, procured, or counseled her boyfriend to murder. *Held:* conviction reversed. "No evidence was adduced to show that appellant intended that Bryan kill Klikna. At best, the inference as to appellant's intent when she egged Bryan to 'do something about it' was that she wanted Bryan to engage in fisticuffs with Klikna.... But, this falls a far cry short of harboring an intent that Bryan kill the deceased. There was no evidence that she aided in the killing; nor that she counseled the killing; nor that she abetted or procured 'such offense ... to be committed.'..." *Casey v. State,* 266 So. 2d 366, 367 (Fla. Dis. Ct. App. 1972).

3. An accessory before the fact or aider and abettor usually will be convicted of the same offense as the principal. This is not invariably the case. In *Moore v. Lowe,* 116 W. Va. 165, 180 S.E. 1 (1935), defendant, the instigator, was convicted of manslaughter although the principal had been convicted of murder.

> The matter is clearly discussed in WHARTON'S CRIMINAL LAW (12th ed.), §§ 269 and 276. In the latter section the author says:
>
> "Under the old law, the defendant was first convicted, and then the accessory was charged with being accessory to the offense which the conviction covered. But now that instigation is a substantive offense, it must be remembered that the offense of the instigator is not necessarily of the same grade as that of the perpetrator. The instigator may act in hot blood, in which case he will be guilty only of manslaughter, while the perpetrator may act coolly, and thus be guilty of murder. The converse, also, may be true; the instigation may be cool and deliberate, the execution in hot blood by a person whom the instigator finds in a condition of unreasoning frenzy. A person desiring coolly to get rid of an enemy, for instance, may employ as a tool someone whom that enemy has aggrieved, and who is infuriated by his grievance. Hence an accessory before the fact (or, to adopt the terms of recent codes, an instigator) may be guilty of murder, while the principal (or perpetrator) may be guilty of manslaughter; or the accessory before the fact (instigator), acting in hot blood, may be guilty of manslaughter, while the perpetrator (principal), acting with deliberate malice, may be guilty of murder." The author uses "instigator" as synonymous with "accessory before the fact." Vide, Section 268.

180 S.E. at 2.

4. The accessory before the fact may be convicted of a lower degree of crime, *supra* note 1, or of a higher degree, depending on the mental element which is proved at the trial of the accessory. In *Oaks v. Patterson,* 278 F. Supp. 703 (D. Colo. 1968), the principal was a 15-year-old youth who fired a shotgun through a storefront window, killing the proprietor. In a separate trial he pleaded guilty to voluntary manslaughter, claiming that the defendant forced him to attempt a robbery of the store by threatening to kill his mother. The defendant, accessory before the fact, was subsequently tried and convicted of first degree murder.

5. In *United States v. Bryan,* 483 F.2d 88 (3d Cir. 1973), appellant and Echols were tried in a nonjury trial. The indictments charged that Echols committed the theft and that Bryan aided and abetted Echols. The evidence revealed that Echols was a mere innocent dupe and he was acquitted. Bryan, who was convicted, argued on appeal that he could not be guilty. Affirmed. " 'It is not [the] prerequisite to the conviction of the aider and abettor that the principal be tried and convicted or in fact even be identified.... Each participant in an illegal venture is required to stand on his own two feet.' " *Id.* at 93.

The court observed "that the distinction between aiders and abettors and principals in cases such as this is to a great extent semantic. Is the driver of the truck the principal because of his physical contact with the stolen goods? Or should he be viewed as the aider and abettor because the plan for taking the goods was conceived by another person? Conversely, is the man who engineered the theft the principal, or rather the aider and abettor? ... Such semantic difficulties were largely eliminated from the Federal Criminal Code by passage of 18 U.S.C. § 2, which makes aiders and abettors punishable as principals." *Id.* at 95.

6. *See* the discussion of *actus reus, supra* Chapter 2, section 2.

UNITED STATES v. RUFFIN
United States Court of Appeals
613 F.2d 408 (2d Cir. 1979)

MANSFIELD, CIRCUIT JUDGE:

William Ruffin appeals from a judgment of the District Court for the Eastern District of New York entered by Judge Mark A. Costantino on September 29, 1978, following a jury trial, convicting Ruffin of three counts charging that he and his co-defendant Olga Defreitas had obtained by fraud from Community Sponsors Inc., Young Mothers Training Program (YMP) monies that were the subject of federal financing under the Economic Opportunity Act of 1964 as amended, all in violation of 42 U.S.C. § 2703. Ruffin was acquitted of a fourth count charging him and Defreitas, YMP's director, with conspiracy in violation of 18 U.S.C. § 371 to obtain the monies by fraud. A fifth count, charging both defendants with a substantive violation of § 2703 was dismissed before the case was submitted to the jury. Appellant's co-defendant Defreitas was acquitted of the four counts submitted to the jury.

The central issue raised on this appeal is whether a person incapable of personally committing a specified crime (in this case because he was not an officer, director, agent or employee of an agency receiving federal financial assistance) who causes an innocent agent meeting the capacity requirements to engage in the proscribed conduct may be punished as a principal under 18 U.S.C. § 2. We hold that he may and affirm.

[The statute under which Ruffin and Defreitas were prosecuted prohibited officers, agents or employees of agencies which received funds under the Economic Opportunity Act of 1964 from embezzling, misapplying, stealing or obtaining by fraud any funds allocated to the agency under the Act. Defreitas was the executive director of an agency which received federal funds. Ruffin, her friend, had no official connection with the agency. Defreitas obtained authority from her board to lease property owned by Ruffin. The property was uninhabitable and unusable for any purpose.]

Although Defreitas was the only defendant who was a "director" and "employee" of an agency receiving federal funds, each of the substantive counts charged that the two defendants jointly, without distinction between them, engaged in the alleged conduct in violation of 42 U.S.C. § 2703 and of 18 U.S.C. § 2, which provides as follows:

> (a) Whoever commits an offense against the United States or aids, abets, counsels, commands, induces or procures its commission, is punishable as a principal.
> (b) Whoever willfully causes an act to be done which if directly performed by him or another would be an offense against the United States, is punishable as a principal.

Discussion

To the extent that Ruffin was charged under 18 U.S.C. § 2(a) as an "aider" and "abettor" of Defreitas' alleged criminal conduct, he could not be found guilty unless Defreitas as a principal had violated 42 U.S.C. § 2703. It is hornbook law that a defendant charged with aiding and abetting the commission of a crime by another cannot be convicted in the absence of proof that the crime was actually committed.

The failure to prosecute or obtain a prior conviction of a principal, such as where he may have been granted immunity or pleaded to a lesser offense, does not preclude conviction of the aider and abettor, as long as the commission of the crime by a principal is proved. Indeed the Third Circuit has recently held that the prior acquittal of the principal in a separate trial does not bar conviction of the aider and abettor if the second jury finds that the principal committed the crime. *United States v. Standefer,* 610 F.2d 1076 (3d Cir. Aug. 12, 1979, Dkt. 78-1909) (en banc).*

It is equally clear that under 18 U.S.C. § 2(b) one who causes another to commit a criminal act may be found guilty as a principal even though the agent who committed the act is innocent or acquitted.... ("It is a general principle of causation in criminal law that an individual (with the necessary intent) may be held liable if he is a cause in fact of the criminal violation, even though the result which the court condemns is achieved through the actions of

---

*Affirmed, Standefer v. United States, 447 U.S. 10 (1980) — Eds.

innocent intermediaries"); *United States v. Ordner,* 554 F.2d 24, 29 (2d Cir.), *cert. denied,* 434 U.S. 824 (1977).

Applying these principles here, the acquittal of Defreitas by the same jury which convicted Ruffin precludes a finding under 18 U.S.C. § 2(a) that Ruffin aided and abetted her commission of the alleged crime, since the jury's verdict amounts to a finding that she had not been proven beyond a reasonable doubt to have knowingly and wilfully committed it. Had Ruffin acted alone, without using Defreitas as an intermediary, he obviously could not have been found guilty of violating 42 U.S.C. § 2703, since he was never an "officer, director, agent or employee of, or connected in any capacity with, any agency receiving financial assistance," the only category of persons to whom the criminal sanction of § 2703 directly applies. However, the record in this case would permit an inference that Ruffin *caused* Defreitas, a person within this category, to engage in the alleged criminal conduct. The issue before us, therefore, narrows down to whether one who would be incapable of violating that law if he acted alone (i.e., Ruffin) may nevertheless be found guilty where he causes the prohibited conduct to be committed by another who has the capacity to violate it (in this case Defreitas) but who has been acquitted. We are persuaded that such a "causer" may be found guilty under § 2(b).

One purpose of 18 U.S.C. § 2 is to enlarge the scope of criminal liability under existing substantive criminal laws so that a person who operates from behind the scenes may be convicted even though he is not expressly prohibited by the substantive statute from engaging in the acts made criminal by Congress. Where the principal is found guilty of a criminal offense, for instance, it is undisputed that a person may be convicted as an aider and abettor under 18 U.S.C. § 2(a) even though he may lack the capacity to violate the substantive criminal statute. We see no logical reason why a person who causes an innocent agent having the capacity to commit a criminal act to do so should not likewise be held criminally responsible under 18 U.S.C. § 2(b) even though the causer lacks the capacity.

Indeed Congress in 1951 amended 18 U.S.C. § 2(b) to insure that a person who manipulates another may not escape criminal responsibility because the manipulator lacks capacity.

Congress, however, removed any doubt about such a person's criminal responsibility by adopting the Act of October 31, 1951, ch. 655, § 17b which, in part, amended, 18 U.S.C. § 2(b) to add the words "or another" so that it now reads:

> (b) Whoever willfully causes an act to be done which if directly performed by him *or another* would be an offense against the United States, is punishable as a principal. (Emphasis added).

The addition of the words "or another" is therefore significant for present purposes because they render criminally liable a person causing another to commit criminal acts where the other, even though innocent, has the capacity to do so and the defendant does not. Prior to the 1951 amendment of § 2(b) it could be argued that in such a case the person causing the criminal act (in this case Ruffin) to be committed by such an innocent agent (in this case Defreitas) could not be punished as a principal for the reason that the act, "if directly performed by him," would not "be an offense against the United States" since he did not fit the description of those persons expressly covered by the substantive statute (i.e., he was not a director, officer or employee). As amended, however, the phrase "which if directly performed ... *by another* would be an offense against the United States" (emphasis added) covers the present case since the criminal act, if committed by "another" (i.e., Defreitas), would be such an offense, even though the other lacked the intent to commit the crime.

Indeed it would be rather incongruous to hold that one lacking the capacity to commit a crime may be held criminally responsible as an "aider and abettor" under 18 U.S.C. § 2(a) but not as a "causer" under § 2(b). In both instances the person committing the criminal act may provide the necessary capacity, whether or not that person has the *mens rea*. In causing an innocent intermediary to commit a criminal act, the causer adopts not only the intermediary's act but his capacity. Moreover, if the causer were required to possess the capacity fixed by the substantive statute, the addition of the words "or another" to § 2(b) would be meaningless surplusage, *see United States v. Menasche,* 348 U.S. 528, 538-39, 75 S.Ct. 513, 99 L.Ed. 615 (1955), since the language of the statute before the 1951 amendment would always have been sufficient to hold him criminally responsible for causing the commission by an innocent intermediary of an act "which if *directly performed by him* would be an offense against the United States." (Emphasis added).

WYATT, DISTRICT JUDGE (dissenting):
Respectfully and with regret, I dissent from the decision expressed in Judge Mansfield's thoughtful opinion. The evidence is more than sufficient to show that Ruffin committed a big fraud and that he should be punished. I do not believe, however, that he can properly be punished in a federal court by conviction for a violation as a principal of 42 U.S.C. § 2971f(a) (formerly 42 U.S.C. § 2703), limited as that section is to those "connected in any capacity" with an agency receiving financial assistance under the Economic Opportunity Act of 1964. Admittedly, Ruffin was not so "connected."

. . . .

There was thus no intention by Section 2(b) to change what had been the law theretofore. If a person uses an innocent intermediary to commit a crime, that person is guilty not as an aider and abettor but as a principal in the first degree. If, however, the offense is one which can only be committed by a specified class of persons — bank employees under 18 U.S.C. § 656, for example — a defendant who uses an innocent intermediary can be prosecuted only if he or she is a member of the specified class. *United States v. Giles,* 300 U.S. 41 (1937), is a good example of the use of an innocent intermediary. A statute made it an offense for an employee of a national bank to make a false entry in its books. Giles was such an employee and was indicted for having made a false entry; he was indicted as a principal. The evidence showed that Giles was a teller who received deposits but held back the records thereof from the bookkeepers, thereby causing the entries by them in the relevant books to be false. Giles argued that he could not be guilty because "[p]ersonally he made no such entry; he did not affirmatively direct one" (300 U.S. at 49). The Supreme Court held that the evidence established his guilt because the substantive statute was "broad enough to include deliberate action from which a false entry by an innocent intermediary necessarily follows." 300 U.S. at 48. *Giles, however, was a bank employee;* he could not otherwise have been prosecuted.

It seems entirely clear to me that a person who lacks the capacity to commit a substantive offense may be prosecuted as an "aider and abettor" under Section 2(a) if there is proof that a principal who did have the capacity was guilty of the offense. At the same time, a person who lacks the capacity to commit a substantive offense may not be prosecuted as a causer under Section 2(b) using an innocent intermediary who does have the capacity. This is not so "incongruous" as the majority thinks. On the contrary, it is the reasonable and logical consequence of settled rules of criminal law, deriving from the classification at common law of parties to crimes and the reasons for that classification.

Before there can be any conviction for any felony offense, there must be at least one guilty principal in the first degree. Where the substantive offense is limited to a specified class — agency employees in the case at bar, bank officers, etc. in 18 U.S.C. § 656 and the like — and an outsider is indicted as an aider and abettor under 18 U.S.C. § 2(a), it is essential for the government to prove that the offense was committed by a principal who, by definition, had the capacity to be such. This was explained in *United States v. Giordano,* 489 F.2d 327, 330 (2d Cir. 1973):

> Cases in which customers of a bank are charged with aiding and abetting a bank officer willfully to misapply money or credit of the bank, 18 U.S.C. § 656, are generally troublesome....
>
> The depositor, not being "connected in any capacity" with the bank cannot be guilty of violating 18 U.S.C. § 656 as a principal.
>
> ....
>
> He can, however, be charged as an accessory under 18 U.S.C. § 2. He may not be convicted as an accessory, however, unless the bank officer, as a principal is himself guilty of violating Section 656.

Where the substantive offense is limited to a specified class, and the causer is not a member of the class, but the innocent intermediary is a member of the class, there can be no conviction of the causer as a principal, by the use of Section 2(b) together with the substantive statute. The causer cannot be a principal because of lack of capacity. The intermediary cannot be a principal because, though possessing capacity, he or she is innocent. Without a principal there can be no violation of the substantive statute.*

NOTES

1. The government would have us believe that the "crimes charged" here are aiding and abetting the possession of heroin with intent to distribute, and that of conspiracy to possess heroin with the intent to distribute.

---

* "In short, one cannot be found guilty of aiding and abetting an official of a carrier if the official is himself not guilty of the underlying offense." United States v. Gregg, 612 F.2d 43, 47 (2d Cir. 1979) — Eds.

… [W]e believe the government's position is unsupportable with respect to the "charge" of aiding and abetting possession with intent to distribute. To be sure, Count Two of the indictment here charged that "the defendant Isaac Daniels aided and abetted by the defendant Paul V. Oates knowingly and intentionally did possess with intent to distribute" heroin. Yet, the simple, although perhaps not immediately apparent, truth of the matter is that the "crime charged" here was possession with intent to distribute, not aiding and abetting possession with intent to distribute. This is so because "aiding and abetting" does not constitute a discrete criminal offense but only serves as a more particularized way of identifying the "persons involved," see *United States v. Campbell,* 426 F.2d 547, 553 (2d Cir. 1970), in the commission of the substantive offense, and serves to describe how those "person[s] involved," committed the substantive offense.

....

… 18 U.S.C. § 2 does not define a crime; rather it makes punishable as a principal one who aids or abets the commission of a substantive crime.

… In other words, one who aids and abets the commission of a crime is not only *punishable* as a principal but is a principal.

United States v. Oates, 560 F.2d 45, 54-55 (2d Cir. 1977).

2. The most well-accepted formulation of the standard of proof for aiding and abetting is that expressed by Judge Learned Hand in *United States v. Peoni,* 100 F.2d 401 (2d Cir. 1938). He wrote that the prosecution must show that the defendant "in some sort associate himself with the venture, that he participate in it as in something that he wishes to bring about, [and] that he seek by his action to make it succeed." *Id.* at 402.

The standard has two prongs — association and participation. *United States v. Greer,* 467 F.2d 1064 (7th Cir. 1972), *cert. denied,* 410 U.S. 929 (1973). To prove association, there must be evidence to establish that the defendant shared in the criminal intent of the principal, *United States v. Smith,* 546 F.2d 1275 (5th Cir. 1977), that is, the state of mind required for the statutory offense must be shown for conviction as an aider and abettor. The defendant, however, need not have the exact intent as the principal. The "community of unlawful intent" does not rise to the level of agreement. *United States v. Lozano,* 511 F.2d 1 (7th Cir.), *cert. denied,* 423 U.S. 850 (1975).

Criminal intent is often difficult to demonstrate by direct proof; it may be inferred from the attendant facts and circumstances. *United States v. Groomer,* 596 F.2d 356, 358 (9th Cir. 1979).

A high level of activity need not be shown to prove participation, the second prong. "The defendant need not have participated in every phase of the criminal venture." *United States v. Diecidue,* 603 F.2d 535, 557 (5th Cir. 1979). Instead, "there must be evidence to establish that the defendant engaged in some affirmative conduct; that is, there must be evidence that [the] defendant committed an overt act designed to aid in the success of the venture." *United States v. Longoria,* 569 F.2d 422, 425 (5th Cir. 1978).

United States v. Beck, 615 F.2d 441, 448-49 (7th Cir. 1980).

3. In the case of *Regina v. Lynch*, the court of criminal appeal observed that a principal in the first degree may be convicted upon proof of "'(a) participation and (b) knowledge that the probable result will be death or serious bodily injury." (citing *Hyam v. D.P.P.*). The court opined that if in *Hyam* "a friend had supplied petrol and matches to Mrs. Hyam or driven her to the scene, or both, in any case knowing that death or serious personal injury was likely to result" then the same instruction should be given to the jury on participation and knowledge as is given in the case of a principal in the first degree. 1975 N. Ir. 35, 53.

> We conclude that, when presence and physical participation are proved, the only element remaining to be established is knowledge that the acts which are to be done will probably result in the death or serious personal injury of a third person. If intention has to be proved, then it is enough to prove intent to assist and this is done ... by proving participation together with the knowledge already mentioned.

Id. at 57. One judge dissented:

> In *National Coal Board v. Gamble* [1959] 1 Q.B. 11, Devlin J. in his judgment at page 20, discusses the essential elements of aiding and abetting:
>
>> A person who supplies the instrument for a crime, or anything essential to its commission aids in the commission of it; and if he does so knowingly and with intent to aid, he abets it as well and is therefore guilty of aiding and abetting.
>
> Again at p. 20 he says:
>
>> Another way of putting the point is to say that aiding and abetting is a crime that requires proof of mens rea, that is to say, of intention to aid as well as of knowledge of the circumstances, and that proof of the intent involves proof of a positive act of assistance voluntarily done.
>
> The word "voluntarily" in this passage should be noted.
>
> In my view assistance plus knowledge is not in itself sufficient to constitute aiding and abetting. Something more is required, namely mens rea.

1975 N. Ir. 60.

4. Is there a difference between "aiding" and "abetting"?

> The word "aid" means "to assist, 'to supplement the efforts of another.'" *People v. Bond,* 13 Cal. App. 175, 185, 109 P.150, 155. "The word 'aid' does not imply guilty knowledge or felonious intent, whereas the definition of the word 'abet' includes knowledge of the wrongful purpose of the perpetrator and counsel and encouragement in the crime." *People v. Dole,* 122 Cal. 486, 492, 55 P. 581, 584. "To 'abet' another in the commission of a crime implies a consciousness of guilt in instigating, encouraging, promoting or aiding the commission of such criminal offense." *People v. Best,* 43 Cal. App. 2d 100, 105, 110 P.2d 504, 507. An aider and abettor is

"guilty only to the extent (1) of his knowledge or (2) of the natural and reasonable consequences of the acts which he aided or encouraged."
People v. Etie, 119 Cal. App. 2d 23, 258 P.2d 1069, 1072 (1953).

5. Agency theories, although exceptions to the general body of criminal law, are occasionally used to extend criminal responsibility to someone who did not himself perpetrate the offense. There is a "procuring agent" theory recognized in some jurisdictions which seems to limit the level of criminal responsibility. In *People v. Roche,* 45 N.Y.2d 78, 379 N.E.2d 208, 407 N.Y.S. 2d 682, *cert. denied,* 439 U.S. 958 (1978), the court held that the underlying theory of the agency defense in drug cases is that one who acts as procuring agent for the buyer alone is a principal or conspirator in the purchase rather than the sale of the contraband. The defense is not available to a middleman who furthers his own interests by serving both buyer and seller, or to one who has some interest in the property or who is an agent of the seller. 379 N.E.2d at 211. The agency defense is not available against a charge of "possession" of drugs.

6. *Can one aid and abet a negligent or reckless act?* In *People v. Pitts,* 84 Mich. App. 656, 270 N.W.2d 482 (1978), defendant argued that a person could not aid or abet a negligent act, in this case reckless discharge of a firearm resulting in death. Conviction affirmed. "[I]n crimes involving lack of care rather than intent, there is no reason to require the latter. It is sufficient if defendant performs acts that aid in the creation of the circumstances or participates in an enterprise, the scope being such that the result is reasonably foreseeable." 270 N.W.2d at 484.

EDITORIAL NOTE ON "KNOWLEDGE"

There is some dispute whether knowingly facilitating the commission of a crime is sufficient to establish accomplice liability in the absence of a purpose to advance the criminal end. Note the similar problem for conspiratorial liability, *infra.* Judge Learned Hand, in *United States v. Peoni,* 100 F.2d 401 (2d Cir. 1938) expressed the view that mere knowledge of a criminal purpose is insufficient for accomplice liability, that there must be a purpose to advance the criminal end. The contrary view was expressed in *Backun v. United States,* 112 F.2d 635, 637 (4th Cir. 1940), where Judge Parker commented that: "One who sells a gun to another knowing that he is buying it to commit a murder, would hardly escape conviction as an accessory to the murder by showing that he received full price for the gun." The early drafts of the Model Penal Code proposed establishing complicity for knowingly rendering substantial aid towards the commission of a crime. The Code ultimately adopted the *Peoni* limitation of "aid with purpose." § 2.06(3)(a). In codifying the Model Penal Code recommendation, New York Penal Law § 20.00 (McKinney 1975) facilitators are punished under the provisions of §§ 115.00 and 115.05 of the Penal Law.

Should it make any difference in resolving the "knowledge" issue if defendant "counseled" or "advised" the principal as to how to commit a crime with no interest in whether the advice or counsel was acted on, or if defendant merely complied with the principal's request for assistance knowing of the principal's purpose but having no interest in whether the principal succeeds? For example, should less be required in terms of "shared purpose" when a person encourages and counsels the principal by providing specific information as to how to commit a complex crime than when a person sells a car to the principal which he or she knows is going to be used to facilitate the commission of a crime? See United States v. Barnett, 667 F.2d 835 (9th Cir. 1982).

See the discussion of *mens rea, supra* Chapter 2, section 1.

NOTES ON ACCESSORIES AFTER THE FACT

1. To be an accessory after the fact requires an affirmative act which reveals an intention to aid the offender to escape arrest, conviction or punishment. Merely denying knowledge of a crime or the whereabouts of the suspect motivated by self-interest will not support a conviction. However, where a person lies to law enforcement officers in order to give the suspect a false alibi, a conviction is proper. *State v. Clifford,* 263 Or. 436, 502 P.2d 1371 (1972).

2. On June 6, Bud Hicks deliberately shot and wounded Thompson Hooker, and fled in an automobile driven by the defendant. Later the same day, defendant and several others attempted to provide a false alibi for Hicks prior to his arrest by police. After all these events, Hooker died on June 7 as a consequence of the gunshot wounds. The defendant was convicted of being an accessory after the fact to the murder. *Held:* conviction reversed. Defendant cannot be convicted of being an accessory after the fact to a felony until the felony has been committed. "Thus, it is held that a person cannot be convicted as an accessory after the fact to a murder because he aided the murderer to escape, when the aid was rendered after the mortal wound was given, but before death ensued, as a murder is not complete until the death results...." The statute provided for punishment of an accessory after the fact to *any felony,* but since no such charge was made in the indictment, the court refrained from expressing an opinion whether the evidence would have supported a conviction for being an accessory after the fact to "secret assault" or assault with intent to kill. *State v. Williams,* 229 N.C. 348, 349, 49 S.E.2d 617, 618 (1948).

3. Mere failure on the part of a witness to a felony, or of one who knows of the commission of a felony, to apprehend the perpetrator or to bring him or her to justice, constitutes the misdemeanor of misprision of felony. See 18 U.S.C. § 4 (1976). Entering into an agreement with anybody, for a valuable consideration, not to prosecute any person for a felony actually committed, or to withhold evidence of felony, constitutes the misdemeanor of compounding a felony. See CAL. PENAL CODE § 153 (West 1971).

MODEL PENAL CODE

§ 242.3. Hindering Apprehension or Prosecution
§ 242.4. Aiding Consummation of Crime
§ 242.5. Compounding

[The text of these sections appears in Appendix A.]

SECTION II. Criminal Liability of Corporations
EDITORIAL NOTE

The subjection of corporations to criminal liability is usually defended on the grounds of deterrence. Note, *Developments in the Law, Corporate Crime: Regulating Corporate Behavior Through Criminal Sanctions*, 92 HARV. L. REV. 1227, 1235 (1978-79) [hereinafter cited as *Developments — Corporate Crime*]. This raises a question of fact. However, the application of the principles of criminal law to "corporate acts" has its share of difficulties. Our criminal law historically was shaped to deal with the crimes of private persons, not complex organizations. Analogizing the corporate person with the natural person creates problems in the areas of *mens rea* and punishment. Friedman, *Some Reflections on the Corporation as a Criminal Defendant*, 55 NOTRE DAME LAW. 173 (1979-80); Braithwaite, *Inegalitarian Consequences of Egalitarian Reforms to Control Corporate Crime*, 53 TEMP. L.Q. 1127, 1130 (1980).

In the wake of this "personalization" of the corporation no comprehensive theory of corporate crime has emerged. For example, no distinctions exist as a matter of law between small family corporations and massive, publicly owned corporations. The problems are compounded because corporate activity includes violations of laws which deal with matters such as antitrust, taxation, securities regulation, environment, health, conservation and consumer protection. "Thus, an informed and intelligent analysis on the general problems of corporate criminal justice administration is retarded by the inherent complexity of a field which requires legal sophistication in a broad range of highly technical areas of law." Orland, *Reflections on Corporate Crime: Law in Search of Theory and Scholarship*, 17 AM. CRIM. L. REV. 501, 504 (1980). The legal approach to corporate crime has often been characterized by the use of strict liability offenses and the reliance on principal-agent rules which have been developed in tort law. See p. 733 *supra*.

A corporation can only act through its officers, agents and employees thereby creating questions as to when it should be held criminally responsible for those acts. When should there be a departure from the usual rule which refuses to apply the doctrine of *respondeat superior* in criminal cases? The subject is given comprehensive treatment in Elkins, *Corporations and the Criminal Law: An Uneasy Alliance*, 65 KY. L.J. 73 (1976).

At common law, a corporation could not be indicted for a crime. 1 W. BLACKSTONE COMMENTARIES 476. Social policy and the prevention of the unjust enrichment of the corporation led to the view that a corporation could be convicted of an offense *malum prohibitum* committed by an employee of the corporation acting in the course and scope of his or her employment. Such liability is imputed through the doctrine of *respondeat superior*. *United States v. E. Brooke Matlack, Inc.*, 149 F. Supp. 814 (D. Md. 1957). The purpose of a regulation prohibiting the carrying of poisonous materials in interstate commerce without the proper labelling of the transport vehicle is to protect the public and provide for punishment of offending businesses. Thus, although there is no evidence of knowledge or intent on the part of directors or officers to violate the regulation, the knowing violation of an employee acting within the course and scope of employment will be imputed to the corporation. *United*

States v. Chicago Express, Inc., 273 F.2d 751 (7th Cir. 1960). There is some authority that the act of the employee will not be imputed to the corporation when the unlawful conduct does not benefit the corporation. "[T]o say that acts done by servants ... were the acts of the very corporations thus sought to be cheated ... would be to disregard every accepted notion of *respondeat superior*." *Standard Oil Co. v. United States*, 307 F.2d 120, 129 (5th Cir. 1962).

Imposition of criminal liability on the corporation for offenses *mala in se* requires that the requisite *mens rea* be imputed to the corporation. The decisions depend upon whether the acts of the corporate employee may be considered to represent the policy of the corporation.

Where acts are committed by members of a corporation's "inner-circle," i.e., officers and managerial agents such as middle management and supervisory personnel, their intent will be imputed to the corporation. As to subordinate employees, where they are ordered or authorized to act by a member of the "inner-circle" or where their acts are acquiesced in by corporate officers or supervisory personnel, the corporation again will be held responsible.

Where there is no "link" to the "inner-circle" most courts, including the federal courts, use a "functional" test in which the criminal act and intent of an employee while performing a function delegated to him will be imputed to the corporation. Under this view *respondeat superior* serves as the basis for determining corporate liability for the acts of all employees. *Elkins, supra,* at 100-08. See also Note, Corporate Homicide: A New Assault on Corporate Decision-Making, 54 NOTRE DAME LAW. 911 (1978-79); Developments — Corporate Crime, *supra,* at 1247-51.

"The general rule now established in the federal courts is that the status of the actor within the corporate hierarchy is not determinative of whether the individual may bring criminal sanctions upon the corporation and that no 'link' is required between the subordinate actor and the 'inner-circle.'" *Elkins, supra,* at 106. See also Developments — Corporate Crime, *supra,* at 1247.

> In general, the federal courts have not attempted to distinguish between welfare offenses and common law crimes such as conspiracy, fraud, and extortion, which have been codified. The courts have employed the same functional test in each case to determine the scope of liability; that is, whether the criminal act was committed within the scope of employment.

Elkins, supra, at 125.

As to crimes *mala in se* which require a specific intent, the Model Penal Code would allow conviction of the corporation if the "commission of the offense was authorized, requested, commanded, performed or recklessly tolerated by the board of directors or by a high managerial agent acting in behalf of the corporation within the scope of his office or employment." § 2.07 (1)(c) (Proposed Official Draft). That position was adopted in *State v. Adjustment Dep't Credit Bureau*, 94 Idaho 156, 483 P.2d 687 (1971). Compare *Commonwealth v. Beneficial Fin. Co.*, 360 Mass. 188, 275 N.E.2d 33 (1971), cert. denied, 407 U.S. 910 (1972), affirming a corporation' conviction for bribery and conspiracy where over a period of seven years the officers and employees of three small loan companies had committed the criminal acts. The court held that criminal responsibility could be imputed to the corporation if the employees were placed in a position of power, responsibility and authority by the corporation. The factors to be considered include the authority of the corporate agent in relation to the offending corporate business, the extent and manner of the use of corporate funds, and the repetition of the conduct.

In *People v. Canadian Fur Trappers' Corp.*, 248 N.Y. 159, 169, 161 N.E. 455, 458 (1928), employees of defendant corporation accepted a $25 deposit on the purchase price of a fur coat from a customer. When the customer later tendered payment in full for the coat, the coat supposedly held for her by the employees had been resold by them. The employees attempted to deliver another coat to the customer, which had been purchased by still another customer and was to be held for him until payment was tendered. The corporation was convicted of grand larceny and fined $5,000. *Held:* judgment reversed. "[T]he defendant corporation was criminally liable only for such felonious acts as it had authorized through the [employees], the officers of the corporation, or for such acts as through a course of business must have been known to the corporation and its officers, and thus authorized by them. The people failed to prove that the officers or any one acting as manager of the Buffalo store, in the place and stead of the officers, had authorized a resale of the complainant's coat; and further that, if the complainant's coat was resold, the resale of purchased coats was a continuous and established practice in the defendant's establishment."

The position adopted by the Model Penal Code and cases which follow that approach has been characterized by Elkins as the "minority view." The majority approach is supported in Seney, *"A Pond as Deep as Hell," Harm, Danger, and Dangerousness in our Criminal Law,* 18 WAYNE L. REV. 569 (1972). The minority view is espoused in Mueller, *Mens Rea and the Corporation,* 19 U. PITT. L. REV. 21 (1957).

As an alternative to these approaches it has been suggested that corporate criminal responsibility should be predicated "on the reasonableness of the corporation's practices and procedures to avert illegal conduct.... The corporation should be required to demonstrate that it employed two kinds of precautions: first, that the illegal conduct had been clearly and convincingly forbidden, and second, that reasonable safeguards designed to prevent corporate crimes had been developed and implemented, including regular procedures for evaluation, detection, and remedy." *Developments — Corporate Crime,* at 1257-58. As an example of this kind of approach, the Texas Penal Code provides that "It is an affirmative defense to prosecution of a corporation or association... that the high managerial agent having supervisory responsibility over the subject matter of the offense employed due diligence to prevent its commission." TEX. PENAL CODE ANN. § 7.24 (West 1975). A "high managerial agent" is defined as a partner in a partnership, an officer of a corporation or association, or an agent of a corporation or association who has duties of such responsibility that his conduct reasonably may be assumed to represent the policy of the corporation or association. TEX. PENAL CODE ANN. § 7.21(2) (West 1973).

Not considered in this section are the policy considerations for imposing criminal liability on corporations and their officers under federal laws which enforce economic regulations. It is indisputable that societal harms which result from antitrust violations, price fixing, industrial pollution and consumer fraud go far beyond the harm resulting from crimes against individuals, which are considered in this section.

MODEL PENAL CODE

§ 2.07. Liability of Corporations, Unincorporated Associations and Persons Acting, or Under a Duty to Act, in Their Behalf.

[The text of this section appears in Appendix A.]

PROPOSED CRIMINAL CODE REFORM ACT OF 1981, § 1630, 97th Congress, 1st Session (1981)

§ 402. Liability of an Organization for Conduct of an Agent

Except as otherwise expressly provided, an organization is criminally liable for an offense if the conduct constituting the offense —

(a) is conduct of its agent, and such conduct —
(1) occurs in the performance of matters within the scope of the agent's employment, or authority, and is intended by the agent to benefit the organization; or
(2) is thereafter ratified or adopted by the organization; or
(b) involves a failure by the organization or its agent to discharge a specific duty of conduct imposed on the organization by law.

§ 403. Liability of an Agent for Conduct of an Organization

(a) Conduct on Behalf of an Organization. — Except as otherwise expressly provided, a person is criminally liable for an offense based upon conduct that he engages in or causes in the name of an organization or on behalf of an organization to the same extent as if he engaged in or caused the conduct in his own name or on his own behalf.

EDITORIAL NOTE ON PERSONAL LIABILITY FOR CORPORATE ACTS

The fact that a corporation may or may not be held criminally responsible for acts committed on behalf of the corporation does not preclude prosecution of the person who committed those acts.

§ 7.23. Criminal Responsibility of Person for Conduct in Behalf of Corporation or Association.

(a) An individual is criminally responsible for conduct that he performs in the name of or in behalf of a corporation or association to the same extent as if the conduct were performed in his own name or behalf.
(b) An agent having primary responsibility for the discharge of a duty to act imposed by law on a corporation or association is criminally responsible for omission to discharge the duty to the same extent as if the duty were imposed by law directly on him.

(c) If an individual is convicted of conduct constituting an offense performed in the name of or on behalf of a corporation or association, he is subject to the sentence authorized by law for an individual convicted of the offense.

TEX. PENAL CODE ANN. § 7.23 (West 1973). Under what circumstances should a corporate officer or employee be held personally responsible for criminal acts of the corporation? Ordinarily, there is no difficulty imposing liability when the defendant himself has committed the prohibited act and satisfied the required culpability.

In more complex situations of shared decisionmaking and delegation of duties, see Note, *Decisionmaking Models and the Control of Corporate Crime*, 85 YALE L.J. 1091 (1975-76). The issue of when corporate officers can be held criminally responsible for acts and omissions of subordinates is considered in *United States v. Park*, supra, pp. 695-699.

SECTION III. Solicitation

PEOPLE v. LUBOW
Court of Appeals of New York
29 N.Y.2d 58, 272 N.E.2d 331 323 N.Y.S.2d 829 (1971)

BERGAN, JUDGE.

The revised Penal Law creates a new kind of offense, simpler in structure than an attempt or a conspiracy, and resting solely on communication without need for any resulting action (art. 100, Criminal Solicitation, part of tit. G, Anticipatory Offenses, L.1965, ch. 1030) Consol.Laws, c. 40. Attempts to commit crimes and conspiracies are continued with some changes as crimes and these, too, are grouped within title G as "Anticipatory Offenses" (art. 105, Conspiracies; art. 110, Attempts).

The basic statutory definition of criminal solicitation is that with intent that another person shall "engage in conduct constituting a crime" the accused "solicits, requests, commands, importunes or otherwise attempts to cause such other person to engage in such conduct." This basic definitory language is continued through three grades of solicitation, the gravity depending on what crime the conduct sought to be induced would effectuate.

....

As it has been noted, nothing need be done under the statute in furtherance of the communication ("solicits, commands, importunes") to constitute the offense. The communication itself with intent the other person engage in the unlawful conduct is enough. It needs no corroboration.

And an attempt at communication which fails to reach the other person may also constitute the offense for the concluding clause "or otherwise attempts to cause such other person to engage in such conduct" would seem literally to embrace as an attempt an undelivered letter or message initiated with the necessary intent.

Appellants have been convicted after a trial by a three-judge panel in the Criminal Court of the City of New York of violation of section 100.05 which describes solicitation to commit a felony....

The evidence showed that complainant Silverman and both defendants were engaged in the jewelry business. It could be found that defendant Lubow owed Silverman $30,000 for diamonds on notes which were unpaid; that Lubow had told Silverman he was associated with a big operator interested in buying diamonds and introduced him to defendant Gissinger.

It could also be found that in October, 1967, Silverman met the two defendants together at their office, demanded his money, and said that because of the amount owed him he was being forced into bankruptcy.

Silverman testified in response to this Lubow said "Well, let's make it a big one, a big bankruptcy," and Gissinger said this was a good idea. When Silverman asked "how it is done" he testified that Lubow, with Gissinger participating, outlined a method by which diamonds would be purchased partly on credit, sold for less than cost, with the proceeds pyramided to boost Silverman's credit rating until very substantial amounts came in, when there was to be a bankruptcy with Silverman explaining that he had lost the cash gambling in Puerto Rico and Las Vegas. The cash would be divided among the three men. The gambling explanation for the disappearance of cash would be made to seem believable by producing credit cards for Puerto Rico and Las Vegas. Silverman testified that Lubow said "we would eventually wind up with a quarter of a million dollars each" and that Gissinger said "maybe millions."

Silverman reported this proposal to the District Attorney in October, 1967 and the following month a police detective equipped Silverman with a tape recorder concealed on his person which was in operation during conversations with defendants on November 16 and which tends to substantiate the charge....

There thus seems sufficient evidence in the record to find that defendants intended Silverman to engage in conduct constituting a felony by defrauding creditors of amounts making out grand larceny and that they importuned Silverman to engage in such conduct. Thus the proof meets the actual terms of the statute.

The statute itself is a valid exercise of legislative power. Commentators closely associated with the drafting of the Model Penal Code of the American Law Institute, from which the New York solicitation statute stems, have observed: "Purposeful solicitation presents dangers calling for preventive intervention and is sufficiently indicative of a disposition towards criminal activity to call for liability. Moreover, the fortuity that the person solicited does not agree to commit or attempt to commit the incited crime plainly should not relieve the solicitor of liability, when otherwise he would be a conspirator or an accomplice."

Solicitation to commit a felony was a misdemeanor at common law (*People v. Bush*, 4 Hill 133, 135; *Rex v. Higgins*, 2 East 5). Summarizing this historical fact Judge Cardozo observed: "So at common law, incitement to a felony, when it did not reach the stage of an attempt, was itself a separate crime, and like conspiracy, which it resembled, was a misdemeanor, not a felony." (*People v. Werblow*, 241 N.Y. 55, 66, 148 N.E. 786, 791, citing *Higgins* and *Rex v. Gregory*, L.R. 1 C.C.R. 77).

...

III. SOLICITATION

Although this Penal Law provision is the first statutory enactment in New York, there have been statutes aimed at criminal solicitation in some other states, notably California.

In commenting on the criminal solicitation enactment of article 100, two lawyers who were active in the work of the State Commission on Revision of the Penal Law and Criminal Code which prepared the present statute observed that article 100 "closes that gap" for those who believe, as apparently the commission and the American Law Institute did, that "solicitation to commit a crime involves sufficient culpability to warrant criminal sanctions."

There are, however, potential difficulties inherent in this penal provision which should be looked at, even though all of them are not decisive in this present case. One, of course, is the absence of any need for corroboration. The tape recording here tends to give some independent support to the testimony of Silverman, but there are types of criminal conduct which might be solicited where there would be a heavy thrust placed on the credibility of a single witness testifying to a conversation. Extraordinary care might be required in deciding when to prosecute; in determining the truth; and in appellate review of the factual decision.

One example would be the suggestion of one person to another that he commit a sexual offense; another is the suggestion that he commit perjury. The Model Penal Code did not require corroboration; but aside from the need for corroboration which is traditional in some sexual offenses, there are dangers in the misinterpretation of innuendos or remarks which could be taken as invitations to commit sexual offenses. These are discussed by Wechsler-Jones-Korn (61 Col.L.Rev., p. 623, *supra*) with the comment that "it is a risk implicit in the punishment of almost all inchoate crimes."....

The California statute is based on a specific list of serious crimes to which criminal solicitation expressly applies; but as to all of them the statute requires that the offense "must be proved by the testimony of two witnesses, or of one witness and corroborating circumstances."

The basic public justification for legislative enactment is, however, very similar to New York's and was developed in the *Burt* [*People v. Burt*, 45 Cal. 2d 311, 288 P.2d 503 (1955)] opinion: "Legislative concern with the proscribed soliciting is demonstrated not only by the gravity of the crimes specified but by the fact that the crime, unlike conspiracy, does not require the commission of any overt act. It is complete when the solicitation is made, and it is immaterial that the object of the solicitation is never consummated, or that no steps are taken toward its consummation." The California Legislature was concerned "not only with the prevention of the harm that would result should the inducements prove successful, but with protecting inhabitants of this state from being exposed to inducements to commit or join in the commission of the crimes specified" (45 Cal. 2d 311, *supra*, p. 314, 288 P.2d 503, p. 505).

[*Affirmed.*]

MODEL PENAL CODE

§ 5.02. Criminal Solicitation

[The text of this section appears in Appendix A.]

NOTES

1. A person cannot be guilty of both solicitation and murder when he or she hires someone to kill another. Guilt for murder is predicated on aiding and abetting, and guilt as an aider and abettor is based on the solicitation. Solicitation merges into the murder. *Lewis v. State,* 285 Md. 705, 404 A.2d 1073 (1979).

2. *See* the discussion of *actus reus, supra* Chapter 2, section 2.

3. In some jurisdictions, the solicitation must be made with the intent to commit a felony of a specified level or degree, and corroboration is required:

§ 15.03. Criminal Solicitation.

>   (a) A person commits an offense if, with intent that a capital felony or felony of the first degree be committed, he requests, commands, or attempts to induce another to engage in specific conduct that, under the circumstances surrounding his conduct as the actor believes them to be, would constitute the felony or make the other a party to its commission.
>
>   (b) A person may not be convicted under this section on the uncorroborated testimony of the person allegedly solicited and unless the solicitation is made under circumstances strongly corroborative of both the solicitation itself and the actor's intent that the other person act on the solicitation.

Tex. Penal Code Ann. § 15.03 (West 1973).

SECTION IV. Criminal Attempt

MODEL PENAL CODE

§ 5.01. Criminal Attempt

[The text of this section appears in Appendix A.]

A. THE HARM

NOTE

"[E]very attempt, although it fail of success, must create alarm, which, of itself, is an injury, and the moral guilt of the offender is the same as if he had succeeded. Moral guilt must be united to injury in order to justify punishment." I Complete Works of Edward Livingston on Criminal Jurisprudence 235 (1873).

"The spirit of any democratic government is utterly abhorrent to anything which tends to corruption in the representatives of the people, or threatens the purity of the administration of the government. And as wealth and power may become powerful forces in this dangerous direction, the protection of equal rights among the people demands that a severe penalty be visited upon any member of the community who gives, or offers to give, anything of value to any representative of the community ... as an inducement to official action. In fine, the gist of the crime is the danger and injury to the community at

B. MENS REA

large. Such being the case, attempts to bribe become clearly indictable, for the state must guard against the tendency to corrupt as well as against actual corruption, both being alike dangerous and injurious to the community at large." *Davis v. State,* 70 Tex. Crim. 524, 158 S.W. 288, 289 (1913).

B. MENS REA

RHODE v. STATE

Court of Appeals of Indiana
391 N.E.2d 666 (1979)

LOWDERMILK, PRESIDING JUDGE.

Issue

We need consider only one issue in reviewing this case: Does Indiana recognize the crime of attempted reckless homicide?

Discussion and Decision

IC 1971, 35-42-1-5 (Burns Code Ed., Repl. 1979) provides as follows:

> A person who recklessly kills another human being commits reckless homicide, a class C felony. However, if the killing results from the operation of a vehicle, the offense is a class D felony....

In arguing that our Legislature has created the crime of attempted reckless homicide, the State places emphasis upon the following portion of IC 1971, 35-41-5-1 (Burns Code Ed., Repl. 1979):

> (a) A person attempts to commit a crime when, *acting with the culpability required for commission of the crime,* he engages in conduct that constitutes a substantial step toward commission of the crime. An attempt to commit a crime is a felony or misdemeanor of the same class as the crime attempted. However, an attempt to commit murder is a class A felony.... (Our emphasis)

IC 1971, 35-41-2-2 (Burns Code Ed., Repl. 1979) provides as follows:

> Culpability. — (a) A person engages in conduct "intentionally" if, when he engages in the conduct, it is his conscious objective to do so.
> (b) A person engages in conduct "knowingly" if, when he engages in the conduct, he is aware of a high probability that he is doing so.
> (c) A person engages in conduct "recklessly" if he engages in the conduct in plain, conscious, and unjustifiable disregard of harm that might result and the disregard involves a substantial deviation from acceptable standards of conduct....

The State maintains that a person attempts reckless homicide when (a) in plain, conscious, and unjustifiable disregard of harm that might result, (b) he engages in conduct which constitutes a substantial step toward the reckless killing of another human being....

The State maintains that our Legislature departed from the element of specific intent and in its place imposed the element of the same culpability required for commission of the crime attempted: intentionally, knowingly, or recklessly.

Indiana's attempt statute includes language comparable to that found in the criminal attempt statute of the American Law Institute's Model Penal Code (§ 5.01, Tent. Draft 10, 1960):

> (1) Definition of attempt. A person is guilty of an attempt to commit a crime if, *acting with the kind of culpability otherwise required for the commission of the crime,* he: ... (Our emphasis)

In the Comments following § 5.01 we note this statement at page 27:

> As previously stated, the proposed definition of attempt follows the conventional pattern of limiting this inchoate crime to purposive conduct. In the language of the courts, there must be "intent in fact" or "specific intent" to commit the crime allegedly attempted.... (Footnote omitted)

At page 30 of the Comments appears a specific declaration that reckless conduct is not encompassed within the criminal attempt statute in the Model Penal Code.

The comments provided by the Indiana Criminal Law Study Commission include the following explanation with regard to Indiana's attempt statute:

> It is, hopefully, clear that the proposed definition of attempt limits this inchoate crime to *intentional conduct.* There must be "intent in fact" or "specific intent" to commit the crime attempted.... (Our emphasis)

Having carefully considered the State's argument, we must hold that our Legislature did not remove the element of specific intent when it drafted Indiana's present attempt statute. Justice Hunter reached this same conclusion when he wrote on behalf of the Supreme Court in the recent case of *Zickefoose v. State,* (1979) Ind., 388 N.E.2d 507, 510:

> ... Although there are somewhat varying definitions of what conduct actually constitutes an attempt, *there is fundamental agreement on the two necessary elements of the crime. First, the defendant must have been acting with a specific intent to commit the crime,* and second, he must have engaged in an overt act which constitutes a substantial step toward the commission of the crime.
>
> ....
>
> Our statute clearly sets out the two elements necessary for an attempt to commit a crime as (1) acting with the required culpability, and (2) engaging in conduct that constitutes a substantial step toward commission of the crime.
>
> ....

The Supreme Court affirmed the conviction for attempted murder in *Zickerfoose, supra;* murder is a crime requiring specific intent. To the contrary, the crime of reckless homicide does not require an intent to accomplish a result which would constitute a crime. IC 35-42-1-5; IC 35-41-2-2; *Beeman v.*

State, (1953) 232 Ind. 683, 115 N.E.2d 919. Recklessness is shown by *a disregard* for the harm that might result. IC 35-41-2-2.

In *State v. Melvin*, (1970) 49 Wis.2d 246, 249-250, 181 N.W.2d 490, 492, Melvin was charged with attempted murder. He argued that the trial court had erred in refusing to read a tendered instruction. The Supreme Court of Wisconsin responded:

> The trial court did not err in refusing to give the requested instruction on attempted homicide by reckless conduct (secs. 940.06 and 939.32, Stats.) because there is no such crime. "An attempt" by sec. 939.32(2) requires that the actor have an intent to perform acts and attain a result which if accomplished would constitute the crime. Acts to constitute an attempt must unequivocally demonstrate that the actor had such intent.... Homicide by reckless conduct does not require any intent to attain a result which if accomplished would constitute a crime; and consequently, one cannot attempt to commit a crime which only requires reckless conduct and not a specific intent. *State v. Carter* (1969), 44 Wis.2d 151, 170 N.W.2d 681.

In closing we quote the following passage from W. LaFave & A. Scott, Handbook on Criminal Law § 59 (1972):

> It has been strongly urged, however, that recklessness or negligence *should* suffice for attempt liability and that therefore it should be possible to attempt such a crime as involuntary manslaughter. "If a pharmacist is grossly negligent in making up a prescription and the patient dies as a result of taking the dosage on the bottle, the pharmacist is clearly guilty of manslaughter. Surely the policy considerations which dictate such a conviction apply equally if, through chance, the negligent error is discovered before any damage is done. There seems to be every reason for a verdict of attempted manslaughter." It may well be that the purposes of the criminal law would be properly served by conviction of the pharmacist for his grossly negligent conduct even though it did not in fact cause harm, but it might be questioned whether this result should be reached by a redefinition of attempt law as opposed to merely making it an offense to engage in negligent or reckless conduct which endangers others. (Original emphasis)

In Indiana our Legislature has done precisely what is recommended in the above treatise. The Legislature has enacted an attempt statute requiring specific intent, and it has also provided IC 1971, 35-42-2-2 (Burns Code Ed., Repl. 1979):

> (a) A person who recklessly, knowingly, or intentionally performs an act that creates a substantial risk of bodily injury to another person commits criminal recklessness, a class B misdemeanor. However, the offense is a class A misdemeanor if the conduct includes the use of a vehicle or deadly weapon....

We now hold that the State of Indiana has no statutory crime of attempted reckless homicide.

The judgment is reversed and the cause is remanded to the trial court for further proceedings consistent with this opinion.

NOTE ON INTENTIONAL AND RECKLESS ATTEMPTS

Paralleling the decisions on assault — in some states an assault must be intentional, while in other states there are also reckless assaults — is the corresponding division regarding criminal attempt. In the United States, the prevailing rule seems to be that an attempt requires a specific intent to commit the proscribed act. In *Thacker v. Commonwealth*, 134 Va. 767, 114 S.E. 504 (1922), a conviction of attempted murder was reversed. The accused, walking down a country road at night while intoxicated and in the company of two other men, fired three pistol shots at a lamp located inside a camping tent occupied by a woman and her children. Two of the shots went through the tent, and one of them narrowly missed striking the woman and one of her children, passing through the head of the bed in which they were sleeping. In reversing, the court said:

> It is not sufficient that his act, had it proved fatal, would have been murder.... For example, if one from a housetop recklessly throws down a billet of wood upon the sidewalk where persons are constantly passing, and it falls upon a person passing by and kills him, this would be the common-law murder, but if, instead of killing, it inflicts only a slight injury, the party could not be convicted of an assault with attempt to commit murder, since, in fact, the murder was not intended.

114 S.E. at 506. *See Groneau v. State*, 201 So. 2d 599, 602 (Fla. 1967).

The New Zealand Law Reform Committee has raised some questions about the logic of punishing reckless behavior which results in death but not similar behavior which creates a risk of death.

> They point out the illogicality of the present law, whereby a minor indiscretion may be turned into a major crime by the occurrence of death, and a bad piece of gross negligence may be no crime at all if its risk of harm fails to materialise. The recommended solution is that criminal liability should depend on the culpable creation of a risk, even if the risk did not materialise. Thus there should be an offence ... of either doing an act "with intent to cause grievous bodily harm to any other person," or "with reckless disregard for the safety of any person or the public" doing something "likely to cause grievous bodily harm" and a lesser offence ... of either doing any act "with intent to injure any other person," or with reckless disregard doing an act "likely to cause injury or endanger safety or health." The "reckless disregard" requirement would be satisfied if the prosecution proved "either that the accused realised that his act might cause harm or that he was grossly negligent in failing to appreciate and guard against the risk."

[1978] CRIM. L. REV. 3.

The Model Penal Code has specific crimes which apply to reckless injury (§ 211.1); recklessly endangering another (§ 211.2); reckless burning

(§ 220.1(2)); recklessly creating a risk of catastrophe (§ 220.0); reckless damage to property by certain dangerous means, reckless tampering with property so as to endanger another, and reckless causing pecuniary loss by deception or threat (§ 220.3).

In some jurisdictions, reckless attempts have been recognized. In *Messer v. State,* 120 Ga. App. 747, 172 S.E.2d 194 (1969), *cert. denied,* 400 U.S. 866 (1970), defendant had beaten her stepchild with boards almost every day for four months, stuck needles in the child, and pushed the child down and stomped her. The child required extensive medical treatment. A conviction of assault with intent to murder was affirmed. "There are wanton or reckless states of mind which are sometimes the equivalent of a specific intention to kill, and which may and should be treated by the jury as amounting to such intention when productive of violence likely to result in the destruction of life, though not so resulting in the given instance." 172 S.E.2d at 195.

In Canada, the Criminal Code has been interpreted so that recklessness is sufficient *mens rea* for a conviction of attempted murder. See *Lajoie v. The Queen,* 33 D.L.R.3d 618, 4 C.C.C.2d 402, 16 C.R.N.S. 180 (1973) and *Regina v. Ritchie,* 3 Ont. R. 417, 5 C.C.C. 336, 16 C.R.N.S. 287 [1970]. Under § 24(1) of the Code, an attempt requires an intent to commit an offense. The court construed the required intent as any of the culpable mental states sufficient for liability under the Criminal Code. Therefore, if death did not result from a reckless infliction of bodily harm likely to cause death, defendant could properly be found guilty of an attempt to murder.

C. PREPARATION AND ATTEMPT

EDITORIAL NOTES

As the following cases and notes illustrate, there is a variety of tests to determine at what point an act has gone beyond the preparation stage. These can be grouped in four categories although these by no means exhaust the possibilities. See MODEL PENAL CODE comments to article 5, pp. 39-47 (Tent. Draft No. 10, 1960).

1. *Proximity.* It is well accepted now that the so-called "last proximate act" test stated by Baron Park in *Regina v. Eagleton,* 169 Eng. Rep. 826 (Crim. App. 1854-55) which indicated in dictum that defendant must have done the last act necessary to commit the crime, has not been followed.

   a. *"Dangerous proximity to success."* Considering the seriousness of the offense, the closeness of the act to completion, and the likelihood that the result will be achieved, has the actor come dangerously close to achieving the criminal objective?

Defendant unlocked his barber shop, admitted a "customer," walked to the barber chair, put on his smock, and offered the chair to the customer. The defendant had laid out his barber tools, and had posted a fraudulent license on the wall of his shop. The "customer" was an agent of the barber's union, and at this point showed the defendant his business card and asked to see defendant's license. A conviction of attempting to practice barbering without a license was affirmed. "The crux of the determination of whether the acts are sufficient to constitute an attempt really is whether, when given the specific intent to commit an offense, the acts taken in furtherance thereof are such that there is a dangerous proximity to success in carrying out the intent." Only the fact that the union man showed the defendant his business card and refused to get into the chair prevented the consummation of the offense. *People v. Paluch,* 78 Ill. App. 2d 356, 222 N.E.2d 508, 510 (1966). The dissent stated that here there was no act which constituted a substantial step towards the commission of the offense. "[I]f [the union man] had sat in the barber chair ... and an overgarment placed upon him, then it could be said that a substantial step toward the commission of the offense charged had taken place — even though not one hair was clipped from his head." 222 N.E.2d at 512.

b. *"Physical proximity."* It is questionable whether this can be regarded as a "test" at all. The term physical proximity means little more than that the courts will look at what remains to be done to complete the offense. Where substantially more remains to be done, courts will conclude that defendant's conduct is not close enough to cause harm and will be regarded as preparation as in the principal case, *People v. Rizzo, infra* pp. 750-751. Varying terminology has been used to express the requirement of "proximity," *e.g.,* an act "tending directly toward" the commission of the offense, "a direct movement toward the commission of the offense," or "the commencement of the consummation." W. LaFave & A. Scott, Handbook on Criminal Law 432 (1972).

2. *Probable desistance.* Has the actor reached the point where it was unlikely that he or she would have voluntarily abandoned his efforts to commit the crime? *State v. Hurley, infra* pp. 754-755.

3. *Res ipsa loquitur or equivocality.* Has the actor's conduct unequivocally manifested an intent to commit a crime? *State v. Gobin, infra,* pp. 757-760.

The use of one test rather than another can lead to different results in similar fact situations as shown in the following abortion cases.

In *Dupuy v. State,* 204 Tenn. 624, 325 S.W.2d 238 (1959), defendant was convicted of attempted abortion. Police had suspected the defendant of committing abortions, and arranged for a woman, who was not pregnant, to contact the defendant with the alleged purpose of procuring an abortion. At the time the police entered and arrested the defendant, he had laid out all of the necessary instruments, turned down the bed, given beer to the woman to aid her in relaxing, and had filled a syringe with penicillin. He had not physically touched the woman, nor did he get closer than five feet to her. *Held:* conviction reversed. The court held that defendant's acts constituted mere preparation, and analogized defendant's acts to the procurement of tools in attempted jailbreak cases. "Preparation consists in devising or arranging the means or measures necessary for the commission of the offense; the attempt to the direct movement toward the commission after the preparations have been made." *Id.* at 240.

The dissent stated that there was sufficient evidence to sustain the jury's finding even in the absence of any physical touching of the woman by the defendant. It is not required that the overt act be such that, if not interrupted, it will result in the commission of the crime. It need only be "something more than mere preparation ... if they are not thus remote, and are done with the specific intent to commit the crime, and directly tend to some substantial degree to accomplish it, they are sufficient." *Id.* at 244 (quoting *State v.*

Dumas, 118 Minn. 77, 136 N.W. 311, at 314). In *People v. MacEwing,* 216 Cal. App. 2d 33, 30 Cal. Rptr. 476 (1963), the defendant made up a bed and gave the girl an inoculation to relax her when the police arrived and arrested the defendant. The court reversed the conviction for attempted abortion, holding that the actions constituted mere preparation.

In *People v. Reed,* 128 Cal. App. 2d 499, 275 P.2d 633, 635 (1954), defendant told a policewoman, masquerading as a patient, to get on an operating table where he would scrape her uterus. He then took a speculum from a sterilizing tray and ran cold water over it. Before the woman positioned herself on the table, and before defendant touched her, police entered and arrested the defendant. Held, that the actions went beyond mere preparation: "Here defendant started to employ means to procure a miscarriage." Conviction of attempted abortion was reversed on other grounds. 128 Cal. App. 2d at 502. In *People v. Berger,* 131 Cal. App. 2d 127, 280 P.2d 136, 139 (1955), the facts were essentially like those in Reed, except that defendant had not picked up an instrument. A conviction of attempted abortion was affirmed.

> It is a matter of common knowledge that the sterilization of the instruments to be used in a surgical operation is the first step taken in the performance of the operation.... In a case where the intent was not clearly established the boiling of surgical instruments might be too equivocal an act to be held to constitute an attempt, but ... since the intent with which this act was done ... is established beyond any doubt, the boiling of the surgical instruments ... was an act done toward the commission of the crime.

131 Cal. App. 2d at 132. *Cf. People v. Tinskey,* 394 Mich. 108, 228 N.W.2d 782 (1975), holding that conspiracy to commit abortion cannot be committed if the woman is not pregnant.

4. *Model Penal Code.* The Model Penal Code uses a "substantial step" test for determining at what point an actor has committed an attempt. Furthermore, the conduct must be "strongly corroborative" of the actor's intent. In adopting the "substantial step" test the Code intends to shift "the emphasis from what remains to be done — the chief concern of the proximity tests — to what the actor *has already done.* The fact that further major steps must be taken before the crime can be completed does not preclude a finding that the steps already undertaken are substantial." MODEL PENAL CODE § 5.01 comment at 47 (Tent. Draft No. 10, 1960). By requiring a "substantial" step "firmness of criminal purpose" will be shown without having to resort to the question of whether the actor probably would have desisted before completing the crime. Finally, the Model Penal Code test requiring "strongly corroborative" facts makes it easier than under *res ipsa loquitur* for the state to prove the actor's intent. Unquestionably, the Model Penal Code has enlarged the scope of criminal attempts. *United States v. Stallworth, infra* pp. 752-754.

In *United States v. Mandujano,* 499 F.2d 370 (5th Cir. 1974), *cert. denied,* 419 U.S. 1114 (1975), the defendant was convicted of an attempt to distribute heroin. The defendant received payment from an undercover agent who represented himself to be a narcotics trafficker. The defendant's efforts consisted of four telephone calls and a search for a contact, all of which was unsuccessful, and he returned the money to the agent. *Held,* conviction affirmed; defendant's acts constituted "a substantial step" toward the commission of the crime.

England has now codified the law of attempt and abolished the common law. The statute applies to "an act which is more than merely preparatory to the commission of the offence." Criminal Attempts Act, 1981. The Act was based on recommendations of the Law Commission. Law Com. Rep. No. 102 (1980). One object of the Act is to broaden the scope of attempt, but it has been criticized as being too imprecise. Dennis, *The Elements of Attempt,* [1980] CRIM. L. REV. 758; Dennis, *The Criminal Attempts 1981,* [1982] CRIM. L. REV. 5.

PEOPLE v. RIZZO

Court of Appeals of New York
246 N.Y. 334, 158 N.E. 888 (1927)

[Charles Rizzo and others were convicted of an attempt to commit robbery in the first degree.]

CRANE, J. ... Charles Rizzo, the defendant, appellant, with three others, Anthony J. Dorio, Thomas Milo, and John Thomasello, on January 14th planned to rob one Charles Rao of a payroll valued at about $1,200 which he was to carry from the bank for the United Lathing Company. These defendants, two of whom had firearms, started out in an automobile, looking for Rao or the man who had the pay roll on that day. Rizzo claimed to be able to identify the man and was to point him out to the others who were to do the actual holding up. The four rode about in their car looking for Rao. They went to the bank from which he was supposed to get the money and to various buildings being constructed by the United Lathing Company. At last they came to One Hundred and Eightieth street and Morris Park avenue. By this time they were watched and followed by two police officers. As Rizzo jumped out of the car and ran into the building, all four were arrested. The defendant was taken out from the building in which he was hiding. Neither Rao nor a man named Previti, who was also supposed to carry a pay roll, were at the place at the time of the arrest. The defendants had not found or seen the man they intended to rob. No person with a pay roll was at any of the places where they had stopped and no one had been pointed out or identified by Rizzo. The four men intended to rob the pay roll man, whoever he was. They were looking for him, but they had not seen or discovered him up to the time they were arrested.

Does this constitute the crime of an attempt to commit robbery in the first degree? The Penal Law, § 2 prescribes:

"An act, done with intent to commit a crime, and tending but failing to effect its commission, is 'an attempt to commit that crime.'"

The word "tending" is very indefinite. It is perfectly evident that there will arise differences of opinion as to whether an act in a given case is one *tending* to commit a crime. "Tending" means to exert activity in a particular direction. Any act in preparation to commit a crime may be said to have a tendency towards its accomplishment. The procuring of the automobile, searching the streets looking for the desired victim, were in reality acts tending toward the commission of the proposed crime. The law, however, has recognized that many acts in the way of preparation are too remote to constitute the crime of attempt. The line has been drawn between those acts which are remote and those which are proximate and near to the consummation. The law must be practical, and, therefore considers those acts only as tending to the commission of the crime which are so near to its accomplishment that in all reasonable probability the crime itself would have been committed but for timely interference. The cases which have been before the courts express this idea in different language, but the idea remains the same. The act or acts must come or advance very near to the accomplishment of the intended crime. In *People v. Mills,* 178 N.Y. 274, 284, it was said:

"Felonious intent alone is not enough, but there must be an overt act shown in order to establish even an attempt. An overt act is one done to carry out the intention, and it must be such as would naturally effect that result, unless prevented by some extraneous cause."

....

The method of committing or attempting crime varies in each case, so that the difficulty, if any, is not with this rule of law regarding an attempt, which is well understood, but with its application to the facts....

How shall we apply this rule of immediate nearness to this case?... The crime of attempt to commit robbery was committed, if these defendants did an act tending to the commission of this robbery. Did the acts above described come dangerously near to the taking of Rao's property? Did the acts come so near the commission of robbery that there was reasonable likelihood of its accomplishment but for the interference? Rao was not found; the defendants were still looking for him; no attempt to rob him could be made, at least until he came in sight; he was not in the building at One Hundred and Eightieth street and Morris Park avenue. There was no man there with the pay roll for the United Lathing Company whom these defendants could rob. Apparently no money had been drawn from the bank for the pay roll by anybody at the time of the arrest. In a word, these defendants had planned to commit a crime and were looking around the city for an opportunity to commit it, but the opportunity fortunately never came. Men would not be guilty of an attempt at burglary if they had planned to break into a building and were arrested while they were hunting about the streets for the building not knowing where it was. Neither would a man be guilty of an attempt to commit murder if he armed himself and started out to find the person whom he had planned to kill but could not find him. So here these defendants were not guilty of an attempt to commit robbery in the first degree when they had not found or reached the presence of the person they intended to rob. *People v. Sullivan,* 173 N.Y. 122, 135.

For these reasons, the judgment of conviction of this defendant appellant, must be reversed and a new trial granted.

UNITED STATES v. STALLWORTH

United States Court of Appeals
543 F.2d 1038 (2d Cir. 1976)

IRVING R. KAUFMAN, CHIEF JUDGE:

Although we affirmed appellants' convictions for attempted bank robbery, 18 U.S.C. § 2113(a),[1] in open court, we believe that since the question is one likely to present itself to district courts not infrequently it is prudent to discuss briefly the perplexing problem of distinguishing "mere preparation" for the commission of a crime from an "attempt."

... Rodney Campbell, a convicted bank robber, agreed to cooperate with the F.B.I. on January 12, 1976 in return for a grant of immunity from prosecution for four armed bank robberies in which he admittedly participated between June and September, 1975. Arrangements were made for Campbell to use an undercover Government vehicle, provided with a tape recorder and monitoring equipment, to assist the authorities in apprehending some of his former accomplices. Campbell consented to the tape recording of all conversations taking place in his car.

After reestablishing contact with individuals named Larry Peterson, Willie Young, and appellant Johnny Sellers, Campbell transported the men in his specially equipped vehicle as they reconnoitered several banks in Queens, New York. The group began actual preparations for a robbery on Wednesday January 21, by stealing ski masks from a department store. Later that day Peterson and Young appropriated surgical gloves from a hospital while Sellers, a recent patient, engaged several nurses in conversation. Finally, Peterson purchased a hacksaw and roofing nails which, he told Campbell, he needed to "fix" a shotgun.

On January 22, Sellers, Peterson, Young and Campbell perfected their plan to rob a branch of the First National City Bank in Whitestone, Queens. Peterson, formerly a factory worker in the neighborhood, advised the group that on Fridays (in this instance, January 23) large amounts of money would be on hand to accommodate industrial employees in cashing their salary checks. Young entered the bank on Thursday afternoon to examine its internal physical structure and reported to his colleagues that the tellers' counters were of average height and security was thin. The participants agreed to recruit appellant Clarence Stallworth to drive the getaway car.

On Friday morning Stallworth joined Young and Sellers, to whom he handed a .38 calibre revolver, and assumed the role of driver. Peterson met his comrades, gave them a sawed-off shotgun and distributed other paraphernalia required for the crime. En route to the bank in Whitestone the occupants of the Government-owned automobile covered their fingers with band-

---

[1] The federal criminal code, unlike some state counterparts, see New York Penal Law § 110.00, does not contain a general provision for the crime of attempt. But see, e.g., Comprehensive Drug Abuse Prevention and Control Act of 1970, Pub. L. 91-513, Title II, § 406, 21 U.S.C. § 846. Attempted bank robbery is, however, an offense under federal law: Whoever, by force and violence, or by intimidation, takes, or attempts to take, from the person or presence of another any property or money or any other thing of value belonging to, or in the care, custody, control, management, or possession of, any bank.... Shall be fined not more than $5,000 or imprisoned not more than twenty years, or both. 18 U.S.C. § 2113(a).

C. PREPARATION AND ATTEMPT

aids, their hands with surgical gloves and donned ski masks. They prepared to destroy the vehicle after the robbery by stuffing gasoline-soaked newspapers under the seats.

The target bank was located in a small shopping center. As the car entered the parking lot, Sellers alighted and strolled past the bank several times, peering inside at each opportunity, as his accomplices circled the shopping center. At approximately 11 A.M., Stallworth stopped the vehicle directly in front of the bank. Sellers, who had stationed himself at an adjacent liquor store, started to approach the bank. Simultaneously, Campbell said, "let's go," and the occupants of the car reached for the doors. At this point, F.B.I. agents and New York City policemen, who had saturated the area as a result of intelligence acquired through the would-be robbers' monitored conversations, arrested the men without incident.

Appellants contend that their conduct, while admittedly sufficient to sustain a conspiracy conviction, punishable by a maximum of five years incarceration, will not support a judgment of attempted bank robbery, carrying a potential twenty-year prison term. They argue that their activities did not transcend a hypothetical fixed point on a spectrum of conduct culminating in the substantive offense of bank robbery. Thus, appellants assert they cannot be convicted of attempted bank robbery because they neither entered the bank nor brandished weapons. We reject this wooden logic. Attempt is a subtle concept that requires a rational and logically sound definition, one that enables society to punish malefactors who have unequivocally set out upon a criminal course without requiring law enforcement officers to delay until innocent bystanders are imperiled.

The classical elements of an attempt are intent to commit a crime, the execution of an overt act in furtherance of the intention, and a failure to consummate the crime. The Fifth Circuit in *United States v. Mandujano,* 499 F.2d 370 (5th Cir. 1974), *cert. denied,* 419 U.S. 1114 (1975), has properly derived from the writings of many distinguished jurists[4] a two-tiered inquiry to determine whether given conduct constitutes an attempt. Initially, the defendant must have been acting with the kind of culpability otherwise required for the commission of the crime he is charged with attempting. Then, the defendant must have engaged in conduct which constitutes a substantial step toward commission of the crime, conduct strongly corroborative of the firmness of the defendant's criminal intent. *Id.,* at 376-77. We note that the Fifth Circuit's analysis conforms closely to the sensible definition of an attempt proffered by the American Law Institute's Model Penal Code. See also ALI's treatment of "reconnoitering the place contemplated for the commission

---

[4] According to Cardozo, a suspect's conduct must "carry the project forward within dangerous proximity to the criminal end to be attained." *People v. Werblow,* 241 N.Y. 55, 148 N.E. 786 (1925). And Learned Hand surveyed the law of attempt in *United States v. Coplon,* 185 F.2d 629, 633 (2d Cir. 1950), cert. denied, 342 U.S. 920, 72 S. Ct. 362, 96 L.Ed. 688 (1952), quoting one of the opinions of Justice Holmes:

> Preparation is not an attempt. But some preparations may amount to an attempt. It is a question of degree. If the preparation comes very near to the accomplishment of the act, the intent to complete it renders the crime so probable that the act will be a misdemeanor, although there is still a locus poenitentiae, in the need of a further exertion of the will to complete the crime. [*Commonwealth v. Peaslee,* 177 Mass. 267, 272, 59 N.E. 55 (1901)].

of the crime" and "possession ... of materials to be employed in the commission of the crime, at or near the place contemplated for its commission, where such possession ... serves no lawful purpose ..." under the subtitle "Conduct Which May Be Held Substantial Step Under Subsection (1)(c)."

Application of the foregoing to the instant case emphasizes the importance of a rule encouraging early police intervention where a suspect is clearly bent on the commission of crime. The undisputed testimony of Campbell and Young established that appellants intended to execute a successful bank robbery. Moreover, Stallworth and Sellers, in furtherance of their plan, took substantial steps that strongly corroborated their criminal intent. They reconnoitered the bank, discussed (on tape) their plan of attack, armed themselves and stole ski masks and surgical gloves. The getaway car was carefully prepared for destruction. As Sellers moved ominously toward the bank and Campbell uttered a verbal signal to his accomplices, a bank robbery was in progress. A jury could properly find that preparation was long since completed. All that stood between appellants and success was a group of F.B.I. agents and police officers. Their timely intervention probably prevented not only a robbery but possible bloodshed in an area crowded with noontime shoppers.

...

Because the conduct of Stallworth and Sellers constituted an attempted bank robbery, the convictions must be affirmed.

STATE v. HURLEY

Supreme Court of Vermont
79 Vt. 28, 64 A. 78 (1906)

MUNSON, J. The respondent is informed against for attempting to break open the jail in which he was confined by procuring to be delivered into his hands 12 steel hack saws, with an intent to break open the jail therewith. The State's evidence tended to show that, in pursuance of an arrangement between the respondent and one Tracy, a former inmate, Tracy attempted to get a bundle of hack saws to the respondent by throwing it to him as he sat behind the bars at an open window, and that the respondent reached through the bars and got the bundle into his hands, but was ordered at that moment by the jailer to drop it, and did so.... All acts done in preparation are, in a sense, acts done toward the accomplishment of the thing contemplated. But most authorities certainly hold, and many of them state specifically, that the act must be something more than mere preparation.

... The exact inquiry presented by the case before us is whether the procurement of the means of committing the offence is to be treated as a preparation for the attempt, or as the attempt itself. In considering this question, it must be remembered that there are some acts, preparatory in their character, which the law treats as substantive offences; for instance, the procuring of tools for the purpose of counterfeiting, and of indecent prints with intent to publish them. Comments upon cases of this character may lead to confusion if not correctly apprehended. Wharton, Cr. Law, § 180, and note 1.

....

C. PREPARATION AND ATTEMPT

The act in question here is the procuring by a prisoner of tools adapted to jail breaking. That act stands entirely unconnected with any further act looking to their use. It is true that the respondent procured them with the design of breaking jail. But he had not put that design into execution and might never have done so. He had procured the means of making the attempt, but the attempt itself was still in abeyance. Its inauguration depended upon the choice of an occasion and a further resolve. That stage was never reached, and the procuring of the tools remained an isolated act. To constitute an attempt, a preparatory act of this nature must be connected with the accomplishment of the intended crime by something more than a general design.

Exceptions sustained, judgment and verdict set aside, demurrer sustained, information held insufficient and quashed, and respondent discharged.

NOTES

1. Is the prisoner guilty of no offense? Would the problem be resolved by a statute which made it an offense for a prison inmate to be in possession of contraband, weapons, or tools? Consider, for example, the following Texas statute:

§ 38.10. Implements for Escape.

(a) A person commits an offense if, with intent to facilitate escape, he introduces into a penal institution, or provides an inmate with, a deadly weapon or anything that may be useful for escape.

(b) An offense under this section is a felony of the third degree unless the actor introduced or provided a deadly weapon, in which event the offense is a felony of the second degree.

TEX. PENAL CODE ANN. § 38.10 (West 1973).

Many states prohibit the possession of weapons, burglary tools, counterfeiting and drug paraphernalia, and other implements of crime with intent to use them criminally. Possession of some weapons is absolutely prohibited without proof of intent, *e.g.*, concealed weapons, sawed-off shotguns, and machine guns. The Model Penal Code provides:

§ 5.06. *Possessing Instruments of Crime; Weapons*

(1) Criminal Instruments Generally. A person commits a misdemeanor if he possesses any instrument of crime with purpose to employ it criminally. "Instrument of crime" means:

(a) anything specially made or specially adapted for criminal use; or

(b) anything commonly used for criminal purposes and possessed by the actor under circumstances which do not negative unlawful purpose.

(2) Presumption of Criminal Purpose from Possession of Weapon. If a person possesses a firearm or other weapon on or about his person, in a vehicle occupied by him, or otherwise readily available for use, it shall be presumed that he had the purpose to employ it criminally, unless:

(a) the weapon is possessed in the actor's home or place of business;

(b) the actor is licensed or otherwise authorized by law to possess such weapon; or

(c) the weapon is a type commonly used in lawful sport.

"Weapon" means anything readily capable of lethal use and possessed under circumstances not manifestly appropriate for lawful uses which it may have; the term includes a firearm which is not loaded or lacks a clip or other component to render it immediately operable, and components which can readily be assembled into a weapon.*

The United States Supreme Court upheld the validity of N.Y. Penal Law § 265.15(3) (McKinney 1975) which in similar language allows a jury to find that presence in a vehicle in which a firearm is found is presumptive evidence of possession. The Court found the presumption to be constitutional because the jury instructions clearly showed that the presumption was not conclusive and that it did not relieve the prosecution of its burden of proof. *County Court v. Allen,* 442 U.S. 140 (1979). *See* p. 59 *supra.*

The subject of presumptions is discussed in Chapter 1, section IV, D, *supra.*

Is the need for such legislation dictated because an attempt requires an act beyond preparation? Where an object has lawful uses, it is only the unlawful possession, that is, for an unlawful purpose, which can be prohibited. *State v. Birdsell,* 235 La. 396, 104 So. 2d 148 (1958) (hypodermic syringe).

2. If, in the principal case, *State v. Hurley,* the prisoner himself was not guilty of attempted escape, what crime, if any, was committed by the person who supplied him with the saw blades? The supplier did not himself try to escape, nor could he be guilty of attempted escape vicariously as an aider and abettor. Can he be convicted of attempting to aid and abet an escape? Is a statute specifically describing his behavior required, such as the Texas Penal Code provision discussed in Note 1, above?

In *State v. Judge,* 81 S.D. 128, 131 N.W.2d 573 (1964), defendant was convicted of assisting prisoners in an attempted escape. Defendant had purchased hacksaw blades and placed them in candy wrappers. He then placed the concealed blades in a paper bag which he hid under the wheels of a county truck parked within the jailhouse grounds. The conviction was affirmed. "The preparatory act of purchasing hacksaw blades which are adapted to a jail break did not in and of itself constitute a crime. Defendant's admissions ... disclosed that he intended to commit a specific crime and that there was an unequivocal act on his part in carrying out such intent when he in furtherance of the

---

*The Model Penal Code facilitates prosecution by providing in § 5.06:

(3) Presumptions as to Possession of Criminal Instruments in Automobiles. Where a weapon or other instrument of crime is found in an automobile, it shall be presumed to be in the possession of the occupant if there is but one. If there is more than one occupant, it shall be presumed to be in the possession of all, except under the following circumstances:

(a) where it is found upon the person of one of the occupants;

(b) where the automobile is not a stolen one and the weapon or instrument is found out of view in a glove compartment, car trunk, or other enclosed customary depository, in which case it shall be presumed to be in the possession of the occupant or occupants who own or have authority to operate the automobile;

(c) in the case of a taxicab, a weapon or instrument found in the passengers' portion of the vehicle shall be presumed to be in the possession of all the passengers, if there are any, and, if not, in the possession of the driver.

C. PREPARATION AND ATTEMPT

understanding with his confederates placed the paper bag containing the hacksaw blades under the county truck. He performed the only further act on his part that would have resulted in accomplishment but for intervening circumstances unknown to him." 131 N.W.2d at 576. It is important to note that the statute prohibited not only assisting an escape or attempted escape, but also carrying or sending or attempting to carry or send into the prison anything useful to aid a prisoner in making his escape, with intent to facilitate the escape.

STATE v. GOBIN

Supreme Court of Kansas
216 Kan. 278, 531 P.2d 16 (1975)

FROMME, JUSTICE:

The appellant, Gary Dean Gobin, was charged and convicted of an attempt to steal swine belonging to Everett Webb of a value of more than $50.00. One of the points raised on appeal concerns the sufficiency of the evidence to establish both the specific criminal intent and the overt act necessary to consummate such a felony.

The evidence established that on December 2, 1973, at 10:20 p.m., Mr. Webb arrived at his swine farm near Jetmore, Kansas to check his hogs. A dead end graveled road led from the highway to a private driveway at the farm. The swine were confined in farrowing houses and in fattening pens located along this private driveway. When Mr. Webb drove into the yard using the private driveway, he saw two people sitting in a pickup truck, equipped with stock racks, parked at the other end of the driveway. He stepped from his car, and the pickup truck sped past him and left the premises. Webb pursued the pickup in his car and was able to obtain the license number during a three mile chase. Webb then drove to Jetmore and reported the incident to the sheriff's office. The pickup was registered in the name of a Mr. Gerald Smith. The sheriff parked his police car at a likely intersection which led to Dodge City and waited. Subsequently two vehicles approached the intersection, one was the pickup truck seen earlier near the swine pens. The sheriff managed to stop the pickup. The appellant Gobin was the sole occupant. The other vehicle was a large truck driven by Mr. Gerald Smith. Both Gobin and Smith were taken to Jetmore and charged with an attempt to exert unauthorized control over swine belonging to Webb, and an attempted felony theft. At the time of the incident there were swine confined in the fattening pens and farrowing houses worth from $20.00 to $300.00 each.

. . . .

The Kansas Criminal Code defines an attempt as follows:

> An attempt is any overt act toward the perpetration of a crime done by a person who intends to commit such crime but fails in the perpetration thereof or is prevented or intercepted in executing such crime. (K.S.A.1973 Supp. 21-3301 [1].)

The Code defines the particular theft charged as being attempted in the present case as follows:

> Theft is any of the following acts done with intent to deprive the owner permanently of the possession, use or benefit of his property:
> *(a)* Obtaining or exerting unauthorized control over property; ..."
> (K.S.A.1973 Supp. 21-3701.)

....

... [I]n order to convict an accused of an attempt to commit a crime an overt act toward consummation of the crime must be established. The overt act necessary must extend beyond mere preparations made by the accused and must approach sufficiently near to consummation of the offense to stand either as the first or some subsequent step in a direct movement towards the completed offense.

Now let us look at our cases on the subject to see where that line has been drawn. In *State v. McCarthy, supra,* the charge was an attempt to commit burglary of a freight car. There was no question of the intent to commit the burglary for the accused explained his plan to a car inspector who agreed to hold the particular train to be robbed long enough for the goods to be removed. The accused and four confederates arrived at the yards in a car and a truck with a pump gun, revolver, ammunition, lanterns, wrenches, screwdriver and a jimmy. Three of the party remained near the scene of their contemplated burglary where they were later arrested. Two went in search of their supposed accomplice, the car inspector. The car inspector testified that the defendant talked with him on the steps of the station and advised that the others were waiting with their vehicles. The accused then left and was arrested a few blocks from the station. The court on appeal concluded that the acts of the defendants went beyond mere preparation for an intended burglary and were steps toward the accomplishment of the crime which justified conviction of an attempt. We note that the overt acts were not necessary to establish an intent to commit the burglary. The accused's intent to commit the crime was independently proven by the testimony of the car inspector.

....

In the present case appellant was charged with an attempt to take swine from Webb. There was convincing evidence that the two persons sitting in the pickup in the driveway never departed from the vehicle. The yard surrounding the vehicle had been freshly dragged and there were no imprints on the surrounding surface except the car and pickup tracks. Mr. Webb testified the pickup was parked 90 feet from the loading chute. A man could have loaded a pig weighing up to 75 pounds without using a chute. The pickup was some distance from both the farrowing houses and the fattening pens. Mr. Webb further testified neither of the persons in the pickup made any movement toward the animals while he was there and that he heard no noise from the swine to indicate that any had been disturbed or lifted. There were no swine in the pickup.

Under such a factual situation there may have been sufficient circumstances, if you include the flight of the pickup, to infer a general unlawful and criminal intent but there are no facts which point to a specific intent to steal

C. PREPARATION AND ATTEMPT

swine. The presence of a strange pickup with stock racks in a private driveway at 10:20 p.m. might well raise a strong suspicion of wrongdoing but its presence and subsequent flight alone does not point to any particular crime intended. The facts are equally susceptible to widely different interpretations, for the known circumstances might be attributable to either an innocent or a criminal cause....

Similarly when we look for an overt act done in an effort to steal the swine the facts and circumstances surrounding the presence of the strange pickup in the driveway are equally susceptible of widely different interpretations. The known circumstances are attributable to either innocent acts or criminal acts in preparation for some crime, possibly theft of pigs or grain or gasoline or equipment. For a felony theft it would have to be inferred that the accused intended to steal at least $50.00 worth of said swine.

Therefore it appears that if this conviction for an attempt to steal swine is upheld both the criminal intent to steal $50.00 worth of swine and the overt act toward the consummation of that theft must be inferred from the presence of two persons in a strange pickup with stock racks parked at 10:20 p.m. in a private driveway between farrowing houses and swine fattening pens.

... This court concludes from all of the facts and circumstances disclosed by the evidence, the jury could not have reasonably drawn a proper inference that the appellant attempted to take from Mr. Webb swine worth over $50.00 with intent to deprive him permanently of the possession, use or benefit of said property. A felony conviction for an attempt to steal swine must be grounded on something more than probabilities, possibilities or suspicions of guilt.

... The judgment of conviction is reversed.

FONTRON, JUSTICE (dissenting):

While I acknowledge the validity of the legal principles set forth in the court's opinion, I arrive at a different destination in applying them to the facts of this case than does the majority. In simple language, I maintain there is sufficient evidence of record to justify a reasonable inference that Mr. Gobin and Mr. Smith, with Smith's two trucks in tow, drove from Dodge City to Everett Webb's pig farm north of Jetmore, a distance of some 35 miles, for the express purpose of pilfering pigs. The driving of the trucks that distance and to that place appears to me as being more than mere preparation; it was, as I see it, an overt act; the first in a series of active moves which would have led directly to consummation of a theft had not the owner fortuitously driven to the farm to shut the door to the farrowing house. The readying of the trucks and stock racks for the journey might well be termed preparation but driving the pickup into a private driveway leading from a dead-end road smack into "the middle of the hog lot" as Mr. Webb put it, at 10:20 p.m. and parking there is more, in my book, than preparation. It is an outward, open manifest act. Neither Mr. Gobin nor Mr. Smith could have "exercised unauthorized control" over the pigs in Mr. Webb's hog lot that night had they remained in Dodge City; they first had to get themselves and the trucks to the pig lot, and that required a moving, purposeful, motivated act.

I find little difficulty in saying the evidence was such that an intent to exert "unauthorized control," or to steal, in other words, might well have been inferred by the jury. The hasty flight of the two men followed by a "cops and robbers" chase of the two trucks over the highways of Hodgeman County belies an honest purpose on their part in parking at the hog lot....

D. ATTEMPT IN RELATION TO SOLICITATION

EDITORIAL NOTE

Where *A* solicits *B* to kill her spouse and *B* does or makes an attempt to, *A* would be guilty of murder or attempted murder, as the case may be, as an aider and abettor. Suppose *B* does not make the attempt, such as where *B* is an undercover police officer, or acting on instructions of the police to pretend to go along with *A*. *A* cannot be guilty of any crime as an aider and abettor because *B* committed no crime. *A* would be guilty of solicitation because it makes no difference whether or not *B* intended to commit the crime. Can *A* be convicted of attempted murder based on her own conduct? Does her act of solicitation constitute an act beyond preparation? Clearly she has the specific intent for her spouse to be killed.

In *State v. Davis,* 319 Mo. 1222, 6 S.W.2d 609 (1928), the court, following what it characterized as the majority view, held that "mere solicitation, unaccompanied by an act moving directly toward the commission of the intended crime, is not an overt act constituting an element of the crime of attempt.... [M]erely soliciting one to commit a crime does not constitute an attempt." 6 S.W.2d at 612. Yet, victim's wife and defendant, her lover, "hired" the undercover officer and paid him. Defendant played an important role in formulating the plan for killing which included providing the assassin with a picture of the victim and telling when and where it was to be done.

Another case, *State v. Gay,* 4 Wash. App. 834, 486 P.2d 341 (1971), upheld a conviction for attempted murder under similar circumstances. The court agreed that solicitation of itself was insufficient for an attempt. Soliciting is one thing; however, hiring the would-be assassin is something else. It is an "act directed toward the commission of the target crime." 486 P.2d at 345. Defendant paid part of the money, furnished pictures of her husband, and described her husband's habits and where he might be found. The court found "that she had done everything there was to be done by her." *Id.* at 346. She had no way of contacting the assassin since he always initiated contact. She could not have stopped him if she had wanted to. "The situation was then beyond her control." *Id.*

In similar situations some courts find that because neither defendant nor the hired "killer" intend to do the act of killing there is no act tending to the accomplishment of the desired result. The subterfuge used by the police prevents defendant's act from ever going beyond the preparatory stage. *People v. Adami,* 36 Cal. App. 3d 452, 111 Cal. Rptr. 544 (1973).

E. ABANDONMENT

EDITORIAL NOTE

Under what circumstances, if any, can a person who has gone beyond preparation reverse course and renounce his or her criminal purpose? *See* MODEL PENAL CODE § 5.01(4) in Appendix A. Some states follow this view. CONN. GEN. STAT. ANN. § 53a-49(c) (West 1972); N.Y. PENAL LAW § 40.10(3) (McKinney 1973); TEX. PENAL CODE ANN. § 15.04 (West 1973).

The Law Commission (England) rejected the Model Penal Code approach, Law Com. Rep., No. 102, pp. 68-69 (1980) and this position is approved by Wasyk, *Abandoning Criminal Attempt,* [1980] CRIM. L. REV. 785: "Once the defendant, with *mens rea,* has committed a proximate rather than a preparatory act in connection with the full offence, he may be arrested, charged and convicted of attempt. Any subsequent change of mind by the defendant, including a quite voluntary decision by him to abandon the attempt, will not excuse him." *See also* G. FLETCHER, RETHINKING CRIMINAL LAW 184-97 (1978).

NOTES

1. Defendants drove to an alley behind a filling station intending to commit robbery. They removed a rifle from their car, loaded it and also removed materials to be used as disguises. They waited until business was slack. One of the defendants approached an attendant and asked for a cigarette. Upon being refused he rejoined his companion and they then tried to summon the courage to commit the crime. At this time an unmarked police car drove into the station. Defendants decided not to go through with their plan and had begun walking away from the station when they were arrested. Defendants were convicted of attempted robbery and appealed on the ground that an instruction on abandonment should have been given. *Held:* unlike some jurisdictions, abandonment is not an affirmative defense. After the prosecution has shown that defendants took a substantial step towards the commission of a crime, their subsequent abandonment of their scheme was irrelevant to the charge of attempt. *State v. Workman,* 90 Wash. 2d 443, 584 P.2d 382 (1978).

2. *Contra* MODEL PENAL CODE § 5.01(4). [The text of this section appears in Appendix A.]

F. "ATTEMPTED" ATTEMPTS

STATE v. WILSON

Supreme Court of Oregon
218 Or. 575, 346 P.2d 115 (1959)

O'CONNELL, JUSTICE. The defendant appeals from a judgment of the circuit court for Multnomah county entered on a verdict pronouncing him guilty of the crime of attempted assault with a dangerous weapon under Count I of the indictment....

... On the afternoon of September 12, 1957, the defendant, Harvey Raymond Wilson, went unarmed to the laundry room of the New Heathman Hotel in Portland, Oregon, where his wife, Frances Ora Wilson, from whom he was separated, was employed. At that time a half dozen or more women, including defendant's wife and a Vivian Smith, were working in the laundry room. Defendant approached his wife. He had been in the same laundry room the previous Saturday and had called her a "yellow bellied son of a bitch" and in addition had said to her, "I'll give you just twenty-four hours to live." This time he stated to his wife: "This is it." Whereupon she ran from the room to an adjoining office where she started to call the police on a telephone. However, the defendant, who had followed her into the room, took the phone from her, tore it loose from the wall and threw it at her. She ducked and the phone hit another woman named Goldie Reed, a co-worker of defendant's wife. Defendant's wife then ran out of that office into another room where she did call the police on another phone.

Meanwhile the defendant went outside the hotel to where his car was parked nearby and got from it a 12-gauge shotgun which was loaded with three shells. He then returned to the laundry room, having only been gone approximately three or four minutes. As he approached the laundry room, with the loaded gun held in a position to shoot directly in front of him, he was walking down a hall which had an open doorway on his right approximately ten feet ahead of him. Almost directly across the hall from this open doorway into the laundry room was another doorway which led into the office where his wife was. At this very time as the defendant was approximately ten feet up the hall from this doorway to the office, his wife started to come out of that doorway into the hall. She then saw the defendant who was also seen at the same time by a Grace Scebeta, another co-worker of the defendant's wife. Miss Scebeta immediately pushed defendant's wife back into the office. The door was quickly shut as was another door leading into the office which now had in it defendant's wife, Grace Scebeta and Goldie Reed.

Defendant meanwhile continued walking down the hall until he came to the doorway of the laundry room. He then entered the laundry room still carrying the loaded shotgun, where he confronted Vivian Smith and Helen Robbins, who also worked in the laundry room. Miss Robbins is a deaf mute. While standing not more than a couple of feet away from these two women, the defendant said to them, "Don't move anyone or I'll shoot you." Shortly after that the defendant turned around and walked away. As he was leaving the building he was apprehended by a police officer who was sent to the hotel as the result of the phone call to the police by defendant's wife.

... In stating his grounds for objecting to the introduction of evidence in proof of the first count counsel for defendant said "... it is the contention of the defendant that there is no such thing as an attempted assault; it is no more than an attempt to inflict an injury or battery, so if a person attempts to assault one then he lacks the attempt to commit the battery."

....

The charge that an attempt to attempt to do an act is beyond understanding, seems at first blush to be justified. It could be interpreted to be the equivalent of a statement that one is guilty of a crime if he proceeds to act in such a way that, if not interrupted, his conduct would result in the commission of an act which if not interrupted would result in a substantive crime.

F. "ATTEMPTED" ATTEMPTS

If we should view criminal assault as a separate substantive crime and not as an attempted battery, the foregoing objection would disappear. If we use the words "assault" and "battery" to express distinct ideas, then criminal assault can mean either (1) an act which causes another to be put in reasonable apprehension of corporal injury and the act is done with the intent of causing either the apprehension or the corporal injury, or (2) an act intended to cause corporal injury by one who has the present ability to carry out such intent. Under the first meaning of assault a crime is committed if the victim is put in apprehension of injury whether there is any actual intent to injure or not. Thus, if the defendant should point an unloaded gun intending only to subject his victim to the apprehension of corporal injury a crime would be committed. The crime is not defined in terms of an attempted battery but as a crime complete in itself. So viewed, there is no logical difficulty in describing as a criminal attempt the acts leading up to the conduct by which the defendant actually places his victim in apprehension.

. . . .

When assault is defined in terms of the victim's apprehension of injury, as many courts do, assault is viewed as a self-contained criminal act rather than as an attempted battery, and yet the definition carries with it the idea that the conduct which causes the apprehension may be, and often is, a step toward the ultimate act of inflicting corporal injury. The fact that the preliminary conduct is described with reference to an act which ordinarily follows, or which is intended to follow, does not preclude us from considering the preliminary conduct as a separate crime distinct from criminal battery, and this is true whether we define assault in terms of the purpose and ability to commit a battery or in terms of putting the victim in fear of corporal injury. Defined either way, the conduct of the actor has advanced to such a stage that his propinquity to the victim's person is in itself a harm either because it generates fear in the victim under one definition, or exposes him to imminent danger of physical injury under the other. That distinct harm can be differentiated from the harm which the law sees at the point where the actor has not yet come upon the scene but has gone far enough to move past the mere preparation phase and into the stage of attempt. Cf. Hall, Principles of Criminal Law (1947), ch. 4. See Note: Is Criminal Assault A Separate Substantive Crime Or Is It An Attempted Battery?, 33 Ky. L.J. 189 (1945). We are of the opinion that criminal assault, even as defined by this court, should be regarded as a distinct crime rather than as an uncompleted battery.

If we should regard assault as an attempted battery, is it reasonable to recognize the crime of attempted assault? It has been categorically asserted that there can be no attempt to commit a crime which is itself merely an attempt. 1 Wharton, Criminal Law and Procedure (Anderson ed.) § 72, p. 154; 1 Burdick, Law of Crime § 135, p. 176 (1946); *State v. Sales*, 1866, 2 Nev. 268; *Wiseman v. Commonwealth*, 1925, 143 Va. 631, 130 S.E. 249, cf., *State v. Underwood*, 1916, 79 Or. 338, 155 P. 194 (suggesting that a charge that defendant was guilty of an attempt to solicit is an "absurdity"). Upon the basis of this premise it is said that there can be no such offense as an attempted assault. 1 Wharton, op. cit. *supra*, § 72 at 154, states that "as an assault is an attempt to commit a battery there can be no attempt to commit an assault."

The same idea is found in Clark & Marshall, Crimes (6th ed.) § 4.07, p. 218....
In none of these sources is it explained why this conclusion is inevitable. It appears to be assumed that logic permits no other conclusion. But is that so? Thurman Arnold, in an article in 40 Yale L.J. 53, 65 (1930) answers as follows:

> ... [It is said that] there can be no attempt at a direct attempt. But the query immediately arises, Why not? We do not punish attempts at ordinary assaults which carry light penalties. But suppose the accused is guilty of conduct tending toward an aggravated assault but which does not seem to require the heavier penalty. The court is confronted with the alternative of either discharging the accused or modifying the penalty to make it more nearly fit his conduct. An easy way to accomplish this is by making attempts at aggravated assaults punishable, and this is frequently done. It is academic to call such cases "wrong" because assault is in the nature of an attempt and hence cannot be attempted, particularly when a common sense result is reached. In short the generalization that there can be no attempt at a crime in the nature of an attempt tells us nothing and tends merely to divert the court's mind from the real issue.

We agree with the foregoing analysis. The mere fact that assault is viewed as preceding a battery should not preclude us from drawing a line on one side of which we require the present ability to inflict corporal injury, denominating this an assault, and on the other side conduct which falls short of a present ability, yet so advanced toward the assault that it is more than mere preparation and which we denominate an attempt.

....

We think that the analysis ... is applicable to the present case. The acts of the defendant after obtaining the gun from his automobile may not have been sufficient to establish that he had the present ability to inflict corporal injury upon his wife who was behind a locked door, but he had proceeded far beyond the stage of preparation and it is reasonable to treat his conduct as an attempt within the meaning of ORS 161.090. It is the function of the law of criminal attempt to permit the courts to adjust the penalty in cases where the conduct falls short of a completed crime. 40 Yale L.J. 53, 74, 75. Our legislature has provided that assault with a dangerous weapon is a crime. ORS 161.090 permits the courts of this state to treat conduct which is short of statutory crimes as a crime, and we regard an attempt to commit an assault as within the intendment of this statute. Support for our position recognizing the crime of attempted assault can be found in other jurisdictions.... The contrary view is little more than a barren logical construct. The recognition of the crime of attempted assault where assault is viewed as a separate substantive crime rather than as an attempted battery indicates that there is no policy against punishing a person who engages in conduct short of an assault. No different policy considerations are presented merely because we view assault as an uncompleted battery rather than as a distinct crime.

....

The judgment of the lower court is affirmed.

NOTES

1. The *Wilson* theory was rejected in *In re M.*, 9 Cal. 3d 517, 510 P.2d 33, 108 Cal. Rptr. 89 (1973), and *Allen v. People*, 175 Colo. 113, 485 P.2d 886 (1971).

2. The subject of "attempted assaults" is also referred to at p. 179 *supra*.

3. Texas designates attempts, conspiracy, and solicitation as "Preparatory Offenses," and provides that "Attempt or conspiracy to commit, or solicitation of, a preparatory offense defined in this chapter [criminal attempt, criminal conspiracy, and criminal solicitation] is not an offense." TEX. PENAL CODE ANN. § 15.05 (West 1973). Hence in that jurisdiction, there can be no "attempted" attempts.

G. IMPOSSIBILITY

1. Of Fact

STATE v. DAMMS

Supreme Court of Wisconsin
9 Wis. 2d 183, 100 N.W.2d 592 (1960)

The defendant Ralph Damms was charged by information with the offense of attempt to commit murder in the first degree contrary to secs. 940.01 and 939.32, Stats. The jury found the defendant guilty as charged, and the defendant was sentenced to imprisonment in the state prison at Waupun for a term of not more than ten years. The defendant has appealed from the judgment of conviction entered May 1, 1959.

The alleged crime occurred on April 6, 1959, near Menomonee Falls in Waukesha county. Prior to that date Marjory Damms, wife of the defendant, had instituted an action for divorce against him and the parties lived apart....

[In an apparent effort to effect a reconciliation, Damms took his wife on a trip. They stopped at a roadside restaurant for a cup of coffee. Damms requested to see his wife's wallet and checkbook.] ... A quarrel ensued between them. Mrs. Damms opened the car door and started to run around the restaurant building screaming, "Help!" Damms pursued her with the pistol in his hand. Mrs. Damms' cries for help attracted the attention of the persons inside the restaurant, including two officers of the State Traffic Patrol who were eating their lunch. One officer rushed out of the front door and the other the rear door. In the meantime, Mrs. Damms had run nearly around three sides of the building. In seeking to avoid colliding with a child, who was in her path, she turned, slipped and fell. Damms crouched down, held the pistol at her head, and pulled the trigger, but nothing happened. He then exclaimed, "It won't fire. It won't fire."

Damms testified that at the time he pulled the trigger the gun was pointing down at the ground and not at Mrs. Damms' head. However, the two traffic patrol officers both testified that Damms had the gun pointed directly at her head when he pulled the trigger. The officers placed Damms under arrest. They found that the pistol was unloaded. The clip holding the cartridges, which clip is inserted in the butt of the gun to load it, they found in the cardboard box in Damms' car together with a box of cartridges.

... Damms stated that he thought the gun was loaded at the time of the alleged attempt to murder. Both the deputy sheriff and the undersheriff testified that Damms had stated to them that he thought the gun was loaded. On the other hand, Damms testified at the trial that he knew at the time of the alleged attempt that the pistol was not loaded.

....

CURRIE, JUSTICE. The ... [question] raised on this appeal ... [is]:
(1) Did the fact that it was impossible for the accused to have committed the act of murder because the gun was unloaded, preclude his conviction of the offense of attempt to commit murder?

....

Sec. 939. 32(2), Stats., provides as follows:

> An attempt to commit a crime requires that the actor have an intent to perform acts and attain a result which, if accomplished, would constitute such crime and that he does acts toward the commission of the crime which demonstrate unequivocally, under all the circumstances, that he formed the intent and would commit the crime *except for the intervention* of another person or *some other extraneous factor.* (Italics supplied.)

The issue ... boils down to whether the impossibility of accomplishment due to the gun being unloaded falls within the statutory words, "except for the intervention of ... some other extraneous factor." We conclude that it does.

Prior to the adoption of the new criminal code of the 1955 legislature the criminal statutes of this state had separate sections making it an offense to assault with intent to do great bodily harm, to murder, to rob, and to rape, etc. The new code did away with these separate sections by creating sec. 939.32, Stats., covering all attempts to commit a battery or felony, and making the maximum penalty not to exceed one-half the penalty imposed for the completed crime, except that, if the penalty for a completed crime is life imprisonment, the maximum penalty for the attempt is thirty years imprisonment.

In an article in 1956 Wisconsin Law Review, 350, 364, by assistant attorney general Platz, who was one of the authors of the new criminal code, explaining such code, he points out that "attempt" is defined therein in a more intelligible fashion than by using such tests as "beyond mere preparation," "*locus poenitentiae*" (the place at which the actor may repent and withdraw), or "dangerous proximity to success." Quoting the author *Ibid*, footnote at p. 364):

"Emphasis upon the dangerous propensities of the actor as shown by his conduct, rather than upon how close he came to succeeding, is more appropriate to the purposes of the criminal law to protect society and reform offenders or render them temporarily harmless."

Robert H. Skilton, in an article entitled, "The Requisite Act in a Criminal Attempt" (1937), 3 University of Pittsburgh Law Review 308, 314, advances the view, that impossibility to cause death because of the attempt to fire a

G. IMPOSSIBILITY

defective weapon at a person, does not prevent the conviction of the actor of the crime of attempted murder:

> [If] the defendant does not know that the gun he fires at B is defective, he is guilty of an attempt to kill B, even though his actions under the circumstances given never come near to killing B .... The possibility of the success of the defendant's enterprise need only be an apparent possibility to the defendant, and not an actual possibility.
>
> ....
>
> It is our considered judgment that the fact, that the gun was unloaded when Damms pointed it at his wife's head and pulled the trigger, did not absolve him of the offense charged, if he actually thought at the time that it was loaded.
>
> ....

Judgment affirmed.

NOTES

1. Conviction of attempted larceny from a coin box does not require that there be any money in the box. If there is any impossibility of success, it is factual rather than legal impossibility. *Gargan v. State,* 436 P.2d 968 (Alaska 1968).

2. In *People v. Siu,* 126 Cal. App. 2d 41, 271 P.2d 575 (1954), a conviction of attempt to possess narcotics was affirmed although the package delivered to defendant contained only talcum powder. "And even though the intended crime could not have been completed, due to some extrinsic fact unknown to the person who intended it, still he is guilty of attempt." 271 P.2d at 576.

3. When the defendant armed himself with a loaded revolver, and went to the window of the room in which he believed John O. Warren was sleeping, from his knowledge acquired by visiting his family, and fired his pistol at the place where he thought Warren was lying, he was attempting to assassinate and murder him. The fact that Warren was not there, as he believed him to be, did not make it any the less an attempt to murder.

State v. Mitchell, 170 Mo. 633, 639, 71 S.W. 175, 177 (1902).

4. There being testimony to the effect that the defendant had heard that the drug was poisonous, and that a very small portion of it — one drop — would kill, it was wholly immaterial to inquire whether the drug was in fact poisonous, or what quantity would be sufficient to endanger life, or cause grievous bodily harm. If the defendant administered the drug with intent to kill, after having heard that it would have that effect, all the elements of the offence charged were present. There was the intent to kill, accompanied by an act which she believed was calculated to effect her intent, and the fact that the act done by her fell short of effecting her intent cannot affect the question.

State v. Glover, 27 S.C. 602, 606, 4 S.E. 564, 565-66 (1888).

2. OF LAW

FOSTER v. COMMONWEALTH

Supreme Court of Appeals of Virginia
96 Va. 306, 31 S.E. 503 (1898)

....

One Foster was convicted of an attempt to commit rape, and he brings error....

RIELY, J. This case presents for decision the important question whether a boy under 14 years of age is capable, under the law, of committing the crime of rape, or of the attempt to commit it.

....

By the common law, a boy under 14 years of age is conclusively presumed to be incapable of committing the offence, whatever be the real fact. Evidence to rebut the presumption is inadmissible. 1 Hale, P. C. 630; 4 Bl. Comm. 212....

In the United States the rule of the common law has not been uniformly followed.

....

The accused being under 14 years of age, and conclusively presumed to be incapable of committing the crime of rape, it logically follows, as a plain legal deduction, that he was also incapable in law of an attempt to commit it.

....

[Reversed.]

PEOPLE v. JAFFE

Court of Appeals of New York
185 N.Y. 497, 78 N.E. 169 (1906)

WILLARD BARTLETT, J. The indictment charged that the defendant on the 6th day of October, 1902, in the county of New York, feloniously received twenty yards of cloth of the value of twenty-five cents a yard belonging to the copartnership of J. W. Goddard & Son, knowing that the said property had been feloniously stolen, taken and carried away from the owners. It was found under section 550 of the Penal Code, which provides that a person who buys or receives any stolen property knowing the same to have been stolen is guilty of criminally receiving such property. The defendant was convicted of an attempt to commit the crime charged in the indictment. The proof clearly showed, and the district attorney conceded upon the trial, that the goods which the defendant attempted to purchase on October 6, 1902, had lost their character as stolen goods at the time when they were offered to the defendant and when he sought to buy them. In fact the property had been restored to the owners and was wholly within their control and was offered to the defendant by their authority and through their agency. The question presented by this appeal, therefore, is whether upon an indictment for receiving goods knowing them to have been stolen the defendant may be convicted of an attempt to commit the crime where it appears without dispute that the property which he sought to receive was not in fact stolen property.

G. IMPOSSIBILITY

The conviction was sustained by the Appellate Division chiefly upon the authority of the numerous cases in which it has been held that one may be convicted of an attempt to commit a crime notwithstanding the existence of facts unknown to him which would have rendered the complete perpetration of the crime itself impossible. Notably among these are what may be called the pickpocket cases, where in prosecutions for attempts to commit larceny from the person by pocket picking it is held not to be necessary to allege or prove that there was anything in the pocket which could be the subject of larceny. *Commonwealth v. McDonald*, 5 Cush. 365; *Rogers v. Commonwealth*, 5 S. & R. 463; *State v. Wilson*, 30 Conn. 500; *People v. Moran*, 123 N.Y. 254. Much reliance was also placed in the opinion of the learned Appellate Division upon the case of *People v. Gardner*, 144 N.Y. 119, where a conviction of an attempt to commit the crime of extortion was upheld, although the woman from whom the defendant sought to obtain money by a threat to accuse her of a crime was not induced to pay the money by fear, but was acting at the time as a decoy for the police, and hence could not have been subjected to the influence of fear.

In passing upon the question here presented for our determination, it is important to bear in mind precisely what it was that the defendant attempted to do. He simply made an effort to purchase certain specific pieces of cloth. He believed the cloth to be stolen property, but it was not such in fact. The purchase, therefore, if it had been completely effected, could not constitute the crime of receiving stolen property, knowing it to be stolen, since there could be no such thing as knowledge on the part of the defendant of a non-existent fact, although there might be a belief on his part that the fact existed. As Mr. Bishop well says, it is a mere truism that there can be no receiving of stolen goods which have not been stolen. (2 Bishop's New Crim. Law, § 1140.) It is equally difficult to perceive how there can be an attempt to receive stolen goods, knowing them to have been stolen, when they have not been stolen in fact.

The crucial distinction between the case before us and the pickpocket cases, and others involving the same principle, lies not in the possibility or impossibility of the commission of the crime, but in the fact that in the present case the act, which it was doubtless the intent of the defendant to commit, would not have been a crime if it had been consummated. If he had actually paid for the goods which he desired to buy and received them into his possession, he would have committed no offense under section 550 of the Penal Code, because the very definition in that section of the offense of criminally receiving property makes it an essential element of the crime that the accused shall have known the property to have been stolen or wrongfully appropriated in such a manner as to constitute larceny. This knowledge being a material ingredient of the offense it is manifest that it cannot exist unless the property has in fact been stolen or larcenously appropriated. No man can know that to be so which is not so in truth and in fact. He may believe it to be so but belief is not enough under this statute. In the present case it appeared not only by the proof but by the express concession of the prosecuting officer that the goods which the defendant intended to purchase had lost their character as stolen goods at the time of the proposed transaction. Hence, no matter what was the motive of the defendant, and no matter what he supposed, he could do no act which was intrinsically adapted to the then present successful perpetration of the crime denounced by this section of the Penal Code, because neither he nor any one in the world could know that the property was stolen property inasmuch as it was not in fact stolen property.

In the pickpocket cases the immediate act which the defendant had in contemplation was an act which if it could have been carried out would have been criminal, whereas in the present case the immediate act which the defendant had in contemplation (to wit, the purchase of the goods which were brought to his place for sale) could not have been criminal under the statute even if the purchase had been completed because the goods had not in fact been stolen but were, at the time when they were offered to him in the custody and under the control of the true owners.

If all which an accused person intends to do would if done constitute no crime it cannot be a crime to attempt to do with the same purpose a part of the thing intended. (1 Bishop's Crim. Law [7th ed.], § 747.) The crime of which the defendant was convicted necessarily consists of three elements: first, the act; second, the intent; and, third, the knowledge of an existing condition. There was proof tending to establish two of these elements, the first and second, but none to establish the existence of the third. This was knowledge of the stolen character of the property sought to be acquired. There could be no such knowledge. The defendant could not know that the property possessed the character of stolen property when it had not in fact been acquired by theft.

The language used by RUGER, CH. J., in *People v. Moran* (123 N.Y. 254), quoted with approval by EARL, J., in *People v. Gardner* (144 N.Y. 119), to the effect that "the question whether an attempt to commit a crime has been made is determinable solely by the condition of the actor's mind and his conduct in the attempted consummation of his design," although accurate in those cases, has no application to a case like this, where, if the accused had completed the act which he attempted to do, he would not be guilty of a criminal offense. A particular belief cannot make that a crime which is not so in the absence of such belief. Take, for example, the case of a young man who attempts to vote, and succeeds in casting his vote under the belief that he is but twenty years of age when he is in fact over twenty-one and a qualified voter. His intent to commit a crime, and his belief that he was committing a crime, would not make him guilty of any offense under these circumstances, although the moral turpitude of the transaction on his part would be just as great as it would if he were in fact under age. So, also, in the case of a prosecution under the statute of this state, which makes it rape in the second degree for a man to perpetrate an act of sexual intercourse with a female not his wife under the age of eighteen years. There could be no conviction if it was established upon the trial that the female was in fact over the age of eighteen years, although the defendant believed her to be younger and intended to commit the crime. No matter how reprehensible would be his act in morals, it would not be the act forbidden by this particular statute. "If what a man contemplates doing would not be in law a crime, he could not be said in point of law to intend to commit the crime. If he thinks his act will be a crime this is a mere mistake of his understanding where the law holds it not to be such, his

G. IMPOSSIBILITY

real intent being to do a particular thing. If the thing is not a crime he does not intend to commit one whatever he may erroneously suppose." (1 Bishop's Crim. Law [7th ed.], § 742.)

The judgment of the Appellate Division and of the Court of General Sessions must be reversed, and the defendant discharged....

PEOPLE v. ROJAS

Supreme Court of California
55 Cal. 2d 252, 358 P.2d 921, 10 Cal. Rptr. 465 (1961)

SCHAUER, JUSTICE.

In a trial by the court, after proper waiver of jury, defendants Rojas and Hidalgo were found guilty of a charge of receiving stolen property....

Defendants urge that they were guilty of no crime (or, at most, of an attempt to receive stolen property) because when they received the property it had been recovered by the police and was no longer in a stolen condition. The attorney general argues that because the thief stole the property pursuant to prearrangement with defendants he took it as their agent, and the crime of receiving stolen property was complete when the thief began its asportation toward defendants and before the police intercepted him and recovered the property. We have concluded that defendants are guilty of attempting to receive stolen goods; that other matters of which they complain do not require a new trial; and that the appeal should be disposed of by modifying the finding that defendants are guilty as charged to a determination that they are guilty of attempting to receive stolen property ....

The offense with which defendants were charged and of which they were convicted was receiving "property which has been *stolen ..., knowing the same to be so stolen.*" Pen.Code, § 496, subd. 1; italics added. Defendants, relying particularly upon *People v. Jaffe* (1906), 185 N.Y. 497, 501 [78 N.E. 169, 9 L.R.A., N.S., 263, 266], urge that they neither received stolen goods nor criminally attempted to do so because the conduit, when defendants received it, was not in a stolen condition but had been recovered by the police. In the *Jaffe* case the stolen property was recovered by the owner while it was en route to the would-be receiver and, by arrangement with the police, was delivered to such receiver as a decoy, not as property in a stolen condition. The New York Court of Appeals held that there was no attempt to receive stolen goods "because neither [defendant] nor anyone else in the world could know that the property was stolen property inasmuch as it was not in fact stolen property.... If all which an accused person intends to do would if done constitute no crime it cannot be a crime to attempt to do with the same purpose a part of the thing intended."

....

As pointed out by the District Court of Appeal in *Faustina v. Superior Court* (1959), 174 Cal.App.2d 830, 833 [1], 345 P.2d 543, "The rule of the Jaffe case has been the subject of much criticism and discussion." *See* Smith, Two Problems in Criminal Attempts (1957), 70 Harv.L.Rev. 422, 439; Sayre, Criminal Attempts (1928), 41 Harv.L.Rev. 821, 853; Keedy, Criminal Attempts at Common Law (1954), 102 Pa.L.Rev. 464, 476; Strahorn, The Effect of Impossibility on Criminal Attempts (1930), 78 Pa.L.Rev. 962, 990; Arnold, Criminal Attempts (1930), 40 Yale L.J. 53, 77; A.L.I. Model Penal Code, Tent. Draft No. 10 (1960), p. 30. In our opinion the following criticism (Hall, General Principles of Criminal Law (1947), p. 127) is sound: "The confusion between what the defendant actually did and his intent is apparent. Intent is in the mind; it is not the external realities to which intention refers. The fact that defendant was mistaken regarding the external realities did not alter his intention, but simply made it impossible to effectuate it."

The situation here is materially like those considered in *People v. Camodeca* (1959), 52 Cal.2d 142, 146-47 [6-9], 338 P.2d 903 (attempted theft by false pretenses), and *People v. Lavine* (1931), 115 Cal.App. 289, 300-301 [11], 1 P.2d 496 (attempted extortion). Each of those cases is decided on the hypothesis that the defendants had the specific intent to commit the substantive offense and that under the circumstances as the defendants reasonably saw them they did the acts necessary to consummate the substantive offense; but because of circumstances unknown to defendants, essential elements of the substantive crime were lacking. Here, the goods did not have the status of stolen property and therefore defendants, although believing them to be stolen, could not have had actual knowledge of that condition. In *People v. Werner* (1940), 16 Cal.2d 216, 225, 105 P.2d 927, overruled by *Camodeca,* the "victim" was not deceived by defendants' false representations and therefore there was no lack of consent to the taking of the property. In the *Lavine* case, supra, the pretending victim was not induced by *fear* to part with any money; rather, the "victim" told the district attorney of the asserted or proposed attempt and by prior arrangement between the district attorney and the "victim" the "extorted" money was paid to defendants who were immediately thereafter arrested by officers who were awaiting the event. It is held (at page 300 [11] of 115 Cal.App., at page 501 of 1 P.2d) that "in attempted extortion the crime depends upon the acts, mind and intent of the person threatening and not upon the effect or result upon the person to be coerced."

In the case at bench the criminality of the attempt is not destroyed by the fact that the goods, having been recovered by the commendably alert and efficient action of the Los Angeles police, had, unknown to defendants, lost their "stolen" status, any more than the criminality of the attempt in the case of *In re Magidson* (1917), 32 Cal.App. 566, 568, 163 P. 689, was destroyed by impossibility caused by the fact that the police had recovered the goods and taken them from the place where the would-be receiver went to get them. In our opinion the consequences of intent and acts such as those of defendants here should be more serious than pleased amazement that because of the timeliness of the police the projected criminality was not merely detected but also wiped out. (*Cf. People v. Jelke* (1956), 1 N.Y.2d 321, 329, 152 N.Y.S.2d 479, 135 N.E.2d 213, explaining the *Jaffe* decision, supra, 185 N.Y. 497, 78 N.E. 169, 9 L.R.A., N.S., 263, as a case "like selling oil stock and being surprised to discover that oil was actually in the ground where the accused vendor had represented but not believed it to be" — conduct which the New York Court of Appeals apparently feels is not criminal.)

We approved the holding of the *Faustina* case (1959), *supra,* at page 834 of 174 Cal.App.2d at page 545 of 345 P.2d that upon a state of facts such as that

G. IMPOSSIBILITY

here, "Even though we say that, technically, the [goods] ... were not 'stolen' nevertheless the defendant did attempt to receive stolen property." The dictum in the *Zimmerman* case (1909), supra, at page 118 of 11 Cal.App., at page 591 of 104 P. that such a state of facts does not constitute a crime is disapproved.

....

Section 1159 of the Penal Code provides that a defendant may be found guilty of an attempt to commit the offense with which he is charged. Section 1181 (subd. 6) provides, "When the ... finding is contrary to law or evidence, but if the evidence shows the defendant to be not guilty of the degree of the crime of which he was convicted, but guilty of a ... lesser crime included therein, the court [the appellate court as well as the trial court] may modify the ... finding or judgment accordingly...." See also Pen.Code, § 1260....

The orders denying defendants' motions for new trial are affirmed. The trial court's finding that defendants are guilty as charged is modified to find them guilty of the offense of attempting to receive stolen property. The judgment and probation order are reversed and the cause is remanded to the trial court for further proceedings not inconsistent with the views hereinabove expressed, and with directions to enter such lawful judgment or order against each defendant, based on the modified finding, as the court deems appropriate.

NOTES

1. In facts similar to *Jaffe* the defendant was convicted of attempting to receive stolen property. *Held:* conviction reversed. The court stated that the confusion that existed because of the diverse rationales as laid down in New York and California was caused by the failure to distinguish between the factual and legal impossibility to commit a crime. Both *Rojas* and *People v. Rollino,* 37 Misc. 2d 14, 233 N.Y.S.2d 580 (1962), which followed the *Jaffe* holding, involved cases of *legal* impossibility. The same impossibility was present on the above facts. Since the property had lost its character as stolen property, the defendant could not properly be convicted of attempting to commit an act which would not have been a crime had the act been consummated. *Booth v. State,* 398 P.2d 863 (Okla. Crim. App. 1964).

2. In *People v. Meyers,* 213 Cal. App. 2d 518, 28 Cal. Rptr. 753 (1963), the rule of *Rojas* was extended to uphold a conviction of attempting to receive stolen property when the property had never had the status as stolen property. Defendant approached an employee of the telephone company and sought to purchase confidential lists of telephone subscribers. The employee notified his employers, who substituted a special agent to make the sale to defendant. The lists were of such a nature that they could not be obtained in any way except by stealing them from the company. After his arrest and conviction, the defendant appealed alleging that *Rojas* could be distinguished as a case of "physical" impossibility, while the present case represented one of "legal" impossibility. In *Rojas,* the goods had been stolen, and a physical intervening force changed their character; in the present case, the goods had never been stolen. The court rejected the argument after discussing the prior

California cases, and restated the California rule: "The rule of the *Jaffe* case, upon which the appellant apparently relies, is not ... the California rule. The courts of this state have not concerned themselves with the niceties of distinction between physical and legal impossibility, but have focused their attention on the question of the specific intent to commit the substantive offense. The hypothesis of the rule established in this state is that the defendant must have the specific intent to commit the substantive offense, and that under the circumstances, as he reasonably sees them, he does the acts necessary to consummate the substantive offense; but because of circumstances unknown to him, essential elements of the substantive crime are lacking.... It is only when the results intended by the actor, if they happened as envisaged by him, would still not be a crime, then and only then, can he not be guilty of an attempt." 213 Cal. App. 2d at 523, 28 Cal. Rptr. at 756.

3. But *cf. Young v. Superior Court,* 253 Cal. App. 2d 848, 61 Cal. Rptr. 355 (1967), which held that *Rojas* did not apply where the goods had never been "stolen" and defendant played no part in the purported theft. This distinction was repudiated subsequently as explained in *People v. Wright,* 105 Cal. App. 3d 329, 331-32, 164 Cal. Rptr. 207, 209 (1980):

> The facts in *People v. Moss* (1976) 55 Cal.App.3d 179, 127 Cal.Rptr. 454 are indistinguishable from the facts in *Young* and in the present case. A state officer sold Moss property which Moss believed was stolen. The merchandise had in fact been acquired by the sheriff's department by purchase or loan for use in the transaction. The *Moss* court expressly rejected the reasoning of *Young,* and adhered to *Rojas* and the line of authority following it. *Moss* holds that it is not necessary to sustain a conviction of attempted receiving stolen property that the People prove the defendant had any prior connection with the thief or that the goods received had ever been stolen.
>
> A detailed analysis of the entire line of cases interpreting and applying the rule of *Rojas* appears in both *Moss* and in *Lupo v. Superior Court* (1973) 34 Cal.App.3d 657, 110 Cal.Rptr. 185. Both Moss and Lupo criticize and reject the reasoning of *Young,* finding it irreconcilable with the rationale of *Rojas.* We agree with these appraisals.
>
> Although as noted in *Young,* the factual situation in *Rojas* was somewhat different in that the goods had actually been stolen, the principle enunciated there is not dependent on that circumstance, but turns upon intent. (*People v. Mayers* [sic] (1963), 213 Cal.App.2d 518, 522, 28 Cal.Rptr. 753.) Thus, a defendant is guilty of an attempt where he has the specific intent to commit the substantive offense and, under the circumstances as he reasonably sees them, does the acts necessary to consummate the substantive offense; however, because of circumstances unknown to him there is an absence of one or more of the essential elements of the substantive crime. (*People v. Rojas, supra,* 55 Cal.2d at p. 257, 10 Cal.Rptr. 465, 358 P.2d 921.) Under the *Rojas* rule, the criminality of the attempt is not dependent on whether the goods had actually been stolen or whether the defendant had any prior connection with the thief. "It is only when the results intended by the actor, *if they happened as envisaged*

by him, would still not be a crime, then and only then, can he not be guilty of an attempt." (Emphasis added; *People v. Mayers,* [sic], *supra,* 213 Cal.App.2d at p. 523, 28 Cal.Rptr. at p. 756.)

4. Defendant had a check upon which was written in words "two and 50/100 dollars." In the right hand corner were the figures "2.50/s100." On the face of the instrument, the words "Ten dollars or less" were stamped. Defendant wrote the figure "1" before the figure "2," thus making the amount "12.50." The conviction of attempted forgery was reversed. The marginal numbers and figures are not part of the instrument. "Our statute ... confines the crime of forgery to instances where 'any person may be affected, bound, or in any way, injured in his person or property.' This is not such a case." *Wilson v. State,* 85 Miss. 687, 38 So. 46, 47 (1904).

5. In *Marley v. State,* 58 N.J.L. 207, 33 A. 208 (1895), the defendants, members of the county board, were indicted for incurring a county obligation in excess of the legal limit. The trial judge charged the jury that under the evidence they could not be convicted of this offense but they were to decide "'whether any of these defendants ... be guilty of an attempt to incur this obligation.'" 33 A. at 209. The trial judge further held that the series of acts done by the defendant did not and could not impose any legal obligation on the county but "were as a matter of law wholly nugatory." *Id.* at 209.

Conviction reversed. "[T]he decision of the trial judge that the facts proved did not show the imposition of an obligation on the county was tantamount to a decision that the indictment itself did not charge any offense, for the facts charged and the facts proved were identical. It would seem to me self-evident that, if the case made by the state was wholly established by the evidence, and the latter, from a legal point of view, was nugatory, it necessarily follows that the case as presented on this record was equally nugatory.... [T]he defendants have been convicted of an attempt to commit a misdemeanor which was a legal impossibility." *Id.* at 210.

6. In *Nell v. State,* 277 So. 2d 1 (Fla. 1973), defendants had been convicted of bribery, in that they paid $1,000 to a county official to influence the granting of a permit to dig a canal. However, because of the proposed location of the canal, a permit was not required. *Held:* conviction quashed. The Florida bribery statute requires the intent to influence the official action of the person to whom the bribe is offered. Furthermore, the statute as construed by the court requires that "the action sought to be influenced must be within the official duties of the official." *Id.* at 6. Since no permit was required, there could be no official matter in which the influence of the official could be sought.

7. Compare the cases arising under 18 U.S.C. § 201(b) (1976). Under that statute, the offense of "giving, offering, or promising a bribe to a public official to influence any official act" is consummated even though the object of the bribe cannot be influenced by the official. Thus, in *Hurley v. United States,* 192 F.2d 297 (4th Cir. 1951), defendant's conviction of bribery was affirmed where he had given money to an Air Force sergeant who was in charge of processing men for induction, for the purpose of avoiding induction into the armed forces. "The cases support the proposition that for a conviction under § 201, it is immaterial that the bribee does not have the power of decision to

accomplish the result which the offerer of the bribe desires." *Id.* at 300. And in *United States v. Lubomski*, 277 F. Supp. 713 (N.D. Ill. 1967), defendant offered a bribe to an employee of the Internal Revenue Service to reduce his tax liability. The employee was merely a technician who had neither the authority nor the power to reduce the taxes. Defendant was nevertheless convicted of bribery.

8. *§ 110.10 Attempt to commit a crime, no defense:*

> If the conduct in which a person engages otherwise constitutes an attempt to commit a crime pursuant to section 110.00, it is no defense to a prosecution for such attempt that the crime charged to have been attempted was, under the attendant circumstances, factually or legally impossible of commission, if such crime could have been committed had the attendant circumstances been as such person believed them to be.

Practice Commentaries, by Arnold D. Hectman

This section seeks to crystallize a subject upon which the former Penal Law was silent, and upon which neither the New York decisions nor American authority in general have been consistent or entirely clear: namely, whether one can "attempt" to commit a crime which, by virtue of particular circumstances, is impossible of actual commission.

"Impossibility" is said to be of two kinds: factual and legal. The classic example of factual impossibility is posed by an attempt to pick a pocket which is in fact empty. Such conduct has been held in New York to constitute attempted larceny. (*People v. Moran*, 1890, 123 N.Y. 254, 25 N.E. 412).

With respect to so-called legal impossibility, it has been held that a person who received goods which he believed to be stolen but which were not such in fact, was not guilty of an attempt to receive stolen goods (*People v. Jaffe*, 1906, 185 N.Y. 497, 500-502, 78 N.E. 169); and that a person who attempted to induce another to commit perjury (materiality of the false testimony being an element of perjury at the time) was not guilty of attempted subornation of perjury because the false testimony sought would not have been material had it been given (*People v. Teal*, 1909, 196 N.Y. 372, 89 N.E. 1086).

While the distinction between factual and legal impossibility is not always clear-cut, the case law of New York appears to have been that factual impossibility did not constitute a defense to a prosecution for attempt, but that legal impossibility did (*People v. Rollino*, 1962, 37 Misc.2d 14, 233 N.Y.S.2d 580).

If such was the law, this section changes it by equally rejecting both brands of impossibility as a defense upon the theory that neither detracts from the offender's culpability.

....

G. IMPOSSIBILITY

This section codifies the recommendation of the American Law Institute. See § 5.01(1)(a) and comments 30-39 (Tentative Draft No. 10, 1960).

N.Y. PENAL LAW § 110.10 (McKinney 1975).

9. *People v. Leichtweis,* 59 A.D.2d 383, 387-88, 399 N.Y.S.2d 439, 441 (1979):

> A person is guilty of burglary in the third degree when he knowingly *enters* or remains *unlawfully* in a building with intent to commit a crime therein." ... On the facts of the instant case, a conviction for burglary would be *legally impossible* because the owner of the hangar, Swissair, had consented to entry by the defendants.
>
> ....
>
> The crime of attempted burglary would constitute a lesser included offense in this case, notwithstanding the legal impossibility of a burglary (see *People v. Dlugash,* 41 N.Y.2d 725, 737, 395 N.Y.S.2d 419, 428, 363 N.E.2d 1155, 1163....
>
> ....
>
> It is noteworthy that prior to the 1967 revision of the Penal Law, legal impossibility as to the commission of the underlying crime was a defense to a charge of attempting to commit the crime (*People v. Jaffe,* 185 N.Y. 497, 78 N.E. 169; *People v. Rollino, supra*). The statutory change in 1967 was apparently based in large part upon the approach of the draftsmen of the Model Penal Code to eliminate the defense of impossibility in virtually all situations. "[T]he code suggested a fundamental change to shift the locus of analysis to the actor's mental frame of reference and away from undue dependence upon external considerations. The basic premise of the code provision is that what was in the actor's own mind should be the standard for determining his dangerousness to society and, hence, his liability for attempting criminal conduct" (*People v. Dlugash, supra,* 41 N.Y.2d p. 734, 395 N.Y.S.2d p. 426, 363 N.E.2d p. 1161). Thus, "[i]n the belief that neither [legal impossibility nor factual impossibility] ... detracts from the offender's moral culpability ... the Legislature substantially carried the code's treatment of impossibility into the 1967 revision of the Penal Law" (*People v. Dlugash, supra,* p. 735, 395 N.Y.S.2d p. 426, 363 N.E.2d p. 1161). Therefore, in the instant case, if the evidence before the Grand Jury was sufficient to establish that respondent *believed* he was entering the hangar unlawfully — *i.e.,* without consent of Swissair — with intent to commit a crime therein, it was error for Criminal Term to have dismissed the indictment for burglary.

UNITED STATES v. BERRIGAN

United States Court of Appeals
482 F.2d 171 (3d Cir. 1973)

ALDISERT, CIRCUIT JUDGE.

Father Philip Berrigan and Sister Elizabeth McAlister appeal from judgments of conviction on seven counts of violating 18 U.S.C. § 1791,[1] as augmented by 28 C.F.R. § 6.1,[2] for sending seven letters into and out of Lewisburg Federal Penitentiary "without the knowledge and consent of the warden." (Counts IV-X.)

....

III

Appellants' contentions that the judgments of conviction on Counts V through X must be reversed because the government failed to prove all elements of the crime presents a very serious and difficult question. In these counts they were charged with and convicted of attempts to violate § 1791. Unlike the circumstances attending Father Berrigan's dispatch of the Count IV letter, which occurred prior to any knowledge on the part of the warden, it is undisputed that the prison officials had prior knowledge of letters embraced by these convictions.[17]

....

Professor Williams asserts that "[i]t should need no demonstration that a person who commits or attempts to commit what is not a crime in law cannot be convicted of attempting to commit a crime, and it makes no difference that he thinks it is a crime."[25] Professor Hall[26] is equally insistent that to make such conduct a criminal attempt would violate the principle of legality.[27]

Moreover, whatever be the approach taken in those jurisdictions utilizing the common law of crimes, except as modified by statute, e.g., Pennsylvania, the interstices of federal criminal law cannot be filled by resort to common

---

[1] 18 U.S.C. § 1791 provides:

Whoever, contrary to any rule or regulation promulgated by the Attorney General, introduces or attempts to introduce into or upon the grounds of any federal penal or correctional institution or takes or attempts to take or send therefrom anything whatsoever, shall be imprisoned not more than ten years.

[2] 28 C.F.R. § 6.1 provides:

The introduction or attempt to introduce into or upon the grounds of any federal penal or correctional institution or the taking or attempt to take or send therefrom anything whatsoever without the knowledge and consent of the warden or superintendent of such federal penal or correctional institution is prohibited.

[17] On cross-examination, Robert L. Hendricks, Associate Warden of Lewisburg, was asked:

Q. Now, did you know that Douglas was carrying letters in and out while he was on study-release, in and out of the penitentiary — unauthorized letters?

A. After we intercepted the first letter, from that point on I knew that he was.

Hendricks reaffirmed this statement several times during his testimony, eventually admitting that after June 3, 1970, he knew Douglas was carrying letters in and out of the prison. All of the letters involved in Counts V to X were exchanged after June 3.

[25] G. Williams, Criminal Law, The General Part, 633 (2d ed. 1961).

[26] J. Hall, General Principles of Criminal Law, 586 (2d ed. 1960).

[27] We have recently emphasized as "the fundament of American law [the principle] 'that no person can be criminally punished except by judicial process and unless the acts for which he was punished were clearly forbidden ....' 'The codification of definite rules in the law of crimes is considered by many in Western democratic societies as a fundamental requirement of liberal democracy.' They take their stand on the principle that no one shall be punished for anything that is not expressly forbidden by law. *Nullum crimen, nulla poena, sine lege.* They regard that principle as their great charter of liberty. 'A. Denning, Freedom Under Law 41 (1949).'" *Levy v. Parker, supra,* 478 F.2d at 791.

law precedents. It cannot be overemphasized that conduct intended to be prohibited by federal law must be explicitly prohibited by statutory authority.

....

B

Indeed, even a decision to analyze impossibility on the basis of what is generally described as the two categories of factual impossibility and legal impossibility presents serious problems unless conceptual distinctions between the two labels are recognized and respected. Generally speaking factual impossibility is said to occur when extraneous circumstances unknown to the actor or beyond his control prevent consummation of the intended crime. The classic example is the man who puts his hand in the coat pocket of another with the intent to steal his wallet and finds the pocket empty. *Regina v. Collins*, 9 Cox Crim. Cas. 497 (1864). Generally, the cases which have imposed criminal liability for attempt where factual circumstances precluded commission of the intended crime have emphasized, as a primary requisite, proof of an intent to commit a specific crime.

Legal impossibility is said to occur where the intended acts, even if completed, would not amount to a crime. Thus, legal impossibility would apply to those circumstances where (1) the motive, desire and expectation is to perform an act in violation of the law; (2) there is intention to perform a physical act; (3) there is a performance of the intended physical act; and (4) the consequence resulting from the intended act does not amount to a crime.[35]

Were intent to break the law the sole criterion to be considered in determining criminal responsibility — and this was the approach utilized by the district court — we could sustain the conviction of appellants on Counts V to X. Clearly, it can be said that Father Berrigan intended to send letters to Sister

---

[35]Intent as used in this connection must be distinguished from motive, desire and expectation. If C by reason of his hatred of A plans to kill him, but mistaking B for A shoots B, his motive, desire and expectation are to kill A but his intent is to kill B. If a married man forcibly has intercourse with a woman whom he believes to be his wife's twin sister, but who in fact is his wife, he is not guilty of rape because his intent was to have intercourse with the woman he attacked, who was in fact his wife. If A takes an umbrella which he believes to belong to B, but which in fact is his own, he does not have the intent to steal, his intent being to take the umbrella he grasps in his hand, which is his own umbrella. If a man, mistaking a dummy in female dress for a woman, tries to ravish it he does not have the intent to commit rape since the ravishment of an inanimate object cannot be rape. If a man mistakes a stump for his enemy and shoots at it, notwithstanding his desire and expectation to shoot his enemy, his intent is to shoot the object aimed at, which is the stump.

Keedy, *supra* note 29, [Criminal Attempts at Common Law, 102 U. Pa.L. Rev. 464 (1954)] at 466-467.

Wharton puts the following case:

Lady Eldon, when traveling with her husband on the Continent, bought what she supposed to be a quantity of French lace, which she hid, concealing it from Lord Eldon in one of the pockets of the coach. The package was brought to light by a custom officer at Dover. The lace turned out to be an English manufactured article, of little value, and of course, not subject to duty. Lady Eldon had bought it at a price vastly above its value, believing it to be genuine....

Wharton opined that Lady Eldon had the intent to smuggle this lace into England and was guilty of an attempt to smuggle. 1 Wharton Criminal Law, 304 n.9 (12th ed. 1932). Professor Keedy suggests: "The fallacy of this argument is found in the fact that the particular lace which Lady Eldon intended to bring into England was not subject to duty and therefore, although there was the wish to smuggle, there was not the intent to do so." Keedy, *Id.*, at 476-477.

McAlister, and vice versa. Normally, of course, the exchange of letters is not a federal offense. Where one of the senders is in prison, however, the sending may or may not be a criminal offense. If the letter is sent within normal channels with the consent and knowledge of the warden it is not a criminal offense. Therefore, an attempt to send a letter through normal channels cannot be considered an attempt to violate the law because none of the intended consequences is in fact criminal. If the letter is sent without the knowledge and consent of the warden, it is a criminal offense and so is the attempt because both the intended consequence and the actual consequence are in fact criminal. Here, we are faced with a third situation where there is a motivation, desire and expectation of sending a letter without the knowledge and consent, and the intended act is performed, but unknown to the sender, the transmittal is accomplished with the knowledge and consent of the warden.

Applying the principles of the law of attempt to the instant case, the writing of the letters, and their copying and transmittal by the courier, Boyd Douglas, constituted the *Act*. This much the government proved. What the government did not prove — and could not prove because it was a legal impossibility — was the "external, objective situation which the substantive law may require to be present," to-wit, absence of knowledge and consent of the warden. Thus, the government failed to prove the *"Circumstances or attendant circumstances"* vital to the offense. Without such proof, the *Consequence* or *Result* did not constitute an offense that violated the federal statute. The warden and the government were aware of the existence of the letters. The courier acted with the consent of the warden. Although there was no entrapment, *United States v. Russell,* 411 U.S. 423 (1973), the public authorities were privy to the *Act* which gave rise to these charges. There are many supporters of the view that irrespective of the absence of a necessary element of the offense prohibited by statute — the "external, objective situation which the substantive law may require be present" — criminal responsibility should attach "if the attendant circumstances were as [the actor] believes them to be." The bills presently before the Congress contain such a provision. But the efforts of the distinguished scholars who drafted these proposals must be kept in perspective; they are recommending changes to fill an apparent void in existing law. They suggest a statutory change which would remove one of the elements of the offense which still must be proved under the present federal statutory law of crimes.

We are also aware that in those jurisdictions which permit the development of elements of the criminal law by the common law tradition of judicial decision, the courts have been willing to change the law through the centuries from an absolute defense of factual impossibility, to a jurisprudential environment which, though extremely complicated and confused, seems to be watering down, if not eliminating, the defense of factual impossibility. But as we have heretofore indicated, we will not fall into the trap of equating *legal* with *factual* impossibility in the law of criminal attempt.[39]

---

[39] Indeed, though it is not before us, we do evidence some concern that the proposed changes in the federal criminal code seem to fashion a new crime where the critical element to be proved is *mens rea simpliciter*. We detect the total lack of objective guidelines in the presentation of such proof or a defense. While *mens rea* is certainly within one's control it is not subject to direct proof;

...

We distinguish between the defense of factual impossibility, which is not involved here, *United States v. Osborn,* 385 U.S. 323 (1966), and legal impossibility, which is. Even were we to concede that factual impossibility of success may not prevent an attempt, there can be no crime of attempt where there is a legal impossibility to commit a crime. Simply stated, attempting to do that which is not a crime is not attempting to commit a crime. Congress has not yet enacted a law that provides that intent plus act plus conduct constitutes the offense of attempt irrespective of legal impossibility. Until such time as such legislative changes in the law take place, this court will not fashion a new non-statutory law of criminal attempt.

Accordingly, the convictions on Counts V-X may not stand.

NOTES

1. In the principal case, *United States v. Berrigan,* "the district court relied on New York Penal Law, McKinney's Consolidated Laws c. 40, § 110.10; *United States v. Thomas,* 13 U.S.C.M.A. 278, 32 C.M.R. 279 (1962); HALL, GENERAL PRINCIPLES OF CRIMINAL LAW, 586 (2d Ed. 1960); PERKINS, CRIMINAL LAW, 489 (1957); and the MODEL PENAL CODE, Art. 5, § 501." 482 F.2d at 185.

In rejecting that approach and reversing the district court, the court of appeals was aware that it was going against the tide: "Indeed, we are informed that elimination of impossibility as a defense to a charge of criminal attempt, as suggested by the Model Penal Code and the proposed federal legislation, is consistent with "'the overwhelming modern view,' and with criminal provisions in such diverse parts as Canada, India and New Zealand." *Id.* at 186.

The matter is discussed in Wechsler, Jones & Korn, *The Treatment of Inchoate Crimes in the Model Penal Code of the American Law Institute: Attempt, Solicitation and Conspiracy,* 61 COLUM. L. REV. 571 (1961); 1 WORKING PAPERS OF THE NATIONAL COMMISSION ON REFORM OF FEDERAL CRIMINAL LAWS 360 (1970).

2. One court has concluded that the terms "legal impossibility" and "factual impossibility" are not very helpful. In *United States v. Oviedo,* 525 F.2d 881 (5th Cir. 1976), defendant had sold a substance he thought to be heroin but which in reality was an uncontrolled substance. Faced with a defense of "legal impossibility," the court remarked:

> These definitions are not particularly helpful here, for they do nothing more than provide a different focus for the analysis. In one sense, the impossibility involved here might be deemed legal, for those *acts* which Oviedo set in motion, the transfer of the substance in his possession, were not a crime. In another sense, the impossibility is factual, for the *objective*

---

it is proved by circumstantial evidence only. More important, it is not subject to direct refutation. It is the subject of inference and speculation. We perceive the danger of potential abuse where the circumstances admit to very little objective measurement. More important, we are unwilling as a court to legislate by judicial fiat a crime consistent only with thought processes, as this is reminiscent of the German law of the Nazi period "that anything is punishable if it is deserving of punishment according 'to the fundamental conceptions of a penal law and sound popular feeling.'" H.L.A. Hart, Law, Liberty and Morality, 12 (1963).

of Oviedo, the sale of heroin, was proscribed by law, and failed only because of a circumstance unknown to Oviedo.[5]

Id. at 883 (emphasis in original).

In formulating its approach the court compared *United States v. Berrigan, supra* with *United States v. Heng Awkak Roman,* 356 F. Supp. 434 (S.D.N.Y.), *aff'd,* 484 F.2d 1271 (2d Cir. 1973), *cert. denied,* 415 U.S. 978 (1974). In *Roman,* defendants' conviction for attempted possession of narcotics with intent to distribute was affirmed although the contents of the suitcase which they tried to sell were soap powder which an informant had substituted for drugs.

The *Oviedo* court rejected both the *Roman* approach which focuses on defendant's criminal objective, and *Berrigan* which looks to the physical act which defendant intended.

> In our view, both *Roman* and *Berrigan* miss the mark, but in opposite directions. A strict application of the Berrigan approach would eliminate any distinction between factual and legal impossibility, and such impossibility would always be a valid defense, since the "intended" physical acts are never criminal.[9] The *Roman* approach turns the attempt statute into a new substantive criminal statute where the critical element to be proved is mens rea simpliciter. It would allow us to punish one's thoughts, desires, or motives, through indirect evidence, without reference to any objective fact.
>
> ....
>
> Thus, we demand that in order for a defendant to be guilty of a criminal attempt, the objective acts performed, without any reliance on the accompanying *mens rea,* mark the defendant's conduct as criminal in nature. The acts should be unique rather than so commonplace that they are engaged in by persons not in violation of the law.
>
> Here we have only two objective facts. First, Oviedo told the agent that the substance he was selling was heroin, and second, portions of the substance were concealed in a television set.

Id. at 884-85. Under the court's approach should Oviedo's conviction have been affirmed or reversed?

EDITORIAL NOTE ON THE IMPOSSIBILITY PROBLEM

There is a rich literature on the subject of impossibility.* The views are diverse and the dispute appears capable of resolution only as a matter of

---

[5] At least one writer has recognized that legal impossibility is logically indistinguishable from factual impossibility. *See* Hall, *Criminal Attempt — A Study of Foundations of Criminal Liability,* 49 YALE L.J. 789, 836 (1940).

[9] If the "intended" physical acts were criminal, the defendant would be guilty of the completed crime, rather than the attempt.

*Weigend, *Why Lady Eldon Should Be Acquitted: The Social Harm in Attempting the Impossible,* 27 DEPAUL L. REV. 231 (1977-78); Elkind, *Impossibility in Criminal Attempts: A Theorist's Headache,* 54 VA. L. REV. 20 (1968); Wechsler, Jones & Korn, *The Treatment of Inchoate Crimes in the Model Penal Code of The American Law Institute: Attempt, Solicitation and Conspiracy,* 61 COLUM. L. REV. 957 (1961); Arnold, *Criminal Attempts — The Rise and Fall of an Abstraction,* 40 YALE L.J. 53 (1930).

G. IMPOSSIBILITY

policy. The question is not which view is correct, but rather what should the correct view be? The problem has been presented in a variety of factual contexts which are collected in Gold, *To "Dream the Impossible Dream": A Problem in Criminal Attempts (and Conspiracy) Revisited,* 21 CRIM. L.Q. 220-26 (1978-79). *See also* Williams, *Attempting the Impossible — A Reply,* 22 CRIM L. Q. 49 (1979-80); 1 WHARTON'S CRIMINAL LAW 304 n.9 (12th ed. 1932).

What is really at the bottom of the dispute over "impossibility"? Is the answer to be found in reexamining the principles of criminal law? Is the legal impossibility defense predicated on a lack of either *actus reus,* or *mens rea,* or a lack of evidence of *mens rea,* or a lack of harm? Does one's position on impossibility depend on one's view of harm? Is the issue broader in the sense that it raises basic questions about the purposes of punishment and the purposes of the criminal law, *i.e.,* is the purpose to protect society from culpable conduct which causes injury or to protect society from dangerous people? The answers are not easy and even settled views are not exempt from reconsideration.

In *Haughton v. Smith,* on facts essentially like those in *Jaffe* and *Rojas,* both the English Court of Appeal, [1973] 2 All E.R. 896, and the House of Lords, [1973] 3 All E.R. 1109, reversed the conviction of attempt, etc.; the Lord Chancellor, Hailsham, specifically disagreeing with *Rojas* and preferring *Jaffe.* The reasoning was much like that of *Jaffe* — if the defendant "set out" to do an act and did it, and committed no crime, he cannot be convicted of an attempt to commit that crime, *i.e.,* the "external" view was accepted. This seemed persuasive because otherwise in the theory and law imposing liability, certain ridiculous conclusions follow, *e.g.,* that a man can be guilty of attempting to kill a dead person. "The law may sometimes be an ass," said Lord Reid, "but it cannot be so asinine as that." [1973] 3 All E.R. at 1121.

In this far-ranging decision, perhaps the most significant result is that the old cases reversing convictions of attempt to pick an empty pocket were held to be sound and that the later cases and long-established decisions that it is criminal to attempt to take property from a pocket which turns out to be empty were criticized. The same result as *Haughton v. Smith* was reached in a conspiracy case. *D.P.P. v. Nock & Alsford,* [1978] A.C. 979.

Under this view impossibility would have been a defense unless the crime failed because of inadequate means. However, the Criminal Attempts Act, 1981, rejected the approach in Haughton and Nock and provided that a person may be guilty of attempt or conspiracy "even though the facts are such that the commission of the offence is impossible." Dennis, *The Criminal Attempts Act 1981,* [1982] CRIM. L. REV. 5.

As a practical matter no one is charged with trying to kill a person known to be dead or to take something from a pocket known to be empty. In *United States v. Thomas & McClellan,* 13 U.S.C.M.A. 278, 32 CMR 278 (1962), two soldiers were held guilty of attempt to rape despite the fact that the medical testimony at the trial established that the woman had died just before the intercourse; admittedly, the defendants thought she was alive when the intercourse occurred. Apparently, there is a common sense view regarding commonplace efforts to pick pockets and there is the "asininity" that common sense applies to such situations viewed in terms of the known actual facts. If the common sense view regarding picking pockets which turn out to be empty prevails as the basic postulate of theories about attempt, the plain implication is that guilt is determined not by the external facts but by the *mens rea* and action going beyond preparation that is intended to actualize the *mens rea*, but which fails to do so because the facts were different from what the defendant thought they were. On the English decisions *see* Buxton, *The Working Paper on Inchoate Offences: Incitement and Attempt*, [1973] Crim. L. Rev. 656.

On the other hand, *Jaffe* and *Haughton v. Smith* have the merit of emphasizing the importance of the principle of legality, and this must be kept in mind in evaluating the proposed solution of the A.L.I. Model Code, enacted in the New York Penal Law. These two decisions also raise questions of policy especially regarding the harms that should be proscribed by criminal law.

There are obvious difficulties in the way of eliminating "legal impossibility" as a defense. For example, if a person believes that destroying food is a crime, doing that or trying to do that is not criminal — the principle of legality bars that. Accordingly, it would seem that the exclusion of "legal impossibility" must be limited so as to not to exclude the principle of legality. How can this be done?

A first approach would seem to focus on the existence of a *mens rea*. But this encounters the same difficulties met in analysis of *error juris*. One who takes property thinking he or she has a legal right to take it is said to lack the required *mens rea*; but one who shoots a trespasser or kills a spouse's lover caught in an act of adultery is said to have the required *mens rea* regardless of an opinion that such an action is legal. If the term "circumstances" in N.Y. Penal Law § 110.10, *supra* p. 776, means "facts," it is still unlikely that those who try to take property mistakenly believed to be theirs will be held criminal for attempted theft, just as it is unlikely that spouses who try to kill adulterers, believing they have a legal right to do so, will escape convictions for criminal attempt.

This suggests that a solution of this problem by reference to *mens rea* depends largely on the meaning of "*mens rea*." It also indicates the difficulties inherent in distinguishing the existence of a law, *e.g.*, governing larceny or homicide, from the question whether in the given "circumstances" the mistake is one of law or of fact. A solution of this problem might therefore take two directions: (1) There must be a relevant law in the sense of satisfying the principle of legality. This implies that the defendant's mistaken belief that such a law exists is not relevant and cannot serve as the ground of liability; and (2) The question of *mens rea* should focus on the distinction between whether the relevant law is part of the *mens rea*, as it is in *animus furandi* (and is treated as "fact") or whether the defendant's position is simply that the law supports what is done, *e.g.*, shooting a trespasser or adulterer. These suggestions should be viewed as a hypothesis and applied to the above cases. This testing should proceed on the assumption that sound policy supports the principle of legality since none of the recent proposals or laws challenge that principle.

PROBLEM

Assume that there is a provision in the United States Code which prohibits the importation or attempted importation of "national treasures" of foreign countries without the approval of the country of origin. The term "national treasure" is defined in part as including "ancient aboriginal artifacts which under the law of the country of origin may not be exported from that country without written permission of the government." A and B go on a vacation together to a foreign country. While there, each, unbeknownst to the other, purchases a statue. Each is told by the respective seller that the statue is an "ancient aboriginal artifact," that the country of origin will not issue an export permit and that the only way to get it out of the country and into the United States is to smuggle it.

A hides his statue in a hidden compartment in his suitcase. B does the same. Neither obtained permission to remove the statues from the country of origin. Upon going through United States customs the secreted statues are discovered. A's statue is a genuine "ancient aboriginal artifact" and of course he may be convicted of smuggling. B's statue, however, is merely an expensive replica which the seller duped her into thinking was genuine. Should B be convicted of attempted smuggling? Would your answer be different if she had succeeded in bringing the statue into the country, and believing it to be genuine, unwittingly bragged to an undercover customs officer how she had declared the item as a replica which she documented with a "false" receipt given to her by the seller which understated the sales price and listed the statue as a replica?

Would your answer in regard to A be different if the following occurred? A thief stole the genuine statue from his suitcase before he departed for the United States and replaced it with a brick. When the custom's officer found the hidden compartment and opened it, A exclaimed, "O.K., You got me! I was trying to smuggle the statue into the country without the proper permit." Later the statue was recovered and the thief confessed to stealing it from A's suitcase.

Finally, suppose after A purchased and hid the statue, but before he returned to the United States, the country where he purchased the statue amended its law so that such items could be removed from the country freely without a permit. A was unaware of the change and when the statue was discovered by a custom's officer in the hidden compartment, A blurted out his "confession." Should he be convicted of attempted smuggling?

SECTION V. Conspiracy

A. CONCEPTUAL MATTERS

1. THE RATIONALE OF CONSPIRACY

INTRODUCTORY NOTE

"[C]ollective criminal agreement — partnership in crime — presents a greater potential threat to the public than individual delicts. Concerted action both increases the likelihood that the criminal object will be successfully attained and decreases the probability that the individuals involved will depart from their path of criminality. Group association for criminal purposes often, if not normally, makes possible the attainment of ends more complex than those which one criminal could accomplish. Nor is the danger of a conspiratorial group limited to the particular end toward which it has embarked. Combination in crime makes more likely the commission of crimes unrelated to the original purpose for which the group was formed. In sum, the danger which a conspiracy generates is not confined to the substantive offense which is the immediate aim of the enterprise." *Callanan v. United States,* 364 U.S. 587, 593-94 (1961).

"The utility of conspiracy theory in the prosecution of organized crime is manifest. No other single substantive legal tool has been as effective in bringing organized crime to book." Blakey & Gettings, *Racketeer Influenced and Corrupt Organizations (RICO): Basic Concepts — Criminal and Civil Remedies,* 53 TEMP. L. Q. 1009, 1010, n.4 (1980).

2. THE DANGERS OF CONSPIRACY PROSECUTIONS

KRULEWITCH v. UNITED STATES
United States Supreme Court
336 U.S. 440 (1949)

MR. JUSTICE JACKSON, concurring in the judgment and opinion of the Court.

This case illustrates a present drift in the federal law of conspiracy which warrants some further comment because it is characteristic of the long evolution of that elastic, sprawling and pervasive offense. Its history exemplifies the "tendency of a principle to expand itself to the limit of its logic." The unavailing protest of courts against the growing habit to indict for conspiracy in lieu of prosecuting for the substantive offense itself or in addition thereto,[2] suggests that loose practice as to this offense constitutes a serious threat to fairness in our administration of justice.

---

[2] The Conference of Senior Circuit Judges, presided over by Chief Justice Taft, in 1925 reported:

> We note the prevalent use of conspiracy indictments for converting a joint misdemeanor into a felony; and we express our conviction that both for this purpose and for the purpose — or at least with the effect — of bringing in much improper evidence, the conspiracy statute is being much abused.
>
> Although in a particular case there may be no preconcert of plan, excepting that necessarily inherent in mere joint action, it is difficult to exclude that situation from the established definitions of conspiracy; yet the theory which permits us to call the aborted plan a greater offense than the completed crime supposes a serious and substantially continued group scheme for cooperative law breaking. We observe so many conspiracy prosecutions which do not have this substantial base that we fear the creation of a general impression, very harmful to law enforcement, that this method of prosecution is used arbitrarily and harshly. Further the rules of evidence in conspiracy cases make them most difficult to try without prejudice to an innocent defendant. Annual Report of the Attorney General for 1925, pp. 5-6.

Fifteen years later Judge Learned Hand observed: "... so many prosecutors seek to sweep within the drag-net of conspiracy all those who have been associated in any degree whatever with the main offenders. That there are opportunities of great oppression in such a doctrine is very plain, and it is only by circumscribing the scope of such all comprehensive indictments that they can be avoided." United States v. Falcone, 109 F.2d 579, 581 (pp. 445-446) [2d Cir. 1940].

A. CONCEPTUAL MATTERS

The modern crime of conspiracy is so vague that it almost defies definition....

The crime comes down to us wrapped in vague but unpleasant connotations. It sounds historical undertones of treachery, secret plotting and violence on a scale that menaces social stability and the security of the state itself. "Privy conspiracy" ranks with sedition and rebellion in the Litany's prayer for deliverance. Conspiratorial movements do indeed lie back of the political assassination, the *coup d'etat,* the *putsch,* the revolution, and seizures of power in modern times, as they have in all history.

But the conspiracy concept also is superimposed upon many concerted crimes having no political motivation. It is not intended to question that the basic conspiracy principle has some place in modern criminal law, because to unite, back of a criminal purpose, the strength, opportunities and resources of many is obviously more dangerous and more difficult to police than the efforts of a lone wrongdoer. It also may be trivialized, as here, where the conspiracy consists of the concert of a loathsome panderer and a prostitute to go from New York to Florida to ply their trade ... and it would appear that a simple Mann Act prosecution would vindicate the majesty of federal law. However, even when appropriately invoked, the looseness and pliability of the doctrine present inherent dangers which should be in the background of judicial thought wherever it is sought to extend the doctrine to meet the exigencies of a particular case.

Conspiracy in federal law aggravates the degree of crime over that of unconcerted offending. The act of confederating to commit a misdemeanor, followed by even an innocent overt act in its execution, is a felony and is such even if the misdemeanor is never consummated.[9] The more radical proposition also is well-established that at common law and under some statutes a combination may be a criminal conspiracy even if it contemplates only acts which are not crimes at all when perpetrated by an individual or by many acting severally.

Thus the conspiracy doctrine will incriminate persons on the fringe of offending who would not be guilty of aiding and abetting or of becoming an accessory, for those charges only lie when an act which is a crime has actually been committed.

When the trial starts, the accused feels the full impact of the conspiracy strategy. Strictly, the prosecution should first establish *prima facie* the conspiracy and identify the conspirators, after which evidence of acts and declarations of each in the course of its execution are admissible against all. But the order of proof of so sprawling a charge is difficult for a judge to control. As a practical matter, the accused often is confronted with a hodgepodge of acts and statements by others which he may never have authorized or intended or even known about, but which help to persuade the jury of existence of the conspiracy itself. In other words, a conspiracy often is proved by evidence that is admissible only upon assumption that conspiracy existed. The naive assump-

---

[9] 18 U.S.C.A. § 371. Until recently, the punishment for such a felony could have been far in excess of that provided for the substantive offense. However, the Act of June 25, 1948, c. 645, 62 Stat. 683, 701, provides that in such a case the punishment for the conspiracy shall not exceed the maximum provided for such misdemeanor. (pp. 448-449.)

tion that prejudicial effects can be overcome by instructions to the jury, ... all practicing lawyers know to be unmitigated fiction.

Currently, federal law provides that "Any person who attempts or conspires to commit any offense defined in this title [Title 18] shall be subject to the same penalties as those prescribed for the offense, the commission of which was the object of the attempt or conspiracy." 18 U.S.C. § 963 (1988).

Some jurisdictions punish conspiracy less severely than the offense which was the object of the conspiracy. For example, the Texas Penal Code provides that "An offense under this section [criminal conspiracy] is one category lower than the most serious felony that is the object of the conspiracy, and if the most serious felony that is the object of the conspiracy is a felony of the third degree, the offense is a Class A misdemeanor." TEX. PENAL CODE ANN. § 15.02(d) (West 1973). In Texas, one of the elements of criminal conspiracy is that the actor must intend that a felony be committed as the object offense. TEX. PENAL CODE ANN. § 15.02(a) (West 1973).

One commentator has urged the abolition of the crime of conspiracy. Johnson, *The Unnecessary Crime of Conspiracy,* 61 CALIF. L. REV. 1137 (1973).

"[I]nsofar as conspiracy adds anything to the attempt provision of the reform codes ..., it adds only overly broad criminal liability. Like its use in every other area of the substantive criminal law, the use of an independent crime of conspiracy to punish inchoate crimes turns out to be unnecessary." *Id.* at 1164. Cf. Misner, *The New Attempt Laws: Unsuspected Threat to the Fourth Amendment,* 33 STAN. L. REV. 201 (1980-81).

Johnson concludes:

> Conspiracy gives the courts a means of deciding difficult questions without thinking about them. The basic objection to the doctrine is not simply that many of its specific rules are bad, but rather that all of them are ill-considered. The first step towards improving a rule of law is to consider the policies it serves. The specific rules of conspiracy, however, are derived more from the logic of an abstract concept than from any realistic assessment of the needs of law enforcement or the legitimate interests of criminal defendants. We need to reconsider the problem of group crime without being distracted by the abstractions that the concept of conspiracy always seems to introduce.

Id. at 1188.

Abolition of the general crime of conspiracy would not necessarily eliminate a need to prohibit certain specific forms of criminal conspiracies or agreements. For example, in some crimes "concert of action" may lie at the core of the harm sought to be avoided. Thus, executives of a single business enterprise can follow policies and practices which maximize profits even though competitors are adversely affected. However, under the federal antitrust laws, which specifically prohibit combinations and conspiracies in restraint of trade, 15 U.S.C. § 1 (1976), executives of two or more enterprises cannot lawfully agree to take concerted action intended to enhance their economic position at the expense of competing enterprises.

B. OVERVIEW

STATE v. CARBONE

Supreme Court of New Jersey
10 N.J. 329, 91 A.2d 571 (1952)

HEHER, J.

[Kalik, a New York bookmaker, introduced Kammerer to a man named Murray and told Kammerer to go with Murray who would "get a phone" for him in New Jersey. Murray took Kammerer to New Jersey and introduced him to Carbone who, in turn, took him to one Franze's apartment. Carbone introduced Kammerer to Franze and showed Kammerer the phone he was to use. Carbone left and had no further contact with Kammerer. Thereafter Kammerer used the apartment on a daily basis receiving bets over the telephone from Kalik's customers, a list of whom he was provided each day by Kalik. Each evening when Kammerer returned to New York he gave the list to a man named Charlie. Charlie gave him the money to pay the telephone bill at Franze's apartment. Carbone, Franze and "John Doe" (Murray) were indicted for conspiracy to violate gambling laws.

[Carbone and Franze were convicted by a jury. On appeal they objected to the introduction at trial of the activities and conversations of Kammerer since he was not charged in the indictment as a defendant or conspirator. Furthermore, they claimed that Kammerer's acts were pursuant to an agreement with Kalik; that taking bets was a furtherance of a conspiracy between Kammerer and Kalik; that neither Carbone nor Franze had "a stake in the venture" which Kammerer was conducting; and that Kammerer's acts in the apartment were performed on behalf of Kalik. In other words, defendants claim not to be part of any conspiracy between Kalik and Kammerer.]

At common law, a conspiracy consists not merely in the intention but in the agreement of two or more persons (not being husband and wife) to do an unlawful act, or to do a lawful act by unlawful means. So long as such a design rests in intention only, it is not indictable. When two agree to carry it into effect, the very plot is an act in itself, and the act of each of the parties, promise against promise, *actus contra actum,* capable of being enforced if lawful, punishable if for a criminal object or for the use of criminal means. The agreement is an advancement of the intention which each has conceived in his mind; the mind proceeds from a secret intention to the overt act of mutual consultation and agreement.... It is not requisite, in order to constitute a conspiracy at common law, that the acts agreed to be done be such as would be criminal if done; it is enough if the acts agreed to be done, although not criminal, be wrongful, *i.e.,* amount to a civil wrong.... The gist of the offense of conspiracy lies, not in doing the act, nor effecting the purpose for which the conspiracy is formed, nor in attempting to do them, nor in inciting others to do them, but in the forming of the scheme or agreement between the parties. 1 East. P.C. 462. The offense depends on the unlawful agreement and not on the act which follows it; the latter is not evidence of the former. 2 Burr.

993; 3 Burr. 1321. The combination itself is vicious and gives the public an interest to interfere by indictment.... The external or overt act of the crime is concert by which initial consent to a common purpose is exchanged.... In order to render one criminally liable for conspiracy at common law, it must be shown that he entered into an agreement as thus defined with one or more persons, whether charged with him in the indictment or not, and whether known or unknown. 1 Hawk., c. 72, § 8; 3 Chitty, Cr.L. 1141.

But it is not essential that there be direct contact between the parties, or that all enter into the conspiratorial agreement at one and the same time. "It may be that the alleged conspirators have never seen each other, and have never corresponded. One may have never heard the name of the other, and yet by the law they may be parties to the same common criminal agreement." ... One who joins a conspiracy after its formation is equally guilty with the original conspirators....

In New Jersey, an agreement or combination between two or more persons to commit a crime constitutes a conspiracy punishable as a misdemeanor, if with certain exceptions there be an overt act in furtherance of the object of the agreement by one or more of the parties. R.S.2:119-1, 2, N.J.S.A. The union is invested with a potentiality for evil that renders the plan criminal in itself, and punishable as such if an act be done to effect its object....

It is a corollary of these common-law principles that the acts and declarations of any of the conspirators in furtherance of the common design may be given in evidence against any other conspirator. And the rule is applicable where it is charged that a crime was committed in pursuance of a conspiracy, whether or not the indictment contains a count for conspiracy....

Where two or more persons have entered into a conspiracy to perpetrate a crime, the acts and declarations of one of the conspirators in furtherance of the common object are deemed in law the acts and declarations of all. This on the theory of a joint or mutual agency ad hoc for the prosecution of the common plan....

... A conspiracy makes each conspirator liable under the criminal law for the acts of every other conspirator done in pursuance of the conspiracy. The admissions of a co-conspirator may be used "to affect the proof against the others, on the same conditions as his acts when used to create their legal liability. The tests ... are the same, whether that which is offered is the act or the admission of the co-conspirator." Wigmore on Evidence (3rd ed.) section 1079. A conspiracy is a partnership in crime. *United States v. Socony-Vacuum Oil Co.,* 310 U.S. 150, 253 (1940). The least degree of concert of action suffices to render the act of one conspirator the act of all. But it is requisite that there be confederacy in fact and that the act be done in the execution of the conspiratorial project. Acts foreign to the common design are not within the principle....

Here, participation in the conspiracy was laid to Kammerer by the overt acts charged in the indictment, although this is not to suggest that the application of the principle is varied by the absence of this circumstance. In the case of *The King v. William Stone,* 6 Durnford & East's Reports 527 (1796), the prisoner was indicted for high treason, for compassing the death of the king and adhering to his enemies. The overt acts charged were 11 in number; but that to which the evidence chiefly applied was the conspiring with John Hurford Stone, William Jackson and others unknown to collect intelligence of the disposition of the king's subjects in case of an invasion of Great Britain or Ireland, and to communicate such intelligence to the enemies of the king. Neither John Hurford Stone nor Jackson was indicted. A letter containing treasonable information dispatched by Jackson with a view of reaching the enemy, in pursuance of the common design, was received in evidence against all engaged in the conspiracy. Grose, J. said: "If a number of persons meet towards one common end, the act of each is evidence against all concerned." And Lawrence, J., added that "evidence having been given sufficient for the jury to consider whether the prisoner was not one engaged in a conspiracy for treasonable purposes with Jackson, if they were of that opinion, Jackson's acts done in pursuance of that conspiracy were in contemplation of law the acts of the prisoner."

The convictions of both defendants are well grounded in the evidence. A conspiracy may be proved by direct evidence, or by circumstances from which the jury may presume it. *R. v. Parsons,* 1 W. Bl. 392; *R. v. Murphy,* 8 C. & P. 297. Proof of the existence of a conspiracy is generally a "matter of inference deduced from certain criminal acts of the parties accused, done in pursuance of an apparent criminal purpose in common between them." ... Though the act of conspiracy is the gist of the offense, "it is not necessary to show an actual association or confederacy, but it may be left to reasonable inference." Chitty, Cr.L., 1141. There is an amplitude of proof of concert of action directed to the furtherance of the common plan charged in the indictment. The inference of guilt is inescapable.

. . . .

Judgment affirmed.

For affirmance: CHIEF JUSTICE VANDERBILT and JUSTICES HEHER, OLIPHANT, BURLING AND BRENAN — 5.

NOTES

1. Recent codes require that the object of the conspiracy be a crime, *e.g.,* N.Y. PENAL LAW § 105.00 (McKinney 1975). In *State v. Smith,* 207 La. 735, 21 So. 2d 890 (1945), the court held that there can be no conspiracy to commit an act which is not a crime under the Louisiana Code. The American Law Institute has adopted the same limitation. MODEL PENAL CODE § 5.03(1), comments 102-104 (Tent. Draft No. 10, 1960). This approach has been adopted in England. Criminal Law Act 1977, Section 1. In Texas, the object of the conspiracy must be a felony. TEX. PENAL CODE ANN. § 15.03(a) (West 1973).

2. Can someone be convicted of conspiracy to attempt a crime? Two United States Court of Appeals decisions have answered in the affirmative. *United States v. Clay,* 495 F.2d 700 (7th Cir.) *cert. denied,* 419 U.S. 937 (1974); *United States v. Meacham,* 626 F.2d 503 (5th Cir. 1980). Texas specifically prohibits this result by statute. TEX. PENAL CODE ANN. § 15.05 (West 1973).

3. It is not necessary that defendants themselves agree to commit a crime. It is sufficient if they agree to aid and abet another in committing a crime.

The line between conspiracy and aiding and abetting is blurred in those cases that uphold convictions of "conspiracy to aid and abet." The criminal objective could be the aiding of several heroin distribution networks. *United States v. Perry,* 643 F.2d 38 (2d Cir.), *cert. denied,* 454 U.S. 835 (1981).

4. Problems of impossibility similar to those discussed in "attempts" *supra,* also arise in regard to conspiracy. In England, the matter has been resolved by statute.

> (1) Subject to the following provisions of this Part of this Act, if a person agrees with any other person or persons that a course of conduct shall be pursued which, if the agreement is carried out in accordance with their intentions, either —
>
> (a) will necessarily amount to or involve the commission of any offence or offences by one or more of the parties to the agreement, or
>
> (b) would do so but for the existence of facts which render the commission of the offence or any of the offences impossible, he is guilty of conspiracy to commit the offence or offences in question.

Criminal Attempts Act 1981, section 5(1), amending the definition of conspiracy.

5. The Model Penal Code, *infra,* and a number of statutes require that an overt act be performed in furtherance of the agreement, but such an act need not be unlawful.

6. *Multiple convictions.*

> The general rule, applied in the majority of jurisdictions, is that conspiracy is not merged into the completed crime that is the object of the conspiracy. Annot., 37 A.L.R. 778 (1925), supplemented by Annot., 75 A.L.R. 1411 (1931).
>
> In *Callanan v. United States,* 364 U.S. 587, 81 S.Ct. 321, 5 L.Ed.2d 312, reh. den., 365 U.S. 825, 81 S.Ct. 687, 5 L.Ed.2d 703 (1961), the United States Supreme Court held that conspiracy and the consummated offense, under the federal statute in question, constituted independent and separate crimes, thus reaffirming the principle approved in *Pinkerton v. United States,* 328 U.S. 640 (1946), and other cases.

Bell v. Commonwealth, 220 Va. 87, 255 S.E.2d 498, 499 (1979).

However, the Model Penal Code § 1.08 precludes conviction for both the conspiracy and the completed offense which is the object of the conspiracy except where the object of the conspiracy was to engage in a course of criminal conduct, that is to commit additional crimes. MODEL PENAL CODE comment 32 (Tent. Draft No. 5, p. 32, 1956).

MODEL PENAL CODE

§ 5.03. Criminal Conspiracy
§ 5.04. Incapacity, Irresponsibility or Immunity of Party to Solicitation or Conspiracy
§ 5.05. Grading of Criminal Attempt, Solicitation and Conspiracy; Mitigation in Cases of Lesser Danger; Multiple Convictions Barred

C. ACTUS REUS

[The text of these sections appears in Appendix A.]

GARCIA v. STATE
Supreme Court of Indiana
394 N.E.2d 106 (1979)

PRETINCE, JUSTICE.

Defendant was convicted in a trial by jury of conspiracy to commit murder, a class A felony, Ind. Code 35-41-5-2 (Burns 1979), and sentenced to twenty years imprisonment. Her sentence was suspended and she was placed on five years probation. On appeal she raises the following issues:

(1) Whether the defendant can be convicted of conspiracy when the only person with whom the defendant conspired was a police informant who only feigned his acquiescence in the scheme.

....

At the close of all of the evidence the defendant moved for a directed verdict of acquittal alleging that the State had failed to prove that there was an "agreement" between the defendant and the alleged co-conspirator. The motion was denied by the trial court, which denial the defendant now assigns as error.

[Defendant asked Young to find someone to kill her husband. Young gave the impression that he would. Instead, he went to the police and after several discussions with defendant introduced a plain-clothes officer to her. Defendant gave the officer $200, a picture of her husband, and a description of his daily habits. She agreed to pay the balance of the contract price. Neither Young nor the police officer ever intended to carry out the plan. They merely feigned acquiescence.]

Issue I

The issue is whether the conspiracy section of our new penal code adopts the Model Penal Code's "unilateral" concept or whether it retains the traditional "bilateral" concept.

The bilateral concept is the traditional view of conspiracy as derived from common law. It is formulated in terms of two or more persons agreeing to commit a crime, each with intent to do so. In cases where the person or persons with whom the defendant conspired only feigned his acquiescence in the plan, the courts have generally held that neither person could be convicted of conspiracy because there was no "conspiratorial agreement."

Reacting to criticism of this viewpoint, the drafters of the Model Penal Code, though not without internal disagreement adopted a "unilateral" concept, as follows:

[The court quotes Model Penal Code §§ 5.03 to 5.04, Appendix A *infra*.] In explanation of their new approach, the Drafters of the Model Penal Code commented:

> Unilateral Approach of the Draft. The definition of the Draft departs from the traditional view of conspiracy as an entirely bilateral or multi-

lateral relationship, the view inherent in the standard formulation cast in terms of "two or more persons" agreeing or combining to commit a crime. Attention is directed instead to each individual's culpability by framing the definition in terms of the conduct which suffices to establish the liability of any given actor, rather than the conduct of a group of which he is charged to be a part — an approach which in this comment we have designated "unilateral."

One consequence of this approach is to make it immaterial to the guilt of a conspirator whose culpability has been established that the person or all of the persons with whom he conspired have not been or cannot be convicted. Present law frequently holds otherwise, reasoning from the definition of conspiracy as an agreement between two or more persons that there must be at least two guilty conspirators or none. The problem arises in a number of contexts.

....

Second: Where the person with whom the defendant conspired secretly intends not to go through with the plan. In these cases it is generally held that neither party can be convicted because there was no "agreement" between two persons. Under the unilateral approach of the Draft, the culpable party's guilt would not be affected by the fact that the other party's agreement was feigned. He has conspired, within the meaning of the definition, in the belief that the other party was with him; apart from the issue of entrapment often presented in such cases, his culpability is not decreased by the other's secret intention. True enough, the project's chances of success have not been increased by the agreement; indeed, its doom may have been sealed by this turn of events. *But the major basis of conspiratorial liability — the unequivocal evidence of a firm purpose to commit a crime — remains the same.* The result would be the same under the Draft if the only co-conspirator established a defense of renunciation under Section 5.03(6). While both the Advisory Committee and the council support the Draft upon this point, it should be noted that the Council vote was 14-11, the dissenting members deeming mutual agreement on the part of two or more essential to the concept of conspiracy. (Our emphasis)

MPC § 5.03, Comments at pp. 104-105.

The Drafters further stated that the only basis for the old rule was a "strict doctrinal approach toward the conception of a conspiracy as a necessarily bilateral relationship." In effect, the Drafters adopted a new definition of conspiracy, one which measures the culpability of each defendant individually.

This concept has been adopted, in whole or in part, in at least 26 states and is under consideration in most of the remaining states. *See*, Note *Conspiracy: Statutory Reform Since the Model Penal Code*, 75 Col.L.R. 1122, 1125 (1975).

In 1976, our Indiana Legislature repealed the existing conspiracy statute and adopted Ind. Code § 35-41-5-2 (Burns 1979), to be effective October 1, 1977, and which reads as follows:

C. ACTUS REUS

35-41-5-2 Conspiracy

[Sec. 2.] (a) A person conspires to commit a felony when, with intent to commit the felony, he agrees with another person to commit the felony. A conspiracy to commit a felony is a felony of the same class as the underlying felony. However, a conspiracy to commit murder is a class A felony.

(b) The state must allege and prove that either the person or the person with whom he agreed performed an overt act in furtherance of the agreement.

(c) It is no defense that the person with whom the accused person is alleged to have conspired:

(1) has not been prosecuted;
(2) has not been convicted;
(3) has been acquitted;
(4) has been convicted of a different crime;
(5) cannot be prosecuted for any reason; or
(6) lacked the capacity to commit the crime.

[As added by Acts 1976, P.L. 148, SEC. 1. Amended by Acts 1977, P.L. 340, SEC. 23.]

Defendant has cited us to numerous cases supporting the bilateral concept requiring "concurrence of sentiment and cooperative conduct in the unlawful and criminal enterprise;" however, those cases were not decided under statutes remotely similar to our own. She has distinguished those cases upholding the unilateral concept upon the basis of better articulated legislative commentary or differences in the wording of the statute under attack which we do not perceive to be material. For example, the Minnesota statute (Minn.St. 609.175, subd. 2) reads "Whoever conspires with another" whereas our own refers to agreeing with another. Her argument that, by definition, an agreement requires the concurrence of sentiment of at least two individuals could be applied with even greater logic to the Minnesota statute and its use of the word "conspires." It is not persuasive in the light of the express wording of the entire enactment.

We find no reversible error. The judgment of the trial court is affirmed.

NOTES

1. A similar result was reached in *State v. St. Christopher,* 305 Minn. 226, 232 N.W.2d 798 (1975):

> Addressing the rule to be applied as a policy issue, a number of commentators have come to the conclusion that there should be no requirement of a meeting of the minds. Thus, Fridman [*Mens Rea in Conspiracy,* 19 Mod. L. Rev. 276] points to cases holding that factual impossibility is no defense to a charge of attempt to commit a crime and argues that, because of close connections between the origins and purposes of the law of conspiracy and of attempt, a similar rule should obtain in conspiracy. Specifically, he argues that "[t]he fact that, unknown to a man who wishes to enter a conspiracy to commit some criminal purpose, the other person has no intention of fulfilling that purpose ought to be irrelevant as long as the first man does intend to fulfill it if he can" because "a man

who believes he is conspiring to commit a crime and wishes to conspire to commit a crime has a guilty mind and has done all in his power to plot the commission of an unlawful purpose." *Id.* at 282, 283.

Professor Glanville Williams makes a somewhat similar argument, basing his opinion on the fact that conspiracy, like attempt, is an inchoate crime and that it is the act of conspiring by a defendant which is the decisive element of criminality, for it makes no difference in logic or public policy that the person with whom the defendant conspires is not himself subject to prosecution. Williams, Criminal Law — The General Part, § 157(a).

232 N.W.2d at 801-02.

Jurisdictions rejecting the "unilateral" approach insist that if there is no "meeting of the minds" between the defendant and at least one other conspirator, then there can be no agreement. If a defendant is dealing with a person he or she believes to be a co-conspirator, but that person is talking with the defendant solely for the purpose of providing information for the police and has no intention whatever of going through with the contemplated conspiracy, then there is no "meeting of the minds," and hence no agreement of the kind required for a criminal conspiracy. *Williams v. State*, 646 S.W.2d 221, 223 (Tex. Crim. App. 1983).

2. "Knowledge" by defendants of each other's unlawful acts does not dispense with the need to prove the "agreement." In *United States v. Ong,* 541 F.2d 331 (2d Cir. 1976), *cert. denied,* 429 U.S. 1075 (1977), operators of gambling establishments offered bribes to INS agents for notice in advance of raids for illegal aliens. Each of the operators was aware of the bribe offers of the others, but there was no evidence of agreement or concerted action. Nevertheless, the government charged them all with a single conspiracy and alleged that their knowledge coupled with their individual activities was sufficient to prove a conspiracy. The court rejected the argument that a "tacit agreement" could be inferred from the fact that each defendant would benefit not only from his own efforts but from the cumulative reduction of raids.

3. *Conspiracy and attempts.*

> [O]ne proves conspiracy to murder by proving that defendant agreed with another to commit murder and by proving some overt act in furtherance of the conspiracy (and courts generally discover an overt act in the slightest action on the part of a conspirator). In order to prove attempt to murder, one must prove that defendant took a substantial step towards, and did more than merely prepare for, the crime — which is something one need not prove in conspiracy. As stated in Sayre, *Criminal Conspiracy,* 35 Harv.L.Rev. 393, 399:
>
> [E]very criminal conspiracy is not an attempt. One may become guilty of conspiracy long before his act has come so dangerously near to completion as to make him criminally liable for the attempted crime. For instance, as Justice Holmes has pointed out, the mere agreement to murder a man fifty miles away could not possibly constitute an attempt, but might easily be indictable as a conspiracy. [*Hyde v. United States,* 225 U.S. 347, 388, 32 S. Ct. 793, 810, 56 L. Ed. 1114, 1134 (1912).]

State v. St. Christopher, 232 N.W.2d at 804.

4. The Florida District Court of Appeal, in what it characterized as a case of first impressions, held that the state's general "attempt" statute does not support a prosecution for "attempted conspiracy." The case arose out of the not unusual situation where defendant attempted to hire a person to kill another and the person approached by defendant reported the incident to the State Attorney's Office. The court relied in part on the basic differences between solicitation and attempt. *Hutchinson v. State,* 315 So. 2d 546 (Fla. Dist. Ct. App. 1975).

D. *MENS REA*

EDITORIAL NOTE

Two "specific intents" must exist before a defendant may be convicted of conspiracy: (1) the intent to agree with another or others to further the enterprise and (2) the intent to commit a crime or an unlawful act.

PEOPLE v. LAURIA

California Court of Appeal
251 Cal. App. 2d 471, 59 Cal. Rptr. 628 (1967)

FLEMING, ASSOCIATE JUSTICE.

In an investigation of call-girl activity the police focused their attention on three prostitutes actively plying their trade on call, each of whom was using Lauria's telephone answering service, presumably for business purposes.

On January 8, 1965, Stella Weeks, a policewoman, signed up for telephone service with Lauria's answering service. Mrs. Weeks, in the course of her conversation with Lauria's office manager, hinted broadly that she was a prostitute concerned with the secrecy of her activities and their concealment from the police. She was assured that the operation of the service was discreet and "about as safe as you can get." It was arranged that Mrs. Weeks need not leave her address with the answering service, but could pick up her calls and pay her bills in person.

On February 11, Mrs. Weeks talked to Lauria on the telephone and told him her business was modelling and she had been referred to the answering service by Terry, one of the three prostitutes under investigation. She complained that because of the operation of the service she had lost two valuable customers, referred to as tricks. Lauria defended his service and said that her friends had probably lied to her about having left calls for her. But he did not respond to Mrs. Weeks' hints that she needed customers in order to make money, other than to invite her to his house for a personal visit in order to get better acquainted. In the course of his talk he said "his business was taking messages."

On February 15, Mrs. Weeks talked on the telephone to Lauria's office manager and again complained of two lost calls, which she described as a $50 and a $100 trick. On investigation the office manager could find nothing wrong, but she said she would alert the switchboard operators about slip-ups on calls.

On April 1, Lauria and the three prostitutes were arrested. Lauria complained to the police that this attention was undeserved, stating that Hollywood Call Board had 60 to 70 prostitutes on its board while his own service had only 9 or 10, that he kept separate records for known or suspected prostitutes for the convenience of himself and the police. When asked if his records were available to police who might come to the office to investigate call girls, Lauria replied that they were whenever the police had a specific name. However, his service didn't "arbitrarily tell the police about prostitutes on our board. As long as they pay their bills we tolerate them." In a subsequent voluntary appearance before the Grand Jury Lauria testified he had always cooperated with the police. But he admitted he knew some of his customers were prostitutes, and he knew Terry was a prostitute because he had personally used her services, and he knew she was paying for 500 calls a month.

Lauria and the three prostitutes were indicated [sic] for conspiracy to commit prostitution, and nine overt acts were specified. Subsequently the trial court set aside the indictment as having been brought without reasonable or probable cause. (Pen.Code, § 995.) The People have appealed, claiming that a sufficient showing of an unlawful agreement to further prostitution was made.

To establish agreement, the People need show no more than a tacit, mutual understanding between coconspirators to accomplish an unlawful act. (*People v. Calhoun*, 50 Cal.2d 137, 144, 323 P.2d 427; *People v. Yeager*, 194 Cal. 452, 484, 229 P. 40.) Here the People attempted to establish a conspiracy by showing that Lauria, well aware that his codefendants were prostitutes who received business calls from customers through his telephone answering service, continued to furnish them with such service. This approach attempts to equate knowledge of another's criminal activity with conspiracy to further such criminal activity, and poses the question of the criminal responsibility of a furnisher of goods or services who knows his product is being used to assist the operation of an illegal business. Under what circumstances does a supplier become a part of a conspiracy to further an illegal enterprise by furnishing goods or services which he knows are to be used by the buyer for criminal purposes?

The two leading cases on this point face in opposite directions. In *United States v. Falcone*, 311 U.S. 205, 61 S.Ct. 204, 85 L.Ed. 128, the sellers of large quantities of sugar, yeast, and cans were absolved from participation in a moonshining conspiracy among distillers who bought from them, while in *Direct Sales Co. v. United States*, 319 U.S. 703, 63 S.Ct. 1265, 87 L.Ed. 1674, a wholesaler of drugs was convicted of conspiracy to violate the federal narcotic laws by selling drugs in quantity to a codefendant physician who was supplying them to addicts. The distinction between these two cases appears primarily based on the proposition that distributors of such dangerous products as drugs are required to exercise greater discrimination in the conduct of their business than are distributors of innocuous substances like sugar and yeast.

In the earlier case, *Falcone*, the sellers' knowledge of the illegal use of the goods was insufficient by itself to make the sellers participants in a conspiracy with the distillers who bought from them. Such knowledge fell short of proof of a conspiracy, and evidence on the volume of sales was too vague to support a jury finding that respondents knew of the conspiracy from the size of the sales alone.

In the later case of *Direct Sales,* the conviction of a drug wholesaler for conspiracy to violate federal narcotic laws was affirmed on a showing that it had actively promoted the sale of morphine sulphate in quantity and had sold codefendant physician, who practiced in a small town in South Carolina, more than 300 times his normal requirements of the drug, even though it had been repeatedly warned of the dangers of unrestricted sales of the drug. The court contrasted the restricted goods involved in *Direct Sales* with the articles of free commerce involved in *Falcone*: "All articles of commerce may be put to illegal ends," said the court. "But all do not have inherently the same susceptibility to harmful and illegal use.... This difference is important for two purposes. One is for making certain that the seller knows the buyer's intended illegal use. The other is to show that by the sale he intends to further, promote and cooperate in it. This intent, when given effect by overt act, is the gist of conspiracy. While it is not identical with mere knowledge that another proposes unlawful action, it is not unrelated to such knowledge.... The step from knowledge to intent and agreement may be taken. There is more than suspicion, more than knowledge, acquiescence, carelessness, indifference, lack of concern. There is informed and interested cooperation, stimulation, instigation. And there is also a 'stake in the venture' which, even if it may not be essential, is not irrelevant to the question of conspiracy." (319 U.S. at 710-713.)

While *Falcone* and *Direct Sales* may not be entirely consistent with each other in their full implications, they do provide us with a framework for the criminal liability of a supplier of lawful goods or services put to unlawful use. Both the element of *knowledge* of the illegal use of the goods or services and the element of *intent* to further that use must be present in order to make the supplier a participant in a criminal conspiracy.

Proof of *knowledge* is ordinarily a question of fact and requires no extended discussion in the present case.... Because Lauria knew in fact that some of his customers were prostitutes, it is a legitimate inference he knew they were subscribing to his answering service for illegal business purposes and were using his service to make assignations for prostitution. On this record we think the prosecution is entitled to claim positive knowledge by Lauria of the use of his service to facilitate the business of prostitution.

The more perplexing issue in the case is the sufficiency of proof of *intent* to further the criminal enterprise. The element of intent may be proved either by direct evidence, or by evidence of circumstances from which an intent to further a criminal enterprise by supplying lawful goods or services may be inferred. Direct evidence of participation, such as advice from the supplier of legal goods or services to the user of those goods or services on their use for illegal purposes, such evidence as appeared in a companion case we decide today, *People v. Roy,* 59 Cal.Rptr. 636, provides the simplest case. When the intent to further and promote the criminal enterprise comes from the lips of the supplier himself, ambiguities of inference from circumstance need not trouble us. But in cases where direct proof of complicity is lacking, intent to further the conspiracy must be derived from the sale itself and its surrounding circumstances in order to establish the supplier's express or tacit agreement to join the conspiracy.

In the case at bench the prosecution argues that since Lauria knew his customers were using his service for illegal purposes but nevertheless continued to furnish it to them, he must have intended to assist them in carrying out their illegal activities. Thus through a union of knowledge and intent he became a participant in a criminal conspiracy. Essentially, the People argue that knowledge alone of the continuing use of his telephone facilities for criminal purposes provided a sufficient basis from which his intent to participate in those criminal activities could be inferred.

In examining precedents in this field we find that sometimes, but not always, the criminal intent of the supplier may be inferred from his knowledge of the unlawful use made of the product he supplies. Some consideration of characteristic patterns may be helpful.

1. Intent may be inferred from knowledge, when the purveyor of legal goods for illegal use has acquired a stake in the venture. (*United State v. Falcone*, 2 Cir., 109 F.2d 579, 581.) For example, in *Regina v. Thomas*, (1957), 2 All E.R. 181, 342, a prosecution for living off the earnings of prostitution, the evidence showed that the accused, knowing the woman to be a convicted prostitute, agreed to let her have the use of his room between the hours of 9 p.m. and 2 a.m. for a charge of $3 a night. The Court of Criminal Appeal refused an appeal from the conviction, holding that when the accused rented a room at a grossly inflated rent to a prostitute for the purpose of carrying on her trade, a jury could find he was living on the earnings of prostitution.

In the present case, no proof was offered of inflated charges for the telephone answering services furnished the codefendants.

2. Intent may be inferred from knowledge, when no legitimate use for the goods or services exists. The leading California case is *People v. McLaughlin*, 111 Cal.App.2d 781, 245 P.2d 1076, in which the court upheld a conviction of the suppliers of horseracing information by wire for conspiracy to promote bookmaking, when it had been established that wire-service information had no other use than to supply information needed by bookmakers to conduct illegal gambling operations.

. . . .

Inflated charges, the sale of goods with no legitimate use, sales in inflated amounts, each may provide a fact of sufficient moment from which the intent of the seller to participate in the criminal enterprise may be inferred. In such instances participation by the supplier of legal goods to the illegal enterprise may be inferred because in one way or another the supplier has acquired a special interest in the operation of the illegal enterprise. His intent to participate in the crime of which he has knowledge may be inferred from the existence of his special interest.

Yet there are cases in which it cannot reasonably be said that the supplier has a stake in the venture or has acquired a special interest in the enterprise, but in which he has been held liable as a participant on the basis of knowledge alone. Some suggestion of this appears in *Direct Sales, supra,* where both the knowledge of the illegal use of the drugs and the intent of the supplier to aid that use were inferred. In *Regina v. Bainbridge* (1959), 3 W.L.R. 656 (CCA 6),

D. MENS REA

a supplier of oxygen-cutting equipment to one known to intend to use it to break into a bank was convicted as an accessory to the crime. In *Sykes v. Director of Public Prosecutions* [1962] A.C. 528, one having knowledge of the theft of 100 pistols, 4 submachine guns, and 1960 rounds of ammunition was convicted of misprision of felony for failure to disclose the theft to the public authorities. It seems apparent from these cases that a supplier who furnishes equipment which he *knows* will be used to commit a serious crime may be deemed from that knowledge alone to have intended to produce the result. Such proof may justify an inference that the furnisher intended to aid the execution of the crime and that he thereby became a participant. For instance, we think the operator of a telephone answering service with positive knowledge that his service was being used to facilitate the extortion of ransom, the distribution of heroin, or the passing of counterfeit money who continued to furnish the service with knowledge of its use, might be chargeable on knowledge alone with participation in a scheme to extort money, to distribute narcotics, or to pass counterfeit money. The same result would follow the seller of gasoline who knew the buyer was using his product to make Molotov cocktails for terroristic use.

Logically, the same reasoning could be extended to crimes of every description. Yet we do not believe an inference of intent drawn from knowledge of criminal use properly applies to the less serious crimes classified as misdemeanors.

With respect to misdemeanors, we conclude that positive knowledge of the supplier that his products or services are being used for criminal purposes does not, without more, establish an intent of the supplier to participate in the misdemeanors. With respect to felonies, we do not decide the converse, viz. that in all cases of felony knowledge of criminal use alone may justify an inference of the supplier's intent to participate in the crime. The implications of Falcone make the matter uncertain with respect to those felonies which are merely prohibited wrongs....

From this analysis of precedent we deduce the following rule: the intent of a supplier who knows of the criminal use to which his supplies are put to participate in the criminal activity connected with the use of his supplies may be established by (1) direct evidence that he intends to participate, or (2) through an inference that he intends to participate based on, (a) his special interest in the activity, or (b) the aggravated nature of the crime itself.

When we review Lauria's activities in the light of this analysis, we find no proof that Lauria took any direct action to further, encourage, or direct the call-girl activities of his codefendants and we find an absence of circumstances from which his special interest in their activities could be inferred. Neither excessive charges for standardized services, nor the furnishing of services without a legitimate use, nor an unusual quantity of business with call girls, are present. The offense which he is charged with furthering is a misdemeanor, a category of crime which has never been made a required subject of positive disclosure to public authority. Under these circumstances, although proof of Lauria's knowledge of the criminal activities of his patrons was sufficient to charge him with that fact, there was insufficient evidence that he intended to further their criminal activities, and hence insufficient proof of his participation in a criminal conspiracy with his codefendants to further prostitution. Since the conspiracy centered around the activities of Lauria's telephone answering service, the charges against his codefendants likewise fail for want of proof.

In absolving Lauria of complicity in a criminal conspiracy we do not wish to imply that the public authorities are without remedies to combat modern manifestations of the world's oldest profession. Licensing of telephone answering services under the police power, together with the revocation of licenses for the toleration of prostitution, is a possible civil remedy. The furnishing of telephone answering service in aid of prostitution could be made a crime. (Cf. Pen.Code, § 316, which makes it a misdemeanor to let an apartment with knowledge of its use for prostitution.) Other solutions will doubtless occur to vigilant public authorities if the problem of call-girl activity needs further suppression.

The order is affirmed.

NOTES ON INTENT TO FURTHER THE OBJECTIVE

1. See discussion of intent, *supra* pp. 669-677.

2. Knowledge of the unlawful objective. *Compare with Lauria, People v. Roy,* 251 Cal. App. 2d 459, 59 Cal. Rptr. 636 (1967). Defendant was an answering service operator who advised a prostitute of precautions which she should take in conducting her business, and introduced her to another prostitute for the purpose of arranging business contacts. The trial court set aside the conspiracy indictment, and the People appealed. *Held:* reversed. The court distinguished *Lauria,* stating: "Had Theresa Roy restricted her activities to the operation of a telephone answering service, even with knowledge that some of her customers were prostitutes ... we agree that she could not have been charged with conspiracy to commit prostitution." 59 Cal. Rptr. at 640.

In *United States v. Falcone,* cited in *Varelli* and *Lauria, supra,* Judge Learned Hand stated: "There are indeed instances of criminal liability ... where the law imposes punishment merely because the accused did not forbear to do that from which the wrong was likely to follow; but in prosecutions for conspiracy or abetting, his attitude towards the forbidden undertaking must be more positive. It is not enough that he does not forego a normally lawful activity, of the fruits of which he knows that others will make an unlawful use; he must in some sense promote their venture himself, make it his own, have a stake in its outcome." 109 F.2d at 581.

3. In *United States v. United States Gypsum Co.,* 438 U.S. 422 (1978), the Supreme Court refused to hold defendants who agreed to certain practices which have anti-competitive effects strictly liable under the antitrust laws for their conduct.

> Our question instead is whether a criminal violation of the antitrust laws requires, in addition to proof of anticompetitive effects, a demonstration that the disputed conduct was undertaken with the "conscious object" of producing such effects, or whether it is sufficient that the conduct is shown to have been undertaken with knowledge that the proscribed effects would most likely follow. While the difference between these formu-

lations is a narrow one, see ALI, Model Penal Code, Comment on § 2.02, p. 125 (Tent. Draft No. 4, 1955), we conclude that action undertaken with knowledge of its probable consequences and having the requisite anticompetitive effects can be a sufficient predicate for a finding of criminal liability under the antitrust laws.[21]

....

Generally this limited distinction between knowledge and purpose has not been considered important since "there is good reason for imposing liability whether the defendant desired or merely knew of the practical certainty of the results." In either circumstance, the defendants are consciously behaving in a way the law prohibits, and such conduct is a fitting object of criminal punishment.

Nothing in our analysis of the Sherman Act persuades us that this general understanding of intent should not be applied to criminal antitrust violations such as charged here. The business behavior which is likely to give rise to criminal antitrust charges is conscious behavior normally undertaken only after a full consideration of the desired results and a weighing of the costs, benefits, and risks. A requirement of proof not only of this knowledge of likely effects, but also of a conscious desire to bring them to fruition or to violate the law would seem, particularly in such a context, both unnecessarily cumulative and unduly burdensome. Where carefully planned and calculated conduct is being scrutinized in the context of a criminal prosecution, the perpetrator's knowledge of the anticipated consequences is a sufficient predicate for a finding of criminal intent.

Id. at 444-46.

4. To be convicted of conspiracy, a defendant must have knowledge of the conspiracy, and must intend to join or associate himself with the objectives of the conspiracy. *United States v. Malatesta*, 590 F.2d 1379, 1381 (5th Cir. 1979) (en banc). Knowledge, actual participation and criminal intent must be proved by the Government. Participation, however, need not be proved by direct evidence; a common purpose and plan may be inferred from a pattern of circumstantial evidence. *Id.*

United States v. Rosado-Fernandez, 614 F.2d 50, 53 (5th Cir. 1980).

5. Some courts have indicated that a greater knowledge of surrounding circumstances may be required to support a conspiracy charge than would be required to convict for commission of the target crime. In *Commonwealth v. Gormley*, 77 Pa. Super. 298, 303 (1921), the court stated that "on the charge of making fraudulent entries on the tally sheet, the defendants had no right to show their intention and ignorance of the law was no answer to the charge." But since such a showing could be a defense to the conspiracy charge, it was

---

[21] In so holding, we do not mean to suggest that conduct undertaken with the purpose of producing anticompetitive effects would not also support criminal liability, even if such effects did not come to pass. Cf. *United States v. Griffith*, 334 U. S. 100, 105 (1948). We hold only that this elevated standard of intent need not be established in cases where anticompetitive effects have been demonstrated; instead, proof that the defendant's conduct was undertaken with knowledge of its probable consequences will satisfy the Government's burden.

error to exclude the evidence. However, more recent cases have held that the intent to further an unlawful act is no greater than that required for the substantive crime. In *United States v. Feola,* 420 U.S. 671 (1975), the Supreme Court stated that "in order to sustain a judgment of conviction on a charge to violate a federal statute, the Government must prove at least the degree of criminal intent necessary for the substantive offense itself." *Id.* at 686. The Court found that on a charge of assaulting a federal officer, knowledge that the individual assaulted was a federal office was immaterial. Therefore, knowledge of identity was not required to establish a conspiracy to assault a federal officer. "Given the level of intent needed to carry out the substantive offense, we fail to see how the agreement is any less blameworthy or constitutes less of a danger solely because the participants are unaware [they are violating federal law]." Id. at 694.

E. SCOPE OF THE CONSPIRATORIAL RELATIONSHIP

EDITORIAL NOTE

Once the elements of agreement and intent have been established it is necessary to determine the *scope* of the conspiracy. That is determined by (1) the party dimension: those parties with whom the defendant agreed and (2) the object dimension: the unlawful acts contemplated or reasonably likely to occur in furtherance of the common design. In a complex situation involving numerous parties and acts it is important to determine whether a single conspiracy or multiple conspiracies existed. Defendants can be charged and convicted only for the "conspiracy" in which they joined. Furthermore, they may be held responsible only for those substantive crimes committed by themselves or by their co-conspirators within the scope of and in furtherance of the conspiracy.

Prosecutors often prefer to group all defendants within a single conspiracy. This facilitates presentation of prosecution proof because evidence admissible against each defendant is heard by the same jury which must determine the guilt of all defendants. Statements made by each co-conspirator during the course of and in furtherance of the conspiracy are admissible to establish the guilt on the substantive charges of all conspirators. Thus, conspirators' statements may incriminate not only themselves but their co-conspirators as well.

Before such testimony is admissible against co-conspirators, the prosecutor must first establish that a conspiracy existed. At one time the trial judge instructed the jury that it must make a preliminary finding that a conspiracy existed before it could use a conspirator's statements against co-conspirators. Today the approach used in most federal courts "requires the Trial Judge to find by a preponderance of the evidence that the government has proved the existence of a conspiracy on the basis of independent evidence. Then, and only then, can the jury rely upon conspirators' statements in assessing the guilt of a non-declarant co-conspirator." S. SALTZBURG & K. REDDEN, FEDERAL RULES OF EVIDENCE MANUAL 506 (3d ed. 1982).

E. SCOPE OF THE CONSPIRATORIAL RELATIONSHIP

The acts (crimes) of each conspirator likewise are attributed to all co-conspirators whether specifically agreed upon or not so long as they were done in furtherance of the objective of the conspiracy and were reasonably foreseeable.

The following cases and notes demonstrate that a defendant's liability for substantive acts committed by co-conspirators may be limited by the finding of several separate conspiracies instead of one large conspiracy. Liability may also be limited by the application of a rule requiring that a defendant actively aid or promote the commission of the target crime, or by a finding that the crime was not committed in furtherance of the conspiracy.

Finally, the defendant may in some cases avoid conviction of conspiracy because of an announced legislative intent not to punish certain "co-conspirators," or by the legal incapacity of the only other alleged co-conspirator.

UNITED STATES v. VARELLI
United States Court of Appeals
407 F.2d 735 (7th Cir. 1969), cert. denied, 405 U.S. 1040 (1972)

KERNER, CIRCUIT JUDGE.

Defendants were indicted and tried together for committing various substantive offenses under Title 18 U.S.C. and for conspiring to commit the offenses. The jury found all the defendants, except two, guilty on all counts and from these convictions all defendants appeal.

. . . .

[On August 23, 1964, defendant Crovedi informed Schang that he knew about a load of Polaroid cameras and equipment located in a trailer in a local freight yard. Schang, a government witness and codefendant, made arrangements with defendants Bambulas, Boscarino, Bratko, Crovedi, Mendola, Nielsen, and Rossi to hijack the Polaroid shipment. That was done the next morning; Nielsen removed the driver from the tractor-trailer, and Schang and Rossi drove it away, followed by Bambulas and Boscarino in another car. The hijacked goods were taken to a garage and placed in several trucks and cars. A few days later, a portion of the goods was sold to defendant Saletko, who knew that the goods had been hijacked. A few weeks later, Schang met defendant Legato who arranged for defendant Infelice to purchase some of the remaining Polaroid equipment. After making his purchase, Infelice sold the merchandise to defendant Gallo, who also knew of the contraband nature of the goods.

On April 18, 1965, defendants Bambulas, Borsellino, Boscarino, and Schang hijacked a truck loaded with silver. The silver was sold to defendant Varelli and was delivered by Bambulas, who parked the truck at a diner and allowed defendant Heckmyer, Varelli's associate, to drive the truck away.

In early May, 1965, Bambulas, Borsellino, Boscarino, and Schang hijacked another truckload of silver and again sold and delivered the goods to Varelli with the aid of Heckmyer.

On October 6, 1965, Schang and Borsellino hijacked another truckload of silver which they sold, with the aid of Bambulas and Boscarino, to Varelli and Heckmyer.]

The defendants have been convicted of a single conspiracy to hijack interstate shipments of merchandise, carry it away and distribute it. The government contends that whether or not a person was involved in the conspiracy is a question of fact for the jury, and since there was evidence to support the jury's finding, the conviction must be upheld. We disagree.

Agreement is the primary element of a conspiracy. The formalities of an agreement are not necessary and are usually lacking since the mark of a successful conspiracy is secrecy. "The agreement may be shown 'if there be concert of action, all the parties working together understandingly, with a single design for the accomplishment of a common purpose.' *Fowler v. United States* (C.C.A.9) 273 F. 15, 19." *Marino v. United States*, 91 F.2d 691-694 (9th Cir. 1937). While the parties to the agreement must know of each other's existence, they need not know each other's identity nor need there be direct contact. The agreement may continue for a long period of time and include the performance of many transactions. New parties may join the agreement at any time while others may terminate their relationship. The parties are not always identical, but this does not mean that there are separate conspiracies. See Developments in the Law — Criminal Conspiracy, 72 Harv.L.Rev. 920, 922-35 (1959).

The distinction must be made between separate conspiracies, where certain parties are common to all and one overall continuing conspiracy with various parties joining and terminating their relationship at different times. Various people knowingly joining together in furtherance of a common design or purpose constitute a single conspiracy. While the conspiracy may have a small group of core conspirators, other parties who knowingly participate with these core conspirators and others to achieve a common goal may be members of an overall conspiracy.

In essence, the question is what is the nature of the agreement. If there is one overall agreement among the various parties to perform different functions in order to carry out the objectives of the conspiracy, the agreement among all the parties constitutes a single conspiracy. However, where various defendants separately conspired with a common conspirator to obtain fraudulent loans from an agency of the United States, the government conceded that there were several conspiracies since there was no overall goal or common purpose. *Kotteakos v. United States*, 328 U.S. 750 (1946). The Supreme Court in *Blumenthal v. United States*, 332 U.S. 539 (1947), where the court found one overall conspiracy, commented on Kotteakos:

> The case therefore is very different from the facts admitted to exist in the *Kotteakos* case. Apart from the much larger number of agreements there involved, no two of those agreements were tied together as stages in the formation of a larger all-inclusive combination, *all directed to achieving a single unlawful end or result.* On the contrary each separate agreement had its own distinct, illegal end. Each loan was an end in itself, separate from all others, although all were alike in having similar illegal objects. Except for Brown, the common figure, no conspirator was interested in whether any loan except his own went through. And none aided in any way, by agreement or otherwise, in procuring another's loan. The conspiracies therefore were distinct and disconnected, not parts of a larger general scheme, both in the phase of agreement with Brown and

E. SCOPE OF THE CONSPIRATORIAL RELATIONSHIP

also in the absence of any aid given to others as well as in specific object and result. There was no drawing of all together in a single, over-all, comprehensive plan. (332 U.S. at 558) [Emphasis added].

Here the government failed to prove one overall general scheme among the parties to hijack trucks passing in interstate commerce, carry away the merchandise and distribute it. Boscarino, Bambulas, Borsellino, Nielsen and Schang had not agreed to join together to hijack various interstate shipments of merchandise. Rather, the evidence only shows two separate conspiracies: one to hijack a shipment of Polaroid equipment and the other to hijack silver shipments from the Handy and Harmon Company. The government contends that while direct evidence of such overall agreement is lacking, there is sufficient evidence from which the existence of an agreement can be inferred. We do not agree with the government that: "The testimony laid bare a sophisticated, complex and highly organized operation geared to the theft and disposal of large amounts of valuable merchandise traveling in interstate commerce."

"Every agreement has two dimensions: the persons privy thereto, and the objectives encompassed therein." Note, Federal Treatment of Multiple Conspiracies, 57 Col.L.Rev. 387 (1957). Schang, Bambulas, Nielsen and Boscarino were the common nucleus of separate conspiracies. The other Polaroid defendants were only involved in the single act of hijacking the Polaroid equipment and were not part of an overall scheme or plan.

> [T]he scope of his [each defendant's] agreement must be determined individually from what was proved as to him. If, in Judge Learned Hand's well-known phrase, in order for a man to be held for joining others in a conspiracy, he "must in some sense promote their venture himself, make it his own," *United States v. Falcone,* 109 F.2d 579, 581 (2 Cir.), aff'd, 311 U.S. 205 (1940), it becomes essential to determine just what he is promoting and making "his own." *United States v. Borelli,* 336 F.2d 376, 385 (2d Cir. 1964).

In *United States v. Aviles,* 274 F.2d 179 (2d Cir. 1960) the court stated:

> A single act may be foundation for drawing the actor within the ambit of a conspiracy.... But, since conviction of conspiracy requires an intent to participate in the unlawful enterprise, the single act must be such that one may reasonably infer from it such an intent. Thus, when two men join together to commit a single robbery, one may infer from their common participation in the robbery that they have conspired to commit the robbery. However, in a multiparty conspiracy of the sort revealed in the present case, with actors performing many different tasks in many places, the inference does not necessarily follow from one contract with one member of the conspiracy. (274 F.2d at 189-190)

We agree with the conclusion in *Aviles* that a single act performed with parties who are involved in more than one conspiracy may be insufficient to draw an inference of the existence of an agreement between the parties in the case of multiple conspiracies. Knowledge of the existence of the other parties to the conspiracies is insufficient....

Schang, Nielsen, Bambulas, Boscarino and Borsellino were involved in many discussions taking place over a long period of time as to the possibility of hijacking silver shipments from the Handy and Harmon Co. There is no evidence of any discussions as to other possible hijackings. The hijacking of the Polaroid equipment did not find its origin in any of these discussions. Rather, Crovedi came to Schang, an admitted hijacker by trade, on August 23, 1964, and said that he knew of a shipment of Polaroid equipment which could be taken. While some of the parties who took part in the Polaroid hijacking were also involved in the silver hijackings, this alone is insufficient to support a finding of one overall continuous conspiracy. The conspirators in the Polaroid hijacking did not contemplate a series of hijackings in which all would partake. Rather, the Polaroid hijacking represented a single transaction with a single purpose. The fact that the object in both the Polaroid hijacking and silver hijackings were similar is insufficient to constitute an overall common conspiracy. Blumenthal v. United States, 332 U.S. 539 (1947). Therefore, we conclude that there was insufficient evidence from which the jury could find a single overall conspiracy.

Purchasers as Conspirators

Varelli, Heckmyer, Saletko, Infelice, Legato and Gallo were all involved with the *distribution* of merchandise stolen in interstate commerce. None of these parties were involved with the *theft* of either the Polaroid equipment or the silver shipments. The relation of buyer and seller even with knowledge of the character of the goods being sold is insufficient to make the buyer a conspirator. In *United States v. Falcone*, 311 U.S. 205 (1940), the Supreme Court held the supplying of sugar to an illicit distiller, with knowledge that party will use the merchandise in furtherance of a conspiracy was insufficient to make the seller a co-conspirator. *Pinkerton v. United States*, 328 U.S. 640 (1946), held that the commission of a substantive offense and a conspiracy to commit it are two separate crimes, but when agreement between two persons is necessary for the completion of the substantive crime, evidence of an additional agreement is required in order to constitute the crime of conspiracy. Cf. *Gebardi v. United States*, 287 U.S. 112 (1932). This Court in *United States v. Ford*, 324 F.2d 950 (7th Cir. 1963), said that the acts of buying and selling of stolen goods without further agreement does [sic] not constitute the crime of conspiracy:

> The relationship of buyer and seller absent any prior or contemporaneous understanding beyond the mere sales agreement does not prove a conspiracy to sell, receive, barter or dispose of stolen property although both parties know of the stolen character of the goods. In such circumstance, the buyer's purpose is to buy; the seller's purpose is to sell. There is no joint objective. (*Id.* at 952.)

....

E. SCOPE OF THE CONSPIRATORIAL RELATIONSHIP

Saletko, Infelice, Legato and Gallo were, at most, purchasers of stolen Polaroid equipment. Each took part in only one single transaction as part of the distribution of the entire truckload of Polaroid cameras and film. There was no evidence of any further agreement, and, therefore, they cannot be charged with conspiracy. Therefore, we find the evidence legally insufficient to convict Saletko, Infelice, Legato and Gallo of conspiracy.

Varelli and Heckmyer became associated with the silver conspiracy. While they acted as purchasers of silver on the first shipment, the evidence is sufficient to conclude that they entered into a further agreement to dispose of future silver shipments. Varelli and Heckmyer by their further agreement became part of the conspiracy in that they agreed to assume a primary role in distributing further silver shipments....

Aiding and Abetting

Infelice, Legato and Gallo were convicted under Count 6 of aiding and abetting in the theft of the Polaroid equipment. Title 18 U.S.C. Section 2, provides that aiders and abettors are punishable as principals. In *Pinkerton v. United States,* 328 U.S. 640 (1946), the court held that evidence of being part of a conspiracy would be sufficient to support conviction on substantive offenses committed in furtherance of the conspiracy. As for the crime of aiding and abetting, the court in *Nye & Nissen v. United States,* 336 U.S. 613, 620 (1949), said:

> And if a conspiracy is also charged, it makes no difference so far as aiding and abetting is concerned whether the substantive offense is done pursuant to the conspiracy. *Pinkerton v. United States* is narrow in its scope. Aiding and abetting rests on a broader base; it states a rule of criminal responsibility for acts which one assists another in performing. The fact that a particular case might conceivably be submitted to the jury on either theory is irrelevant. It is sufficient if the proof adduced and the basis on which it was submitted were sufficient to support the verdict.

Too, as the court held in Pereira v. United States, 347 U.S. 1, 11 (1954):

> Aiding, abetting, and counseling are not terms which presuppose the existence of an agreement. Those terms have a broader application, making the defendant a principal when he consciously shares in a criminal act, regardless of the existence of a conspiracy.

We conclude that the evidence does not support conviction for aiding and abetting. Judge Learned Hand in *United States v. Peoni,* 100 F.2d 401, 402 (2d Cir. 1938), said that the crime of aiding and abetting requires that defendant "in some sort associate himself with the venture, that he participate in it as in something that he wishes to bring about, that he seek by his action to make it succeed." Here the defendants' roles are similar to that of defendant Bollenbach in *Bollenbach v. United States,* 326 U.S. 607 (1946), (Bollenbach helped to dispose of securities in New York which were stolen in Minneapolis). In both cases defendants were accessories after the fact and cannot be made principals under § 2: "[T]o constitute one an aider and abettor, he must not only be on the ground, and by his presence aid, encourage, or incite the principal to commit the crime, but he must share the criminal intent or purpose of the principal." *Morei v. United States,* 127 F.2d 827, 831 (6th Cir. 1942). Here defendants entered the scheme or plan too late to be considered aiders or abettors in the commission of the theft of Polaroid equipment.

....

For the above stated reasons, we reverse and remand for new trials the convictions of Crovedi, Nielsen, Bratko, Rossi, Saletko, Bambulas, Borsellino, Varelli, Heckmyer and Cardenas, and reverse and dismiss Infelice, Legato and Gallo.

NOTES

1. A purchaser of stolen goods is not liable as an aider and abettor of the theft because of his status as a buyer, but because he enters the plan too late. *United States v. Varelli,* 407 F.2d 735 (7th Cir. 1969). See also *United States v. Gallagher,* 565 F.2d 981 (7th Cir. 1977) (willing buyer not an aider and abettor of possession of stolen securities). The gravamen of the offense is the theft, not what happens to the goods afterwards. If the defendant does not aid the theft itself, he does not commit an act that aids the commission of the offense.

United States v. Beck, 615 F.2d at 450 (7th Cir. 1980).

2. In this case, the government alleges a single objective: to illegally locate and obtain information in the possession of the United States which relates to the Church of Scientology and to individuals, organizations, and agencies perceived to be enemies of the Church of Scientology. The alleged conspirators are all allegedly members of the Church. Their interest in advancing the Church's interest would be assisted in each of the three conspiracies as described by the defendants. Accordingly, there is a sufficient stake by each defendant in the entire venture or conspiracy.

United States v. Hubbard, 474 F. Supp. 64, 72 (D.D.C. 1979).

3. In discussing single versus multiple conspiracies the courts have metaphorically designated some as "wheels" and others as "chains." These were described in *United States v. Elliott,* 571 F.2d 880, cert. denied, 439 U.S. 953 (1978):

A. *Prior Law: Wheels and Chains*

1. *Kotteakos and the Wheel Conspiracy Rationale*: The Court in *Kotteakos* held that proof of multiple conspiracies under an indictment alleging a single conspiracy constituted a material variance requiring reversal where a defendant's substantial rights had been affected. At issue was "the right not to be tried en masse for the conglomeration of distinct and separate offenses committed by others." 328 U.S. at 775. *Kotteakos* thus protects against the "spill-over effect," the transference of guilt from members of one conspiracy to members of another. *United States v. Bertolotti,* 529 F.2d 149, 156 (2d Cir. 1975).

The facts of *Kotteakos* have been summarized by this court as follows:

E. SCOPE OF THE CONSPIRATORIAL RELATIONSHIP

In that case, one where the indictment charged but one overall conspiracy, the government's proof at trial, by its own admission, showed that there were eight separate conspiracies involving some thirty-two persons. The key figure in the scheme, which involved the obtaining of government loans by making fraudulent representations, was a man named Brown, who was a part of, and directed each of the eight conspiracies. Brown was the only element common to the eight otherwise completely separate undertakings, no other person taking part in, nor having knowledge of the other conspiracies. Though each of the conspiracies had similar illegal objects, none depended upon, was aided by, or had any interest in the success of the others.

United States v. Perez, 489 F.2d 51, 60 (5th Cir. 1973). These facts led the Court to speak in terms of a "wheel conspiracy," in which one person, the "hub" of the wheel, was accused of conspiring with several others, the "spokes" of the wheel. As we explained in *United States v. Levine,* 546 F.2d 658, 663 (5th Cir. 1977):

> For a [single] wheel conspiracy to exist those people who form the wheel's spokes must have been aware of each other and must do something in furtherance of some single, illegal enterprise. Otherwise the conspiracy lacks "the rim of the wheel to enclose the spokes." If there is not some interaction between those conspirators who form the spokes of the wheel as to at least one common illegal object, the "wheel" is incomplete, and two conspiracies rather than one are charged. [Citations omitted.]

2. Blumenthal *and the Chain Conspiracy Rationale*: The impact of *Kotteakos* was soon limited by the Court in *Blumenthal v. United States,* 332 U.S. 539 (1947), where the indictment charged a single conspiracy to sell whiskey at prices above the ceiling set by the Office of Price Administration. The owner of the whiskey, through a series of middlemen, had devised an intricate scheme to conceal the true amount he was charging for the whiskey. Although some of the middlemen had no contact with each other and did not know the identity of the owner, they had to have realized that they were indispensable cogs in the machinery through which this illegal scheme was effectuated. The Court concluded that "in every practical sense the unique facts of this case reveal a single conspiracy of which the several agreements were essential and integral steps." *Id.* at 559. Thus the "chain conspiracy" rational evolved.

The essential element of a chain conspiracy — allowing persons unknown to each other and never before in contact to be jointly prosecuted as co-conspirators — is interdependence. The scheme which is the object of the conspiracy must depend on the successful operation of each link in the chain. "An individual associating himself with a "chain' conspiracy knows that it has a "scope' and that for its success it requires an organization wider than may be disclosed by his personal participation" *United States v. Agueci,* 310 F.2d 817, 827 (2d Cir. 1962), cert. denied, 372 U.S. 959 (1963). "Thus, in a 'chain' conspiracy prosecution, the requisite element — knowledge of the existence of remote links — may be inferred solely from the nature of the enterprise." *United States v. Perez, supra,* 489 F.2d at 59 n. 10.

571 F.2d at 900-01.

4. The chain conspiracy was carried to an extreme in *United States v. Bruno,* 105 F.2d 921 (2d Cir.), *rev'd on other grounds,* 308 U.S. 287 (1939). There 88 persons were indicted for conspiracy to import, sell and possess narcotics. The group included

> smugglers, who imported the drugs; middlemen who paid the smugglers, and distributed to retailers; and two groups of retailers — one in New York and one in Texas and Louisiana — who supplied the addicts.... The evidence did not disclose any cooperation or communication between the smugglers and either group of retailers, or between the two groups of retailers themselves; however, the smugglers knew that the middlemen must sell to retailers, and the retailers knew that the middlemen must buy of importers of one sort or another. Thus the conspirators at one end of the chain knew that the unlawful business would not, and could not, stop with their buyers; and those at the other end knew that it had not begun with their sellers. That being true, a jury might have found that all the accused were embarked upon a venture, in all parts of which each was a participant, and an abettor in the sense that the success of that part with which he was immediately concerned, was dependent upon the success of the whole.

105 F.2d at 922.

The court dismissed the contention that the New York retailers were not co-conspirators with the Texas and Louisiana retailers:

> Clearly, quoad the smugglers, there was but one conspiracy, for it was of no moment to them whether the middlemen sold to one or more groups of retailers, provided they had a market somewhere. So too of any retailer; he knew that he was a necessary link in a scheme of distribution, and the others, whom he knew to be convenient to its execution, were as much parts of a single undertaking or enterprise as two salesmen in the same shop.

Id. at 923.

What about the addicts on the street who purchased the drugs from the retailers; could they be included as co-conspirators? See Note, *infra* p. 820.

5. A single act may be sufficient to draw one into a broad conspiracy. However, there must be independent evidence which establishes that the actor had some knowledge of the broader conspiracy or the act itself must support an inference of such knowledge. In *United States v. Sperling,* 506 F.2d 1323 (2d Cir. 1974), *cert. denied,* 420 U.S. 962 (1975), where a large number of defendants were prosecuted for a single conspiracy to purchase, process and resell hard narcotics, two of the defendants who participated in a single isolated transaction could not be linked to the conspiracy on the basis of the single act

E. SCOPE OF THE CONSPIRATORIAL RELATIONSHIP

in question. The court cautioned the government on its use of the single conspiracy theory:

> In view of the frequency with which the single conspiracy vs. multiple conspiracies claim is being raised on appeals before this court ... we take this occasion to caution the government with respect to future prosecutions that it may be unnecessarily exposing itself to reversal by continuing the indictment format reflected in this case. While it is obviously impractical and inefficient for the government to try conspiracy cases one defendant at a time, it has become all too common for the government to bring indictments against a dozen or more defendants and endeavor to force as many of them as possible to trial in the same proceeding on the claim of a single conspiracy when the criminal acts could be more reasonably regarded as two or more conspiracies, perhaps with a link at the top.

506 F.2d at 1340-41.

6. Before agreement can be shown, it must appear that the defendant knew of the conspiracy: "[A] defendant may enter the ranks of the conspirators subsequently to the inception of the agreement and yet be guilty of conspiracy. Neither is it necessary for him to know all of the conspirators, or be cognizant of all of the ramifications of the illegal combination. It must appear, however, that he know of the existence of the conspiracy and took some part in furthering it, in order to justify his conviction. 'Those having no knowledge of the conspiracy are not conspirators.'" *United States v. Speed,* 78 F. Supp. 366, 370 (D.D.C. 1948) *citing United v. Falcone,* 311 U.S. 205 (1948)).

In *State v. Dressel,* 85 N.M. 450, 513 P.2d 187 (1973), defendant devised a scheme whereby he could deliver less grain than his weight tickets indicated, and sell the surplus grain for his own profit. He was convicted of conspiracy, on evidence which showed that his only alleged co-conspirator met him on the night that the grain was to be sold, followed defendant in her car, and gave him a ride back into town. Defendant then made a second trip alone to sell the grain, and received a check in the name of the alleged co-conspirator in payment, which she never received. Held: conviction reversed. "One does not become a party to a conspiracy by aiding and abetting it unless one knows of the conspiracy.... There is no evidence that [the alleged co-conspirator] had any knowledge whatsoever of defendant's scheme. Although she was present with him while he was effectuating his scheme, there is nothing to suggest that she was or should have been aware of it." 513 P.2d at 188. Since the case failed against the only other alleged co-conspirator, defendant's conviction was reversed.

7. *Aiding without agreement — joint action.* In *State ex rel. Martin v. Tally,* 102 Ala. 25, 15 So. 722 (1893), (an impeachment proceeding) defendant had sent a telegram to delay a warning which had been sent to the victim of a conspiracy to murder. The conspirators had no knowledge of the defendant or his assistance, but with the aid of the defendant, the murder was accomplished. The court found that defendant was an accomplice to the murder, but not as a conspirator. *See also Harris v. State,* 177 Ala. 17, 59 So. 205 (1912); *Espy v. State,* 54 Wyo. 291, 92 P.2d 549 (1939).

State v. Madden, 61 N.J. 377, 294 A.2d 609 (1972), arose from a racial riot, during which a mob pursued a police officer and beat him to death. Two of the participants were convicted of murder in the first degree. The prosecution proceeded on two alternative theories: that the defendants participated in the fatal beating, or that they aided and abetted the killing. The trial court instructions on aiding and abetting included an instruction on the liability of coconspirators for the acts done in furtherance of a conspiracy. *Held:* conviction reversed. "The crime of conspiracy requires an actual agreement for the commission of the substantive crime, and unless the agreement in fact existed, each defendant is liable with respect to the substantive offense on the basis of his own conduct with respect to that substantive offense.... [W]hen, as here, there is no proof of an actual prior agreement and each defendant's liability inevitably depends upon what that defendant did at the time and place of the homicide, the case is unnecessarily encumbered by the introduction of an instruction upon conspiracy." 294 A.2d at 617-18. The court also noted: "Of course, one may be liable as a principal under our aiding or abetting statute even though no conspiracy existed between him and the immediate perpetrator of the substantive crime. And the immediate perpetrator does not become a conspirator with another merely because the other aided or abetted him." *Id.* at 617.

8. Counts One and Twenty-three charge the defendants with conspiracy. The Count One conspiracy charges each of the defendants except Wolfe with conspiring to collect, by covert means, data relating to the Church of Scientology, its founder L. Ron Hubbard, and other Church members, which was in the possession of the United States Department of Justice, the Department of the Treasury's Internal Revenue Service, and the Office of the United States Attorney for the District of Columbia. Count Twenty-three alleges that the defendants, except for Thomas, conspired to cover up the scope of these activities after two agents of the Church, Michael J. Meisner and Wolfe, were caught inside the United States Courthouse with fake IRS credentials.

....

Two key factors control the contours of a conspiratorial agreement: "the persons privy thereto, and the objectives encompassed therein." Note, Federal Treatment of Multiple Conspiracies, 57 COL. L. REV. 387, 387 (1957) (citations omitted), *cited in United States v. Varelli*, 407 F.2d at 743. In this case, there is a large overlap between the people involved in the "three conspiracies" as claimed by the defendants. Of the ten defendants named in Count One, only one has no involvement in the first conspiracy as defined by the defendants; only one has no involvement in the second conspiracy as defined by the defendants; and only three have no involvement in the third conspiracy as defined by the defendants. Since so many of the same people are engaged in each of these three supposedly separate conspiracies, it is logical to conclude that distinct agreements were not made but, rather, a single agreement encompassing each of the distinct objectives was made by each conspirator.

The second factor, which as previously indicated, often demonstrates a linkage between individuals so that an agreement can be inferred is the objectives encompassed by the behavior of the conspirators....

United States v. Hubbard, 474 F. Supp. 64, 70, 72 (D.D.C. 1979).

E. SCOPE OF THE CONSPIRATORIAL RELATIONSHIP

PINKERTON v. UNITED STATES
United States Supreme Court
328 U.S. 640 (1946)

[W. Daniel Pinkerton and Walter G. Pinkerton were convicted of unlawfully removing, depositing, and concealing certain commodities subject to tax by the United States with intent to defraud the United States of such tax and with conspiracy so to do. Judgments of conviction were affirmed by the Circuit Court of Appeals, 151 F.2d 499 (5th Cir. 1945) and defendants brought certiorari.]

MR. JUSTICE DOUGLAS delivered the opinion of the Court.
....
A single conspiracy was charged and proved. Some of the overt acts charged in the conspiracy count were the same acts charged in the substantive counts. Each of the substantive offenses found was committed pursuant to the conspiracy. Petitioners therefore contend that the substantive counts became merged in the conspiracy count, and that only a single sentence not exceeding the maximum two-year penalty provided by the conspiracy statute (Criminal Code § 37, 18 U.S.C. § 88) ... could be imposed. Or to state the matter differently, they contend that each of the substantive counts became a separate conspiracy count but since only a single conspiracy was charged and proved, only a single sentence for conspiracy could be imposed. They rely on *Braverman v. United States*, 317 U.S. 49....

In the *Braverman* case the indictment charged no substantive offense. Each of the several counts charged a conspiracy to violate a different statute. But only one conspiracy was proved. We held that a single conspiracy, charged under the general conspiracy statute, however diverse its objects may be, violates but a single statute and no penalty greater than the maximum provided for one conspiracy may be imposed. That case is not apposite here. For the offenses charged and proved were not only a conspiracy but substantive offenses as well.

Nor can we accept the proposition that the substantive offenses were merged in the conspiracy.... The common law rule that the substantive offense, if a felony, was merged in the conspiracy, has little vitality in this country. It has been long and consistently recognized by the Court that the commission of the substantive offense and a conspiracy to commit it are separate and distinct offenses. The power of Congress to separate the two and to affix to each a different penalty is well established. *Clune v. United States*, 159 U.S. 590, 594-595.... A conviction for the conspiracy may be had though the substantive offense was completed. See *Heike v. United States*, 227 U.S. 131, 144.... And the plea of double jeopardy is no defense to a conviction for both offenses....
....
Moreover, it is not material that overt acts charged in the conspiracy counts were also charged and proved as substantive offenses. As stated in *Sneed v. United States*, ... [298 Fed. 911, 913], "If the overt act be the offense which was the object of the conspiracy, and is also punished, there is not a double

punishment of it." The agreement to do an unlawful act is even then distinct from the doing of the act.

It is contended that there was insufficient evidence to implicate Daniel in the conspiracy. But we think there was enough evidence for submission of the issue to the jury.

There is, however, no evidence to show that Daniel participated directly in the commission of the substantive offenses on which his conviction has been sustained, although there was evidence to show that these substantive offenses were in fact committed by Walter in furtherance of the unlawful agreement or conspiracy existing between the brothers. The question was submitted to the jury on the theory that each petitioner could be found guilty of the substantive offenses, if it was found at the time those offenses were committed petitioners were parties to an unlawful conspiracy and the substantive offenses charged were in fact committed in furtherance of it.

Daniel relies on *United States v. Sall*, ... [116 F.2d 745]. That case held participation in the conspiracy was not itself enough to sustain a conviction for the substantive offense even though it was committed in furtherance of the conspiracy. The court held that, in addition to evidence that the offense was in fact committed in furtherance of the conspiracy, evidence of direct participation in the commission of the substantive offense or other evidence from which participation might fairly be inferred was necessary.

We take a different view. We have here a continuous conspiracy. There is here no evidence of the affirmative action on the part of Daniel which is necessary to establish his withdrawal from it. *Hyde v. United States*, 225 U.S. 347, 369.... As stated in that case, "Having joined in an unlawful scheme, having constituted agents for its performance, scheme and agency to be continuous until full fruition be secured, until he does some act to disavow or defeat the purpose he is in no situation to claim the delay of the law. As the offense has not been terminated or accomplished he is still offending. And we think, consciously offending, offending as certainly, as we have said, as at the first moment of his confederation, and consciously through every moment of its existence." *Id.*, p. 369.... And so long as the partnership in crime continues, the partners act for each other in carrying it forward. It is settled that "an overt act of one partner may be the act of all without any new agreement specifically directed to that act." *United States v. Kissel*, 218 U.S. 601, 608.... Motive or intent may be proved by the acts or declarations of some of the conspirators in the furtherance of the common objective. *Wiborg v. United States*, 163 U.S. 632, 657-658.... A scheme to use the mails to defraud, which is joined in by more than one person, is a conspiracy. *Cochran v. United States*, ... 41 F.2d 193, 199-200. Yet all members are responsible, though only one did the mailing. *Cochran v. United States, supra; Mackett v. United States*, ... 90 F.2d 462, 464; *Baker v. United States*, ... 115 F.2d 533, 540; *Blue v. United States*, ... 138 F.2d 351, 359. The governing principle is the same when the substantive offense is committed by one of the conspirators in furtherance of the unlawful project. *Johnson v. United States*, ... 62 F.2d 32, 34. The criminal intent to do the act is established by the formation of the conspiracy. Each conspirator instigated the commission of the crime. The unlawful agreement contemplated precisely what was done. It was formed for the purpose. The act done was in execution of the enterprise. The rule which holds responsible one who counsels, procures, or commands another to commit a crime is founded on the same principle. That principle is recognized in the law of conspiracy when the overt act of one partner in crime is attributable to all. An overt act is an essential ingredient of the crime of conspiracy under § 37 of the Criminal Code, 18 U.S.C. § 88.... If that can be supplied by the act of one conspirator, we fail to see why the same or other acts in furtherance of the conspiracy are likewise not attributable to the others for the purpose of holding them responsible for the substantive offense.

A different case would arise if the substantive offense committed by one of the conspirators was not in fact done in furtherance of the conspiracy, did not fall within the scope of the unlawful project, or was merely a part of the ramifications of the plan which could not be reasonably foreseen as a necessary or natural consequence of the unlawful agreement. But as we read this record, that is not this case.

Affirmed.

MR. JUSTICE RUTLEDGE, dissenting in part.

The judgment concerning Daniel Pinkerton should be reversed. In my opinion it is without precedent here and is a dangerous precedent to establish.

Daniel and Walter, who were brothers living near each other, were charged in several counts with substantive offenses, and then a conspiracy count was added naming those offenses as overt acts. The proof showed that Walter alone committed the substantive crimes. There was none to establish that Daniel participated in them, aided and abetted Walter in committing them, or knew that he had done so. Daniel in fact was in the penitentiary, under sentence for other crimes, when some of Walter's crimes were done.

There was evidence, however, to show that over several years Daniel and Walter had confederated to commit similar crimes concerned with unlawful possession, transportation, and dealing in whiskey, in fraud of the federal revenues. On this evidence both were convicted of conspiracy. Walter also was convicted on the substantive counts on the proof of his committing the crimes charged. Then, on that evidence without more than the proof of Daniel's criminal agreement with Walter and the latter's overt acts, which were also the substantive offenses charged, the court told the jury they could find Daniel guilty of those substantive offenses. They did so.

I think this ruling violates both the letter and the spirit of what Congress did when it separately defined the three classes of crime, namely, (1) completed substantive offenses; (2) aiding, abetting or counseling another to commit them; and (3) conspiracy to commit them. Not only does this ignore the distinctions Congress has prescribed shall be observed. It either convicts one man for another's crime or punishes the man convicted twice for the same offense.

The three types of offense are not identical. *Bollenbach v. United States*, 326 U.S. 607, 611 ...; *United States v. Sall*, ... 116 F.2d 745. Nor are their differences merely verbal. *Ibid.* The gist of conspiracy is the agreement; that of aiding, abetting or counseling is in consciously advising or assisting another to commit particular offenses, and thus becoming a party to them; that of substantive crime, going a step beyond mere aiding, abetting, counseling to completion of the offense.

The general differences are well understood. But when conspiracy has ripened into completed crime, or has advanced to the stage of aiding and abetting, it becomes easy to disregard their differences and loosely to treat one as identical with the other, that is, for every purpose except the most vital one of imposing sentence. And thus the substance, if not the technical effect, of double jeopardy or multiple punishment may be accomplished. Thus also may one be convicted of an offense not charged or proved against him, on evidence showing he committed another.

The old doctrine of merger of conspiracy in the substantive crime has not obtained here. But the dangers for abuse, which in part it sought to avoid, in applying the law of conspiracy have not altogether disappeared. Cf. *Kotteakos v. United States*, ... [328 U.S. 750]. There is some evidence that they may be increasing. The looseness with which the charge may be proved, the almost unlimited scope of vicarious responsibility for others' acts which follows once agreement is shown, the psychological advantages of such trials for securing conviction by attributing to one proof against another, these and other inducements require that the broad limits of discretion allowed to prosecuting officers in relation to such charges and trials be not expanded into new, wider and more dubious areas of choice.

... Daniel has been held guilty of the substantive crimes committed only by Walter on proof that he did no more than conspire with him to commit offenses of the same general character. There was no evidence that he counseled, advised or had knowledge of those particular acts or offenses. There was, therefore, none that he aided, abetted or took part in them. There was only evidence sufficient to show that he had agreed with Walter at some past time to engage in such transactions generally. As to Daniel this was only evidence of conspiracy, not of substantive crime.

The Court's theory seems to be that Daniel and Walter became general partners in crime by virtue of their agreement and because of that agreement without more on his part Daniel became criminally responsible as a principal for everything Walter did thereafter in the nature of a criminal offense of the general sort the agreement contemplated, so long as there was not clear evidence that Daniel had withdrawn from or revoked the agreement. Whether or not his commitment to the penitentiary had that effect, the result is a vicarious criminal responsibility as broad as, or broader than, the vicarious civil liability of a partner for acts done by a co-partner in the course of the firm's business.

Such analogies from private commercial law and the law of torts are dangerous, in my judgment, for transfer to the criminal field. See Sen. Rep. No. 163, 72d Cong., 1st Sess., 20. Guilt there with us remains personal, not vicarious, for the more serious offenses. It should be kept so. The effect of Daniel's conviction in this case, to repeat, is either to attribute to him Walter's guilt or to punish him twice for the same offense, namely, agreeing with Walter to engage in crime. Without the agreement Daniel was guilty of no crime on this record. With it and no more, so far as his own conduct is concerned, he was guilty of two.

PEOPLE v. McGEE

Court of Appeals of New York
49 N.Y.2d 48, 399 N.E.2d 1177, 424 N.Y.S.2d 157,
cert. denied, 446 U.S. 942 (1980)

Opinion of the Court

COOKE, CHIEF JUDGE.

....

McGee argues that the Trial Judge erred in charging the jury that he could be found guilty of the substantive offense of bribery by virtue of his status as a conspirator. After determining that there was sufficient evidence of an agreement among the defendants to go to the jury on the conspiracy count, the court charged that each conspirator could be convicted of bribery on the basis of acts of any one of the coconspirators committed in furtherance of the conspiracy (see *Pinkerton v. United States,* 328 U.S. 640). The court also charged that McGee alone could be convicted of the bribery if he solicited, requested, commanded, importuned or intentionally aided another to engage in that offense (see Penal Law, § 20.00). McGee is correct in his contention that the portion of the charge concerning conspirator liability was erroneous. It is held that liability for the substantive offense may not be independently predicated upon defendant's participation in an underlying conspiracy. As there was no evidence of McGee's complicity in the bribery counts submitted to the jury, and thus no basis for accomplice liability, there must be a reversal of the conviction of bribery and a dismissal of the indictment as to those counts.

In rejecting the notion that one's status as a conspirator standing alone is sufficient to support a conviction for a substantive offense committed by a coconspirator, it is noted that the Legislature has defined the conduct that will render a person criminally responsible for the act of another. Conspicuously absent from section 20.00 of the Penal Law is reference to one who conspires to commit an offense. That omission cannot be supplied by construction. Conduct that will support a conviction for conspiracy will not perforce give rise to accessorial liability (compare Penal Law, § 105.05, with § 20.00). True, a conspirator's conduct in many instances will suffice to establish liability as an accomplice, but the concepts are, in reality, analytically distinct. To permit mere guilt of conspiracy to establish the defendant's guilt of the substantive crime without any evidence of further action on the part of the defendant, would be to expand the basis of accomplice liability beyond the legislative design.

The crime of conspiracy is an offense separate from the crime that is the object of the conspiracy. Once an illicit agreement is shown, the overt act of any conspirator may be attributed to other conspirators to establish the offense of conspiracy (cf. *People v. Salko,* 47 N.Y.2d 230, 417 N.Y.S.2d 894, 391 N.E.2d 976; *People v. Sher,* 68 Misc.2d 917, 329 N.Y.S.2d 202) and that act may be the object crime. But the overt act itself is not the crime in a conspiracy prosecution; it is merely an element of the crime that has as its basis the agreement (cf. *People v. Hines,* 284 N.Y. 93, 29 N.E.2d 483). It is not offensive to permit a conviction of conspiracy to stand on the overt act committed by another, for the act merely provides corroboration of the existence of the agreement and indicates that the agreement has reached a point where it poses a sufficient threat to society to impose sanctions (see 72 Harv.L.Rev. 920, 998; 16 Ford.L.Rev. 275, 277). But it is repugnant to our system of jurisprudence, where guilt is generally personal to the defendant (see Sayre, Criminal Responsibility for the Acts of Another, 43 Harv.L.Rev. 689), to impose punishment, not for the socially harmful agreement to which the defendant is a party, but for substantive offense in which he did not participate (*Commonwealth v. Stasiun*, 349 Mass. 38, 206 N.E.2d 672; see, generally, 56 Yale L.J. 371).

We refuse to sanction such a result and thus decline to follow the rule adopted for Federal prosecutions in *Pinkerton v. United States*, 328 U.S. 640, *supra*. Accessorial conduct may not be equated with mere membership in a conspiracy and the State may not rely solely on the latter to prove guilt of the substantive offense.[3]

EDITORIAL NOTE

"*Strict liability.*" In *People v. Luciano*, 277 N.Y. 348, 14 N.E.2d 433, cert. denied, 305 U.S. 620 (1938), the defendants were convicted of sixty-two separate counts of compulsory prostitution, after proof that they were the directors and controllers of a vice ring. The American Law Institute raised the question whether, under similar circumstances, the *Pinkerton* rule could be invoked to convict the conspiring prostitutes of the acts committed by other members of the conspiracy. The conclusion was that "[l]aw would lose all sense of just proportion if in virtue of that one crime, each were held accountable for thousands of offenses that he did not influence at all." MODEL PENAL CODE comment at 21 (Tent. Draft No. 1, 1953).

Massachusetts courts have refused to follow the *Pinkerton* rule, and hold that liability for a substantive offense committed in furtherance of the conspiracy cannot be based solely on membership in the conspiracy. "To be liable for the substantive offense, a co-conspirator must participate or aid in the commission of it.... Long ago this court cautioned that the proof of conspiracy, without more, did not justify a finding that a conspirator had committed the offence which was the object of the conspiracy." *Commonwealth v. Stasiun*, 349 Mass. 38, 206 N.E.2d 672, 678-79 (1965). Cf. *Commonwealth v. Perry*, *supra*, and *Commonwealth v. Mangula*, 2 Mass. App. Ct. 785, 322 N.E.2d 177 (1975), holding that accomplice liability requires that aid or assistance be rendered in the commission of the target offense, and mere agreement to commit a crime is insufficient for conviction.

However, several statutes provide that accomplice liability may be predicated solely upon a showing of membership in the conspiracy, e.g., MINN.

---

[3] We are not unmindful of cases indicating that "[e]ach conspirator is liable ... for the acts of every associate done in the effort to carry the conspiracy into effect" (e.g., People v. Collins, 234 N.Y. 355, 361, 137 N.E. 753, 755; see also, People v. Luciano, 277 N.Y. 348, 14 N.E.2d 433; People v. Michalow, 229 N.Y. 325, 128 N.E. 228; People v. McKane, 143 N.Y. 455, 38 N.E. 950). Those cases, however, do not support extending the agency rationale to impose liability for the substantive offense solely on the basis of liability for the agreement. Indeed, closer examination of each of them reveals that the defendant had actively participated to a degree sufficient to impose accessorial liability.

STAT. ANN. § 609.05(1) (1963); WIS. STAT. ANN. § 939.05(2)(c) (West 1981). The American Law Institute adopted the position that accomplice liability should not be based solely on the fact of membership in a conspiracy. MODEL PENAL CODE § 2.04(3), comment at 20-24 (Tent. Draft No. 1, 1953); § 5.03(6), comment at 143 (Tent. Draft No. 10, 1960). The Institute also recommended that the scope of conspiratorial liability be limited to those crimes which defendants intended to promote or facilitate, and to acts of co-conspirators with whom he agreed or whom they agreed or who they knew were engaged in the conspiracy. MODEL PENAL CODE § 5.03(1)(2), comment at 117-26 (Tent. Draft No. 10, 1960).

See Perkins, *The Act of One Conspirator,* 26 HASTINGS L.J. 337 (1974), discussing the rule of the *Pinkerton* case and concluding that it is sound insofar as the conspirators actually aided and abetted the commission of the target crime. In a small-scale conspiracy, co-conspirators will often be accomplices under the traditional law of parties. Such rules will seldom be applicable, however, when a "complex and sprawling network of crime" is the product of the conspiracy.

F. JOINT LIABILITY — PROCEDURAL PROBLEMS

GARDNER v. STATE

Court of Appeals of Maryland
286 Md. 520, 408 A.2d 1317 (1979)

COLE, JUDGE.

In this case, the primary issue we are asked to decide is whether one conspirator's conviction may stand where the sole co-conspirator is acquitted at a subsequent trial.

The facts are not in substantial dispute and may be set forth briefly. Gardner was a contract killer who conspired with Ralph Lubow to murder Morton Hollander and Alvin Blum. Gardner decided to subcontract the killing of Blum to one Timothy McDonald for $10,000. Gardner had several meetings with McDonald and gave him $60.00 for expense money, a gun, and ammunition to effect the killing. Gardner also told McDonald that he (Gardner) would first kill Hollander and that if this did not create the desired result, McDonald would be directed to kill Blum. However, if McDonald was not called upon to kill Blum, McDonald would be paid $3,000 in any event. McDonald later learned from Gardner that Ralph Lubow was directing the operation and met with Lubow who promised to pay him $2,500. At a subsequent meeting, he did in fact pay McDonald $500.00. Gardner and Lubow were arrested and charged with criminal misconduct in a five count indictment which included two counts of conspiracy to commit murder, two counts of solicitation to commit murder and a handgun violation. Gardner requested a separate trial and was tried without a jury, several months before Lubow in the Circuit Court for Howard County. As part of his defense, Gardner offered expert testimony in an effort to prove that Lubow was insane at the time of the alleged conspiracy and hence there could be no conspiracy. The State in rebuttal presented expert and lay testimony. The trial judge, after denying Gardner's motions for judgment of acquittal, specifically rejected Gardner's defense that Lubow was legally insane and that there was no meeting of the minds. The trial judge then found Gardner guilty (1) of conspiring with Lubow to commit the murder of one Morton Hollander, (2) conspiring with Lubow to commit the murder of Alvin Blum, and (3) soliciting Timothy McDonald to commit the murder of one Alvin Blum. On March 21, 1978 Gardner was sentenced to a term of five (5) years imprisonment on each of the three counts, to be served concurrently. He appealed to the Court of Special Appeals.

Several months later, Lubow was tried before a jury in the Circuit Court for Howard County. The trial judge granted Lubow's motion for acquittal as to the count charging conspiracy with Gardner to commit the murder of Morton Hollander; the jury found Lubow not guilty by reason of insanity on the remaining counts of conspiracy to commit the murder of Alvin Blum and solicitation to commit the murder of Alvin Blum.

... We granted his petition for certiorari to review ...:

1. Whether the subsequent acquittal of Gardner's alleged co-conspirator, Ralph Lubow, renders null and void Gardner's conviction for conspiracy.

....

I

The crime of conspiracy requires "a combination of two or more persons, [who] by some concerted action [seek] to accomplish some criminal or unlawful purpose; or to accomplish some purpose, not in itself criminal or unlawful, by criminal or unlawful means." *Lanasa v. State,* 109 Md. 602, 607, 71 A. 1058, 1060 (1909); *State v. Buchanan,* 5 H. & J. 259 (1821).

....

Thus, it is settled that the crime of conspiracy necessarily requires the participation of at least two people. Where the participation of only one is shown the crime is incomplete and a conviction as to him is void. This proposition is recognized in the law as the rule of consistency: that "As one person alone cannot be guilty of conspiracy, when all but one conspirator are acquitted, conviction of the remaining conspirator cannot stand." *Hurwitz v. State,* 200 Md. 578, 92 A.2d 575, 581 (1952). The rule developed many years ago when the practice was to try all persons charged with the crime of conspiracy together. Under such circumstances, common sense dictated that verdicts based on the same evidence and circumstances should be consistent. Accordingly the rule has developed primarily regarding joint trials....

However, while the evidence at the trial of a conspirator must show that he and at least another are guilty of forming an illegal scheme, it is not necessary that more than one person be convicted. Thus, the quantum of proof is sufficient at the trial of A when the evidence convinces the trier of fact beyond a reasonable doubt that A and B agreed with one another to accomplish some criminal purpose or to accomplish some purpose, not in itself criminal, by criminal or unlawful means. The rule of consistency has been held not to apply when A has been convicted of conspiracy and B has been granted immunity, or when B is dead, unknown, untried, unapprehended, or unindicted. [Citations omitted.] In these and other situations in which there has been no judicial determination of the guilt or innocence of the alleged co-conspirators,

F. JOINT LIABILITY—PROCEDURAL PROBLEMS

i.e., no adjudication on the merits, there is nothing incongruous or inconsistent about convicting a sole defendant if there is sufficient evidence of the conspiracy....

....

In *United States v. Bruno,* 333 F.Supp. 570 (E.D.Pa. 1971) the court held that the prior acquittal of all of the other co-conspirators precludes conviction of the remaining conspirator. See *Eyman v. Deutsch,* 92 Ariz. 82, 373 P.2d 716 (1962); *People v. Levy,* 299 Ill.App. 453, 20 N.E.2d 171 (1939). We note, however, that Gardner was actually tried and convicted prior to Lubow's "acquittal," a fact which serves to distinguish the instant case from ... *Bruno.*

Other courts, however, have held that the rule of consistency does not apply to separate trials of co-conspirators. In *United States v. Musgrave,* 483 F.2d 327 (5th Cir. 1973), the United States Court of Appeals held that an alleged conspirator could be convicted even though his alleged co-conspirator had been previously acquitted. A California court of appeals has made a similar holding. *People v. Superior Court,* 44 Cal.App.3d 494, 118 Cal.Rptr. 702 (1975). Other courts have held that a prior guilty plea or plea of non vult will stand despite the later acquittal of all of the alleged co-conspirators. *United States v. Strother,* 458 F.2d 424 (5th Cir. 1972); *Rosecrans v. United States,* 378 F.2d 561 (5th Cir. 1967); *State v. Oats,* 32 N.J.Super. 435, 108 A.2d 641 (Super.Ct.App.Div. 1954).

Two cases involving the same chronological pattern as the instant case are particularly instructive. In *People v. Holzer,* 25 Cal.App.3d 456, 102 Cal.Rptr. 11, 13 (Ct.App. 1972), the court declared:

> But a jury trying X alone, can find that X and Y were co-conspirators and can properly convict X. The fact that Y is later acquitted of conspiracy with X by a different jury on a different presentation of evidence, cannot affect the validity of the first conviction. [(citations omitted)].

The most persuasive reasons for not applying the rule to separate trials were set forth in *Platt v. State,* 143 Neb. 131, 8 N.W.2d 849 (1943). There the Supreme Court of Nebraska said:

> We think that the verdict of a jury on a separate trial, finding one of two persons charged with conspiracy to be guilty, concludes also the guilt of the other for the purposes of that trial, otherwise no conviction could have been had. The guilt of the codefendant was found as against the convicted defendant. This element of the crime having been established as against the convicted defendant, the crime was complete and the conviction final as to him, irrespective of what some other jury on different evidence might decide. The rule cannot logically be otherwise. The subsequent acquittal of the other necessarily amounts to no more than that there was a failure of proof as to him. But if they were tried together, a failure of proof as to one would amount to a failure of proof as to both because the evidence was the same. *It seems to us that reason and sound logic do not support the rule where one of two conspirators is convicted in a separate trial, that he shall be discharged because the second may be acquitted for a multitude of reasons having nothing to do with his guilt.* The acquittal of

the second conspirator could well result from the death or absence of an important state witness, the incompetency of a confession of the convicted conspirator in the second trial, the incompetency of a plea of guilty entered by the convicted conspirator at his trial, or for any other reason that would amount to a failure of proof. [8 N.W.2d at 855 (emphasis added)].

We believe that *Platt* represents the better reasoned point of view, and we adopt it.

....

Judgment affirmed; appellant to pay the costs.

NOTES

1. Unfortunately, we do not provide, as do some foreign countries, for a third verdict, *i.e.,* something such as "guilt not proven beyond a reasonable doubt." If we did, we would know when a verdict was or was not a "declaration of innocence."

    Why would a jury acquit except where it found the defendant innocent? There are a myriad of reasons. For example, the prosecutor may have done a poor job, or defense counsel may have done an exceptionally good job, or the witnesses for the State may have testified poorly, or the quantum or quality of the evidence offered by the State may have been inferior. One could go on and on. But it is clear that it is unrealistic to equate a verdict of "not guilty" with a "declaration of innocence."

State v. Hacker, 167 N.J. Super. 166, 172-73, 400 A.2d 567, 570 (1979).

2. The Model Penal Code attempted to balance the policies against inconsistent verdicts with those against an acquittal because of miscarriage of justice. In the complicity draft, the Code provides that "an accomplice may be convicted on proof of the commission of the crime and his complicity therein, though the person claimed to have committed the crime has not been prosecuted or convicted or has been convicted of a different crime or degree of crime or has been acquitted." § 2.06(6) (Tent. Draft No. 4, 1955).

    The Code defines conspiracy in terms of an actor agreeing *with* another to commit a crime, rather than as an agreement between two or more persons. The Code describes this as a "unilateral" approach, in an effort to avoid the problems inherent in a "meeting of the minds." Under such a definition, the problems of immunity, incapacity, failure of agreement, and inconsistent separate trials would be avoided. Section 5.03(1) comment at 104-06 (Tent. Draft No. 10, 1960).

    In neither case, however, does the American Law Institute take a position on the effect of inconsistent verdicts in joint complicity or conspiracy trials.

    See Note, *Conspiracy: Statutory Reform Since the Model Penal Code,* 75 COLUM. L. REV. 1122 (1975).

3. *Incapacity.* A defense of incapacity available to a principal will not exonerate an accomplice. In *People v. Jones,* 184 Colo. 96, 518 P.2d 819 (1974), the defendant obtained a pistol for the purpose of robbing homosexuals. His codefendant killed a man with the pistol in the course of a robbery, and the felony-murder rule was invoked to charge the defendant with first degree

F. JOINT LIABILITY—PROCEDURAL PROBLEMS

murder. The principal was found not guilty by reason of insanity, and the defendant was convicted of murder. The conviction was affirmed. In *Babcock v. State,* 485 S.W.2d 85, 89 (Mo. 1972), an accomplice's guilty plea was upheld despite the principal's previously having been found not guilty by reason of insanity. To hold otherwise "would permit one to use an insane person as his agent of destruction."

However, conspiracy requires an agreement or "meeting of the minds," and an actor is incapable of entering into a conspiracy if incapable of committing a crime. In *Regle v. State,* 9 Md. App. 346, 264 A.2d 119 (1970), defendant's conviction of conspiracy to commit robbery was reversed because the only other conspirator had been insane at the time of the alleged agreement.

> By its nature, conspiracy is a joint or group offense requiring a concert of free wills, and the union of the minds of at least two persons is a prerequisite to the commission of the offense.... [W]e hold that where only two persons are implicated in a conspiracy, and one is shown to have been insane at the time the agreement was concluded ... there is no punishable criminal conspiracy, the requisite joint criminal intent being absent.

264 A.2d at 124. *Contra, Jones v. State,* 31 Ala. App. 504, 19 So. 2d 81 (1944). *But see* N.Y. PENAL LAW § 105.30 (McKinney 1975), providing that the incapacity of all other co-conspirators offers no defense to the conviction of the remaining conspirator. *See Garcia v. State, supra* pp. 793-795.

Where there is a demonstrated legislative intent that the victims of crime are to remain unpunished, such persons are incapable of conspiring to commit the crime. Thus, in *Nigro v. United States,* 117 F.2d 624 (8th Cir. 1941), a doctor had agreed to issue fictitious prescriptions to a drug addict so that the addict could purchase drugs. The court reversed a conviction of conspiracy to violate the Harrison Anti-Narcotics Act because of a demonstrated congressional intent not to punish addicted purchasers of drugs. Similarly, an expressed legislative intent not to punish a woman who acquiesced in her transportation across state lines for immoral purposes under the Mann Act precluded charging her with conspiracy to violate the Mann Act. *Gebardi v. United States,* 287 U.S. 112 (1932).

Distinguish, however, cases where personal defenses of other conspirators not amounting to legal incapacity to commit crime will not protect a defendant conspirator who does not enjoy the same immunity from prosecution. In *Farnsworth v. Zerbst,* 98 F.2d 541 (5th Cir. 1938), the court affirmed a conviction of conspiracy to violate the Espionage Act. Defendant had sold classified information to Japanese diplomats; co-conspirators who were representatives of the Japanese government and thus immune from prosecution.

4. The *"Wharton Rule."*

> An agreement between two persons to commit an offense does not constitute conspiracy when the target offense is so defined that it can be committed only by the participation of two persons, or, to use common statutory language, the offense is so defined "that the defendant's conduct is inevitably incident to its commission." Thus, there can be no conspiracy between the giver and receiver of a bribe; the giver and receiver of an

illegal rebate; a prostitute and a pimp or panderer; the parties to adultery; or a fugitive from justice and the person concealing him.

4 C. TORCIA, WHARTON'S CRIMINAL LAW AND PROCEDURE § 741, p. 545 (14th ed. 1981).

In *Iannelli v. United States,* 420 U.S. 770 (1975), defendants were convicted of conspiring to violate and violating 18 U.S.C. § 1955 (1976), a federal gambling statute making it a crime for five or more persons to direct or supervise a gambling business prohibited by state law. The defendants appealed, alleging that the "five or more" requirement prohibited their prosecution for conspiracy. They thus asserted that the recognized "third party exception," which renders Wharton's Rule inapplicable when the conspiracy involves a greater number of persons than is required for commission of the substantive offense, did not apply in their case. The Supreme Court granted certiorari to resolve a conflict in the circuits, and affirmed the conviction. Justice Powell, writing for the majority, reviewed the history of the rule and concluded "it has current vitality only as a judicial presumption, to be applied in the absence of legislative intent to the contrary. The classic Wharton's Rule offenses ... are crimes that are characterized by the general congruence of the agreement and the completed substantive offense. The parties to the agreement are the only persons who participate in commission of the substantive offense, and the immediate consequences of the crime rest on the parties themselves rather than on society at large. *Id.* at 782-83. In the present case, gambling activity has consequences which reach far beyond the effects on the immediate organizers. The legislative history of the Organized Crime Control Act and § 1955 evidenced Congress' concern with widespread gambling and indicated no intent that the separate substantive crimes of conspiracy to violate § 1955 and violation of § 1955 should be merged. Finally, said the Court, the "five or more" limitation in the statute merely demonstrated the legislative intent to concern the federal courts with large-scale gambling enterprises in an effort to combat organized crime revenue raising devices, leaving small-scale operations to local law enforcement. Mr. Justice Douglas dissented: "The rule that a conspiracy remains separable from the completed crime, thus permitting simultaneous conviction for both, rests on the assumption that the act of conspiring presents special dangers the legislature did not address in defining the substantive crime and that are not adequately checked by its prosecution.... Wharton's Rule teaches that where the substantive crime itself is aimed at the evils traditionally addressed by the law of conspiracy, separability should not be found unless the clearest legislative statement demands it. In my view this case fits the rationale of Wharton's Rule, and there is no legislative statement justifying the inference that Congress intended to permit multiple convictions." *Id.* at 793-94.

G. ORGANIZED CRIME

INTRODUCTORY NOTE

In the twentieth century attempts to cope with organized crime have been frustrated by the necessity to adhere to the basic principles of criminal law

G. ORGANIZED CRIME

which are dealt with in Chapter 1. There is no difficulty in responding to specific antisocial acts. There are difficulties when the criminal law is used to deal with an organized criminal group as an entity or with a member of an organized criminal group, primarily because of membership in the group.

The evolution of a far reaching conspiracy doctrine represents a unique aspect of the common law. In present statutory form it has been used as a tool against organized crime. Conspiracy, however, requires proof of an agreement and an intent to further the objectives of the agreement. Contemporary efforts to deal with organized crime have attempted to focus on the status of being involved in an organized criminal group.

Lanzetta v. New Jersey, 306 U.S. 451 (1939), invalidated a statute which created the crime of "gangsterism." Under the statute: "Any person not engaged in any lawful occupation, known to be a member of any gang consisting of two or more persons, who has been convicted at least three times of being a disorderly person, or who has been convicted of any crime in this or in any other state is declared to be a gangster." The state court had upheld the statute because "[t]he evident aim of this provision was to render penal the association of criminals for the pursuit of criminal enterprises." *Id.* at 455. In holding the statute unconstitutional because of vagueness the United States Supreme Court stated: "The challenged provision condemns no act or omission; ...." *Id.* at 458.

More recent federal statutes have attempted to avoid the problems of the Lanzetta statute. For example, 18 U.S.C. § 1955 (1976) makes it a federal crime, to conduct, etc., an illegal gambling business. Under the act —

> (1) [An] illegal gambling business means a gambling business which
> (i) is in violation of the law of a statute or political subdivision in which it is conducted;
> (ii) involves five or more persons who conduct, finance, manage, supervise, direct, or own all or part of such business; and
> (iii) has been or remains in substantially continuous operation for a period in excess of thirty days or has a gross revenue of $2,000 in any single day....

The Supreme Court in *Iannelli v. United States,* 420 U.S. 770 (1975), held that it was permissible to prosecute both under § 1955 and for conspiracy to violate § 1955.

EDITORIAL NOTE ON TRANSITION FROM "CONSPIRACY" TO "ENTERPRISE"

Until recently the crime of conspiracy has been used as a tool against organized crime. In 1976, Congress enacted the Racketeer Influenced and Corrupt Organizations Act (RICO), 18 U.S.C. §§ 1961 to 1968, which introduced the notion of a criminal "enterprise."

Under RICO, it is unlawful for a person to use income derived from a pattern of racketeering to acquire or invest in an enterprise, 18 U.S.C. § 1962(a); to acquire or maintain an interest in an enterprise through a pattern of racketeering activity, 18 U.S.C. § 1962(b); to conduct the affairs of an enterprise through a pattern of racketeering activity, 18 U.S.C. § 1962(c); to conspire to commit any of these acts, 18 U.S.C. § 1962(d). *See* the portions of *United States v. Turkette,* 452 U.S. 576 (1981), *supra* pp. 22-23; Blakey & Gettings, *Racketeer Influenced and Corrupt Organizations (RICO): Basic Concepts — Criminal and Civil Remedies,* 53 TEMP. L.Q. 1009 (1980); Blakey & Goldstock, *"On the Waterfront": RICO and Labor Racketeering,* 17 AM. CRIM. L. REV. 341 (1980).

Enterprise "includes any individual, partnership, corporation, association, or other legal entity, and any union or group of individuals associated in fact though not a legal entity." 18 U.S.C. § 1961(4) (1976). Racketeering is an act that violates one of over forty enumerated federal and state laws. The pattern of racketeering activity requires at least two acts of racketeering committed within ten years of each other. Survey, *White Collar Crime: Racketeering Influenced and Corrupt Organizations (RICO),* 18 AM. CRIM. L. REV. 308 (1980).

> Courts have determined that the general federal conspiracy law makes a common agreement or objective an essential element of a single conspiracy. As a consequence, there is a diminished likelihood that multi-faceted, syndicated criminal activity would be found to be one conspiracy. RICO removes this prosecutorial barrier by formulating racketeering offenses which support the connection between crimes and parties that courts had previously been less willing to recognize. RICO extends the reach of prior conspiracy law by criminalizing the maintenance or infiltration of an "enterprise" through a pattern of racketeering activity. Section (d) then allows the prosecution of the huge and diversified pattern as a single conspiracy. As a result, section (d) suggests the concept of an "enterprise" conspiracy in addition to the more limited "wheel" and "chain" type conspiracies.
>
> Because of the breadth of the "enterprise" offenses, it is less essential for the court to discover a specific uniform objective on the part of interdependent conspirators. It is sufficient if there exists a broad conspiratorial objective to become involved in and conduct an enterprise through a pattern of corrupt activities....
>
> ... Conspiracy can therefore be established where the defendants have agreed to participate in the furtherance of an enterprise's affairs by committing the underlying offenses. That the underlying offenses may be totally unrelated need not be a barrier to a successful prosecution for conspiracy under RICO. Instead, the key element is proof that the various crimes were performed in order to assist the enterprise's involvement in corrupt endeavors. Since the broad objective necessary to establish an enterprise conspiracy allows the tying together of seemingly unrelated crimes, section (d) has added an important weapon to the prosecutorial arsenal and filled a void left by the narrowness of the general conspiracy statute.

Blakey & Goldstock, 17 Am. Crim. L. Rev. at 360-61.

It has been asserted that:

> RICO is not a criminal statute; it does not make criminal conduct that before its enactment was not already prohibited, since its application depends on the existence of "racketeering activity" that violates an independent criminal statute. In addition, its standards of unlawful, *i.e.*, criminal or civil, conduct are sanctioned by both criminal and civil remedies. RICO, in short, is a "remedial" statute.

Blakey & Gettings, 53 Temp. L.Q. at 1021.

UNITED STATES v. ELLIOTT

United States Court of Appeals
571 F.2d 880 (5th Cir.), *cert. denied*, 439 U.S. 953 (1978)

Simpson, Circuit Judge:

In this case we deal with the question of whether and, if so, how a free society can protect itself when groups of people, through division of labor, specialization, diversification, complexity of organization, and the accumulation of capital, turn crime into an ongoing business. Congress fired a telling shot at organized crime when it passed the Racketeer Influenced and Corrupt Organizations Act of 1970, popularly known as RICO. 18 U.S.C. §§ 1961 et seq. (1970). Since the enactment of RICO, the federal courts, guided by constitutional and legislative dictates, have been responsible for perfecting the weapons in society's arsenal against criminal confederacies.

Today we review the convictions of six persons accused of conspiring to violate the RICO statute, two of whom were also accused and convicted of substantive RICO violations. The government admits that in this prosecution it has attempted to achieve a broader application of RICO than has heretofore been sanctioned. Predictably, the government and the defendants differ as to what this case is about. According to the defendants, what we are dealing with is a leg, a tail, a trunk, an ear — separate entities unaffected by RICO proscriptions. The government, on the other hand, asserts that we have come eyeball to eyeball with a single creature of behemoth proportions, securely within RICO's grasp. After a careful, if laborious study of the facts and the law, we accept, with minor exceptions, the government's view. Because of the complicated nature of this case, both factually and doctrinally, a detailed explication of the facts and of the reasoning underlying our conclusions must be undertaken.

[The court then described in detail the testimony involving twenty different criminal episodes. These include, in part:

> A. Foster told Gunnells that he paid J. C. Hawkins and his brother Recea Hawkins $4500 to burn down a nursing home in which Foster had an interest. The nursing home was burned down on December 3, 1970.
>
> B. From 1971 through 1974, J. C. Hawkins, Delph and Taylor furnished counterfeit titles to and helped sell cars stolen by a major car theft ring in and near Atlanta, Georgia.

C. A truckload of Hormel meat was stolen on April 1, 1972 in Smyrna, Georgia while en route to Atlanta. On the night of April 1, 1972 J. C. Hawkins visited Flanders at his grocery store and asked if he could store meat in the cooler. During the next few days J. C. stored 40 to 50 boxes of meat there. Later that month he offered to sell a truckload of meat to Sykes for $7,000. Codefendant Elliott sold a 50-pound piece of Hormel meat to Joe Fuchs. Flanders was charged later with possession of stolen meat. J. C. later told Gunnells that it had been his meat and that he and his brother Recea purchased it for $10,000.

D. Immediately preceding Flanders' trial on the possession charge, early in May, 1973, he met with J. C. Hawkins, Gunnells and others. The jury list for the trial was passed around. J. C. recognized one of the names and said he was certain that person would cooperate. That person did in fact sit on the jury. He voted for acquittal although the other 11 jurors voted for conviction.

[There were numerous other transactions involving stolen goods, e.g., a front end loader and a dump truck, Swift Premium meats and dairy products. There was intimidation of a witness and the killing of one. There were also numerous separate drug transactions.

[All six defendants were charged with having conspired to violate RICO from December 3, 1970 until June, 1976. Count 2 charged only J. C. and Recea Hawkins with a substantive violation of RICO. The remaining counts charge specific acts of misconduct, *e.g.*, possession of stolen Hormel meat, corruptly endeavoring to obstruct justice in the Flanders prosecution, possession of stolen Swift Premium meats and dairy products.]

III. The Substantive RICO Violation

J. C. and Recea Hawkins contend that their acts, while arguably violative of other criminal statutes, are not proscribed by the substantive RICO provision under which they were charged, 18 U.S.C. § 1962(c), in that they were not committed in furtherance of the affairs of an "enterprise" as required by the Act. At best, they say, the facts disclosed that two brothers confederated to commit a few, isolated criminal acts over a period of six years. Neither the facts nor the law support this contention.

Because this prosecution was based on a novel and recently enacted criminal statute, we must, at the outset, determine exactly what that statute denounces as illegal, as relevant to this case. Section 1962(c) provides:

> It shall be unlawful for any person employed by or associated with any enterprise engaged in, or the activities of which affect, interstate or foreign commerce, to conduct or participate, directly or indirectly, in the conduct of such enterprise's affairs through a pattern of racketeering activity or collection of unlawful debt.

This section must be read in the context of the statutory definitions of its key terms. "Enterprise," as used in the Act, "includes any individual, partnership, corporation, association, or other legal entity, and any union or group of individuals associated in fact although not a legal entity." 18 U.S.C. § 1961(4). As relevant to this case, a "pattern of racketeering activity" simply requires at least two acts of "racketeering activity" committed within ten years of each other. 18 U.S.C. § 1961(5). "Racketeering activity" includes three broad categories of crimes: (A) any of several specified "act[s] or threat[s] ... chargeable under State law and punishable by imprisonment for more than one year," including, as relevant here, murder and arson, (B) any act which is indictable under any of several specified sections of Title 18, U.S.C., including, as relevant here, § 659 (felonious theft from interstate shipment), § 1503 (obstruction of justice), and § 2315 (interstate shipment of stolen or counterfeit securities) or (C) federal offenses involving narcotics or other dangerous drugs. 18 U.S.C. § 1961(1).

Reduced to its bare essentials, the charge against J. C. and Recea may be restated as follows:

> Being associated with a group of individuals who were associated in fact, J. C. and Recea Hawkins each directly and indirectly participated in the group's affairs through the commission of two or more predicate crimes.

The gist of J. C.'s and Recea's objection to their conviction on Count Two is that there was no group of individuals associated in fact — no enterprise — in whose affairs they could have participated, directly or indirectly. We disagree.

In *United States v. Hawes,* 529 F.2d 472, 479 (5th Cir. 1976), we noted that "Congress gave the term 'enterprise' a very broad meaning." On its face and in light of its legislative history, the Act clearly encompasses "not only legitimate businesses but also enterprises which are from their inception organized for illicit purposes." *United States v. McLaurin,* 557 F.2d 1064, 1073 (5th Cir. 1977).[17] Similarly, we are persuaded that "enterprise" includes an informal, de facto association such as that involved in this case. In defining "enterprise," Congress made clear that the statute extended beyond conventional business organizations to reach "*any ...* group of individuals" whose association, however loose or informal, furnishes a vehicle for the commission of two or more predicate crimes. The statute demands only that there be association "in fact" when it cannot be implied in law. There is no distinction, for "enterprise" purposes, between a duly formed corporation that elects officers and holds annual meetings and an amoeba-like infra-structure that controls a secret criminal network.

---

[17] The dispute over whether the Act reaches illegitimate businesses stems from dicta in Iannelli v. United States, 420 U.S. 770, 95 S.Ct. 1284, 43 L.Ed.2d 616 (1975). Although that case did not involve a prosecution under the RICO statute, the Court, in footnote 19, noted: "[RICO] seeks to prevent the infiltration of legitimate business operations affecting interstate commerce by individuals who have obtained investment capital from a pattern of racketeering activity." As we explained in United States v. McLaurin, *supra,* 557 F.2d at 1073, there is no indication that the dicta was intended to describe fully the ambit of the Act's coverage. Furthermore, the Act on its face draws no distinction between legitimate and illegitimate businesses, and the legislative history supports the broad application inherent in the words of the statute. See "Congressional Statement of Findings and Purpose," Pub.L.No. 91 — 452, § 1, 84 Stat. 922 (1970); United States v. Brown, 555 F.2d 407, 415-16 (5th Cir. 1977). "[W]e do not believe that it is normally a proper judicial function to try to cabin in the plain language of a statute, even a criminal statute, by limiting its coverage to the primary activity Congress had in mind when it acted." United States v. Mandel, 415 F.Supp. 997, 1019 (D. Md. 1976), quoting United States v. LeFaivre, 507 F.2d 1288, 1295 (4th Cir. 1974), cert. denied, 420 U.S. 1004, 95 S.Ct. 1446, 43 L.Ed.2d 762 (1975).

Here, the government proved beyond a reasonable doubt the existence of an enterprise comprised of at least five of the defendants. This enterprise can best be analogized to a large business conglomerate. Metaphorically speaking, J. C. Hawkins was the chairman of the board, functioning as the chief executive officer and overseeing the operations of many separate branches of the corporation. An executive committee in charge of the "Counterfeit Title, Stolen Car, and Amphetamine Sales Department" was comprised of J. C., Delph, and Taylor, who supervised the operations of lower level employees such as Farr, the printer, and Green, Boyd, and Jackson, the car thieves. Another executive committee, comprised of J. C., Recea and Foster, controlled the "Thefts From Interstate Commerce Department," arranging the purchase, concealment, and distribution of such commodities as meat, dairy products, "Career Club" shirts, and heavy construction equipment. An offshoot of this department handled subsidiary activities, such as murder and obstruction of justice, intended to facilitate the smooth operation of its primary activities. Each member of the conglomerate, with the exception of Foster, was responsible for procuring and wholesaling whatever narcotics could be obtained. The thread tying all of these departments, activities, and individuals together was the desire to make money.

. . . .

A jury is entitled to infer the existence of an enterprise on the basis of largely or wholly circumstantial evidence. Like a criminal conspiracy, a RICO enterprise cannot be expected to maintain a high profile in the community. Its affairs are likely to be conducted in secrecy and to involve a minimal amount of necessary contact between participants. Thus, direct evidence of association may be difficult to obtain; a jury should be permitted to draw the natural inference arising from circumstantial evidence of association.[19]

. . . .

Additionally, although the target of the RICO statute is not "sporadic activity," we find nothing in the Act excluding from its ambit an enterprise engaged in diversified activity.

. . . .

IV. The RICO Conspiracy Count

All six defendants were convicted under 18 U.S.C. § 1962(d) of having conspired to violate a substantive RICO provision, § 1962(c). In this appeal, all defendants, with the exception of Foster, argue that while the indictment alleged but one conspiracy, the government's evidence at trial proved the existence of several conspiracies, resulting in a variance which substantially prejudiced their rights and requires reversal, citing *Kotteakos v. United States*, 328 U.S. 750, 66 S.Ct. 1239, 90 L.Ed. 1557 (1946). Prior to the enactment of the RICO statute, this argument would have been more persuasive. However, as we explain below, RICO has displaced many of the legal precepts

---

[19] In conspiracy cases, we allow the jury to infer agreement on the basis of "the acts and conduct of the alleged conspirators themselves." United States v. Morado, 454 F.2d 167, 174 (5th Cir. 1972). In this case, it is apparent that the enterprise operated in a manner calculated to minimize direct evidence of association. See notes 13 and 14, *supra*, and accompanying text.

traditionally applied to concerted criminal activity. Its effect in this case is to free the government from the strictures of the multiple conspiracy doctrine and to allow the joint trial of many persons accused of diversified crimes.

[The court described "wheel" and "chain" types of conspiracies. *See* pp. 810-811 *supra.*]

... Generally, where the government has shown that a number of otherwise diverse activities were performed to achieve a single goal, courts have been willing to find a single conspiracy. This "common objective" test has most often been used to connect the many facets of drug importation and distribution schemes. The rationale falls apart, however, where the remote members of the alleged conspiracy are not truly interdependent or where the various activities sought to be tied together cannot reasonably be said to constitute a unified scheme....

Applying pre-RICO conspiracy concepts to the facts of this case, we doubt that a single conspiracy could be demonstrated.

....

B. RICO to the Rescue: The Enterprise Conspiracy

In enacting RICO, Congress found that "organized crime continues to grow" in part "because the sanctions and remedies available to the Government are unnecessarily limited in scope and impact." Thus, one of the express purposes of the Act was "to seek the eradication of organized crime ... by establishing new penal prohibitions, and by providing enhanced sanctions and new remedies to deal with the unlawful activities of those engaged in organized crime." Pub.L.91 — 452, § 1, 84 Stat. 922 (1970). Against this background, we are convinced that, through RICO, Congress intended to authorize the single prosecution of a multi-faceted, diversified conspiracy by replacing the inadequate "wheel" and "chain" rationales with a new statutory concept: the enterprise.

To achieve this result, Congress acted against the backdrop of hornbook conspiracy law. Under the general federal conspiracy statute,

> the precise nature and extent of the conspiracy must be determined by reference to the agreement which embraces and defines its objects. Whether the object of a single agreement is to commit one or many crimes, it is in either case that agreement which constitutes the conspiracy which the statute punishes. *Braverman v. United States,* 317 U.S. 49, 53 (1942).

In the context of organized crime, this principle inhibited mass prosecutions because a single agreement or "common objective" cannot be inferred from the commission of highly diverse crimes by apparently unrelated individuals. RICO helps to eliminate this problem by creating a substantive offense which ties together these diverse parties and crimes. Thus, the object of a RICO conspiracy is to violate a substantive RICO provision — here, to conduct or participate in the affairs of an enterprise through a pattern of racketeering activity — and not merely to commit each of the predicate crimes necessary to demonstrate a pattern of racketeering activity. The gravamen of the conspiracy charge in this case is not that each defendant agreed to commit arson, to steal goods from interstate commerce, to obstruct justice, and to sell narcotics; rather, it is that each agreed to participate, directly or indirectly, in the affairs of the enterprise by committing two or more predicate crimes. Under the statute, it is irrelevant that each defendant participated in the enterprise's affairs through different, even unrelated crimes, so long as we may reasonably infer that each crime was intended to further the enterprise's affairs. To find a single conspiracy, we still must look for agreement on an overall objective. What Congress did was to define that objective through the substantive provisions of the Act.

C. *Constitutional Considerations*

The "enterprise conspiracy" is a legislative innovation in the realm of individual liability for group crime. We need to consider whether this innovation comports with the fundamental demand of due process that guilt remain "individual and personal." *Kotteakos, supra,* 328 U.S. at 722.

The substantive proscriptions of the RICO statute apply to insiders *and outsiders* — those merely "associated with" an enterprise — who participate directly *and indirectly* in the enterprise's affairs through a pattern of racketeering activity. 18 U.S.C. § 1962(c). Cf. *United States v. Forsythe,* 560 F.2d 1127, 1135-36 (3d Cir. 1977). Thus, the RICO net is woven tightly to trap even the smallest fish, those peripherally involved with the enterprise. This effect is enhanced by principles of conspiracy law also developed to facilitate prosecution of conspirators at all levels. Direct evidence of agreement is unnecessary: "proof of such an agreement may rest upon inferences drawn from relevant and competent circumstantial evidence — ordinarily the acts and conduct of the alleged conspirators themselves." *United States v. Morado, supra,* 454 F.2d at 174. Additionally, once the conspiracy has been established, the government need show only "slight evidence" that a particular person was a member of the conspiracy. *Id.* at 175. Of course, "a party to a conspiracy need not know the identity, or even the number, of his confederates." *United States v. Andolschek,* 142 F.2d 503, 507 (2d Cir. 1944).

Undeniably, then, under the RICO conspiracy provision, remote associates of an enterprise may be convicted as conspirators on the basis of purely circumstantial evidence. We cannot say, however, that this section of the statute demands inferences that cannot reasonably be drawn from circumstantial evidence or that it otherwise offends the rule that guilt be individual and personal. The Act does not authorize that individuals "be tried en masse for the conglomeration of distinct and separate offenses committed by others." *Kotteakos, supra.* Nor does it punish mere association with conspirators or knowledge of illegal activity; its proscriptions are directed against conduct, not status. *United States v. Forsythe, supra,* 560 F.2d at 1136. To be convicted as a member of an enterprise conspiracy, an individual, by his words or actions, must have objectively manifested an agreement to participate, directly or indirectly, in the affairs of an enterprise through the commission of two or more predicate crimes. One whose agreement with the members of an enterprise did not include this vital element cannot be convicted under the Act. Where, as here, the evidence establishes that each defendant, over a period of years, committed several acts of racketeering activity in furtherance of the enterprise's affairs, the inference of an agreement to do so is unmistakable.

....

VII. Conclusion

Through RICO, Congress defined a new separate crime to help snare those who make careers of crime. Participation in the affairs of an enterprise through the commission of two or more predicate crimes is now an offense separate and distinct from those predicate crimes. So too is conspiracy to commit this new offense a crime separate and distinct from conspiracy to commit the predicate crimes. The necessity which mothered this statutory invention was caused by the inability of the traditional criminal law to punish and deter organized crime.

The realistic view of group crime which inspired Congress to enact RICO should also guide the courts in construing RICO. Thus, in this case, we are satisfied that the evidence, circumstantial and indirect though it largely was, proved the existence of both an enterprise committed to profiting from criminal activity and an agreement among five of the defendants to participate in the affairs of the enterprise through a pattern of racketeering activity.

As explained above, we find the evidence insufficient to sustain James Elliott's conviction on Count One and reverse as to him. We find that the other defendants were properly convicted and affirm in each of their cases. Those five, Delph, Foster, Recea Hawkins, John Clayburn Hawkins, Jr. a/k/a J. C., and Taylor received their just desserts [sic] by the verdict of the jury in a fair trial free from prejudicial error.

Affirmed in part; reversed in part.

NOTES

1. The Supreme Court has interpreted the enterprise element in the RICO statute as including not only legitimate entities, but also those associations which are formed solely to achieve criminal objectives, *United States v. Turkette,* 452 U.S. 576 (1981). A gang of thieves, extortionists, etc. could qualify as an "enterprise." In reversing the court of appeals, the Court explained the element and proof required under RICO:

> That a wholly criminal enterprise comes within the ambit of the statute does not mean that a "pattern of racketeering activity" is an "enterprise." In order to secure a conviction under RICO, the Government must prove both the existence of an "enterprise" and the connected "pattern of racketeering activity." The enterprise is an entity, for present purposes a group of persons associated together for a common purpose of engaging in a course of conduct. The pattern of racketeering activity is, on the other hand, a series of criminal acts as defined by the statute. 18 U.S.C. § 1961(1). The former is proved by evidence of an ongoing organization, formal or informal, and by evidence that the various associates function as a continuing unit. The latter is proved by evidence of the requisite number of acts of racketeering committed by the participants in the en-

terprise. While the proof used to establish these separate elements may in particular cases coalesce, proof of one does not necessarily establish the other. The "enterprise" is not the "pattern of racketeering activity"; it is an entity separate and apart from the pattern of activity in which it engages. The existence of an enterprise at all times remains a separate element which must be proved by the Government.

Id. at 583. *See also* discussion of the *Turkette* case, *supra* pp. 22-24.

2. The Seventh Circuit has stated that the application of RICO "is not restricted to members of organized crime." *United States v. Aleman,* 609 F.2d 298, 303 (7th Cir. 1979), *cert. denied,* 445 U.S. 946 (1980). That court, as well as most others which have ruled on the issue, also included public entities, such as a police department, within the definition of "enterprise." *United States v. Grzywacz,* 603 F.2d 682 (7th Cir. 1979). *But see United States v. Mandel,* 415 F. Supp. 997 (D. Md. 1976) (State of Maryland not an "enterprise").

3. Many difficult problems in interpreting RICO are discussed in Bradley, Racketeers, Congress and the Courts: An Analysis of RICO, 65 IOWA L. REV. 837 (1979-80).

Some commentators are not particularly supportive of RICO:

> RICO was passed by Congress with a laudable motive: the elimination of organized crime. But in an effort to catch all possible members of organized crime and to avoid the constitutional problem of making a crime out of the status of being a member of organized crime, Congress passed a sweeping Act which intrudes on state power and has great potential for abuse against individual defendants.
>
> No constitutional challenges to RICO have, as yet, been upheld. Constitutional challenges may, however, still be mounted on several grounds. These grounds include vagueness, double jeopardy and cruel and unusual punishment. Such challenges are more likely to be successful the more abusive a particular RICO prosecution appears to be.

Atkinson, *"Racketeer Influenced and Corrupt Organizations,"* 18 U.S.C. §§ 1961-68: Broadest of the Federal Criminal Statutes, 69 J. CRIM. L. & CRIMINOLOGY 1, 18 (1978).

PART FOUR
SANCTIONS

A

Chapter 11
PURPOSES, CONSTITUTIONALITY AND FORMS OF CRIMINAL SANCTIONS

SECTION I. General Purposes of Sanctioning

EDITORIAL NOTE — VIEWS ON PUNISHMENT

Retribution

Punishment under a retributive view is imposed on people, not to achieve some specific aim, but simply because they have committed crimes. Retribution is premised on a theory of "justice." Unquestionably, it is "unjust" to punish those who have not violated the law. As a corollary, if the term "justice" is to have meaning, persons who have violated the criminal law must be punished. Hence, not only is punishment permissible; it is right and necessary as a matter of elemental justice. Because people are held accountable for their actions, they should receive the just deserts of their criminal acts.

Retribution is a concept of ancient origin rooted in notions of revenge and expiation. The *lex talionis* decreed an eye for an eye and a tooth for a tooth. Nevertheless, implicit in this statement is a notion of proportionality: The phrase imports limits on punishment, so that only one tooth, not a mouthful of teeth, can be extracted in vengeance.

The retributive view, at least in its original formulation, does not rest on grounds of social utility, but rather on notions of a community's right or obligation to punish those who violate its criminal ordinances. Consequently, it needs no further justification, in contrast to the theories of deterrence and rehabilitation discussed below. Yet that very advantage yields a disadvantage, namely, the criticism that retribution is nothing more than the primitive reaction of inflicting pain for the sake of pain.

Does the retributive view necessarily exclude from its ambit any dimension of social value? One may well conclude that it does not. Even in a contemporary and humanistic society, experience suggests that retribution may be justified on bases other than revenge or expiation. Imposition of punishment may serve as a safety valve for community fears and hostilities generated as a consequence of criminal acts. Punishment, one may well argue, reinforces community norms and values by demonstrating in a dramatic fashion that certain standards of conduct are so important to society that it will inflict pain on those within it who contravene them. Finally, punishment administered to offenders through the agencies of government sublimates deep-seated demands for revenge held widely among the citizenry and so blunts the impetus to wreak private vengeance.

Prevention: Deterrence, Incapacitation, and Rehabilitation

Concepts of punishment, other than retribution, are premised on their utility in preventing crime. Accordingly, utilitarian theories of sanctioning accept punishment if the costs it imposes do not outweigh the benefits it produces. In other words, for punishment to be justifiable (and just), society must experience good results from infliction of punishment significantly greater than the harms generated by withholding it. Punishment can be used in different ways under a utilitarian concept. If it is invoked to affect the future conduct of persons other than offenders, by making examples of the latter and thus discouraging the former from duplicating past criminal activity, it seeks to achieve *general deterrence*. To the extent sanctions are imposed to order to change the personal behavior of offenders through official intimidation, they work *special deterrence*. If imprisonment is the selected sanction (or, as an ultimate measure, offenders are executed), thereby forestalling opportunities to commit new crimes, the consequence is *incapacitation*. Finally, if one or more forms of control and reformation are utilized for the purpose of changing an offender's future behavior, the aim is *rehabilitation*.

General Deterrence

General deterrence rests on the assumption that most people are rational and hedonistic, seeking to gain pleasure and to avoid pain. Because society punishes those who break its laws, and punishment is painful, its members will endeavor to avoid punishment by conforming their conduct to the requirements of law. Crimes are committed for gain, whether in the form of material goods, as in theft, or psychological satisfaction, as when persons strike those who have insulted them. In essence, invocation of sanctions through the operation of a system of criminal justice is designed to create within the minds of those who may be tempted to commit crimes a counterweight, based on the deprivations and unpleasantness which will flow from perpetration of offenses and subsequent apprehension, prosecution, and conviction. In assessing the functional significance of "prospects of punishment," however, severity of punishment, although an important consideration from the standpoint of those contemplating commission of crimes, is overbalanced by the likelihood, i.e. the statistical probability, that they will later be apprehended, adjudicated, and in fact punished to some extent. To illustrate, if only 100 out of 10,000 burglars ever serve time in prison, general deterrent effect is slight. Thus, the efficacy of general deterrence is very much dependent on public perceptions of the efficiency of law-enforcement agencies and the criminal justice system generally.

General deterrence has been criticized on various grounds. (1) Obviously, people continue to commit crimes; therefore, general deterrence does not work. In response, one may note that we have no way to determine how many more crimes might have been committed were there no punishment. In other words, although it is relatively easy to identify those who have not been deterred, it is exceedingly difficult to ascertain the number of those who were in fact deterred. (2) Also, it has been said that certain people cannot be deterred at all, or deterred from committing certain crimes, e.g. crimes of passion. But this does not mean that most people cannot be deterred from committing all or almost all crimes, or that certain kinds of crime, like economic crimes, cannot be deterred. (3) Finally, the morality has been questioned of using persons as objects, as "its" rather than "thous" in the words of Martin Buber,* i.e. as means to manipulate the conduct of others. There is probably no "answer" to such an objection, resting as it does in theology and moral philosophy. All that one can say is that persons adhering to such a premise will react strongly against sanctions authorized or invoked under a general deterrence theory.

There is another way of looking at general deterrence. Imposing punishment is part of a process which helps create and shape societal values. The process of apprehending, adjudicating, and punishing offenders reinforces the sense of right and wrong held within the community as a whole, at least for those of its members sufficiently socialized to feel guilt over breaking rules. Punishment clearly and demonstrably draws a line between good and evil. In the end, the administration of justice, including punishment, plays an important, indeed an indispensable, role in making people law-abiding.

Special Deterrence

The concept of special deterrence likewise assumes that people are rational. Hence, it is reasonable to expect that individuals who have been subjected to the pain of punishment will seek to avoid equivalent unpleasant experiences in the future by refraining from repeated criminal activities.

Criticism of special deterrence rests usually on the fact of recidivism, especially the high rate manifested by those who already have been very severely punished. Again, as in the context of general deterrence, one may respond that recidivism rates probably would have been even higher had there been no punishment. Also, those who are most severely punished have committed the most serious crimes, are among the most irresponsible members of society, and consequently are relatively unlikely to have experienced anything sufficient to cause them to wish to change their future conduct. In contrast, recidivism rates almost always are relatively low among those who have received less severe sentences or placed on probation. Admittedly, though, it is impossible to demonstrate statistically that those who prove not to be repeat offenders have been motivated by a desire to avoid future punishment like that they have experienced in the past.

The dimension of proportionality is important in special (and general) deterrence. More severe sanctions than are needed to change future behavior have no utilitarian justification and, therefore, must be denominated unjust. It is on this basis that the concept of least-restrictive alternative in the imposition of sanctions rests.** But there is also a risk that inadequate sanctions will if anything encourage commission of crimes. To illustrate, if a prostitute can earn $2,000 weekly, is likely to be arrested no more than once a month, will be released on personal recognizance within two or three hours, and will pay at most a fine of $200 upon conviction, the criminal justice system at most

---

*See MARTIN BUBER, I AND THOU (2d ed. 1958) *passim.*
**See *infra,* pp. 844-852.

imposes a special tax on the occupation of prostitution; prostitutes still net more income through their illicit activities than they lose through punishment. A similar conclusion might be drawn concerning a major corporate polluter of the environment, if cost of emission control equipment is $10 million, but the maximum fine which can be imposed is $10,000. Or to illustrate further, if the only penalty to be imposed upon me should I park unlawfully in the business district of a major city is a fine of $15.00, I will have to pay $25 at a commercial parking structure, and conformity to legal requirements is not an overriding consideration to me, I have a direct economic inducement to park my car illegally. That inducement is even greater if I know or believe that only a few scofflaws are ever apprehended and sanctioned. If, in contrast, police tow trucks are visibly present cruising downtown streets, cars are swiftly towed to a remote location from which they can be recovered only upon immediate payment of a $200 fine and towing charges of $75, or if officers install a so-called "Denver boot" so that I cannot use my car until I have paid $125 in fine and costs, I am likely to park my car off the street or use taxis or public transportation if I must go into the city. Thus, the dimension of proportionality cannot be ignored in evaluating deterrence theory in application.*

Incapacitation

Incapacitation is founded on the basic premise that those who are removed from a community, particularly through incarceration, cannot victimize society during a time of physical separation. The prototype of incapacitation was banishment; the English sanction of transportation of convicted convicts to penal colonies in Australia and North America is also a historical example, as is the Russian tradition, coming into the recent past, of assigning criminals and political dissidents to Siberian penal colonies. In modern times, however, walls and bars create the physical separation once provided by the seas or sheer distance.

It is difficult to quarrel with the premise underlying the theory of incapacitation. Nevertheless, it is not without its intrinsic difficulties. Implicit within it is an assumption that those who violate the law once will do so again. That cannot be true in all cases. Some people will not commit future offenses even if left free within a community, and thus do not require incapacitation. Accordingly, the first question has to be, which offenders should be incapacitated? To answer this, a criminal justice system must predict future conduct, which requires sufficient sound data on which to rest an acceptably accurate prediction. A second question is, for how long should an individual be incapacitated? This, too, can be answered only through predictive standards supported by sufficient reliable criteria, on the basis of which future conduct, dangerous or

---

*Reflecting concerns like those expressed in the text, Congress enacted the Criminal Fines Improvements Act of 1987 that included a substantial revision of 18 U.S.C.A. § 3571 (West Supp. 1993). Under § 3572(d), fines for federal offenses may be increased by an amount reflecting up to twice the gross gain realized by a defendant from the underlying offense, or up to twice the loss experienced by anyone other than the defendant from the commission of the offense. If the amount of a fine computed in that manner is higher than the statutory amount otherwise applicable, it sets the maximum fine. Id. § 3571(b)(2), (c)(2). However, an alternative fine should not be set by a federal district court if the computation and imposition would unduly complicate or prolong the sentencing process. Id. § 3571(d), final sentence.

nondangerous, can be forecast. Therefore, despite the surface appeal of incarceration as a justification for penal sanctions, one must conclude that society does not now possess sufficient data and proven criteria to allow accurate predictions about future conduct dangerous to a community.

One also must ask a third question: How can incapacitation accommodate the rule of proportionality? In other words, should those who commit relatively minor offenses, and who are likely to recidivate, be incarcerated for long periods of time because they and their projected recurring acts are considered to be dangerous?

Two other issues emerge particularly in regard to incapacitation. The economic costs of imprisonment are high, perhaps too high in relation to demonstrable achievements to survive a cost-benefit analysis. Moreover, incarcerating people for long periods exacts substantial costs from prisoners' families and the communities to which prisoners will return, which must be added to the high direct costs of a prison system itself.

Rehabilitation

Rehabilitation, like other preventive theories, has an immediate appeal stemming from the apparent logic of its underlying premises. To be specific, if society is committed to punishment, it might as well structure penal sanctions in the form of treatment modalities that can cure the causes of criminal conduct at the same time as offenders experience penal sanctions. Thus, the theory goes, rehabilitative treatment not only will prevent crimes, but will benefit offenders by changing their attitudes through education, vocational training, counseling, medical and psychological treatment, and the like.

The rehabilitative view, or "ideal" as it sometimes has been denominated in recognition that it is a goal to be pursued and not a proven theory to be implemented, has been severely criticized as, indeed, have all rationales for punishment. The frequently invoked analogy of treating illness (a medical model) has doubtful validity as a justification for treating criminality. The causes of crime are complex, varied and difficult to isolate. They tend to be rooted deeply within a society or a culture, so that to cure crime in fact requires first that society itself be cured. This logical difficulty aside, however, the most telling criticism of the rehabilitative premise is that it has not worked, at least to the extent to and ways in which it has been applied. Modern societies seem not to posses sufficient knowledge about methods of behavior modification or proven techniques for reforming those who violate the criminal law to render rehabilitative theory just in its applications.

In addition, some criticize strongly on moral grounds a premise that individuals and their attitudes should be changed against their will. In the view of such critics, "treatment," however euphemized, is involuntarily imposed and thus properly to be viewed by its recipients as punishment. Another difficulty inherent in the rehabilitative view is that, like incapacitation, it focuses on predicted future conduct of offenders, and thus lacks proportionality. Indeed, the problem of want of proportion is more acute in the setting of rehabilitation than in that of incapacitation, in that there is a strong temptation to prescribe "stiff medicine" for even minor offenders because, after all, it is for their own good.

A final question concerning rehabilitation, one which is usually not addressed because of the imperfect state of our collective knowledge, may in the end be the most cogent: Even if we possessed the knowledge and means to modify offender behavior, would we as a society be justified in using them? As one noted scholar, the late Professor Herbert Packer, noted:

> I am impelled to ask whether a theory of punishment that requires acquiescence in a compelled personality change can ever be squared with long-cherished ideals of human autonomy.*

For additional reading see NORVAL MORRIS, THE FUTURE OF IMPRISONMENT (1974); HERBERT PACKER, THE LIMITS OF THE CRIMINAL SANCTION 37-58 (1968); THEORIES OF PUNISHMENT (S. Grupp ed. 1971). For a different perspective on rehabilitation, see FRANCIS A. ALLEN, THE DECLINE OF THE REHABILITATIVE IDEAL (1981). As to inability to demonstrate the efficacy of deterrence and incapacitation, see ALFRED BLUMSTEIN ET AL., DETERRENCE AND INCAPACITATION: ESTIMATING THE EFFECTS OF CRIMINAL SANCTIONS ON CRIME RATES 7 (1978) ("In summary, therefore, we cannot yet assert that the evidence warrants an affirmative conclusion regarding deterrence.... Our reluctance to draw stronger conclusions does not imply support for a position that deterrence does not exist, since the evidence certainly favors a proposition supporting deterrence more than it favors one asserting that deterrence in absent.").

HENRY M. HART, THE AIMS OF THE CRIMINAL LAW, 23 Law and Contemporary Problems 401 (1958)**

I

Introduction

... A penal code that reflected only a single basic principle would be a very bad one. Social purposes can never be single or simple, or held unqualifiedly to the exclusion of all other social purposes; and an effort to make them so can result only in the sacrifice of other values which also are important. Thus, to take only one example, the purpose of preventing any particular kind of crime, or crimes generally, is qualified always by the purposes of avoiding the conviction of the innocent and of enhancing that sense of security throughout the society which is one of the prime functions of the manifold safeguards of American criminal procedure. And the same thing would be true even if the dominant purpose of the criminal law were thought to be the rehabilitation of offenders rather than the prevention of offenses.

Examination of the purposes commonly suggested for the criminal law will show that each of them is complex and that none may be thought of as wholly excluding the others. Suppose, for example, that the deterrence of offenses is

---

*HERBERT PACKER, THE LIMITS OF THE CRIMINAL SANCTION 57-58 (1968).

**Reprinted, with permission, from a symposium on Sentencing appearing in Law and Contemporary Problems (Vol. 23, No. 3, Summer 1958), published by the Duke University School of Law, Durham, North Carolina. Copyright, 1958 by Duke University.

taken to be the chief end. It will still be necessary to recognize that the rehabilitation of offenders, the disablement of offenders, the sharpening of the community's sense of right and wrong, and the satisfaction of the community's sense of just retribution may all serve this end by contributing to an ultimate reduction in the number of crimes. Even socialized vengeance may be accorded a marginal role, if it is understood as the provision of an orderly alternative to mob violence.

The problem, accordingly, is one of the priority and relationship of purposes as well as of their legitimacy — of multivalued rather than of single-valued thinking.[2]

There is still another range of complications which are ignored if an effort is made to formulate any single "theory" or set of "principles" of criminal law. The purpose of having principles and theories is to help in organizing thought. In the law, the ultimate purpose of thought is to help in deciding upon a course of action. In the criminal law, as in all law, questions about the action to be taken do not present themselves for decision in an institutional vacuum. They arise rather in the context of some established and specific procedure of decision: in a constitutional convention; in a legislature; in a prosecuting attorney's office; in a court charged with the determination of guilt or innocence; in a sentencing court; before a parole board; and so on. This means that each agency of decision must take account always of its own place in the institutional system and of what is necessary to maintain the integrity and workability of the system as a whole. A complex of institutional ends must be served, in other words, as well as a complex of substantive social ends.[3]

. . . .

II

The Perspective of Constitution Makers

We can get our broadest view of the aims of the criminal law if we look at them from the point of view of the makers of a constitution — of those who are seeking to establish sound foundations for a tolerable and durable social order. From this point of view, these aims can be most readily seen, as they need to be seen, in their relation to the aims of the good society generally.

In this setting, the basic question emerges: Why should the good society make use of the method of the criminal law at all?

A. *What the Method of the Criminal Law Is*

The question posed raises preliminarily an even more fundamental inquiry: What do we mean by "crime" and "criminal"? Or, put more accurately, what should we understand to be "the method of the criminal law," the use of which is in question? This latter way of formulating the preliminary inquiry is more accurate, because it pictures the criminal law as a process, a way of doing

---

[2] *See* Herbert Wechsler & Jerome Michael, *A Rationale of the Law of Homicide II*, 37 COLUM. L. REV. 1261, 1262 (1937).

[3] See Note on Organized Societies and the Principle of Institutional Settlement, in HENRY M. HART, JR. & ALBERT M. SACKS, THE LEGAL PROCESS: BASIC PROBLEMS IN THE MAKING AND APPLICATION OF LAW I (mim. ed. 1957).

something, which is what it is. A great deal of intellectual energy has been misspent in an effort to develop a concept of crime as "a natural and social phenomenon"[4] abstracted from the functioning system of institutions which make use of the concept and give it impact and meaning.[5] But the criminal law, like all law, is concerned with the pursuit of human purposes through the forms and modes of social organization, and it needs always to be thought about in that context as a method or process of doing something.

....

What then are the characteristics of this method.

1. The method operates by means of a series of directions, or commands, formulated in general terms, telling people what they must or must not do. Mostly, the commands of the criminal law are "must-nots," or prohibitions, which can be satisfied by inaction. "Do not murder, rape, or rob." But some of them are "musts," or affirmative requirements, which can be satisfied only by taking a specifically, or relatively specifically, described kind of action. "Support your wife and children," and "File your income tax return."

2. The commands are taken as valid and binding upon all those who fall within their terms when the time comes for complying with them, whether or not they have been formulated in advance in a single authoritative set of words. They speak to members of the community, in other words, in the community's behalf, with all the power and prestige of the community behind them.

3. The commands are subject to one or more sanctions for disobedience which the community is prepared to enforce.

Thus far, it will be noticed, nothing has been said about the criminal law which is not true also of a large part of the noncriminal, or civil, law. The law of torts, the law of contracts, and almost every other branch of private law that can be mentioned operate, too, with general directions prohibiting or requiring described types of conduct, and the community's tribunals enforce these commands.[8] What, then, is distinctive about the method of the criminal law?

Can crimes be distinguished from civil wrongs on the ground that they constitute injuries to society generally which society is interested in preventing? The difficulty is that society is interested also in the due fulfillment of contracts and the avoidance of traffic accidents and most of the other stuff of civil litigation. The civil law is framed and interpreted and enforced with a constant eye to these social interests. Does the distinction lie in the fact that proceedings to enforce the criminal law are instituted by public officials other

---

[4] See the discussion of the Italian positivists and their influence in American criminology in JEROME HALL, GENERAL PRINCIPLES OF CRIMINAL LAW 539-51 (1947), especially at p. 549.

[5] *Cf.* Karl Llewellyn, *Law and the Social Sciences — Especially Sociology*, 62 HARV. L. REV. 1286, 1287 (1949): "When I was younger I used to hear smuggish assertions among my sociological friends, such as: 'I take the sociological, not the legal, approach to crime'; and I suspect an inquiring reporter could still hear much of the same (perhaps with 'psychiatric' often substituted for 'sociological') — though it is surely somewhat obvious that when you take 'the legal' out, you also take out 'crime'."

[8] Many of the duties of the civil law, of course, are open-ended, the specific nature of what is to be done being privately determined, as in contracts, and wills. In the criminal law, in contrast, officials bear the whole burden of prescribing the details of private conduct. But the same thing is true, for the most part, in the law of torts and other areas of civil law.

I. GENERAL PURPOSES OF SANCTIONING

than private complainants? The difficulty is that public officers may also bring many kinds of "civil" enforcement actions — for an injunction, for the recovery of a "civil" penalty or even for the detention of the defendant by public authority.[9] Is the distinction, then, in the peculiar character of what is done to people who are adjudged to be criminals? The difficulty is that, with the possible exception of death, exactly the same kinds of unpleasant consequences, objectively considered, can be and are visited upon unsuccessful defendants in civil proceedings.[10]

If one were to judge from the notions apparently underlying many judicial opinions, and the overt language even of some of them, the solution of the puzzle is simply that a crime is anything which is called a crime, and a criminal penalty is simply the penalty provided for doing anything which has been given that name. So vacant a concept is a betrayal of intellectual bankruptcy. Certainly, it poses no intelligible issue for a constitution-maker concerned to decide whether to make use of "the method of the criminal law." Moreover, it is false to popular understanding, and false also to the understanding embodied in existing constitutions. By implicit assumptions that are more impressive than any explicit assertions, these constitutions proclaim that a conviction for crime is a distinctive and serious matter — a something, and not a nothing. What is that something?

4. What distinguishes a criminal from a civil sanction and all that distinguishes it, is ventured, is the judgment of community condemnation which accompanies and justifies its imposition....

If this is what a "criminal" penalty is, then we can say readily enough what a "crime" is. It is not simply anything which a legislature chooses to call a "crime." It is not simply antisocial conduct which public officers are given a responsibility to suppress. It is not simply any conduct to which a legislature chooses to attach a "criminal" penalty. It is conduct which, if duly shown to have taken place, will incur a formal and solemn pronouncement of the moral condemnation of the community.

5. The method of the criminal law, of course, involves something more than the threat (and, on due occasion, the expression) of community condemnation of antisocial conduct. It involves, in addition, the threat (and, on due occasion, the imposition) of unpleasant physical consequences, commonly called punishment. But ... these added consequences take their character as punishment from the condemnation which precedes them and serves as the warrant for their infliction. Indeed, the condemnation plus the added consequences may well be considered, compendiously, as constituting the punishment. Otherwise, it would be necessary to think of a convicted criminal as going unpunished if the imposition or execution of his sentence is suspended.

In traditional thought and speech, the ideas of crime and punishment have been inseparable; the consequences of conviction for crime have been de-

---

[9] In many legal systems, moreover, private persons may institute criminal proceedings, as, of course, they could in the English common law and still can in contemporary England.

[10] Thus, debtors were once imprisoned. Insane persons, aliens held for deportation, and recalcitrant witnesses still are. Juvenile delinquents are put on probation. A judgment for the payment of money, which objectively considered is all that a fine is, is, of course, the characteristic civil judgment. And the amount of the civil judgment may be "punitive," and not merely compensatory or restorative.

scribed as a matter of course as "punishment." The Constitution of the United States and its amendments, for example, use this word or its verb form in relation to criminal offenses no less than six times. Today, "treatment" has become a fashionable euphemism for the older, ugly word. This bowdlerizing of the Constitution and of conventional speech may serve a useful purpose in discouraging unduly harsh sentences and emphasizing that punishment is not an end in itself. But to the extent that it dissociates the treatment of criminals from the social condemnation of their conduct which is implicit in their conviction, there is danger that it will confuse thought and do a disservice.

At least under existing law, there is a vital difference between the situation of a patient who has been committed to a mental hospital and the situation of an inmate of a state penitentiary. The core of the difference is precisely that the patient has not incurred the moral condemnation of his community, whereas the convict has.[15]

B. The Utility of the Method

We are in a position now to restate the basic question confronting our hypothetical constitution-makers. The question is whether to make use, in the projected social order, of the method of discouraging undesired conduct and encouraging desired conduct by means of the threat — and, when necessary, the fulfillment of the threat — of the community's condemnation of an actor's violation of law and of punishment, or treatment, of the actor as blameworthy for having committed the violation.

The question, like most legal questions, is one of alternatives. Perhaps the leading alternative, to judge from contemporary criticism of the penal law, would be to provide that people who behave badly should simply be treated as sick people to be cured, rather than as bad people to be condemned and punished. A constitutional guarantee to accomplish this could be readily drafted: "No person shall be subjected to condemnation or punishment for violation of law, but only to curative-rehabilitative treatment." Would the establishment of this new constitutional liberty be well-advised?

. . . .

Any theory of criminal justice which emphasizes the criminal rather than the crime encounters an initial and crucial difficulty when it is sought to be applied at the stage of legislative enactment, where the problem in the first instance is to define and grade the crime. How *can* a conception of multiple causation and curative-rehabilitative treatment predominate in the definition and grading of crimes, let alone serve as the sole guide?[17] But even if it were

---

[15] For a convincing statement that the difference does not lie in the necessarily greater gentleness of the treatment administered in the hospital, see Edward de Grazia, *The Distinction of Being Mad*, 22 U. CHI. L. REV. 339, 348-55 (1955). Of course, there are also differences in the legal provisions governing the possibility of release, but these are mostly corollaries of the basic difference in the nature of the judgment directing detention.

[17] Is the correlation between describable types of conduct (acts or omissions), on the one hand, and the need for cure and rehabilitation of those who engage in them, on the other hand, so close that the need can be taken as a reliable index of the types of conduct to be forbidden and the differentiation among offenses to be made? These determinations must be made in advance and in general terms. In making them, the extent of the depravity of character characteristically manifested by particular types of behavior ought, of course, to be taken into account so far as it can be.

possible to gauge in advance the types of conduct to be forbidden by the expected need for reformation of those who will thereafter engage in them, would it be sensible to try to do so? Can the content of the law's commands be rationally determined with an eye singly or chiefly to the expected deficiencies of character of those who will violate them? Obviously not. The interests of society in having certain things not done or done are also involved.

Precisely because of the difficulties of relating the content of the law's commands to the need for reformation of those who violate them, a curative-rehabilitative theory of criminal justice tends always to depreciate, if not to deny, the significance of these general formulations and to focus attention instead on the individual defendant at the time of his apprehension, trial, and sentence. This has in it always a double danger — to the individual and to society. The danger to the individual is that he will be punished, or treated, for what he is or is believed to be, rather than for what he has done. If his offense is minor but the possibility of his reformation is thought to be slight, the other side of the coin of mercy can become cruelty.[19] The danger to society is that the effectiveness of the general commands of the criminal law as instruments for influencing behavior so as to avoid the necessity for enforcement proceedings will be weakened.

This brings us to the crux of the issue confronting our supposed constitution-makers. The commands of the criminal law are commands which the public interest requires people to comply with. This being so, will the public interest be adequately protected if the legislature is allowed only to say to people, "If you do not comply with any of these commands, you will merely be considered to be sick and subjected to officially-imposed rehabilitative treatment in an effort to cure you"? Can it be adequately protected if the legisla-

---

But this is a factor which is peculiarly difficult to appraise ahead of time by a generalized judgment. Depravity of character and the need of the individual for cure and rehabilitation are essentially personal matters, as the whole modern theory of the individualization of correctional treatment bears witness. A fortiori, the susceptibility of the individual to rehabilitation is personal.

[19] So, two contemporary advocates of "a rational approach to crime repression" who urge reformation as the central objective in the treatment of criminals are led to follow out the apparent logic of their position by saying that "those who cannot be reformed ... must be segregated for life — but not necessarily punished — irrespective of the crimes they have committed." (Emphasis added.) HARRY E. BARNES & NEGLEY K. TEETERS, NEW HORIZONS IN CRIMINOLOGY: THE AMERICAN CRIME PROBLEM 953 (rev. ed. 1945).

Speaking of the school of positivism which has dominated American criminology in recent years, Professor Jerome Hall says: "Its dogmas biased not only theories concerning prevention but also, combined with its determinism, stigmatized punishment as vengeance — at the same time opening the door to unmitigated cruelty in the name of 'measures of safety'." Jerome Hall, *op. cit., supra* note 4, at 551.

The rash of so-called "sexual psychopath" laws which disgrace the statute books of many states illustrate the possibilities to which this streak of cruelty may lead. See Frederick J. Hacker & Marcel Frym, *The Sexual Psychopath Act in Practice: A Critical Discussion,* 43 CALIF. L. REV. 766 (1955); Alan Guttmacher & Henry Weihofen, *Sex Offenses,* 43 J. CRIM. L., C. & P.S. 153 (1952). For the shock of a concrete example of what may happen in the administration of such laws, until the courts correct it, read *In re* Maddox, 88 N.W. 2d 470 (Mich. 1958), where the state hospital psychiatrist insisted on assuming the truth of unproved police charges in his treatment of one who had been civilly committed as a "sexual psychopath" and, when his victim kept protesting his innocence, had him transferred to state prison on the ground that this refusal to admit guilt made him "an adamant patient" lacking "the desire to get well" which was necessary to make him amenable to hospital care. Consider also the possibilities implicit in the Maryland Defective Delinquent Law, Md. Ann. Code art. 31B (1951).

ture is required to say, "If you do not comply, your own personal need for cure and rehabilitation will be the predominating factor in determining what happens to you"? Or should the legislature be enabled to say, "If you violate any of these laws and the violation is culpable, your conduct will receive the formal and solemn condemnation of the community as morally blameworthy, and you will be subjected to whatever punishment, or treatment, is appropriate to vindicate the law and to further its various purposes"?

On the sheerly pragmatic ground of the need for equipping the proposed social order with adequate tools to discourage undesired conduct, a responsible constitution-maker assuredly would hesitate long before rejecting the third of these possibilities in favor of either of the first two. To be sure, the efficacy of criminal punishment as a deterrent has often been doubted. But it is to be observed that the doubts are usually expressed by those who are thinking from the retrospective, sanction-imposing point of view. From this point of view, it is natural to be impressed by the undoubted fact that many people do become criminals, and will continue to do so, in spite of all the threats of condemnation and of treatment-in-consequence-of-condemnation that society can offer. But the people who do not commit crimes need to be taken into account, too. A constitution-maker, thinking from the prospective point of view of the primary, as distinguished from the remedial, law has especially to think of them, if he is to see his problem whole. So doing, he will be likely to regard the desire of the ordinary man to avoid the moral condemnation of his community, as well as the physical pains and inconveniences of punishment, as a powerful factor in influencing human behavior which can scarcely with safety be dispensed with.[21] Whether he is right or wrong in this conclusion, he will align himself, in reaching it, with the all but universal judgment, past and present, of mankind.

Moreover, there are other and larger considerations to be weighed in the balance. The case against a primarily rehabilitative theory of criminal justice is understated if it is rested solely on the need for the threat of criminal conviction as an instrument of deterrence of antisocial conduct. Deterrence, it is ventured, ought not to be thought of as the overriding and ultimate purpose of the criminal law, important though it is. For deterrence is negative, whereas the purpose of law is positive. And the practical fact must be faced that many crimes, as just recognized, are undeterrable. The grim negativism and the frequent seeming futility of the criminal law when it is considered simply as a means of preventing undesired behavior no doubt help to explain

---

[21] *Cf.* RANYARD WEST, CONSCIENCE AND SOCIETY 165 (1945): "It is upon the fact of the potential criminal in every man that I would give to law its psychological grounding."

Compare the valuable analysis by a Norwegian scholar, Johannes Andenaes, in *General Prevention — Illusion or Reality?*, 43 J. CRIM. L., C. & P.S. 176, 179-80 (1952). Professor Andenaes distinguishes between individual prevention ("the effect of punishment on the punished") and general prevention ("the ability of the criminal law and its enforcement to make citizens law-abiding"). He further distinguishes "three sorts of general-preventive effects": first, a "deterrent" effect (used in the narrow sense of "the mere frightening ... effect of punishment — the risk of discovery outweighing the temptation to commit the crime"); second, a "moralizing" effect (punishment helping "to form and to strengthen the public's moral code" and so to create "conscious or unconscious inhibitions against committing crime"); and, third, a habit-forming effect (arousing "unconscious inhibitions against committing forbidden acts ... without appealing to the individual's concepts of morality").

I. GENERAL PURPOSES OF SANCTIONING

why sensitive people, working at close hand with criminals, tend so often to embrace the more hopeful and positive tenets of a curative-rehabilitative philosophy.

However, a different view is possible if an effort is made to fit the theory of criminal justice into a theory of social justice — to see the purposes of the criminal law in their relation to the purposes of law as a whole. Man is a social animal, and the function of law is to enable him to realize his potentialities as a human being through the forms and modes of social organization. It is important to consider how the criminal law serves this ultimate end.

Human beings, of course, realize their potentialities in part through enjoyment of the various satisfactions of human life, both tangible and intangible, which existing social resources and their own individual capacities make available to them. Yet, the social resources of the moment are always limited, and human capacities for enjoyment are limited also. Social resources for providing the satisfactions of life and human capacities for enjoying them, however, are always susceptible of enlargement, so far as we know, without eventual limit. Man realizes his potentialities most significantly in the very process of developing these resources and capacities — by making himself a functioning and participating member of his community, contributing to it as well as drawing from it.

What is crucial in this process is the enlargement of each individual's capacity for effectual and responsible decision. For it is only through personal, self-reliant participation, by trial and error, in the problems of existence, both personal and social, that the capacity to participate effectively can grow. Man learns wisdom in choosing by being confronted with choices and by being made aware that he must abide the consequences of his choice. In the training of a child in the small circle of the family, this principle is familiar enough. It has the same validity in the training of an adult in the larger circle of the community.

Seen in this light, the criminal law has an obviously significant and, indeed, a fundamental role to play in the effort to create the good society. For it is the criminal law which defines the minimum conditions of man's responsibility to his fellows and holds him to that responsibility. The assertion of social responsibility has value in the treatment even of those who have become criminals.[23] It has far greater value as a stimulus to the great bulk of mankind to abide by the law and to take pride in so abiding.

This, then, is the critical weakness of the two alternative constitutional provisions that have been discussed — more serious by far than losing or damaging a useful, even if imperfect, instrument of deterrence. The provisions would undermine the foundation of a free society's effort to build up each

---

[23] WALTON HAMILTON MOBERLY, RESPONSIBILITY: THE CONCEPT IN PSYCHOLOGY, IN THE LAW, AND IN THE CHRISTIAN FAITH 23 (1956): "Recite a delinquent's disabilities and handicaps in front of him in open court and you are doing something to confirm them; you are impairing that self-respect and sense of responsibility which is the chief incentive to effort. Treat him as sane and responsible and as a whole man and you give him the best chance of rising to this level. In many circumstances to expect and to exact a high standard is the most likely way to get it."
See also the discussion of the problem of growth in responsibility in Wilber G. Katz, *Law, Psychiatry, and Free Will*, 22 U. CHI. L. REV. 397 (1955).

individual's sense of responsibility as a guide and a stimulus to the constructive development of his capacity for effectual and fruitful decision.[24]

HINTZ v. STATE

Supreme Court of Alaska
627 P.2d 207 (1981)

CONNOR, JUSTICE.

Hintz appeals his sentence as excessive. As we noted at the outset of this opinion, Hintz was sentenced to life imprisonment for kidnapping, twenty years for rape, to be served consecutively to the life sentence, and ten years for each of two counts of armed robbery, to be served concurrently with each other and with the rape sentence.

A life sentence is the maximum sentence allowable for kidnapping. Likewise, twenty years is the maximum sentence for rape. We have stated on numerous occasions that a maximum sentence is not appropriate unless the defendant can be characterized as a "worst offender."

By "worst offender" we mean that the defendant must be the worst type of offender "within the group of persons committing the offense in question." *Wilson v. State*, 582 P.2d 154, 157 n.3 (Alaska 1978). In evaluating whether a particular defendant is a worst offender we look at the manner in which the crime was committed, as well as the character and background of the defendant. *Moore v. State*, 597 P.2d 975, 976 n.4 (Alaska 1979); *Saganna v. State*, 594 P.2d 69 (Alaska 1979). In *State v. Wortham*, 537 P.2d 1117, 1120 (Alaska 1975), we listed several factors the court has looked to in order to support a characterization as worst offender: prior criminal convictions, age, military records, employment history, drug or alcohol addiction, presentence report evaluations and predictions, and the possible presence of antisocial tendencies which pose a clear risk to the public.

In the present case, although the sentencing judge concluded that appellant was a "professional criminal," we find no justification for such a conclusion. The record discloses that appellant was 21 years old at the time the offense was committed. He had no history of drug abuse and termed himself a "social drinker." His only prior offense was a 1975 conviction for burglary not in a dwelling. Although appellant's psychological evaluation noted some antisocial tendencies, these were termed only "moderate" and the examining psychiatrist conjectured that such tendencies might be modified by the simple process of aging. In short, there is nothing particularly unique about appellant's past

---

[24] See generally Moberly, op. cit. *supra* note 23, and especially the opening lecture on "The Concept [Of Responsibility] in Psychology and Law." There are other agencies of social discipline, of course, than the criminal law. But the criminal law is the only one which speaks to the individual formally and solemnly in behalf of the whole society. In what the criminal law says to the individual, moreover, much more is involved than training simply in the observance of the specific and mostly elementary standards of conduct which the law seeks directly to enforce. Limits of some kind upon the scope of permissible choice perform an indispensable psychological role in the development of personal capacity for successful social adjustment. By fixing even minimal limits, the law thus develops capacities which are transferable to the more complex problems of social existence. This is especially so to the extent that the individual is made conscious of the moral basis and social rationale of the law's commands, for the principles of social living underlying them have far wider relevance than the commands themselves.

or, for that matter, his future, which calls for classification as a worst offender.

Nor do we think that the manner in which the crimes were carried out justifies such a classification. On two previous occasions, we have affirmed maximum sentences for kidnapping in a kidnapping-rape situation. In each case, however, the defendant's background or character was such as would justify classification as a "worst offender" or the crime was committed in a particularly heinous manner. In *Morrell v. State,* 575 P.2d 1200 (Alaska 1978), the victim was confined, and often physically bound, for a period of eight days. And in Post v. State, 580 P.2d 304 (Alaska 1978), the victim was held for over 20 hours and regained her freedom only by escaping. Moreover, in Post, the defendant possessed a lengthy criminal record and had "highly dangerous potentialities," 580 P.2d at 310 (concurring opinion of Boochever, C. J.).

In the present case, we find no such aggravating factors. While we do not mean to minimize the seriousness of the crimes involved, we do not believe that appellant's conduct in this case can be put on a par with that in Morrell and Post.

In *State v. Chaney,* 477 P.2d 441, 444 (Alaska 1970), we recognized the following goals of criminal sanctions: (1) rehabilitation of the convicted offender into a non-criminal member of society; (2) isolation of the offender from society to prevent criminal conduct during the period of confinement; (3) deterrence of other members of the community who might have tendencies toward criminal conduct similar to those of the offender; (4) deterrence of the offender himself after release; (5) community condemnation of the individual offender, or in other words, the affirmation of societal norms for the purpose of maintaining respect for the norms themselves.

Applying these standards to the present case, it is clear that a substantial period of incarceration is warranted. As we noted in *Post v. State,* 580 P.2d 304, 309 (Alaska 1978), the kidnap-rape situation is often associated with serious injury or death to the victim and must be strongly condemned. Nevertheless, in the circumstances of the present case, we think that a sentence of life plus twenty years is clearly mistaken and, therefore, excessive. Such an extraordinarily long sentence completely disregards any hope of rehabilitation. Moreover, we think whatever added deterrence such a sentence would have is minimal at best. In our view a sentence of 20 years for kidnapping, and a sentence of 10 years for rape, to be served consecutively to the sentence for kidnapping, is appropriate. The two sentences of 10 years for armed robbery, to be served concurrently with each other and with the rape sentence shall remain unchanged.

MODEL PENAL CODE § 1.02(2)

[The text of this section appears in Appendix A.]

NOTES

1. N.J. STAT. ANN. § 2C:1-2(b) (West 1982):

   (1) To prevent and condemn the commission of offenses;

   (2) To promote the correction and rehabilitation of offenders;

   (3) To insure the public safety by preventing the commission of offenses through the deterrent influence of sentences imposed and the confinement of offenders when required in the interest of public protection;

   (4) To safeguard offenders against excessive, disproportionate or arbitrary punishment;

   (5) To give fair warning of the nature of the sentences that may be imposed on conviction of an offense;

   (6) To differentiate among offenders with a view to a just individualization in their treatment; and

   (7) To advance the use of generally accepted scientific methods and knowledge in sentencing offenders.

2. N.Y. PENAL LAW § 1.05 (McKinney 1987):

   The general purposes of the provisions of this chapter are:

   ....

   (6) To insure the public safety by preventing the commission of offenses through the deterrent influence of the sentences authorized, the rehabilitation of those convicted, and their confinement when required in the interests of public protection.

SECTION II. Constitutional Restrictions: Cruel and Unusual Punishment

A. GENERALLY

Changes in the Supreme Court's composition in recent years had engendered some doubt as to whether the Court's five-to-four decision in *Solem v. Helm*,[1] would long survive. *Harmelin v. Michigan*,[2] seemed to be a likely candidate for an overruling; Harmelin attacked a mandatory life term without possibility of parole imposed on him as a recidivist controlled substances trafficker.[3] As it turned out, although a majority of the Justices voted to affirm a Michigan Court of Appeals determination that the Michigan statute was not violative of Eighth Amendment disproportionality standards, there was a doctrinal majority only on the premise that a mandatory sentencing scheme like that in the Michigan legislation does not violate the Eighth Amendment; a penal statute does not have to set forth an array of alternative

---

[1] 463 U.S. 277 (1983), holding that noncapital sentences could be disproportionate and therefore constitute cruel and unusual punishment under the eighth amendment (Helm had received a mandatory life sentence for four nonviolent property felonies arguably caused by his alcoholism, without any legal possibility of parole or realistic expectation of executive clemency). The criteria for disproportionality review are (1) the gravity of an offense and the harshness of the penalty, (2) the sentences imposed on other criminals for other offenses in the same jurisdiction, and (3) sentences assessed in other jurisdictions for the same crime. *Solem*, 463 U.S. at 291-92.

[2] 111 S. Ct. 2680 (1991).

[3] *Id.* at 2684 (plurality opinion).

sanctions to be constitutional.[4] A perusal of the two opinions on which the judgmental majority is based and the dissenting opinions[5] supports a conclusion that for the time being *Solem v. Helm* does not totter on the brink of extinction, but may be simplified in its detail.

NOTES

1. Review Note on Robinson v. California and Powell v. Texas, *supra* Chapter 8, pp. 659-660.

2. The Eighth Amendment governs prison conditions. As the Supreme Court noted in *Rhodes v. Chapman*, 452 U.S. 337, 345-47 (1981):

> The Eighth Amendment, in only three words, imposes the constitutional limitation upon punishments: They cannot be "cruel and unusual." The Court has interpreted these words "in a flexible and dynamic manner," *Gregg v. Georgia*, 428 U.S. 153 (1976) (joint opinion), and has extended the Amendment's reach beyond the barbarous physical punishments at issue in the Court's earliest cases.... Today, the Eighth Amendment prohibits punishments which, although not physically barbarous, "involve the unnecessary and wanton infliction of pain," *Gregg v. Georgia, supra*, at 173, or are grossly disproportionate to the severity of the crime.... Among "unnecessary and wanton" inflictions of pain are those "totally without penological justification."...
>
> No static "test" can exist by which courts determine whether conditions of confinement are cruel and unusual, for the Eighth Amendment "must draw its meaning from the evolving standards of decency that mark the progress of a maturing society." *Trop v. Dulles*, 356 U.S. 86, 101 (1957) (plurality opinion). The Court has held, however, that "Eighth Amendment judgments should neither be nor appear to be merely the subjective views" of judges. *Rummel v. Estelle*, 445 U.S. 263, 275 (1980)....
>
> ... Conditions must not involve the wanton and unnecessary infliction of pain, nor may they be grossly disproportionate to the severity of the crime warranting imprisonment.... Conditions ..., alone or in combination, may deprive inmates of the minimal civilized measure of life's necessities. Such conditions could be cruel and unusual under the contemporary standard of decency that we recognized in [*Estelle v.*] *Gamble*, 429 U.S. [97, 103-04 (1976)]. But conditions that cannot be said to be cruel and unusual under contemporary standards are not unconstitutional. To the extent that such conditions are restrictive and even harsh, they are

---

[4] *Id.* at 2701-02. Any form of life imprisonment is less than capital punishment, and individualized sentencing is required constitutionally only in death penalty cases. *Id.* at 2702.

[5] Justice Scalia's doctrinal discussion, according to which the eighth amendment requires that punishment be *both* "cruel" *and* "unusual," thus precluding proportionality review comparing the seriousness of a crime and length of sentencing, *id.* at 2684-2701, was endorsed only by Chief Justice Rehnquist, *id.* at 2683. Justices Kennedy, O'Connor, and Souter, *id.* at 2702-09, disagreed with Justice Scalia's reasoning, and indicated clearly that proportionality review is required under the eighth amendment in noncapital as well as capital cases, but would have abandoned the *Solem v. Helm* three-factor test in favor of a single standard of "gross disproportionality." *Id.* at 2705. The dissenters (Justice White joined by Justices Blackmun and Stevens, *id.* at 2709, Justice Marshall, *id.* at 2719, and Justice Stevens joined by Justice Blackmun, *id.*) clearly reject the Kennedy single standard and endorse a continuation of the *Helm* three-factor test.

part of the penalty that criminal offenders pay for their offenses against society.

3. *See generally* RONALD GOLDFARB & LINDA SINGER, AFTER CONVICTION (1973); SHELDON KRANTZ, LAW OF CORRECTIONS AND PRISONERS' RIGHTS (1973); AMERICAN BAR ASSOCIATION STANDARDS FOR CRIMINAL JUSTICE, LEGAL STATUS OF PRISONERS (2d ed. 1983); AMERICAN CORRECTIONAL ASSOCIATION, STANDARDS FOR ADULT CORRECTIONAL INSTITUTIONS (3d ed. 1991); U.S. NAT'L ADVISORY COMM'N ON CRIMINAL JUSTICE STANDARDS & GOALS, CORRECTIONS REPORT (1973).

See also Note, *Creatures, Persons, and Prisoners; Evaluating Prison Conditions Under the Eighth Amendment*, 55 S. CAL. L. REV. 1099 (1982); Note, *Complex Enforcement; Unconstitutional Prison Conditions*, 94 HARV. L. REV. 627 (1980-81).

4. People v. Kelly, 117 Cal. App. 3d 943, 173 Cal. Rptr. 106, 110 (1981):

> Appellant also contends life imprisonment without possibility of parole for an unintentional homicide constitutes cruel and unusual punishment under article I, section 17, of the California Constitution.[5] It is urged that although the method of punishment, in the abstract, is not cruel and unusual, the punishment offends article I, section 17, because it is so disproportionate to the offense committed it shocks the conscience and offends fundamental notions of human dignity. (*In re Lynch* (1972) 8 Cal.3d 410, 423-424, 105 Cal.Rptr. 217, 503 P.2d 921.)

Lynch sets forth three distinct techniques to determine whether a given punishment is disproportionate to the offense committed.

First, consideration must be given to the nature of the offense and/or offender, with particular regard to the degree of danger both present to society. Relevant to the question of proportionality is whether the offense is of a violent nature, and whether there are rational gradations of culpability that can be made on the basis of the injury to the victim. (*In re Lynch, supra,* at pp. 425-426, 105 Cal.Rptr. 217, 503 P.2d 921.)

The second technique enunciated by *Lynch* is to compare the challenged penalty with the punishments prescribed in the same jurisdiction for different offenses which would be deemed more serious. If among them there are found more serious crimes that are punished less severely than the offense in question, the challenged penalty is to that extent suspect. (*Id.* at p. 426, 105 Cal.Rptr. 217, 503 P.2d 921.)

The third technique used in this inquiry is a comparison of the challenged penalty with the punishment prescribed by other jurisdictions for the same offense having an identical or similar constitutional provision. If the challenged penalty is found to exceed the punishments set by a significant number of those jurisdictions, the disparity is a further measure of its excessiveness. (*Id.* at p. 427, 105 Cal.Rptr. 217, 503 P.2d 921.)

Underlying the three criteria prescribed by Lynch is the primary concern of the social utility of the particular penalty. (*In re Matson* (1973) 33 Cal.App.3d

---

[5] "Cruel and unusual punishment may not be inflicted or excessive fines imposed." (Cal. Const., art 1, § 17.)

559, 562, 109 Cal.Rptr. 164.) The initial purpose or necessity of a given penalty is determined by the Legislature. As emphasized by *Matson,* courts should pay particular attention to whether there was a rational basis for the Legislature's choice of a particular penalty. If a rational basis exists, courts should hesitate to call the penalty cruel and unusual. (*Kelly* at p. 562, 109 Cal.Rptr. 164.)

5. Various criteria have been advanced to govern the disproportionality dimensions of the eighth amendment or an equally or more explicit state constitutional provision. (On the significance of greater specificity, see *State v. Goode,* 380 So. 2d 1361, 1363-64 (La. 1980) invalidating a statute mandating a minimum additional sentence of five consecutive years of imprisonment without benefit of parole, probation, or suspension of sentence for certain crimes committed against victims age 65 or older, because such a mandatory penalty could produce a sentence disproportionate to the severity of particular crimes). See, e.g., *People v. Truett,* 178 Cal. Rptr. 535, 537 (Cal. Ct. App. 1981): "(1) the 'proportionality' of the punishment to the offense — is a severe punishment prescribed for a serious crime, or is it an 'extraordinary penalty' for 'a crime of ordinary gravity committed under ordinary circumstances'" ... (2) comparison of the punishment with penalties provided for similar offenses within the same jurisdiction; and (3) comparison of the punishment with that prescribed for the same offense in other jurisdictions"; *State v. Williams,* 397 So. 2d 1287, 1294 (La. 1981): "A punishment is 'excessive' and unconstitutional if it (1) makes no measurable contribution to acceptable goals of punishment and hence is nothing more than the purposeless and needless imposition of pain and suffering; and (2) is grossly out of proportion to the severity of the crime"; *State v. Fain,* 617 P.2d 720, 726 (Wash. 1980): "(1) the nature of the offense; (2) the legislative purpose behind the ... statute; (3) the punishment defendant would have received in other jurisdictions for the same offense; and (4) the punishment meted out for other offenses in the same jurisdiction"; *Wanstreet v. Bordenkircher,* 276 S.E.2d 205 (W. Va. 1981). See also Martin R. Gardner, *The Determinate Sentencing Movement and the Eighth Amendment: Excessive Punishment Before and After Rummel v. Estelle,* 1980 DUKE L.J. 1103.

6. The constitutionality of capital punishment is covered in Part B. below.

7. Mandatory life sentences for first-degree murder generally have been sustained in the face of attacks based on the proportionality doctrine. *See, e.g., State v. Farrow,* 386 A.2d 808 (N.H. 1978); *Commonwealth v. Sourbeer,* 422 A.2d 116 (Pa. 1980); *State ex rel. Leach v. Hamilton,* 280 S.E.2d 62 (W.Va. 1980).

8. Mandatory life sentences under an habitual offender statute, even for minor felonies involving property have been maintained in the face of challenges under the Eighth and Fourteenth Amendments. *See Rummel v. Estelle,* 445 U.S. 263 (1980).

9. Racial discrimination in assessing penal sentences violates equal protection. *Britton v. Rogers,* 631 F.2d 572, 577 (8th Cir. 1980) (but defendant failed to establish necessary factual basis).

B. CAPITAL PUNISHMENT

EDITORIAL NOTE

(a) *Introduction.* In 1972, the Supreme Court invalidated all traditional capital penalty legislation as violative of the Eighth and Fourteenth Amendments.[1] Four years later, in 1976, the Court reworked its constitutional rationale in a series of holdings,[2] so that death penalty legislation could be constitutional if proper substantive criteria were set forth in legislation and procedural safeguards accorded defendants so that arbitrary and capricious invocation of the death penalty might be forestalled. A substantial majority of states thereafter revised their statutes to meet the Supreme Court's expectations; although there has been massive litigation concerning capital punishment, there is no room at the present time to attack the constitutionality of capital punishment itself.

In the Anti-Drug Abuse Act of 1988 Congress reintroduced capital punishment into federal law in the context of the Controlled Substances Act.[3] It must be stressed that because of the placement of the death penalty provision in Title 21, it has no applicability to the general body of federal crimes in Title 18; a separate provision enacted later would be necessary to reinstate capital punishment in that context, where no viable provisions currently exist.

(b) *Constitutional Limitations on Capital Punishment.*

(1) Substantive Criteria.

(i) Vagueness and indefiniteness. Legislatures must define the aggravating circumstances that legitimate the death penalty with sufficient precision to satisfy due process of law; vague legislation is unconstitutional because it fails to give fair notice as to what conduct is acceptable and what is not, and invites arbitrary and discriminatory enforcement because of its failure to establish reasonably clear guidelines for law enforcement officials and triers of fact.[4] On that basis the Supreme Court has struck down such statutory usages in death-penalty legislation as "especially heinous, atrocious, or cruel"[5] and "outrageously or wantonly vile, horrible or inhuman" involving "depravity of mind."[6] However, suitably restrictive instructions to juries can overcome the impact of legislative language that, standing alone, would be vague and indefinite.[7]

---

[1] Furman v. Georgia, 408 U.S. 238 (1972) (per curiam). There was no majority opinion; instead, each Justice wrote separately.

[2] Gregg v. Georgia, 428 U.S. 153 (1976), is the lead decision although, once again, there was no majority opinion. The contemporaneous decisions were Roberts v. Louisiana, 428 U.S. 325 (1976); Woodson v. North Carolina, 428 U.S. 280 (1976); Jurek v. Texas, 428 U.S. 262 (1976); Proffitt v. Florida, 428 U.S. 242 (1976). None presented a majority opinion.

[3] 21 U.S.C.A. § 848(e) (West Supp. 1993).

[4] On the general principle, *see, e.g.*, Boos v. Berry, 485 U.S. 312 (1988); City of Houston v. Hill, 482 U.S. 451 (1987); Smith v. Goguen, 415 U.S. 566 (1974).

[5] Maynard v. Cartwright, 486 U.S. 356 (1988).

[6] Godfrey v. Georgia, 446 U.S. 420 (1980).

[7] Walton v. Arizona, 497 U.S. 639 (1990).

(ii) Constitutional scope of capital crimes. A safe conclusion appears to be that the death penalty cannot be authorized constitutionally for any crime but an aggravated form of murder. In *Coker v. Georgia*,[8] a majority of the Court joined in reversing a death sentence for rape; the plurality Justices indicated a substantial doubt as to whether the death penalty ever can be imposed on defendants who themselves have not taken human life.

(iii) Accomplices to Aggravated Murder. Accomplices to aggravated murder are not automatically eligible for capital punishment, even though they may be convicted of the predicate crime on principles of accomplice criminality. This would be most evident in instances in which the felony-murder rule has been invoked against an accomplice to the underlying felony who did not directly participate in the killing. Thus, in *Enmund v. Florida*,[9] the Court ruled that such an accomplice cannot be sentenced to death in the absence of proof beyond a reasonable doubt that she or he killed, attempted to kill or intended to kill.

If an accomplice is more actively involved in the lethal transaction, however, even though not as an actual killer, the death penalty is an available sanction, as demonstrated in *Tison v. Arizona*.[10] In that case, the Court affirmed a capital sentence against two accomplices to kidnaping and intentional murder committed in the course of a prison escape they helped engineer; they had played major roles in the transaction and had manifested a culpable mental state of reckless indifference to human life. The Court thought that an "intent to kill" standard is not a highly satisfactory means of determining the most culpable and dangerous murders:

> Therefore, a reckless disregard for human life implicit in knowingly engaging in criminal activities known to carry a grave risk of death represents a highly culpable mental state ... that may be taken into account in making a capital sentencing judgment when that conduct causes its natural, though also not inevitable, lethal result.[11]

In short, "major participation in the felony committed, combined with reckless indifference to human life, is sufficient to satisfy the *Enmund* culpability requirement."[12]

(iv) Mandatory capital punishment. The unfailing objective of the Court in its death-penalty jurisprudence has been to require a careful, reasoned selection of death over life. Accordingly, no form of intentional murder can be made a mandatory basis for assessment of the death penalty; that rule has been strongly confirmed in *Sumner v. Shuman*.[13] In that case, Nevada required invocation of the death sanction against life-term prisoners who committed murder while in prison. The Court struck down the statute, holding

---

[8] 433 U.S. 584 (1977).
[9] 458 U.S. 782 (1982).
[10] 481 U.S. 137 (1987).
[11] *Id.* at 157-58.
[12] *Id.* at 158.
[13] 483 U.S. 66 (1987). *See also* McDougall v. Dixon, 921 F.2d 518, 523-27 (4th Cir. 1990), *cert. denied*, 111 S. Ct. 2840 (1992) (rejecting contention that trial court's instruction had converted the statute into a mandatory death penalty).

that a properly guided and regulated discretion is an absolute prerequisite for capital punishment in every murder case.

(v) *Juvenile murder.* The Supreme Court has found nothing in the federal Constitution to bar the execution of persons who were minors at the time they committed their lethal acts. That had been the judgmental result in *Thompson v. Oklahoma*,[14] in which five of the eight participating Justices had vacated a death sentence imposed on a juvenile aged 15 when he committed murder. In 1989, a doctrinal majority held to the same effect in two cases involving a 16-year-old[15] and a 17-year-old.[16] The Court's holding, of course, related only to the constitutionality of legislation authorizing the imposition of the death penalty; it did not diminish in any way the Court's holding that any mitigating data, including age, must be allowed before the jury deliberating on the death penalty.[17]

(b) *Disproportionality.* The Supreme Court has not been hospitable toward claims that the death penalty cannot be invoked consistently. In its initial holding in point, *Maggio v. Williams*,[18] it rejected a contention that there had to be district-wide rather than statewide proportionality review of state death sentences. That holding, however, was absorbed in the broader ruling of *Pulley v. Harris*.[19] A number of state death penalty statutes require proportionality review, according to which sentencing courts must examine the background of a given defendant and the circumstances of the slaying concerning which a conviction has been entered, and then compare them with those of other defendants, some of whom received the death penalty and some of whom received life imprisonment. The Supreme Court, however, refused to make that a requirement under the Eighth Amendment. A mandatory state high court review, plenary in character, is a sufficient guarantee against disproportionate election of the death penalty, and the Supreme Court would not go beyond that.

In *McCleskey v. Kemp*,[20] the Court did not find that scientific studies purporting to show that blacks received the death penalty in a disproportionate ratio to whites were sufficient to support a threshold showing that the Georgia death penalty statute violated the Equal Protection Clause. The state had no opportunity to rebut the principal study, which of itself was inadequate to place on it the responsibility to explain an apparent denial of equal protection. There likewise was no Eighth Amendment violation because the statute was essentially the same as the one already approved by the Court as constitutional in *Gregg v. Georgia*.[21]

---

[14] 487 U.S. 815 (1988). *See also* Sochor v. Florida, 112 S. Ct. 2114 (1992) (trial court erred in considering as an aggravating circumstance a "coldness factor," *i.e.*, that the murder was committed in a cold, calculated and premeditated manner, when that was unsupported by the evidence).
[15] Wilkins v. Missouri, 492 U.S. 361 (1989).
[16] Stanford v. Kentucky, 492 U.S. 361 (1989).
[17] *See* Eddings v. Oklahoma, 456 U.S. 904 (1981).
[18] 464 U.S. 46 (1983).
[19] 465 U.S. 37 (1984).
[20] 481 U.S. 279 (1987).
[21] 428 U.S. 153 (1976).

(c) *Procedural Issues.*

(i) State Subvention of Defense Preparation. In *Ake v. Oklahoma*,[22] the Court held that the defense of mental nonresponsibility [insanity] is so significant that the state must provide expert psychiatric resources for financially-unable defendants.

(ii) Voir dire examination. In its doctrinal statements since 1976, the Court has confirmed that the institution of so-called "death-qualified juries," first laid down in *Witherspoon v. Illinois*,[23] continues to the present time. Under *Witherspoon*, venirepersons who are so unalterably opposed to capital punishment that they will not vote for the death penalty no matter how strong the state's case, are subject to exclusion for cause; the test for determining whether venirepersons can serve is whether their views would "prevent or substantially impair the performance of [their] duties as a juror in accordance with [their] instructions and oath."[24] No specific voir dire question is critical; the issue is whether venirepersons have been made sufficiently aware of the test for juror eligibility in capital cases.[25] The *Witherspoon* inquiry can be made at the voir dire of the trial jury that decides both guilt and sanction in a unitary trial,[26] and it is not prejudicial to death-qualify a jury that will try a capital co-defendant when the objecting defendant is not the target of a death sentence;[27] the Court was not persuaded that a death-qualified jury lacks impartiality.

Because due process requires that juries engaged in capital sentencing be impartial and indifferent and, therefore, capital defendants may challenge for cause prospective jurors who automatically would vote to impose a death sentence upon conviction of a capital offense, the Sixth Amendment right to a fair jury trial impels a trial court on voir dire, at a defendant's request, to inquire into prospective jurors' views on capital punishment in order to identify unqualified jurors.[28]

(iii) Trial evidence. The Court has adhered to its position that a prosecution psychiatric expert witness cannot testify in support of the death penalty on the basis of a court-ordered psychiatric examination of which defense counsel was not notified in advance or at which counsel was not either present or absent following a valid waiver of the right of representation.[29]

There is no bar to the use of otherwise valid psychiatric evidence, however, for purposes of predicting dangerousness, or of hypothetical questions to elicit expert opinion.[30]

During a relatively brief time span, the Supreme Court by a slim majority held it prejudicial for jurors in a capital case to consider a victim impact

---

[22] 470 U.S. 68 (1985).
[23] 391 U.S. 510 (1968).
[24] Wainwright v. Witt, 469 U.S. 412, 424 (1985) (quoting Adams v. Texas, 448 U.S. 38, 45 [1980]).
[25] Darden v. Wainwright, 477 U.S. 168 (1986).
[26] Lockhart v. McCree, 476 U.S. 162 (1986).
[27] Buchanan v. Kentucky, 483 U.S. 402 (1987).
[28] Morgan v. Illinois, 112 S. Ct. 2222 (1992) (a trial court's general fairness and "follow the law" questions on voir dire were insufficient to detect venirepersons who would automatically impose death and who should have been disqualified).
[29] Satterwhite v. Texas, 486 U.S. 249 (1988); Estelle v. Smith, 451 U.S. 454 (1981).
[30] Barefoot v. Estelle, 463 U.S. 880 (1983).

statement (VIS) at the death-penalty phase.[31] Although in 1989 the Court reaffirmed its *Booth* doctrine,[32] four Justices indicated at that time their dissatisfaction with *Booth* and their readiness to overturn it. Soon thereafter, Justice Brennan retired from the Court and Justice Souter joined the Court; that in fact produced a changed alignment among the Court's members that resulted in a repudiation of the Court's *Booth-Gathers* doctrine, in *Payne v. Tennessee*.[33]

According to the *Payne* Court, *Booth* and *Gathers* had been based on two premises: (a) evidence relative to a particular victim or to the harm a capital defendant causes a victim's family does not in general reflect on a defendant's "blameworthiness"; and (b) only evidence relating to "blameworthiness" is relevant to a capital sentencing decision. The Court rejected those premises in *Payne*. It noted that the *Federal Sentencing Guidelines* consider harm inflicted by defendants' acts in calculating sentences, and that the Court's death-penalty jurisprudence required that jurors in death-penalty cases be allowed to consider all relevant mitigating data.

Although capital defendants are entitled to individualized consideration, that does not mean they are entitled to individualized consideration wholly apart from the crimes they are charged with committing. Victim-impact evidence is relevant to the circumstances of a capital offense, and the Court no longer saw any likelihood that defense efforts to rebut it would turn into a "mini-trial" on a victim's character. Such evidence, in short, is simply an alternative way to show jurors the specific harm inflicted by the crime in question. If VIS-based evidence should prove unduly prejudicial in a particular case, the due process clause is always available to provide a remedy. Accordingly, states may conclude that, in order for juries to assess meaningfully the moral culpability and blameworthiness of capital defendants, they are to be allowed to have before them during the sentencing phase of capital cases evidence concerning the specific harm caused by a defendant.[34]

In *Johnson v. Mississippi*,[35] the Supreme Court ruled that when a sister-state felony conviction, relied on by the forum state's sentencing jury in determining the existence of a statutory aggravating circumstance supporting the death penalty, is reversed after completion of regular forum-state appellate review, and the reversal is asserted as a ground for forum-state postconviction review, the death penalty sentence must be vacated and the matter remanded for resentencing.

(d) *Mechanisms for Determining the Death Penalty*

(i) *Allocation of Responsibility*. A death penalty procedural statute may either provide for a bifurcation of trial proceedings, the first phase of which determines guilt or innocence on the underlying charges and the second of which addresses the penalty to be assessed against a convicted defendant,[36] or specify a unitary trial in which a single jury determines both guilt of the

---

[31] 482 U.S. 496 (1987).
[32] 490 U.S. 805 (1989).
[33] 111 S. Ct. 2597 (1991).
[34] The *Payne* majority also reversed the *Gathers* holding, and ruled that the Eighth Amendment does not bar *per se* prosecutors from arguing to jurors the human cost of a capital crime.
[35] 486 U.S. 578 (1988).
[36] Marshall v. Lonberger, 459 U.S. 422 (1983).

predicate offense and eligibility for the death penalty.[37] Conversely, there is no objection to allowing trial courts and not juries to select between life and death, once a jury has found guilt of a capital offense beyond a reasonable doubt,[38] or authorizing trial courts to find the aggravating circumstances authorizing imposition of a death sentence after juries have unanimously recommended a death sentence.[39] The existence of aggravating factors is not an element of the capital offense, but instead is a sentencing factor coming into play after guilt has been determined. Accordingly, it is not within the Sixth Amendment jury trial right.[40]

The Court has considered on several occasions the relative responsibilities of trial juries and trial judges in determining the election between life imprisonment and capital punishment; several alternative approaches have survived constitutional attack, as long as the Court concludes that each forestalls "an arbitrary or freakish sentence forbidden by the Eighth Amendment."[41]

There is, first of all, no constitutional impediment to a system which allows the jury to consider initially whether one or more of several statutory aggravating factors are present, as a device to screen capital from noncapital cases.[42] The Court in *Zant v. Stephens* indicated that if a statute requires a balancing of aggravating factors against mitigating data, and one or more of the aggravating criteria were unconstitutional, then an ensuing death sentence might be invalid. However, if the jury should find that one valid aggravating circumstance existed (as the jury did in *Stephens*), that would be sufficient to move the case forward into the phase of consideration at which an election between death and life imprisonment would be made. In other words, under such a form of capital sentencing, an aggravating circumstance, established beyond a reasonable doubt, is a condition precedent to selection of the death penalty. It does not matter, constitutionally speaking, whether the aggravating factors are contained in the first-degree (capital) murder statute or are set forth in the portion of the procedural statutes or rules regulating the adjudication of sentences in death-penalty cases.[43]

A legislature is free to determine whether a jury holding in favor of life imprisonment is binding. In *Spaziano v. Florida*,[44] the Court held that although a strong majority of death penalty jurisdictions indeed make such a jury finding conclusive, thus precluding judicial entry of a death sentence, Florida did not violate the sixth amendment right to jury trial by withholding from a jury the ultimate power to opt for life imprisonment.

There is no objection, either, to a mandate that a jury enter a verdict of death after finding guilt on the predicate capital murder charge, as long as

---

[37] Walton v. Arizona, 497 U.S. 639, 647-49 (1990); Cabana v. Bullock, 474 U.S. 376 (1986).
[38] Cabana v. Bullock, 474 U.S. 376 (1986).
[39] Hildwin v. Florida, 490 U.S. 638 (1989) (per curiam).
[40] *Id.* at 640-41 (relying on doctrinal statements in McMillan v. Pennsylvania, 477 U.S. 79 (1986), relating to a mandatory minimum sentence based on possession of a firearm during commission of a felony). Accordingly, if a jury determines that at least one of the statutory aggravating factors is present, it need not thereafter weigh further or refine the aggravating factor(s) it has determined to exist. Blystone v. Pennsylvania, 494 U.S. 299 1083 (1990).
[41] Wainwright v. Goode, 464 U.S. 78, 87 (1983).
[42] Zant v. Stephens, 462 U.S. 862 (1983).
[43] Lowenfield v. Phelps, 484 U.S. 231 (1988).
[44] 468 U.S. 447 (1984).

the trial court exercises discretion as to whether to confirm the death penalty verdict or substitute a sentence of life imprisonment.[45]

As long as juries have a role in the screening process, trial courts must exercise care in instructing them, lest they be led to shirk their responsibilities. Accordingly, for example, a jury responsible for making an initial death penalty determination cannot be led to believe that some other entity, *i.e.*, the trial court or an appellate court on mandatory review, will make the actual determination of sentence.[46] In *Caldwell*, the point was made by the prosecutor in closing argument and the trial court confirmed the prosecutor's contention in a statement made to the jury in relation to a defense objection to the prosecutor's remarks.

Juries also must be given instructions on lesser-included offenses, so that their choice is not restricted to acquittal or conviction of the charged capital offense. However, that does not hold true if there are no available lesser-included offenses, as the Court held in *Spaziano v. Florida*.[47] In that case, the Court found *Beck* inapplicable because there was no lesser-included offense charge still extant; the statute of limitations on it had run and Spaziano refused to waive its protection, insisting instead on a *Beck* instruction. The Court held that he could not follow that course; he would have either to waive the statute of limitations or forgo the *Beck* instruction.

In *Schad v Arizona*,[48] the Court ruled that a defendant charged with first-degree (capital) murder by either premeditation or by felony-murder premised on a robbery is not constitutionally entitled to a lesser-included offense instruction on robbery. Schad's jury had been given a second-degree murder instruction, which seemingly satisfied *Beck* concerns.

However, the Court found nothing unconstitutional in a mandated instruction that the state governor could grant a reprieve, pardon or commutation for any sentence, including a mandatory life sentence.[49] Ramos had objected that the instruction had asserted pressure on the jury to return a death verdict and that the instruction was erroneous in that it did not apprise the jury that a death sentence also could be commuted. In deciding on its sentence, the jury properly could consider Ramos's future dangerousness, the Court thought, and weigh it against the possibility that he might be returned to the community. The Court noted, however, that states can prevent juries from becoming aware of and considering the gubernatorial power of commutation, as many indeed have done.

In a related fashion, the Court believed that an instruction that jurors "must not be swayed by mere sentiment, conjecture, sympathy, passion, prejudice, public opinion or public feeling" did not prevent the jurors from considering any "sympathy factor" favorable to the defendant, and thus reversed the state supreme court holding that it had.[50]

---

[45] Baldwin v. Alabama, 472 U.S. 372 (1985).
[46] Caldwell v. Mississippi, 472 U.S. 320 (1985).
[47] 468 U.S. 447 (1984).
[48] Schad v. Arizona, 111 S. Ct. 2491 (1991).
[49] California v. Ramos, 463 U.S. 992 (1983).
[50] California v. Brown, 479 U.S. 538 (1987).

(ii) Aggravating Data Considered by Trial Courts. The Constitution seemingly does not bar trial courts from considering factors, not embodied in the statutory list of aggravating circumstances constituting the threshold for death eligibility, in deciding whether to confirm or enter a death sentence.[51] Although there was no majority opinion in the case, a review of the multiple opinions seems to confirm that trial judges, after receiving a jury recommendation against the death penalty, can consider a variety of factors before deciding to invoke that sanction. In other words, state law can authorize a judge to ignore a jury recommendation of life imprisonment and consider other factors in favor of capital punishment, provided there is plenary supreme court review of a death sentence.

In further elaboration of the basic principle, the Supreme Court in *Espinosa v. Florida*[52] held that when a capital sentencer weighs aggravating and mitigating circumstances, its use of an invalid aggravating circumstance[53] violates the Eighth Amendment; if the sentencing authority is placed in two actors rather than one, neither can be permitted to weigh invalid aggravating circumstances.

In *Dawson v. Delaware*,[54] the Court concluded that although the first amendment does not *per se* bar evidence of affiliation and beliefs bearing on capital sentencing, the receipt into evidence at death-sentence proceedings of the defendant's membership in a white racist prison gang was constitutional error because the evidence was irrelevant to any issues addressed at Dawson's hearing.

(iii) Mitigating Data. Beginning with its holding in *Lockett v. Ohio*,[55] the Court has ruled that capital defendants have a constitutional right to put before the jury all mitigating data, whether or not they conform to a list of mitigating circumstances set out in a death penalty statute; in particular, that extends to aspects of a defendant's character and the circumstances of the underlying offense.[56] Thus, in *Eddings v. Oklahoma*,[57] a youth charged with the murder of a police officer had to be allowed to put in evidence of the defendant's brutal and sordid family environment that might have accounted for his acts, even though there was no "home" for that sort of proof in the statutory listing of mitigating factors. In *Skipper v. South Carolina*,[58] the defendant's rights in this regard were impaired by a trial court ruling disallowing testimony by jailers and a "regular visitor" to the jail where Skipper had been held pending trial that he had made a good adjustment to prison life;

---

[51] Barclay v. Florida, 463 U.S. 939 (1983).

[52] 112 S. Ct. 2926 (1992) (per curiam).

[53] In *Espinosa*, the legislative statement of the aggravating circumstance was unconstitutionally vague and indefinite.

[54] 112 S. Ct. 1093 (1992).

[55] 438 U.S. 586 (1978).

[56] The Court reaffirmed this premise in Blystone v. Pennsylvania, 494 U.S. 299, 305 (1990). The state statute contained a "catchall" provision allowing jury consideration of any other evidence of mitigation concerning the character and record of the defendant and the circumstances of the offense, which the Pennsylvania Supreme Court had construed as not limiting mitigating data in any way. The Supreme Court confirmed that mitigating evidence must be admitted whether or not it fits within the literal language of such a residual provision. *Id.* at 305 & n.2.

[57] 456 U.S. 904 (1982).

[58] 476 U.S. 1 (1986).

the prosecutor argued to the jury that Skipper probably would rape other prisoners if imprisoned for life. In *Penry v. Lynaugh*,[59] the Court reversed the death sentence against a severely mentally-retarded capital defendant because the state procedures in place at the time the death penalty was imposed prevented the jury from giving adequate consideration to Penry's moral culpability in light of his retardation.

After aggravating and mitigating data have been heard by the jury, its discretion to consider mitigating data cannot be restricted by instructions of law, whether founded on statute[60] or standard jury instructions.[61] Nevertheless, the instructions given in a particular case are to be evaluated in the context of the proceeding to determine whether there was a reasonable likelihood that the jury applied a challenged instruction in a way that prevented consideration of constitutionally relevant evidence.[62] That premise, established in *Mills v. Maryland*,[63] was confirmed in *McKay v. North Carolina*.[64]

The Sixth Amendment right to jury trial is not infringed if appellate courts exercise the power of reviewing valid aggravating circumstances against mitigating data in determining whether to vacate and remand a death sentence.[65] Nothing in a system of appellate weighing or reweighing of aggravating and mitigating circumstances is at odds with contemporary standards of fairness, or inherently unreliable and likely to result in an arbitrary assessment of the death penalty.[66] Written jury findings are no more necessary to aid appellate courts than they are to assist trial judges.[67]

The basic *Lockett* rule is violated if jury members are led to believe that they are not allowed to consider any mitigating evidence unless they agree unanimously that a particular mitigating circumstance existed — the holding of *Mills v. Maryland*.[68] A jury response form (a type of questionnaire) in use at the time of Mills' trial might have infringed *Lockett* and *Eddings*, the Court thought, because it disabled reasonable jurors from considering mitigating data that some but not all of them agreed had existed.

(iv) Double Jeopardy Considerations. If a first jury trial results in an assessment of life imprisonment rather than death and the defendant successfully appeals the predicate conviction, the state is barred from seeking the death penalty at the conclusion of the retrial at which a new conviction is obtained;[69] the first jury's rejection of the death penalty is as conclusive as would be a finding of guilt on a lesser-included offense, which serves as an

---

[59] 492 U.S. 302 (1989).

[60] Blystone v. Pennsylvania, 494 U.S. 299 1084 (1990). The issue can be advanced whether or not a defendant offered mitigating data at the penalty phase of the proceeding. *Id.* at 1083. *See also* Boyde v. California, 494 U.S. 370 (1990).

[61] Boyde v. California, 494 U.S. 370 (1990).

[62] *Id.* at 383-84. In so holding, the Court abandoned the standard discernible in its earlier precedents based on "how a single hypothetical, 'reasonable' juror could or might have interpreted the instruction." *Id.* at 380.

[63] 486 U.S. 367 (1988).

[64] 494 U.S. 433 (1990).

[65] Clemons v. Mississippi, 494 U.S. 738 (1990).

[66] *Clemons*, 494 U.S. at 750.

[67] *Id.*

[68] 486 U.S. 367 (1988).

[69] Bullington v. Missouri, 451 U.S. 430 (1981).

implied acquittal of the greater offense.[70] The same result obtains if a trial court assessed life imprisonment, even though on the basis of an erroneous judicial interpretation of a statutory aggravating factor; double jeopardy bars a reconsideration of the initial ruling.[71]

However, if the trial court assessed the death penalty and an appellate court reversed because the aggravating factors relied on by the trial court did not cover the case, but retrial established one or more applicable aggravating factors and the trial court again assessed the death penalty, *Rumsey* is not violated; a trial court finding that one aggravating factor applies is not an implied finding that none of the others existed.[72]

(v) *Fair Notice of Possibility of Death Sentence.* Before commencing death-penalty proceedings, a trial court must see that a defendant is adequately apprised that a death sentence is a possibility.[73] In *Lankford*, the defendant had been advised at arraignment that the charge of first-degree murder carried a maximum punishment of life imprisonment or death. A later plea bargain excluding the death penalty was rejected by the trial court, and Lankford was convicted. Before the sentencing proceeding commenced, the prosecution submitted a statement to the court that it was not seeking the death penalty, and the trial court gave no indication whatever that it considered the death penalty a live alternative; no evidence of either aggravating or mitigating circumstances was offered by either side. The court at the penultimate sentencing hearing indicated that it had before it, and was considering, sentences of imprisonment. At the final hearing, however, the court assessed the death penalty. The Supreme Court held that Lankford's due process rights had been violated because of the trial court's failure at any time to give adequate notice to the defendant that he might be sentenced to death.

(e) *Mandatory Appellate Review; Postconviction Review.* A common thread running through many of the Supreme Court's death penalty cases is that the ultimate safeguard against freakish, capricious and erratic capital decisions is a plenary review by the highest court of the jurisdiction; that factor was prominent, for example, in the Court's consideration of allegations of racial discrimination in the administration of capital legislation in *McCleskey v. Kemp*,[74] in which it noted several safeguards against "arbitrariness and caprice" in the Georgia system, including an automatic appeal of death sentences to the state supreme court.[75]

Meaningful appellate review consists of an individualized determination of the appropriateness of the death penalty based on the capital defendant's character and the circumstances of the capital crime. If the state's highest court finds there is insufficient evidence to support some of the aggravating circumstances underlying a death sentence, meaningful appellate review allows it either to reweigh the aggravating and mitigating factors or to conduct an acceptable harmless-error analysis. If, however, it refuses to do either, but

---

[70] *See, e.g.,* Green v. United States, 355 U.S. 184 (1957).
[71] Arizona v. Rumsey, 467 U.S. 203 (1984).
[72] Poland v. Arizona, 476 U.S. 147 (1986).
[73] Lankford v. Idaho, 111 S. Ct. 1723 (1991).
[74] 481 U.S. 279 (1987).
[75] *McCleskey*, 481 U.S. at 303. *See also* Pulley v. Harris, 465 U.S. 37 (1984); Spaziano v. Florida, 468 U.S. 447, 465-67 (1984); Wainwright v. Goode, 464 U.S. 78 (1983) (per curiam).

accepts instead the trial court judge's weighing, the death sentence must be vacated on federal grounds.[76]

However, once the plenary review in the state's highest court has been completed, postconviction review proceedings can be subjected to procedural requirements, including those governing federal habeas corpus review.[77] If a state court system allows postconviction review, however, it cannot exclude from its consideration anything that militates in favor of a vacation of a capital sentence and renewed capital sentencing proceedings.[78]

Following plenary review, death-row inmates appear to have an "election to die," as indicated at least indirectly by the Court's position that relatives and counsel cannot pursue postconviction review procedures and appeals to stay or invalidate capital warrants if the inmates have disavowed such efforts.[79]

(f) *Execution of Mentally-Impaired Capital Convicts.* In *Ford v. Wainwright*,[80] a majority of the Court held that mentally-ill capital convicts cannot be executed. However, there was no majority holding addressing the procedures to be followed in making the determination and no firm indication of the responsibility test to be used to screen such cases. Nevertheless, in 1989 there was a narrow, but clear, doctrinal majority in *Penry v. Lynaugh*[81] supporting the constitutionality of legislation that allows mentally-retarded convicts to be executed. However, Penry's conviction was reversed because the

---

[76] *Parker v. Dugger*, 111 S. Ct. 731 (1991).

[77] *See Barefoot v. Estelle*, 463 U.S. 880 (1983), for procedures to be followed in expediting the review of capital habeas proceedings in federal courts of appeals.

Death penalty litigants must take account of *McCleskey v. Zant*, 111 S. Ct. 1454 (1991), in which a majority of the Court established quite stringent limitations on second or later applications for habeas corpus lodged by or on behalf of death-row inmates. Claims not included in an earlier petition are subject to dismissal unless an applicant can meet the "cause-and-prejudice" standard: (a) some objective factor external to the defense impeded counsel's effort to raise the claim on the (or an) earlier occasion; and (b) actual prejudice flowed from the complained-of error(s). However, federal courts may consider constitutional errors not excusable under the cause-and-prejudice standard if the result was a fundamental miscarriage of justice.

Also relevant is *Coleman v. Thompson*, 111 S. Ct. 2546 (1991), in which the Court held that dismissal of a state appeal (it happened to be in the context of an appeal from a refusal to grant state habeas corpus relief to a death-row inmate) based on a failure to make a timely filing, constitutes an independent state ground that precludes later review in federal courts. Again, such a preclusion doctrine will be bypassed if a would-be appellant meets the cause-and-prejudice standard or shows that a failure to review a federal claim will result in a fundamental miscarriage of justice. According to *Sawyer v. Whitley*, 112 S. Ct. 2514 (1992), to qualify under the latter exception, habeas petitioners must establish by clear and convincing evidence that they are actually innocent of their crimes or ineligible for the death sentence imposed on them; capital defendants must show that no reasonable juror would have found them death-eligible under the state statutes governing criminality and the existence of aggravating circumstances.

The cause-and-prejudice standard, and not the "deliberate bypass" standard, determines whether habeas corpus petitioners' failure to develop material facts in earlier state proceedings will be excused; failures to do so can be excused and hearings held, based on a showing that a fundamental miscarriage of justice will flow from a failure to hold a federal evidentiary hearing. *Keeney v. Tamayo-Reyes*, 112 S. Ct. 1715 (1992).

[78] *See Johnson v. Mississippi*, 486 U.S. 578 (1988).

[79] *See Whitmore v. Arkansas*, 495 U.S. 149 (1990) (invoking "case or controversy" requirement of Const. art. III as precluding a third party from challenging the validity of a death sentence imposed on a capital defendant who has elected to forgo the right of appeal); *Demosthenes v. Baal*, 495 U.S. 731 (1990) (per curiam) (applying the same rationale to efforts to invoke federal habeas corpus); *Hammett v. Texas*, 448 U.S. 725 (1980); *Gilmore v. Utah*, 429 U.S. 1012 (1976).

[80] 477 U.S. 399 (1986).

[81] 492 U.S. 302 (1989).

jury had been prevented from considering Penry's mental retardation as it bore on his moral culpability.[82]

SECTION III. Patterns of Sentencing

A. INDETERMINATE SENTENCES: THE REHABILITATIVE IDEAL

AMERICAN BAR ASSOCIATION STANDARDS FOR CRIMINAL JUSTICE (2d ed. 1981) SENTENCING ALTERNATIVES AND PROCEDURES

§ 18-2.1. *Commentary pp. 18-33 to 18-35.*

Penal Code Revision

The starting point for sentencing reform must be rationalization of the penalty structure of the penal code. Uniformly, serious critiques of the contemporary sentencing process have pointed to the inconsistency and irrationality present in many penal codes. The original edition took notice of numerous instances where the severity of the penalty was almost inversely proportional to the gravity of the offense. Thus, for example, the offender convicted of first-degree murder might in some instances be required to serve a minimum sentence of ten years while one convicted of a lesser degree of murder could be forced to serve fifteen years or more. In another case, the penalty for stealing a car was ten years, but as much as fifteen years if instead only its glove compartment were broken into. Almost as irrational is the prevalence of inconsistent penal evaluations by the legislature of substantially the same conduct. Broadly drafted or overlapping penal statutes often proscribe identical conduct, but prescribe widely variant penalties, punishing the conduct in question in one instance by up to five years imprisonment and in another by ten. The result is not only to produce unwarranted disparities, but to erode the moral coherence of the criminal law and generate cynicism on the part of those closest to its operation (including not least of all the offender).

The causes of such *reductio ad absurdum* results are not hard to discern. Criminal legislation is more often than not "the product of ad hoc responses to particular situations extending over an enormous time period." At each legislative session, penal statutes are passed — often in response to a notorious crime or a perceived wave of a particular type of offense — without attention being given to integrating the penalties so adopted with those provided for other offenses of greater or lesser severity. Inevitably, both inconsistency and statutory clutter result as a proliferation of different penalties come into existence over the decades. In one jurisdiction, a study found as many as 466 different penalty types, each different from the other and each specified by at least one of 1,413 often overlapping penal statutes.

The remedy for this lack of coherence so evident in many penal codes also seems clear: (1) integrate all sentencing provisions of the penal code within a

---

[82] A proposed legislative standard governing competency for purposes of execution may be found in ABA STANDARDS FOR CRIMINAL JUSTICE § 7-5.6(b) (rev. ed. 1989).

separate section of that code; (2) establish a rationally graded penalty structure consisting of a limited number of crime categories; and (3) encourage new penal statutes to prescribe penalties only by reference to those crime categories. Thus, as new penal statutes are enacted, they would be less likely to distort the desired proportionality of the penalty structure....

§ 18-4.1. *Commentary pp. 18-241 to 18-246.*

Indeterminacy Reconsidered

Beginning in the late 1960's, a steady progression of critics have been challenging the rationale underlying the indeterminate sentencing structure.[1] The elements of this critique are now well known and can be briefly summarized:

1. The failure to impose a sentence establishing within a relatively narrow range the date on which the offender would be released aggravates the disparate treatment accorded similarly situated offenders. Although in theory parole boards might individualize as well as the sentencing court, they in practice are so overloaded that erratic, random results become inevitable.[2]

2. The psychological impact of uncertainty upon the offender produces intense and unnecessary anxiety. The "inmate experiences as cruel and degrading the command that he remain in custody for some uncertain period, while his keepers study him, grade him in secret, and decide if and when he may be let go."[3] In turn, his anxiety produces sham efforts at rehabilitation and play

---

[1] For an overview of the various statutory patterns of indeterminate sentencing, see Comment, *The Indeterminate Sentence: Judicial Intervention in the Correctional Process*, 21 BUFFALO L. REV. 935 (1972). *See also* RONALD GOLDFARB & LINDA SINGER, AFTER CONVICTION 167-169 (1973). For a review of the history of the indeterminate sentence, see Marvin Zalman, *The Rise and Fall of the Indeterminate Sentence*, 24 WAYNE L. REV. 45, 857 (1977-1978).

An example of the third and probably most common variety of the indeterminate sentence (e.g., judicially set maximums and minimums) is New York's statute. See N.Y. PENAL LAW § 70.00 (McKinney [1987]). In contrast, the Model Penal Code contemplates that the court would impose the minimum sentence and the legislature the maximum. ALI, MODEL PENAL CODE § 6.06. At the opposite end of the spectrum from the New York approach, the former California statute (amended in 1977) legislatively established both the maximum and the minimum terms and the court simply sentenced the offender to the term "prescribed by law." In effect, this meant that the California Adult Authority determined the date of release and was the operative dispositional decision maker. *See* former CAL. PENAL CODE §§ 1168, 3041 (West Cum. Supp. 1966). Although the California statute was frequently cited as the extreme example of sentencing indeterminacy, many sexual psychopath statutes present equally extreme examples, because typically the offender is sentenced under them to an open-ended term "until cured." *See* D.C. CODE §§ 22-3504 to 22-3509 (1973) (discharge "when the Superintendent of Saint Elizabeth's Hospital finds that [the offender] was sufficiently recovered so as to not be dangerous to other persons").

[2] Among the well-known works that have brought this critique to the public's attention, the following stand out: AMERICAN FRIENDS SERVICE COMMITTEE, STRUGGLE FOR JUSTICE (1971); MARVIN FRANKEL, CRIMINAL SENTENCES (1973); JESSICA MITFORD, KIND AND USUAL PUNISHMENT (1973); KENNETH CULP DAVIS, DISCRETIONARY JUSTICE: A PRELIMINARY INQUIRY (1969). Prof. Davis, a noted legal scholar, has concluded simply: "[t]he performance of the Parole Board seems on the whole about as low in quality as anything I have seen in the federal government." *Id.* at 133. For the leading exposition of the virtues of an indeterminate sentencing structure, see Herbert Wechsler, *Sentencing, Corrections and the Model Penal Code*, 109 U. PA. L. REV. 465 (1961).

[3] *See* MARVIN FRANKEL, *supra* note 2, at 96.

acting for the parole board. Whatever effect well-meaning treatment programs might otherwise have is thereby undercut.[4]

3. Indeterminacy results in discretion being exercised to a greater degree by low-visibility lower-echelon administrative personnel. The potential for abuse is thereby heightened. In particular as Kenneth Culp Davis has pointed out, "*the power to be lenient is the power to discriminate.*"[5]

4. Unless carefully confined, indeterminacy tends in practice to be inconsistent with the quest for proportionality. It invites the legislature and the sentencing court to omit specifying the maximum penalty that is "deserved" for the offense or, at least, to specify a more severe penalty. Time is thus "added on," and the result in some cases is an unjust amount of punishment purely in proportion to the illegal act committed, even without regard to the cases of other offenders.[6]

These criticisms in the main parallel the attack on the rehabilitative model, of which the indeterminate sentencing structure is the primary legislative means of implementation. As the pendulum has swung, repeated calls for the abolition of parole and a return to determinate sentencing have been voiced. To a considerable degree, both the Model Sentencing and Corrections Act and S. 1437 have heeded these calls.[7] With them, this edition agrees that the extent of the indeterminacy in many, if not most, state penal codes is excessive. Unlike them, however, this edition continues to believe that an independent parole agency should be retained and thus that some element of indeterminacy should remain. This position is taken in the belief that there are other frequently overlooked arguments for the retention of a measure of indeterminacy that are unrelated to the rehabilitative model and should not be abandoned with it. These arguments are outlined below.

The Proper Functions of Indeterminacy

In consideration of the full range of functions that an indeterminate *sentencing* structure performs and that this edition sees as justifying a scaled-down form of indeterminacy, it must above all be understood that the question of flat time versus indeterminate sentencing necessarily overlaps with the question whether there should be a single agency determining the length of

---

[4] This theme has, of course, been popularized by Jessica Mitford (*supra* note 2), but essentially the same message comes through in more dispassionate studies. *See* Cressey, *Adult Felons in Prison,* in PRISONERS IN AMERICA 117 (Lloyd Ohlin ed. 1973); NORVAL MORRIS, THE FUTURE OF IMPRISONMENT 1-27 (1974); AMERICAN FRIENDS SERVICE COMMITTEE, *supra* note 2, at 97-99; PIERCE O'DONNELL, MICHAEL CHURGIN, & DENNIS CURTIS, TOWARD A JUST AND EFFECTIVE SENTENCING SYSTEM: AGENDA FOR LEGISLATIVE REFORM 68 (1977) ("uncertainty deprives a prisoner of the incentive to prepare seriously for release and fosters self-defeating despair").

[5] KENNETH CULP DAVIS, *supra* note 2, at 170 (emphasis in original).

[6] This criticism that the optimistic language of treatment and rehabilitation could serve as a cloak under which greater intervention could be justified in the lives of offenders than under a frankly punitive rationale was first and most forcefully articulated by Prof. Francis Allen. *See* FRANCIS A. ALLEN, THE BORDERLAND OF CRIMINAL JUSTICE (1964)....

[7] *See* S. 1437, §§ 3824, 3831 (which would effectively subject the United States Parole Commission to the policies established by the United States Sentencing Commission). The Model Sentencing and Corrections Act contains no provisions authorizing parole release. *See* NCCUSL, MODEL SENTENCING AND CORRECTIONS ACT, prefatory note to art. 3. Parole release has been recently eliminated by the legislature in Indiana, Illinois, California, Maine, and Minnesota (as of 1980)....

confinement to be served or whether this responsibility should be shared. Even after the rehabilitative model is abandoned, valid justifications persist for favoring a "check and balance" system under which the authority to determine the actual time to be served is allocated between dual agencies. Briefly, the following arguments have a collective validity that causes this edition to continue to endorse a degree of indeterminacy, albeit for different reasons than the prior edition.

The "humanizing" function of parole

As unjustifiable as the gap is today between the length of sentences imposed by the court and the length actually served, a worse alternative would be a system under which the excessive sentences imposed were actually required to be served in full. A fair evaluation is the following one: "Whatever its defects, the parole board has performed one essential function: it transforms lengthy judicial sentences into more realistic terms of actual confinement."[8] This conclusion, excerpted from a recent study by leading proponents of a retributive system of punishment, has been similarly reached by other commentators who have focused not on what a sentencing system should ideally be but on what is realistically likely to occur under existing circumstances if parole were abolished. Underlying this conclusion are several common themes. First, a parole agency has historically been able to mitigate the severity of the penalty structure. In part, this has probably been attributable to the lower political visibility that the parole agency has in comparison with either the legislature or the sentencing court. Public acceptance of the idea that individuals change, or at least mature, over time has also produced less resistance to an early release system than to short sentences in the first instance, even if the practical results are the same under both systems. Whatever the reason, the parole board's relative political insulation from public pressure for unrealistically long sentences should not be lightly abandoned, particularly in the absence of any knowledge of the pressures that would accumulate on the agency that replaces it. A second theme in this debate is the argument that, if parole were abolished, sentencing courts would thereafter still focus on the average length of sentences as they were previously imposed, rather than on the period of confinement that had actually been served. Inertia is a powerful force. Accustomed for decades to a system of "dual time" under which long sentences are imposed but not served, courts (and any guideline drafting agency that constructs a descriptive model of their practices) may begin their deliberations from a point of reference that looks at past sentencing practices. In any event, the transition from "dual time" to "single time" under which only one agency prescribes guidelines may make it difficult for guideline ranges to be reduced even to the actual average length of confinement now served in such situations. For example, if the guideline drafting agency were to issue a three-year guideline for a crime for which the average sentence previously imposed by courts was seven years, objections might be voiced about excessive leniency — even though three years might have been the

---

[8] Andrew von Hirsch & Kathleen J. Hanrahan, Abolish Parole?, at ii (1977).

actual average length of confinement and seem comparatively severe by European standards.

The function of disparity reduction

As impressive as the case is for sentencing guidelines, it cannot yet be safely concluded that guidelines alone are sufficient to reduce sentencing disparities to a tolerable level. Conversely, parole guidelines as administered by the United States Parole Commission have proven efficacy. A realistic appreciation of the tendency for change to be gradual leads this edition to recommend that, for at least a transitional period, exclusive reliance should not be placed on sentencing guidelines. First, to use the federal system as a model, parole guidelines are implemented by a relatively small body of specialized hearing examiners who deal exclusively with parole decisions, make decisions in panels, and are subject to administrative review. In contrast, there are today roughly 500 federal judges deciding cases individually and for whom sentencing is only one of many difficult responsibilities. Consistency seems, then, more likely to be attained through a centralized parole agency than through a decentralized judicial system. Also, because appellate review of sentences will often be to intermediate appellate courts, some disparity among circuits remains likely. To these objective differences must be added a more subjective one: the tradition of "rugged individualism" that exists among judges on the topic of sentencing. These combined factors have led some commentators to warn of judicial resistance to policies aimed at greater accountability in sentencing and to recommend continued reliance on a modified parole system.

Such warnings may be unduly pessimistic. Guidelines may well be welcomed by many judges as pathmarks out of the current sentencing morass. Nonetheless, as experience does not yet exist with the implementation of guidelines on a group as large or geographically diffuse as the trial court judiciary of most state jurisdictions, it seems premature to abandon parole guidelines at this juncture.

A final consideration in evaluating the relative ability of sentencing and parole guidelines to reduce disparity is the greater ability of the latter to deal with the disparities caused by plea bargaining. Without endorsing "real offense" sentencing, it still must be recognized that the parole agency is in a better position to detect the disparities that result from plea bargaining and is less compelled to accept them since it is remote from the day-to-day pressures of caseload management.

The need to respond to subsequent developments

The rejection of rehabilitation as a factor to be considered at sentencing does not mean that only factors existing at the moment of sentencing should affect the date of release. First and perhaps most obviously, prison overcrowding and other basic limitations on our capacity to institutionalize need to be considered and hence make necessary some mechanism for early release. Second and at least as important, social attitudes toward different crimes change over time. By definition, any change in sentencing guideline ranges will create "intertemporal disparities between offenders sentenced before and those sentenced after the change — unless some means exist to adjust the former sentences. S. 1437 recognizes this need and so retains a parole agency to perform basically this limited function. Once the decision is made to retain such an agency, however, the arguments multiply for expanding its role. Although these standards do not address the question of the extent to which the needs of institutional discipline should affect the release decision, it is obvious that this is another area where a parole agency *could* consider factors beyond the cognizance of the sentencing court. Finally, although rehabilitation is rejected as a guide, these standards reject the doctrinaire attitude that fails to admit the existence of exceptional cases. The offender who matures beyond the age of potential dangerousness, the offender who pursues graduate study in prison and who could perform significant services for society, the terminally ill offender, the offender who deserves to be rewarded for some act of heroism, such as foiling an attempt to take hostages — all these are cases in which it would be either pointlessly punitive or dangerously rigid to abolish any means for recognizing exceptional circumstances.

§ *18-2.2. Commentary pp. 18-67 to 18-70.*

The Role of Equality in Sentencing

This edition gives a qualified endorsement to the goal of sentencing equality. Basically, it conceives of equality as a side constraint upon the pursuit of the end purposes of a system of criminal sanctions and upon the degree to which distinction should be made among offenders in terms of their predicted future behavior. The goal of equality is not, however, elevated to the status of an independent justification for confinement.[33]

In part, this restricted role for equality is motivated by the recognition that a tension inevitably exists between the goal of equality and the least restrictive alternative principle. For example, to the extent that we can differentiate between high-risk and low-risk offenders, there are obvious reasons why the high-risk offenders should be incapacitated for a longer period. But confinement based on predicted risk is a troubling concept. Conversely, to confine the lower-risk offender for a similarly extended period on the grounds that those who are equally culpable should receive equal treatment offends the least drastic means concept (since no preventive purpose is thereby furthered, at least not in a way that minimizes the use of confinement as that principle requires). This apparent conflict between liberty and equality is troubling in principle, but may be substantially avoidable in reality. The collision can be averted because to a substantial extent the factors that best distinguish high-risk from low-risk offenders also are factors that make the former group more culpable than the latter (*e.g.,* prior convictions, prior incarcerations, etc.). To

---

[33] In short, it is not intended that the sentence given one offender be extended because earlier or subsequent offenders received longer terms or a contemporary offender received an exemplary sentence. The overzealous pursuit of absolute equality leads ultimately to the unfortunate end result of a sentencing structure where all sentences are made consecutive (since the multiple offender is not "equal" with the offender who has committed only a single crime) and where enhancements for aggravating factors are made mandatory rather than discretionary....

the extent that the former group is more culpable, the goal of sentencing equality is not violated by confining the former marginally longer, since the two groups do not represent "like cases." Admittedly, high-risk and low-risk groups may also be distinguished by socioeconomic factors, relating principally to their social stability, which involve no element of culpability. Here, however, standard 18-3.2(a)(vi) instructs sentencing authorities that predictions of future recidivism should only be founded upon verified instances of past or present criminal conduct and never upon "factors relating primarily to the offender's social or economic status." The reasons for such a restriction are discussed in that standard, but here the important point is that such a limitation minimizes the troubling tension between the values of equality and liberty.

Conceptually, the phrase "sentencing equality" masks two quite different claims. First is the claim of the individual offender that he or she should be treated no more harshly than others equally culpable. Second is the claim that punishment should not be allocated in a manner that systematically prejudices some classes of offenders while other classes of equal blameworthiness receive leniency. Essentially, this latter claim asserts that sentencing presents issues of distributive justice. Thus, not only the offender directly affected but others within society generally might object, for example, to a penalty structure that imposed fixed fines on all offenders and then imprisoned those unable to pay.

These standards endorse this second interpretation of sentencing equality as a species of distributive justice, finding it more modest in scope, more capable of realization, and closer to the source of the public's discontent with current sentencing practices. It is not random variations in sentencing but very nonrandom differences under which some seem always to escape imprisonment that most alarm the public. Standard 18-3.2(a)(vi) speaks directly to this goal of eliminating institutionalized bias by prohibiting the use of socioeconomic criteria (such as the offender's education level or employment history). Standard 18-3.2(a)(ii) states a more general principle and asks sentencing authorities to provide special justification and to minimize the resulting disparity when compelling reasons do require different sentences assigned offenders of equal culpability.

In so doing, these standards at least implicitly decline to accept the first claim discussed above that the offender should never be treated more harshly than others who have committed crimes of similar gravity. This position is reached with some reluctance (as standard 18-3.2(a)(ii) makes evident) but in the belief that such a moral imperative would prove overly confining and would also commit sentencing authorities to the pursuit of an illusory goal. Even if sentencing were ideally fair, practices such as plea bargaining, pretrial diversion, and prosecutorial discretion would still interfere with realization of absolute equality (not to mention the effect of low rates of apprehension). More important, the preventive ends of criminal justice can justify some deviation from such a strict view of equality, for example, where one of two equally culpable offenders was a member of organized crime and so was more likely to return to crime upon release or where a given crime had recently reached epidemic proportions so as to necessitate an enhanced penalty. Other considerations arguably may merit similar deviations, for example, the effect of a sentence on the offender's dependents or on the health of the offender. At least in the abstract, these standards are unwilling to restrict society's ability to maximize crime prevention within the limits of the proportionality principle by grafting inflexible limits onto the allocation of punishment which invariably require that the equally culpable be treated exactly alike. In truth, to accept such a rigid principle is as a practical matter to accept the just deserts model earlier rejected. In general, jurisprudential writers have agreed, arguing that where a strict interpretation of the requirements of equality conflicts with the preventive ends of criminal justice, the former should yield to the latter.

Instances of principled sentencing disparities represent the exception rather than the rule. More often, the tendency toward inequality in sentencing has no such defensible foundation and is the result of random variation or worse. Accordingly, because the focus of these standards is on practice rather than theory, their basic recommendation is that differences in treatment accorded those of equal culpability should be scrutinized closely. These standards conclude then with what is intended more as a prudential rule than a jurisprudential law: "Like cases" should be treated alike in the absence of strong reasons to the contrary, because unexplained disparities erode our society's professed ideal that all are equal before the law.

The case for sentencing equality can be founded on the need to protect not only the fairness of our criminal justice system but also its efficiency. A less noticed consequence of sentencing disparities is their tendency to produce both delay and court congestion as counsel seek to postpone sentencings until they can be heard before a judge thought to be lenient. In turn, appeals of a conviction may often be based less on any substantial error in the trial than on the belief, sometimes justified, that an overly harsh sentence may motivate the appellate court to reverse on an error it would otherwise consider harmless. In short, when a system permits itself to be manipulated, it is predictable that it will be manipulated. In the end, the consequence is to reduce the deterrent potential of the criminal law from that which would prevail if the hope of "beating the game" did not loom so large. In short, to be either just or effective, our criminal justice system must recognize the importance of sentencing equality.

NOTES

1. Techniques of behavior modification, whether in prisons or mental hospitals, arouse substantial controversy. *See generally* Michael H. Shapiro, *Legislating the Control of Behavior Control: Autonomy and the Coercive Use of Organic Therapies,* 47 S. CAL. L. REV. 237 (1974). Nonconsensual psychotropic medication raises federal constitutional problems. *Scott v. Plante,* 532 F.2d 939 (3d Cir. 1976), and *cf. Riggins v. Nevada,* 112 S. Ct. 1810 (1992) (constitutional error to order that a defendant be administered antipsychotic drugs over his objection, without finding that no less intrusive measures were available, and that the medication was both medically appropriate and essential for the sake of the defendant's safety or the safety of others). Administrative

due process concerns must be met before convulsive or coma therapy may be used. *Aden v. Younger,* 129 Cal. Rptr. 535 (Cal. Ct. App. 1976). *Price v. Sheppard,* 239 N.W.2d 905 (Minn. 1976). There also is authority that patients capable of consent must agree to shock therapy, *New York City Health & Hospital Corp. v. Stein,* 335 N.Y.S.2d 461 (N.Y. Sup. Ct. 1972), and that hospital personnel who administer shock therapy and chemotherapy without consent are civilly liable. *Mackey v. Procunier,* 477 F.2d 877 (9th Cir. 1973).

2. Sterilization of mental patients has been ruled constitutional. *North Carolina Ass'n for Retarded Children v. North Carolina,* 420 F. Supp. 451 (M.D.N.C. 1976) (three-judge court); *In re Moore,* 221 S.E.2d 307 (N.C. 1976), based on *Buck v. Bell,* 274 U.S. 200 (1927), and distinguishing *Skinner v. Oklahoma ex rel. Williamson,* 316 U.S. 535 (1942).

3. The Supreme Court apparently accepted the concept of "least restrictive alternative," *i.e.,* that only the minimum degree of restraint on liberty and rigor of therapeutic regimen justified by a patient's mental condition is constitutionally allowable. *O'Connor v. Donaldson,* 422 U.S. 563 (1975). Donaldson sued for damages the former superintendent of a state mental hospital who had refused him outpatient status despite the willingness of responsible citizens to undertake his supervision. The Court noted, "[i]n short, a State cannot constitutionally confine without more a nondangerous individual who is capable of surviving safely in freedom by himself or with the help of willing and responsible family members or friends." *Id.* at 576.

B. PRESUMPTIVE SENTENCING: "JUST DESERTS" THEORY

AMERICAN BAR ASSOCIATION STANDARDS FOR CRIMINAL JUSTICE SENTENCING ALTERNATIVES AND PROCEDURES (2d ed. 1981)

§ *18-2-2. Commentary pp. 18-59 to 18-63.*

The "Just Deserts" Model

Concern about the pervasive existence of sentencing disparities, particularly between those assigned white collar and blue collar offenders, has lately led a number of commentators to recommend a return to a retributive model of punishment under which the sentence imposed is to be exclusively based on the gravity of the offense.[7] A trend toward legislative acceptance of this "principle of commensurate deserts" is evident. The recent California Determinate Sentencing Act expresses, for example, the view that "the purposes [sic] of imprisonment for crime is punishment."[8] The Model Sentencing and

---

[7] ANDREW VON HIRSCH, DOING JUSTICE (1976); AMERICAN FRIENDS SERVICE COMMITTEE, STRUGGLE FOR JUSTICE (1971); Norval Morris, *Persons and Punishment,* 52 MONIST 475 (1968); DAVID FOGEL, "WE ARE THE LIVING PROOF..." (1975). For assessments of these theories, *see* Martin R. Gardner, *The Renaissance of Retribution — An Examination of Doing Justice,* 1976 WIS. L. REV. 781; JUSTICE AND PUNISHMENT (Jerry B. Cederblom & William L. Blizek ed. 1977).

[8] CAL. PENAL CODE § 1170(a)(1) (West Cum. Supp. 1979).

Corrections Act also adopts such a punishment rationale,[9] as have several states.[10]

Nonetheless, the use of a punishment rationale as the ideological base upon which to build a more equitable sentencing structure seems both unnecessary and unsound. To a degree, the attractions of such a model must be acknowledged. A punishment rationale provides principled guidance to sentencing authorities and so may tend to reduce disparities; in addition, the use of the concept of "deserved punishment" as an outer limiting principle places a desirable limit on the maximum punishment that may be imposed for a particular offense (a ceiling that a wholly rehabilitative orientation tends to ignore). Without question, all criminal justice systems give some weight to the desirability of administering to the culpable their "just deserts," and no doubt this will continue. Thus, it is not the intent of this edition to reject retribution as a sometimes relevant consideration in the allocation of punishment; rather, the recommendation is that the role it is allowed to play be kept modest. Even conceding that its resurgence is attributable to obvious deficiencies in our contemporary system of sentencing requiring reform, the concern here is that the remedy may prove worse than the disease. That is, the guidance provided by a retributive theory may fundamentally misdirect our criminal justice system, both in theory and in operation. Among our reservations about an approach focusing primarily on how much punishment is "deserved" by the offense are the following.

1. Danger exists once the criminal justice system strays very far from a preventive rationale which keys the use of punishment to the need to prevent even greater suffering from befalling future victims.[11] Such a utilitarian focus is itself an important limiting principle on the use of punishment and is the foundation for the least drastic means concept enunciated in this standard. To expand the least drastic means principle so that it encompasses the idea of punishing the offender simply because the offender "deserves" punishment ultimately inflates that principle into meaninglessness. If the idea of "least drastic means" is to have a limiting effect, it must mean that a socially useful purpose should underlie the imposition of punishment.

---

[9] NCCUSL, Model Sentencing and Corrections Act §§ 3-101, 3-102. Section 3-101 begins: "The purposes of this Article are to ... punish a criminal defendant by assuring the imposition of a sentence he deserves in relation to the seriousness of his offense...." Section 3-102(1) then uses the just deserts principle differently by employing it as a ceiling on the allocation of punishment. These standards are in accord with the second manner in which the principle is used but not the first.

[10] Since 1976, the following determinate, or flat time, sentencing statutes have been adopted: Ind. Code Ann. §§ 35-50-2-4 et seq. (Burns 1979); Ill. Rev. Stat. ch. 38, §§ 1005-5-1 et seq. (Cum. Supp. 1978); Minn. Stat. Ann. §§ 244.01 et seq. (West Cum. Supp. 1979); Ariz. Rev. Stat. §§ 13-601 et seq. (1978); Me. Rev. Stat. tit. 17A, §§ 4, 4-A (1978). Other jurisdictions, most notably New Jersey and Oregon, have paralleled this trend through the adoption of presumptive guidelines and the concomitant abolition of most forms of early release.

[11] Until the rebirth of interest in retribution, a consensus seemed to exist among most jurisprudential writers that prevention of criminal conduct was the primary aim of the criminal law. See Henry L.A. Hart, Punishment and Responsibility 3-4, 8-12, 172-173 (1968); Herbert Packer, The Limits of the Criminal Sanction 66 (1968); see also John C. Coffee, Jr., *The Repressed Issues of Sentencing: Accountability, Predictability, and Equality in the Era of the Sentencing Commission*, 66 Geo. L.J. 975, 1056-1080 (1978).

B. PRESUMPTIVE SENTENCING: "JUST DESERTS" THEORY

2. Legitimizing retribution may have an inflationary effect on the length of criminal sentences, both as authorized and as imposed. This is clearly unintended by most academic proponents of such reforms, but courts and legislatures may be made unduly susceptible to public pressures for "tough" penalties by such a rationale and, in any event, may have vastly different views of what level of punishment is deserved for a given offense than the original proponents of such reform. In short, once Pandora's box is opened, there are signs it will not easily again be shut.[12] This danger arises not simply because of the possibility that the legislature may overreact to the stimulus that a "just deserts" model provides, but also because the internal logic of such a model seems inherently to require a constantly escalating punishment scale under which enhancement of the sentence for aggravating factors becomes mandatory. An example of this (discussed *infra* in standard 18-4.5) is the requirement of the Model Sentencing and Corrections Act that multiple sentences run consecutively rather than concurrently. In contrast, these standards favor a presumption supporting concurrent sentences (as do most states today), because they take a significantly different view of the nature of the claim underlying the goal of sentencing equality.

3. A purely retributive model for punishment would have many of the characteristics of a straitjacket, since it would deny the criminal justice system the flexibility to respond to the need for increased general deterrence or for special deterrence or incapacitation in a special case, or to adjust penalties in keeping with changing community attitudes.

4. The point has been well made by others that the central touchstone of culpability used by retributive models is inherently no less subjective than the elusive concepts employed by rehabilitative or other models to guide punishment allocation. It may tell us that crime X is more grave than crime Y, but it fails to supply a satisfactory mechanism for measuring the degree of difference between them.[13]

---

[12] As Prof. Zimring has written: "Once a determinate sentencing bill is before a legislative body, it takes only an eraser and pencil to make a one-year presumptive sentence into a six-year sentence for the same offense." Franklin E. Zimring, *A Consumer's Guide to Sentencing Reform — Making the Punishment Fit the Crime,* in REFORM OF THE FEDERAL CRIMINAL LAWS: HEARINGS ON S. 1437 BEFORE THE SUBCOMMITTEE ON CRIMINAL LAWS AND PROCEDURES OF THE COMMITTEE ON THE JUDICIARY, PT. 13, 95TH CONG., 1ST SESS. 9428 (1977)....

Although the academic proponents of a just deserts model have advocated a reduction in the length of authorized sentences, legislatures that have followed their suggestions in other respects have deviated at this point. The recent Indiana penal code revisions provide a sober example: sixty- and fifty-year sentences were authorized at the same time the parole system was eliminated. Specifically, a maximum sentence of death or forty years was provided for the crime of murder, which sentence might be further increased to sixty years or decreased to thirty years if certain aggravating or mitigating factors were found to be present (IND. CODE ANN. § 35-50-2-3 (Burns 1979)). For class A felonies, the presumptive term was made thirty years, but again, because of the effect given to aggravating and mitigating factors, the effective range becomes twenty to fifty years (§ 35-50-2-4). For class B felonies, the effective range, computed on the same basis, is six to twenty years (§ 35-50-2-5); for class C, two to eight years (§ 35-50-2-6); and for class D, two to four years (§ 35-50-2-7). Suspended sentences were prohibited in specified circumstances (§ 35-50-2-2), and consecutive sentences and special habitual offender sentences were made mandatory in other circumstances (§§ 35-50-1-2, 35-50-2-8). Both the Arizona and the Illinois statutes roughly parallel Indiana. *See* ARIZ. REV. STAT., §§ 13-701 *et seq.* (1978); ILL. REV. STAT. ch. 38, §§ 1005-8-1 *et seq.* (Cum. Supp. 1978).

[13] *See* comments of Prof. Joseph Goldstein in the appendix to ANDREW VON HIRSCH, *supra* note 7, at 174. Goldstein objects that a just deserts sentencing system "will prove to be just another

5. The proposition that people "deserve" punishment for their misdeeds may reinforce the "we/they" perception of the offender as qualitatively different and so impede the offender's reintegration into society.[14] In any event, a harsher, more vengeful tone is given the criminal law by the assertion that punishment is deserved than by the alternative justification endorsed here that incarceration is necessary because no other less drastic alternative will suffice to prevent more suffering.

6. An ulterior motive influencing some to adopt a retributive rationale may lie in the greater degree to which it seems likely to prevent sentencing disparities among those convicted of offenses of similar gravity. If so, a more direct, less ideological approach to these same goals is both possible and preferable. As a means to greater equality, "just deserts" is something of a fifth wheel and may fundamentally confuse the pursuit of that goal. It insists on obedience to a strict and formal theory of punishment which may reduce some instances of unjustified disparity but never directly addresses the tendency for social and economic cleavages to underlie differences in sentencing patterns. In contrast, these standards emphasize procedural reforms aimed at structuring discretion in the belief that most instances of unwarranted sentencing disparity can be reduced without the need for society to commit itself to so confining a substantive theory.

In summary, these standards agree with the apt observation of one critic of the new retributive theorists that they have "rediscovered 'sin' in the absence of a better alternative." In the view of these standards, structuring discretion is probably the better alternative, and certainly the less drastic one.

These standards do accept the concept of a retributive limit on punishment (*see* standard 18-3.2(a)) but disfavor the concept of a retribution justification for punishment. This limited acceptance of retributive is, however, consistent with the least drastic means principle and does not authorize any attempt to match the level of the sanction imposed to the level of the harm caused.

One qualification on this rejection of the newly popular retributive models must be noted. It continues to be recognized that occasions can arise in which the gravity of the offense would be "inconsistent with a sanction other than imprisonment." In these relatively rare instances — often involving a crime committed by a person occupying a position of public trust — the failure to impose some period of confinement could undercut important denunciatory functions of the criminal law and promote social anomie. As others have ably expressed it, the criminal law must function as an educational and socially cohesive force whose purposes are not exhausted simply by the deterrence of potential offenders. To say this, however, is not to deviate from an essentially

---

discretionary sentencing system with a new and protean slogan for justifying retributive excesses under a vaguely articulated "moral claim,' in place of a "do-gooder' claim to cure the sick offender."

[14] Albert L. Porterfield, *The "We-They" Fallacy in Thinking About Delinquents and Criminals*, in BEHAVIORAL SCIENCE AND MODERN PENOLOGY (William H. Lyle & Thetus W. Horner ed. 1973). Prof. Leonard Orland has similarly argued that the total abandonment of a rehabilitative model in favor of a retributive one would in the long run have a profoundly adverse effect on the quality of services provided within institutions: "The risk is that if correctional officers do not consider rehabilitation their goal, they will not make rehabilitation their goal; if correctional officers are told that their business is to punish, they will punish." Leonard Orland, *Is Determinate Sentencing an Illusory Reform?*, 62 JUDICATURE 381, 385 (1979).

B. PRESUMPTIVE SENTENCING: "JUST DESERTS" THEORY

preventive theory of criminal sanctions. The distinction in part is that where a retributive model might require a corresponding level of punishment, a preventive rationale should require only the minimum level of punishment necessary to prevent the social harm foreseen. Theoretical as such a dividing line may seem, it has considerable relevance to the position taken hereafter in standards 18-2.4 and 18-3.1(c)(i) that society can express its condemnation of criminal conduct through means other than total confinement. Sometimes the symbolic punishment inherent in conviction will be adequate. This position would be untenable, however, if the first principle of sentencing were that the offender deserved to suffer in a manner corresponding to the severity of the crime.

JUNEBY v. STATE
Alaska Court of Appeals
641 P.2d 823 (1982)

[Juneby pleaded nolo contendere to charges of first-degree burglary and first-degree sexual assault (rape). He was given the maximum sentence of twenty years allowed for the latter offence, and appealed, contending that the sentencing court gave undue weight to aggravating circumstances and thus imposed an excessive punishment.]

BRYNER, CHIEF JUDGE.

I. The Presumptive Sentencing Provisions of the Alaska Revised Criminal Code

At his sentencing, it was undisputed that Juneby had previously been convicted of grand larceny, a felony. Accordingly, upon his conviction of burglary and sexual assault, Juneby became subject to presumptive sentencing as a second felony offender under the provisions of the Alaska Revised Criminal Code. The presumptive sentencing provisions specifically applicable to Juneby are contained in AS 12.55.125(c)(2) and (d)(1); these provisions state, in pertinent part:

> (c) A defendant convicted of a class A felony may be sentenced to a definite term of imprisonment of not more than 20 years, and shall be sentenced to the following presumptive terms ....
>
> ....
>
> (2) if the offense is a second felony conviction, 10 years;
>
> ....
>
> (d) A defendant convicted of a class B felony may be sentenced to a definite term of imprisonment of not more than 10 years, and shall be sentenced to the following presumptive terms ....
>
> (1) if the offense is a second felony conviction, four years ....

Accordingly, Juneby was subject to presumptive terms of ten years for his sexual assault and four years for his burglary. In the absence of extraordinary circumstances, these presumptive sentences were mandatory, and the sentencing court was bound to impose them, subject only to adjustment for aggravating or mitigating factors in accordance with AS 12.55.155.

In this appeal, Juneby challenges the sentencing court's interpretation and application of the provisions of AS 12.55.155 permitting adjustment of presumptive sentences upon proof of aggravating or mitigating factors. He further contends that Judge Van Hoomissen incorrectly concluded that the aggravating factors established in his case justified increasing his sentence for first degree sexual assault from the ten-year presumptive sentence prescribed under AS 12.55.125(c)(2) to the maximum twenty-year term for the offense.

Before we attempt to consider the merits of Juneby's claims, we must address two threshold matters. First, we believe that discussion of the basic structure and purposes of Alaska's presumptive sentencing scheme, with specific reference to the legislature's commentary on the code's sentencing provisions, will be helpful in providing a background for review of the sentencing court's decision. Second, we must consider the manner in which the revised code's presumptive sentencing provisions alter the previously existing scope of review in sentence appeals.

A. Structure and Purposes of the Presumptive Sentencing Statutes

In 1977, when the Alaska Legislature began its consideration of a comprehensive revision of the former criminal code, there was a strong perception that the sentencing structure of Alaska's criminal statutes lacked coherence.... Furthermore, based on the results of sentencing studies in Alaska, the legislature was concerned with eliminating disparity in the sentencing of similarly situated offenders and making criminal sentencing a predictable, internally consistent process....

Decisions of the Alaska Supreme Court in sentence appeals had given little significance to uniformity as a goal of sentencing or of appellate review of sentences. The markedly different approach to sentencing taken by the Alaska Legislature in enacting the Alaska Revised Criminal Code is made explicit in the first section of the new code's chapter dealing with sentencing. AS 12.55.125 provides, in relevant part:

> *Declaration of Purpose.* The purpose of this chapter is to provide the means for determining the appropriate sentence to be imposed upon conviction of an offense. *The legislature finds that the elimination of unjustified disparity in sentences and the attainment of reasonable uniformity in sentences can best be achieved through a sentencing framework fixed by statute as provided in this chapter.* [Emphasis added.]

The presumptive sentencing provisions of the Revised Criminal Code, contained in AS 12.55.125 and 12.55.155, thus reflect the legislature's intent to assure predictability and uniformity in sentencing by the use of fixed and relatively inflexible sentences, statutorily prescribed, for persons convicted of second or subsequent felony offenses.

Under the provisions of AS 12.55.125, courts sentencing individuals convicted of their first felony offense are not expressly limited in the sentence

B. PRESUMPTIVE SENTENCING: "JUST DESERTS" THEORY

that can be imposed; thus, much of the traditionally broad discretion to decide what kind of a sentence to impose in each case is retained. For second and subsequent felony offenders, however, the legislature has evidenced a strong resolution to restrict judicial discretion and to assure that, as a general rule, statutorily mandated sentences would be imposed. AS 12.55.125(c)(2), (c)(3), (d)(1), (d)(2), (e)(1), and (e)(2), establish presumptive sentences to be imposed upon persons convicted of class A, B, and C felonies when their convictions are for second or subsequent felonies. Under the provisions of AS 12.55.125(g), these presumptive terms may not be suspended or reduced, nor is an offender who is subject to presumptive sentencing eligible to receive a suspended imposition of sentence.

Only two methods are provided for a sentencing judge to deviate from a presumptive sentence established under AS 12.55.125. One occurs when the judge concludes that extraordinary circumstances exist, so that manifest injustice would result if normal presumptive sentencing procedures, as set forth in AS 12.55.125 and 12.55.155, were followed. Upon reaching such a conclusion, the judge must refer the case for sentencing to a specially constituted three-judge panel, which is empowered to impose a sentence without regard to the presumptive terms provided for under AS 12.55.125. See AS 12.55.165 and 12.55.175. The second alternative, provided for in AS 12.55.155, allows a sentencing judge to adjust a presumptive term upward or downward based on a finding of aggravating or mitigating factors. Under AS 12.55.155(c), eighteen aggravating factors are enumerated; thirteen mitigating factors are listed under AS 12.55.155(d).[13] Only the factors specifically stated may be

---

[13] Because its provisions are crucial to the disposition of this case, the text of AS 12.55.155 will be set out in full:

Factors in aggravation and mitigation. (a) If a defendant is convicted of an offense and is subject to sentencing under AS 12.55.125(c)(1), (c)(2), (c)(3), (d)(1), (d)(2), (e)(1), or (e)(2) of this chapter and

(1) the presumptive term is four years or less, the court may decrease the presumptive term by an amount as great as the presumptive term for factors in mitigation or may increase the presumptive term up to the maximum term of imprisonment for factors in aggravation;

(2) the presumptive term of imprisonment is more than four years the court may decrease the presumptive term by an amount as great as 50 per cent of the presumptive term for factors in mitigation or may increase the presumptive term up to the maximum term of imprisonment for factors in aggravation.

(b) Sentence increments and decrements under this section shall be based on the totality of the aggravating and mitigating factors set out in (c) and (d) of this section.

(c) The following factors shall be considered by the sentencing court and may aggravate the presumptive terms set out in AS 12.55.125:

(1) a person, other than an accomplice, sustained physical injury as a direct result of the defendant's conduct;

(2) the defendant's conduct during the commission of the offense manifested deliberate cruelty to another person;

(3) the defendant was the leader of a group of three or more persons who participated in the offense;

(4) the defendant employed a dangerous instrument in furtherance of the offense;

(5) the defendant knew or reasonably should have known that the victim of the offense was particularly vulnerable or incapable of resistance due to advanced age, disability, ill health, or extreme youth or was for any other reason substantially incapable of exercising normal physical or mental powers of resistance;

(6) the defendant's conduct created a risk of imminent physical injury to three or more persons, other than accomplices;

(7) a prior felony conviction considered for the purpose of invoking the presumptive terms of this chapter was of a more serious class of offense than the present offense;

(8) the defendant has a criminal history consisting of prior convictions for offenses, including misdemeanors, that involved aggravated or repeated instances of assaultive behavior;

(9) the defendant knew that the offense involved more than one victim;

(10) the conduct constituting the offense was among the most serious conduct included in the definition of the offense;

(11) the defendant committed the offense pursuant to an agreement that he either pay or be paid for the commission of the offense, and the pecuniary incentive was beyond that inherent in the offense itself;

(12) the defendant was on release under AS 12.30.020 or 12.30.040 for another felony charge or conviction or for a misdemeanor charge or conviction having assault as a necessary element;

(13) the defendant knowingly directed the conduct constituting the offense at an active officer of the court or at an active or former judicial officer, prosecuting attorney, law enforcement officer, correctional employee, or fireman during or because of the exercise of his official duties;

(14) the defendant was a member of an organized group of five or more persons, and the offense was committed to further the criminal objectives of the group;

(15) the defendant has three or more prior felony convictions;

(16) the defendant's criminal conduct was designed to obtain substantial pecuniary gain and the risk of prosecution and punishment for the conduct is slight;

(17) the offense was one of a continuing series of criminal offenses committed in furtherance of illegal business activities from which the defendant derives a major portion of his income;

(18) the offense was a crime specified in AS 11.41 and was committed against a spouse, a former spouse, or a member of the social unit comprised of those living together in the same dwelling as the defendant.

(d) The following factors shall be considered by the sentencing court and may mitigate the presumptive terms set out in AS 12.55.125:

(1) the offense was principally accomplished by another person, and the defendant manifested extreme caution or sincere concern for the safety or well-being of the victim;

(2) the defendant, although an accomplice, played only a minor role in the commission of the offense;

(3) the defendant committed the offense under some degree of duress, coercion, threat, or compulsion insufficient to constitute a complete defense, but which significantly affected his conduct;

(4) the conduct of a youthful defendant was substantially influenced by another person more mature than the defendant;

(5) the conduct of an aged defendant was substantially a product of physical or mental infirmities resulting from his age;

(6) in a conviction for assault under AS 11.41.200 — 11.41.230, the defendant acted with serious provocation from the victim;

(7) except in the case of a crime defined by AS 11.41.410 — 11.41.470, the victim provoked the crime to a significant degree;

(8) a prior felony conviction considered for the purpose of invoking the presumptive terms of this chapter was of a less serious class of offense than the present offense;

(9) the conduct constituting the offense was among the least serious conduct included in the definition of the offense;

(10) before the defendant knew that his criminal conduct had been discovered, he fully compensated or made a good faith effort to fully compensate the victim of his criminal conduct for any damage or injury sustained;

(11) the defendant was motivated to commit the offense solely by an overwhelming compulsion to provide for emergency necessities for his immediate family;

(12) the defendant assisted authorities to detect or apprehend other persons who committed the offense with him;

(13) the facts surrounding the commission of the offense and any previous offenses by the defendant establish that the harm caused by the defendant's conduct is consistently minor and inconsistent with the imposition of a substantial period of imprisonment.

(e) If a factor in aggravation is a necessary element of the present offense, that factor may not be used to aggravate the presumptive term. If a factor in mitigation is raised at trial as a defense reducing the offense charged to a lesser included offense, that factor may not be used to mitigate the presumptive term.

B. PRESUMPTIVE SENTENCING: "JUST DESERTS" THEORY

considered by the court in determining whether a presumptive sentence should be adjusted.

It is manifest that the legislature did not intend aggravating and mitigating circumstances to be lightly found. This is reflected in AS 12.55.155(f), which states, in pertinent part: "Factors in aggravation and factors in mitigation must be established by clear and convincing evidence ...." The requirement of proof by clear and convincing evidence is a strong indication of the legislature's intent to prohibit frequent and substantial departure by sentencing judges from the presumptive sentences that it statutorily prescribed. The legislature emphasized this intent in commenting upon the clear and convincing evidence requirement of AS 12.55.155(f):

> Factors in aggravation or mitigation must be proven by "clear and convincing" evidence so that deviation from the presumptive sentence does not occur routinely.

The presumptive terms set out in AS 12.55.125 were thus intended as appropriate for imposition in most cases, without significant upward or downward adjustment. The commentary to AS 12.55.125 lends further support to this conclusion:

> A presumptive sentence is a legislative determination of the term of imprisonment *the average defendant convicted of an offense should be sentenced to*, absent the presence of legislatively prescribed factors in aggravation or mitigation or extraordinary circumstances.

Commentary on the Alaska Revised Criminal Code, *supra* at 153 (emphasis added). Under the view espoused by the legislature, a presumptive term represents the appropriate sentence for cases that fall within the middle-ground between the opposing extremes of the most and least serious conduct for a given crime. It is to be expected, then, that sentences equalling or varying only slightly from the presumptive terms will generally be suitable when presumptive sentencing applies. Minor adjustments for aggravating or mitigating circumstances might be appropriate in a significant number of cases; only in unusual cases, however, can it be anticipated that substantial deviation from the presumptive term will be called for.

When viewed in the light of the fundamental goals of the new sentencing statutes, the rationale for this relatively inflexible sentencing framework is readily understood. If sentencing courts were permitted, under the presumptive sentencing scheme, to deviate routinely and substantially from the presumptive terms prescribed by law, the fundamental purposes of eliminating

---

(f) If the state seeks to establish a factor in aggravation at sentencing or if the defendant seeks to establish a factor in mitigation at sentencing, written notice must be served on the opposing party and filed with the court not later than 10 days before the date set for imposition of sentence. Factors in aggravation and factors in mitigation must be established by clear and convincing evidence before the court sitting without a jury. All findings must be set out with specificity.

(g) Voluntary alcohol or other drug intoxication or chronic alcoholism or other drug addiction may not be considered an aggravating or mitigating factor.

(h) As used in this section, "serious provocation" has the meaning ascribed to it in AS 11.41.115(f).

disparity and establishing reasonable uniformity in sentencing would be completely undermined. Unless the provisions of AS 12.55.155 are adhered to strictly, and unless a measured and restrained approach is taken in the adjustment of presumptive sentences for both aggravating and mitigating factors, then the prospect of attaining the statutory goal of uniform treatment for similarly situated offenders would quickly be eroded, the potential for irrational disparity in sentencing would threaten to become reality, and the revised code's carefully fashioned system of escalating penalties for repeat offenders would be rendered utterly ineffective.

B. Standard of Review for Appeals from Presumptive Sentences

We next address the question of the appropriate scope of appellate review in sentence appeals evolving from cases in which presumptive sentences are imposed. The state has argued that, in deciding Juneby's sentence appeal, this court "is limited to an inquiry of whether the sentence imposed by the trial judge was clearly mistaken." We disagree.

The "clearly mistaken" standard was established for resolution of sentence appeals in *McClain v. State*, 519 P.2d 811, 813-14 (Alaska 1974), well before the presumptive sentencing provisions of the Alaska Revised Criminal Code were adopted. Application of the "clearly mistaken" standard was appropriate under our former sentencing provisions in order to determine whether the sentencing court properly exercised its discretion in light of the broad sentencing goals enumerated in *State v. Chaney*, 477 P.2d 441, 444 (Alaska 1970). However, when the presumptive sentencing provisions of AS 12.55.125 and 12.55.155 apply, neither the *Chaney* criteria nor the "clearly mistaken" standard of appellate review will suffice to assure accurate resolution of sentence appeals.

This is not to say that the *Chaney* criteria and the "clearly mistaken" standard of review on appeal will be wholly irrelevant in sentence appeals involving presumptive sentences. Once a sentencing court has correctly interpreted and applied the presumptive sentencing provisions of the code and has properly determined the existence of aggravating or mitigating factors, then it will have the discretion to adjust the presumptive sentence for the particular offense, within the limits prescribed by AS 12.55.155(a)(1) and (2). In such instances the *Chaney* criteria, as stated in AS 12.55.005(2)-(6), will be relevant to the sentencing court's determination of the amount by which the presumptive term should be adjusted. Thus, in sentence appeals involving presumptive sentences, it is only when we are called upon to decide if the sentencing court properly exercised its discretion to adjust a presumptive term for aggravating or mitigating factors that the "clearly mistaken" standard of review will continue to govern.

[The court concluded that the trial court record was insufficient to support a finding of aggravating factors sufficient to support the sentence imposed, and remanded for a new sentencing hearing. It noted its "belief that the legislature's paramount goals of eliminating disparity and achieving reasonable uniformity in sentencing can best be attained by adopting a measured and restrained approach toward adjustment of presumptive sentences for both aggravating and mitigating factors." *Id.* at 847.]

NOTE

See generally Albert Alschuler, *Sentencing Reform and Prosecutorial Power: A Critique of Recent Proposals for "Fixed" and "Presumptive" Sentencing*, 126 U. PA. L. REV. 550 (1978); Norval Morris, *Toward Principled Sentencing*, 37 MD. L. REV. 267, 281-84 (1977); Richard Singer, *In Favor of "Presumptive Sentences" Set by a Sentencing Commission*, 24 CRIME & DELINQ. 40 (1978).

NOTE ON THE FEDERAL SENTENCING GUIDELINES AND THEIR APPLICATION

(a) *Inception of the Federal Sentencing Guidelines.* In the Sentencing Reform Act of 1984, Congress established the United States Sentencing Commission, charged with the responsibility to prepare and present to Congress for approval federal sentencing guidelines, to be developed within parameters fixed by Congress.[1] The Commission transmitted its proposed guidelines to Congress; because Congress interposed no objection to them, they went into force on November 1, 1987. Since then, amendments have become effective annually since 1988.

(b) *Charge Offense Sentencing.* The Commission viewed its charge from Congress to be the achievement of honesty, uniformity, and proportionality in sentencing.[2] It also acknowledged that it had been urged from various quarters to adopt a controlling principle or rationale for punishment from among those invoked in classical penal law; deterrence, incapacitation, retribution and rehabilitation. In the end, it declined to do so because to do so might impede the general acceptability of the guidelines.[3] The Commission, however, did resolve certain policy issues in ways that may or may not prove valid in the long run. The first related to the choice between real offense sentencing (the actual conduct in which defendants engaged, whatever the charges on which they were indicted or convicted) and charge offense sentencing (the conduct corresponding to the material elements of the crimes of which defendants have been convicted or to which they plead guilty).[4] After experimentation with a real offense system, the Commission thought the goal of sentencing based on real offenses to be unattainable, and therefore went in the direction of a charge offense system. However, the Commission's work has certain elements of reality; as an illustration, it has utilized generic conduct rather than the elements of a multiplicity of narrow federal criminal statutes.[5] The Sentencing Guidelines also reflect important real offense elements, commonly

---

[1] 28 U.S.C. §§ 991-998 (1988).
[2] U.S. SENTENCING COMM'N, SENTENCING GUIDELINES AND POLICY STATEMENTS 1.2 (West 1993 ed.) [hereinafter Sentencing Guidelines].
[3] *Id.* at 1.3-1.4. For a critical view of that omission, *see* Andrew von Hirsch, FEDERAL SENTENCING GUIDELINES: THE UNITED STATES AND CANADIAN SCHEMES COMPARED, 4 OCCASIONAL PAPERS FROM THE CENTER FOR RESEARCH IN CRIME AND JUSTICE, NEW YORK UNIVERSITY SCHOOL OF LAW 3-6 (1988) [hereinafter VON HIRSCH].
[4] *See* Sentencing Guidelines, *supra* note 2, at 1.5.
[5] *Id.* at 1.5-1.6.

encountered, *e.g.*, role in the commission of an offense, presence of firearms and the amount of money taken.[6]

(c) *Judicial Departures From Guideline Sentences.*

(i) *Congressional objectives.* The second basic policy adopted by the Commission related to judicial freedom to depart from guideline sentences. It took a relatively relaxed view of the matter by not invoking the congressional allocation of power to courts to depart from standard sentences only when the Sentencing Commission had not taken into account an aggravating or mitigating circumstance.[7] It denominated each of its guidelines as a "'heartland,' a set of typical cases embodying the conduct that each guideline describes."[8] Although it has specified some factors that cannot be taken as grounds for departure, the courts can consider any ground for departure that is presented "in an unusual case."[9] The Commission took that view for two reasons. One is the difficulty of capturing the vast range of potential human conduct in a single set of guidelines. The second is an assumption that federal courts will not depart frequently from guidelines, even though they are legally empowered to do so.[10] If that assumption should prove wrong in application, the Commission can address it through modifications in guidelines.[11]

(ii) *Guideline coverage.* The Sentencing Guidelines acknowledge two patterns of judicial departure from guidelines: (1) An authorized departure based on analogy or other numerical or nonnumerical suggestions contained in commission policy statements.[12] The Commission anticipated that most departures would reflect its suggestions, and that departures outside those parameters might well be viewed as unreasonable by federal courts of appeals.[13] (2) Departures for which no commission guidelines exist.[14] The Commission has listed some grounds for departure,[15] but believed that other grounds for departure may well be encountered, although they should be highly unusual.[16]

(d) *Multiple Count Convictions.* The guidelines address the problem of multiple violations of federal criminal law, each of which is reflected in separate counts of indictments or informations. They do not, however, simply multiply the penalties appropriate for an individual count by a factor reflecting the number of aggregate counts, but rather provide for a measured augmentation.[17] The principles, as summarized by the Commission, are rather straightforward: (1) If conduct involves fungible items like amounts of controlled substances or items of money or property, the amounts are cumulated and the

---

[6]*Id.* at 1.6. The Commission thought the functional differences between real and charge offense systems would not be great in practice because the bulk of federal criminal sentencing relates to a rather short list of federal crimes that in effect allows defendants to be charged with the conduct in which they actually have engaged. *Id.*

[7] 18 U.S.C.A. § 3553(b) (West Supp. 1993).

[8] Sentencing Guidelines, *supra* note 2, at 1.6.

[9]*Id.* at 1.6-1.7.

[10]*Id.* at 1.7.

[11]*Id.*

[12]*Id.* at 8.

[13]*Id.*

[14]*Id.*

[15]*Id.* Ch. 5, Part H.

[16]*Id.* Ch. 1, Part A at 8.

[17]*Id.* Ch. 1, Part. A at 8.

B. PRESUMPTIVE SENTENCING: "JUST DESERTS" THEORY

guidelines apply to the total amount.[18] (2) In other instances, the offense level for the most serious conduct is increased on a somewhat diminishing scale to reflect the fact of conviction on the remaining counts.[19] If, however, a single transaction has arbitrarily been charged in multiple counts, the usual augmentation will not occur by virtue of a judicial exercise of the power to depart from guidelines in order to generate a mitigated sentence.[20]

(e) *Sentencing Ranges.* The Commission used as its starting point for determining sentencing ranges the estimated average sentences being served within each category of offense, believing that wide disparity would be eliminated through application of the guidelines.[21] Critics, however, have maintained that in fact the guideline ranges have resulted in an increase in the severity of federal sentences.[22] The Commission did not anticipate any significant impact on federal prison population, because it thought increases would be attributable to other factors;[23] again, critics have disagreed with that assessment.[24]

(f) *The Sentencing Table.* The core of the Commission's system is its sentencing table,[25] the vertical axis of which rests on 43 levels of offenses and the horizontal axis of which consists of six criminal history categories [*see* Table I]. The junction of the two axes indicates the normal range of sentences that is appropriate in counterpart cases. Each level overlaps to a certain extent with the levels in the preceding and succeeding rows, as a means to discourage unnecessary litigation, because a difference in adjacent levels may generate no sentencing differences.[26]

TABLE I

SENTENCING TABLE
(in months of imprisonment)

Criminal History Category (Criminal History Points)

Offense Level	I (0 or 1)	II (2 or 3)	III (4, 5, 6)	IV (7, 8, 9)	V (10, 11, 12)	VI (13 or more)
1	0-6	0-6	0-6	0-6	0-6	0-6
2	0-6	0-6	0-6	0-6	0-6	1-7
3	0-6	0-6	0-6	0-6	2-8	3-9
4	0-6	0-6	0-6	2-8	4-10	6-12
5	0-6	0-6	1-7	4-10	6-12	9-15
6	0-6	1-7	2-8	6-12	9-15	12-18
7	0-6	2-8	4-10	8-14	12-18	15-21
8	0-6	4-10	6-12	10-16	15-21	18-24
9	4-10	6-12	8-14	12-18	18-24	21-27

---

[18] *Id.*
[19] *Id.*
[20] *Id.*
[21] *Id.* at 9.
[22] *See* von Hirsch, *supra* note 3, at 7-9.
[23] *See* Sentencing Guidelines, *supra* note 2, at 9.
[24] *See* von Hirsch, *supra* note 3, at 6-7.
[25] *See Sentencing Guidelines* at 5.2. The table is reproduced on the following two pages.
[26] *See* Sentencing Guidelines, *supra* note 2, Ch. 5, Part. A.

Offense Level	I (0 or 1)	II (2 or 3)	III (4, 5, 6)	IV (7, 8, 9)	V (10, 11, 12)	VI (13 or more)
10	6-12	8-14	10-16	15-21	21-27	24-30
11	8-14	10-16	12-18	18-24	24-30	27-33
12	10-16	12-18	15-21	21-27	27-33	30-37
13	12-18	15-21	18-24	24-30	30-37	33-41
14	15-21	18-24	21-27	27-33	33-41	37-46
15	18-24	21-27	24-30	30-37	37-46	41-51
16	21-27	24-30	27-33	33-41	41-51	46-57
17	24-30	27-33	30-37	37-46	46-57	51-63
18	27-33	30-37	33-41	41-51	51-63	57-71
19	30-37	33-41	37-46	46-57	57-71	63-78
20	33-41	37-46	41-51	51-63	63-78	70-87
21	37-46	41-51	46-57	57-71	70-87	77-96
22	41-51	46-57	51-63	63-78	77-96	84-105
23	46-57	51-63	57-71	70-87	84-105	92-115
24	51-63	57-71	63-78	77-96	92-115	100-125
25	57-71	63-78	70-87	84-105	100-125	110-137
26	63-78	70-87	78-97	92-115	110-137	120-150
27	70-87	78-97	87-108	100-125	120-150	130-162
28	78-97	87-108	97-121	110-137	130-162	140-175
29	87-108	97-121	108-135	121-151	140-175	151-188
30	97-121	108-135	121-151	135-168	151-188	168-210
31	108-135	121-151	135-168	151-188	168-210	188-235
32	121-151	135-168	151-188	168-210	188-235	210-262
33	135-168	151-188	168-210	188-235	210-262	235-293
34	151-188	168-210	188-235	210-262	235-293	262-327
35	168-210	188-235	210-262	235-293	262-327	292-365
36	188-235	210-262	235-293	262-327	292-365	324-405
37	210-262	235-293	262-327	292-365	324-405	360-life
38	235-293	262-327	292-365	324-405	360-life	360-life
39	262-327	292-365	324-405	360-life	360-life	360-life
40	292-365	324-405	360-life	360-life	360-life	360-life
41	324-405	360-life	360-life	360-life	360-life	360-life
42	360-life	360-life	360-life	360-life	360-life	360-life
43	life	life	life	life	life	life

(g) *Constitutionality of Sentencing Guidelines.* In *Mistretta v. United States*,[27] the Supreme Court affirmed the basic constitutional validity of the United States Sentencing Commission and its work. The Court described the century-old modified indeterminate sentencing system in force in the federal jurisdiction, directed at the rehabilitation of offenders. Both sentencing and parole were "predictive and discretionary," as the Court itself had characterized them.[28] To the Court, federal sentencing had never been thought to be assigned by the Constitution to the exclusive jurisdiction of any one of the three branches of government. Congress has the power to fix the sentences for

---

[27] 488 U.S. 361 (1989).
[28] *Mistretta*, 488 U.S. at 364 (quoting Morrissey v. Brewer, 408 U.S. 471, 480 (1972)).

B. PRESUMPTIVE SENTENCING: "JUST DESERTS" THEORY

federal crimes and the scope of judicial discretion concerning sentencing, but nevertheless had long since abandoned a system of fixed penalties for each federal crime in favor of almost unfettered judicial discretion to assess sentence within the broad limits established through penal legislation; that broad judicial discretion had been enhanced further through the power of sentencing courts to suspend sentences and order probation. Paroling authority, however, had been placed by Congress in the executive branch.[29]

Congressional dissatisfaction with the "outmoded rehabilitation model" and the serious disparities in sentencing generated through indeterminate sentencing had led Congress to institute a system of mandatory sentencing guidelines to be generated by the new United States Sentencing Commission established through CCCA. Mistretta had argued that by delegating its powers to the Commission, Congress had managed an excessive assignment of its discretionary powers that violated the nondelegation doctrine derived from the Constitution.

The Court, however, disagreed. The nondelegation doctrine does not bar Congress from obtaining assistance from its coordinate branches of government; indeed, "our jurisprudence has been driven by a practical understanding that in our increasingly complex society, replete with ever changing and more technical problems, Congress cannot do its job absent an ability to delegate power under broad general directives."[30] The Constitution simply requires that Congress clearly delineate the general policy, the public agency which is to apply it and the boundaries of the delegated authority.[31] Congress had achieved that quite satisfactorily in the Sentencing Reform Act of 1984 by setting three goals and four purposes which it required the Commission to pursue. Beyond that, it had fixed the general range within which minimum and maximum terms comprehended in a sentencing guideline could allow sentencing discretion, using then-existing average federal sentences as a starting point, and had expressed its views concerning a number of factors that the Commission either was or was not to consider in setting offense and offender categories.

At the same time, the Court recognized, as Mistretta had urged, that the Commission had significant discretion in setting its guidelines, for example, in determining the relative severity of federal crimes, assessing the relative weight of offender characteristics listed by Congress, determining which crimes had been punished too leniently in the past and which too severely, and ascertaining the types of crimes and criminals that should be considered similar for purposes of sentencing.[32] Nevertheless, the Court thought that the processes of developing proportionate penalties for hundreds of separate crimes committed by a virtually limitless array of offenders constitute "precisely the sort of intricate, labor-intensive task for which delegation to an expert body is especially appropriate."[33] Hence, Congress had not delegated power to the Commission in an unconstitutional fashion.

---

[29] *Id.* at 364-65.
[30] *Id.* at 372.
[31] *Id.* at 372-73.
[32] *Id.* at 377.
[33] *Id.* at 379.

The *Mistretta* Court then looked at the defense contention that the Commission and its work violated the separation of powers principle, an issue which the Court had addressed in the preceding term in the context of the constitutionality of the independent counsel (special prosecutor) provisions of federal ethics legislation.[34] The Court, therefore, had rejected the notion that the three branches of government must be entirely separate and distinct; instead, security against governmental tyranny over which the Founders were concerned, *i.e.*, the accumulation of excessive authority in a single branch, does not lie "in a hermetic division between the Branches, but in a carefully crafted system of checked and balanced power within each Branch."[35] In light of that constitutional principle, the Court found no merit in Mistretta's contentions that the Sentencing Commission and its activities had breached the separation of powers doctrine.

First, it noted the placement of the Commission within the judicial branch even though it is not a court and exercises no judicial power. Anomaly or innovation, however, does not violate the separation of powers theory. Location of the Commission in the judicial branch would not be unconstitutional unless Congress had vested in it powers that either are more appropriately performed by the other branches or undermine the integrity of the judiciary.[36] The judicial branch has been entrusted with nonadjudicatory functions, including judicial rulemaking and the administration of the federal probation service, but that is not unconstitutional if extrajudicial activities bear a close relationship to the central mission of the judiciary, are consonant with its integrity and are not more appropriately to be exercised by either of the two other branches.[37] On that basis, the Court found no impediment to establishing within the judicial branch a sentencing commission to develop guidelines bearing on the clear judicial function of sentencing in criminal cases.[38]

If federal judges are bound by those guidelines, so are they bound by procedural rules; the Court found no difference between the two, even though it acknowledged Mistretta's point that rule-making and guideline-determining are not precisely analogous. Nevertheless, the significantly political character of the Commission's work did not render unconstitutional the placement of the Commission within the judicial branch. The Commission's powers were not united with the powers of the judiciary in a way significant to a separation-of-powers analysis. Nor was the power of the judicial branch enhanced at the expense of the other branches because of the placement of the Commission there. In short, the creation within the judicial arm of an entity responsible to develop sentencing guidelines could not possibly be construed as preventing the judiciary from accomplishing its constitutionally-assigned functions; despite the substantive nature of its work, the Commission was neither incongruous with nor inappropriate to the judiciary. Neither did it involve a degree of political authority unsuitable for a nonpolitical branch, since guidelines do not bind or regulate the primary conduct of the public or vest in the judiciary

---

[34] Morrison v. Olson, 487 U.S. 654 (1988).
[35] *Mistretta*, 488 U.S. at 381.
[36] *Id.* at 385.
[37] *Id.*
[38] *Id.* at 388-89.

B. PRESUMPTIVE SENTENCING: "JUST DESERTS" THEORY

the legislative responsibility to establish minimum or maximum penalties for every crime; instead, they only fetter the discretion of judges to impose sentences within the broad limits established by Congress.[39]

The Court then addressed the matter of the composition of the Commission, which embraces both federal judges and nonjudges. It found no bar to the performance by federal judges of nonjudicial services, as illustrated by the many historical occurrences during which they had done so. Although some conceivable forms of extrajudicial service might be incompatible with or inappropriate to continuing service on the bench, that would be because they would undermine the integrity of the judicial branch. The Court did not believe that service on the Commission was forced on any individual federal judges; the judicial members of the Commission were volunteers in a functional sense, and there was no real basis to expect that those judicial members would have to recuse themselves frequently in the course of their strictly judicial functions, thus affecting the work of the judiciary adversely. The Court was somewhat more troubled by Mistretta's contention that the political work of the Commission, in which its judicial members would participate, would undermine public confidence in the disinterestedness of the judiciary, but thought that on balance there was an insufficient danger of such a consequence that it would outweigh the need for judicial participation in the Commission's work as a means of presenting "a uniquely judicial view on the uniquely judicial subject of sentencing."[40]

Finally, the Court focused on the issue of whether presidential control over the nomination and removal of commissioners would prevent the judicial branch from performing its constitutionally-assigned functions. To the Court, however, the notion that a power of appointing judges to the Commission (subject to confirmation by the Senate) would give the President an actual or potential influence over the judiciary in performing its judicial functions was "fanciful."[41] If judicial integrity were that frail, the Court thought, it would have failed long since. The power to remove commissioners likewise posed "a similarly negligible threat to judicial independence."[42] Because the President lacks a power to affect the tenure or compensation of Article III judges, removal of judges serving as commissioners would create no ability to coerce those judges in the exercise of their judicial duties, particularly because they can be removed only for good cause.[43]

As the Court summarized its *Mistretta* holding: [I]n creating the Sentencing Commission — an unusual hybrid in structure and authority — Congress neither delegated excessive legislative power nor upset the constitutionally mandated balance of powers among the coordinate Branches. The Constitution's structural protections do not prohibit Congress from delegating to an expert body located within the Judicial Branch the intricate task of formulating sentencing guidelines consistent with such significant statutory direction as is present here. Nor does our system of checked and balanced authority

---
[39] *Id.* at 396-97.
[40] *Id.* at 408.
[41] *Id.* at 409.
[42] *Id.* at 410.
[43] *Id.* at 411.

prohibit Congress from calling upon the accumulated wisdom and experience of the Judicial Branch in creating policy on a matter uniquely within the ken of judges....[44]

(b) *Determining Applicable Guidelines.*

(i) *Offense guideline determination.* The first step is to ascertain an offense guideline section for the specific offense, based on and in the order listed in Chapter Two of the *Sentencing Guidelines*;[45] if the statute underlying the conviction embraces a variety of conduct which might implicate the guidelines, the court is to select the appropriate one, based upon the nature of the offense conduct charged against the defendant.[46] A lengthy list of federal offenses constitutes the body of Chapter Two, each carrying a designated base offense level. However, stipulations to additional offenses in the context of a plea of guilty or nolo contendere are to be treated as if the defendant had been convicted of separate counts charging those offenses.[47]

(ii) *Determining applicable guideline range.* Next, the court should determine the applicable guideline range, set out in general in § 1B1.3 of the *Sentencing Guidelines*, governing relevant conduct, *i.e.*, factors that determine the guideline range for given offenses. Basically, the conduct relevant to determining the applicable guideline range includes the following factors. For purposes of Chapters Two (offense conduct) and Three (adjustments), unless otherwise specified, the base offense level where the guideline specifies more than one base offense level; specific offense characteristics, cross references in Chapter Two and adjustments in Chapter Three are determined on the following bases:

(1) All acts or omissions committed, aided, abetted counseled, commanded or procured by the defendant that otherwise were in furtherance of that offense and, in the instance of jointly undertaken criminal activity, all reasonably foreseeable acts and omissions of others in furtherance of the jointly undertaken criminal activity.[48]

(2) Solely with respect to offenses of a character for which § 3D1.2(d) requires grouping of multiple counts, all acts and omissions that were part of the same course of conduct or common scheme or plan as the offense of conviction.[49]

(3) All harm or risk of harm resulting in the preceding two subparagraphs, if the harm or risk was caused intentionally, recklessly or by criminal negligence, and all harm or risk that was the object of those acts or omissions.[50]

(4) Other information specified in the applicable guideline.[51]

In determining the criminal history category and the applicability of the career offender and criminal livelihood guidelines, courts are to consider all

---

[44] *Id.* at 412.
[45] Sentencing Guidelines, *supra* note 2, § 1B1.2(a).
[46] *Id.* § 8B1.2, comment (n.1).
[47] *Id.* § 1B1.2(a). *See also id.* § 1B1.2, comment (n.1).
[48] *Id.* § 1B1.3(a)(1).
[49] *Id.* § 1B1.3(a)(2).
[50] *Id.* § 1B1.3(a)(3). "Harm" includes bodily injury, monetary loss, property damage and any resulting harm. *Id.* § 1B1.3, comment (n.3). Harm that is risked is not to be treated as harm inflicted unless a guideline specifies the contrary. *Id.*, (n.4).
[51] *Id.* § 1B1.3(a)(4).

conduct relevant to a determination of the factors enumerated in the various guidelines in Chapter Four.[52]

Once the guideline range has been ascertained preliminarily, the court may consider, for purposes either of determining the sentence to be imposed within that range or of departing from the guideline range, all information about the background, character and conduct of the defendant, unless the information otherwise is prohibited by law.[53]

AMERICAN BAR ASSOCIATION STANDARDS FOR CRIMINAL JUSTICE (2d ed. 1981) SENTENCING ALTERNATIVES AND PROCEDURES

§ 18-3.1 and Commentary pp. 18-187 to 18-191.

Standard 18-3.1. Sentencing guidelines

(a) The legislature should establish a guideline drafting agency in the judicial branch empowered to promulgate presumptively appropriate sentencing ranges within the statutory limits. The creation of such a body is recommended because:

> (i) unstructured judicial discretion tends to produce unwarranted sentencing disparities among similarly situated offenders;
>
> (ii) guidelines ranges facilitate a reduction in the excessive indeterminacy that now characterizes many penal codes; and
>
> (iii) the administrative agency approach makes possible greater flexibility, specificity, and oversight than the legislature could achieve directly.

(b) The proper function of sentencing guidelines is to shape and structure judicial discretion, not replace it with mechanical rules. Accordingly, the legislature should counterbalance this delegation of authority to such an agency with a clear statement of the responsibility of the sentencing court to depart from the applicable guideline range when substantial mitigating or aggravating factors are present that were not adequately taken into consideration by the guideline drafting agency.

(c) The following standards should apply to sentencing guidelines or any similar system of presumptive sentencing:

> (i) In recognition that deserved punishment need not necessarily take the form of institutional confinement, a system of guidelines should take into account a variety of sentencing alternatives, including probation, "split sentences," fines, community service, and other intermediate sanctions;
>
> (ii) Except in the case of short-term sentences (where a single guideline range may be appropriate), separate guidelines ranges should generally be promulgated for both the maximum and minimum terms to be imposed by the court, since use of such a dual guideline approach reduces the

---
[52]*Id.* § 1B1.3(b).
[53]*Id.* § 1B1.4

possibility that factors affecting the determination of one term of the sentence will arbitrarily influence the setting of the other term. Different considerations also should apply with respect to the desirable breadth of these two guideline ranges. The guideline range for the maximum term should be relatively narrow and as a general rule should not exceed two years; in contrast, in the case of guidelines applicable to the minimum term, the governing consideration should be to ensure that minimum terms do not so closely approach the maximum so as to prevent the effective operation of an independent system of early release administered by parole or correctional authorities. This question of the desirable degree of indeterminacy which should exist between minimum and maximum terms is more specifically addressed in standards 18-4.1 to 18-4.3, and a scale dependent on the length of the maximum term is there recommended;

(iii) Guidelines should focus on more than the offense of conviction alone, and should seek to relate combinations of offense-offender characteristics to presumptive sentencing ranges; and

(iv) Guidelines should seek to reflect a current community consensus about the relative gravity of offenses. In order to achieve proportionality among offenses, the guideline drafting agency should not rely simply upon historical sentencing averages, but should instead seek to construct a normative ranking of offenses consistent with contemporary community attitudes, subject to the limits imposed by the crime categories established by the legislature (standard 18-2.1(a)). Periodic review of any such offense severity scale in light of changing societal values should also be required.

Commentary

Background

Nowhere is the problem of sentence disparity more acute than in the American judicial system. Wide sentencing frames, almost complete discretion of the sentencing judge within those frames, and the lack of effective guidelines allow sentences to differ widely for no other reason than that the one was set by Judge A and the other by Judge B.[1]

So opens one of the most recent and authoritative studies in the burgeoning literature on the problem of sentencing disparity.[2] Responsibility for the

---

[1] Hans Zeisel & Shari Seidman Diamond, *Search for Sentencing Equity: Sentence Review in Massachusetts and Connecticut,* 1977 A.B.F. RES. J. 881, 883-884.

[2] For other significant studies of sentencing disparities, see ANTHONY PARTRIDGE & WILLIAM ELDRIDGE, THE SECOND CIRCUIT SENTENCING STUDY (1974); JOHN HOGARTH, SENTENCING AS A HUMAN PROCESS (1971); EDWARD GREEN, JUDICIAL ATTITUDES IN SENTENCING (1961); R. HOOD, SENTENCING IN MAGISTRATES' COURTS (1962); Lawrance P. Tiffany, Yakov Avichai & Geoffrey W. Peters, *A Statistical Analysis of Sentencing in Federal Courts: Defendants Convicted After Trial, 1967-1968,* 4 J. LEGAL STUD. 369 (1975); Whitney North Seymour, Jr. *1972 Sentencing Study for the Southern District of New York,* 45 N.Y. ST. B.J. 163 (1973), reprinted in CONGRESSIONAL RECORD, H.R. 1313, March 1, 1973; INSTITUTE FOR LAW AND SOCIAL RESEARCH, INTERIM REPORT ON SENTENCING IN THE SUPERIOR COURT OF THE DISTRICT OF COLUMBIA (1977); MARVIN ZALMAN, CHARLES OSTROM, PHILLIP GULLIAMS & GARRET PEASLEE, SENTENCING IN MICHIGAN (1979).

B. PRESUMPTIVE SENTENCING: "JUST DESERTS" THEORY

erratic, indeed sometimes random, variations in the sentences assigned similar defendants must to a substantial extent be ascribed to the legislature, which has permitted a vacuum of standards to exist at sentencing, with the result that inconsistent policies and philosophies will of necessity be pursued by individual judges who have nothing to guide them.

How should this vacuum be filled? In overview, two basic responses are possible: (a) the legislature could adopt either mandatory penalties or narrow sentencing ranges under which penalties are fixed in advance for the crime, or (b) an administrative agency mechanism could be developed to promulgate and revise guidelines on a continuing basis. The dangers of the first approach have already been stressed: (1) Inflation of the penalty structure and an increase in average time served seem likely to result. (2) Some loss of the criminal justice system's capacity for individualization, either to mitigate the severity of the penal code or to respond to special needs and exceptional factors, also seems inevitable. (3) Legislatively fixed sentences, once established, are likely to remain static for years despite changes in community attitudes about the severity of the crime or new developments in criminological research concerning the prediction of recidivism. (4) When legislative changes do come, they are more apt to be an ad hoc response to a notorious crime or to short-term political pressures, and thus the danger of overreactions that distort the penalty structure is increased. (5) The legislature is too remote from both the sentencing process and the criminal justice system generally to understand the factors underlying existing sentencing practices or to be able to respond to special circumstances and conditions (e.g., prison overcrowding or patterns of evasion that may develop through plea bargaining). Given these disadvantages, this edition has elected to steer a middle course between the extremes of flat time sentencing and open-ended indeterminacy by recommending greater reliance on an administrative agency to draft sentencing guidelines. This position is taken not just because of the advantages such an approach offers but because there simply is no acceptable alternative.

Many of the advantages such an administrative agency approach offers are not immediately obvious. First among these is the relative ability of such an agency to assess, synthesize, and respond to far greater amounts of information than the legislature can.[3] The capacity of legislative bodies to undertake research, make empirical findings, and tailor reforms to detailed policy considerations is frankly limited. There is merit to the observation of others that the legislature must ultimately rely "on its collective intuition" in framing a sentencing policy and cannot respond with adequate subtlety to the diversity of offense-offender combinations that come before the sentencing court.[4] No

---

[3] In particular, an administrative agency can take cognizance of prison populations and existing sentencing practices, can respond to new crime patterns and the possible need for additional deterrence, and can incorporate new evidence about the factors associated with recidivism into its guideline table. In short, these standards agree with the following conclusion reached by the leading study on sentencing guidelines: "A dynamic criminal justice system ... requires a sentencing agency to possess the flexibility to change with changed circumstances. Adaptability to changes in population concentrations, societal attitudes to given offenses, or prison conditions is the hallmark of informed, on-the-spot, timely, judicial sentencing and not that of a distant legislature." LESLIE T. WILKINS, JACK M. KRESS, DONALD M. GOTTFREDSON, JOSEPH C. CALPIN, & ARTHUR M. GELMAN, SENTENCING GUIDELINES: STRUCTURING JUDICIAL DISCRETION 4 (1978).

[4] *Id.* (noting also the inability of the legislature to develop any empirically derived data base).

doubt the legislature must make some moral evaluations, particularly about the relative gravity of offenses, in order to express the collective judgment of the community. Standard 18-2.1 recognizes this need and calls upon the legislature to reorder and rationalize the penal code into a limited number of graded categories. But to urge the legislature to go further and prescribe penalties with greater specificity is to overextend its role unrealistically and in so doing preempt the judicial system from any meaningful opportunity to shape sentencing policy. As others have concluded, there are significant reasons for believing that any such attempt to eliminate judicial discretion, rather than only structure it, will be resisted and ultimately thwarted. In the process, sentencing disparities may even be aggravated as implicit policies develop that conflict with the explicit sentencing policy adopted by the legislature.[5]

Beyond the obvious virtues — greater sophistication, specificity, and flexibility — that a judicial sentencing agency can bring to the formulation of sentencing policies, there is a second major reason for preferring such an approach to a legislative model for reform. Unlike legislatively fixed or restricted sentences, guidelines do not represent a retreat from the goal of individualization. On the contrary, their adoption offers a means of achieving better individualization because they provide a framework within which more information can be brought to bear, more variables considered, and the exercise of discretion thus qualitatively improved. In short, they not only assist the judge in avoiding unwarranted disparities but, by in effect providing the court with a checklist of factors that should be considered, they can also serve to enhance the court's consciousness of factors which indicate that differences in treatment are indeed thoroughly warranted.

A fundamental misconception that tends to haunt discussions of guideline systems is the idea that the goals of individualization and reduction of unwarranted disparities are necessarily inconsistent. Empirically, social scientists studying dispositional decisions have found that only a relatively small number of items of information are typically used by decision makers,[6] in part because of the difficulties the human mind has in absorbing more than a limited quantity of data at a time or in suspending judgment until all the relevant information has been collectively appraised.[7] In addition, related studies have shown that different decision makers "process" information in different ways, each seeking different kinds of information and evaluating it according to a personal calculus.[8] Further complicating the problems of en-

---

[5] Judicial opposition to mandatory sentences and other means of reducing judicial discretion has been noted by a number of commentators and lends further support to a compromise guideline approach that factors existing sentencing practices into the guideline table and seeks to accommodate the understandable desire of the judiciary to preserve their autonomy. See Gerald Robin, *Judicial Resistance to Sentencing Accountability*, 21 CRIME & DELINQUENCY 201 (1975); Marvin Zalman, *A Commission Model of Sentencing*, 53 NOTRE DAME LAW. 266, 284-285 (1977); RICHARD NIMMER, THE NATURE OF SYSTEM CHANGE 189-192 (1978) (discussing the limited impact of mandatory reforms at sentencing and elsewhere).

[6] Sentencing Guidelines, *supra* note 3, at 25; LESLIE T. WILKINS, EVALUATION OF PENAL MEASURES 106 (1969); *see also id.*, at 12-15.

[7] John Hogarth, *supra* note 2, at 249, 261, 302-303, 390; Leslie T. Wilkins, *Information Overload: Peace or War with the Computer*, in PAROLE (W. Amos & C. Newman eds. 1975).

[8] This literature is reviewed in John C. Coffee, Jr. *The Repressed Issues of Sentencing: Accountability, Predictability, and Equality in the Era of the Sentencing Commission*, 66 GEO. L.J. 975, 983-987 (1978).

suring reasonable consistency has been the finding made in several studies of presentence reports of a tendency toward inconsistency. Aspects of an offender discussed in one presentence report may be ignored in a report on another offender, although the same factors, whether positive or negative, are present in the case of both offenders.[9] The result, of course, is a false comparison. Guideline systems should at least partially alleviate each of these problems. They assist the decision maker to factor more information into the personal sentencing equation. They similarly increase the accountability of the process by providing greater assurance that variables society considers important will be given attention by the sentencing court. Finally, by expressly identifying factors that should be at least considered in every case and giving them some form of numerical weight, guidelines should improve the consistency of the informational resources utilized at sentencing.

Guidelines are not by themselves a substantive sentencing policy. Rather, they are a procedural means of making explicit a basic set of sentencing principles and of translating rhetoric into reality. By highlighting decisions that appear to deviate from the sentencing policy underlying the guidelines, such a system facilitates the task of appellate review and in the long run should tend to minimize the covert forms of evasion to which flat time sentencing proposals remain vulnerable. Although these standards do endorse some limited sentencing principles in standards 18-2.2 and 18-3.2, a guideline system could equally well be utilized to implement a sentencing policy oriented toward retribution or rehabilitation (directions that these standards clearly reject)....

NOTE

The requirement of guided discretion in capital cases, discussed in the editorial note *supra* pp. 858-869, rests on the uniqueness, especially the utter irrevocability, of the death penalty. Hence, the rule of guided discretion does not extend to require sentencing guidelines for noncapital sanctions. *Britton v. Rogers,* 631 F.2d 571, 578-79 (8th Cir. 1980).

SECTION IV. Forms of Sanctions
A. PROBATION

MODEL PENAL CODE, § 7.01

[The text of this section appears in Appendix A.]

TITLE 18, UNITED STATES CODE (1988)

Section 3551

....

---

[9] *See, e.g.,* Yona Cohn, *Criteria for the Probation Officer's Recommendations to the Juvenile Court Judge,* 9 CRIME & DELINQUENCY 262 (1963); Robert M. Carter & Leslie T. Wilkins, *Some Factors in Sentencing Policy,* 58 J. CRIM. L.C. & P.S. 503-511 (1967); Robert M. Carter, *The Presentence Report and the Decision-making Process,* 4 J. RES. CRIME & DELINQUENCY 203 (1967).

(b) INDIVIDUALS. — An individual found guilty of an offense shall be sentenced, in accordance with the provisions of section 3553, to —

(1) a term of probation as authorized by subchapter B;
(2) a fine as authorized by subchapter C; or
(3) a term of imprisonment as authorized by subchapter D....

(c) ORGANIZATIONS. — An organization found guilty of an offense shall be sentenced, in accordance with the provisions of section 3553, to —

(1) a term of probation as authorized by subchapter B; or
(2) a fine as authorized by subchapter C....

Section 3561

(a) IN GENERAL. — A defendant who has been found guilty of an offense may be sentenced to a term of probation unless —

(1) the offense is a Class A or Class B felony;
(2) the offense is an offense for which probation has been expressly precluded; or
(3) the defendant is sentenced at the same time to a term of imprisonment for the same or a different offense.

The liability of a defendant for any unexecuted fine or other punishment imposed as to which probation is granted shall be fully discharged by the fulfillment of the terms and conditions of probation.

(b) AUTHORIZED TERMS. — The authorized terms of probation are —

(1) for a felony, not less than one nor more than five years;
(2) for a misdemeanor, not more than five years; and
(3) for an infraction, not more than one year.

NOTE

Probation revocation procedures are subject to procedural due process requirements, albeit less onerous ones than govern criminal proceedings generally. *See* Gagnon v. Scarpelli, 411 U.S. 778 (1973); *cf.* Morrissey v. Brewer, 408 U.S. 471 (1972) (parole revocation procedures).

BEARDEN v. GEORGIA

Supreme Court of the United States
461 U.S. 660 (1983)

JUSTICE O'CONNOR delivered the opinion of the Court.

The question in this case is whether the Fourteenth Amendment prohibits a State from revoking an indigent defendant's probation for failure to pay a fine and restitution. Its resolution involves a delicate balance between the acceptability, and indeed wisdom, of considering all relevant factors when determining an appropriate sentence for an individual and the impermissibility of imprisoning a defendant solely because of his lack of financial resources. We conclude that the trial court erred in automatically revoking probation because petitioner could not pay his fine, without determining that petitioner had not made sufficient bona fide efforts to pay or that adequate alternative forms of punishment did not exist. We therefore reverse the judgment of the Georgia Court of Appeals upholding the revocation of probation, and remand for a new sentencing determination.

I

In September 1980, petitioner was indicted for the felonies of burglary and theft by receiving stolen property. He pleaded guilty, and was sentenced on October 8, 1980. Pursuant to the Georgia First Offender's Act, the trial court did not enter a judgment of guilt, but deferred further proceedings and sentenced petitioner to three years on probation for the burglary charge and a concurrent one year on probation for the theft charge. As a condition of probation, the trial court ordered petitioner to pay a $500 fine and $250 in restitution. Petitioner was to pay $100 that day, $100 the next day, and the $550 balance within four months.

Petitioner borrowed money from his parents and paid the first $200. About a month later, however, petitioner was laid off from his job. Petitioner, who has only a ninth grade education and cannot read, tried repeatedly to find other work but was unable to do so. The record indicates that petitioner had no income or assets during this period.

Shortly before the balance of the fine and restitution came due in February 1981, petitioner notified the probation office he was going to be late with his payment because he could not find a job. In May 1981, the State filed a petition in the trial court to revoke petitioner's probation because he had not paid the balance. After an evidentiary hearing, the trial court revoked probation for failure to pay the balance of the fine and restitution, entered a conviction, and sentenced petitioner to serve the remaining portion of the probationary period in prison. The Georgia Court of Appeals, relying on earlier Georgia Supreme Court cases, rejected petitioner's claim that imprisoning him for inability to pay the fine violated the Equal Protection Clause of the Fourteenth Amendment. The Georgia Supreme Court denied review. Since other courts have held that revoking the probation of indigents for failure to pay fines does not violate the Equal Protection Clause, we granted certiorari to resolve this important issue in the administration of criminal justice....

The question presented here is whether a sentencing court can revoke a defendant's probation for failure to pay the imposed fine and restitution, absent evidence and findings that the defendant was somehow responsible for the failure or that alternative forms of punishment were inadequate. The parties ... have argued the question primarily in terms of equal protection, and debate vigorously whether strict scrutiny or rational basis is the appropriate standard of review. There is no doubt that the State has treated the petitioner differently from a person who did not fail to pay the imposed fine and therefore did not violate probation. To determine whether this differential treatment violates the Equal Protection Clause, one must determine whether, and under what circumstances, a defendant's indigent status may be considered in the decision whether to revoke probation. This is substantially similar to asking directly the due process question of whether and when it is fundamentally unfair or arbitrary for the State to revoke probation when an indigent is unable to pay the fine. Whether analyzed in terms of equal protection or due process, the issue cannot be resolved by resort to easy slogans or pigeonholes analysis, but rather requires a careful inquiry into such factors as "the nature of the individual interest affected, the extent to which it is affected, the rationality of the connection between legislative means and purpose, [and] the existence of alternative means for effectuating the purpose ...." *Williams v. Illinois,* [399 U.S. 235, 260 (1970)] (Harlan, J., concurring).

In analyzing this issue, of course, we do not write on a clean slate, for both *Williams* and *Tate* analyzed similar situations. The reach and limits of their holdings are vital to a proper resolution of the issue here. In *Williams*, a defendant was sentenced to the maximum prison term and fine authorized under the statute. Because of his indigency he could not pay the fine. Pursuant to another statute equating a $5 fine with a day in jail, the defendant was kept in jail for 101 days beyond the maximum prison sentence to "work out" the fine. The Court struck down the practice, holding that "[o]nce the State has defined the outer limits of incarceration necessary to satisfy its penological interests and policies, it may not then subject a certain class of convicted defendants to a period of imprisonment beyond the statutory maximum solely by reason of their indigency." 399 U.S., at 233-234. In *Tate v. Short,* 401 U.S. 395 (1971), we faced a similar situation, except that the statutory penalty there permitted only a fine. Quoting from a concurring opinion in *Morris v. Schoonfield,* 399 U.S. 508, 509 (1970), we reasoned that "the same constitutional defect condemned in *Williams* also inheres in jailing an indigent for failing to make immediately payment of any fine, whether or not the fine is accompanied by a jail term and whether or not the jail term of the indigent extends beyond the maximum term that may be imposed on a person willing and able to pay a fine." 401 U.S. at 398.

The rule of *Williams* and *Tate,* then, is that the State cannot "impos[e] a fine as a sentence and then automatically conver[t] it into a jail term solely because the defendant is indigent and cannot forthwith pay the fine in full." *Tate, supra,* at 398. In other words, if the State determines a fine or restitution to be the appropriate and adequate penalty for the crime, it may not thereafter imprison a person solely because he lacked the resources to pay it. Both *Williams* and *Tate* carefully distinguished this substantive limitation on the imprisonment of indigents from the situation where a defendant was at fault in failing to pay the fine. As the Court made clear in *Williams,* nothing in our decision today precludes imprisonment for willful refusal to pay a fine or court costs." 399 U.S., at 242, n.19. Likewise in *Tate,* the Court "emphasize[d] that our holding today does not suggest any constitutional infirmity in imprisonment of a defendant with the means to pay a fine who refuses or neglects to do so." 401 U.S., at 400.

This distinction, based on the reasons for non-payment, is of critical importance here. If the probationer has willfully refused to pay the fine or restitution when he has the means to pay, the State is perfectly justified in using
ment as a sanction to enforce collection.... Similarly, a probationer's
make sufficient bona fide efforts to seek employment or borrow

money in order to pay the fine or restitution may reflect an insufficient concern for paying the debt he owes to society for his crime. In such a situation, the State is likewise justified in revoking probation and using imprisonment as an appropriate penalty for the offense. But if the probationer has made all reasonable efforts to pay the fine or restitution, and yet cannot do so through no fault of his own, it is fundamentally unfair to revoke probation automatically without considering whether adequate alternative methods of punishing the defendant are available. This lack of fault provides a "substantial reaso[n] which justifie[s] or mitigate[s] the violation and make[s] revocation inappropriate."...

The State, of course, has a fundamental interest in appropriately punishing persons — rich and poor — who violate its criminal laws. A defendant's poverty in no way immunizes him from punishment. Thus, when determining initially whether the State's penological interests require imposition of a term of imprisonment, the sentencing court can consider the entire background of the defendant, including his employment history and financial resources.... As we said in *Williams v. Illinois,* "[a]fter having taken into consideration the wide range of factors underlying the exercise of his sentencing function, nothing we now hold precludes a judge from imposing on an indigent, as on any defendant, the maximum penalty prescribed by law." 399 U.S., at 243.

The decision to place the defendant on probation, however, reflects a determination by the sentencing court that the State's penological interests do not require imprisonment.... A probationer's failure to make reasonable efforts to repay his debt to society may indicate that this original determination needs reevaluation, and imprisonment may now be required to satisfy the State's interests. But a probationer who has made sufficient bona fide efforts to pay his fine and restitution, and who has complied with the other conditions of probation, has demonstrated a willingness to pay his debt to society and an ability to conform his conduct to social norms. The State nevertheless asserts three reasons why imprisonment is required to further its penal goals.

First, the State argues that revoking probation furthers its interest in ensuring that restitution be paid to the victims of crime. A rule that imprisonment may befall the probationer who fails to make sufficient bona fide efforts to pay restitution may indeed spur probationers to try hard to pay, thereby increasing the number of probationers who make restitution. Such a goal is fully served, however, by revoking probation only for persons who have not made sufficient bona fide efforts to pay. Revoking the probation of someone who through no fault of his own is unable to make restitution will not make restitution suddenly forthcoming. Indeed, such a policy may have the perverse effect of inducing the probationer to use illegal means to acquire funds to pay in order to avoid revocation.

Second, the State asserts that its interest in rehabilitating the probationer and protecting society requires it to remove him from the temptation of committing other crimes. This is no more than a naked assertion that a probationer's poverty by itself indicates he may commit crimes in the future and thus that society needs for him to be incapacitated. We have already indicated that a sentencing court can consider a defendant's employment history and financial resources in setting an initial punishment. Such considerations are a necessary part of evaluating the entire background of the defendant in order to tailor an appropriate sentence for the defendant and crime. But it must [be] remembered that the State is seeking here to use as the *sole* justification for imprisonment the poverty of a probationer who, by assumption, has demonstrated sufficient bona fide efforts to find a job and pay the fine and whom the State initially thought it unnecessary to imprison. Given the significant interest of the individual in remaining on probation, ... the State cannot justify incarcerating a probationer who has demonstrated sufficient bona fide efforts to repay his debt to society, solely by lumping him together with other poor persons and thereby classifying him as dangerous. This would be little more than punishing a person for his poverty.

Third, and most plausibly, the State argues that its interests in punishing the lawbreaker and deterring others from criminal behavior require it to revoke probation for failure to pay a fine or restitution. The State clearly has an interest in punishment and deterrence, but this interest can often be served fully by alternative means. As we said in *Williams,* 399 U.S., at 244, and reiterated in *Tate,* 401 U.S., at 399, "[t]he State is not powerless to enforce judgments against those financially unable to pay a fine." For example, the sentencing court could extend the time for making payments, or reduce the fine, or direct that the probationer perform some form of labor or public service in lieu of the fine. Justice Harlan appropriately observed in his concurring opinion in *Williams* that "the deterrent effect of a fine is apt to derive more from its pinch on the purse than the time of payment." *Ibid.,* at 265. Indeed, given the general flexibility of tailoring fines to the resources of a defendant, or even permitting the defendant to do specified work to satisfy the fine, see *Williams, supra,* at 244, n. 21, a sentencing court can often establish a reduced fine or alternate public service in lieu of a fine that adequately serves the State's goals of punishment and deterrence, given the defendant's diminished financial resources. Only if the sentencing court determines that alternatives to imprisonment are not adequate in a particular situation to meet the State's interest in punishment and deterrence may the State imprison a probationer who has made sufficient bona fide efforts to pay.

We hold, therefore, that in revocation proceedings for failure to pay a fine or restitution, a sentencing court must inquire into the reasons for the failure to pay. If the probationer willfully refused to pay or failed to make sufficient bona fide efforts legally to acquire the resources to pay, the court may revoke probation and sentence the defendant to imprisonment within the authorized range of its sentencing authority. If the probationer could not pay despite sufficient bona fide efforts to acquire the resources to do so, the court must consider alternate measures of punishment other than imprisonment. Only if alternate measures are not adequate to meet the State's interests in punishment and deterrence may the court imprison a probationer who has made sufficient bona fide efforts to pay. To do otherwise would deprive the probationer of his conditional freedom simply because, through no fault of his own, he cannot pay the fine. Such a deprivation would be contrary to the fundamental fairness required by the Fourteenth Amendment.

III

We return to the facts of this case. At the probation revocation hearing, the petitioner and his wife testified about their lack of income and assets and of his repeated efforts to obtain work. While the sentencing court commented on the availability of odd jobs such as lawnmowing, it made no finding that the petitioner had not made sufficient bona fide efforts to find work, and the record as it presently stands would not justify such a finding. This lack of findings is understandable, of course, for under the rulings of the Georgia Supreme Court such an inquiry would have been irrelevant to the constitutionality of revoking probation. The State argues that the sentencing court determined that the petitioner was no longer a good probation risk. In the absence of a determination that the petitioner did not make sufficient bona fide efforts to pay or to obtain employment in order to pay, we cannot read the opinion of the sentencing court as reflecting such a finding. Instead, the court curtly rejected counsel's suggestion that the time for making the payments be extended, saying that "the fallacy in that argument" is that the petitioner has long known he had to pay the $550 and yet did not comply with the court's prior order to pay. App. 45. The sentencing judge declared that "I don't know any way to enforce the prior orders of the Court but one way," which was to sentence him to imprisonment. *Ibid.*

The focus of the court's concern, then, was that the petitioner had disobeyed a prior court order to pay the fine, and for that reason must be imprisoned. But this is no more than imprisoning a person solely because he lacks funds to pay the fine, a practice we condemned in *Williams* and *Tate*. By sentencing petitioner to imprisonment simply because he could not pay the fine, without considering the reasons for the inability to pay or the propriety of reducing the fine or extending the time for payments or making alternative orders, the court automatically turned a fine into a prison sentence.

We do not suggest by our analysis of the present record that the State may not place the petitioner in prison. If, upon remand, the Georgia courts determine that petitioner did not make sufficient bona fide efforts to pay his fine, or determine that alternate punishment is not adequate to meet the State's interests in punishment and deterrence, imprisonment would be a permissible sentence. Unless such determinations are made, however, fundamental fairness requires that the petitioner remain on probation.

IV

The judgment is reversed, and the case is remanded for further proceedings not inconsistent with this opinion.

It is so ordered.

NOTE ON RESTITUTION

(a) *Authority to require restitution.* As part of the Victim and Witness Protection Act of 1982,[1] federal courts can enter orders of restitution in connec-

---

[1] 18 U.S.C. §§ 3579–3580 (1982 ed.), redesignated as §§ 3664–3665 (1988).

tion with sentencing. The 1984 statute[2] confirms that orders of restitution may be (but are not required to be) entered in connection with sentences imposed for any Title 18 offense or violations of certain provisions of the Federal Aviation Act of 1958.[3] It should be noted also that federal courts are now required to impose on all convicted felons who are placed on probation a condition of paying either (i) a fine or (ii) restitution, or (iii) performing community service.[4] If a probationer is sentenced to pay restitution, but does not perform, he or she violates probation.[5] Finally, an order of restitution can be made a condition governing a term of supervised release to follow imprisonment.[6]

The United States Sentencing Commission has issued policy statements affecting judicial use of restitution orders.[7]

(b) *Procedures preliminary to restitution orders.* Before a court orders restitution, it is required to give notice to both the defendant and the government prosecutor that it is considering that action.[8] On the motion of either side or on the court's own motion, the sentencing court must allow the parties to submit affidavits and written memoranda on matters relevant to the restitution decision,[9] afford counsel an opportunity in open court to make oral representations concerning the appropriateness of a restitution order,[10] and include in the statement of reasons it is required to make at sentencing coverage of the restitution dimension of its sentence.[11] The sentencing court also has discretion to employ additional procedures that will not unduly complicate or prolong the sentencing process, on the motion of either party or on the court's own motion.[12]

(c) *Implementation of restitution order.* An order of restitution must require a defendant either to make restitution directly to the victim or other person eligible to receive restitution, or to deliver the amount or property due in restitution to the Attorney General for transfer to the victim or ultimate recipient.[13]

(d) *Dischargeability in bankruptcy.* Whether a restitution order is dischargeable in bankruptcy is entirely a matter of statute. As the federal bankruptcy statutes have been construed by the United States Supreme Court, whether a discharge in bankruptcy extends to restitution orders in criminal cases turns on the form of the bankruptcy proceedings. In *Kelly v. Robinson*,[14] the Court concluded that the language of § 523(a)(7) of the Bankruptcy Code, protecting against discharge of any debt that reflects "a fine, penalty, or forfeiture payable to and for the benefit of a governmental unit, and ... not

---

[2] 18 U.S.C. § 3556 (1988).
[3] 49 U.S.C. § 1742(h), (*i*), (j), (n) (1988).
[4] 18 U.S.C. § 3563(a)(2) (1988).
[5] *Id.* §§ 3565, 3663(g).
[6] *Id.* § 3583(d).
[7] UNITED STATES SENTENCING COMMISSION, FEDERAL SENTENCING GUIDELINES § 5E1.1 (1993 ed.)
[8] 18 U.S.C. § 3553(d) (1988).
[9] *Id.* § 3553(d)(1).
[10] *Id.* § 3553(d)(2).
[11] *Id.* § 3553(d)(3).
[12] *Id.* § 3553(d)(4).
[13] *Id.* § 3663(f)(4).
[14] 479 U.S. 36 (1986).

compensation for actual pecuniary loss," does not compel a conclusion that restitution orders fall outside its provisions, particularly in the absence of clear preenactment materials confirming that conclusion. Criminal judgments imposing restitution do not operate primarily for the benefit of victims but for society as a whole and are directed at both punishment and rehabilitation. Victims have no control over the decision to impose a restitution requirement on convicted defendants or the amount of restitution. Moreover, restitution is governed not by measurable harm to victims but rather penal goals and each defendant's circumstances. An exclusion of restitution orders from discharges in bankruptcy, the Court believed, would best effectuate the will of Congress.[15]

However, a contrary conclusion pertains if the discharge in bankruptcy falls within Chapter 13 of the Bankruptcy Code[16] — the Court's holding in *Pennsylvania Department of Public Welfare v. Davenport*.[17] The Bankruptcy Code[18] defines "debt" as a "liability on a claim." A claim, in turn, is defined as a "right to payment, whether or not such a right is reduced to judgment, liquidated, unliquidated, fixed, contingent, matured, unmatured, disputed, undisputed, legal, equitable, secured, or unsecured."[19] The state argued that a restitution order was not a "right to payment" because there was no traditional debtor-creditor relationship with a criminal offender. The Court, however, disavowed any such statements as determinative in a Chapter 13 proceeding. *Kelly v. Robinson*, related exclusively to § 523(a)(7), which in turn related to the purpose of required compensation. The key term under § 1328(a) is a claim *qua* right to payment, and the state restitution obligation fits the definition.

The Supreme Court did not have the last word, however. Congress responded to *Davenport* by amending the bankruptcy statute[20] to add a provision excepting from discharge criminal restitution debts.

B. FINES

MODEL PENAL CODE § 7.02

[The text of this Section appears in Appendix A.]

TITLE 18, UNITED STATES CODE

Section 3551(b)-(c)

[The text of this Section appears at pp. 899-900 *supra*.]

Section 3571. Sentence of fine

(a) IN GENERAL. — A defendant who has been found guilty of an offense may be sentenced to pay a fine.

---

[15] *Id.* at 53.
[16] 11 U.S.C. § 1301 *et seq.* (1988).
[17] 495 U.S. 552 (1990).
[18] 11 U.S.C. § 101(11) (1988).
[19] *Id.* § 101(4)(A).
[20] 11 U.S.C.A. § 1328(a) (West Supp. 1993).

(b) FINES FOR INDIVIDUALS. — Except as provided in subsection (e) of this section, an individual who has been found guilty of an offense may be fined not more than the greatest of —

(1) the amount specified in the law setting forth the offense;
(2) the applicable amount under subsection (d) of this section;
(3) for a felony, not more than $250,000;
(4) for a misdemeanor resulting in death, not more than $250,000;
(5) for a Class A misdemeanor that does not result in death, not more than $100,000;
(6) for a Class B or C misdemeanor that does not result in death, not more than $5,000; or
(7) for an infraction, not more than $5,000.

(c) FINES FOR ORGANIZATIONS. — Except as provided in subsection (e) of this section, an organization that has been found guilty of an offense may be fined not more than the greatest of —

(1) the amount specified in the law setting forth the offense;
(2) the applicable amount under subsection (d) of this section;
(3) for a felony, not more than $500,000;
(4) for a misdemeanor resulting in death, not more than $500,000;
(5) for a Class A misdemeanor that does not result in death, not more than $200,000;
(6) for a Class B or C misdemeanor that does not result in death, not more than $10,000; or
(7) for an infraction, not more than $10,000.

(d) ALTERNATIVE FINE BASED ON GAIN OR LOSS. — If any person derives pecuniary gain from the offense, or if the offense results in pecuniary loss to a person other than the defendant, the defendant may be fined not more than the greater of twice the gross gain or twice the gross loss, unless imposition of a fine under this subsection would unduly complicate or prolong the sentencing process.

(e) SPECIAL RULE FOR LOWER FINE SPECIFIED IN SUBSTANTIVE PROVISION. — If a law setting forth an offense specifies no fine or a fine that is lower than the fine otherwise applicable under this section and such law by specific reference exempts the offense from the applicability of the fine otherwise applicable under this section, the defendant may not be fined more than the amount specified in the law setting forth the offense.

NOTES

1. On the impact of indigency on sentences to fines, review *Bearden v. Georgia, supra* at pp. 900-905.

2. Under the federal legislation, the following factors are to govern the imposition of sentences to pay fines:

(a) The defendant's income, earning capacity and financial resources.[1]

---

[1] 18 U.S.C.A. § 3572(a)(1) (West Supp. 1993).

B. FINES 909

(b) The burden a fine will impose on a defendant, any person financially dependent on the defendant, or any other person (including a government) that would be responsible for the welfare of any person financially dependent on the defendant, relative to the burden that alternative punishments would impose.[2]

(c) Pecuniary loss inflicted on others as a result of the offense.[3]

(d) Restitution, if ordered, and the amount of restitution.[4]

(e) The need to deprive the defendant of gains illegally obtained from the offense.[5]

(f) The ability of a defendant to pass along the expense of a fine to consumers or other persons.[6]

(g) In instances of organizations, the size of the organization, and measures taken by the organization to discipline the officers, directors, employees or agents responsible for the offense and to prevent a recurrence of the offense.[7]

The language of the statute is mandatory ("the court shall consider").[8] That has raised the issue of whether this has created a checklist to which sentencing courts must refer specifically in their statements of facts underlying sentences, or whether courts need refer only to the elements in the list they believe to be pertinent to their sentences. Precedents appear to be in some disarray on the point.[9]

NOTE ON ENFORCEMENT OF FINES

(a) *Finality of Sentences to a Fine.* Under the 1987 federal statute, a judgment that includes a sentence to a fine is a final judgment.[10] There are three circumstances, however, in which the basic premise does not operate. One is when a fine is modified or remitted under Section 3573.[11] The second is when a judgment containing a fine is corrected under Federal Rule of Criminal Procedure 35 and § 3742.[12] The third is when such a judgment is appealed and modified.[13]

(b) *Alternative Sentence Precluded.* Under classic penal legislation providing for both fines and imprisonment, courts could impose a sentence that

---

[2] *Id.* § 3572(a)(2).
[3] *Id.* § 3572(a)(3).
[4] *Id.* § 3572(a)(4). The obvious legislative policy is to give victim restitution a clear priority over fines and penalties for the benefit of the federal fisc. This is explicit in § 3572(b):

> If, as a result of a conviction, the defendant has the obligation to make restitution to a victim of the offense, the court shall impose a fine or other monetary penalty only to the extent that such fine or penalty will not impair the ability of the defendant to make restitution.

[5] *Id.* § 3572(a)(5).
[6] *Id.* § 3572(a)(6).
[7] *Id.* § 3572(a)(7).
[8] *Id.* § 3572(a), first sentence.
[9] Indicating that the statute created a checklist, see, *e.g.,* United States v. Pilgrim Market Corp., 944 F.2d 14, 21-22 (1st Cir. 1991). Indicating no need to articulate the factors, see, *e.g.,* United States v. Marquez, 941 F.2d 60, 65 (2d Cir. 1991). Articulation is necessary of at least one of the factors, however, United States v. Radix Laboratories, Inc., 963 F.2d 1034, 1043-44 (7th Cir. 1992).
[10] *Id.* § 3752(c), final sentence.
[11] *Id.* § 3572(c)(1).
[12] *Id.* § 3752(c)(2).
[13] *Id.* § 3572(c)(3).

required the payment of a fine, but then provide for a period of incarceration if the fine were not paid, the classic "thirty dollars or thirty days" sentence. That is not necessarily an unconstitutional sentence under current federal constitutional doctrine,[14] but Congress has forestalled the problem by providing that:

> At the time a defendant is sentenced to pay a fine, the court may not impose an alternative sentence to be carried out if the fine is not paid.

The consequences of nonpayment are addressed below, but it is clear that they cannot be anticipated and incorporated in the original sentence.

(c) *Stay Pending Appeal.* A sentence to pay a fine, like other criminal sentences, can be stayed if the statutory and rule requirements are met. Congress has stated expressly that, unless exceptional circumstances exist as determined by the sentencing court,[15] that a sentencing federal court must include in its order of stay one of the following alternatives: (i) Require that the defendant deposit in the district court registry any amount of the fine that is due.[16] (ii) Require that the defendant provide a bond or other security to ensure payment of the fine.[17] (iii) Restrain the defendant from transferring or dissipating assets.[18]

(d) *Modification or Remission of Fines.*

(i) *Initiation of proceedings.* Under current federal procedure, only the government may initiate proceedings to modify or remit a sentence to a fine.[19] The defense no longer has the power to do so.[20]

. . . .

(iii) *Venue of motion.* A petition for modification or remission must be filed in the court that imposed the original sentence.[21]

(iv) *Prerequisite showing.* The government must show that reasonable efforts to collect a fine or special assessment "are not likely to be effective."[22] The court then has discretion to modify or remit the sentence in question if that is "in the interests of justice."[23]

(v) *Contents of order.* The court may enter an order embracing any of the following alternatives: (A) Remission of all or part of the unpaid portion of a fine or special assessment, including interest and penalties.[24] (B) Deferral of payment of a fine or special assessment to a date certain, or according to an installment schedule.[25] (C) Extension of a date certain or an installment schedule previously ordered.[26]

---

[14] Bearden v. Georgia, 461 U.S. 660 (1983). *Bearden* appears at pp. 900-905 *supra.*
[15] 18 U.S.C.A. § 3572(g) (West Supp. 1993), first sentence.
[16] *Id.* § 3572(g)(1).
[17] *Id.* § 3572(g)(2).
[18] *Id.* § 3572(g)(3).
[19] *Id.* § 3573, first sentence.
[20] *See* United States v. Linker, 920 F.2d 1 (7th Cir. 1990).
[21] 18 U.S.C.A. § 3573 (West Supp. 1993), final sentence. That court, however, may transfer jurisdiction to another court if it wishes. *Id.*
[22] *Id.*, first sentence.
[23] *Id.*
[24] *Id.* § 3573(1).
[25] *Id.* § 3573(2).
[26] *Id.* § 3573(3).

(e) *Effect of Sentence to Pay a Fine.*

(i) Immediate obligation to pay. When a sentence to pay a fine or other monetary penalty has been pronounced, the defendant is obliged to pay the entire amount immediately.[27] However, in the interest of justice, the sentencing court may specify payment of the entire amount at a later designated time ("payment on a date certain") or in installments.[28]

(ii) Installment payments. If a court allows installment payments, payment must be in equal monthly amounts over a period set by the court. However, the court has the power to establish a different schedule of payments. Nevertheless, no period of extended payments can exceed five years from the date of sentence, excluding any period during which the defendant is serving a sentence of imprisonment for the offense.[29]

(iii) Individual responsibility for monetary obligations of organizations. Under the federal statute, the responsibility rests on individuals to pay amounts assessed against convicted organizations as fines, special assessments, or other monetary obligations including interest.[30] Under such circumstances, each individual authorized to make disbursements for the organization is under a duty to pay the obligation to the federal government from the assets of the organization. However, if the obligation is imposed on directors, officers, shareholders, employees, or agents of organizations, it cannot be discharged, directly or indirectly, from organizational resources, but instead must be satisfied by the individuals concerned, unless the federal court finds that payments from organizational funds are expressly allowed under applicable state law.[31]

(f) *Payment a Condition of Probation and Supervised Release.* If a court imposes a sentence to a fine and also sentences the defendant to probation, payment of the fine or adherence to the court-established installment schedule constitutes a mandatory condition of probation.[32] Payment also can be imposed as a condition to supervised release following imprisonment.[33]

(g) *Delinquency and Default.* Fines are delinquent if payment is more than 30 days late.[34] A fine is in default after payment has been delinquent for more than 90 days.[35] In that event, the entire amount of the fine becomes payable within 30 days following notification of default, without regard to whatever installment schedule the court might have authorized at sentencing.[36]

(h) *Payment of Fines.* Under § 3611,[37] the Director of the Administrative Office of the United States Courts specifies whether fines and other amounts

---

[27] *Id.* § 3572(d).

[28] *Id.* If a sentencing court does not refer expressly to installment payments, the entire amount of the fine is payable immediately. *See, e.g.,* United States v. Gresham, 964 F.2d 1426, 1429 (4th Cir. 1992).

[29] 18 U.S.C.A. § 3572(d) (West Supp. 1993).

[30] *Id.* § 3572(f).

[31] *Id.*

[32] *Id.* § 3563(a), final sentence. Conditions of probation are to include payment of fines. 18 U.S.C. § 3563(b)(2) (1988).

[33] 18 U.S.C.A. § 3583(d) (West Supp. 1993).

[34] 18 U.S.C.A. § 3572(h) (West Supp. 1993).

[35] *Id.* § 3572(i).

[36] *Id.*

[37] *Id.* § 3611.

are to be paid to the clerk of the sentencing court, or are to be processed as provided for in Title 28, § 604(a)(18).[38]

(i) Collection of Fines.

(ii) Notification. Under the current the statute,[39] the clerk or a person designated under Title 28, § 604(a)(18), is to notify the Attorney General of each payment as it is received. Notice is to be provided in whatever manner is agreed on between the Attorney General and the Director of the Administrative Office of the United States Courts,[40] and must occur within either 15 days after receipt or any other time period determined jointly by the Attorney General and the Director of the Administrative Office of the United States Courts.[41]

(iii) Contents of judgment relating to notification. The notice requirements apply only to judgments or orders imposing, modifying, or remitting fines of more than $100.[42] The required contents of judgments or orders imposing, modifying or remitting fines exceeding $100 have been expanded somewhat to include all of the following: (A) The defendant's name, social security account number, mailing address, and residence address.[43] (B) The docket number of the case.[44] (C) The original amount of the fine and the amount that is owing and unpaid.[45] (D) The schedule of payments, if other than immediate payment has been permitted under § 3572(d).[46] (E) A description of any modification or remission.[47] (F) If other than immediate payment has been permitted, a requirement that the defendant notify the Attorney General of any change in the defendant's mailing or residence address, not later than 30 days after the change has occurred.[48]

(iv) Certified copy of judgment. The sentencing court is required to transmit to the Attorney General a certified copy of the judgment or order, not later than ten days after entry.[49]

(v) Responsibility for collection. The Attorney General is responsible for the collection of unpaid fines concerning which certifications have been issued.[50]

(vi) Notifications of delinquency and default. The Attorney General (Department of Justice) must notify persons whose fines are delinquent of the delinquency within ten working days after the delinquency occurs.[51] Within ten days after default, a similar notice must be given to the defaulter, includ-

---

[38] This provides that the Director will perform other duties as assigned by the Supreme Court or the Judicial Conference of the United States. A similar amendment governs receipt of restitution payments by courts. 18 U.S.C.A. § 3663(f)(4) (West Supp. 1993).

[39] § 3612(a) (West Supp. 1993).

[40] *Id.* § 3612(a)(1).

[41] *Id.* § 3612(a)(2). If the fifteenth day falls on a Saturday, Sunday, or legal public holiday, then notification is to be accomplished no later than the next day that is not a Saturday, Sunday or legal holiday. *Id.* § 3612(a), final sentence.

[42] *Id.* § 3612(b)(1).

[43] *Id.* § 3612(b)(1)(A).

[44] *Id.* § 3612(b)(1)(B).

[45] *Id.* § 3612(b)(1)(C).

[46] *Id.* § 3612(b)(1)(D).

[47] *Id.* § 3612(b)(1)(E).

[48] *Id.* § 3612(b)(1)(F).

[49] *Id.* § 3612(b)(2).

[50] 18 U.S.C. § 3612(c) (1988). An order of restitution entered under *id.* § 3556 creates no right of action against the United States by persons to whom restitution has been ordered paid. *Id.*

[51] 18 U.S.C.A. § 3612(d) (West Supp. 1993).

ing advice that the entire unpaid balance, including interest and penalties, is due within 30 days.[52]

(vii) Accrual and computation of interest on fines. The interest provisions of federal law apply only to fines in excess of $2,500. Interest begins to accrue on fines larger than $2,500 on the fifteenth day after the date of the judgment.[53] Interest accrues on a daily basis from the first day on which liability for interest attaches,[54] and is to be computed at a rate equal to the coupon issue yield equivalent, determined by the Secretary of the Treasury, of the average accepted auction price for the last auction of 52-week United States Treasury bills settled before the first day on which a defendant becomes liable for interest under Section 3612(f)(1).[55]

(viii) Modification of interest by court action. If the sentencing court determines that a defendant cannot pay interest as ordinarily computed, it may in its discretion grant any of the following to the defendant: (A) Waiver of the interest requirement.[56] (B) Specification of a total dollar amount limiting the interest that the defendant must pay.[57] (C) A limitation of the period of time during which interest will accrue.[58]

(ix) Penalty for delinquent fine. If a fine becomes delinquent, a defendant must pay a penalty equivalent to ten percent of the principal amount (but not interest) that is delinquent.[59] If delinquency ripens into default, a defendant must pay an additional penalty equal to 15 percent of the principal amount that is in default.[60]

(x) Waiver of interest or penalty. The Attorney General may waive all or part of accrued interest or penalties on the basis of a determination that reasonable efforts to collect the amount owed is not likely to be effective.[61]

(xi) Application of payments. Payments relating to fines are to be applied first to principal, second to costs, third to interest, and fourth to penalties.[62]

(j) *Liens to Enforce Fines.*

(i) *Coverage of current legislative provisions.* Under § 3613(c), tax assessment and lien procedures are to be used for purposes of collecting unpaid fines, as modified by Department of Justice (Attorney General) regulations reflecting the differences between the two enforcement contexts. Under current statute, a judgment becomes a lien on property[63] in favor of the United States when a notice is filed equivalent to notice of a tax lien under the Internal Revenue Code.[64] This enhances the government's ability to collect fines by giving it greater standing than other judgment creditors, and serves

---

[52] *Id.* § 3612(e).
[53] *Id.* § 3612(f)(1). If that day falls on a Saturday, Sunday or legal public holiday, liability commences at the next day that is not a Saturday, Sunday or legal holiday. *Id.*
[54] *Id.* § 3612(f)(2)(A).
[55] *Id.* § 3612(f)(2)(B).
[56] *Id.* § 3612(f)(3)(A).
[57] *Id.* § 3612(f)(3)(B).
[58] *Id.* § 3612(f)(3)(C).
[59] *Id.* § 3612(g). A fine is delinquent if more than 30 days late. *Id.* § 3572(h).
[60] *Id.* § 3612(g).
[61] *Id.* § 3612(h).
[62] *Id.* § 3612(i).
[63] *Id.* § 3613(d).
[64] 26 U.S.C.A. § 6323(f) (West Supp. 1993).

to make much more property available for federal levy than had been true when state law governed, as it did under legislation before 1987.

(ii) Date and duration of lien. The lien in favor of the United States arises at the time of entry of the judgment imposing a fine, and continues until the liability is satisfied, remitted or set aside, or until it becomes unenforceable through expiration.[65]

(iii) Certificate of release or discharge. A defendant can apply to the Attorney General for either of the following two administrative actions[66] to relieve the hardship of a lien filing: (A) A certificate of release[67] pursuant to the Attorney General's acceptance of a bond[68] as established under the Internal Revenue Code.[69] (B) A certificate of discharge under the Internal Revenue Code[70] covering any part of the fair market value of the liened property that the Attorney General determines to exceed at least three times the amount of the fine.[71]

(iv) Expiration of lien. A lien becomes unenforceable, and a defendant's liability to pay a fine expires under either of the following circumstances: (A) Upon the elapse of 20 years after the entry of the judgment.[72] (B) The death of the individual fined.[73]

(k) *Discharge of Debts Inapplicable.* The statute[74] forbids a discharge of debts in bankruptcy to render a lien under § 3613 unenforceable or to discharge the liability to pay a fine.

(l) *Alternative Enforcement.* A judgment imposing a fine also can be enforced through execution against the convicted defendant's property as if it were a civil judgment;[75] the administrative lien provisions are not preclusive. However, liability can never be extended[76] beyond the period of time a lien would be valid.[77]

(m) *Resentencing a Delinquent Defendant.* A defendant who was sentenced to pay a fine, but knowingly failed to do so, can be resentenced to any sentence that originally might have been imposed.[78] However, imprisonment cannot be assessed unless the court determines that either: (A) The defendant either willfully refused to pay the delinquent fine or to make sufficient bona fide efforts to pay it.[79] (B) In light of the nature of the offense and characteristics of

---

[65] 18 U.S.C. § 3613(a) (1988).
[66] *Id.*
[67] Under Internal Revenue Code § 6325, 26 U.S.C.A. § 6325 (West Supp. 1993).
[68] 18 U.S.C. § 3613(a)(1) (1988).
[69] Section 6325(a)(2), 26 U.S.C.A. § 6325(a)(2) (West Supp. 1993).
[70] *Id.* § 6325.
[71] 18 U.S.C. § 3613(a)(2) (1988).
[72] *Id.* § 3613(b)(1). However, the period can be extended before its expiration through a written agreement between the person fined and the Attorney General. *Id.* § 3613(b), final paragraph. The period also is suspended during any interval in which the period of limitations governing collection of tax liabilities also would be suspended under cited provisions of the Internal Revenue Code. *Id.*
[73] *Id.* § 3613(b), final paragraph.
[74] *Id.* § 3613(f).
[75] *Id.* § 3613(e).
[76] *Id.*
[77] *Id.* § 3613(b).
[78] 18 U.S.C. § 3614(a) (1988).
[79] *Id.* § 3614(b)(1).

the defendant, alternatives to imprisonment are not adequate to serve the purposes of punishment and deterrence.[80]

(n) *Criminal Default.* Congress in 1984 established a crime of willful default in paying a criminal fine, punishable by a fine the greater of $10,000 or not more than twice the unpaid balance of the fine, imprisonment for not more than one year, or both.[81]

C. FORFEITURES

1. COLLATERAL PROFITS OF CRIME

SIMON & SCHUSTER V. NEW YORK CRIME VICTIMS BOARD

Supreme Court of the United States
112 S. Ct. 501 (1991)

[The New York so-called "Son of Sam" statute[1] defined the term "person convicted of a crime" to include "any person convicted of a crime in this state either by entry of a plea of guilty or by conviction after trial *and any person who has voluntarily and intelligently admitted the commission of a crime for which such person is not prosecuted.*"[2] The statute was construed not to apply to victimless crimes.[3] The *Simon & Schuster* litigation arose when the Crime Victims Board became aware of a contract between Simon & Schuster and an admitted organized crime figure, Henry Hill, who had been placed in a safe location under the federal witness protection program. According to the publication contract, Hill would collaborate with an established author, Nicholas Pileggi, in the creation of biography.[4] The Board ordered Simon & Schuster to provide it with copies of its contract with Hill and an accounting of its payments to Hill under the contract.[5] The Board determined that the Simon & Schuster contract fell within § 632-a and that Simon & Schuster had violated the law by making payments to Hill. Therefore, it ordered the publisher to turn over all money still held or to be held for Hill's benefit, and ordered Hill to remit the amounts he already had received.

---

[80] *Id.* § 3614(b)(2).

[81] 18 U.S.C. § 3615 (1988).

[1] Over the years, a number of notorious criminals realized substantial profits from the sales of books they had written or had ghost-written. One of the most publicized instances was that of David Berkowitz, tried in New York City for several murders. He claimed that his spiritual father, "Sam," had ordered him to kill. Berkowitz signed lucrative contracts for publication of his memoirs, and the New York legislature responded by authorizing the forfeiture of contract proceeds for purposes of victim compensation. N.Y. EXEC. LAW § 632-a (McKinney 1982 & Supp. 1993). This so-called "Son-of-Sam" statute became the prototype of statutes in a number of states. *See* REPORT OF THE COMMITTEE ON THE JUDICIARY, UNITED STATES SENATE, ON S. 2423, REPORT NO. 98-497, 98TH CONG., 2D SESS. 6 n.12 (1984) (noting that 25 states had such legislation as of 1984); Note, *Publication Rights Agreements in Sensational Criminal Cases: A Response to the Problem,* 68 CORNELL L. REV. 686 (1983); Note, *State Appellate Court Interpretations of Victim Compensation Statutes,* 10 NEW ENG. J. ON CRIM. & CIV. CONFINEMENT 87, 114-15 (1984).

[2] N.Y. EXEC. LAW § 632-a(10)(b) (McKinney 1982 & Supp. 1992) (emphasis added).

[3] Children of Bedford, Inc. v. Petromelis, 77 N.Y.2d 713, 726, 573 N.E.2d 541, 548, 570 N.Y.S.2d 453, 460 (1991), *vacated on other grounds,* 112 S. Ct. 889, *on reh'g,* 79 N.Y.2d 972, 592 N.E.2d 796, 583 N.Y.S.2d 188 (1992).

[4] Ultimately published as NICHOLAS PILEGGI, WISEGUY: LIFE IN A MAFIA FAMILY (1985). The book, a commercial best-seller, became the basis of a 1990 award-winning film, "Goodfellas."

[5] By that time, the publisher had paid $96,250 in advances and royalties to Hill's agent, and was holding an additional amount of $27,958 for future payment to Hill.

Simon & Schuster responded by commencing a Federal Civil Rights Act-based action,[6] seeking a declaratory judgment that the New York statute violated the First Amendment, and an injunction against enforcement of the statute by the Board. The district court sustained the constitutionality of the statute, and a divided panel of the Second Circuit affirmed. Because of equivalent federal legislation and legislation in most of the states, and because of the likelihood that the same significant issue would recur, the Supreme Court granted certiorari.]

JUSTICE O'CONNOR delivered the opinion of the Court.

. . .

A statute is presumptively inconsistent with the First Amendment if it imposes a financial burden on speakers because of the content of their speech. *Leathers v. Medlock,* 111 S. Ct. 1438, 1443-1444 (1991). As we emphasized in invalidating a content-based magazine tax, "official scrutiny of the content of publications as the basis for imposing a tax is entirely incompatible with the First Amendment's guarantee of freedom of the press." *Arkansas Writers' Project, Inc. v. Ragland,* 481 U.S. 221, 230 (1987).

This is a notion so engrained in our First Amendment jurisprudence that last Term we found it so "obvious" as to not require explanation. *Leathers, supra,* 111 S. Ct., at 1444. It is but one manifestation of a far broader principle: "Regulations which permit the Government to discriminate on the basis of the content of the message cannot be tolerated under the First Amendment." *Regan v. Time, Inc.,* 468 U.S. 641, 648-649 (1984).... In the context of financial regulations, it bears repeating, as we did in *Leathers,* that the Government's ability to impose content-based burdens on speech raises the specter that the Government may effectively drive certain ideas or viewpoints from the marketplace.... The First Amendment presumptively places this sort of discrimination beyond the power of the Government. As we reiterated in *Leathers,* "'The constitutional right of free expression is ... intended to remove governmental restraints from the arena of public discussion, putting the decision as to what views shall be voiced largely in the hands of each one of us ... in the belief that no other approach would comport with the premise of individual dignity and choice upon which our political system rests.'" *Id.* at 1444 (quoting *Cohen v. California,* 403 U.S. 15, 24 (1971)).

The Son of Sam law is such a content-based statute. It singles out income derived from expressive activity for a burden the State places on no other income, and it is directed only at works with a specified content. Whether the First Amendment "speaker" is considered to be Henry Hill, whose income the statute places in escrow because of the story he has told, or Simon & Schuster, which can publish books about crime with the assistance of only those criminals willing to forgo remuneration for at least five years, the statute plainly imposes a financial disincentive only on speech of a particular content.

[The Board then asserted that discriminatory financial treatment is suspect under the first amendment only if there is a legislative purpose to suppress certain ideas. That, however, was incompatible with the Court's precedents,[7]

---

[6] 42 U.S.C. § 1983 (1988).

[7] *E.g.,* Minneapolis Star & Tribune Co. v. Minnesota Comm'r of Revenue, 460 U.S. 575, 592 (1983).

C. FORFEITURES

stating that "[i]llicit legislative intent is not the *sine qua non*" of first-amendment infringements. The Court rejected as well the Board's efforts to distinguish its foundational legislation from statutes and regulations earlier invalidated by the Court, based on a claimed general burden, not on media as such, but on entities that contracted with convicted persons to transmit their speech. In the Court's analysis, any entity contracting to transmit speech becomes by definition a medium of communication; in any event, characterization of entities as within "the media" or not is irrelevant to the unconstitutionality of content-based financial disincentives on speech. Because the Son of Sam law established a financial disincentive to create or publish works of particular content, it was unconstitutional unless the state could show that the regulation was necessary to serve a compelling state interest and was narrowly drawn to achieve that end.]

... The Board thus does not assert any interest in limiting whatever anguish Henry Hill's victims may suffer from reliving their victimization.

There can be little doubt, on the other hand, that the State has a compelling interest in ensuring that victims of crime are compensated by those who harm them. Every State has a body of tort law serving exactly this interest. The State's interest in preventing wrongdoers from dissipating their assets before victims can recover explains the existence of the State's statutory provisions for prejudgment remedies and orders of restitution....

The State likewise has an undisputed compelling interest in ensuring that criminals do not profit from their crimes.... The force of this interest is evidenced by the State's statutory provisions for the forfeiture of the proceeds and instrumentalities of crime.... [The Court assumed without deciding that the income escrowed under the statute represented fruits of crime.]

The Board attempts to define the State's interest more narrowly, as "ensuring that criminals do not profit from storytelling about their crimes before their victims have a meaningful opportunity to be compensated for their injuries." ... Here the Board is on far shakier ground. The Board cannot explain why the State should have any greater interest in compensating victims from the proceeds of such "storytelling" than from any of the criminal's other assets. Nor can the Board offer any justification for a distinction between this expressive activity and any other activity in connection with its interest in transferring the fruits of crime from criminals to their victims. Thus even if the State can be said to have an interest in classifying a criminal's assets in this manner, that interest is hardly compelling.... The distinction drawn by the Son of Sam law has nothing to do with the State's interest in transferring the proceeds of crime from criminals to their victims....

In short, the State has a compelling interest in compensating victims from the fruits of the crime, but little if any interest in limiting such compensation to the proceeds of the wrongdoer's speech about the crime. We must therefore determine whether the Son of Sam law is narrowly tailored to advance the former, not the latter, objective.

[The Court then concluded that the law was not sufficiently circumscribed, but instead was overinclusive. The statute extended to works on any subject, provided they embraced thoughts or recollections about a crime, however tangentially or incidentally. It also defined the phrase "person convicted of a crime" to include those who admitted in their writings to criminal conduct, whether or not they were ever accused in fact or convicted of that conduct. In the Court's view, that definition would have embraced *The Autobiography of Malcolm X,* Henry Thoreau's *Civil Disobedience* and *The Confessions of Saint Augustine,* as well as a lengthy bibliography of works by American prisoners and former prisoners including Emma Goldman, Martin Luther King, Jr., Jesse Jackson and Bertrand Russell. A statute that could impound for five years all the royalties from an autobiographical work, written late in life, admitting to a minor theft committed "as a youthful prank" was not narrowly enough drawn to achieve a state objective to compensate crime victims from the profits of the crimes that had harmed them.

The Court naturally did not purport to address the constitutionality of all Son of Sam laws, the language of which might vary from that of New York's legislation. The New York statute, however, violated the first amendment by singling out speech addressed to a particular subject matter for the imposition of a financial burden imposed on no other speech and no other income, and by not narrowly tailoring its statute to address the acceptable state interest in compensating victims from the fruits of crimes committed against them.]

2. FORFEITURES AS A CRIMINAL SANCTION

TITLE 18, UNITED STATES CODE

Section 1963. Criminal penalties

(a) Whoever violates any provision of section 1962 of this chapter ... shall forfeit to the United States, irrespective of any provision of State law —

(1) any interest the person has acquired or maintained in violation of section 1962;

(2) any —

   (A) interest in;
   (B) security of;
   (C) claim against; or
   (D) property[1] or contractual right of any kind affording a source of influence over

any enterprise which the person has established, operated, controlled, conducted, or participated in the conduct of in violation of section 1962; and

(3) any property constituting, or derived from, any proceeds which the person obtained, directly or indirectly, from racketeering activity or unlawful debt[2] collection in violation of section 1962....

...

---

[1] The statute, 18 U.S.C.A. § 1963(b) (West Supp. 1993), defines "property" to include: (a) real property, including things growing on, affixed to and found in land; (b) tangible and intangible personal property, including rights, privileges, interests, claims and securities, *id.* § 1963(b)(2).

[2] The term "unlawful debt" is generally defined in the statute, 18 U.S.C. § 1961(6) (1988), to include (a) gambling debts (i) incurred or contracted in illegal gambling activity and (ii) in the course of an unlawful gambling enterprise, or (b) debts incurred in the course of the business of lending money or things of value at a rate usurious under state or federal law, if the usurious rate is at least twice the legally enforceable rate.

(c) All right, title, and interest in property described in subsection (a) vests in the United States upon the commission of the act giving rise to forfeiture under this section. Any such property that is subsequently transferred to a person other than the defendant may be the subject of a special verdict of forfeiture and thereafter shall be ordered forfeited to the United States, unless the transferee establishes in a hearing pursuant to subsection (*l*) that he [or she] is a bona fide purchaser for value of such property who at the time of purchase was reasonably without cause to believe that the property was subject to forfeiture under this section.

. . .

NOTE ON FORFEITURE PROCEDURES

(a) *Temporary Restraining Orders.*

(i) *Authority to seek restraining order.* A United States Attorney responsible for a RICO case is empowered to apply to the federal district court in which criminal prosecution is or will be pending for (A) a restraining order, (B) an injunction, (C) an order for the execution of a satisfactory performance bond, or (D) judicial action of any other kind to preserve the availability of forfeitable property.[3]

(ii) *Post-indictment applications.* A United States Attorney can seek any of the above remedies whenever an indictment or information has been filed (A) charging a RICO violation and (B) alleging that property, in the event of conviction, is subject to forfeiture under Section 1963.[4]

(iii) *Preindictment applications.* More elaborate requirements pertain to a government application submitted to a federal district court before an indictment has been returned or an information filed. In that event, the following prerequisites must be met: (A) Notice must be given to persons having an interest in the property.[5] However, no notice need be given if the government establishes probable cause to believe there is danger that the property to be affected by an order of forfeiture will not be available if notice is given.[6] (B) A hearing must be held after notice has been given.[7] As in the matter of notice, no hearing need be held if the government establishes probable cause to believe that the property to be subjected to forfeiture is in jeopardy of being unavailable if a hearing is held.[8] However, a hearing must be held before the time limit for an ex parte restraining order has expired.[9] (C) The government must establish the following three matters: (1) Substantial probability that the government will prevail on the issue of forfeiture.[10] (2) Substantial probability that a failure to enter an order will result in the destruction or removal of the property from the jurisdiction of the court, or its unavailability for any other reason.[11] (3) The need to preserve the availability of the property

---

[3] 18 U.S.C.A. § 1963(d)(1) (West Supp. 1993).
[4] *Id.* § 1963(d)(1)(A).
[5] *Id.* § 1963(d)(1)(B).
[6] *Id.* § 1963(d)(2).
[7] *Id.* § 1963(d)(1)(B).
[8] *Id.* § 1963(d)(2).
[9] *Id.*
[10] *Id.* § 1963(d)(1)(B)(i).
[11] *Id.*

through entry of the requested order outweighs the hardship experienced by any party against whom the order will be entered.[12] (D) The court is not bound by the rules of trial evidence at a hearing under the provision, so that evidence and information inadmissible under the Federal Rules of Evidence may be used in reaching the required determination.[13] (E) The court may enter an appropriate order[14] if it finds the statutory prerequisites to have been met. (4) A temporary order after notice and hearing is effective for not more than ninety days, but may be extended for good cause shown.[15] In the case of a preindictment order entered without advance notice and hearing, an order can be entered for ten days only, but the period between entry and hearing can be extended for good cause shown, and a party affected by the seizure can consent to a postponement of hearing for a longer period.[16] The return of an indictment or the filing of an information also serves to extend the effectiveness of an order until completion of criminal proceedings.[17]

(b) *Order of Forfeiture.*

(i) Procedural prerequisites. An indictment or information must allege the extent of the interest or property subject to forfeiture, if a valid forfeiture order ultimately is to be entered.[18] The criminal trial jury also must return a special verdict covering the extent of the interest or property, if any, subject to forfeiture.[19] On the basis of such a special verdict, the court is to enter a judgment of criminal forfeiture[20] supplemented by an order that the defendant will forfeit the described property to the United States.[21] Both the order and judgment authorize the Attorney General to seize the specified property, subject to whatever terms and conditions the court includes in its judgment and order.[22]

(ii) Jurisdiction. The jurisdiction of district courts to enter orders authorized under § 1963 is not determined according to the location of any property which may be subject to forfeiture under the section or has been ordered forfeited.[23]

(c) *Seizure of Forfeited Property.*

(i) Protective orders. After the entry of a forfeiture order, the government can apply for (i) appropriate restraining orders or injunctions; (ii) the execution of satisfactory performance bonds on the part of the defendant; (iii) appointment of receivers, conservators, appraisers, accountants or trustees; or (iv) any other action appropriate to protect the interest of the United States in the forfeited property.[24] If an enterprise or an interest in an enterprise has been ordered forfeited, income accruing to or derived from it is to be used to

---

[12] *Id.* § 1963(d)(1)(B)(ii).
[13] *Id.* § 1963(d)(3).
[14] *Id.* § 1963(d)(1).
[15] *Id.* § 1963(d)(1), proviso.
[16] *Id.* § 1963(d)(2).
[17] *Id.* § 1963(d)(1), proviso.
[18] FED. R. CRIM. P. 7(c)(2).
[19] *Id.* R. 31(e).
[20] 18 U.S.C.A. § 1963(e) (West Supp. 1993); FED. R. CRIM. P. 32(b)(2).
[21] 18 U.S.C.A. § 1963(a) (West Supp. 1993), final sentence.
[22] 18 U.S.C.A. § 1963(e) (West Supp. 1993); FED. R. CRIM. P. 32(b)(2).
[23] 18 U.S.C.A. § 1963(j) (West Supp. 1993).
[24] *Id.* § 1963(e).

C. FORFEITURES

offset ordinary and necessary expenses of the enterprise either (1) required by law, or (2) necessary to protect the interests of the United States or third parties.[25]

(ii) Depositions to facilitate seizure. The government, if it is confronted with a need to facilitate the identification or location of property ordered forfeited, may apply to the issuing court for a deposition order affecting a witness who may have relevant information.[26] A recipient may be directed at the time and place of the deposition proceeding to produce designated books, papers, documents, records, recording or other material not protected by privilege.[27] Otherwise, usual deposition practice[28] governs in this context as well.[29]

(iii) Safeguarding seized property. The Attorney General[30] is authorized to take appropriate measures to safeguard and maintain property ordered to be forfeited under § 1963, pending its final disposition.[31]

(d) *Remission or Mitigation of Forfeiture.*

(i) Notice to possible claimants. Whenever a forfeiture order has been entered, the government is required to publish notice of the order and of its intent to dispose of the forfeited property for at least seven successive court days.[32] In addition, the government may provide direct written notice, to the extent practicable, to anyone known to have an alleged interest in the property subject to a forfeiture order; actual notice serves as a substitute for published notice as far as a recipient is concerned.[33]

(ii) Administrative remission or modification. The statute authorizes the Attorney General, pursuant to administrative regulations,[34] to take several measures concerning forfeitures without the necessity of advance judicial authorization: (A) Grant petitions for mitigation or remission of forfeiture.[35] (B) Restore forfeited property to victims of a violation of the underlying criminal activity.[36] (C) Take any other action to protect the rights of innocent persons in the interest of justice, if not inconsistent with other provisions governing forfeitures.[37] (D) Compromise claims arising under § 1963.[38] (E) Award compensation to persons providing information resulting in a forfeiture under § 1963.[39]

---

[25] *Id.*
[26] *Id.* § 1963(k).
[27] *Id.*
[28] FED. R. CRIM. P. 15, 17(f).
[29] 18 U.S.C.A. § 1963(k) (West Supp. 1993).
[30] The Attorney General is authorized under the RICO statute to delegate authority conferred under the statute to designated categories of Department of Justice officials. 18 U.S.C.A. § 1961(10) (West Supp. 1993).
[31] *Id.* § 1963(g)(5).
[32] *Id.* § 1963(*l*)(1).
[33] *Id.*
[34] *Id.* § 1963(h)(2)-(3) authorizes Department of Justice regulations governing granting petitions for remission or mitigation of forfeiture and the restitution of property to victims of an offense petitioning for remission or mitigation of forfeiture under the provision. Activities to be conducted by the "Attorney General" under RICO can be delegated to other designated Department of Justice officials. *See id.* § 1961(10).
[35] *Id.* § 1963(g)(1).
[36] *Id.*
[37] *Id.*
[38] *Id.* § 1963(g)(2).
[39] *Id.* § 1963(g)(3).

(e) *Judicial Hearings to Preserve Third-Party Interests.*

(i) Limitation on judicial avenues of redress. The statute forbids parties claiming interests in forfeited property from pursuing either of the following procedural avenues to assert their claims: (A) Intervention in the trial or appeal of the criminal case pursuant to which forfeiture was ordered.[40] (B) Institution of a law or equity action concerning the validity of an alleged interest in property subject to forfeiture, if the action is begun after the filing of an indictment or information alleging that the property is forfeitable under § 1963.[41] Consequently, the only avenue provided under the legislation to assert a property interest in matter subjected to forfeiture is a special proceeding set forth in § 1963 itself.[42]

(ii) Theoretical basis for subsection (l) proceedings. A criminal forfeiture order or proceeding (including one under RICO) is *in personam.* Accordingly, a forfeiture order properly may reach only a defendant's property unless a transfer to a third party is voidable. Consequently, if a third party can demonstrate that his or her interest in the forfeited property is exclusive of or superior to the interest of the defendant, the third party's claim renders that portion of the order of forfeiture reaching that interest invalid.

(iii) Procedures to assert third-party claims to forfeited property. The statutory notice procedures[43] are intended to give claimants the needed awareness of seizures for purposes of forfeiture that otherwise they may lack. The procedures they must pursue are the following: (A) A claimant other than the criminal defendant, who asserts a legal interest in forfeited property, may petition for a hearing to adjudicate the claimed interest.[44] The petition must be submitted within 30 days after the last of the required notices by publication.[45] Defendants are excluded from subsection (m) relief because the proceeding is intended to protect third parties only, and a defendant has ample remedies in the form of an appeal against a forfeiture order.[46] The petition must be signed by the petitioner under penalty of perjury, and must specify: (i) the nature and extent of the petitioner's right, title or interest in the property; (ii) the time and circumstances of the petitioner's acquisition of the right, title or interest; (iii) any additional facts supporting the petitioner's claim; and (iv) the relief sought.[47] (B) Upon receipt of a valid petition, the recipient court (which is the court that tried the criminal case and ordered the forfeiture[48]) conducts a hearing without a jury.[49] (C) The hearing must be held within 30 days after a petition has been filed.[50] (D) If there are two or more petitions relating to the forfeited property (excluding any attack by the criminal defendant), the recipient court has discretion to conduct a consolidated

---

[40] *Id.* § 1963(i)(1).
[41] *Id.* § 1963(i)(2).
[42] *Id.* § 1963(*l*)(2)-(6).
[43] 18 U.S.C.A. § 1963(*l*)(1) (West Supp. 1993).
[44] *Id.* § 1963(*l*)(2).
[45] *Id.*
[46] *Id.* § 3742(a)(1), (d)(1).
[47] *Id.* § 1963(*l*)(3).
[48] *Id.* § 1963(j).
[49] *Id.* § 1963(*l*)(2).
[50] *Id.* § 1963(*l*)(4).

C. FORFEITURES 923

hearing on all of them.[51] (E) The petitioner is authorized to testify and present evidence and witnesses on his or her behalf, and has the right to cross-examine government witnesses.[52] (F) The government may present evidence and witnesses to rebut a petitioner's case and to defend its claim to the property; it also may cross-examine petitioner witnesses.[53] (G) The court is required to consider all the evidence submitted by a petitioner and the government, as well as the relevant portions of the criminal case records underlying the order of forfeiture.[54] (H) On the basis of those data, the court is to give appropriate relief if it finds by a preponderance of the evidence[55] that a petitioner has established either of the following: (i) The petitioner has a legal right, title or interest in the property that renders the order of forfeiture wholly or partially invalid because the petitioner's right, title or interest either (a) was vested in him, her, or it and not the defendant, or (b) was superior to the defendant's right, title or interest at the time of the commission of the criminal acts underlying the forfeiture order.[56] (ii) A petitioner is a bona fide purchaser for value of the right, title or interest in the property, and was at the time of purchase without reasonable cause to believe the property was subject to forfeiture under § 1963.[57]

(iv) Judicial order. If the court makes the requisite findings by a preponderance that a petitioner's claim to forfeited property is better than the government's, it is to amend the original order of forfeiture accordingly. If seized property is ordered to be returned, the government cannot be ordered to pay a monetary award equivalent to an amount by which the property has decreased in value while in government custody.[58]

(f) *Disposal of Forfeited Property.*

(i) Methods of disposition. After property has been ordered forfeited, the Attorney General under Department of Justice regulations[59] may dispose of the property by sale or other commercially feasible method, but must make due provision for the rights of innocent persons who may be affected.[60] The defendant or anyone acting in concert with or on behalf of the defendant is, however, ineligible to purchase the property.[61]

(ii) Stay of disposition. The court that authorized the forfeiture is empowered to grant a stay of disposition pending appeal of the criminal conviction underlying the forfeiture order, on the application of a person other than the defendant or someone acting in concert with or on behalf of the defendant.[62] An eligible applicant bears the burden of establishing that sale or disposition

---

[51] *Id.*
[52] *Id.* § 1963(*l*)(5).
[53] *Id.*
[54] *Id.*
[55] *Id.* § 1963(*l*)(6).
[56] *Id.* § 1963(*l*)(6)(A).
[57] *Id.* § 1963(*l*)(6)(B).
[58] *Id.* § 1963(*l*)(6).
[59] *Id.* § 1963(g)(4).
[60] *Id.* § 1963(f).
[61] *Id.*
[62] *Id.* § 1963(f).

of the property in the interim will result in irreparable injury, harm or loss to the applicant.[63]

(iii) Proceeds. The usual federal statutory rule is that government officials or agents who receive money for the government from any source are required to deposit it in the Treasury as soon as practical "without deduction for any charge or claim."[64] Because of its concern over the impact of that rule on agency budgets, Congress expressly abrogated the § 3302(b) requirement that gross receipts be deposited, by allowing the proceeds from the enforcement of a forfeiture to be used to pay "all proper expenses for the forfeiture and the sale, including expenses of seizure, maintenance and custody of the property pending its disposition, advertising and court costs."[65] Any remaining residue then is to be deposited in the Treasury under the direction of the Attorney General.[66]

(iv) Warranty of title. If no subsection (m) petitions have been filed, or if the government prevails in whole or in part after a subsection (m) petition has been disposed of finally, the United States is confirmed to have clear title to property that is the subject of a forfeiture order, and may warrant good title to subsequent purchasers or transferees.[67]

3. FORFEITURE OF ATTORNEY'S FEES

The United States Supreme Court sustained the constitutionality of the forfeitability of property constituting or derived from the proceeds of drug-law violations,[68] even though defendants desire to use that property for the purpose of retaining defense counsel, in *Caplin & Drysdale, Chartered v. United States.*[69] The Court first rejected the petitioner's contention that forfeiture before conviction of funds that could be used to retain private counsel violated the sixth amendment right to counsel. Consonant with the Court's statements in *Wheat v. United States*[70] that defendants may not insist on representation by attorneys they cannot afford, the Court found no impermissible burden wrought by forfeiture on the criminal defendant's (Reckmeyer's) ability to achieve representation.

The Court commented that defendants may have other nonforfeitable assets from which they can pay counsel fees, or may find attorneys willing to represent them in the expectation of future payment of fees following an acquittal. Nevertheless, even if there were a measurable burden through forfeiture on the freedom of a defendant who had insufficient nonforfeitable assets to retain counsel of choice, the government's interests embodied in the forfeiture statute outweighed it, the Court thought. That legislation[71] incorporates the "ap-

---

[63] *Id.*
[64] 31 U.S.C. § 3302(b) (1988).
[65] 18 U.S.C.A. § 1963(g) (West Supp. 1993).
[66] *Id.*
[67] *Id.* § 1963(*l*)(7).
[68] The forfeiture provisions of the federal Controlled Substances Act, 21 U.S.C.A. §§ 853, 967 (West Supp. 1993), are precise counterparts of the Title 18 RICO-related legislation discussed above.
[69] 491 U.S. 617 (1989).
[70] 486 U.S. 153, 159 (1988).
[71] 21 U.S.C.A. § 853(c) (West Supp. 1993).

plication of the long-recognized and lawful practice of vesting title to any forfeitable assets, in the United States, at the time of the criminal act giving rise to forfeiture."[72] Because, under the taint theory on which the legislation rests, the government acquired title to Reckmeyer's property at the time of his offenses, no constitutional principle required that Reckmeyer be allowed to give the government's property to a third party (defense counsel), even if Reckmeyer were doing so in the exercise of a constitutional right.

The petitioner had argued that the governmental objective underlying the forfeiture legislation would be accomplished if the proceeds of crime were paid to defense counsel, because that would dispossess drug dealers or racketeers of the proceeds of their wrongdoing. The Court rejected that premise as deprecating the government's actual interest in forfeitable assets. First, those assets would go into the Department of Justice Assets Forfeiture Fund which supports law-enforcement efforts in a variety of important and useful ways — a significant governmental interest. Second, rightful owners of forfeited property can claim its return. The Court likened that dimension of federal forfeiture proceedings to the status of bank robbers who might wish to use stolen funds to retain counsel but would not be permitted to do so against the claims of the victim banks to a return of their property. Third, a major objective of both RICO and CCE [Continuing Criminal Enterprise statute] forfeitures is to reduce the economic power of organized crime and narcotics enterprises, an objective furthered by denying the economic power to hire counsel of choice and to finance an expensive defense.[73] Accordingly, the Court rejected the claim that the sixth amendment right to counsel incorporates a right to use government assets to pay retained counsel from the portion of those assets still in a defendant's possession.[74]

The final premise relied on by the petitioner was that forfeiture denied due process of law because it upset the "balance of forces" between accused persons and their accuser.[75] The Court doubted that the fifth amendment due process clause added protections beyond those inherent in the sixth amendment right to counsel. It noted, however, even on the contrary assumption, that the petitioner had established no infringement in its case. The fact that government prosecutors might abuse their powers under the forfeiture statute in other contexts, for example, by attempting to impose the forfeiture sanction on persons who should not be subjected to it, does not benefit defendants or others whose own rights have not been infringed.[76]

The same constitutional doctrines also governed *Monsanto*.[77] However, the Court discussed at some length, as a preliminary matter, the issue of whether Section 853 requires the forfeiture of assets intended to be used by defendants

---

[72] *Caplin & Drysdale*, 491 U.S. at 627.

[73] *Id*. at 630. The Court noted that IRS jeopardy assessments are constitutional even though a freeze on assets to cover potential tax liability impairs the ability to retain counsel. "Criminal defendants ... are not exempted from federal, state, and local taxation simply because these financial levies may deprive them of resources that could be used to hire an attorney." *Id*. at 630-32.

[74] *Id*. at 632.

[75] 491 U.S. at 633 (citing Wardius v. Oregon, 412 U.S. 470, 474 [1973]).

[76] *Id*. at 634.

[77] United States v. Monsanto, 491 U.S. 600 (1989).

to pay their retained counsel. The Court concluded that the provision is plain and unambiguous, and mandates the forfeiture of all assets within its provisions, without exception; there is no basis to exclude assets used or to be used to pay attorney's fees from the statutory term "property." Nothing in the legislative history led to a contrary conclusion. The Court noted that in part of the same enactment creating the Criminal Forfeitures Act (CFA), namely, the Victims of Crime ("Son of Sam") Act, Congress had expressly exempted from forfeiture payments for legal representation; that suggested to the Court that Congress knew quite well what it was accomplishing through CFA.[78]

Monsanto had argued the additional point that, although § 853(a) contained no exemption of funds for use in retaining counsel, the portion of the statute governing pretrial restraining orders[79] should be read to include it under principles of equity, because district courts are endowed with discretion concerning the issuance of such orders. The Court, however, found no validity in that distinction. Section 853(a) requires forfeiture, and § 853(e)(1)(A), designed to implement forfeiture, could not be construed to grant discretion to dissipate assets that should be forfeited. Any contrary holding would substantially infringe the "relation-back" theory on which the forfeiture provision rested, the Court thought. If that result is harsh, nevertheless, that is what Congress intended in its effort to give force to the old adage that crime does not pay; the Court would not rewrite the "nostrum" to read "crime does not pay, except for attorney's fees."[80]

D. IMPRISONMENT

1. CIRCUMSTANCES OF IMPRISONMENT

AMERICAN BAR ASSOCIATION STANDARDS FOR CRIMINAL JUSTICE LEGAL STATUS OF PRISONERS (Supp. 1983)

Standard 23-1.1. General principle

Prisoners retain the rights of free citizens except:
(a) as specifically provided to the contrary in these standards; or
(b) when restrictions are necessary to assure their orderly confinement and interaction; or
(c) when restrictions are necessary to provide reasonable protection for the rights and physical safety of all members of the prison system and the general public.

Commentary

This standard accomplishes two things. First, it articulates the basic benchmark for measuring the legal rights of prisoners as they are detailed throughout this chapter. Second, it provides a residual guideline for evolving legal rights of prisoners which will inexorably need to be defined as future experi-

---

[78] *Id.* at 611.
[79] 21 U.S.C.A. § 853(e)(1)(A) (West Supp. 1993).
[80] *Monsanto*, 491 U.S. at 613-14. The Court utilized this portion of its *Monsanto* rationale in rejecting an identical claim made in *Caplin & Drysdale*, 461 U.S. at 623.

D. IMPRISONMENT

ence accumulates. Thus, according to the principle that the specific overrules the general, this standard should be viewed as superseded by each individual standard in this chapter for the subject matter it addresses. Under the same rationale, each standard is intended to embody the spirit of the general principle as it applies to the specific context.

The United States Supreme Court has enunciated four principles delineating the constitutional status of both convicted prisoners and persons in pretrial confinement:[1]

> 1. Prison residents do not forfeit all their constitutional protections. "There is no iron curtain drawn between the Constitution and the prisons of this country."[2]
>
> 2. Constitutional rights of prisoners, however, are subject to restrictions and limitations "justified by the considerations underlying our penal system."[3] A prisoner "simply does not possess the full range of freedoms of an unincarcerated individual."[4]
>
> 3. Essential goals of maintaining institutional security and preserving internal order and discipline may require limitation or retraction of constitutional rights retained by persons in confinement. "Prison officials must be free to take appropriate action to ensure the safety of inmates and corrections personnel and to prevent escape or unauthorized entry."[5] Even practices infringing constitutional rights as important as those under the first amendment are to be evaluated "in the light of the central objective of prison administration, safeguarding institutional security."[6]
>
> 4. Because penal administration is inherently difficult, prison administrators "should be accorded wide-ranging deference in the adoption and execution of policies and practices that in their judgment are needed to preserve internal order and discipline and to maintain institutional security."[7]

The first three elements of this constitutional doctrine are incorporated in this standard and establish guidelines for the application of the more detailed provisions of the standards that follow. The fourth is not incorporated because it functions to allocate a burden of persuasion in litigation and thus lies outside the ambit of these standards. Incarceration, whatever its theoretical justification, constitutes and is viewed by those undergoing it as punishment. It should not be augmented by a wholesale deprivation of civil rights. Nevertheless, limitations on prisoners' civil rights flow from three sources under these standards.

---

[1] Bell v. Wolfish, 441 U.S. 520, 544-48 (1979).
[2] Wolff v. McDonnell, 418 U.S. 539, 555-56 (1974).
[3] Bell v. Wolfish, 441 U.S. at 546 (quoting Price v. Johnson, 334 U.S. 266, 285 [1948]). *See also* Rhodes v. Chapman, 452 U.S. 337, 347 (1981) ("[t]o the extent that [prison] conditions are restrictive and even harsh, they are part of the penalty that criminal offenders pay for their offenses against society").
[4] Bell v. Wolfish, 441 U.S. at 546.
[5] *Id.*
[6] *Id.* at 547.
[7] *Id.*

One source of limitations is the detailed provisions of the standards themselves as they are implemented through statutes and administrative regulations. Specific provisions control the general statement of principle in this standard.[8]

A second source is the legal provisions based on considerations of confinement of prisoners and interaction between prisoners and correctional personnel. Constructive interaction and communication between staff and residents are essential to institutional programming and effective administration.[9] Nevertheless, the two bodies, staff and residents, are not equals who engage in arm's-length negotiations.[10] Restrictions may be imposed to ensure that interaction as well as confinement is orderly.

A third source is the laws and regulations instituted to safeguard the legal rights and physical safety of all persons within a prison system (staff, residents, visitors, etc.) and of the general public. Individual claims must give way to collective safety in specific instances.

The standard does not expressly touch on procedural burdens, which can best be dealt with through judicial decisions.[11] It does, however, provide a conceptual background against which important procedural concerns can be resolved. Prisoners have the same rights to challenge administrative actions as do other members of the public, *but have no greater rights of challenge*. In that process, burdens of pleading, going forward, and persuasion inevitably will be delineated.[12] Purely procedural concerns aside, litigation cannot resolve the bulk of problems arising in prison settings. A degree of accommodation between competing individuals and groups must be achieved. If, against the general principle advocated in this standard, the compelling circumstances of specific cases can be recognized and not rejected through rote reliance on the letter of institutional regulations, a suitable outcome of most if not all disputes can be anticipated.

2. EXTENDED TERMS OF IMPRISONMENT; HABITUAL OFFENDER STATUTES

MODEL PENAL CODE §§ 6.07, 7.03, 7.04

[The text of these sections appears in Appendix A.]

---

[8] For an overview of these standards, *see* B.J. George, *Standards Governing Legal Status of Prisoners,* 59 DEN. L.J. 93 (1981).

[9] *See* Standard 23-7.1(a); ACA, STANDARDS FOR ADULT CORRECTIONAL INSTITUTIONS 2-4015, -4018, -4342 (2d ed. 1981).

[10] Jones v. North Carolina Prisoners' Labor Union, Inc., 433 U.S. 119 (1977).

[11] The concept of "deference" enunciated in Bell v. Wolfish, text accompanying note 7 *supra*, indicates the allocation of the burden of persuasion in federal litigation. Such a burden may be significantly more than the preponderance test. In Jones v. North Carolina Prisoners' Labor Union, Inc., 433 U.S. at 132, correctional administrators who believed prisoner unionization would be detrimental to institutional order and security had "not been conclusively shown to be wrong in this."

[12] *Cf.* Santosky v. Kramer, 455 U.S. 745, 762-70 (1982) (burden of persuasion in proceedings to terminate parental rights is "clear and convincing proof"); Addington v. Texas, 441 U.S. 418 (1979) (same burden of persuasion in civil commitment proceedings).

D. IMPRISONMENT

UNITED STATES NATIONAL ADVISORY COMMISSION ON CRIMINAL JUSTICE STANDARDS AND GOALS, CORRECTIONS REPORT (1973)

Standard 5.3

Sentencing to Extended Terms

State penal code revisions should contain separate provisions for sentencing offenders when, in the interest of public protection, it is considered necessary to incapacitate them for substantial periods of time.

The following provisions should be included:

1. Authority for the judicial imposition of an extended term of confinement of not more than 25 years, except for murder, when the court finds the incarceration of the defendant for a term longer than 5 years is required for the protection of the public and that the defendant is (a) a persistent felony offender, (b) a professional criminal, or (c) a dangerous offender.

2. Definition of a persistent felony offender as a person over 21 years of age who stands convicted of a felony for the third time. At least one of the prior felonies should have been committed within the 5 years preceding the commission of the offense for which the offender is being sentenced. At least two of the three felonies should be offenses involving the infliction, or attempted or threatened infliction, of serious bodily harm on another.

3. Definition of a professional criminal as a person over 21 years of age, who stands convicted of a felony that was committed as part of a continuing illegal business in which he acted in concert with other persons and occupied a position of management, or was an executor of violence. An offender should not be found to be a professional criminal unless the circumstances of the offense for which he stands convicted show that he has knowingly devoted himself to criminal activity as a major source of his livelihood or unless it appears that he has substantial income or resources that do not appear to be from a source other than criminal activity.

4. Definition of a dangerous offender as a person over 21 years of age whose criminal conduct is found by the court to be characterized by: (a) a pattern of repetitive behavior which poses a serious threat to the safety of others, (b) a pattern of persistent aggressive behavior with heedless indifference to the consequences, or (c) a particularly heinous offense involving the threat or infliction of serious bodily injury.

5. Authority for the court to impose a minimum sentence to be served prior to eligibility for parole. The minimum sentence should be limited to those situations in which the community requires reassurance as to the continued confinement of the offender. It should not exceed one-third of the maximum sentence imposed or more than three years.

6. Authority for the sentencing court to permit the parole of an offender sentenced to a minimum term prior to service of that minimum upon request of the board of parole.

7. Authority for the sentencing court in lieu of the imposition of a minimum to recommend to the board of parole at the time of sentencing that the offender not be paroled until a given period of time has been served.

Commentary

The arguments for incapacitating the "dangerous offender" are threefold:

1. Modern American statutes contain excessively high maximum sentencing provisions largely aimed at controlling the "dangerous" offender, but unfortunately often ensnare the nondangerous offender as well, needlessly increasing the period of his incarceration.

2. Current attempts to classify the "dangerous" offender in terms of sexual crimes or by "habitual offender" laws are undeniably ineffective and have become so distorted in their application as to be meaningless.

3. Clear authority to sentence the "dangerous offender" to a long term of incapacitation may induce the legislature to agree more readily to a significantly shorter sentence for the nondangerous offender.

....

Virtually every State has a "habitual offender" law. Approximately half have special provisions dealing with sexual offenders or "sexual psychopaths." The goals of these statutes are similar and raise similar problems. They provide for extended incarceration, often life, often without eligibility for parole; they require a finding that the defendant fits within the specified category; they seek to prevent the return to the community of persons deemed especially dangerous. In the case of the sexual offender, specific psychiatric findings are required, while in the case of the recidivist, the danger is presumed from the fact of his repeated criminality.

"Sexual psychopath" laws follow a general pattern: they accept as a premise the theory that a "sexual" criminal is likely to repeat his crime unless removed from society for many years. The laws have been criticized for vagueness, overbreadth in application, and as imposing cruel and unusual punishment. Nevertheless, a majority of States now have sexual psychopath laws of one kind or another.

Both "recidivist" and "sexual psychopath" laws are aimed at the removal of potentially dangerous offenders from the society they otherwise might harass and damage. But each is grossly overbroad, poorly defined, often resulting in mismanagement and distortion of the criminal process and perpetuation of the arcane concept that the recidivist is *automatically* a danger to society, while the first offender is not. A repeater bad-check artist is hardly to be considered as dangerous to society as the professional killer who has been apprehended for the first time in his life. Within the spectrum between those two extremes lies an infinite variety of combinations of dangerousness and recidivism.

....

The standard authorizes extended maximum sentences beyond 5 years if the court finds that the defendant is a danger to the public *and* he fits within one of the three categories of offenders to which the standard is applicable: persistent offenders, professional criminals, and dangerous offenders.

The "persistent offender" definition should replace the broad, all-encompassing, and often abused "habitual offender" provisions existing in many States. The defendant must have been convicted of three felonies. One of the prior felonies must have been committed within 5 years of the third convic-

D. IMPRISONMENT

tion. This is to avoid instances where two felony convictions separated by 10, 15, or 20 years from the third result in extended confinement. There is little in such a situation to indicate that the offender is really dangerous. The persistent offender problem centers not so much on the number of offenses as on the pattern of continued criminal behavior with no indication of reform. Likewise it is required that two of the three convictions be for offenses involving serious bodily harm, either actual or contemplated. The interest of society in lengthy incapacitation of those who persist in acts dangerous to life or limb is clear. However, it is less clear why an extended term should be imposed for bad-check passing or like felonies not involving personal safety of others. On balance, the general 5-year maximum authorized by Standard 5.2 would appear sufficient.

The definition of professional criminal is directed toward persons involved in organized crime. The nature of the activity suggests that normal approaches to criminal sentencing are inappropriate. The professional criminal is not susceptible to correctional programming. His activity is based on the calculations appropriate to a business enterprise. The lengthy incapacitation of such offenders not only is justified but is perhaps the only appropriate sanction.

The definition of dangerous offender is an attempt to avoid psychiatric definitions of mental abnormality, which are not necessarily accurate and whose terminology may produce judicial reactions that can result in highly inappropriate sentencing. The history of the offender as contained in the presentence report should indicate whether or not he has a longstanding pattern of behavior threatening to the public. As stated in Standard 5.19, the court should be required to state in writing the reasons for the sentence imposed.

This standard also authorizes, in addition to an extended maximum term, the imposition of a judicial minimum. While mandatory legislative minimums are not recommended because of their inflexibility, in rare instances a court may find it desirable to impose a minimum sentence to preclude early parole. When the advisory committee which studied sentencing for the American Bar Association split on the issue of judicial control of the minimum sentence, the majority recognized that in some instances a court may feel the community needs reassurance as to the incapacitation of a particularly dangerous offender. The standard authorizes such imposition for that purpose, with the restriction that the minimum may not exceed 3 years or one-third of the maximum imposed.

To avoid the rigidity of the minimum sentence, the standard would allow the court to authorize parole for the offender prior to expiration of his minimum sentence if requested to do so by the paroling authority.

The standard also provides that in lieu of such judicial imposition of a minimum sentence, the court be authorized to recommend to the board of parole at time of sentencing that parole be denied for a given period of time. This would allow the court to express community feelings without making the sentence unduly rigid.

NOTES

1. Habitual criminal legislation is constitutional. *See Rummel v. Estelle,* 445 U.S. 263 (1980), discussed at p. 857 *supra; Graham v. West Virginia,* 224 U.S. 616 (1912); *Holley v. State,* 397 So. 2d 211 (Ala. Crim. App. 1981); *People v. Gutierrez,* 622 P.2d 547 (Colo. 1981).

2. Defendants have a constitutional claim to notice and hearing, *Oyler v. Boles,* 368 U.S. 448 (1962), and counsel, *Chewning v. Cunningham,* 368 U.S. 443 (1962), before habitual offender penalties may be enhanced, and data must be placed in a trial court record sufficient to support assessment of enhanced penalties. *State v. Wilson,* 627 P.2d 1185 (Kan. App. 1981). The full panoply of constitutional safeguards applicable to criminal trials need not govern recidivist penalty hearings, however. *See Eutsey v. Florida,* 383 So. 2d 219 (Fla. 1980) (discussing authorities); *Cavanaugh v. Crist,* 615 P.2d 890 (Mont. 1980).

3. A prosecutor's office classification system based on "high impact" crimes, requiring habitual criminal proceedings against perpetrators with two valid prior convictions, did not violate due process or equal protection. *State v. Rowe,* 609 P.2d 1348 (Wash. 1980).

4. Under a "central monitoring case" (CMC) system, the Federal Bureau of Prisons imposes stricter controls over some prisoners than others because of their criminal careers. Attacks have been lodged on assignments to such a status without a prior administrative hearing, with varying results. *Cf. Pugliese v. Nelson,* 617 F.2d 916 (2d Cir. 1980) (no hearing required), *with Bryant v. Carlson,* 489 F. Supp. 1075 (M.D. Pa. 1980) (hearing required).

NOTE ON FEDERAL SENTENCING GUIDELINES PROVISIONS RELATING TO CRIMINAL HISTORY AND LIVELIHOOD AND CAREER OFFENDERS

(a) *Criminal History.* As will be recalled, the normal sentence range for a given offense is determined by the placement of that offense within a grid, the vertical axis of which rests on offense level and the horizontal axis of which reflects an offender's criminal history.[1] The criminal history category for an offender is determined according to the total points cumulated according to the following factors:[2]

(1) Three points are added for each prior sentence of imprisonment exceeding one year and one month.[3] There is no limit to the number of points that can be compiled under this guideline.[4]

---

[1] *See* pp. 889-890 *supra.*

[2] *Federal Sentencing Guidelines,* § 4A1.1.

[3] *Id.* § 4A1.1(a). Sentences specifying fines or other nonmonetary incarcerative dispositions as an alternative to a term of imprisonment (*e.g.,* $1,000 fine or 90 days' imprisonment), are to be treated as nonimprisonment sentences. *Id.* § 4A1.2 comment (n.4).

[4] *Id.* § 4A1.1(a), comment (n.1). For purposes of this subparagraph, confinement requires that time have been served, or in instances of escape would have been served. The stated maximum term determines the applicability of the subsection, not the time actually served. *Id.* § 4A1.2, comment (n.2). There are, however, limitations on the availability of certain prior sentences under the guideline:

D. IMPRISONMENT

(2) Two points are added for each prior sentence of imprisonment of at least 60 days not counted in (1).[5]

(3) One point is added for each prior sentence not included in (1) or (2), but no more than four points can be added on the basis of this subsection.[6]

(4) Two points are to be added if a defendant committed the instant offense while under any criminal justice sentence, including probation, parole, supervised release, imprisonment, work release or escape status.[7]

(5) Two points are added if a defendant committed the instant offense less than two years after release from imprisonment on a sentence counted under (1) or (2); if two points have been added for item (4), only one additional point can be assessed under this subparagraph.[8]

(6) One point is added for each sentence resulting from a conviction of a crime of violence that has not been counted in (1)-(3) above.[9]

---

(1) Sentences imposed more than 15 years before defendant's commencement of the instant offense are not counted unless the defendant's incarceration extended into that 15-year period. *Id.* § 4A1.2(e), comment (n.1), cross-referring to *id.* § 4A1.2(e).

(2) Sentences imposed for offenses committed before a defendant's eighteenth birthday are counted only if they were imposed for convictions as an adult. *Id.* § 4A1.1, comment (n.1), cross-referring to *id.* § 4A1.2(d).

(3) Sentences based on foreign convictions, convictions that have been expunged or invalid convictions are not counted. *Id.* § 4A1.1, comment (n.2), cross-referring to *id.* § 4A1.2(h), (j) and Commentary to § 4A1.2.

[5]*Id.* § 4A1.1(b). For purposes of this subparagraph, confinement requires that time have been served, or in instances of escape would have been served. The stated maximum term determines the applicability of the subsection, not the time actually served. *Id.* § 4A1.2, comment (n.2). There are, however, limitations on the availability of certain prior sentences under the guideline:

(1) Sentences imposed more than ten years before defendant's commencement of the instant offense are not counted unless the defendant's incarceration extended into that 15-year period. *Id.*, cross-referring to *id.* § 4A1.2(e).

(2) Sentences imposed for offenses committed before a defendant's eighteenth birthday are counted only if the defendant's incarceration extended into a five-year period preceding the commencement of the instant offense. *Id.*, cross-referring to *id.* § 4A1.2(d).

(3) Sentences for nonfelony offenses listed in *id.* § 4A1.2(c)(2) are never counted.

(4) Sentences based on foreign convictions, convictions that have been expunged or invalid convictions are not counted. *Id.* § 4A1.1, comment (n.2), cross-referring to *id.* § 4A1.2(h), (j).

[6]*Federal Sentencing Guidelines*, § 4A1.1(c). There are, however, limitations on the availability of certain prior sentences under the guideline:

(1) Sentences imposed more than ten years before defendant's commencement of the instant offense are not counted. *Id.*, cross-referring to *id.* § 4A1.2(e).

(2) Sentences imposed for offenses committed before a defendant's eighteenth birthday are counted only if imposed within five years of the defendant's commencement of the instant offense. *Id.*, cross-referring to *id.* § 4A1.2(d).

(3) Sentences for certain specified nonfelony offenses are counted only if they resulted in a term of probation of at least one year or a term of imprisonment of at least 30 days, or if the prior offense was similar to an instant offense. *Id.*, cross-referring to *id.* § 4A1.2(c)(1).

(4) Sentences for nonfelony offenses listed in *id.* § 4A1.2(c)(2) are never counted.

(5) Diversionary dispositions are counted only if there has been a finding or admission of guilt in a judicial proceeding. *Id.*, cross-referring to *id.* § 4A1.2(f).

(6) Sentences based on foreign convictions, convictions that have been expunged or invalid convictions are not counted. *Id.*, cross-referring to *id.* § 4A1.2(h), (j) and Commentary to § 4A1.2.

(7) Military sentences are counted only if imposed by a general or special court martial. *Id.*, cross-referring to *id.* § 4A1.2(g). *Id.* § 4A1.2, comment (n.3).

[7]*Id.* § 4A1.1(d). The term **criminal justice sentence** means a sentence countable under *id.* § 4A1.2. *Id.* § 4A1.1(d), comment (n.4).

[8]*Id.* § 4A1.1(e). The subsection applies if a defendant committed any part of the instant offense, that is, any relevant conduct, or if the defendant committed the instant offense while in imprisonment or escape status under such a sentence. *Id.* § 4A1.1(e), comment (n.5).

[9]*Id.* § 4A1.1(f).

Prior convictions may represent convictions in the federal system, 50 state systems, District of Columbia, territories and foreign, tribal and military courts.[10] Juvenile delinquency adjudications can be used for purposes of a determination of a federal criminal history category,[11] even though they are not available for a like purpose under state law.[12]

(b) *Departures from Criminal History Categories.* The United States Sentencing Commission chose to utilize a policy statement rather than a guideline to set forth the circumstances under which departures can occur from the criminal history categories determined under the more specific guidelines.[13] It recognized that criminal history scores do not necessarily reflect all the variations in the seriousness of criminal histories that may occur.[14]

Essentially, if reliable information indicates that a criminal history category does not adequately reflect the seriousness of the defendant's past criminal conduct or the likelihood that the defendant will commit other crimes, a court may consider imposing a sentence departing from the otherwise applicable guideline range. The Commission set forth a nonconclusive list of factors that might be relevant in that way: (1) Prior sentence(s) not used in computing the criminal history category, *e.g.*, sentences for foreign and tribal offenses. (2) Prior sentence(s) of substantially more than one year imposed as a result of independent crimes committed on different occasions. (3) Prior similar misconduct established by a civil adjudication or a failure to comply with an administrative order. (4) The fact of whether a defendant was pending trial, sentencing or appeal on another charge at the time of the instant offense. (5) Prior similar adult criminal conduct not resulting in a criminal conviction.

Courts are warranted in departing upward from the guidelines if the criminal history category significantly underrepresents the seriousness of the actual criminal history or the likelihood of recidivism.[15] A prior arrest record,

---

[10] *Id.* § 4A1.1, comment (backg'd). The Commission selected a criterion of maximum imposed terms of imprisonment, rather than designations as felonies and misdemeanors; it thought that imposition of a maximum sentence exceeding a year and one month usually reflects a judicial assessment that the underlying criminal conduct was serious. *Id.*

[11] United States v. Mackbee, 894 F.2d 1057, 1058 (9th Cir.) (*per curiam*), *cert. denied*, 495 U.S. 962 (1990).

[12] United States v. Kirby, 893 F.2d 867, 868 (6th Cir. 1990) (*per curiam*).

[13] *Federal Sentencing Guidelines* § 4A1.3.

[14] *Sentencing Guidelines* § 4A1.3, comment. For example, a defendant with an extensive record of serious assaultive conduct who had received what might later be considered extremely lenient treatment in the past might have the same criminal history category as a defendant with a record of less serious conduct. Nevertheless, the first defendant's history clearly may be the more serious. The Commission believed this might be particularly true in instances of defendants in their early twenties or younger, who are more likely to have received repeated lenient treatment, but in fact may pose a greater risk of serious recidivism than older defendants. The policy statement authorizes the consideration of a departure from the guidelines in the limited circumstances in which reliable information indicates that the criminal history category does not adequately reflect the seriousness of the defendant's criminal history or likelihood of recidivism, and provides guidance for the judicial consideration of such departures. *Id.*

[15] *Id.* § 4A1.3. Examples include defendants who (1) had several previous foreign sentences for serious offenses, (2) had received a prior consolidated sentence of ten years for a series of serious assaults, (3) had a similar instance of large scale fraudulent misconduct established by an adjudication in a SEC enforcement proceeding; (4) committed the instant offense while on bail or

D. IMPRISONMENT

standing alone, is not sufficient, however, in the Commission's view.[16]

Departures can be downward, if a court concludes that a criminal history category overrepresents the seriousness of a criminal history or the likelihood of repeated criminality.[17]

In utilizing the policy statement, courts should find an alternative criminal history category, the defendants falling within which in general resemble the defendant in question.

(c) *Career Offenders.* Defendants count as career offenders if: (1) They were at least 18 years old at the time of the instant offense. (2) The instant offense of conviction is a felony that is either a crime of violence or a controlled substance offense. (3) They have at least two prior felony convictions of either a crime of violence or a controlled substance offense.[18]

In such cases, a career offender's criminal history category must be Category VI.[19] In addition, a contingent reevaluation of the offense level should be conducted based on the following table:

Offense	Statutory Penalty	Maximum Offense Level
(A)	Life	37
(B)	25 years or more	34
(C)	20 years or more, but less than 25 years	32
(D)	15 years or more, but less than 20 years	29
(E)	10 years or more, but less than 15 years	24
(F)	5 years or more, but less than 10 years	17
(G)	More than 1 year, but less than 5 years	12

Either the score according to the table or the base offense level, whichever is higher, will then be used.

If an adjustment based on acceptance of responsibility[20] applies, the otherwise applicable offense level is to be decreased by two levels.[21]

---

pretrial release for another serious offense, or (5) appropriate reasons like cooperation of other defendants. *Id.*

[16] *Id.*

[17] The Commission offered as an example a defendant with two minor misdemeanor convictions close to ten years before the instant offense, and no other evidence of prior criminal behavior in the intervening period. *Id.*

[18] *Id.* § 4B1.1.

[19] *Id.*

[20] Pursuant to *id.* § 3E1.1.

[21] *Id.* § 4B1.1, comment (n.2). The term "offense statutory maximum" as used in the guideline refers to the maximum term of imprisonment authorized for the offense of conviction that is a crime of violence or controlled substance offense; if more than one count of conviction is a crime of violence or controlled substance offense, the maximum authorized term of imprisonment for the count that authorizes the greatest maximum term of imprisonment is to be used in the computation. *Id.* The term "crime of violence" is defined according to Title 18, § 16. The term "controlled substance offense" is defined according to designated sections of the Controlled Substances Act. *Id.* § 4B1.2(2) (referring to 21 U.S.C.A. §§ 841, 952(a), 955, 955a, 959, 405B, 416 (West Supp. 1993)). The term "prior felony conviction" means a prior adult federal or state conviction for an offense punishable by death or imprisonment for a term exceeding one year, whether or not such

(d) *Criminal Livelihood.* The offense level for defendants who committed an offense as part of a pattern of criminal conduct [22] from which they derived a substantial portion of their income [23] shall not be less than 13; such defendants are ineligible for probation.[24]

(e) *Armed Career Criminal.* In 1990, the Commission added a new basis for determining criminal history categories, based on a defendant's status as an armed career criminal.[25] The offense level for an armed career criminal is the greatest of the following: (1) The offense level applicable under the general principles set out in Chapters 2 and 3 of the *Federal Sentencing Guidelines*.[26] (2) The offense level determined on the basis of being a career offender [27] if applicable.[28] (3) An offense level of 34 if the defendant used or possessed the firearm or ammunition in connection with a crime of violence or controlled substance offense [29] or if the firearm was of a type described in 26 U.S.C. § 5845(a) (1988).[30] (4) An offense level of 33, if no other provision governs.[31]

In instances falling within the latter two categories, if the provisions governing acceptance of responsibility [32] apply, the level is to be reduced by two levels.[33]

The criminal history category for an armed career criminal is the greatest from among the following: (1) The criminal history category from Chapter 4, Part A, or Section 4B1.1 (career offenders), if applicable.[34] (2) Category VI if

---

an offense is specifically designated as a felony and without regard to the sentence actually imposed. *Id.* § 4B1.2, comment (n.3). The term "two prior felony convictions" has two dimensions. The first is that the defendant committed the instant offense after sustaining at least two felony convictions of a crime of violence or a controlled substance offense. That would include two crimes of violence, two controlled substance offenses or one crime of violence and one controlled substance offense. *Id.* § 4B1.2(3). The second is that the sentences for at least two of the felony convictions count separately under the provisions of Part A (criminal history under § 4A1.1). *Id.* The date a defendant sustained a conviction is the date the judgment of conviction was entered. *Id.*

[22] The term "pattern of criminal conduct" means planned criminal acts occurring over a substantial period of time; those acts may involve a single course of conduct or be independent offenses. *Id.* § 4B1.3, comment.

[23] The term "engaged in as a livelihood" means that (1) a defendant derived income from the pattern of criminal conduct that in any 12-month period exceeded 2,000 times the then-existing hourly minimum wage under federal law, and (2) the totality of circumstances shows that the criminal conduct was the defendant's primary occupation in that 12-month period (*e.g.*, the defendant engaged in criminal conduct rather than regular, legitimate employment, or the defendant's legitimate employment was merely a front for the criminal conduct). *Id.* § 4B1.3, comment (n.2).

[24] *Id.* § 4B1.3.

[25] *Id.* § 4B1.4(a) defines as "an armed career criminal" a person who is subject to an enhanced sentence under 18 U.S.C. § 924(e) (1988). That in turn covers persons convicted of committing the federal firearms offense defined in *id.* § 922(g) by a person who has at least three prior convictions for either a violent felony or a serious drug offense, or both, committed on occasions different from one another. The terms "violent felony" and "serious drug offense" are defined in *id.* § 924(e)(2) (which definitions are not identical with those otherwise provided for sentencing purposes in *Federal Sentencing Guidelines* § 4B1.1; neither are the time periods for counting prior sentences under *id.* § 4A1.2 the same). *See id.* § 4B1.4, comment (n.1).

[26] *Federal Sentencing Guidelines* § 4B1.4(b)(1).

[27] Under *id.* § 4B1.1.

[28] *Id.* § 4B1.4(b)(2).

[29] As defined in *id.* § 4B1.2(1).

[30] *Id.* § 4B1.4(b)(3)(A).

[31] *Id.* § 4B1.4(b)(3)(B).

[32] Under *id.* § 3E1.1.

[33] *Id.* § 4B1.4 note*.

[34] *Id.* § 4B1.4(c)(1).

the defendant used or possessed the firearm or ammunition in connection with a crime of violence or controlled substance offense[35] or if the firearm was of a type described in 26 U.S.C. § 5845(a) (1988).[36] (3) Category IV.[37]

3. MULTIPLE SENTENCES

MODEL PENAL CODE § 7.06

[The text of this section appears in Appendix A.]

UNITED STATES NATIONAL ADVISORY COMMISSION ON CRIMINAL JUSTICE STANDARDS AND GOALS, CORRECTIONS REPORT (1973)

Standard 5.6

Multiple Sentences

State legislatures should authorize sentencing courts to make disposition of offenders convicted of multiple offenses, as follows:

1. Under normal circumstances, when an offender is convicted of multiple offenses separately punishable, or when an offender is convicted of an offense while under sentence on a previous conviction, the court should be authorized to impose concurrent sentences.

2. Where the court finds on substantial evidence that the public safety requires a longer sentence, the court should be authorized to impose consecutive sentences. However, a consecutive sentence should not be imposed if the result would be a maximum sentence more than double the maximum sentence authorized for the most serious of the offenses involved.

3. The sentencing court should have authority to allow a defendant to plead guilty to any other offenses he has committed within the State, after the concurrence of the prosecutor and after determination that the plea is voluntarily made. The court should take each of these offenses into account in setting the sentence. Thereafter, the defendant should not be held further accountable for the crimes to which he has pleaded guilty.

4. The sentencing court should be authorized to impose a sentence that would run concurrently with out-of-State sentences, even though the time will be served in an out-of-State institution. When apprised of either pending charges or outstanding detainers against the defendant in other jurisdictions, the court should be given by interstate agreements the authority to allow the defendant to plead to those charges and to be sentenced, as provided for in the case of intrastate criminal activity.

Commentary

A perplexing problem, in terms of both substantive criminal law and sentencing policy, has been presented by the "multiple" offender. Several situa-

---

[35] As defined in *id.* § 4B1.2(1).
[36] *Id.* § 4B1.4(c)(2).
[37] *Id.* § 4B1.4(c)(3).

tions, each distinct, but each raising the same basic point, can be hypothesized:

1. The offender commits one criminal "act," but it causes two injuries, such as detonation of a bomb that causes both personal and property damage.

2. The offender commits the same offense several times, as when a bank teller embezzles a large sum of money over a period of time.

3. The offender commits several separate acts, all within the same "transaction," as (a) entering a bank with the intent to steal, (b) stealing, and (c) escaping in a (d) stolen car (e) across State lines.

4. The offender commits one "act," punishable by two or more jurisdictions, as when a defendant robs a federally insured bank, which is both a Federal and a State crime.

5. The offender commits different crimes, at different times, in different jurisdictions.

The problem of the multiple offender is complicated by a number of factors and legal doctrines that come into play when an offender is charged with more than one offense within the same jurisdiction. Depending on the circumstances, the prosecuting attorney may wish to consolidate all related offenses into one action to make efficient use of prosecution and judicial resources. The defendant, on the other hand, may believe himself to be prejudiced by having too many offenses consolidated in the same trial, reasoning that the jury may believe that, with so many charges, one or more has to be true.

However, the opposite attitudes may prevail. The prosecutor may wish to sever the trial of related offenses in order to have more than one chance of conviction, or because, although prepared for one offense, he lacks evidence for support of the other. In addition, the prosecution may seek to obtain consecutive sentences with more than one trial to increase the punishment. The defendant may wish to consolidate all offenses either to avoid having to suffer through more than one trial or in the belief that he will receive a lesser sentence if all offenses are tried together.

Multiple offenses that cross jurisdictional lines are even more complex. When two jurisdictions are involved, there generally are two prosecutors and two courts that must decide the extent to which offenses can be consolidated. And where two separate States are involved, resolution of the issue may depend on the availability of interstate agreements authorizing consolidation. The allocation of the expense of the trial and eventual correctional program also are factors that make interjurisdictional consolidation of offenses difficult.

Whatever justification there may be for severing various offenses for separate trial, from the correctional standpoint the consolidation of trials would result in more appropriate sentences. An offender standing trial for additional offenses is not likely to be receptive to correctional programs. Also a plan for reintegrating the offender into the community is not practicable if he faces further confinement in another jurisdiction or further trial on pending charges.

One result of multiple trials is the potential for consecutive sentences. An offender sentenced to one term of years subsequently is sentenced to another term to be served after completion of the first. There is little justification for this result other than to extend the period of confinement. Such an extension, if based solely on the fact that more than one offense was committed, regardless of the needs of the particular offender or the requirements of public safety, amounts to the imposition of sanction purely for punishment purposes.

....

The presumption should be in favor of concurrent sentences for multiple offenses. This report has recognized the need for extended terms for certain dangerous offenders in Standard 5.3. Sentences beyond the maximum of 5 years normally should be imposed only where the recommendations and specific findings of Standard 5.3 are met.

4. MANDATORY MINIMUM SENTENCES

AMERICAN BAR ASSOCIATION STANDARDS FOR CRIMINAL JUSTICE (2d Ed. 1981) SENTENCING ALTERNATIVES AND PROCEDURES

§ 4.3. Commentary pp. 18-267 to 18-271.

Legislative Minimums

In overview, four basic arguments can be made in opposition to legislatively required minimum sentences: (1) they result in injustice in a significant number of cases; (2) they may actually aggravate the disparity problem; (3) they do not accomplish the ends for which they were designed and, indeed, may be counterproductive to them; and (4) less drastic means exist to accomplish those ends, and such means will probably prove more successful as well.

The basic argument about injustice has already been made in connection with the disapproval in Standard 18-2.1(c) of mandatory sentences and requires little further elaboration. Legislative overbreadth is inevitable; the most severe crimes tend to be the least homogeneous. Thus, as a predictable result, mandatory minimums will result in the imposition of far more punishment in some cases than would seem appropriate to even the sternest of retributionists.

The second argument — that mandatory minimums can actually exacerbate the disparity problem — may seem paradoxical, since the intent of many such statutes has been to assure fair and certain punishment for all who have committed the same offense. Yet, for two reasons this may not occur. First, of course, are the familiar problems of plea bargaining. The "offense of conviction" may be less severe than the "real offense" for any of a variety of reasons. Second, proposals for mandatory minimums overlook the steady growth in recent years of pretrial diversion programs under which offenders whose guilt is either acknowledged as a condition of participation or established at a relatively informal hearing are diverted from the criminal justice system before trial. The existence of a mandatory minimum widens the gap between those informally diverted and those formally adjudicated, since the former will typically receive a form of probation-like supervision while the latter will be confined. Given the volume of the cases that courts in many jurisdictions must process, proposals to curtail or abolish either plea bargaining or informal diversion must still be described as more heroic than realistic. The upshot, then, is a system of criminal disposition that is neither fair nor certain but has increased rigidity.

The third argument — that mandatory minimums generally prove counterproductive — is perhaps even more surprising, but careful empirical studies have reached this conclusion. A noteworthy example is the study conducted by the Association of the Bar of the City of New York in connection with the Drug Abuse Council, Inc., of New York's particularly severe drug offense laws.[11] Adopted in 1973, these statutes established a mandatory minimum of between fifteen and twenty-five years for persons convicted of selling one or more ounces of heroin or of possession of more than two ounces.[12] Lesser penalties involving minimums of between six and eight and one-third years and a maximum of life were established for those selling or possessing lesser quantities.[13] The impact of these statutes on both the criminal justice system and the crime rate was closely studied over a three-year period, and the following conclusions were reached: (1) illegal use of drugs was more widespread at the end of the period than at the beginning; (2) serious property crimes of the sort associated with heroin users had increased sharply; and (3) the special recidivist sentencing provisions of these statutes did not appear to have deterred significantly even the prior felony offenders, who were subjected by their operation to lengthy mandatory sentences if reconvicted.[14]

What accounted for these disappointing results? It was concluded that the criminal justice system as a whole had failed to increase the threat to the offender, even though a single variable — the penalty structure — had been significantly enhanced. Particularly in New York City, the time required to process drug law cases had lengthened dramatically. Demands for trials had risen and the productivity of the new courts established by these laws had not matched that of the judicial system as a whole. Most important, the risk of imprisonment for persons having one or more prior felony convictions had actually fallen after the 1973 statutes took effect. Why? To begin with, the rate had been higher than the legislature probably realized (84 percent of those convicted of a second crime already were in the process of receiving a prison term in 1971 before the 1973 statute went into force),[15] but after 1973, both the percentage of felony arrests resulting in indictments and the percentage of indictments leading to conviction declined for these prior offenders (in the former case from 40 to 24 percent and in the latter from 90 to 71 percent).[16] The net result was that where 24 percent of prior felons newly arrested for a felony had been ultimately sent to prison, the new rate was only 16 percent.[17] In short, the "tough" law had produced a perversely illogical (although perhaps foreseeable) result.

---

[11] ASSOCIATION OF THE BAR OF THE CITY OF NEW YORK AND DRUG ABUSE COUNCIL, THE NATION'S TOUGHEST DRUG LAW (1977).

[12] N.Y. PENAL LAW § 70.00 (McKinney 1975). Such acts were made class A-I felonies.

[13] These penalties were made applicable to class A-II felonies, which were defined to include middle-level drug dealers who sold one-eighth of an ounce or more or possessed one to two ounces.

[14] The Nation's Toughest Drug Law, *supra* note 11, at 7-11.

[15] *Id.* at 67. In short, although the intent of the statute was to incapacitate the "career" criminal who had previous convictions, the evidence in New York was that this offender was not escaping confinement on a second conviction.

[16] *Id.* at 68.

[17] *Id.*

Such a study does not disprove the theory of deterrence; rather, it shows the difficulties of implementation and the likelihood of hidden variables, which the legislature tends to ignore or underestimate, such as court congestion and prosecutorial plea bargaining practices. Other studies have not always been as dramatic in their findings. Indeed, a study of the Bartley-Fox Law in Massachusetts (which imposes a considerably shorter mandatory term of one year for possession of an unregistered firearm) found significant reduction in the number of firearms violations and no overall pattern of prosecutorial or judicial nullification.[18] There, however, the penalty was short and compliance was uniquely possible because firearms could be registered without great difficulty. Nonetheless, only 62 percent of Bartley-Fox defendants were convicted.[19] A fair generalization, still, is that the overall response to such mandatory minimums has been one of judicial resistance and prosecutorial evasion.

Still another perspective on the efficacy of mandatory minimum sentences has been supplied by a Federal Judicial Center study conducted in 1977.[20] Examining recent federal proposals for mandatory minimums, the study asked how such proposals, if enacted, would change existing sentencing practices in the federal courts. After a careful study of pre-sentence reports to detect the presence or absence of the factors that these proposals (six in all) would have employed to require a mandatory minimum, it reported that "few sentences were found that conflicted with the legislative proposals."[21] What mandatory minimum proposals seem to ignore is that sentencing disparity is most aggravated in the intermediate-gravity ranges, and it is not these offenses but the more serious ones on which legislative proposals tend to focus. In so doing, they overlook the high probability that the vast majority of such serious offenses already result in imprisonment.

A final reason for rejecting mandatory minimums exists today that was absent at the time of the first edition of these standards: a system of presumptive guidelines can achieve the same anticipated benefits as mandatory minimums were thought to offer, but with less adverse consequences in terms of overbreadth, delay, and disparity. As existing practice shows, guidelines will not be written on a blank slate, but will probably begin with existing sentencing averages. Thus, adequate provision will be made for the serious offense or the dangerous offender. Even as modified, little valid reason exists to suspect that a guideline drafting agency will adamantly resist a clear legislative

---

[18] Beha, "And Nobody Can Get You Out": The Impact of a Mandatory Prison Sentence for the Illegal Carrying of a Firearm on the Use of Firearms and on the Administration of Criminal Justice in Boston (pt. 1), 57 B.U. L. Rev. 96 (1977). *See also* MASS. ANN. LAWS, ch. 269, § 10 (Michie/Law Co-op Cum. Supp. 1979) (the Bartley-Fox Act).

[19] Although there was a material decline in the conviction rate after the adoption of the mandatory penalty, the Harvard study attributes this to more vigorous defense work, rather than to judicial evasion of the law. The effectiveness of the mandatory minimum in reducing the use of firearms seems also to have been enhanced by the considerable publicity surrounding its adoption and the relative lack of severity of the penalty.

[20] J. EAGLIN & A. PARTRIDGE, AN EVALUATION OF THE PROBABLE IMPACT OF SELECTED PROPOSALS FOR IMPOSING MANDATORY MINIMUM SENTENCES IN THE FEDERAL COURTS (1977).

[21] *Id.* at 14. For some serious crimes, *e.g.*, bank robbery and aggravated assault however, significant deviations between actual sentences and the proposed mandatory minimums were found.

desire that the dangerous offender be isolated or that a grave offense be appropriately punished.

Table of Cases

References are to pages. Principal cases and pages where they appear are in italics.

A

Abbott v. The Queen, 566
Addington v. Texas, 625, 627, 642
Aden v. Younger, 877
Agnew v. State, 374
Ake v. Oklahoma, 861
Aldrich v. People, 378
Allen v. People, 765
Allen v. State, 371
Anderson v. State, 113
Application of Jones, 625
Arizona v. Manypenny, 64
Arnold v. United States, 217

B

Babcock v. State, 825
Backun v. United States, 733
Bailey v. Commonwealth, 525
Banton v. State, 31
Barnes v. United States, 468
Baxstrom v. Herold, 643
Beard v. United States, 524
Bearden v. Georgia, 900, 908, 910
Beardsley, 119
Beausoliel v. United States, 191
Bell v. Commonwealth, 792
Blondheim v. State, 667
Blumenthal v. United States, 811
Bolling v. Sharpe, 49
Booth v. State, 773
Bordenkircher v. Hayes, 51
Bowers v. Hardwick, 51
Bowring v. Godwin, 642
Bradley v. United States, 31
Brewster v. State, 50
Britton v. Rogers, 858, 899
Brooks v. State, 379, 618
Brown v. United States, 524
Bruce v. Estelle, 637
Bryant v. Carlson, 932
Buck v. Bell, 877
Buckingham v. State, 15
Bullock v. United States, 274
Bundren v. State, 172
Burchett v. Bower, 643
Butterfield v. State, 558, 559
Butts v. Commonwealth, 447
Byrum v. State, 404

C

Calder v. Bull, 26
Calhoun v. State, 385
Callanan v. United States, 786
Cannon v. State, 349
Caplin & Drysdale, Chartered v. United States, 924, 925
Carella v. California, 60
Carey v. State, 371
Carlson v. Greene, 642
Carr v. Clark County Sheriff, 128
Cascio v. State, 194
Casey v. State, 725
Castle v. United States, 560
Cavanaugh v. Crist, 932
Chambers v. Mississippi, 655
Chapman v. State, 163
Chappell v. United States, 358
Chavez v. United States, 630, 636
Chewning v. Cunningham, 932
Christensen v. State, 179
Christian v. Commonwealth, 263
City of Chicago v. Wilson, 26, 43
City of Dallas v. Stanglin, 49
City of Lorain v. Tomasic, 63
City of Portland v. Dollarhide, 14
City of Seattle v. Buchanan, 49
City of Spokane v. Portch, 63
City of Tacoma v. Luvene, 37, 46
Cladd v. State, 492
Clemons, 866
Coker v. Georgia, 859
Coleman v. State, 513
Collins v. Youngblood, 26
Coloutti v. Franklin, 234
Colten v. Kentucky, 34
Commonwealth v. Adams, 709
Commonwealth v. Balliro, 313
Commonwealth v. Barky, 630
Commonwealth v. Benders, 724
Commonwealth v. Beneficial Fin. Co., 736
Commonwealth v. Benesch, 710
Commonwealth v. Bomersbach, 416
Commonwealth v. Bowden, 309
Commonwealth v. Bridge, 653
Commonwealth v. Buckley, 126
Commonwealth v. Burke, 218
Commonwealth v. Cheatham, 109
Commonwealth v. Colandro, 322

Commonwealth v. Davis, 177
Commonwealth v. Dodge, 52
Commonwealth v. Emmons, 536
Commonwealth v. Farrar, 471
Commonwealth v. French, 548
Commonwealth v. Froelich, 488
Commonwealth v. Gallison, 119
Commonwealth v. Gerulis, 453
Commonwealth v. Godin, 121
Commonwealth v. Gormley, 803
Commonwealth v. Gregory, 190, 512, 524
Commonwealth v. Henson, 173
Commonwealth v. Hicks, 653, 654
Commonwealth v. Hill, 629
Commonwealth v. Howard, 256
Commonwealth v. Jennings, 321
Commonwealth v. Johnston, 523
Commonwealth v. Kendrick, 511
Commonwealth v. King, 52
Commonwealth v. Klein, 548
Commonwealth v. Koczwara, 700
Commonwealth v. Konz, 26
Commonwealth v. Koons, 558, 559
Commonwealth v. Lee, 125
Commonwealth v. Lewis, 266
Commonwealth v. Lombardi, 630, 637
Commonwealth v. Malone, 286
Commonwealth v. Mangula, 820
Commonwealth v. Mochan, 4
Commonwealth v. Moon, 179
Commonwealth v. Moreira, 548
Commonwealth v. Mutnik, 449
Commonwealth v. Ostolaza, 476
Commonwealth v. Perry, 723, 820
Commonwealth v. Rementer, 241
Commonwealth v. Rogers, 585
Commonwealth v. Root, 256
Commonwealth v. Rosenberg, 672
Commonwealth v. Shaffer, 524
Commonwealth v. Skufca, 257
Commonwealth v. Sleighter, 484
Commonwealth v. Sourbeer, 857
Commonwealth v. Spallone, 303
Commonwealth v. Stasiun, 820
Commonwealth v. Tilley, 496
Commonwealth v. Travis, 626
Commonwealth v. White, 367
Commonwealth v. Williams, 339
Commonwealth v. Youngkin, 257
Commonwealth v. Yourawski, 426
Compton v. State, 362
Connecticut v. Menillo, 234
County Court of Ulster County v. Allen, 59, 449, 468, 756
Craig v. Boren, 49
Crutcher v. State, 379
Crutchfield v. State, 62

Cruzan v. Director, Missouri Department of Health, 190, 241
Cummings v. Commonwealth, 379
Curry v. State, 621

D

Davis, 178
Davis v. Alaska, 655
Davis v. State, 630, 675, 677, 743
Dawson v. Delaware, 865
DeBettencourt v. State, 502
DeKaplany v. Enomoto, 630
Director of Pub. Prosecution v. Smith, 288, 290
Director of Pub. Prosecutions v. Majewski, 650
Doe v. Bolton, 233, 234
Don Moran v. People, 219
Dorsey v. Solomon, 626
Dotson v. State, 679
Douglas v. Seacoast Products, Inc., 63
Dowling v. United States, 21
D.P.P. v. Morgan, 203, 669, 677
D.P.P. v. Nock & Alsford, 783
Dunlavey v. Commonwealth, 372
Dupuy v. State, 748

E

Eddings v. Oklahoma, 865
Edwards v. State, 167, 484
Eisenstadt v. Baird, 53
Employment Div., Dep't of Human Resources of Ore. v. Smith, 71
Enmund v. Florida, 859
Espinosa v. Florida, 865
Espy v. State, 813
Estate of Hofferber, 638
Estelle v. Gamble, 642, 855
Estelle v. Smith, 616
Eutsey v. Florida, 932
Evans v. Commonwealth, 458
Ex parte Boetscher, 50
Ex Parte Fraley, 318
Ex Parte Guerrero, 32
Ex parte Hagans, 629
Ex parte Heigho, 246
Ex parte Kent, 637

F

Farnsworth v. Zerbst, 825
Federov v. United States, 51
Fenster v. Leary, 657
Fitzpatrick v. State, 195
Flippo v. State, 119
Flohr v. Territory, 408
Ford v. Wainwright, 868
Foster v. Commonwealth, 768

TABLE OF CASES

Fowler v. State, 525
Francis v. Franklin, 54, 60, 449, 468, 682
Frank v. State, 79
Frendak v. United States, 615
Frisby v. Schultz, 78
Frolik v. State, 49
Fugate v. Commonwealth, 362
Fulcher v. State, 603
Fulton v. State, 350

G

Gaetano v. United States, 78
Garcia v. State, 793, 825
Gardner v. State, 595, 821
Gargan v. State, 767
Gebardi v. United States, 825
Gibbs v. Helgemoe, 627
Gibson v. Commonwealth, 524
Goddard v. State, 655
Gonzales v. State, 195
Gooding v. Wilson, 34
Gordon v. State, 678, 679
Government of the Virgin Islands v. Fredericks, 600, *618*
Government of Virgin Islands v. Williams, 10
Graham v. State, 618
Graham v. West Virginia, 932
Grayned v. City of Rockford, 36
Green v. State, 270
Gregg v. Georgia, 860
Groneau v. State, 746
Groomes v. United States, 432
Guerin v. State, 468

H

H. L. v. Matheson, 234
H.L. Sykes v. Director of Public Prosecutions, 7
Haines v. Wisconsin, 78
Hall v. State, 60
Hall v. United States, 218
Hamburg v. State, 125
Hammontree v. Phelps, 344
Hancock v. Commonwealth, 502
Harmelin v. Michigan, 854
Harrell v. State, 653, 654
Harris v. McCrae, 234
Harris v. State, 449, 562, 813
Haughton v. Smith, 783
Hays v. People, 191
Head v. New Mexico Board of Examiners in Optometry, 63
Heath v. Alabama, 375
Hernandez v. Commonwealth, 46
Hetherton v. Sears, Roebuck & Co., 50
Hintz v. State, 852

Hite v. State, 309
Hodges v. Commonwealth, 375
Hodgson v. Minnesota, 234
Hoffman v. State, 301
Holland v. State, 9
Holley v. State, 932
Hopkins v. State, 683
Howe v. Smith, 66
Humphrey v. Cady, 642
Hurley v. United States, 775
Hutchinson v. State, 797
Hyam v. D.P.P., 732

I

Iannelli v. United States, 826, 827
In re Appeal No. 631 (77) From the District Court of Montgomery County, Juvenile Div., 497
In re D.W.J., Jr., 169
In re Davis, 637, 638
In re G.L., 492
In re Greene, 10
In re Hurt, 643
In re J.N., Jr., 142, 248
In re Lewis, 627
In re Lynch, 856
In re M., 765
In re M.E., 493
In re Matson, 856
In re Moore, 877
In re Moye, 626
In re Powell, 61
In re Pray, 638
In re Ramon M., 603, *656*
In re Torsney, 625, 627
In the Matter of Anthony M., 245
Inmates of Allegheny County Jail v. Peirce, 642

J

Jackson v. Indiana, 630
Jackson v. State, 305
Jacobson v. United States, 577
Jaffe, 783
Jarrett v. State, 475
Jenkins v. State, 125
Jennings v. United States, 493
Johnson v. Mississippi, 862
Johnson v. State, 125, 447
Jones v. State, 825
Jones v. United States, 119
Jordan v. State, 468
Juneby v. State, 881

K

Kanteles v. Wheelock, 641
Kelley v. People, 404

Kelly v. Robinson, 906, 907
Kelner v. United States, 182
Kesselbrenner v. Anonymous, 643
Ketchum v. Commonwealth, 452
Ketchum v. Ward, 691
Kimoktoak v. State, 94
Kind v. State, 621
King v. Commonwealth, 341
King v. State, 172
Kleinbart v. United States, 617
Krulewitch v. United States, 786

L

Labor v. Gibson, 614
Lajoie v. The Queen, 747
Lake v. State, 404
Lamb v. State, 172
Lambert v. California, 710
Landen v. United States, 709
Lane v. State, 628, 638
Lanzetta v. New Jersey, 33, 827
Law v. State, 542
Lawson v. Commonwealth, 496
Lee v. State, 431
Lewis v. Commonwealth, 11
Lewis v. State, 721, 742
Liles v. Ward, 643
Linne v. State, 435
Liparota v. United States, 709
Litton v. Commonwealth, 491
Lockett v. Ohio, 865, 866
Lockland v. State, 536
Locklear v. State, 449
Long v. State, 692
Love v. State, 560
Lovelace v. State, 113
Lupo v. United States, 637
Lutz v. United States, 52
Lynch v. D.P.P., 566

M

Mack v. State, 448
Mackey v. Procunier, 877
Madison v. State, 195
Maggio v. Williams, 860
Marley v. State, 775
Marthall v. State, 178
Martin v. Estelle, 637
Martin v. Ohio, 513
Martin v. State, 313
Mason v. State, 129
Massachusetts v. Westcott, 63
Matter of Lewis, 623
McClellan v. Commonwealth, 332
McCleskey v. Kemp, 860, 867
McCreary v. State, 351
McElroy v. United States, 471

McKay v. North Carolina, 866
McQuirk v. State, 218, 219
Meazel v. State, 274
Messer v. State, 747
Michael M. v. Superior Court of Sonoma County, 224
Miller v. California, 47
Miller v. Florida, 27
Mills v. Maryland, 866
Miranda v. Arizona, 616, 630
Mistretta v. United States, 890, 892, 893
Mitchell v. Territory, 386
Monsanto, 925
Montague v. State, 617
Montgomery v. Commonwealth, 534
Moore v. Lowe, 725
Morissette v. United States, 69, 703, 719
Morris v. State, 179
Morrison v. Commonwealth, 527
Morrow v. State, 630
Moskal v. United States, 17
Mullaney v. Wilbur, 447

N

Neely v. State, 577
Nell v. State, 775
New York City Health & Hospital Corp. v. Stein, 877
Newlon v. Bennett, 375
Nigro v. United States, 825
Nixon v. State, 350
Noble v. State, 617
Norris v. State, 653
North Carolina Ass'n for Retarded Children v. North Carolina, 877
Norton v. State, 408
Novosel v. Helgemoe, 617, 641

O

Oaks v. Patterson, 726
O'Connor v. Donaldson, 877
Ohio v. Akron Center for Reproductive Health, 234
Olden v. Kentucky, 213
O'Leary v. State, 653, 654
Oyler v. Boles, 932

P

Partain v. State, 403
Patterson v. New York, 324, 513, 627
Patty v. State, 623
Payne v. Commonwealth, 224
Payne v. Kentucky, 224
Payne v. Tennessee, 862
Pennsylvania Department of Public Welfare v. Davenport, 907
Pennsylvania v. Nelson, 63

TABLE OF CASES

Penry v. Lynaugh, 866, 868
People ex rel. Myers v. Briggs, 638
People ex rel. Russel v. District Court, 294
People in Interest of C.M., 34
People v. Aaron, 299, 314
People v. Abbot, 208
People v. Adami, 760
People v. Ah Gee, 722
People v. Anderson, 285
People v. Andrews, 452
People v. Antick, 308
People v. Ashley, 414
People v. Ashworth, 358
People v. Beardsley, 117
People v. Becker, 390
People v. Berger, 749
People v. Best, 732
People v. Bettis, 348
People v. Blackwell, 625
People v. Bond, 732
People v. Borchers, 322
People v. Boss, 302
People v. Brackett, 254
People v. Bradovich, 432
People v. Brown, 204, 260
People v. Brucato, 349
People v. Burns, 426
People v. Burton, 313
People v. Cable and Godbee, 245
People v. Cage, 412
People v. Calvaresi, 348
People v. Campbell, 238
People v. Canadian Fur Trappers' Corp., 737
People v. Carlson, 349
People v. Ceballos, 536
People v. Chapman, 177
People v. Chesler, 447
People v. Churchill, 419
People v. Clayton, 361
People v. Conley, 285
People v. Couch, 546, 551
People v. Davis, 416, 667
People v. DelGuidice, 653
People v. Dillon, 357, 377
People v. Dole, 732
People v. Drew, 595, 622
People v. Driver, 237
People v. Dubrin, 385
People v. Elkhatib, 395
People v. Etie, 733
People v. Eulo, 249
People v. Ferguson, 683
People v. Flack, 709
People v. Flannel, 332, 527
People v. Franco, 358
People v. Futterman, 99

People v. Gaines, 603
People v. Gann, 627
People v. Gauze, 493
People v. Gilbert, 63, 308
People v. Glover, 79
People v. Goodman, 132
People v. Gorshen, 285
People v. Grant, 603
People v. Green, 205
People v. Greer, 172
People v. Guthreau, 196, 204
People v. Guthrie, 232
People v. Gutierrez, 932
People v. Guzman, 484
People v. Hamrick, 246
People v. Haney, 345, 348
People v. Hanselman, 363, 396
People v. Hardin, 621
People v. Hecker, 525
People v. Hernandez, 220, 205
People v. Hickman, 309
People v. Hocquard, 576
People v. Hood, 171
People v. Jaffe, 768
People v. Jones, 348, 667, 824
People v. Kendrick, 302
People v. King, 496
People v. Krist, 480
People v. Kunkin, 464
People v. Kyllonen, 465
People v. Lafka, 369
People v. Lamirato, 468
People v. LaRose, 411
People v. Lauria, 797
People v. Leichtweis, 777
People v. Lewis, 251
People v. Lopez, 262, 312
People v. Lovercamp, 576
People v. Lubow, 739
People v. Luciano, 820
People v. Luongo, 376, 445
People v. MacEwing, 749
People v. Marcy, 295
People v. Marrero, 684
People v. Matheson, 630
People v. Mayberry, 203, 204
People v. McCullum, 637
People v. Mcgee, 819
People v. McQuillan, 625
People v. Menagas, 358
People v. Merrill, 194
People v. Meyers, 773
People v. Mijares, 125
People v. Miller, 313
People v. Mirmirani, 182
People v. Mitten, 722
People v. Moore, 559
People v. Myers, 261

People v. Newsom, 362
People v. Nieto-Bewitez, 312
People v. Ogg, 343
People v. Oliver, 31
People v. Olivo, 377, 428
People v. Palmer, 496
People v. Paluch, 748
People v. Pape, 167
People v. Patterson, 312
People v. Pavlic, 315
People v. Pitts, 733
People v. Poddar, 285
People v. Pomeroy, 109
People v. Powell, 709
People v. Privitera, 53
People v. Reed, 749
People v. Register, 291
People v. Reid, 481
People v. Rincon-Pineda, 205, 208, 209, 217, 218
People v. Rizzo, 748, 750
People v. Robbins, 24, 121
People v. Robles, 496
People v. Roche, 733
People v. Rodriguez, 342, 349
People v. Rojas, 771
People v. Rollino, 773
People v. Ross, 178
People v. Rossi, 29
People v. Roy, 802
People v. Rubin, 127
People v. Saille, 285, 334
People v. Salas, 302
People v. Samuel, 637
People v. Samuels, 190
People v. Satchell, 312
People v. Schmidt, 592
People v. Shelton, 332
People v. Siu, 767
People v. Skelton, 477
People v. Smith, 164
People v. Stamp, 246
People v. Stamps, 248
People v. Stewart, 248, 261, 408
People v. Stiso, 78
People v. Stuart, 336
People v. Tanner, 594
•People v. Taylor, 308
People v. Thomson, 621
People v. Tijerina, 432
People v. Tinskey, 749
People v. Toland, 496
People v. Tomlins, 524
People v. Truett, 857
People v. Turner, 725
People v. Valdez, 627
People v. Vogel, 692

People v. Walsh, 302
People v. Washburn, 442
People v. Washington, 308, 314
People v. Watson, 350, 351
People v. Weaver, 86
People v. Wells, 285, 349
People v. Wetmore, 285
People v. Whitfield, 351
People v. Whitty, 551
People v. Wielograf, 471
People v. Williams, 509
People v. Wilson, 313
People v. Wood, 308
People v. Wright, 774
People v. Yannett, 396
People v. Young, 9
People v. Yslas, 162
People v. Yukl, 594
People v. Yutt, 94
People v. Zahn, 637
People v. Zierlion, 722
People v. Zinke, 358
Perrin v. United States, 10
Petty v. People, 125
Pfeifer v. United States Bureau of Prisons, 63
Phelps v. State, 408
Pinkerton v. United States, 815
Pizano v. Superior Court of Tulare County, 308
Planned Parenthood v. Casey, 234
Plas v. State, 49
Pope v. State, 7, *115*
Postell v. United States, 169
Powell v. Texas, 659
Price v. Sheppard, 877
Pugliese v. Nelson, 932
Pulley v. Harris, 860
Purvis v. State, 49

Q

Queen v. Clarence, 192
Queen v. Flattery, 219

R

R. v. Howe, 566
Raithel v. State, 637
Reg. v. Barratt, 218
Reg. v. Fletcher, 218
Reg. v. Pressy, 219
Reg. v. Ryan, 218
Regina v. Barrow, 219
Regina v. Caldwell, 344
Regina v. Dee, 220
Regina v. Dudley & Stephens, 552, 559
Regina v. Eagleton, 747
Regina v. Easom, 445

TABLE OF CASES

Regina v. Hudson & Taylor, 570
Regina v. Hyam, 291
Regina v. Kindon, 369
Regina v. Lamb, 288
Regina v. Lynch, 732
Regina v. Pembliton, 85
Regina v. Riley, 368
Regina v. Ritchie, 747
Regina v. Tolson, 692
Regina v. Wheat, 692
Regle v. State, 825
Rex v. Arnold, 585
Rex v. Turvey, 362, 396
Reyes v. United States, 713
Rhode v. State, 743
Rhodes v. Chapman, 855
Riggins v. Nevada, 876
Robinson v. California, 167, 659
Robinson v. State, 385
Robinson v. United States, 164, 171
Roe v. Wade, 53, 233, 234
Rogers v. People, 414
Rojas, 783
Rosado v. Civiletti, 63, 64
Ross v. State, 526
Rowe v. United States, 524
Rozell v. State, 205
Rummel v. Estelle, 855, 857, 932
Rusk v. State, 196, 202
Russell v. Smith, 385
Russell v. United States, 20

S

Saddler v. United States, 629
Salas v. State, 667
Sanchez v. State, 617
Sanditen v. State, 379
Sandstrom v. Montana, 449, 468, 682
Schad v Arizona, 864
Scott v. Plante, 637, 876
Scott v. State, 683
Sears v. State, 51
Shaw v. Director of Public Prosecutions, 4
Sheppard v. State, 321
Sherman v. United States, 581
Sikes v. Commonwealth, 512
Simon & Schuster v. New York Crime Victims Bd., 915
Skinner v. Oklahoma ex rel. Williamson, 877
Skipper v. South Carolina, 865
Slay v. State, 390
Smith v. California, 713
Smith v. State, 379, 445
Solem v. Helm, 854, 855
Sorrells v. United States, 581

Spataro v. State, 125
Spaziano v. Florida, 863, 864
Speidel v. State, 452
Staley v. State, 692
Standard Oil Co. v. United States, 736
State ex rel. Allen v. Radack, 627
State ex rel. Arbogast v. Mohn, 31
State ex rel. Deisinger v. Treffert, 638
State ex rel. Haskins v. County Court, 638
State ex rel. Juvenile Dep't of Multnomah County v. Anderson, 96
State ex rel. Leach v. Hamilton, 857
State ex rel. Martin v. Tally, 813
State ex rel. Matalik v. Schubert, 638
State ex rel. Pope v. Superior Court, 208, 212
State ex rel. Porter v. Wolke, 637
State ex rel. Smith v. Scott, 641
State ex rel. Walker v. Jenkins, 636, 638
State ex rel. Williams v. Whitman, 683
State v. Abbott, 519
State v. Adjustment Dep't Credit Bureau, 736
State v. Agnew, 172
State v. Aguillard, 78
State v. Akers, 113
State v. Albert, 490
State v. Allen, 168, 169
State v. Alto, 627
State v. Anderson, 350
State v. Asberry, 127
State v. Ashby, 471
State v. Atkins, 219
State v. Barclay, 496
State v. Batten, 499
State v. Baublits, 349
State v. Bauer, 629
State v. Bell, 204
State v. Bender, 62
State v. Bias, 452
State v. Bingham, 275
State v. Birdsell, 756
State v. Blier, 637
State v. Boggs, 125
State v. Bowers, 178
State v. Boyd, 621, 630
State v. Boyett, 680
State v. Bradbury, 536
State v. Bragg, 617
State v. Brown, 68, *186*, 189, 233, *405*
State v. Buggs, 228
State v. Burroff, 83
State v. Butler, 480
State v. Byers, 218
State v. Cabral, 218
State v. Campbell, 94
State v. Cann, 25

State v. Carbone, 789
State v. Carson, 9
State v. Carswell, 376
State v. Chavez, 350
State v. Chiarello, 529
State v. Church, 163
State v. Claibon, 623
State v. Clark, 449
State v. Clifford, 734
State v. Clothier, 536, 551
State v. Clowes, 561
State v. Cogdell, 9
State v. Collis, 179
State v. Coombs, 369
State v. Cooper, 388
State v. Correra, 655
State v. Courtsol, 386
State v. Coville, 637
State v. Cox, 524
State v. Craig, 305
State v. Crenshaw, 591
State v. Crocker, 244
State v. Crowe, 441
State v. Cutshaw, 703
State v. D'Amico, 83, 653
State v. Damms, 765
State v. Davis, 169, 760
State v. Dechand, 468
State v. Degrenier, 37
State v. DeMeo, 693
State v. Diebold, 301
State v. Dirker, 452
State v. Doherty, 433
State v. Donnelly, 524
State v. Dorsey, 78, *560*
State v. Dougall, 62
State v. Dougherty, 496
State v. Doyle, 258, 618
State v. Dressel, 813
State v. Dumas, 749
State v. Duncan, 220
State v. Dunning, 547
State v. Durant, 501
State v. Egan, 8
State v. Ehlers, 69
State v. Elder, 547
State v. Elliott, 328
State v. Ely, 219
State v. Ervin, 492
State v. Everhardt, 178
State v. F.W. Post No. 3722, 683
State v. Fain, 857
State v. Farrow, 857
State v. Fearon, 667
State v. Fields, 627
State v. Fierro, 237
State v. Flaherty, 125, 204
State v. Fox, 629

State v. Frazier, 334
State v. Freitas, 654
State v. Gay, 760
State v. Gelinas, 531
State v. Gisclair, 446
State v. Glidden, 195
State v. Glover, 295, 630, 767
State v. Gobin, 748, 757
State v. Gokey, 621
State v. Goode, 857
State v. Graham, 512
State v. Graves, 533
State v. Green, 209, 630
State v. Guest, 223
State v. Gunter, 703
State v. Gunzelman, 180
State v. Gyles, 233
State v. Hacker, 824
State v. Hallett, 253
State v. Hamann, 589, 593, 621
State v. Hamm, 409
State v. Hammond, 496
State v. Hancock, 638
State v. Harris, 313
State v. Harrison, 594
State v. Hatch, 714
State v. Hayes, 638
State v. Helderle, 219
State v. Henker, 125
State v. Hennum, 517
State v. Hetzel, 179
State v. Hill, 495
State v. Hintz, 349
State v. Hodgdon, 351
State v. Hooper, 23
State v. Horton, 335
State v. Hudson, 59
State v. Hunt, 379
State v. Hunter, 562
State v. Hurley, 748, 754, 756
State v. Hyams, 179
State v. Ivicsics, 541
State v. Jacquith, 392
State v. Jenkins, 247
State v. Jewett, 219
State v. Johnson, 179, 227, 496, 561
State v. Jojola, 638
State v. Jordan, 61
State v. Judge, 756
State v. Keian, 709
State v. Kelly, 391
State v. Kim, 351
State v. Knowles, 432
State v. Korell, 605
State v. Kvale, 484
State v. La Goy, 615
State v. Laborde, 377
State v. Lamb, 403

TABLE OF CASES

State v. Langford, 381
State v. Langis, 390
State v. Lankford, 192
State v. Larsen, 484
State v. Larson, 495
State v. Laufenberg, 130
State v. Law, 591, 638
State v. Lawrence, 468
State v. LeCompte, 15
State v. Leos, 512
State v. Lofton, 125
State v. Lopez, 637
State v. Lowe, 123
State v. Lowery, 309
State v. Lozier, 493
State v. Madden, 814
State v. Madry, 484
State v. Malumphy, 592
State v. Marley, 534, 561
State v. Marthall, 179
State v. Martin, 205, 484
State v. Matthews, 559
State v. Mauck, 449
State v. Mauldin, 302
State v. Mayberry, 526
State v. McClose, 251, 256
State v. McCoy, 59
State v. McCray, 358
State v. McGraw, 458
State v. McKenzie, 621
State v. Melendez, 516
State v. Mercer, 630
State v. Meyer, 12, 449
State v. Migliorino, 78
State v. Milam, 637, 641
State v. Miles, 350
State v. Miller, 541
State v. Milsaps, 163
State v. Mishne, 653
State v. Mitchell, 169, 468, 767
State v. Moe, 562
State v. Moore, 224, 280, 623
State v. Morey, 274
State v. Morris, 637
State v. Moss, 408
State v. Muhammad, 194
State v. Mulvihill, 548
State v. Murphy, 638
State v. Myers, 248
State v. Nargashian, 575
State v. Navarro, 219
State v. Nevares, 319
State v. Nielson, 627
State v. O'Brien, 78
State v. O'Neil, 683
State v. Odom, 391
State v. Oliver, 5, 232
State v. Ollens, 275

State v. Olson, 235
State v. Ottwell, 576
State v. Oxendine, 503
State v. Patton, 379
State v. Pearson, 683
State v. Pickus, 416
State v. Pine, 264
State v. Piper, 408
State v. Plaspohl, 352
State v. Ponce, 321
State v. Post, 474
State v. Quarles, 524
State v. Quinnam, 131
State v. Randolph, 223
State v. Riggs, 369
State v. Rivera, 49
State v. Robinson, 323, 414
State v. Rodriguez, 61
State v. Rosencrans, 495
State v. Ross, 315
State v. Rossier, 621
State v. Roush, 245
State v. Rowe, 932
State v. Roy, 623
State v. Rullis, 536
State v. Sahr, 561
State v. Sanchez, 618
State v. Sanders, 618
State v. Saucier, 389
State v. Sauter, 247
State v. Schaaf, 441
State v. Schulz, 654
State v. Searcy, 605
State v. Shaffer, 237
State v. Shaw, 500
State v. Shipp, 672
State v. Sidway, 92
State v. Smith, 204, 361, 403, 600, 621, 791
State v. St. Christopher, 795, 797
State v. Stacy, 638
State v. Stahl, 400
State v. Standiford, 276
State v. Stasio, 643
State v. Strubberg, 617
State v. Taft, 107
State v. Talbert, 203
State v. Tarr, 218
State v. Taylor, 59, 401
State v. Thomas, 112
State v. Thompson, 313, 480
State v. Tindall, 468
State v. Toppan, 126
State v. Toscano, 566
State v. Troiano, 502
State v. Ulin, 248
State v. Van Antwerp, 672
State v. Vance, 266

State v. Vollmer, 341, 351, 352
State v. Wagenius, 446
State v. Wanrow, 516
State v. Warbritton, 172
State v. Ward, 618
State v. Webb, 426
State v. Weddle, 274
State v. Wenger, 533
State v. Westlund, 548
State v. Whitcomb, 692
State v. Wilkerson, 262
State v. Williams, 59, 103, 119, 344, 448, 452, 496, 734, 857
State v. Willis, 496
State v. Wilson, 761, 932
State v. Woll, 433
State v. Wood, 208
State v. Workman, 761
State v. Zangrilli, 177
Steele v. State, 617
Stewart v. Commonwealth, 362
Sumner v. Shuman, 859
Suzuki v. Yuen, 625
Swafford v. State, 237, 266

T

Tanner v. State, 496
Taylor v. Commonwealth, 12
Tennessee v. Garner, 542, 551
Terrebonne v. Blackburn, 857, 932
Thacker v. Commonwealth, 746
The Antelope, 63
Thompson v. Oklahoma, 860
Thompson v. State, 351
Thoreson v. State, 480
Tison v. Arizona, 859
Touby v. United States, 61
Trice v. United States, 71
Trop v. Dulles, 855
Turner v. Commonwealth, 269, 274

U

United v. Falcone, 813
United States v. Agueci, 811
United States v. Alberico, 395
United States v. Aleman, 836
United States v. Arthur, 487
United States v. Aulet, 671
United States v. Bailey, 571, 575
United States v. Barker, 684
United States v. Bass, 618
United States v. Batchelder, 50
United States v. Beck, 732, 810
United States v. Bell, 484
United States v. Benson, 411
United States v. Bergman, 150

United States v. Berrigan, 77, 534, 777, 781, 782
United States v. Bright, 669, 677
United States v. Bruno, 812
United States v. Bryan, 726
United States v. Chicago Express, Inc., 736
United States v. Clay, 791
United States v. Currens, 600
United States v. DeBellis, 638
United States v. Diecidue, 731
United States v. DiGiglio, 464
United States v. DiGilio, 394, 425, 637
United States v. E. Brooke Matlack, Inc., 735
United States v. Eichman, 43
United States v. Elliott, 810, 829
United States v. Engler, 719
United States v. Falcone, 802
United States v. Feola, 172, 804
United States v. Freed, 714, 719
United States v. Gilliss, 603
United States v. Girard, 425
United States v. Goodwin, 51
United States v. Greenbaum, 693
United States v. Greene, 48
United States v. Greer, 731
United States v. Groomer, 731
United States v. Grzywacz, 836
United States v. Halper, 144
United States v. Hayes, 51, 638
United States v. Hendrix, 621
United States v. Heng Awkak Roman, 782
United States v. Henry, 615, 616
United States v. Holmes, 555, 559
United States v. Hubbard, 810
United States v. International Minerals & Chemicals Corp., 715
United States v. Jackson, 625
United States v. Johnson, 629
United States v. Kabat, 561
United States v. Kehoe, 358
United States v. Kozminski, 21, 41
United States v. Levine, 811
United States v. Longoria, 731
United States v. Lozano, 731
United States v. Lubomski, 776
United States v. Malatesta, 803
United States v. Mandel, 836
United States v. Mandujano, 749
United States v. Martinez, 684
United States v. Masthers, 630
United States v. Meacham, 791
United States v. Monasterski, 459
United States v. Moore, 660
United States v. Morales, 672
United States v. Myers, 486

TABLE OF CASES

United States v. Oates, 731
United States v. Ong, 796
United States v. Oviedo, 781
United States v. Pardue, 638
United States v. Park, 695, 739
United States v. Peoni, 731, 733
United States v. Perez, 811, 812
United States v. Perry, 474, 792
United States v. Powell, 404
United States v. Randall, 559
United States v. Robert Wulff, 715
United States v. Rodgers, 20
United States v. Rogers, 385
United States v. Rosado-Fernandez, 803
United States v. Ruffin, 113, *726*
United States v. Sanchez-Robles, 89
United States v. Santore, 125
United States v. Sheffield, 390
United States v. Simpson, 561
United States v. Smith, 731
United States v. Speed, 813
United States v. Sperling, 812
United States v. Squires, 691
United States v. Stallworth, 749, *752*
United States v. Stancil, 452
United States v. Swanson, 629
United States v. Thomas & McClellan, 783
United States v. Thomas, 781
United States v. Thornton, 203
United States v. Turkette, 22, 486, 828, 835
United States v. Turley, 464
United States v. Tyler, 621, 623
United States v. United States Gypsum Co., 67, 709, 802
United States v. Varelli, 805
United States v. Wiley, 214, 217, 225
United States v. Williams, 719
United States ex rel. Goddard v. Vaughn, 655
United States ex rel. Little v. Twomey, 638
United States ex rel. McGough v. Hewitt, 629

V

Vasquez v. State, 223
Vick v. State, 667
Video Software Dealers Ass'n v. Webster, 47
Vitek v. Jones, 642
Vogel v. Brown, 709

W

Walker v. Butterworth, 621
Walker v. State, 496
Waller v. Florida, 375
Wanstreet v. Bordenkircher, 857
Warner v. State, 627
Warren v. State, 36
Watkins v. State, 9
Weaver v. Graham, 28
Webster v. Reproductive Health Servs., 234
Wheat v. United States, 924
White v. Commonwealth, 512
Williams v. State, 121, 618, 637, 796
Williams v. United States, 411
Wilson v. State, 625, 775
Witherspoon v. Illinois, 861
Wolff v. McDonnell, 642
Woodall v. Foti, 642
Wooten v. State, 274

Y

Young v. Superior Court, 774
Youngblood, 26
Younie v. State, 375

Z

Zamora v. State, 593
Zangrilli, 178
Zant v. Stephens, 863

Index

A

ABANDONMENT.
Attempt, p. 761.

ACCESSORIES.
Parties to crime, pp. 721 to 734.

ACQUITTAL.
By reason of mental condition.
  Commitment procedures, pp. 623 to 626.
  Release, pp. 626, 627.

ACTUS REUS.
Concurrence of mens rea and actus reus, pp. 127 to 130.
Conspiracy, pp. 793 to 797.
Criminal conduct.
  See CRIMINAL CONDUCT.
Theft and related offenses.
  Asportation, pp. 376 to 379.
  Deception, theft by, pp. 434 to 440.
  Embezzlement, pp. 396 to 405.
  False pretenses, obtaining title to property by, pp. 409 to 414.
  Lost or mislaid goods and mistakenly transferred goods, pp. 379 to 386.
  Misappopriation of property, pp. 433, 434.
  Receiving stolen property, pp. 468 to 471.
  Robbery, pp. 475 to 481.
  Trespass and continuing trespass, pp. 367 to 376.
  Unauthorized control of property, pp. 426 to 433.

AGGRAVATING DATA.
Death penalty, p. 865.

ALI TESTS.
Acquittals by reason of mental condition.
  Consequences of acquittals, pp. 623 to 627.
Bifurcated proceedings, p. 617.
Burden of persuasion, pp. 622, 623.
Diagnostic commitments and reports, pp. 615 to 617.
Jury instructions, pp. 618 to 621.
Legal tests for responsibility, pp. 595 to 603.
Pleading the defence, pp. 614, 615.
Psychiatric and lay opinion evidence, pp. 617, 618.

APPELLATE REVIEW.
Capital punishment, pp. 867, 868.
Presumptive sentences, pp. 886, 887.

ARMED ROBBERY, pp. 477 to 481.

ARREST.
Prevention of crime, pp. 542 to 551.

ARSON, pp. 499 to 503.

ASPORTATION.
Actus reus of larceny, pp. 376 to 379.

ASSAULT AND BATTERY.
Aggravated assaults, pp. 173 to 179.
Common law.
  Definitions of assault and battery, pp. 161 to 169.
Consent, pp. 186 to 192.
Definitions.
  Common law and modern views, pp. 161 to 169.
Grading of offenses, pp. 173 to 179.
Harassment, pp. 184, 185.
Intent to commit specific crimes.
  Assaults with, pp. 178, 179.
Mens rea, pp. 169 to 172.
Stalking, pp. 185, 186.
Terroristic threats, pp. 179 to 184.
Weapons.
  Dangerous and deadly weapons, pp. 177, 178.

ATTEMPT.
Abandonment, p. 761.
"Attempted" attempts, pp. 761 to 765.
Impossibility of fact, pp. 765 to 767.
Impossibility of law, pp. 768 to 785.
Mens rea, pp. 743 to 747.
Preparation and attempt, pp. 747 to 760.
Solicitation, p. 760.
The "harm," pp. 742, 743.

ATTORNEYS' FEES.
Forfeitures, pp. 924 to 926.

AUTOMOBILES, UNAUTHORIZED USE, pp. 449 to 452.

B

BAD CHECKS, pp. 448, 449.

BATTERED WIVES.
Self-defense, pp. 517 to 519.

BATTERY.
See ASSAULT AND BATTERY.

BIFURCATED PROCEEDINGS.
Mental condition.
  Administration of legal tests for responsibility, p. 617.

BOOTSTRAPPING.
Homicide, pp. 313, 314.

BRAIN DEATH.
Homicide, pp. 235 to 238.

BRAINWASHING.
Duress, pp. 562 to 677.

BRIBERY OF PUBLIC OFFICIALS, pp. 486 to 489.

BURDEN OF PERSUASION.
Mental condition.
  Administration of legal tests for responsibility, pp. 622, 623.

BURGLARY, pp. 489 to 497.

C

CAPITAL PUNISHMENT, pp. 858 to 869.
Accomplices to aggravated murder, p. 859.
Aggravating data, p. 865.
Allocation of responsibility, pp. 862 to 864.
Appellate review, pp. 867, 868.
Disproportionality, p. 860.
Double jeopardy considerations, pp. 866, 867.
Execution of mentally-impaired capital convicts, pp. 868, 869.
Insane indigent defendants.
   Expert psychiatric resources, p. 861.
Jurors' qualifications, p. 861.
Juvenile murder, p. 860.
Mandatory capital punishment, pp. 859, 860.
Mitigating data, pp. 865, 866.
Notice of possibility of death sentence.
   Fair notice requirement, p. 867.
Psychiatric evidence, pp. 861, 862.

CAREER CRIMINALS.
See PROFESSIONAL CRIMINALS.

CAUSATION, pp. 138 to 143.
Homicide.
   Culpability in relation to causation, pp. 253 to 258.
   Direct, intervening and supervening cause, pp. 241 to 252.
   "Year and a day" rule, pp. 264 to 266.

COERCIVE PERSUASION.
Duress, pp. 562 to 577.

COMMON LAW, pp. 4 to 11.
Assault and battery.
   Definitions of assault and battery, pp. 161 to 169.
Homicide.
   "Year and a day" rule, pp. 264 to 266.

COMPUTER CRIMES, pp. 453 to 458.

CONDITION OR STATUS.
Incapacity, pp. 657 to 668.

CONSENT.
Assault and battery, pp. 186 to 192.

CONSOLIDATION.
Theft and related offenses.
   Contemporary statutory patterns, pp. 419 to 422.

CONSPIRACY.
Actus reus, pp. 793 to 797.
Conceptual matters, pp. 785, 786.
Dangers of conspiracy prosecutions, pp. 786 to 789.
Joint liability.
   Procedure problems, pp. 821 to 826.
Mens rea, pp. 797 to 804.
Organized crime, pp. 826 to 836.
Overt act, pp. 789 to 793.
Procedure problems.
   Joint liability, pp. 821 to 826.
Prosecutions.
   Dangers of conspiracy prosecutions, pp. 786 to 789.
Rational of conspiracy, pp. 785, 786.

CONSPIRACY—Cont'd
Scope of conspiratorial relationship, pp. 804 to 821.

CONSTITUTIONAL LAW.
Cruel and unusual punishment, pp. 854 to 869.
Equal protection.
  Capital punishment and disproportionality, p. 860.
Fines.
  Alternative sentence of imprisonment for nonpayment of fine, pp. 909, 910.
Indefiniteness.
  Capital punishment restrictions, p. 858.
Interpretation of penal legislation.
  Constitutional basis for attacking legislation.
    Separation of powers, pp. 60 to 62.
  Constitutional basis for attacking penal legislation.
    Burden of proof and presumptions, pp. 53 to 60.
    Equal protection.
      Discriminatory enforcement, pp. 50, 51.
      Irrational legislative classification, pp. 48 to 50.
    Ex post facto clause, pp. 26 to 32.
    First amendment, pp. 43 to 48.
    Occupation of the field, pp. 62, 63.
    Right of privacy, pp. 51 to 53.
    State and federal crimes, p. 62.
    Vagueness, pp. 32 to 37.
  Overbreadth, pp. 37 to 43.
Probation revocation procedures, pp. 900 to 905.
Psychotropic medication.
  Restrictions, pp. 876, 877.
Son of Sam laws, pp. 915 to 918.
Vagueness.
  Capital punishment restrictions, p. 858.

CONSTRUCTION AND INTERPRETATION.
Legislation.
  See LEGALITY.

CONSTRUCTIVE POSSESSION.
Criminal conduct, p. 134.

CORPORATE CRIME.
Criminal liability of corporations, pp. 735 to 739.

CORPORATIONS.
Parties to crime.
  Criminal liability of corporations, pp. 735 to 739.

CORROBORATION.
Rape, pp. 214 to 218.

CREDIT CARD MISUSE, pp. 447, 448.

CRIMINAL CONDUCT.
Causation, pp. 138 to 143.
Culpability.
  Concurrence of mens rea and actus reus, pp. 127 to 130.
  General provisions.
    See CULPABILITY.
Harm.
  Generally, pp. 130 to 138.
Innocent agent, pp. 112 to 114.
Omission to act, pp. 115 to 122.
Possession, pp. 123 to 126.

INDEX

CRIMINAL CONDUCT—Cont'd
Solicitation, p. 127.
Voluntariness, pp. 103 to 112.

CRUEL AND UNUSUAL PUNISHMENT, pp. 854 to 869.

CULPABILITY.
Criminal conduct.
   Concurrence of mens rea and actus reus, pp. 127 to 130.
Homicide.
   Causation.
      Culpability in relation to causation, pp. 253 to 258.
      "Year and a day" rule, pp. 264 to 266.
Intent or purpose, pp. 79 to 88.
Motive.
   Culpability distinguished from motive, pp. 69 to 79.
Negligence, pp. 98 to 103.
Non facit reum nisi mens sit rea, pp. 67 to 69.
Purpose or intent, pp. 79 to 88.
Recklessness, pp. 95 to 98.

D

DEATH.
Brain death, pp. 235 to 238.

DEATH PENALTY, pp. 858 to 869.
Aggravated murder.
   Accomplices, p. 859.
Aggravating data, p. 865.
Allocation of responsibility, pp. 862 to 864.
Appellate review, pp. 867, 868.
Disproportionality, p. 860.
Double jeopardy considerations, pp. 866, 867.
Execution of mentally-impaired capital convicts, pp. 868, 869.
Insane indigent defendents.
   Expert psychiatric resources, p. 861.
Jurors' qualifications, p. 861.
Juvenile murder, p. 860.
Mandatory capital punishment, pp. 859, 860.
Mitigating data, pp. 865, 866.
Notice of possibility of death sentence.
   Fair notice requirement, p. 867.
Psychiatric evidence, pp. 861, 862.

DECEPTION, THEFT BY, pp. 434 to 440.

DEFENSE OF OTHERS, pp. 527 to 534.

DEFENSE OF PROPERTY, pp. 534 to 542.

DEFENSES.
Condition or status, pp. 657 to 668.
Defense of others, pp. 527 to 534.
Defense of property, pp. 534 to 542.
Duress, pp. 562 to 577.
Entrapment, pp. 577 to 582.
Ignorance and mistake of fact, pp. 669 to 680.
Ignorance and mistake of law, pp. 680 to 719.
Immaturity, pp. 655 to 657.
Intoxication, pp. 643 to 655.

DEFENSES—Cont'd
Mental condition.
  Generally, pp. 583 to 643.
    See MENTAL CONDITION.
Necessity, pp. 551 to 562.
Pleading.
  Mental condition.
    Administration of legal tests for responsibility, pp. 614, 615.
Prevention of crime, pp. 542 to 551.
Self-defense, pp. 508 to 527.

DEFINITIONS.
Assault and battery.
  Common law and modern views, pp. 161 to 169.
Homicide.
  By another, pp. 238 to 241.
  Causation.
    "Year and a day" rule, pp. 264 to 266.
  Death, pp. 235 to 238.
  Life in being, pp. 232 to 234.
Rape.
  Forcible rape, pp. 193 to 205.
  Modern redefinition of rape and other sexual offenses, pp. 225 to 230.
Rule of law, p. 3.

DETERRENCE.
Views on punishment, pp. 840 to 842.

DIAGNOSTIC COMMITMENTS AND REPORTS.
Mental condition.
  Administration of legal tests for responsibility, pp. 615 to 617.

DIMINISHED RESPONSIBILITY.
Acquittals by reason of mental condition.
  Consequences of acquittals, pp. 623 to 627.
Bifurcated proceedings, p. 617.
Burden of persuasion, pp. 622, 623.
Diagnostic commitments and reports, pp. 615 to 617.
Jury instructions, pp. 618 to 621.
Legal test for responsibility, pp. 279 to 286.
Pleading the defense, pp. 614, 615.
Psychiatric and lay opinion evidence, pp. 617, 618.

DOMESTIC VIOLENCE.
Self-defense.
  Battered wives, pp. 517 to 519.

DOUBLE JEOPARDY, pp. 144 to 150.
Death penalty cases, pp. 866, 867.

DUE PROCESS.
Interpretation of penal legislation.
  Overbreadth, pp. 37 to 43.
  Vagueness, pp. 32 to 37.
Probation revocation procedures, pp. 900 to 905.
Psychotropic medication.
  Use, pp. 876, 877.

DURESS, pp. 562 to 577.

INDEX 961

E

EJUSDEM GENERIS CLAUSES.
Interpretation of penal legislation, pp. 22 to 24.

EMBEZZLEMENT, pp. 396 to 408.
Actus reus, pp. 396 to 405.
Mens rea, pp. 405 to 408.

ENTRAPMENT, pp. 577 to 582.

EQUAL PROTECTION.
Capital punishment and disproportionality, p. 860.
Constitutional basis for attacking penal legislation.
  Discriminatory enforcement, pp. 50, 51.
  Irrational legislative classification, pp. 48 to 50.

EVIDENCE.
Death penalty cases.
  Psychiatric evidence, pp. 861, 862.
Homicide, pp. 258 to 264.
Psychiatric evidence.
  Death penalty cases, pp. 861, 862.

EXCUSE.
Condition or status, pp. 657 to 668.
Defense of others, pp. 527 to 534.
Defense of property, pp. 534 to 542.
Duress, pp. 562 to 577.
Entrapment, pp. 577 to 582.
Ignorance and mistake of fact, pp. 669 to 680.
Ignorance and mistake of law, pp. 680 to 719.
Immaturity, pp. 655 to 657.
Intoxication, pp. 643 to 655.
Justification distinguished, p. 507.
Mental condition.
  Generally, pp. 583 to 563.
    See MENTAL CONDITION.
Necessity, pp. 551 to 562.
Prevention of crime, pp. 542 to 551.
Self-defense, pp. 508 to 527.

EXPERT TESTIMONY.
Mental condition.
  Administration of legal tests for responsibility, pp. 617, 618.

EX POST FACTO LEGISLATION.
Prohibition against, pp. 26 to 32.

EXTORTION, p. 485.

F

FALSE PRETENSES, OBTAINING TITLE TO PROPERTY BY, pp. 409 to 419.
Actus reus.
  False representations, pp. 412 to 416.
  "Title," pp. 409 to 412.
Mens rea, pp. 416 to 419.

FEDERAL SENTENCING GUIDELINES, pp. 887 to 895.

FELONY-MURDER, pp. 295 to 315.

FETUS.
Homicide.
  Born alive, pp. 232 to 234.

FINES, pp. 907 to 915.
Constitutional law.
  Alternative sentence of imprisonment for nonpayment of fine, pp. 909, 910.
Delinquency and default, p. 911.
  Criminal default, p. 915.
  Resentencing a delinquent defendant, pp. 914, 915.
Effect of sentence to pay, pp. 910, 911.
Finality of sentence to a fine, p. 909.
Indigent defendants, pp. 908, 909.
Individuals, p. 908.
Modification or remission, p. 910.
Organizations, pp. 908, 909.
Payment, pp. 911 to 913.
Probation.
  Payment as condition of probation, p. 911.
Stay pending appeal, p. 910.

FOREIGN PENAL ADJUDICATIONS.
Legislation.
  Nonenforcement, pp. 63 to 66.

FORFEITURES, pp. 915 to 926.
As a criminal sanction, pp. 918, 919.
Attorneys' fees, pp. 924 to 926.
Collateral profits from crime, pp. 915 to 918.
Disposal of forfeited property, pp. 923, 924.
Order of forfeiture, p. 920
Remission or mitigation, p. 921.
Seizure of forfeited property, pp. 920, 921.
Temporary restraining orders, pp. 919, 920.
Third-party interests.
  Judicial hearings to preserve, pp. 922, 923.

FORMER JEOPARDY.
Death penalty cases, pp. 866, 867.

FRAUD.
Rape.
  Nonforcible rape, pp. 219, 220.

FREE SPEECH.
Son of Sam laws, pp. 915 to 918.

FUNDS RECEIVED, THEFT OF, p. 447.

G

GUILTY BUT MENTALLY ILL.
Acquittals by reason of mental condition.
  Consequences of acquittals, pp. 623 to 627.
Bifurcated proceedings, p. 617.
Burden of persuasion, pp. 622, 623.
Diagnostic commitments and reports, pp. 615 to 617.
Jury instructions, pp. 618 to 621.
Legal test for responsibility, pp. 612 to 614.
Pleading the defense, pp. 614, 615.
Psychiatric and lay opinion evidence, pp. 617, 618.

INDEX 963

H

HABITUAL OFFENDERS.
See PROFESSIONAL CRIMINALS.

HARASSMENT.
Assault and battery, pp. 184, 185.

HARM.
Generally, pp. 130 to 138.
Victimless crimes, pp. 133 to 138.

HOMICIDE.
Bootstrapping, pp. 313, 314.
Brain death, pp. 235 to 238.
By another, pp. 238 to 241.
Causation.
   Culpability in relation to causation, pp. 253 to 258.
   Direct, intervening and supervening cause, pp. 241 to 252.
   "Year and a day" rule, pp. 264 to 266.
Classification.
   Mens rea.
      Classification in terms of, pp. 266 to 270.
Common law.
   "Year and a day" rule, pp. 264 to 266.
Culpability.
   Causation.
      Culpability in relation to causation, pp. 253 to 258.
      Direct, intervening and supervening cause, pp. 241 to 252.
      "Year and a day" rule, pp. 264 to 266.
Definitions.
   By another, pp. 238 to 241.
   Causation.
      "Year and a day" rule, pp. 264 to 266.
   Death, pp. 235 to 238.
   Life in being, pp. 232 to 234.
Diminished responsibility, pp. 279 to 286.
Evidence, pp. 258 to 264.
Felony-murder, pp. 295 to 315.
Fetus.
   Born alive, pp. 232 to 234.
Intent of murder, pp. 270 to 286.
Involuntary manslaughter.
   Criminal negligence, pp. 342 to 352.
   Unlawful acts, pp. 334 to 342.
Manslaughter.
   Involuntary manslaughter. See within this heading, "Involuntary manslaughter."
   Voluntary manslaughter. See within this heading, "Voluntary manslaughter."
Mens rea.
   Classification in terms of mens rea, pp. 266 to 270.
   Diminished responsibility, pp. 279 to 286.
Mitigating circumstances.
   Diminished responsibility, pp. 279 to 286.
   Extreme emotional disturbance, pp. 324 to 332.
   Provocation, pp. 315 to 324.
   Self-defense.
      Imperfect self-defense, pp. 332 to 334.
Negligence.
   Criminal-negligent involuntary manslaughter, pp. 342 to 352.
Premeditation, pp. 270 to 279.

HOMICIDE—Cont'd
Provocation.
   Voluntary manslaughter, pp. 315 to 324.
Recklessness.
   Extreme recklessness, pp. 286 to 295.
Self-defense.
   Mitigating circumstances.
     Imperfect self-defense, pp. 332 to 334.
Unintended killings.
   "Depraved heart," pp. 286 to 295.
   Recklessness.
     Extreme recklessness, pp. 286 to 295.
Vehicular homicide, pp. 350 to 352.
Voluntary manslaughter.
   Extreme emotional disturbance, pp. 324 to 332.
   Imperfect self-defense, pp. 332 to 334.
   Provocation, pp. 315 to 324.
"Year and a day" rule, pp. 264 to 266.

I

IGNORANCE AND MISTAKE OF FACT, pp. 669 to 680.
Negating "mens rea," pp. 668 to 680.
Negating required intent, pp. 669 to 677.

IGNORANCE AND MISTAKE OF LAW, pp. 680 to 719.
Strict liability, pp. 693 to 719.

IMMATURITY, pp. 655 to 657.

IMPOSSIBILITY OF FACT.
Attempt, pp. 765 to 767.

IMPOSSIBILITY OF LAW.
Attempt, pp. 768 to 785.

IMPRISONMENT.
Circumstances of, pp. 926 to 928.
Extended terms for habitual offenders, pp. 928 to 937.
Life imprisonment without possibility of parole.
   As cruel and unusual punishment, pp. 854 to 857.
Mandatory minimum sentences, pp. 939 to 942.
Multiple sentences for multiple offenses, pp. 937 to 939.

INCAPACITATION AS PURPOSE OF PUNISHMENT, pp. 842, 843.

INCAPACITY.
Condition or status, pp. 657 to 668.
Immaturity, pp. 655 to 657.
Intoxication, pp. 643 to 655.
Mental condition.
   Generally, pp. 583 to 643.
     See MENTAL CONDITION.

INCOMPETENCY TO STAND TRIAL, pp. 628 to 638.
"Chemical competence," p. 638.
Constitutional standards, pp. 628 to 630.
Procedure requirements, pp. 630 to 638.

INDETERMINATE SENTENCES, pp. 869 to 877.

INDIGENT DEFENDANTS.
Insanity defense.
   Capital cases, p. 861.

INNOCENT AGENT.
Criminal conduct, pp. 112 to 114.

IN PARI MATERIA.
Interpretation of penal legislation, pp. 24 to 26.

INSANITY DEFENSE.
Indigent defendants.
  Capital cases, p. 861.

INTENT.
Culpability.
  Intent or purpose, pp. 79 to 88.
Homicide, pp. 270 to 286.
Ignorance and mistake of fact.
  Negating required intent, pp. 669 to 677.

INTOXICATION, pp. 643 to 655.

IRRESISTIBLE IMPULSE.
"Control" tests.
  Acquittals by reason of mental condition.
    Consequences of acquittals, pp. 623 to 627.
  Bifurcated proceedings, p. 617.
  Burden of proof, pp. 622, 623.
  Diagnostic commitments and reports, pp. 615 to 617.
  Jury instructions, pp. 618 to 621.
  Legal tests for responsibility, pp. 593 to 595.
  Pleading the defense, pp. 614, 615.
  Psychiatric and lay opinion evidence, pp. 617, 618.

J

JOYRIDING, pp. 449 to 452.

JURORS' QUALIFICATIONS.
Death penalty cases, p. 861.

JURY INSTRUCTIONS.
Mental condition.
  Administration of legal tests for responsibility, pp. 618 to 621.
Rape.
  Cautionary instruction, pp. 205 to 207.

JUST DESSERTS THEORY OF SENTENCING, pp. 877 to 899.

JUSTIFICATION AND EXCUSE.
Condition or status, pp. 657 to 668.
Defense of others, pp. 527 to 534.
Defense of property, pp. 534 to 542.
Defenses to criminal prosecution, p. 507.
Distinguished, p. 507.
Duress, pp. 562 to 577.
Entrapment, pp. 577 to 582.
Ignorance and mistake of fact, pp. 669 to 680.
Ignorance and mistake of law, pp. 680 to 719.
Immaturity, pp. 655 to 657.
Intoxication, pp. 643 to 655.
Introductory notes, pp. 507, 508.
Mental condition.
  Generally, pp. 583 to 643.
    See MENTAL CONDITION.
Necessity, pp. 551 to 562.
Prevention of crime, pp. 542 to 551.

JUSTIFICATION AND EXCUSE—Cont'd
Self-defense, pp. 508 to 527.

JUVENILE MURDER.
Capital punishment, p. 860.

K

KIDNAPPING.
Rape.
    Definitions, pp. 228 to 230.

KNOWLEDGE.
Culpability, pp. 89 to 95.

L

LARCENY.
Generally, pp. 353 to 396.
    See THEFT AND RELATED OFFENSES.

LAY OPINION EVIDENCE.
Mental condition.
    Administration of legal tests for responsibility, pp. 617, 618.

LEGALITY.
Basic concept, p. 4.
Common law, pp. 4 to 11.
Due process.
    Interpretation of penal legislation.
        Overbreadth, pp. 37 to 43.
        Vagueness, pp. 32 to 37.
Ex post facto legislation.
    Prohibition against, pp. 26 to 32.
Interpretation of penal legislation. See within this heading, "Legislation."
Legislation.
    Equal protection.
        Constitutional basis for attacking penal legislation.
            Discriminatory enforcement, pp. 50, 51.
            Irrational legislative classification, pp. 48 to 50.
    Interpretation of penal legislation.
        Burden of proof, pp. 53 to 60.
        Constitutional basis for attacking penal legislation.
            Due process.
                Overbreadth, pp. 37 to 43.
                Vagueness, pp. 32 to 37.
            Equal protection.
                Discriminatory enforcement, pp. 50, 51.
                Irrational legislative classification, pp. 48 to 50.
        Ex post facto clause, pp. 26 to 32.
        First amemdment, pp. 43 to 48.
        Occupation of the field, pp. 62, 63.
        Overbreadth, pp. 37 to 43.
        Presumptions, pp. 53 to 60.
        Right of privacy, pp. 51 to 53.
        Separation of powers, pp. 60 to 62.
        State and federal crimes, p. 62.
        Vagueness, pp. 32 to 37.
    Ejusdem generis clauses, pp. 22 to 24.

LEGALITY—Cont'd
Legislation—Cont'd
  Interpretation of penal legislation—Cont'd
    Equal protection.
      Discriminatory enforcement, pp. 50, 51.
      Irrational legislative classification, pp. 48 to 50.
    Federal legislation, pp. 17 to 22.
    General principles, p. 16.
    In pari materia, pp. 24 to 26.
    Lenity, pp. 17 to 22.
    Nulla poena sine lege, pp. 14, 15.
    Nullum crimen sine lege, pp. 11 to 14.
    Occupation of the field, pp. 62, 63.
    Overbreadth, pp. 37 to 43.
    Presumptions, pp. 53 to 60.
    Privacy.
      Right of privacy, pp. 51 to 53.
    Separation of powers, pp. 60 to 62.
    Vagueness.
      Constitutional basis for attacking penal legislation, pp. 32 to 37.
Nulla poena sine lege, pp. 14, 15.
Nullum crimen sine lege, pp. 11 to 14.
Rule of law, p. 3.

LEGAL TESTS FOR RESPONSIBILITY.
Intoxication.
  Incapacity by mental condition.
    Generally, pp. 583 to 643.
      See MENTAL CONDITION.

LEGISLATION.
Foreign penal adjudications.
  Nonenforcement, pp. 63 to 66.
Legality.
  See LEGALITY.

LENITY.
Doctrine of lenity.
  Supreme court construction of legislation, pp. 17 to 22.

LIFE IMPRISONMENT WITHOUT POSSIBILITY OF PAROLE.
As cruel and unusual punishment, pp. 854 to 857.

LOST OR MISLAID GOODS.
Actus reus of larceny, pp. 379 to 386.

M

MANDATORY LIFE SENTENCES.
As cruel and unusual punishment, p. 857.

MANDATORY MINIMUM SENTENCES, pp. 939 to 942.

MANSLAUGHTER.
Homicide generally.
  See HOMICIDE.
Involuntary manslaughter.
  Criminal negligence, pp. 342 to 352.
  Unlawful acts, pp. 334 to 342.
Voluntary manslaughter.
  Extreme emotional disturbance, pp. 324 to 332.
  Imperfect self-defense, pp. 332 to 334.

MANSLAUGHTER—Cont'd
Voluntary manslaughter—Cont'd
　Provocation, pp. 315 to 324.

MENS REA.
Assault and battery, pp. 169 to 172.
Attempt, pp. 743 to 747.
Concurrence of mens rea and actus reus, pp. 127 to 130.
Conspiracy, pp. 797 to 804.
Culpability generally.
　See CULPABILITY.
Homicide.
　Classification in terms of mens rea, pp. 266 to 270.
　Diminished responsibility, pp. 279 to 286.
Ignorance and mistake of fact.
　Negating "mens rea," pp. 668 to 680.
Rape.
　Forcible rape, pp. 202 to 204.
Theft and related offenses.
　Claim of right, pp. 391, 392.
　　Contemporary legislation, pp. 445, 446.
　Embezzlement, pp. 405 to 408.
　False pretenses, obtaining title to property by, pp. 416 to 419.
　General concept, pp. 386 to 391.
　　Contemporary legislation, pp. 442 to 445.
　Receiving stolen property, pp. 471 to 474.
　Robbery, pp. 481 to 484.

MENS REA OR ABOLITION TESTS.
Acquittals by reason of mental condition.
　Consequences of acquittals, pp. 623 to 627.
Bifurcated proceedings, p. 617.
Burden of persuasion, pp. 622, 623.
Diagnostic commitments and reports, pp. 615 to 617.
Jury instructions, pp. 618 to 621.
Legal tests for responsibility, pp. 604 to 613.
Pleading the defense, pp. 614, 615.
Psychiatric and lay opinion evidence, pp. 617, 618.

MENTAL CONDITION, pp. 583 to 643.
Acquittals by reason of mental condition.
　Commitment procedures, pp. 623 to 626.
　Consequences of acquittals, pp. 623 to 627.
　Release, pp. 626, 627.
Administration of legal tests for responsibility, pp. 614 to 623.
ALI test, pp. 595 to 603.
Bifurcated proceedings, p. 617.
Burden of persuasion, pp. 622, 623.
Constitutional standards.
　Incompetency to stand trial, pp. 628 to 630.
"Control tests."
　Irresistible impulse, pp. 593 to 595.
Diagnostic commitments and reports, pp. 615 to 617.
Diminished responsibility, pp. 279 to 286.
Diversion of mentally-ill arrestees and defendants, pp. 639 to 642.
"Guilty but mentally ill," pp. 612 to 614.
　Consequences of acquittals, pp. 623 to 627.
Homicide.
　Diminished responsibility, pp. 279 to 286.

INDEX

MENTAL CONDITION—Cont'd
Incompetency to stand trial, pp. 628 to 638.
  "Chemical competence," p. 638.
  Constitutional standards, pp. 628 to 630.
  Procedure requirements, pp. 630 to 638.
Intoxication, pp. 643 to 655.
Irresistible impulse, pp. 593 to 595.
Jury instructions, pp. 618 to 621.
"Mens rea" or abolition test, pp. 604 to 612.
Mentally-ill arrestees and defendants.
  Screening and diversion, pp. 639 to 642.
Mentally-ill prisoners, pp. 642, 643.
M'Naghten rule, pp. 585 to 593.
Pleading the defense, pp. 614, 615.
Procedure requirements.
  Incompetency to stand trial, pp. 630 to 638.
Psychiatric and lay opinion evidence, pp. 617, 618.
Screening of mentally-ill arrestees and defendants, pp. 639 to 642.

MENTALLY RETARDED.
Executions, pp. 868, 869.

MISAPPROPRIATION OF PROPERTY, pp. 433, 434.

MISTAKENLY TRANSFERRED GOODS.
Actus reus of larceny, pp. 379 to 386.

MITIGATING CIRCUMSTANCES.
Homicide.
  Extreme emotional disturbance, pp. 324 to 332.
  Provocation, pp. 315 to 324.
  Self-defense.
    Imperfect self-defense, pp. 332 to 334.

MITIGATING DATA.
Death penalty, pp. 865, 866.

M'NAGHTEN RULE.
Acquittals by reason of mental condition.
  Consequences of acquittals, pp. 623 to 627.
Bifurcated proceedings, p. 617.
Burden of persuasion, pp. 622, 623.
Diagnostic commitments and reports, pp. 615 to 617.
Jury instructions, pp. 618 to 621.
Legal test for responsibility, pp. 585 to 593.
Pleading the defense, pp. 614, 615.
Psychiatric and lay opinion evidence, pp. 617, 618.

MOTIVE.
Culpability.
  Culpability distinguished from motive, pp. 69 to 79.

MOTOR VEHICLES.
Vehicular homicide, pp. 350 to 352.

MOTOR VEHICLES, UNAUTHORIZED USE, pp. 449 to 452.

MURDER.
Aggravated murder.
  Death penalty for accomplices, p. 859.
Death penalty, pp. 858 to 869.
General provisions.
  See HOMICIDE.

MURDER—Cont'd
Juvenile murder.
  Capital punishment, p. 860.

N

NECESSITY, pp. 551 to 562.

NEGLIGENCE.
Culpability, pp. 98 to 103.
Homicide.
  Criminal-negligence involuntary manslaughter, pp. 342 to 352.

NO-ACCOUNT CHECK LEGISLATION, pp. 448, 449.

O

OCCUPATION OF THE FIELD.
Constitutional basis for attacking penal legislation, pp. 62, 63.

OMISSION TO ACT.
Criminal conduct, pp. 115 to 122.

ORGANIZED CRIME.
Conspiracy, pp. 826 to 836.

OVERBREADTH.
Interpretation of penal legislation, pp. 37 to 43.

P

PAROLE.
Humanizing function, pp. 872, 873.

PARTIES.
Rape, pp. 204, 205.

PARTIES TO CRIME.
Conspiracy.
  Generally, pp. 785 to 836.
    See CONSPIRACY.
Corporate criminal liability, pp. 735 to 739.
Principals and accessories, pp. 721 to 734.
Solicitation, pp. 739 to 742.

POSSESSION.
Criminal conduct, pp. 123 to 126.

POSTCONVICTION REVIEW.
Capital punishment, pp. 867, 868.

PRESUMPTIONS.
Interpretation of penal legislation, pp. 53 to 60.

PRESUMPTIVE SENTENCING, pp. 877 to 899.

PREVENTION OF CRIME, pp. 542 to 551.

PRINCIPALS AND ACCESSORIES.
Parties to crime, pp. 721 to 734.

PRINCIPLES.
Unifying principles, p. 3.

PRISON TERMS.
Generally, pp. 926 to 942.
  See IMPRISONMENT.

PRISON TERMS—Cont'd
Life imprisonment without possibility of parole.
  As cruel and unusual punishment, pp. 854 to 857.

PRIVACY.
Right of privacy.
  Constitutional basis for attacking penal legislation, pp. 51 to 53.

PROBATION, pp. 899 to 907.
Fines.
  Payment as condition of probation, p. 911.
Revocation procedures, pp. 900 to 905.

PROFESSIONAL CRIMINALS.
Maximum punishment, pp. 852, 853.
  Constitutional restrictions, pp. 854 to 869.
Prison terms.
  Extension, pp. 928 to 937.

PROFITS FROM CRIME.
Forfeiture of collateral profits, pp. 915 to 918.
Forfeitures generally.
  See FORFEITURES.

PROPERTY CRIMES.
Theft and related offenses.
  Generally, pp. 353 to 503.
    See THEFT AND RELATED OFFENSES.

PROVOCATION.
Homicide.
  Voluntary manslaughter, pp. 315 to 324.

PSYCHIATRIC EVIDENCE.
Death penalty cases, pp. 861, 862.

PSYCHOTROPIC MEDICATION.
Sanctions, pp. 876, 877.

PUNISHMENT, pp. 839 to 942.
Capital punishment, pp. 858 to 869.
Constitutional restrictions, pp. 854 to 869.
Double jeopardy, pp. 144 to 150.
Fines, pp. 907 to 915.
Forfeitures, pp. 915 to 926.
Forms of, pp. 899 to 942.
Imprisonment, pp. 926 to 942.
  See IMPRISONMENT.
Maximum punishment, pp. 852, 853.
  Constitutional restrictions, pp. 854 to 869.
Model penal code.
  Purposes of punishment, p. 854.
Principles generally, pp. 144 to 158.
Probation, pp. 899 to 907.
Psychotropic medication, pp. 876, 877.
Purposes, pp. 839 to 854.
Restitution, pp. 905 to 907.
Sentencing, pp. 869 to 899.
  See SENTENCING.

R

RAPE.
Corroboration, pp. 214 to 218.

RAPE—Cont'd
Definitions.
   Forcible rape, pp. 193 to 205.
   Modern redefinition of rape and other sexual offenses, pp. 225 to 230.
Forcible rape.
   Generally, pp. 193 to 205.
   Mens rea, pp. 202 to 204.
   Parties, pp. 204, 205.
   Proof.
     Cautionary instruction, pp. 205 to 207.
     Corroboration, pp. 214 to 218.
     Prior acts of unchastity, pp. 208 to 213.
   Resistance.
     Utmost resistance, pp. 194 to 202.
Fraud.
   Nonforcible rape, pp. 219, 220.
"Incidental" offenses, pp. 227, 228.
Jury instructions.
   Cautionary instruction, pp. 205 to 207.
Kidnapping.
   Definitions, pp. 228 to 230.
Mens rea.
   Forcible rape, pp. 202 to 204.
Nonforcible rape.
   Fraud, pp. 219, 220.
   Lack of capacity, pp. 218, 219.
Parties, pp. 204, 205.
Rape shield law, pp. 208 to 213.
Resistance.
   Utmost resistance, pp. 194 to 202.
Statutory rape, pp. 220 to 225.
Unchastity.
   Prior acts of unchastity, pp. 208 to 213.

RAPE SHIELD LAW, pp. 208 to 213.

RECEIVING STOLEN PROPERTY, pp. 458 to 474.
Actus reus, pp. 468 to 471.
Generally, pp. 458, 459.
Grading, p. 474.
Harm involved.
   "Stolen," pp. 459 to 468.
Mens rea, pp. 471 to 474.

RECIVIDISTS.
See PROFESSIONAL CRIMINALS.

RECKLESSNESS.
Culpability, pp. 95 to 98.
Homicide.
   Extreme recklessness, pp. 286 to 295.

REHABILITATION.
Purpose of punishment, pp. 843, 844.

REPEAT OFFENDERS.
See PROFESSIONAL CRIMINALS.

RESISTANCE.
Rape.
   Utmost resistance, pp. 194 to 202.

RESTITUTION, pp. 905 to 907.

INDEX

RETARDED PERSON.
Executions, pp. 868, 869.

RETRIBUTION.
"Just desserts" theory of sentencing, pp. 877 to 899.
Views on punishment, p. 839.

RETROACTIVE LAWS, pp. 26 to 32.

ROBBERY, pp. 474 to 484.
Actus reus, pp. 475 to 481.
Gradation, p. 484.
Harm, p. 474.
Mens rea, pp. 481 to 484.

RULE OF LAW.
Definitions, p. 3.
Legality, p. 3.

S

SANCTIONS, pp. 839 to 942.
Capital punishment, pp. 858 to 869.
Cruel and unusual punishment, pp. 854 to 869.
Double jeopardy, pp. 144 to 150.
Fines, pp. 907 to 915.
Forfeitures, pp. 915 to 926.
Forms of, pp. 899 to 942.
Imprisonment, pp. 926 to 942.
  See IMPRISONMENT.
Maximum punishment, pp. 852, 853.
  Constitutional restrictions, pp. 854 to 869.
Model penal code.
  Purposes of sanctioning, p. 854.
Principles generally, pp. 144 to 158.
Probation, pp. 899 to 907.
Psychotropic medication, pp. 876, 877.
Purposes, pp. 839 to 854.
Restitution, pp. 905 to 907.
Sentencing, pp. 869 to 899.
  See SENTENCING.

SEIZURE OF FORFEITED PROPERTY, pp. 920, 921.

SELF DEFENSE, pp. 508 to 527.
Homicide.
  Mitigating circumstances.
    Imperfect self-defense, pp. 332 to 334.

SENTENCING, pp. 869 to 899.
ABA guidelines, pp. 895 to 899.
Appellate review.
  Presumptive sentences, pp. 886, 887.
Death penalty.
  See DEATH PENALTY.
Equality in, pp. 874 to 876.
Federal sentencing guidelines, pp. 887 to 895.
Indeterminate sentences, pp. 869 to 877.
Presumptive sentencing, pp. 877 to 899.

SEPARATION OF POWERS.
Constitutional basis for attacking penal legislation, pp. 60 to 62.

SERVICES, THEFT OF, pp. 446, 447.

SEXUAL OFFENSES.
Rape.
  See RAPE.

SOLICITATION.
Attempt, p. 760.
Criminal conduct, p. 127.
Parties to crime, pp. 739 to 742.

SON OF SAM LAWS, pp. 915 to 918.

SPOUSAL PROPERTY.
Theft, p. 440.

STALKING.
Assault and battery, pp. 185, 186.

STATUTORY RAPE, pp. 220 to 225.

STOLEN PROPERTY, RECEIVING, pp. 458 to 474.
See RECEIVING STOLEN PROPERTY.

STRICT LIABILITY.
Ignorance and mistake of law, pp. 693 to 719.

T

TEMPORARY RESTRAINING ORDERS.
Forfeitures, pp. 919, 920.

TERRORISTIC THREATS.
Assault and battery, pp. 179 to 184.

THEFT AND RELATED OFFENSES, pp. 353 to 503.
Actus reus.
  Asportation, pp. 376 to 379.
  Deception, theft by, pp. 434 to 440.
  Embezzlement, pp. 396 to 405.
  False pretenses, obtaining title to property by, pp. 409 to 414.
  Lost or mislaid goods and mistakenly transferred goods, pp. 379 to 386.
  Misappropriation of property, pp. 433, 434.
  Receiving stolen property, pp. 468 to 471.
  Robbery, pp. 475 to 481.
  Trespass and continuing trespass, pp. 367 to 376.
  Unauthorized control of property, pp. 426 to 433.
Bad checks, pp. 448, 449.
Bribery of public officials, pp. 486 to 489.
Burglary, pp. 489 to 497.
Computer crimes, pp. 453 to 458.
Consolidation, pp. 440, 441.
  Contemporary statutory patterns, pp. 419 to 422.
Contemporary legislation, pp. 419 to 474.
Credit card misuse, pp. 447, 448.
Criminal trespass, pp. 497 to 499.
Deception, theft by, pp. 434 to 440.
Development of traditional theft offenses, pp. 357, 358.
Embezzlement, pp. 396 to 408.
Extortion, p. 485.
False pretenses, obtaining title to property by, pp. 409 to 419.
Funds received, p. 447.
Grading (value), pp. 392 to 395.
  Contemporary legislation, pp. 440 to 442.
  Receiving stolen property, p. 474.
  Robbery, p. 484.

INDEX

THEFT AND RELATED OFFENSES—Cont'd
Harm involved.
  Protected values behind contemporary legislation, pp. 422 to 426.
  Receiving stolen property.
    "Stolen," pp. 459 to 468.
  Robbery, p. 474.
  Traditional forms of criminality, pp. 358 to 367.
Intangibles.
  Subject matter of theft, p. 358.
Mens rea.
  Claim of right, pp. 391, 392.
    Contemporary legislation, pp. 445, 446.
  Embezzlement, pp. 405 to 408.
  False pretenses, obtaining title to property by, pp. 416 to 419.
  General concept, pp. 386 to 391.
    Contemporary legislation, pp. 442 to 445.
  Receiving stolen property, pp. 471 to 474.
  Robbery, pp. 481 to 484.
Misappropriation of property, pp. 433, 434.
Movable and immovable property defined under contemporary legislation, pp. 424 to 426.
Personal property.
  Traditional subject matter of theft, pp. 353 to 357.
Property of another defined under contemporary legislation, pp. 422 to 424.
Realty and things savoring of realty.
  Subject matter of theft, p. 358.
Receiving stolen property, pp. 458 to 474.
Robbery, pp. 474 to 484.
Services, pp. 446, 447.
Spousal property, p. 440.
Subject matter of theft.
  Traditional forms of criminality, pp. 353 to 358.
Traditional forms of criminality, pp. 353 to 419.
Unlawful taking or unlawful control, pp. 426 to 433.
Unlawful vehicle use, pp. 449 to 452.
Value, things of.
  Subject matter of theft, p. 358.
White collar crime, pp. 485 to 489.

THREATS.
Terroristic threats.
  Assault and battery, pp. 180 to 184.

TRESPASS AND CONTINUING TRESPASS.
Actus reus of larceny, pp. 367 to 376.
Criminal trespass, pp. 497 to 499.

U

UNAUTHORIZED CONTROL OF PROPERTY, pp. 426 to 433.

UNCHASTITY.
Rape.
  Prior acts of unchastity, pp. 208 to 213.

V

VAGUENESS.
Interpretation of penal legislation, pp. 32 to 37.

VEHICLES, UNAUTHORIZED USE, pp. 449 to 452.

VEHICULAR HOMICIDE.
Homicide, pp. 350 to 352.

VICTIMLESS CRIMES, pp. 133 to 138.

VOLUNTARINESS.
Criminal conduct, pp. 103 to 112.

VOLUNTARY MANSLAUGHTER.
Homicide.
   Extreme emotional disturbance, pp. 324 to 332.
   Imperfect self-defense, pp. 332 to 334.
   Provocation, pp. 315 to 324.

W

WEAPONS.
Assault and battery.
   Dangerous and deadly weapons, pp. 177, 178.

WHITE COLLAR CRIMES, pp. 485 to 489.

WORST OFFENDER STATUS.
Maximum punishment, pp. 852, 853.

Y

YEAR AND A DAY RULE.
Homicide, pp. 264 to 266.

9184